COLLINS
ENGLISH
Mini
THESAURUS

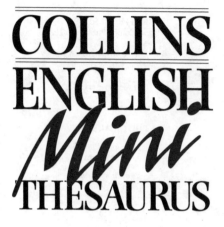

COLLINS
ENGLISH
Mini
THESAURUS

HarperCollins*Publishers*

First Published 1993
© HarperCollins Publishers 1993

ISBN 0 00 470287 - 5

EDITORIAL STAFF

Senior Editor
Lorna Knight

Editorial Assistance
Anne Young

A catalogue record for this book is
available from the British Library.

Entered words that we have reason to
believe constitute trademarks have been
designated as such. However, neither the
presence nor absence of such designation
should be regarded as affecting the legal
status of any trademark.

Computer typeset by Barbers Ltd
Wrotham, England

Printed in Great Britain by
HarperCollins *Manufacturing*
~ PO Box, Glasgow G4 0NB

CONTENTS

INTRODUCTION

The word "thesaurus" comes from a Greek word meaning "treasury" or "storehouse", and a thesaurus is a treasury or storehouse of words for you to draw on. It provides lists of synonyms - words which mean the same, or almost the same, as the one you already have in mind, so that you can choose an alternative.

There are many reasons why you might want to look for a different word to use. Perhaps you want to avoid using the same word more than once, or perhaps the one that comes to mind first is not precise enough to convey the exact meaning of what you want to say, or is too informal for the style in which you are writing.

The **Collins English Mini Thesaurus** is arranged in a single alphabetical list of main-entry words, like a dictionary. To find exactly the right word for your purpose, look up the word which is your starting point. There, you will find a selection of alternatives which can be used to replace it. If the original word has more than one meaning, the alternative words are grouped in separate numbered lists. For many basic words you will also find antonyms, words that mean the opposite. All the main-entry words and the numbers that identify different senses are printed in red so that it is quick and easy to find what you are looking for.

In addition to giving practical everyday help in all contexts and situations where good English is required, the thesaurus, especially when used in conjunction with one of the Collins range of dictionaries, will enable you to broaden your command of the language.

EXPLANATORY NOTES

1. Under each main entry word, the synonyms are arranged alphabetically. When a word has distinctly separate meanings, separate numbered lists are given for the different senses, eg

      distinct 1. apparent, clear, clear-cut ...
         2. detached, different,   discrete ...

2. Where it is helpful to distinguish between different parts of speech, labels have been added as follows: *n.* (noun), *v.* (verb), *adj.* (adjective), *adv.* (adverb), *pron.* (pronoun), *conj.* (conjunction), *prep.* (preposition), *interj.* (interjection). When a headword has more than one meaning and can function as more than one part of speech, a new part-of-speech function is shown by a large swung dash (~), eg

      local *adj.* **1.** community, district ...
         2. confined, limited ... ~ *n.*
         3. character (*Inf.*), inhabitant ...

3. Usually the synonyms for a particular part of speech are grouped together. For instance, in the entry *catch* synonyms for all the verb senses are given first, followed by synonyms for all the noun senses. Sometimes, however, noun and verb functions are very closely associated in specific meanings, and where this is the case the synonyms are grouped by meanings, as in the entry for *cover*.

4. Much-used phrases appear as main entries; for instance, *act for* comes after *act*. Expressions such as *en route*, and compounds such as *high-spirited*, are also given as main entries within the alphabetical listing. Short idiomatic phrases are entered under their key word and are to be found either at the end of the entry or immediately following the sense with which they are associated. Thus, the phrase *have a shot* appears as sense 5 of the entry *shot*, since the synonyms in sense 4 most closely approximate to the meaning of the phrase.

5. Plural forms that have a distinctly separate meaning, such as *provisions*, are entered at their own alphabetical position, while those with a less distinct difference, such as *extremities*, are given as a separate sense under the singular form, eg

> **extremity** ... **2.** ... *Plural* ...

6. A label in brackets applies only to the synonym preceding it, while one which is not bracketed relates to the whole of that particular sense. Labels have been abbreviated when a readily understandable shortened form exists, such as *Sl.* (Slang), *Inf.* (Informal), and *Fig.* (Figurative).

7. The antonym lists which follow many entries are arranged alphabetically, and, where appropriate, treated according to the rules given for synonyms.

8. The small swung dash symbol (~) is used to show that a word has been broken merely because it happens to fall at the end of a line, while the conventional sign (-) is used to distinguish a word which is always written with a hyphen, as in the entry for *airy*:

> **airy 1.** blowy, breezy, draughty, fresh, gusty, light, lofty, open, spacious, uncluttered, well-ventilated, windy **2.** aerial, deli~cate, ethereal, fanciful, flimsy

A

abandon v. 1. desert, forsake, jilt, leave, leave behind 2. evacuate, quit, vacate, withdraw from ~n. 3. careless freedom, dash, recklessness, unrestraint, wantonness, wild impulse, wildness
Antonyms v. defend, keep, maintain, take, uphold ~n. control, moderation, restraint

abandonment dereliction, desertion, forsaking, jilting, leaving

abbey cloister, convent, friary, monastery, nunnery, priory

abdicate abandon, abjure, abnegate, cede, forgo, give up, quit, relinquish, renounce, resign, retire, surrender, vacate, waive, yield

abduct carry off, kidnap, make off with, run away with, run off with, seize, snatch (*Sl.*)

abhor abominate, detest, execrate, hate, loathe, recoil from, regard with repugnance *or* horror, shrink from, shudder at

abhorrent abominable, detestable, disgusting, distasteful, execrable, hated, hateful, heinous, horrible, horrid, loathsome, obnoxious, odious, offensive, repellent, repugnant, repulsive, revolting

abide 1. accept, bear, brook, endure, put up with, stand, stomach, submit to, suffer, tolerate 2. continue, endure, last, persist, remain, survive

abide by 1. acknowledge, agree to, comply with, conform to, follow, obey, observe, submit to 2. adhere to, carry out, discharge, fulfil, hold to, keep to, persist in, stand by

ability adeptness, aptitude, capability, capacity, competence, competency, dexterity, endowment, energy, expertise, expertness, facility, faculty, flair, force, gift, knack, know-how (*Inf.*), potentiality, power, proficiency, qualification, skill, talent
Antonyms inability, incapability, incapacity, incompetence, powerlessness, weakness

ablaze 1. afire, aflame, alight, blazing, burning, fiery, flaming, ignited, lighted, on fire 2. aglow, brilliant, flashing, gleaming, glowing, illuminated, incandescent, luminous, radiant, sparkling

able accomplished, adept, adequate, adroit, capable, clever, competent, effective, efficient, experienced, expert, fit, fitted, gifted, highly endowed, masterful, masterly, powerful, practised, proficient, qualified, skilful, skilled, strong, talented
Antonyms amateurish, inadequate, incapable, incompetent, ineffective, inefficient, inept, mediocre, unfit, unskilful, weak

able-bodied firm, fit, hale, hardy, healthy, hearty, lusty, powerful, robust, sound, staunch, stout, strapping, strong, sturdy, vigorous
Antonyms ailing, debilitated, feeble, fragile, frail, sickly, tender, weak

abnormal aberrant, anomalous, atypical, curious, deviant, eccentric, erratic, exceptional, extraordinary, irregular, monstrous, odd, peculiar, queer, singular, strange, uncommon, unexpected, unnatural, untypical, unusual, weird
Antonyms common, conventional, customary, familiar, natural, normal, ordinary, regular, unexceptional, usual

abnormality aberration, anomaly, atypicalness, bizarreness, deformity, deviation, eccentricity, exception, extraordinariness, flaw, irregularity, monstrosity, oddity, peculiarity, queerness, singularity, strangeness, uncommonness, unexpectedness, unnaturalness, untypicalness, unusualness, weirdness

abolish abrogate, annihilate, annul, blot out, cancel, destroy, do away with, eliminate, end, eradicate, expunge, exterminate, extinguish, extirpate, invalidate, nullify, obliterate, overthrow, overturn, put an end to, quash, repeal, repudiate, rescind, revoke, stamp out, subvert, suppress, terminate, vitiate, void, wipe out

Antonyms authorize, continue, create, establish, found, institute, introduce, legalize, promote, reinstate, reintroduce, restore, revive, sustain

abolition abrogation, annihilation, annulment, blotting out, cancellation, destruction, elimination, end, ending, eradication, expunction, extermination, extinction, extirpation, invalidation, nullification, obliteration, overthrow, overturning, quashing, repeal, repudiation, rescission, revocation, stamping out, subversion, suppression, termination, vitiation, voiding, wiping out, withdrawal

abominable abhorrent, accursed, atrocious, base, contemptible, despicable, detestable, disgusting, execrable, foul, hateful, heinous, hellish, horrible, horrid, loathsome, nauseous, obnoxious, odious, repellent, reprehensible, repugnant, repulsive, revolting, terrible, vile, villainous, wretched

abomination abhorrence, antipathy, aversion, detestation, disgust, distaste, execration, hate, hatred, horror, loathing, odium, repugnance, revulsion

abound be jammed with, be packed with, be plentiful, crowd, flourish, increase, infest, luxuriate, overflow, proliferate, super-

abound, swarm, swell, teem, thrive

abounding abundant, bountiful, copious, filled, flourishing, flowing, flush, full, lavish, luxuriant, overflowing, plenteous, plentiful, profuse, prolific, rank, replete, rich, superabundant, teeming

about prep. 1. anent (Scot.), as regards, concerning, connected with, dealing with, on, re, referring to, regarding, relating to, relative to, respecting, touching, with respect to 2. adjacent, beside, circa (used with dates), close to, near, nearby 3. around, encircling, on all sides, round, surrounding 4. all over, over, through, throughout ~adv. 5. almost, approaching, approximately, around, close to, more or less, nearing, nearly, roughly

above 1. prep. atop, beyond, exceeding, higher than, on top of, over, upon 2. adj. aforementioned, aforesaid, earlier, foregoing, preceding, previous, prior

Antonyms prep. below, beneath, under, underneath

abrasive annoying, biting, caustic, cutting, galling, grating, hurtful, irritating, nasty, rough, sharp, unpleasant

abreast acquainted, au courant, au fait, conversant, familiar, informed, in touch, knowledgeable, up to date

abridge abbreviate, abstract, clip, compress, concentrate, condense, contract, curtail, cut, cut down, decrease, digest, diminish, epitomize, lessen, précis, reduce, shorten, summarize, synopsize (U.S.), trim

Antonyms amplify, augment, enlarge, expand, extend, go into detail, lengthen, prolong, protract, spin out, stretch out

abroad beyond the sea, in foreign lands, out of the country, overseas

abrupt 1. blunt, brisk, brusque, curt, direct, discourteous, gruff, impolite, rough, rude, short,

snappish, snappy, terse, uncer~
emonious, uncivil, ungracious 2.
precipitous, sharp, sheer, steep,
sudden

Antonyms (*sense 1*) civil, cour~
teous, gracious, polite (*sense 2*)
gradual

absence 1. absenteeism, non-
appearance, nonattendance, tru~
ancy 2. default, defect, deficien~
cy, lack, need, nonexistence,
omission, privation, unavailabil~
ity, want

absent *adj.* 1. away, elsewhere,
gone, lacking, missing, nonat~
tendant, nonexistent, not present,
out, truant, unavailable, wanting
2. absent-minded, absorbed, ab~
stracted, bemused, blank, daydreaming, distracted, dreamy,
empty, faraway, heedless, inat~
tentive, musing, oblivious, preoc~
cupied, unaware, unconscious,
unheeding, unthinking, vacant,
vague

Antonyms (*sense 1*) attendant, in
attendance, present (*sense 2*)
alert, attentive, aware, conscious,
thoughtful

absent-minded absent, ab~
sorbed, abstracted, bemused,
distracted, dreaming, dreamy,
engrossed, faraway, forgetful,
heedless, in a brown study, inat~
tentive, musing, oblivious, preoc~
cupied, unaware, unconscious,
unheeding, unthinking

Antonyms alert, awake, obser~
vant, on one's toes, on the ball,
perceptive, quick, vigilant, wary,
wide-awake

absolute 1. complete, consum~
mate, downright, entire, out-and-
out, perfect, pure, sheer,
thorough, total, unadulterated,
unalloyed, unmitigated, unmixed,
unqualified, utter 2. actual, cat~
egorical, certain, conclusive, de~
cided, decisive, definite, exact,
genuine, infallible, positive, pre~
cise, sure, unambiguous, un~
equivocal, unquestionable 3. ab~
solutist, arbitrary, autarchical,
autocratic, autonomous, despotic,
dictatorial, full, peremptory,

sovereign, supreme, tyrannical,
unbounded, unconditional, un~
limited, unqualified, unquestion~
able, unrestrained, unrestricted

absolutely 1. completely, con~
summately, entirely, fully, per~
fectly, purely, thoroughly, totally,
unmitigatedly, utterly, wholly 2.
actually, categorically, certainly,
conclusively, decidedly, deci~
sively, definitely, exactly, genu~
inely, infallibly, positively, pre~
cisely, surely, truly, unambigu~
ously, unequivocally, unques~
tionably 3. arbitrarily, autocrati~
cally, autonomously, despotical~
ly, dictatorially, fully, peremp~
torily, sovereignly, supremely, ty~
rannically, unconditionally, un~
questionably, unrestrainedly,
without qualification

Antonyms conditionally, fairly,
probably, reasonably, somewhat

absolution acquittal, amnesty,
deliverance, discharge, dispen~
sation, exculpation, exemption,
exoneration, forgiveness, freeing,
indulgence, liberation, mercy,
pardon, release, remission, set~
ting free, shriving, vindication

absolve acquit, clear, deliver,
discharge, exculpate, excuse, ex~
empt, exonerate, forgive, free,
let off, liberate, loose, pardon,
release, remit, set free, shrive,
vindicate

Antonyms blame, censure,
charge, condemn, convict, damn,
denounce, pass sentence on, rep~
rehend, reproach, reprove, sen~
tence, upbraid

absorb 1. assimilate, consume,
devour, digest, drink in, exhaust,
imbibe, incorporate, ingest, os~
mose, receive, soak up, suck up,
take in 2. captivate, engage, en~
gross, enwrap, fascinate, fill, fill
up, fix, hold, immerse, monopo~
lize, occupy, preoccupy, rivet

absorbing arresting, captivating,
engrossing, fascinating, gripping,
interesting, intriguing, preoccu~
pying, riveting, spellbinding

abstain avoid, cease, decline,
deny (oneself), desist, forbear,

forgo, give up, keep from, refrain, refuse, renounce, shun, stop, withhold
Antonyms abandon oneself, give in, indulge, partake, yield

abstention abstaining, abstinence, avoidance, desistance, eschewal, forbearance, nonindulgence, refraining, refusal, self-control, self-denial, self-restraint

abstinence abstemiousness, asceticism, avoidance, continence, forbearance, moderation, refraining, self-denial, self-restraint, soberness, sobriety, teetotalism, temperance
Antonyms abandon, acquisitiveness, covetousness, excess, gluttony, greediness, indulgence, self-indulgence, wantonness

abstinent abstaining, abstemious, continent, forbearing, moderate, self-controlled, self-denying, self-restraining, sober, temperate

abstract *adj.* 1. abstruse, arcane, complex, conceptual, deep, general, generalized, hypothetical, indefinite, intellectual, nonconcrete, occult, philosophical, profound, recondite, separate, subtle, theoretic, theoretical, unpractical, unrealistic ~*n.* 2. abridgment, compendium, condensation, digest, epitome, essence, outline, précis, recapitulation, résumé, summary, synopsis ~*v.* 3. abbreviate, abridge, condense, digest, epitomize, outline, précis, shorten, summarize, synopsize (*U.S.*) 4. detach, dissociate, extract, isolate, remove, separate, steal, take away, take out, withdraw
Antonyms actual, concrete, definite, factual, material, real, specific ~*n.* enlargement, expansion ~*v.* (*sense 4*) add, combine, inject

absurd crazy (*Inf.*), daft (*Inf.*), farcical, foolish, idiotic, illogical, incongruous, irrational, laughable, ludicrous, meaningless, nonsensical, preposterous, ridiculous, senseless, silly, stupid, unreasonable

Antonyms intelligent, logical, prudent, rational, reasonable, sagacious, sensible, smart, wise

absurdity craziness (*Inf.*), daftness (*Inf.*), farce, farcicality, farcicalness, folly, foolishness, idiocy, illogicality, illogicalness, incongruity, irrationality, joke, ludicrousness, meaninglessness, nonsense, preposterousness, ridiculousness, senselessness, silliness, stupidity, unreasonableness

abundance 1. affluence, ampleness, bounty, copiousness, exuberance, fullness, heap (*Inf.*), plenitude, plenteousness, plenty, profusion 2. affluence, fortune, opulence, riches, wealth
Antonyms dearth, deficiency, lack, need, paucity, scantiness, scarcity, sparseness

abundant ample, bounteous, bountiful, copious, exuberant, filled, full, lavish, luxuriant, overflowing, plenteous, plentiful, profuse, rank, rich, teeming, well-provided, well-supplied
Antonyms deficient, few, few and far between, inadequate, in short supply, insufficient, lacking, rare, scanty, scarce, short, sparse

abuse *v.* 1. damage, exploit, harm, hurt, ill-treat, impose upon, injure, maltreat, manhandle, mar, misapply, misuse, oppress, spoil, take advantage of, wrong 2. calumniate, castigate, curse, defame, disparage, insult, inveigh against, libel, malign, revile, scold, slander, smear, swear at, traduce, upbraid, vilify, vituperate ~*n.* 3. damage, exploitation, harm, hurt, ill-treatment, imposition, injury, maltreatment, manhandling, misapplication, misuse, oppression, spoiling, wrong 4. blame, calumniation, castigation, censure, contumely, curses, cursing, defamation, derision, disparagement, insults, invective, libel, opprobrium, reproach, revilement, scolding, slander, swearing, tirade, traducement, upbraiding, vilification, vituperation

Antonyms *v. (sense 1)* care for, protect *(sense 2)* acclaim, commend, compliment, extol, flatter, praise, respect

abusive 1. calumniating, castigating, censorious, contumelious, defamatory, derisive, disparaging, insulting, invective, libellous, maligning, offensive, opprobrious, reproachful, reviling, rude, scathing, scolding, slanderous, traducing, upbraiding, vilifying, vituperative **2.** brutal, cruel, destructive, harmful, hurtful, injurious, rough

Antonyms *(sense 1)* approving, complimentary, eulogistic, flattering, laudatory, panegyrical, praising

academic *adj.* **1.** bookish, campus, college, collegiate, erudite, highbrow, learned, lettered, literary, scholarly, scholastic, school, studious, university **2.** abstract, conjectural, hypothetical, impractical, notional, speculative, theoretical ~*n.* **3.** academician, don, fellow, lecturer, master, professor, pupil, scholar, scholastic, schoolman, student, tutor

accede 1. accept, acquiesce, admit, agree, assent, comply, concede, concur, consent, endorse, grant, yield **2.** assume, attain, come to, enter upon, inherit, succeed, succeed to *(as heir)*

accelerate advance, expedite, forward, further, hasten, hurry, pick up speed, precipitate, quicken, speed, speed up, spur, step up *(Inf.)*, stimulate

Antonyms decelerate, delay, hinder, impede, obstruct, slow down

accent *n.* **1.** beat, cadence, emphasis, force, pitch, rhythm, stress, timbre, tonality **2.** articulation, enunciation, inflection, intonation, modulation, pronunciation, tone ~*v.* **3.** accentuate, emphasize, stress, underline, underscore

accept 1. acquire, gain, get, have, obtain, receive, secure, take **2.** accede, acknowledge, acquiesce, admit, adopt, affirm, agree to, approve, believe, concur with, consent to, cooperate with, recognize, swallow *(Inf.)* **3.** bear, bow to, brook, defer to, put up with, stand, submit to, suffer, take, yield to **4.** acknowledge, admit, assume, avow, bear, take on, undertake

Antonyms decline, deny, disown, refuse, reject, repudiate, spurn

acceptable 1. agreeable, delightful, grateful, gratifying, pleasant, pleasing, welcome **2.** adequate, admissible, all right, fair, moderate, passable, satisfactory, so-so *(Inf.)*, standard, tolerable

Antonyms unacceptable, unsatisfactory, unsuitable

acceptance 1. accepting, acquiring, gaining, getting, having, obtaining, receipt, securing, taking **2.** accedence, accession, acknowledgement, acquiescence, admission, adoption, affirmation, agreement, approbation, approval, assent, belief, compliance, concession, concurrence, consent, cooperation, credence, O.K. *(Inf.)*, permission, recognition, stamp or seal of approval **3.** deference, standing, submission, taking, yielding **4.** acknowledgment, admission, assumption, avowal, taking on, undertaking

accepted acceptable, acknowledged, admitted, agreed, agreed upon, approved, authorized, common, confirmed, conventional, customary, established, normal, received, recognized, regular, sanctioned, standard, time-honoured, traditional, universal, usual

Antonyms abnormal, irregular, unconventional, uncustomary, unorthodox, unusual, unwonted

access admission, admittance, approach, avenue, course, door, entering, entrance, entrée, entry, gateway, key, passage, passage-way, path, road

accessible 1. achievable, at hand, attainable, available, get-at-able (*Inf.*), handy, near, near-by, obtainable, on hand, possible, reachable, ready **2.** affable, approachable, available, conversable, cordial, friendly, informal **3.** exposed, liable, open, subject, susceptible, vulnerable, wide-open

Antonyms far-off, hidden, inaccessible, secreted, unapproachable, unavailable, unobtainable, unreachable

accessory *n.* **1.** abettor, accomplice, assistant, associate (*in crime*), colleague, confederate, helper, partner **2.** accent, accompaniment, addition, adjunct, adornment, aid, appendage, attachment, component, convenience, decoration, extension, extra, frill, help, supplement, trim, trimming

accident 1. blow, calamity, casualty, chance, collision, crash, disaster, misadventure, mischance, misfortune, mishap, pile-up **2.** chance, fate, fluke, fortuity, fortune, hazard, luck

accidental adventitious, casual, chance, contingent, fortuitous, haphazard, inadvertent, incidental, inessential, nonessential, random, uncalculated, uncertain, unessential, unexpected, unforeseen, unintended, unintentional, unlooked-for, unplanned, unpremeditated, unwitting

Antonyms calculated, designed, expected, foreseen, intended, intentional, planned, prepared

accidentally adventitiously, by accident, by chance, by mistake, casually, fortuitously, haphazardly, inadvertently, incidentally, randomly, unconsciously, undesignedly, unexpectedly, unintentionally, unwittingly

Antonyms by design, consciously, deliberately, designedly, on purpose, wilfully

acclaim 1. *v.* applaud, approve,

celebrate, cheer, clap, commend, eulogize, exalt, extol, hail, honour, laud, praise, salute, welcome **2.** *n.* acclamation, applause, approbation, approval, celebration, cheering, clapping, commendation, eulogizing, exaltation, honour, laudation, plaudits, praise, welcome

Antonyms *n.* bad press, brickbats, censure, criticism, disparagement, fault-finding, flak (*Inf.*), panning (*Inf.*), vituperation

acclimatize accommodate, acculture, accustom, adapt, adjust, become seasoned to, get used to, habituate, inure, naturalize

accommodate 1. billet, board, cater for, entertain, harbour, house, lodge, put up, quarter, shelter **2.** afford, aid, assist, furnish, help, oblige, provide, serve, supply **3.** accustom, adapt, adjust, comply, compose, conform, fit, harmonize, modify, reconcile, settle

accommodating complaisant, considerate, cooperative, friendly, helpful, hospitable, kind, obliging, polite, unselfish, willing

Antonyms disobliging, inconsiderate, rude, uncooperative, unhelpful

accommodation board, digs (*Inf.*), harbouring, house, housing, lodging(s), quartering, quarters, shelter, sheltering

accompany attend, chaperon, conduct, convoy, escort, go with, squire, usher

accompanying accessory, added, additional, appended, associate, associated, attached, attendant, complementary, concomitant, concurrent, connected, fellow, joint, related, supplemental, supplementary

accomplice abettor, accessory, ally, assistant, associate, coadjutor, collaborator, colleague, confederate, helper, henchman, partner

accomplish achieve, attain, bring about, bring off (*Inf.*), carry out, complete, conclude, con-

summate, do, effect, effectuate, execute, finish, fulfil, manage, perform, produce, realize
Antonyms fail, fall short, forsake, give up

accomplished adept, consummate, cultivated, expert, gifted, masterly, polished, practised, proficient, skilful, skilled, talented
Antonyms amateurish, incapable, incompetent, inexpert, unestablished, unproven, unrealized, unskilled, untalented

accomplishment 1. achievement, attainment, bringing about, carrying out, completion, conclusion, consummation, doing, effecting, execution, finishing, fulfilment, management, performance, production, realization **2.** achievement, act, attainment, coup, deed, exploit, feat, stroke, triumph **3.** ability, achievement, art, attainment, capability, gift, proficiency, skill, talent

according to 1. as believed by, as maintained by, as stated by, in the light of, on the authority of, on the report of **2.** after, after the manner of, consistent with, in accordance with, in compliance with, in conformity with, in harmony with, in keeping with, in line with, in obedience to, in step with, in the manner of, obedient to

account n. **1.** chronicle, description, detail, explanation, history, narration, narrative, recital, record, relation, report, statement, story, tale, version **2.** Commerce balance, bill, book, books, charge, computation, inventory, invoice, ledger, reckoning, register, score, statement, tally **3.** basis, cause, consideration, ground, grounds, interest, motive, reason, regard, sake, score (Inf.) ~v. **4.** appraise, assess, believe, calculate, compute, consider, count, deem, esteem, estimate, explain, gauge, hold, judge, rate, reckon, regard, think, value, weigh

accountability answerability, chargeability, culpability, liability, responsibility

accountable amenable, answerable, charged with, liable, obligated, obliged, responsible

account for answer for, clarify, clear up, elucidate, explain, illuminate, justify, rationalize

accredit appoint, authorize, certify, commission, depute, empower, endorse, entrust, guarantee, license, recognize, sanction, vouch for

accumulate accrue, amass, build up, collect, cumulate, gather, grow, hoard, increase, pile up, stockpile, store

accumulation aggregation, augmentation, build-up, collection, conglomeration, gathering, growth, heap, hoard, increase, mass, pile, stack, stock, stockpile, store

accuracy accurateness, authenticity, carefulness, closeness, correctness, exactitude, exactness, faithfulness, faultlessness, fidelity, meticulousness, niceness, nicety, precision, strictness, truth, truthfulness, veracity, verity
Antonyms carelessness, erroneousness, imprecision, inaccuracy, incorrectness, inexactitude

accurate authentic, careful, close, correct, exact, faithful, faultless, just, meticulous, nice, precise, proper, regular, right, scrupulous, spot-on (Inf.), strict, true, truthful, unerring, veracious
Antonyms careless, defective, faulty, imperfect, imprecise, inaccurate, incorrect, inexact, slovenly, wrong

accurately authentically, carefully, closely, correctly, exactly, faithfully, faultlessly, justly, meticulously, nicely, precisely, properly, regularly, rightly, scrupulously, strictly, truly, truthfully, unerringly, veraciously

accusation allegation, arraignment, attribution, charge, citation, complaint, denunciation, impeachment, imputation, incrimination, indictment, recrimination

accuse allege, arraign, attribute, blame, censure, charge, cite, denounce, impeach, impute, incriminate, indict, recriminate, tax

Antonyms absolve, answer, defend, deny, exonerate, plea, reply, vindicate

accustom acclimatize, acquaint, adapt, discipline, exercise, familiarize, habituate, inure, season, train

accustomed 1. acclimatized, acquainted, adapted, disciplined, exercised, familiar, familiarized, given to, habituated, in the habit of, inured, seasoned, trained, used **2.** common, conventional, customary, established, everyday, expected, fixed, general, habitual, normal, ordinary, regular, routine, set, traditional, usual, wonted

Antonyms (*sense 1*) unaccustomed, unfamiliar, unused (*sense 2*) abnormal, infrequent, occasional, odd, peculiar, rare, strange, unaccustomed, uncommon, unfamiliar, unusual

ache *v.* hurt, pain, pound, smart, suffer, throb, twinge

achieve accomplish, acquire, attain, bring about, carry out, complete, consummate, do, earn, effect, execute, finish, fulfil, gain, get, obtain, perform, procure, reach, realize, win

achievement accomplishment, acquirement, attainment, completion, execution, fulfilment, performance, production, realization

acid acerbic, acidulous, acrid, biting, pungent, sharp, sour, tart, vinegarish, vinegary

acidity acerbity, acidulousness, acridity, acridness, bitterness, pungency, sharpness, sourness, tartness, vinegariness, vinegarishness

acknowledge 1. accede, accept,

acquiesce, admit, allow, concede, confess, declare, grant, own, profess, recognize, yield **2.** answer, notice, react to, recognize, reply to, respond to, return

Antonyms (*sense 1*) contradict, deny, disclaim, reject, renounce, repudiate (*sense 2*) deny, disavow, disdain, disregard, ignore, reject, snub, spurn

acknowledged accepted, accredited, admitted, answered, approved, conceded, confessed, declared, professed, recognized, returned

acknowledgment 1. acceptance, accession, acquiescence, admission, allowing, confession, declaration, profession, realization, yielding **2.** answer, appreciation, credit, gratitude, reaction, recognition, reply, response, return, thanks

acquaint advise, announce, apprise, disclose, divulge, enlighten, familiarize, inform, let (someone) know, notify, reveal, tell

acquaintance associate, colleague, contact

Antonyms buddy, good friend, intimate, stranger

acquainted alive to, apprised of, au fait, aware of, cognizant of, conscious of, conversant with, experienced in, familiar with, informed of, in on, knowledgeable about, privy to, versed in

acquiesce accede, accept, agree, allow, approve, assent, bow to, comply, concur, conform, consent, give in, go along with, submit, yield

Antonyms balk at, contest, demur, disagree, dissent, fight, object, protest, refuse, resist, veto

acquiescence acceptance, accession, agreement, approval, assent, compliance, concurrence, conformity, consent, giving in, obedience, submission, yielding

acquire achieve, amass, attain, buy, collect, earn, gain, gather, get, obtain, pick up, procure, realize, receive, secure, win

Antonyms be deprived of, forfeit,

forgo, give up, lose, relinquish, renounce, renounce, waive

acquisition buy, gain, possession, prize, property, purchase

acquisitive avaricious, avid, covetous, grabbing, grasping, greedy, predatory, rapacious

acquit absolve, clear, deliver, discharge, exculpate, exonerate, free, fulfil, liberate, release, relieve, vindicate

Antonyms blame, charge, condemn, convict, damn, find guilty, sentence

acquittal absolution, clearance, deliverance, discharge, exculpation, exoneration, freeing, liberation, release, relief, vindication

acrimonious acerbic, astringent, biting, bitter, caustic, censorious, churlish, crabbed, cutting, irascible, mordant, peevish, petulant, pungent, rancorous, sarcastic, severe, sharp, spiteful, splenetic, tart, testy, trenchant

act *n.* **1.** accomplishment, achievement, action, blow, deed, doing, execution, exertion, exploit, feat, move, operation, performance, step, stroke, undertaking **2.** bill, decree, edict, enactment, law, measure, ordinance, resolution, statute **3.** performance, routine, show, sketch, turn ~*v.* **4.** acquit, bear, behave, carry, carry out, comport, conduct, do, enact, execute, exert, function, go about, make, move, operate, perform, react, serve, strike, take effect, undertake, work **5.** affect, assume, counterfeit, dissimulate, feign, imitate, perform, pose, posture, pretend, put on, seem, sham **6.** act out, characterize, enact, impersonate, mime, mimic, perform, personate, personify, play, play or take the part of, portray, represent

act for cover for, deputize for, fill in for, function in place of, replace, represent, serve, stand in for, substitute for, take the place of

acting *adj.* **1.** interim, *pro tem*, provisional, substitute, surrogate, temporary ~*n.* **2.** characterization, dramatics, enacting, impersonation, performance, performing, playing, portrayal, portraying, stagecraft, theatre **3.** assuming, counterfeiting, dissimulation, feigning, imitating, imitation, imposture, play-acting, posing, posturing, pretence, pretending, putting on, seeming, shamming

action 1. accomplishment, achievement, act, blow, deed, exercise, exertion, exploit, feat, move, operation, performance, step, stroke, undertaking **2.** activity, energy, force, liveliness, spirit, vigour, vim, vitality **3.** battle, combat, conflict, fighting, warfare **4.** case, cause, lawsuit, litigation, proceeding, prosecution, suit

actions bearing, behaviour, comportment, conduct, demeanour, deportment, manners, ways

active 1. acting, astir, at work, doing, effectual, functioning, in action, in force, in operation, live, moving, operative, running, stirring, working **2.** bustling, busy, engaged, full, hard-working, involved, occupied, on the go (*Inf.*), on the move, strenuous **3.** alert, animated, diligent, energetic, industrious, lively, nimble, on the go (*Inf.*), quick, spirited, sprightly, spry, vibrant, vigorous, vital, vivacious

Antonyms dormant, dull, idle, inactive, inoperative, lazy, sedentary, slow, sluggish, torpid, unimaginative, unoccupied

activity 1. action, activeness, animation, bustle, enterprise, exercise, exertion, hurly-burly, hustle, labour, life, liveliness, motion, movement, stir, work **2.** act, avocation, deed, endeavour, enterprise, hobby, interest, job, labour, occupation, pastime, project, pursuit, scheme, task, undertaking, venture, work

Antonyms (*sense 1*) dullness, idleness, immobility, inaction, inactivity, indolence, inertia, lethargy, passivity, sluggishness, torpor

actor actress, dramatic artist, leading man, performer, play-actor, player, Thespian, tragedian, trouper

actress actor, dramatic artist, leading lady, performer, play-actor, player, starlet, Thespian, tragedienne, trouper

actual 1. absolute, categorical, certain, concrete, corporeal, definite, factual, indisputable, indubitable, physical, positive, real, substantial, tangible, undeniable, unquestionable **2.** current, existent, extant, live, living, present, present-day, prevailing

Antonyms (*sense 1*) fictitious, hypothetical, made-up, probable, supposed, theoretical, unreal, untrue

actually absolutely, as a matter of fact, de facto, essentially, indeed, in fact, in point of fact, in reality, in truth, literally, really, truly, veritably

acute 1. astute, canny, clever, discerning, discriminating, incisive, ingenious, insightful, intuitive, keen, observant, penetrating, perceptive, perspicacious, piercing, sensitive, sharp, smart, subtle **2.** cuspate, needle-shaped, peaked, pointed, sharp, sharpened

adamant determined, firm, fixed, immovable, inexorable, inflexible, insistent, intransigent, obdurate, resolute, rigid, set, stiff, stubborn, unbending, uncompromising, unrelenting, unshakable, unyielding

Antonyms compliant, compromising, easy-going, flexible, lax, pliant, receptive, responsive, susceptible, tractable, yielding

adapt acclimatize, accommodate, adjust, alter, apply, change, comply, conform, familiarize, fashion, fit, habituate, harmonize, make, match, modify, prepare, qualify, remodel, shape, suit, tailor

adaptable adjustable, alterable, changeable, compliant, conformable, convertible, easy-going, flexible, malleable, modifiable, plastic, pliant, resilient, variable, versatile

adaptation adjustment, alteration, change, conversion, modification, refitting, remodelling, reworking, shift, transformation, variation, version

add 1. adjoin, affix, amplify, annex, append, attach, augment, enlarge by, include, increase by, supplement **2.** add up, compute, count up, reckon, sum up, total, tot up

Antonyms deduct, diminish, lessen, reduce, remove, subtract, take away, take from

addict dope-fiend (*Sl.*), fiend (*Inf.*), freak (*Sl.*), head (*Inf.*), junkie (*Sl.*), user (*Inf.*)

addicted absorbed, accustomed, dedicated, dependent, devoted, disposed, fond, habituated, hooked (*Sl.*), inclined, obsessed, prone

addiction craving, dependence, enslavement, habit, obsession

addition 1. accession, adding, adjoining, affixing, amplification, annexation, attachment, augmentation, enlargement, extension, inclusion, increasing **2.** addendum, additive, adjunct, affix, appendage, appendix, extension, extra, gain, increase, increment, supplement

Antonyms deduction, detachment, diminution, lessening, reduction, removal, subtraction

additional added, affixed, appended, extra, fresh, further, increased, more, new, other, over-and-above, spare, supplementary

address *n.* **1.** abode, domicile, dwelling, home, house, location, lodging, place, residence, situation, whereabouts **2.** direction, inscription, superscription **3.** discourse, disquisition, dissertation, harangue, lecture, oration, sermon, speech, talk **4.** accost, apostrophize, approach, greet, hail, invoke, salute, speak to, talk to **5.** discourse, give a speech, give a talk, harangue, lecture, orate, sermonize, speak, talk

add up add, compute, count, count up, reckon, sum up, total, tot up

adept able, accomplished, adroit, dexterous, expert, masterful, masterly, practised, proficient, skilful, skilled, versed

adequacy capability, commensurateness, competence, fairness, requisiteness, satisfactoriness, sufficiency, suitability, tolerability

adequate capable, commensurate, competent, enough, fair, passable, requisite, satisfactory, sufficient, suitable, tolerable
Antonyms deficient, inadequate, insufficient, lacking, meagre, short, unsatisfactory, unsuitable

adhere attach, cement, cleave, cling, cohere, fasten, fix, glue, glue on, hold fast, paste, stick, stick fast, unite

adhesive 1. *adj.* adhering, attaching, clinging, cohesive, gluey, glutinous, gummy, holding, mucilaginous, sticking, sticky, tacky, tenacious **2.** *n.* cement, glue, gum, mucilage, paste

adjacent abutting, adjoining, alongside, beside, bordering, close, contiguous, near, neighbouring, next door, touching
Antonyms distant, far away, remote, separated

adjoining abutting, adjacent, bordering, connecting, contiguous, impinging, interconnecting, joined, joining, near, neighbouring, next door, touching, verging

adjourn defer, delay, discontinue, interrupt, postpone, prorogue, put off, recess, stay, suspend
Antonyms assemble, continue, convene, gather, open, remain, reopen, stay

adjournment deferment, deferral, delay, discontinuation, interruption, postponement, prorogation, putting off, recess, stay, suspension

adjudicate adjudge, arbitrate, decide, determine, judge, referee, settle, umpire

adjudication adjudgment, arbitration, conclusion, decision, determination, finding, judgment, pronouncement, ruling, settlement, verdict

adjust acclimatize, accommodate, accustom, adapt, alter, arrange, compose, dispose, fit, fix, harmonize, make conform, measure, modify, order, reconcile, rectify, redress, regulate, remodel, set, settle, suit, tune (up)

adjustable adaptable, alterable, flexible, malleable, modifiable, mouldable, movable, tractable

adjustment adaptation, alteration, arrangement, arranging, fitting, fixing, modification, ordering, rectification, redress, regulation, remodelling, setting, tuning

ad-lib *v.* extemporize, improvise, make up, speak extemporaneously, speak impromptu, speak off the cuff

administer conduct, control, direct, govern, manage, oversee, run, superintend, supervise

administration 1. administering, application, conduct, control, direction, dispensation, distribution, execution, governing, government, management, overseeing, performance, provision, running, superintendence, supervision **2.** executive, governing body, government, management, ministry, term of office

admirable choice, commendable, estimable, excellent, exquisite, fine, laudable, meritorious, praiseworthy, rare, superior, valuable, wonderful, worthy
Antonyms bad, commonplace, deplorable, disappointing, displeasing, mediocre, worthless

admiration adoration, affection, amazement, appreciation, approbation, approval, astonishment, delight, esteem, pleasure, praise, regard, respect, surprise, veneration, wonder, wonderment

admire adore, appreciate, approve, esteem, idolize, look up to, praise, prize, respect, think highly of, value, venerate, worship
Antonyms contemn, deride, despise, look down on, look down one's nose at (*Inf.*), misprize, scorn, sneer at, spurn, undervalue

admirer 1. beau, boyfriend, lover, suitor, sweetheart, wooer **2.** adherent, devotee, disciple, enthusiast, fan, follower, partisan, supporter, votary, worshipper

admissible acceptable, allowable, allowed, passable, permissible, permitted, tolerable, tolerated
Antonyms disallowed, inadmissible, intolerable, unacceptable

admission 1. acceptance, access, admittance, entrance, entrée, entry, ingress, initiation, introduction **2.** acknowledgment, admitting, affirmation, allowance, avowal, concession, confession, declaration, disclosure, divulgence, profession, revelation

admit 1. accept, allow, allow to enter, give access, initiate, introduce, let in, receive, take in **2.** acknowledge, affirm, avow, concede, confess, declare, disclose, divulge, profess, reveal **3.** agree, allow, grant, let, permit, recognize
Antonyms (*sense 1*) exclude, keep out (*senses 2 & 3*) deny, dismiss, forbid, negate, prohibit, reject

adolescence 1. boyhood, girlhood, juvenescence, minority, teens, youth **2.** boyishness, childishness, girlishness, immaturity, juvenility, puerility, youthfulness

adolescent 1. adj. boyish, girlish, growing, immature, juvenile, puerile, teenage, young, youthful **2.** n. juvenile, minor, teenager, youngster, youth

adopt 1. accept, appropriate, approve, assume, choose, embrace, endorse, espouse, follow, maintain, ratify, select, support, take on, take over, take up **2.** foster, take in
Antonyms (*sense 1*) abandon, abnegate, cast aside, cast off, disavow, disclaim, disown, forswear, give up, reject, renounce, repudiate, spurn, wash one's hands of

adoption 1. acceptance, approbation, appropriation, approval, assumption, choice, embracing, endorsement, espousal, following, maintenance, ratification, selection, support, taking on, taking over, taking up **2.** adopting, fosterage, fostering, taking in

adore admire, bow to, cherish, dote on, esteem, exalt, glorify, honour, idolize, love, revere, reverence, venerate, worship
Antonyms abhor, abominate, despise, detest, execrate, hate, loathe

adorn array, beautify, bedeck, deck, decorate, embellish, emblazon, enhance, enrich, garnish, grace, ornament, trim

adornment accessory, decoration, embellishment, frill, frippery, ornament, trimming

adult 1. adj. full grown, fully developed, fully grown, grown-up, mature, of age, ripe **2.** n. grown or grown-up person (man or woman), grown-up, person of mature age

advance v. **1.** accelerate, bring forward, bring up, come forward, elevate, go ahead, go forward, go on, hasten, move onward, move up, press on, proceed, progress, speed, upgrade **2.** adduce, allege, cite, offer, present, proffer, put forward, submit, suggest **3.** increase (*price*), lend, pay beforehand, raise (*price*), supply on credit ~n. **4.** advancement, betterment, breakthrough, furtherance, gain, growth, improvement, progress, promotion, step **5.** appreciation, credit, deposit, down payment, increase (*in price*), loan, prepay-

ment, retainer, rise (*in price*) **6.**
advances approach, approaches,
moves, overtures, proposals,
proposition ~*adj.* **7.** beforehand,
early, foremost, forward, in front,
leading, prior
Antonyms v. (*sense 1*) demote,
hold back, impede, move back,
regress, retard, retreat, set back,
withdraw (*sense 2*) hide, hold
back, suppress, withhold (*sense
3*) defer payment, withhold payment

advanced ahead, avant-garde,
extreme, foremost, forward,
higher, late, leading, precocious,
progressive
Antonyms backward, behind,
retarded, underdeveloped, undeveloped

advantage aid, ascendancy, asset, assistance, avail, benefit,
blessing, boon, convenience,
dominance, edge, gain, good,
help, interest, lead, precedence,
pre-eminence, profit, service,
start, superiority, sway, upper
hand, use, utility, welfare
Antonyms curse, difficulty, disadvantage, drawback, handicap,
hindrance, inconvenience

advantageous 1. dominant,
dominating, favourable, superior
2. beneficial, convenient, helpful,
of service, profitable, useful,
valuable, worthwhile
Antonyms detrimental, unfavourable, unfortunate, unhelpful,
useless

adventure *n.* chance, contingency, enterprise, experience, exploit, hazard, incident, occurrence, risk, speculation, undertaking, venture

adventurous adventuresome,
audacious, bold, dangerous,
daredevil, daring, enterprising,
foolhardy, hazardous, headstrong, intrepid, rash, reckless,
risky, temerarious (*Rare*),
venturesome
Antonyms careful, cautious,
chary, circumspect, hesitant,
prudent, tentative, timid, timorous, safe, unadventurous, wary

adverse antagonistic, conflicting,
contrary, detrimental, disadvantageous, hostile, inexpedient, inimical, injurious, inopportune,
negative, opposing, opposite, reluctant, repugnant, unfavourable,
unfortunate, unfriendly, unlucky,
unpropitious, unwilling
Antonyms advantageous, auspicious, beneficial, favourable, fortunate, helpful, lucky, opportune,
promising, propitious, suitable

adversity affliction, bad luck, calamity, catastrophe, disaster,
distress, hardship, hard times, ill-
fortune, ill-luck, misery, misfortune, mishap, reverse, sorrow,
suffering, trial, trouble, woe,
wretchedness

advertise advise, announce, apprise, blazon, declare, display,
flaunt, inform, make known, notify, plug (*Inf.*), praise, proclaim,
promote, promulgate, publicize,
publish, puff, push (*Inf.*), tout

advertisement ad (*Inf.*), advert
(*Inf.*), announcement, bill, blurb,
circular, commercial, display,
notice, placard, plug (*Inf.*), poster, promotion, publicity, puff

advice admonition, caution,
counsel, guidance, help, injunction, opinion, recommendation,
suggestion, view

advisable appropriate, apt, desirable, expedient, fit, fitting, judicious, politic, profitable, proper, prudent, recommended,
seemly, sensible, sound, suggested, suitable, wise
Antonyms ill-advised, impolitic,
improper, imprudent, inappropriate, inexpedient, injudicious,
silly, stupid, undesirable, unfitting, unprofitable, unseemly, unsound, unsuitable, unwise

advise admonish, caution, commend, counsel, enjoin, recommend, suggest, urge

adviser aide, authority, coach,
confidant, consultant, counsel,
counsellor, guide, helper, lawyer,
mentor, right-hand man, solicitor, teacher, tutor

advocate 1. *v.* advise, argue for,

campaign for, champion, countenance, defend, encourage, favour, hold a brief for (*Inf.*), justify, plead for, press for, promote, propose, recommend, speak for, support, uphold, urge 2. *n.* apologist, apostle, backer, campaigner, champion, counsellor, defender, pleader, promoter, proponent, proposer, speaker, spokesman, supporter, upholder

Antonyms *v.* contradict, oppose, resist, speak against, take a stand against, take issue with

affable amiable, amicable, approachable, benevolent, benign, civil, congenial, cordial, courteous, friendly, genial, good-humoured, good-natured, gracious, kindly, mild, obliging, pleasant, sociable, urbane, warm

affair 1. activity, business, circumstance, concern, episode, event, happening, incident, interest, matter, occurrence, proceeding, project, question, subject, transaction, undertaking 2. amour, intrigue, liaison, relationship, romance

affect 1. act on, alter, bear upon, change, concern, impinge upon, influence, interest, involve, modify, prevail over, regard, relate to, sway, transform 2. adopt, aspire to, assume, contrive, counterfeit, feign, imitate, pretend, put on, sham, simulate

affectation act, affectedness, appearance, artificiality, assumed manners, façade, fakery, false display, insincerity, mannerism, pose, pretence, pretension, pretentiousness, sham, show, simulation, unnatural imitation

affected artificial, assumed, conceited, contrived, counterfeit, feigned, insincere, la-di-da (*Inf.*), mannered, mincing, phoney (*Inf.*), pompous, precious, pretended, pretentious, put-on, sham, simulated, spurious, stiff, studied, unnatural

Antonyms genuine, natural, real, unaffected

affection amity, attachment, care, desire, feeling, fondness, friendliness, good will, inclination, kindness, liking, love, passion, propensity, tenderness, warmth

affectionate attached, caring, devoted, doting, fond, friendly, kind, loving, tender, warm, warm-hearted

Antonyms cold, cool, glacial, indifferent, stony, uncaring, undemonstrative, unfeeling, unresponsive

affinity alliance, analogy, closeness, compatibility, connection, correspondence, kinship, likeness, relation, relationship, resemblance, similarity

affirm assert, asseverate, attest, aver, avouch, avow, certify, confirm, declare, maintain, pronounce, ratify, state, swear, testify

Antonyms deny, disallow, refute, reject, renounce, repudiate, rescind

affirmation assertion, asseveration, attestation, averment, avouchment, avowal, certification, confirmation, declaration, oath, pronouncement, ratification, statement, testimony

affirmative agreeing, approving, assenting, concurring, confirming, consenting, corroborative, favourable, positive

Antonyms denying, disagreeing, disapproving, dissenting, negating, negative

afflict beset, burden, distress, grieve, harass, hurt, oppress, pain, plague, rack, smite, torment, trouble, try, wound

affluence abundance, exuberance, fortune, opulence, plenty, profusion, prosperity, riches, wealth

affluent loaded (*Sl.*), moneyed, opulent, prosperous, rich, wealthy, well-heeled (*Inf.*), well-off, well-to-do

afford bear, spare, stand, sustain

afraid alarmed, anxious, apprehensive, cowardly, faint-hearted, fearful, frightened, intimidated, nervous, reluctant, scared, suspicious, timid, timorous

Antonyms audacious, bold, fearless, inappropriate, indifferent, unafraid

after afterwards, behind, below, following, later, subsequently, succeeding, thereafter

Antonyms before, earlier, in advance, in front, previously, prior to, sooner

again 1. afresh, anew, another time, once more **2.** also, besides, furthermore, in addition, moreover, on the contrary, on the other hand

against 1. counter, hostile to, in contrast to, in defiance of, in opposition to, in the face of, opposed to, opposing, resisting, versus **2.** abutting, close up to, facing, fronting, in contact with, on, opposite to, touching, upon

age n. **1.** date, day(s), duration, epoch, era, generation, lifetime, period, span, time **2.** advancing years, decline (of life), majority, maturity, old age, senescence, senility, seniority ~v. **3.** decline, deteriorate, grow old, mature, mellow, ripen

Antonyms n. (sense 2) adolescence, boyhood, childhood, girlhood, immaturity, juvenescence, salad days, young days, youth

aged age-old, ancient, antiquated, antique, elderly, getting on, grey, hoary, old, senescent, superannuated

Antonyms adolescent, boyish, childish, girlish, immature, juvenile, young, youthful

agency bureau, business, department, office, organization

agent 1. advocate, deputy, emissary, envoy, factor, go-between, negotiator, rep (Inf.), representative, substitute, surrogate **2.** agency, cause, force, instrument, means, power, vehicle

aggravate 1. exacerbate, exaggerate, heighten, increase, inflame, intensify, magnify, make worse, worsen **2.** Inf. annoy, exasperate, get on one's nerves

(Inf.), irk, irritate, needle (Inf.), nettle, pester, provoke, tease, vex

Antonyms (sense 1) alleviate, assuage, calm, diminish, ease, improve, lessen, mitigate, smooth (sense 2) assuage, calm, pacify, please

aggression assault, attack, encroachment, injury, invasion, offence, offensive, onslaught, raid

aggressive belligerent, destructive, hostile, offensive, pugnacious, quarrelsome

Antonyms friendly, mild, peaceful, quiet, retiring, submissive

agile active, acute, alert, brisk, clever, limber, lithe, lively, nimble, prompt, quick, quick-witted, sharp, sprightly, spry, supple, swift

Antonyms awkward, clumsy, heavy, lumbering, ponderous, slow, slow-moving, stiff, ungainly, unsupple

agitate 1. beat, churn, convulse, disturb, rock, rouse, shake, stir, toss **2.** alarm, arouse, confuse, disconcert, disquiet, distract, disturb, excite, ferment, fluster, incite, inflame, perturb, rouse, ruffle, stimulate, trouble, upset, work up, worry

Antonyms (sense 2) appease, assuage, calm, calm down, mollify, pacify, placate, quiet, quieten, soothe, still, tranquillize

agitation 1. churning, convulsion, disturbance, rocking, shake, shaking, stir, stirring, tossing, turbulence **2.** alarm, arousal, clamour, commotion, confusion, discomposure, disquiet, distraction, disturbance, excitement, ferment, flurry, fluster, incitement, lather (Inf.), outcry, stimulation, trouble, tumult, turmoil, upset, worry

agitator agent provocateur, demagogue, firebrand, inciter, instigator, rabble-rouser, revolutionary, troublemaker

agony affliction, anguish, distress, misery, pain, pangs, suffering, throes, torment, torture, woe

agree 1. accede, acquiesce, admit, allow, assent, be of the same mind, comply, concede, concur, consent, engage, grant, permit, see eye to eye, settle **2.** accord, answer, chime, coincide, conform, correspond, fit, get on (together), harmonize, match, square, suit, tally
Antonyms contradict, deny, differ, disagree, dispute, dissent, refute

agreeable 1. acceptable, delightful, enjoyable, gratifying, pleasant, pleasing, pleasurable, satisfying, to one's liking, to one's taste **2.** acquiescent, amenable, approving, complying, concurring, consenting, in accord, responsive, sympathetic, well-disposed, willing
Antonyms (*sense 1*) disagreeable, displeasing, offensive, unlikeable, unpleasant

agreement 1. accord, accordance, affinity, analogy, compatibility, compliance, concert, concord, concurrence, conformity, congruity, consistency, correspondence, harmony, similarity, suitableness, union **2.** arrangement, bargain, compact, contract, covenant, deal (*Inf.*), pact, settlement, treaty, understanding
Antonyms (*sense 1*) altercation, argument, clash, conflict, difference, discord, discrepancy, disparity, dispute, dissent, dissimilarity, diversity, division, falling-out, incompatibility, incongruity, quarrel, squabble, strife, tiff, wrangle

agriculture agronomics, agronomy, cultivation, culture, farming, husbandry, tillage

aground ashore, beached, foundered, grounded, high and dry, on the rocks, stranded, stuck

ahead along, at an advantage, at the head, before, forwards, in advance, in front, in the foreground, in the lead, in the vanguard, leading, on, onwards, to the fore, winning

aid *v.* **1.** abet, assist, befriend, encourage, favour, help, promote, relieve, second, serve, subsidize, succour, support, sustain ~*n.* **2.** assistance, benefit, encouragement, favour, help, relief, service, succour, support **3.** abettor, adjutant, aide, aide-de-camp, assistant, helper, second, supporter
Antonyms *v.* detract from, harm, hinder, hurt, impede, obstruct, oppose, thwart ~*n.* hindrance

aim 1. *v.* aspire, attempt, design, direct, draw a bead (on), endeavour, intend, level, mean, plan, point, propose, purpose, resolve, seek, set one's sights on, sight, strive, take aim (at), train, try, want, wish **2.** *n.* ambition, aspiration, course, design, desire, direction, end, goal, intent, intention, mark, object, objective, plan, purpose, scheme, target, wish

aimless chance, directionless, erratic, frivolous, goalless, haphazard, pointless, purposeless, random, stray, undirected, unguided, unpredictable, vagrant, wayward
Antonyms decided, deliberate, determined, firm, fixed, positive, purposeful, resolute, resolved, settled, single-minded

air *n.* **1.** atmosphere, heavens, sky **2.** blast, breath, breeze, draught, puff, waft, whiff, wind, zephyr **3.** ambience, appearance, atmosphere, aura, bearing, character, demeanour, effect, feeling, flavour, impression, look, manner, mood, quality, style, tone **4.** circulation, display, dissemination, exposure, expression, publicity, utterance, vent, ventilation **5.** aria, lay, melody, song, tune ~*v.* **6.** aerate, expose, freshen, ventilate **7.** circulate, communicate, declare, disclose, display, disseminate, divulge, exhibit, expose, express, give vent to, make known, make public, proclaim, publicize, reveal, tell, utter, ventilate, voice

airing 1. aeration, drying, fresh~

ening, ventilation **2.** excursion, jaunt, outing, promenade, stroll, walk **3.** circulation, display, dissemination, exposure, expression, publicity, utterance, vent, ventilation

airless breathless, close, heavy, muggy, oppressive, stale, stifling, stuffy, suffocating, sultry, unventilated

Antonyms airy, blowy, breezy, draughty, fresh, gusty, light, open, spacious, well-ventilated

airs affectation, affectedness, arrogance, haughtiness, hauteur, pomposity, pretensions, superciliousness, swank (*Inf.*)

airy 1. blowy, breezy, draughty, fresh, gusty, light, lofty, open, spacious, uncluttered, well-ventilated, windy **2.** aerial, delicate, ethereal, fanciful, flimsy, illusory, imaginary, immaterial, incorporeal, insubstantial, light, vaporous, visionary, weightless, wispy **3.** animated, blithe, buoyant, cheerful, cheery, debonair, frolicsome, gay, graceful, happy, high-spirited, jaunty, light, light-hearted, lively, merry, nonchalant, sprightly

Antonyms (*sense 1*) airless, close, heavy, muggy, oppressive, stale, stifling, stuffy, suffocating, unventilated (*sense 2*) concrete, corporeal, material, real, realistic, substantial, tangible (*sense 3*) cheerless, dismal, gloomy, glum, melancholy, miserable, morose, sad

alarm *v.* **1.** daunt, dismay, distress, frighten, give (someone) a turn (*Inf.*), panic, put the wind up (someone) (*Inf.*), scare, startle, terrify, unnerve **2.** alert, arouse, signal, warn ~*n.* **3.** anxiety, apprehension, consternation, dismay, distress, fear, fright, nervousness, panic, scare, terror, trepidation, unease, uneasiness **4.** alarm-bell, alert, bell, danger signal, distress signal, siren, tocsin, warning

Antonyms *v.* (*sense 1*) assure, calm, comfort, reassure, relieve,

soothe ~*n.* (*sense 3*) calm, calmness, composure, sang-froid, serenity

alarming daunting, dismaying, distressing, disturbing, dreadful, frightening, scaring, shocking, startling, terrifying, unnerving

alcoholic *n.* bibber, boozer (*Inf.*), dipsomaniac, drunk, drunkard, hard drinker, inebriate, soak (*Inf.*), sot, sponge (*Inf.*), tippler, toper, tosspot (*Inf.*), wino (*Inf.*)

alert 1. *adj.* active, agile, attentive, brisk, careful, circumspect, heedful, lively, nimble, observant, on guard, on one's toes, on the ball (*Inf.*), on the lookout, on the watch, perceptive, quick, ready, spirited, sprightly, vigilant, wary, watchful, wide-awake **2.** *n.* alarm, signal, siren, warning **3.** *v.* alarm, forewarn, inform, notify, signal, warn

Antonyms *adj.* careless, heedless, inactive, languid, lethargic, listless, oblivious, slow, unaware, unconcerned, unwary ~*n.* all clear ~*v.* lull

alias 1. *adv.* also called, also known as, otherwise, otherwise known as **2.** *n.* assumed name, nom de guerre, nom de plume, pen name, pseudonym, stage name

alibi defence, excuse, explanation, justification, plea, pretext, reason

alien 1. *adj.* adverse, conflicting, contrary, estranged, exotic, foreign, inappropriate, incompatible, incongruous, not native, not naturalized, opposed, outlandish, remote, repugnant, separated, strange, unfamiliar **2.** *n.* foreigner, newcomer, outsider, stranger

alight[1] *v.* come down, come to rest, descend, disembark, dismount, get down, get off, land, light, perch, settle, touch down

Antonyms ascend, climb, float up, fly up, go up, lift off, mount, move up, rise, scale, soar, take off

alight[2] *adj.* ablaze, aflame, blazing, burning, fiery, flaming, flaring, ignited, lighted, lit, on fire

alike *adj.* akin, analogous, corresponding, duplicate, equal, equivalent, even, identical, parallel, resembling, similar, the same, uniform
Antonyms different, dissimilar, diverse, separate, unlike

alive 1. animate, breathing, having life, in the land of the living (*Inf.*), living, subsisting 2. active, existent, existing, extant, functioning, in existence, in force, operative, unquenched 3. active, alert, animated, awake, brisk, cheerful, eager, energetic, full of life, lively, quick, spirited, sprightly, spry, vigorous, vital, vivacious, zestful
Antonyms (*sense 1*) dead, deceased, departed, expired, extinct, gone, inanimate, lifeless (*sense 2*) extinct, inactive, inoperative, lost (*sense 3*) apathetic, dull, inactive, lifeless, spiritless

all *adj.* 1. every bit of, the complete, the entire, the sum of, the totality of, the total of, the whole of 2. each, each and every, every, every one of, every single 3. complete, entire, full, greatest, perfect, total, utter ~*n.* 4. aggregate, entirety, everything, sum, sum total, total, total amount, totality, utmost, whole, whole amount ~*adv.* 5. altogether, completely, entirely, fully, totally, utterly, wholly

allergic affected by, hypersensitive, sensitive, sensitized, susceptible

alley alleyway, backstreet, lane, passage, passageway, pathway, walk

alliance affiliation, affinity, agreement, association, coalition, combination, compact, concordat, confederacy, confederation, connection, federation, league, marriage, pact, partnership, treaty, union
Antonyms alienation, breach, break, disaffection, dissociation, disunion, disunity, division, rupture, separation, severance, split, split-up

allied affiliated, amalgamated, associated, bound, combined, confederate, connected, hand in glove (*Inf.*), in cahoots (*U.S. inf.*), in league, joined, joint, kindred, leagued, linked, married, related, unified, united, wed

allot allocate, apportion, appropriate, assign, budget, designate, earmark, mete, set aside, share out

allotment 1. allocation, allowance, apportionment, appropriation, grant, lot, measure, portion, quota, ration, share, stint 2. kitchen garden, patch, plot, tract

all-out complete, determined, exhaustive, full, full-scale, maximum, optimum, resolute, supreme, thorough, thoroughgoing, total, undivided, unlimited, unremitting, unrestrained, unstinted, utmost
Antonyms careless, cursory, half-hearted, negligent, off-hand, perfunctory, unenthusiastic

allow 1. acknowledge, acquiesce, admit, concede, confess, grant, own 2. approve, authorize, bear, brook, endure, give leave, let, permit, put up with (*Inf.*), sanction, stand, suffer, tolerate
Antonyms (*sense 1*) contradict, deny, disagree with, gainsay, oppose (*sense 2*) ban, disallow, forbid, prohibit, proscribe, refuse

allowance 1. allocation, allotment, amount, annuity, apportionment, grant, lot, measure, pension, portion, quota, ration, remittance, share, stint, stipend, subsidy 2. admission, concession, sanction, sufferance, toleration 3. concession, deduction, discount, rebate, reduction

allow for arrange for, consider, foresee, keep in mind, make allowances for, make concessions for, make provision for, plan for, provide for, set (something) aside for, take into account, take into consideration

all right 1. *adj.* acceptable, adequate, average, fair, O.K. (*Inf.*), passable, satisfactory, standard,

unobjectionable 2. *adv.* accept-
ably, adequately, O.K. (*Inf.*),
passably, satisfactorily, unobjec-
tionably, well enough

Antonyms *adj.* bad, inadequate,
not good enough, not up to
scratch (*Inf.*), objectionable,
poor, unacceptable, unsatisfactory

allusion casual remark, glance,
hint, implication, indirect reference, innuendo, insinuation, intimation, mention, suggestion

ally *n.* abettor, accessory, accomplice, associate, coadjutor, collaborator, colleague, confederate, co-worker, friend, helper,
partner

Antonyms adversary, antagonist,
competitor, enemy, foe, opponent, rival

almighty absolute, all-powerful,
invincible, omnipotent, supreme,
unlimited

almost about, all but, approximately, as good as, close to, just
about, nearly, not far from, not
quite, on the brink of, practically,
virtually, well-nigh

alone abandoned, apart, by itself,
by oneself, deserted, desolate,
detached, forlorn, forsaken, isolated, lonely, lonesome, only,
separate, single, single-handed,
sole, solitary, unaccompanied,
unaided, unassisted, unattended,
uncombined, unconnected, unescorted

Antonyms accompanied, aided,
among others, assisted, escorted,
helped, jointly, together

aloud audibly, clearly, distinctly,
intelligibly, out loud, plainly

already as of now, at present,
before now, by now, by that time,
by then, by this time, even now,
heretofore, just now, previously

also additionally, along with, and,
as well, as well as, besides, further, furthermore, in addition,
including, into the bargain,
moreover, on top of that, plus, to
boot, too

alter adapt, adjust, amend,
change, convert, diversify,
metamorphose, modify, recast,
reform, remodel, reshape, revise,
shift, transform, transmute, turn,
vary

alteration adaptation, adjustment, amendment, change, conversion, difference, diversification, metamorphosis, modification, reformation, remodelling, reshaping, revision, shift,
transformation, transmutation,
variance, variation

alternate 1. *v.* act reciprocally,
alter, change, follow in turn, follow one another, interchange,
intersperse, oscillate, rotate,
substitute, take turns, vary 2. *adj.*
alternating, every other, every
second, interchanging, rotating

alternative *n.* choice, option,
other (*of two*), preference, recourse, selection, substitute

although albeit, despite the fact
that, even if, even supposing,
even though, notwithstanding,
though, while

altogether 1. absolutely, completely, fully, perfectly, quite,
thoroughly, totally, utterly, wholly 2. all in all, all things considered, as a whole, collectively,
generally, in general, *in toto*, on
the whole 3. all told, everything
included, in all, in sum, *in toto*,
taken together

Antonyms (*sense 1*) halfway, incompletely, in part, in some
measure, not fully, partially,
relatively, slightly, somewhat, to
a certain degree *or* extent, up to
a certain point

always consistently, constantly,
continually, eternally, ever,
everlastingly, evermore, every
time, forever, *in perpetuum*, invariably, perpetually, repeatedly,
unceasingly, without exception

Antonyms hardly, hardly ever,
infrequently, once in a blue
moon, once in a while, only now
and then, on rare occasions,
rarely, scarcely ever, seldom

amass accumulate, aggregate,
assemble, collect, compile, gar-

ner, gather, heap up, hoard, pile up, rake up, scrape together

amateur dabbler, dilettante, layman, nonprofessional

amaze alarm, astonish, astound, bewilder, bowl over (*Inf.*), confound, daze, dumbfound, electrify, flabbergast, shock, stagger, startle, stun, stupefy, surprise

amazement admiration, astonishment, bewilderment, confusion, marvel, perplexity, shock, stupefaction, surprise, wonder

ambassador agent, consul, deputy, diplomat, emissary, envoy, legate, minister, plenipotentiary, representative

ambiguous cryptic, doubtful, dubious, enigmatic, enigmatical, equivocal, inconclusive, indefinite, indeterminate, obscure, puzzling, uncertain, unclear, vague
Antonyms clear, definite, explicit, obvious, plain, simple, specific, unequivocal, unmistakable, unquestionable

ambition 1. aspiration, avidity, desire, drive, eagerness, enterprise, get-up-and-go (*Inf.*), hankering, longing, striving, yearning, zeal 2. aim, aspiration, desire, dream, end, goal, hope, intent, objective, purpose, wish

ambitious aspiring, avid, desirous, driving, eager, enterprising, hopeful, intent, purposeful, striving, zealous
Antonyms apathetic, lazy, unambitious, unaspiring

ambush *n.* ambuscade, concealment, cover, hiding, hiding place, lying in wait, retreat, shelter, trap, waylaying

amenable able to be influenced, acquiescent, agreeable, open, persuadable, responsive, susceptible, tractable
Antonyms inflexible, intractable, mulish, obdurate, obstinate, pigheaded, recalcitrant, stiff-necked, stubborn, unbending, unyielding

amend alter, ameliorate, better, change, correct, enhance, fix, improve, mend, modify, rectify, reform, remedy, repair, revise

amendment 1. alteration, amelioration, betterment, change, correction, enhancement, improvement, mending, modification, rectification, reform, remedy, repair, revision 2. addendum, addition, adjunct, alteration, attachment, clarification

amenity advantage, comfort, convenience, facility, service

amiable affable, agreeable, attractive, benign, charming, cheerful, delightful, engaging, friendly, genial, good-humoured, good-natured, kind, kindly, lovable, obliging, pleasant, pleasing, sociable, sweet-tempered, winning, winsome

ammunition armaments, cartridges, explosives, materiel, munitions, powder, rounds, shells, shot, shot and shell

among, amongst 1. amid, in association with, in the middle of, in the midst of, in the thick of, midst, surrounded by, together with, with 2. between, to each of 3. in the class of, in the company of, in the group of, in the number of, out of 4. by all of, by the joint action of, by the whole of, mutually, with one another

amount 1. bulk, expanse, extent, lot, magnitude, mass, measure, number, quantity, supply, volume 2. addition, aggregate, entirety, extent, lot, sum, sum total, total, whole

amount to add up to, aggregate, become, come to, develop into, equal, grow, mean, purport, total

ample abounding, abundant, big, bountiful, broad, capacious, commodious, copious, enough and to spare, expansive, extensive, full, generous, great, large, lavish, liberal, plenteous, plentiful, plenty, profuse, rich, roomy, spacious, substantial, unrestricted, voluminous, wide

amuse beguile, charm, cheer, delight, divert, enliven, entertain, gladden, gratify, interest, occupy,

please, recreate, regale, tickle (*Inf.*)
Antonyms be tedious, bore, jade, pall on, send to sleep, tire, weary

amusement 1. beguilement, cheer, delight, diversion, enjoyment, entertainment, fun, gladdening, gratification, hilarity, interest, laughter, merriment, mirth, pleasing, pleasure, recreation, regalement, sport 2. distraction, diversion, entertainment, game, hobby, joke, lark, pastime, prank, recreation, sport
Antonyms boredom, displeasure, monotony, sadness, tedium

amusing charming, cheerful, cheering, comical, delightful, diverting, droll, enjoyable, entertaining, facetious, funny, gladdening, gratifying, humorous, interesting, jocular, laughable, lively, merry, pleasant, pleasing, rib-tickling, witty

analyse 1. assay, estimate, evaluate, examine, interpret, investigate, judge, test 2. anatomize, break down, consider, dissect, dissolve, divide, resolve, separate, study, think through

analysis 1. anatomization, anatomy, assay, breakdown, dissection, dissolution, division, enquiry, examination, investigation, resolution, scrutiny, separation, sifting, test 2. estimation, evaluation, finding, interpretation, judgment, opinion, reasoning, study

ancestor forebear, forefather, forerunner, precursor, predecessor, progenitor
Antonyms descendant, inheritor, issue, offspring, progeny, successor

ancient aged, age-old, antediluvian, antiquated, antique, archaic, bygone, early, hoary, obsolete, old, olden, old-fashioned, outmoded, out-of-date, primeval, primordial, superannuated, timeworn
Antonyms current, fresh, in vogue, late, modern, modish, new, newfangled, new-fashioned,

novel, recent, state-of-the-art, up-to-date, with-it (*Sl.*), young

and along with, also, as well as, furthermore, in addition to, including, moreover, plus, together with

anecdote reminiscence, short story, sketch, story, tale, yarn

angel archangel, cherub, divine messenger, guardian spirit, seraph, spiritual being

anger 1. *n.* annoyance, antagonism, choler, displeasure, exasperation, fury, ill humour, ill temper, indignation, ire, irritability, irritation, outrage, passion, pique, rage, resentment, spleen, temper, vexation, wrath 2. *v.* affront, annoy, antagonize, displease, enrage, exasperate, excite, fret, gall, incense, infuriate, irritate, madden, nettle, offend, outrage, pique, provoke, rile, vex
Antonyms *n.* acceptance, amiability, approval, calmness, forgiveness, goodwill, gratification, liking, patience, peace, pleasure ~*v.* appease, calm, pacify, placate, please, soothe

angle *n.* 1. bend, corner, crook, crotch, cusp, edge, elbow, intersection, knee, nook, point 2. approach, aspect, outlook, perspective, point of view, position, side, slant, standpoint, viewpoint ~*v.* 3. cast, fish

angry annoyed, antagonized, choleric, displeased, enraged, exasperated, furious, heated, hot, hot under the collar (*Inf.*), illtempered, incensed, indignant, infuriated, irascible, irate, ireful, irritable, irritated, mad (*Inf.*), nettled, outraged, passionate, piqued, provoked, raging, resentful, riled, splenetic, tumultuous, uptight (*Sl.*), wrathful
Antonyms agreeable, amiable, calm, friendly, gratified, happy, loving, mild, peaceful, pleasant, pleased

animal 1. *n.* beast, brute, creature 2. *adj.* bestial, bodily, brutish, carnal, fleshly, gross, physical, sensual

animate v. activate, embolden, encourage, energize, enliven, excite, fire, gladden, impel, incite, inspire, inspirit, instigate, invigorate, kindle, move, quicken, revive, rouse, spark, spur, stimulate, stir, urge, vitalize, vivify

Antonyms check, curb, deaden, deter, devitalize, discourage, dull, inhibit, kill, make lifeless, put a damper on, restrain

animosity acrimony, animus, antagonism, antipathy, bad blood, bitterness, enmity, hate, hatred, hostility, ill will, malevolence, malice, malignity, rancour, resentment, virulence

annihilate abolish, destroy, eradicate, erase, exterminate, extinguish, extirpate, liquidate, nullify, obliterate, root out, wipe out

announce advertise, broadcast, declare, disclose, divulge, give out, intimate, make known, proclaim, promulgate, propound, publish, report, reveal, tell

Antonyms bury, conceal, cover up, hide, hold back, hush, hush up, keep back, keep quiet, keep secret, suppress, withhold

announcement advertisement, broadcast, bulletin, communiqué, declaration, disclosure, divulgence, intimation, proclamation, promulgation, publication, report, revelation, statement

annoy anger, badger, bedevil, bore, bother, bug (*Inf.*), displease, disturb, exasperate, gall, get (*Inf.*), harass, harry, incommode, irk, irritate, madden, molest, needle (*Inf.*), nettle, peeve, pester, plague, provoke, rile, ruffle, tease, trouble, vex

Antonyms appease, calm, comfort, console, mollify, solace, soothe

annoyance aggravation, anger, bedevilment, bother, displeasure, disturbance, exasperation, har-

assment, irritation, nuisance, provocation, trouble, vexation

annoying aggravating, bedevilling, boring, bothersome, displeasing, disturbing, exasperating, galling, harassing, irksome, irritating, maddening, peeving (*Inf.*), provoking, teasing, troublesome, vexatious

Antonyms agreeable, amusing, charming, delightful, diverting, enjoyable, entertaining, gratifying, pleasant

anomaly aberration, abnormality, departure, deviation, eccentricity, exception, incongruity, inconsistency, irregularity, oddity, peculiarity, rarity

anonymous incognito, innominate, nameless, unacknowledged, unattested, unauthenticated, uncredited, unidentified, unknown, unnamed, unsigned

Antonyms accredited, acknowledged, attested, authenticated, credited, identified, known, named, signed

answer 1. n. acknowledgment, comeback, defence, explanation, plea, reaction, refutation, rejoinder, reply, report, resolution, response, retort, return, riposte, solution, vindication 2. v. acknowledge, explain, react, refute, rejoin, reply, resolve, respond, retort, return, solve

Antonyms n. inquiry, interrogation, query, question ~v. ask, inquire, interrogate, query, question

answerable accountable, amenable, chargeable, liable, responsible, subject, to blame

answer for be accountable for, be answerable for, be chargeable for, be liable for, be responsible for, be to blame for, take the rap for (*Sl.*)

antagonism antipathy, competition, conflict, contention, discord, dissension, friction, hostility, opposition, rivalry

Antonyms accord, agreement, amity, friendship, harmony, love, peacefulness, sympathy

antagonize alienate, anger, annoy, disaffect, estrange, insult, irritate, offend, repel, rub (someone) up the wrong way (*Inf.*)
Antonyms appease, calm, conciliate, disarm, mollify, pacify, placate, propitiate, soothe, win over

anthem canticle, chant, chorale, hymn, psalm

anticipate 1. apprehend, await, count upon, expect, forecast, foresee, foretell, hope for, look for, look forward to, predict, prepare for **2.** antedate, beat (someone) to it (*Inf.*), forestall, intercept, prevent

anticipation apprehension, awaiting, expectancy, expectation, foresight, foretaste, forethought, hope, preconception, premonition, prescience, presentiment

anticlimax bathos, comedown (*Inf.*), disappointment, letdown
Antonyms climax, culmination, height, highlight, high point, peak, summit, top, zenith

antipathy abhorrence, animosity, animus, antagonism, aversion, bad blood, contrariety, disgust, dislike, distaste, enmity, hatred, hostility, ill will, incompatibility, loathing, opposition, rancour, repugnance, repulsion

antique *adj.* **1.** aged, ancient, elderly, old, superannuated **2.** archaic, obsolete, old-fashioned, outdated ~*n.* **3.** bygone, heirloom, object of virtu, relic

antiquity 1. age, ancientness, elderliness, old age, oldness **2.** ancient times, distant past, olden days, time immemorial

antiseptic 1. *adj.* aseptic, clean, germ-free, hygienic, pure, sanitary, sterile, uncontaminated, unpolluted **2.** *n.* bactericide, disinfectant, germicide, purifier
Antonyms *adj.* contaminated, dirty, impure, infected, insanitary, polluted, septic, unhygienic

antisocial alienated, asocial, misanthropic, reserved, retiring, uncommunicative, unfriendly, unsociable, withdrawn
Antonyms companionable, friendly, gregarious, philanthropic, sociable, social

anxiety angst, apprehension, care, concern, disquiet, disquietude, distress, foreboding, fretfulness, misgiving, nervousness, restlessness, solicitude, suspense, tension, unease, uneasiness, watchfulness, worry
Antonyms assurance, calmness, confidence, contentment, relief, security, serenity

anxious apprehensive, careful, concerned, disquieted, distressed, disturbed, fearful, fretful, in suspense, nervous, overwrought, restless, solicitous, taut, tense, troubled, uneasy, unquiet (*Chiefly literary*), watchful, worried
Antonyms assured, calm, certain, collected, composed, confident, cool, nonchalant, unperturbed

apart 1. afar, alone, aloof, aside, away, by itself, by oneself, cut off, distant, distinct, divorced, excluded, independent, independently, isolated, piecemeal, separate, separated, separately, singly, to itself, to oneself, on one side **2.** asunder, in bits, in pieces, into parts, to bits, to pieces **3.** **apart from** aside from, besides, but, except for, excluding, not counting, other than, save

apartment accommodation, chambers, compartment, flat, living quarters, penthouse, quarters, room, rooms, suite

apathetic cold, cool, emotionless, impassive, indifferent, insensible, listless, passive, phlegmatic, sluggish, stoic, stoical, torpid, unconcerned, unemotional, unfeeling, uninterested, unmoved, unresponsive
Antonyms active, anxious, aroused, bothered, caring, committed, concerned, emotional, enthusiastic, excited, interested, moved, passionate, responsive, troubled, worried, zealous

apathy coldness, coolness, emotionlessness, impassibility, impassivity, indifference, insensibility, listlessness, passiveness, passivity, phlegm, sluggishness, stoicism, torpor, unconcern, unfeelingness, uninterestedness, unresponsiveness
Antonyms anxiety, attention, concern, emotion, enthusiasm, feeling, interest, zeal

apologetic contrite, penitent, regretful, remorseful, rueful, sorry

apologize ask forgiveness, beg pardon, express regret, say one is sorry, say sorry

apology acknowledgment, confession, defence, excuse, explanation, extenuation, justification, plea, vindication

appal alarm, astound, daunt, dishearten, dismay, frighten, harrow, horrify, intimidate, outrage, petrify, scare, shock, terrify, unnerve

appalling alarming, astounding, awful, daunting, dire, disheartening, dismaying, dreadful, fearful, frightening, frightful, ghastly, grim, harrowing, hideous, horrible, horrid, horrific, horrifying, intimidating, petrifying, scaring, shocking, terrible, terrifying, unnerving

apparatus appliance, contraption (*Inf.*), device, equipment, gear, implements, machine, machinery, materials, means, mechanism, outfit, tackle, tools, utensils

apparent clear, conspicuous, discernible, distinct, evident, indubitable, manifest, marked, obvious, open, overt, patent, plain, understandable, unmistakable, visible
Antonyms ambiguous, doubtful, dubious, hazy, indefinite, indistinct, obscure, uncertain, unclear, vague

apparently it appears that, it seems that, on the face of it, ostensibly, outwardly, seemingly, speciously, superficially

apparition 1. appearance, manifestation, materialization, presence, vision, visitation 2. chimera, ghost, phantom, revenant, shade (*Literary*), spectre, spirit, spook (*Inf.*), visitant, wraith

appeal *n.* 1. adjuration, application, entreaty, invocation, petition, plea, prayer, request, solicitation, suit, supplication 2. allure, attraction, attractiveness, beauty, charm, engagingness, fascination, interestingness, pleasingness ~*v.* 3. adjure, apply, ask, beg, beseech, call, call upon, entreat, implore, petition, plead, pray, refer, request, resort to, solicit, sue, supplicate 4. allure, attract, charm, engage, entice, fascinate, interest, invite, please, tempt
Antonyms *n.* (*sense 1*) denial, refusal, rejection, repudiation (*sense 2*) repulsiveness ~*v.* (*sense 3*) deny, refuse, reject, repudiate (*sense 4*) alienate, bore, repulse, revolt

appear 1. arise, arrive, attend, be present, come forth, come into sight, come into view, come out, come to light, crop up (*Inf.*), develop, emerge, issue, loom, materialize, occur, show (*Sl.*), show up (*Inf.*), surface, turn out, turn up 2. look (*like or* as if), occur, seem, strike one as 3. be apparent, be clear, be evident, be manifest, be obvious, be patent, be plain 4. become available, be created, be developed, be invented, be published, come into being, come into existence, come out 5. act, be exhibited, come on, come onstage, enter, perform, play, play a part, take part
Antonyms be doubtful, be unclear, disappear, vanish

appearance 1. advent, appearing, arrival, coming, debut, emergence, introduction, presence, showing up (*Inf.*), turning up 2. air, aspect, bearing, demeanour, expression, face, figure, form, image, look, looks, manner, mien (*Literary*) 3. front, guise, illusion, image, impression, outward show, pretence, semblance

appendix addendum, addition, adjunct, appendage, codicil, postscript, supplement

appetite appetence, appetency, craving, demand, desire, hankering, hunger, inclination, liking, longing, passion, proclivity, propensity, relish, stomach, taste, willingness, yearning, zeal, zest

appetizing appealing, delicious, inviting, mouthwatering, palatable, savoury, scrumptious (*Inf.*), succulent, tasty, tempting

applaud acclaim, approve, cheer, clap, commend, compliment, encourage, eulogize, extol, laud, magnify (*Archaic*), praise
Antonyms boo, censure, condemn, criticize, decry, deprecate, deride, disparage, hiss, pan (*Sl.*), ridicule, run down, slag (*Sl.*), vilify

applause acclaim, acclamation, accolade, approbation, approval, cheering, cheers, commendation, eulogizing, hand, hand-clapping, laudation, ovation, plaudit, praise

appliance apparatus, device, gadget, implement, instrument, machine, mechanism, tool

applicable apposite, appropriate, apropos, apt, befitting, fit, fitting, germane, pertinent, relevant, suitable, suited, to the point, to the purpose, useful

applicant aspirant, candidate, claimant, inquirer, petitioner, postulant, suitor, suppliant

application 1. appositeness, exercise, function, germaneness, pertinence, practice, purpose, relevance, use, value 2. appeal, claim, inquiry, petition, request, requisition, solicitation, suit 3. assiduity, attention, attentiveness, commitment, dedication, diligence, effort, hard work, industry, perseverance, study

apply 1. administer, assign, bring into play, bring to bear, carry out, employ, engage, execute, exercise, implement, practise, put to use, use, utilize 2. apper-

tain, be applicable, be appropriate, bear upon, be fitting, be relevant, fit, pertain, refer, relate, suit 3. anoint, bring into contact with, cover with, lay on, paint, place, put on, smear, spread on, touch to 4. appeal, claim, inquire, make application, petition, put in, request, requisition, solicit, sue 5. address, be assiduous, be diligent, be industrious, buckle down (*Inf.*), commit, concentrate, dedicate, devote, direct, give, make an effort, pay attention, persevere, study, try, work hard

appoint 1. allot, arrange, assign, choose, decide, designate, determine, establish, fix, set, settle 2. assign, choose, commission, delegate, elect, install, name, nominate, select
Antonyms (*sense 1*) cancel (*sense 2*) discharge, dismiss, fire, give the sack, sack

appointed 1. allotted, arranged, assigned, chosen, decided, designated, determined, established, fixed, set, settled 2. assigned, chosen, commissioned, delegated, elected, installed, named, nominated, selected

appointment 1. arrangement, assignation, consultation, date, engagement, interview, meeting, rendezvous, session, tryst (*Archaic*) 2. assignment, berth (*Inf.*), job, office, place, position, post, situation, station

apportion allocate, allot, assign, deal, dispense, distribute, divide, dole out, measure out, mete out, parcel out, ration out, share

appreciate 1. be appreciative, be grateful for, be indebted, be obliged, be thankful for, give thanks for 2. acknowledge, be alive to, be aware (cognizant, conscious) of, comprehend, estimate, know, perceive, realize, recognize, sympathize with, take account of, understand 3. admire, cherish, enjoy, esteem, like, prize, rate highly, regard, relish, respect, savour, treasure, value 4.

enhance, gain, grow, improve, increase, inflate, raise the value of, rise

Antonyms (*sense 1*) be ungrateful (*sense 2*) be unaware, misunderstand, underrate (*sense 3*) belittle, disdain, disparage, scorn (*sense 4*) deflate, depreciate, devaluate, fall

appreciation 1. acknowledgment, gratefulness, gratitude, indebtedness, obligation, thankfulness, thanks 2. admiration, appraisal, assessment, awareness, cognizance, comprehension, enjoyment, esteem, estimation, knowledge, liking, perception, realization, recognition, regard, relish, respect, responsiveness, sensitivity, sympathy, understanding, valuation 3. enhancement, gain, growth, improvement, increase, inflation, rise 4. acclamation, criticism, critique, notice, praise, review, tribute

Antonyms (*sense 1*) ingratitude (*sense 2*) antipathy, dislike, ignorance, incomprehension (*sense 3*) decline, depreciation, devaluation, fall

appreciative 1. beholden, grateful, indebted, obliged, thankful 2. admiring, aware, cognizant, conscious, enthusiastic, in the know (*Inf.*), knowledgeable, mindful, perceptive, pleased, regardful, respectful, responsive, sensitive, supportive, sympathetic, understanding

apprehend 1. arrest, bust (*Inf.*), capture, catch, collar (*Inf.*), nab (*Inf.*), nick (*Sl.*), pinch (*Inf.*), run in (*Sl.*), seize, take, take prisoner 2. appreciate, believe, comprehend, conceive, grasp, imagine, know, perceive, realize, recognize, think, understand

apprehension 1. alarm, anxiety, apprehensiveness, concern, disquiet, doubt, dread, fear, foreboding, misgiving, mistrust, premonition, suspicion, unease, uneasiness, worry 2. arrest, capture, catching, seizure, taking 3. awareness, comprehension,

grasp, intellect, intelligence, ken, knowledge, perception, understanding 4. belief, concept, conception, conjecture, idea, impression, notion, opinion, sentiment, thought, view

Antonyms (*sense 1*) assurance, composure, confidence, nonchalance, serenity, unconcern (*sense 2*) discharge, liberation, release (*sense 3*) incomprehension

apprehensive afraid, alarmed, anxious, concerned, disquieted, doubtful, fearful, foreboding, mistrustful, suspicious, uneasy, worried

Antonyms assured, at ease, composed, confident, nonchalant, unafraid

apprentice beginner, learner, neophyte, novice, probationer, pupil, student, tyro

Antonyms ace (*Inf.*), adept, dab hand (*Inf.*), expert, master, past master, pro

approach v. 1. advance, catch up, come close, come near, come to, draw near, gain on, meet, move towards, near, push forward, reach 2. appeal to, apply to, broach the matter with, make advances to, make a proposal to, make overtures to, sound out 3. approximate, be comparable to, be like, come close to, come near to, compare with, resemble ~n. 4. access, advance, advent, arrival, avenue, coming, drawing near, entrance, nearing, passage, road, way 5. approximation, likeness, semblance 6. *Often plural* advance, appeal, application, invitation, offer, overture, proposal, proposition 7. attitude, course, manner, means, method, mode, modus operandi, procedure, style, technique, way

appropriate *adj.* 1. adapted, applicable, apposite, appurtenant, apropos, apt, becoming, befitting, belonging, congruous, correct, felicitous, fit, fitting, germane, meet (*Archaic*), opportune, pertinent, proper, relevant, right, seemly, suitable, to the point, to the purpose, well-suited, well-timed ~ *v.* **2.** annex, arrogate, assume, commandeer, confiscate, expropriate, impound, preempt, seize, take, take over, take possession of, usurp **3.** embezzle, filch, misappropriate, pilfer, pocket, steal

Antonyms *adj.* improper, inappropriate, incompatible, incorrect, inopportune, irrelevant, unfitting, unsuitable, untimely ~ *v.* cede, donate, give, relinquish, withhold

approval 1. acquiescence, agreement, assent, authorization, blessing, compliance, concurrence, confirmation, consent, countenance, endorsement, imprimatur, leave, licence, mandate, O.K. (*Inf.*), permission, ratification, recommendation, sanction, the go-ahead (*Inf.*), the green light (*Inf.*), validation **2.** acclaim, admiration, applause, appreciation, approbation, commendation, esteem, favour, good opinion, liking, praise, regard, respect

Antonyms disapproval, dislike, disparagement, displeasure, dissatisfaction, objection

approve 1. acclaim, admire, applaud, appreciate, be pleased with, commend, esteem, favour, have a good opinion of, like, praise, regard highly, respect, think highly of **2.** accede to, accept, advocate, agree to, allow, assent to, authorize, bless, concur in, confirm, consent to, countenance, endorse, give the go-ahead (*Inf.*), give the green light (*Inf.*), go along with, mandate, O.K. (*Inf.*), pass, permit, ratify, recommend, sanction, second, subscribe to, uphold, validate

Antonyms (*sense 1*) blame, censure, condemn, deplore, deprecate, disapprove, dislike, find unacceptable, frown on, look down one's nose at (*Inf.*), object to, take exception to (*sense 2*) disallow, discountenance, veto

approximate *adj.* **1.** almost accu-

rate, almost exact, close, near **2.** estimated, inexact, loose, rough **3.** approach, border on, come close, come near, reach, resemble, touch, verge on

Antonyms *adj.* (*senses 1 & 2*) accurate, correct, definite, exact, precise, specific

approximately about, almost, around, circa (*used with dates*), close to, generally, in the neighbourhood of, in the region of, in the vicinity of, just about, loosely, more or less, nearly, not far off, relatively, roughly

approximation conjecture, estimate, estimation, guess, guesswork, rough calculation, rough idea

apt 1. applicable, apposite, appropriate, apropos, befitting, correct, fit, fitting, germane, meet (*Archaic*), pertinent, proper, relevant, seemly, suitable, timely, to the point, to the purpose **2.** disposed, given, inclined, liable, likely, of a mind, prone, ready **3.** astute, bright, clever, expert, gifted, ingenious, intelligent, prompt, quick, sharp, skilful, smart, talented, teachable

Antonyms (*sense 1*) ill-fitted, ill-suited, ill-timed, improper, inapplicable, inapposite, inappropriate, infelicitous, inopportune, irrelevant, unsuitable, untimely (*sense 3*) awkward, clumsy, dull, gauche, incompetent, inept, inexpert, maladroit, slow, stupid

arbitrary capricious, chance, discretionary, erratic, fanciful, inconsistent, optional, personal, random, subjective, unreasonable, whimsical, wilful

Antonyms consistent, judicious, logical, objective, rational, reasonable, reasoned, sensible, sound

arbitrate adjudge, adjudicate, decide, determine, judge, pass judgment, referee, settle, sit in judgment, umpire

arbitration adjudication, arbitrament, decision, determination, judgment, settlement

arbitrator adjudicator, arbiter, judge, referee, umpire

arc arch, bend, bow, crescent, curve, half-moon

arch n. archway, curve, dome, span, vault

archetype classic, exemplar, form, ideal, model, original, paradigm, pattern, prime example, prototype, standard

architect designer, master builder, planner

archives annals, chronicles, documents, papers, records, registers, rolls

ardent avid, eager, enthusiastic, fervent, fervid, fierce, fiery, hot, hot-blooded, impassioned, intense, keen, lusty, passionate, spirited, vehement, warm, warm-blooded, zealous

ardour avidity, devotion, eagerness, earnestness, enthusiasm, feeling, fervour, fierceness, fire, heat, intensity, keenness, passion, spirit, vehemence, warmth, zeal

arduous backbreaking, burdensome, difficult, exhausting, fatiguing, formidable, gruelling, hard, harsh, heavy, laborious, onerous, painful, punishing, rigorous, severe, steep, strenuous, taxing, tiring, toilsome, tough, troublesome, trying

area 1. district, domain, locality, neighbourhood, patch, plot, realm, region, sector, sphere, stretch, territory, tract, zone 2. part, portion, section, sector 3. sunken space, yard

arena 1. amphitheatre, bowl, coliseum, field, ground, park (*Inf.*), ring, stadium, stage 2. area, battlefield, battleground, domain, field, field of conflict, lists, province, realm, scene, scope, sector, sphere, territory, theatre

argue 1. altercate, bandy words, bicker, disagree, dispute, fall out (*Inf.*), feud, fight, have an argument, quarrel, squabble, wrangle 2. assert, claim, contend, controvert, debate, discuss, dispute, ex-

postulate, hold, maintain, plead, question, reason, remonstrate 3. demonstrate, denote, display, evince, exhibit, imply, indicate, manifest, point to, show, suggest

argument 1. altercation, barney (*Inf.*), bickering, clash, controversy, difference of opinion, disagreement, dispute, falling out (*Inf.*), feud, fight, quarrel, row, squabble, wrangle 2. assertion, claim, contention, debate, discussion, dispute, expostulation, plea, pleading, questioning, remonstrance, remonstration 3. argumentation, case, defence, dialectic, ground(s), line of reasoning, logic, polemic, reason, reasoning
Antonyms (*senses 1 & 2*) accord, agreement, concurrence, rebuttal, refutation, response

argumentative belligerent, combative, contentious, contrary, disputatious, litigious, opinionated, quarrelsome
Antonyms accommodating, amenable, complaisant, compliant, conciliatory, easy-going, obliging

arid barren, desert, dried up, dry, moistureless, parched, sterile, waterless
Antonyms fertile, fruitful, lush, rich, verdant

arise 1. appear, begin, come into being, come to light, commence, crop up (*Inf.*), emanate, emerge, ensue, follow, happen, issue, occur, originate, proceed, result, set in, spring, start, stem 2. ascend, climb, lift, mount, move upward, rise, soar, tower

aristocracy body of nobles, elite, gentry, *haut monde*, nobility, noblesse (*Literary*), patricians, patriciate, peerage, ruling class, upper class, upper crust (*Inf.*)
Antonyms commoners, common people, hoi polloi, lower classes, masses, plebeians, plebs (*Sl.*), proles (*Sl.*), proletariat, working classes

aristocrat grandee, lady, lord,

noble, nobleman, noblewoman, patrician, peer, peeress

aristocratic blue-blooded, elite, gentle (*Archaic*), gentlemanly, highborn, lordly, noble, patrician, titled, upper-class, well-born
Antonyms common, lower-class, plebeian, proletarian, working-class

arm[1] *n.* 1. appendage, limb, upper limb 2. bough, branch, department, detachment, division, extension, offshoot, projection, section, sector

arm[2] *v.* 1. *Esp. with weapons* accoutre, array, deck out, equip, furnish, issue with, outfit, provide, rig, supply 2. mobilize, muster forces, prepare for war, take up arms

armed accoutred, arrayed, carrying weapons, equipped, fitted out, forearmed, fortified, furnished, girded, guarded, in arms, prepared, primed, protected, provided, ready, rigged out, strengthened, supplied, under arms

arms 1. armaments, firearms, guns, instruments of war, ordnance, weaponry, weapons 2. blazonry, crest, escutcheon, heraldry, insignia

army 1. armed force, host (*Archaic*), land forces, legions, military, military force, soldiers, soldiery, troops 2. *Fig.* array, horde, host, multitude, pack, swarm, throng, vast number

aroma bouquet, fragrance, odour, perfume, redolence, savour, scent, smell

aromatic balmy, fragrant, odoriferous, perfumed, pungent, redolent, savoury, spicy, sweet-scented, sweet-smelling

around *prep.* 1. about, encircling, enclosing, encompassing, environing, on all sides of, on every side of, surrounding 2. about, approximately, circa (*used with dates*), roughly ~*adv.* 3. about, all over, everywhere, here and there, in all directions, on all sides, throughout, to and fro 4. at

hand, close, close at hand, close by, near, nearby, nigh (*Archaic or dialect*)

arouse agitate, animate, awaken, call forth, enliven, excite, foment, foster, goad, incite, inflame, instigate, kindle, move, provoke, quicken, rouse, sharpen, spark, spur, stimulate, stir up, summon up, waken, wake up, warm, whet, whip up
Antonyms allay, alleviate, assuage, calm, dampen, dull, end, lull, pacify, quell, quench, still

arrange 1. align, array, class, classify, dispose, file, form, group, line up, marshal, order, organize, position, put in order, range, rank, set out, sort, sort out (*Inf.*), systematize, tidy 2. adjust, agree to, come to terms, compromise, construct, contrive, determine, devise, fix up (*Inf.*), organize, plan, prepare, schedule, settle 3. adapt, instrument, orchestrate, score
Antonyms (*senses 1 & 2*) disarrange, disorganize, disturb, mess up, scatter

arrangement 1. alignment, array, classification, design, display, disposition, form, grouping, line-up, marshalling, order, ordering, organization, ranging, rank, setup (*Inf.*), structure, system 2. adaptation, instrumentation, interpretation, orchestration, score, version

array *n.* arrangement, collection, display, disposition, exhibition, formation, line-up, marshalling, muster, order, parade, show, supply

arrest 1. *v.* apprehend, bust (*Inf.*), capture, catch, collar (*Inf.*), detain, lay hold of, nab (*Inf.*), nick (*Sl.*), pinch (*Inf.*), run in (*Sl.*), seize, take, take into custody, take prisoner 2. *n.* apprehension, bust (*Inf.*), capture, cop (*Sl.*), detention, seizure
Antonyms *v.* free, let go, release, set free ~*n.* freeing, release

arrival advent, appearance, ar~

riving, coming, entrance, happening, occurrence, taking place

arrive appear, attain, befall, come, enter, get to, happen, occur, reach, show up (*Inf.*), take place, turn up

Antonyms depart, disappear, exit, go, go away, leave, retire, take (one's) leave, vanish, withdraw

arrogance bluster, conceit, conceitedness, contemptuousness, disdainfulness, haughtiness, hauteur, high-handedness, imperiousness, insolence, loftiness, lordliness, overweeningness, pomposity, pompousness, presumption, pretension, pretentiousness, pride, scornfulness, superciliousness, swagger, uppishness (*Brit. inf.*)

arrogant assuming, blustering, conceited, contemptuous, disdainful, haughty, high and mighty (*Inf.*), high-handed, imperious, insolent, lordly, overbearing, overweening, pompous, presumptuous, pretentious, proud, scornful, supercilious, swaggering, uppish (*Brit. inf.*)

Antonyms bashful, deferential, diffident, humble, modest, polite, servile, shy, unassuming

arsenal ammunition dump, armoury, arms depot, magazine, ordnance depot, stock, stockpile, store, supply

art adroitness, aptitude, artifice (*Archaic*), artistry, craft, craftsmanship, dexterity, expertise, facility, ingenuity, knack, knowledge, mastery, method, profession, skill, trade, virtuosity

artful adept, adroit, clever, crafty, cunning, deceitful, designing, dexterous, foxy, ingenious, intriguing, masterly, politic, proficient, resourceful, scheming, sharp, shrewd, skilful, sly, smart, subtle, tricky, wily

Antonyms artless, clumsy, frank, ingenuous, open, simple, straightforward, unadept, unskilled, untalented

article 1. commodity, item, object, piece, substance, thing, unit **2.** composition, discourse, essay, feature, item, paper, piece, story, treatise

articulate 1. *adj.* clear, coherent, comprehensible, eloquent, expressive, fluent, intelligible, lucid, meaningful, understandable, vocal, well-spoken **2.** *v.* enounce, enunciate, express, pronounce, say, speak, state, talk, utter, verbalize, vocalize, voice

Antonyms *adj.* dumb, faltering, halting, hesitant, incoherent, incomprehensible, indistinct, mumbled, mute, poorly-spoken, silent, speechless, stammering, stuttering, tongue-tied, unclear, unintelligible, voiceless

artificial 1. man-made, manufactured, non-natural, plastic, synthetic **2.** bogus, counterfeit, ersatz, fake, imitation, mock, phoney (*Inf.*), sham, simulated, specious, spurious

Antonyms authentic, frank, genuine, honest, natural, sincere, true, unaffected

artistic aesthetic, beautiful, creative, cultivated, cultured, decorative, elegant, exquisite, graceful, imaginative, ornamental, refined, sensitive, stylish, tasteful

as *conj.* **1.** at the time that, during the time that, just as, when, while **2.** in the manner that, in the way that, like **3.** that which, what **4.** because, considering that, seeing that, since **5.** in the same manner with, in the same way that, like **6.** for instance, like, such as ~*prep.* **7.** being, in the character of, in the role of, under the name of **8.** **as for** as regards, in reference to, on the subject of, with reference to, with regard to, with respect to **9. as it were** in a manner of speaking, in a way, so to say, so to speak

ascend climb, float up, fly up, go up, lift off, mount, move up, rise, scale, slope upwards, soar, take off, tower

Antonyms alight, descend, dip, drop, fall, go down, incline, move down, plummet, plunge, sink, slant, slope, subside, tumble

ascent 1. ascending, ascension, clambering, climb, climbing, mounting, rise, rising, scaling, upward movement 2. acclivity, gradient, incline, ramp, rise, rising ground, upward slope

ascribe assign, attribute, charge, credit, impute, put down, refer, set down

ashamed abashed, bashful, blushing, chagrined, conscience-stricken, crestfallen, discomfited, distressed, embarrassed, guilty, humbled, humiliated, mortified, prudish, reluctant, remorseful, shamefaced, sheepish, shy, sorry

Antonyms gratified, honoured, pleased, proud, satisfied, unashamed, vain

aside *adv.* alone, alongside, apart, away, beside, in isolation, in reserve, on one side, out of mind, out of the way, privately, separately, to one side, to the side

ask 1. inquire, interrogate, query, question, quiz 2. appeal, apply, beg, beseech, claim, crave, demand, entreat, implore, petition, plead, pray, request, seek, solicit, sue, supplicate 3. bid, invite, summon

Antonyms (*sense 1*) answer, reply, respond

asleep crashed out (*Sl.*), dead to the world (*Inf.*), dormant, dozing, fast asleep, napping, sleeping, slumbering, snoozing (*Inf.*), sound asleep

aspect 1. air, appearance, attitude, bearing, condition, countenance, demeanour, expression, look, manner, mien (*Literary*) 2. angle, facet, feature, side

aspiration aim, ambition, craving, desire, dream, eagerness, endeavour, goal, hankering, hope, longing, object, objective, wish, yearning

aspire aim, be ambitious, be eager, crave, desire, dream, hanker, hope, long, pursue, seek, wish, yearn

aspiring *adj.* ambitious, aspirant,

eager, endeavouring, hopeful, longing, striving, wishful, would-be

assassin eliminator (*Sl.*), executioner, hatchet man (*Sl.*), hit man (*Sl.*), killer, liquidator, murderer, slayer

assassinate eliminate (*Sl.*), hit (*U.S. sl.*), kill, liquidate, murder, slay

assault 1. *n.* aggression, attack, charge, incursion, invasion, offensive, onset, onslaught, storm, storming, strike 2. *v.* assail, attack, beset, charge, fall upon, invade, lay into, set about, set upon, storm, strike at

assemble 1. accumulate, amass, bring together, call together, collect, come together, congregate, convene, convoke, flock, forgather, gather, marshal, meet, muster, rally, round up, summon 2. build up, connect, construct, erect, fabricate, fit together, join, make, manufacture, piece together, put together, set up

Antonyms adjourn, break up (*Inf.*), disassemble, disband, dismiss, disperse, distribute, divide, scatter, take apart

assembly 1. accumulation, aggregation, assemblage, body, collection, company, conclave, conference, congregation, convocation, council, crowd, diet, flock, gathering, group, mass, meeting, multitude, rally, synod, throng 2. building up, connecting, construction, erection, fabrication, fitting together, joining, manufacture, piecing together, putting together, setting up

assent 1. *v.* accede, accept, acquiesce, agree, allow, approve, comply, concur, consent, fall in with, go along with, grant, permit, sanction, subscribe 2. *n.* acceptance, accession, accord, acquiescence, agreement, approval, compliance, concurrence, consent, permission, sanction

assert affirm, allege, asseverate, attest, aver, avouch (*Archaic*), avow, contend, declare, main-

tain, predicate, profess, pronounce, state, swear
Antonyms deny, disavow, disclaim, refute
assess 1. appraise, compute, determine, estimate, evaluate, fix, gauge, judge, rate, size up (*Inf.*), value, weigh **2.** demand, evaluate, fix, impose, levy, rate, tax, value
assessment 1. appraisal, computation, determination, estimate, estimation, evaluation, judgment, rating, valuation **2.** charge, demand, duty, evaluation, fee, impost, levy, rate, rating, tariff, tax, taxation, toll, valuation
asset 1. advantage, aid, benefit, blessing, boon, help, resource, service **2.** *Plural* capital, estate, funds, goods, holdings, means, money, possessions, property, reserves, resources, valuables, wealth
Antonyms (*sense 1*) burden, disadvantage, drag, drawback, encumbrance, handicap, hindrance, impediment, liability, millstone, minus (*Inf.*), nuisance
assign 1. appoint, choose, delegate, designate, name, nominate, select **2.** allocate, allot, apportion, consign, distribute, give, give out, grant, make over
assignment appointment, charge, commission, duty, job, mission, position, post, responsibility, task
assist abet, aid, back, benefit, boost, collaborate, cooperate, expedite, facilitate, further, help, reinforce, relieve, second, serve, succour, support, sustain, work for, work with
Antonyms frustrate, hamper, handicap, hinder, hold back, hold up, impede, obstruct, resist, thwart, work against
assistance abetment, aid, backing, benefit, boost, collaboration, cooperation, furtherance, help, helping hand, reinforcement, relief, service, succour, support, sustenance
assistant abettor, accessory, accomplice, aide, aider, ally, associate, auxiliary, backer, coadjutor (*Rare*), collaborator, colleague, confederate, cooperator, helper, helpmate, henchman, partner, right-hand man, second, supporter
associate 1. *v.* affiliate, ally, combine, confederate, conjoin, connect, correlate, couple, identify, join, league, link, lump together, mix, pair, relate, think of together, unite, yoke **2.** *n.* ally, collaborator, colleague, companion, compeer, comrade, confederate, confrère, co-worker, follower, friend, mate, partner
Antonyms *v.* detach, disconnect, dissociate, distance, distinguish, divorce, isolate, segregate, separate, set apart
association 1. affiliation, alliance, band, clique, club, coalition, combine, company, confederacy, confederation, cooperative, corporation, federation, fraternity, group, league, organization, partnership, society, syndicate, union **2.** blend, bond, combination, concomitance, connection, correlation, identification, joining, juxtaposition, linkage, linking, lumping together, mixing, mixture, pairing, relation, tie, union, yoking
assorted different, diverse, diversified, heterogeneous, miscellaneous, mixed, motley, sundry, varied, variegated, various
Antonyms alike, homogeneous, identical, like, same, similar, uniform, unvaried
assortment array, choice, collection, diversity, farrago, hotchpotch, jumble, medley, *mélange*, miscellany, mishmash, mixed bag (*Inf.*), mixture, potpourri, salmagundi, selection, variety
assume 1. accept, believe, expect, fancy, guess (*Inf.*, *chiefly U.S.*), imagine, infer, presume, presuppose, suppose, surmise, suspect, take for granted, think **2.** adopt, affect, counterfeit, feign, imitate, impersonate, mimic,

pretend to, put on, sham, simulate 3. accept, acquire, attend to, begin, don, embark upon, embrace, enter upon, put on, set about, shoulder, take on, take over, take responsibility for, take up, undertake
Antonyms (*sense 1*) know, prove (*sense 3*) give up, hand over, leave, put aside, relinquish

assumed affected, bogus, counterfeit, fake, false, feigned, fictitious, imitation, made-up, make-believe, phoney (*Inf.*), pretended, pseudonymous, sham, simulated, spurious
Antonyms actual, authentic, known, natural, positive, real, stated, true

assumption acceptance, belief, conjecture, expectation, fancy, guess, hypothesis, inference, postulate, postulation, premise, premiss, presumption, presupposition, supposition, surmise, suspicion, theory

assurance 1. affirmation, assertion, declaration, guarantee, oath, pledge, profession, promise, protestation, vow, word, word of honour 2. aggressiveness, assuredness, boldness, certainty, certitude, confidence, conviction, coolness, courage, faith, firmness, nerve, poise, positiveness, security, self-confidence, self-reliance, sureness
Antonyms (*sense 1*) falsehood, lie (*sense 2*) apprehension, diffidence, distrust, doubt, self-doubt, self-effacement, shyness, timidity, uncertainty

assure 1. comfort, convince, embolden, encourage, hearten, persuade, reassure, soothe 2. affirm, attest, certify, confirm, declare confidently, give one's word to, guarantee, pledge, promise, swear, vow 3. clinch, complete, confirm, ensure, guarantee, make certain, make sure, seal, secure

astonish amaze, astound, bewilder, confound, daze, dumbfound, flabbergast (*Inf.*), stagger, stun, stupefy, surprise

astonishing amazing, astounding, bewildering, breathtaking, impressive, staggering, striking, stunning, stupefying, surprising

astonishment amazement, awe, bewilderment, confusion, consternation, stupefaction, surprise, wonder, wonderment

astute adroit, artful, bright, calculating, canny, clever, crafty, cunning, discerning, foxy, insightful, intelligent, keen, knowing, penetrating, perceptive, politic, sagacious, sharp, shrewd, sly, subtle, wily

asylum 1. harbour, haven, preserve, refuge, retreat, safety, sanctuary, shelter 2. *Old-fashioned* funny farm (*Sl.*), hospital, institution, loony bin (*Sl.*), madhouse (*Inf.*), mental hospital, nuthouse (*Sl.*), psychiatric hospital

atheism disbelief, freethinking, godlessness, heathenism, infidelity, irreligion, nonbelief, paganism, scepticism, unbelief

atheist disbeliever, freethinker, heathen, infidel, irreligionist, nonbeliever, pagan, sceptic, unbeliever

athlete competitor, contender, contestant, games player, gymnast, player, runner, sportsman, sportswoman

athletic 1. *adj.* able-bodied, active, brawny, energetic, fit, herculean, husky (*Inf.*), lusty, muscular, powerful, robust, sinewy, strapping, strong, sturdy, vigorous, well-proportioned 2. *pl. n.* contests, exercises, games of strength, gymnastics, races, sports, track and field events
Antonyms (*sense 1*) delicate, feeble, frail, puny, sickly, weedy (*Inf.*)

atmosphere 1. aerosphere, air, heavens, sky 2. air, ambience, aura, character, climate, environment, feel, feeling, flavour, mood, quality, spirit, surroundings, tone

atrocious barbaric, brutal, cruel, diabolical, fiendish, flagrant, heinous, infamous, infernal, inhuman, monstrous, nefarious, ruthless, savage, vicious, villainous, wicked

atrocity abomination, act of savagery, barbarity, brutality, crime, cruelty, enormity, evil, horror, monstrosity, outrage, villainy

attach add, adhere, affix, annex, append, bind, connect, couple, fasten, fix, join, link, make fast, secure, stick, subjoin, tie, unite
Antonyms detach, disconnect, loosen, remove, separate, untie

attached affectionate towards, devoted, fond of, full of regard for, possessive

attachment adapter, bond, clamp, connection, connector, coupling, fastener, fastening, joint, junction, link, tie

attack *n.* 1. aggression, assault, charge, foray, incursion, inroad, invasion, offensive, onset, onslaught, raid, rush, strike 2. abuse, blame, calumny, censure, criticism, denigration, impugnment, vilification 3. access, bout, convulsion, fit, paroxysm, seizure, spasm, spell, stroke ~*v.* 4. assail, assault, charge, fall upon, invade, lay into, raid, rush, set about, set upon, storm, strike (at) 5. abuse, berate, blame, censure, criticize, impugn, malign, revile, vilify
Antonyms *n.* defence, retreat, support, vindication, withdrawal ~*v.* defend, guard, protect, retreat, support, sustain, vindicate, withdraw

attain accomplish, achieve, acquire, arrive at, bring off, complete, earn, effect, fulfil, gain, get, grasp, obtain, procure, reach, realize, reap, secure, win

attempt 1. *n.* assault, attack, bid, crack (*Inf.*), effort, endeavour, essay, experiment, go, shot (*Inf.*), trial, try, undertaking, venture 2. *v.* endeavour, essay, experiment, have a crack (go, shot) (*Inf.*),

seek, strive, tackle, take on, try, try one's hand at, undertake, venture

attend 1. appear, be at, be here, be present, be there, frequent, go to, haunt, make one (*Inf.*), put in an appearance, show up (*Inf.*), turn up, visit 2. follow, hear, hearken (*Archaic*), heed, listen, look on, mark, mind, note, notice, observe, pay attention, pay heed, regard, take to heart, watch 3. *With* to apply oneself to, concentrate on, devote oneself to, get to work on, look after, occupy oneself with, see to, take care of 4. accompany, chaperon, companion, convoy, escort, guard, squire, usher
Antonyms (*sense 1*) be absent, miss, play truant (*senses 2 & 3*) disregard, ignore, neglect

attendance audience, crowd, gate, house, number present, turnout

attendant *n.* aide, assistant, auxiliary, chaperon, companion, custodian, escort, flunky, follower, guard, guide, helper, lackey, menial, servant, steward, underling, usher, waiter

attention 1. concentration, consideration, contemplation, deliberation, heed, heedfulness, intentness, mind, scrutiny, thinking, thought, thoughtfulness 2. awareness, consciousness, consideration, notice, observation, recognition, regard 3. care, concern, looking after, ministration, treatment
Antonyms carelessness, disregard, distraction, inattention, negligence, thoughtlessness, unconcern

attentive alert, awake, careful, concentrating, heedful, intent, listening, mindful, observant, regardful, studious, watchful
Antonyms absent-minded, careless, distracted, dreamy, heedless, inattentive, neglectful, negligent, preoccupied, remiss, thoughtless, unheeding, unmindful

attitude 1. approach, disposition, frame of mind, mood, opinion, outlook, perspective, point of view, position, posture, stance, standing, view 2. air, aspect, bearing, carriage, condition, demeanour, manner, mien (*Literary*), pose, position, posture, stance

attract allure, appeal to, bewitch, captivate, charm, decoy, draw, enchant, endear, engage, entice, fascinate, incline, induce, interest, invite, lure, pull (*Inf.*), tempt
Antonyms disgust, give one the creeps (*Inf.*), put one off, repel, repulse, revolt, turn one off (*Inf.*)

attraction allure, appeal, attractiveness, bait, captivation, charm, come-on (*Inf.*), draw, enchantment, endearment, enticement, fascination, inducement, interest, invitation, lure, magnetism, pull (*Inf.*), temptation, temptingness

attractive agreeable, alluring, appealing, beautiful, captivating, charming, comely, engaging, enticing, fair, fascinating, fetching, good-looking, gorgeous, handsome, interesting, inviting, lovely, magnetic, pleasant, pleasing, prepossessing, pretty, seductive, tempting, winning, winsome
Antonyms disagreeable, displeasing, distasteful, offensive, repulsive, ugly, unappealing, unbecoming, uninviting, unlikeable, unpleasant, unsightly

attribute 1. *v.* apply, ascribe, assign, blame, charge, credit, impute, lay at the door of, put down to, refer, set down to, trace to 2. *n.* aspect, character, characteristic, facet, feature, idiosyncrasy, indication, mark, note, peculiarity, point, property, quality, quirk, sign, symbol, trait, virtue

audacious adventurous, bold, brave, courageous, daredevil, daring, dauntless, death-defying, enterprising, fearless, intrepid, rash, reckless, risky, valiant, venturesome

audacity 1. adventurousness, audaciousness, boldness, bravery, courage, daring, dauntlessness, enterprise, fearlessness, guts (*Sl.*), intrepidity, nerve, rashness, recklessness, valour, venturesomeness 2. audaciousness, brass neck (*Inf.*), cheek, defiance, disrespectfulness, effrontery, forwardness, gall (*Inf.*), impertinence, impudence, insolence, nerve, pertness, presumption, rudeness, shamelessness

audible clear, detectable, discernible, distinct, hearable, perceptible
Antonyms faint, imperceptible, inaudible, indistinct, low, out of earshot

audience 1. assemblage, assembly, congregation, crowd, gallery, gathering, house, listeners, onlookers, spectators, turnout, viewers 2. consultation, hearing, interview, meeting, reception

auspicious bright, encouraging, favourable, felicitous, fortunate, happy, hopeful, lucky, opportune, promising, propitious, prosperous, rosy, timely

austere 1. cold, exacting, forbidding, formal, grave, grim, hard, harsh, inflexible, rigorous, serious, severe, solemn, stern, stiff, strict, stringent, unfeeling, unrelenting 2. abstemious, abstinent, ascetic, chaste, continent, economical, exacting, puritanical, rigid, self-denying, self-disciplined, sober, solemn, Spartan, strait-laced, strict, unrelenting

austerity 1. coldness, exactingness, forbiddingness, formality, gravity, grimness, hardness, harshness, inflexibility, rigour, seriousness, severity, solemnity, sternness, stiffness, strictness 2. abstemiousness, abstinence, asceticism, chasteness, chastity, continence, economy, exactingness, puritanism, rigidity, self-denial, self-discipline, sobriety, solemnity, Spartanism, strictness

authentic accurate, actual, authoritative, bona fide, certain,

dependable, factual, faithful, genuine, legitimate, original, pure, real, reliable, simon-pure (*Rare*), true, true-to-life, trustworthy, valid, veritable
Antonyms counterfeit, fake, false, fictititious, fraudulent, hypothetical, imitation, misleading, mock, spurious, supposed, synthetic, unfaithful, unreal, untrue

authenticity accuracy, actuality, authoritativeness, certainty, dependability, factualness, faithfulness, genuineness, legitimacy, purity, realness, reliability, trustworthiness, truth, truthfulness, validity, veritableness, verity

author architect, composer, creator, designer, doer, fabricator, father, founder, framer, initiator, inventor, maker, mover, originator, parent, planner, prime mover, producer, writer

authoritarian *adj.* absolute, autocratic, despotic, dictatorial, disciplinarian, doctrinaire, dogmatic, domineering, harsh, imperious, rigid, severe, strict, tyrannical, unyielding
Antonyms broad-minded, democratic, flexible, indulgent, lenient, liberal, permissive, tolerant

authority 1. ascendancy, charge, command, control, domination, dominion, force, government, influence, jurisdiction, might, power, prerogative, right, rule, say-so, strength, supremacy, sway, weight **2.** authorization, justification, licence, permission, permit, sanction, say-so, warrant **3.** arbiter, bible, connoisseur, expert, judge, master, professional, scholar, specialist, textbook

authorize 1. accredit, commission, empower, enable, entitle, give authority **2.** accredit, allow, approve, confirm, countenance, give authority for, give leave, license, permit, ratify, sanction, vouch for, warrant
Antonyms ban, debar, disallow, exclude, forbid, outlaw, preclude, prohibit, proscribe, rule out, veto

automatic 1. automated, mechanical, mechanized, push-button, robot, self-acting, self-activating, self-moving, self-propelling, self-regulating **2.** habitual, kneejerk, mechanical, perfunctory, routine, unconscious
Antonyms (*sense 1*) done by hand, hand-operated, human, manual, physical (*sense 2*) conscious, deliberate, intentional, voluntary

autonomous free, independent, self-determining, self-governing, self-ruling, sovereign

auxiliary *adj.* accessory, aiding, ancillary, assisting, back-up, emergency, helping, reserve, secondary, subsidiary, substitute, supplementary, supporting

available accessible, applicable, at hand, at one's disposal, attainable, convenient, free, handy, obtainable, on hand, on tap, ready, ready for use, to hand, vacant
Antonyms busy, engaged, inaccessible, in use, occupied, spoken for, taken, unattainable, unavailable, unobtainable

avalanche 1. landslide, landslip, snow-slide, snow-slip **2.** barrage, deluge, flood, inundation, torrent

avaricious acquisitive, close-fisted, covetous, grasping, greedy, mean, miserable, miserly, niggardly, parsimonious, penny-pinching, penurious, rapacious, stingy

avenge even the score for, get even for, punish, repay, requite, retaliate, revenge, take satisfaction for, take vengeance

avenue access, alley, approach, boulevard, channel, course, drive, driveway, entrance, entry, pass, passage, path, pathway, road, route, street, thoroughfare, way

average *n.* **1.** common run, mean, medium, midpoint, norm, normal, par, rule, run, run of the mill, standard ~*adj.* **2.** common, commonplace, fair, general, indifferent, mediocre, middling,

moderate, normal, not bad, ordinary, passable, regular, run-of-the-mill, so-so (Inf.), standard, tolerable, typical, undistinguished, unexceptional, usual 3. intermediate, mean, median, medium, middle
Antonyms adj. abnormal, awful, bad, different, exceptional, great, maximum, memorable, minimum, outstanding, remarkable, special, terrible, unusual

averse antipathetic, backward, disinclined, hostile, ill-disposed, indisposed, inimical, loath, opposed, reluctant, unfavourable, unwilling
Antonyms agreeable, amenable, disposed, eager, favourable, inclined, keen, sympathetic, willing

avid ardent, devoted, eager, enthusiastic, fanatical, fervent, intense, keen, passionate, zealous

avoid avert, bypass, circumvent, dodge, duck (out of) (Inf.), elude, escape, eschew, evade, fight shy of, keep aloof from, keep away from, prevent, refrain from, shirk, shun, sidestep, steer clear of
Antonyms approach, confront, contact, face, find, invite, pursue, seek out, solicit

await 1. abide, anticipate, expect, look for, look forward to, stay for, wait for 2. attend, be in readiness for, be in store for, be prepared for, be ready for, wait for

awake alert, alive, aroused, attentive, awakened, aware, conscious, heedful, not sleeping, observant, on guard, on the alert, on the lookout, vigilant, wakeful, waking, watchful, wide-awake
Antonyms asleep, crashed out (Sl.), dead to the world (Inf.), dormant, dozing, inattentive, napping, sleeping, unaware, unconscious

awaken activate, alert, animate, arouse, awake, call forth, enliven, excite, fan, incite, kindle, provoke, revive, rouse, stimulate, stir up, vivify, wake

award v.1. accord, adjudge, allot,

apportion, assign, bestow, confer, decree, distribute, endow, gift, give, grant, present, render ~n. 2. adjudication, allotment, bestowal, conferment, conferral, decision, decree, endowment, gift, order, presentation 3. decoration, gift, grant, prize, trophy, verdict

aware acquainted, alive to, appreciative, apprised, attentive, au courant, cognizant, conscious, conversant, enlightened, familiar, hip (Sl.), informed, knowing, knowledgeable, mindful, sensible, sentient, wise (Inf.)
Antonyms ignorant, insensible, oblivious, unaware, unfamiliar with, unknowledgeable

awareness acquaintance, appreciation, attention, cognizance, consciousness, enlightenment, familiarity, knowledge, mindfulness, perception, realization, recognition, sensibility, sentience, understanding

away adv. 1. abroad, elsewhere, from here, from home, hence, off 2. apart, at a distance, far, remote 3. aside, out of the way, to one side ~adj. 4. abroad, absent, elsewhere, gone, not at home, not here, not present, not there, out

awful alarming, appalling, deplorable, dire, distressing, dreadful, fearful, frightful, ghastly, gruesome, harrowing, hideous, horrendous, horrible, horrific, horrifying, nasty, shocking, terrible, tremendous, ugly, unpleasant, unsightly
Antonyms amazing, brilliant, excellent, fabulous (Inf.), fantastic, great (Inf.), magnificent, marvellous, miraculous, sensational, smashing (Inf.), super (Inf.), superb, terrific, tremendous, wonderful

awfully badly, disgracefully, disreputably, dreadfully, inadequately, reprehensibly, shoddily, unforgivably, unpleasantly, wickedly, woefully, wretchedly

awkward 1. all thumbs, artless,

blundering, bungling, clownish, clumsy, coarse, gauche, gawky, graceless, ham-fisted, ham-handed, ill-bred, inelegant, inept, inexpert, lumbering, maladroit, oafish, rude, skill-less, stiff, unco-ordinated, uncouth, ungainly, ungraceful, unpolished, unrefined, unskilful, unskilled **2.** cumbersome, difficult, inconvenient, troublesome, unhandy, unmanageable, unwieldy **3.** annoying, bloody-minded (*Inf.*), difficult, disobliging, exasperating, hard to handle, intractable, irritable, perverse, prickly, stubborn, touchy, troublesome, trying, uncooperative, unhelpful, unpredictable, vexatious, vexing

Antonyms (*sense 1*) adept, adroit, dexterous, graceful, skilful (*sense 2*) convenient, easy, handy

awkwardness 1. artlessness, clownishness, clumsiness, coarseness, gaucheness, gaucherie, gawkiness, gracelessness, ill-breeding, inelegance, ineptness, inexpertness, maladroitness, oafishness, rudeness, skill-lessness, stiffness, uncoordination, uncouthness, ungainliness, unskilfulness, unskilledness **2.** cumbersomeness, difficulty, inconvenience, troublesomeness, unhandiness, unmanageability, unwieldiness **3.** delicacy, difficulty, discomfort, embarrassment, inconvenience, inopportuneness, painfulness, perplexingness, stickiness (*Inf.*), thorniness, ticklishness, unpleasantness, untimeliness **4.** bloody-mindedness (*Inf.*), difficulty, disobligingness, intractability, irritability, perversity, prickliness, stubbornness, touchiness, uncooperativeness, unhelpfulness, unpredictability

axiom adage, aphorism, apophthegm, dictum, fundamental, gnome, maxim, postulate, precept, principle, truism

axiomatic 1. absolute, accepted, apodictic, assumed, certain, fundamental, given, granted, indubitable, manifest, presupposed, self-evident, understood, unquestioned **2.** aphoristic, apophthegmatic, epigrammatic, gnomic, pithy, terse

axis axle, centre line, pivot, shaft, spindle

axle arbor, axis, mandrel, pin, pivot, rod, shaft, spindle

B

baby 1. *n.* babe, bairn (*Scot.*), child, infant, newborn child **2.** *adj.* diminutive, dwarf, little, midget, mini, miniature, minute, pygmy, small, tiny, wee

babyish baby, childish, foolish, immature, infantile, juvenile, namby-pamby, puerile, silly, sissy, soft (*Inf.*), spoiled
Antonyms adult, grown-up, mature, of age

back *v.* **1.** abet, advocate, assist, champion, countenance, encourage, endorse, favour, finance, sanction, second, side with, sponsor, subsidize, support, sustain, underwrite **2.** backtrack, go back, move back, regress, retire, retreat, reverse, turn tail, withdraw ~*n.* **3.** backside, end, far end, hind part, hindquarters, posterior, rear, reverse, stern, tail end ~*adj.* **4.** end, hind, hindmost, posterior, rear, tail
Antonyms *v.* (*sense 1*) attack, combat, hinder, thwart, undermine, weaken (*sense 2*) advance, approach, move forward, progress ~*n.* face, fore, front, head ~*adj.* advance, fore, front

backer advocate, angel (*Inf.*), benefactor, patron, promoter, second, sponsor, subscriber, supporter, underwriter, well-wisher

backfire boomerang, disappoint, fail, flop, miscarry, rebound, recoil

background breeding, circumstances, credentials, culture, education, environment, experience, grounding, history, milieu, preparation, qualifications, tradition, upbringing

backing abetment, accompaniment, advocacy, aid, assistance, championing, encouragement, endorsement, funds, grant, moral support, patronage, sanction, seconding, sponsorship, subsidy, support

backlash backfire, boomerang, counteraction, counterblast, kickback, reaction, recoil, repercussion, resentment, resistance, response, retaliation, retroaction

backlog accumulation, build-up, excess, hoard, reserve, reserves, resources, stock, supply

back out abandon, cancel, chicken out (*Inf.*), give up, go back on, recant, renege, resign, retreat, withdraw

backslider apostate, deserter, recidivist, recreant, renegade, reneger, turncoat

back up aid, assist, bolster, confirm, corroborate, reinforce, second, stand by, substantiate, support

backward *adj.* **1.** bashful, diffident, hesitating, late, reluctant, shy, sluggish, tardy, unwilling, wavering **2.** behind, behindhand, dense, dull, retarded, slow, stupid, subnormal, underdeveloped, undeveloped ~*adv.* **3.** aback, behind, in reverse, rearward
Antonyms *adj.* advanced, ahead, bold, brash, eager, forward, willing ~*adv.* correctly, forward, frontward, properly

bad 1. defective, deficient, erroneous, fallacious, faulty, imperfect, inadequate, incorrect, inferior, poor, substandard, unsatisfactory **2.** damaging, dangerous, deleterious, detrimental, harmful, hurtful, injurious, ruinous, unhealthy **3.** base, corrupt, criminal, delinquent, evil, immoral, mean, sinful, vile, villainous, wicked, wrong **4.** disobedient, mischievous, naughty, unruly **5.** decayed, mouldy, off, putrid, rancid, rotten, sour, spoiled **6.** ailing, diseased, ill, sick, unwell **7.**

adverse, discouraged, discouraging, distressed, distressing, gloomy, grim, melancholy, troubled, troubling, unfortunate, unpleasant

Antonyms (*sense 1*) adequate, fair, satisfactory (*sense 2*) agreeable, beneficial, good, healthful, safe, sound, wholesome (*sense 3*) ethical, fine, first-rate, good, moral, righteous, virtuous (*sense 4*) biddable, docile, good, obedient, well-behaved

badge brand, device, emblem, identification, insignia, mark, sign, stamp, token

badly 1. carelessly, defectively, erroneously, faultily, imperfectly, inadequately, incorrectly, ineptly, poorly, shoddily, wrong, wrongly 2. unfavourably, unfortunately, unsuccessfully 3. criminally, evilly, immorally, improperly, naughtily, shamefully, unethically, wickedly

Antonyms ably, competently, correctly, ethically, morally, properly, righteously, rightly, satisfactorily, splendidly, well

bag *v.* acquire, capture, catch, gain, get, kill, land, shoot, take, trap

baggage accoutrements, bags, belongings, equipment, gear, impedimenta, luggage, paraphernalia, suitcases, things

baggy billowing, bulging, droopy, floppy, ill-fitting, loose, oversize, roomy, sagging, seated, slack

Antonyms close, close-fitting, constricted, cramped, narrow, snug, stretched, taut, tight, tight-fitting

bail[1] *n.* bond, guarantee, guaranty, pledge, security, surety, warranty

bail[2], **bale** *v.* dip, drain off, ladle, scoop

bait 1. *n.* allurement, attraction, bribe, decoy, enticement, inducement, lure, snare, temptation 2. *v.* annoy, gall, harass, hound, irk, irritate, needle (*Inf.*), persecute, provoke, tease, torment

baked arid, desiccated, dry, parched, scorched, seared, sunbaked

balance *v.* 1. level, match, parallel, poise, stabilize, steady 2. adjust, compensate for, counteract, counterbalance, counterpoise, equalize, equate, make up for, neutralize, offset ~*n.* 3. correspondence, equilibrium, equipoise, equity, equivalence, evenness, parity, symmetry 4. composure, equanimity, poise, self-control, self-possession, stability, steadiness 5. difference, remainder, residue, rest, surplus

Antonyms *v.* outweigh, overbalance, upset ~*n.* disproportion, instability, shakiness, unbalance, uncertainty

bald 1. baldheaded, baldpated, depilated, glabrous (*Biol.*), hairless 2. barren, bleak, exposed, naked, stark, treeless, uncovered

balk 1. demur, dodge, evade, flinch, hesitate, jib, recoil, refuse, resist, shirk, shrink from 2. baffle, bar, check, counteract, defeat, disconcert, foil, forestall, frustrate, hinder, obstruct, prevent, thwart

ball drop, globe, globule, orb, pellet, sphere, spheroid

ballast balance, counterbalance, counterweight, equilibrium, sandbag, stability, stabilizer, weight

ballot election, poll, polling, vote, voting

ballyhoo babble, commotion, fuss, hubbub, hue and cry, hullabaloo, noise, racket, to-do

ban 1. *v.* banish, bar, debar, disallow, exclude, forbid, interdict, outlaw, prohibit, proscribe, restrict, suppress 2. *n.* boycott, censorship, embargo, interdiction, prohibition, proscription, restriction, stoppage, suppression, taboo

Antonyms *v.* allow, approve, authorize, let, permit, sanction ~*n.* allowance, approval, permission, sanction

banal clichéd, cliché-ridden,

commonplace, everyday, hackneyed, humdrum, old hat, ordinary, pedestrian, platitudinous, stale, stereotyped, stock, threadbare, tired, trite, unimaginative, unoriginal, vapid
Antonyms challenging, distinctive, fresh, imaginative, interesting, new, novel, original, stimulating, unique, unusual

band[1] *n.* bandage, belt, binding, bond, chain, cord, fetter, fillet, ligature, manacle, ribbon, shackle, strap, strip, tie

band[2] *n.* 1. assembly, association, body, clique, club, company, coterie, crew (*Inf.*), gang, horde, party, society, troop 2. combo, ensemble, group, orchestra

bandage 1. *n.* compress, dressing, gauze, plaster 2. *v.* bind, cover, dress, swathe

bandit brigand, crook, desperado, footpad, freebooter, gangster, gunman, highwayman, hijacker, marauder, outlaw, pirate, racketeer, robber, thief

bang *n.* 1. boom, burst, clang, clap, clash, detonation, explosion, peal, pop, report, shot, slam, thud, thump 2. blow, box, bump, cuff, hit, knock, punch, smack, stroke, wallop (*Inf.*), whack ~*v.* 3. bash (*Inf.*), beat, bump, clatter, crash, hammer, knock, pound, pummel, rap, slam, strike, thump

banish deport, drive away, eject, evict, exclude, excommunicate, exile, expatriate, expel, ostracize, outlaw, shut out, transport
Antonyms accept, admit, embrace, hail, invite, offer hospitality to, receive, welcome

banishment deportation, exile, expatriation, expulsion, proscription, transportation

bank[1] 1. *n.* accumulation, depository, fund, hoard, repository, reserve, reservoir, savings, stock, stockpile, store, storehouse 2. *v.* deal with, deposit, keep, save, transact business with

bank[2] *n.* 1. banking, embankment, heap, mass, mound, pile, ridge 2. brink, edge, margin, shore, side

~*v.* 3. amass, heap, mass, mound, pile, stack 4. camber, cant, incline, pitch, slant, slope, tilt, tip

bank[3] *n.* array, file, group, line, rank, row, sequence, series, succession, tier, train

bankrupt broke (*Inf.*), depleted, destitute, exhausted, failed, impoverished, insolvent, lacking, ruined, spent
Antonyms in the money (*Inf.*), on the up and up, prosperous, solvent, sound, wealthy

banquet dinner, feast, meal, repast, revel, treat

baptism 1. christening, immersion, purification, sprinkling 2. beginning, debut, dedication, initiation, introduction, launching, rite of passage

bar *n.* 1. batten, crosspiece, paling, pole, rail, rod, shaft, stake, stick 2. barricade, barrier, deterrent, hindrance, impediment, obstacle, obstruction, rail, railing, stop 3. boozer (*Inf.*), canteen, counter, inn, lounge, pub (*Inf.*), public house, saloon, tavern 4. bench, court, courtroom, dock, law court 5. *Law* barristers, body of lawyers, counsel, court, judgment, tribunal ~*v.* 6. barricade, bolt, fasten, latch, lock, secure 7. ban, exclude, forbid, hinder, keep out, obstruct, prevent, prohibit, restrain
Antonyms *n.* (*sense 2*) aid, benefit, help ~*v.* (*sense 2*) accept, admit, allow, clear, let, open, permit, receive

barbarian *n.* 1. brute, hooligan, lout, lowbrow, ned (*Sl.*), ruffian, savage, vandal, yahoo 2. bigot, boor, ignoramus, illiterate, lowbrow, philistine

barbaric primitive, rude, uncivilized, wild
Antonyms civilized, cultivated, cultured, gentlemanly, gracious, humane, refined, sophisticated, urbane

bare 1. denuded, exposed, naked, nude, peeled, shorn, stripped, unclad, unclothed, uncovered,

undressed 2. barren, blank, empty, lacking, mean, open, poor, scanty, scarce, unfurnished, vacant, void, wanting
Antonyms abundant, adorned, attired, clad, clothed, concealed, covered, dressed, full, hidden, plentiful, profuse, well-stocked

bargain n. 1. agreement, arrangement, business, compact, contract, convention, engagement, negotiation, pact, pledge, promise, stipulation, transaction, treaty, understanding 2. (cheap) purchase, discount, giveaway, good buy, good deal, good value, reduction, snip (Inf.) ~v. 3. agree, contract, covenant, negotiate, promise, stipulate, transact 4. barter, buy, deal, haggle, sell, trade, traffic

bark n./v. bay, growl, howl, snarl, woof, yap, yelp

barmy Also **balmy** crazy, daft, dippy, doolally (Sl.), foolish, idiotic, insane, loony (Sl.), nuts (Sl.), nutty (Sl.), odd, silly, stupid
Antonyms all there (Inf.), in one's right mind, of sound mind, rational, reasonable, sane, sensible

barrage battery, bombardment, cannonade, curtain of fire, fusillade, gunfire, salvo, shelling, volley

barren 1. childless, infecund, infertile, sterile, unprolific 2. arid, desert, desolate, dry, empty, unfruitful, unproductive, waste
Antonyms fecund, fertile, fruitful, lush, productive, profitable, rich, useful

barrier 1. bar, barricade, blockade, boundary, ditch, fence, fortification, obstacle, obstruction, railing, rampart, stop, wall 2. Fig. check, difficulty, drawback, handicap, hindrance, hurdle, impediment, limitation, obstacle, restriction, stumbling block

barter bargain, exchange, haggle, sell, swap, trade, traffic

base¹ n. 1. bed, bottom, foot, foundation, groundwork, pedestal, rest, stand, support 2. basis,

core, essence, essential, fundamental, heart, key, origin, principal, root, source 3. camp, centre, headquarters, home, post, settlement, starting point, station ~v. 4. build, construct, depend, derive, establish, found, ground, hinge, locate, station
Antonyms (sense 1) apex, crown, peak, summit, top, vertex

baseless groundless, unconfirmed, uncorroborated, unfounded, ungrounded, unjustifiable, unjustified, unsubstantiated, unsupported
Antonyms authenticated, confirmed, corroborated, proven, substantiated, supported, validated, verified, well-founded

bashful abashed, blushing, confused, constrained, coy, diffident, easily embarrassed, nervous, overmodest, reserved, reticent, retiring, self-conscious, self-effacing, shamefaced, sheepish, shrinking, shy, timid, timorous
Antonyms aggressive, arrogant, bold, brash, conceited, confident, egoistic, fearless, forward, immodest, impudent, intrepid, self-assured

basic central, elementary, essential, fundamental, indispensable, inherent, intrinsic, key, necessary, primary, underlying, vital
Antonyms complementary, minor, peripheral, secondary, supplementary, supporting, trivial, unessential

basics brass tacks (Inf.), core, essentials, facts, fundamentals, hard facts, necessaries, nitty-gritty (Sl.), nuts and bolts (Inf.), practicalities, principles, rudiments

basis base, bottom, footing, foundation, ground, groundwork, support

bastard 1. n. illegitimate (child), love child, natural child, whoreson (Archaic) 2. adj. adulterated, baseborn, counterfeit, false, illegitimate, imperfect, impure, inferior, irregular, misbegotten, sham, spurious

bastion bulwark, citadel, defence, fastness, fortress, mainstay, prop, rock, stronghold, support, tower of strength

bat bang, hit, rap, smack, strike, swat, thump, wallop (*Inf.*), whack

batch accumulation, aggregation, amount, assemblage, bunch, collection, crowd, group, lot, pack, quantity, set

bath 1. *n.* ablution, cleansing, douche, douse, scrubbing, shower, soak, soaping, sponging, tub, wash, washing 2. *v.* bathe, clean, douse, lave (*Archaic*), scrub down, shower, soak, soap, sponge, tub, wash

bathe 1. *v.* cleanse, cover, dunk, flood, immerse, moisten, rinse, soak, steep, suffuse, wash, wet 2. *n.* dip, dook (*Scot.*), swim, wash

baton club, mace, rod, staff, stick, truncheon, wand

batter 1. assault, bash, beat, belabour, break, buffet, dash against, lash, pelt, pound, pummel, smash, smite, thrash, wallop (*Inf.*) 2. bruise, crush, deface, demolish, destroy, disfigure, hurt, injure, mangle, mar, maul, ruin, shatter, shiver

battery assault, attack, beating, mayhem, onslaught, physical violence, thumping

battle *n.* action, attack, combat, encounter, engagement, fight, fray, hostilities, skirmish, war, warfare **Antonyms** accord, agreement, armistice, ceasefire, concord, entente, peace, suspension of hostilities, truce

batty barmy (*Sl.*), bats (*Sl.*), bonkers (*Sl.*), cracked (*Sl.*), crackers (*Sl.*), cranky (*Inf.*), crazy, daft, dotty (*Sl.*), eccentric, insane, loony (*Sl.*), lunatic, mad, nuts (*Sl.*), nutty (*Sl.*), odd, off one's rocker (*Sl.*), peculiar, potty (*Inf.*), queer, screwy (*Inf.*), touched

bazaar 1. exchange, market, marketplace, mart 2. bring-and-buy, fair, fête, sale of work

be 1. be alive, breathe, exist,

inhabit, live 2. abide, continue, endure, last, obtain, persist, prevail, remain, stand, stay, survive

beach coast, lido, littoral, margin, plage, sands, seaboard (*Chiefly U.S.*), seashore, seaside, shingle, shore, strand, water's edge

beacon beam, bonfire, flare, lighthouse, pharos, rocket, sign, signal, signal fire, smoke signal, watchtower

beak 1. bill, mandible, neb (*Archaic or dialect*), nib 2. nose, proboscis, snout 3. *Naut.* bow, prow, ram, rostrum, stem

beam *n.* 1. girder, joist, plank, rafter, spar, support, timber 2. bar, emission, gleam, glimmer, glint, glow, radiation, ray, shaft, streak, stream ~*v.* 3. broadcast, emit, glare, gleam, glitter, glow, radiate, shine, transmit 4. grin, laugh, smile

bear 1. bring, carry, convey, move, take, tote, transport 2. abide, admit, allow, brook, endure, permit, put up with (*Inf.*), stomach, suffer, tolerate, undergo 3. beget, breed, bring forth, develop, engender, generate, give birth to, produce, yield

bearable admissible, endurable, manageable, passable, sufferable, supportable, sustainable, tolerable **Antonyms** insufferable, insupportable, intolerable, oppressive, too much (*Inf.*), unacceptable, unbearable, unendurable

bearer agent, carrier, conveyor, messenger, porter, runner, servant

bearing 1. air, aspect, attitude, behaviour, carriage, demeanour, deportment, manner, mien, posture 2. *Naut.* course, direction, point of compass 3. application, connection, import, pertinence, reference, relation, relevance, significance **Antonyms** (*sense 3*) inappositeness, inappropriateness, inaptness, inconsequence, irrelevance, irrelevancy, non sequitur

bear out confirm, corroborate,

endorse, justify, prove, substantiate, support, uphold, vindicate

bear with be patient, forbear, make allowances, put up with (*Inf.*), suffer, tolerate, wait

beast 1. animal, brute, creature 2. barbarian, brute, fiend, monster, ogre, sadist, savage, swine

beastly 1. barbarous, bestial, brutal, brutish, coarse, cruel, depraved, inhuman, monstrous, repulsive, sadistic, savage 2. awful, disagreeable, foul, mean, nasty, rotten, terrible, unpleasant

beat *v.* 1. bang, batter, break, bruise, buffet, cane, cudgel, drub, flog, hit, knock, lash, maul, pelt, pound, punch, strike, thrash, thwack, whip 2. best, conquer, defeat, excel, outdo, outrun, outstrip, overcome, overwhelm, subdue, surpass, vanquish ~ *n.* 3. blow, hit, lash, punch, shake, slap, strike, swing, thump 4. flutter, palpitation, pulsation, pulse, throb 5. accent, cadence, measure, metre, rhythm, stress, time 6. circuit, course, path, rounds, route, way

beaten 1. baffled, cowed, defeated, disappointed, disheartened, frustrated, overcome, overwhelmed, thwarted, vanquished 2. blended, foamy, frothy, mixed, stirred, whipped, whisked

beautiful alluring, appealing, attractive, charming, comely, delightful, exquisite, fair, fine, good-looking, gorgeous, graceful, handsome, lovely, pleasing, radiant, ravishing, stunning (*Inf.*)
Antonyms awful, bad, hideous, repulsive, terrible, ugly, unattractive, unpleasant, unsightly

beautify adorn, array, bedeck, deck, decorate, embellish, enhance, garnish, gild, glamorize, grace, ornament

beauty 1. allure, attractiveness, bloom, charm, comeliness, elegance, exquisiteness, fairness, glamour, grace, handsomeness, loveliness, pulchritude, seemliness, symmetry 2. belle, charmer, cracker (*Sl.*), goddess, good-

looker, lovely (*Sl.*), stunner (*Inf.*), Venus
Antonyms flaw, repulsiveness, ugliness, unpleasantness, unseemliness

because as, by reason of, in that, on account of, owing to, since, thanks to

beckon bid, gesticulate, gesture, motion, nod, signal, summon, wave at

become 1. alter to, be transformed into, change into, develop into, evolve into, grow into, mature into, metamorphose into, ripen into 2. embellish, enhance, fit, flatter, grace, harmonize, ornament, set off, suit

becoming attractive, comely, enhancing, flattering, graceful, neat, pretty, tasteful
Antonyms ugly, unattractive, unbecoming

bed *n.* 1. bedstead, berth, bunk, cot, couch, divan, pallet 2. area, border, garden, patch, plot, row, strip

bedridden confined, confined to bed, flat on one's back, incapacitated, laid up (*Inf.*)

bedrock bed, bottom, foundation, nadir, rock bottom, substratum, substructure

beef *Inf.* brawn, flesh, heftiness, muscle, physique, robustness, sinew, strength

befitting appropriate, becoming, fit, fitting, meet (*Archaic*), proper, right, seemly, suitable
Antonyms improper, inappropriate, irrelevant, unbecoming, unfit, unsuitable, wrong

before 1. *adv.* ahead, earlier, formerly, in advance, in front, previously, sooner 2. *prep.* earlier than, in advance of, in front of, in the presence of, prior to
Antonyms *adv.* after, afterwards, behind, later, subsequently, thereafter ~ *prep.* after, behind, following, succeeding

beforehand ahead of time, already, before, before now, earlier, in advance, in anticipation, previously, sooner

befriend advise, aid, assist, back, benefit, encourage, favour, help, patronize, side with, stand by, succour, support, sustain, uphold, welcome

beg 1. beseech, crave, desire, entreat, implore, importune, petition, plead, pray, request, solicit, supplicate **2.** cadge, call for alms, scrounge, seek charity, solicit charity, sponge on
Antonyms (*sense 1*) apportion, award, bestow, commit, confer, contribute, donate, give, grant, impart, present (*sense 2*) claim, demand, exact, extort, insist on

beggar *n.* cadger, mendicant, scrounger (*Inf.*), sponger (*Inf.*), supplicant, tramp, vagrant

begin commence, embark on, inaugurate, initiate, instigate, institute, prepare, set about, set on foot, start
Antonyms cease, complete, end, finish, stop, terminate

beginner amateur, apprentice, cub, fledgling, freshman, greenhorn (*Inf.*), initiate, learner, neophyte, novice, recruit, starter, student, tenderfoot, trainee, tyro
Antonyms authority, expert, master, old hand, old stager, oldtimer, past master, past mistress, pro (*Inf.*), professional, trouper, veteran

beginning birth, commencement, inauguration, inception, initiation, onset, opening, origin, outset, preface, prelude, rise, rudiments, source, start, starting point
Antonyms closing, completion, conclusion, end, ending, finish, termination

begrudge be jealous, be reluctant, be stingy, envy, grudge, resent

behave 1. act, function, operate, perform, run, work **2.** act correctly, conduct oneself properly, mind one's manners
Antonyms act up (*Inf.*), be bad, be insubordinate, be naughty, carry on (*Inf.*), get up to mis-

chief, misbehave, muck about (*Brit. sl.*)

behaviour 1. actions, bearing, carriage, comportment, conduct, demeanour, deportment, manner, manners, ways **2.** action, functioning, operation, performance

behind *prep.* **1.** after, at the back of, at the rear of, following, later than **2.** at the bottom of, causing, initiating, instigating, responsible for **3.** backing, for, in agreement, on the side of, supporting ~*adv.* **4.** after, afterwards, following, in the wake (of), next, subsequently **5.** behindhand, in arrears, in debt, overdue
Antonyms (*sense 1*) earlier than, in advance of, in front of, in the presence of, prior to (*sense 4*) ahead, earlier, formerly, in advance, previously, sooner

behold *v.* consider, contemplate, discern, eye, look at, observe, perceive, regard, scan, survey, view, watch, witness

being 1. actuality, animation, existence, life, living, reality **2.** entity, essence, nature, soul, spirit, substance **3.** animal, beast, body, creature, human being, individual, living thing, mortal, thing
Antonyms nihility, nonbeing, nonexistence, nothingness, nullity, oblivion

belated behindhand, behind time, delayed, late, overdue, tardy

belief 1. admission, assent, assurance, confidence, conviction, credit, feeling, impression, judgment, notion, opinion, persuasion, presumption, reliance, theory, trust, view **2.** credence, credo, creed, doctrine, dogma, faith, ideology, principles, tenet
Antonyms disbelief, distrust, doubt, dubiety, incredulity, mistrust, scepticism

believe 1. accept, be certain of, be convinced of, count on, credit, depend on, have faith in, hold, place confidence in, presume true, rely on, swear by, trust **2.** assume, conjecture, consider,

gather, guess, imagine, judge, maintain, postulate, presume, reckon, speculate, suppose, think
Antonyms disbelieve, distrust, doubt, know, question

believer adherent, convert, devotee, disciple, follower, proselyte, supporter, upholder, zealot
Antonyms agnostic, atheist, disbeliever, doubting Thomas, infidel, sceptic, unbeliever

belong 1. With to be at the disposal of, be held by, be owned by, be the property of 2. With to be affiliated to, be allied to, be a member of, be associated with, be included in 3. attach to, be connected with, be fitting, be part of, fit, go with, have as a proper place, pertain to, relate to

belongings accoutrements, chattels, effects, gear, goods, paraphernalia, personal property, possessions, stuff, things

beloved admired, adored, cherished, darling, dear, dearest, loved, pet, precious, prized, revered, sweet, treasured, worshipped

below 1. adv. beneath, down, lower, under, underneath 2. prep. inferior, lesser, lesser than, subject, subordinate, unworthy of

belt band, cincture, cummerbund, girdle, girth, sash, waistband

bemused absent-minded, bewildered, confused, dazed, engrossed, fuddled, half-drunk, muddled, perplexed, preoccupied, stunned, stupefied, tipsy

bench 1. form, pew, seat, settle, stall 2. board, counter, table, trestle table, workbench, worktable 3. court, courtroom, judge, judges, judiciary, magistrate, magistrates, tribunal

bend 1. v. bow, buckle, contort, crouch, curve, deflect, diverge, flex, incline, incurvate, lean, stoop, swerve, turn, twist, veer, warp 2. n. angle, arc, bow, corner, crook, curve, hook, loop, turn, twist, zigzag

beneath 1. adv. below, in a lower place, underneath 2. prep. below,

inferior to, less than, lower than, unbefitting, underneath, unworthy of
Antonyms (sense 2) above, atop, beyond, exceeding, higher than, on top of, over, upon

beneficial advantageous, benign, favourable, gainful, healthful, helpful, profitable, salubrious, salutary, serviceable, useful, valuable, wholesome
Antonyms detrimental, disadvantageous, harmful, pernicious, useless

benefit 1. n. advantage, aid, asset, assistance, avail, betterment, blessing, boon, favour, gain, good, help, interest, profit, use 2. v. advance, advantage, aid, ameliorate, assist, avail, better, enhance, further, improve, profit, promote, serve
Antonyms n. damage, detriment, disadvantage, harm, impairment, injury, loss ~ v. damage, deprive, detract from, harm, impair, injure, worsen

bent adj. 1. angled, arched, bowed, crooked, curved, hunched, stooped, twisted 2. With on determined, disposed, fixed, inclined, insistent, predisposed, resolved, set
Antonyms (sense 1) aligned, erect, even, horizontal, in line, level, perpendicular, plumb, smooth, square, straight, true, upright, vertical

bequest bequeathal, bestowal, dower, endowment, estate, gift, heritage, inheritance, legacy, settlement, trust

bereavement affliction, death, deprivation, loss, misfortune, tribulation

berserk amok, crazy, enraged, frantic, frenzied, insane, mad, maniacal, manic, rabid, raging, uncontrollable, violent, wild

berth n. 1. bed, billet, bunk, cot (Naut.) hammock 2. anchorage, dock, harbour, haven, pier, port, quay, slip, wharf

beseech adjure, ask, beg, call upon, crave, entreat, implore, importune, petition, plead, pray, solicit, sue, supplicate

beside abreast of, adjacent to, alongside, at the side of, close to, near, nearby, neighbouring, next door to, next to, overlooking

besides *adv.* also, as well, further, furthermore, in addition, moreover, otherwise, too, what's more

besiege beleaguer, beset, blockade, confine, encircle, encompass, environ, hedge in, hem in, invest (*Rare*), lay siege to, shut in, surround

best *adj.* **1.** chief, finest, first, first-class, first-rate, foremost, highest, leading, most excellent, outstanding, perfect, pre-eminent, principal, superlative, supreme, unsurpassed **2.** advantageous, apt, correct, golden, most desirable, most fitting, right **3.** greatest, largest, most ~*adv.* **4.** advantageously, attractively, excellently, most fortunately **5.** extremely, greatly, most deeply, most fully, most highly ~*n.* **6.** choice, cream, elite, favourite, finest, first, flower, pick, prime, top

bestial animal, barbaric, barbarous, beastlike, beastly, brutal, brutish, carnal, degraded, depraved, gross, inhuman, low, savage, sensual, sordid, vile

bestow accord, allot, apportion, award, commit, confer, donate, entrust, give, grant, honour with, impart, lavish, present, render to

Antonyms acquire, attain, come by, earn, gain, get, make, net, obtain, procure, secure

bet 1. *n.* ante, gamble, hazard, long shot, pledge, risk, speculation, stake, venture, wager **2.** *v.* chance, gamble, hazard, pledge, punt (*Brit.*), put money on, risk, speculate, stake, venture, wager

betray 1. be disloyal (treacherous, unfaithful), break one's promise, break with, double-cross (*Inf.*), inform on *or* against, sell down the river (*Inf.*), sell out (*Inf.*) **2.** blurt out, disclose, divulge, evince, expose, give away, lay bare, let slip, manifest, reveal, show, tell, tell on, uncover, unmask **3.** abandon, desert, forsake, jilt, walk out on

betrayal 1. deception, disloyalty, double-cross (*Inf.*), double-dealing, duplicity, falseness, perfidy, sell-out (*Inf.*), treachery, treason, trickery, unfaithfulness **2.** blurting out, disclosure, divulgence, giving away, revelation, telling

Antonyms (*sense 1*) allegiance, constancy, devotion, faithfulness, fealty, fidelity, loyalty, steadfastness, trustiness, trustworthiness (*sense 2*) guarding, keeping, keeping secret, preserving, safeguarding

better *adj.* **1.** bigger, excelling, finer, fitter, greater, higher-quality, larger, more appropriate (desirable, expert, fitting, suitable, useful, valuable), preferable, superior, surpassing, worthier **2.** cured, fitter, fully recovered, healthier, improving, less ill, mending, more healthy, on the mend (*Inf.*), progressing, recovering, stronger, well **3.** bigger, greater, larger, longer ~*adv.* **4.** in a more excellent manner, in a superior way, more advantageously (attractively, competently, completely, effectively, thoroughly), to a greater degree

Antonyms *adj.* inferior, lesser, smaller, substandard, worse ~*adv.* worse

between amidst, among, betwixt, halfway, in the middle of, mid

bewail bemoan, cry over, deplore, express sorrow, grieve for, keen, lament, moan, mourn, regret, repent, rue, wail, weep over

beware avoid, be careful (cautious, wary), guard against, heed, look out, mind, refrain from, shun, steer clear of, take heed, watch out

bewilder baffle, befuddle, bemuse, confound, confuse, daze, mix up, mystify, perplex, puzzle, stupefy

bewitch allure, attract, beguile, captivate, charm, enchant, enrapture, entrance, fascinate, hypnotize, spellbind

beyond above, apart from, at a distance, away from, before, farther, out of range, out of reach, over, past, remote, superior to, yonder

bias n. bent, bigotry, favouritism, inclination, intolerance, leaning, narrow-mindedness, one-sidedness, partiality, penchant, predilection, predisposition, prejudice, proclivity, proneness, propensity, tendency, turn, unfairness

Antonyms equality, equity, fairness, impartiality, neutrality, objectivity, open-mindedness

biased distorted, embittered, jaundiced, one-sided, partial, predisposed, prejudiced, slanted, swayed, twisted, warped, weighted

bicker argue, disagree, dispute, fight, quarrel, row (Inf.), scrap (Inf.), spar, squabble, wrangle

bid v. 1. offer, proffer, propose, submit, tender 2. call, greet, say, tell, wish 3. ask, call, charge, command, desire, direct, enjoin, instruct, invite, require, solicit, summon, tell ~n. 4. advance, amount, offer, price, proposal, proposition, submission, sum, tender 5. attempt, crack (Inf.), effort, endeavour, try, venture

bidding behest, call, charge, command, demand, direction, injunction, instruction, invitation, order, request, summons

big 1. bulky, burly, colossal, considerable, enormous, extensive, gigantic, great, huge, hulking, immense, large, mammoth, massive, ponderous, prodigious, sizable, spacious, substantial, vast, voluminous 2. eminent, important, influential, leading, main, momentous, paramount, powerful, prime, principal, prominent, serious, significant, valuable, weighty 3. altruistic, benevolent, generous, gracious,

heroic, magnanimous, noble, princely, unselfish 4. arrogant, boastful, bragging, conceited, haughty, inflated, pompous, pretentious, proud

Antonyms (sense 1) diminutive, insignificant, little, mini, miniature, petite, pint-sized (Inf.), pocket-sized, small, tiny, wee (sense 2) humble, ignoble, insignificant, minor, modest, ordinary, unimportant, unknown

bill[1] n. 1. account, charges, invoice, note of charge, reckoning, score, statement, tally 2. advertisement, broadsheet, bulletin, circular, handbill, handout, leaflet, notice, placard, playbill, poster 3. measure, piece of legislation, projected law, proposal ~v. 4. charge, debit, figure, invoice, reckon, record

bill[2] beak, mandible, neb (Archaic or dialect), nib

billet 1. n. accommodation, barracks, lodging, quarters 2. v. accommodate, berth, quarter, station

billow n. 1. breaker, crest, roller, surge, swell, tide, wave 2. cloud, deluge, flood, outpouring, rush, surge, wave ~v. 3. balloon, belly, puff up, rise up, roll, surge, swell

bind v. 1. attach, fasten, glue, hitch, lash, paste, rope, secure, stick, strap, tie, tie up, truss, wrap 2. compel, constrain, engage, force, necessitate, obligate, oblige, prescribe, require 3. confine, detain, hamper, hinder, restrain, restrict 4. bandage, cover, dress, encase, swathe, wrap 5. border, edge, finish, hem, trim

Antonyms (senses 1 & 3) free, loosen, release, unbind, undo, unfasten, untie

binding adj. compulsory, conclusive, imperative, indissoluble, irrevocable, mandatory, necessary, obligatory, unalterable

Antonyms discretionary, free, noncompulsory, optional, uncompelled, unconstrained, unforced, voluntary

birth 1. childbirth, delivery, nativity, parturition 2. beginning, emergence, fountainhead, genesis, origin, rise, source 3. ancestry, background, blood, breeding, derivation, descent, extraction, forebears, genealogy, line, lineage, nobility, noble extraction, parentage, pedigree, race, stock, strain

Antonyms (senses 1 & 2) death, demise, end, extinction, passing, passing away or on

bisect bifurcate, cross, cut across, cut in half, cut in two, divide in two, halve, intersect, separate, split, split down the middle

bit atom, chip, crumb, fragment, grain, iota, jot, mite, morsel, mouthful, part, piece, scrap, segment, slice, small piece, speck, tittle, whit

bite v. 1. champ, chew, clamp, crunch, crush, cut, gnaw, grip, hold, masticate, nibble, nip, pierce, pinch, rend, seize, snap, tear, wound ~n. 2. itch, nip, pinch, prick, smarting, sting, tooth marks, wound 3. food, light meal, morsel, mouthful, piece, refreshment, snack, taste 4. edge, kick (Inf.), piquancy, punch (Inf.), pungency, spice

bitter 1. acid, acrid, astringent, sharp, sour, tart, unsweetened, vinegary 2. acrimonious, begrudging, crabbed, embittered, hostile, morose, rancorous, resentful, sore, sour, sullen, with a chip on one's shoulder

Antonyms appreciative, bland, friendly, gentle, grateful, happy, mellow, mild, pleasant, sugary, sweet, thankful

bitterness 1. acerbity, acidity, sharpness, sourness, tartness, vinegariness 2. animosity, grudge, hostility, pique, rancour, resentment

bizarre abnormal, comical, curious, eccentric, extraordinary, fantastic, freakish, grotesque, ludicrous, odd, oddball (Inf.), offbeat, outlandish, outré, peculiar,

queer, ridiculous, strange, unusual, way-out (Inf.), weird

Antonyms common, customary, normal, ordinary, regular, routine, standard, typical

black adj. 1. coal-black, dark, dusky, ebony, inky, jet, murky, pitchy, raven, sable, starless, stygian, swarthy 2. Fig. atrocious, depressing, dismal, distressing, doleful, foreboding, funereal, gloomy, hopeless, horrible, lugubrious, mournful, ominous, sad, sombre 3. bad, evil, iniquitous, nefarious, villainous, wicked ~v. 4. ban, bar, blacklist, boycott

blacken 1. befoul, begrime, cloud, darken, grow black, make black, smudge, soil 2. calumniate, decry, defame, defile, denigrate, dishonour, malign, slander, smear, smirch, stain, sully, taint, tarnish, traduce, vilify

blacklist v. ban, bar, blackball, boycott, debar, exclude, expel, ostracize, preclude, proscribe, reject, repudiate, snub, vote against

black magic black art, diabolism, necromancy, sorcery, voodoo, witchcraft, wizardry

blackmail n. bribe, exaction, extortion, hush money (Sl.), intimidation, milking, pay-off (Inf.), protection (Inf.), ransom, slush fund

blackness darkness, duskiness, gloom, inkiness, melanism, murkiness, nigrescence, nigritude (Rare), swarthiness

Antonyms brightness, brilliance, effulgence, incandescence, lambency, light, lightness, luminescence, luminosity, phosphorescence, radiance

blackout n. 1. coma, faint, loss of consciousness, oblivion, swoon, syncope (Pathology), unconsciousness 2. power cut, power failure

black sheep disgrace, dropout, ne'er-do-well, outcast, prodigal, renegade, reprobate, wastrel

blame n. 1. accountability, culpability, fault, guilt, incrimination, liability, onus, rap (*Inf.*), responsibility 2. accusation, castigation, censure, charge, complaint, condemnation, criticism, recrimination, reproach, reproof ~*v.* 3. accuse, admonish, censure, charge, chide, condemn, criticize, disapprove, express disapprobation, find fault with, hold responsible, reprehend, reproach, reprove, tax, upbraid

Antonyms *n.* absolution, acclaim, alibi, commendation, credit, excuse, exoneration, honour, praise, tribute, vindication ~*v.* absolve, acclaim, acquit, approve of, clear, commend, compliment, excuse, exonerate, forgive, praise, vindicate

blameless above suspicion, clean, faultless, guiltless, immaculate, impeccable, innocent, in the clear, irreproachable, perfect, stainless, unblemished, unimpeachable, unoffending, unspotted, unsullied, untarnished, upright, virtuous

Antonyms at fault, censurable, culpable, guilty, reprovable, responsible, to blame

bland 1. boring, dull, flat, humdrum, insipid, monotonous, tasteless, tedious, undistinctive, unexciting, uninspiring, uninteresting, unstimulating, vapid, weak 2. affable, amiable, congenial, courteous, friendly, gentle, gracious, smooth, suave, unemotional, urbane

Antonyms (*sense 1*) distinctive, exciting, inspiring, interesting, rousing, stimulating, turbulent, volatile

blank *adj.* 1. bare, clean, clear, empty, plain, spotless, uncompleted, unfilled, unmarked, void, white 2. at a loss, bewildered, confounded, confused, disconcerted, dumbfounded, muddled, nonplussed, uncomprehending ~*n.* 3. emptiness, empty space, gap, nothingness, space, tabula rasa, vacancy, vacuity, vacuum, void

blanket *n.* 1. afghan, cover, cov-

erlet, rug 2. carpet, cloak, coat, coating, covering, envelope, film, layer, mantle, sheet, wrapper, wrapping ~*v.* 3. cloak, cloud, coat, conceal, cover, eclipse, hide, mask, obscure, suppress, surround

blare blast, boom, clamour, clang, honk, hoot, peal, resound, roar, scream, sound out, toot, trumpet

blasphemous godless, impious, irreligious, irreverent, profane, sacrilegious, ungodly

Antonyms devout, God-fearing, godly, pious, religious, respectful, reverent, reverential

blasphemy cursing, desecration, execration, impiety, impiousness, indignity (*to God*), irreverence, profanation, profaneness, profanity, sacrilege, swearing

blast *n./v.* 1. blare, blow, clang, honk, peal, scream, toot, wail ~*n.* 2. bang, blow-up, burst, crash, detonation, discharge, eruption, explosion, outburst, salvo, volley ~*v.* 3. blow up, break up, burst, demolish, destroy, explode, ruin, shatter

blatant bald, brazen, conspicuous, flagrant, flaunting, glaring, naked, obtrusive, obvious, ostentatious, outright, overt, prominent, pronounced, sheer, unmitigated

Antonyms agreeable, cultured, dignified, hidden, inconspicuous, refined, subtle, tasteful, unnoticeable, unobtrusive, wellmannered

blaze *n.* 1. bonfire, conflagration, fire, flame, flames 2. beam, brilliance, flare, flash, glare, gleam, glitter, glow, light, radiance ~*v.* 3. beam, burn, fire, flame, flare, flash, glare, gleam, glow, shine 4. boil, explode, flare up, fume, seethe

bleak 1. bare, barren, chilly, cold, desolate, exposed, gaunt, open, raw, unsheltered, weatherbeaten, windswept, windy 2. cheerless, comfortless, depressing, discouraging, disheartening, dismal, dreary, gloomy, grim, hopeless, joyless, sombre, unpromising

Antonyms cheerful, cosy, encouraging, promising, protected, sheltered, shielded

blemish n. blot, blotch, blur, defect, disfigurement, disgrace, dishonour, fault, flaw, imperfection, mark, smudge, speck, spot, stain, taint

Antonyms enhancement, improvement, ornament, perfection, purity, refinement

blend v. 1.amalgamate, coalesce, combine, compound, fuse, intermix, meld, merge, mingle, mix, synthesize, unite 2. complement, fit, go well, go with, harmonize, suit ~n. 3. alloy, amalgam, amalgamation, combination, composite, compound, concoction, fusion, meld, mix, mixture, synthesis, union

bless 1. anoint, consecrate, dedicate, exalt, extol, give thanks to, glorify, hallow, invoke happiness on, magnify, ordain, praise, sanctify, thank 2. bestow, endow, favour, give, grace, grant, provide

Antonyms (*sense 1*) accuse, anathematize, curse, damn, excommunicate, execrate, fulminate, imprecate (*sense 2*) afflict, blight, burden, curse, destroy, doom, plague, scourge, torment, trouble, vex

blessed 1. adored, beatified, divine, hallowed, holy, revered, sacred, sanctified 2. endowed, favoured, fortunate, granted, lucky

blessing 1. benediction, benison, commendation, consecration, dedication, grace, invocation, thanksgiving 2. approbation, approval, backing, concurrence, consent, favour, good wishes, leave, permission, regard, sanction, support 3. advantage, benefit, boon, bounty, favour, gain, gift, godsend, good fortune, help, kindness, profit, service, windfall

Antonyms condemnation, curse, damage, deprivation, disadvantage, disapproval, disfavour,

drawback, harm, malediction, misfortune, objection, reproof

blight n. 1.canker, decay, disease, fungus, infestation, mildew, pest, pestilence, rot ~v. 2. blast, destroy, injure, nip in the bud, ruin, shrivel, taint with mildew, wither 3. *Fig.* annihilate, crush, dash, disappoint, frustrate, mar, nullify, ruin, spoil, wreck

blind adj. 1. destitute of vision, eyeless, sightless, stone-blind, unseeing, unsighted, visionless 2. *Fig.* careless, heedless, ignorant, inattentive, inconsiderate, indifferent, indiscriminate, injudicious, insensitive, morally darkened, neglectful, oblivious, prejudiced, thoughtless, unaware of, unconscious of, uncritical, undiscerning, unmindful of, unobservant, unreasoning 3. hasty, impetuous, irrational, mindless, rash, reckless, senseless, uncontrollable, uncontrolled, unthinking, violent, wild ~n. 4. camouflage, cloak, cover, façade, feint, front, mask, masquerade, screen, smoke screen

Antonyms adj. alive to, attentive, aware, concerned, conscious, discerning, heedful, knowledgeable, noticeable, observant, obvious, seeing, sighted

bliss beatitude, blessedness, blissfulness, ecstasy, euphoria, felicity, gladness, happiness, heaven, joy, paradise, rapture

Antonyms affliction, anguish, distress, grief, heartbreak, misery, mourning, regret, sadness, sorrow, unhappiness, woe, wretchedness

blissful delighted, ecstatic, elated, enchanted, enraptured, euphoric, happy, heavenly (*Inf.*), in ecstasies, joyful, joyous, rapturous

blithe animated, buoyant, carefree, cheerful, cheery, debonair, gay, gladsome, happy, jaunty, light-hearted, merry, mirthful, sprightly, sunny, vivacious

blizzard blast, gale, snowstorm, squall, storm, tempest

block *n.* 1. bar, brick, cake, chunk, cube, hunk, ingot, lump, mass, piece, square 2. bar, barrier, blockage, hindrance, impediment, jam, obstacle, obstruction, stoppage ~*v.* 3. bung up (*Inf.*), choke, clog, close, obstruct, plug, stop up 4. arrest, bar, check, deter, halt, hinder, impede, obstruct, stop, thwart

Antonyms *v.* (*sense 3*) clear, open, unblock, unclog (*sense 4*) advance, aid, expedite, facilitate, foster, further, lend support to, promote, push, support

blockade barricade, barrier, closure, encirclement, hindrance, impediment, obstacle, obstruction, restriction, siege, stoppage

blood 1. gore, lifeblood, vital fluid 2. ancestry, birth, consanguinity, descendants, descent, extraction, family, kindred, kinship, lineage, noble extraction, relations

bloodshed blood bath, bloodletting, butchery, carnage, gore, killing, massacre, murder, slaughter, slaying

bloodthirsty barbarous, brutal, cruel, ferocious, inhuman, murderous, ruthless, savage, vicious, warlike

bloody 1. bleeding, blood-soaked, blood-spattered, bloodstained, gaping, raw, unstaunched 2. cruel, ferocious, fierce, sanguinary, savage

bloom *n.* 1. blossom, blossoming, bud, efflorescence, flower, opening (*of flowers*) 2. *Fig.* beauty, blush, flourishing, flush, freshness, glow, health, heyday, lustre, perfection, prime, radiance, rosiness, vigour ~*v.* 3. blossom, blow, bud, burgeon, open, sprout

Antonyms *v.* (*sense 2*) bloodlessness, paleness, pallor, wanness, whiteness ~*v.* (*sense 3*) decay, die, droop, fade, perish, shrink, shrivel, waste, wilt, wither

blossom *n.* 1. bloom, bud, floret, flower, flowers ~*v.* 2. bloom, burgeon, flower 3. *Fig.* bloom, develop, flourish, grow, mature, progress, prosper, thrive

blot *n.* 1. blotch, mark, patch, smear, smudge, speck, splodge, spot 2. blemish, blur, defect, disgrace, fault, flaw, spot, stain, taint

blow¹ *v.* 1. blast, breathe, exhale, fan, pant, puff, waft 2. flow, rush, stream, whirl 3. bear, buffet, drive, fling, flutter, sweep, waft, whirl, whisk 4. blare, mouth, pipe, play, sound, toot, trumpet, vibrate ~*n.* 5. blast, draught, flurry, gale, gust, puff, strong breeze, tempest, wind

blow² *n.* 1. bang, bash (*Inf.*), belt (*Inf.*), buffet, clomp (*Sl.*), clout (*Inf.*), clump (*Sl.*), knock, punch, rap, slosh (*Sl.*), smack, sock (*Sl.*), stroke, thump, wallop (*Inf.*), whack 2. *Fig.* affliction, bolt from the blue, bombshell, calamity, catastrophe, comedown (*Inf.*), disappointment, disaster, jolt, misfortune, reverse, setback, shock, upset

blow up 1. blast, distend, enlarge, expand, fill, inflate, puff up, pump up, swell 2. blast, bomb, burst, detonate, dynamite, explode, go off, rupture, shatter 3. enlarge, enlarge on, exaggerate, heighten, magnify, overstate

blue 1. azure, cerulean, cobalt, cyan, navy, sapphire, sky-coloured, ultramarine 2. *Fig.* dejected, depressed, despondent, dismal, downcast, down-hearted, down in the dumps (*Inf.*), fed up, gloomy, glum, low, melancholy, sad, unhappy

blueprint design, draft, layout, outline, pattern, pilot scheme, plan, project, prototype, scheme, sketch

bluff¹ *v.* deceive, defraud, delude, fake, feign, humbug, lie, mislead, pretend, sham 2. *n.* bluster, boast, braggadocio, bragging, bravado, deceit, deception, fake, feint, fraud, humbug, idle boast, lie, mere show, pretence, sham, show, subterfuge

blunder 1. *n.* error, fault, inaccuracy, mistake, oversight, slip,

slip-up (*Inf.*) **2.** *v.* botch, bungle, err, slip up (*Inf.*)

Antonyms *n.* accuracy, achievement, correctness, success ~*v.* be correct, get it right

blunt *adj.* **1.** dull, dulled, edgeless, pointless, rounded, unsharpened **2.** *Fig.* bluff, brusque, discourteous, explicit, forthright, frank, impolite, outspoken, plainspoken, rude, straightforward, tactless, trenchant, uncivil, unpolished

Antonyms acute, courteous, diplomatic, keen, pointed, sensitive, sharp, subtle, tactful

blur *v.* **1.** becloud, bedim, befog, cloud, darken, dim, fog, make hazy, make indistinct, make vague, mask, obscure, soften **2.** blot, smear, smudge, spot, stain ~*n.* **3.** blear, blurredness, cloudiness, confusion, dimness, fog, haze, indistinctness, obscurity

blush *v.* colour, crimson, flush, redden, turn red, turn scarlet

Antonyms blanch, blench, drain, fade, pale, turn pale, whiten

bluster **1.** *v.* boast, brag, bulldoze, bully, domineer, hector, rant, roar, roister, storm, swagger, swell, vaunt **2.** *n.* bluff, boasting, boisterousness, bombast, bragging, bravado, crowing, swagger, swaggering

board *n.* **1.** panel, piece of timber, plank, slat, timber **2.** daily meals, food, meals, provisions, victuals **3.** advisers, advisory group, committee, conclave, council, directorate, directors, panel, trustees ~*v.* **4.** embark, embus, enplane, enter, entrain, mount **5.** accommodate, feed, house, lodge, put up, quarter, room

Antonyms (*sense 4*) alight, arrive, disembark, dismount, get off, go ashore, land

boast *v.* **1.** blow one's own trumpet, bluster, brag, crow, exaggerate, puff, strut, swagger, talk big (*Sl.*), vaunt **2.** be proud of, congratulate oneself on, exhibit, flatter oneself, possess, pride oneself on, show off ~*n.* **3.** avowal, brag, gasconade (*Rare*), rodomontade (*Literary*), swank (*Inf.*), vaunt **4.** gem, joy, pride, pride and joy, source of pride, treasure

boastful bragging, cocky, conceited, crowing, egotistical, puffed-up, swaggering, swanky (*Inf.*), swollen-headed, vainglorious, vaunting

Antonyms deprecating, humble, modest, self-belittling, self-effacing, unassuming

body **1.** build, figure, form, frame, physique, shape, torso, trunk **2.** cadaver, carcass, corpse, dead body, relics, remains, stiff (*Sl.*) **3.** bulk, essence, main part, mass, material, matter, substance **4.** association, band, bloc, collection, company, confederation, congress, corporation, society **5.** crowd, horde, majority, mass, mob, multitude, throng

bog fen, marsh, marshland, mire, morass, moss (*Northern Eng. & Scot.*), peat bog, quagmire, slough, swamp, wetlands

bogus artificial, counterfeit, dummy, fake, false, forged, fraudulent, imitation, phoney (*Sl.*), pseudo (*Inf.*), sham, spurious

bohemian *adj.* alternative, artistic, arty (*Inf.*) avant-garde, eccentric, exotic, left-bank, nonconformist, offbeat, unconventional, unorthodox, way-out (*Inf.*)

Antonyms bourgeois, conservative, conventional, square (*Inf.*), straight (*Sl.*), straight-laced, stuffy

boil *v.* agitate, bubble, churn, effervesce, fizz, foam, froth, seethe

boisterous bouncy, clamorous, disorderly, impetuous, loud, noisy, obstreperous, riotous, rollicking, rowdy, rumbustious, unrestrained, unruly, uproarious, vociferous, wild

Antonyms calm, controlled, peaceful, quiet, restrained, self-controlled, subdued

bold **1.** adventurous, audacious, brave, courageous, daring,

dauntless, enterprising, fearless, gallant, heroic, intrepid, lion-hearted, valiant, valorous **2.** bright, colourful, conspicuous, eye-catching, flashy, forceful, lively, loud, prominent, pronounced, showy, spirited, striking, strong, vivid
Antonyms conservative, cool, courteous, cowardly, dull, faint-hearted, fearful, ordinary, pale, soft, timid, timorous, unimaginative

bolt *n.* **1.** bar, catch, fastener, latch, lock, sliding bar **2.** peg, pin, rivet, rod **3.** bound, dart, dash, escape, flight, rush, spring, sprint **4.** arrow, dart, missile, projectile, shaft, thunderbolt ~*v.* **5.** bar, fasten, latch, lock, secure **6.** cram, devour, gobble, gorge, gulp, guzzle, stuff, swallow whole, wolf **7.** abscond, bound, dash, escape, flee, fly, hurtle, jump, leap, make a break (for it), run, run for it, rush, spring, sprint

bomb 1. *n.* bombshell, charge, device, explosive, grenade, mine, missile, projectile, rocket, shell, torpedo **2.** *v.* attack, blow up, bombard, destroy, shell, strafe, torpedo

bona fide actual, authentic, genuine, honest, kosher (*Inf.*), lawful, legal, legitimate, real, true

bond *n.* **1.** band, binding, chain, cord, fastening, fetter, ligature, link, manacle, shackle, tie **2.** affiliation, affinity, attachment, connection, link, relation, tie, union **3.** agreement, compact, contract, covenant, guarantee, obligation, pledge, promise, word ~*v.* **4.** bind, connect, fasten, fix together, fuse, glue, gum, paste

bonus benefit, bounty, commission, dividend, extra, gift, gratuity, hand-out, honorarium, perk (*Inf.*), plus, premium, prize, reward

book *n.* **1.** manual, publication, roll, scroll, textbook, tome, tract, volume, work **2.** album, diary, exercise book, jotter, notebook,

pad ~*v.* **3.** arrange for, bill, charter, engage, line up, make reservations, organize, procure, programme, reserve, schedule

boom *v.* **1.** bang, blast, crash, explode, resound, reverberate, roar, roll, rumble, thunder **2.** develop, expand, flourish, gain, grow, increase, intensify, prosper, spurt, strengthen, succeed, swell, thrive ~*n.* **3.** bang, blast, burst, clap, crash, explosion, roar, rumble, thunder **4.** advance, boost, development, expansion, gain, growth, improvement, increase, jump, push, spurt, upsurge, upswing, upturn
Antonyms *v.* (*sense 2*) crash, fail, fall, slump ~*n.* (*sense 4*) bust (*Inf.*), collapse, crash, decline, depression, downturn, failure, hard times, recession, slump

boon *n.* advantage, benefaction, benefit, blessing, donation, favour, gift, godsend, grant, gratuity, present, windfall

boost *n.* **1.** encouragement, help, hype (*Inf.*), improvement, praise, promotion **2.** heave, hoist, lift, push, raise, shove, thrust **3.** addition, expansion, improvement, increase, increment, jump, rise ~*v.* **4.** advance, advertise, assist, encourage, foster, further, hype (*Inf.*), improve, inspire, plug (*Inf.*), praise, promote, support, sustain **5.** elevate, heave, hoist, lift, push, raise, shove, thrust

border *n.* **1.** bound, boundary, bounds, brim, brink, confine, confines, edge, hem, limit, limits, lip, margin, rim, skirt, verge **2.** borderline, boundary, frontier, line, march

borderline *adj.* ambivalent, doubtful, equivocal, indecisive, indefinite, indeterminate, inexact, marginal, unclassifiable

bore¹ 1. *v.* burrow, drill, gouge out, mine, penetrate, perforate, pierce, sink, tunnel **2.** *n.* borehole, calibre, drill hole, hole, shaft, tunnel

bore² 1. *v.* annoy, be tedious, bother, exhaust, fatigue, jade, pall on, pester, send to sleep, tire, trouble, vex, wear out, weary, worry 2. v. bother, drag (SL), dullard, dull person, headache (Inf.), nuisance, pain (Inf.), pain in the neck (Inf.), pest, tiresome person, wearisome talker, yawn (Inf.)

Antonyms v. amuse, divert, engross, excite, fascinate, hold the attention of, interest, stimulate

boredom apathy, doldrums, dullness, ennui, flatness, irksomeness, monotony, sameness, tediousness, tedium, weariness, world-weariness

boring dead, dull, flat, humdrum, insipid, monotonous, repetitious, routine, stale, tedious, tiresome, tiring, unexciting, uninteresting, unvaried, wearisome

borrow 1. cadge, scrounge (Inf.), take and return, take on loan, use temporarily 2. acquire, adopt, appropriate, copy, filch, imitate, obtain, pilfer, pirate, plagiarize, simulate, steal, take, use, usurp

Antonyms advance, give, lend, loan, provide, return, supply

bosom n. 1. breast, bust, chest 2. affections, emotions, feelings, heart, sentiments, soul, spirit, sympathies ~adj. 3. boon, cherished, close, confidential, intimate, very dear

boss n. administrator, chief, director, employer, executive, foreman, gaffer (Inf.), governor (Inf.), head, leader, manager, master, overseer, owner, superintendent, supervisor

botch v. balls up (Taboo sl.), blunder, bungle, butcher, cobble, cock up (Brit. sl.), fumble, mar, mend, mess, mismanage, muff, patch, screw up (Inf.), spoil

bother 1. v. alarm, annoy, concern, dismay, distress, disturb, harass, inconvenience, irritate, molest, nag, pester, plague, put out, trouble, upset, vex, worry 2. n. aggravation, annoyance, bustle, difficulty, flurry, fuss, inconvenience, irritation, molestation, nuisance, perplexity, pest, problem, strain, trouble, vexation, worry

bottom n. 1. base, basis, bed, deepest part, depths, floor, foot, foundation, groundwork, lowest part, pedestal, support 2. lower side, sole, underneath, underside ~adj. 3. base, basement, basic, fundamental, ground, last, lowest, undermost

Antonyms n. cover, crown, height, lid, peak, summit, surface, top ~adj. higher, highest, top, upper

bounce v. 1. bob, bound, bump, jounce, jump, leap, rebound, recoil, resile, ricochet, spring, thump ~n. 2. bound, elasticity, give, rebound, recoil, resilience, spring, springiness 3. animation, dynamism, energy, go (Inf.), life, liveliness, pep, vigour, vitality, vivacity, zip (Inf.)

bound¹ adj. 1. cased, fastened, fixed, pinioned, secured, tied, tied up 2. certain, destined, doomed, fated, sure 3. beholden, committed, compelled, constrained, duty-bound, forced, obligated, obliged, pledged, required

bound² v./n. bob, bounce, caper, frisk, gambol, hurdle, jump, leap, pounce, prance, skip, spring, vault

bound³ n. Usually plural border, boundary, confine, edge, extremity, fringe, limit, line, march, margin, pale, periphery, rim, termination, verge

boundary barrier, border, borderline, bounds, brink, confines, edge, extremity, fringe, frontier, limits, march, margin, precinct, termination, verge

boundless endless, illimitable, immeasurable, immense, incalculable, inexhaustible, infinite, limitless, measureless, unbounded, unconfined, unending, unlimited, untold, vast

Antonyms bounded, confined, limited, little, restricted, small

bountiful 1. abundant, ample, bounteous, copious, exuberant, lavish, luxuriant, plenteous, plentiful, prolific **2.** beneficent, bounteous, generous, liberal, magnanimous, munificent, open-handed, princely, unstinting

bout battle, boxing match, competition, contest, encounter, engagement, fight, match, set-to, struggle

bow v. **1.** bend, bob, droop, genuflect, incline, make obeisance, nod, stoop **2.** accept, acquiesce, comply, concede, defer, give in, kowtow, relent, submit, surrender, yield ~n. **3.** bending, bob, genuflexion, inclination, kowtow, nod, obeisance, salaam

box n. carton, case, chest, container, pack, package, portmanteau, receptacle, trunk

boy fellow, junior, lad, schoolboy, stripling, youngster, youth

boycott ban, bar, black, blackball, blacklist, embargo, exclude, ostracize, outlaw, prohibit, proscribe, refrain from, refuse, reject, spurn
Antonyms accept, advocate, back, champion, defend, help, patronize, promote, support, welcome

boyfriend admirer, beau, date, follower, lover, man, steady, suitor, swain, sweetheart, toy boy, young man

bracing brisk, chilly, cool, crisp, energizing, exhilarating, fortifying, fresh, invigorating, lively, refreshing, restorative, reviving, rousing, stimulating, tonic, vigorous
Antonyms debilitating, draining, enervating, exhausting, fatiguing, sapping, soporific, taxing, tiring, weakening

brainless foolish, idiotic, inept, mindless, senseless, stupid, thoughtless, unintelligent, witless

brake 1. n. check, constraint, control, curb, rein, restraint **2.** v. check, decelerate, halt, moderate, reduce speed, slacken, slow, stop

branch 1. arm, bough, limb, offshoot, prong, ramification, shoot, spray, sprig **2.** chapter, department, division, local office, office, part, section, subdivision, subsection, wing

brand n. **1.** cast, class, grade, kind, make, quality, sort, species, type, variety **2.** emblem, hallmark, label, mark, marker, sign, stamp, symbol, trademark ~v. **3.** burn, burn in, label, mark, scar, stamp **4.** censure, denounce, discredit, disgrace, expose, mark, stigmatize

brandish display, exhibit, flaunt, flourish, parade, raise, shake, swing, wield

bravado bluster, boast, boastfulness, boasting, braggadocio, braggadocio, fanfaronade (Rare), swagger, swaggering, swashbuckling, vaunting

brave adj. bold, courageous, daring, dauntless, fearless, gallant, heroic, intrepid, plucky, resolute, undaunted, valiant, valorous
Antonyms afraid, cowardly, craven, faint-hearted, fearful, frightened, scared, shrinking, timid

bravery balls (Sl.), boldness, bravura, courage, daring, dauntlessness, doughtiness, fearlessness, fortitude, gallantry, grit, guts (Inf.), hardihood, hardiness, heroism, indomitability, intrepidity, mettle, pluck, pluckiness, spirit, spunk (Inf.), valour
Antonyms cowardice, faint-heartedness, fearfulness, fright, timidity

brawl 1. n. affray (Law), altercation, argument, battle, broil, clash, disorder, dispute, donnybrook, fight, fracas, fray, free-for-all (Inf.), melee, punch-up (Sl.), quarrel, row (Inf.), ruckus (Inf.), rumpus, scrap (Inf.), scuffle, squabble, tumult, uproar, wrangle **2.** v. altercate, argue, battle, dispute, fight, quarrel, row (Inf.), scrap (Inf.), scuffle, tussle, wrangle, wrestle

breach 1. aperture, break, chasm, cleft, crack, fissure, gap, hole, opening, rent, rift, rupture, split **2.** contravention, disobedience, infraction, infringement, non-compliance, nonobservance, offence, transgression, trespass, violation

bread aliment, diet, fare, food, necessities, nourishment, nutriment, provisions, subsistence, sustenance, staff of life, victuals

breadth 1. beam (of a ship), broadness, latitude, span, spread, wideness, width 2. broadmindedness, freedom, latitude, liberality, open-mindedness, openness, permissiveness

break v. 1. batter, burst, crack, crash, demolish, destroy, disintegrate, divide, fracture, fragment, part, rend, separate, sever, shatter, shiver, smash, snap, splinter, split, tear 2. breach, contravene, disobey, disregard, infract (Law), infringe, renege on, transgress, violate 3. cow, cripple, demoralize, dispirit, enervate, enfeeble, impair, incapacitate, subdue, tame, undermine, weaken 4. Of a record, etc. beat, better, cap (Inf.), exceed, excel, go beyond, outdo, outstrip, surpass, top 5. appear, burst out, come forth suddenly, emerge, erupt, happen, occur 6. cut and run (Inf.), dash, escape, flee, fly, get away, run away ~n. 7. breach, cleft, crack, division, fissure, fracture, gap, gash, hole, opening, rent, rift, rupture, split, tear 8. breather (Inf.), halt, hiatus, interlude, intermission, interruption, interval, let-up (Inf.), lull, pause, recess, respite, rest, suspension 9. alienation, breach, disaffection, dispute, divergence, estrangement, rift, rupture, schism, separation, split

Antonyms (sense 1) attach, bind, connect, fasten, join, repair, unite (sense 2) abide by, adhere to, conform, discharge, follow, obey, observe

breakdown 1. collapse, crackup (Inf.), disintegration, disruption, failure, mishap, stoppage 2. analysis, categorization, classifi-

cation, detailed list, diagnosis, dissection, itemization

break off 1. detach, divide, part, pull off, separate, sever, snap off, splinter 2. cease, desist, discontinue, end, finish, halt, pause, stop, suspend, terminate

break out 1. appear, arise, begin, commence, emerge, happen, occur, set in, spring up, start 2. abscond, bolt, break loose, burst out, escape, flee, get free 3. burst out, erupt

breakthrough advance, development, discovery, find, gain, improvement, invention, leap, progress, quantum leap, step forward

break-up breakdown, breaking, crackup (Inf.), disintegration, dispersal, dissolution, divorce, ending, parting, rift, separation, split, splitting, termination, wind-up (Inf., chiefly U.S.)

break up adjourn, disband, dismantle, disperse, disrupt, dissolve, divide, divorce, end, part, scatter, separate, sever, split, stop, suspend, terminate

breath 1. air, animation, breathing, exhalation, gasp, gulp, inhalation, pant, respiration, wheeze 2. aroma, odour, smell, vapour, whiff 3. faint breeze, flutter, gust, puff, sigh, slight movement, waft, zephyr 4. hint, murmur, suggestion, suspicion, undertone, whisper

breathe 1. draw in, gasp, gulp, inhale and exhale, pant, puff, respire, wheeze 2. articulate, express, murmur, say, sigh, utter, voice, whisper

breathless 1. choking, exhausted, gasping, gulping, out of breath, panting, short-winded, spent, wheezing, winded 2. agog, anxious, astounded, avid, eager, excited, flabbergasted (Inf.), on tenterhooks, open-mouthed, thunderstruck, with bated breath

breathtaking amazing, astonishing, awe-inspiring, awesome, exciting, heart-stirring, impressive, magnificent, moving, overwhelming, stunning (*Inf.*), thrilling

breed v. 1. bear, beget, bring forth, engender, generate, hatch, multiply, originate, procreate, produce, propagate, reproduce 2. bring up, cultivate, develop, discipline, educate, foster, instruct, nourish, nurture, raise, rear ~n. 3. brand, class, extraction, family, ilk, kind, line, lineage, pedigree, progeny, race, sort, species, stamp, stock, strain, type, variety

breeding 1. ancestry, cultivation, development, lineage, nurture, raising, rearing, reproduction, training, upbringing 2. civility, conduct, courtesy, cultivation, culture, gentility, manners, polish, refinement, urbanity

breeze n. air, breath of wind, capful of wind, current of air, draught, flurry, gust, light wind, puff of air, waft, whiff, zephyr

brevity 1. conciseness, concision, condensation, crispness, curtness, economy, pithiness, succinctness, terseness 2. briefness, ephemerality, impermanence, shortness, transience, transitoriness

Antonyms (*sense 1*) circuity, diffuseness, discursiveness, longwindedness, prolixity, rambling, redundancy, tautology, tediousness, verbiage, verboseness, verbosity, wordiness

brew v. 1. boil, ferment, infuse (*tea*), make (*beer*), prepare by fermentation, seethe, soak, steep, stew 2. breed, concoct, contrive, develop, devise, excite, foment, form, gather, hatch, plan, plot, project, scheme, start, stir up

bribe 1. n. allurement, backhander (*Sl.*), boodle (*Sl., chiefly U.S.*), corrupting gift, enticement, graft, hush money (*Sl.*), incentive, inducement, kickback (*U.S.*), pay-off (*Inf.*), payola (*Inf.*), reward for treachery 2. v. buy off, corrupt, get at, grease the palm or hand of (*Sl.*), influence by gifts, lure, oil the palm of

(*Inf.*), pay off (*Inf.*), reward, square, suborn

bribery buying off, corruption, graft, inducement, palm-greasing (*Sl.*), payola (*Inf.*), protection, subornation

bridge n. 1. arch, flyover, overpass, span, viaduct 2. band, bond, connection, link, tie ~v. 3. arch over, attach, bind, connect, couple, cross, cross over, extend across, go over, join, link, reach across, span, traverse, unite

bridle v. check, constrain, control, curb, govern, keep in check, master, moderate, repress, restrain, subdue

brief adj. 1. compendious, compressed, concise, crisp, curt, laconic, limited, pithy, short, succinct, terse, thumbnail, to the point 2. ephemeral, fast, fleeting, hasty, little, momentary, quick, short, short-lived, swift, temporary, transitory 3. abrupt, blunt, brusque, curt, sharp, short, surly ~n. 4. abridgment, abstract, digest, epitome, outline, precis, sketch, summary, synopsis 5. argument, case, contention, data, defence, demonstration ~v. 6. advise, explain, fill in (*Inf.*), gen up (*Brit. inf.*), give (someone) a rundown, give (someone) the gen (*Brit. inf.*), inform, instruct, prepare, prime, put (someone) in the picture (*Inf.*)

Antonyms adj. circuitous, detailed, diffuse, extensive, lengthy, long, long-drawn-out, long-winded, protracted

briefing conference, directions, guidance, information, instruction, instructions, meeting, preamble, preparation, priming, rundown

briefly abruptly, briskly, casually, concisely, cursorily, curtly, fleetingly, hastily, hurriedly, in a few words, in a nutshell, in brief, in outline, in passing, momentarily, precisely, quickly, shortly, temporarily

bright 1. beaming, blazing, brilliant, dazzling, effulgent, flashing,

gleaming, glistening, glittering, glowing, illuminated, intense, lambent, luminous, lustrous, radiant, resplendent, scintillating, shimmering, shining, sparkling, twinkling, vivid **2.** clear, clement, cloudless, fair, limpid, lucid, pellucid, pleasant, sunny, translucent, transparent, unclouded **3.** acute, astute, aware, brainy, brilliant, clear-headed, clever, ingenious, intelligent, inventive, keen, quick, quick-witted, sharp, smart, wide-awake **4.** auspicious, encouraging, excellent, favourable, golden, good, hopeful, optimistic, palmy, promising, propitious, prosperous, rosy **5.** cheerful, gay, genial, glad, happy, jolly, joyful, joyous, light-hearted, lively, merry, sparky, vivacious
Antonyms (senses 1 & 2) cloudy, dark, dim, dusky, gloomy, grey, overcast, poorly lit (sense 3) dense, dim, dim-witted (Inf.), dull, dumb, foolish, idiotic, ignorant, retarded, simple, slow, stupid, thick, unintelligent, witless

brighten 1. clear up, enliven, gleam, glow, illuminate, lighten, light up, make brighter, shine **2.** become cheerful, buck up (Inf.), buoy up, cheer, encourage, enliven, gladden, hearten, make happy, perk up
Antonyms (sense 1) becloud, blacken, cloud over or up, dim, dull, obscure, overshadow, shade, shadow (sense 2) become angry, become gloomy, blacken, cloud, deject, depress, dispirit, look black, sadden

brilliance, brilliancy 1. blaze, brightness, dazzle, effulgence, gleam, glitter, intensity, luminosity, lustre, radiance, refulgence, resplendence, sheen, sparkle, vividness **2.** acuity, aptitude, braininess, cleverness, distinction, excellence, genius, giftedness, greatness, inventiveness, talent, wisdom **3.** éclat, glamour, gorgeousness, grandeur, illustriousness, magnificence, pizzazz or pzazz (Inf.), splendour

Antonyms darkness, dimness, dullness, folly, idiocy, inanity, incompetence, ineptitude, obscurity, paleness, silliness, simplemindedness, stupidity, thickness

brilliant 1. ablaze, bright, coruscating, dazzling, glittering, glossy, intense, luminous, lustrous, radiant, refulgent, resplendent, scintillating, shining, sparkling, vivid **2.** celebrated, eminent, exceptional, famous, glorious, illustrious, magnificent, outstanding, splendid, superb **3.** accomplished, acute, astute, brainy, clever, discerning, expert, gifted, intellectual, intelligent, inventive, masterly, penetrating, profound, quick, talented
Antonyms (sense 1) dark, dim, dull, gloomy, obscure (senses 2 & 3) dim, dull, ordinary, run-of-the-mill, simple, slow, stupid, unaccomplished, unexceptional, untalented

brim n. border, brink, circumference, edge, lip, margin, rim, skirt, verge

bring 1. accompany, bear, carry, conduct, convey, deliver, escort, fetch, gather, guide, import, lead, take, transfer, transport, usher **2.** cause, contribute to, create, effect, engender, inflict, occasion, produce, result in, wreak

bring about accomplish, achieve, bring to pass, cause, compass, create, effect, effectuate, generate, give rise to, make happen, manage, occasion, produce, realize

bring off accomplish, achieve, bring home the bacon (Inf.), bring to pass, carry off, carry out, discharge, execute, perform, pull off, succeed

bring up breed, develop, educate, form, nurture, raise, rear, support, teach, train

brink border, boundary, brim, edge, fringe, frontier, limit, lip, margin, point, rim, skirt, threshold, verge

brisk active, agile, alert, animat-

ed, bustling, busy, energetic, lively, nimble, no-nonsense, quick, sparky, speedy, sprightly, spry, vigorous, vivacious
Antonyms boring, dull, enervating, heavy, lazy, lethargic, slow, sluggish, tiring, unenergetic, wearisome

bristle 1. n. barb, hair, prickle, spine, stubble, thorn, whisker **2.** be angry, be infuriate, be maddened, bridle, flare up, get one's dander up (Sl.), rage, see red, seethe, spit (Inf.)

brittle breakable, crisp, crumbling, crumbly, delicate, fragile, frail, frangible, friable, shatterable, shivery
Antonyms durable, elastic, flexible, infrangible, nonbreakable, resistant, rugged, shatterproof, strong, sturdy, toughened

broad 1. ample, beamy (of a ship), capacious, expansive, extensive, generous, large, roomy, spacious, vast, voluminous, wide, widespread **2.** all-embracing, catholic, comprehensive, encyclopedic, far-reaching, general, global, inclusive, nonspecific, sweeping, undetailed, universal, unlimited, wide, wide-ranging **3.** broad-minded, liberal, open, permissive, progressive, tolerant, unbiased
Antonyms close, confined, constricted, cramped, limited, meagre, narrow, restricted, tight

broadcast v **1.** air, beam, cable, put on the air, radio, relay, show, televise, transmit **2.** advertise, announce, circulate, disseminate, make public, proclaim, promulgate, publish, report, spread ~n. **3.** programme, show, telecast, transmission

broaden augment, develop, enlarge, expand, extend, fatten, increase, open up, spread, stretch, supplement, swell, widen
Antonyms circumscribe, constrain, diminish, narrow, reduce, restrict, simplify, tighten

broad-minded catholic, cosmopolitan, dispassionate, flexible,

free-thinking, indulgent, liberal, open-minded, permissive, responsive, tolerant, unbiased, unbigoted, undogmatic, unprejudiced
Antonyms biased, bigoted, closed-minded, dogmatic, inflexible, intolerant, narrow-minded, prejudiced, uncharitable

brochure advertisement, booklet, circular, folder, handbill, handout, leaflet, mailshot, pamphlet

broken 1. burst, demolished, destroyed, fractured, fragmented, rent, ruptured, separated, severed, shattered, shivered **2.** defective, exhausted, feeble, imperfect, kaput (Inf.), not functioning, out of order, ruined, rundown, spent, weak **3.** disconnected, discontinuous, disturbed, erratic, fragmentary, incomplete, intermittent, interrupted, spasmodic **4.** beaten, browbeaten, crippled, crushed, defeated, demoralized, humbled, oppressed, overpowered, subdued, tamed, vanquished

broken-down collapsed, dilapidated, in disrepair, inoperative, kaput (Inf.), not functioning, not in working order, old, on the blink (Inf.), out of commission, out of order, worn out

broker agent, dealer, factor, go-between, intermediary, middleman, negotiator

brood 1. v. agonize, dwell upon, fret, meditate, mope, mull over, muse, ponder, repine, ruminate, think upon **2.** n. breed, chicks, children, clutch, family, hatch, infants, issue, litter, offspring, progeny, young

brook beck, burn, gill (Dialect), rill, rivulet, runnel (Literary), stream, streamlet, watercourse

brother 1. blood brother, kin, kinsman, relation, relative, sibling **2.** associate, chum (Inf.), colleague, companion, comper, comrade, confrère, fellow member, mate, pal (Inf.), partner **3.** cleric, friar, monk, regular, religious

brotherhood 1. brotherliness, camaraderie, companionship, comradeship, fellowship, friendliness, kinship 2. alliance, association, clan, clique, community, coterie, fraternity, guild, league, society, union

brotherly affectionate, altruistic, amicable, benevolent, cordial, fraternal, friendly, kind, neighbourly, philanthropic, sympathetic

browbeat badger, bulldoze (*Inf.*), bully, coerce, cow, domineer, dragoon, hector, intimidate, lord it over, oppress, overawe, overbear, threaten, tyrannize
Antonyms beguile, cajole, coax, entice, flatter, inveigle, lure, manoeuvre, seduce, sweet talk, tempt, wheedle

brown *adj.* auburn, bay, brick, bronze, bronzed, browned, brunette, chestnut, chocolate, coffee, dark, donkey brown, dun, dusky, fuscous, ginger, hazel, rust, sunburnt, tan, tanned, tawny, toasted, umber

browse 1. dip into, examine cursorily, flip through, glance at, leaf through, look round, look through, peruse, scan, skim, survey 2. crop, eat, feed, graze, nibble, pasture

bruise 1. *v.* blacken, blemish, contuse, crush, damage, deface, discolour, injure, mar, mark, pound, pulverize 2. *n.* black-and-blue mark, black mark, blemish, contusion, discoloration, injury, mark, swelling

brush[1] *n.* 1. besom, broom, sweeper 2. clash, conflict, confrontation, encounter, fight, fracas, scrap (*Inf.*), set-to (*Inf.*), skirmish, slight engagement, spot of bother (*Inf.*), tussle ~*v.* 3. buff, clean, paint, polish, sweep, wash 4. caress, contact, flick, glance, graze, kiss, scrape, stroke, sweep, touch

brush[2] *n.* brushwood, bushes, copse, scrub, shrubs, thicket, undergrowth, underwood

brutal 1. barbarous, bloodthirsty, cruel, ferocious, heartless, inhuman, merciless, pitiless, remorseless, ruthless, savage, uncivilized, vicious 2. beastly, bestial, brute, brutish, carnal, coarse, crude, sensual
Antonyms civilized, gentle, humane, kind, merciful, polite, refined, sensitive, soft-hearted

brute *n.* 1. animal, beast, creature, wild animal 2. barbarian, beast, devil, fiend, monster, ogre, sadist, savage, swine

bubble *n.* 1. air ball, bead, blister, blob, drop, droplet, globule, vesicle ~*v.* 2. boil, effervesce, fizz, foam, froth, percolate, seethe, sparkle 3. babble, burble, gurgle, murmur, purl, ripple, trickle, trill

buckle *n.* 1. catch, clasp, clip, fastener, hasp ~*v.* 2. catch, clasp, close, fasten, hook, secure 3. bend, bulge, cave in, collapse, contort, crumple, distort, fold, twist, warp

bud 1. *n.* embryo, germ, shoot, sprout 2. *v.* burgeon, burst forth, develop, grow, pullulate, shoot, sprout

budding beginning, burgeoning, developing, embryonic, fledgling, flowering, germinal, growing, incipient, nascent, potential, promising

budge 1. dislodge, give way, inch, move, propel, push, remove, roll, shift, slide, stir 2. bend, change, convince, give way, influence, persuade, sway, yield

budget 1. *n.* allocation, allowance, cost, finances, financial statement, fiscal estimate, funds, means, resources 2. *v.* allocate, apportion, cost, cost out, estimate, plan, ration

buffer bulwark, bumper, cushion, fender, intermediary, safeguard, screen, shield, shock absorber

buffet 1. *v.* bang, batter, beat, box, bump, clobber (*Sl.*), cuff, flail, knock, pound, pummel, push, rap, shove, slap, strike, thump, wallop (*Inf.*) 2. *n.* bang, blow, box, bump, cuff, jolt, knock, push, rap, shove, slap, smack, thump, wallop (*Inf.*)

bug 1. *n.* *Inf.* bacterium, disease, germ, infection, microorganism, virus **2.** *v.* eavesdrop, listen in, spy, tap, wiretap

build *v.* **1.** assemble, construct, erect, fabricate, form, make, put up, raise **2.** base, begin, constitute, establish, formulate, found, inaugurate, initiate, institute, originate, set up, start ~*n.* **3.** body, figure, form, frame, physique, shape, structure

Antonyms *v.* debilitate, demolish, dismantle, end, finish, harm, impair, lower, relinquish, sap, suspend, tear down

building 1. domicile, dwelling, edifice, fabric, house, pile, structure **2.** architecture, construction, erection, fabricating, raising

build-up 1. accumulation, development, enlargement, escalation, expansion, gain, growth, increase **2.** accretion, accumulation, heap, load, mass, stack, stockpile, store

bulge *n.* **1.** bump, lump, projection, protrusion, protuberance, swelling **2.** boost, increase, intensification, rise, surge ~*v.* **3.** bag, dilate, distend, enlarge, expand, project, protrude, puff out, sag, stand out, stick out, swell, swell out

Antonyms bowl, cave, cavity, concavity, crater, dent, depression, hole, hollow, indentation, pit, trough

bulk *n.* **1.** amplitude, bigness, dimensions, immensity, largeness, magnitude, massiveness, size, substance, volume, weight **2.** better part, body, generality, lion's share, main part, majority, major part, mass, most, nearly all, plurality, preponderance

bulldoze demolish, flatten, level, raze

bullet ball, missile, pellet, projectile, shot, slug

bulletin account, announcement, communication, communiqué, dispatch, message, news flash, notification, report, statement

bulwark bastion, buttress, defence, embankment, fortification, outwork, partition, rampart, redoubt

bumbling awkward, blundering, botching, bungling, clumsy, incompetent, inefficient, inept, lumbering, maladroit, muddled, stumbling

Antonyms able, brisk, capable, competent, efficient, equal, fit

bump *v.* **1.** bang, collide (with), crash, hit, knock, slam, smash into, strike **2.** bounce, jar, jerk, jolt, jostle, jounce, rattle, shake ~*n.* **3.** bang, blow, collision, crash, hit, impact, jar, jolt, knock, rap, shock, smash, thud, thump **4.** bulge, contusion, hump, knob, knot, lump, node, nodule, protuberance, swelling

bump into chance upon, come across, encounter, happen upon, light upon, meet, meet up with, run across, run into

bunch 1. *n.* assortment, batch, bouquet, bundle, clump, cluster, collection, heap, lot, mass, number, parcel, pile, quantity, sheaf, spray, stack, tuft **2.** *v.* assemble, bundle, cluster, collect, congregate, cram together, crowd, flock, group, herd, huddle, mass, pack

bundle *n.* **1.** accumulation, assortment, batch, bunch, collection, group, heap, mass, pile, quantity, stack **2.** bag, bale, box, carton, crate, pack, package, packet, pallet, parcel, roll ~*v.* **3.** bale, bind, fasten, pack, package, palletize, tie, tie together, tie up, truss, wrap

bungle blunder, bodge (*Inf.*), botch, butcher, cock up (*Brit. sl.*), foul up, fudge, louse up (*Sl.*), make a mess of, mar, mess up, miscalculate, mismanage, muff, ruin, screw up (*Inf.*), spoil

Antonyms accomplish, achieve, carry off, effect, fulfil, succeed, triumph

bungling awkward, blundering, botching, cack-handed (*Inf.*), clumsy, ham-fisted (*Inf.*), ham-handed (*Inf.*), incompetent, inept, maladroit, unskilful

buoy *n.* beacon, float, guide, marker, signal

buoyant 1. afloat, floatable, floating, light, weightless **2.** animated, blithe, bouncy, breezy, bright, carefree, cheerful, debonair, happy, jaunty, joyful, lighthearted, lively, peppy (*Inf.*), sunny, sparky, vivacious

burden 1. *n.* affliction, anxiety, care, clog, encumbrance, grievance, load, millstone, obstruction, onus, responsibility, sorrow, strain, stress, trial, trouble, weight, worry **2.** *v.* bother, encumber, handicap, load, oppress, overload, overwhelm, saddle with, strain, tax, weigh down, worry

bureau 1. desk, writing desk **2.** agency, branch, department, division, office, service

bureaucracy administration, authorities, civil service, corridors of power, directorate, government, ministry, officialdom, officials, the system

bureaucrat administrator, apparatchik, civil servant, functionary, mandarin, minister, officeholder, officer, official, public servant

burglar cat burglar, filcher, housebreaker, picklock, pilferer, robber, sneak thief, thief

burial burying, entombment, exequies, funeral, inhumation, interment, obsequies, sepulture

buried 1. coffined, consigned to the grave, entombed, interred, laid to rest **2.** dead and buried, dead and gone, in the grave, long gone, pushing up the daisies, six feet under **3.** covered, forgotten, hidden, repressed, sunk in oblivion, suppressed **4.** cloistered, concealed, hidden, private, sequestered, tucked away **5.** caught up, committed, concentrating, devoted, engrossed, immersed, intent, lost, occupied, preoccupied, rapt

burlesque 1. *n.* caricature, mock,

mockery, parody, satire, send-up (*Brit. inf.*), spoof (*Inf.*), takeoff (*Inf.*), travesty **2.** *v.* ape, caricature, exaggerate, imitate, lampoon, make fun of, mock, parody, ridicule, satirize, send up (*Brit. inf.*), spoof (*Inf.*), take off (*Inf.*), travesty

burly beefy, big, brawny, bulky, hefty, hulking, muscular, powerful, Ramboesque, stocky, stout, strapping, strong, sturdy, thickset, well-built

Antonyms lean, puny, scraggy, scrawny, slight, spare, thin, weak, weedy (*Inf.*), wimpish or wimpy (*Inf.*)

burn 1. be ablaze, be on fire, blaze, flame, flare, flash, flicker, glow, smoke **2.** brand, calcine, char, ignite, incinerate, kindle, light, parch, reduce to ashes, scorch, set on fire, shrivel, singe, toast, wither

burning 1. blazing, fiery, flaming, flashing, gleaming, glowing, hot, illuminated, scorching, smouldering **2.** all-consuming, ardent, eager, earnest, fervent, fervid, frantic, frenzied, impassioned, intense, passionate, vehement, zealous

Antonyms apathetic, calm, cool, cooling, faint, indifferent, mild, numbing, passive, soothing

burrow 1. *n.* den, hole, lair, retreat, shelter, tunnel **2.** *v.* delve, dig, excavate, hollow out, scoop out, tunnel

burst 1. *v.* blow up, break, crack, disintegrate, explode, fly open, fragment, puncture, rend asunder, rupture, shatter, shiver, split, tear apart **2.** *n.* bang, blast, blasting, blowout, blow-up, breach, break, crack, discharge, explosion, rupture, split

bury 1. consign to the grave, entomb, inearth, inhume, inter, lay to rest, sepulchre **2.** conceal, cover, cover up, enshroud, hide, secrete, shroud, stow away **3.** drive in, embed, engulf, implant, sink, submerge

Antonyms (*senses 1 & 2*) bring to

light, dig up, discover, disinter, dredge up, exhume, expose, find, reveal, turn up, uncover, unearth

bush 1. hedge, plant, shrub, shrubbery, thicket 2. backwoods, brush, scrub, scrubland, the wild, woodland

business 1. calling, career, craft, employment, function, job, line, métier, occupation, profession, pursuit, trade, vocation, work 2. company, concern, corporation, enterprise, establishment, firm, organization, venture 3. bargaining, commerce, dealings, industry, manufacturing, merchandising, selling, trade, trading, transaction

businesslike correct, efficient, matter-of-fact, methodical, orderly, organized, practical, professional, regular, routine, systematic, thorough, well-ordered, workaday
Antonyms careless, disorderly, disorganized, frivolous, impractical, inefficient, irregular, sloppy, unprofessional, unsystematic, untidy

businessman, businesswoman capitalist, employer, entrepreneur, executive, financier, *homme d'affaires*, industrialist, merchant, tradesman, tycoon

bust bosom, breast, chest, torso

bustle 1. *v.* bestir, dash, flutter, fuss, hasten, hurry, rush, scamper, scramble, scurry, scuttle, stir, tear 2. *n.* activity, ado, agitation, commotion, excitement, flurry, fuss, haste, hurly-burly, hurry, pother, stir, to-do, tumult

busy *adj.* 1. active, assiduous, brisk, diligent, employed, engaged, engrossed, hard at work, industrious, in harness, occupied, on duty, persevering, slaving, working 2. active, energetic, exacting, full, hectic, hustling, lively, on the go (*Inf.*), restless, strenuous, tireless, tiring

Antonyms idle, inactive, indolent, lackadaisical, lazy, off duty, relaxed, shiftless, slothful, unoccupied

but 1. *sentence connector* further, however, moreover, nevertheless, on the contrary, on the other hand, still, yet 2. *conj.* bar, barring, except, excepting, excluding, notwithstanding, save, with the exception of 3. *adv.* just, merely, only, simply, singly, solely

butcher *n.* 1. destroyer, killer, murderer, slaughterer, slayer ~*v.* 2. carve, clean, cut, cut up, dress, joint, prepare, slaughter 3. assassinate, cut down, destroy, exterminate, kill, liquidate, massacre, put to the sword, slaughter, slay 4. bodge (*Inf.*), botch, destroy, mess up, mutilate, ruin, spoil, wreck

butt[1] haft, handle, hilt, shaft, shank, stock

butt[2] Aunt Sally, dupe, laughing stock, mark, object, point, subject, target, victim

butt[3] *v./n.* With or of the head or horns buck, buffet, bump, bunt, jab, knock, poke, prod, punch, push, ram, shove, thrust

buy 1. *v.* acquire, get, invest in, obtain, pay for, procure, purchase, shop for 2. *n.* acquisition, bargain, deal, purchase
Antonyms *v.* auction, barter, retail, sell, vend

by *prep.* 1. along, beside, by way of, close to, near, next to, over, past, via 2. through, through the agency of, under the aegis of ~*adv.* 3. aside, at hand, away, beyond, close, handy, in reach, near, past, to one side

bystander eyewitness, looker-on, observer, onlooker, passer-by, spectator, viewer, watcher, witness
Antonyms contributor, partaker, participant, party

C

cab hackney, hackney carriage, minicab, taxi, taxicab

cabin 1. berth, bothy, chalet, cot, cottage, crib, hovel, hut, lodge, shack, shanty, shed **2.** berth, compartment, deckhouse, quarters, room

cabinet 1. case, chiffonier, closet, commode, cupboard, dresser, escritoire, locker **2.** administration, assembly, council, counsellors, ministry

café cafeteria, coffee bar, coffee shop, lunchroom, restaurant, snack bar, tearoom

cage v. confine, coop up, fence in, immure, impound, imprison, incarcerate, lock up, mew, restrain, shut up

cajole beguile, coax, decoy, dupe, entice, entrap, flatter, inveigle, lure, manoeuvre, mislead, seduce, sweet-talk (*U.S. inf.*), tempt, wheedle

cake n. bar, block, cube, loaf, lump, mass, slab

calamity adversity, affliction, cataclysm, catastrophe, disaster, distress, downfall, hardship, misadventure, mischance, misfortune, mishap, reverse, ruin, scourge, tragedy, trial, tribulation, woe, wretchedness

calculate adjust, compute, consider, count, determine, enumerate, estimate, figure, gauge, judge, rate, reckon, value, weigh, work out

calculation answer, computation, estimate, estimation, figuring, forecast, judgment, reckoning, result

calibre 1. bore, diameter, gauge, measure **2.** *Fig.* ability, capacity, distinction, endowment, faculty, force, gifts, merit, parts, quality, scope, stature, strength, talent, worth

call v. **1.** announce, arouse, awaken, cry, cry out, hail, halloo, proclaim, rouse, shout, waken, yell **2.** assemble, bid, collect, contact, convene, convoke, gather, invite, muster, phone, rally, ring up, summon, telephone **3.** christen, denominate, describe as, designate, dub, entitle, label, name, style, term ~n. **4.** cry, hail, scream, shout, signal, whoop, yell **5.** announcement, appeal, command, demand, invitation, notice, order, plea, request, ring (*Brit. inf.*), summons, supplication, visit
Antonyms v. (*sense 1*) be quiet, be silent, murmur, mutter, speak softly, whisper (*sense 2*) call off, cancel, dismiss, disperse, excuse, release ~n. (*sense 4*) murmur, mutter, whisper (*sense 5*) dismissal, release

call for demand, entail, involve, necessitate, need, occasion, require, suggest

calling business, career, employment, life's work, line, métier, mission, occupation, profession, province, pursuit, trade, vocation, walk of life, work

callous apathetic, case-hardened, cold, hard-bitten, hard-boiled (*Inf.*), hardened, hardhearted, heartless, indifferent, indurated (*Rare*), insensate, insensible, insensitive, inured, obdurate, soulless, thick-skinned, torpid, uncaring, unfeeling, unresponsive, unsusceptible, unsympathetic
Antonyms caring, compassionate, considerate, gentle, sensitive, soft, sympathetic, tender, understanding

calm adj. **1.** balmy, halcyon, mild, pacific, peaceful, placid, quiet,

restful, serene, smooth, still, tranquil, windless 2. collected, composed, cool, dispassionate, equable, impassive, imperturbable, relaxed, sedate, self-possessed, undisturbed, unemotional, unexcitable, unexcited, unflappable (*Inf.*), unmoved, unruffled ~*n.* 3. hush, mollify, placate, quieten, relax, soothe
Antonyms *adj.* agitated, aroused, discomposed, disturbed, emotional, excited, fierce, frantic, heated, perturbed, rough, shaken, stormy, troubled, wild, worried ~*v.* aggravate, agitate, arouse, disturb, excite, irritate, stir

calmness 1. calm, composure, equability, hush, motionlessness, peace, peacefulness, placidity, quiet, repose, restfulness, serenity, smoothness, stillness, tranquillity 2. composure, cool (*Sl.*), coolness, dispassion, equanimity, impassivity, imperturbability, poise, sang-froid, self-possession

camouflage 1. *n.* blind, cloak, concealment, cover, deceptive markings, disguise, false appearance, front, guise, mask, masquerade, mimicry, protective colouring, screen, subterfuge 2. *v.* cloak, conceal, cover, disguise, hide, mask, obfuscate, obscure, screen, veil
Antonyms *v.* bare, display, exhibit, expose, reveal, show, uncover, unmask, unveil

camp bivouac, camping ground, camp site, cantonment (*Mil.*), encampment, tents

campaign attack, crusade, drive, expedition, jihad (*Rare*), movement, offensive, operation, push

cancel abolish, abort, abrogate, annul, blot out, call off, countermand, cross out, delete, do away with, efface, eliminate, erase, expunge, obliterate, quash, repeal, repudiate, rescind, revoke

cancer blight, canker, carcinoma (*Pathol.*), corruption, evil, growth, malignancy, pestilence, rot, sickness, tumour

candid blunt, fair, forthright,

frank, free, guileless, impartial, ingenuous, just, open, outspoken, plain, sincere, straightforward, truthful, unbiased, unequivocal, unprejudiced

candidate applicant, aspirant, claimant, competitor, contender, contestant, entrant, nominee, possibility, runner, solicitant, suitor

candour artlessness, directness, fairness, forthrightness, frankness, guilelessness, honesty, impartiality, ingenuousness, naïveté, openness, outspokenness, simplicity, sincerity, straightforwardness, truthfulness, unequivocalness
Antonyms bias, cunning, deceit, diplomacy, dishonesty, flattery, insincerity, prejudice, subtlety

canny acute, artful, astute, careful, cautious, circumspect, clever, judicious, knowing, perspicacious, prudent, sagacious, sharp, shrewd, subtle, wise, worldly-wise

canter *n.* amble, dogtrot, easy gait, jog, lope

canvass 1. *v.* analyse, campaign, electioneer, examine, inspect, investigate, poll, scan, scrutinize, sift, solicit, solicit votes, study, ventilate 2. *n.* examination, investigation, poll, scrutiny, survey, tally

cap *v.* beat, better, complete, cover, crown, eclipse, exceed, excel, finish, outdo, outstrip, overtop, surpass, top, transcend

capability ability, capacity, competence, facility, faculty, means, potential, potentiality, power, proficiency, qualification(s), wherewithal
Antonyms inability, incompetence, inefficiency, ineptitude, powerlessness

capable able, accomplished, adapted, adept, adequate, apt, clever, competent, efficient, experienced, fitted, gifted, intelligent, masterly, proficient, qualified, skilful, suited, susceptible, talented

Antonyms incapable, incompetent, ineffective, inept, inexpert, unqualified, unskilled

capacious ample, broad, comfortable, commodious, comprehensive, expansive, extended, extensive, generous, liberal, roomy, sizable, spacious, substantial, vast, voluminous, wide
Antonyms confined, constricted, cramped, enclosed, incommodious, insubstantial, limited, narrow, poky, restricted, small, tight, tiny, uncomfortable, ungenerous

capacity 1. amplitude, compass, dimensions, extent, magnitude, range, room, scope, size, space, volume **2.** ability, aptitude, aptness, brains, capability, cleverness, competence, competency, efficiency, facility, faculty, forte, genius, gift, intelligence, power, readiness, strength **3.** appointment, function, office, position, post, province, role, service, sphere

cape chersonese (*Poetic*), head, headland, ness (*Archaic*), peninsula, point, promontory

caper *v.* bounce, bound, cavort, dance, frisk, frolic, gambol, hop, jump, leap, romp, skip, spring

capital *adj.* **1.** cardinal, central, chief, controlling, essential, foremost, important, leading, main, major, overruling, paramount, pre-eminent, primary, prime, principal, prominent, vital **2.** excellent, fine, first, first-rate, prime, splendid, superb ~*n.* **3.** assets, cash, finance, finances, financing, funds, investment(s), means, money, principal, property, resources, stock, wealth, wherewithal

capitalism free enterprise, *laissez faire*, private enterprise, private ownership

capitulate come to terms, give in, give up, relent, submit, succumb, surrender, yield

capsize invert, keel over, overturn, tip over, turn over, turn turtle, upset

captain boss, chief, chieftain, commander, head, leader, master, number one (*Inf.*), officer, (senior) pilot, skipper

captivate allure, attract, beguile, bewitch, charm, dazzle, enamour, enchant, enrapture, enslave, ensnare, enthral, entrance, fascinate, hypnotize, infatuate, lure, mesmerize, seduce, win

captive 1. *n.* bondservant, convict, detainee, hostage, internee, prisoner, prisoner of war, slave **2.** *adj.* caged, confined, enslaved, ensnared, imprisoned, incarcerated, locked up, penned, restricted, subjugated

captivity bondage, confinement, custody, detention, durance (*Archaic*), duress, enthralment, imprisonment, incarceration, internment, restraint, servitude, slavery, thraldom, vassalage

capture 1. *v.* apprehend, arrest, bag, catch, collar (*Inf.*), lift (*Sl.*), nab (*Inf.*), secure, seize, take, take into custody, take prisoner **2.** *n.* apprehension, arrest, catch, imprisonment, seizure, taking, taking captive, trapping
Antonyms *v.* free, let go, let out, liberate, release, set free, turn loose

car auto (*U.S.*), automobile, jalopy (*Inf.*), machine, motor, motorcar, vehicle

carcass body, cadaver (*Medical*), corpse, corse (*Archaic*), dead body, framework, hulk, remains, shell, skeleton

cardinal capital, central, chief, essential, first, foremost, fundamental, greatest, highest, important, key, leading, main, paramount, pre-eminent, primary, prime, principal
Antonyms dispensable, least important, lowest, secondary, subordinate, unessential

care 1. affliction, anxiety, burden, concern, disquiet, hardship, interest, perplexity, pressure, responsibility, solicitude, stress, tribulation, trouble, vexation, woe, worry **2.** attention, carefulness, caution, circumspection, consideration, direction, forethought, heed, management, meticulousness, pains, prudence, regard, vigilance, watchfulness **3.** charge, control, custody, guardianship, keeping, management, ministration, protection, supervision, ward

Antonyms (*sense 1*) pleasure, relaxation (*sense 2*) abandon, carelessness, heedlessness, inattention, indifference, neglect, negligence, unconcern

career n. calling, employment, life work, livelihood, occupation, pursuit, vocation

care for 1. attend, foster, look after, mind, minister to, nurse, protect, provide for, tend, watch over **2.** be fond of, desire, enjoy, find congenial, like, love, prize, take to, want

careful 1. accurate, attentive, cautious, chary, circumspect, conscientious, discreet, fastidious, heedful, painstaking, precise, prudent, punctilious, scrupulous, thoughtful, thrifty **2.** alert, concerned, judicious, mindful, particular, protective, solicitous, vigilant, wary, watchful

Antonyms abandoned, careless, casual, inaccurate, inattentive, inexact, neglectful, negligent, reckless, remiss, slovenly, thoughtless, unconcerned, untroubled

careless 1. absent-minded, cursory, forgetful, hasty, heedless, incautious, inconsiderate, indiscreet, negligent, perfunctory, regardless, remiss, thoughtless, unconcerned, unguarded, unmindful, unthinking **2.** inaccurate, irresponsible, lackadaisical, neglectful, offhand, slapdash, slipshod, sloppy (*Inf.*)

Antonyms accurate, alert, anxious, attentive, careful, cautious, concerned, correct, neat, on the ball (*Inf.*), orderly, painstaking, tidy, wary, watchful

caress 1. v. cuddle, embrace, fondle, hug, kiss, nuzzle, pet,

stroke **2.** n. cuddle, embrace, fondling, hug, kiss, pat, stroke

caretaker n. concierge, curator, custodian, janitor, keeper, porter, superintendent, warden, watchman

cargo baggage, consignment, contents, freight, goods, lading, load, merchandise, shipment, tonnage, ware

caricature 1. n. burlesque, cartoon, distortion, farce, lampoon, mimicry, parody, pasquinade, satire, send-up (*Brit. inf.*), takeoff (*Inf.*), travesty **2.** v. burlesque, distort, lampoon, mimic, mock, parody, ridicule, satirize, send up (*Brit. inf.*), take off (*Inf.*)

carnival celebration, fair, festival, fête, fiesta, gala, holiday, jamboree, jubilee, Mardi Gras, merry-making, revelry

carriage 1. carrying, conveyance, conveying, delivery, freight, transport, transportation **2.** cab, coach, conveyance, vehicle **3.** *Fig.* air, bearing, behaviour, comportment, conduct, demeanour, deportment, gait, manner, mien, posture, presence

carry 1. bear, bring, conduct, convey, fetch, haul, lift, lug, move, relay, take, transfer, transmit, transport **2.** bear, hold up, maintain, shoulder, stand, suffer, support, sustain, underpin, uphold

carry on continue, endure, keep going, last, maintain, perpetuate, persevere, persist

carry out accomplish, achieve, carry through, consummate, discharge, effect, execute, fulfil, implement, perform, realize

carton box, case, container, pack, package, packet

cartoon animated cartoon, animated film, animation, caricature, comic strip, lampoon, parody, satire, sketch, takeoff (*Inf.*)

cartridge charge, round, shell

carve chip, chisel, cut, divide, engrave, etch, fashion, form, grave, hack, hew, incise, indent, mould, sculpt, sculpture, slash, slice, whittle

cascade *n.* avalanche, cataract, deluge, falls, flood, fountain, outpouring, shower, torrent, waterfall

case 1. box, cabinet, canister, capsule, carton, cartridge, casket, chest, compact, container, crate, holder, receptacle, shell, suitcase, tray, trunk **2.** circumstance(s), condition, context, contingency, dilemma, event, plight, position, predicament, situation, state **3.** example, illustration, instance, occasion, occurrence, specimen **4.** *Law* action, cause, dispute, lawsuit, proceedings, process, suit, trial

cash banknotes, bread (*Sl.*), bullion, charge, coin, coinage, currency, dosh (*Brit. sl.*), dough (*Sl.*), funds, money, notes payment, ready (*Inf.*), ready money, resources, specie, wherewithal

cashier *n.* accountant, bank clerk, banker, bursar, clerk, purser, teller, treasurer

cast *v.* **1.** chuck, drive, drop, fling, hurl, impel, launch, lob, pitch, project, shed, shy, sling, throw, thrust, toss ~*n.* **2.** fling, lob, throw, thrust, toss **3.** actors, characters, company, dramatis personae, players, troupe

cast down deject, depress, desolate, discourage, dishearten, dispirit

castle chateau, citadel, donjon, fastness, fortress, keep, mansion, palace, peel, stronghold, tower

casual 1. accidental, chance, contingent, fortuitous, incidental, irregular, occasional, random, serendipitous, uncertain, unexpected, unforeseen, unintentional, unpremeditated **2.** apathetic, blasé, cursory, indifferent, informal, insouciant, lackadaisical, nonchalant, offhand, perfunctory, relaxed, unconcerned
Antonyms (*sense 1*) arranged, expected, deliberate, fixed, foreseen, intentional, planned, premeditated (*sense 2*) committed,

concerned, direct, enthusiastic, passionate, serious, systematic

casualty loss, sufferer, victim

catalogue *n.* directory, gazetteer, index, inventory, list, record, register, roll, roster, schedule

catastrophe adversity, affliction, blow, calamity, cataclysm, devastation, disaster, failure, fiasco, ill, meltdown (*Inf.*), mischance, misfortune, mishap, reverse, tragedy, trial, trouble

catch *v.* **1.** apprehend, arrest, capture, clutch, ensnare, entangle, entrap, grab, grasp, grip, lay hold of, nab (*Inf.*), seize, snare, snatch, take **2.** detect, discover, expose, find out, surprise, take unawares, unmask ~*n.* **3.** bolt, clasp, clip, fastener, hasp, hook, hook and eye, latch, sneck, snib (*Scot.*) **4.** disadvantage, drawback, fly in the ointment, hitch, snag, stumbling block, trap, trick
Antonyms *v.* (*sense 1*) drop, free, give up, liberate, loose, release ~*n.* (*sense 4*) advantage, benefit, bonus, boon, reward

catching communicable, contagious, infectious, infective, transferable, transmittable
Antonyms incommunicable, noncatching, non-contagious, noninfectious, non-transmittable

categorical absolute, direct, downright, emphatic, explicit, express, positive, unambiguous, unconditional, unequivocal, unqualified, unreserved
Antonyms bigoted, conditioned, hesitant, illiberal, indefinite, qualified, questionable, uncertain, vague

category class, classification, department, division, grade, grouping, head, heading, list, order, rank, section, sort, type

cater furnish, outfit, provide, provision, purvey, supply, victual

cattle beasts, bovines, cows, kine (*Archaic*), livestock, neat (*Archaic*), stock

catty backbiting, bitchy (*Sl.*), illnatured, malevolent, malicious, mean, rancorous, snide, spiteful, venomous

Antonyms benevolent, charitable, compassionate, considerate, generous, kind, pleasant

cause n. 1. agent, beginning, creator, genesis, mainspring, maker, origin, originator, prime mover, producer, root, source, spring 2. account, agency, aim, basis, consideration, end, grounds, incentive, inducement, motivation, motive, object, purpose, reason ~v. 3. begin, bring about, compel, create, effect, engender, generate, give rise to, incite, induce, lead to, motivate, occasion, precipitate, produce, provoke, result in

Antonyms n. consequence, effect, end, outcome, result ~v. deter, foil, inhibit, prevent, stop

caustic acrid, astringent, biting, burning, corroding, corrosive, keen, mordant

Antonyms bland, gentle, mild, soft, temperate

caution n. 1. alertness, care, carefulness, circumspection, deliberation, discretion, forethought, heed, heedfulness, prudence, vigilance, watchfulness 2. admonition, advice, counsel, injunction, warning ~v. 3. admonish, advise, tip off, urge, warn

cautious alert, cagey (Inf.), careful, chary, circumspect, discreet, guarded, heedful, judicious, prudent, tentative, vigilant, wary, watchful

Antonyms adventurous, bold, careless, daring, foolhardy, heedless, impetuous, inattentive, incautious, indiscreet, madcap, rash, reckless, unguarded, unheeedful, venturesome, venturous

cave cavern, cavity, den, grotto, hollow

cavern cave, hollow, pothole

cavity crater, dent, gap, hole, hollow, pit

cease break off, bring or come to an end, conclude, culminate, desist, die away, discontinue, end,

fail, finish, halt, leave off, refrain, stay, stop, terminate

Antonyms begin, commence, continue, initiate, start

ceaseless constant, continual, continuous, endless, eternal, everlasting, incessant, indefatigable, interminable, never-ending, nonstop, perennial, perpetual, unending, unremitting, untiring

Antonyms broken, erratic, intermittent, irregular, occasional, periodic, spasmodic, sporadic

celebrate bless, commemorate, commend, drink to, eulogize, exalt, extol, glorify, honour, keep, laud, observe, perform, praise, proclaim, publicize, rejoice, reverence, solemnize, toast

celebrated acclaimed, distinguished, eminent, famed, famous, glorious, illustrious, lionized, notable, outstanding, popular, preeminent, prominent, renowned, revered, well-known

Antonyms dishonoured, forgotten, insignificant, obscure, trivial, unacclaimed, undistinguished, unknown, unnotable, unpopular

celebration carousal, festival, festivity, gala, jollification, jubilee, junketing, merrymaking, party, revelry

celebrity big name, big shot (Sl.), bigwig (Sl.), celeb (Inf.), dignitary, lion (Inf.), luminary, name, personage, personality, star, superstar, V.I.P.

Antonyms has-been, nobody, unknown

cell cavity, chamber, compartment, cubicle, dungeon, stall

cement v. attach, bind, bond, cohere, combine, glue, gum, join, plaster, seal, solder, stick together, unite, weld

cemetery burial ground, churchyard, God's acre, graveyard, necropolis

censure 1. v. abuse, berate, blame, castigate, chide, condemn, criticize, denounce, rebuke, reprehend, reprimand, reproach, reprove, scold, upbraid 2.

n. blame, castigation, condemnation, criticism, disapproval, dressing down (*Inf.*), obloquy, rebuke, remonstrance, reprehension, reprimand, reproach, reproof, stricture

Antonyms *v.* applaud, commend, compliment, laud (*Literary*) ~*n.* approval, commendation, compliment, encouragement

central chief, essential, focal, fundamental, inner, interior, key, main, mean, median, mid, middle, primary, principal

Antonyms exterior, minor, outer, outermost, secondary, subordinate, subsidiary

centre *n.* bull's-eye, core, crux, focus, heart, hub, mid, middle, midpoint, nucleus, pivot

Antonyms border, boundary, brim, circumference, edge, fringe, limit, lip, margin, perimeter, periphery, rim

ceremonial 1. *adj.* formal, liturgical, ritual, ritualistic, solemn, stately **2.** *n.* ceremony, formality, rite, solemnity

Antonyms *adj.* casual, informal, relaxed, simple

ceremony commemoration, function, observance, parade, rite, ritual, service, show, solemnities

certain 1. assured, confident, convinced, positive, satisfied, sure **2.** ascertained, conclusive, incontrovertible, indubitable, irrefutable, known, plain, true, undeniable, undoubted, unequivocal, unmistakable, valid **3.** decided, definite, established, fixed, settled

Antonyms disputable, doubtful, dubious, equivocal, fallible, indefinite, questionable, uncertain, unconvinced, undecided, unlikely, unsettled, unsure

certainty assurance, authoritativeness, certitude, confidence, conviction, faith, indubitableness, inevitability, positiveness, sureness, trust, validity

Antonyms disbelief, doubt, inde-

cision, qualm, scepticism, uncertainty, unsureness

certificate authorization, credential(s), diploma, document, licence, testimonial, voucher, warrant

certify ascertain, assure, attest, authenticate, aver, avow, confirm, corroborate, declare, endorse, guarantee, notify, show, testify, validate, verify, vouch, witness

chain *v.* **1.** bind, confine, enslave, fetter, gyve (*Archaic*), handcuff, manacle, restrain, shackle, tether, trammel, unite ~*n.* **2.** bond, coupling, fetter, link, manacle, shackle, union **3.** concatenation, progression, sequence, series, set, string, succession, train

challenge *v.* accost, arouse, beard, brave, call out, claim, confront, dare, defy, demand, dispute, impugn, investigate, object to, provoke, question, require, stimulate, summon, tax, test, throw down the gauntlet, try

chamber apartment, bedroom, cavity, compartment, cubicle, enclosure, hall, hollow, room

champion *n.* backer, challenger, conqueror, defender, guardian, hero, nonpareil, patron, protector, title holder, upholder, victor, vindicator, warrior, winner

chance *n.* **1.** liability, likelihood, occasion, odds, opening, opportunity, possibility, probability, prospect, scope, time **2.** accident, casualty, coincidence, contingency, destiny, fate, fortuity, fortune, luck, misfortune, peril, providence **3.** gamble, hazard, jeopardy, risk, speculation, uncertainty ~*v.* **4.** befall, betide, come about, come to pass, fall out, happen, occur **5.** endanger, gamble, go out on a limb (*Inf.*), hazard, jeopardize, risk, stake, try, venture, wager

Antonyms *n.* certainty, design, impossibility, improbability, intention, surety, unlikelihood

change *v.* **1.** alter, convert, diversify, fluctuate, metamor-

phose, moderate, modify, mutate, reform, remodel, reorganize, restyle, shift, transform, transmute, vacillate, vary, veer 2. alternate, barter, convert, displace, exchange, interchange, remove, replace, substitute, swap (*Inf.*), trade, transmit ~*n.* 3. alteration, difference, innovation, metamorphosis, modification, mutation, permutation, revolution, transformation, transition, transmutation, vicissitude 4. conversion, exchange, interchange, substitution, trade
Antonyms *v.* hold, keep, remain, stay ~*n.* constancy, permanence, stability, uniformity

changeable capricious, changeful, chequered, erratic, fickle, fitful, fluid, inconstant, irregular, kaleidoscopic, labile (*Chem.*), mercurial, mobile, mutable, protean, shifting, uncertain, unpredictable, unreliable, unsettled, unstable, unsteady, vacillating, variable, versatile, volatile, wavering
Antonyms constant, invariable, irreversible, regular, reliable, stable, steady, unchangeable

channel 1. *n.* canal, chamber, conduit, duct, fluting, furrow, groove, gutter, main, passage, route, strait 2. *v.* conduct, convey, direct, guide, transmit

chant 1. *n.* carol, chorus, melody, psalm, song 2. *v.* carol, chorus, croon, descant, intone, recite, sing, warble

chaos anarchy, bedlam, confusion, disorder, disorganization, entropy, lawlessness, pandemonium, tumult
Antonyms neatness, orderliness, organization, tidiness

chapter clause, division, episode, part, period, phase, section, stage, topic

character 1. attributes, bent, calibre, cast, complexion, constitution, disposition, individuality, kidney, make-up, marked traits, nature, personality, quality, reputation, temper, tempera-

ment, type 2. honour, integrity, rectitude, strength, uprightness 3. card (*Inf.*), eccentric, oddball (*Inf.*), odd bod (*Inf.*), oddity, original, queer fish (*Inf.*) 4. part, persona, portrayal, role

characteristic 1. *adj.* distinctive, distinguishing, idiosyncratic, individual, peculiar, representative, singular, special, specific, symbolic, symptomatic, typical 2. *n.* attribute, faculty, feature, idiosyncrasy, mark, peculiarity, property, quality, quirk, trait
Antonyms *adj.* rare, uncharacteristic, unrepresentative, unusual

charge *v.* 1. accuse, arraign, blame, impeach, incriminate, indict, involve ~*n.* 2. accusation, allegation, imputation, indictment 3. assault, attack, onset, onslaught, rush, sortie 4. burden, care, concern, custody, duty, office, responsibility, safekeeping, trust, ward 5. amount, cost, damage (*Inf.*), expenditure, expense, outlay, payment, price, rate ~*v.* 6. bid, command, enjoin, exhort, instruct, order, require
Antonyms *v.* (*sense 1*) absolve, acquit, clear, exonerate, pardon ~*n.* (*sense 2*) absolution, acquittal, clearance, exoneration, pardon, reprieve (*sense 3*) retreat, withdrawal

charity alms-giving, assistance, benefaction, contributions, donations, endowment, fund, gift, hand-out, philanthropy, relief
Antonyms miserliness, selfishness, stinginess, uncharitableness

charm 1. *v.* allure, attract, beguile, bewitch, cajole, captivate, delight, enamour, enchant, enrapture, entrance, fascinate, mesmerize, please, win, win over 2. *n.* allure, allurement, appeal, attraction, desirability, enchantment, fascination, magic, magnetism, sorcery, spell
Antonyms *v.* alienate, repel, repulse ~*n.* repulsiveness, unattractiveness

charming appealing, attractive,

chart 73 **cheer**

bewitching, captivating, delec~ table, delightful, engaging, eye-catching, fetching, irresistible, lovely, pleasant, pleasing, seductive, winning, winsome

Antonyms disgusting, repulsive, unappealing, unattractive, unlikeable, unpleasant, unpleasing

chart 1. *n.* blueprint, diagram, graph, map, plan, table, tabulation **2.** *v.* delineate, draft, graph, map out, outline, plot, shape, sketch

charter *n.* bond, concession, contract, deed, document, franchise, indenture, licence, permit, prerogative, privilege, right

chase *v.* course, drive, drive away, expel, follow, hound, hunt, pursue, put to flight, run after, track

chaste austere, decent, decorous, elegant, immaculate, incorrupt, innocent, modest, moral, neat, pure, quiet, refined, restrained, simple, unaffected, uncontaminated, undefiled, unsullied, vestal, virginal, virtuous, wholesome

Antonyms blemished, corrupt, dirty, dishonourable, gaudy, immoral, impure, married, ornate, promiscuous, self-indulgent, tainted, unchaste, unclean, unrestrained, wanton

chat 1. *n.* chatter, chinwag (*Brit. inf.*), confab (*Inf.*), gossip, heart-to-heart, natter, talk, tête-à-tête **2.** *v.* chatter, chew the rag *or* fat (*Sl.*), gossip, jaw (*Sl.*), natter, rabbit (on) (*Brit. sl.*), talk

chatter *n./v.* babble, blather, chat, gab (*Inf.*), gossip, jabber, natter, prate, prattle, tattle, twaddle

cheap 1. bargain, cheapo (*Inf.*), cut-price, economical, economy, inexpensive, keen, low-cost, low-priced, reasonable, reduced, sale **2.** common, inferior, paltry, poor, second-rate, shoddy, tatty, tawdry, worthless **3.** base, contemptible, despicable, low, mean, scurvy, sordid, vulgar

Antonyms (*sense 1*) costly, dear, expensive, pricey (*Inf.*), steep

(*senses 2 & 3*) admirable, charitable, decent, elegant, generous, good, high-class, honourable, superior, tasteful, valuable

cheat *v.* **1.** bamboozle (*Inf.*), beguile, bilk, con (*Sl.*), deceive, defraud, diddle (*Inf.*), do (*Sl.*), double-cross (*Inf.*), dupe, finagle (*Inf.*), fleece, fool, gull (*Archaic*), hoax, hoodwink, mislead, rip off (*Sl.*), swindle, take for a ride (*Inf.*), take in (*Inf.*), thwart, trick, victimize **2.** baffle, check, defeat, deprive, foil, frustrate, prevent, thwart ~*n.* **3.** charlatan, cheater, con man (*Inf.*), deceiver, dodger, double-crosser (*Inf.*), impostor, knave (*Archaic*), rogue, shark, sharper, swindler, trickster

check *v.* **1.** check out (*Inf.*), compare, confirm, enquire into, examine, inspect, investigate, look at, look over, make sure, monitor, note, probe, scrutinize, study, test, tick, verify **2.** arrest, bar, bridle, control, curb, delay, halt, hinder, impede, inhibit, limit, nip in the bud, obstruct, pause, repress, restrain, retard, stop, thwart ~*n.* **3.** examination, inspection, investigation, research, scrutiny, test **4.** constraint, control, curb, damper, hindrance, impediment, inhibition, limitation, obstruction, restraint, stoppage

Antonyms *v.* (*sense 1*) disregard, ignore, neglect, overlook, pass over, pay no attention to (*sense 2*) accelerate, advance, begin, encourage, further, give free rein, help, release, start

cheer *v.* **1.** animate, brighten, buoy up, cheer up, comfort, console, elate, elevate, encourage, enliven, exhilarate, gladden, hearten, incite, inspirit, solace, uplift, warm **2.** acclaim, applaud, clap, hail, hurrah ~*n.* **3.** animation, buoyancy, cheerfulness, comfort, gaiety, gladness, glee, hopefulness, joy, liveliness, merriment, merry-making, mirth, optimism, solace

Antonyms *v.* (*sense 1*) darken,

depress, discourage, dishearten, sadden (*sense 2*) blow a raspberry, boo, hiss, jeer, ridicule

cheerful animated, blithe, bright, bucked (*Inf.*), buoyant, cheery, contented, enlivening, enthusiastic, gay, glad, gladsome (*Archaic*), happy, hearty, jaunty, jolly, joyful, light-hearted, lightsome (*Archaic*), merry, optimistic, pleasant, sparkling, sprightly, sunny

Antonyms cheerless, dejected, depressed, depressing, despondent, dismal, down, downcast, down in the dumps (*Inf.*), dull, gloomy, lifeless, melancholy, miserable, morose, pensive, sad, unhappy, unpleasant

cheerfulness buoyancy, exuberance, gaiety, geniality, gladness, good cheer, good humour, high spirits, jauntiness, joyousness, light-heartedness

cheerless austere, bleak, comfortless, dark, dejected, depressed, desolate, despondent, disconsolate, dismal, dolorous, drab, dreary, dull, forlorn, gloomy, grim, joyless, melancholy, miserable, mournful, sad, sombre, sorrowful, sullen, unhappy, woebegone, woeful

Antonyms cheerful, cheery, elated, happy, jolly, joyful, light-hearted, merry

cherish care for, cleave to, cling to, comfort, cosset, encourage, entertain, foster, harbour, hold dear, nourish, nurse, nurture, prize, shelter, support, sustain, treasure

Antonyms abandon, desert, despise, disdain, dislike, forsake, hate, neglect

chest box, case, casket, coffer, crate, strongbox, trunk

chew bite, champ, crunch, gnaw, grind, masticate, munch

chief 1. *adj.* capital, cardinal, central, especial, essential, foremost, grand, highest, key, leading, main, most important, outstanding, paramount, predominant, pre-eminent, premier, prevailing, primary, prime, principal, superior, supreme, uppermost, vital **2.** *n.* boss (*Inf.*), captain, chieftain, commander, director, governor, head, leader, lord, manager, master, principal, ringleader, ruler, superintendent, suzerain

Antonyms *adj.* least, minor, subordinate, subsidiary ~*n.* follower, subject, subordinate

chiefly above all, especially, essentially, in general, in the main, mainly, mostly, on the whole, predominantly, primarily, principally, usually

child babe, baby, bairn (*Scot.*), brat, chit, descendant, infant, issue, juvenile, kid (*Inf.*), little one, minor, nipper (*Inf.*), nursling, offspring, progeny, suckling, toddler, tot, wean (*Scot.*), youngster

childhood boyhood, girlhood, immaturity, infancy, minority, schooldays, youth

childlike artless, credulous, guileless, ingenuous, innocent, naive, simple, trustful, trusting, unfeigned

chill 1. *adj.* biting, bleak, chilly, cold, freezing, frigid, raw, sharp, wintry **2.** *v.* congeal, cool, freeze, refrigerate

chilly 1. blowy, breezy, brisk, cool, crisp, draughty, fresh, nippy, penetrating, sharp **2.** frigid, hostile, unfriendly, unresponsive, unsympathetic, unwelcoming

Antonyms (*sense 1*) balmy, hot, mild, scorching, sunny, sweltering, warm (*sense 2*) affable, chummy (*Inf.*), congenial, cordial, friendly, responsive, sociable, sympathetic, warm, welcoming

chip *n.* dent, flake, flaw, fragment, nick, notch, paring, scrap, scratch, shard, shaving, sliver, wafer

chivalrous bold, brave, courageous, courteous, courtly, gallant, gentlemanly, heroic, high-minded, honourable, intrepid, knightly, magnanimous, true, valiant

Antonyms boorish, cowardly, cruel, dishonourable, disloyal, rude, uncourtly, ungallant, unmannerly

chivalry courage, courtesy, courtliness, gallantry, gentlemanliness, knight-errantry, knighthood, politeness

choice 1. *n.* alternative, discrimination, election, option, pick, preference, say, selection, variety 2. *adj.* bad (*Sl.*), best, crucial (*Sl.*), dainty, def (*Sl.*), elect, elite, excellent, exclusive, exquisite, hand-picked, nice, precious, prime, prize, rare, select, special, superior, uncommon, unusual, valuable

choke asphyxiate, bar, block, clog, close, congest, constrict, dam, obstruct, occlude, overpower, smother, stifle, stop, strangle, suffocate, suppress, throttle

choose adopt, cull, designate, desire, elect, espouse, fix on, opt for, pick, predestine, prefer, see fit, select, settle upon, single out, take, wish

Antonyms decline, dismiss, exclude, forgo, leave, refuse, reject, throw aside

chore burden, duty, errand, fag (*Inf.*), job, task

chorus 1. choir, choristers, ensemble, singers, vocalists 2. burden, refrain, response, strain

christen baptize, call, designate, dub, name, style, term, title

chronicle 1. *n.* account, annals, diary, history, journal, narrative, record, register, story 2. *v.* enter, narrate, put on record, record, recount, register, relate, report, set down, tell

chuck cast, discard, fling, heave, hurl, pitch, shy, sling, throw, toss

churlish boorish, brusque, crabbed, harsh, ill-tempered, impolite, loutish, morose, oafish, rude, sullen, surly, uncivil, unmannerly, vulgar

cinema big screen (*Inf.*), films, flicks (*Sl.*), motion pictures, movies, pictures

circle *n.* 1. band, circumference, coil, cordon, cycle, disc, globe, lap, loop, orb, perimeter, periphery, revolution, ring, round, sphere, turn 2. area, bounds, circuit, compass, domain, enclosure, field, orbit, province, range, realm, region, scene, sphere 3. assembly, class, clique, club, company, coterie, crowd, fellowship, fraternity, group, school, set, society ~ *v.* 4. belt, circumnavigate, circumscribe, coil, compass, curve, encircle, enclose, encompass, envelop, gird, hem in, pivot, revolve, ring, rotate, surround, tour, whirl

circuit area, compass, course, journey, orbit, perambulation, revolution, round, route, tour, track

circulate broadcast, diffuse, disseminate, distribute, issue, make known, promulgate, propagate, publicize, publish, spread

circulation 1. currency, dissemination, distribution, spread, transmission, vogue 2. circling, flow, motion, rotation

circumference border, boundary, bounds, circuit, edge, extremity, fringe, limits, outline, perimeter, periphery, rim, verge

circumstance accident, condition, contingency, detail, element, event, fact, factor, happening, incident, item, occurrence, particular, position, respect, situation

circumstances life style, means, position, resources, situation, state, state of affairs, station, status, times

cite 1. adduce, advance, allude to, enumerate, evidence, extract, mention, name, quote, specify 2. *Law* call, subpoena, summon

citizen burgess, burgher, denizen, dweller, freeman, inhabitant, ratepayer, resident, subject, townsman

city *n.* conurbation, megalopolis, metropolis, municipality

civil 1. civic, domestic, home, interior, municipal, political 2. accommodating, affable, civilized, complaisant, courteous, courtly, obliging, polished, polite, refined, urbane, well-bred, well-mannered

Antonyms (*sense 1*) military, religious, state (*sense 2*) discourteous, ill-mannered, impolite, rude, uncivil, unfriendly, ungracious, unpleasant

civilization 1. advancement, cultivation, culture, development, education, enlightenment, progress, refinement, sophistication **2.** community, nation, people, polity, society

civilize cultivate, educate, enlighten, humanize, improve, polish, refine, sophisticate, tame

civilized cultured, educated, enlightened, humane, polite, sophisticated, tolerant, urbane

Antonyms barbarous, green, ignorant, naive, primitive, simple, uncivilized, uncultivated, uncultured, undeveloped, uneducated, unenlightened, unsophisticated, untutored, wild

claim 1. v. allege, ask, assert, call for, challenge, collect, demand, exact, hold, insist, maintain, need, pick up, profess, require, take, uphold **2.** n. affirmation, allegation, application, assertion, call, demand, petition, pretension, privilege, protestation, request, requirement, right, title

clan band, brotherhood, clique, coterie, faction, family, fraternity, gens, group, house, race, sect, sept, set, society, sodality, tribe

clap acclaim, applaud, cheer

Antonyms blow a raspberry, boo, catcall, hiss, jeer

clarify clear up, elucidate, explain, illuminate, make plain, resolve, simplify, throw or shed light on

clarity clearness, comprehensibility, definition, explicitness, intelligibility, limpidity, lucidity, obviousness, precision, simplicity, transparency

Antonyms cloudiness, complex-

ity, complication, dullness, haziness, imprecision, intricacy, murkiness, obscurity

clash 1. v. conflict, cross swords, feud, grapple, quarrel, war, wrangle **2.** n. brush, collision, conflict, confrontation, difference of opinion, disagreement, fight, showdown (*Inf.*)

clasp 1. v. attack, clutch, concatenate, connect, embrace, enfold, fasten, grapple, grasp, grip, hold, hug, press, seize, squeeze **2.** n. brooch, buckle, catch, clip, fastener, fastening, grip, hasp, hook, pin, press stud, snap

class n. caste, category, classification, collection, denomination, department, division, genre, genus, grade, group, grouping, kind, league, order, rank, set, sort, species, sphere, status, type, value

classic adj. **1.** best, consummate, finest, first-rate, masterly **2.** archetypal, definitive, exemplary, ideal, master, model, paradigmatic, quintessential, standard **3.** abiding, ageless, deathless, enduring, immortal, lasting, undying ~n. **4.** exemplar, masterpiece, masterwork, model, paradigm, prototype, standard

Antonyms adj. inferior, modern, poor, second-rate, terrible, unrefined, unrepresentative ~n. trash

classical 1. chaste, elegant, harmonious, pure, refined, restrained, symmetrical, understated, well-proportioned **2.** Attic, Augustan, Grecian, Greek, Hellenic, Latin, Roman

classification analysis, arrangement, cataloguing, categorization, codification, grading, sorting, taxonomy

classify arrange, catalogue, categorize, codify, dispose, distribute, file, grade, pigeonhole, rank, sort, systematize, tabulate

clause 1. article, chapter, condition, paragraph, part, passage, section **2.** heading, item, point, provision, proviso, specification, stipulation

claw *n.* nail, nipper, pincer, talon, tentacle, unguis

clean *adj.* **1.** faultless, flawless, fresh, hygienic, immaculate, laundered, pure, sanitary, spotless, unblemished, unsoiled, unspotted, unstained, unsullied, washed **2.** chaste, decent, exemplary, good, honourable, innocent, moral, pure, respectable, undefiled, upright, virtuous ~*v.* **3.** bath, cleanse, deodorize, disinfect, do up, dust, launder, lave, mop, purge, purify, rinse, sanitize, scour, scrub, sponge, swab, sweep, vacuum, wash, wipe
Antonyms *adj.* (*sense 1*) dirty, filthy, mucky, soiled, sullied, unwashed (*sense 2*) dishonourable, immoral, impure, indecent, unchaste ~*v.* adulterate, defile, dirty, disorder, disorganize, infect, mess up, pollute, soil, stain

clear[1] *adj.* **1.** bright, cloudless, fair, fine, halcyon, light, luminous, shining, sunny, unclouded, undimmed **2.** apparent, articulate, audible, coherent, comprehensible, conspicuous, definite, distinct, evident, explicit, express, incontrovertible, intelligible, lucid, manifest, obvious, palpable, patent, perceptible, plain, pronounced, recognizable, unambiguous, unequivocal, unmistakable, unquestionable **3.** empty, free, open, smooth, unhampered, unhindered, unimpeded, unlimited, unobstructed **4.** certain, convinced, decided, definite, positive, resolved, satisfied, sure
Antonyms (*sense 1*) cloudy, dark, dull, foggy, hazy, misty, murky, overcast, stormy (*sense 2*) ambiguous, confused, doubtful, equivocal, hidden, inarticulate, inaudible, incoherent, indistinct, inexplicit, obscured, unrecognizable (*sense 3*) barricaded, blocked, closed, engaged, hampered, impeded, obstructed

clear[2] *v.* **1.** clean, cleanse, erase, purify, refine, sweep away, tidy (up), wipe **2.** break up, brighten, clarify, lighten **3.** absolve, acquit, excuse, exonerate, justify, vindicate **4.** jump, leap, miss, pass over, vault
Antonyms (*sense 3*) accuse, blame, charge, condemn, convict, find guilty

clear-cut definite, explicit, plain, precise, specific, straightforward, unambiguous, unequivocal

clearly beyond doubt, distinctly, evidently, incontestably, incontrovertibly, markedly, obviously, openly, undeniably, undoubtedly

clear up 1. answer, clarify, elucidate, explain, resolve, solve, straighten out, unravel **2.** order, rearrange, tidy (up)

clergyman chaplain, cleric, curate, divine, father, man of God, man of the cloth, minister, padre, parson, pastor, priest, rabbi, rector, reverend (*Inf.*), vicar

clever able, adroit, apt, astute, brainy (*Inf.*), bright, canny, capable, cunning, deep, dexterous, discerning, expert, gifted, ingenious, intelligent, inventive, keen, knowing, knowledgeable, quick, quick-witted, rational, resourceful, sagacious, sensible, shrewd, skilful, smart, talented, witty
Antonyms awkward, boring, clumsy, dense, dull, ham-fisted (*Inf.*), inept, inexpert, maladroit, slow, stupid, thick, unaccomplished, unimaginative, witless

client applicant, buyer, consumer, customer, dependant, habitué, patient, patron, protégé, shopper

clientele business, clients, customers, following, market, patronage, regulars, trade

cliff bluff, crag, escarpment, face, overhang, precipice, rock face, scar, scarp

climate 1. clime, country, region, temperature, weather **2.** ambience, disposition, feeling, mood, temper, tendency, trend

climax *n.* acme, apogee, culmination, head, height, highlight, high spot (*Inf.*), ne plus ultra, pay-off (*Inf.*), peak, summit, top, zenith

climb ascend, clamber, mount, rise, scale, shin up, soar, top

cling adhere, attach to, be true to, clasp, cleave to, clutch, embrace, fasten, grasp, grip, hug, stick, twine round

clip[1] *v.* crop, curtail, cut, cut short, pare, prune, shear, shorten, snip, trim

clip[2] *v.* attach, fasten, fix, hold, pin, staple

cloak 1. *v.* camouflage, conceal, cover, disguise, hide, mask, obscure, screen, veil 2. *n.* blind, cape, coat, cover, front, mantle, mask, pretext, shield, wrap

clog *v.* block, burden, congest, dam up, hamper, hinder, impede, jam, obstruct, occlude, shackle, stop up

close[1] *v.* 1. bar, block, choke, clog, confine, cork, fill, lock, obstruct, plug, seal, secure, shut, shut up, stop up 2. cease, complete, conclude, culminate, discontinue, end, finish, mothball, shut down, terminate, wind up (*Inf.*)

Antonyms (*sense 1*) clear, free, open, release, unblock, unclog, uncork, unstop, widen (*sense 2*) begin, commence, initiate, open, start

close[2] 1. adjacent, adjoining, approaching, at hand, handy, hard by, imminent, impending, near, nearby, neighbouring, nigh 2. compact, congested, cramped, cropped, crowded, dense, impenetrable, jam-packed, packed, short, solid, thick, tight 3. attached, confidential, dear, devoted, familiar, inseparable, intimate, loving 4. airless, confined, frowsty, fuggy, heavy, humid, muggy, oppressive, stale, stifling, stuffy, suffocating, sweltering, thick, unventilated 5. illiberal, mean, mingy (*Inf.*), miserly, near, niggardly, parsimonious, penurious, stingy, tight-fisted, ungenerous

Antonyms (*sense 1*) distant, far, far away, far off, future, outlying, remote (*sense 2*) dispersed, empty, free, loose, penetrable, porous, uncongested, uncrowded (*sense 3*) alienated, aloof, chilly, cold, cool, distant, indifferent, standoffish, unfriendly (*sense 4*) airy, fresh, refreshing, roomy, spacious (*sense 5*) charitable, extravagant, generous, lavish, liberal, magnanimous, unstinting

cloth dry goods, fabric, material, stuff, textiles

clothe accoutre, apparel, array, attire, bedizen (*Archaic*), caparison, cover, deck, doll up (*Sl.*), drape, dress, endow, enwrap, equip, fit out, garb, habit, invest, outfit, rig, robe, swathe

Antonyms disrobe, divest, expose, strip, strip off, unclothe, uncover, undress

clothes, clothing apparel, attire, clobber (*Brit. sl.*), costume, dress, duds (*Inf.*), ensemble, garb, garments, gear (*Inf.*), get-up (*Inf.*), glad rags (*Inf.*), habits, outfit, raiment, rigout (*Inf.*), togs (*Inf.*), vestments, vesture, wardrobe, wear

cloud 1. *n.* billow, darkness, fog, gloom, haze, mist, murk, nebula, nebulosity, obscurity, vapour 2. *v.* becloud, darken, dim, eclipse, obfuscate, obscure, overcast, overshadow, shade, shadow, veil

cloudy blurred, confused, dark, dim, dismal, dull, dusky, emulsified, gloomy, hazy, indistinct, leaden, lowering, muddy, murky, nebulous, obscure, opaque, overcast, sombre, sullen, sunless

Antonyms bright, clear, distinct, fair, obvious, plain, sunny, uncloudy

clown 1. *n.* buffoon, comedian, dolt, fool, harlequin, jester, joker, merry-andrew, mountebank, pierrot, prankster, punchinello 2. *v.* act the fool, act the goat, jest, mess about

club *n.* 1. bat, bludgeon, cosh, cudgel, stick, truncheon 2. association, circle, clique, company, fraternity, group, guild, lodge, order, set, society, sodality, union

clue evidence, hint, indication, inkling, intimation, lead, pointer, sign, suggestion, suspicion, tip, tip-off, trace

clumsy awkward, blundering, bumbling, bungling, butter-fingered (*Inf.*), cack-handed (*Inf.*), gauche, gawky, ham-fisted (*Inf.*), ham-handed (*Inf.*), heavy, ill-shaped, inept, inexpert, lumbering, maladroit, ponderous, uncoordinated, uncouth, ungainly, unhandy, unskilful, unwieldy
Antonyms adept, adroit, competent, deft, dexterous, expert, graceful, handy, proficient, skilful

cluster 1. *n.* assemblage, batch, bunch, clump, collection, gathering, group, knot 2. *v.* assemble, bunch, collect, flock, gather, group

clutch catch, clasp, cling to, embrace, fasten, grab, grapple, grasp, grip, seize, snatch

coach *n.* 1. bus, car, carriage, charabanc, vehicle 2. instructor, teacher, trainer, tutor ~*v.* 3. cram, drill, instruct, prepare, train, tutor

coalition affiliation, alliance, amalgam, amalgamation, association, bloc, combination, compact, confederacy, confederation, conjunction, fusion, integration, league, merger, union

coarse boorish, brutish, coarse-grained, foul-mouthed, gruff, loutish, rough, rude, uncivil
Antonyms civilized, cultured, elegant, genteel, pleasant, polite, proper, urbane, well-bred, well-mannered

coarseness bawdiness, boorishness, crudity, earthiness, indelicacy, offensiveness, poor taste, ribaldry, roughness, smut, smuttiness, uncouthness, unevenness

coast 1. *n.* beach, border, coastline, littoral, seaboard, seaside, shore, strand 2. *v.* cruise, drift, freewheel, get by, glide, sail, taxi

coat *n.* 1. fleece, fur, hair, hide,

pelt, skin, wool 2. coating, covering, layer, overlay ~*v.* 3. apply, Artex (*Trademark*), cover, plaster, smear, spread

coax allure, beguile, cajole, decoy, entice, flatter, inveigle, persuade, prevail upon, soft-soap (*Inf.*), soothe, sweet-talk (*Inf.*), talk into, wheedle
Antonyms browbeat, bully, coerce, force, harass, intimidate, pressurize, threaten

cocky arrogant, brash, cocksure, conceited, egotistical, lordly, swaggering, swollen-headed, vain
Antonyms hesitant, lacking confidence, modest, self-effacing, uncertain, unsure

code 1. cipher, cryptograph 2. canon, convention, custom, ethics, etiquette, manners, maxim, regulations, rules, system

coil convolute, curl, entwine, loop, snake, spiral, twine, twist, wind, wreathe, writhe

coincide 1. be concurrent, coexist, occur simultaneously, synchronize 2. accord, harmonize, match, quadrate, square, tally
Antonyms be inconsistent, be unlike, contradict, differ, disagree, diverge, divide, part, separate

coincidence accident, chance, eventuality, fluke, fortuity, happy accident, luck, stroke of luck

cold *adj.* 1. arctic, biting, bitter, bleak, brumal, chill, chilly, cool, freezing, frigid, frosty, frozen, gelid, icy, inclement, raw, wintry 2. benumbed, chilled, chilly, freezing, frozen to the marrow, numbed, shivery 3. aloof, apathetic, cold-blooded, dead, distant, frigid, glacial, indifferent, inhospitable, lukewarm, passionless, phlegmatic, reserved, spiritless, standoffish, stony, undemonstrative, unfeeling, unmoved, unresponsive, unsympathetic ~*n.* 4. chill, chilliness, coldness, frigidity, frostiness, iciness, inclemency
Antonyms (*sense 1*) balmy, heated, hot, mild, sunny, warm

(sense 3) alive, animated, caring, compassionate, conscious, demonstrative, emotional, friendly, loving, open, passionate, responsive, spirited, sympathetic, warm

collaborate cooperate, coproduce, join forces, participate, team up, work together

collaborator associate, colleague, confederate, co-worker, partner, team-mate

collapse 1. *v.* break down, cave in, come to nothing, crack up *(Inf.)*, crumple, fail, faint, fall, fold, founder, give way, subside **2.** *n.* breakdown, cave-in, disintegration, downfall, exhaustion, failure, faint, flop *(Sl.)*, prostration, subsidence

colleague aider, ally, assistant, associate, auxiliary, coadjutor *(Rare)*, collaborator, companion, comrade, confederate, confrère, fellow worker, helper, partner, team-mate, workmate

collect 1. accumulate, aggregate, amass, assemble, gather, heap, hoard, save, stockpile **2.** assemble, cluster, congregate, convene, converge, flock together, rally
Antonyms disperse, distribute, scatter, spread, strew

collected calm, composed, confident, cool, placid, poised, self-possessed, serene, together *(Sl.)*, unperturbable, unperturbed, unruffled

collection 1. accumulation, anthology, compilation, congeries, heap, hoard, mass, pile, set, stockpile, store **2.** assemblage, assembly, assortment, cluster, company, congregation, convocation, crowd, gathering, group **3.** alms, contribution, offering, offertory

collide clash, come into collision, conflict, crash, meet head-on

collision accident, bump, crash, impact, pile-up, prang *(Inf.)*, smash

colony community, dependency, dominion, outpost, possession, province, satellite state, settlement, territory

colossal Brobdingnagian, elephantine, enormous, gargantuan, gigantic, ginormous, herculean, huge, immense, mammoth, massive, monstrous, monumental, mountainous, prodigious, titanic, vast

colour *n.* **1.** colorant, coloration, complexion, dye, hue, paint, pigment, pigmentation, shade, tincture, tinge, tint **2.** animation, bloom, blush, brilliance, flush, glow, liveliness, rosiness, ruddiness, vividness ~*v.* **3.** colourwash, dye, paint, stain, tinge, tint **4.** *Fig.* disguise, distort, embroider, exaggerate, falsify, garble, gloss over, misrepresent, pervert, prejudice, slant, taint **5.** blush, burn, crimson, flush, go crimson, redden

colourful 1. bright, brilliant, Dayglo *(Trademark)*, intense, jazzy *(Sl.)*, kaleidoscopic, motley, multicoloured, psychedelic, rich, variegated, vibrant, vivid **2.** characterful, distinctive, graphic, interesting, lively, picturesque, rich, stimulating, unusual, vivid
Antonyms *(sense 1)* colourless, dark, drab, dreary, dull, faded, pale, washed out *(sense 2)* boring, characterless, dull, flat, lifeless, monotonous, unexciting, uninteresting, unvaried

colourless characterless, dreary, insipid, lacklustre, tame, uninteresting, unmemorable, vacuous, vapid
Antonyms animated, bright, colourful, compelling, distinctive, exciting, interesting, unusual

column 1. cavalcade, file, line, list, procession, queue, rank, row, string, train **2.** caryatid, obelisk, pilaster, pillar, post, shaft, support, upright

coma drowsiness, insensibility, lethargy, oblivion, somnolence, stupor, torpor, trance, unconsciousness

comb *v.* **1.** arrange, curry, dress, groom, untangle **2.** *Fig.* go through with a fine-tooth comb, hunt, rake, ransack, rummage, scour, screen, search, sift, sweep

combat n. action, battle, conflict, contest, encounter, engagement, fight, skirmish, struggle, war, warfare

Antonyms agreement, armistice, peace, surrender, truce

combination 1. amalgam, amalgamation, blend, coalescence, composite, connection, mix, mixture 2. alliance, association, cabal, cartel, coalition, combine, compound, confederacy, confederation, consortium, conspiracy, federation, merger, syndicate, unification, union

combine amalgamate, associate, bind, blend, bond, compound, connect, cooperate, fuse, incorporate, integrate, join (together), link, marry, merge, mix, pool, put together, synthesize, unify, unite

Antonyms detach, dissociate, dissolve, disunite, divide, part, separate, sever

come 1. advance, appear, approach, arrive, become, draw near, enter, happen, materialize, move, move towards, near, occur, originate, show up (Inf.), turn out, turn up (Inf.) 2. appear, arrive, attain, enter, materialize, reach, show up (Inf.), turn up (Inf.) 3. fall, happen, occur, take place 4. arise, emanate, emerge, end up, flow, issue, originate, result, turn out 5. extend, reach

come about arise, befall, come to pass, happen, occur, result, take place, transpire (Inf.)

come across bump into (Inf.), chance upon, discover, encounter, find, happen upon, hit upon, light upon, meet, notice, stumble upon, unearth

come apart break, come unstuck, crumble, disintegrate, fall to pieces, give way, separate, split, tear

comeback rally, rebound, recovery, resurgence, return, revival, triumph

come back reappear, recur, re-enter, return

comedown anticlimax, blow, decline, deflation, demotion, disappointment, humiliation, letdown, reverse

comedy chaffing, drollery, facetiousness, farce, fun, hilarity, humour, jesting, joking, light entertainment, sitcom (Inf.), slapstick, wisecracking, witticisms

Antonyms high drama, melancholy, melodrama, opera, sadness, seriousness, serious play, soap opera, solemnity, tragedy

come in appear, arrive, cross the threshold, enter, finish, reach, show up (Inf.)

come out 1. appear, be published (announced, divulged, issued, released, reported, revealed) 2. conclude, end, result, terminate

come through 1. accomplish, achieve, prevail, succeed, triumph 2. endure, survive, weather the storm, withstand

comfort v. 1. alleviate, assuage, cheer, commiserate with, compassionate (Archaic), console, ease, encourage, enliven, gladden, hearten, inspirit, invigorate, reassure, refresh, relieve, solace, soothe, strengthen ~n. 2. aid, alleviation, cheer, compensation, consolation, ease, encouragement, enjoyment, help, relief, satisfaction, succour, support 3. cosiness, creature comforts, ease, luxury, opulence, snugness, wellbeing

comfortable 1. adequate, agreeable, ample, commodious, convenient, cosy, delightful, easy, enjoyable, homely, loose, loose-fitting, pleasant, relaxing, restful, roomy, snug 2. affluent, prosperous, well-off, well-to-do

Antonyms (sense 1) disagreeable, inadequate, skin-tight, tight, tight-fitting, uncomfortable, unpleasant

comic adj. amusing, comical, droll, facetious, farcical, funny, humorous, jocular, joking, light, rich, waggish, witty

Antonyms depressing, melancholy, pathetic, sad, serious, solemn, touching, tragic

coming 1. *adj.* approaching, at hand, due, en route, forthcoming, future, imminent, impending, in store, in the wind, near, next, nigh **2.** *n.* accession, advent, approach, arrival

command *v.* **1.** bid, charge, compel, demand, direct, enjoin, order, require **2.** control, dominate, govern, head, lead, manage, reign over, rule, supervise, sway ~*n.* **3.** behest, bidding, commandment, decree, direction, directive, edict, fiat, injunction, instruction, mandate, order, precept, requirement, ultimatum
Antonyms (*sense 1*) appeal (to), ask, beg, beseech, plead, request, supplicate (*sense 2*) be inferior, be subordinate, follow

commander boss, captain, chief, C in C, C.O., commander-in-chief, commanding officer, director, head, leader, officer, ruler

commanding advantageous, controlling, decisive, dominant, dominating, superior
Antonyms retiring, shrinking, submissive, timid, weak

commemorate celebrate, honour, immortalize, keep, memorialize, observe, pay tribute to, remember, salute, solemnize
Antonyms disregard, forget, ignore, omit, overlook, pass over, take no notice of

commemoration ceremony, honouring, memorial service, observance, remembrance, tribute

commence begin, embark on, enter upon, inaugurate, initiate, open, originate, start
Antonyms bring *or* come to an end, cease, complete, conclude, desist, end, finish, halt, stop, terminate, wind up

commend acclaim, applaud, approve, compliment, eulogize, extol, praise, recommend, speak highly of
Antonyms attack, censure, condemn, criticize, denounce, disapprove, knock (*Inf.*), slam

comment *v.* **1.** animadvert, interpose, mention, note, observe, opine, point out, remark, say **2.** annotate, criticize, elucidate, explain, interpret ~*n.* **3.** animadversion, observation, remark, statement **4.** annotation, commentary, criticism, elucidation, explanation, exposition, illustration, note

commentary analysis, critique, description, exegesis, explanation, narration, notes, review, treatise, voice-over

commentator commenter, reporter, special correspondent, sportscaster

commerce business, dealing, exchange, merchandising, trade, traffic

commercial business, mercantile, profit-making, sales, trade, trading

commission *n.* **1.** appointment, authority, charge, duty, employment, errand, function, mandate, mission, task, trust, warrant **2.** allowance, brokerage, compensation, cut, fee, percentage, rake-off (*Sl.*) **3.** board, body of commissioners, commissioners, committee, delegation, deputation, representative ~*v.* **4.** appoint, authorize, contract, delegate, depute, empower, engage, nominate, order, select, send

commit carry out, do, enact, execute, perform, perpetrate

commitment 1. duty, engagement, liability, obligation, responsibility, tie **2.** assurance, guarantee, pledge, promise, undertaking, vow, word
Antonyms disavowal, indecisiveness, negation, vacillation, wavering

common 1. average, commonplace, conventional, customary, daily, everyday, familiar, frequent, general, habitual, humdrum, obscure, ordinary, plain, regular, routine, run-of-the-mill, simple, standard, stock, usual, workaday **2.** accepted, general, popular, prevailing, prevalent, universal, widespread **3.** coarse, hackneyed, inferior, low, pedestrian, plebeian, stale, trite, undistinguished, vulgar

Antonyms (*sense 1*) abnormal, distinguished, famous, formal, important, infrequent, noble, outstanding, rare, scarce, sophisticated, strange, superior, uncommon, unknown, unpopular, unusual (*sense 3*) cultured, gentle, refined, sensitive

commotion ado, agitation, brouhaha, bustle, disorder, disturbance, excitement, ferment, furore, fuss, hubbub, hullabaloo, hurly-burly, perturbation, racket, riot, rumpus, to-do, tumult, turmoil, uproar

communal collective, communistic, community, general, joint, neighbourhood, public, shared

Antonyms exclusive, individual, personal, private, single, unshared

communicate acquaint, announce, be in contact, be in touch, connect, convey, correspond, declare, disclose, disseminate, divulge, impart, inform, make known, pass on, phone, proclaim, publish, report, reveal, ring up, signify, spread, transmit, unfold

Antonyms conceal, cover up, hold back, hush up, keep back, keep secret, keep under wraps, repress, sit on (*Inf.*), suppress, whitewash (*Inf.*), withhold

communication 1. connection, contact, conversation, correspondence, dissemination, intercourse, link, transmission **2.** announcement, disclosure, dispatch, information, intelligence, message, news, report, statement, word

communism Bolshevism, collectivism, Marxism, socialism, state socialism

community association, body politic, brotherhood, commonwealth, company, district, general public, locality, people, populace, population, public, residents, society, state

compact *adj.* **1.** close, compressed, condensed, dense, firm, impenetrable, impermeable, pressed together, solid, thick **2.** brief, compendious, concise, epigrammatic, laconic, pithy, pointed, succinct, terse, to the point

Antonyms (*sense 1*) dispersed, large, loose, roomy, scattered, spacious, sprawling (*sense 2*) circumlocutory, garrulous, lengthy, long-winded, prolix, rambling, verbose, wordy

companion 1. accomplice, ally, associate, buddy (*Inf.*), colleague, comrade, confederate, consort, crony, friend, mate (*Inf.*), partner **2.** complement, counterpart, fellow, match, mate, twin

companionship amity, camaraderie, company, comradeship, conviviality, esprit de corps, fellowship, fraternity, friendship, rapport, togetherness

company 1. assemblage, assembly, band, body, circle, collection, community, concourse, convention, coterie, crew, crowd, ensemble, gathering, group, league, party, set, throng, troop, troupe, turnout **2.** association, business, concern, corporation, establishment, firm, house, partnership, syndicate

compare *With* with balance, collate, contrast, juxtapose, set against, weigh

comparison 1. collation, contrast, distinction, juxtaposition **2.** analogy, comparability, correlation, likeness, resemblance, similarity

compartment alcove, bay, berth, booth, carrel, carriage, cell, chamber, cubbyhole, cubicle, locker, niche, pigeonhole, section

compassion charity, clemency, commiseration, compunction, condolence, fellow feeling, heart, humanity, kindness, mercy, ruth (*Archaic*), soft-heartedness, sorrow, sympathy, tender-heartedness, tenderness

Antonyms apathy, cold~heartedness, indifference, mer~cilessness, unconcern

compel bulldoze (*Inf.*), coerce, constrain, dragoon, drive, en~force, exact, force, hustle (*Sl.*), impel, make, necessitate, oblige, restrain, squeeze, urge

compensate 1. atone, indemnify, make good, make restitution, recompense, refund, reimburse, remunerate, repay, requite, re~ward, satisfy 2. balance, cancel (out), counteract, countervail, make amends, make up for, offset, redress

compensation amends, atone~ment, damages, indemnification, indemnity, payment, recom~pense, reimbursement, remu~neration, reparation, requital, restitution, reward, satisfaction

compete be in the running, chal~lenge, contend, contest, emulate, fight, pit oneself against, rival, strive, struggle, vie

competent able, adapted, ad~equate, appropriate, capable, clever, endowed, equal, fit, perti~nent, proficient, qualified, suffi~cient, suitable

Antonyms inadequate, inca~pable, incompetent, inexperi~enced, inexpert, undependable, unqualified, unskilled

competition 1. contention, con~test, emulation, one-upmanship (*Inf.*), opposition, rivalry, strife, struggle 2. championship, con~test, event, puzzle, quiz, tourna~ment

competitor adversary, antago~nist, challenger, competition, contestant, emulator, opponent, opposition, rival

compile accumulate, amass, an~thologize, collect, cull, garner, gather, marshal, organize, put together

complacent contented, gratified, pleased, pleased with oneself, satisfied, self-assured, self-contented, self-righteous, self-satisfied, serene, smug, un~concerned

Antonyms discontent, dissatis~fied, insecure, rude, troubled, un~easy, unsatisfied

complain beef (*Sl.*), bellyache (*Sl.*), bemoan, bewail, bitch (*Sl.*), carp, deplore, find fault, fuss, grieve, gripe (*Inf.*), groan, grouse, growl, grumble, kick up a fuss (*Inf.*), lament, moan, whine

complaint 1. accusation, annoy~ance, beef (*Sl.*), bitch (*Sl.*), charge, criticism, dissatisfaction, fault-finding, grievance, gripe (*Inf.*), grouse, grumble, lament, moan, plaint, remonstrance, trouble, wail 2. affliction, ail~ment, disease, disorder, illness, indisposition, malady, sickness, upset

complete adj. 1. all, entire, fault~less, full, intact, integral, plenary, unabridged, unbroken, undivided, unimpaired, whole 2. accom~plished, achieved, concluded, ended, finished 3. absolute, con~summate, dyed-in-the-wool, per~fect, thorough, thoroughgoing, total, utter ~v. 4. accomplish, achieve, cap, close, conclude, crown, discharge, do, end, ex~ecute, fill in, finalize, finish, fulfil, perfect, perform, realize, round off, settle, terminate, wrap up (*Inf.*)

Antonyms deficient, imper~fect, incomplete, inconclusive, partial, spoilt, unaccomplished, unfinished, unsettled ~v. begin, commence, initiate, mar, spoil, start

completely absolutely, altogeth~er, down to the ground, en masse, entirely, from A to Z, from be~ginning to end, fully, heart and soul, hook, line and sinker, in full, *in toto*, perfectly, quite, root and branch, solidly, thoroughly, to~tally, utterly, wholly

complex adj. circuitous, compli~cated, convoluted, Daedalian (*Literary*), intricate, involved, knotty, labyrinthine, mingled, mixed, tangled, tortuous

complicate confuse, entangle,

interweave, involve, make intricate, muddle, snarl up

complicated 1. Byzantine (*of attitudes, etc.*), complex, convoluted, elaborate, interlaced, intricate, involved, labyrinthine 2. difficult, involved, perplexing, problematic, puzzling, troublesome
Antonyms clear, easy, simple, straightforward, uncomplicated, undemanding, understandable, uninvolved, user-friendly

complication *n.* combination, complexity, confusion, entanglement, intricacy, mixture, web

compliment 1. *n.* admiration, bouquet, commendation, congratulations, courtesy, eulogy, favour, flattery, honour, praise, tribute 2. *v.* commend, congratulate, extol, felicitate, flatter, laud, pay tribute to, praise, salute, sing the praises of, speak highly of, wish joy to
Antonyms *n.* complaint, condemnation, criticism, disparagement, insult, reproach ~*v.* condemn, criticize, decry, disparage, insult, reprehend, reproach

comply abide by, accede, accord, acquiesce, adhere to, agree to, conform to, consent to, defer, discharge, follow, fulfil, obey, observe, perform, respect, satisfy, submit, yield
Antonyms break, defy, disobey, disregard, fight, ignore, oppose, refuse to obey, reject, repudiate, resist, spurn, violate

component *n.* constituent, element, ingredient, item, part, piece, unit

compose build, compound, comprise, constitute, construct, fashion, form, make, make up, put together

composition 1. arrangement, configuration, constitution, design, form, formation, layout, make-up, organization, structure 2. creation, essay, exercise, literary work, opus, piece, study, work, writing

composure aplomb, calm, calm-

ness, collectedness, cool (*Sl.*), coolness, dignity, ease, equanimity, imperturbability, placidity, poise, sang-froid, sedateness, self-assurance, self-possession, serenity, tranquillity
Antonyms agitation, discomposure, excitability, impatience, nervousness, perturbation, uneasiness

compound 1. *v.* amalgamate, blend, coalesce, combine, concoct, fuse, intermingle, mingle, mix, synthesize, unite 2. *n.* alloy, amalgam, blend, combination, composite, composition, conglomerate, fusion, medley, mixture, synthesis 3. *adj.* complex, composite, conglomerate, intricate, multiple, not simple
Antonyms *v.* divide, part, segregate ~*n.* element ~*adj.* pure, simple, single, unmixed

comprehend apprehend, assimilate, conceive, discern, fathom, grasp, know, make out, perceive, see, take in, understand

comprehension conception, discernment, grasp, intelligence, judgment, knowledge, perception, realization, sense, understanding

compress abbreviate, compact, concentrate, condense, constrict, contract, cram, crowd, crush, press, shorten, squash, squeeze, summarize, wedge

comprise be composed of, comprehend, consist of, contain, embrace, encompass, include, take in

compromise 1. *v.* adjust, agree, arbitrate, compose, compound, concede, give and take, go fifty-fifty (*Inf.*), meet halfway, settle, strike a balance 2. *n.* accommodation, accord, adjustment, agreement, concession, give-and-take, half measures, middle ground, settlement, trade-off
Antonyms *v.* argue, contest, differ, disagree ~*n.* contention, controversy, difference, disagreement, dispute, quarrel

compulsive besetting, compelling, driving, irresistible, obsessive, overwhelming, uncontrollable, urgent

compulsory binding, de rigueur, forced, imperative, mandatory, obligatory, required, requisite
Antonyms discretionary, non-obligatory, non-requisite, optional, unimperative, unnecessary

comrade ally, associate, buddy (Inf.), colleague, companion, compatriot, compeer, confederate, co-worker, crony, fellow, friend, mate (Inf.), pal (Inf.), partner

conceal bury, camouflage, cover, disguise, dissemble, hide, keep dark, keep secret, mask, obscure, screen, secrete, shelter
Antonyms disclose, display, divulge, expose, lay bare, reveal, show, uncover, unmask, unveil

conceit amour-propre, arrogance, complacency, egotism, narcissism, pride, self-importance, self-love, swagger, vainglory, vanity

conceited arrogant, bigheaded (Inf.), cocky, egotistical, immodest, narcissistic, overweening, puffed up, self-important, stuck up (Inf.), swollen-headed, vain, vainglorious
Antonyms humble, modest, self-effacing, unassuming

conceivable believable, credible, imaginable, possible, thinkable
Antonyms inconceivable, incredible, unbelievable, unimaginable, unthinkable

conceive 1. appreciate, apprehend, believe, comprehend, envisage, fancy, grasp, imagine, realize, suppose, understand 2. contrive, create, design, develop, devise, form, formulate, produce, project, purpose, think up

concentrate 1. be engrossed in, consider closely, focus attention on, give all one's attention to, put one's mind to, rack one's brains 2. bring to bear, centre, cluster, converge, focus
Antonyms (sense 1) disregard,

let one's mind wander, lose concentration, pay no attention to, pay no heed to (sense 2) deploy, diffuse, disperse, dissipate, scatter, spread out

concentrated 1. all-out (Inf.), deep, hard, intense, intensive 2. boiled down, condensed, evaporated, reduced, rich, thickened, undiluted

concept abstraction, conception, conceptualization, hypothesis, idea, image, impression, notion, theory, view

concern v. 1. affect, apply to, bear on, be relevant to, interest, involve, pertain to, regard, touch ~n. 2. affair, business, charge, deportment, field, interest, involvement, job, matter, mission, occupation, responsibility, task, transaction ~v. 3. bother, disquiet, distress, disturb, make anxious, make uneasy, perturb, trouble, worry ~n. 4. anxiety, apprehension, attention, burden, care, consideration, disquiet, disquietude, distress, heed, responsibility, solicitude, worry 5. business, company, corporation, enterprise, establishment, firm, house, organization

concerned 1. active, implicated, interested, involved, mixed up, privy to 2. anxious, bothered, distressed, disturbed, exercised, troubled, uneasy, upset, worried
Antonyms aloof, carefree, detached, indifferent, neglectful, unconcerned, uninterested, untroubled, without a care

concerning about, anent (Scot.), apropos of, as regards, as to, in the matter of, on the subject of, re, regarding, relating to, respecting, touching, with reference to

concise brief, compact, compendious, compressed, condensed, epigrammatic, laconic, pithy, short, succinct, summary, synoptic, terse, to the point
Antonyms diffuse, discursive, garrulous, lengthy, long-winded, prolix, rambling, verbose, wordy

conclude 1. bring down the curtain, cease, close, come to an end, complete, draw to a close, end, finish, round off, terminate, wind up (*Inf.*) **2.** assume, decide, deduce, gather, infer, judge, reckon (*Inf.*), sum up, suppose, surmise
Antonyms (*sense 1*) begin, commence, extend, initiate, open, protract, start

conclusion 1. close, completion, end, finale, finish, result, termination **2.** consequence, culmination, issue, outcome, result, upshot **3.** agreement, conviction, decision, deduction, inference, judgment, opinion, resolution, settlement, verdict

conclusive clinching, convincing, decisive, definite, definitive, final, irrefutable, ultimate, unanswerable, unarguable
Antonyms contestable, disputable, doubtful, dubious, impeachable, inconclusive, indecisive, indefinite, questionable, refutable, unconvincing, vague

concrete *adj.* actual, definite, explicit, factual, material, real, sensible, specific, substantial, tangible
Antonyms abstract, immaterial, indefinite, insubstantial, intangible, theoretical, unspecified, vague

condemn 1. blame, censure, damn, denounce, disapprove, reprehend, reproach, reprobate, reprove, upbraid **2.** convict, damn, doom, pass sentence on, proscribe, sentence
Antonyms (*sense 1*) acclaim, applaud, approve, commend, compliment, condone, praise (*sense 2*) acquit, free, liberate

condemnation 1. blame, censure, denouncement, denunciation, disapproval, reproach, reprobation, reproof, stricture **2.** conviction, damnation, doom, judgment, proscription, sentence

condense 1. abbreviate, abridge, compact, compress, concentrate, contract, curtail, encapsulate, epitomize, précis, shorten, summarize
Antonyms elaborate, enlarge, expand, expatiate, increase, lengthen, pad out, spin out

condensed abridged, compressed, concentrated, curtailed, shortened, shrunken, slimmed down, summarized

condescend 1. be courteous, bend, come down off one's high horse (*Inf.*), deign, humble *or* demean oneself, lower oneself, see fit, stoop, submit, unbend (*Inf.*), vouchsafe **2.** patronize, talk down to

condescending disdainful, lofty, lordly, patronizing, snobbish, snooty (*Inf.*), supercilious, superior, toffee-nosed (*Sl.*)

condition *n.* **1.** case, circumstances, plight, position, predicament, shape, situation, state, state of affairs, *status quo* **2.** arrangement, article, demand, limitation, modification, prerequisite, provision, proviso, qualification, requirement, requisite, restriction, rule, stipulation, terms **3.** fettle, fitness, health, kilter, order, shape, state of health, trim ~*v.* **4.** accustom, adapt, educate, equip, habituate, inure, make ready, prepare, ready, tone up, train, work out

conditional contingent, dependent, limited, provisional, qualified, subject to, with reservations
Antonyms absolute, categorical, unconditional, unrestricted

conditions circumstances, environment, milieu, situation, surroundings, way of life

conduct *n.* **1.** administration, control, direction, guidance, leadership, management, organization, running, supervision ~*v.* **2.** administer, carry on, control, direct, govern, handle, lead, manage, organize, preside over, regulate, run, supervise ~*n.* **3.** attitude, bearing, behaviour, carriage, comportment, demeanour, deportment, manners, mien (*Literary*), ways

confederacy alliance, bund, coalition, compact, confederation, conspiracy, covenant, federation, league, union

confer consult, converse, deliberate, discourse, parley, talk

conference colloquium, congress, consultation, convention, convocation, discussion, forum, meeting, seminar, symposium, teach-in

confess 1. acknowledge, admit, allow, blurt out, come clean (*Inf.*), concede, confide, disclose, divulge, grant, make a clean breast of, own, own up, recognize **2.** affirm, assert, attest, aver, confirm, declare, evince, manifest, profess, prove, reveal

confession acknowledgment, admission, avowal, disclosure, divulgence, exposure, revelation, unbosoming

confide admit, breathe, confess, disclose, divulge, impart, reveal, whisper

confidence 1. belief, credence, dependence, faith, reliance, trust **2.** aplomb, assurance, boldness, courage, firmness, nerve, self-possession, self-reliance **3. in confidence** between you and me (and the gatepost), confidentially, in secrecy, privately
Antonyms (*sense 1*) disbelief, distrust, doubt, misgiving, mistrust (*sense 2*) apprehension, fear, self-doubt, shyness, uncertainty

confident 1. certain, convinced, counting on, positive, satisfied, secure, sure **2.** assured, bold, dauntless, fearless, self-assured, self-reliant
Antonyms (*sense 1*) doubtful, dubious, not sure, tentative, uncertain, unconvinced, unsure (*sense 2*) afraid, hesitant, insecure, jittery, lacking confidence, mousy, nervous, scared, self-doubting, unsure

confidential classified, hush-hush (*Inf.*), intimate, off the record, private, privy, secret

confine *v.* bind, bound, cage, circumscribe, enclose, hem in, hold back, immure, imprison, incarcerate, intern, keep, limit, repress, restrain, restrict, shut up

confirm 1. assure, buttress, clinch, establish, fix, fortify, reinforce, settle, strengthen **2.** approve, authenticate, bear out, corroborate, endorse, ratify, sanction, substantiate, validate, verify

confirmation 1. authentication, corroboration, evidence, proof, substantiation, testimony, validation, verification **2.** acceptance, agreement, approval, assent, endorsement, ratification, sanction
Antonyms (*sense 1*) contradiction, denial, disavowal, repudiation (*sense 2*) annulment, cancellation, disapproval, refusal, rejection

confirmed chronic, dyed-in-the-wool, habitual, hardened, ingrained, inured, inveterate, long-established, rooted, seasoned

conflict *n.* **1.** battle, clash, collision, combat, contention, contest, encounter, engagement, fight, fracas, set-to (*Inf.*), strife, war, warfare **2.** antagonism, bad blood, difference, disagreement, discord, dissension, divided loyalties, friction, hostility, interference, opposition, strife, variance ~*v.* **3.** be at variance, clash, collide, combat, contend, contest, differ, disagree, fight, interfere, strive, struggle
Antonyms *n.* accord, agreement, harmony, peace, treaty, truce ~*v.* agree, coincide, harmonize, reconcile

confuse 1. baffle, bemuse, bewilder, darken, mystify, obscure, perplex, puzzle **2.** abash, addle, demoralize, discomfit, discompose, disconcert, discountenance, disorient, embarrass, fluster, mortify, nonplus, rattle (*Inf.*), shame, throw off balance, upset

confused 1. at a loss, at sea, at sixes and sevens, baffled, bewildered, dazed, discombobulated

(*Inf., chiefly U.S.*), disorganized, disorientated, flummoxed, muddled, muzzy (*U.S. inf.*), nonplussed, not with it (*Inf.*), perplexed, puzzled, taken aback, thrown off balance, upset **2.** at sixes and sevens, chaotic, disarranged, disordered, disorderly, disorganized, higgledy-piggledy (*Inf.*), hugger-mugger (*Archaic*), in disarray, jumbled, mistaken, misunderstood, mixed up, out of order, topsy-turvy, untidy

Antonyms arranged, aware, enlightened, informed, in order, on the ball (*Inf.*), organized, tidy, with it (*Inf.*)

confusion 1. befuddlement, bemusement, bewilderment, disorientation, mystification, perplexity, puzzlement **2.** bustle, chaos, clutter, commotion, disarrangement, disorder, disorganization, hotchpotch, jumble, mess, muddle, shambles, tangle, turmoil, untidiness, upheaval

Antonyms (*sense 1*) clarification, composure, enlightenment, explanation, solution (*sense 2*) arrangement, neatness, order, organization, tidiness

congenial adapted, agreeable, companionable, compatible, complaisant, favourable, fit, friendly, genial, kindly, kindred, like-minded, pleasant, pleasing, suitable, sympathetic, well-suited

congested blocked-up, clogged, crammed, crowded, jammed, overcrowded, overfilled, overflowing, packed, stuffed, stuffed-up, teeming

Antonyms clear, empty, free, half-full, uncongested, uncrowded, unhampered, unhindered, unimpeded, unobstructed

congratulate compliment, felicitate, wish joy to

congratulations best wishes, compliments, felicitations, good wishes, greetings

congregate assemble, collect, come together, concentrate, convene, converge, convoke, flock, forgather, gather, mass,

meet, muster, rally, rendezvous, throng

Antonyms break up, dispel, disperse, dissipate, part, scatter, separate, split up

congregation assembly, brethren, crowd, fellowship, flock, host, laity, multitude, parish, parishioners, throng

congress assembly, chamber of deputies, conclave, conference, convention, convocation, council, delegates, diet, legislative assembly, legislature, meeting, parliament, representatives

connect affix, ally, associate, cohere, combine, couple, fasten, join, link, relate, unite

Antonyms detach, disconnect, dissociate, divide, part, separate, sever, unfasten

connected affiliated, akin, allied, associated, banded together, bracketed, combined, coupled, joined, linked, related, united

connection 1. alliance, association, attachment, coupling, fastening, junction, link, tie, union **2.** affinity, association, bond, commerce, communication, correlation, correspondence, intercourse, interrelation, link, marriage, relation, relationship, relevance, tie-in **3.** acquaintance, ally, associate, contact, friend, sponsor

connoisseur aficionado, appreciator, arbiter, authority, buff (*Inf.*), cognoscente, devotee, expert, judge, maven (*U.S.*), savant, specialist

conquer beat, checkmate, crush, defeat, discomfit, get the better of, humble, master, overcome, overpower, overthrow, prevail, quell, rout, subdue, subjugate, succeed, surmount, triumph, vanquish

Antonyms be defeated, capitulate, give in, give up, lose, quit, submit, surrender, throw in the towel, yield

conqueror champion, conquistador, defeater, hero, lord, master, subjugator, vanquisher, victor, winner

conquest 1. defeat, discomfiture, mastery, overthrow, rout, triumph, vanquishment, victory **2.** acquisition, annexation, appropriation, coup, invasion, occupation, subjection, subjugation, takeover

conscience moral sense, principles, scruples, sense of right and wrong, still small voice

conscientious careful, diligent, exact, faithful, meticulous, painstaking, particular, punctilious, thorough
Antonyms careless, irresponsible, negligent, remiss, slack, thoughtless, unconscientious, unreliable

conscious 1. alert, alive to, awake, aware, cognizant, percipient, responsive, sensible, sentient, wise to (*Sl.*) **2.** calculated, deliberate, intentional, knowing, premeditated, rational, reasoning, reflective, responsible, self-conscious, studied, wilful
Antonyms (*sense 1*) ignorant, insensible, oblivious, unaware, unconscious (*sense 2*) accidental, uncalculated, unintended, unintentional, unplanned, unpremeditated, unwitting

consciousness apprehension, awareness, knowledge, realization, recognition, sensibility

consecrate dedicate, devote, exalt, hallow, ordain, sanctify, set apart, venerate

consecutive chronological, following, in sequence, in turn, running, sequential, seriatim, succeeding, successive, uninterrupted

consent 1. *v.* accede, acquiesce, agree, allow, approve, assent, comply, concede, concur, permit, yield **2.** *n.* acquiescence, agreement, approval, assent, compliance, concession, concurrence, go-ahead (*Inf.*), O.K. (*Inf.*), permission, sanction
Antonyms *v.* decline, demur, disagree, disapprove, dissent,

refuse, resist ~*n.* disagreement, disapproval, dissent, refusal, unwillingness

consequence effect, end, event, issue, outcome, repercussion, result, upshot

conservation custody, economy, guardianship, husbandry, maintenance, preservation, protection, safeguarding, safekeeping, saving, upkeep

conservative *adj.* cautious, conventional, die-hard, guarded, hidebound, middle-of-the-road, moderate, quiet, reactionary, right-wing, sober, tory, traditional
Antonyms imaginative, innovative, liberal, progressive, radical

conserve go easy on (*Inf.*), hoard, husband, keep, nurse, preserve, protect, save, store up, take care of, use sparingly

consider 1. chew over, cogitate, consult, contemplate, deliberate, discuss, examine, meditate, mull over, muse, ponder, reflect, revolve, ruminate, study, think about, turn over in one's mind, weigh **2.** bear in mind, care for, keep in view, make allowance for, reckon with, regard, remember, respect, take into account

considerable 1. abundant, ample, appreciable, comfortable, goodly, great, large, lavish, marked, much, noticeable, plentiful, reasonable, sizable, substantial, tidy, tolerable **2.** distinguished, important, influential, noteworthy, renowned, significant, venerable
Antonyms insignificant, insubstantial, meagre, ordinary, paltry, small, unimportant, unremarkable

considerate attentive, charitable, circumspect, concerned, discreet, forbearing, kind, kindly, mindful, obliging, patient, tactful, thoughtful, unselfish
Antonyms heedless, inconsiderate, selfish, thoughtless

consideration 1. analysis, attention, cogitation, contemplation, deliberation, discussion, examination, reflection, regard, review, scrutiny, study, thought **2.** concern, considerateness, friendliness, kindliness, kindness, respect, solicitude, tact, thoughtfulness

considering all in all, all things considered, insomuch as, in the light of, in view of

consignment *Something consigned* batch, delivery, goods, shipment

consist *With of* be composed of, be made up of, amount to, comprise, contain, embody, include, incorporate, involve

consistent constant, dependable, persistent, regular, steady, true to type, unchanging, undeviating
Antonyms changing, deviating, erratic, inconsistent, irregular

consolation alleviation, assuagement, cheer, comfort, ease, easement, encouragement, help, relief, solace, succour, support

console assuage, calm, cheer, comfort, encourage, express sympathy for, relieve, solace, soothe
Antonyms aggravate, agitate, annoy, discomfort, distress, hurt, sadden, torment, trouble, upset

consolidate fortify, reinforce, secure, stabilize, strengthen

conspicuous apparent, clear, discernible, easily seen, evident, manifest, noticeable, obvious, patent, perceptible, visible
Antonyms concealed, hidden, imperceptible, inconspicuous, indiscernible, invisible, obscure, unnoticeable

conspiracy cabal, collusion, confederacy, frame-up (*Sl.*), intrigue, league, machination, plot, scheme, treason

conspire cabal, confederate, contrive, devise, hatch treason, intrigue, machinate, manoeuvre, plot, scheme

constant 1. continual, even, firm, fixed, habitual, immutable, invariable, permanent, perpetual,

regular, stable, steadfast, steady, unalterable, unbroken, uniform, unvarying **2.** ceaseless, continual, continuous, endless, eternal, everlasting, incessant, interminable, never-ending, nonstop, perpetual, persistent, relentless, sustained, uninterrupted, unrelenting, unremitting
Antonyms changeable, changing, deviating, erratic, inconstant, intermittent, irregular, occasional, random, uneven, unstable, unsustained, variable

constantly all the time, always, continually, continuously, endlessly, everlastingly, incessantly, interminably, invariably, morning, noon and night, night and day, nonstop, perpetually, persistently, relentlessly
Antonyms (every) now and then, every so often, from time to time, intermittently, irregularly, now and again, occasionally, off and on, periodically, sometimes

consternation alarm, amazement, anxiety, awe, bewilderment, confusion, dismay, distress, dread, fear, fright, horror, panic, shock, terror, trepidation

constituent 1. *adj.* basic, component, elemental, essential, integral **2.** *n.* component, element, essential, factor, ingredient, part, principle, unit

constitute compose, comprise, create, enact, establish, fix, form, found, make, make up, set up

constitution composition, establishment, formation, organization

constrain bind, coerce, compel, drive, force, impel, necessitate, oblige, pressure, pressurize, urge

constraint 1. coercion, compulsion, force, necessity, pressure, restraint **2.** check, curb, damper, deterrent, hindrance, limitation, restriction

construct assemble, build, compose, create, design, elevate, engineer, erect, establish, fabricate, fashion, form, formulate, found, frame, make, manufacture, organize, put up, raise, set up, shape

Antonyms bulldoze, demolish, destroy, devastate, dismantle, flatten, knock down, level, pull down, raze, tear down

construction assembly, building, composition, creation, edifice, erection, fabric, fabrication, figure, form, formation, shape, structure

constructive helpful, positive, practical, productive, useful, valuable

Antonyms destructive, futile, ineffective, limp-wristed, negative, unhelpful, unproductive, useless, vain, worthless

consult ask, ask advice of, commune, compare notes, confer, consider, debate, deliberate, interrogate, question, refer to, take counsel, turn to

consultant adviser, authority, specialist

consultation appointment, conference, council, deliberation, dialogue, discussion, examination, hearing, interview, meeting, session

consume absorb, deplete, dissipate, drain, eat up, employ, exhaust, expend, finish up, fritter away, lavish, lessen, spend, squander, use, use up, utilize, vanish, waste, wear out

consumer buyer, customer, purchaser, shopper, user

contact *n.* 1. approximation, contiguity, junction, juxtaposition, touch, union 2. acquaintance, connection ~*v.* 3. approach, call, communicate with, get *or* be in touch with, get hold of, phone, reach, ring (up), speak to, write to

contain accommodate, enclose, have capacity for, hold, incorporate, seat

container holder, receptacle, repository, vessel

contemplate 1. brood over, consider, deliberate, meditate, meditate on, mull over, muse over, observe, ponder, reflect

upon, revolve *or* turn over in one's mind, ruminate (upon), study 2. aspire to, consider, design, envisage, expect, foresee, have in view *or* in mind, intend, mean, plan, propose, think of

contemporary *adj.* 1. coetaneous (*Rare*), coeval, coexistent, coexisting, concurrent, contemporaneous, synchronous 2. à la mode, current, in fashion, latest, modern, newfangled, present, present-day, recent, trendy (*Brit. inf.*), ultramodern, up-to-date, up-to-the-minute, with it (*Inf.*) ~*n.* 3. compeer, fellow, peer

Antonyms *adj.* antecedent, antique, early, obsolete, old, old-fashioned, out-of-date, passé, succeeding

contempt condescension, contumely, derision, despite (*Archaic*), disdain, disregard, disrespect, mockery, neglect, scorn, slight

Antonyms admiration, esteem, honour, liking, regard, respect

contend 1. clash, compete, contest, cope, emulate, grapple, jostle, litigate, skirmish, strive, struggle, vie 2. affirm, allege, argue, assert, aver, avow, debate, dispute, hold, maintain

content[1] 1. *v.* appease, delight, gladden, gratify, humour, indulge, mollify, placate, please, reconcile, satisfy, suffice 2. *n.* comfort, contentment, ease, gratification, peace, peace of mind, pleasure, satisfaction 3. *adj.* agreeable, at ease, comfortable, contented, fulfilled, satisfied, willing to accept

content[2] burden, essence, gist, ideas, matter, meaning, significance, substance, text, thoughts

contented at ease, at peace, cheerful, comfortable, complacent, content, glad, gratified, happy, pleased, satisfied, serene, thankful

Antonyms annoyed, discontented, displeased, dissatisfied, troubled, uncomfortable, uneasy

contentment comfort, complacency, content, contentedness,

ease, equanimity, fulfilment, gladness, gratification, happiness, peace, pleasure, repletion, satisfaction, serenity
Antonyms discomfort, discontent, discontentment, displeasure, dissatisfaction, uneasiness, unhappiness
contents 1. constituents, elements, ingredients, load 2. chapters, divisions, subject matter, subjects, themes, topics
contest *n.* 1. competition, game, match, tournament, trial ~*v.* 2. compete, contend, fight, fight over, strive, vie 3. argue, call in *or* into question, challenge, debate, dispute, doubt, litigate, object to, oppose, question
contestant aspirant, candidate, competitor, contender, entrant, participant, player
context background, connection, frame of reference, framework, relation
continual constant, continuous, endless, eternal, everlasting, frequent, incessant, interminable, oft-repeated, perpetual, recurrent, regular, repeated, repetitive, unceasing, uninterrupted, unremitting
Antonyms broken, ceasing, erratic, fluctuating, fragmentary, infrequent, intermittent, interrupted, irregular, occasional, periodic, spasmodic, sporadic, terminable
continually all the time, always, constantly, endlessly, eternally, everlastingly, forever, incessantly, interminably, nonstop, persistently, repeatedly
continuation addition, extension, furtherance, postscript, sequel, supplement
continue abide, carry on, endure, last, live on, persist, remain, rest, stay, stay on, survive
Antonyms abdicate, leave, quit, resign, retire, step down
continuity cohesion, connection, flow, interrelationship, progression, sequence, succession, whole
continuous connected, constant,

continued, extended, prolonged, unbroken, unceasing, undivided, uninterrupted
Antonyms broken, disconnected, ending, inconstant, intermittent, interrupted, occasional, passing, severed, spasmodic
contract *v.* 1. abbreviate, abridge, compress, condense, confine, constrict, curtail, dwindle, epitomize, lessen, narrow, purse, reduce, shrink, shrivel, tighten, wither, wrinkle 2. agree, arrange, bargain, clinch, close, come to terms, commit oneself, covenant, engage, enter into, negotiate, pledge, stipulate ~*n.* 3. agreement, arrangement, bargain, bond, commission, commitment, compact, concordat, convention, covenant, deal (*Inf.*), engagement, pact, settlement, stipulation, treaty, understanding
Antonyms (*sense 1*) broaden, develop, distend, enlarge, expand, grow, increase, inflate, multiply, spread, stretch, swell, widen (*sense 2*) decline, disagree, refuse, turn down
contradict be at variance with, belie, challenge, contravene, controvert, counter, counteract, deny, dispute, gainsay (*Archaic*), impugn, negate, oppose
Antonyms affirm, agree, authenticate, confirm, defend, endorse, support, verify
contradiction conflict, confutation, contravention, denial, incongruity, inconsistency, negation, opposite
contradictory antagonistic, antithetical, conflicting, contrary, discrepant, incompatible, inconsistent, irreconcilable, opposed, opposite, paradoxical, repugnant
contrary *adj.* adverse, antagonistic, clashing, contradictory, counter, discordant, hostile, inconsistent, inimical, opposed, opposite, paradoxical
Antonyms accordant, congruous, consistent, harmonious, in agreement, parallel, unopposed
contrast 1. *n.* comparison,

contrariety, difference, differentiation, disparity, dissimilarity, distinction, divergence, foil, opposition 2. *v.* compare, differ, differentiate, distinguish, oppose, set in opposition, set off

contribute add, afford, bestow, chip in (*Inf.*), donate, furnish, give, provide, subscribe, supply

contribution addition, bestowal, donation, gift, grant, input, offering, subscription

contributor 1. backer, bestower, conferrer, donor, giver, patron, subscriber, supporter 2. correspondent, freelance, freelancer, journalist, reporter

contrite chastened, conscience-stricken, humble, in sackcloth and ashes, penitent, regretful, remorseful, repentant, sorrowful, sorry

contrive concoct, construct, create, design, devise, engineer, fabricate, frame, improvise, invent, wangle (*Inf.*)

contrived artificial, elaborate, forced, laboured, overdone, planned, recherché, strained, unnatural
Antonyms genuine, natural, relaxed, spontaneous, unaffected, unconstrained, unfeigned, unforced, unpretentious

control *v.* 1. boss (*Inf.*), call the tune, command, conduct, direct, dominate, govern, have charge of, hold the purse strings, lead, manage, manipulate, oversee, pilot, reign over, rule, steer, superintend, supervise 2. bridle, check, constrain, contain, curb, hold back, limit, master, rein in, repress, restrain, subdue ~*n.* 3. authority, charge, command, direction, discipline, government, guidance, jurisdiction, management, mastery, oversight, rule, superintendence, supervision, supremacy 4. brake, check, curb, limitation, regulation, restraint

controversial at issue, contended, contentious, controvertible, debatable, disputable, disputed, open to question, under discussion

controversy altercation, argument, contention, debate, discussion, dispute, dissension, polemic, quarrel, squabble, strife, wrangle, wrangling

convene assemble, bring together, call, come together, congregate, convoke, gather, meet, muster, rally, summon

convenience accessibility, appropriateness, availability, fitness, handiness, opportuneness, serviceability, suitability, usefulness, utility
Antonyms inconvenience, uselessness

convenient 1. adapted, appropriate, beneficial, commodious, fit, fitted, handy, helpful, labour-saving, opportune, seasonable, serviceable, suitable, suited, timely, useful, well-timed 2. accessible, at hand, available, close at hand, handy, just round the corner, nearby, within reach
Antonyms awkward, distant, inaccessible, inconvenient, out-of-the-way, unsuitable, useless

convention 1. assembly, conference, congress, convocation, council, delegates, meeting, representatives 2. code, custom, etiquette, formality, practice, propriety, protocol, tradition, usage

converge coincide, combine, come together, concentrate, focus, gather, join, meet, merge, mingle

conversation chat, chinwag (*Brit. inf.*), colloquy, communication, communion, confab (*Inf.*), confabulation, conference, converse, dialogue, discourse, discussion, exchange, gossip, intercourse, powwow, talk, tête-à-tête

converse *n.* antithesis, contrary, obverse, opposite, other side of the coin, reverse

conversion 1. change, metamorphosis, transfiguration, transformation, transmogrification (*Jocular*), transmutation 2. adaptation, alteration, modification, reconstruction, remodelling, re~organization **3.** change of heart, proselytization, rebirth, refor~mation, regeneration

convert v. **1.** alter, change, inter~change, metamorphose, trans~form, transmogrify (Jocular), transmute, transpose, turn **2.** adapt, apply, appropriate, modi~fy, remodel, reorganize, restyle, revise

convey bear, bring, carry, con~duct, fetch, forward, grant, guide, move, send, support, transmit, transport

convict 1. v. condemn, find guilty, imprison, pronounce guilty, sen~tence **2.** n. con (Sl.), criminal, culprit, felon, jailbird, malefac~tor, old lag (Sl.), prisoner

conviction assurance, certainty, certitude, confidence, earnest~ness, fervour, firmness, reliance

convince assure, bring round, gain the confidence of, persuade, prevail upon, prove to, satisfy, sway, win over

cool adj. **1.** chilled, chilling, chilly, coldish, nippy, refreshing **2.** calm, collected, composed, de~liberate, dispassionate, imper~turbable, laid-back (Inf.), level-headed, placid, quiet, relaxed, self-controlled, self-possessed, serene, together (Sl.), unemo~tional, unexcited, unruffled **3.** aloof, apathetic, distant, frigid, incurious, indifferent, lukewarm, offhand, reserved, standoffish, uncommunicative, unconcerned, unenthusiastic, unfriendly, unin~terested, unresponsive, unwel~coming ~v. **4.** chill, cool off, freeze, lose heat, refrigerate **5.** abate, allay, assuage, calm (down), dampen, lessen, moder~ate, quiet, temper

Antonyms adj. (sense 1) luke~warm, moderately hot, sunny, tepid, warm (sense 2) agitated, delirious, excited, impassioned, nervous, overwrought, perturbed, tense, troubled (sense 3) amiable, chummy (Inf.), cordial, friendly, outgoing, receptive, responsive,

sociable, warm ~v. (sense 4) heat, reheat, take the chill off, thaw, warm, warm up

cooperate abet, aid, assist, col~laborate, combine, concur, con~duce, conspire, contribute, coor~dinate, go along with, help, join forces, pitch in, play ball (Inf.), pool resources, pull together, work together

Antonyms conflict, contend with, fight, hamper, hamstring, hinder, impede, obstruct, oppose, pre~vent, put the mockers on (Inf.), resist, struggle against, stymie, thwart

cooperation assistance, collabo~ration, combined effort, concert, concurrence, esprit de corps, give-and-take, helpfulness, par~ticipation, responsiveness, team~work, unity

Antonyms discord, dissension, hindrance, opposition, rivalry

cooperative accommodating, helpful, obliging, responsive, supportive

coordinate v. correlate, harmo~nize, integrate, match, mesh, or~ganize, relate, synchronize, sys~tematize

cope 1. carry on, get by (Inf.), hold one's own, make out (Inf.), make the grade, manage, rise to the occasion, struggle through, survive **2. cope with** contend, deal, dispatch, encounter, grap~ple, handle, struggle, tangle, tus~sle, weather, wrestle

copious abundant, ample, boun~teous, bountiful, extensive, exu~berant, full, generous, lavish, lib~eral, luxuriant, overflowing, plenteous, plentiful, profuse, rich, superabundant

copy n. **1.** archetype, carbon copy, counterfeit, duplicate, fac~simile, fake, fax, forgery, image, imitation, likeness, model, pat~tern, photocopy, Photostat (Trademark), print, replica, rep~lication, representation, repro~duction, transcription, Xerox (Trademark) ~v. **2.** counterfeit, duplicate, photocopy, Photostat

(*Trademark*), replicate, reproduce, transcribe, Xerox (*Trademark*) **3.** ape, echo, emulate, follow, follow suit, follow the example of, imitate, mimic, mirror, parrot, repeat, simulate
Antonyms *n.* model, original, pattern, prototype, the real thing ~*v.* create, originate

cord line, rope, string, twine

cordial affable, affectionate, agreeable, cheerful, earnest, friendly, genial, heartfelt, hearty, invigorating, sociable, warm, warm-hearted, welcoming, wholehearted

core centre, crux, essence, gist, heart, kernel, nub, nucleus, pith

corner *n.* **1.** angle, bend, crook, joint **2.** cavity, cranny, hideaway, hide-out, hidey-hole (*Inf.*), niche, nook, recess, retreat ~*v.* **3.** bring to bay, run to earth, trap

corny banal, commonplace, dull, feeble, hackneyed, maudlin, mawkish, old-fashioned, old hat, sentimental, stale, stereotyped, trite

corpse body, cadaver, carcass, remains, stiff (*Sl.*)

correct *v.* **1.** adjust, amend, cure, emend, improve, rectify, redress, reform, regulate, remedy, right **2.** admonish, chasten, chastise, chide, discipline, punish, reprimand, reprove ~*adj.* **3.** accurate, equitable, exact, faultless, flawless, just, O.K. (*Inf.*), precise, regular, right, strict, true
Antonyms *v.* (*sense 1*) damage, harm, impair, ruin, spoil (*sense 2*) compliment, excuse, praise ~*adj.* false, inaccurate, incorrect, untrue, wrong

correction 1. adjustment, alteration, amendment, improvement, modification, rectification, righting **2.** admonition, castigation, chastisement, discipline, punishment, reformation, reproof

correctly accurately, aright, perfectly, precisely, properly, right, rightly

correctness accuracy, exactitude, exactness, faultlessness, fidelity, preciseness, precision, regularity, truth

correspond 1. accord, agree, be consistent, coincide, complement, conform, correlate, dovetail, fit, harmonize, match, square, tally **2.** communicate, exchange letters, keep in touch, write
Antonyms be at variance, be dissimilar, be inconsistent, belie, be unlike, differ, disagree, diverge, vary

correspondence 1. agreement, analogy, coincidence, comparability, comparison, concurrence, conformity, congruity, correlation, fitness, harmony, match, relation, similarity **2.** communication, letters, mail, post, writing

correspondent *n.* **1.** letter writer, pen friend *or* pal **2.** contributor, gazetteer (*Archaic*), journalist, reporter, special correspondent

corresponding analogous, answering, complementary, correlative, correspondent, equivalent, identical, interrelated, matching, reciprocal, similar, synonymous

corridor aisle, hallway, passage, passageway

corrode canker, consume, corrupt, deteriorate, eat away, erode, gnaw, impair, oxidize, rust, waste, wear away

corrosive acrid, biting, caustic, consuming, corroding, erosive, virulent, wasting, wearing

corrupt *adj.* **1.** bent (*Sl.*), bribable, crooked (*Inf.*), dishonest, fraudulent, rotten, shady (*Inf.*), unethical, unprincipled, unscrupulous, venal ~*v.* **2.** bribe, buy off, debauch, demoralize, deprave, entice, fix (*Inf.*), grease (someone's) palm (*Sl.*), lure, pervert, square (*Inf.*), suborn, subvert ~*adj.* **3.** adulterated, altered, contaminated, decayed, defiled, distorted, doctored, falsified, infected, polluted, putrescent, putrid, rotten, tainted

Antonyms *adj.* (*sense 1*) ethical, honest, honourable, moral, noble, principled, righteous, scrupulous, straight, undefiled, upright, virtuous ~*v.* (*sense 2*) correct, purify, reform

corruption 1. breach of trust, bribery, bribing, crookedness (*Inf.*), demoralization, dishonesty, extortion, fiddling (*Inf.*), fraud, fraudulency, graft, jobbery, profiteering, shadiness, shady dealings (*Inf.*), unscrupulousness, venality 2. baseness, decadence, degeneration, degradation, depravity, evil, immorality, impurity, iniquity, perversion, profligacy, sinfulness, turpitude, vice, viciousness, wickedness

cosmetic *adj.* beautifying, non-essential, superficial, surface, touching-up

cosmopolitan *adj.* broad-minded, catholic, open-minded, sophisticated, universal, urbane, well-travelled, worldly, worldly-wise

cost *n.* 1. amount, charge, damage (*Inf.*), expenditure, expense, figure, outlay, payment, price, rate, worth 2. damage, deprivation, detriment, expense, harm, hurt, injury, loss, penalty, sacrifice, suffering ~*v.* 3. come to, command a price of, sell at, set (someone) back (*Inf.*)

costly 1. dear, excessive, exorbitant, expensive, extortionate, highly-priced, steep (*Inf.*), stiff, valuable 2. gorgeous, lavish, luxurious, opulent, precious, priceless, rich, splendid, sumptuous

Antonyms (*sense 1*) cheap, cheapo (*Inf.*), dirt-cheap, economical, fair, inexpensive, low-priced, reasonable, reduced

costume apparel, attire, clothing, dress, ensemble, garb, get-up (*Inf.*), livery, national dress, outfit, robes, uniform

cosy comfortable, comfy (*Inf.*), cuddled up, homely, intimate, secure, sheltered, snug, snuggled down, tucked up, warm

council assembly, board, cabinet, chamber, committee, conclave, conference, congress, convention, convocation, diet, governing body, ministry, panel, parliament, synod

counsel *n.* 1. admonition, advice, caution, consideration, consultation, deliberation, direction, forethought, guidance, information, recommendation, suggestion, warning 2. advocate, attorney, barrister, lawyer, legal adviser, solicitor ~*v.* 3. admonish, advise, advocate, caution, exhort, instruct, recommend, urge, warn

count *v.* 1. add (up), calculate, cast up, check, compute, enumerate, estimate, number, reckon, score, tally, tot up 2. carry weight, cut any ice (*Inf.*), enter into consideration, matter, rate, signify, tell, weigh

counter 1. *adv.* against, at variance with, contrarily, contrariwise, conversely, in defiance of, versus 2. *adj.* adverse, against, conflicting, contradictory, contrary, contrasting, obverse, opposed, opposing, opposite 3. *v.* answer, hit back, meet, offset, parry, resist, respond, retaliate, return, ward off

counterbalance balance, compensate, counterpoise, countervail, make up for, offset, set off

counterfeit 1. *v.* copy, fabricate, fake, feign, forge, imitate, impersonate, pretend, sham, simulate 2. *adj.* bogus, copied, ersatz, faked, false, feigned, forged, fraudulent, imitation, phoney (*Sl.*), pseud (*Inf.*), pseudo (*Inf.*), sham, simulated, spurious, suppositious 3. *n.* copy, fake, forgery, fraud, imitation, phoney (*Sl.*), reproduction, sham

Antonyms authentic, genuine, good, original, real, the real thing

counterpart complement, copy, correlative, duplicate, equal, fellow, match, mate, opposite number, supplement, tally, twin

countless endless, immeasurable, incalculable, infinite, innumerable, legion, limitless, meas-

ureless, multitudinous, myriad, numberless, uncounted, untold
Antonyms finite, limited, restricted

count on *or* **upon** bank on, believe (in), depend on, lean on, pin one's faith on, reckon on, rely on, take for granted, take on trust, trust

country n. **1.** commonwealth, kingdom, nation, people, realm, sovereign state, state **2.** fatherland, homeland, motherland, nationality, native land, *patria* **3.** land, part, region, terrain, territory **4.** citizenry, citizens, community, electors, grass roots, inhabitants, nation, people, populace, public, society, voters **5.** backwoods, boondocks (*U.S. sl.*), countryside, farmland, green belt, outback (*Australian & New Zealand*), outdoors, provinces, rural areas, sticks (*Inf.*), the back of beyond, the middle of nowhere, wide open spaces (*Inf.*)
Antonyms (*sense 5*) city, metropolis, town

count up add, reckon up, sum, tally, total

coup accomplishment, action, deed, exploit, feat, manoeuvre, masterstroke, stratagem, stroke, stroke of genius, stunt, *tour de force*

couple 1. n. brace, duo, item, pair, span (*of horses or oxen*), twain (*Archaic*), twosome **2.** v. buckle, clasp, conjoin, connect, hitch, join, link, marry, pair, unite, wed, yoke

courage balls (*Sl.*), boldness, bottle (*Sl.*), bravery, daring, dauntlessness, fearlessness, firmness, fortitude, gallantry, grit, guts (*Inf.*), hardihood, heroism, intrepidity, lion-heartedness, mettle, nerve, pluck, resolution, spunk (*Inf.*), valour
Antonyms cowardice, faintheartedness, fear, timidity

courageous audacious, bold, brave, daring, dauntless, fearless, gallant, hardy, heroic, indomitable, intrepid, lion-hearted,

plucky, resolute, stouthearted, valiant, valorous
Antonyms chicken (*Sl.*), chicken-hearted, cowardly, craven, dastardly, faint-hearted, gutless (*Inf.*), lily-livered, pusillanimous, scared, spineless, timid, timorous, yellow (*Inf.*)

course n. **1.** advance, advancement, continuity, development, flow, furtherance, march, movement, order, progress, progression, sequence, succession, unfolding **2.** channel, direction, line, orbit, passage, path, road, route, tack, track, trail, trajectory, way **3.** duration, lapse, passage, passing, sweep, term, time **4.** behaviour, conduct, manner, method, mode, plan, policy, procedure, programme, regimen **5.** cinder track, circuit, lap, race, racecourse, round **6.** classes, course of study, curriculum, lectures, programme, schedule, studies **7.** **of course** certainly, definitely, indubitably, naturally, obviously, undoubtedly, without a doubt

court n. **1.** cloister, courtyard, piazza, plaza, quad (*Inf.*), quadrangle, square, yard **2.** hall, manor, palace **3.** attendants, cortege, entourage, retinue, royal household, suite, train **4.** bar, bench, court of justice, lawcourt, seat of judgment, tribunal ∼ v. **5.** chase, date, go (out) with, go steady with (*Inf.*), keep company with, make love to, pay court to, pay one's addresses to, pursue, run after, serenade, set one's cap at, sue (*Archaic*), take out, walk out with, woo **6.** cultivate, curry favour with, fawn upon, flatter, pander to, seek, solicit

courteous affable, attentive, ceremonious, civil, courtly, elegant, gallant, gracious, mannerly, polished, polite, refined, respectful, urbane, well-bred, well-mannered
Antonyms discourteous, disrespectful, ill-mannered, impolite, insolent, rude, uncivil, ungracious, unkind

courtesy affability, civility, courteousness, courtliness, elegance, gallantness, gallantry, good breeding, good manners, graciousness, polish, politeness, urbanity

courtier attendant, follower, henchman, liegeman, pursuivant (*Historical*), squire, train-bearer

courtyard area, enclosure, peristyle, playground, quad, quadrangle, yard

covenant *n.* **1.** arrangement, bargain, commitment, compact, concordat, contract, convention, pact, promise, stipulation, treaty, trust **2.** bond, deed

cover *v.* **1.** camouflage, cloak, conceal, cover up, curtain, disguise, eclipse, enshroud, hide, hood, house, mask, obscure, screen, secrete, shade, shroud, veil ~*n.* **2.** cloak, cover-up, disguise, façade, front, mask, pretence, screen, smoke screen, veil, window-dressing ~*v.* **3.** defend, guard, protect, reinforce, shelter, shield, watch over ~*n.* **4.** camouflage, concealment, defence, guard, hiding place, protection, refuge, sanctuary, shelter, shield, undergrowth, woods **5.** double for, fill in for, relieve, stand in for, substitute, take over, take the rap for (*Sl.*) **6.** describe, detail, investigate, narrate, recount, relate, report, tell of, write up ~*n.* **7.** compensation, indemnity, insurance, payment, protection, reimbursement
Antonyms *v.* (*sense 1*) exhibit, expose, reveal, show, unclothe, uncover, unmask, unwrap

covering 1. *n.* blanket, casing, clothing, coating, cover, housing, layer, overlay, protection, shelter, top, wrap, wrapper, wrapping **2.** *adj.* accompanying, descriptive, explanatory, introductory

cover up conceal, cover one's tracks, feign ignorance, hide, hush up, keep dark, keep secret, keep silent about, keep under

one's hat (*Inf.*), repress, stonewall, suppress, whitewash (*Inf.*)

covet aspire to, begrudge, crave, desire, envy, fancy (*Inf.*), hanker after, have one's eye on, long for, lust after, thirst for, yearn for

covetous acquisitive, avaricious, close-fisted, envious, grasping, greedy, jealous, mercenary, rapacious, yearning

coward caitiff (*Archaic*), craven, dastard (*Archaic*), faint-heart, funk (*Inf.*), poltroon, recreant (*Archaic*), renegade, scaredy-cat (*Inf.*), skulker, sneak, yellow-belly (*Sl.*)

cowardly base, caitiff (*Archaic*), chicken (*Sl.*), chicken-hearted, craven, dastardly, faint-hearted, fearful, gutless (*Inf.*), lily-livered, pusillanimous, recreant (*Archaic*), scared, shrinking, soft, spineless, timorous, weak, weak-kneed (*Inf.*), white-livered, yellow (*Inf.*)
Antonyms audacious, bold, brave, courageous, daring, dauntless, doughty, intrepid, plucky, valiant

cower cringe, crouch, draw back, fawn, flinch, grovel, quail, shrink, skulk, sneak, tremble, truckle

coy arch, backward, bashful, coquettish, demure, evasive, flirtatious, kittenish, modest, overmodest, prudish, reserved, retiring, self-effacing, shrinking, shy, skittish, timid
Antonyms bold, brash, brass-necked (*Inf.*), brassy (*Inf.*), brazen, flip (*Inf.*), forward, impertinent, impudent, pert, pushy (*Inf.*), saucy, shameless

crack *v.* **1.** break, burst, chip, chop, cleave, crackle, craze, fracture, rive, snap, splinter, split ~*n.* **2.** breach, break, chink, chip, cleft, cranny, crevice, fissure, fracture, gap, interstice, rift **3.** burst, clap, crash, explosion, pop, report, snap ~*v.* **4.** break down, collapse, give way, go to pieces, lose control, succumb, yield ~*n.* **5.** *Inf.* attempt, go, opportunity, stab, try **6.** *Sl.* dig, funny remark, gag, insult, jibe, joke, quip, smart-alecky remark, wisecrack, witticism ~*adj.* 7. *Sl.* ace, choice, elite, excellent, first-class, first-rate, hand-picked, superior

crack up break down, collapse, come apart at the seams (*Inf.*), freak out (*Inf.*), go berserk, go crazy (*Inf.*), go off one's rocker (*Sl.*), go out of one's mind, go to pieces, have a breakdown, throw a wobbly (*Sl.*)

craft 1. ability, aptitude, art, artistry, cleverness, dexterity, expertise, expertness, ingenuity, knack, know-how (*Inf.*), skill, technique, workmanship 2. artfulness, artifice, contrivance, craftiness, cunning, deceit, duplicity, guile, ruse, scheme, shrewdness, stratagem, subterfuge, subtlety, trickery, wiles 3. business, calling, employment, handicraft, handiwork, line, occupation, pursuit, trade, vocation, work 4. aircraft, barque, boat, plane, ship, spacecraft, vessel

craftsman artificer, artisan, maker, master, skilled worker, smith, technician, wright

crafty artful, astute, calculating, canny, cunning, deceitful, designing, devious, duplicitous, foxy, fraudulent, guileful, insidious, knowing, scheming, sharp, shrewd, sly, subtle, tricksy, tricky, wily
Antonyms candid, ethical, frank, honest, ingenuous, innocent, naive, open, simple

cram compact, compress, crowd, crush, fill to overflowing, force, jam, overcrowd, overfill, pack, pack in, press, ram, shove, squeeze, stuff

cramp[1] *v.* check, circumscribe, clog, confine, constrain, encumber, hamper, hamstring, handicap, hinder, impede, inhibit, obstruct, restrict, shackle, stymie, thwart

cramp[2] *n.* ache, contraction, convulsion, crick, pain, pang, shooting pain, spasm, stiffness, stitch, twinge

cramped awkward, circum-

scribed, closed in, confined, congested, crowded, hemmed in, jammed in, narrow, overcrowded, packed, restricted, squeezed, uncomfortable
Antonyms capacious, commodious, large, open, roomy, sizable, spacious, uncongested, uncrowded

cranny breach, chink, cleft, crack, crevice, fissure, gap, hole, interstice, nook, opening

crash *n.* 1. bang, boom, clang, clash, clatter, clattering, din, racket, smash, smashing, thunder ~*v.* 2. come a cropper (*Inf.*), dash, fall, fall headlong, give way, hurtle, lurch, overbalance, pitch, plunge, precipitate oneself, sprawl, topple 3. bang, bump (into), collide, crash-land (*an aircraft*), drive into, have an accident, hit, hurtle into, plough into, run together, wreck ~*n.* 4. accident, bump, collision, jar, jolt, pile-up (*Inf.*), prang (*Inf.*), smash, smash-up, thud, thump, wreck 5. bankruptcy, collapse, debacle, depression, downfall, failure, ruin, smash

crate 1. *n.* box, case, container, packing case, tea chest 2. *v.* box, case, encase, enclose, pack, pack up

crater depression, dip, hollow, shell hole

crave 1. be dying for, cry out for (*Inf.*), desire, fancy (*Inf.*), hanker after, hunger after, long for, lust after, need, pant for, pine for, require, sigh for, thirst for, want, yearn for 2. ask, beg, beseech, entreat, implore, petition, plead for, pray for, seek, solicit, supplicate

crawl 1. advance slowly, creep, drag, go on all fours, inch, move at a snail's pace, move on hands and knees, pull *or* drag oneself along, slither, worm one's way, wriggle, writhe 2. abase oneself, cringe, fawn, grovel, humble oneself, toady, truckle
Antonyms (*sense 1*) dart, dash,

fly, hasten, hurry, race, run, rush, sprint, step on it (*Inf.*), walk

craze *n.* enthusiasm, fad, fashion, infatuation, mania, mode, novelty, passion, preoccupation, rage, the latest (*Inf.*), thing, trend, vogue

crazy 1. *Inf.* a bit lacking upstairs (*Inf.*), barmy (*Sl.*), batty (*Sl.*), berserk, bonkers (*Sl.*), crazed (*Sl.*), cuckoo (*Inf.*), daft (*Sl.*), delirious, demented, deranged, idiotic, insane, lunatic (*Inf. or archaic*), mad, mad as a hatter, mad as a March hare, maniacal, mental (*Sl.*), not all there (*Inf.*), nuts (*Sl.*), nutty (*Sl.*), nutty as a fruitcake (*Inf.*), off one's head (*Sl.*), of unsound mind, potty (*Inf.*), round the bend (*Sl.*), touched, unbalanced, unhinged **2.** bizarre, eccentric, fantastic, odd, outrageous, peculiar, ridiculous, silly, strange, weird

Antonyms (*sense 1*) all there (*Inf.*), compos mentis, down-to-earth, in one's right mind, intelligent, mentally sound, practical, prudent, rational, reasonable, sane, sensible, smart, wise (*sense 2*) common, conventional, normal, ordinary, orthodox, regular, usual

creak *v.* grate, grind, groan, rasp, scrape, scratch, screech, squeak, squeal

cream *n.* **1.** cosmetic, emulsion, essence, liniment, lotion, oil, ointment, paste, salve, unguent **2.** best, *crème de la crème*, elite, flower, pick, prime

crease 1. *v.* corrugate, crimp, crinkle, crumple, double up, fold, pucker, ridge, ruck up, rumple, screw up, wrinkle **2.** *n.* bulge, corrugation, fold, groove, line, overlap, pucker, ridge, ruck, tuck, wrinkle

create beget, bring into being *or* existence, coin, compose, concoct, design, develop, devise, dream up (*Inf.*), form, formulate, generate, give birth to, give life to, hatch, initiate, invent, make, originate, produce, spawn

Antonyms annihilate, close, demolish, destroy

creation 1. conception, formation, generation, genesis, making, procreation, siring **2.** constitution, development, establishment, formation, foundation, inception, institution, laying down, origination, production, setting up **3.** achievement, brainchild (*Inf.*), chef-d'oeuvre, concept, concoction, handiwork, invention, magnum opus, pièce de résistance, production

creative artistic, clever, fertile, gifted, imaginative, ingenious, inspired, inventive, original, productive, stimulating, visionary

creator architect, author, begetter, designer, father, framer, God, initiator, inventor, maker, originator, prime mover

creature animal, beast, being, brute, critter (*U.S. dialect*), dumb animal, living thing, lower animal, quadruped

credentials attestation, authorization, card, certificate, deed, diploma, docket, letter of recommendation *or* introduction, letters of credence, licence, missive, passport, recommendation, reference(s), testament, testimonial, title, voucher, warrant

credibility believability, believableness, integrity, plausibility, reliability, tenability, trustworthiness

credible believable, conceivable, imaginable, likely, plausible, possible, probable, reasonable, supposable, tenable, thinkable

Antonyms doubtful, implausible, inconceivable, incredible, questionable, unbelievable, unlikely

credit *n.* **1.** acclaim, acknowledgment, approval, commendation, fame, glory, honour, kudos, merit, praise, recognition, thanks, tribute ~*v.* **2.** *With* with accredit, ascribe to, assign to, attribute to, chalk up to (*Inf.*), impute to, refer to **3.** accept, bank on, believe, buy (*Inf.*), depend on, fall

creditable admirable, commendable, deserving, estimable, exemplary, honourable, laudable, meritorious, praiseworthy, reputable, respectable, worthy

credulity blind faith, credulousness, gullibility, naiveté, silliness, simplicity, stupidity

creed articles of faith, belief, canon, catechism, confession, credo, doctrine, dogma, persuasion, principles, profession (of faith), tenet

creek bay, bight, cove, firth or frith (Scot.), inlet

creep v. 1. crawl, crawl on all fours, glide, insinuate, slither, squirm, worm, wriggle, writhe 2. approach unnoticed, skulk, slink, sneak, steal, tiptoe 3. crawl, dawdle, drag, edge, inch, proceed at a snail's pace

crescent n. half-moon, meniscus, new moon, old moon, sickle, sickle-shape

crest apex, crown, head, height, highest point, peak, pinnacle, ridge, summit, top

crestfallen chapfallen, dejected, depressed, despondent, disappointed, disconsolate, discouraged, disheartened, downcast, downhearted

crevice chink, cleft, crack, cranny, fissure, fracture, gap, hole, interstice, opening, rent, rift, slit, split

crew 1. hands, (ship's) company, (ship's) complement 2. company, corps, gang, party, posse, squad, team, working party

crib v. Inf. cheat, pass off as one's own work, pilfer, pirate, plagiarize, purloin, steal

crime atrocity, fault, felony, malfeasance, misdeed, misdemeanour, offence, outrage, transgression, trespass, unlawful act, violation, wrong

criminal 1. n. con (Sl.), con man (Inf.), convict, crook (Inf.), culprit, delinquent, evildoer, felon, jailbird, lawbreaker, malefactor, offender, sinner, transgressor 2. adj. bent (Sl.), corrupt, crooked (Inf.), culpable, felonious, illegal, illicit, immoral, indictable, iniquitous, lawless, nefarious, peccant (Rare), unlawful, unrighteous, vicious, villainous, wicked, wrong
Antonyms commendable, honest, honourable, innocent, lawabiding, lawful, legal, right

cripple v. debilitate, disable, enfeeble, hamstring, incapacitate, lame, maim, mutilate, paralyse, weaken

crippled bedridden, deformed, disabled, enfeebled, handicapped, housebound, incapacitated, laid up (Inf.), lame, paralysed

crisis 1. climacteric, climax, confrontation, critical point, crunch (Inf.), crux, culmination, height, moment of truth, point of no return, turning point 2. catastrophe, critical situation, dilemma, dire straits, disaster, emergency, exigency, extremity, meltdown (Inf.), mess, plight, predicament, quandary, strait, trouble

crisp 1. brittle, crispy, crumbly, crunchy, firm, fresh, unwilted 2. bracing, brisk, fresh, invigorating, refreshing 3. brief, brusque, clear, incisive, pithy, short, succinct, tart, terse
Antonyms (sense 1) drooping, droopy, flaccid, floppy, limp, soft, wilted, withered (sense 2) balmy, clement, mild, pleasant, warm

criterion bench mark, canon, gauge, measure, norm, principle, proof, rule, standard, test, touchstone, yardstick

critic 1. analyst, arbiter, authority, commentator, connoisseur, expert, expositor, judge, pundit, reviewer 2. attacker, carper, caviller, censor, censurer, detractor, fault-finder, knocker (Inf.), Momus, reviler, vilifier

critical 1. captious, carping, cavilling, censorious, derogatory, disapproving, disparaging, faultfinding, nagging, niggling, nit-picking (*Inf.*) **2.** accurate, analytical, diagnostic, discerning, discriminating, fastidious, judicious, penetrating, perceptive, precise **3.** all-important, crucial, dangerous, deciding, decisive, grave, hairy (*Sl.*), high-priority, momentous, perilous, pivotal, precarious, pressing, psychological, risky, serious, urgent, vital **Antonyms** appreciative, approving, complimentary, permissive, safe, secure, settled, uncritical, undiscriminating, unimportant

criticism 1. animadversion, bad press, brickbats (*Inf.*), censure, critical remarks, disapproval, disparagement, fault-finding, flak (*Inf.*), knocking (*Inf.*), panning (*Inf.*), slam (*Sl.*), slating (*Inf.*), stricture **2.** analysis, appraisal, appreciation, assessment, comment, commentary, critique, elucidation, evaluation, judgment, notice, review

criticize animadvert on *or* upon, carp, censure, condemn, disapprove of, disparage, excoriate, find fault with, give (someone *or* something) a bad press, knock (*Inf.*), nag at, pan (*Inf.*), pass strictures upon, pick to pieces, slam (*Sl.*), slate (*Inf.*) **Antonyms** commend, compliment, extol, laud (*Literary*), praise

crook *n. Inf.* cheat, criminal, knave (*Archaic*), racketeer, robber, rogue, shark, swindler, thief, villain

crooked I. anfractuous, bent, bowed, crippled, curved, deformed, deviating, disfigured, distorted, hooked, irregular, meandering, misshapen, out of shape, tortuous, twisted, twisting, warped, winding, zigzag **2.** angled, askew, asymmetric, at an angle, awry, lopsided, off-centre, slanted, slanting, squint, tilted, to one side, uneven, unsymmetrical **3.** *Inf.* bent (*Sl.*), corrupt, crafty, criminal, deceitful, dishonest, dishonourable, dubious, fraudulent, illegal, knavish, nefarious,

questionable, shady (*Inf.*), shifty, treacherous, underhand, unlawful, unprincipled, unscrupulous **Antonyms** (*sense 1*) flat, straight (*sense 3*) ethical, fair, honest, honourable, lawful, legal, straight, upright

crop 1. *n.* fruits, gathering, harvest, produce, reaping, season's growth, vintage, yield **2.** *v.* clip, curtail, cut, lop, mow, pare, prune, reduce, shear, shorten, snip, top, trim

crop up appear, arise, emerge, happen, occur, spring up, turn up

cross *adj.* **1.** angry, annoyed, cantankerous, captious, churlish, crotchety (*Inf.*), crusty, disagreeable, fractious, fretful, grouchy (*Inf.*), grumpy, ill-humoured, ill-tempered, impatient, in a bad mood, irascible, irritable, out of humour, peeved (*Inf.*), peevish, pettish, petulant, put out, querulous, shirty (*Sl.*), short, snappish, snappy, splenetic, sullen, surly, testy, vexed, waspish ~*v.* **2.** bridge, cut across, extend over, ford, meet, pass over, ply, span, traverse, zigzag **3.** crisscross, intersect, intertwine, lace, lie athwart of **4.** blend, crossbreed, cross-fertilize, cross-pollinate, hybridize, interbreed, intercross, mix, mongrelize ~*n.* **5.** crucifix, rood **6.** crossing, crossroads, intersection, junction **7.** amalgam, blend, combination, crossbreed, cur, hybrid, hybridization, mixture, mongrel, mutt (*Sl.*) ~*adj.* **8.** crosswise, intersecting, oblique, transverse **Antonyms** (*sense 1*) affable, agreeable, calm, cheerful, civil, congenial, even-tempered, genial, good-humoured, good-natured, nice, placid, pleasant, sweet

cross-examine catechize, grill (*Inf.*), interrogate, pump, question, quiz

cross out *or* **off** blue-pencil, cancel, delete, eliminate, strike off *or* out

crouch bend down, bow, duck, hunch, kneel, squat, stoop

crow bluster, boast, brag, exult, flourish, gloat, glory in, strut, swagger, triumph, vaunt

crowd n. **1.** army, assembly, company, concourse, flock, herd, horde, host, mass, mob, multitude, pack, press, rabble, swarm, throng, troupe **2.** attendance, audience, gate, house, spectators ~ v. **3.** cluster, congregate, cram, flock, forgather, gather, huddle, mass, muster, press, push, stream, surge, swarm, throng

crowded busy, congested, cramped, crushed, full, huddled, jam-packed, mobbed, overflowing, packed, populous, swarming, teeming, thronged

crown n. **1.** chaplet, circlet, coronal (*Poetic*), coronet, diadem, tiara **2.** bays, distinction, garland, honour, kudos, laurels, laurel wreath, prize, trophy **3.** emperor, empress, king, monarch, monarchy, queen, *rex*, royalty, ruler, sovereign, sovereignty ~ v. **4.** adorn, dignify, festoon, honour, invest, reward **5.** be the climax or culmination of, cap, complete, consummate, finish, fulfil, perfect, put the finishing touch to, round off, surmount, terminate, top

crucial central, critical, decisive, pivotal, psychological, searching, testing, trying

crude 1. boorish, coarse, crass, dirty, gross, indecent, lewd, obscene, smutty, tactless, tasteless, uncouth, vulgar **2.** natural, raw, unmilled, unpolished, unprepared, unprocessed, unrefined **3.** clumsy, makeshift, outline, primitive, rough, rough-hewn, rude, rudimentary, sketchy, undeveloped, unfinished, unformed, unpolished
Antonyms (*sense 1*) genteel, polished, refined, subtle, tasteful (*sense 2*) fine, fine-grained, polished, prepared, processed, refined

crudity coarseness, crudeness,

impropriety, indecency, indelicacy, lewdness, loudness, lowness, obscenity, obtrusiveness, smuttiness, vulgarity

cruel 1. atrocious, barbarous, bitter, bloodthirsty, brutal, brutish, callous, cold-blooded, depraved, excruciating, fell (*Archaic*), ferocious, fierce, flinty, grim, hard, hard-hearted, harsh, heartless, hellish, implacable, inclement, inexorable, inhuman, inhumane, malevolent, painful, poignant, Ramboesque, ravening, raw, relentless, remorseless, sadistic, sanguinary, savage, severe, spiteful, stony-hearted, unfeeling, unkind, unnatural, vengeful, vicious **2.** merciless, pitiless, ruthless, unrelenting
Antonyms benevolent, caring, compassionate, gentle, humane, kind, merciful, sympathetic, warm-hearted

cruelty barbarity, bestiality, bloodthirstiness, brutality, brutishness, callousness, depravity, ferocity, fiendishness, hardheartedness, harshness, heartlessness, inhumanity, mercilessness, murderousness, ruthlessness, sadism, savagery, severity, spite, spitefulness, venom, viciousness

cruise 1. v. coast, sail, voyage **2.** n. boat trip, sail, sea trip, voyage

crumb atom, bit, grain, mite, morsel, particle, scrap, shred, sliver, snippet, *soupçon*, speck

crumble 1. bruise, crumb, crush, fragment, granulate, grind, pound, powder, pulverize, triturate **2.** break up, collapse, come to dust, decay, decompose, degenerate, deteriorate, disintegrate, fall apart, go to pieces (*Inf.*), go to wrack and ruin, moulder, perish, tumble down

crumple 1. crease, crush, pucker, rumple, screw up, wrinkle **2.** break down, cave in, collapse, fall, give way, go to pieces

crusade campaign, cause, drive, holy war, jihad, movement, push

crush v. **1.** bray, break, bruise,

comminute, compress, contuse, crease, crumble, crumple, crunch, mash, pound, pulverize, rumple, smash, squeeze, wrinkle **2.** conquer, extinguish, overcome, overpower, overwhelm, put down, quell, stamp out, subdue, vanquish

crust caking, coat, coating, concretion, covering, film, incrustation, layer, outside, scab, shell, skin, surface

cry *v.* **1.** bawl, bewail, blubber, boohoo, greet (*Scot.*), howl one's eyes out, keen, lament, mewl, pule, shed tears, snivel, sob, wail, weep, whimper, whine, whinge (*Inf.*), yowl ~*n.* **2.** bawling, blubbering, crying, greet (*Scot.*), howl, keening, lament, lamentation, plaint (*Archaic*), snivel, snivelling, sob, sobbing, sorrowing, wailing, weep, weeping ~*v.* **3.** bawl, bellow, call, call out, ejaculate, exclaim, hail, halloo, holler (*Inf.*), howl, roar, scream, screech, shout, shriek, sing out, vociferate, whoop, yell
Antonyms (*sense 1*) chortle, chuckle, giggle, laugh, snicker, snigger, twitter

cry off back out, beg off, excuse oneself, quit, withdraw, withdraw from

cub 1. offspring, whelp, young **2.** babe (*Inf.*), beginner, fledgling, greenhorn (*Inf.*), lad, learner, puppy, recruit, tenderfoot, trainee, whippersnapper, youngster

cue catchword, hint, key, nod, prompting, reminder, sign, signal, suggestion

culminate climax, close, come to a climax, come to a head, conclude, end, end up, finish, rise to a crescendo, terminate, wind up (*Inf.*)

culprit criminal, delinquent, evildoer, felon, guilty party, malefactor, miscreant, offender, person responsible, rascal, sinner, transgressor, wrongdoer

cult 1. body, church, clique, denomination, faction, faith, following, party, religion, school, sect **2.** admiration, craze, devotion, idolization, reverence, veneration, worship

cultivate 1. bring under cultivation, farm, fertilize, harvest, plant, plough, prepare, tend, till, work **2.** ameliorate, better, bring on, cherish, civilize, develop, discipline, enrich, foster, improve, polish, promote, refine, train

cultivation advancement, advocacy, development, encouragement, enhancement, fostering, furtherance, help, nurture, patronage, promotion, support

cultural artistic, broadening, civilizing, developmental, edifying, educational, educative, elevating, enlightening, enriching, humane, humanizing, liberal, liberalizing

culture 1. civilization, customs, life style, mores, society, stage of development, the arts, way of life **2.** accomplishment, breeding, education, elevation, enlightenment, erudition, gentility, good taste, improvement, polish, politeness, refinement, urbanity

cultured accomplished, advanced, educated, enlightened, erudite, genteel, highbrow, knowledgeable, polished, refined, scholarly, urbane, versed, well-bred, well-informed, well-read
Antonyms coarse, common, inelegant, uncultivated, uneducated, unpolished, unrefined, vulgar

cumbersome awkward, bulky, burdensome, clumsy, cumbrous, embarrassing, heavy, hefty (*Inf.*), incommodious, inconvenient, oppressive, unmanageable, unwieldy, weighty
Antonyms compact, convenient, easy to use, handy, manageable, practical, serviceable, wieldy

cunning 1. *adj.* artful, astute, canny, crafty, devious, foxy, guileful, knowing, Machiavellian, sharp, shifty, shrewd, subtle, sly, wily **2.** *n.* artfulness, astuteness, craftiness, deceitfulness, devi-

ousness, foxiness, guile, shrewdness, slyness, trickery, wiliness
Antonyms adj. artless, dull, ethical, frank, honest, ingenuous ~n.
candour, ingenuousness, sincerity

curb 1. v. bite back, bridle, check,
constrain, contain, control, hinder, impede, inhibit, moderate,
muzzle, repress, restrain, restrict, retard, subdue, suppress 2.
n. brake, bridle, check, control,
deterrent, limitation, rein, restraint

cure v. 1. alleviate, correct, ease,
heal, help, make better, mend,
rehabilitate, relieve, remedy, restore, restore to health ~n. 2.
alleviation, antidote, corrective,
healing, medicine, panacea, recovery, remedy, restorative,
specific, treatment ~v. 3. dry,
kipper, pickle, preserve, salt,
smoke

curiosity 1. inquisitiveness, interest, nosiness (Inf.), prying,
snooping (Inf.) 2. celebrity, freak,
marvel, novelty, oddity, phenomenon, rarity, sight, spectacle,
wonder

curious 1. inquiring, inquisitive,
interested, puzzled, questioning,
searching 2. inquisitive, meddling, nosy (Inf.), peeping, peering, prying, snoopy (Inf.) 3. bizarre, exotic, extraordinary,
marvellous, mysterious, novel,
odd, peculiar, puzzling, quaint,
queer, rare, singular, strange,
unconventional, unexpected,
unique, unorthodox, unusual,
wonderful
Antonyms (senses 1 & 2) incurious, indifferent, uninquisitive,
uninterested (sense 3) common,
everyday, familiar, ordinary

curl v. bend, coil, convolute, corkscrew, crimp, crinkle, crisp,
curve, entwine, frizz, loop, meander, ripple, spiral, turn, twine,
twirl, twist, wind, wreathe,
writhe

currency bills, coinage, coins,
dosh (Brit. sl.), medium of exchange, money, notes

current adj. 1. accepted, circulat-
ing, common, common knowl-
edge, customary, general, going
around, in circulation, in progress, in the air, in the news,
ongoing, popular, present, prevailing, prevalent, rife, widespread 2. contemporary, fashionable, in, in fashion, in vogue,
now (Inf.), present-day, sexy
(Inf.), trendy (Inf.), up-to-date,
up-to-the-minute ~n. 3. course,
draught, flow, jet, progression,
river, stream, tide
Antonyms (sense 2) archaic, obsolete, old-fashioned, outmoded,
out-of-date, passé, past

curse n. 1. blasphemy, expletive,
oath, obscenity, swearing,
swearword 2. anathema, ban,
denunciation, evil eye, excom-
munication, execration, imprecation, jinx, malediction, malison
(Archaic) 3. affliction, bane, burden, calamity, cross, disaster,
evil, misfortune, ordeal, plague,
scourge, torment, tribulation,
trouble, vexation ~v. 4. be foul-
mouthed, blaspheme, cuss (Inf.),
swear, take the Lord's name in
vain, turn the air blue (Inf.), use
bad language 5. accurse, anathematize, damn, excommunicate,
execrate, fulminate, imprecate

cursed 1. accursed, bedevilled,
blighted, cast out, confounded,
damned, doomed, excommunicate, execrable, fey (Scot.), fore-
doomed, ill-fated, star-crossed,
unholy, unsanctified, villainous 2.
abominable, damnable, detestable, devilish, fell (Archaic),
fiendish, hateful, infamous, infernal, loathsome, odious, pernicious, pestilential, vile
Antonyms (sense 1) blessed,
charmed, favoured, fortunate,
lucky

curt abrupt, blunt, brief, brusque,
concise, gruff, offhand, pithy,
rude, sharp, short, snappish, succinct, summary, tart, terse, unceremonious, uncivil, ungracious

curtail abbreviate, abridge, contract, cut, cut back, cut short,

decrease, dock, lessen, lop, pare down, reduce, retrench, shorten, trim, truncate

curtain 1. *n.* drape (*Chiefly U.S.*), hanging **2.** *v.* conceal, drape, hide, screen, shroud, shut off, shutter, veil

curve 1. *v.* arc, arch, bend, bow, coil, hook, inflect, spiral, swerve, turn, twist, wind **2.** *n.* arc, bend, camber, curvature, half-moon, loop, trajectory, turn

curved arced, arched, bent, bowed, crooked, humped, rounded, serpentine, sinuous, sweeping, turned, twisted

custody arrest, confinement, detention, durance (*Archaic*), duress, imprisonment, incarceration

custom habit, habitude (*Rare*), manner, mode, procedure, routine, way, wont

customary accepted, accustomed, acknowledged, common, confirmed, conventional, established, everyday, familiar, fashionable, general, habitual, normal, ordinary, popular, regular, routine, traditional, usual, wonted **Antonyms** exceptional, infrequent, irregular, occasional, rare, uncommon, unusual

customer buyer, client, consumer, habitué, patron, prospect, purchaser, regular (*Inf.*), shopper

customs duty, import charges, tariff, taxes, toll

cut *v.* **1.** chop, cleave, divide, gash, incise, lacerate, nick, notch, penetrate, pierce, score, sever, slash, slice, slit, wound **2.** carve, chip, chisel, chop, engrave, fashion, form, saw, sculpt, sculpture, shape, whittle **3.** contract, cut back, decrease, ease up on, lower, rationalize, reduce, slash, slim (down) **4.** abbreviate, abridge, condense, curtail, delete, edit out, excise, precis, shorten **5.** gash, graze, groove, incision, laceration, nick, rent, rip, slash, slit,

stroke, wound **6.** cutback, decrease, decrement, diminution, economy, fall, lowering, reduction, saving **Antonyms** (*sense 4*) add to, augment, enlarge, expand, extend, fill out, increase

cutback cut, decrease, economy, lessening, reduction, retrenchment

cut down fell, hew, level, lop, raze

cut in break in, butt in, interpose, interrupt, intervene, intrude, move in (*Inf.*)

cut off 1. disconnect, intercept, interrupt, intersect **2.** isolate, separate, sever

cut out cease, delete, extract, give up, refrain from, remove, sever, stop

cut-price bargain, cheap, cheapo (*Inf.*), cut-rate (*Chiefly U.S.*), reduced, sale

cut short abort, break off, bring to an end, check, halt, interrupt, leave unfinished, postpone, stop, terminate

cutting *adj.* biting, bitter, chill, keen, numbing, penetrating, piercing, raw, sharp, stinging **Antonyms** balmy, pleasant, soothing

cut up *v.* **1.** carve, chop, dice, divide, mince, slice **2.** injure, knife, lacerate, slash, wound

cycle aeon, age, circle, era, period, phase, revolution, rotation, round (*of years*)

cynic doubter, misanthrope, misanthropist, pessimist, sceptic, scoffer

cynical contemptuous, derisive, distrustful, ironic, misanthropic, misanthropical, mocking, pessimistic, sarcastic, sardonic, sceptical, scoffing, scornful, sneering, unbelieving **Antonyms** credulous, green, gullible, hopeful, optimistic, trustful, trusting, unsceptical, unsuspecting

D

daily *adj.* **1.** circadian, diurnal, everyday, quotidian **2.** common, commonplace, day-to-day, everyday, ordinary, quotidian, regular, routine ~*adv.* **3.** constantly, day after day, day by day, every day, often, once a day, per diem, regularly

dainty *adj.* charming, delicate, elegant, exquisite, fine, graceful, neat, petite, pretty
Antonyms awkward, clumsy, coarse, gauche, inelegant, maladroit, uncouth, ungainly

dam 1. *n.* barrage, barrier, embankment, hindrance, obstruction, wall **2.** *v.* barricade, block, block up, check, choke, confine, hold back, hold in, obstruct, restrict

damage *n.* **1.** destruction, detriment, devastation, harm, hurt, impairment, injury, loss, mischief, mutilation, suffering **2.** *Plural* compensation, fine, indemnity, reimbursement, reparation, satisfaction ~*v.* **3.** deface, harm, hurt, impair, incapacitate, injure, mar, mutilate, ruin, spoil, tamper with, weaken, wreck
Antonyms *n.* gain, improvement, reparation ~*v.* better, fix, improve, mend, repair

damaging deleterious, detrimental, disadvantageous, harmful, hurtful, injurious, prejudicial, ruinous
Antonyms advantageous, favourable, healthful, helpful, profitable, salutary, useful, valuable, wholesome

damn *v.* **1.** blast, castigate, censure, condemn, criticize, denounce, denunciate, excoriate, inveigh against, pan (*Inf.*), slam (*Sl.*), slate (*Inf.*) **2.** abuse, anathematize, blaspheme, curse, execrate, imprecate, revile, swear

3. condemn, doom, sentence ~*n.* **4.** brass farthing, hoot, iota, jot, tinker's curse *or* damn (*Sl.*), two hoots, whit

damned 1. accursed, anathematized, condemned, doomed, infernal, lost, reprobate, unhappy **2.** *Sl.* confounded, despicable, detestable, hateful, infamous, infernal, loathsome, revolting

damp *n.* **1.** clamminess, dampness, darkness, dew, drizzle, fog, humidity, mist, moisture, muzziness, vapour ~*adj.* **2.** clammy, dank, dewy, dripping, drizzly, humid, misty, moist, muggy, sodden, soggy, sopping, vaporous, wet ~*v.* **3.** dampen, moisten, wet **4.** *Fig.* allay, check, chill, cool, curb, dash, deaden, deject, depress, diminish, discourage, dispirit, dull, inhibit, moderate, restrain, stifle
Antonyms *n.* aridity, dryness ~*adj.* arid, dry, watertight ~*v.* (*sense 4*) encourage, hearten, inspire

dance 1. *v.* bob up and down, caper, frolic, gambol, hop, jig, prance, rock, skip, spin, sway, swing, whirl **2.** *n.* ball, dancing party, disco, discotheque, hop (*Inf.*), knees-up (*Inf.*), social

danger endangerment, hazard, insecurity, jeopardy, menace, peril, precariousness, risk, threat, venture, vulnerability

dangerous alarming, breakneck, chancy (*Inf.*), exposed, hairy (*Sl.*), hazardous, insecure, menacing, nasty, parlous (*Archaic*), perilous, precarious, risky, threatening, treacherous, ugly, unchancy (*Scot.*), unsafe, vulnerable
Antonyms harmless, innocuous, OK *or* okay (*Inf.*), out of danger,

dangle

out of harm's way, protected, safe, safe and sound, secure

dangle v. 1. depend, flap, hang, hang down, sway, swing, trail 2. brandish, entice, flaunt, flourish, lure, tantalize, tempt, wave

dare v. 1. challenge, defy, goad, provoke, taunt, throw down the gauntlet 2. adventure, brave, endanger, gamble, hazard, make bold, presume, risk, stake, venture ~n. 3. challenge, defiance, provocation, taunt

daring 1. adj. adventurous, audacious, bold, brave, daredevil, fearless, game (Inf.), impulsive, intrepid, plucky, rash, reckless, valiant, venturesome 2. n. audacity, balls (Sl.), boldness, bottle (Sl.), bravery, courage, derring-do (Archaic), fearlessness, grit, guts (Inf.), intrepidity, nerve (Inf.), pluck, rashness, spirit, spunk (Inf.), temerity
Antonyms adj. anxious, careful, cautious, cowardly, faint-hearted, fearful, timid, wary, uncourageous ~n. anxiety, caution, cowardice, fear, timidity

dark adj. 1. black, brunette, dark-skinned, dusky, ebony, sable, swarthy 2. cloudy, darksome (Literary), dim, dingy, indistinct, murky, overcast, pitch-black, pitchy, shadowy, shady, sunless, unlit 3. abstruse, arcane, concealed, cryptic, deep, enigmatic, hidden, mysterious, mystic, obscure, occult, puzzling, recondite, secret 4. bleak, cheerless, dismal, doleful, drab, gloomy, grim, joyless, morbid, morose, mournful, sombre 5. angry, dour, forbidding, frowning, glowering, glum, ominous, scowling, sulky, sullen, threatening ~n. 6. darkness, dimness, dusk, gloom, murk, murkiness, obscurity, semi-darkness 7. evening, night, nightfall, night-time, twilight
Antonyms (sense 1) blond, blonde, fair, fair-haired, flaxen-haired, light, light-complexioned, towheaded (senses 2 & 4) bright,

cheerful, clear, genial, glad, hopeful, pleasant, sunny

darkness blackness, dark, dimness, dusk, duskiness, gloom, murk, murkiness, nightfall, obscurity, shade, shadiness, shadows

darling n. 1. beloved, dear, dearest, love, sweetheart, truelove 2. apple of one's eye, blue-eyed boy, fair-haired boy (U.S.), favourite, pet, spoiled child ~adj. 3. adored, beloved, cherished, dear, precious, treasured

darn v. cobble up, mend, patch, repair, sew up, stitch

dart bound, dash, flash, flit, fly, race, run, rush, scoot, shoot, spring, sprint, start, tear, whistle (Inf.), whiz

dash v. 1. break, crash, destroy, shatter, shiver, smash, splinter 2. cast, fling, hurl, slam, sling, throw 3. bolt, bound, dart, fly, haste, hasten, hurry, race, run, rush, speed, spring, sprint, tear 4. abash, chagrin, confound, dampen, disappoint, discomfort, discourage ~n. 5. brio, élan, flair, flourish, panache, spirit, style, verve, vigour, vivacity
Antonyms v. crawl, dawdle, enhance, improve, walk

dashing bold, daring, debonair, exuberant, gallant, lively, plucky, spirited, swashbuckling

data details, documents, dope (Inf.), facts, figures, info (Inf.), information, input, materials, statistics

date n. 1. age, epoch, era, period, stage, time 2. appointment, assignation, engagement, meeting, rendezvous, tryst

dated antiquated, archaic, démodé, obsolete, old-fashioned, old hat, out, outdated, outmoded, out of date, passé, unfashionable, untrendy
Antonyms à la mode, all the rage, chic, cool (Inf.), current, hip (Inf.), in vogue, latest, modern, modish, popular, stylish, trendy (Inf.), up to date

daub v. coat, cover, paint, plaster, slap on (*Inf.*), smear

daunt alarm, appal, cow, dismay, frighten, frighten off, intimidate, overawe, scare, subdue, terrify
Antonyms cheer, comfort, hearten, reassure, support

dawdle dally, delay, dilly-dally (*Inf.*), fritter away, hang about, idle, lag, loaf, loiter, potter, trail, waste time
Antonyms fly, get a move on (*Inf.*), hasten, hurry, lose no time, make haste, rush, scoot, step on it (*Inf.*)

dawn 1. n. aurora (*Literary*), cockcrow, crack of dawn, dawning, daybreak, daylight, dayspring (*Poetic*), morning, sunrise, sunup 2. v. break, brighten, gleam, glimmer, grow light, lighten

day 1. daylight, daylight hours, daytime, twenty-four hours, working day 2. date, particular day, point in time, set time, time

daydream n. 1. dream, imagining, musing, reverie, stargazing, vision, woolgathering 2. castle in the air or in Spain, dream, fancy, fantasy, figment of the imagination, fond hope, pipe dream, wish ~v. 3. dream, envision, fancy, fantasize, hallucinate, imagine, muse, stargaze

daylight 1. light of day, sunlight, sunshine 2. broad day, daylight hours, daytime 3. full view, light of day, openness, public attention

daze v. 1. benumb, numb, paralyse, shock, stun, stupefy 2. amaze, astonish, astound, befog, bewilder, blind, confuse, dazzle, dumbfound, flabbergast (*Inf.*), perplex, stagger, startle, surprise ~n. 3. bewilderment, confusion, distraction, shock, stupor, trance, trancelike state

dazed baffled, bemused, bewildered, confused, disorientated, dizzy, dopey (*Sl.*), flabbergasted (*Inf.*), fuddled, groggy (*Inf.*), lightheaded, muddled, nonplussed, numbed, perplexed, punch-drunk,

shocked, staggered, stunned, stupefied, woozy (*Inf.*)

dazzle v. 1. bedazzle, blind, blur, confuse, daze 2. amaze, astonish, awe, bowl over (*Inf.*), fascinate, hypnotize, impress, overawe, overpower, overwhelm, strike dumb, stupefy

dead adj. 1. deceased, defunct, departed, extinct, gone, inanimate, late, lifeless, passed away, perished 2. apathetic, callous, cold, dull, frigid, glassy, glazed, indifferent, inert, lukewarm, numb, paralysed, spiritless, torpid, unresponsive, wooden 3. boring, dead-and-alive, dull, flat, insipid, stale, tasteless, uninteresting, vapid
Antonyms active, alive, animate, animated, effective, existing, in use, lively, living, responsive, vivacious

deadlock cessation, dead heat, draw, full stop, halt, impasse, stalemate, standoff, standstill, tie

deadly 1. baleful, baneful, dangerous, death-dealing, deathly, destructive, fatal, lethal, malignant, mortal, noxious, pernicious, poisonous, venomous 2. cruel, grim, implacable, mortal, ruthless, savage, unrelenting 3. accurate, effective, exact, on target, precise, sure, true, unerring, unfailing

deaf 1. hard of hearing, stone deaf, without hearing 2. indifferent, oblivious, unconcerned, unhearing, unmoved

deafening booming, dinning, earpiercing, ear-splitting, intense, overpowering, piercing, resounding, ringing, thunderous

deal v. 1. bargain, buy and sell, do business, negotiate, sell, stock, trade, traffic, treat (with) ~n. 2. *Inf.* agreement, arrangement, bargain, buy (*Inf.*), contract, pact, transaction, understanding ~v. 3. allot, apportion, assign, bestow, dispense, distribute, divide, dole out, give, mete out, reward, share

dealer chandler, marketer, mer-

chandiser, merchant, trader, tradesman, wholesaler

dear *adj.* **1.** beloved, cherished, close, darling, esteemed, familiar, favourite, intimate, precious, prized, respected, treasured **2.** at a premium, costly, expensive, high-priced, overpriced, pricey (*Inf.*) ~*n.* **3.** angel, beloved, darling, loved one, precious, treasure

Antonyms cheap, common, disliked, hated, inexpensive, worthless

dearly extremely, greatly, profoundly, very much

death 1. bereavement, cessation, curtains (*Inf.*), decease, demise, departure, dissolution, dying, end, exit, expiration, loss, passing, quietus, release **2.** annihilation, destruction, downfall, eradication, extermination, extinction, finish, grave, obliteration, ruin, ruination, undoing

Antonyms beginning, birth, emergence, genesis, growth, origin, rise, source

deathless eternal, everlasting, immortal, imperishable, incorruptible, timeless, undying

Antonyms corporeal, earthly, ephemeral, human, mortal, passing, temporal, transient, transitory

deathly 1. cadaverous, deathlike, gaunt, ghastly, grim, haggard, pale, pallid, wan **2.** deadly, extreme, fatal, intense, mortal, terrible

debase abase, cheapen, degrade, demean, devalue, disgrace, dishonour, drag down, humble, humiliate, lower, reduce, shame

Antonyms elevate, enhance, exalt, improve, uplift

debatable arguable, borderline, controversial, disputable, doubtful, dubious, in dispute, moot, open to question, problematical, questionable, uncertain, undecided, unsettled

debate *v.* **1.** argue, contend, contest, controvert, discuss, dispute, question, wrangle ~*n.* **2.** alter-

cation, argument, contention, controversy, discussion, disputation, dispute, polemic **3.** cogitation, consideration, deliberation, meditation, reflection

debris bits, brash, detritus, dross, fragments, litter, pieces, remains, rubbish, rubble, ruins, waste, wreck, wreckage

debt arrears, bill, claim, commitment, debit, due, duty, liability, obligation, score

debtor borrower, defaulter, insolvent, mortgagor

debunk cut down to size, deflate, disparage, expose, lampoon, mock, puncture, ridicule, show up

debut beginning, bow, coming out, entrance, first appearance, inauguration, initiation, introduction, launching, presentation

decadent corrupt, debased, debauched, decaying, declining, degenerate, degraded, depraved, dissolute, immoral, self-indulgent

decay *v.* **1.** atrophy, crumble, decline, degenerate, deteriorate, disintegrate, dissolve, dwindle, moulder, shrivel, sink, spoil, wane, waste away, wear away, wither **2.** corrode, decompose, mortify, perish, putrefy, rot

Antonyms expand, flourish, flower, grow, increase

deceased *adj.* dead, defunct, departed, expired, finished, former, gone, late, lifeless, lost

deceit artifice, cheating, chicanery, craftiness, cunning, deceitfulness, deception, dissimulation, double-dealing, duplicity, fraud, fraudulence, guile, hypocrisy, imposition, pretence, slyness, treachery, trickery, underhandedness

Antonyms candour, frankness, honesty, openness, sincerity, truthfulness

deceitful counterfeit, crafty, deceiving, deceptive, designing, dishonest, disingenuous, double-dealing, duplicitous, fallacious, false, fraudulent, guileful, hypocritical, illusory, insincere, knavish (*Archaic*), sneaky, treacherous, tricky, two-faced, underhand, untrustworthy

deceive bamboozle (*Inf.*), beguile, betray, cheat, con (*Sl.*), cozen, delude, disappoint, double-cross (*Inf.*), dupe, ensnare, entrap, fool, hoax, hoodwink, impose upon, lead (someone) on (*Inf.*), mislead, outwit, pull a fast one (*Sl.*), pull the wool over (someone's) eyes, swindle, take for a ride (*Inf.*), take in (*Inf.*), trick

decency appropriateness, civility, correctness, courtesy, decorum, etiquette, fitness, good form, good manners, modesty, propriety, respectability, seemliness

decent appropriate, becoming, befitting, chaste, comely, *comme il faut*, decorous, delicate, fit, fitting, modest, nice, polite, presentable, proper, pure, respectable, seemly, suitable

deception craftiness, cunning, deceit, deceitfulness, deceptiveness, dissimulation, duplicity, fraud, fraudulence, guile, hypocrisy, imposition, insincerity, legerdemain, treachery, trickery
Antonyms artlessness, candour, fidelity, frankness, honesty, openness, scrupulousness, straightforwardness, trustworthiness, truthfulness

deceptive ambiguous, deceitful, delusive, dishonest, fake, fallacious, false, fraudulent, illusory, misleading, mock, specious, spurious, unreliable

decide adjudge, adjudicate, choose, come to a conclusion, commit oneself, conclude, decree, determine, elect, end, make a decision, make up one's mind, purpose, reach *or* come to a decision, resolve, settle
Antonyms be indecisive, be unable to decide, blow hot and cold (*Inf.*), dither, falter, fluctuate, hesitate, hum and haw, seesaw, shillyshally (*Inf.*), swither (*Scot.*), vacillate

decipher construe, crack, decode, deduce, explain, figure out (*Inf.*), interpret, make out, read, reveal, solve, understand, unfold, unravel

decision arbitration, conclusion, finding, judgment, outcome, resolution, result, ruling, sentence, settlement, verdict

decisive 1. absolute, conclusive, critical, crucial, definite, definitive, fateful, final, influential, momentous, positive, significant **2.** decided, determined, firm, forceful, incisive, resolute, strong-minded, trenchant
Antonyms doubtful, hesitant, hesitating, indecisive, in two minds (*Inf.*), irresolute, pussy-footing (*Inf.*), uncertain, undecided, vacillating

deck v. adorn, apparel (*Archaic*), array, attire, beautify, bedeck, bedight (*Archaic*), bedizen (*Archaic*), clothe, decorate, dress, embellish, festoon, garland, grace, ornament, trim

declaim harangue, hold forth, lecture, orate, perorate, proclaim, rant, recite, speak, spiel (*Inf.*)

declaration 1. acknowledgment, affirmation, assertion, attestation, averment, avowal, deposition, disclosure, protestation, revelation, statement, testimony **2.** announcement, edict, manifesto, notification, proclamation, profession, promulgation, pronouncement, pronunciamento

declare affirm, announce, assert, attest, aver, avow, certify, claim, confirm, maintain, proclaim, profess, pronounce, state, swear, testify, validate

decline v. **1.** avoid, deny, forgo, refuse, reject, say 'no', send one's regrets, turn down **2.** decrease, diminish, dwindle, ebb, fade, fail, fall, fall off, flag, lessen, shrink, sink, wane ~n. **3.** abatement, diminution, downturn, dwindling, falling off, lessening, recession, slump
Antonyms v. accept, agree, con-

sent, improve, increase, rise ~*n.* improvement, rise, upswing

decorate 1. adorn, beautify, bedeck, deck, embellish, enrich, grace, ornament, trim **2.** colour, do up (*Inf.*), furbish, paint, paper, renovate, wallpaper **3.** cite, honour, pin a medal on

decoration 1. adornment, beautification, elaboration, embellishment, enrichment, garnishing, ornamentation, trimming **2.** arabesque, bauble, curlicue, falderal, flounce, flourish, frill, furbelow, garnish, ornament, scroll, spangle, trimmings, trinket **3.** award, badge, colours, emblem, garter, medal, order, ribbon, star

decorum behaviour, breeding, courtliness, decency, deportment, dignity, etiquette, gentility, good grace, good manners, gravity, politeness, politesse, propriety, protocol, punctilio, respectability, seemliness

Antonyms bad manners, churlishness, impoliteness, impropriety, indecorum, rudeness, unseemliness

decoy 1. *n.* attraction, bait, ensnarement, enticement, inducement, lure, pretence, trap **2.** *v.* allure, bait, deceive, ensnare, entice, entrap, inveigle, lure, seduce, tempt

decrease 1. *v.* abate, contract, curtail, cut down, decline, diminish, drop, dwindle, ease, fall off, lessen, lower, peter out, reduce, shrink, slacken, subside, wane **2.** *n.* abatement, contraction, cutback, decline, diminution, downturn, dwindling, ebb, falling off, lessening, loss, reduction, shrinkage, subsidence

Antonyms *v.* enlarge, expand, extend, increase, rise ~*n.* expansion, extension, growth

decree 1. *n.* act, command, dictum, edict, enactment, law, mandate, order, ordinance, precept, proclamation, regulation, ruling, statute **2.** *v.* command, decide, determine, dictate, enact, lay

down, ordain, order, prescribe, proclaim, pronounce, rule

decrepit aged, crippled, debilitated, doddering, effete, feeble, frail, incapacitated, infirm, superannuated, wasted, weak

dedicate commit, devote, give over to, pledge, surrender

dedicated committed, devoted, enthusiastic, given over to, purposeful, single-minded, sworn, wholehearted, zealous

deduce conclude, derive, draw, gather, glean, infer, reason, take to mean, understand

deduct decrease by, knock off (*Inf.*), reduce by, remove, subtract, take away, take from, take off, take out, withdraw

deduction 1. assumption, conclusion, consequence, corollary, finding, inference, reasoning, result **2.** abatement, allowance, decrease, diminution, discount, reduction, subtraction, withdrawal

deed achievement, act, action, exploit, fact, feat, performance, reality, truth

deep *adj.* **1.** abyssal, bottomless, broad, far, profound, unfathomable, wide, yawning **2.** extreme, grave, great, intense, profound **3.** *Of a sound* bass, booming, full-toned, low, low-pitched, resonant, sonorous ~*adv.* **4.** deeply, far down, far into, late

Antonyms *adj.* high, shallow, sharp, superficial

default 1. *n.* absence, defect, deficiency, dereliction, failure, fault, lack, lapse, neglect, non-payment, omission, want **2.** *v.* bilk, defraud, dodge, evade, fail, levant (*Brit.*), neglect, rat, swindle, welsh (*Sl.*)

defeat 1. *v.* beat, conquer, crush, overpower, overthrow, overwhelm, quell, repulse, rout, subdue, subjugate, vanquish **2.** *n.* beating, conquest, debacle, overthrow, repulse, rout, trouncing, vanquishment

Antonyms *v.* bow, lose, submit, succumb, surrender, yield ~*n.* success, triumph, victory

defect 1. *n.* blemish, blotch, error, failing, fault, flaw, foible, imperfection, mistake, spot, taint, want 2. *v.* abandon, apostatize, break faith, change sides, desert, go over, rebel, revolt, tergiversate, walk out on (*Inf.*)

defective broken, deficient, faulty, flawed, imperfect, inadequate, incomplete, insufficient, not working, out of order, scant, short

Antonyms adequate, intact, perfect, whole, working

defence 1. armament, cover, deterrence, guard, immunity, protection, resistance, safeguard, security, shelter 2. apologia, apology, argument, excuse, exoneration, explanation, extenuation, justification, plea, vindication 3. *Law* alibi, case, declaration, denial, plea, pleading, rebuttal, testimony

defend 1. cover, fortify, guard, keep safe, preserve, protect, safeguard, screen, secure, shelter, shield, ward off, watch over 2. assert, champion, endorse, espouse, justify, maintain, plead, speak up for, stand by, stand up for, support, sustain, uphold, vindicate

defender 1. bodyguard, escort, guard, protector 2. advocate, champion, patron, sponsor, supporter, vindicator

defer adjourn, delay, hold over, postpone, procrastinate, prorogue, protract, put off, put on ice, set aside, shelve, suspend, table

defiance challenge, confrontation, contempt, contumacy, disobedience, disregard, insolence, insubordination, opposition, provocation, rebelliousness, recalcitrance, spite

Antonyms accordance, acquiescence, compliance, deference, obedience, observance, regard, respect, subservience

deficiency defect, demerit, failing, fault, flaw, frailty, imperfection, shortcoming, weakness

deficit arrears, default, deficiency, loss, shortage, shortfall

define characterize, describe, designate, detail, determine, explain, expound, interpret, specify, spell out

definite clear, clear-cut, clearly defined, determined, exact, explicit, express, fixed, marked, obvious, particular, precise, specific

Antonyms confused, fuzzy, general, hazy, ill-defined, imprecise, indefinite, indeterminate, indistinct, inexact, loose, obscure, unclear, undetermined, vague

definitely absolutely, beyond any doubt, categorically, certainly, clearly, decidedly, easily, far and away, finally, indubitably, obviously, plainly, positively, surely, undeniably, unequivocally, unmistakably, unquestionably, without doubt, without fail, without question

definition clarification, description, elucidation, explanation, exposition, statement of meaning

deflate 1. collapse, contract, empty, exhaust, flatten, puncture, shrink, void 2. chasten, dash, debunk (*Inf.*), disconcert, dispirit, humble, humiliate, mortify, put down (*Sl.*), squash, take the wind out of (someone's) sails

Antonyms aerate, amplify, balloon, blast, blow up, boost, dilate, distend, enlarge, exaggerate, expand, increase, inflate, puff up *or* out, pump up, swell

deflect bend, deviate, diverge, glance off, ricochet, shy, sidetrack, slew, swerve, turn, turn aside, twist, veer, wind

defraud beguile, bilk, cheat, con (*Sl.*), cozen, delude, diddle (*Inf.*), do (*Sl.*), dupe, embezzle, fleece, gull (*Archaic*), gyp (*Sl.*), outwit, pilfer, pull a fast one on (*Inf.*), rip off (*Sl.*), rob, rook (*Sl.*), swindle, trick

deft able, adept, adroit, agile, clever, dexterous, expert, handy, neat, nimble, proficient, skilful

defy beard, brave, challenge,

confront, contemn, dare, despise, disregard, face, flout, hurl defiance at, provoke, scorn, slight, spurn

degenerate 1. adj. base, corrupt, debased, debauched, decadent, degenerated, degraded, depraved, deteriorated, dissolute, fallen, immoral, low, mean, perverted **2.** v. decay, decline, decrease, deteriorate, fall off, lapse, regress, retrogress, rot, sink, slip, worsen

degrade cheapen, corrupt, debase, demean, deteriorate, discredit, disgrace, dishonour, humble, humiliate, impair, injure, pervert, shame, vitiate
Antonyms dignify, enhance, ennoble, honour, improve

degree 1. class, grade, level, order, position, rank, standing, station, status **2.** calibre, extent, intensity, level, measure, proportion, quality, quantity, range, rate, ratio, scale, scope, severity, standard

dejected blue, cast down, crestfallen, depressed, despondent, disconsolate, disheartened, dismal, doleful, down, downcast, downhearted, gloomy, glum, low, low-spirited, melancholy, miserable, morose, sad, woebegone, wretched
Antonyms blithe, cheerful, encouraged, happy, joyous, light-hearted

delay v. **1.** defer, hold over, postpone, procrastinate, prolong, protract, put off, shelve, stall, suspend, table, temporize ~n. **2.** deferment, postponement, procrastination, stay, suspension **3.** check, detention, hindrance, hold-up, impediment, interruption, interval, obstruction, setback, stoppage, wait
Antonyms accelerate, precipitate, press, promote, urge

delegate n. agent, ambassador, commissioner, deputy, envoy, legate, representative, vicar

delegation commission, contin-

gent, deputation, embassy, envoys, legation, mission

delete blot out, blue-pencil, cancel, cross out, cut out, dele, edit, edit out, efface, erase, expunge, obliterate, remove, rub out, strike out

deliberate 1. v. cogitate, consider, consult, debate, discuss, meditate, mull over, ponder, reflect, think, weigh **2.** adj. calculated, conscious, considered, designed, intentional, planned, prearranged, premeditated, purposeful, studied, thoughtful, wilful
Antonyms adj. accidental, inadvertent, unconscious, unintended, unpremeditated, unthinking

deliberation calculation, care, carefulness, caution, circumspection, cogitation, consideration, coolness, forethought, meditation, prudence, purpose, reflection, speculation, study, thought, wariness

delicacy 1. accuracy, daintiness, elegance, exquisiteness, fineness, lightness, nicety, precision, subtlety **2.** discrimination, fastidiousness, finesse, purity, refinement, sensibility, sensitiveness, sensitivity, tact, taste **3.** bonne bouche, dainty, luxury, relish, savoury, titbit, treat

delicate 1. ailing, debilitated, flimsy, fragile, frail, sickly, slender, slight, tender, weak **2.** accurate, deft, detailed, minute, precise, skilled **3.** considerate, diplomatic, discreet, sensitive, tactful **4.** critical, difficult, precarious, sensitive, sticky (Inf.), ticklish, touchy
Antonyms harsh, healthy, inconsiderate, insensitive, strong

delicately carefully, daintily, deftly, elegantly, exquisitely, fastidiously, finely, gracefully, lightly, precisely, sensitively, skilfully, softly, subtly, tactfully

delicious ambrosial, appetizing, choice, dainty, delectable, luscious, mouthwatering, nectareous, palatable, savoury, scrumptious (*Inf.*), tasty, toothsome, yummy (*Sl.*)

delight 1. *n.* ecstasy, enjoyment, felicity, gladness, gratification, happiness, joy, pleasure, rapture, transport **2.** *v.* amuse, charm, cheer, divert, enchant, gratify, please, ravish, rejoice, satisfy, thrill
Antonyms *n.* disapprobation, disfavour, dislike, displeasure, dissatisfaction, distaste ~*v.* disgust, displease, dissatisfy, gall, irk, offend, upset, vex

delighted captivated, charmed, ecstatic, elated, enchanted, gladdened, happy, joyous, jubilant, overjoyed, pleased, thrilled

delightful agreeable, amusing, captivating, charming, congenial, delectable, enchanting, engaging, enjoyable, entertaining, fascinating, gratifying, heavenly, pleasant, pleasing, pleasurable, rapturous, ravishing, thrilling
Antonyms disagreeable, displeasing, distasteful, nasty, unpleasant

deliver 1. bear, bring, carry, cart, convey, distribute, transport **2.** cede, commit, give up, grant, hand over, make over, relinquish, resign, surrender, transfer, turn over, yield **3.** acquit, discharge, emancipate, free, liberate, loose, ransom, redeem, release, rescue, save

delivery 1. consignment, conveyance, dispatch, distribution, handing over, surrender, transfer, transmission, transmittal **2.** deliverance, escape, liberation, release, rescue

delude bamboozle (*Inf.*), beguile, cheat, con (*Sl.*), cozen, deceive, dupe, fool, gull (*Archaic*), hoax, hoodwink, impose on, lead up the garden path (*Inf.*), misguide, mislead, take in (*Inf.*), trick

deluge *n.* cataclysm, downpour, flood, inundation, overflowing, spate, torrent

de luxe choice, costly, elegant, exclusive, expensive, grand, luxurious, opulent, palatial, plush

(*Inf.*), rich, select, special, splendid, sumptuous, superior

demand *v.* **1.** ask, challenge, inquire, interrogate, question, request **2.** call for, cry out for, involve, necessitate, need, require, take, want ~*n.* **3.** bidding, charge, inquiry, interrogation, order, question, request, requisition
Antonyms *v.* come up with, contribute, furnish, give, grant, produce, provide, supply, yield

demanding challenging, difficult, exacting, exhausting, exigent, hard, taxing, tough, trying, wearing
Antonyms a piece of cake (*Inf.*), child's play (*Inf.*), easy, effortless, facile, no bother, painless, simple, straightforward, uncomplicated, undemanding

demeanour air, bearing, behaviour, carriage, comportment, conduct, deportment, manner, mien

democracy commonwealth, government by the people, representative government, republic

democratic autonomous, egalitarian, popular, populist, representative, republican, self-governing

demolish 1. bulldoze, destroy, dismantle, flatten, knock down, level, overthrow, pulverize, raze, ruin, tear down **2.** *Fig.* annihilate, defeat, destroy, overthrow, overturn, undo, wreck
Antonyms build, construct, create, repair, restore, strengthen

demonstrable attestable, axiomatic, certain, evident, evincible, incontrovertible, indubitable, irrefutable, obvious, palpable, positive, provable, self-evident, undeniable, unmistakable, verifiable

demonstrate 1. display, establish, evidence, evince, exhibit, indicate, manifest, prove, show, testify to **2.** describe, explain, illustrate, make clear, show how, teach **3.** march, parade, picket, protest, rally

demonstration 1. affirmation, confirmation, display, evidence, exhibition, expression, illustration, manifestation, proof, substantiation, testimony, validation **2.** description, explanation, exposition, presentation, test, trial **3.** march, mass lobby, parade, picket, protest, rally, sit-in

demure decorous, diffident, grave, modest, reserved, reticent, retiring, sedate, shy, sober, staid, unassuming
Antonyms brash, brazen, forward, immodest, impudent, shameless

den 1. cave, cavern, haunt, hideout, hole, lair, shelter **2.** cloister, cubbyhole, hideaway, retreat, sanctuary, sanctum, snuggery, study

denial adjuration, contradiction, disavowal, disclaimer, dismissal, dissent, negation, prohibition, rebuff, refusal, rejection, renunciation, repudiation, repulse, retraction, veto
Antonyms acknowledgment, admission, affirmation, avowal, confession, declaration, disclosure, divulgence, profession, revelation

denomination 1. belief, communion, creed, persuasion, religious group, school, sect **2.** grade, size, unit, value

denote betoken, designate, express, imply, import, indicate, mark, mean, show, signify, typify

denounce accuse, arraign, attack, brand, castigate, censure, condemn, declaim against, decry, denunciate, impugn, proscribe, revile, stigmatize, vilify

dense close, close-knit, compact, compressed, condensed, heavy, impenetrable, opaque, solid, substantial, thick, thickset
Antonyms light, scattered, sparse, thin, transparent

dent 1. *n.* chip, concavity, crater, depression, dimple, dip, hollow, impression, indentation, pit **2.** *v.*

depress, dint, gouge, hollow, imprint, make a dent in, make concave, press in, push in

deny 1. contradict, disagree with, disprove, gainsay, oppose, rebuff, refute **2.** abjure, disavow, discard, disclaim, disown, recant, renounce, repudiate, revoke
Antonyms acknowledge, admit, affirm, agree, concede, confirm, recognize

depart absent (oneself), decamp, disappear, escape, exit, go, go away, leave, make tracks, quit, remove, retire, retreat, set forth, start out, take (one's) leave, vanish, withdraw
Antonyms arrive, remain, show up (*Inf.*), stay, turn up

department 1. district, division, province, region, sector **2.** branch, bureau, division, office, section, station, subdivision, unit **3.** area, domain, function, line, province, realm, responsibility, speciality, sphere

departure 1. exit, exodus, going, going away, leave-taking, leaving, removal, retirement, withdrawal **2.** branching out, change, difference, innovation, novelty, shift
Antonyms advent, appearance, arrival, coming, entrance, return

depend 1. bank on, build upon, calculate on, confide in, count on, lean on, reckon on, rely upon, trust in, turn to **2.** be based on, be contingent on, be determined by, be subject to, be subordinate to, hang on, hinge on, rest on, revolve around

dependent *adj.* **1.** counting on, defenceless, helpless, immature, reliant, relying on, vulnerable, weak **2.** conditional, contingent, depending, determined by, liable to, relative, subject to
Antonyms autarkic, autonomous, independent, self-determining, self-governing, self-reliant

deplete bankrupt, consume, decrease, drain, empty, evacuate, exhaust, expend, impoverish, lessen, milk, reduce, use up

Antonyms add to, augment, enhance, expand, increase, raise, step up (*Inf.*), swell

deplorable 1. calamitous, dire, disastrous, distressing, grievous, heartbreaking, lamentable, melancholy, miserable, pitiable, regrettable, sad, unfortunate, wretched 2. blameworthy, disgraceful, dishonourable, disreputable, execrable, opprobrious, reprehensible, scandalous, shameful
Antonyms A1 (*Inf.*), admirable, bad (*Sl.*), brilliant, excellent, fantastic, great (*Inf.*), laudable, marvellous, notable, outstanding, praiseworthy, super (*Inf.*), superb

deplore 1. bemoan, bewail, grieve for, lament, mourn, regret, rue, sorrow over 2. abhor, censure, condemn, denounce, deprecate, disapprove of, object to

depose break, cashier, degrade, demote, dethrone, dismiss, displace, downgrade, oust, remove from office

deposit 1. *v.* drop, lay, locate, place, precipitate, put, settle, sit down 2. *n.* down payment, instalment, money (*in bank*), part payment, pledge, retainer, security, stake, warranty

depot 1. depository, repository, storehouse, warehouse 2. *Military* arsenal, dump 3. bus station, garage, terminus

depraved abandoned, corrupt, debased, debauched, degenerate, degraded, dissolute, evil, immoral, lascivious, lewd, licentious, perverted, profligate, shameless, sinful, vicious, vile, wicked
Antonyms chaste, decent, ethical, good, honourable, innocent, moral, principled, proper, pure, upright, virtuous, wholesome

depreciate decrease, deflate, devaluate, devalue, lessen, lose value, lower, reduce
Antonyms add to, augment, appreciate, enhance, enlarge, expand, grow, increase, rise

depreciation 1. deflation, depression, devaluation, drop, fall, slump 2. belittlement, deprecation, derogation, detraction, disparagement, pejoration

depress cast down, chill, damp, daunt, deject, desolate, discourage, dishearten, dispirit, make despondent, oppress, sadden, weigh down
Antonyms cheer, elate, hearten, strengthen, uplift

depressed blue, crestfallen, dejected, despondent, discouraged, dispirited, down, downcast, downhearted, down in the dumps (*Inf.*), fed up, glum, low, low-spirited, melancholy, moody, morose, pessimistic, sad, unhappy

depressing black, bleak, daunting, dejecting, depressive, discouraging, disheartening, dismal, dispiriting, distressing, dreary, gloomy, heartbreaking, hopeless, melancholy, sad, saddening, sombre

depression 1. dejection, despair, despondency, dolefulness, downheartedness, dumps (*Inf.*), gloominess, hopelessness, low spirits, melancholia, melancholy, sadness, the blues 2. *Commerce* dullness, economic decline, hard or bad times, inactivity, lowness, recession, slump, stagnation

deprive bereave, despoil, dispossess, divest, expropriate, rob, strip, wrest

deprived bereft, denuded, destitute, disadvantaged, forlorn, in need, in want, lacking, necessitous, needy, poor
Antonyms born with a silver spoon in one's mouth, favoured, fortunate, golden, happy, having a charmed life, lucky, prosperous, sitting pretty (*Inf.*), successful, well-off

depth 1. abyss, deepness, drop, extent, measure, profoundness, profundity 2. *Often plural* abyss, bowels of the earth, deepest (furthest, innermost, most intense, remotest) part, middle, midst, slough of despond

Antonyms (*sense 1*) apex, apogee, crest, crown, height, peak, pinnacle, summit, top, vertex, zenith

deputation commission, delegates, delegation, deputies, embassy, envoys, legation

deputize act for, stand in for, take the place of, understudy

deputy *n.* agent, ambassador, commissioner, delegate, legate, lieutenant, nuncio, proxy, representative, second-in-command, substitute, surrogate, vicegerent

deranged berserk, crazed, crazy, delirious, demented, distracted, frantic, frenzied, insane, irrational, lunatic, mad, maddened, unbalanced, unhinged

derelict *adj.* abandoned, deserted, dilapidated, discarded, forsaken, neglected, ruined

deride chaff, contemn, detract, disdain, disparage, flout, gibe, insult, jeer, knock (*Inf.*), mock, pooh-pooh, ridicule, scoff, scorn, sneer, taunt

derivation ancestry, basis, beginning, descent, etymology, foundation, genealogy, origin, root, source

derive collect, deduce, draw, elicit, extract, follow, gain, gather, get, glean, infer, obtain, procure, receive, trace

descend 1. alight, dismount, drop, fall, go down, move down, plummet, plunge, sink, subside, tumble 2. dip, gravitate, incline, slant, slope 3. be handed down, be passed down, derive, issue, originate, proceed, spring

Antonyms ascend, climb, go up, mount, rise, scale, soar

descent 1. coming down, drop, fall, plunge, swoop 2. ancestry, extraction, family tree, genealogy, heredity, lineage, origin, parentage

describe characterize, define, depict, detail, explain, express, illustrate, narrate, portray, recount, relate, report, specify, tell

description account, characterization, delineation, depiction, detail, explanation, narration, narrative, portrayal, report, representation, sketch

desert[1] 1. *n.* solitude, waste, wasteland, wilderness, wilds 2. *adj.* arid, bare, barren, desolate, infertile, lonely, solitary, uncultivated, uninhabited, unproductive, untilled, waste, wild

desert[2] *v.* abandon, abscond, betray, decamp, defect, forsake, give up, go over the hill (*Military sl.*), jilt, leave, leave high and dry, leave (someone) in the lurch, leave stranded, maroon, quit, rat (on), relinquish, renounce, resign, run out on (*Inf.*), strand, throw over, vacate, walk out on (*Inf.*)

Antonyms be a source of strength to, look after, maintain, provide for, succour, sustain, take care of

deserted abandoned, bereft, cast off, derelict, desolate, empty, forlorn, forsaken, godforsaken, isolated, left in the lurch, left stranded, lonely, neglected, solitary, unfriended, unoccupied, vacant

deserter absconder, apostate, defector, escapee, fugitive, rat (*Inf.*), renegade, runaway, traitor, truant

deserve be entitled to, be worthy of, earn, gain, justify, merit, procure, rate, warrant, win

deserved appropriate, condign, due, earned, fair, fitting, just, justifiable, justified, meet (*Archaic*), merited, proper, right, rightful, suitable, warranted, well-earned

design *v.* 1. delineate, describe, draft, draw, outline, plan, sketch, trace ~*n.* 2. blueprint, delineation, draft, drawing, model, outline, plan, scheme, sketch ~*v.* 3. conceive, create, fabricate, fashion, invent, originate, think up 4. aim, contrive, destine, devise, intend, make, mean, plan, project, propose, purpose, scheme, tailor ~*n.* 5. aim, end, goal, intent,

intention, meaning, object, objective, point, purport, purpose,
target, view

designation denomination, description, epithet, label, name,
name, title

designer architect, artificer,
couturier, creator, deviser, inventor, originator, stylist

desirable 1. advantageous, advisable, agreeable, beneficial,
covetable, eligible, enviable,
good, pleasing, preferable, profitable, worthwhile 2. adorable,
alluring, attractive, fascinating,
fetching, seductive, sexy (*Inf.*)
Antonyms disagreeable, distasteful, unacceptable, unappealing, unattractive, undesirable, unpleasant, unpopular,
unsexy (*Inf.*)

desire v. 1. aspire to, covet,
crave, desiderate, fancy, hanker
after, long for, set one's heart on,
want, wish for, yearn for ~n. 2.
appetite, aspiration, craving,
hankering, longing, need, want,
wish, yearning, yen (*Inf.*) ~v. 3.
ask, entreat, importune, petition,
request, solicit ~n. 4. appetite,
concupiscence, lasciviousness,
lechery, libido, lust, lustfulness,
passion

desist abstain, break off, cease,
discontinue, end, forbear, give
over (*Inf.*), give up, have done
with, leave off, pause, refrain
from, stop, suspend

desolate adj. 1. bare, barren,
bleak, desert, dreary, ruined,
solitary, unfrequented, uninhabited, waste, wild 2. abandoned,
bereft, cheerless, comfortless,
companionless, dejected, depressing, despondent, disconsolate, dismal, downcast, forlorn,
forsaken, gloomy, lonely, melancholy, miserable, wretched
Antonyms adj. cheerful, happy,
inhabited, joyous, light-hearted,
populous

desolation destruction, devastation, havoc, ravages, ruin, ruination

despair 1. v. despond, give up,

lose heart, lose hope 2. n. anguish, dejection, depression, des-
peration, despondency, disheart-
enment, gloom, hopelessness,
melancholy, misery, wretchedness

despairing anxious, broken-
hearted, dejected, depressed,
desperate, despondent, disconsolate, downcast, frantic, grief-
stricken, hopeless, inconsolable,
melancholy, miserable, suicidal,
wretched

desperate 1. audacious, dangerous, daring, death-defying, determined, foolhardy, frantic, furious,
hasty, hazardous, headstrong,
impetuous, madcap, precipitate,
rash, reckless, risky, violent, wild
2. despairing, despondent, forlorn, hopeless, inconsolable, irrecoverable, irremediable, irretrievable, wretched

desperately badly, dangerously,
gravely, perilously, seriously, severely

despise abhor, contemn, deride,
detest, disdain, disregard, flout,
loathe, look down on, neglect,
revile, scorn, slight, spurn,
undervalue
Antonyms admire, adore, be
fond of, be keen on, cherish, dig
(*Sl.*), esteem, fancy (*Inf.*), love,
relish, revel in, take to

despite against, even with, in
contempt of, in defiance of, in
spite of, in the face of, in the
teeth of, notwithstanding, regardless of, undeterred by

despondent blue, dejected, depressed, despairing, disconsolate,
discouraged, disheartened, dispirited, doleful, down, downcast,
downhearted, gloomy, glum,
hopeless, in despair, low, low-
spirited, melancholy, miserable,
morose, sad, sorrowful, woebegone, wretched
Antonyms buoyant, cheerful,
cheery, happy, hopeful, glad,
joyful, light-hearted, optimistic

despotism absolutism, autarchy,
autocracy, dictatorship, monoc-

racy, oppression, totalitarianism, tyranny

destination harbour, haven, journey's end, landing-place, resting-place, station, stop, terminus

destined bound, certain, designed, doomed, fated, foreordained, ineluctable, inescapable, inevitable, intended, meant, ordained, predestined, unavoidable

destiny cup, divine decree, doom, fate, fortune, karma, kismet, lot, portion

destitute distressed, down and out, impecunious, impoverished, indigent, insolvent, moneyless, necessitous, needy, on one's uppers, on the breadline (*Inf.*), penniless, penurious, poor, poverty-stricken

destroy annihilate, blow to bits, break down, crush, demolish, desolate, devastate, dismantle, dispatch, eradicate, extinguish, extirpate, gut, kill, ravage, raze, ruin, shatter, slay, smash, torpedo, trash (*Sl.*), waste, wipe out, wreck

destruction annihilation, crushing, demolition, devastation, downfall, end, eradication, extermination, extinction, havoc, liquidation, massacre, overthrow, overwhelming, ruin, ruination, shattering, slaughter, undoing, wreckage, wrecking

destructive baleful, baneful, calamitous, cataclysmic, catastrophic, damaging, deadly, deleterious, detrimental, devastating, fatal, harmful, hurtful, injurious, lethal, noxious, pernicious, ruinous

detach cut off, disconnect, disengage, disentangle, disjoin, disunite, divide, free, isolate, loosen, remove, segregate, separate, sever, tear off, uncouple, unfasten, unhitch
Antonyms attach, bind, connect, fasten

detachment aloofness, coolness, indifference, remoteness, unconcern

detail 1. *n.* aspect, component, count, element, fact, factor, feature, item, particular, point, respect, specific, technicality 2. *v.* allocate, appoint, assign, charge, commission, delegate, detach, send

detailed blow-by-blow, circumstantial, comprehensive, elaborate, exact, exhaustive, full, intricate, itemized, meticulous, minute, particular, particularized, specific, thorough

detain 1. check, delay, hinder, hold up, impede, keep, keep back, retard, slow up (*or* down), stay, stop 2. arrest, confine, hold, intern, restrain

detect 1. ascertain, catch, descry, distinguish, identify, note, notice, observe, recognize, scent, spot 2. catch, disclose, discover, expose, find, reveal, track down, uncover, unmask

detective busy (*Sl.*), C.I.D. man, constable, cop (*Sl.*), copper (*Sl.*), dick (*Sl., chiefly U.S.*), gumshoe (*U.S. sl.*), investigator, private eye, private investigator, sleuth (*Inf.*), tec (*Sl.*)

detention confinement, custody, delay, hindrance, holding back, imprisonment, incarceration, keeping in, quarantine, restraint, withholding

deter caution, check, damp, daunt, debar, discourage, dissuade, frighten, hinder, inhibit from, intimidate, prevent, prohibit, put off, restrain, stop, talk out of

deteriorate 1. corrupt, debase, decline, degenerate, degrade, deprave, depreciate, go downhill (*Inf.*), go to pot, go to the dogs (*Inf.*), impair, injure, lower, slump, spoil, worsen 2. be the worse for wear (*Inf.*), crumble, decay, decline, decompose, disintegrate, ebb, fade, fall apart, lapse, weaken, wear away
Antonyms advance, ameliorate, get better, improve, upgrade

determination backbone, constancy, conviction, dedication, doggedness, drive, firmness, fortitude, indomitability, perseverance, persistence, resoluteness, resolution, resolve, single-mindedness, steadfastness, tenacity, willpower

Antonyms doubt, hesitancy, hesitation, indecision, instability, irresolution, vacillation

determine 1. arbitrate, conclude, decide, end, finish, fix upon, ordain, regulate, settle, terminate 2. ascertain, certify, check, detect, discover, find out, learn, verify, work out

determined bent on, constant, dogged, firm, fixed, intent, persevering, persistent, purposeful, resolute, set on, single-minded, steadfast, strong-minded, strong-willed, tenacious, unflinching, unwavering

deterrent n. check, curb, defensive measures, determent, discouragement, disincentive, hindrance, impediment, obstacle, restraint

Antonyms bait, carrot (Inf.), enticement, incentive, inducement, lure, motivation, spur, stimulus

detest abhor, abominate, despise, dislike intensely, execrate, feel aversion (disgust, hostility, repugnance) towards, hate, loathe, recoil from

Antonyms adore, cherish, dig (Sl.), dote on, love, relish

detour bypass, byway, circuitous route, deviation, diversion, indirect course, roundabout way

detract devaluate, diminish, lessen, lower, reduce, take away from

Antonyms add to, augment, boost, complement, enhance, improve, reinforce, strengthen

detriment damage, disadvantage, disservice, harm, hurt, impairment, injury, loss, mischief, prejudice

detrimental adverse, baleful, damaging, deleterious, destructive, disadvantageous, harmful, inimical, injurious, mischievous, pernicious, prejudicial, unfavourable

Antonyms advantageous, beneficial, efficacious, favourable, good, helpful, salutary

devastate demolish, desolate, despoil, destroy, lay waste, level, pillage, plunder, ravage, raze, ruin, sack, spoil, waste, wreck

devastating caustic, cutting, deadly, destructive, effective, incisive, keen, mordant, overpowering, overwhelming, ravishing, sardonic, satirical, savage, stunning, trenchant, withering

develop 1. advance, cultivate, evolve, flourish, foster, grow, mature, progress, promote, prosper, ripen 2. amplify, augment, broaden, dilate upon, elaborate, enlarge, expand, unfold, work out 3. be a direct result of, break out, come about, ensue, follow, happen, result

development 1. advance, advancement, evolution, expansion, growth, improvement, increase, maturity, progress, progression, spread, unfolding, unravelling 2. change, circumstance, event, happening, incident, issue, occurrence, outcome, phenomenon, result, situation, turn of events, upshot

deviate avert, bend, deflect, depart, differ, digress, diverge, drift, err, part, stray, swerve, turn, turn aside, vary, veer, wander

deviation aberration, alteration, change, deflection, departure, digression, discrepancy, disparity, divergence, fluctuation, inconsistency, irregularity, shift, variance, variation

device 1. apparatus, appliance, contraption, contrivance, gadget, gimmick, gizmo (Sl.), implement, instrument, invention, tool, utensil 2. artifice, design, dodge, expedient, gambit, improvisation, manoeuvre, plan, ploy, project, purpose, ruse, scheme, shift, stratagem, strategy, stunt, trick, wile

devil 1. *Sometimes cap.* Apollyon, archfiend, Beelzebub, Belial, Clootie (*Scot.*), demon, fiend, Lucifer, Old Harry (*Inf.*), Old Nick (*Inf.*), Prince of Darkness, Satan **2.** beast, brute, demon, monster, ogre, rogue, savage, terror, villain

devious calculating, crooked (*Inf.*), deceitful, dishonest, double-dealing, evasive, indirect, insidious, insincere, not straightforward, scheming, sly, surreptitious, treacherous, tricky, underhand, wily

devise arrange, conceive, concoct, construct, contrive, design, dream up, form, formulate, frame, imagine, invent, plan, plot, prepare, project, scheme, think up, work out

devoid barren, bereft, deficient, denuded, destitute, empty, free from, lacking, sans (*Archaic*), vacant, void, wanting, without

devote allot, apply, appropriate, assign, commit, concern oneself, consecrate, dedicate, enshrine, give, occupy oneself, pledge, reserve, set apart

devoted ardent, caring, committed, concerned, constant, dedicated, devout, faithful, fond, loving, loyal, staunch, steadfast, true **Antonyms** disloyal, inconstant, indifferent, uncommitted, undedicated, unfaithful

devour bolt, consume, cram, dispatch, eat, gobble, gorge, gulp, guzzle, polish off (*Inf.*), stuff, swallow, wolf

devout godly, holy, orthodox, pious, prayerful, pure, religious, reverent, saintly **Antonyms** impious, irreligious, irreverent, sacrilegious

dexterity adroitness, artistry, deftness, effortlessness, expertise, facility, finesse, handiness, knack, mastery, neatness, nimbleness, proficiency, skill, smoothness, touch **Antonyms** clumsiness, gaucheness, incompetence, uselessness

diagnose analyse, determine, distinguish, identify, interpret, investigate, pinpoint, pronounce, recognize

diagnosis 1. analysis, examination, investigation, scrutiny **2.** conclusion, interpretation, opinion, pronouncement

diagonal *adj.* angled, catercornered (*U.S. inf.*), cornerways, cross, crossways, crosswise, oblique, slanting

diagonally aslant, at an angle, cornerwise, crosswise, obliquely, on the bias, on the cross

diagram chart, drawing, figure, layout, outline, plan, representation, sketch

dialect accent, idiom, jargon, language, lingo (*Inf.*), localism, patois, pronunciation, provincialism, speech, tongue, vernacular

dialogue 1. colloquy, communication, confabulation, conference, conversation, converse, discourse, discussion, duologue, interlocution **2.** conversation, lines, script, spoken part

diary appointment book, chronicle, daily record, day-to-day account, engagement book, Filofax (*Trademark*), journal

dictate *v.* **1.** read out, say, speak, transmit, utter **2.** command, decree, direct, enjoin, impose, lay down, ordain, order, prescribe, pronounce

dictator absolute ruler, autocrat, despot, oppressor, tyrant

diction 1. expression, language, phraseology, phrasing, style, usage, vocabulary, wording **2.** articulation, delivery, elocution, enunciation, fluency, inflection, intonation, pronunciation, speech

dictionary concordance, encyclopedia, glossary, lexicon, vocabulary, wordbook

die 1. breathe one's last, decease, depart, expire, finish, give up the ghost, hop the twig (*Sl.*), kick the bucket (*Sl.*), pass away, perish, snuff it (*Sl.*) **2.** decay, decline, disappear, dwindle, ebb, end, fade, lapse, pass, sink, subside,

vanish, wane, wilt, wither **3.** break down, fade out *or* away, fail, fizzle out, halt, lose power, peter out, run down, stop
Antonyms be born, begin, build, come to life, exist, flourish, grow, increase, live, survive

die-hard 1. *n.* fanatic, intransigent, old fogy, reactionary, stick-in-the-mud (*Inf.*), ultraconservative, zealot **2.** *adj.* dyed-in-the-wool, immovable, inflexible, intransigent, reactionary, ultraconservative, uncompromising, unreconstructed (*Chiefly U.S.*)

diet 1. *n.* abstinence, dietary, fast, regime, regimen **2.** aliment, comestibles, commons, edibles, fare, food, nourishment, nutriment, provisions, rations, subsistence, sustenance, viands, victuals ~ *v.* **3.** abstain, eat sparingly, fast, lose weight, reduce, slim
Antonyms *v.* get fat, glut, gobble, gormandize, guzzle, indulge, overindulge, pig out (*Sl.*), stuff oneself

differ be dissimilar, be distinct, contradict, contrast, depart from, diverge, run counter to, stand apart, vary
Antonyms accord, acquiesce, coincide, concur, harmonize

difference 1. alteration, change, contrast, deviation, differentiation, discrepancy, disparity, dissimilarity, distinction, distinctness, divergence, diversity, unlikeness, variation, variety **2.** distinction, exception, idiosyncrasy, particularity, peculiarity, singularity **3.** argument, clash, conflict, contention, contrariety, contretemps, controversy, debate, disagreement, discordance, dispute, quarrel, set-to (*Inf.*), strife, tiff, wrangle
Antonyms affinity, agreement, comparability, concordance, conformity, congruence, likeness, relation, resemblance, sameness, similarity, similitude

different 1. altered, at odds, at variance, changed, clashing, contrasting, deviating, discrep-

ant, disparate, dissimilar, divergent, diverse, inconsistent, opposed, unlike **2.** assorted, divers (*Archaic*), diverse, manifold, many, miscellaneous, multifarious, numerous, several, some, sundry, varied, various

differentiate contrast, discern, discriminate, distinguish, make a distinction, mark off, separate, set off *or* apart, tell apart

difficult 1. arduous, burdensome, demanding, formidable, hard, laborious, no picnic (*Inf.*), onerous, painful, strenuous, toilsome, uphill, wearisome **2.** demanding, fastidious, fractious, fussy, hard to please, intractable, obstreperous, perverse, refractory, rigid, tiresome, troublesome, trying, unaccommodating, unamenable, unmanageable
Antonyms accommodating, amenable, co-operative, easy, light, manageable, pleasant

difficulty 1. arduousness, awkwardness, hardship, laboriousness, labour, pain, painfulness, strain, strenuousness, tribulation **2.** deep water, dilemma, distress, embarrassment, fix (*Inf.*), hot water, jam (*Inf.*), mess, perplexity, pickle (*Inf.*), plight, predicament, quandary, spot (*Inf.*), straits, trial, trouble

diffident backward, bashful, constrained, distrustful, doubtful, hesitant, insecure, meek, modest, reluctant, reserved, self-conscious, self-effacing, sheepish, shrinking, shy, suspicious, timid, timorous, unassertive, unassuming, unobtrusive, unsure, withdrawn

dig *v.* **1.** break up, burrow, delve, excavate, gouge, grub, hoe, hollow out, mine, penetrate, pierce, quarry, scoop, till, tunnel, turn over **2.** delve, dig down, go into, investigate, probe, research, search ~ *n.* **3.** jab, poke, prod, punch, thrust **4.** crack (*Sl.*), cutting remark, gibe, insult, jeer, quip, sneer, taunt, wisecrack (*Inf.*)

digest v. 1. absorb, assimilate, concoct, dissolve, incorporate, macerate 2. absorb, assimilate, con, consider, contemplate, grasp, master, meditate, ponder, study, take in, understand

dignified august, decorous, distinguished, exalted, formal, grave, honourable, imposing, lofty, lordly, noble, reserved, solemn, stately, upright
Antonyms crass, inelegant, unbecoming, undignified, unseemly, vulgar

dignitary n. bigwig (Inf.), celeb (Inf.), high-up (Inf.), notability, notable, personage, pillar of society (the church, the state), public figure, V.I.P., worthy

dignity courtliness, decorum, grandeur, gravity, hauteur, loftiness, majesty, nobility, propriety, solemnity, stateliness

digress be diffuse, depart, deviate, diverge, drift, expatiate, get off the point or subject, go off at a tangent, ramble, stray, turn aside, wander

dilapidated battered, broken-down, crumbling, decayed, decaying, decrepit, fallen in, falling apart, gone to wrack and ruin, in ruins, neglected, ramshackle, rickety, ruined, ruinous, run-down, shabby, shaky, tumble-down, uncared for, worn-out

dilemma difficulty, embarrassment, fix (Inf.), jam (Inf.), mess, perplexity, pickle (Inf.), plight, predicament, problem, puzzle, quandary, spot (Inf.), strait, tight corner or spot

diligence activity, application, assiduity, assiduousness, attention, attentiveness, care, constancy, earnestness, heedfulness, industry, intentness, laboriousness, perseverance, sedulousness

diligent active, assiduous, attentive, busy, careful, conscientious, constant, earnest, hard-working, indefatigable, industrious, laborious, painstaking, persevering, persistent, sedulous, studious, tireless

Antonyms careless, dilatory, inconstant, indifferent, lazy

dilute v. adulterate, cut, make thinner, thin (out), water down, weaken
Antonyms concentrate, condense, intensify, strengthen, thicken

dim adj. 1. caliginous (Archaic), cloudy, dark, darkish, dusky, grey, overcast, poorly lit, shadowy, tenebrous, unilluminated 2. bleary, blurred, faint, fuzzy, ill-defined, indistinct, obscured, shadowy, unclear 3. dense, doltish, dull, dumb (Inf.), obtuse, slow, slow on the uptake (Inf.), stupid, thick 4. bedim, blur, cloud, darken, dull, fade, lower, obscure, tarnish, turn down
Antonyms (sense 1) bright, clear, cloudless, fair, limpid, pleasant, sunny, unclouded (sense 2) bright, brilliant, clear, distinct, limpid, palpable (sense 3) acute, astute, aware, brainy, bright, clever, intelligent, keen, quick-witted, sharp, smart

diminish abate, contract, curtail, cut, decrease, lessen, lower, reduce, retrench, shrink, weaken
Antonyms amplify, augment, enhance, enlarge, expand, increase

diminutive adj. bantam, Lilliputian, little, midget, mini, miniature, minute, petite, pocket (-sized), pygmy, small, tiny, undersized, wee

din n. babel, clamour, clangour, clash, clatter, commotion, crash, hubbub, hullabaloo, noise, outcry, pandemonium, racket, row, shout, uproar
Antonyms calm, calmness, hush, peace, quiet, quietness, silence, tranquillity

dingy bedimmed, colourless, dark, dim, dirty, discoloured, drab, dreary, dull, dusky, faded, gloomy, grimy, murky, obscure, seedy, shabby, soiled, sombre, tacky

dinner banquet, beanfeast (Inf.), blowout (Sl.), collation, feast, main meal, meal, refection, repast, spread

dip *v.* 1. bathe, douse, duck, dunk, immerse, plunge, rinse, souse 2. ladle, scoop, spoon 3. *With in or into* draw upon, reach into ~ *n.* 4. douche, drenching, ducking, immersion, plunge, soaking 5. bathe, dive, plunge, swim 6. concoction, dilution, infusion, mixture, preparation, solution, suspension 7. basin, concavity, depression, hole, hollow, incline, slope 8. decline, fall, lowering, sag, slip, slump

diplomacy 1. international negotiation, statecraft, statesmanship 2. artfulness, craft, delicacy, discretion, finesse, savoir faire, skill, subtlety, tact
Antonyms awkwardness, clumsiness, ineptness, tactlessness, thoughtlessness

diplomat conciliator, go-between, mediator, moderator, negotiator, politician, public relations expert, tactician

diplomatic adept, discreet, polite, politic, prudent, sensitive, subtle, tactful
Antonyms impolitic, insensitive, rude, tactless, thoughtless, undiplomatic, unsubtle

dire 1. alarming, appalling, awful, calamitous, cataclysmic, catastrophic, cruel, disastrous, horrible, horrid, ruinous, terrible, woeful 2. dismal, dreadful, fearful, gloomy, grim, ominous, portentous

direct¹ *v.* 1. administer, advise, conduct, control, dispose, govern, guide, handle, lead, manage, mastermind, oversee, preside over, regulate, rule, run, superintend, supervise 2. bid, charge, command, dictate, enjoin, instruct, order 3. guide, indicate, lead, point in the direction of, point the way, show

direct² *adj.* 1. candid, frank, honest, man-to-man, matter-of-fact, open, outspoken, plain-spoken, sincere, straight, straightforward 2. absolute, blunt, categorical,

downright, explicit, express, plain, point-blank, unambiguous, unequivocal 3. nonstop, not crooked, shortest, straight, through, unbroken, undeviating, uninterrupted
Antonyms ambiguous, circuitous, crooked, devious, indirect, mediated, sly, subtle

direction 1. administration, charge, command, control, government, guidance, leadership, management, order, oversight, superintendence, supervision 2. aim, bearing, course, line, path, road, route, track way

directly 1. by the shortest route, exactly, in a beeline, precisely, straight, unswervingly, without deviation 2. candidly, face-to-face, honestly, in person, openly, personally, plainly, point-blank, straightforwardly, truthfully, unequivocally, without prevarication

director administrator, boss (*Inf.*), chairman, chief, controller, executive, governor, head, leader, manager, organizer, principal, producer, supervisor

dirt 1. dust, excrement, filth, grime, grot (*Sl.*), impurity, mire, muck, mud, slime, smudge, stain, tarnish 2. clay, earth, loam, soil

dirty *adj.* 1. begrimed, filthy, foul, grimy, grotty (*Sl.*), grubby, grungy (*Sl., chiefly U.S.*), messy, mucky, muddy, nasty, polluted, soiled, sullied, unclean 2. corrupt, crooked, dishonest, fraudulent, illegal, treacherous, unfair, unscrupulous, unsporting
Antonyms clean, honest, pleasant, reputable, respectable, upright

disability affliction, ailment, complaint, defect, disablement, disorder, handicap, impairment, infirmity, malady

disable cripple, damage, debilitate, enfeeble, hamstring, handicap, immobilize, impair, incapacitate, paralyse, prostrate, put out of action, render *hors de* *combat*, render inoperative, unfit, unman, weaken

disabled bedridden, crippled, handicapped, incapacitated, infirm, lame, maimed, mangled, mutilated, paralysed, weak, weakened, wrecked
Antonyms able-bodied, fit, hale, healthy, hearty, robust, sound, strong, sturdy

disadvantage damage, detriment, disservice, harm, hurt, injury, loss, prejudice
Antonyms advantage, aid, benefit, gain, help

disagree 1. be discordant, be dissimilar, conflict, contradict, counter, depart, deviate, differ, diverge, run counter to, vary 2. argue, bicker, clash, contend, contest, debate, differ (in opinion), dispute, dissent, fall out (*Inf.*), have words (*Inf.*), object, oppose, quarrel, take issue with, wrangle
Antonyms accord, agree, coincide, concur, get on (together), harmonize

disagreeable bad-tempered, brusque, churlish, contrary, cross, difficult, disobliging, ill-natured, irritable, nasty, peevish, rude, surly, unfriendly, ungracious, unlikable, unpleasant
Antonyms agreeable, congenial, delightful, enjoyable, friendly, good-natured, lovely, nice, pleasant

disagreement 1. difference, discrepancy, disparity, dissimilarity, dissimilitude, divergence, diversity, incompatibility, incongruity, unlikeness, variance 2. altercation, argument, clash, conflict, debate, difference, discord, dispute, dissent, division, falling out, misunderstanding, quarrel, squabble, strife, wrangle
Antonyms accord, agreement, correspondence, harmony, similarity, unity

disappear 1. be lost to view, depart, drop out of sight, ebb, escape, evanesce, fade away, flee, fly, go, pass, recede, retire,

vanish from sight, wane, withdraw 2. cease, cease to be known, die out, dissolve, end, evaporate, expire, fade, leave no trace, melt away, pass away, perish, vanish
Antonyms appear, arrive, materialize, reappear

disappearance departure, desertion, disappearing, disappearing trick, eclipse, evanescence, evaporation, fading, flight, going, loss, melting, passing, vanishing, vanishing point

disappoint chagrin, dash, deceive, delude, disenchant, disgruntle, dishearten, disillusion, dismay, dissatisfy, fail, let down, sadden, vex

disappointed balked, cast down, depressed, despondent, discontented, discouraged, disenchanted, disgruntled, disillusioned, dissatisfied, distressed, downhearted, foiled, frustrated, let down, saddened, thwarted, upset
Antonyms content, contented, fulfilled, happy, pleased, satisfied

disappointment chagrin, discontent, discouragement, disenchantment, disillusionment, displeasure, dissatisfaction, distress, failure, frustration, ill-success, mortification, regret, unfulfilment

disapproval censure, condemnation, criticism, denunciation, deprecation, disapprobation, displeasure, dissatisfaction, objection, reproach

disapprove 1. *Often with of* blame, censure, condemn, deplore, deprecate, discountenance, dislike, find unacceptable, frown on, look down one's nose at (*Inf.*), object to, reject, take exception to 2. disallow, set aside, spurn, turn down, veto

disarrange confuse, derange, discompose, disorder, disorganize, disturb, jumble (up), mess (up), scatter, shake (up), shuffle, unsettle, untidy

disarray 1. confusion, discomposure, disharmony, dismay, disorder, disorderliness, disorganization, disunity, indiscipline, unruliness, upset **2.** chaos, clutter, dishevelment, jumble, mess, mix-up, muddle, shambles, tangle, untidiness

Antonyms arrangement, harmony, method, neatness, order, orderliness, organization, pattern, plan, regularity, symmetry, system, tidiness

disaster accident, act of God, adversity, blow, calamity, cataclysm, catastrophe, misadventure, mischance, misfortune, mishap, reverse, ruin, ruination, stroke, tragedy, trouble

disastrous adverse, calamitous, cataclysmal, cataclysmic, catastrophic, destructive, detrimental, devastating, dire, dreadful, fatal, hapless, harmful, ill-fated, ill-starred, ruinous, terrible, tragic, unfortunate, unlucky, unpropitious, untoward

disbelief distrust, doubt, dubiety, incredulity, mistrust, scepticism, unbelief

Antonyms belief, credence, credulity, faith, trust

discard abandon, cast aside, dispense with, dispose of, ditch (*Sl.*), drop, dump (*Inf.*), get rid of, jettison, reject, relinquish, remove, repudiate, scrap, shed, throw away *or* out

Antonyms hang *or* hold on to, hold back, keep, reserve, retain, save

discharge *v.* **1.** absolve, acquit, allow to go, clear, exonerate, free, liberate, pardon, release, set free ~*n.* **2.** acquittal, clearance, exoneration, liberation, pardon, release, remittance ~*v.* **3.** cashier, discard, dismiss, eject, expel, fire, (*Inf.*), give (someone) the sack (*Inf.*), oust, remove, sack (*Inf.*) ~*v.* **4.** detonate, explode, fire, let off, set off, shoot ~*n.* **5.** blast, burst, detonation, discharging, explosion, firing, fusillade, report, salvo, shot, volley ~*v.* **6.** accomplish, carry out, do, execute, fulfil, observe, perform

7. clear, honour, meet, pay, relieve, satisfy, settle, square up

disciple adherent, apostle, believer, catechumen, convert, devotee, follower, learner, partisan, proselyte, pupil, student, supporter, votary

Antonyms guru, leader, master, swami, teacher

disciplinarian authoritarian, despot, drill sergeant, hard master, martinet, stickler, strict teacher, taskmaster, tyrant

discipline *n.* **1.** drill, exercise, method, practice, regimen, regulation, training **2.** conduct, control, orderliness, regulation, restraint, self-control, strictness **3.** castigation, chastisement, correction, punishment ~*v.* **4.** break in, bring up, check, control, drill, educate, exercise, form, govern, instruct, inure, prepare, regulate, restrain, train

disclose broadcast, communicate, confess, divulge, impart, leak, let slip, make known, make public, publish, relate, reveal, spill the beans (*Inf.*), tell, unveil, utter

Antonyms conceal, dissemble, keep secret, secrete

discolour fade, mar, mark, rust, soil, stain, streak, tarnish, tinge

discomfort *n.* ache, annoyance, disquiet, distress, hardship, hurt, inquietude, irritation, malaise, nuisance, pain, soreness, trouble, uneasiness, unpleasantness, vexation

disconcert abash, agitate, bewilder, discompose, disturb, flurry, fluster, nonplus, perplex, perturb, put out of countenance, rattle (*Inf.*), ruffle, shake up (*Inf.*), take aback, throw off balance, trouble, unbalance, unsettle, upset, worry

disconcerting alarming, awkward, baffling, bewildering, bothersome, confusing, dismaying, distracting, disturbing, embarrassing, off-putting (*Brit. inf.*), perplexing, upsetting

disconnect cut off, detach, disengage, divide, part, separate, sever, take apart, uncouple

disconsolate crushed, dejected, desolate, despairing, forlorn, gloomy, grief-stricken, heart-broken, hopeless, inconsolable, melancholy, miserable, sad, unhappy, woeful, wretched

discontinue abandon, break off, cease, drop, end, finish, give up, halt, interrupt, leave off, pause, put an end to, quit, refrain from, stop, suspend, terminate

discord 1. clashing, conflict, contention, difference, disagreement, discordance, dispute, dissension, disunity, division, friction, incompatibility, lack of concord, opposition, rupture, strife, variance, wrangling **2.** cacophony, din, disharmony, dissonance, harshness, jangle, jarring, racket, tumult
Antonyms accord, agreement, concord, euphony, friendship, harmony, melody, peace, tunefulness, understanding, unity

discount *v.* **1.** brush off, disbelieve, disregard, ignore, leave out of account, overlook, pass over **2.** deduct, lower, mark down, rebate, reduce, take off ~*n.* **3.** abatement, allowance, concession, cut, cut price, deduction, drawback, percentage (*Inf.*), rebate, reduction

discourage abash, awe, cast down, cow, damp, dampen, dash, daunt, deject, demoralize, depress, dishearten, dismay, dispirit, frighten, intimidate, overawe, put a damper on, scare, unman, unnerve

discouraged crestfallen, dashed, daunted, deterred, disheartened, dismayed, dispirited, downcast, down in the mouth, glum, pessimistic, put off

discouragement cold feet (*Inf.*), dejection, depression, despair, despondency, disappointment, discomfiture, dismay, downheartedness, hopelessness, loss of confidence, low spirits, pessimism

discouraging dampening, daunting, depressing, disappointing, disheartening, dispiriting, offputting (*Brit. inf.*), unfavourable, unpropitious

discourse 1. *n.* chat, communication, conversation, converse, dialogue, discussion, speech, talk **2.** *v.* confer, converse, debate, declaim, discuss, expatiate, hold forth, speak, talk

discourteous abrupt, bad-mannered, boorish, brusque, curt, disrespectful, ill-bred, ill-mannered, impolite, insolent, offhand, rude, uncivil, uncourteous, ungentlemanly, ungracious, unmannerly
Antonyms civil, courteous, courtly, gracious, mannerly, polite, respectful, well-mannered

discover 1. bring to light, come across, come upon, dig up, find, light upon, locate, turn up, uncover, unearth **2.** ascertain, descry, detect, determine, discern, disclose, espy, find out, get wise to (*Inf.*), learn, notice, perceive, realize, recognize, reveal, see, spot, turn up, uncover

discovery 1. ascertainment, detection, disclosure, espial, exploration, finding, introduction, locating, location, origination, revelation, uncovering **2.** bonanza, breakthrough, coup, find, findings, godsend, innovation, invention, secret

discreet careful, cautious, circumspect, considerate, diplomatic, discerning, guarded, judicious, politic, prudent, reserved, sagacious, sensible, tactful, wary
Antonyms incautious, indiscreet, injudicious, rash, tactless, undiplomatic, unthinking, unwise

discrepancy conflict, contrariety, difference, disagreement, discordance, disparity, dissimilarity, dissonance, divergence, incongruity, inconsistency, variance, variation

discretion acumen, care, carefulness, caution, circumspection, consideration, diplomacy, dis-

cernment, good sense, heedful~
ness, judgment, judiciousness,
maturity, prudence, sagacity,
tact, wariness
Antonyms carelessness, indis~
cretion, insensitivity, rashness,
tactlessness, thoughtlessness
discriminate 1. disfavour, favour,
show bias, show prejudice, single
out, treat as inferior, treat differ~
ently, victimize **2.** assess, differ~
entiate, discern, distinguish, draw
a distinction, evaluate, segregate,
separate, sift, tell the difference
discriminating acute, astute,
critical, cultivated, discerning,
fastidious, keen, particular, re~
fined, selective, sensitive, tasteful
Antonyms careless, desultory,
general, hit or miss (*Inf.*), indis~
criminate, random, undiscrimi~
nating, unselective, unsystematic
discrimination bias, bigotry, fa~
vouritism, inequity, intolerance,
prejudice, unfairness
discuss argue, confer, consider,
consult with, converse, debate,
deliberate, examine, exchange
views on, get together (*Inf.*), go
into, reason about, review, sift,
talk about, thrash out, ventilate,
weigh up the pros and cons
discussion analysis, argument,
colloquy, confabulation, confer~
ence, consideration, consultation,
conversation, debate, delibera~
tion, dialogue, discourse, exami~
nation, exchange, review, scruti~
ny, symposium
disdain *n.* arrogance, contempt,
contumely, derision, dislike,
haughtiness, hauteur, indiffer~
ence, scorn, sneering, snobbish~
ness, superciliousness
disease affliction, ailment, com~
plaint, condition, disorder, ill
health, illness, indisposition, in~
fection, infirmity, malady, sick~
ness, upset
diseased ailing, infected, rotten,
sick, sickly, tainted, unhealthy,
unsound, unwell, unwholesome
disembark alight, arrive, get off,
go ashore, land, step out of
disentangle detach, disconnect,

disengage, extricate, free, loose,
separate, sever, unfold, unravel,
unsnarl, untangle, untwist
disfavour disapprobation, disap~
proval, dislike, displeasure
disfigure blemish, damage, de~
face, deform, disfeature, distort,
injure, maim, make ugly, mar,
mutilate, scar
disgrace *n.* **1.** baseness, degrada~
tion, dishonour, disrepute, igno~
miny, infamy, odium, oppro~
brium, shame **2.** aspersion,
blemish, blot, defamation, re~
proach, scandal, slur, stain, stig~
ma **3.** contempt, discredit, dises~
teem, disfavour, obloquy ~*v.* **4.**
abase, bring shame upon, de~
fame, degrade, discredit, disfa~
vour, dishonour, disparage, hu~
miliate, reproach, shame, slur,
stain, stigmatization, sully, taint
Antonyms *n.* credit, esteem, fa~
vour, grace, honour, repute ~*v.*
credit, grace, honour
disgraceful blameworthy, con~
temptible, degrading, detestable,
discreditable, dishonourable, dis~
reputable, ignominious, infa~
mous, low, mean, opprobrious,
scandalous, shameful, shocking,
unworthy
disgruntled annoyed, cheesed off
(*Brit. sl.*), discontented, dis~
pleased, dissatisfied, grumpy, ir~
ritated, malcontent, peeved,
peevish, petulant, pissed off (*Sl.*),
put out, sulky, sullen, testy, vexed
disguise *v.* **1.** camouflage, cloak,
conceal, cover, hide, mask,
screen, secrete, shroud, veil **2.**
deceive, dissemble, dissimulate,
fake, falsify, fudge, gloss over,
misrepresent ~*n.* **3.** camouflage,
cloak, costume, cover, get-up
(*Inf.*), mask, screen, veil
disgust 1. *v.* cause aversion, dis~
please, fill with loathing, nau~
seate, offend, outrage, put off,
repel, revolt, sicken, turn one's
stomach **2.** *n.* abhorrence,
abomination, antipathy, aversion,
detestation, dislike, distaste,
hatefulness, hatred, loathing,

nausea, repugnance, repulsion, revulsion

Antonyms *v.* delight, impress, please ~*n.* liking, love, pleasure, satisfaction, taste

disgusted appalled, nauseated, offended, outraged, repelled, repulsed, scandalized, sick and tired of (*Inf.*), sickened, sick of (*Inf.*)

disgusting abominable, detestable, distasteful, foul, gross, grotty (*Sl.*), hateful, loathsome, nasty, nauseating, nauseous, objectionable, obnoxious, odious, offensive, repellent, repugnant, revolting, shameless, sickening, stinking, vile, vulgar

dish *n.* 1. bowl, plate, platter, salver 2. fare, food, recipe

dishearten cast down, crush, damp, dampen, dash, daunt, deject, depress, deter, discourage, dismay, dispirit, put a damper on

Antonyms cheer up, buck up (*Inf.*), encourage, hearten, lift, perk up, rally

dishonest bent (*Sl.*), cheating, corrupt, crafty, crooked (*Inf.*), deceitful, deceiving, deceptive, designing, disreputable, doubledealing, false, fraudulent, guileful, knavish (*Archaic*), lying, mendacious, perfidious, shady (*Inf.*), swindling, treacherous, unfair, unprincipled, unscrupulous, untrustworthy, untruthful

Antonyms honest, honourable, law-abiding, lawful, principled, true, trustworthy, upright

dishonesty cheating, chicanery, corruption, craft, criminality, crookedness, deceit, duplicity, falsehood, falsity, fraud, fraudulence, graft, improbity, mendacity, perfidy, sharp practice, stealing, treachery, trickery, unscrupulousness, wiliness

dishonour 1. *v.* abase, blacken, corrupt, debase, debauch, defame, degrade, discredit, disgrace, shame, sully 2. *n.* abasement, degradation, discredit, disfavour, disgrace, disrepute, ignominy, infamy, obloquy, odium,

opprobrium, reproach, scandal, shame

Antonyms *v.* esteem, exalt, respect, revere, worship ~*n.* decency, goodness, honour, integrity, morality, principles, rectitude

dishonourable base, contemptible, despicable, discreditable, disgraceful, ignoble, ignominious, infamous, scandalous, shameful

disillusioned disabused, disappointed, disenchanted, enlightened, indifferent, out of love, sadder and wiser, undeceived

disinclination alienation, antipathy, aversion, demur, dislike, hesitance, lack of desire, lack of enthusiasm, loathness, objection, opposition, reluctance, repugnance, resistance, unwillingness

disinclined antipathetic, averse, balking, hesitating, indisposed, loath, not in the mood, opposed, reluctant, resistant, unwilling

disinfect clean, cleanse, decontaminate, deodorize, fumigate, purify, sanitize, sterilize

disinfectant antiseptic, germicide, sanitizer, sterilizer

disinherit cut off, cut off without a penny, disown, dispossess, oust, repudiate

disintegrate break apart, break up, crumble, disunite, fall apart, fall to pieces, reduce to fragments, separate, shatter, splinter

disinterested candid, detached, dispassionate, equitable, evenhanded, free from self-interest, impartial, impersonal, neutral, outside, unbiased, uninvolved, unprejudiced, unselfish

Antonyms biased, involved, partial, prejudiced, selfish

dislike 1. *n.* animosity, animus, antagonism, antipathy, aversion, detestation, disapprobation, disapproval, disgust, disinclination, displeasure, distaste, enmity, hatred, hostility, loathing, repugnance 2. *v.* abhor, abominate, be averse to, despise, detest, disapprove, disfavour, disrelish, hate, have no taste *or* stomach for, loathe, not be able to bear *or* abide, object to, scorn, shun

Antonyms *n.* admiration, attraction, delight, esteem, inclination, liking ~ *v.* esteem, favour, like

disloyal apostate, disaffected, faithless, false, perfidious, seditious, subversive, traitorous, treacherous, treasonable, two-faced, unfaithful, unpatriotic, untrustworthy

Antonyms constant, dependable, dutiful, faithful, loyal, steadfast, true, trustworthy, trusty

disloyalty betrayal of trust, breach of trust, breaking of faith, deceitfulness, double-dealing, falseness, falsity, inconstancy, infidelity, perfidy, Punic faith, treachery, treason, unfaithfulness

dismal black, bleak, cheerless, dark, depressing, despondent, discouraging, dolorous, dreary, forlorn, funereal, gloomy, gruesome, lonesome, lowering, lugubrious, melancholy, sad, sombre, sorrowful

Antonyms bright, cheerful, cheery, glad, happy, joyful, light-hearted, sunny

dismay 1. *v.* affright, alarm, appal, distress, fill with consternation, frighten, horrify, paralyse, scare, terrify, unnerve **2.** *n.* agitation, alarm, anxiety, apprehension, consternation, distress, dread, fear, fright, horror, panic, terror, trepidation

dismiss 1. axe (*Inf.*), cashier, discharge, fire (*Inf.*), give notice to, lay off, oust, remove, sack (*Inf.*), send packing (*Inf.*) **2.** disband, disperse, dissolve, free, let go, release, send away

dismissal 1. adjournment, congé, end, freedom to depart, permission to go, release **2.** discharge, expulsion, marching orders (*Inf.*), notice, one's books *or* cards, removal, the boot (*Sl.*), the heave-ho (*Sl.*), the push (*Sl.*), the sack (*Inf.*)

disobedience indiscipline, infraction, insubordination, mutiny,

noncompliance, nonobservance, recalcitrance, revolt, unruliness, waywardness

disobedient contrary, contumacious, defiant, disorderly, froward, insubordinate, intractable, mischievous, naughty, noncompliant, nonobservant, obstreperous, refractory, undisciplined, unruly, wayward, wilful

Antonyms biddable, compliant, dutiful, manageable, obedient, submissive, well-behaved

disobey contravene, defy, disregard, flout, go counter to, ignore, infringe, overstep, rebel, refuse to obey, resist, transgress, violate

disorderly 1. chaotic, confused, disorganized, higgledy-piggledy (*Inf.*), indiscriminate, irregular, jumbled, messy, shambolic (*Inf.*), unsystematic, untidy **2.** boisterous, disruptive, indisciplined, lawless, obstreperous, rebellious, refractory, riotous, rowdy, stormy, tumultuous, turbulent, ungovernable, unlawful, unmanageable, unruly

Antonyms arranged, neat, orderly, organized, tidy

disown abandon, abnegate, cast off, deny, disallow, disavow, disclaim, refuse to acknowledge *or* recognize, reject, renounce, repudiate

dispassionate calm, collected, composed, cool, imperturbable, moderate, quiet, serene, sober, temperate, unemotional, unexcitable, unexcited, unmoved, unruffled

Antonyms ardent, emotional, excited, fervent, impassioned, intense, passionate

dispatch, despatch 1. *v.* conclude, discharge, dispose of, expedite, finish, make short work of (*Inf.*), perform, settle **2.** *n.* account, bulletin, communication, communiqué, document, instruction, item, letter, message, missive, news, piece, report, story

dispense 1. allocate, allot, apportion, assign, deal out, disburse, distribute, dole out, mete out, share 2. administer, apply, carry out, direct, discharge, enforce, execute, implement, operate, undertake

disperse 1. broadcast, circulate, diffuse, disseminate, dissipate, distribute, scatter, spread, strew 2. break up, disappear, disband, dismiss, dispel, dissolve, rout, scatter, send off, separate, vanish Antonyms amass, assemble, collect, concentrate, congregate, convene, gather, muster, pool

dispirited crestfallen, dejected, depressed, despondent, discouraged, disheartened, down, downcast, gloomy, glum, in the doldrums, low, morose, sad

displace 1. derange, disarrange, disturb, misplace, move, shift, transpose 2. crowd out, oust, replace, succeed, supersede, supplant, take the place of

display v. 1. betray, demonstrate, disclose, evidence, evince, exhibit, expose, manifest, open, open to view, present, reveal, show, unveil 2. expand, extend, model, open out, spread out, stretch out, unfold, unfurl ~n. 3. array, demonstration, exhibition, exposition, exposure, manifestation, presentation, revelation, show 4. flourish, ostentation, pageant, parade, pomp, show, spectacle
Antonyms v. conceal, cover, hide, keep dark, keep secret, mask, secrete, veil

displease aggravate (Inf.), anger, annoy, disgust, dissatisfy, exasperate, gall, incense, irk, irritate, nettle, offend, pique, provoke, put out, rile, upset, vex

displeasure anger, annoyance, disapprobation, disapproval, disfavour, disgruntlement, dislike, dissatisfaction, distaste, indignation, irritation, offence, pique, resentment, vexation, wrath
Antonyms approval, endorsement, pleasure, satisfaction

disposal 1. clearance, discarding, dumping (Inf.), ejection, jettison-

ing, parting with, relinquishment, removal, riddance, scrapping, throwing away 2. arrangement, array, dispensation, disposition, distribution, grouping, placing, position

dispose adjust, arrange, array, determine, distribute, fix, group, marshal, order, place, put, range, rank, regulate, set, settle, stand

dispose of 1. deal with, decide, determine, end, finish with, settle 2. bestow, give, make over, part with, sell, transfer 3. destroy, discard, dump (Inf.), get rid of, jettison, scrap, throw out or away, unload

disposition character, constitution, make-up, nature, spirit, temper, temperament

disproportion asymmetry, discrepancy, disparity, imbalance, inadequacy, inequality, insufficiency, lopsidedness, unevenness, unsuitableness
Antonyms balance, congruity, harmony, proportion, symmetry

disproportionate excessive, incommensurate, inordinate, out of proportion, too much, unbalanced, unequal, uneven, unreasonable

disprove confute, contradict, controvert, discredit, expose, give the lie to, invalidate, negate, prove false, rebut, refute
Antonyms ascertain, bear out, confirm, evince, prove, show, substantiate, verify

dispute v. 1. altercate, argue, brawl, clash, contend, debate, discuss, quarrel, squabble, wrangle 2. challenge, contest, contradict, controvert, deny, doubt, impugn, question ~n. 3. altercation, argument, brawl, conflict, disagreement, discord, disturbance, feud, friction, quarrel, strife, wrangle

disqualification 1. disability, disablement, incapacitation, incapacity, unfitness 2. debarment, disenablement, disentitlement, elimination, exclusion, incompetence, ineligibility, rejection

disqualify 1. disable, incapacitate, invalidate, unfit (*Rare*) **2.** debar, declare ineligible, disentitle, preclude, prohibit, rule out

disquiet *n.* alarm, angst, anxiety, concern, disquietude, distress, disturbance, fear, foreboding, fretfulness, nervousness, restlessness, trouble, uneasiness, unrest, worry

disregard *v.* **1.** brush aside *or* away, discount, disobey, ignore, laugh off, leave out of account, make light of, neglect, overlook, pass over, pay no attention to, pay no heed to, take no notice of, turn a blind eye to **2.** brush off (*Sl.*), cold-shoulder, contemn, despise, disdain, disparage, slight, snub
Antonyms attend, heed, listen to, mind, note, pay attention to, regard, respect, take into consideration, take notice of

disreputable base, contemptible, derogatory, discreditable, disgraceful, dishonourable, disorderly, ignominious, infamous, louche, low, mean, notorious, opprobrious, scandalous, shady (*Inf.*), shameful, shocking, unprincipled, vicious, vile
Antonyms decent, reputable, respectable, respected, upright, worthy

disrepute discredit, disesteem, disfavour, disgrace, dishonour, ignominy, ill favour, ill repute, infamy, obloquy, shame, unpopularity

disrespect contempt, discourtesy, dishonour, disregard, impertinence, impoliteness, impudence, incivility, insolence, irreverence, lack of respect, lesemajesty, rudeness, unmannerliness
Antonyms esteem, regard, respect

disrespectful bad-mannered, cheeky, contemptuous, discourteous, ill-bred, impertinent, impolite, impudent, insolent, insulting, irreverent, misbehaved, rude, uncivil

disrupt agitate, confuse, disorder, disorganize, disturb, spoil, throw into disorder, upset

dissatisfaction annoyance, chagrin, disappointment, discomfort, discontent, dislike, dismay, displeasure, distress, exasperation, frustration, irritation, regret, resentment, unhappiness

dissatisfied disappointed, discontented, disgruntled, displeased, fed up, frustrated, not satisfied, unfulfilled, ungratified, unhappy, unsatisfied
Antonyms content, contented, pleased, satisfied

dissect anatomize, cut up *or* apart, dismember, lay open

disseminate broadcast, circulate, diffuse, disperse, dissipate, distribute, proclaim, promulgate, propagate, publicize, publish, scatter, sow, spread

dissension conflict, conflict of opinion, contention, difference, disagreement, discord, discordance, dispute, dissent, friction, quarrel, strife, variance

dissent 1. *v.* decline, differ, disagree, object, protest, refuse, withhold assent *or* approval **2.** *n.* difference, disagreement, discord, dissension, dissidence, nonconformity, objection, opposition, refusal, resistance

dissertation critique, discourse, disquisition, essay, exposition, thesis, treatise

disservice bad turn, disfavour, harm, ill turn, injury, injustice, unkindness, wrong
Antonyms courtesy, good turn, indulgence, kindness, obligation (*Scot. or Archaic*), service

dissident 1. *adj.* differing, disagreeing, discordant, dissentient, dissenting, heterodox, nonconformist, schismatic **2.** *n.* agitator, dissenter, protestor, rebel, recusant

dissimilar different, disparate, divergent, diverse, heterogeneous, mismatched, not alike, not capable of comparison, not similar, unlike, unrelated, various

Antonyms alike, comparable, congruous, corresponding, in agreement, much the same, resembling, uniform

dissipate burn up, consume, deplete, expend, fritter away, indulge oneself, lavish, misspend, run through, spend, squander, waste

dissociate 1. break up, disband, disrupt, part company, quit **2.** detach, disconnect, distance, divorce, isolate, segregate, separate, set apart

dissolute abandoned, corrupt, debauched, degenerate, depraved, dissipated, immoral, lax, lewd, libertine, licentious, loose, profligate, rakish, unrestrained, vicious, wanton, wild

Antonyms chaste, clean-living, good, moral, upright, virtuous

dissolution breaking up, disintegration, division, divorce, parting, resolution, separation

dissolve 1. deliquesce, flux, fuse, liquefy, melt, soften, thaw **2.** crumble, decompose, diffuse, disappear, disintegrate, disperse, dissipate, dwindle, evanesce, evaporate, fade, melt away, perish, vanish, waste away

dissuade advise against, deter, discourage, disincline, divert, expostulate, persuade not to, put off, remonstrate, talk out of, urge not to, warn

Antonyms bring round (*Inf.*), coax, convince, persuade, sway, talk into

distance 1. *n.* absence, extent, gap, interval, lapse, length, range, reach, remoteness, remove, separation, space, span, stretch, width **2.** *v.* dissociate oneself, put in proportion, separate oneself

distant 1. abroad, afar, far, far-away, far-flung, far-off, outlying, out-of-the-way, remote, removed **2.** aloof, ceremonious, cold, cool, formal, haughty, reserved, restrained, reticent, standoffish,

stiff, unapproachable, unfriendly, withdrawn

Antonyms (*sense 1*) adjacent, adjoining, at hand, close, handy, imminent, near, nearby, neighbouring, nigh (*sense 2*) close, friendly, intimate, warm

distaste abhorrence, antipathy, aversion, detestation, disfavour, disgust, disinclination, dislike, displeasure, disrelish, dissatisfaction, horror, loathing, repugnance, revulsion

distasteful abhorrent, disagreeable, displeasing, loathsome, nauseous, objectionable, obnoxious, offensive, repugnant, repulsive, undesirable, uninviting, unpalatable, unpleasant, unsavoury

Antonyms agreeable, charming, enjoyable, pleasing, pleasurable

distil condense, draw out, evaporate, express, extract, press out, purify, rectify, refine, sublimate, vaporize

distinct 1. apparent, clear, clear-cut, decided, definite, evident, lucid, manifest, marked, noticeable, obvious, palpable, patent, plain, recognizable, sharp, unambiguous, unmistakable, well-defined **2.** detached, different, discrete, dissimilar, individual, separate, unconnected

Antonyms common, connected, fuzzy, identical, indefinite, indistinct, obscure, similar, unclear, vague

distinction 1. differentiation, discernment, discrimination, penetration, perception, separation **2.** contrast, difference, differential, division, separation **3.** account, celebrity, consequence, credit, eminence, excellence, fame, greatness, honour, importance, merit, name, note, prominence, quality, rank, renown, reputation, repute, superiority, worth

distinguish 1. ascertain, decide, determine, differentiate, discriminate, judge, tell apart, tell between, tell the difference **2.** discern, know, make out, perceive, pick out, recognize, see, tell 3. celebrate, dignify, honour, immortalize, make famous, signalize

distinguished acclaimed, celebrated, conspicuous, eminent, famed, famous, illustrious, notable, noted, renowned, well-known

distort 1. bend, buckle, contort, deform, disfigure, misshape, twist, warp, wrench, wrest 2. bias, colour, falsify, garble, misrepresent, pervert, slant, twist

distract 1. divert, draw away, sidetrack, turn aside 2. agitate, bewilder, confound, confuse, derange, discompose, disconcert, disturb, harass, madden, perplex, puzzle, torment, trouble

distracted 1. agitated, bemused, bewildered, confounded, confused, flustered, harassed, in a flap (*Inf.*), perplexed, puzzled, troubled 2. crazy, deranged, distraught, frantic, frenzied, grief-stricken, insane, mad, over-wrought, raving, wild

distraction 1. abstraction, agitation, bewilderment, commotion, confusion, discord, disorder, disturbance 2. amusement, beguilement, diversion, divertissement, entertainment, pastime, recreation

distress 1. *n.* affliction, agony, anguish, anxiety, desolation, discomfort, grief, heartache, misery, pain, sadness, sorrow, suffering, torment, torture, woe, worry, wretchedness 2. *v.* afflict, agonize, bother, disturb, grieve, harass, harrow, pain, perplex, sadden, torment, trouble, upset, worry, wound

distressed afflicted, agitated, anxious, distracted, distraught, saddened, tormented, troubled, upset, worried, wretched

distressing affecting, afflicting, distressful, disturbing, grievous, heart-breaking, hurtful, lamentable, nerve-racking, painful, sad, upsetting, worrying

distribute administer, allocate,

allot, apportion, assign, deal, dispense, dispose, divide, dole out, give, measure out, mete, share

distribution 1. allocation, allotment, apportionment, dispensation, division, dole, partition, sharing 2. *Commerce* dealing, delivery, handling, mailing, marketing, trading, transport, transportation

district area, community, locale, locality, neighbourhood, parish, quarter, region, sector, vicinity, ward

distrust 1. *v.* be sceptical of, be suspicious of, be wary of, disbelieve, discredit, doubt, misbelieve, mistrust, question, smell a rat (*Inf.*), suspect, wonder about 2. *n.* disbelief, doubt, lack of faith, misgiving, mistrust, qualm, question, scepticism, suspicion, wariness
Antonyms *v.* believe, depend, have confidence, have faith, trust ~*n.* confidence, faith, reliance, trust

disturb 1. bother, butt in on, disrupt, interfere with, interrupt, intrude on, pester, rouse, startle 2. agitate, alarm, annoy, confound, discompose, distract, distress, excite, fluster, harass, perturb, ruffle, shake, trouble, unsettle, upset, worry
Antonyms calm, compose, lull, pacify, quiet, quieten, reassure, relax, relieve, settle, soothe

disturbance 1. agitation, annoyance, bother, confusion, derangement, disorder, distraction, hindrance, interruption, intrusion, molestation, perturbation, upset 2. bother (*Inf.*), brawl, commotion, disorder, fracas, fray, hubbub, riot, ruckus (*Inf.*), ruction (*Inf.*), tumult, turmoil, uproar

disuse abandonment, decay, desuetude, discontinuance, idleness, neglect, non-employment, nonuse
Antonyms application, employment, practice, service, usage, use

ditch n. 1. channel, drain, dyke, furrow, gully, moat, trench, watercourse ~v. 2. dig, drain, excavate, gouge, trench 3. Sl. abandon, discard, dispose of, drop, dump (Inf.), get rid of, jettison, scrap, throw out or overboard

dither v. faff about (Brit. inf.), falter, haver, hesitate, oscillate, shillyshally (Inf.), swither (Scot.), teeter, vacillate, waver

dive 1. v. descend, dip, disappear, drop, duck, fall, go underwater, jump, leap, nose-dive, pitch, plummet, plunge, submerge, swoop 2. n. dash, header (Inf.), jump, leap, lunge, nose dive, plunge, spring

diverge bifurcate, branch, divaricate, divide, fork, part, radiate, separate, split, spread

diverse 1. assorted, diversified, miscellaneous, of every description, several, sundry, varied, various 2. different, differing, discrete, disparate, dissimilar, distinct, divergent, separate, unlike, varying

diversion 1. alteration, change, deflection, departure, detour, deviation, digression, variation 2. amusement, beguilement, delight, distraction, divertissement, enjoyment, entertainment, game, gratification, pastime, play, pleasure, recreation, relaxation, sport

diversity assortment, difference, dissimilarity, distinctiveness, divergence, diverseness, diversification, heterogeneity, medley, multiplicity, range, unlikeness, variance, variegation, variety

divert avert, deflect, redirect, switch, turn aside

divide 1. bisect, cleave, cut (up), detach, disconnect, part, partition, segregate, separate, sever, shear, split, subdivide, sunder 2. allocate, allot, apportion, deal out, dispense, distribute, divvy (up) (Inf.), dole out, measure out, portion, share

Antonyms (sense 1) combine,

come together, connect, join, knit, marry, splice, unite

dividend bonus, cut (Inf.), divvy (Inf.), extra, gain, plus, portion, share, surplus

divine adj. 1. angelic, celestial, godlike, heavenly, holy, spiritual, superhuman, supernatural 2. Inf. beautiful, excellent, glorious, marvellous, perfect, splendid, superlative, wonderful ~v. 3. apprehend, conjecture, deduce, discern, foretell, guess, infer, intuit, perceive, prognosticate, suppose, surmise, suspect, understand

divinity 1. deity, divine nature, godhead, godhood, godliness, holiness, sanctity 2. daemon, deity, genius, god, goddess, guardian spirit, spirit 3. religion, religious studies, theology

divisible dividable, fractional, separable, splittable

division 1. bisection, cutting up, detaching, dividing, partition, separation, splitting up 2. allotment, apportionment, distribution, sharing 3. border, boundary, demarcation, divide, divider, dividing line, partition 4. branch, category, class, compartment, department, group, head, part, portion, section, sector, segment

divorce 1. n. annulment, breach, break, decree nisi, dissolution, disunion, rupture, separation, severance, split-up 2. v. annul, disconnect, dissociate, dissolve (marriage), disunite, divide, part, separate, sever, split up, sunder

divulge betray, communicate, confess, declare, disclose, exhibit, expose, impart, leak, let slip, make known, proclaim, promulgate, publish, reveal, spill (Inf.), tell, uncover

Antonyms conceal, hide, keep secret

dizzy faint, giddy, light-headed, off balance, reeling, shaky, staggering, swimming, vertiginous, weak at the knees, wobbly, woozy (Inf.)

do v. 1. accomplish, achieve, act,

carry out, complete, conclude, discharge, end, execute, perform, produce, transact, undertake, work **2.** answer, be adequate, be enough, be of use, be sufficient, pass muster, satisfy, serve, suffice, suit **3.** adapt, render, translate, transpose **4.** bear oneself, behave, carry oneself, comport oneself, conduct oneself **5.** fare, get along, get on, make out, manage, proceed **6.** bring about, cause, create, effect, produce **7.** *Sl.* cheat, con (*Sl.*), cozen, deceive, defraud, dupe, fleece, hoax, swindle, take (someone) for a ride (*Inf.*), trick ~*n.* **8.** *Inf.* affair, event, function, gathering, occasion, party

do away with 1. bump off (*Sl.*), destroy, do in (*Sl.*), exterminate, kill, liquidate, murder, slay **2.** abolish, discard, discontinue, eliminate, get rid of, put an end to, remove

docile amenable, biddable, compliant, ductile, manageable, obedient, pliant, submissive, teachable (*Rare*), tractable
Antonyms difficult, intractable, obstreperous, troublesome, trying, uncooperative, unmanageable

docility amenability, biddableness, compliance, ductility, manageability, meekness, obedience, pliancy, submissiveness, tractability

dock **1.** *n.* harbour, pier, quay, waterfront, wharf **2.** *v.* anchor, berth, drop anchor, land, moor, put in, tie up

doctor *n.* **1.** general practitioner, G.P., medic (*Inf.*), medical practitioner, physician ~*v.* **2.** apply medication to, give medical treatment to, treat **3.** botch, cobble, do up (*Inf.*), fix, mend, patch up, repair **4.** alter, change, disguise, falsify, fudge, misrepresent, pervert, tamper with

doctrine article, article of faith, belief, canon, concept, conviction, creed, dogma, opinion, precept, principle, teaching, tenet

document **1.** *n.* certificate, instrument, legal form, paper, record, report **2.** *v.* authenticate, back up, certify, cite, corroborate, detail, give weight to, instance, particularize, substantiate, support, validate, verify

dodge *v.* **1.** dart, duck, shift, side-step, swerve, turn aside **2.** avoid, deceive, elude, equivocate, evade, fend off, fudge, get out of, hedge, parry, shirk, shuffle, trick ~*n.* **3.** contrivance, device, feint, machination, ploy, ruse, scheme, stratagem, subterfuge, trick, wheeze (*Sl.*), wile

dog **1.** *n.* bitch, canine, cur, hound, man's best friend, mongrel, mutt (*Sl.*), pooch (*Sl.*), pup, puppy, tyke **2.** *v.* haunt, hound, plague, pursue, shadow, tail (*Inf.*), track, trail, trouble

dogged determined, firm, indefatigable, obstinate, persevering, persistent, pertinacious, resolute, single-minded, staunch, steadfast, steady, stubborn, tenacious, unflagging, unshakable, unyielding

dogma article, article of faith, belief, credo, creed, doctrine, opinion, precept, principle, teachings, tenet

dogmatic arbitrary, arrogant, assertive, categorical, dictatorial, doctrinaire, downright, emphatic, imperious, magisterial, obdurate, opinionated, overbearing, peremptory

doldrums apathy, blues, boredom, depression, dullness, dumps (*Inf.*), ennui, gloom, inertia, lassitude, listlessness, malaise, stagnation, tedium, torpor

dole **1.** *n.* allowance, alms, benefit, donation, gift, grant, gratuity, modicum, parcel, pittance, portion, quota, share **2.** *v. Usually with* **out** administer, allocate, allot, apportion, assign, deal, dispense, distribute, divide, give, hand out, mete, share

dolt ass, blockhead, booby, chump (*Inf.*), clot (*Sl.*), dimwit (*Inf.*), dope (*Sl.*), dullard, dunce, fool, idiot, ignoramus, nitwit, nurd

(*Sl.*), plonker (*Sl.*), simpleton, thickhead, wally (*Sl.*)

domestic *adj.* 1. domiciliary, family, home, household, private 2. domesticated, house, house-trained, pet, tame, trained 3. indigenous, internal, native, not foreign

dominant ascendant, assertive, authoritative, commanding, controlling, governing, leading, presiding, ruling, superior, supreme **Antonyms** ancillary, auxiliary, inferior, junior, lesser, lower, minor, secondary, subservient, subsidiary

dominate 1. control, direct, domineer, govern, have the upper hand over, have the whip hand over, keep under one's thumb, lead, lead by the nose (*Inf.*), master, monopolize, overbear, rule, tyrannize 2. bestride, loom over, overlook, stand head and shoulders above, stand over, survey, tower above

domination ascendancy, authority, command, control, influence, mastery, power, rule, superiority, supremacy, sway

domineer bluster, boss around *or* about (*Inf.*), browbeat, bully, hector, intimidate, lord (*It.*) over, menace, overbear, ride roughshod over, swagger, threaten, tyrannize

dominion ascendancy, authority, command, control, domination, government, jurisdiction, mastery, power, rule, sovereignty, supremacy, sway

don clothe oneself in, dress in, get into, pull on, put on, slip on *or* into

donate bequeath, bestow, chip in (*Inf.*), contribute, gift, give, make a gift of, present, subscribe

donation alms, benefaction, boon, contribution, gift, grant, gratuity, largess, offering, present, subscription

done *adj.* 1. accomplished, completed, concluded, consummated, ended, executed, finished, over, perfected, realized, terminated,

through 2. cooked, cooked enough, cooked sufficiently, cooked to a turn, ready 3. depleted, exhausted, finished, spent, used up 4. acceptable, conventional, *de rigueur*, proper

donor almsgiver, benefactor, contributor, donator, giver, grantor (*Law*), philanthropist **Antonyms** assignee, beneficiary, inheritor, legatee, payee, receiver, recipient

doom 1. *n.* catastrophe, death, destiny, destruction, downfall, fate, fortune, lot, portion, ruin 2. *v.* condemn, consign, damn, decree, destine, foreordain, judge, predestine, sentence, threaten

doomed bedevilled, bewitched, condemned, cursed, fated, hopeless, ill-fated, ill-omened, luckless, star-crossed

door doorway, egress, entrance, entry, exit, ingress, opening

dope *n.* drugs, narcotic, opiate

dormant asleep, comatose, fallow, hibernating, inactive, inert, inoperative, latent, quiescent, sleeping, sluggish, slumbering, suspended, torpid **Antonyms** active, alert, aroused, awake, awakened, conscious, wakeful, wide-awake

dose dosage, draught, drench, measure, portion, potion, prescription, quantity

dot *n.* atom, circle, dab, fleck, full stop, iota, jot, mark, mite, mote, point, speck, spot

dotage decrepitude, feebleness, imbecility, old age, second childhood, senility, weakness

dote on *or* **upon** admire, adore, hold dear, idolize, lavish affection on, prize, treasure

double 1. *adj.* binate (*Botany*), coupled, doubled, dual, duplicate, in pairs, paired, twice, twin, twofold 2. *v.* duplicate, enlarge, fold, grow, increase, magnify, multiply, plait, repeat

double-cross betray, cheat, defraud, hoodwink, mislead, swindle, trick, two-time (*Inf.*)

doubt *v.* 1. discredit, distrust, fear,

lack confidence in, misgive, mistrust, query, question, suspect ~n. **2.** apprehension, disquiet, distrust, fear, incredulity, lack of faith, misgiving, mistrust, qualm, scepticism, suspicion ~v. **3.** be dubious, be uncertain, demur, fluctuate, hesitate, scruple, vacillate, waver ~n. **4.** ambiguity, confusion, difficulty, dilemma, perplexity, problem, quandary
Antonyms v. accept, believe, have faith in, trust ~n. belief, certainty, confidence, conviction, trust

doubtful 1. ambiguous, debatable, dubious, equivocal, hazardous, inconclusive, indefinite, indeterminate, obscure, precarious, problematic, questionable, unclear, unconfirmed, unsettled, vague **2.** distrustful, hesitating, in two minds (Inf.), irresolute, perplexed, sceptical, suspicious, tentative, uncertain, unconvinced, undecided, unresolved, unsettled, unsure, vacillating, wavering
Antonyms certain, decided, definite, indubitable, positive, resolute

doubtless 1. assuredly, certainly, clearly, indisputably, of course, precisely, surely, truly, undoubtedly, unquestionably, without doubt **2.** apparently, most likely, ostensibly, presumably, probably, seemingly, supposedly

dour dismal, dreary, forbidding, gloomy, grim, morose, sour, sullen, unfriendly

dowdy dingy, drab, frowzy, frumpish, frumpy, ill-dressed, old-fashioned, scrubby (Inf.), shabby, slovenly, tacky (U.S. inf.), unfashionable
Antonyms chic, dressy, fashionable, neat, smart, spruce, trim, well-dressed

do without abstain from, dispense with, forgo, get along without, give up, manage without

down adj. blue, dejected, depressed, disheartened, downcast, low, miserable, sad, unhappy

down and out adj. derelict, destitute, impoverished, penniless, ruined

downcast cheerless, crestfallen, daunted, dejected, depressed, despondent, disappointed, disconsolate, discouraged, disheartened, dismayed, dispirited, miserable, sad, unhappy
Antonyms cheerful, cheery, contented, elated, happy, joyful, light-hearted, optimistic

downfall breakdown, collapse, comedown, comeuppance (Sl.), debacle, descent, destruction, disgrace, fall, overthrow, ruin, undoing

downgrade degrade, demote, humble, lower or reduce in rank, take down a peg (Inf.)
Antonyms advance, ameliorate, better, elevate, enhance, improve, promote, raise, upgrade

downhearted blue, chapfallen, crestfallen, dejected, depressed, despondent, discouraged, disheartened, dismayed, dispirited, downcast, low-spirited, sad, sorrowful, unhappy

downpour cloudburst, deluge, flood, inundation, rainstorm, torrential rain

down-to-earth common-sense, hard-headed, matter-of-fact, mundane, no-nonsense, plainspoken, practical, realistic, sane, sensible, unsentimental

downward adj. declining, descending, earthward, heading down, sliding, slipping

doze v. catnap, drop off (Inf.), drowse, kip (Sl.), nap, nod, nod off (Inf.), sleep, sleep lightly, slumber, snooze (Inf.), zizz (Inf.)

drab cheerless, colourless, dingy, dismal, dreary, dull, flat, gloomy, grey, lacklustre, shabby, sombre, uninspired, vapid
Antonyms bright, cheerful, colourful, jazzy (Sl.), vibrant, vivid

draft 1. v. compose, delineate, design, draw, draw up, formulate, outline, plan, sketch **2.** n. abstract, delineation, outline, plan, preliminary form, rough, sketch, version

drag v. draw, hale, haul, lug, pull, tow, trail, tug, yank

drain v. 1. bleed, draw off, dry, empty, evacuate, milk, pump off or out, remove, tap, withdraw 2. consume, deplete, dissipate, empty, exhaust, sap, strain, tax, use up, weary ~n. 3. channel, conduit, culvert, ditch, duct, outlet, pipe, sewer, sink, trench, watercourse 4. depletion, drag, exhaustion, expenditure, reduction, sap, strain, withdrawal

drama 1. dramatization, play, show, stage play, stage show, theatrical piece 2. acting, dramatic art, dramaturgy, stagecraft, theatre, Thespian art 3. crisis, dramatics, excitement, histrionics, scene, spectacle, theatrics, turmoil

dramatic 1. dramaturgic, dramaturgical, theatrical, Thespian 2. breathtaking, climactic, electrifying, emotional, exciting, melodramatic, sensational, startling, sudden, suspenseful, tense, thrilling
Antonyms ordinary, run-of-the-mill, undramatic, unexceptional, unmemorable

dramatist dramaturge, playwright, screen-writer, script-writer

dramatize act, exaggerate, lay it on (thick) (Sl.), make a performance of, overdo, overstate, play-act, play to the gallery

drastic desperate, dire, extreme, forceful, harsh, radical, severe, strong

draught 1. Of air current, flow, influx, movement, puff 2. cup, dose, drench, drink, potion, quantity

draw v. 1. drag, haul, pull, tow, tug 2. delineate, depict, design, map out, mark out, outline, paint, portray, sketch, trace 3. allure, attract, bring forth, call forth, elicit, engage, entice, evoke, induce, influence, invite, persuade 4. attenuate, elongate, extend,

lengthen, stretch 5. breathe in, drain, inhale, inspire, puff, pull, respire, suck 6. compose, draft, formulate, frame, prepare, write n. 7. Inf. attraction, enticement, lure, pull (Inf.) 8. dead heat, deadlock, impasse, stalemate, tie

drawback defect, deficiency, detriment, difficulty, disadvantage, fault, flaw, fly in the ointment (Inf.), handicap, hindrance, hitch, impediment, imperfection, nuisance, obstacle, snag, stumbling block, trouble
Antonyms advantage, asset, benefit, gain, help, service, use

drawing cartoon, delineation, depiction, illustration, outline, picture, portrayal, representation, sketch, study

drawn fatigued, fraught, haggard, harassed, harrowed, pinched, sapped, strained, stressed, taut, tense, tired, worn

draw out drag out, extend, lengthen, make longer, prolong, prolongate, protract, spin out, stretch, string out
Antonyms curtail, cut, cut short, dock, pare down, reduce, shorten, trim, truncate

dread 1. v. anticipate with horror, cringe at, fear, have cold feet (Inf.), quail, shrink from, shudder, tremble 2. n. affright, alarm, apprehension, aversion, awe, dismay, fear, fright, funk (Inf.), heebie-jeebies (Sl.), horror, terror, trepidation

dreadful alarming, appalling, awful, dire, distressing, fearful, formidable, frightful, ghastly, grievous, hideous, horrendous, horrible, monstrous, shocking, terrible, tragic, tremendous

dream n. 1. daydream, delusion, fantasy, hallucination, illusion, imagination, pipe dream, reverie, speculation, trance, vagary, vision 2. ambition, aspiration, design, desire, goal, hope, notion, wish ~v. 3. build castles in the air or in Spain, conjure up, daydream, envisage, fancy, fantasize, hallucinate, have dreams, imagine, stargaze, think, visualize

dreamy 1. chimerical, dreamlike, fantastic, intangible, misty, phantasmagoric, phantasmagorical, shadowy, unreal 2. absent, abstracted, daydreaming, far-away, in a reverie, musing, pensive, preoccupied, with one's head in the clouds
Antonyms down-to-earth, feet-on-the-ground, pragmatic, realistic

dreary 1. bleak, cheerless, comfortless, depressing, dismal, doleful, downcast, drear, forlorn, gloomy, glum, joyless, lonely, lonesome, melancholy, mournful, sad, solitary, sombre, sorrowful, wretched 2. boring, colourless, drab, dull, humdrum, lifeless, monotonous, routine, tedious, uneventful, uninteresting, wearisome
Antonyms bright, cheerful, happy, interesting, joyful

dregs deposit, draff, dross, grounds, lees, residue, residuum, scourings, scum, sediment, trash, waste

drench v. drown, duck, flood, imbrue, inundate, saturate, soak, souse, steep, wet

dress n. 1. costume, ensemble, frock, garment, get-up (Inf.), gown, outfit, rigout (Inf.), robe, suit 2. apparel, attire, clothes, clothing, costume, garb, garments, gear (Sl.), guise, habiliment, raiment (Archaic), togs, vestment ~v. 3. attire, change, clothe, don, garb, put on, robe, slip on or into 4. bandage, bind up, plaster, treat
Antonyms (sense 3) disrobe, divest oneself of, peel off (Sl.), shed, strip, take off one's clothes

dressmaker couturier, modiste, seamstress, sewing woman, tailor

dress up beautify, do oneself up, embellish, gild, improve, titivate, trick out or up

dribble drip, drop, fall in drops, leak, ooze, run, seep, trickle

drift v. be carried along, coast, float, go (aimlessly), meander, stray, waft, wander

drill v. 1. coach, discipline, exercise, instruct, practise, rehearse, teach, train ~n. 2. discipline, exercise, instruction, practice, preparation, repetition, training ~v. 3. bore, penetrate, perforate, pierce, puncture, sink in ~n. 4. bit, borer, boring-tool, gimlet, rotary tool

drink v. 1. absorb, drain, gulp, guzzle, imbibe, partake of, quaff, sip, suck, sup, swallow, swig, swill, toss off, wash down, wet one's whistle (Inf.) 2. booze (Inf.), carouse, go on a binge or bender (Inf.), hit the bottle (Inf.), indulge, pub-crawl (Chiefly Brit. sl.), revel, tipple, tope, wassail ~n. 3. beverage, liquid, potion, refreshment, thirst quencher 4. alcohol, booze (Inf.), hooch (Sl.), liquor, spirits, the bottle (Inf.)

drip 1. v. dribble, drizzle, drop, exude, filter, plop, splash, sprinkle, trickle 2. n. dribble, dripping, drop, leak, trickle

drive v. 1. herd, hurl, impel, propel, push, send, urge 2. direct, go, guide, handle, manage, motor, operate, ride, steer, travel ~n. 3. excursion, hurl (Scot.), jaunt, journey, outing, ride, run, spin (Inf.), trip, turn 4. ambition, effort, energy, enterprise, get-up-and-go (Inf.), initiative, motivation, pressure, push (Inf.), vigour, zip (Inf.)

driving compelling, dynamic, energetic, forceful, galvanic, sweeping, vigorous, violent

drizzle 1. n. fine rain, Scotch mist, smir (Scot.) 2. v. mizzle (Dialect), rain, shower, spot or spit with rain, spray, sprinkle

droll amusing, clownish, comic, comical, diverting, eccentric, entertaining, farcical, funny, humorous, jocular, laughable, ludicrous, odd, quaint, ridiculous, risible, waggish, whimsical

droop bend, dangle, drop, fall down, hang (down), sag, sink

drop n. 1. bead, bubble, driblet, drip, droplet, globule, pearl, tear 2. dab, dash, mouthful, nip, pinch, shot (*Inf.*), sip, spot, taste, tot, trace, trickle 3. cut, decline, decrease, deterioration, downturn, fall-off, lowering, reduction, slump ~v. 4. decline, depress, descend, diminish, dive, droop, fall, lower, plummet, plunge, sink, tumble 5. abandon, cease, desert, discontinue, forsake, give up, kick (*Inf.*), leave, quit, relinquish, remit, terminate

drop out abandon, back out, forsake, give up, leave, quit, renege, stop, withdraw

drought aridity, dehydration, drouth (*Archaic or Scot.*), dryness, dry spell, dry weather, parchedness
Antonyms deluge, downpour, flood, flow, outpouring, rush, stream, torrent

drove collection, company, crowd, flock, gathering, herd, horde, mob, multitude, press, swarm, throng

drown deluge, drench, engulf, flood, go down, go under, immerse, inundate, sink, submerge, swamp

drudge n. dogsbody (*Inf.*), factotum, hack, maid *or* man of all work, menial, plodder, scullion (*Archaic*), servant, skivvy, slave, toiler, worker

drudgery chore, donkey-work, fag (*Inf.*), grind (*Inf.*), hack work, hard work, labour, menial labour, skivvying, slavery, slog, sweat (*Inf.*), sweated labour, toil

drug n. 1. medicament, medication, medicine, physic, poison, remedy 2. dope (*Sl.*), narcotic, opiate, stimulant ~v. 3. administer a drug, dope (*Sl.*), dose, medicate, treat

drunk 1. adj. bacchic, canned (*Sl.*), drunken, fu (*Scot.*), fuddled, half seas over (*Inf.*), inebriated, intoxicated, loaded (*Sl., chiefly U.S. & Canada*), maudlin, merry (*Inf.*), pickled (*Inf.*), pie-eyed (*Sl.*), pissed (*Sl.*), plastered (*Sl.*), sloshed (*Sl.*), soaked (*Inf.*), steamboats (*Sl.*), stewed (*Sl.*), stoned (*Sl.*), tanked up (*Sl.*), tiddly (*Sl.*), tight (*Inf.*), tipsy, tired and emotional (*Euphemistic*), under the influence (*Inf.*), well-oiled (*Sl.*) 2. n. boozer (*Inf.*), drunkard, inebriate, lush (*Sl.*), soak (*Sl.*), sot, toper, wino (*Sl.*)

drunkenness alcoholism, bibulousness, dipsomania, inebriety, insobriety, intemperance, intoxication, sottishness, tipsiness

dry adj. 1. arid, barren, dehydrated, desiccated, dried up, juiceless, moistureless, parched, sapless, thirsty, torrid, waterless 2. Fig. boring, dreary, dull, monotonous, plain, tedious, tiresome, uninteresting ~v. 3. dehumidify, dehydrate, desiccate, drain, make dry, parch, sear
Antonyms adj. damp, entertaining, humid, interesting, lively, moist, wet ~v. moisten, wet

dual binary, coupled, double, duplex, duplicate, matched, paired, twin, twofold

dubious 1. doubtful, hesitant, iffy (*Inf.*), sceptical, uncertain, unconvinced, undecided, unsure, wavering 2. ambiguous, debatable, doubtful, equivocal, indefinite, indeterminate, obscure, problematical, unclear, unsettled 3. fishy (*Inf.*), questionable, shady (*Inf.*), suspect, suspicious, undependable, unreliable, untrustworthy
Antonyms certain, definite, dependable, obvious, positive, reliable, sure, trustworthy

duck 1. bend, bob, bow, crouch, dodge, drop, lower, stoop 2. Inf. avoid, dodge, escape, evade, shirk, shun, sidestep

due adj. 1. in arrears, outstanding, owed, owing, payable, unpaid 2. appropriate, becoming, bounden, deserved, fit, fitting, just, justified, merited, obligatory, proper, requisite, right, rightful, suitable, well-earned 3. expected, expected to arrive, scheduled ~adv. 4.

dead, direct, directly, exactly, straight, undeviatingly

duel *n.* 1. affair of honour, single combat 2. clash, competition, contest, encounter, engagement, fight, rivalry

dues charge, charges, fee, levy

dull *adj.* 1. dense, dim, dim-witted (*Inf.*), doltish, slow, stolid, stupid, thick, unintelligent 2. apathetic, blank, callous, dead, empty, heavy, indifferent, insensible, insensitive, lifeless, listless, passionless, slow, sluggish, unresponsive, unsympathetic, vacuous 3. boring, commonplace, dreary, dry, flat, humdrum, monotonous, plain, prosaic, run-of-the-mill, tedious, tiresome, unimaginative, uninteresting, vapid 4. cloudy, dim, dismal, gloomy, leaden, opaque, overcast, turbid **Antonyms** bright, clever, exciting, intelligent, interesting, lively

duly 1. accordingly, appropriately, befittingly, correctly, decorously, deservedly, fittingly, properly, rightfully, suitably 2. at the proper time, on time, punctually

dumb at a loss for words, inarticulate, mum, mute, silent, soundless, speechless, tongue-tied, voiceless, wordless

dummy *n.* 1. figure, form, lay figure, manikin, mannequin, model 2. copy, counterfeit, duplicate, imitation, sham, substitute ~*adj.* 3. artificial, bogus, fake, false, imitation, mock, phoney (*Sl.*), sham, simulated

dump *v.* 1. deposit, drop, fling down, let fall, throw down ~*n.* 2. coup, junkyard, refuse heap, rubbish heap, rubbish tip, tip 3. *Inf.* hole (*Inf.*), hovel, joint (*Sl.*), mess, pigsty, shack, shanty, slum

dungeon cage, cell, donjon, lock-up, oubliette, prison, vault

duplicate 1. *adj.* corresponding, identical, matched, matching, twin, twofold 2. *n.* carbon copy, clone, copy, double, facsimile, fax, likeness, lookalike, match, mate, photocopy, Photostat

(*Trademark*), replica, reproduction, ringer (*Sl.*), twin, Xerox (*Trademark*) 3. *v.* clone, copy, double, echo, fax, photocopy, Photostat (*Trademark*), repeat, replicate, reproduce, Xerox (*Trademark*)

durable abiding, constant, dependable, enduring, fast, firm, fixed, hard-wearing, lasting, long-lasting, permanent, persistent, reliable, resistant, sound, stable, strong, sturdy, substantial, tough **Antonyms** breakable, brittle, delicate, fragile, impermanent, perishable, weak

dusk dark, evening, eventide, gloaming, nightfall, sundown, sunset, twilight **Antonyms** aurora (*Literary*), cockcrow, dawn, dawning, daybreak, daylight, morning, sunlight, sunup

dusky dark, dark-complexioned, dark-hued, sable, swarthy

dust *n.* 1. fine fragments, grime, grit, particles, powder, powdery dirt 2. dirt, earth, ground, soil

dusty dirty, grubby, sooty, unclean, undusted, unswept

dutiful compliant, conscientious, deferential, devoted, docile, duteous (*Archaic*), filial, obedient, punctilious, respectful, reverential, submissive **Antonyms** disobedient, disrespectful, insubordinate, remiss, uncaring

duty 1. assignment, business, calling, charge, engagement, function, mission, obligation, office, onus, province, responsibility, role, service, task, work 2. customs, due, excise, impost, levy, tariff, tax, toll 3. **off duty** at leisure, free, off, off work, on holiday 4. **on duty** at work, busy, engaged

dwarf 1. *n.* bantam, homunculus, hop-o'-my-thumb, Lilliputian, manikin, midget, pygmy, Tom Thumb 2. *adj.* baby, bonsai, diminutive, dwarfed, Lilliputian, miniature, petite, pocket, small, tiny, undersized 3. *v.* dim, dimin-

ish, dominate, minimize, over~
shadow, tower above or over
dwell abide, establish oneself,
hang out (*Inf.*), inhabit, live,
lodge, quarter, remain, reside,
rest, settle, sojourn, stay, stop
dwelling abode, domicile, dwell~
ing house, establishment, habita~
tion, home, house, lodging, quar~
ters, residence
dye 1. *n.* colorant, colour, colour~
ing, pigment, stain, tinge, tint **2.**
v. colour, pigment, stain, tinc~
ture, tinge, tint

dying at death's door, ebbing,
expiring, fading, failing, final,
going, *in extremis*, moribund,
mortal, passing, perishing, sink~
ing

dynamic active, driving, electric,
energetic, forceful, go-ahead, go-
getting (*Inf.*), high-powered, live~
ly, magnetic, powerful, vigorous,
vital, zippy (*Inf.*)

dynasty ascendancy, dominion,
empire, government, house, re~
gime, rule, sovereignty, sway

E

each 1. *adj.* every **2.** *pron.* each and every one, each one, every one, one and all **3.** *adv.* apiece, for each, from each, individually, per capita, per head, per person, respectively, singly, to each

eager agog, anxious, ardent, athirst, avid, earnest, enthusiastic, fervent, fervid, greedy, hot, hungry, impatient, intent, keen, longing, raring, vehement, yearning, zealous
Antonyms apathetic, blasé, impassive, indifferent, lazy, nonchalant, opposed, unambitious, unconcerned, unenthusiastic, unimpressed, uninterested

early 1. *adj.* advanced, forward, premature, untimely **2.** *adv.* ahead of time, beforehand, betimes (*Archaic*), in advance, in good time, prematurely, too soon
Antonyms *adv.* behind, belated, late, overdue, tardy

earn 1. bring in, collect, draw, gain, get, gross, make, net, obtain, procure, realize, reap, receive **2.** acquire, attain, be entitled to, be worthy of, deserve, merit, rate, warrant, win

earnest *adj.* close, constant, determined, firm, fixed, grave, intent, resolute, resolved, serious, sincere, solemn, stable, staid, steady, thoughtful
Antonyms *adj.* flippant, frivolous, indifferent, insincere, light, slack, trifling, unstable

earnings emolument, gain, income, pay, proceeds, profits, receipts, remuneration, return, reward, salary, stipend, takings, wages

earth 1. globe, orb, planet, sphere, terrestrial sphere, world **2.** clay, clod, dirt, ground, land, loam, mould, sod, soil, topsoil, turf

earthenware ceramics, crock-

ery, crocks, pots, pottery, terra cotta

earthly 1. mundane, sublunary, tellurian, telluric, terrene, terrestrial, worldly **2.** human, material, mortal, non-spiritual, profane, secular, temporal, worldly
Antonyms ethereal, heavenly, immaterial, immortal, otherwordly, spiritual, supernatural, unearthly

ease 1. *n.* affluence, calmness, comfort, content, contentment, enjoyment, happiness, leisure, peace, peace of mind, quiet, quietude, relaxation, repose, rest, restfulness, serenity, tranquillity **2.** *v.* abate, allay, alleviate, appease, assuage, calm, comfort, disburden, lessen, lighten, mitigate, moderate, mollify, pacify, palliate, quiet, relax, relent, relieve, slacken, soothe, still, tranquillize
Antonyms *n.* discomfort, hardship, pain, poverty, tension ~*v.* aggravate, discomfort, exacerbate, hinder, irritate, make nervous, make uneasy, retard, worsen

easily comfortably, effortlessly, facilely, readily, simply, smoothly, with ease, without difficulty, without trouble

easy a piece of cake (*Inf.*), a pushover (*Sl.*), child's play (*Inf.*), clear, effortless, facile, light, no bother, not difficult, no trouble, painless, simple, smooth, straightforward, uncomplicated, undemanding
Antonyms arduous, complex, demanding, difficult, exacting, exhausting, hard, impossible, onerous

easy-going amenable, calm, carefree, casual, complacent, easy, even-tempered, flexible, happy-go-lucky, indulgent, insouciant, laid-back (*Inf.*), lenient, liberal, mild, moderate, nonchalant, permissive, placid, relaxed, serene, tolerant, unconcerned, uncritical, undemanding, unhurried

Antonyms anxious, edgy, fussy, hung-up (*Inf.*), intolerant, irritated, nervy, on edge, strict, tense, uptight (*Inf.*)

eat 1. chew, consume, devour, gobble, ingest, munch, scoff (*Sl.*), swallow 2. break bread, dine, feed, have a meal, take food, take nourishment

eavesdrop bug (*Inf.*), listen in, monitor, overhear, snoop (*Inf.*), spy, tap (*Inf.*)

ebb v. 1. abate, fall away, fall back, flow back, go out, recede, retire, retreat, retrocede, sink, subside, wane, withdraw 2. decay, decline, decrease, degenerate, deteriorate, diminish, drop, dwindle, fade away, fall away, flag, lessen, peter out, shrink, sink, slacken, weaken

eccentric adj. aberrant, abnormal, anomalous, bizarre, capricious, erratic, freakish, idiosyncratic, irregular, odd, outlandish, peculiar, queer (*Inf.*), quirky, singular, strange, uncommon, unconventional, weird, whimsical

Antonyms average, conventional, normal, ordinary, regular, run-of-the-mill, straightforward, typical

eccentricity aberration, abnormality, anomaly, bizarreness, caprice, capriciousness, foible, freakishness, idiosyncrasy, irregularity, nonconformity, oddity, oddness, outlandishness, peculiarity, queerness (*Inf.*), quirk, singularity, strangeness, unconventionality, waywardness, weirdness, whimsicality, whimsicalness

ecclesiastic n. churchman, clergyman, cleric, divine, holy man, man of the cloth, minister, parson, priest

echo v. 1. repeat, resound, reverberate ~n. 2. answer, repetition, reverberation 3. copy, imitation, mirror image, parallel, reflection, reiteration, reproduction, ringing

eclipse v. 1. blot out, cloud, darken, dim, extinguish, obscure, overshadow, shroud, veil ~n. 2. darkening, dimming, extinction, obscuration, occultation, shading 3. decline, diminution, failure, fall, loss

economic 1. business, commercial, financial, industrial, mercantile, trade 2. money-making, productive, profitable, profit-making, remunerative, solvent, viable 3. bread-and-butter (*Inf.*), budgetary, financial, fiscal, material, monetary, pecuniary

economical 1. cost-effective, efficient, money-saving, sparing, time-saving, unwasteful, work-saving 2. careful, economizing, frugal, prudent, saving, scrimping, sparing, thrifty

Antonyms extravagant, generous, imprudent, lavish, loss-making, profligate, spendthrift, uneconomical, unprofitable, unthrifty, wasteful

economize be economical, be frugal, be sparing, cut back, husband, retrench, save, scrimp, tighten one's belt

Antonyms be extravagant, push the boat out (*Inf.*), spend, splurge, squander

economy frugality, husbandry, parsimony, providence, prudence, restraint, retrenchment, saving, sparingness, thrift, thriftiness

ecstasy bliss, delight, elation, enthusiasm, euphoria, exaltation, fervour, frenzy, joy, rapture, ravishment, rhapsody, seventh heaven, trance, transport

Antonyms affliction, agony, anguish, distress, hell, misery, pain, suffering, torment, torture

ecstatic blissful, delirious, elated, enraptured, enthusiastic, entranced, euphoric, fervent, frenzied, in exaltation, in transports of delight, joyful, joyous, on cloud nine (*Inf.*), overjoyed, rapturous, rhapsodic, transported

eddy 1. *n.* counter-current, counterflow, swirl, vortex, whirlpool **2.** *v.* swirl, whirl

edge *n.* **1.** border, bound, boundary, brim, brink, contour, fringe, limit, line, lip, margin, outline, perimeter, periphery, rim, side, threshold, verge **2.** acuteness, animation, bite, effectiveness, force, incisiveness, interest, keenness, point, pungency, sharpness, sting, urgency, zest

edible comestible (*Rare*), digestible, eatable, esculent, fit to eat, good, harmless, palatable, wholesome

Antonyms baneful, harmful, indigestible, inedible, noxious, pernicious, poisonous, uneatable

edict act, command, decree, dictate, dictum, enactment, fiat, injunction, law, mandate, manifesto, order, ordinance, proclamation, pronouncement, pronunciamento, regulation, ruling, statute, ukase (*Rare*)

edit adapt, annotate, censor, check, condense, correct, emend, polish, redact, rephrase, revise, rewrite

edition copy, impression, issue, number, printing, programme (*TV, Radio*), version, volume

educate civilize, coach, cultivate, develop, discipline, drill, edify, enlighten, exercise, foster, improve, indoctrinate, inform, instruct, mature, rear, school, teach, train, tutor

educated civilized, cultivated, cultured, enlightened, experienced, informed, knowledgeable, learned, literary, polished, refined, tasteful

Antonyms benighted, lowbrow, philistine, uncultivated, uncultured, uneducated

education breeding, civilization, coaching, cultivation, culture, development, discipline, drilling, edification, enlightenment, eru-

dition, improvement, indoctrination, instruction, knowledge, nurture, scholarship, schooling, teaching, training, tuition, tutoring

eerie awesome, creepy (*Inf.*), eldritch (*Poetic*), fearful, frightening, ghostly, mysterious, scary (*Inf.*), spectral, spooky (*Inf.*), strange, uncanny, unearthly, uneasy, weird

effect *n.* **1.** aftermath, conclusion, consequence, event, fruit, issue, outcome, result, upshot **2. in effect** actually, effectively, essentially, for practical purposes, in actuality, in fact, in reality, in truth, really, to all intents and purposes, virtually **3. take effect** become operative, begin, come into force, produce results, work ~*v.* **4.** accomplish, achieve, actuate, bring about, carry out, cause, complete, consummate, create, effectuate, execute, fulfil, give rise to, initiate, make, perform, produce

effective 1. able, active, adequate, capable, competent, effectual, efficacious, efficient, energetic, operative, productive, serviceable, useful **2.** active, actual, current, in effect, in execution, in force, in operation, operative, real

Antonyms feeble, inactive, inadequate, incompetetent, ineffective, ineffectual, inefficient, inoperative, unproductive, useless, vain, weak, worthless

effects belongings, chattels, furniture, gear, goods, movables, paraphernalia, possessions, property, things, trappings

effervesce bubble, ferment, fizz, foam, froth, sparkle

effervescent 1. bubbling, bubbly, carbonated, fermenting, fizzing, fizzy, foaming, foamy, frothing, frothy, sparkling **2.** animated, bubbly, buoyant, ebullient, enthusiastic, excited, exhilarated, exuberant, gay, in high spirits, irrepressible, lively, merry, vital, vivacious, zingy (*Inf.*)

Antonyms boring, dull, flat, flavourless, insipid, jejune, lacklustre, lifeless, spiritless, stale, unexciting, vapid, watery, weak

efficacious active, adequate, capable, competent, effective, effectual, efficient, energetic, operative, potent, powerful, productive, serviceable, successful, useful

efficiency ability, adeptness, capability, competence, economy, effectiveness, efficacy, power, productivity, proficiency, readiness, skilfulness, skill

efficient able, adept, businesslike, capable, competent, economic, effective, effectual, organized, powerful, productive, proficient, ready, skilful, well-organized, workmanlike

Antonyms disorganized, incompetent, ineffectual, inefficient, inept, slipshod, sloppy, unbusinesslike, unproductive, wasteful

effort 1. application, endeavour, energy, exertion, force, labour, pains, power, strain, stress, stretch, striving, struggle, toil, travail (*Literary*), trouble, work

effortless easy, facile, painless, simple, smooth, uncomplicated, undemanding, untroublesome

Antonyms demanding, difficult, formidable, hard, onerous, uphill

effusion discharge, effluence, efflux, emission, gush, outflow, outpouring, shedding, stream

effusive demonstrative, ebullient, enthusiastic, expansive, extravagant, exuberant, free-flowing, fulsome, gushing, lavish, overflowing, profuse, talkative, unreserved, unrestrained, wordy

egocentric egoistic, egotistical, egotistic, egotistical, self-centred, selfish

egoism egocentricity, egomania, egotism, narcissism, self-absorption, self-centredness, self-importance, self-interest, selfishness, self-love, self-regard, self-seeking

egotist bighead (*Inf.*), blowhard

(*Inf.*), boaster, braggadocio, braggart, egoist, egomaniac, self-admirer, swaggerer

eject 1. cast out, discharge, disgorge, emit, expel, spew, spout, throw out, vomit 2. discharge, dislodge, dismiss, fire (*Inf.*), get rid of, kick out (*Inf.*), oust, sack (*Inf.*), throw out

elaborate *adj.* 1. careful, detailed, exact, intricate, laboured, minute, painstaking, perfected, precise, skilful, studied, thorough 2. complex, complicated, decorated, detailed, extravagant, fancy, fussy, involved, ornamented, ornate, ostentatious, showy ~v. 3. add detail, amplify, complicate, decorate, develop, devise, embellish, enhance, enlarge, expand (upon), flesh out, garnish, improve, ornament, polish, produce, refine, work out

Antonyms *adj.* basic, minimal, modest, plain, simple, unadorned, unembellished, unfussy ~v. abbreviate, condense, put in a nutshell, reduce to essentials, simplify, streamline, summarize, truncate

elapse glide by, go, go by, lapse, pass, pass by, roll by, roll on, slip away, slip by

elastic ductile, flexible, plastic, pliable, pliant, resilient, rubbery, springy, stretchable, stretchy, supple, yielding

Antonyms firm, immovable, inflexible, intractable, rigid, set, stiff, unyielding

elated animated, blissful, cheered, delighted, ecstatic, elevated, euphoric, excited, exhilarated, exultant, gleeful, in high spirits, joyful, joyous, jubilant, overjoyed, proud, puffed up, roused

Antonyms dejected, depressed, discouraged, dispirited, downcast, down in the dumps (*Inf.*), miserable, sad, unhappy, woebegone

elbow 1. *n.* angle, bend, corner, joint, turn 2. *v.* bump, crowd, hustle, jostle, knock, nudge, push, shoulder, shove

elder 1. *adj.* ancient, earlier born, first-born, older, senior **2.** *n.* older person, senior

elect *v.* appoint, choose, decide upon, designate, determine, opt for, pick, pick out, prefer, select, settle on, vote

election appointment, choice, choosing, decision, determination, judgment, preference, selection, vote, voting

elector chooser, constituent, selector, voter

electric *Fig.* charged, dynamic, exciting, rousing, stimulating, stirring, tense, thrilling

electrify *Fig.* amaze, animate, astonish, astound, excite, fire, galvanize, invigorate, jolt, rouse, shock, startle, stimulate, stir, take one's breath away, thrill
Antonyms be tedious, bore, fatigue, jade, send to sleep, weary

elegance beauty, courtliness, dignity, gentility, grace, gracefulness, grandeur, luxury, polish, politeness, refinement, sumptuousness

elegant à la mode, artistic, beautiful, chic, choice, comely, courtly, cultivated, delicate, exquisite, fashionable, fine, genteel, graceful, handsome, luxurious, modish, nice, polished, refined, stylish, sumptuous, tasteful
Antonyms awkward, clumsy, coarse, gauche, graceless, inelegant, misshapen, plain, tasteless, tawdry, ugly, uncouth, undignified, ungraceful, unrefined

element basis, component, constituent, essential factor, factor, feature, hint, ingredient, member, part, section, subdivision, trace, unit

elementary 1. clear, easy, facile, plain, rudimentary, simple, straightforward, uncomplicated **2.** basic, elemental, fundamental, initial, introductory, original, primary, rudimentary
Antonyms advanced, complex, complicated, higher, highly-

developed, progressive, secondary, sophisticated

elements basics, essentials, foundations, fundamentals, principles, rudiments

elevate 1. heighten, hoist, lift, lift up, raise, uplift, upraise **2.** advance, aggrandize, exalt, prefer, promote, upgrade

elevation 1. altitude, height **2.** acclivity, eminence, height, hill, hillock, mountain, rise, rising ground **3.** exaltedness, grandeur, loftiness, nobility, nobleness, sublimity

elicit bring forth, bring out, bring to light, call forth, cause, derive, draw out, educe, evoke, evolve, exact, extort, extract, give rise to, obtain, wrest

eligible acceptable, appropriate, desirable, fit, preferable, proper, qualified, suitable, suited, worthy
Antonyms inappropriate, ineligible, unacceptable, unqualified, unsuitable, unsuited

eliminate cut out, dispose of, do away with, eradicate, exterminate, get rid of, remove, stamp out, take out

elite *n.* aristocracy, best, cream, *crème de la crème*, elect, flower, gentry, high society, nobility, pick, upper class
Antonyms dregs, hoi polloi, rabble, riffraff

elocution articulation, declamation, delivery, diction, enunciation, oratory, pronunciation, public speaking, rhetoric, speech, speechmaking, utterance, voice production

elope abscond, bolt, decamp, disappear, escape, leave, run away, run off, slip away, steal away

eloquence expression, expressiveness, fluency, forcefulness, oratory, persuasiveness, rhetoric, way with words

eloquent articulate, fluent, forceful, graceful, moving, persuasive, silver-tongued, stirring, well-expressed
Antonyms faltering, halting,

hesitant, inarticulate, speechless, stumbling, tongue-tied, wordless

elsewhere abroad, absent, away, hence (*Archaic*), in *or* to another place, not here, not present, somewhere else

elucidate annotate, clarify, clear up, explain, explicate, expound, gloss, illuminate, illustrate, interpret, make plain, shed *or* throw light upon, spell out, unfold

elude avoid, circumvent, dodge, duck (*Inf.*), escape, evade, flee, get away from, outrun, shirk, shun

elusive difficult to catch, shifty, slippery, tricky

emaciated atrophied, attenuate, attenuated, cadaverous, gaunt, haggard, lank, lean, meagre, pinched, scrawny, skeletal, thin, undernourished, wasted

emanate arise, come forth, derive, emerge, flow, issue, originate, proceed, spring, stem

emancipate deliver, discharge, disencumber, disenthral, enfranchise, free, liberate, manumit, release, set free, unchain, unfetter, unshackle
Antonyms bind, capture, enchain, enslave, enthral, fetter, shackle, subjugate, yoke

emancipation deliverance, discharge, enfranchisement, freedom, liberation, liberty, manumission, release
Antonyms bondage, captivity, confinement, detention, enthralment, imprisonment, servitude, slavery, thraldom

embargo *n.* ban, bar, barrier, blockage, check, hindrance, impediment, interdict, interdiction, prohibition, proscription, restraint, restriction, stoppage

embark 1. board ship, go aboard, put on board, take on board, take ship 2. *With* on *or* upon begin, broach, commence, engage, enter, initiate, launch, plunge into, set about, set out, start, take up, undertake
Antonyms (*sense 1*) alight, ar-

rive, get off, go ashore, land, step out of

embarrass abash, chagrin, confuse, discomfit, discompose, disconcert, discountenance, distress, fluster, mortify, put out of countenance, shame, show up (*Inf.*)

embarrassing awkward, blushmaking, compromising, discomfiting, disconcerting, distressing, humiliating, mortifying, sensitive, shameful, shaming, touchy, tricky, uncomfortable

embarrassment awkwardness, bashfulness, chagrin, confusion, discomfiture, discomposure, distress, humiliation, mortification, self-consciousness, shame, showing up (*Inf.*)

embellish adorn, beautify, bedeck, deck, decorate, dress up, elaborate, embroider, enhance, enrich, exaggerate, festoon, garnish, gild, grace, ornament, tart up (*Sl.*), varnish

embezzle abstract, appropriate, defalcate (*Law*), filch, have one's hand in the till (*Inf.*), misapply, misappropriate, misuse, peculate, pilfer, purloin, rip off (*Sl.*), steal

embitter alienate, anger, disaffect, disillusion, envenom, make bitter *or* resentful, poison, sour

emblem badge, crest, device, figure, image, insignia, mark, representation, sigil (*Rare*), sign, symbol, token, type

embrace *v.* 1. canoodle (*Sl.*), clasp, cuddle, encircle, enfold, grasp, hold, hug, seize, squeeze, take *or* hold in one's arms 2. accept, adopt, avail oneself of, espouse, grab, make use of, receive, seize, take up, welcome ~*n.* 3. clasp, clinch (*Sl.*), cuddle, hug, squeeze

embroil complicate, compromise, confound, confuse, disorder, disturb, encumber, enmesh, ensnare, entangle, implicate, incriminate, involve, mire, mix up, muddle, perplex, trouble

embryo beginning, germ, nucleus, root, rudiment

emend amend, correct, edit, improve, rectify, redact, revise

emerge 1. appear, arise, become visible, come forth, come into view, come out, come up, emanate, issue, proceed, rise, spring up, surface **2.** become apparent, become known, come out, come to light, crop up, develop, materialize, transpire, turn up
Antonyms depart, disappear, enter, fade, fall, recede, retreat, sink, submerge, vanish from sight, wane, withdraw

emergency crisis, danger, difficulty, exigency, extremity, necessity, pass, pinch, plight, predicament, quandary, scrape (*Inf.*), strait

emigrate migrate, move, move abroad, remove

eminence celebrity, dignity, distinction, esteem, fame, greatness, illustriousness, importance, notability, note, pre-eminence, prestige, prominence, rank, renown, reputation, repute, superiority

eminent celebrated, conspicuous, distinguished, elevated, esteemed, exalted, famous, grand, great, high, high-ranking, illustrious, important, notable, noted, noteworthy, outstanding, paramount, pre-eminent, prestigious, prominent, renowned, signal, superior, well-known
Antonyms anonymous, commonplace, infamous, lowly, ordinary, undistinguished, unheard-of, unimportant, unknown, unremarkable, unsung

emission diffusion, discharge, ejaculation, ejection, emanation, exhalation, exudation, issuance, issue, radiation, shedding, transmission, utterance, venting

emit breathe forth, cast out, diffuse, discharge, eject, emanate, exhale, exude, give off, give out, give vent to, issue, radiate, send forth, send out, shed, throw out, transmit, utter, vent

Antonyms absorb, assimilate, consume, devour, digest, drink in, incorporate, ingest, receive, soak up, suck up, take in

emotion agitation, ardour, excitement, feeling, fervour, passion, perturbation, sensation, sentiment, vehemence, warmth

emotional 1. demonstrative, excitable, feeling, hot-blooded, passionate, responsive, sensitive, sentimental, susceptible, temperamental, tender, warm **2.** ardent, enthusiastic, fervent, fervid, fiery, heated, impassioned, passionate, roused, stirred, zealous
Antonyms apathetic, cold, detached, dispassionate, insensitive, phlegmatic, undemonstrative, unemotional, unenthusiastic, unexcitable, unfeeling

emphasis accent, accentuation, attention, decidedness, force, importance, impressiveness, insistence, intensity, moment, positiveness, power, pre-eminence, priority, prominence, significance, strength, stress, underscoring, weight

emphasize accent, accentuate, dwell on, give priority to, highlight, insist on, lay stress on, play up, press home, put the accent on, stress, underline, underscore, weight
Antonyms gloss over, make light of, make little of, minimize, play down, soft-pedal (*Inf.*), underplay

emphatic absolute, categorical, certain, decided, definite, direct, distinct, earnest, energetic, forceful, forcible, important, impressive, insistent, marked, momentous, positive, powerful, pronounced, resounding, significant, striking, strong, telling, unequivocal, unmistakable, vigorous

empire commonwealth, domain, imperium (*Rare*), kingdom, realm

employ *v.* **1.** commission, engage, enlist, hire, retain, take on **2.** engage, fill, keep busy, make use of, occupy, spend, take up, use up

employed active, busy, engaged, in a job, in employment, in work, occupied, working
Antonyms idle, jobless, laid off, on the dole (*Brit. Inf.*), out of a job, out of work, redundant, unoccupied

employee hand, job-holder, staff member, wage-earner, worker, workman

employer boss (*Inf.*), business, company, establishment, firm, gaffer (*Inf., chiefly Brit.*), organization, outfit (*Inf.*), owner, patron, proprietor

employment 1. engagement, enlistment, hire, retaining, taking on **2.** application, exercise, exertion, use, utilization **3.** avocation (*Archaic*), business, calling, craft, employ, job, line, métier, occupation, profession, pursuit, service, trade, vocation, work

empower allow, authorize, commission, delegate, enable, entitle, license, permit, qualify, sanction, warrant

emptiness 1. bareness, blankness, desertedness, desolation, destitution, vacancy, vacuum, void, waste **2.** cheapness, hollowness, idleness, insincerity, triviality, trivialness

empty adj. **1.** bare, blank, clear, deserted, desolate, destitute, hollow, unfurnished, uninhabited, unoccupied, untenanted, vacant, void, waste **2.** aimless, banal, bootless, frivolous, fruitless, futile, hollow, inane, ineffective, meaningless, purposeless, senseless, silly, unreal, unsatisfactory, unsubstantial, vain, valueless, worthless **3.** absent, blank, expressionless, unintelligent, vacant, vacuous ∼v. **4.** clear, consume, deplete, discharge, drain, dump, evacuate, exhaust, gut, pour out, unburden, unload, use up, vacate, void
Antonyms adj. busy, fulfilled, inhabited, interesting, meaningful, occupied, purposeful, satisfying, serious, significant, useful, valu-

able, worthwhile ∼v. cram, fill, pack, replenish, stock, stuff

enable allow, authorize, capacitate, commission, empower, facilitate, fit, license, permit, prepare, qualify, sanction, warrant
Antonyms bar, block, hinder, impede, obstruct, prevent, stop, thwart

enact authorize, command, decree, establish, legislate, ordain, order, pass, proclaim, ratify, sanction

enamoured bewitched, captivated, charmed, crazy about (*Inf.*), enchanted, enraptured, entranced, fascinated, fond, infatuated, in love, nuts on or about (*Sl.*), smitten, swept off one's feet, taken, wild about (*Inf.*)

enchant beguile, bewitch, captivate, cast a spell on, charm, delight, enamour, enrapture, enthral, fascinate, hypnotize, mesmerize, spellbind

enchanting alluring, appealing, attractive, bewitching, captivating, charming, delightful, endearing, entrancing, fascinating, lovely, pleasant, ravishing, winsome

enclose 1. bound, circumscribe, cover, encase, encircle, encompass, environ, fence, hedge, hem in, pen, shut in, wall in, wrap **2.** include, insert, put in, send with

encompass 1. circle, circumscribe, encircle, enclose, envelop, environ, girdle, hem in, ring, surround **2.** bring about, cause, contrive, devise, effect, manage

encounter v. **1.** bump into (*Inf.*), chance upon, come upon, confront, experience, face, happen on or upon, meet, run across, run into (*Inf.*) **2.** attack, clash with, combat, come into conflict with, contend, cross swords with, do battle with, engage, fight, grapple with, strive, struggle ∼n. **3.** brush, confrontation, meeting, rendezvous

encourage animate, buoy up, cheer, comfort, console, embolden, hearten, incite, inspire, inspirit, rally, reassure, rouse, stimulate

Antonyms daunt, depress, deter, discourage, dishearten, dispirit, dissuade, scare

encouragement advocacy, aid, boost, cheer, consolation, favour, help, incitement, inspiration, inspiritment, promotion, reassurance, stimulation, stimulus, succour, support, urging

encouraging bright, cheerful, cheering, comforting, good, heartening, hopeful, promising, reassuring, rosy, satisfactory, stimulating

Antonyms daunting, depressing, disappointing, discouraging, disheartening, dispiriting, offputting (*Inf.*), unfavourable, unpropitious

encroach appropriate, arrogate, impinge, infringe, intrude, invade, make inroads, overstep, trench, trespass, usurp

end *n.* **1.** bound, boundary, edge, extent, extreme, extremity, limit, point, terminus, tip **2.** attainment, cessation, close, closure, completion, conclusion, consequence, consummation, culmination, denouement, ending, expiration, expiry, finale, finish, issue, outcome, resolution, result, stop, termination, upshot, wind-up **3.** aim, aspiration, design, drift, goal, intent, intention, object, objective, point, purpose, reason **4.** annihilation, death, demise, destruction, dissolution, doom, extermination, extinction, ruin, ruination ~*v.* **5.** bring to an end, cease, close, complete, conclude, culminate, dissolve, expire, finish, resolve, stop, terminate, wind up

Antonyms *n.* beginning, birth, commencement, inception, launch, opening, origin, outset, prelude, source, start ~*v.* begin, come into being, commence, initiate, launch, originate, start

endanger compromise, hazard, imperil, jeopardize, put at risk, put in danger, risk, threaten

Antonyms defend, guard, preserve, protect, safeguard, save, secure

endeavour 1. *n.* aim, attempt, crack (*Inf.*), effort, enterprise, essay, go, shot (*Inf.*), stab (*Inf.*), trial, try, undertaking, venture **2.** *v.* aim, aspire, attempt, do one's best, essay, have a go (crack, shot, stab), labour, make an effort, strive, struggle, take pains, try, undertake

ending catastrophe, cessation, close, completion, conclusion, consummation, culmination, denouement, end, finale, finish, resolution, termination, wind-up

Antonyms birth, commencement, inauguration, inception, onset, opening, origin, preface, source, start, starting point

endless 1. boundless, ceaseless, constant, continual, eternal, everlasting, immortal, incessant, infinite, interminable, limitless, measureless, perpetual, unbounded, unbroken, undying, unending, uninterrupted, unlimited **2.** interminable, monotonous, overlong **3.** continuous, unbroken, undivided, whole

Antonyms bounded, brief, circumscribed, finite, limited, passing, restricted, temporary, terminable, transient, transitory

endorse, indorse advocate, affirm, approve, authorize, back, champion, confirm, favour, ratify, recommend, sanction, subscribe to, support, sustain, vouch for, warrant

endow award, bequeath, bestow, confer, donate, endue, enrich, favour, finance, fund, furnish, give, grant, invest, leave, make over, provide, settle on, supply, will

endurance bearing, fortitude, patience, perseverance, persistence, pertinacity, resignation, resolution, stamina, staying power, strength, submission, sufferance, tenacity, toleration

endure 1. bear, brave, cope with, experience, go through, stand, stick it out (*Inf.*), suffer, support, sustain, take it (*Inf.*), thole

(*Scot.*), undergo, weather, withstand 2. abide, allow, bear, brook, countenance, permit, put up with, stand, stick (*Sl.*), stomach, submit to, suffer, swallow, take patiently, tolerate

enemy adversary, antagonist, competitor, foe, opponent, rival, the opposition, the other side
Antonyms ally, confederate, friend, supporter

energetic active, animated, brisk, dynamic, forceful, forcible, high-powered, indefatigable, lively, potent, powerful, spirited, strenuous, strong, tireless, vigorous, zippy (*Inf.*)
Antonyms debilitated, dull, enervated, inactive, lazy, lethargic, lifeless, listless, slow, sluggish, torpid, weak

energy activity, animation, ardour, brio, drive, efficiency, élan, exertion, fire, force, forcefulness, get-up-and-go (*Inf.*), go (*Inf.*), intensity, life, liveliness, pluck, power, spirit, stamina, strength, strenuousness, verve, vigour, vim (*Sl.*), vitality, vivacity, zeal, zest, zip (*Inf.*)

enforce administer, apply, carry out, coerce, compel, constrain, exact, execute, implement, impose, insist on, oblige, prosecute, put in force, put into effect, reinforce, require, urge

engage 1. appoint, commission, employ, enlist, enrol, hire, retain, take on 2. bespeak, book, charter, hire, lease, prearrange, rent, reserve, secure 3. absorb, busy, engross, grip, involve, occupy, preoccupy, tie up 4. *Military* assail, attack, combat, come to close quarters with, encounter, fall on, fight with, give battle to, join battle with, meet, take on 5. activate, apply, bring into operation, energize, set going, switch on 6. dovetail, interact, interconnect, interlock, join, mesh
Antonyms (*sense 1*) axe (*Inf.*), discharge, dismiss, fire (*Inf.*), give notice to, lay off, oust, remove, sack (*Inf.*)

engaged affianced, betrothed (*Archaic*), pledged, promised, spoken for
Antonyms available, fancy-free, free, unattached, uncommitted, unengaged

engagement 1. assurance, betrothal, bond, compact, contract, oath, obligation, pact, pledge, promise, troth (*Archaic*), undertaking, vow, word 2. appointment, arrangement, commitment, date, meeting 3. action, battle, combat, conflict, confrontation, contest, encounter, fight

engineer 1. *n.* architect, contriver, designer, deviser, director, inventor, manager, manipulator, originator, planner, schemer 2. *v.* bring about, cause, concoct, contrive, control, create, devise, effect, encompass, finagle (*Inf.*), manage, manoeuvre, mastermind, originate, plan, plot, scheme, wangle (*Inf.*)

engrave carve, chase, chisel, cut, enchase (*Rare*), etch, grave (*Archaic*), inscribe

engrossed absorbed, captivated, caught up, deep, enthralled, fascinated, gripped, immersed, intent, intrigued, lost, preoccupied, rapt, riveted

enjoy 1. appreciate, be entertained by, be pleased with, delight in, like, rejoice in, relish, revel in, take joy in, take pleasure in *or* from 2. be blessed *or* favoured with, experience, have, have the benefit of, have the use of, own, possess, reap the benefits of, use
Antonyms (*sense 1*) abhor, despise, detest, dislike, hate, have no taste *or* stomach for, loathe

enjoyable agreeable, amusing, delectable, delicious, delightful, entertaining, gratifying, pleasant, pleasing, pleasurable, satisfying, to one's liking
Antonyms despicable, disagreeable, displeasing, hateful, loathsome, obnoxious, offensive, repugnant, unenjoyable, unpleasant, unsatisfying, unsavoury

enjoyment amusement, delectation, delight, diversion, entertainment, fun, gladness, gratification, gusto, happiness, indulgence, joy, pleasure, recreation, relish, satisfaction, zest

enlarge add to, amplify, augment, blow up (*Inf.*), broaden, diffuse, dilate, distend, elongate, expand, extend, grow, heighten, increase, inflate, lengthen, magnify, make *or* grow larger, multiply, stretch, swell, wax, widen
Antonyms abbreviate, abridge, compress, condense, curtail, decrease, diminish, lessen, narrow, reduce, shorten, shrink, trim, truncate

enlighten advise, apprise, cause to understand, civilize, counsel, edify, educate, inform, instruct, make aware, teach

enlist engage, enrol, enter (into), gather, join up, muster, obtain, procure, recruit, register, secure, sign up, volunteer

enliven animate, brighten, buoy up, cheer, cheer up, excite, exhilarate, fire, gladden, hearten, inspire, inspirit, invigorate, pep up, perk up, quicken, rouse, spark, stimulate, vitalize, vivify, wake up
Antonyms chill, dampen, deaden, depress, put a damper on, repress, subdue

enmity acrimony, animosity, animus, antagonism, antipathy, aversion, bad blood, bitterness, hate, hatred, hostility, ill will, malevolence, malice, malignity, rancour, spite, venom
Antonyms affection, amity, cordiality, friendliness, friendship, geniality, goodwill, harmony, love, warmth

enormity atrociousness, atrocity, depravity, disgrace, evilness, heinousness, monstrousness, nefariousness, outrageousness, turpitude, viciousness, vileness, villainy, wickedness

enormous astronomic, Brobdingnagian, colossal, excessive, gargantuan, gigantic, gross, huge, immense, jumbo (*Inf.*), mammoth, massive, monstrous, mountainous, prodigious, titanic, tremendous, vast
Antonyms diminutive, dwarf, infinitesimal, insignificant, Lilliputian, little, meagre, microscopic, midget, minute, petite, pint-sized (*Inf.*), small, tiny, trivial, wee

enough 1. *adj.* abundant, adequate, ample, plenty, sufficient **2.** *adv.* abundantly, adequately, amply, fairly, moderately, passably, reasonably, satisfactorily, sufficiently, tolerably

enquire 1. ask, query, question, request information, seek information **2.** *Also* **inquire** conduct an inquiry, examine, explore, inspect, investigate, look into, make inquiry, probe, scrutinize, search

enquiry *Also* **inquiry** examination, exploration, inquest, inspection, investigation, probe, research, scrutiny, search, study, survey

enrage aggravate (*Inf.*), anger, exasperate, incense, incite, inflame, infuriate, irritate, madden, make one's blood boil, make one see red (*Inf.*), provoke
Antonyms appease, assuage, calm, conciliate, mollify, pacify, placate, soothe

en route in transit, on *or* along the way, on the road

ensue arise, attend, be consequent on, befall, come after, come next, come to pass (*Archaic*), derive, flow, follow, issue, proceed, result, stem, succeed, supervene, turn out *or* up

entail bring about, call for, cause, demand, encompass, give rise to, impose, involve, lead to, necessitate, occasion, require, result in

entangle 1. catch, compromise, embroil, enmesh, ensnare, entrap, foul, implicate, involve, knot, mat, mix up, ravel, snag, snare, tangle, trammel, trap **2.** bewilder, complicate, confuse, jumble, mix up, muddle, perplex, puzzle, snarl, twist

Antonyms (*sense 1*) detach, disconnect, disengage, disentangle, extricate, free, loose, separate, sever, unfold, unravel, unsnarl, untangle, untwist (*sense 2*) clarify, clear (up), resolve, simplify, work out

enter 1. arrive, come *or* go in *or* into, insert, introduce, make an entrance, pass into, penetrate, pierce 2. become a member of, begin, commence, commit oneself to, embark upon, enlist, enrol, join, participate in, set about, set out on, sign up, start, take part in, take up 3. inscribe, list, log, note, record, register, set down, take down 4. offer, present, proffer, put forward, register, submit, tender

Antonyms depart, drop out, exit, go, issue from, leave, pull out, resign, retire, take one's leave, withdraw

enterprise 1. adventure, effort, endeavour, essay, operation, plan, programme, project, undertaking, venture 2. activity, adventurousness, alertness, audacity, boldness, daring, dash, drive, eagerness, energy, enthusiasm, get-up-and-go (*Inf.*), gumption (*Inf.*), initiative, push (*Inf.*), readiness, resource, resourcefulness, spirit, vigour, zeal 3. business, company, concern, establishment, firm, operation

enterprising active, adventurous, alert, audacious, bold, daring, dashing, eager, energetic, enthusiastic, go-ahead, intrepid, keen, ready, resourceful, spirited, stirring, up-and-coming, venturesome, vigorous, zealous

entertain 1. amuse, charm, cheer, delight, divert, occupy, please, recreate (*Rare*), regale 2. accommodate, be host to, harbour, have company, have guests *or* visitors, lodge, put up, show hospitality to, treat

entertainment amusement, cheer, distraction, diversion, enjoyment, fun, good time, leisure activity, pastime, play, pleasure,

recreation, satisfaction, sport, treat

enthusiasm ardour, avidity, devotion, eagerness, earnestness, excitement, fervour, frenzy, interest, keenness, passion, relish, vehemence, warmth, zeal, zest

enthusiast admirer, aficionado, buff (*Inf.*), devotee, fan, fanatic, fiend (*Inf.*), follower, freak (*Sl.*), lover, supporter, zealot

enthusiastic ardent, avid, devoted, eager, earnest, ebullient, excited, exuberant, fervent, fervid, forceful, hearty, keen, lively, passionate, spirited, unqualified, unstinting, vehement, vigorous, warm, wholehearted, zealous

Antonyms apathetic, blasé, bored, cool, dispassionate, halfhearted, indifferent, nonchalant, unconcerned, unenthusiastic, uninterested

entice allure, attract, beguile, cajole, coax, decoy, draw, inveigle, lead on, lure, persuade, prevail on, seduce, tempt, wheedle

entire complete, full, gross, total, whole

entirely absolutely, altogether, completely, fully, in every respect, perfectly, thoroughly, totally, unreservedly, utterly, wholly, without exception, without reservation

Antonyms incompletely, moderately, partially, partly, piecemeal, slightly, somewhat, to a certain extent *or* degree

entitle 1. accredit, allow, authorize, empower, enable, enfranchise, fit for, license, make eligible, permit, qualify for, warrant 2. call, characterize, christen, denominate, designate, dub, label, name, style, term, title

entrance[1] *n.* 1. access, avenue, door, doorway, entry, gate, ingress, inlet, opening, passage, portal, way in 2. appearance, arrival, coming in, entry, ingress, introduction 3. access, admission, admittance, entrée, entry, ingress, permission to enter

Antonyms departure, egress,

exit, exodus, leave-taking, outlet, way out

entrance² *v.* bewitch, captivate, charm, delight, enchant, enrapture, enthral, fascinate, gladden, ravish, spellbind, transport
Antonyms bore, disenchant, irritate, offend, put off, turn off

entrant 1. beginner, convert, initiate, neophyte, newcomer, new member, novice, probationer, tyro **2.** candidate, competitor, contestant, entry, participant, player

entrust, intrust assign, authorise, charge, commend, commit, confide, consign, delegate, deliver, give custody of, hand over, invest, trust, turn over

entry 1. appearance, coming in, entering, entrance, initiation, introduction **2.** access, avenue, door, doorway, entrance, gate, ingress, inlet, opening, passage, passageway, portal, way in **3.** access, admission, entrance, entrée, free passage, permission to enter **4.** attempt, candidate, competitor, contestant, effort, entrant, participant, player, submission
Antonyms departure, egress, exit, leave, leave-taking, withdrawal

envelop blanket, cloak, conceal, cover, embrace, encase, encircle, enclose, encompass, enfold, engulf, enwrap, hide, obscure, sheathe, shroud, surround, swaddle, swathe, veil, wrap

envelope case, casing, coating, cover, covering, jacket, sheath, shell, skin, wrapper, wrapping

enviable advantageous, blessed, covetable, desirable, favoured, fortunate, lucky, much to be desired, privileged

envious begrudging, covetous, green-eyed, green with envy, grudging, jaundiced, jealous, malicious, resentful, spiteful

environment atmosphere, background, conditions, context, domain, element, habitat, locale,

medium, milieu, scene, setting, situation, surroundings, territory

envoy agent, ambassador, courier, delegate, deputy, diplomat, emissary, intermediary, legate, messenger, minister, plenipotentiary, representative

envy 1. *n.* covetousness, enviousness, grudge, hatred, ill will, jealousy, malice, malignity, resentfulness, resentment, spite, the green-eyed monster (*Inf.*) **2.** *v.* be envious (of), begrudge, be jealous (of), covet, grudge, resent

epidemic 1. *adj.* general, pandemic, prevailing, prevalent, rampant, rife, sweeping, wide-ranging, widespread **2.** *n.* contagion, growth, outbreak, plague, rash, spread, upsurge, wave

epigram aphorism, *bon mot*, quip, witticism

epilogue afterword, coda, concluding speech, conclusion, postscript
Antonyms exordium, foreword, introduction, preamble, preface, prelude, prologue

episode 1. adventure, affair, business, circumstance, event, experience, happening, incident, matter, occurrence **2.** chapter, instalment, part, passage, scene, section

epistle communication, letter, message, missive, note

epitome archetype, embodiment, essence, exemplar, personification, quintessence, representation, type, typical example

equable 1. agreeable, calm, composed, easy-going, even-tempered, imperturbable, level-headed, placid, serene, temperate, unexcitable, unflappable (*Inf.*), unruffled **2.** consistent, constant, even, smooth, stable, steady, temperate, tranquil, unchanging, uniform, unvarying

equal *adj.* **1.** alike, commensurate, equivalent, identical, like, one and the same, proportionate, tantamount, the same, uniform **2.** balanced, corresponding, egalitarian, even, evenly balanced, evenly matched, evenly proportioned, fifty-fifty (*Inf.*), level pegging (*Brit. inf.*), matched, regular, symmetrical, uniform, unvarying **3.** able, adequate, capable, competent, fit, good enough, ready, strong enough, suitable, up to ~*n.* **4.** brother, compeer, counterpart, equivalent, fellow, match, mate, parallel, peer, rival, twin

Antonyms *adj.* different, disproportionate, dissimilar, diverse, inadequate, inequitable, irregular, unbalanced, unequal, uneven, unlike, unmatched

equality balance, coequality, correspondence, egalitarianism, equal opportunity, equatability, equivalence, evenness, fairness, identity, likeness, parity, sameness, similarity, uniformity

Antonyms bias, discrimination, disparity, imparity, inequality, lack of balance, prejudice, unevenness, unfairness

equate agree, balance, be commensurate, compare, correspond with *or* to, equalize, liken, make *or* be equal, match, offset, pair, parallel, square, tally, think of together

equation agreement, balancing, comparison, correspondence, equality, equalization, equating, equivalence, likeness, match, pairing, parallel

equilibrium **1.** balance, counterpoise, equipoise, evenness, rest, stability, steadiness, symmetry **2.** calm, calmness, collectedness, composure, coolness, equanimity, poise, self-possession, serenity, stability, steadiness

equip accoutre, arm, array, attire, deck out, dress, endow, fit out, fit up, furnish, kit out, outfit, prepare, provide, rig, stock, supply

equipment accoutrements, apparatus, appurtenances, baggage, equipage, furnishings, furniture, gear, materiel, outfit, paraphernalia, rig, stuff, supplies, tackle, tools

equivalence agreement, alikeness, conformity, correspondence, equality, evenness, identity, interchangeableness, likeness, match, parallel, parity, sameness, similarity, synonymy

equivalent *adj.* alike, commensurate, comparable, correspondent, corresponding, equal, even, homologous, interchangeable, of a kind, same, similar, synonymous, tantamount

equivocal ambiguous, ambivalent, doubtful, dubious, evasive, indefinite, indeterminate, misleading, oblique, obscure, prevaricating, questionable, suspicious, uncertain, vague

era aeon, age, cycle, date, day *or* days, epoch, generation, period, stage, time

eradicate abolish, annihilate, deracinate, destroy, efface, eliminate, erase, expunge, exterminate, extinguish, extirpate, obliterate, remove, root out, stamp out, uproot, weed out, wipe out

erect **1.** *adj.* elevated, firm, perpendicular, pricked-up, raised, rigid, standing, stiff, straight, upright, vertical **2.** *v.* build, construct, elevate, lift, mount, pitch, put up, raise, rear, set up, stand up

Antonyms *adj.* bent, flaccid, horizontal, leaning, limp, prone, recumbent, relaxed, supine ~*v.* demolish, destroy, dismantle, raze, tear down

erode abrade, consume, corrode, destroy, deteriorate, disintegrate, eat away, grind down, spoil, wear down *or* away

err be inaccurate, be incorrect, be in error, blunder, go astray, go wrong, make a mistake, misapprehend, miscalculate, misjudge, mistake, slip up (*Inf.*)

errand charge, commission, job, message, mission, task

erratic aberrant, abnormal, capricious, changeable, desultory, eccentric, fitful, inconsistent, irregular, shifting, unpredictable, unreliable, unstable, variable, wayward

Antonyms certain, consistent, constant, dependable, invariable, natural, normal, predictable, regular, reliable, stable, steady, straight, unchanging, undeviating

erroneous amiss, fallacious, false, faulty, flawed, inaccurate, incorrect, inexact, invalid, mistaken, spurious, unfounded, unsound, untrue, wrong

error bloomer (*Inf.*), blunder, boner (*Sl.*), boob (*Sl.*), delusion, erratum, fallacy, fault, flaw, howler (*Inf.*), inaccuracy, misapprehension, miscalculation, misconception, mistake, oversight, slip, solecism

erudite cultivated, cultured, educated, knowledgeable, learned, lettered, literate, scholarly, well-educated, well-read

Antonyms ignorant, illiterate, shallow, uneducated, uninformed, unlettered, unschooled, untaught, unthinking

erupt be ejected, belch forth, blow up, break out, burst forth, burst into, burst out, discharge, explode, flare up, gush, pour forth, spew forth *or* out, spit out, spout, throw off, vent, vomit

eruption discharge, ejection, explosion, flare-up, outbreak, outburst, sally, venting

escalate amplify, ascend, be increased, enlarge, expand, extend, grow, heighten, increase, intensify, magnify, mount, raise, rise, step up

Antonyms abate, contract, decrease, descend, diminish, fall, lessen, limit, lower, shrink, wane, wind down

escapade adventure, antic, caper, fling, lark (*Inf.*), mischief, prank, romp, scrape (*Inf.*), spree, stunt, trick

escape *v.* 1. abscond, bolt, break free *or* out, decamp, do a bunk (*Sl.*), flee, fly, get away, make *or* effect one's escape, make one's getaway, run away *or* off, skip,

slip away ~*n.* 2. bolt, break, break-out, decampment, flight, getaway ~*v.* 3. avoid, circumvent, dodge, duck, elude, evade, pass, shun, slip ~*n.* 4. avoidance, circumvention, elusion, evasion ~*v.* 5. discharge, drain, emanate, flow, gush, issue, leak, pour forth, seep, spurt ~*n.* 6. discharge, drain, effluence, efflux, emanation, emission, gush, leak, leakage, outflow, outpour, seepage, spurt

escort 1. *n.* bodyguard, company, convoy, cortege, entourage, guard, protection, retinue, safeguard, train 2. *v.* accompany, chaperon, conduct, convoy, guard, guide, lead, partner, protect, shepherd, squire, usher

especially chiefly, conspicuously, exceptionally, extraordinarily, mainly, markedly, notably, outstandingly, principally, remarkably, signally, specially, strikingly, supremely, uncommonly, usually

essay article, composition, discourse, disquisition, dissertation, paper, piece, tract

essence 1. being, core, crux, entity, heart, kernel, life, lifeblood, meaning, nature, pith, principle, quiddity, quintessence, significance, soul, spirit, substance 2. concentrate, distillate, elixir, extract, spirits, tincture

essential *adj.* 1. crucial, important, indispensable, necessary, needed, requisite, vital 2. basic, cardinal, constitutional, elemental, elementary, fundamental, inherent, innate, intrinsic, key, main, principal ~*n.* 3. basic, fundamental, must, necessity, prerequisite, principle, requisite, rudiment, *sine qua non*, vital part **Antonyms** accessory, dispensable, expendable, extra, extraneous, incidental, inessential, lesser, minor, nonessential, option, secondary, superfluous, surplus, trivial, unimportant, unnecessary

establish base, constitute, create,

decree, enact, ensconce, entrench, fix, form, found, ground, implant, inaugurate, install, institute, organize, plant, root, secure, settle, set up, start

establishment 1. business, company, concern, corporation, enterprise, firm, house, institute, institution, organization, outfit (*Inf.*), setup (*Inf.*), structure, system **2. the Establishment** established order, institutionalized authority, ruling class, the powers that be, the system

estate area, demesne, domain, holdings, lands, manor, property

esteem 1. *v.* admire, be fond of, cherish, honour, like, love, prize, regard highly, respect, revere, reverence, think highly of, treasure, value, venerate **2.** *n.* admiration, consideration, credit, estimation, good opinion, honour, regard, respect, reverence, veneration

estimate *v.* **1.** appraise, assess, calculate roughly, evaluate, gauge, guess, judge, number, reckon, value **2.** assess, believe, conjecture, consider, form an opinion, guess, judge, rank, rate, reckon, surmise, think ~*n.* **3.** appraisal, appraisement, approximate calculation, assessment, evaluation, guess, guesstimate (*Inf.*), judgment, reckoning, valuation

estuary creek, firth, fjord, inlet, mouth

et cetera and others, and so forth, and so on, and the like, and the rest, et al.

eternal abiding, ceaseless, constant, deathless, endless, everlasting, immortal, infinite, interminable, never-ending, perennial, perpetual, sempiternal (*Literary*), timeless, unceasing, undying, unending, unremitting, without end

Antonyms changing, ephemeral, evanescent, finite, fleeting, infrequent, irregular, occasional, random, rare, temporal, transient, transitory

ethical conscientious, correct, decent, fair, fitting, good, honest, honourable, just, moral, principled, proper, right, righteous, upright, virtuous

Antonyms dishonourable, disreputable, immoral, improper, indecent, low-down, underhand, unethical, unfair, unscrupulous, unseemly

ethics conscience, moral code, morality, moral philosophy, moral values, principles, rules of conduct, standards

etiquette civility, code, convention, courtesy, customs, decorum, formalities, good *or* proper behaviour, manners, politeness, politesse, propriety, protocol, rules, usage

evacuate abandon, clear, decamp, depart, desert, forsake, leave, move out, pull out, quit, relinquish, remove, vacate, withdraw

evade avoid, circumvent, decline, dodge, duck, elude, escape, escape the clutches of, get away from, shirk, shun, sidestep, steer clear of

Antonyms brave, confront, encounter, face, meet, meet face to face

evaluate appraise, assay, assess, calculate, estimate, gauge, judge, rank, rate, reckon, size up (*Inf.*), value, weigh

evaporate 1. dehydrate, desiccate, dry, dry up, vaporize **2.** dematerialize, disappear, dispel, disperse, dissipate, dissolve, evanesce, fade, fade away, melt, melt away, vanish

evasion artifice, avoidance, circumvention, cop-out (*Sl.*), cunning, dodge, elusion, equivocation, escape, evasiveness, excuse, fudging, obliqueness, pretext, prevarication, ruse, shift, shirking, shuffling, sophism, sophistry, subterfuge, trickery, waffle (*Inf.*)

eve day before, night before, vigil

even *adj.* **1.** flat, flush, horizontal, level, parallel, plane, plumb, smooth, steady, straight, true, uniform 2. calm, composed, cool, equable, equanimous, even-tempered, imperturbable, peaceful, placid, serene, stable, steady, tranquil, undisturbed, un-excitable, unruffled, well-balanced 3. balanced, disinterested, dispassionate, equitable, fair, fair and square, impartial, just, unbiased, unprejudiced ~adv. 4. all the more, much, still, yet

Antonyms (sense 1) asymmetrical, awry, bumpy, curving, different, odd, rough, twisting, undulating, uneven, wavy (sense 2) agitated, changeable, emotional, excitable, quick-tempered, unpredictable (sense 3) biased, partial, prejudiced, unbalanced, unequal, unfair

event adventure, affair, business, circumstance, episode, experience, fact, happening, incident, matter, milestone, occasion, occurrence

eventful active, busy, consequential, critical, crucial, decisive, exciting, fateful, full, historic, important, lively, memorable, momentous, notable, noteworthy, remarkable, significant

Antonyms commonplace, dull, humdrum, insignificant, ordinary, trivial, uneventful, unexceptional, unexciting, unimportant, uninteresting, unremarkable

eventually after all, at the end of the day, finally, in the course of time, in the end, in the long run, one day, some day, some time, sooner or later, ultimately, when all is said and done

ever 1. at all, at any time (period, point), by any chance, in any case, on any occasion 2. always, at all times, constantly, continually, endlessly, eternally, everlastingly, evermore, for ever, incessantly, perpetually, relentlessly, to the end of time, unceasingly, unendingly

everlasting abiding, deathless, endless, eternal, immortal, imperishable, indestructible, infinite, interminable, never-ending, perpetual, timeless, undying

Antonyms brief, ephemeral, fleeting, impermanent, passing, short-lived, temporary, transient, transitory

evermore always, eternally, ever, for ever, in perpetuum, to the end of time

everyday accustomed, common, common or garden (Inf.), commonplace, conventional, customary, dull, familiar, frequent, habitual, informal, mundane, ordinary, routine, run-of-the-mill, stock, unexceptional, unimaginative, usual, wonted, workaday

Antonyms best, exceptional, exciting, extraordinary, incidental, individual, infrequent, interesting, irregular, now and then, occasional, original, outlandish, periodic, special, uncommon, unusual

evict boot out (Inf.), chuck out (Inf.), dislodge, dispossess, eject, expel, kick out (Inf.), oust, put out, remove, show the door (to), throw on to the streets, throw out, turf out (Inf.), turn out

evidence n. affirmation, attestation, averment, confirmation, corroboration, data, declaration, demonstration, deposition, grounds, indication, manifestation, mark, proof, sign, substantiation, testimony, token, witness

evident apparent, clear, conspicuous, incontestable, incontrovertible, indisputable, manifest, noticeable, obvious, palpable, patent, perceptible, plain, tangible, unmistakable, visible

Antonyms ambiguous, concealed, doubtful, dubious, hidden, imperceptible, obscure, questionable, secret, uncertain, unclear, unknown, vague

evidently apparently, it seems, it would seem, ostensibly, outwardly, seemingly, to all appearances

evil adj. 1. bad, base, corrupt,

depraved, heinous, immoral, iniquitous, maleficent, malevolent, malicious, malignant, nefarious, reprobate, sinful, vicious, vile, villainous, wicked, wrong ~*n.* **2.** badness, baseness, corruption, curse, depravity, heinousness, immorality, iniquity, malefactor, cence, malignity, sin, sinfulness, turpitude, vice, viciousness, villainy, wickedness, wrong, wrongdoing ~*adj.* **3.** baneful (*Archaic*), calamitous, catastrophic, deleterious, destructive, detrimental, dire, disastrous, harmful, hurtful, inauspicious, injurious, mischievous, painful, pernicious, ruinous, sorrowful, unfortunate, unlucky, woeful

evoke 1. arouse, awaken, call, excite, give rise to, induce, recall, rekindle, stimulate, stir up, summon up **2.** call forth, educe (*Rare*), elicit, produce, provoke

evolution development, enlargement, evolvement, expansion, growth, increase, maturation, progress, progression, unfolding, unrolling, working out

evolve develop, disclose, educe, elaborate, enlarge, expand, grow, increase, mature, open, progress, unfold, unroll, work out

exact *adj.* **1.** accurate, careful, correct, definite, explicit, express, faithful, faultless, identical, literal, methodical, orderly, particular, precise, right, specific, true, unequivocal, unerring, veracious, very **2.** careful, exacting, meticulous, painstaking, punctilious, rigorous, scrupulous, severe, strict ~*v.* **3.** call for, claim, command, compel, demand, extort, extract, force, impose, insist upon, require, squeeze, wrest, wring

Antonyms *adj.* approximate, careless, imprecise, inaccurate, incorrect, indefinite, inexact, loose, rough, slovenly

exactly *adv.* **1.** accurately, carefully, correctly, definitely, explicitly, faithfully, faultlessly, literally, methodically, precisely,

rigorously, scrupulously, severely, strictly, truly, truthfully, unequivocally, unerringly, veraciously **2.** absolutely, bang, explicitly, expressly, indeed, in every respect, just, particularly, precisely, quite, specifically

exactness accuracy, carefulness, correctness, exactitude, faithfulness, faultlessness, nicety, orderliness, painstakingness, preciseness, precision, promptitude, regularity, rigorousness, rigour, scrupulousness, strictness, truth, unequivocalness, veracity

Antonyms imprecision, inaccuracy, incorrectness, inexactness, unfaithfulness

exaggerate amplify, embellish, embroider, emphasize, enlarge, exalt, hyperbolize, inflate, lay it on thick (*Inf.*), magnify, overdo, overemphasize, overestimate, overstate

exaggeration amplification, embellishment, emphasis, enlargement, exaltation, excess, extravagance, hyperbole, inflation, magnification, overemphasis, overestimation, overstatement, pretension, pretentiousness

Antonyms litotes, meiosis, restraint, underplaying, understatement

exalt advance, aggrandize, dignify, elevate, ennoble, honour, promote, raise, upgrade

exalted august, dignified, elevated, eminent, grand, high, highranking, honoured, lofty, prestigious

examination analysis, assay, catechism, checkup, exploration, inquiry, inquisition, inspection, interrogation, investigation, observation, perusal, probe, questioning, quiz, research, review, scrutiny, search, study, survey, test, trial

examine analyse, appraise, assay, check, check out, consider, explore, go over *or* through, inspect, investigate, look over, pe-

example 164 **exchange**

ruse, ponder, pore over, probe, review, scan, scrutinize, sift, study, survey, take stock of, test, vet, weigh

example 1. case, case in point, exemplification, illustration, instance, sample, specimen **2. for example** as an illustration, by way of illustration, e.g., *exempli gratia*, for instance, to cite an instance, to illustrate

exasperate aggravate (*Inf.*), anger, annoy, bug (*Inf.*), embitter, enrage, exacerbate, excite, gall, get (*Inf.*), incense, inflame, infuriate, irk, irritate, madden, needle (*Inf.*), nettle, peeve (*Inf.*), pique, provoke, rankle, rile (*Inf.*), rouse, try the patience of, vex

exasperation aggravation (*Inf.*), anger, annoyance, exacerbation, fury, ire (*Literary*), irritation, passion, pique, provocation, rage, vexation, wrath

excavate burrow, cut, delve, dig, dig out, dig up, gouge, hollow, mine, quarry, scoop, trench, tunnel, uncover, unearth

exceed beat, be superior to, better, cap (*Inf.*), eclipse, excel, go beyond, outdistance, outdo, outreach, outrun, outshine, outstrip, overtake, pass, surmount, surpass, top, transcend

excel beat, be superior, better, cap (*Inf.*), eclipse, exceed, go beyond, outdo, outrival, outshine, pass, surmount, surpass, top, transcend

excellence distinction, eminence, fineness, goodness, greatness, high quality, merit, perfection, pre-eminence, purity, superiority, supremacy, transcendence, virtue, worth

excellent A1 (*Inf.*), admirable, brilliant (*Inf.*), capital, champion, choice, distinguished, estimable, exemplary, exquisite, fine, first-class, first-rate, good, great, meritorious, notable, noted, outstanding, prime, select, sterling, superb, superior, superlative, tiptop, top-notch (*Inf.*), worthy
Antonyms bad, dreadful, faulty,

imperfect, incompetent, inexpert, inferior, lousy (*Sl.*), mediocre, poor, rotten (*Inf.*), secondclass, second-rate, substandard, terrible, unskilled

except, except for apart from, bar, barring, besides, but, excepting, excluding, exclusive of, omitting, other than, save (*Archaic*), saving, with the exception of

exception anomaly, departure, deviation, freak, inconsistency, irregularity, oddity, peculiarity, quirk, special case

exceptional excellent, extraordinary, marvellous, outstanding, phenomenal, prodigious, remarkable, special, superior
Antonyms average, awful, bad, lousy (*Sl.*), mediocre, ordinary, second-rate, unexceptional, unremarkable

excess n. **1.** glut, leftover, overabundance, overdose, overflow, overload, plethora, remainder, superabundance, superfluity, surfeit, surplus, too much **2.** debauchery, dissipation, dissoluteness, exorbitance, extravagance, immoderation, intemperance, overindulgence, prodigality, unrestraint ~*adj.* **3.** extra, leftover, redundant, remaining, residual, spare, superfluous, surplus
Antonyms (*sense 1*) dearth, deficiency, insufficiency, lack, shortage, want (*sense 2*) moderation, restraint, self-control, selfdiscipline, self-restraint, temperance

excessive disproportionate, enormous, exaggerated, exorbitant, extravagant, extreme, immoderate, inordinate, intemperate, needless, overdone, overmuch, prodigal, profligate, superfluous, too much, unconscionable, undue, unreasonable

exchange 1. *v.* bandy, barter, change, commute, convert into, interchange, reciprocate, swap (*Inf.*), switch, trade, truck **2.** *n.* barter, dealing, interchange, quid pro quo, reciprocity, substitution, swap (*Inf.*), switch, tit for tat, trade, traffic, truck

excitable edgy, emotional, hasty, highly strung, hot-headed, hot-tempered, irascible, mercurial, nervous, passionate, quick-tempered, sensitive, susceptible, temperamental, testy, touchy, uptight (*Inf.*), violent, volatile
Antonyms calm, cool, cool-headed, even-tempered, imperturbable, laid-back (*Inf.*), placid, unexcitable, unruffled

excite agitate, animate, arouse, awaken, discompose, disturb, electrify, elicit, evoke, fire, foment, galvanize, incite, inflame, inspire, instigate, kindle, move, provoke, quicken, rouse, stimulate, stir up, thrill, titillate, waken, whet

excitement action, activity, ado, adventure, agitation, animation, commotion, discomposure, elation, enthusiasm, ferment, fever, flurry, furore, heat, kicks (*Inf.*), passion, perturbation, thrill, tumult, warmth

exciting electrifying, exhilarating, inspiring, intoxicating, moving, provocative, rip-roaring (*Inf.*), rousing, sensational, stimulating, stirring, thrilling, titillating
Antonyms boring, dreary, dull, flat, humdrum, monotonous, unexciting, uninspiring, uninteresting

exclaim call, call out, cry, cry out, declare, ejaculate, proclaim, shout, utter, vociferate, yell

exclamation call, cry, ejaculation, expletive, interjection, outcry, shout, utterance, vociferation, yell

exclude 1. ban, bar, blackball, debar, disallow, embargo, forbid, interdict, keep out, ostracize, prohibit, proscribe, refuse, shut out, veto 2. count out, eliminate, except, ignore, leave out, omit, pass over, preclude, reject, repudiate, rule out, set aside
Antonyms accept, admit, allow, count, include, let in, permit, receive, welcome

exclusive 1. aristocratic, chic, choice, clannish, classy (*Sl.*), cliquish, closed, discriminative, elegant, fashionable, limited, narrow, posh (*Inf.*), private, restricted, restrictive, select, selfish, snobbish 2. confined, limited, peculiar, restricted, unique
Antonyms common, communal, open, popular, public, sociable, unrestricted

excommunicate anathematize, ban, banish, cast out, denounce, eject, exclude, expel, proscribe, remove, repudiate, unchurch

excursion airing, day trip, expedition, jaunt, journey, outing, pleasure trip, ramble, tour, trip

excuse *v.* 1. absolve, acquit, bear with, exculpate, exonerate, extenuate, forgive, indulge, make allowances for, overlook, pardon, pass over, tolerate, turn a blind eye to, wink at 2. absolve, discharge, exempt, free, let off, liberate, release, relieve, spare ~*n.* 3. apology, defence, explanation, grounds, justification, mitigation, plea, pretext, reason, vindication
Antonyms *v.* accuse, arraign, blame, censure, charge, chasten, chastise, criticize, compel, condemn, convict, correct, hold responsible, indict, oblige, punish, sentence ~*n.* accusation, charge, imputation, indictment

execute behead, electrocute, guillotine, hang, kill, put to death, shoot

execution 1. accomplishment, achievement, administration, carrying out, completion, consummation, discharge, effect, enactment, enforcement, implementation, operation, performance, prosecution, realization, rendering 2. capital punishment, hanging, killing

executive *n.* 1. administrator, director, manager, official 2. administration, directorate, directors, government, hierarchy, leadership, management ~*adj.*

3. administrative, controlling, decision-making, directing, governing, managerial

exemplary admirable, commendable, correct, estimable, excellent, good, honourable, ideal, laudable, meritorious, model, praiseworthy, punctilious, sterling

exemplify demonstrate, depict, display, embody, evidence, exhibit, illustrate, instance, manifest, represent, serve as an example of, show

exempt 1. *v.* absolve, discharge, except, excuse, exonerate, free, grant immunity, let off, liberate, release, relieve, spare 2. *adj.* absolved, clear, discharged, excepted, excused, favoured, free, immune, liberated, not liable, not subject, privileged, released, spared
Antonyms *adj.* accountable, answerable, chargeable, liable, obligated, responsible, subject

exercise *v.* 1. apply, bring to bear, employ, enjoy, exert, practise, put to use, use, utilize, wield 2. discipline, drill, habituate, inure, practise, train, work out ~*n.* 3. action, activity, discipline, drill, drilling, effort, labour, toil, training, work, work-out 4. drill, lesson, practice, problem, schooling, schoolwork, task, work

exert bring into play, bring to bear, employ, exercise, expend, make use of, put forth, use, utilize, wield

exertion action, application, attempt, effort, employment, endeavour, exercise, industry, labour, pains, strain, stretch, struggle, toil, travail (*Literary*), trial, use, utilization

exhaust 1. bankrupt, cripple, debilitate, disable, drain, enervate, enfeeble, fatigue, impoverish, prostrate, sap, tire, tire out, weaken, wear out 2. consume, deplete, dissipate, expend, finish, run through, spend, squander, use up, waste 3. drain, dry, empty, strain, void

exhausted 1. all in (*Sl.*), beat (*Sl.*), crippled, dead (*Inf.*), dead beat (*Inf.*), dead tired, debilitated, disabled, dog-tired (*Inf.*), done in (*Inf.*), drained, enervated, enfeebled, fatigued, jaded, knackered (*Sl.*), out on one's feet, prostrated, ready to drop, sapped, spent, tired out, wasted, weak, worn out 2. at an end, consumed, depleted, dissipated, done, expended, finished, gone, spent, squandered, used up, wasted
Antonyms active, animated, conserved, enlivened, invigorated, kept, preserved, refreshed, rejuvenated, replenished, restored, revived, stimulated

exhausting arduous, back-breaking, crippling, debilitating, difficult, draining, enervating, fatiguing, gruelling, hard, laborious, punishing, sapping, strenuous, taxing, testing, tiring

exhibit 1. *v.* air, demonstrate, disclose, display, evidence, evince, expose, express, flaunt, indicate, make clear *or* plain, manifest, offer, parade, present, put on view, reveal, show 2. *n.* display, exhibition, illustration, model, show

exhort admonish, advise, beseech, bid, call upon, caution, counsel, encourage, enjoin, entreat, goad, incite, persuade, press, spur, urge, warn

exile *n.* 1. banishment, deportation, expatriation, expulsion, ostracism, proscription, separation 2. deportee, émigré, expatriate, outcast, refugee ~*v.* 3. banish, deport, drive out, eject, expatriate, expel, ostracize, oust, proscribe

exist abide, be, be extant, be living, be present, breathe, continue, endure, happen, last, live, obtain, occur, prevail, remain, stand, survive

existence actuality, animation, being, breath, continuance, continuation, duration, endurance, life, subsistence, survival

exit *n.* door, egress, gate, outlet, passage out, vent, way out
Antonyms entrance, entry, ingress, inlet, opening, way in

expand amplify, augment, bloat, blow up, broaden, develop, dilate, distend, enlarge, extend, fatten, fill out, grow, heighten, increase, inflate, lengthen, magnify, multiply, prolong, protract, swell, thicken, wax, widen
Antonyms abbreviate, close, condense, contract, decrease, reduce, shorten, shrink

expanse area, breadth, extent, field, plain, range, space, stretch, sweep, tract

expansive affable, communicative, easy, effusive, free, friendly, garrulous, genial, loquacious, open, outgoing, sociable, talkative, unreserved, warm

expect 1. assume, believe, calculate, conjecture, forecast, foresee, imagine, presume, reckon, suppose, surmise, think, trust **2.** anticipate, await, bargain for, contemplate, envisage, hope for, look ahead to, look for, look forward to, predict, watch for

expectation assumption, assurance, belief, calculation, confidence, conjecture, forecast, likelihood, presumption, probability, supposition, surmise, trust

expediency, expedience advantageousness, advisability, appropriateness, aptness, benefit, convenience, desirability, effectiveness, fitness, helpfulness, judiciousness, meetness, practicality, pragmatism, profitability, properness, propriety, prudence, suitability, usefulness, utilitarianism, utility

expedient *adj.* advantageous, advisable, appropriate, beneficial, convenient, desirable, effective, fit, helpful, judicious, meet, opportune, politic, practical, pragmatic, profitable, proper, prudent, suitable, useful, utilitarian, worthwhile
Antonyms detrimental, disadvantageous, futile, harmful, ill-advised, impractical, imprudent, inadvisable, inappropriate, ineffective, inexpedient, unwise, wrong

expedition enterprise, excursion, exploration, journey, mission, quest, safari, tour, trek, trip, undertaking, voyage

expel 1. belch, cast out, discharge, dislodge, drive out, eject, remove, spew, throw out **2.** ban, banish, bar, blackball, discharge, dismiss, drum out, evict, exclude, exile, expatriate, oust, proscribe, send packing, throw out, turf out (*Inf.*)
Antonyms (*sense 2*) admit, allow to enter, give access, let in, receive, take in, welcome

expend consume, disburse, dissipate, employ, exhaust, fork out (*Sl.*), go through, lay out (*Inf.*), pay out, shell out (*Inf.*), spend, use (up)

expendable dispensable, inessential, nonessential, replaceable, unimportant, unnecessary
Antonyms crucial, essential, indispensable, key, necessary, vital

expenditure application, charge, consumption, cost, disbursement, expense, outgoings, outlay, output, payment, spending, use

expense charge, consumption, cost, disbursement, expenditure, loss, outlay, output, payment, sacrifice, spending, toll, use

expensive costly, dear, excessive, exorbitant, extravagant, high-priced, inordinate, lavish, overpriced, rich, steep (*Inf.*), stiff
Antonyms bargain, budget, cheap, cut-price, economical, inexpensive, low-cost, low-priced, reasonable

experience *n.* **1.** contact, doing, evidence, exposure, familiarity, involvement, know-how (*Inf.*), knowledge, observation, participation, practice, proof, training, trial, understanding **2.** adventure, affair, encounter, episode, event, happening, incident, occurrence, ordeal, test, trial ~*v.* **3.** apprehend, become familiar with, behold, encounter, endure, face, feel, go through, have, know, live through, meet, observe, participate in, perceive, sample, sense, suffer, sustain, taste, try, undergo

experienced accomplished, adept, capable, competent, expert, familiar, knowledgeable, master, practised, professional, qualified, seasoned, skilful, tested, trained, tried, veteran, well-versed

Antonyms apprentice, green, incompetent, inexperienced, new, unqualified, unskilled, untrained, untried

experiment 1. *n.* assay, attempt, examination, experimentation, investigation, procedure, proof, research, test, trial, trial and error, trial run, venture **2.** *v.* assay, examine, investigate, put to the test, research, sample, test, try, verify

experimental empirical, exploratory, pilot, preliminary, probationary, provisional, speculative, tentative, test, trial, trial-and-error

expert 1. *n.* ace (*Inf.*), adept, authority, connoisseur, dab hand (*Inf.*), master, past master, pro (*Inf.*), professional, specialist, virtuoso, wizard **2.** *adj.* able, adept, adroit, apt, clever, deft, dexterous, experienced, facile, handy, knowledgeable, master, masterly, practised, professional, proficient, qualified, skilful, skilled, trained, virtuoso

Antonyms *n.* amateur, dabbler, ham, layman, nonprofessional, novice ~ *adj.* amateurish, cack-handed (*Inf.*), clumsy, incompetent, inexperienced, unpractised, unqualified, unskilled, untrained

expertise ableness, adroitness, aptness, cleverness, command, deftness, dexterity, expertness, facility, judgment, knack, know-how (*Inf.*), knowledge, masterliness, mastery, proficiency, skilfulness, skill

expire 1. cease, close, come to an end, conclude, end, finish, lapse,

run out, stop, terminate **2.** decease, depart, die, kick the bucket (*Inf.*), pass away *or* on, perish

explain clarify, clear up, define, demonstrate, describe, disclose, elucidate, explicate (*Formal*), expound, illustrate, interpret, make clear *or* plain, resolve, solve, teach, unfold

explanation 1. clarification, definition, demonstration, description, elucidation, explication, exposition, illustration, interpretation, resolution **2.** account, answer, cause, excuse, justification, meaning, mitigation, motive, reason, sense, significance, vindication

explicit absolute, categorical, certain, clear, definite, direct, distinct, exact, express, frank, open, outspoken, patent, plain, positive, precise, specific, stated, straightforward, unambiguous, unequivocal, unqualified, unreserved

Antonyms ambiguous, cryptic, general, implicit, implied, indefinite, indirect, inexact, obscure, suggested, uncertain, vague

explode 1. blow up, burst, detonate, discharge, erupt, go off, set off, shatter, shiver **2.** belie, debunk, discredit, disprove, give the lie to, invalidate, refute, repudiate

exploit 1. *n.* accomplishment, achievement, adventure, attainment, deed, feat, stunt **2.** *v.* abuse, impose upon, manipulate, milk, misuse, play on *or* upon, take advantage of

exploration analysis, examination, inquiry, inspection, investigation, probe, research, scrutiny, search, study

explore analyse, examine, inquire into, inspect, investigate, look into, probe, prospect, research, scrutinize, search

explosion bang, blast, burst, clap, crack, detonation, discharge, outburst, report

explosive 1. unstable, volatile **2.**

fiery, stormy, touchy, vehement, violent

exponent advocate, backer, champion, defender, promoter, propagandist, proponent, spokesman, spokeswoman, supporter, upholder

expose 1. display, exhibit, manifest, present, put on view, reveal, show, uncover, unveil 2. air, betray, bring to light, denounce, detect, disclose, divulge, lay bare, let out, make known, reveal, show up, smoke out, uncover, unearth, unmask
Antonyms conceal, cover, hide, keep secret, screen

exposed 1. bare, exhibited, laid bare, made manifest, made public, on display, on show, on view, revealed, shown, unconcealed, uncovered, unveiled 2. open, open to the elements, unprotected, unsheltered

exposure 1. baring, display, exhibition, manifestation, presentation, publicity, revelation, showing, uncovering, unveiling 2. airing, betrayal, denunciation, detection, disclosure, divulgence, divulging, exposé, revelation, unmasking

expound describe, elucidate, explain, explicate (*Formal*), illustrate, interpret, set forth, spell out, unfold

express *v.* 1. articulate, assert, asseverate, communicate, couch, declare, enunciate, phrase, pronounce, put, put across, put into words, say, speak, state, tell, utter, verbalize, voice, word ~*adj.* 2. clearcut, especial, particular, singular, special 3. direct, fast, high-speed, nonstop, quick, rapid, speedy, swift

expression 1. announcement, assertion, asseveration, communication, declaration, enunciation, mention, pronouncement, speaking, statement, utterance, verbalization, voicing 2. demonstration, embodiment, exhibition, indication, manifestation, representation, show, sign, symbol, to-

ken 3. choice of words, delivery, diction, emphasis, execution, intonation, language, phraseology, phrasing, speech, style, wording 4. idiom, locution, phrase, remark, set phrase, term, turn of phrase, word

expressly especially, exactly, intentionally, on purpose, particularly, precisely, purposely, specially, specifically

expulsion banishment, debarment, discharge, dislodgment, dismissal, ejection, eviction, exclusion, exile, expatriation, extrusion, proscription, removal

exquisite 1. beautiful, dainty, delicate, elegant, fine, lovely, precious 2. attractive, beautiful, charming, comely, lovely, pleasing, striking
Antonyms ill-favoured, ugly, unattractive, unlovely, unsightly

extend 1. carry on, continue, drag out, draw out, elongate, lengthen, make longer, prolong, protract, spin out, spread out, stretch, unfurl, unroll 2. add to, amplify, augment, broaden, develop, dilate, enhance, enlarge, expand, increase, spread, supplement, widen
Antonyms abbreviate, abridge, condense, contract, curtail, cut, decrease, limit, reduce, restrict, shorten

extension addendum, addition, adjunct, annexe, appendage, appendix, branch, ell, supplement, wing

extensive all-inclusive, broad, capacious, commodious, comprehensive, expanded, extended, far-flung, far-reaching, general, great, huge, large, large-scale, lengthy, long, pervasive, prevalent, protracted, spacious, sweeping, thorough, universal, vast, voluminous, wholesale, wide, widespread
Antonyms circumscribed, confined, constricted, limited, narrow, restricted, tight

extent 1. bounds, compass, play, range, reach, scope, sphere, sweep **2.** amount, amplitude, area, breadth, bulk, degree, duration, expanse, expansion, length, magnitude, measure, quantity, size, stretch, term, time, volume, width

exterior 1. *n.* appearance, aspect, coating, covering, façade, face, finish, outside, shell, skin, surface **2.** *adj.* external, outer, outermost, outside, outward, superficial, surface

Antonyms *n.* inner, inside, interior ~*adj* inherent, inside, interior, internal, intrinsic

exterminate abolish, annihilate, destroy, eliminate, eradicate, extirpate

external apparent, exterior, outer, outermost, outside, outward, superficial, surface, visible

Antonyms inherent, inner, inside, interior, internal, intrinsic

extinct dead, defunct, gone, lost, vanished

Antonyms existing, extant, flourishing, living, surviving, thriving

extinction abolition, annihilation, death, destruction, dying out, eradication, excision, extermination, extirpation, obliteration, oblivion

extinguish 1. blow out, douse, put out, quench, smother, snuff out, stifle **2.** abolish, annihilate, destroy, eliminate, end, eradicate, erase, expunge, exterminate, extirpate, kill, obscure, remove, suppress, wipe out

extol acclaim, applaud, celebrate, commend, cry up, eulogize, exalt, glorify, laud, magnify (*Archaic*), panegyrize, pay tribute to, praise, sing the praises of

extort blackmail, bleed (*Inf.*), bully, coerce, exact, extract, force, squeeze, wrest, wring

extra 1. *adj.* accessory, added, additional, ancillary, auxiliary, fresh, further, more, new, other, supplemental, supplementary **2.** *n.* accessory, addendum, addition, adjunct, affix, appendage, appurtenance, attachment, bonus, complement, extension, supernumerary, supplement **3.** *adv.* especially, exceptionally, extraordinarily, extremely, particularly, remarkably, uncommonly, unusually

Antonyms *n.* essential, must, necessity, precondition, prerequisite, requirement, requisite

extract *v.* **1.** draw, extirpate, pluck out, pull, pull out, remove, take out, uproot, withdraw **2.** bring out, derive, draw, elicit, evoke, exact, gather, get, glean, obtain, reap, wrest, wring ~*n.* **3.** concentrate, decoction, distillate, distillation, essence, juice **4.** abstract, citation, clipping, cutting, excerpt, passage, quotation, selection

extraordinary amazing, bizarre, curious, exceptional, fantastic, marvellous, odd, outstanding, particular, peculiar, phenomenal, rare, remarkable, singular, special, strange, surprising, uncommon, unfamiliar, unheard-of, unique, unprecedented, unusual, unwonted, weird, wonderful

Antonyms common, commonplace, customary, everyday, ordinary, unexceptional, unremarkable, usual

extravagance improvidence, lavishness, overspending, prodigality, profligacy, profusion, squandering, waste, wastefulness

extravagant 1. excessive, improvident, imprudent, lavish, prodigal, profligate, spendthrift, wasteful **2.** costly, excessive, exorbitant, expensive, extortionate, inordinate, overpriced, steep (*Inf.*), unreasonable

Antonyms careful, conservative, economical, frugal, miserly, prudent, restrained, sensible, sober, sparing, thrifty, tight-fisted (*Inf.*)

extreme *adj.* **1.** acute, great, greatest, high, highest, intense, maximum, severe, supreme, ultimate, utmost, uttermost, worst **2.** faraway, far-off, farthest, final, last, most distant, outermost, remotest, terminal, ultimate, utmost, uttermost ~*n.* **3.** acme, apex, apogee, boundary, climax, consummation, depth, edge, end, excess, extremity, height, limit, maximum, minimum, nadir, pinnacle, pole, termination, top, ultimate, zenith

Antonyms *adj.* nearest

extremely acutely, awfully (*Inf.*), exceedingly, exceptionally, excessively, extraordinarily, greatly, highly, inordinately, intensely, markedly, quite, severely, terribly, *to or* in the extreme, ultra, uncommonly, unusually, utterly, very

extremity 1. acme, apex, apogee, border, bound, boundary, brim, brink, edge, end, extreme, frontier, limit, margin, maximum, minimum, nadir, pinnacle, pole, rim, terminal, termination, terminus, tip, top, ultimate, verge, zenith **2.** *Plural* fingers and toes, hands and feet, limbs

extricate clear, deliver, disembarrass, disengage, disentangle, free, get out, get (someone) off the hook (*Sl.*), liberate, release, relieve, remove, rescue, withdraw, wriggle out of

exuberance 1. animation, buoyancy, cheerfulness, eagerness, ebullience, effervescence, energy, enthusiasm, excitement, exhilaration, high spirits, life, liveliness, spirit, sprightliness, vigour, vitality, vivacity, zest **2.** abundance, copiousness, lavishness, lushness, luxuriance, plenitude, profusion, rankness, richness, superabundance, teemingness

exuberant 1. animated, buoyant, cheerful, eager, ebullient, effervescent, elated, energetic, enthusiastic, excited, exhilarated, full of life, high-spirited, in high

spirits, lively, sparkling, spirited, sprightly, vigorous, vivacious, zestful **2.** abundant, copious, lavish, lush, luxuriant, overflowing, plenteous, plentiful, profuse, rank, rich, superabundant, teeming

exult be delighted, be elated, be in high spirits, be joyful, be jubilant, be overjoyed, celebrate, jubilate, jump for joy, make merry, rejoice

eye *n.* **1.** eyeball, optic (*Inf.*), orb (*Poetic*), peeper (*Sl.*) **2.** appreciation, discernment, discrimination, judgment, perception, recognition, taste **3. keep an** *or* **one's eye on** guard, keep in view, keep tabs on (*Inf.*), keep under surveillance, look after, look out for, monitor, observe, pay attention to, regard, scrutinize, supervise, survey, watch, watch over **4. see eye to eye** accord, agree, back, be in unison, coincide, concur, fall in, get on, go along, harmonize, jibe (*Inf.*), subscribe to **5. up to one's eyes** busy, caught up, engaged, flooded out, fully occupied, inundated, overwhelmed, up to here, up to one's elbows, wrapped up in ~*v.* **6.** contemplate, gaze at, glance at, have *or* take a look at, inspect, look at, peruse, regard, scan, scrutinize, stare at, study, survey, view, watch

eyesight observation, perception, range of vision, sight, vision

eyesore atrocity, blemish, blight, blot, disfigurement, disgrace, horror, mess, monstrosity, sight (*Inf.*), ugliness

eyewitness bystander, looker-on, observer, onlooker, passer-by, spectator, viewer, watcher, witness

F

fabric 1. cloth, material, stuff, textile, web **2.** constitution, construction, foundations, framework, infrastructure, make-up, organization, structure

fabulous n. **1.** amazing, astounding, breathtaking, fictitious, immense, inconceivable, incredible, legendary, phenomenal, unbelievable **2.** apocryphal, fantastic, fictitious, imaginary, invented, legendary, made-up, mythical, unreal
Antonyms actual, common, commonplace, credible, genuine, natural, ordinary, real

façade appearance, exterior, face, front, frontage, guise, mask, pretence, semblance, show, veneer

face n. **1.** clock (Sl.), countenance, dial (Sl.), features, kisser (Sl.), lineaments, mug (Sl.), phiz or phizog (Sl.), physiognomy, visage **2.** appearance, aspect, expression, frown, grimace, look, moue, pout, scowl, smirk **3. face to face** à deux, confronting, eyeball to eyeball, in confrontation, opposite, tête-à-tête, vis-à-vis **4. on the face of it** apparently, at first sight, seemingly, to all appearances, to the eye ~v. **5.** be confronted by, brave, come up against, confront, cope with, deal with, defy, encounter, experience, meet, oppose **6.** be opposite, front onto, give towards or onto, look onto, overlook

facet angle, aspect, face, part, phase, plane, side, slant, surface

facetious amusing, comical, droll, flippant, frivolous, funny, humorous, jesting, jocose, jocular, merry, playful, pleasant, tongue in cheek, unserious, waggish, witty
Antonyms earnest, genuine,

grave, lugubrious, pensive, sedate, serious, sincere, sober, thoughtful

face up to accept, acknowledge, come to terms with, confront, cope with, deal with, meet head on

facile adept, adroit, dexterous, easy, effortless, fluent, light, proficient, quick, ready, simple, skilful, smooth, uncomplicated
Antonyms awkward, careful, clumsy, difficult, intractable, maladroit, slow, unskilful

facilitate assist the progress of, ease, expedite, forward, further, help, make easy, promote, smooth the path of, speed up
Antonyms delay, encumber, frustrate, hamper, handicap, hinder, hold up or back, impede, obstruct, prevent, restrain, thwart

facility ability, adroitness, dexterity, ease, efficiency, effortlessness, expertness, fluency, gift, knack, proficiency, quickness, readiness, skilfulness, skill, smoothness, talent
Antonyms awkwardness, clumsiness, difficulty, hardship, ineptness, maladroitness, pains

facing adj. fronting, opposite, partnering

facsimile carbon, carbon copy, copy, duplicate, fax, photocopy, Photostat (Trademark), print, replica, reproduction, transcript, Xerox (Trademark)

fact 1. act, deed, event, fait accompli, happening, incident, occurrence, performance **2.** actuality, certainty, gospel (truth), naked truth, reality, truth **3. in fact** actually, indeed, in point of fact, in reality, in truth, really, truly
Antonyms delusion, fable, fabri-

cation, falsehood, fiction, invention, lie, tall story, untruth, yarn (*Inf.*)

faction bloc, cabal, camp, caucus, clique, coalition, combination, confederacy, contingent, coterie, division, gang, ginger group, group, junta, lobby, minority, party, pressure group, section, sector, set, splinter group

factor aspect, cause, circumstance, component, consideration, determinant, element, influence, item, part, point, thing

factory manufactory, mill, plant, works

facts data, details, gen (*Inf.*), info (*Inf.*), information, the lowdown (*Inf.*), the score (*Inf.*), the whole story

factual accurate, authentic, circumstantial, close, correct, credible, exact, faithful, genuine, literal, matter-of-fact, objective, precise, real, sure, true, true-to-life, unadorned, unbiased, veritable

Antonyms embellished, fanciful, fictitious, fictive, figurative, imaginary, unreal

faculty 1. branch of learning, department, discipline, profession, school, teaching staff (*Chiefly U.S.*) **2.** authorization, licence, prerogative, privilege, right

fad affectation, craze, fancy, fashion, mania, mode, rage, trend, vogue, whim

fade 1. blanch, bleach, blench, dim, discolour, dull, grow dim, lose colour, lose lustre, pale, wash out **2.** decline, die away, die out, dim, disappear, disperse, dissolve, droop, dwindle, ebb, etiolate, evanesce, fail, fall, flag, languish, melt away, perish, shrivel, vanish, vanish into thin air, wane, waste away, wilt, wither

faded bleached, dim, discoloured, dull, etiolated, indistinct, lustreless, pale, washed out

fading declining, decreasing, disappearing, dying, on the decline, vanishing

fail 1. be defeated, be found lacking *or* wanting, be in vain, be unsuccessful, break down, come a cropper (*Inf.*), come to grief, come to naught, come to nothing, fall, fall short, fall short of, fall through, fizzle out (*Inf.*), flop (*Inf.*), founder, go astray, go down, go up in smoke (*Inf.*), meet with disaster, miscarry, misfire, miss, not make the grade (*Inf.*), run aground, turn out badly **2.** abandon, break one's word, desert, disappoint, forget, forsake, let down, neglect, omit

Antonyms bloom, flourish, grow, pass, prosper, strengthen, succeed, thrive, triumph

failing *n.* blemish, blind spot, defect, deficiency, drawback, error, failure, fault, flaw, foible, frailty, imperfection, lapse, miscarriage, misfortune, shortcoming, weakness

Antonyms advantage, asset, forte, metier, speciality, strength, strong suit

failure 1. abortion, breakdown, collapse, defeat, downfall, fiasco, frustration, lack of success, miscarriage, overthrow, wreck **2.** black sheep, dead duck (*Inf.*), disappointment, dud (*Inf.*), flop (*Inf.*), incompetent, loser, ne'er-do-well, no-good, no-hoper (*Chiefly Aust.*), nonstarter, washout (*Inf.*) **3.** default, deficiency, dereliction, neglect, negligence, nonobservance, nonperformance, nonsuccess, omission, remissness, shortcoming, stoppage **4.** breakdown, decay, decline, deterioration, failing, loss **5.** bankruptcy, crash, downfall, folding (*Inf.*), insolvency, ruin

Antonyms adequacy, care, effectiveness, fortune, observance, prosperity, strengthening, success, triumph

faint *adj.* **1.** bleached, delicate, dim, distant, dull, faded, faltering, feeble, hazy, hushed, ill-defined, indistinct, light, low, muffled, muted, soft, subdued, thin, vague, whispered **2.** feeble, remote,

slight, unenthusiastic, weak **3.** dizzy, drooping, enervated, exhausted, faltering, fatigued, giddy, languid, lethargic, light-headed, muzzy, vertiginous, weak, woozy (*Inf.*) ~v. **4.** black out, collapse, fade, fail, flake out (*Inf.*), keel over (*Inf.*), languish, lose consciousness, pass out, swoon (*Literary*), weaken
Antonyms *adj.* bold, brave, bright, clear, conspicuous, courageous, distinct, energetic, fresh, hearty, loud, powerful, strong, vigorous

faintly feebly, in a whisper, indistinctly, softly, weakly
Antonyms audacious, bold, brave, courageous, daring, dauntless, fearless, game (*Inf.*), intrepid, plucky, stouthearted

fair¹ *adj.* **1.** above board, according to the rules, clean, disinterested, dispassionate, equal, equitable, even-handed, honest, honourable, impartial, just, lawful, legitimate, objective, on the level (*Inf.*), proper, square, trustworthy, unbiased, unprejudiced, upright **2.** blond, blonde, fair-haired, flaxen-haired, light, light-complexioned, tow-haired, tow-headed **3.** adequate, all right, average, decent, mediocre, middling, moderate, not bad, O.K. (*Inf.*), passable, reasonable, respectable, satisfactory, so-so (*Inf.*), tolerable **4.** beauteous, beautiful, bonny, comely, handsome, lovely, pretty, well-favoured
Antonyms (*sense 1*) bad, biased, bigoted, discriminatory, dishonest, inequitable, partial, partisan, prejudiced, one-sided, unfair, unjust (*sense 4*) homely, plain, ugly

fair² *n.* bazaar, carnival, expo (*Inf.*), exposition, festival, fête, gala, market, show

fairly 1. adequately, moderately, pretty well, quite, rather, reasonably, somewhat, tolerably **2.** deservedly, equitably, justly, objectively, properly, without fear or favour

fairness decency, disinterestedness, equitableness, equity, impartiality, justice, legitimacy, rightfulness, uprightness

fairy brownie, elf, hob, leprechaun, pixie, Robin Goodfellow, sprite

fairy tale *or* **fairy story 1.** folk tale, romance **2.** cock-and-bull story (*Inf.*), fabrication, fantasy, fiction, invention, lie, tall story, untruth

faith 1. assurance, confidence, conviction, credence, credit, dependence, reliance, trust **2.** allegiance, constancy, faithfulness, fealty, fidelity, loyalty, truth, truthfulness
Antonyms agnosticism, apprehension, denial, disbelief, distrust, doubt, incredulity, infidelity, misgiving, mistrust, rejection, scepticism, suspicion, uncertainty

faithful 1. attached, constant, dependable, devoted, loyal, reliable, staunch, steadfast, true, true-blue, trusty, truthful, unswerving, unwavering **2.** accurate, close, exact, just, precise, strict, true
Antonyms disloyal, doubting, faithless, false, false-hearted, fickle, inconstant, perfidious, recreant (*Archaic*), traitorous, treacherous, unbelieving, unfaithful, unreliable, untrue, untrustworthy, untruthful

faithless disloyal, doubting, false, fickle, inconstant, perfidious, traitorous, treacherous, unbelieving, unfaithful, unreliable, untrue, untrustworthy, untruthful

fake 1. *v.* affect, assume, copy, counterfeit, fabricate, feign, forge, pretend, put on, sham, simulate **2.** *n.* charlatan, copy, forgery, fraud, hoax, imitation, impostor, mountebank, phoney (*Sl.*), reproduction, sham

fall *v.* **1.** be precipitated, cascade, collapse, crash, descend, dive, drop, drop down, go head over heels, keel over, nose-dive, pitch, plummet, plunge, settle, sink, stumble, subside, topple, trip, trip

over, tumble **2.** abate, become lower, decline, decrease, depreciate, diminish, dwindle, ebb, fall off, flag, go down, lessen, slump, subside **3.** be overthrown, be taken, capitulate, give in *or* up, give way, go out of office, pass into enemy hands, resign, succumb, surrender, yield ~*n.* **4.** descent, dive, drop, nose dive, plummet, plunge, slip, spill, tumble **5.** cut, decline, decrease, diminution, dip, drop, dwindling, falling off, lessening, lowering, reduction, slump **6.** capitulation, collapse, death, defeat, destruction, downfall, failure, overthrow, resignation, ruin, surrender **7.** declivity, descent, downgrade, incline, slant, slope
Antonyms (*sense 1*) ascend, climb, go up, increase, mount, rise, scale, soar, wax (*sense 2*) advance, appreciate, climb, escalate, extend, heighten, increase (*sense 3*) endure, hold out, prevail, survive, triumph

fallacy casuistry, deceit, deception, delusion, error, falsehood, faultiness, flaw, illusion, inconsistency, misapprehension, misconception, mistake, sophism, sophistry, untruth

fall apart break up, crumble, disband, disintegrate, disperse, dissolve, fall to bits, go *or* come to pieces, lose cohesion, shatter

fall asleep doze off, drop off (*Inf.*), go to sleep, nod off (*Inf.*)

fall back on call upon, employ, have recourse to, make use of, press into service, resort to

fall behind be in arrears, drop back, get left behind, lag, lose one's place, trail

fallible erring, frail, ignorant, imperfect, mortal, prone to error, uncertain, weak
Antonyms divine, faultless, impeccable, infallible, omniscient, perfect, superhuman, unerring, unimpeachable

fall out altercate, argue, clash, differ, disagree, fight, quarrel, squabble

fallow dormant, idle, inactive, inert, resting, uncultivated, undeveloped, unplanted, untilled, unused

false 1. concocted, erroneous, faulty, fictitious, improper, inaccurate, incorrect, inexact, invalid, mistaken, unfounded, unreal, wrong **2.** lying, mendacious, truthless, unreliable, unsound, untrue, untrustworthy, untruthful **3.** artificial, bogus, counterfeit, ersatz, fake, feigned, forged, imitation, mock, pretended, sham, simulated, spurious, synthetic
Antonyms authentic, bona fide, correct, exact, faithful, genuine, honest, loyal, real, right, sincere, sound, true, trustworthy, valid

falsehood 1. deceit, deception, dishonesty, dissimulation, inveracity (*Rare*), mendacity, perjury, prevarication, untruthfulness **2.** fabrication, fib, fiction, lie, misstatement, story, untruth

falsify alter, belie, cook (*Sl.*), counterfeit, distort, doctor, fake, forge, garble, misrepresent, misstate, pervert, tamper with

falter break, hesitate, shake, speak haltingly, stammer, stumble, stutter, totter, tremble, vacillate, waver

fame celebrity, credit, eminence, glory, honour, illustriousness, name, prominence, public esteem, renown, reputation, repute, stardom
Antonyms disgrace, dishonour, disrepute, ignominy, infamy, oblivion, obscurity, shame

familiar 1. accustomed, common, common *or* garden (*Inf.*), conventional, customary, domestic, everyday, frequent, household, mundane, ordinary, recognizable, repeated, routine, stock, well-known **2.** familiar with, abreast of, acquainted with, at home with, *au courant*, *au fait*, aware of, conscious of, conversant with, introduced, knowledgeable, no stranger to, on speaking terms with, versed in, well up in **3.** amicable, chummy

(*Inf.*), close, confidential, cordial, easy, free, free-and-easy, friendly, hail-fellow-well-met, informal, intimate, near, open, relaxed, unceremonious, unconstrained, unreserved

Antonyms aloof, cold, detached, distant, formal, ignorant, infrequent, unaccustomed, unacquainted, uncommon, unfamiliar, unfriendly, uninformed, unknown, unskilled, unusual

familiarity 1. acquaintance, acquaintanceship, awareness, experience, grasp, understanding **2.** absence of reserve, closeness, ease, fellowship, freedom, friendliness, friendship, informality, intimacy, naturalness, openness, sociability, unceremoniousness

Antonyms constraint, decorum, distance, formality, ignorance, inexperience, propriety, reserve, respect, unfamiliarity

family brood, children, descendants, folk (*Inf.*), household, issue, kin, kindred, kinsmen, kith and kin, ménage, offspring, one's nearest and dearest, one's own flesh and blood, people, progeny, relations, relatives

famine dearth, destitution, hunger, scarcity, starvation

famous acclaimed, celebrated, conspicuous, distinguished, eminent, excellent, far-famed, glorious, honoured, illustrious, legendary, lionized, much-publicized, notable, noted, prominent, remarkable, renowned, signal, well-known

Antonyms forgotten, mediocre, obscure, uncelebrated, undistinguished, unexceptional, unknown, unremarkable

fanatic *n.* activist, addict, bigot, devotee, enthusiast, extremist, militant, visionary, zealot

fancy *v.* **1.** be inclined to think, believe, conceive, conjecture, guess, imagine, infer, reckon, suppose, surmise, think, think likely **2.** be attracted to, crave, desire, dream of, hanker after,

have a yen for, long for, relish, wish for, would like, yearn for ~*adj.* **3.** baroque, decorated, decorative, elaborate, elegant, embellished, extravagant, fanciful, intricate, ornamental, ornamented, ornate

Antonyms *adj.* basic, cheap, common, inferior, ordinary, plain, simple, unadorned, undecorated

fantastic comical, eccentric, exotic, fanciful, freakish, grotesque, imaginative, odd, outlandish, peculiar, phantasmagorical, quaint, queer, rococo, strange, unreal, weird, whimsical

Antonyms common, everyday, moderate, normal, ordinary, sensible, typical

far *adv.* **1.** afar, a good way, a great distance, a long way, deep, miles **2.** considerably, decidedly, extremely, greatly, incomparably, much, very much **3. so far** thus far, to date, until now, up to now, up to the present ~*adj.* **4.** distant, faraway, far-flung, far-off, far-removed, long, outlying, out-of-the-way, remote, removed

Antonyms adjacent, adjoining, alongside, at close quarters, beside, bordering, close, contiguous, near, nearby, neighbouring

farce 1. broad comedy, buffoonery, burlesque, comedy, satire, slapstick **2.** absurdity, joke, mockery, nonsense, parody, ridiculousness, sham, travesty

fare *n.* **1.** charge, passage money, price, ticket money, transport cost **2.** commons, diet, eatables, food, meals, menu, provisions, rations, sustenance, table, victuals ~*v.* **3.** do, get along, get on, make out, manage, prosper

farewell adieu, adieux *or* adieus, departure, goodbye, leave-taking, parting, sendoff (*Inf.*), valediction

far-fetched doubtful, dubious, fantastic, hard to swallow (*Inf.*), implausible, improbable, incredible, preposterous, strained, unbelievable, unconvincing, unlikely, unnatural, unrealistic

Antonyms acceptable, authentic, believable, credible, feasible, imaginable, likely, plausible, possible, probable, realistic, reasonable

farm 1. *n.* acreage, acres, croft (*Scot.*), farmstead, grange, holding, homestead, land, plantation, ranch (*Chiefly North American*), smallholding, station (*Aust. & New Zealand*) **2.** *v.* bring under cultivation, cultivate, operate, plant, practise husbandry, till the soil, work

far-reaching broad, extensive, important, momentous, pervasive, significant, sweeping, widespread

fascinate absorb, allure, beguile, bewitch, captivate, charm, delight, enamour, enchant, engross, enrapture, enravish, enthral, entrance, hold spellbound, hypnotize, infatuate, intrigue, mesmerize, rivet, spellbind, transfix
Antonyms alienate, bore, disenchant, disgust, irritate, jade, put one off, sicken, turn one off

fascination allure, attraction, charm, enchantment, glamour, lure, magic, magnetism, pull, sorcery, spell

fashion *n.* **1.** convention, craze, custom, fad, latest, latest style, look, mode, prevailing taste, rage, style, trend, usage, vogue **2.** attitude, demeanour, manner, method, mode, style, way ~*v.* **3.** construct, contrive, create, design, forge, form, make, manufacture, mould, shape, work

fashionable à la mode, all the go (*Inf.*), all the rage, chic, cool (*Sl.*), current, customary, genteel, hip (*Sl.*), in (*Inf.*), in vogue, latest, modern, modish, popular, prevailing, smart, stylish, trendsetting, trendy (*Inf.*), up-to-date, up-to-the-minute, usual, voguish (*Inf.*), with it (*Inf.*)
Antonyms behind the times, dated, frumpy, obsolete, old-fashioned, old-hat, outmoded, out of date, uncool (*Sl.*), unfashion-

able, unpopular, unstylish, untrendy (*Inf.*)

fast[1] *adj.* **1.** accelerated, brisk, fleet, flying, hasty, hurried, mercurial, nippy (*Inf.*), quick, rapid, speedy, swift, winged ~*adv.* **2.** apace, hastily, hell for leather, hurriedly, in haste, like a bat out of hell (*Inf.*), like a flash, like a shot (*Inf.*), posthaste, presto, quickly, rapidly, speedily, swiftly, with all haste ~*adj.* **3.** dissipated, dissolute, extravagant, gadabout, giddy, immoral, intemperate, licentious, loose, profligate, promiscuous, rakish, reckless, self-indulgent, wanton, wild ~*adv.* **4.** extravagantly, intemperately, loosely, promiscuously, rakishly, recklessly, wildly
Antonyms (*sense 1*) leisurely, plodding, slow, slow moving, unhurried (*sense 2*) at a snail's pace, at one's leisure, gradually, leisurely, slowly, steadily, unhurriedly

fast[2] **1.** *v.* abstain, deny oneself, go hungry, go without food, practise abstention, refrain from food or eating **2.** *n.* abstinence, fasting

fasten affix, anchor, attach, bind, bolt, chain, connect, fix, grip, join, lace, link, lock, make fast, make firm, seal, secure, tie, unite

fat *adj.* **1.** beefy (*Inf.*), broad in the beam (*Inf.*), corpulent, elephantine, fleshy, gross, heavy, obese, overweight, plump, podgy, portly, roly-poly, rotund, solid, stout, tubby **2.** adipose, fatty, greasy, oily, oleaginous, suety ~*n.* **3.** adipose tissue, blubber, bulk, cellulite, corpulence, fatness, flab, flesh, obesity, overweight, paunch, weight problem
Antonyms angular, bony, gaunt, lank, lean, scanty, scarce, scrawny, skinny, slender, slight, slim, spare, thin

fatal 1. deadly, destructive, final, incurable, killing, lethal, malignant, mortal, pernicious, terminal **2.** baleful, baneful, calamitous, catastrophic, disastrous, lethal, ruinous

Antonyms beneficial, benign, harmless, inconsequential, innocuous, inoffensive, minor, non-lethal, non-toxic, salutary, vitalizing, wholesome

fate 1. chance, destiny, divine will, fortune, kismet, nemesis, predestination, providence, weird (*Archaic*) 2. end, future, issue, outcome, upshot

fated destined, doomed, foreordained, ineluctable, inescapable, inevitable, marked down, predestined, pre-elected, preordained, sure, written

fateful critical, crucial, decisive, important, portentous, significant **Antonyms** inconsequential, insignificant, nugatory, ordinary, unimportant

father *n*. 1. begetter, dad (*Inf.*), daddy (*Inf.*), governor (*Inf.*), old boy (*Inf.*), old man (*Inf.*), pa (*Inf.*), pater, paterfamilias, patriarch, pop (*Inf.*), sire 2. ancestor, forebear, forefather, predecessor, progenitor 3. abbé, confessor, curé, padre (*Inf.*), pastor, priest ~ *v*. 4. beget, get, procreate, sire

fatherly affectionate, benevolent, benign, forbearing, indulgent, kind, kindly, paternal, patriarchal, protective, supportive, tender

fatigue 1. *v*. drain, drain of energy, exhaust, fag (out) (*Inf.*), jade, knacker (*Inf.*), overtire, poop (*Inf.*), take it out of (*Inf.*), tire, weaken, wear out, weary, whack (*Inf.*) 2. *n*. debility, ennui, heaviness, languor, lethargy, listlessness, overtiredness, tiredness **Antonyms** *n*. alertness, animation, energy, freshness, get up and go, go, indefatigability, life, vigour, zest ~ *v*. refresh, rejuvenate, relieve, rest, revive, stimulate

fault *n*. 1. blemish, defect, deficiency, drawback, failing, flaw, imperfection, infirmity, lack, shortcoming, snag, weakness, weak point 2. delinquency, frailty, lapse, misconduct, misdeed, misdemeanour, offence, peccadillo, sin, transgression, trespass, wrong

Antonyms (*sense 1*) asset, attribute, credit, goodness, merit, perfection, strength, virtue

fault-finding *adj*. captious, carping, censorious, critical, hypercritical, pettifogging

Antonyms complimentary, easily pleased, indiscriminate, uncritical, undiscerning, unexacting, unfussy, unperceptive

faultless 1. accurate, classic, correct, exemplary, faithful, flawless, foolproof, impeccable, model, perfect, unblemished 2. above reproach, blameless, guiltless, immaculate, innocent, irreproachable, pure, sinless, spotless, stainless, unblemished, unspotted, unsullied

faulty bad, blemished, broken, damaged, defective, erroneous, fallacious, flawed, impaired, imperfect, imprecise, inaccurate, incorrect, invalid, malfunctioning, not working, out of order, unsound, weak, wrong

favour *n*. 1. approbation, approval, backing, bias, championship, esteem, favouritism, friendliness, good opinion, good will, grace, kindness, kind regard, partiality, patronage, support 2. benefit, boon, courtesy, good turn, indulgence, kindness, obligement (*Scot. or Archaic*), service 3. **in favour of** all for (*Inf.*), backing, for, on the side of, pro, supporting, to the benefit of ~ *v*. 4. be partial to, esteem, have in one's good books, indulge, pamper, pull strings for (*Inf.*), reward, side with, smile upon, spoil, treat with partiality, value

Antonyms *n*. animosity, antipathy, disapproval, disfavour, disservice, harm, ill will, injury, malevolence, wrong ~ *v*. disapprove, disdain, dislike

favourable advantageous, appropriate, auspicious, beneficial, convenient, encouraging, fair, fit, good, helpful, hopeful, opportune, promising, propitious, suitable, timely

Antonyms disadvantageous, ill-disposed, inauspicious, unfavourable, unhelpful, unpromising, useless

favourably advantageously, auspiciously, conveniently, fortunately, opportunely, profitably, to one's advantage, well

favourite 1. *adj.* best-loved, choice, dearest, esteemed, favoured, preferred **2.** *n.* beloved, blue-eyed boy (*Inf.*), choice, darling, dear, idol, pet, pick, preference, teacher's pet, the apple of one's eye

fawn *v.* Often with *on* or *upon* be obsequious, be servile, bow and scrape, court, crawl, creep, cringe, curry favour, dance attendance, flatter, grovel, ingratiate oneself, kneel, kowtow, lick (someone's) boots, pay court, toady, truckle

fear *n.* **1.** alarm, apprehensiveness, awe, blue funk (*Inf.*), consternation, cravenness, dismay, dread, fright, horror, panic, qualms, terror, timidity, tremors, trepidation **2.** *bête noire*, bogey, bugbear, horror, nightmare, phobia, spectre ~*v.* **3.** apprehend, be apprehensive (afraid, frightened, scared), be in a blue funk (*Inf.*), dare not, dread, have a horror of, have a phobia about, have butterflies in one's stomach (*Inf.*), have qualms, live in dread of, shake in one's shoes, shudder at, take fright, tremble at

fearful 1. afraid, alarmed, anxious, apprehensive, diffident, faint-hearted, frightened, hesitant, intimidated, jittery (*Inf.*), jumpy, nervous, nervy, panicky, pusillanimous, scared, shrinking, tense, timid, timorous, uneasy **2.** appalling, atrocious, awful, dire, distressing, dreadful, frightful, ghastly, grievous, grim, gruesome, hair-raising, hideous, horrendous, horrible, horrific, mon-

strous, shocking, terrible, unspeakable

Antonyms (*sense 1*) bold, brave, confident, courageous, daring, dauntless, doughty, gallant, game (*Inf.*), gutsy (*Sl.*), heroic, indomitable, intrepid, lion-hearted, plucky, unabashed, unafraid, undaunted, unflinching, valiant, valorous

fearless bold, brave, confident, courageous, daring, gallant, heroic, indomitable, intrepid, plucky, unafraid, valiant, valorous

feasible achievable, attainable, likely, possible, practicable, realizable, reasonable, viable, workable

Antonyms impossible, impracticable, inconceivable, unreasonable, untenable, unviable, unworkable

feast *n.* banquet, barbecue, bean-feast (*Brit. inf.*), beano (*Brit. sl.*), blowout (*Sl.*), carousal, carouse, dinner, entertainment, festive board, jollification, junket, repast, revels, slap-up meal (*Brit. inf.*), spread (*Inf.*), treat

feat accomplishment, achievement, act, attainment, deed, exploit, performance

feathers down, plumage, plumes

feature *n.* **1.** aspect, attribute, characteristic, facet, factor, hallmark, mark, peculiarity, point, property, quality, trait **2.** article, column, comment, item, piece, report, story ~*v.* **3.** accentuate, call attention to, emphasize, give prominence to, · give the full works (*Sl.*), headline, play up, present, promote, set off, spotlight, star

federation alliance, amalgamation, association, *Bund*, coalition, combination, confederacy, co-partnership, entente, federacy, league, syndicate, union

fed up (with) annoyed, blue, bored, brassed off (*Inf.*), browned-off (*Inf.*), depressed, discontented, dismal, dissatisfied, down, gloomy, glum, sick and tired of (Inf.), tired of, weary of

fee account, bill, charge, compensation, emolument, hire, honorarium, pay, payment, recompense, remuneration, reward, toll

feeble debilitated, delicate, doddering, effete, enervated, enfeebled, etiolated, exhausted, failing, faint, frail, infirm, languid, powerless, puny, shilpit (Scot.), sickly, weak, weakened, weedy (Sl.) **Antonyms** ardent, effective, energetic, forceful, hale, healthy, hearty, lusty, robust, stalwart, strong, sturdy, successful, vigorous

feebleness debility, delicacy, effeteness, enervation, etiolation, exhaustion, frailness, frailty, incapacity, infirmity, lack of strength, languor, lassitude, sickliness, weakness

feed v. 1. cater for, nourish, provide for, provision, supply, sustain, victual, wine and dine 2. Sometimes with **on** devour, eat, exist on, fare, graze, live on, nurture, partake of, pasture, subsist, take nourishment

feel v. 1. caress, finger, fondle, handle, manipulate, maul, paw, run one's hands over, stroke, touch 2. be aware of, be sensible of, endure, enjoy, experience, go through, have, have a sensation of, know, notice, observe, perceive, suffer, take to heart, undergo 3. explore, fumble, grope, sound, test, try 4. be convinced, feel in one's bones, have a hunch, have the impression, intuit, sense 5. believe, be of the opinion that, consider, deem, hold, judge, think & appear, resemble, seem, strike one as 7. **feel like** could do with, desire, fancy, feel inclined, feel the need for, feel up to, have the inclination, want

feeling 1. feel, perception, sensation, sense, sense of touch, touch 2. apprehension, consciousness, hunch, idea, impression, inkling, notion, presentiment, sense, suspicion 3. inclination, instinct, opinion, point of view

feelings ego, emotions, self-esteem, sensitivities, susceptibilities

fell v. cut, cut down, demolish, flatten, floor, hew, knock down, level, prostrate, raze, strike down

fellow n. 1. bloke (Inf.), boy, chap (Inf.), character, customer (Inf.), guy (Inf.), individual, man, person, punter (Sl.) 2. associate, colleague, companion, compeer, comrade, co-worker, equal, friend, member, partner, peer

fellowship amity, brotherhood, camaraderie, communion, companionability, companionship, familiarity, fraternization, intercourse, intimacy, kindliness, sociability

feminine delicate, gentle, girlish, graceful, ladylike, modest, soft, tender, womanly **Antonyms** indelicate, rough, unladylike, unwomanly

fen bog, holm (Dialect), marsh, morass, moss (Scot.), quagmire, slough, swamp

fence 1. n. barbed wire, barricade, barrier, defence, guard, hedge, paling, palisade, railings, rampart, shield, stockade, wall 2. v. Often with **in** or **off** bound, circumscribe, confine, coop, defend, encircle, enclose, fortify, guard, hedge, pen, protect, restrict, secure, separate, surround

ferment v. 1. boil, brew, bubble, concoct, effervesce, foam, froth, heat, leaven, rise, seethe, work 2. Fig. agitate, boil, excite, fester, foment, heat, incite, inflame, provoke, rouse, seethe, smoulder, stir up ~n. 3. Fig. agitation, brouhaha, commotion, disruption, excitement, fever, frenzy, furore, glow, heat, hubbub, imbroglio, state of unrest, stew, stir, tumult, turbulence, turmoil, unrest, uproar **Antonyms** n. calmness, hush, peacefulness, quiet, restfulness, stillness, tranquillity

ferocious feral, fierce, predatory, rapacious, ravening, savage, violent, wild

Antonyms calm, docile, gentle, mild, subdued, submissive, tame

ferocity barbarity, bloodthirstiness, brutality, cruelty, ferociousness, fierceness, inhumanity, rapacity, ruthlessness, savageness, savagery, viciousness, wildness

ferry 1. *n.* ferryboat, packet, packet boat 2. *v.* carry, chauffeur, convey, run, ship, shuttle, transport

fertile abundant, fat, fecund, flowering, flowing with milk and honey, fruit-bearing, fruitful, generative, luxuriant, plenteous, plentiful, productive, prolific, rich, teeming, yielding

Antonyms barren, dry, impotent, infecund, infertile, poor, sterile, unfruitful, unimaginative, uninventive, unproductive

fertility abundance, fecundity, fruitfulness, luxuriance, productiveness, richness

fervent, fervid animated, ardent, devout, eager, earnest, ecstatic, emotional, enthusiastic, excited, fiery, heartfelt, impassioned, intense, perfervid (*Literary*), vehement, warm, zealous

fervour animation, ardour, eagerness, earnestness, enthusiasm, excitement, fervency, intensity, passion, vehemence, warmth, zeal

festival 1. anniversary, commemoration, feast, fête, fiesta, holiday, holy day, saint's day 2. carnival, celebration, entertainment, festivities, fête, field day, gala, jubilee, treat

festive back-slapping, carnival, celebratory, cheery, Christmassy, convivial, festal, gala, gay, gleeful, happy, hearty, holiday, jolly, jovial, joyful, joyous, jubilant, light-hearted, merry, mirthful, sportive

Antonyms depressing, drab, dreary, funereal, gloomy, lugubrious, mournful, sad

festoon *v.* array, bedeck, beribbon, deck, decorate, drape, garland, hang, swathe, wreathe

fetch 1. bring, carry, conduct, convey, deliver, escort, get, go for, lead, obtain, retrieve, transport 2. draw forth, elicit, give rise to, produce 3. bring in, earn, go for, make, realize, sell for, yield

feud 1. *n.* argument, bad blood, bickering, broil, conflict, contention, disagreement, discord, dissension, enmity, estrangement, faction, falling out, grudge, hostility, quarrel, rivalry, strife, vendetta 2. *v.* be at daggers drawn, be at odds, bicker, brawl, clash, contend, dispute, duel, fall out, quarrel, row, squabble, war

fever *Fig.* agitation, delirium, ecstasy, excitement, ferment, fervour, flush, frenzy, heat, intensity, passion, restlessness, turmoil, unrest

few 1. *adj.* hardly any, inconsiderable, infrequent, insufficient, meagre, negligible, not many, rare, scant, scanty, scarce, scarcely any, scattered, sparse, sporadic, thin 2. *pron.* handful, scarcely any, scattering, small number, some

Antonyms *adj.* abundant, bounteous, divers (*Archaic*), inexhaustible, manifold, many, multifarious, plentiful, sundry

fiancé, fiancée betrothed, intended, prospective spouse, wife- *or* husband-to-be

fiasco catastrophe, debacle, disaster, failure, flap (*Inf.*), mess, rout, ruin, washout (*Inf.*)

fib *n.* fiction, lie, prevarication, story, untruth, white lie, whopper (*Inf.*)

fibre 1. fibril, filament, pile, staple, strand, texture, thread 2. *Fig.* essence, nature, quality, spirit, substance

fickle blowing hot and cold, capricious, changeable, faithless, fitful, flighty, inconstant, irresolute, mercurial, mutable, quicksilver, unfaithful, unpredictable, unstable, unsteady, vacillating, variable, volatile

Antonyms changeless, constant, faithful, firm, invariable, loyal, reliable, resolute, settled, stable, staunch, steadfast, true, trustworthy

fiction 1. fable, fantasy, legend, myth, novel, romance, story, storytelling, tale, work of imagination, yarn (*Inf.*) 2. cock and bull story (*Inf.*), concoction, fabrication, falsehood, fancy, fantasy, figment of the imagination, imagination, improvisation, invention, lie, tall story, untruth

fictitious apocryphal, artificial, assumed, bogus, counterfeit, fabricated, false, fanciful, feigned, imaginary, imagined, improvised, invented, made-up, make-believe, mythical, spurious, unreal, untrue

Antonyms actual, authentic, genuine, legitimate, real, true, truthful, veracious, veritable

fidelity 1. allegiance, constancy, dependability, devotedness, devotion, faith, faithfulness, fealty, integrity, lealty (*Archaic or Scot.*), loyalty, staunchness, true-heartedness, trustworthiness 2. accuracy, adherence, closeness, correspondence, exactitude, exactness, faithfulness, preciseness, precision, scrupulousness

Antonyms disloyalty, faithlessness, falseness, inaccuracy, inexactness, infidelity, perfidiousness, treachery, unfaithfulness, untruthfulness

fidget *v.* be like a cat on hot bricks (*Inf.*), bustle, chafe, fiddle, fret, jiggle, jitter (*Inf.*), move restlessly, squirm, twitch, worry

fidgety impatient, jerky, jittery (*Inf.*), jumpy, nervous, on edge, restive, restless, twitchy, uneasy

field 1. *n.* grassland, green, greensward (*Archaic*), lea (*Literary*), mead (*Archaic*), meadow, pasture 2. *v.* catch, pick up, retrieve, return, stop

fiend 1. demon, devil, evil spirit,

hellhound 2. *Inf.* addict, enthusiast, fanatic, freak (*Sl.*), maniac

fierce barbarous, brutal, cruel, dangerous, fell (*Archaic*), feral, ferocious, fiery, menacing, murderous, passionate, savage, threatening, tigerish, truculent, uncontrollable, untamed, vicious, wild

Antonyms affectionate, calm, civilized, cool, docile, domesticated, gentle, harmless, kind, mild, peaceful, submissive, tame, tranquil

fiercely ferociously, frenziedly, furiously, in a frenzy, like cat and dog, menacingly, passionately, savagely, tempestuously, tigerishly, tooth and nail, uncontrolledly, viciously, with bared teeth, with no holds barred

fight *v.* 1. assault, battle, bear arms against, box, brawl, carry on war, clash, close, combat, come to blows, conflict, contend, cross swords, do battle, engage, engage in hostilities, exchange blows, feud, go to war, grapple, joust, scrap (*Inf.*), spar, struggle, take the field, take up arms against, tilt, tussle, wage war, war, wrestle 2. contest, defy, dispute, make a stand against, oppose, resist, stand up to, strive, struggle, withstand 3. argue, bicker, dispute, fall out (*Inf.*), squabble, wrangle 4. carry on, conduct, engage in, prosecute, wage ~n. 5. action, affray (*Law*), altercation, battle, bout, brawl, brush, clash, combat, conflict, contest, dispute, dissension, dogfight, duel, encounter, engagement, exchange of blows, fracas, fray, free-for-all (*Inf.*), hostilities, joust, melee, passage of arms, riot, row, rumble (*U.S. sl.*), scrap (*Inf.*), scuffle, set-to (*Inf.*), skirmish, sparring match, struggle, tussle, war

fighter 1. fighting man, man-at-arms, soldier, warrior 2. boxer, bruiser (*Inf.*), prize fighter, pugilist

fighting *adj.* aggressive, argumentative, bellicose, belligerent, combative, contentious, disputatious, hawkish, martial, militant, pugnacious, sabre-rattling, truculent, warlike

fight off beat off, keep or hold at bay, repel, repress, repulse, resist, stave off, ward off

figure n. 1. character, cipher, digit, number, numeral, symbol 2. amount, cost, price, sum, total, value 3. form, outline, shadow, shape, silhouette 4. body, build, chassis (Sl.), frame, physique, proportions, shape, torso 5. celebrity, character, dignitary, force, leader, notability, notable, personage, personality, presence, somebody, worthy

figurehead cipher, dummy, front man (Inf.), leader in name only, man of straw, mouthpiece, name, nonentity, puppet, straw man (Chiefly U.S.), titular or nominal head, token

figure out 1. calculate, compute, reckon, work out 2. comprehend, decipher, fathom, make head or tail of (Inf.), make out, resolve, see, understand

file[1] v. abrade, burnish, furbish, polish, rasp, refine, rub, rub down, scrape, shape, smooth

file[2] 1. n. case, data, documents, dossier, folder, information, portfolio 2. v. document, enter, pigeonhole, put in place, record, register, slot in

fill brim over, cram, crowd, furnish, glut, gorge, inflate, pack, pervade, replenish, sate, satiate, satisfy, stock, store, stuff, supply, swell
Antonyms diminish, drain, empty, exhaust, shrink, subside, vacate, void

fill in 1. answer, complete, fill out (U.S.), fill up 2. deputize, replace, represent, stand in, sub, substitute, take the place of

filling 1. n. contents, filler, innards (Inf.), inside, insides, padding, stuffing, wadding 2. adj. ample, heavy, satisfying, square, substantial

film n. 1. coat, coating, covering, dusting, gauze, integument, layer, membrane, pellicle, scum, skin, tissue 2. flick (Sl.), motion picture, movie (U.S. inf.) ~v. 3. photograph, shoot, take, video, videotape

filter 1. v. clarify, filtrate, purify, refine, screen, sieve, sift, strain, winnow 2. n. gauze, membrane, mesh, riddle, sieve, strainer

filth 1. carrion, contamination, defilement, dirt, dung, excrement, excreta, faeces, filthiness, foul matter, foulness, garbage, grime, muck, nastiness, ordure, pollution, putrefaction, putrescence, refuse, sewage, slime, sludge, squalor, uncleanness 2. corruption, dirty-mindedness, impurity, indecency, obscenity, pornography, smut, vileness, vulgarity

filthy 1. dirty, faecal, feculent, foul, nasty, polluted, putrid, scummy, slimy, squalid, unclean, vile 2. begrimed, black, blackened, grimy, grubby, miry, mucky, muddy, mud-encrusted, smoky, sooty, unwashed 3. bawdy, coarse, corrupt, depraved, dirty-minded, foul, foulmouthed, impure, indecent, lewd, licentious, obscene, pornographic, smutty, suggestive

final 1. closing, concluding, end, eventual, last, last-minute, latest, terminal, terminating, ultimate 2. absolute, conclusive, decided, decisive, definite, definitive, determinate, finished, incontrovertible, irrevocable, settled
Antonyms earliest, first, initial, introductory, maiden, opening, original, precursory, prefatory, premier, preparatory

finalize agree, clinch (Inf.), complete, conclude, decide, settle, sew up (Inf.), tie up, work out, wrap up (Inf.)

finally at last, at length, at long last, at the last, at the last moment, eventually, in the end, in the long run, lastly, ultimately, when all is said and done

finance 1. *n.* accounts, banking, business, commerce, economics, financial affairs, investment, money, money management 2. *v.* back, bankroll (*U.S.*), float, fund, guarantee, pay for, provide security for, set up in business, subsidize, support, underwrite

finances affairs, assets, capital, cash, financial condition, funds, money, resources, wherewithal

financial budgeting, economic, fiscal, monetary, money, pecuniary

find *v.* 1. catch sight of, chance upon, come across, come up with, descry, discover, encounter, espy, expose, ferret out, hit upon, lay one's hand on, light upon, locate, meet, recognize, run to earth, spot, stumble upon, track down, turn up, uncover, unearth 2. get back, recover, regain, repossess, retrieve ~*n.* 3. acquisition, asset, bargain, catch, discovery, good buy
Antonyms (*sense 1*) lose, miss, overlook, mislay, misplace

find out detect, discover, learn, note, observe, perceive, realize

fine¹ *adj.* 1. accomplished, admirable, beautiful, choice, excellent, exceptional, exquisite, first-class, first-rate, great, magnificent, masterly, ornate, outstanding, rare, select, showy, skilful, splendid, superior, supreme 2. balmy, bright, clear, clement, cloudless, dry, fair, pleasant, sunny 3. dainty, delicate, elegant, expensive, exquisite, fragile, quality 4. abstruse, acute, critical, discriminating, fastidious, hairsplitting, intelligent, keen, minute, nice, precise, quick, refined, sensitive, sharp, subtle, tasteful, tenuous 5. clear, pure, refined, solid, sterling, unadulterated, unalloyed, unpolluted 6. acceptable, agreeable, all right, convenient, good, O.K. (*Inf.*), satisfactory, suitable
Antonyms (*sense 1*) indifferent, inferior, poor, second rate, substandard (*sense 2*) cloudy, dull,

overcast, unpleasant (*senses 3 & 4*) blunt, coarse, crude, dull, heavy, rough, uncultured, unfinished, unrefined

fine² 1. *v.* amerce (*Archaic*), mulct, penalize, punish 2. *n.* amercement (*Archaic*), damages, forfeit, penalty, punishment

finesse *n.* 1. adeptness, adroitness, artfulness, cleverness, craft, delicacy, diplomacy, discretion, know-how (*Inf.*), polish, quickness, savoir-faire, skill, sophistication, subtlety, tact 2. artifice, bluff, feint, manoeuvre, ruse, stratagem, trick, wile

finger *v.* feel, fiddle with (*Inf.*), handle, manipulate, maul, meddle with, paw (*Inf.*), play about with, touch, toy with

finish *v.* 1. accomplish, achieve, bring to a close *or* conclusion, carry through, cease, close, complete, conclude, culminate, deal with, discharge, do, end, execute, finalize, fulfil, get done, get out of the way, make short work of, put the finishing touch(es) to, round off, settle, stop, terminate, wind up (*Inf.*), wrap up (*Inf.*) 2. *Often with* administer *or* give the coup de grâce, annihilate, best, bring down, defeat, destroy, dispose of, drive to the wall, exterminate, get rid of, kill, overcome, overpower, put an end to, rout, ruin, worst ~*n.* 3. cessation, close, closing, completion, conclusion, culmination, dénouement, end, ending, finale, last stage(s), termination, winding up (*Inf.*), wind-up (*Inf.*, *chiefly U.S.*) 4. annihilation, bankruptcy, curtains (*Inf.*), death, defeat, end, end of the road, liquidation, ruin ~*v.* 5. elaborate, perfect, polish, refine ~*n.* 6. cultivation, culture, elaboration, perfection, polish, refinement ~*v.* 7. coat, face, gild, lacquer, polish, smooth off, stain, texture, veneer, wax ~*n.* 8. appearance, grain, lustre, patina, polish, shine, smoothness, surface, texture

Antonyms *v.* begin, commence, create, embark on, instigate, start, undertake ~*n.* beginning, birth, commencement, conception, genesis, inauguration, inception, instigation, preamble, preface, prologue

finished 1. accomplished, classic, consummate, cultivated, elegant, expert, flawless, impeccable, masterly, perfected, polished, professional, proficient, refined, skilled, smooth, urbane 2. accomplished, achieved, closed, complete, completed, concluded, done, ended, entire, final, finalized, full, in the past, over, over and done with, sewed up (*Inf.*), shut, terminated, through, tied up, wrapped up (*Inf.*) 3. done, drained, empty, exhausted, gone, played out (*Inf.*), spent, used up 4. bankrupt, defeated, devastated, done for (*Inf.*), doomed, gone, liquidated, lost, ruined, through, undone, washed up (*Inf., chiefly U.S.*), wiped out, wound up, wrecked

Antonyms basic, begun, coarse, crude, imperfect, inartistic, incomplete, inelegant, inexperienced, raw, rough, unfinished, unrefined, unskilled, unsophisticated

finite bounded, circumscribed, conditioned, delimited, demarcated, limited, restricted, subject to limitations, terminable

Antonyms boundless, endless, eternal, everlasting, immeasurable, infinite, interminable, limitless, perpetual, unbounded

fire *n.* 1. blaze, combustion, conflagration, flames, inferno 2. barrage, bombardment, cannonade, flak, fusillade, hail, salvo, shelling, sniping, volley 3. **on fire a.** ablaze, aflame, alight, blazing, burning, fiery, flaming, in flames **b.** ardent, eager, enthusiastic, excited, inspired, passionate ~*v.* 4. enkindle, ignite, kindle, light, put a match to, set ablaze, set aflame, set alight, set fire to, set on fire 5. detonate, discharge, eject, explode, hurl, launch, let off, loose, pull the trigger, set off, shell, shoot, touch off

firm[1] *adj.* 1. close-grained, compact, compressed, concentrated, congealed, dense, hard, inelastic, inflexible, jelled, jellified, rigid, set, solid, solidified, stiff, unyielding 2. anchored, braced, cemented, embedded, fast, fastened, fixed, immovable, motionless, riveted, robust, rooted, secure, secured, stable, stationary, steady, strong, sturdy, taut, tight, unfluctuating, unmoving, unshakable 3. adamant, constant, definite, fixed, inflexible, obdurate, resolute, resolved, set on, settled, staunch, steadfast, strict, true, unalterable, unbending, unfaltering, unflinching, unshakable, unshaken, unswerving, unwavering, unyielding

Antonyms flabby, flaccid, flimsy, inconstant, insecure, irresolute, limp, loose, shaky, soft, unreliable, unstable, unsteady, wavering

firm[2] *n.* association, business, company, concern, conglomerate, corporation, enterprise, house, organization, outfit (*Inf.*), partnership

firmly 1. enduringly, immovably, like a rock, motionlessly, securely, steadily, tightly, unflinchingly, unshakably 2. determinedly, resolutely, staunchly, steadfastly, strictly, through thick and thin, unchangeably, unwaveringly, with a rod of iron, with decision

firmness 1. compactness, density, fixedness, hardness, inelasticity, inflexibility, resistance, rigidity, solidity, stiffness 2. immovability, soundness, stability, steadiness, strength, tautness, tensile strength, tension, tightness 3. constancy, fixedness, fixity of purpose, inflexibility, obduracy, resolution, resolve, staunchness, steadfastness, strength of will, strictness

first *adj.* 1. chief, foremost, head, highest, leading, pre-eminent, prime, principal, ruling 2. earliest, initial, introductory, maiden, opening, original, premier, primeval, primitive, primordial, pristine 3. basic, cardinal, elementary, fundamental, key, primary, rudimentary ~*adv.* 4. at the beginning, at the outset, before all else, beforehand, firstly, initially, in the first place, to begin with, to start with

first-rate admirable, A-one (*Inf.*), crack (*Sl.*), elite, excellent, exceptional, exclusive, first class, outstanding, prime, second to none, superb, superlative, tiptop, top, topnotch (*Inf.*), tops (*Sl.*)

fissure breach, break, chink, cleavage, cleft, crack, cranny, crevice, fault, fracture, gap, hole, interstice, opening, rent, rift, rupture, slit, split

fit *adj.* 1. able, adapted, adequate, appropriate, apt, becoming, capable, competent, convenient, correct, deserving, equipped, expedient, fitted, fitting, good enough, meet (*Archaic*), prepared, proper, qualified, ready, right, seemly, suitable, trained, well-suited, worthy 2. able-bodied, hale, healthy, in good condition, in good shape, in good trim, robust, strapping, toned up, trim, well ~*v.* 3. accord, agree, be consonant, belong, concur, conform, correspond, dovetail, go, interlock, join, match, meet, suit, tally 4. adapt, adjust, alter, arrange, dispose, fashion, modify, place, position, shape

Antonyms (*sense 1*) amiss, ill-fitted, ill-suited, improper, inadequate, inappropriate, unfit, unprepared, unseemly, unsuitable, untimely (*sense 2*) flabby, in poor condition, out of shape, out of trim, unfit, unhealthy

fitful broken, desultory, disturbed, erratic, flickering, fluctuating, haphazard, impulsive, intermittent, irregular, spasmodic, sporadic, unstable, variable

Antonyms constant, equable, even, orderly, predictable, regu- lar, steady, systematic, unchanging, uniform

fitness 1. adaptation, applicability, appropriateness, aptness, competence, eligibility, pertinence, preparedness, propriety, qualifications, readiness, seemliness, suitability 2. good condition, good health, health, robustness, strength, vigour

fitting 1. *adj.* appropriate, becoming, *comme il faut*, correct, decent, decorous, desirable, meet (*Archaic*), proper, right, seemly, suitable 2. *n.* accessory, attachment, component, connection, part, piece, unit

Antonyms *adj.* ill-suited, improper, unfitting, unseemly, unsuitable

fix *v.* 1. anchor, embed, establish, implant, install, locate, place, plant, position, root, set, settle 2. attach, bind, cement, connect, couple, fasten, glue, link, make fast, pin, secure, stick, tie 3. agree on, appoint, arrange, arrive at, conclude, decide, define, determine, establish, limit, name, resolve, set, settle, specify ~*n.* 4. *Inf.* difficult situation, difficulty, dilemma, embarrassment, hole (*Sl.*), jam (*Inf.*), mess, pickle (*Inf.*), plight, predicament, quandary, spot (*Inf.*), ticklish situation

fixed 1. anchored, attached, established, immovable, made fast, permanent, rigid, rooted, secure, set 2. agreed, arranged, decided, definite, established, planned, resolved, settled

Antonyms inconstant, mobile, motile, moving, pliant, unfixed, varying, wavering

fix up agree on, arrange, fix, organize, plan, settle, sort out

flabbergasted abashed, amazed, astonished, astounded, bowled over (*Inf.*), confounded, dazed, disconcerted, dumbfounded, nonplussed, overcome, overwhelmed, rendered speechless, speechless, staggered, struck dumb, stunned

flag[1] *v.* abate, decline, die, droop,

ebb, fade, fail, faint, fall, fall off, feel the pace, languish, peter out, pine, sag, sink, slump, succumb, taper off, wane, weaken, weary, wilt

flag² n. banderole, banner, colours, ensign, gonfalon, jack, pennant, pennon, standard, streamer

flagrant arrant, atrocious, awful, barefaced, blatant, bold, brazen, crying, dreadful, egregious, enormous, flagitious, flaunting, glaring, heinous, immodest, infamous, notorious, open, ostentatious, out-and-out, outrageous, scandalous, shameless, undisguised

flail v. beat, thrash, thresh, windmill

flair 1. ability, accomplishment, aptitude, faculty, feel, genius, gift, knack, mastery, talent 2. chic, dash, discernment, elegance, panache, style, stylishness, taste

flamboyant 1. baroque, elaborate, extravagant, florid, ornate, ostentatious, over the top (*Inf.*), rich, rococo, showy, theatrical 2. brilliant, colourful, dashing, dazzling, exciting, glamorous, swashbuckling

flame v. 1. blaze, burn, flare, flash, glare, glow, shine ∼n. 2. blaze, brightness, fire, light 3. *Fig.* affection, ardour, enthusiasm, fervency, fervour, fire, intensity, keenness, passion, warmth

flaming 1. ablaze, afire, blazing, brilliant, burning, fiery, glowing, ignited, in flames, raging, red, red-hot 2. angry, ardent, aroused, frenzied, hot, impassioned, intense, raging, scintillating, vehement, vivid

flap 1. v. agitate, beat, flail, flutter, shake, swing, swish, thrash, thresh, vibrate, wag, wave 2. n. apron, cover, fly, fold, lapel, lappet, overlap, skirt, tab, tail

flare v. blaze, burn up, dazzle, flicker, flutter, glare, waver

flash v. 1. blaze, coruscate, flare, flicker, glare, gleam, glint, glisten, glitter, light, scintillate, shimmer, sparkle, twinkle ∼n. 2.

blaze, burst, coruscation, dazzle, flare, flicker, gleam, ray, scintillation, shaft, shimmer, spark, sparkle, streak, twinkle ∼v. 3. bolt, dart, dash, fly, race, shoot, speed, sprint, streak, sweep, whistle, zoom ∼n. 4. instant, jiffy (*Inf.*), moment, second, shake, split second, trice, twinkling, twinkling of an eye, two shakes of a lamb's tail (*Inf.*)

flashy cheap, cheap and nasty, flamboyant, flaunting, garish, gaudy, glittery, glitzy, in poor taste, jazzy (*Inf.*), loud, meretricious, ostentatious, over the top (*Inf.*), showy, snazzy (*Inf.*), tasteless, tawdry, tinselly

Antonyms downbeat, low-key, modest, natural, plain, unaffected, understated

flat¹ adj. 1. even, horizontal, level, levelled, low, planar, plane, smooth, unbroken 2. laid low, lying full length, outstretched, prostrate, reclining, recumbent, supine 3. boring, dead, dull, flavourless, insipid, jejune, lacklustre, lifeless, monotonous, pointless, prosaic, spiritless, stale, tedious, uninteresting, vapid, watery, weak

Antonyms (*sense 1*) broken, hilly, irregular, rolling, rough, rugged, slanting, sloping, uneven, up and down (*sense 2*) on end, perpendicular, straight, upright, vertical (*sense 3*) bubbly, effervescent, exciting, fizzy, palatable, sparkling, tasty, zestful

flat² apartment, rooms

flatly absolutely, categorically, completely, positively, unhesitatingly

flatness 1. evenness, horizontality, levelness, smoothness, uniformity 2. dullness, emptiness, insipidity, monotony, staleness, tedium, vapidity

flatten compress, even out, iron out, level, plaster, raze, roll, smooth off, squash, trample

flatter blandish, butter up, cajole, compliment, court, fawn, flannel (*Inf.*), humour, inveigle, lay it on (thick) (*Sl.*), praise, puff, soft-soap (*Inf.*), sweet-talk (*U.S. inf.*), wheedle

flattering adulatory, complimentary, fawning, fulsome, gratifying, honeyed, honey-tongued, ingratiating, laudatory, sugary
Antonyms blunt, candid, honest, straight, uncomplimentary, warts and all

flattery adulation, blandishment, blarney, cajolery, false praise, fawning, flannel (*Inf.*), fulsomeness, honeyed words, obsequiousness, servility, soft-soap (*Inf.*), sweet-talk (*U.S. inf.*), sycophancy, toadyism

flavour 1. *n.* aroma, essence, extract, flavouring, odour, piquancy, relish, savour, seasoning, smack, tang, taste, zest, zing (*Inf.*) **2.** *v.* ginger up, imbue, infuse, lace, leaven, season, spice
Antonyms *n.* blandness, flatness, insipidity, odourlessness, tastelessness, vapidity

flaw 1. blemish, defect, disfigurement, failing, fault, imperfection, speck, spot, weakness, weak spot **2.** breach, break, cleft, crack, crevice, fissure, fracture, rent, rift, scission, split, tear

flawed blemished, broken, chipped, cracked, damaged, defective, erroneous, faulty, imperfect, unsound

flee abscond, avoid, beat a hasty retreat, bolt, cut and run (*Inf.*), decamp, depart, escape, fly, get away, leave, make a quick exit, make off, make oneself scarce (*Inf.*), make one's escape, make one's getaway, run away, scarper (*Sl.*), shun, skedaddle (*Inf.*), split (*Sl.*), take flight, take off (*Inf.*), take to one's heels, vanish

fleet *n.* argosy, armada, flotilla, naval force, navy, sea power, squadron, task force, vessels, warships

fleeting brief, ephemeral, evanescent, flitting, flying, fugacious, fugitive, here today, gone tomorrow, momentary, passing, short,

short-lived, temporary, transient, transitory
Antonyms abiding, continuing, durable, enduring, imperishable, lasting, long-lasting, long-lived, permanent

flesh 1. beef (*Inf.*), body, brawn, fat, fatness, food, meat, tissue, weight **2.** animality, body, carnality, flesh and blood, human nature, physicality, physical nature, sensuality

flexibility adaptability, adjustability, complaisance, elasticity, give (*Inf.*), pliability, pliancy, resilience, springiness, tensility

flexible bendable, ductile, elastic, limber, lithe, mouldable, plastic, pliable, pliant, springy, stretchy, supple, tensile, whippy, willowy, yielding **2.** adaptable, adjustable, discretionary, open, variable **3.** amenable, biddable, complaisant, compliant, docile, gentle, manageable, responsive, tractable
Antonyms absolute, determined, fixed, inexorable, inflexible, immovable, intractable, obdurate, rigid, staunch, stiff, tough, unyielding

flicker *v.* **1.** flutter, quiver, vibrate, waver ~*n.* **2.** flare, flash, gleam, glimmer, spark **3.** atom, breath, drop, glimmer, iota, spark, trace, vestige

flight[1] **1.** flying, mounting, soaring, winging **2.** *Of air travel* journey, trip, voyage **3.** cloud, flock, formation, squadron, swarm, unit, wing

flight[2] departure, escape, exit, exodus, fleeing, getaway, retreat, running away

flimsy 1. delicate, fragile, frail, gimcrack, insubstantial, makeshift, rickety, shaky, shallow, slight, superficial, unsubstantial **2.** feeble, frivolous, implausible, inadequate, poor, thin, transparent, trivial, unconvincing, unsatisfactory, weak
Antonyms durable, heavy, robust, serious, solid, sound, stout, strong, sturdy, substantial

flinch baulk, blench, cower, cringe, draw back, duck, flee, quail, recoil, retreat, shirk, shrink, shy away, start, swerve, wince, withdraw

fling v. cast, catapult, chuck (*Inf.*), heave, hurl, jerk, let fly, lob (*Inf.*), pitch, precipitate, propel, send, shy, sling, throw, toss

flippant cheeky, disrespectful, flip (*Inf., chiefly U.S.*), frivolous, glib, impertinent, impudent, irreverent, offhand, pert, rude, saucy, superficial

flirt 1. v. chat up (*Inf.*), coquet, dally, lead on, make advances, make eyes at, philander 2. n. coquette, heart-breaker, philanderer, tease, trifler, wanton

float v. 1. be or lie on the surface, be buoyant, displace water, hang, hover, poise, rest on water, stay afloat 2. bob, drift, glide, move gently, sail, slide, slip along 3. get going, launch, promote, push off, set up

floating 1. afloat, buoyant, buoyed up, nonsubmersible, ocean-going, sailing, swimming, unsinkable 2. fluctuating, free, migratory, movable, unattached, uncommitted, unfixed, variable, wandering

flock v. 1. collect, congregate, converge, crowd, gather, group, herd, huddle, mass, throng, troop ~n. 2. colony, drove, flight, gaggle, herd, skein 3. assembly, bevy, collection, company, congregation, convoy, crowd, gathering, group, herd, host, mass, multitude, throng

flog 1. beat, castigate, chastise, flagellate, flay, lash, scourge, thrash, trounce, whack, whip 2. drive, oppress, overexert, overtax, overwork, punish, push, strain, tax

flood v. 1. brim over, deluge, drown, immerse, inundate, overflow, pour over, submerge, swamp 2. engulf, flow, gush, overwhelm, rush, surge, swarm, sweep 3. choke, fill, glut, oversupply, saturate ~n. 4. deluge,

downpour, flash flood, freshet, inundation, overflow, spate, tide, torrent 5. abundance, flow, glut, multitude, outpouring, profusion, rush, stream, torrent

floor 1. n. level, stage, storey, tier 2. v. *Fig.* baffle, beat, bewilder, bowl over (*Inf.*), bring up short, confound, conquer, defeat, discomfit, disconcert, dumbfound, knock down, nonplus, overthrow, perplex, prostrate, puzzle, stump, throw (*Inf.*)

florid 1. blowzy, flushed, high-coloured, high-complexioned, rubicund, ruddy 2. baroque, busy, embellished, euphuistic, figurative, flamboyant, flowery, fussy, grandiloquent, high-flown, ornate, overelaborate

Antonyms anaemic, bare, bloodless, dull, pale, pallid, pasty, plain, unadorned, wan, washed out

flounder v. be in the dark, blunder, fumble, grope, muddle, plunge, struggle, stumble, thrash, toss, tumble, wallow

flourish 1. v. bear fruit, be in one's prime, be successful, be vigorous, bloom, blossom, boom, burgeon, develop, do well, flower, get ahead, get on, go great guns (*Sl.*), go up in the world, grow, grow fat, increase, prosper, succeed, thrive 2. n. brandishing, dash, display, fanfare, parade, shaking, show, showy gesture, twirling, wave

Antonyms decline, diminish, dwindle, fade, fail, grow less, pine, shrink, wane

flourishing blooming, burgeoning, doing well, going strong, in the pink, in top form, lush, luxuriant, mushrooming, on the up and up (*Inf.*), prospering, rampant, successful, thriving

flow v. circulate, course, glide, gush, move, pour, purl, ripple, roll, run, rush, slide, surge, sweep, swirl, whirl

flower n. 1. bloom, blossom, efflorescence, *Fig.* best, choicest part, cream, elite, freshness, greatest *or* finest point, height, pick, vigour ~*v.* 3. bloom, blossom, blow, burgeon, effloresce, flourish, mature, open, unfold

flowery baroque, embellished, euphuistic, fancy, figurative, florid, high-flown, ornate, overwrought, rhetorical

flowing continuous, cursive, easy, fluent, smooth, unbroken, uninterrupted

fluctuate alter, alternate, change, ebb and flow, go up and down, hesitate, oscillate, rise and fall, seesaw, shift, swing, undulate, vacillate, vary, veer, waver

fluency articulateness, assurance, command, control, ease, facility, glibness, readiness, slickness, smoothness, volubility

fluent articulate, easy, effortless, facile, flowing, glib, natural, ready, smooth, smooth-spoken, voluble, well-versed
Antonyms faltering, halting, hesitant, hesitating, inarticulate, stammering, stumbling, terse, tongue-tied

fluid *adj.* 1. aqueous, flowing, in solution, liquefied, liquid, melted, molten, running, runny, watery 2. adaptable, adjustable, changeable, flexible, floating, fluctuating, indefinite, mercurial, mobile, mutable, protean, shifting ~*n.* 3. liquid, liquor, solution
Antonyms *adj.* definite, firm, fixed, hard, immobile, immutable, rigid, set, solid

flurry *n. Fig.* ado, agitation, bustle, commotion, disturbance, excitement, ferment, flap, fluster, flutter, furore, fuss, hurry, stir, to-do, tumult, whirl

flush[1] 1. *v.* blush, burn, colour, colour up, crimson, flame, glow, go red, redden, suffuse 2. *n.* bloom, blush, colour, freshness, glow, redness, rosiness

flush[2] *adj.* 1. even, flat, level, plane, square, true 2. abundant, affluent, full, generous, lavish, liberal, overflowing, prodigal ~*adv.* 3. even with, hard against,

in contact with, level with, squarely, touching

fluster 1. *v.* agitate, bother, bustle, confound, confuse, disturb, excite, flurry, hassle (*Inf.*), heat, hurry, make nervous, perturb, rattle (*Inf.*), ruffle, throw off balance, upset 2. *n.* agitation, bustle, commotion, disturbance, dither, flap (*Inf.*), flurry, flutter, furore, perturbation, ruffle, state (*Inf.*), turmoil

flutter 1. *v.* agitate, bat, beat, flap, flicker, flit, flitter, fluctuate, hover, palpitate, quiver, ripple, ruffle, shiver, tremble, vibrate, waver 2. *n.* palpitation, quiver, quivering, shiver, shudder, tremble, tremor, twitching, vibration

fly 1. *v.* flit, flutter, hover, mount, sail, soar, take to the air, take wing, wing 2. aviate, be at the controls, control, manoeuvre, operate, pilot 3. display, flap, float, flutter, show, wave 4. elapse, flit, glide, pass, pass swiftly, roll on, run its course, slip away 5. be off like a shot (*Inf.*), bolt, career, dart, dash, hare (*Inf.*), hasten, hurry, race, rush, scamper, scoot, shoot, speed, sprint, tear, whiz (*Inf.*), zoom

flying *adj.* 1. brief, fleeting, fugacious, hasty, hurried, rushed, short-lived, transitory 2. express, fast, fleet, mercurial, mobile, rapid, speedy, winged

foam 1. *n.* bubbles, froth, head, lather, spray, spume, suds 2. *v.* boil, bubble, effervesce, fizz, froth, lather

focus *n.* bull's eye, centre, centre of activity, centre of attraction, core, cynosure, focal point, headquarters, heart, hub, meeting place, target

foe adversary, antagonist, enemy, foeman (*Archaic*), opponent, rival
Antonyms ally, companion, comrade, confederate, friend, partner

fog *n.* gloom, miasma, mist, murk,

murkiness, peasouper (*Inf.*), smog

foggy blurred, brumous (*Rare*), cloudy, dim, grey, hazy, indistinct, misty, murky, nebulous, obscure, smoggy, soupy, vaporous
Antonyms accurate, bright, clear, distinct, palpable, sharp, undimmed

foil¹ v. baffle, balk, check, checkmate, circumvent, counter, defeat, disappoint, elude, frustrate, nip in the bud, nullify, outwit, put a spoke in (someone's) wheel (*Brit.*), stop, thwart

foil² antithesis, background, complement, contrast, setting

fold v. **1.** bend, crease, crumple, dog-ear, double, double over, gather, intertwine, overlap, pleat, tuck, turn under ~n. **2.** bend, crease, double thickness, folded portion, furrow, knife-edge, layer, overlap, pleat, turn, wrinkle ~v. **3.** do up, enclose, enfold, entwine, envelop, wrap, wrap up

folder binder, envelope, file, portfolio

folk clan, ethnic group, family, kin, kindred, people, race, tribe

follow 1. come after, come next, step into the shoes of, succeed, supersede, supplant, take the place of **2.** chase, dog, hound, hunt, pursue, run after, shadow, stalk, tail, track, trail **3.** act in accordance with, be guided by, comply, conform, give allegiance to, heed, mind, note, obey, observe, regard, watch
Antonyms abandon, avoid, desert, disobey, flout, forsake, give up, guide, ignore, lead, precede, shun, steer

follower adherent, admirer, apostle, backer, believer, convert, devotee, disciple, fan, fancier, habitué, partisan, pupil, representative, supporter, votary, worshipper
Antonyms guru, leader, mentor, teacher, tutor, svengali, swami

following adj. coming, consequent, consequential, ensuing, later, next, specified, subsequent, succeeding, successive

folly absurdity, daftness, fatuity, foolishness, idiocy, imbecility, imprudence, indiscretion, irrationality, lunacy, madness, nonsense, preposterousness, rashness, recklessness, silliness, stupidity
Antonyms judgment, level-headedness, moderation, prudence, rationality, reason, sanity, sense, wisdom

fond adoring, affectionate, amorous, caring, devoted, doting, indulgent, loving, tender, warm
Antonyms aloof, austere, averse, disinterested, indifferent, rational, sensible, unaffectionate, unconcerned, undemonstrative

fondle caress, cuddle, dandle, pat, pet, stroke

fondly affectionately, dearly, indulgently, lovingly, possessively, tenderly, with affection

fondness attachment, fancy, liking, love, partiality, penchant, predilection, preference, soft spot, susceptibility, taste, weakness
Antonyms antagonism, antipathy, aversion, contempt, dislike, hatred, hostility, loathing, repugnance, repulsion

food aliment, board, bread, chow (*Inf.*), comestibles, commons, cooking, cuisine, diet, eatables (*Sl.*), edibles, eats (*Sl.*), foodstuffs, grub (*Sl.*), larder, meat, menu, nosh (*Sl.*), nourishment, nutriment, nutrition, pabulum (*Rare*), provender, provisions, rations, refreshment, scoff (*Sl.*), stores, subsistence, sustenance, table, tuck (*Inf.*), viands, victuals

fool n. **1.** ass, bird-brain (*Inf.*), blockhead, bonehead (*Sl.*), chump (*Inf.*), clodpate (*Archaic*), clot (*Inf.*), dimwit (*Inf.*), dolt, dope (*Sl.*), dunce, dunderhead, fat-head (*Inf.*), goose (*Inf.*), half-wit, idiot, ignoramus, illiterate, imbecile (*Inf.*), jackass, loon, mooncalf, moron, nincompoop,

ninny, nit (*Inf.*), nitwit, numskull, pillock (*Sl.*), plonker (*Sl.*), prat (*Sl.*), sap (*Sl.*), silly, simpleton, twerp (*Inf.*), twit (*Inf.*) **2.** buffoon, clown, comic, harlequin, jester, merry-andrew, motley, pierrot, punchinello ~*v.* **3.** bamboozle, beguile, bluff, cheat, con (*Sl.*), deceive, delude, dupe, gull (*Archaic*), have (someone) on, hoax, hoodwink, kid (*Inf.*), make a fool of, mislead, play a trick on, put one over on (*Inf.*), take in, trick **4.** act the fool, cut capers, feign, jest, joke, kid (*Inf.*), make believe, pretend, tease
Antonyms expert, genius, master, sage, savant, scholar, wise man

foolhardy adventurous, bold, hot-headed, impetuous, imprudent, incautious, irresponsible, madcap, precipitate, rash, reckless, temerarious, venturesome, venturous

foolish 1. absurd, ill-advised, ill-considered, ill-judged, imprudent, incautious, indiscreet, injudicious, nonsensical, senseless, short-sighted, silly, unintelligent, unreasonable, unwise **2.** brainless, crazy, daft (*Inf.*), doltish, fatuous, half-baked (*Inf.*), half-witted, harebrained, idiotic, imbecilic, ludicrous, mad, moronic, potty (*Brit. inf.*), ridiculous, senseless, silly, simple, stupid, weak, witless
Antonyms bright, cautious, clever, commonsensical, intelligent, judicious, prudent, rational, sagacious, sane, sensible, sharp, smart, sound, thoughtful, wise

foolishly absurdly, idiotically, ill-advisedly, imprudently, incautiously, indiscreetly, injudiciously, like a fool, mistakenly, short-sightedly, stupidly, unwisely, without due consideration

foolishness absurdity, folly, imprudence, inanity, indiscretion, irresponsibility, silliness, stupidity, weakness

foolproof certain, guaranteed, infallible, never-failing, safe, sure-fire (*Inf.*), unassailable, unbreakable

footing basis, establishment, foothold, foundation, ground, groundwork, installation, settlement

footstep 1. footfall, step, tread **2.** footmark, footprint, trace, track

forage *n. Cattle, etc.* feed, fodder, food, foodstuffs, provender

forbear abstain, avoid, cease, decline, desist, eschew, hold back, keep from, omit, pause, refrain, resist the temptation to, restrain oneself, stop, withhold

forbearance indulgence, leniency, lenity, longanimity (*Rare*), long-suffering, mildness, moderation, patience, resignation, restraint, self-control, temperance, tolerance
Antonyms anger, impatience, impetuosity, intolerance, irritability, shortness

forbearing clement, easy, forgiving, indulgent, lenient, long-suffering, merciful, mild, moderate, patient, tolerant

forbid ban, debar, disallow, exclude, hinder, inhibit, interdict, outlaw, preclude, prohibit, proscribe, rule out, veto
Antonyms allow, approve, authorize, bid, endorse, grant, let, license, O.K. *or* okay (*Inf.*), order, permit, sanction

forbidden banned, outlawed, out of bounds, prohibited, proscribed, taboo, *verboten*, vetoed

force *n.* **1.** dynamism, energy, impact, impulse, life, might, momentum, muscle, potency, power, pressure, stimulus, strength, stress, vigour **2.** arm-twisting (*Inf.*), coercion, compulsion, constraint, duress, enforcement, pressure, violence **3.** bite, cogency, effect, effectiveness, efficacy, influence, persuasiveness, power, punch (*Inf.*), strength, validity, weight **4.** drive, emphasis, fierceness, intensity, persistence, vehemence, vigour ~*v.* **5.** bring pressure to bear upon, coerce, compel, constrain, drive, impel,

impose, make, necessitate, obligate, oblige, overcome, press, press-gang, pressure, pressurize, put the squeeze on (*Inf.*), strongarm (*Inf.*), urge 6. blast, break open, prise, propel, push, thrust, use violence on, wrench, wrest 7. drag, exact, extort, wring
Antonyms *n.* debility, enervation, feebleness, fragility, frailty, impotence, ineffectiveness, irresolution, powerlessness, weakness ~ *v.* coax, convince, induce, persuade, prevail, talk into

forced 1. compulsory, conscripted, enforced, involuntary, mandatory, obligatory, slave, unwilling 2. affected, artificial, contrived, false, insincere, laboured, stiff, strained, unnatural, wooden
Antonyms easy, natural, simple, sincere, spontaneous, unforced, unpretending, voluntary

forceful cogent, compelling, convincing, dynamic, effective, persuasive, pithy, potent, powerful, telling, vigorous, weighty
Antonyms enervated, exhausted, faint, feeble, frail, powerless, spent, weak

forcible active, cogent, compelling, effective, efficient, energetic, forceful, impressive, mighty, potent, powerful, strong, telling, valid, weighty

forebear ancestor, father, forefather, forerunner, predecessor, progenitor

foreboding anxiety, apprehension, apprehensiveness, chill, dread, fear, misgiving, premonition, presentiment

forecast 1. *v.* anticipate, augur, calculate, divine, estimate, foresee, foretell, plan, predict, prognosticate, prophesy 2. *n.* anticipation, conjecture, foresight, forethought, guess, outlook, planning, prediction, prognosis, projection, prophecy

forefather ancestor, father, forebear, forerunner, predecessor, primogenitor, procreator, progenitor

foregoing above, antecedent, anterior, former, preceding, previous, prior

foreign alien, borrowed, distant, exotic, external, imported, outlandish, outside, overseas, remote, strange, unfamiliar, unknown
Antonyms customary, domestic, familiar, native, well-known

foreigner alien, immigrant, incomer, newcomer, outlander, stranger

foremost chief, first, front, headmost, highest, inaugural, initial, leading, paramount, pre-eminent, primary, prime, principal, supreme

forerunner ancestor, announcer, envoy, forebear, foregoer, harbinger, herald, precursor, predecessor, progenitor, prototype

foresee anticipate, divine, envisage, forebode, forecast, foretell, predict, prophesy

foreshadow adumbrate, augur, betoken, bode, forebode, imply, indicate, portend, predict, prefigure, presage, promise, prophesy, signal

foresight anticipation, care, caution, circumspection, farsightedness, forethought, precaution, premeditation, preparedness, prescience, prevision (*Rare*), provision, prudence
Antonyms carelessness, hindsight, imprudence, inconsideration, lack of foresight, neglect, retrospection, thoughtlessness, unpreparedness

foretell adumbrate, augur, bode, forebode, forecast, foreshadow, foreshow, forewarn, portend, predict, presage, prognosticate, prophesy, signify, soothsay

forethought anticipation, farsightedness, foresight, precaution, providence, provision, prudence
Antonyms carelessness, imprudence, impulsiveness, inconsideration, neglect, unpreparedness

forewarn admonish, advise, alert, apprise, caution, dissuade, give fair warning, put on guard, put on the qui vive, tip off

forfeit 1. *n.* amercement (*Obsolete*), damages, fine, forfeiture, loss, mulct, penalty **2.** *v.* be deprived of, be stripped of, give up, lose, relinquish, renounce, surrender

forge *v.* coin, copy, counterfeit, fake, falsify, feign, imitate

forget leave behind, lose sight of, omit, overlook

forgive absolve, accept (someone's) apology, acquit, bear no malice, condone, excuse, exonerate, let bygones be bygones, let off (*Inf.*), pardon, remit
Antonyms blame, censure, charge, condemn, find fault with, reproach, reprove

forgiving clement, compassionate, forbearing, humane, lenient, magnanimous, merciful, mild, soft-hearted, tolerant

forgo, forego abandon, abjure, cede, do without, give up, leave alone *or* out, relinquish, renounce, resign, sacrifice, surrender, waive, yield

forgotten blotted out, buried, bygone, consigned to oblivion, gone (clean) out of one's mind, left behind *or* out, lost, obliterated, omitted, past, past recall, unremembered

forlorn abandoned, bereft, cheerless, comfortless, deserted, desolate, destitute, disconsolate, forgotten, forsaken, friendless, helpless, homeless, hopeless, lonely, lost, miserable, pathetic, pitiable, pitiful, unhappy, woebegone, wretched
Antonyms busy, cheerful, happy, hopeful, optimistic, thriving

form¹ *v.* **1.** assemble, bring about, build, concoct, construct, contrive, create, devise, establish, fabricate, fashion, forge, found, invent, make, manufacture, model, mould, produce, put together, set up, shape **2.** arrange, combine, design, dispose, draw up, frame, organize, pattern, plan, think up

form² *n.* **1.** appearance, cast, configuration, construction, cut, fashion, formation, model, mould, pattern, shape, structure **2.** format, framework, harmony, order, orderliness, organization, plan, proportion, structure, symmetry **3.** application, document, paper, sheet

formal approved, ceremonial, explicit, express, fixed, lawful, legal, methodical, official, prescribed, *pro forma*, regular, rigid, ritualistic, set, solemn, strict
Antonyms informal, unofficial

formality 1. ceremony, convention, conventionality, custom, form, gesture, matter of form, procedure, red tape, rite, ritual **2.** ceremoniousness, correctness, decorum, etiquette, politesse, protocol, punctilio

formation 1. accumulation, compilation, composition, constitution, crystallization, development, establishment, evolution, forming, generation, genesis, manufacture, organization, production **2.** arrangement, configuration, design, disposition, figure, grouping, pattern, rank, structure

former 1. ancient, bygone, departed, long ago, long gone, of yore, old, old-time, past **2.** above, aforementioned, aforesaid, first mentioned, foregoing, preceding
Antonyms coming, current, ensuing, following, future, latter, modern, present, present-day, subsequent, succeeding

formerly aforetime (*Archaic*), already, at one time, before, heretofore, lately, once, previously

formidable 1. appalling, dangerous, daunting, dismaying, dreadful, fearful, frightful, horrible, intimidating, menacing, shocking, terrifying, threatening **2.** arduous, challenging, colossal, difficult, mammoth, onerous, overwhelming, staggering, toilsome
Antonyms cheering, comforting,

easy, encouraging, genial, heartening, pleasant, reassuring

formula 1. form of words, formulary, rite, ritual, rubric **2.** blueprint, method, modus operandi, precept, prescription, principle, procedure, recipe, rule, way

formulate codify, define, detail, express, frame, give form to, particularize, set down, specify, systematize

forsake abandon, cast off, desert, disown, jettison, jilt, leave, leave in the lurch, quit, repudiate, throw over

forsaken abandoned, cast off, deserted, destitute, disowned, forlorn, friendless, ignored, isolated, jilted, left behind, left in the lurch, lonely, marooned, outcast, solitary

fort blockhouse, camp, castle, citadel, fastness, fortification, fortress, garrison, redoubt, station, stronghold

forth ahead, away, forward, into the open, onward, out, out of concealment, outward

forthcoming 1. approaching, coming, expected, future, imminent, impending, prospective **2.** chatty, communicative, expansive, free, informative, open, sociable, talkative, unreserved

forthright above-board, blunt, candid, direct, frank, open, outspoken, plain-spoken, straightforward, straight from the shoulder (*Inf.*)
Antonyms dishonest, furtive, secret, secretive, sneaky, underhand, untruthful

forthwith at once, directly, immediately, instantly, quickly, right away, straightaway, *tout de suite*, without delay

fortification bastion, bulwark, castle, citadel, defence, fastness, fort, fortress, keep, protection, stronghold

fortify brace, cheer, confirm, embolden, encourage, hearten, invigorate, reassure, stiffen, strengthen, sustain

Antonyms demoralize, dishearten, sap the strength of, weaken

fortress castle, citadel, fastness, fort, redoubt, stronghold

fortunate born with a silver spoon in one's mouth, bright, favoured, golden, happy, having a charmed life, in luck, lucky, prosperous, rosy, sitting pretty (*Inf.*), successful, well-off
Antonyms hapless, ill-fated, illstarred, miserable, poor, unfortunate, unhappy, unlucky, unsuccessful, wretched

fortunately by a happy chance, by good luck, happily, luckily, providentially

fortune 1. affluence, gold mine, opulence, possessions, property, prosperity, riches, treasure, wealth **2.** accident, chance, contingency, destiny, fate, fortuity, hap (*Archaic*), hazard, kismet, luck, providence
Antonyms (*sense 1*) destitution, hardship, indigence, penury, poverty, privation

forward *adj.* **1.** advanced, advancing, early, forward-looking, onward, precocious, premature, progressive, well-developed ~*adv.* **2.** *Also* **forwards** ahead, forth, on, onward ~*v.* **3.** advance, aid, assist, back, encourage, expedite, favour, foster, further, hasten, help, hurry, promote, speed, support
Antonyms *adj.* backward, diffident, modest, regressive, retiring, shy ~ *adv.* backward(s) ~*v.* bar, block, hinder, hold up, impede, obstruct, retard, thwart

foster 1. cultivate, encourage, feed, foment, nurture, promote, stimulate, support, uphold **2.** bring up, mother, nurse, raise, rear, take care of **3.** accommodate, cherish, entertain, harbour, nourish, sustain
Antonyms combat, curb, curtail, hold out against, inhibit, oppose, resist, restrain, subdue, suppress, withstand

foul *adj.* **1.** contaminated, dirty, disgusting, fetid, filthy, grotty

(*Sl.*), grungy (*Sl.*, chiefly *U.S.*), impure, loathsome, malodorous, mephitic, nasty, nauseating, noisome, offensive, polluted, putrid, rank, repulsive, revolting, rotten, squalid, stinking, sullied, tainted, unclean **2.** bad, blustery, disagreeable, foggy, murky, rainy, rough, stormy, wet, wild ~*v.* **3.** begrime, besmear, besmirch, contaminate, defile, dirty, pollute, smear, soil, stain, sully, taint **Antonyms** clean, clear, fair, fragrant, fresh, spotless, undefiled ~*v.* clean, cleanse, clear, honour, purge, purify, sanitize

found bring into being, constitute, construct, create, endow, erect, establish, fix, inaugurate, institute, organize, originate, plant, raise, settle, set up, start

foundation 1. base, basis, bedrock, bottom, footing, groundwork, substructure, underpinning **2.** endowment, establishment, inauguration, institution, organization, setting up, settlement

founder[1] *n.* architect, author, beginner, benefactor, builder, constructor, designer, establisher, father, framer, generator, initiator, institutor, inventor, maker, organizer, originator, patriarch

founder[2] *v.* be lost, go down, go to the bottom, sink, submerge

fountain font, fount, jet, reservoir, spout, spray, spring, well

foyer antechamber, anteroom, entrance hall, lobby, reception area, vestibule

fracas affray (*Law*), aggro (*Sl.*), brawl, disturbance, donnybrook, fight, free-for-all (*Inf.*), melee, quarrel, riot, row, rumpus, scrimmage, scuffle, trouble, uproar

fractious awkward, captious, crabby, cross, fretful, froward, grouchy (*Inf.*), irritable, peevish, pettish, petulant, querulous, recalcitrant, refractory, testy, touchy, unruly

fracture 1. *n.* breach, break, cleft, crack, fissure, gap, opening, rent, rift, rupture, schism, split **2.** *v.*

break, crack, rupture, splinter, split

fragile breakable, brittle, dainty, delicate, feeble, fine, flimsy, frail, frangible, infirm, slight, weak **Antonyms** durable, elastic, flexible, hardy, lasting, reliable, resilient, robust, strong, sturdy, tough

fragment *n.* bit, chip, fraction, morsel, part, particle, piece, portion, remnant, scrap, shiver, sliver

fragmentary bitty, broken, disconnected, discrete, disjointed, incoherent, incomplete, partial, piecemeal, scattered, scrappy, sketchy, unsystematic

fragrance aroma, balm, bouquet, fragrancy, perfume, redolence, scent, smell, sweet odour **Antonyms** effluvium, miasma, offensive smell, pong (*Inf.*), reek, smell, stink, whiff

fragrant ambrosial, aromatic, balmy, odoriferous, odorous, perfumed, redolent, sweet-scented, sweet-smelling **Antonyms** fetid, foul-smelling, malodorous, noisome, pongy (*Inf.*), reeking, smelling, smelly, stinking

frail breakable, brittle, decrepit, delicate, feeble, flimsy, fragile, frangible, infirm, insubstantial, puny, slight, tender, unsound, vulnerable, weak, wispy **Antonyms** hale, healthy, robust, sound, stalwart, strong, sturdy, substantial, tough, vigorous

frailty fallibility, feebleness, frailness, infirmity, peccability, puniness, susceptibility, weakness

frame *v.* **1.** assemble, build, constitute, construct, fabricate, fashion, forge, form, institute, invent, make, manufacture, model, mould, put together, set up **2.** block out, compose, conceive, concoct, contrive, cook up, devise, draft, draw up, form, formulate, hatch, map out, plan, shape, sketch **3.** case, enclose, mount, surround ~*n.* **4.** casing, construction, fabric, form,

framework, scheme, shell, structure, system 5. anatomy, body, build, carcass, morphology, physique, skeleton **6.** mount, mounting, setting

framework core, fabric, foundation, frame, frame of reference, groundwork, plan, schema, shell, skeleton, structure, the bare bones

frank artless, blunt, candid, direct, downright, forthright, free, honest, ingenuous, open, outright, outspoken, plain, plain-spoken, sincere, straightforward, straight from the shoulder (*Inf.*), transparent, truthful, unconcealed, undisguised, unreserved, unrestricted
Antonyms artful, crafty, cunning, evasive, indirect, inscrutable, reserved, reticent, secretive, shifty, shy, underhand

frantic at one's wits' end, berserk, beside oneself, distracted, distraught, fraught (*Inf.*), frenetic, frenzied, furious, hectic, mad, overwrought, raging, raving, uptight (*Inf.*), wild
Antonyms calm, collected, composed, cool, laid-back, poised, self-possessed, together (*Sl.*), unruffled

fraternity association, brotherhood, camaraderie, circle, clan, club, companionship, company, comradeship, fellowship, guild, kinship, league, set, sodality, union

fraud 1. artifice, cheat, chicane, chicanery, craft, deceit, deception, double-dealing, duplicity, guile, hoax, humbug, imposture, sharp practice, spuriousness, stratagems, swindling, treachery, trickery **2.** bluffer, charlatan, cheat, counterfeit, double-dealer, fake, forgery, hoax, hoaxer, impostor, mountebank, phoney (*Inf.*), pretender, quack, sham, swindler
Antonyms (*sense I*) fairness, good faith, honesty, integrity, probity, rectitude, trustworthiness, virtue

fraudulent counterfeit, crafty, criminal, crooked (*Inf.*), deceitful, deceptive, dishonest, double-dealing, duplicitous, false, knavish, phoney (*Inf.*), sham, spurious, swindling, treacherous
Antonyms above board, genuine, honest, honourable, lawful, principled, true, trustworthy, upright

fray *v.* become threadbare, chafe, fret, rub, wear, wear away, wear thin

freak 1. *n.* aberration, abnormality, abortion, anomaly, grotesque, malformation, monster, monstrosity, mutant, oddity, queer fish (*Inf.*), *rara avis*, sport, teratism, weirdo or weirdie (*Inf.*) **2.** *adj.* aberrant, abnormal, atypical, bizarre, erratic, exceptional, fluky (*Inf.*), fortuitous, odd, queer, unaccountable, unexpected, unforeseen, unparalleled, unpredictable, unusual

free *adj.* **1.** complimentary, for free (*Inf.*), for nothing, free of charge, gratis, gratuitous, on the house, unpaid, without charge **2.** at large, at liberty, footloose, independent, liberated, loose, off the hook (*Inf.*), on the loose, uncommitted, unconstrained, unengaged, unfettered, unrestrained **3.** able, allowed, clear, disengaged, loose, open, permitted, unattached, unengaged, unhampered, unimpeded, unobstructed, unregulated, unrestricted, untrammelled **4.** With of above, beyond, deficient in, devoid of, exempt from, immune to, lacking (in), not liable to, safe from, sans (*Archaic*), unaffected by, unencumbered by, untouched by, without **5.** autarchic, autonomous, democratic, emancipated, independent, self-governing, self-ruling, sovereign **6.** at leisure, available, empty, extra, idle, not tied down, spare, unemployed, uninhabited, unoccupied, unused, vacant **7.** big (*Inf.*), bounteous, bountiful, charitable, eager, generous, hospitable, lavish, liberal, munificent, open-handed, prodi-

gal, unsparing, unstinting, willing **8. free and easy** casual, easy-going, informal, laid-back (*Inf.*), lax, lenient, liberal, relaxed, tolerant, unceremonious ~*adv.* **9.** at no cost, for love, gratis, without charge **10.** abundantly, copiously, freely, idly, loosely ~*v.* **11.** deliver, discharge, disenthrall, emancipate, let go, let out, liberate, loose, manumit, release, set at liberty, set free, turn loose, uncage, unchain, unfetter, unleash, untie **12.** clear, cut loose, deliver, disengage, disentangle, exempt, extricate, ransom, redeem, relieve, rescue, rid, unburden, undo, unshackle
Antonyms (*senses 2 & 3*) bound, captive, confined, dependent, fettered, immured, incarcerated, occupied, restrained, restricted, secured (*sense 7*) close, mean, mingy (*Inf.*), stingy, tight, ungenerous (*senses 11 & 12*) confine, imprison, incarcerate, inhibit, limit, restrain, restrict

freedom 1. autonomy, deliverance, emancipation, home rule, independence, liberty, manumission, release, self-government **2.** exemption, immunity, impunity, privilege **3.** ability, carte blanche, discretion, elbowroom, facility, flexibility, free rein, latitude, leeway, licence, opportunity, play, power, range, scope
Antonyms bondage, captivity, dependence, imprisonment, limitation, restriction, servitude, slavery, thraldom

freely 1. of one's own accord, of one's own free will, spontaneously, voluntarily, willingly, without prompting **2.** candidly, frankly, openly, plainly, unreservedly, without reserve **3.** as you please, unchallenged, without let or hindrance, without restraint **4.** abundantly, amply, bountifully, copiously, extravagantly, lavishly, liberally, like water, open-handedly, unstintingly, with a free hand

freeze 1. benumb, chill, congeal,

glaciate, harden, ice over *or* up, stiffen **2.** fix, hold up, inhibit, peg, stop, suspend

freezing arctic, biting, bitter, chill, chilled, cutting, frost-bound, frosty, glacial, icy, numbing, penetrating, polar, raw, Siberian, wintry

freight *n.* bales, bulk, burden, cargo, consignment, contents, goods, haul, lading, load, merchandise, payload, tonnage

frenzied agitated, all het up (*Inf.*), convulsive, distracted, distraught, excited, feverish, frantic, frenetic, furious, hysterical, mad, maniacal, rabid, uncontrolled, wild

frequent[1] *adj.* common, constant, continual, customary, everyday, familiar, habitual, incessant, numerous, persistent, recurrent, recurring, reiterated, repeated, usual
Antonyms few, few and far between, infrequent, occasional, rare, scanty, sporadic

frequent[2] *v.* attend, be a regular customer of, be found at, hang out at (*Inf.*), haunt, patronize, resort, visit
Antonyms avoid, keep away, shun, spurn

frequently commonly, customarily, habitually, many a time, many times, much, not infrequently, oft (*Literary*), often, oftentimes (*Archaic*), over and over again, repeatedly, thick and fast, very often
Antonyms hardly ever, infrequently, occasionally, once in a blue moon (*Inf.*), rarely, seldom

fresh 1. different, latest, modern, modernistic, new, new-fangled, novel, original, recent, this season's, unconventional, unusual, up-to-date **2.** added, additional, auxiliary, extra, further, more, other, renewed, supplementary **3.** bracing, bright, brisk, clean, clear, cool, crisp, invigorating, pure, refreshing, spanking, sparkling, stiff, sweet, unpolluted **4.** blooming, clear, fair, florid, glowing, good, hardy, healthy, rosy, ruddy, wholesome 5. artless, callow, green, inexperienced, natural, new, raw, uncultivated, untrained, untried, youthful

Antonyms experienced, musty, old, ordinary, sickly, stale, stereotyped, trite, warm

freshen enliven, freshen up, liven up, refresh, restore, revitalize, rouse, spruce up, titivate

fret affront, agonize, anguish, annoy, brood, chagrin, goad, grieve, harass, irritate, lose sleep over, provoke, ruffle, torment, upset *or* distress oneself, worry

friction abrasion, attrition, chafing, erosion, fretting, grating, irritation, rasping, resistance, rubbing, scraping, wearing away

friend Achates, alter ego, boon companion, bosom friend, buddy (*Inf.*), china (*Sl.*), chum (*Inf.*), companion, comrade, confidant, crony, familiar, intimate, mate (*Inf.*), pal, partner, playmate, soul mate

Antonyms adversary, enemy, foe

friendliness affability, amiability, companionability, congeniality, conviviality, geniality, kindliness, mateyness (*Brit. inf.*), neighbourliness, open arms, sociability, warmth

friendly affable, affectionate, amiable, amicable, attached, attentive, auspicious, beneficial, benevolent, benign, chummy (*Inf.*), close, clubby, companionable, comradely, conciliatory, confiding, convivial, cordial, familiar, favourable, fond, fraternal, genial, good, helpful, intimate, kind, kindly, matey (*Brit. inf.*), neighbourly, on good terms, on visiting terms, outgoing, peaceable, propitious, receptive, sociable, sympathetic, thick (*Inf.*), welcoming, well-disposed

Antonyms antagonistic, belligerent, cold, contentious, distant, inauspicious, sinister, uncongenial, unfriendly

friendship affection, affinity, alliance, amity, attachment, benevolence, closeness, concord, familiarity, fondness, friendliness, good-fellowship, good will, harmony, intimacy, love, rapport, regard

Antonyms animosity, antagonism, antipathy, aversion, conflict, enmity, hatred, hostility, resentment, strife, unfriendliness

fright alarm, apprehension, (blue) funk (*Inf.*), cold sweat, consternation, dismay, dread, fear, fear and trembling, horror, panic, quaking, scare, shock, terror, the shivers, trepidation

frighten affright (*Archaic*), alarm, appal, cow, daunt, dismay, freeze one's blood, intimidate, make one's blood run cold, make one's hair stand on end (*Inf.*), make (someone) jump out of his skin (*Inf.*), petrify, put the wind up (someone) (*Inf.*), scare, scare (someone) stiff, scare the living daylights out of (someone) (*Inf.*), shock, startle, terrify, terrorize, throw into a fright, throw into a panic, unman, unnerve

Antonyms allay, assuage, calm, comfort, encourage, hearten, reassure, soothe

frightened abashed, affrighted (*Archaic*), afraid, alarmed, cowed, dismayed, frozen, in a cold sweat, in a panic, in fear and trepidation, numb with fear, panicky, petrified, scared, scared stiff, startled, terrified, terrorized, terror-stricken, unnerved

frightening alarming, appalling, bloodcurdling, daunting, dismaying, dreadful, fearful, fearsome, hair-raising, horrifying, intimidating, menacing, scary (*Inf.*), shocking, spooky (*Inf.*), terrifying, unnerving

frightful alarming, appalling, awful, dire, dread, dreadful, fearful, ghastly, grim, grisly, gruesome, harrowing, hideous, horrendous, horrible, horrid, lurid, macabre, petrifying, shocking, terrible, terrifying, traumatic, unnerving, unspeakable

frigid 1. arctic, chill, cold, cool, frost-bound, frosty, frozen, gelid, glacial, hyperboreal, icy, Siberian, wintry **2.** aloof, austere, cold-hearted, forbidding, formal, icy, lifeless, passionless, passive, repellent, rigid, stiff, unapproachable, unbending, unfeeling, unloving, unresponsive
Antonyms ardent, cordial, friendly, hospitable, hot, impassioned, passionate, responsive, sensual, stifling, sweltering, warm

frills additions, affectation(s), bits and pieces, decoration(s), dressing up, embellishment(s), extras, fanciness, fandangles, finery, frilliness, frippery, fuss, gewgaws, jazz (*Sl.*), mannerisms, nonsense, ornamentation, ostentation, superfluities, tomfoolery, trimmings

fringe *n.* **1.** binding, border, edging, hem, tassel, trimming **2.** borderline, edge, limits, march, marches, margin, outskirts, perimeter, periphery

frisk bounce, caper, cavort, curvet, dance, frolic, gambol, hop, jump, play, prance, rollick, romp, skip, sport, trip

fritter (away) dally away, dissipate, fool away, idle (away), misspend, run through, spend like water, squander, waste

frivolity childishness, flightiness, flippancy, flummery, folly, frivolousness, fun, gaiety, giddiness, jest, levity, light-heartedness, lightness, nonsense, puerility, shallowness, silliness, superficiality, trifling, triviality
Antonyms earnestness, gravity, humourlessness, importance, sedateness, seriousness, significance, soberness, sobriety

frivolous childish, dizzy, empty-headed, flighty, flip (*Inf.*), flippant, foolish, giddy, idle, ill-considered, juvenile, light-minded, nonserious, puerile, silly, superficial
Antonyms earnest, mature, responsible, sensible, serious, solemn

frolic *v.* **1.** caper, cavort, cut capers, frisk, gambol, lark, make merry, play, rollick, romp, sport ~*n.* **2.** antic, escapade, gambado, gambol, game, lark, prank, revel, romp, spree **3.** amusement, drollery, fun, fun and games, gaiety, high jinks, merriment, skylarking (*Inf.*), sport

front *n.* **1.** anterior, exterior, façade, face, facing, foreground, forepart, frontage, obverse **2.** beginning, fore, forefront, front line, head, lead, top, van, vanguard **3.** blind, cover, cover-up, disguise, façade, mask, pretext, show **4. in front** ahead, before, first, in advance, in the lead, in the van, leading, preceding, to the fore ~*adj.* **5.** first, foremost, head, headmost, lead, leading, topmost ~*v.* **6.** face (onto), look over *or* onto, overlook
Antonyms (*senses 1 & 2*) aft, back, back end, behind, hindmost, nethermost, rear

frontier borderland, borderline, bound, boundary, confines, edge, limit, marches, perimeter, verge

frosty 1. chilly, cold, frozen, hoar (*Rare*), ice-capped, icicled, icy, rimy, wintry **2.** discouraging, frigid, off-putting, standoffish, unenthusiastic, unfriendly, unwelcoming

frown 1. give a dirty look, glare, glower, knit one's brows, look daggers, lower, scowl **2.** *With on or upon* disapprove of, discountenance, discourage, dislike, look askance at, not take kindly to, show disapproval *or* displeasure, take a dim view of, view with disfavour

frozen 1. arctic, chilled, chilled to the marrow, frigid, frosted, icebound, ice-cold, ice-covered, icy, numb **2.** fixed, pegged (*of prices*), petrified, rooted, stock-still, stopped, suspended, turned to stone

frugal abstemious, careful, cheeseparing, economical, mea~

gre, niggardly, parsimonious, penny-wise, provident, prudent, saving, sparing, thrifty
Antonyms excessive, extravagant, imprudent, lavish, luxurious, prodigal, profligate, spendthrift, wasteful

fruit 1. crop, harvest, produce, product, yield **2.** advantage, benefit, consequence, effect, outcome, profit, result, return, reward

fruitful 1. fecund, fertile, fructiferous **2.** abundant, copious, flush, plenteous, plentiful, productive, profuse, prolific, rich, spawning
Antonyms barren, fruitless, infertile, scarce, unfruitful, unproductive

fruitless abortive, barren, bootless, futile, idle, ineffectual, in vain, pointless, profitless, to no avail, to no effect, unavailing, unfruitful, unproductive, unprofitable, unprolific, unsuccessful, useless, vain

frustrate baffle, balk, block, check, circumvent, confront, counter, defeat, disappoint, foil, forestall, inhibit, neutralize, nullify, render null and void, stymie, thwart
Antonyms advance, cheer, encourage, endorse, forward, further, hearten, promote, satisfy, stimulate

frustrated carrying a chip on one's shoulder (*Inf.*), disappointed, discontented, discouraged, disheartened, embittered, foiled, irked, resentful

fuel *n. Fig.* ammunition, encouragement, fodder, food, incitement, material, means, nourishment, provocation

fugitive *n.* deserter, escapee, refugee, runagate (*Archaic*), runaway

fulfil accomplish, achieve, answer, bring to completion, carry out, complete, comply with, conclude, conform to, discharge, effect, execute, fill, finish, keep, meet, obey, observe, perfect, perform, realise, satisfy

Antonyms disappoint, dissatisfy, fail in, fail to meet, fall short of, neglect

fulfilment accomplishment, achievement, attainment, carrying out *or* through, completion, consummation, crowning, discharge, discharging, effecting, end, implementation, observance, perfection, realization

full 1. brimful, brimming, complete, entire, filled, gorged, intact, loaded, replete, sated, satiated, satisfied, saturated, stocked, sufficient **2.** abundant, adequate, all-inclusive, ample, broad, comprehensive, copious, detailed, exhaustive, extensive, generous, maximum, plenary, plenteous, plentiful, thorough, unabridged **3.** chock-a-block, chock-full, crammed, crowded, in use, jammed, occupied, packed, taken
Antonyms abridged, blank, devoid, empty, exhausted, incomplete, limited, partial, vacant, void

full-grown adult, developed, full-fledged, grown-up, in one's prime, marriageable, mature, nubile, of age, ripe
Antonyms adolescent, green, premature, undeveloped, unfledged, unformed, unripe, untimely, young

fullness broadness, completeness, comprehensiveness, entirety, extensiveness, plenitude, totality, vastness, wealth, wholeness

full-scale all-encompassing, all-out, comprehensive, exhaustive, extensive, full-dress, in-depth, major, proper, sweeping, thorough, thoroughgoing, wide-ranging

fully 1. absolutely, altogether, completely, entirely, every inch, from first to last, heart and soul, in all respects, intimately, perfectly, positively, thoroughly, totally, utterly, wholly **2.** abundantly, adequately, amply, comprehensively, enough, plentifully, satisfactorily, sufficiently

fulsome

fulsome adulatory, cloying, excessive, extravagant, fawning, gross, immoderate, ingratiating, inordinate, insincere, nauseating, overdone, saccharine, sickening, smarmy (Inf.), sycophantic, unctuous

fumble botch, bungle, make a hash of (Inf.), mess up, misfield, mishandle, mismanage, muff, spoil

fume Fig. v. boil, chafe, champ at the bit (Inf.), get hot under the collar (Inf.), get steamed up about (Sl.), rage, rant, rave, seethe, smoulder, storm

fumes effluvium, exhalation, exhaust, gas, haze, miasma, pollution, reek, smog, smoke, stench, vapour

fumigate clean out or up, cleanse, disinfect, purify, sanitize, sterilize

fun n. amusement, cheer, distraction, diversion, enjoyment, entertainment, frolic, gaiety, good time, high jinks, jollification, jollity, joy, junketing, living it up, merriment, merrymaking, mirth, pleasure, recreation, romp, sport, treat, whoopee (Inf.)
Antonyms depression, desolation, despair, distress, gloom, grief, melancholy, misery, sadness, sorrow, unhappiness, woe

function n. 1. activity, business, capacity, charge, concern, duty, employment, exercise, job, mission, occupation, office, operation, part, post, province, purpose, raison d'être, responsibility, role, situation, task ~v. 2. act the part of, behave, be in commission, be in operation or action, be in running order, do duty, go, officiate, operate, perform, run, serve, serve one's turn, work ~n. 3. affair, do (Inf.), gathering, reception, social occasion

functional hard-wearing, operative, practical, serviceable, useful, utilitarian, utility, working

fund n. 1. capital, endowment, foundation, kitty, pool, reserve,

stock, store, supply 2. hoard, mine, repository, reserve, reservoir, source, storehouse, treasury, vein ~v. 3. capitalize, endow, finance, float, pay for, promote, stake, subsidize, support

fundamental adj. basic, cardinal, central, constitutional, crucial, elementary, essential, first, important, indispensable, integral, intrinsic, key, necessary, organic, primary, prime, principal, rudimentary, underlying, vital
Antonyms advanced, back-up, extra, incidental, lesser, secondary, subsidiary, superfluous

funds bread (Sl.), capital, cash, dough (Sl.), finance, hard cash, money, ready money, resources, savings, the ready (Inf.), the wherewithal

funeral burial, inhumation, interment, obsequies

funny adj. 1. absurd, amusing, a scream (card, caution) (Inf.), comic, comical, diverting, droll, entertaining, facetious, farcical, hilarious, humorous, jocose, jocular, jolly, killing (Inf.), laughable, ludicrous, rich, ridiculous, riotous, risible, side-splitting, silly, slapstick, waggish, witty 2. curious, dubious, mysterious, odd, peculiar, perplexing, puzzling, queer, remarkable, strange, suspicious, unusual, weird
Antonyms (sense 1) grave, humourless, melancholy, serious, sober, solemn, stern, unfunny

furious angry, beside oneself, boiling, enraged, frantic, frenzied, fuming, incensed, infuriated, in high dudgeon, livid (Inf.), mad, maddened, on the warpath (Inf.), raging, up in arms, wrathful, wroth (Archaic)
Antonyms calm, dispassionate, impassive, imperturbable, mild, placated, pleased, serene, tranquil

furnish 1. appoint, decorate, equip, fit (out, up), outfit, provide, provision, rig, stock, store, supply 2. afford, bestow, endow, give,

furniture appliances, appointments, chattels, effects, equipment, fittings, furnishings, goods, household goods, movable property, movables, possessions, things (*Inf.*)

furrow *n.* channel, corrugation, crease, crow's-foot, fluting, groove, hollow, line, rut, seam, trench, wrinkle

further 1. *adj.* additional, extra, fresh, more, new, other, supplementary **2.** *adv.* additionally, also, as well as, besides, furthermore, in addition, moreover, on top of, over and above, to boot, what's more, yet **3.** *v.* advance, aid, assist, champion, contribute to, encourage, expedite, facilitate, forward, foster, hasten, help, lend support to, patronize, plug (*Inf.*), promote, push, speed, succour, work for

Antonyms *v.* foil, frustrate, hinder, impede, obstruct, oppose, prevent, retard, stop, thwart

furthermore additionally, as well, besides, further, in addition, into the bargain, moreover, not to mention, to boot, too, what's more

furthest extreme, farthest, furthermost, most distant, outermost, outmost, remotest, ultimate, uttermost

furtive clandestine, cloaked, conspiratorial, covert, hidden, secret, secretive, skulking, slinking, sly, sneaking, sneaky, stealthy, surreptitious, underhand, under-the-table

Antonyms above-board, candid, forthright, frank, open, public, straightforward, undisguised, unreserved

fury 1. anger, frenzy, impetuosity, ire, madness, passion, rage, wrath **2.** ferocity, fierceness, force, intensity, power, savagery,

grant, offer, present, provide, reveal, supply

severity, tempestuousness, turbulence, vehemence, violence

Antonyms calm, calmness, composure, equanimity, hush, peace, peacefulness, serenity, stillness, tranquillity

fuss *n.* **1.** ado, agitation, bother, bustle, commotion, confusion, excitement, fidget, flap (*Inf.*), flurry, fluster, flutter, hurry, palaver, pother, stir, storm in a teacup (*Brit.*), to-do, upset, worry **2.** altercation, argument, bother, complaint, difficulty, display, furore, hassle (*Inf.*), objection, row, squabble, trouble, unrest, upset ~*v.* **3.** bustle, chafe, fidget, flap (*Inf.*), fret, fume, get in a stew (*Inf.*), get worked up, labour over, make a meal of (*Inf.*), make a thing of (*Inf.*), niggle, take pains, worry

fussy choosy (*Inf.*), dainty, difficult, discriminating, exacting, faddish, faddy, fastidious, finicky, hard to please, nit-picking (*Inf.*), old-maidish, old womanish, overparticular, particular, pernickety, squeamish

futile abortive, barren, bootless, empty, forlorn, fruitless, hollow, ineffectual, in vain, nugatory, profitless, sterile, to no avail, unavailing, unproductive, unprofitable, unsuccessful, useless, vain, valueless, worthless

Antonyms constructive, effective, fruitful, profitable, purposeful, significant, successful, useful, valuable, worthwhile

future 1. *n.* expectation, hereafter, outlook, prospect, time to come **2.** *adj.* approaching, coming, destined, eventual, expected, fated, forthcoming, impending, in the offing, later, prospective, subsequent, to be, to come, ultimate, unborn

Antonyms *adj.* bygone, erstwhile, ex-, former, late, past, preceding, previous, quondam

G

gadget appliance, contraption (*Inf.*), contrivance, device, gimmick, gizmo (*Sl., chiefly U.S.*), invention, novelty, thing, tool

gag *v.* curb, muffle, muzzle, quiet, silence, stifle, still, stop up, suppress, throttle

gaiety animation, blitheness, blithesomeness (*Literary*), cheerfulness, effervescence, elation, exhilaration, glee, good humour, high spirits, hilarity, *joie de vivre*, jollity, joviality, joyousness, light-heartedness, liveliness, merriment, mirth, sprightliness, vivacity
Antonyms despondency, gloom, melancholy, misery, sadness

gaily blithely, cheerfully, gleefully, happily, joyfully, lightheartedly, merrily

gain *v.* **1.** achieve, acquire, advance, attain, bag, build up, capture, collect, enlist, gather, get, glean, harvest, improve, increase, net, obtain, pick up, procure, profit, realize, reap, secure, win, win over **2.** acquire, bring in, clear, earn, get, make, net, obtain, produce, realize, win, yield ~*n.* **3.** accretion, achievement, acquisition, advance, advancement, advantage, attainment, benefit, dividend, earnings, emolument, growth, headway, improvement, income, increase, increment, lucre, proceeds, produce, profit, progress, return, rise, winnings, yield
Antonyms *v.* fail, forfeit, lose, worsen ~*n.* damage, forfeiture, injury, loss, privation

gains booty, earnings, gainings, pickings, prize, proceeds, profits, revenue, takings, winnings

gait bearing, carriage, pace, step, stride, tread, walk

gala *n.* carnival, celebration, festival, festivity, fête, jamboree, pageant, party

gale blast, cyclone, hurricane, squall, storm, tempest, tornado, typhoon

gallant *adj.* **1.** bold, brave, courageous, daring, dashing, dauntless, doughty, fearless, game (*Inf.*), heroic, high-spirited, honourable, intrepid, lion-hearted, manful, manly, mettlesome, noble, plucky, valiant, valorous **2.** attentive, chivalrous, courteous, courtly, gentlemanly, gracious, magnanimous, noble, polite ~*n.* **3.** admirer, beau, boyfriend, escort, lover, paramour, suitor, wooer
Antonyms churlish, cowardly, discourteous, fearful, ignoble, ill-mannered, impolite, rude

gallantry audacity, boldness, bravery, courage, courageousness, daring, dauntlessness, derring-do (*Archaic*), fearlessness, heroism, intrepidity, manliness, mettle, nerve, pluck, prowess, spirit, valiance, valour
Antonyms cowardice, irresolution

galling aggravating (*Inf.*), annoying, bitter, bothersome, exasperating, harassing, humiliating, irksome, irritating, nettlesome, plaguing, provoking, rankling, vexatious, vexing

gallop bolt, career, dart, dash, fly, hasten, hie (*Archaic*), hurry, race, run, rush, scud, shoot, speed, sprint, tear along, zoom

gamble *v.* **1.** back, bet, game, have a flutter (*Inf.*), lay *or* make a bet, play, punt, stake, try one's luck, wager **2.** back, chance, hazard, put one's faith *or* trust in, risk, speculate, stake, stick one's neck out (*Inf.*), take a chance, venture ~*n.* **3.** chance, leap in

the dark, lottery, risk, speculation, uncertainty, venture 4. bet,
flutter (*Inf.*), punt, wager
Antonyms (*sense 3*) certainty,
foregone conclusion, safe bet,
sure thing

gambol v. caper, cavort, curvet,
cut a caper, frisk, frolic, hop,
jump, prance, rollick, skip

game¹ n. 1. amusement, distraction, diversion, entertainment,
frolic, fun, jest, joke, lark, merriment, pastime, play, recreation,
romp, sport 2. competition, contest, event, match, meeting,
round, tournament 3. chase, prey,
quarry, wild animals
Antonyms business, chore, duty,
job, labour, toil, work

game² adj. bold, brave, courageous, dauntless, dogged, fearless, gallant, heroic, intrepid,
persevering, persistent, plucky,
resolute, spirited, unflinching,
valiant, valorous
Antonyms cowardly, fearful, irresolute

gang band, circle, clique, club,
company, coterie, crew (*Inf.*),
crowd, group, herd, horde, lot,
mob, pack, party, ring, set, shift,
squad, team, troupe

gangster bandit, brigand, crook
(*Inf.*), desperado, gang member,
hood (*U.S. sl.*), hoodlum (*Chiefly
U.S.*), mobster (*U.S. sl.*), racketeer, robber, ruffian, thug, tough

gap blank, breach, break, chink,
cleft, crack, cranny, crevice, dis-
continuity, divide, hiatus, hole,
interlude, intermission, interruption, interstice, interval, lacuna,
lull, opening, pause, recess, rent,
rift, space, vacuity, void

gape 1. gawk, gawp (*Brit. sl.*),
goggle, stare, wonder 2. crack,
open, split, yawn

gaping broad, cavernous, great,
open, vast, wide, wide open,
yawning

garbage bits and pieces, debris,
detritus, junk, litter, odds and
ends, rubbish, scraps

garble 1. confuse, jumble, mix up
2. corrupt, distort, doctor, falsify,

misinterpret, misquote, misreport, misrepresent, misstate,
mistranslate, mutilate, pervert,
slant, tamper with, twist
Antonyms clarify, decipher,
make intelligible

garish brassy, brummagem,
cheap, flash (*Inf.*), flashy, flaunting, gaudy, glaring, glittering,
loud, meretricious, raffish,
showy, tasteless, tawdry, vulgar
Antonyms conservative, elegant,
modest, plain, refined, sedate,
sombre, unobtrusive

garland n. bays, chaplet, coronal,
crown, festoon, honours, laurels,
wreath

garments apparel, array, articles
of clothing, attire, clothes, clothing, costume, dress, duds (*Inf.*),
garb, gear (*Sl.*), habiliment, habit,
outfit, raiment (*Archaic*), robes,
togs, uniform, vestments, wear

garner v. accumulate, amass, assemble, collect, deposit, gather,
hoard, husband, lay in *or* up, put
by, reserve, save, stockpile,
store, stow away, treasure

garnish v. adorn, beautify, bedeck, deck, decorate, embellish,
enhance, grace, ornament, set
off, trim
Antonyms denude, spoil, strip

garrison n. 1. armed force, command, detachment, troops, unit 2.
base, camp, encampment, fort,
fortification, fortress, post, station, stronghold

gash 1. v. cleave, cut, gouge,
incise, lacerate, rend, slash, slit,
split, tear, wound 2. n. cleft, cut,
gouge, incision, laceration, rent,
slash, slit, split, tear, wound

gasp 1. v. blow, catch one's
breath, choke, fight for breath,
gulp, pant, puff 2. n. blow, ejaculation, exclamation, gulp, pant,
puff

gate access, barrier, door, doorway, egress, entrance, exit, gateway, opening, passage, port
(*Scot.*), portal

gather 1. accumulate, amass, assemble, bring *or* get together,
collect, congregate, convene,

flock, forgather, garner, group, heap, hoard, marshal, mass, muster, pile up, round up, stack up, stockpile 2. assume, be led to believe, conclude, deduce, draw, hear, infer, learn, make, surmise, understand 3. crop, cull, garner, glean, harvest, pick, pluck, reap, select

Antonyms diffuse, disperse, dissipate, scatter, separate

gathering assemblage, assembly, company, conclave, concourse, congregation, congress, convention, convocation, crowd, flock, get-together (*Inf.*), group, knot, meeting, muster, party, rally, throng, turnout

gauche awkward, clumsy, graceless, ignorant, ill-bred, inmannered, inelegant, inept, insensitive, lacking in social graces, maladroit, tactless, uncultured, unpolished, unsophisticated

gaudy bright, brilliant, brummagem, flash (*Inf.*), flashy, florid, garish, gay, glaring, loud, meretricious, ostentatious, raffish, showy, tasteless, tawdry, vulgar

Antonyms colourless, conservative, dull, elegant, modest, quiet, refined, sedate, subtle, tasteful

gauge v. 1. ascertain, calculate, check, compute, count, determine, measure, weigh 2. adjudge, appraise, assess, estimate, evaluate, guess, judge, rate, reckon, value ~n. 3. basis, criterion, example, exemplar, guide, guideline, indicator, measure, meter, model, pattern, rule, sample, standard, test, touchstone, yardstick 4. bore, capacity, degree, depth, extent, height, magnitude, measure, scope, size, span, thickness, width

gaunt angular, attenuated, bony, cadaverous, emaciated, haggard, lank, lean, meagre, pinched, rawboned, scraggy, scrawny, skeletal, skinny, spare, thin, wasted

Antonyms chubby, corpulent, fat, obese, plump, stout, well-fed

gawky awkward, clownish, clumsy, gauche, loutish, lumbering, lumpish, maladroit, oafish, uncouth, ungainly

Antonyms elegant, graceful, self-assured, well-coordinated

gay *adj.* 1. animated, blithe, carefree, cheerful, debonair, glad, gleeful, happy, hilarious, insouciant, jolly, jovial, joyful, joyous, light-hearted, lively, merry, sparkling, sunny, vivacious 2. bright, brilliant, colourful, flamboyant, flashy, fresh, garish, gaudy, rich, showy, vivid

Antonyms (*sense 1*) cheerless, colourless, conservative, drab, dull, grave, grim, melancholy, miserable, sad, sedate, serious, sober, solemn, sombre, unhappy

gaze 1. v. contemplate, gape, look, look fixedly, regard, stare, view, watch, wonder 2. n. fixed look, look, stare

gear n. 1. cog, cogwheel, gearwheel, toothed wheel 2. accessories, accoutrements, apparatus, equipment, harness, instruments, outfit, paraphernalia, rigging, supplies, tackle, tools, trappings 3. baggage, belongings, effects, kit, luggage, stuff, things

gem 1. jewel, precious stone, semiprecious stone, stone 2. flower, jewel, masterpiece, pearl, pick, prize, treasure

general 1. accepted, broad, common, extensive, popular, prevailing, prevalent, public, universal, widespread 2. accustomed, conventional, customary, everyday, habitual, normal, ordinary, regular, typical, usual 3. approximate, ill-defined, imprecise, inaccurate, indefinite, inexact, loose, undetailed, unspecific, vague

Antonyms definite, distinctive, exact, exceptional, extraordinary, individual, infrequent, particular, peculiar, precise, rare, special, specific, unusual

generally 1. almost always, as a rule, by and large, conventionally, customarily, for the most part, habitually, in most cases, mainly,

normally, on average, on the whole, ordinarily, regularly, typically, usually **2.** commonly, extensively, popularly, publicly, universally, widely
Antonyms especially, individually, occasionally, particularly, rarely, unusually

generate beget, breed, bring about, cause, create, engender, form, give rise to, initiate, make, originate, procreate, produce, propagate, spawn, whip up
Antonyms annihilate, crush, destroy, end, extinguish, kill, terminate

generation 1. begetting, breeding, creation, engenderment, formation, genesis, origination, procreation, production, propagation, reproduction **2.** age, day, days, epoch, era, period, time, times

generosity beneficence, benevolence, bounteousness, bounty, charity, kindness, liberality, munificence, open-handedness

generous 1. beneficent, benevolent, bounteous, bountiful, charitable, free, hospitable, kind, lavish, liberal, munificent, open-handed, princely, ungrudging, unstinting **2.** big-hearted, disinterested, good, high-minded, lofty, magnanimous, noble, unselfish
Antonyms avaricious, cheap, close-fisted, greedy, mean, minimal, miserly, parsimonious, scanty, selfish, small, stingy, tight, tiny

genial affable, agreeable, amiable, cheerful, cheery, congenial, convivial, cordial, easygoing, enlivening, friendly, glad, good-natured, happy, hearty, jolly, jovial, joyous, kind, kindly, merry, pleasant, sunny, warm, warm-hearted
Antonyms cheerless, cool, discourteous, frigid, morose, rude, sardonic, sullen, unfriendly, ungracious, unpleasant

genius 1. adept, brain (*Inf.*), expert, intellect (*Inf.*), maestro,

master, master-hand, mastermind, virtuoso **2.** ability, aptitude, bent, brilliance, capacity, creative power, endowment, faculty, flair, gift, inclination, knack, propensity, talent, turn
Antonyms dolt, dunce, fool, half-wit, idiot, imbecile, nincompoop, simpleton

genteel aristocratic, civil, courteous, courtly, cultivated, cultured, elegant, fashionable, formal, gentlemanly, ladylike, mannerly, polished, polite, refined, respectable, stylish, urbane, well-bred, well-mannered
Antonyms discourteous, ill-bred, impolite, inelegant, low-bred, natural, plebeian, rude, unaffected, uncultured, unmannerly, unpolished, unrefined

gentility civility, courtesy, courtliness, cultivation, culture, decorum, elegance, etiquette, formality, good breeding, good manners, mannerliness, polish, politeness, propriety, refinement, respectability, urbanity

gentle 1. amiable, benign, bland, compassionate, dove-like, humane, kind, kindly, lenient, meek, merciful, mild, pacific, peaceful, placid, quiet, soft, sweet-tempered, tender **2.** balmy, calm, clement, easy, light, low, mild, moderate, muted, placid, quiet, serene, slight, smooth, soft, soothing, temperate, tranquil, untroubled
Antonyms aggressive, cruel, fierce, hard, harsh, heartless, impolite, powerful, rough, savage, sharp, strong, unkind, violent, wild

gentlemanly civil, civilized, courteous, cultivated, gallant, genteel, gentlemanlike, honourable, mannerly, noble, obliging, polished, polite, refined, reputable, suave, urbane, well-bred, well-mannered

genuine actual, authentic, bona fide, honest, legitimate, natural, original, pure, real, sound, ster-

ling, true, unadulterated, unalloyed, veritable
Antonyms artificial, bogus, counterfeit, fake, false, feigned, fraudulent, hypocritical, imitation, phoney, sham, simulated, spurious
germ 1. bacterium, bug (*Inf.*), microbe, microorganism, virus 2. beginning, bud, cause, embryo, origin, root, rudiment, seed, source, spark
germinate bud, develop, generate, grow, originate, pullulate, shoot, sprout, swell, vegetate
gesture 1. *n.* action, gesticulation, indication, motion, sign, signal 2. *v.* gesticulate, indicate, motion, sign, signal, wave
get 1. achieve, acquire, attain, bag, bring, come by, come into possession of, earn, fall heir to, fetch, gain, glean, inherit, make, net, obtain, pick up, procure, realize, reap, receive, secure, succeed to, win 2. arrest, capture, collar (*Inf.*), grab, lay hold of, seize, take, trap 3. become, come to be, grow, turn, wax 4. arrive, come, make it (*Inf.*), reach 5. arrange, contrive, fix, manage, succeed, wangle (*Inf.*) 6. coax, convince, induce, influence, persuade, prevail upon, sway, talk into, wheedle, win over
get ahead advance, be successful, do well, flourish, get on, make good, progress, prosper, succeed, thrive
get along 1. agree, be compatible, be friendly, get on, harmonize, hit it off (*Inf.*) 2. cope, develop, fare, get by (*Inf.*), make out (*Inf.*), manage, progress, shift
get at 1. acquire, attain, come to grips with, gain access to, get, get hold of, reach 2. hint, imply, intend, lead up to, mean, suggest 3. annoy, attack, blame, carp, criticize, find fault with, irritate, nag, pick on, taunt
get down alight, bring down, climb down, descend, disembark, dismount, get off, lower, step down

get off alight, depart, descend, disembark, dismount, escape, exit, leave
get on 1. ascend, board, climb, embark, mount 2. advance, cope, fare, get along, make out (*Inf.*), manage, progress, prosper, succeed 3. agree, be compatible, be friendly, concur, get along, harmonize, hit it off (*Inf.*)
get over 1. cross, ford, get across, pass, pass over, surmount, traverse 2. come round, get better, mend, pull through, recover from, revive, survive 3. communicate, convey, get or put across, impart, make clear or understood
get round 1. bypass, circumvent, edge, evade, outmanoeuvre, skirt 2. *Inf.* cajole, coax, convert, persuade, prevail upon, talk round, wheedle, win over
get up arise, ascend, climb, increase, mount, rise, scale, stand
ghastly ashen, cadaverous, deathlike, deathly pale, dreadful, frightful, grim, grisly, gruesome, hideous, horrendous, horrible, horrid, livid, loathsome, pale, pallid, repellent, shocking, spectral, terrible, terrifying, wan
Antonyms appealing, attractive, beautiful, blooming, charming, healthy, lovely, pleasing
ghost apparition, manes, phantasm, phantom, revenant, shade (*Literary*), soul, spectre, spirit, spook (*Inf.*), wraith
ghostly eerie, ghostlike, illusory, insubstantial, phantasmal, phantom, spectral, spooky (*Inf.*), supernatural, uncanny, unearthly, weird, wraithlike
giant 1. *n.* behemoth, colossus, Hercules, leviathan, monster, titan 2. *adj.* Brobdingnagian, colossal, elephantine, enormous, gargantuan, gigantic, huge, immense, jumbo (*Inf.*), large, mammoth, monstrous, prodigious, titanic, vast
Antonyms *adj.* dwarf, Lilliputian, miniature, pygmy, tiny
gibberish babble, balderdash,

blather, double talk, drivel, gab~
ble, gobbledegook (*Inf.*), jabber,
jargon, mumbo jumbo, nonsense,
prattle, twaddle, yammer (*Inf.*)

gibe, jibe 1. *v.* deride, flout, jeer,
make fun of, mock, poke fun at,
ridicule, scoff, scorn, sneer,
taunt, twit **2.** *n.* crack (*Sl.*), cut~
ting remark, derision, dig, jeer,
mockery, ridicule, sarcasm,
scoffing, sneer, taunt

giddiness dizziness, faintness,
light-headedness, vertigo

giddy dizzy, dizzying, faint, light-
headed, reeling, unsteady, ver~
tiginous

gift 1. benefaction, bequest, bo~
nus, boon, bounty, contribution,
donation, grant, gratuity, largess,
legacy, offering, present **2.** abil~
ity, aptitude, attribute, bent, ca~
pability, capacity, endowment,
faculty, flair, genius, knack,
power, talent, turn

gifted able, accomplished, adroit,
brilliant, capable, clever, expert,
ingenious, intelligent, masterly,
skilled, talented
Antonyms amateur, backward,
dull, incapable, inept, retarded,
slow, talentless, unskilled

gigantic Brobdingnagian, colos~
sal, Cyclopean, elephantine,
enormous, gargantuan, giant,
herculean, huge, immense,
mammoth, monstrous, prodi~
gious, stupendous, titanic, tre~
mendous, vast
Antonyms diminutive, insignifi~
cant, little, miniature, puny,
small, tiny, weak

giggle *v./n.* cackle, chortle,
chuckle, laugh, snigger, tee-hee,
titter, twitter

gimmick contrivance, device,
dodge, gadget, gambit, gizmo (*Sl.*,
chiefly *U.S.*), ploy, scheme,
stratagem, stunt, trick

gird 1. belt, bind, girdle **2.** block~
ade, encircle, enclose, encom~
pass, enfold, engird, environ,
hem in, pen, ring, surround

girdle 1. *n.* band, belt, cincture,
cummerbund, fillet, sash, waist~
band **2.** *v.* bind, bound, encircle,

enclose, encompass, engird, en~
viron, gird, hem, ring, surround

girl bird (*Sl.*), chick (*Sl.*), colleen
(*Irish*), damsel (*Archaic*), daugh~
ter, female child, lass, lassie
(*Inf.*), maid (*Archaic*), maiden
(*Archaic*), miss, wench

girth bulk, circumference, meas~
ure, size

gist bulk, drift, essence, force,
idea, import, marrow, meaning,
nub, pith, point, quintessence,
sense, significance, substance

give 1. accord, administer, allow,
award, bestow, commit, confer,
consign, contribute, deliver, do~
nate, entrust, furnish, grant, hand
over *or* out, make over, permit,
present, provide, supply, vouch~
safe **2.** demonstrate, display, evi~
dence, indicate, manifest, offer,
proffer, provide, set forth, show
3. allow, cede, concede, devote,
grant, hand over, lend, relin~
quish, surrender, yield
Antonyms accept, get, hold,
keep, receive, take, withdraw

give away betray, disclose, di~
vulge, expose, inform on, leak, let
out, let slip, reveal, uncover

give in admit defeat, capitulate,
collapse, comply, concede, quit,
submit, surrender, yield

give off discharge, emit, exhale,
exude, produce, release, send
out, smell of, throw out, vent

give out discharge, emit, exhale,
exude, produce, release, send
out, smell of, throw out, vent

give up abandon, capitulate,
cease, cede, cut out, desist, des~
pair, forswear, hand over, leave
off, quit, relinquish, renounce,
resign, stop, surrender, throw in
the towel, waive

glad blithesome (*Literary*),
cheerful, chuffed (*Sl.*), contented,
delighted, gay, gleeful, gratified,
happy, jocund, jovial, joyful,
overjoyed, pleased, willing
Antonyms depressed, discon~
tented, displeased, melancholy,
miserable, sad, sorrowful, un~
happy

gladden cheer, delight, elate, en~

liven, exhilarate, gratify, hearten, please, rejoice

gladly cheerfully, freely, gaily, gleefully, happily, jovially, joyfully, joyously, merrily, readily, willingly, with (a) good grace, with pleasure
Antonyms dolefully, grudgingly, reluctantly, sadly, unenthusiastically, unwillingly

gladness animation, blitheness, cheerfulness, delight, felicity, gaiety, glee, happiness, high spirits, hilarity, jollity, joy, joyousness, mirth, pleasure

glamorous alluring, attractive, beautiful, bewitching, captivating, charming, dazzling, elegant, enchanting, entrancing, exciting, fascinating, glittering, glossy, lovely, prestigious, smart
Antonyms colourless, dull, unattractive, unexciting, unglamorous

glamour allure, appeal, attraction, beauty, bewitchment, charm, enchantment, fascination, magnetism, prestige, ravishment, witchery

glance v. 1. gaze, glimpse, look, peek, peep, scan, view ~n. 2. brief look, dekko (Sl.), glimpse, look, peek, peep, quick look, squint, view 3. flash, gleam, glimmer, glint, reflection, sparkle, twinkle 4. allusion, passing mention, reference
Antonyms v. peruse, scrutinize, study ~n. (sense 2) examination, good look, inspection, perusal

glare v. 1. frown, give a dirty look, glower, look daggers, lower, scowl, stare angrily ~n. 2. angry stare, black look, dirty look, frown, glower, lower, scowl 3. blaze, brilliance, dazzle, flame, flare, glow

glaring audacious, blatant, conspicuous, egregious, flagrant, gross, manifest, obvious, open, outrageous, outstanding, overt, patent, rank, unconcealed, visible

glassy clear, glossy, icy, shiny,

slick, slippery, smooth, transparent

glaze 1. v. burnish, coat, enamel, furbish, gloss, lacquer, polish, varnish 2. n. coat, enamel, finish, gloss, lacquer, lustre, patina, polish, shine, varnish

gleam 1. n. beam, flash, glimmer, glow, ray, sparkle 2. v. coruscate, flare, flash, glance, glimmer, glint, glisten, glitter, glow, scintillate, shimmer, shine, sparkle

glee cheerfulness, delight, elation, exhilaration, exuberance, exultation, fun, gaiety, gladness, hilarity, jocularity, jollity, joviality, joy, joyfulness, joyousness, liveliness, merriment, mirth, sprightliness, triumph, verve
Antonyms depression, gloom, melancholy, misery, sadness

gleeful cheerful, cock-a-hoop, delighted, elated, exuberant, exultant, gay, gratified, happy, jocund, jovial, joyful, joyous, jubilant, merry, mirthful, overjoyed, pleased, triumphant

glib artful, easy, fast-talking, fluent, garrulous, insincere, plausible, quick, ready, slick, slippery, smooth, smooth-tongued, suave, talkative, voluble
Antonyms halting, hesitant, implausible, sincere, tongue-tied

glide coast, drift, float, flow, fly, roll, run, sail, skate, skim, slide, slip, soar

glimmer 1. v. blink, flicker, gleam, glisten, glitter, glow, shimmer, shine, sparkle, twinkle 2. n. blink, flicker, gleam, glow, ray, shimmer, sparkle, twinkle

glimpse 1. n. brief view, glance, look, peek, peep, quick look, sight, sighting, squint 2. v. catch sight of, descry, espy, sight, spot, spy, view

glint 1. v. flash, gleam, glimmer, glitter, shine, sparkle, twinkle 2. n. flash, gleam, glimmer, glitter, shine, sparkle, twinkle, twinkling

glisten coruscate, flash, glance, glare, gleam, glimmer, glint, glitter, scintillate, shimmer, shine, sparkle, twinkle

glitter 1. *v.* coruscate, flare, flash, glare, gleam, glimmer, glint, glisten, scintillate, shimmer, shine, sparkle, twinkle 2. *n.* beam, brightness, brilliance, flash, glare, gleam, lustre, radiance, scintillation, sheen, shimmer, shine, sparkle

gloat crow, exult, glory, relish, revel in, rub it in (*Inf.*), triumph, vaunt

global 1. international, pandemic, planetary, universal, world, worldwide 2. all-encompassing, all-inclusive, all-out, comprehensive, encyclopedic, exhaustive, general, thorough, total, unbounded, unlimited
Antonyms (*sense 2*) limited, narrow, parochial, restricted, sectional

globe ball, earth, orb, planet, round, sphere, world

globule bead, bubble, drop, droplet, particle, pearl, pellet

gloom 1. blackness, cloud, cloudiness, dark, darkness, dimness, dullness, dusk, duskiness, gloominess, murk, murkiness, obscurity, shade, shadow, twilight 2. blues, dejection, depression, desolation, despair, despondency, downheartedness, low spirits, melancholy, misery, sadness, sorrow, unhappiness, woe
Antonyms brightness, cheerfulness, daylight, delight, happiness, high spirits, jollity, joy, light, mirth, radiance

gloomy 1. black, crepuscular, dark, dim, dismal, dreary, dull, dusky, murky, obscure, overcast, shadowy, sombre, Stygian, tenebrous 2. bad, black, cheerless, comfortless, depressing, disheartening, dispiriting, dreary, joyless, sad, saddening, sombre 3. blue, chapfallen, cheerless, crestfallen, dejected, despondent, dismal, dispirited, down, downcast, downhearted, down in the dumps (*Inf.*), down in the mouth, glum, in low spirits, melancholy,

miserable, moody, morose, pessimistic, sad, saturnine, sullen
Antonyms blithe, bright, brilliant, cheerful, happy, high-spirited, jolly, jovial, light, merry, radiant, sunny

glorify 1. add lustre to, adorn, aggrandize, augment, dignify, elevate, enhance, ennoble, illuminate, immortalize, lift up, magnify, raise 2. celebrate, cry up (*Inf.*), eulogize, extol, hymn, laud, lionize, magnify, panegyrize, praise, sing *or* sound the praises of
Antonyms condemn, debase, defile, degrade, desecrate, dishonour, humiliate, mock

glorious 1. celebrated, distinguished, elevated, eminent, excellent, famed, famous, grand, honoured, illustrious, magnificent, majestic, noble, noted, renowned, sublime, triumphant 2. *Inf.* delightful, enjoyable, excellent, fine, great, heavenly (*Inf.*), marvellous, pleasurable, splendid, wonderful

glory *n.* 1. celebrity, dignity, distinction, eminence, exaltation, fame, honour, illustriousness, immortality, kudos, praise, prestige, renown 2. adoration, benediction, blessing, gratitude, homage, laudation, praise, thanksgiving, veneration, worship 3. grandeur, greatness, magnificence, majesty, nobility, pageantry, pomp, splendour, sublimity, triumph ~*v.* 4. boast, crow, exult, gloat, pride oneself, relish, revel, take delight, triumph

gloss[1] 1. *n.* brightness, brilliance, burnish, gleam, lustre, polish, sheen, shine, varnish, veneer 2. *v.* camouflage, conceal, cover up, disguise, hide, mask, smooth over, veil, whitewash (*Inf.*)

gloss[2] *n.* annotation, comment, commentary, elucidation, explanation, footnote, interpretation, note, scholium, translation

glossy bright, brilliant, burnished, glassy, glazed, lustrous,

polished, sheeny, shining, shiny, silken, silky, sleek, smooth
Antonyms drab, dull, mat *or* matt, subfusc

glow *n.* **1.** burning, gleam, glimmer, incandescence, lambency, light, luminosity, phosphorescence **2.** brilliance, brilliance, effulgence, radiance, splendour, vividness **3.** ardour, earnestness, enthusiasm, excitement, fervour, gusto, impetuosity, intensity, passion, vehemence, warmth ~*v.* **4.** brighten, burn, gleam, glimmer, redden, shine, smoulder **5.** be suffused, blush, colour, fill, flush, radiate, thrill, tingle

glower *v.* frown, give a dirty look, glare, look daggers, lower, scowl

glowing aglow, beaming, bright, flaming, florid, flushed, lambent, luminous, red, rich, ruddy, suffused, vibrant, vivid, warm
Antonyms colourless, cool, dull, grey, pale, pallid, wan

glue *n.* adhesive, cement, gum, mucilage, paste **2.** *v.* affix, agglutinate, cement, fix, gum, paste, seal, stick

glum chapfallen, churlish, crabbed, crestfallen, crusty, dejected, doleful, down, gloomy, gruff, grumpy, ill-humoured, low, moody, morose, pessimistic, saturnine, sour, sulky, sullen, surly
Antonyms cheerful, cheery, jolly, joyful, merry

glut *n.* excess, overabundance, oversupply, saturation, superabundance, superfluity, surfeit, surplus
Antonyms dearth, lack, paucity, scarcity, shortage, want

glutton gannet (*Sl.*), gobbler, gorger, gormandizer, gourmand, pig (*Inf.*)

gluttony gormandizing, gourmandism, greed, greediness, piggishness, rapacity, voraciousness, voracity

gnaw 1. bite, chew, munch, nibble, worry **2.** consume, devour, eat away *or* into, erode, fret, wear away *or* down

go *v.* **1.** advance, decamp, depart,

fare (*Archaic*), journey, leave, make for, move, move out, pass, proceed, repair, set off, travel, withdraw **2.** function, move, operate, perform, run, work **3.** develop, eventuate, fall out, fare, happen, proceed, result, turn out, work out **4.** die, expire, give up the ghost, pass away, perish **5.** elapse, expire, flow, lapse, pass, slip away ~*n.* **6.** attempt, bid, crack (*Inf.*), effort, essay, shot (*Inf.*), stab, try, turn, whack (*Inf.*), whirl (*Inf.*)
Antonyms *v.* (*sense 1*) arrive, halt, reach, remain, stay, stop (*sense 2*) break (down), fail, malfunction, stop

goad 1. *n.* impetus, incentive, incitement, irritation, motivation, pressure, spur, stimulation, stimulus, urge **2.** *v.* annoy, arouse, drive, egg on, exhort, harass, hound, impel, incite, instigate, irritate, lash, prick, prod, prompt, propel, spur, stimulate, sting, urge, worry

goal aim, ambition, design, destination, end, intention, limit, mark, object, objective, purpose, target

go along acquiesce, agree, assent, concur, cooperate, follow

go away decamp, depart, exit, leave, move out, recede, withdraw

go back return, revert

gobble bolt, cram, devour, gorge, gulp, guzzle, stuff, swallow, wolf

go-between agent, broker, dealer, factor, intermediary, liaison, mediator, medium, middleman

go by 1. elapse, exceed, flow on, move onward, pass, proceed **2.** adopt, be guided by, follow, heed, judge from, observe, take as guide

godforsaken abandoned, backward, bleak, deserted, desolate, dismal, dreary, forlorn, gloomy, lonely, neglected, remote, wretched

godless atheistic, depraved, evil, impious, irreligious, profane, ungodly, unprincipled, unrighteous, wicked

godly devout, god-fearing, good, holy, pious, religious, righteous, saintly

godsend blessing, boon, manna, stroke of luck, windfall

go far advance, be successful, do well, get ahead (*Inf.*), get on (*Inf.*), make a name for oneself, progress, succeed

go for 1. clutch at, fetch, obtain, reach, seek, stretch for 2. assail, assault, attack, launch oneself at, rush upon, set about or upon, spring upon

go in (for) adopt, embrace, engage in, enter, espouse, practise, pursue, take up, undertake

go into analyse, consider, delve into, discuss, examine, inquire into, investigate, look into, probe, pursue, review, scrutinize, study

gone 1. elapsed, ended, finished, over, past 2. absent, astray, away, lacking, lost, missing, vanished 3. dead, deceased, defunct, departed, extinct, no more 4. consumed, done, finished, spent, used up

good adj. 1. acceptable, admirable, agreeable, bad (*Sl.*), capital, choice, commendable, crucial (*Sl.*), excellent, fine, first-class, first-rate, great, pleasant, pleasing, positive, precious, satisfactory, splendid, super (*Inf.*), superior, tiptop, valuable, wicked (*Sl.*), worthy 2. admirable, estimable, ethical, exemplary, honest, honourable, moral, praiseworthy, right, righteous, trustworthy, upright, virtuous, worthy 3. able, accomplished, adept, adroit, capable, clever, competent, dexterous, efficient, expert, first-rate, proficient, reliable, satisfactory, serviceable, skilled, sound, suitable, talented, thorough, useful 4. authentic, bona fide, dependable, genuine, honest, legitimate, proper, real, reliable, sound, true, trustworthy, valid 5. decorous, dutiful, mannerly, obedient, orderly, polite, proper, seemly, well-behaved,

well-mannered 6. adequate, ample, complete, considerable, entire, extensive, full, large, long, sizable, solid, substantial, sufficient, whole ~n. 7. advantage, avail, behalf, benefit, gain, interest, profit, service, use, usefulness, welfare, wellbeing, worth 8. excellence, goodness, merit, morality, probity, rectitude, right, righteousness, uprightness, virtue, worth

Antonyms adj. (*sense 1*) awful, bad, boring, disagreeable, dull, inadequate, rotten, tedious, unpleasant (*sense 2*) bad, base, corrupt, dishonest, dishonourable, evil, immoral, improper, sinful (*sense 3*) bad, incompetent, inefficient, unsatisfactory, unskilled (*sense 4*) counterfeit, false, fraudulent, invalid, phoney (*sense 5*) ill-mannered, mischievous, naughty, rude, unkind (*sense 6*) scant, short ~n. (*sense 7*) detriment, disadvantage, failure, ill-fortune, loss (*sense 8*) badness, baseness, corruption, cruelty, dishonesty, evil, immorality, meanness, wickedness

goodbye adieu, farewell, leave-taking, parting

good-for-nothing 1. *n.* black sheep, idler, layabout, ne'er-do-well, profligate, rapscallion, scapegrace, waster, wastrel 2. *adj.* feckless, idle, irresponsible, useless, worthless

good-humoured affable, amiable, cheerful, congenial, genial, good-tempered, happy, pleasant

good-looking attractive, comely, fair, handsome, personable, pretty, well-favoured

good-natured agreeable, benevolent, friendly, good-hearted, helpful, kind, kindly, tolerant, warm-hearted, well-disposed, willing to please

goodness 1. excellence, merit, quality, superiority, value, worth 2. beneficence, benevolence, friendliness, generosity, good will, graciousness, humaneness, kind-heartedness, kindliness, kindness, mercy, obligingness 3. honesty, honour, integrity, merit, morality, probity, rectitude, righteousness, uprightness, virtue

Antonyms badness, corruption, dishonesty, evil, immorality, wickedness, worthlessness

goods 1. appurtenances, belongings, chattels, effects, furnishings, furniture, gear, movables, paraphernalia, possessions, property, things, trappings 2. commodities, merchandise, stock, stuff, wares

good will amity, benevolence, favour, friendliness, friendship, heartiness, kindliness, zeal

go off 1. blow up, detonate, explode, fire 2. *Inf.* go bad, go stale, rot

go on continue, endure, happen, last, occur, persist, proceed, stay

go out 1. depart, exit, leave 2. be extinguished, die out, expire, fade out

go over 1. examine, inspect, rehearse, reiterate, review, revise, study 2. peruse, read, scan, skim

gorge¹ *n.* canyon, cleft, clough (*Dialect*), defile, fissure, pass, ravine

gorge² *v.* bolt, cram, devour, feed, fill, glut, gobble, gormandize, gulp, guzzle, overeat, raven, sate, satiate, stuff, surfeit, swallow, wolf

gorgeous beautiful, brilliant, dazzling, elegant, glittering, grand, luxuriant, magnificent, opulent, ravishing, resplendent, showy, splendid, stunning (*Inf.*), sumptuous, superb

Antonyms cheap, dismal, dreary, dull, gloomy, homely, plain, repulsive, shabby, shoddy, sombre, ugly, unattractive, unsightly

gossamer *adj.* airy, delicate, diaphanous, fine, flimsy, gauzy, light, sheer, silky, thin, transparent

gossip *n.* 1. blether, chinwag (*Brit. inf.*), chitchat, clishmaclaver (*Scot.*), hearsay, idle talk, jaw (*Sl.*), newsmongering (*Old-*

fashioned), prattle, scandal, small talk, tittle-tattle 2. babbler, blatherskite, blether, busybody, chatterbox (*Inf.*), chatterer, flibbertigibbet, gossipmonger, newsmonger (*Old-fashioned*), prattler, quidnunc, scandalmonger, tattler, telltale ~ *v.* 3. blather, blether, chat, gabble, jaw (*Sl.*), prate, prattle, tattle

go through 1. bear, brave, endure, experience, suffer, tolerate, undergo, withstand 2. consume, exhaust, squander, use 3. check, examine, explore, hunt, look, search

govern 1. administer, be in power, command, conduct, control, direct, guide, hold sway, lead, manage, order, oversee, pilot, reign, rule, steer, superintend, supervise 2. decide, determine, guide, influence, rule, sway, underlie

government 1. administration, authority, dominion, execution, governance, law, polity, rule, sovereignty, state, statecraft 2. administration, executive, ministry, powers-that-be, regime 3. authority, command, control, direction, domination, guidance, management, regulation, restraint, superintendence, supervision, sway

governor administrator, boss (*Inf.*), chief, commander, comptroller, controller, director, executive, head, leader, manager, overseer, ruler, superintendent, supervisor

go with accompany, agree, blend, complement, concur, correspond, fit, harmonize, match, suit

go without abstain, be denied, be deprived of, deny oneself, do without, go short, lack, want

gown costume, dress, frock, garb, garment, habit, robe

grab bag, capture, catch, catch *or* take hold of, clutch, grasp, grip, latch on to, nab (*Inf.*), pluck, seize, snap up, snatch

grace *n.* 1. attractiveness, beauty, charm, comeliness, ease, elegance, finesse, gracefulness, loveliness, pleasantness, poise, polish, refinement, shapeliness, tastefulness 2. benefaction, beneficence, benevolence, favour, generosity, goodness, good will, kindliness, kindness 3. breeding, consideration, cultivation, decency, decorum, etiquette, mannerliness, manners, propriety, tact 4. charity, clemency, compassion, forgiveness, indulgence, leniency, lenity, mercy, pardon, quarter, reprieve 5. benediction, blessing, prayer, thanks, thanksgiving ~v. 6. adorn, beautify, bedeck, deck, decorate, dignify, distinguish, elevate, embellish, enhance, enrich, favour, garnish, glorify, honour, ornament, set off **Antonyms** n. awkwardness, bad manners, clumsiness, condemnation, disfavour, harshness, ill will, inelegance, stiffness, tactlessness, tastelessness, ugliness, ungainliness ~v. desecrate, dishonour, insult, ruin, spoil

graceful agile, beautiful, becoming, charming, comely, easy, elegant, fine, flowing, gracile (*Rare*), natural, pleasing, smooth, symmetrical, tasteful
Antonyms awkward, clumsy, gawky, inelegant, plain, ponderous, stiff, ugly, ungainly, ungraceful

gracious accommodating, affable, amiable, beneficent, benevolent, benign, benignant, charitable, chivalrous, civil, compassionate, considerate, cordial, courteous, courtly, friendly, hospitable, indulgent, kind, kindly, lenient, loving, merciful, mild, obliging, pleasing, polite, wellmannered
Antonyms brusque, cold, discourteous, gruff, haughty, impolite, mean, remote, rude, surly, unfriendly, ungracious, unpleasant

grade 1. n. brand, category, class, condition, degree, echelon, group, level, mark, notch, order, place, position, quality, rank,

rung, size, stage, station, step 2. v. arrange, brand, class, classify, evaluate, group, order, range, rank, rate, sort, value

gradient acclivity, bank, declivity, grade, hill, incline, rise, slope

gradual continuous, even, gentle, graduated, moderate, piecemeal, progressive, regular, slow, steady, successive, unhurried
Antonyms abrupt, broken, instantaneous, overnight, sudden

gradually bit by bit, by degrees, drop by drop, evenly, gently, little by little, moderately, piece by piece, piecemeal, progressively, slowly, steadily, step by step, unhurriedly

graduate v. calibrate, grade, mark off, measure out, proportion, regulate

grain 1. cereals, corn 2. grist, kernel, seed

grand 1. ambitious, august, dignified, elevated, eminent, exalted, fine, glorious, grandiose, great, haughty, illustrious, imposing, impressive, large, lofty, lordly, luxurious, magnificent, majestic, monumental, noble, opulent, ostentatious, palatial, pompous, pretentious, princely, regal, splendid, stately, striking, sublime, sumptuous 2. admirable, excellent, fine, first-class, firstrate, great (*Inf.*), marvellous (*Inf.*), outstanding, smashing (*Inf.*), splendid, super (*Inf.*), superb, terrific (*Inf.*), very good, wonderful
Antonyms awful, bad, base, common, contemptible, inferior, insignificant, little, mean, petty, poor, secondary, small, terrible, trivial, undignified, unimportant, unimposing, worthless

grandeur augustness, dignity, greatness, importance, loftiness, magnificence, majesty, nobility, pomp, splendour, state, stateliness, sublimity

grandiose affected, ambitious, bombastic, extravagant, flamboyant, high-flown, ostentatious, pompous, pretentious, showy

Antonyms humble, modest, un~
pretentious

grant 1. *v.* accede to, accord,
acknowledge, admit, agree to,
allocate, allot, allow, assign,
award, bestow, cede, concede,
confer, consent to, donate, give,
impart, permit, present, vouch~
safe, yield **2.** *n.* admission, allo~
cation, allotment, allowance,
award, benefaction, bequest,
boon, bounty, concession, dona~
tion, endowment, gift, present,
subsidy

grasp *v.* **1.** catch, clasp, clinch,
clutch, grab, grapple, grip, hold,
lay *or* take hold of, seize, snatch
2. catch *or* get the drift of, catch
on, comprehend, follow, get, re~
alize, see, take in, understand
~*n.* **3.** clasp, clutches, embrace,
grip, hold, possession, tenure **4.**
awareness, comprehension, ken,
knowledge, mastery, perception,
realization, understanding

grasping acquisitive, avaricious,
close-fisted, covetous, greedy,
mean, miserly, niggardly, penny-
pinching (*Inf.*), rapacious, selfish,
stingy, tightfisted, usurious, venal
Antonyms altruistic, generous,
unselfish

grate *v.* **1.** creak, grind, rasp, rub,
scrape, scratch **2.** annoy, chafe,
exasperate, fret, gall, get one
down, get on one's nerves (*Inf.*),
irk, irritate, jar, nettle, peeve,
rankle, rub one up the wrong
way, set one's teeth on edge, vex
grateful appreciative, beholden,
indebted, obliged, thankful

gratify cater to, delight, favour,
fulfil, give pleasure, gladden, hu~
mour, indulge, please, recom~
pense, requite, satisfy, thrill

gratitude appreciation, grateful~
ness, indebtedness, obligation,
recognition, sense of obligation,
thankfulness, thanks
Antonyms ingratitude, ungrate~
fulness, unthankfulness

gratuitous complimentary, free,
spontaneous, unasked-for, un~
paid, unrewarded, voluntary

grave¹ *n.* burying place, crypt,

last resting place, mausoleum,
pit, sepulchre, tomb, vault

grave² 1. dignified, dour, dull,
earnest, gloomy, grim-faced,
heavy, leaden, long-faced, muted,
quiet, sage (*Obsolete*), sedate,
serious, sober, solemn, sombre,
staid, subdued, thoughtful, un~
smiling **2.** acute, critical, crucial,
dangerous, exigent, hazardous,
important, life-and-death, mo~
mentous, of great consequence,
perilous, pressing, serious, se~
vere, significant, threatening,
urgent, vital, weighty
Antonyms carefree, exciting,
flippant, frivolous, happy, insig~
nificant, joyous, merry, mild, tri~
fling, undignified, unimportant

graveyard boneyard (*Inf.*), burial
ground, cemetery, charnel house,
churchyard, God's acre (*Liter~
ary*), necropolis

gravity acuteness, consequence,
exigency, hazardousness, impor~
tance, moment, momentousness,
perilousness, pressingness, seri~
ousness, severity, significance,
urgency, weightiness
Antonyms inconsequentiality,
insignificance, levity, triviality,
unimportance

greasy 1. fatty, oily, slick, slimy,
slippery **2.** fawning, glib, grovel~
ling, ingratiating, oily, slick,
smarmy (*Brit. inf.*), smooth,
sycophantish, toadying, unctuous

great 1. big, bulky, colossal, enor~
mous, extensive, gigantic, huge,
immense, large, mammoth, pro~
digious, stupendous, tremendous,
vast, voluminous **2.** extended,
lengthy, long, prolonged, pro~
tracted **3.** capital, chief, grand,
leading, main, major, paramount,
primary, principal, prominent,
superior **4.** considerable, decided,
excessive, extravagant, extreme,
grievous, high, inordinate, prodi~
gious, pronounced, strong **5.** con~
sequential, critical, crucial,
grave, heavy, important, mo~
mentous, serious, significant,
weighty **6.** celebrated, distin~
guished, eminent, exalted, excel~

lent, famed, famous, glorious, illustrious, notable, noteworthy, outstanding, prominent, remarkable, renowned, superlative, talented 7. august, chivalrous, dignified, distinguished, exalted, fine, glorious, grand, heroic, highminded, idealistic, impressive, lofty, magnanimous, noble, princely, sublime 8. active, devoted, enthusiastic, keen, zealous 9. able, adept, adroit, crack (Sl.), expert, good, masterly, proficient, skilful, skilled 10. Inf. admirable, excellent, fantastic (Inf.), fine, first-rate, good, marvellous (Inf.), terrific (Inf.), tremendous (Inf.), wonderful
Antonyms average, bad, base, diminutive, hateful, ignoble, inconsequential, inconsiderable, inferior, inhumane, insignificant, little, mean, mild, petty, poor, secondary, second-rate, small, terrible, trivial, undistinguished, unimportant, unkind, unnotable, unskilled, weak

greatly abundantly, by leaps and bounds, by much, considerably, enormously, exceedingly, extremely, highly, hugely, immensely, markedly, mightily, much, notably, powerfully, remarkably, tremendously, vastly, very much

greatness 1. bulk, enormity, hugeness, immensity, largeness, length, magnitude, mass, prodigiousness, size, vastness 2. gravity, heaviness, import, importance, moment, momentousness, seriousness, significance, urgency, weight 3. celebrity, distinction, eminence, fame, glory, grandeur, illustriousness, lustre, note, renown

greed, greediness 1. edacity, esurience, gluttony, gormandizing, hunger, insatiableness, ravenousness, voracity 2. acquisitiveness, avidity, covetousness, craving, cupidity, desire, eagerness, graspingness, longing, rapacity, selfishness
Antonyms altruism, benevo-

lence, generosity, munificence, self-restraint, unselfishness

greedy 1. edacious, esurient, gluttonous, gormandizing, hoggish, hungry, insatiable, piggish, ravenous, voracious 2. acquisitive, avaricious, avid, covetous, craving, desirous, eager, grasping, hungry, impatient, rapacious, selfish
Antonyms altruistic, apathetic, benevolent, full, generous, indifferent, munificent, self-restrained, unselfish

green adj. 1. blooming, budding, flourishing, fresh, grassy, leafy, new, undecayed, verdant, verdurous 2. fresh, immature, new, raw, recent, unripe ~n. 3. common, grassplot, lawn, sward, turf

greet accost, address, compliment, hail, meet, nod to, receive, salute, tip one's hat to, welcome

greeting address, hail, reception, salutation, salute, welcome

grey 1. ashen, bloodless, colourless, livid, pale, pallid, wan 2. cheerless, cloudy, dark, depressing, dim, dismal, drab, dreary, dull, foggy, gloomy, misty, murky, overcast, sunless 3. aged, ancient, elderly, experienced, hoary, mature, old, venerable

grief affliction, agony, anguish, bereavement, dejection, distress, grievance, heartache, heartbreak, misery, mournfulness, mourning, pain, regret, remorse, sadness, sorrow, suffering, trial, tribulation, trouble, woe
Antonyms cheer, comfort, consolation, delight, gladness, happiness, joy, rejoicing, solace

grievance affliction, beef (Sl.), complaint, damage, distress, grief, gripe (Inf.), hardship, injury, injustice, resentment, sorrow, trial, tribulation, trouble, unhappiness, wrong

grieve 1. ache, bemoan, bewail, complain, deplore, lament, mourn, regret, rue, sorrow, suffer, wail, weep 2. afflict, agonize, break the heart of, crush, distress, hurt, injure, make one's heart bleed, pain, sadden, wound **Antonyms** cheer, comfort, console, ease, gladden, please, rejoice, solace

grievous 1. afflicting, calamitous, damaging, distressing, dreadful, grave, harmful, heavy, hurtful, injurious, lamentable, oppressive, painful, severe, wounding **2.** appalling, atrocious, deplorable, dreadful, egregious, flagrant, glaring, heinous, intolerable, lamentable, monstrous, offensive, outrageous, shameful, shocking, unbearable **Antonyms** delightful, insignificant, mild, pleasant, trivial, unimportant

grim cruel, ferocious, fierce, forbidding, formidable, frightful, ghastly, grisly, gruesome, harsh, hideous, horrible, horrid, implacable, merciless, morose, relentless, resolute, ruthless, severe, shocking, sinister, stern, sullen, surly, terrible, unrelenting, unyielding **Antonyms** amiable, attractive, benign, cheerful, easy, genial, gentle, happy, kind, pleasant, soft, sympathetic

grimace n. face, frown, mouth, scowl, sneer, wry face

grime dirt, filth, smut, soot

grimy begrimed, besmeared, besmirched, dirty, filthy, foul, grubby, smutty, soiled, sooty, unclean

grind v. **1.** abrade, comminute, crush, granulate, grate, kibble, mill, pound, powder, pulverize, triturate **2.** gnash, grate, grit, scrape ~n. **3.** Inf. chore, drudgery, hard work, labour, sweat (Inf.), task, toil

grip n. **1.** clasp, handclasp (U.S.), purchase **2.** clutches, comprehension, control, domination, grasp, hold, influence, keeping, mastery, perception, possession, power, tenure, understanding ~v. **3.** clasp, clutch, grasp, hold, latch on to, seize, take hold of **4.** catch up, compel, engross, en-

thral, entrance, fascinate, hold, involve, mesmerize, rivet, spellbind

gripping compelling, compulsive, engrossing, enthralling, entrancing, exciting, fascinating, riveting, spellbinding, thrilling, unputdownable (Inf.)

grisly abominable, appalling, awful, dreadful, frightful, ghastly, grim, gruesome, hideous, horrible, horrid, macabre, shocking, sickening, terrible, terrifying

grit n. **1.** dust, gravel, pebbles, sand **2.** backbone, courage, determination, doggedness, fortitude, gameness, guts (Inf.), hardihood, mettle, nerve, perseverance, pluck, resolution, spirit, tenacity, toughness

groan 1. n. cry, moan, sigh, whine **2.** v. cry, moan, sigh, whine

groggy befuddled, confused, dazed, dizzy, faint, muzzy, punch-drunk, reeling, shaky, staggering, stunned, stupefied, unsteady, weak, wobbly, woozy (Inf.)

groom n. **1.** currier (Rare), hostler or ostler (Archaic), stableboy, stableman ~v. **2.** clean, dress, get up (Inf.), preen, primp, smarten up, spruce up, tidy, turn out **3.** coach, drill, educate, make ready, nurture, prepare, prime, ready, train

groove channel, cut, cutting, flute, furrow, gutter, hollow, indentation, rebate, rut, score, trench

grope cast about, feel, finger, fish, flounder, fumble, grabble, scrabble, search

gross adj. **1.** big, bulky, corpulent, dense, fat, great, heavy, hulking, large, lumpish, massive, obese, overweight, thick **2.** aggregate, before deductions, before tax, entire, total, whole **3.** coarse, crude, improper, impure, indecent, indelicate, lewd, low, obscene, offensive, ribald, rude, sensual, smutty, unseemly, vulgar **4.** boorish, callous, coarse, crass, dull, ignorant, imperceptive, insensitive, tasteless, uncultured, undiscriminating, unfeeling, unrefined, unsophisticated

Antonyms adj. cultivated, decent, delicate, elegant, little, net, partial, petite, proper, pure, qualified, refined, slim, small, svelte, thin

grotesque absurd, bizarre, deformed, distorted, extravagant, fanciful, fantastic, freakish, incongruous, ludicrous, malformed, misshapen, odd, outlandish, preposterous, ridiculous, strange, unnatural, weird, whimsical

Antonyms average, classic, graceful, natural, normal, realistic

ground n. 1. clod, dirt, dry land, dust, earth, field, land, loam, mould, sod, soil, terra firma, terrain, turf 2. *Often plural* area, country, district, domain, estate, fields, gardens, habitat, holding, land, property, realm, terrain, territory, tract 3. arena, field, park (*Inf.*), pitch, stadium ~v. 4. base, establish, fix, found, set, settle 5. acquaint with, coach, familiarize with, inform, initiate, instruct, prepare, teach, train, tutor

groundless baseless, chimerical, empty, false, idle, illusory, imaginary, unauthorized, uncalled-for, unfounded, unjustified, unprovoked, unsupported, unwarranted

Antonyms justified, logical, proven, real, reasonable, substantial, supported, true, well-founded

groundwork base, basis, cornerstone, footing, foundation, fundamentals, preliminaries, preparation, spadework, underpinnings

group 1. n. aggregation, assemblage, association, band, batch, bunch, category, circle, class, clique, clump, cluster, collection, company, congregation, coterie, crowd, faction, formation, gang, gathering, organization, pack, party, set, troop 2. v. arrange, assemble, associate, assort, bracket, class, classify, dispose, gather, marshal, order, organize, put together, range, sort

grow 1. develop, enlarge, expand, extend, fill out, get bigger, get taller, heighten, increase, multiply, spread, stretch, swell, thicken, widen 2. develop, flourish, germinate, shoot, spring up, sprout, vegetate 3. advance, expand, flourish, improve, progress, prosper, succeed, thrive 4. breed, cultivate, farm, nurture, produce, propagate, raise

Antonyms decline, decrease, diminish, dwindle, fail, lessen, shrink, subside

grown-up adj. adult, fully-grown, mature, of age

growth 1. aggrandizement, augmentation, development, enlargement, evolution, expansion, extension, growing, heightening, increase, multiplication, proliferation, stretching, thickening, widening 2. crop, cultivation, development, germination, produce, production, shooting, sprouting, vegetation 3. advance, advancement, expansion, improvement, progress, prosperity, rise, success

Antonyms decline, decrease, dwindling, failure, lessening, retreat, shrinkage, slackening, subsiding

grubby besmeared, dirty, filthy, frowzy, grimy, manky (*Scot. dialect*), mean, messy, mucky, scruffy, seedy, shabby, slovenly, smutty, soiled, sordid, squalid, unkempt, untidy, unwashed

grudge 1. n. animosity, animus, antipathy, aversion, bitterness, dislike, enmity, grievance, hard feelings, hate, ill will, malevolence, malice, pique, rancour, resentment, spite, venom 2. v. begrudge, be reluctant, complain, covet, envy, hold back, mind, resent, stint

gruelling arduous, backbreaking, brutal, crushing, demanding, difficult, exhausting, fatiguing, fierce, grinding, hard, harsh, la-

borious, punishing, severe, stiff, strenuous, taxing, tiring, trying
Antonyms cushy (*Inf.*), easy, enjoyable, light, pleasant, undemanding

gruesome abominable, awful, fearful, ghastly, grim, grisly, hideous, horrendous, horrible, horrid, horrific, horrifying, loathsome, macabre, repugnant, repulsive, shocking, spine-chilling, terrible
Antonyms appealing, benign, cheerful, pleasant, sweet

gruff bad-tempered, bearish, blunt, brusque, churlish, crabbed, crusty, curt, discourteous, grouchy (*Inf.*), grumpy, ill-humoured, ill-natured, impolite, rough, rude, sour, sullen, surly, uncivil, ungracious, unmannerly
Antonyms courteous, good-tempered, gracious, kind, mellifluous, pleasant, polite, smooth, sweet

grumble 1. *v.* beef (*Sl.*), bellyache (*Sl.*), bitch (*Sl.*), carp, complain, find fault, gripe (*Inf.*), grouch (*Inf.*), grouse, moan, repine, whine **2.** *n.* beef (*Sl.*), complaint, grievance, gripe (*Inf.*), grouch (*Inf.*), grouse, moan, objection

guarantee 1. *n.* assurance, bond, certainty, collateral, covenant, earnest, guaranty, pledge, promise, security, surety, undertaking, warranty, word, word of honour **2.** *v.* answer for, assure, certify, ensure, insure, maintain, make certain, pledge, promise, protect, secure, stand behind, swear, vouch for, warrant

guard *v.* **1.** cover, defend, escort, keep, mind, oversee, patrol, police, preserve, protect, safeguard, save, screen, secure, shelter, shield, supervise, tend, watch, watch over ~*n.* **2.** custodian, defender, lookout, picket, protector, sentinel, sentry, warder, watch, watchman **3.** buffer, bulwark, bumper, defence, pad, protection, rampart, safeguard, screen, security, shield **4.** atten-

tion, care, caution, heed, vigilance, wariness, watchfulness

guardian attendant, champion, curator, custodian, defender, escort, guard, keeper, preserver, protector, trustee, warden, warder

guess 1. *v.* conjecture, estimate, fathom, hypothesize, penetrate, predict, solve, speculate, work out **2.** *n.* conjecture, feeling, hypothesis, judgment, notion, prediction, reckoning, speculation, supposition, surmise, suspicion, theory
Antonyms *v.* know, prove, ~*n.* certainty, fact

guest boarder, caller, company, lodger, visitant, visitor

guidance advice, auspices, conduct, control, counsel, counselling, direction, government, help, instruction, intelligence, leadership, management, teaching

guide *v.* **1.** accompany, attend, conduct, convoy, direct, escort, lead, pilot, shepherd, show the way, steer, usher **2.** command, control, direct, handle, manage, manoeuvre, steer **3.** advise, counsel, educate, govern, influence, instruct, oversee, regulate, rule, superintend, supervise, sway, teach, train ~*n.* **4.** adviser, attendant, chaperon, cicerone, conductor, controller, counsellor, director, escort, leader, mentor, monitor, pilot, steersman, teacher, usher **5.** catalogue, directory, guidebook, handbook, instructions, key, manual, vade mecum

guild association, brotherhood, club, company, corporation, fellowship, fraternity, league, lodge, order, organization, society, union

guile art, artfulness, artifice, cleverness, craft, craftiness, cunning, deceit, deception, duplicity, gamesmanship (*Inf.*), knavery, ruse, sharp practice, slyness, treachery, trickery, trickiness, wiliness
Antonyms candour, frankness, honesty, sincerity, truthfulness

guilt 1. blame, blameworthiness, criminality, culpability, delinquency, guiltiness, iniquity, misconduct, responsibility, sinfulness, wickedness, wrong, wrongdoing **2.** bad conscience, contrition, disgrace, dishonour, guiltiness, guilty conscience, infamy, regret, remorse, self-condemnation, self-reproach, shame, stigma
Antonyms blamelessness, honour, innocence, pride, righteousness, self-respect, sinlessness, virtue

guiltless blameless, clean (*Sl.*), clear, immaculate, impeccable, innocent, irreproachable, pure, sinless, spotless, unimpeachable, unsullied, untainted, untarnished

guilty at fault, blameworthy, convicted, criminal, culpable, delinquent, erring, evil, felonious, iniquitous, offending, reprehensible, responsible, sinful, to blame, wicked, wrong
Antonyms blameless, innocent, moral, proud, righteous, virtuous

gulf 1. bay, bight, sea inlet **2.** abyss, breach, chasm, cleft, gap, opening, rent, rift, separation, split, void, whirlpool

gullible born yesterday, credulous, easily taken in, foolish, green, innocent, naive, silly, simple, trusting, unsceptical, unsophisticated, unsuspecting
Antonyms cynical, sophisticated, suspicious, untrusting, worldly

gulp 1. *v.* bolt, devour, gobble, guzzle, knock back (*Inf.*), quaff, swallow, swig (*Inf.*), swill, toss off, wolf **2.** *n.* draught, mouthful, swallow, swig (*Inf.*)

gum *n.* adhesive, cement, exudate, glue, mucilage, paste, resin

gumption ability, acumen, astuteness, cleverness, common sense, discernment, enterprise, get-up-and-go (*Inf.*), horse sense, initiative, mother wit, nous (*Brit. sl.*), resourcefulness, sagacity, savvy (*Sl.*), shrewdness, spirit, wit(s)

gurgle 1. *v.* babble, bubble, burble, crow, lap, murmur, plash, purl, ripple, splash **2.** *n.* babble, murmur, purl, ripple

gush 1. *v.* burst, cascade, flood, flow, jet, pour, run, rush, spout, spurt, stream **2.** *n.* burst, cascade, flood, flow, jet, outburst, outflow, rush, spout, spurt, stream, torrent

gust *n.* blast, blow, breeze, flurry, gale, puff, rush, squall

gusto appetite, appreciation, brio, delight, enjoyment, enthusiasm, exhilaration, fervour, liking, pleasure, relish, savour, verve, zeal, zest
Antonyms apathy, coolness, disinterest, distaste

guts audacity, backbone, boldness, bottle (*Sl.*), courage, daring, forcefulness, grit, hardihood, mettle, nerve, pluck, spirit, spunk (*Inf.*), willpower

gutter channel, conduit, ditch, drain, duct, pipe, sluice, trench, trough, tube

guttural deep, gravelly, gruff, hoarse, husky, low, rasping, rough, thick, throaty

guy 1. *n.* *Inf.* bloke (*Brit. inf.*), cat (*Sl.*), chap, fellow, lad, man, person, youth **2.** *v.* caricature, make (a) game of, make fun of, mock, poke fun at, rib (*Inf.*), ridicule, send up (*Brit inf.*), take off (*Inf.*)

H

habit *n.* **1.** bent, custom, disposition, manner, mannerism, practice, proclivity, propensity, quirk, tendency, way **2.** convention, custom, mode, practice, routine, rule, second nature, usage, wont **3.** apparel, dress, garb, garment, habiliment, riding dress

habitation abode, domicile, dwelling, dwelling house, home, house, living quarters, lodging, quarters, residence

habitual accustomed, common, customary, familiar, fixed, natural, normal, ordinary, regular, routine, standard, traditional, usual, wonted

Antonyms abnormal, exceptional, infrequent, irregular, occasional, rare, strange, uncommon, unusual

hack[1] *v.* chop, cut, gash, hew, kick, lacerate, mangle, mutilate, notch, slash

hack[2] *adj.* **1.** banal, mediocre, pedestrian, poor, stereotyped, tired, undistinguished, uninspired, unoriginal ~*n.* **2.** Grub Street writer, literary hack, penny-a-liner, scribbler **3.** drudge, plodder, slave

hackneyed banal, clichéd, common, commonplace, overworked, pedestrian, played out (*Inf.*), run-of-the-mill, stale, stereotyped, stock, threadbare, timeworn, tired, trite, unoriginal, worn-out

Antonyms fresh, imaginative, new, novel, original, striking, unusual

hag beldam (*Archaic*), crone, fury, harridan, Jezebel, shrew, termagant, virago, vixen, witch

haggard careworn, drawn, emaciated, gaunt, ghastly, hollow-eyed, pinched, shrunken, thin, wan, wasted, wrinkled

Antonyms bright-eyed, brisk,

energetic, hale, robust, sleek, vigorous

haggle **1.** bargain, barter, beat down, chaffer, dicker (*Chiefly U.S.*), higgle, palter **2.** bicker, dispute, quarrel, squabble, wrangle

hail[1] *Fig.* **1.** *n.* barrage, bombardment, pelting, rain, shower, storm, volley **2.** *v.* barrage, batter, beat down upon, bombard, pelt, rain, rain down on, shower, storm, volley

hail[2] acclaim, acknowledge, applaud, cheer, exalt, glorify, greet, honour, salute, welcome

Antonyms boo, condemn, criticize, hiss, insult, jeer

hair **1.** head of hair, locks, mane, mop, shock, tresses **2. split hairs** cavil, find fault, overrefine, pettifog, quibble

hair-raising alarming, bloodcurdling, breathtaking, creepy, exciting, frightening, horrifying, petrifying, scary, shocking, spine-chilling, startling, terrifying, thrilling

hale able-bodied, blooming, fit, flourishing, healthy, hearty, in fine fettle, in the pink, robust, sound, strong, vigorous, well

half **1.** *n.* bisection, division, equal part, fifty per cent, fraction, hemisphere, portion, section **2.** *adj.* divided, fractional, halved, incomplete, limited, moderate, partial **3.** *adv.* after a fashion, all but, barely, inadequately, incompletely, in part, partially, partly, pretty nearly, slightly

half-hearted apathetic, cool, indifferent, lacklustre, listless, lukewarm, neutral, passive, perfunctory, spiritless, tame, unenthusiastic, uninterested

Antonyms ambitious, animated, avid, concerned, determined, eager, emotional, energetic, enthusiastic, excited, spirited, warm, whole-hearted, zealous

halfway adv. 1. midway, to or in the middle, to the midpoint 2. incompletely, moderately, nearly, partially, partly, rather ~adj. 3. central, equidistant, intermediate, mid, middle, midway

half-witted addle-brained, barmy (Sl.), batty (Sl.), crazy, doltish, dull, dull-witted, feeble-minded, flaky (U.S. sl.), foolish, idiotic, moronic, nurdish (Sl.), silly, simple, simple-minded, stupid

hall 1. corridor, entrance hall, entry, foyer, hallway, lobby, passage, passageway, vestibule 2. assembly room, auditorium, chamber, concert hall, meeting place

halt¹ v. 1. break off, call it a day, cease, close down, come to an end, desist, draw up, pull up, rest, stand still, stop, wait 2. arrest, block, bring to an end, check, curb, cut short, end, hold back, impede, terminate ~n. 3. arrest, break, close, end, impasse, interruption, pause, stand, standstill, stop, stoppage, termination

Antonyms v. aid, begin, boost, commence, continue, encourage, forward, go ahead, maintain, proceed, resume, start ~n. beginning, commencement, continuation, resumption, start

halt² v. 1. be defective, falter, hobble, limp, stumble 2. be unsure, boggle, dither, haver, hesitate, pause, stammer, swither (Scot. dialect), think twice, waver

halting awkward, faltering, hesitant, imperfect, laboured, stammering, stumbling, stuttering

halve v. bisect, cut in half, divide equally, reduce by fifty per cent, share equally, split in two

hammer v. 1. bang, beat, drive, hit, knock, strike, tap 2. beat out, fashion, forge, form, make, shape

hamper v. bind, cramp, curb, embarrass, encumber, entangle, fetter, frustrate, hamstring,

handicap, hinder, hold up, impede, interfere with, obstruct, prevent, restrain, restrict, slow down, thwart, trammel

Antonyms aid, assist, boost, encourage, expedite, forward, further, help, promote, speed

hand n. 1. fist, mitt (Sl.), palm, paw (Inf.) 2. agency, direction, influence, part, participation, share 3. aid, assistance, help, support 4. artificer, artisan, craftsman, employee, hired man, labourer, operative, worker, workman 5. in hand a. in order, receiving attention, under control b. available for use, in reserve, put by, ready ~ v. 6. deliver, hand over, pass 7. aid, assist, conduct, convey, give, guide, help, lead, present, transmit

handbook Baedeker, guide, guidebook, instruction book, manual, vade mecum

handcuff v. fetter, manacle, shackle

hand down or **on** bequeath, give, grant, pass on or down, transfer, will

handful few, small number, small quantity, smattering, sprinkling

Antonyms a lot, crowd, heaps, horde, large number, large quantity, loads (Inf.), masses (Inf.), mob, plenty, scores, stacks

handicap n. 1. barrier, block, disadvantage, drawback, encumbrance, hindrance, impediment, limitation, millstone, obstacle, restriction, shortcoming, stumbling block 2. advantage, edge, head start, odds, penalty, upper hand 3. defect, disability, impairment

Antonyms (sense 1) advantage, asset, benefit, boost, edge

handicraft art, artisanship, craft, craftsmanship, handiwork, skill, workmanship

handiwork achievement, artefact, creation, design, invention, product, production, result

handle n. 1. grip, haft, handgrip, helve, hilt, knob, stock ~ v. 2. feel, finger, fondle, grasp, hold, maul, paw (*Inf.*), pick up, poke, touch **3.** control, direct, guide, manage, manipulate, manoeuvre, operate, steer, use, wield **4.** administer, conduct, cope with, deal with, manage, supervise, take care of, treat

hand-out 1. alms, charity, dole **2.** bulletin, circular, free sample, leaflet, literature (*Inf.*), mailshot, press release

hand out deal out, disburse, dish out (*Inf.*), dispense, disseminate, distribute, give out, mete

hand over deliver, donate, fork out *or* up (*Sl.*), present, release, surrender, transfer, turn over, yield

handsome admirable, attractive, becoming, comely, dishy (*Inf., chiefly Brit.*), elegant, fine, good-looking, gorgeous, graceful, majestic, personable, stately, well-proportioned
Antonyms inelegant, tasteless, ugly, unattractive, unprepossessing, unsightly

handsomely abundantly, amply, bountifully, generously, liberally, magnanimously, munificently, plentifully, richly

handwriting calligraphy, chirography, fist, hand, longhand, penmanship, scrawl, script

handy 1. accessible, at *or* on hand, available, close, convenient, near, nearby, within reach **2.** convenient, easy to use, helpful, manageable, neat, practical, serviceable, useful, user-friendly **3.** adept, adroit, clever, deft, dexterous, expert, nimble, proficient, ready, skilful, skilled
Antonyms awkward, clumsy, ham-fisted, inaccessible, incompetent, inconvenient, inept, inexpert, maladroit, out of the way, unaccomplished, unavailable, unskilful, unskilled, unwieldy, useless

hang *v.* **1.** be pendent, dangle, depend, droop, incline, suspend **2.** execute, gibbet, send to the gallows, string up (*Inf.*) **3.** adhere, cling, hold, rest, stick **4.** attach,

cover, deck, decorate, drape, fasten, fix, furnish

hang about *or* **around** dally, linger, loiter, roam, tarry, waste time

hang back be backward, be reluctant, demur, hesitate, hold back, recoil

hanger-on dependant, follower, freeloader, chance (*Sl.*), lackey, leech, ligger (*Sl.*), minion, parasite, sponger (*Inf.*), sycophant

hanging *adj.* dangling, drooping, flapping, flopping, floppy, loose, pendent, suspended, swinging, unattached, unsupported

hang on carry on, continue, endure, go on, hold on, hold out, persevere, persist, remain

hank coil, length, loop, piece, roll, skein

hankering craving, desire, hunger, itch, longing, pining, thirst, urge, wish, yearning, yen (*Inf.*)

haphazard 1. accidental, arbitrary, chance, fluky (*Inf.*), random **2.** aimless, careless, casual, disorderly, disorganized, hit or miss (*Inf.*), indiscriminate, slapdash, slipshod, unmethodical, unsystematic
Antonyms arranged, careful, considered, deliberate, methodical, orderly, organized, planned, systematic, thoughtful

happen 1. appear, arise, come about, come off (*Inf.*), come to pass, crop up (*Inf.*), develop, ensue, eventuate, follow, materialize, occur, present itself, result, take place, transpire (*Inf.*) **2.** become of, befall, betide **3.** chance, fall out, have the fortune to be, supervene, turn out

happening accident, adventure, affair, case, chance, episode, event, experience, incident, occasion, occurrence, phenomenon, proceeding, scene

happily 1. agreeably, contentedly, delightedly, enthusiastically, freely, gladly, heartily, willingly, with pleasure **2.** blithely, cheerfully, gaily, gleefully, joyfully, joyously, merrily **3.** auspiciously, favourably, fortunately, luckily, opportunely, propitiously, providentially, seasonably **4.** appropriately, aptly, felicitously, gracefully, successfully

happiness beatitude, blessedness, bliss, cheer, cheerfulness, cheeriness, contentment, delight, ecstasy, elation, enjoyment, exuberance, felicity, gaiety, gladness, high spirits, joy, jubilation, light-heartedness, merriment, pleasure, prosperity, satisfaction, wellbeing

Antonyms annoyance, bane, depression, despondency, distress, grief, low spirits, misery, misfortune, sadness, sorrow, unhappiness

happy blessed, blest, blissful, blithe, cheerful, content, contented, delighted, ecstatic, elated, glad, gratified, jolly, joyful, joyous, jubilant, merry, overjoyed, over the moon (*Inf.*), pleased, sunny, thrilled, walking on air (*Inf.*)

Antonyms depressed, despondent, discontented, displeased, down in the dumps, forlorn, gloomy, joyless, melancholy, miserable, mournful, sad, sombre, sorrowful, sorry, unfortunate, unhappy, unlucky

happy-go-lucky blithe, carefree, casual, devil-may-care, easygoing, heedless, improvident, insouciant, irresponsible, lighthearted, nonchalant, unconcerned, untroubled

Antonyms careworn, cheerless, gloomy, melancholy, morose, sad, serious, unhappy

harass annoy, badger, bait, beleaguer, bother, chivvy (*Brit.*), devil (*Inf.*), disturb, exasperate, exhaust, fatigue, harry, hassle (*Inf.*), hound, perplex, persecute, pester, plague, tease, tire, torment, trouble, vex, weary, worry

harbour *n.* **1.** anchorage, destination, haven, port **2.** asylum, covert, haven, refuge, retreat, sanctuary, sanctum, security, shelter ~*v.* **3.** conceal, hide, lodge, protect, provide refuge, relieve, secrete, shelter, shield

hard *adj.* **1.** compact, dense, firm, impenetrable, inflexible, rigid, rocklike, solid, stiff, stony, strong, tough, unyielding **2.** arduous, backbreaking, burdensome, exacting, exhausting, fatiguing, formidable, Herculean, laborious, rigorous, strenuous, toilsome, tough, uphill, wearying **3.** baffling, complex, complicated, difficult, intricate, involved, knotty, perplexing, puzzling, tangled, thorny, unfathomable **4.** callous, cold, cruel, exacting, grim, hardhearted, harsh, implacable, obdurate, pitiless, ruthless, severe, stern, strict, stubborn, unfeeling, unjust, unkind, unrelenting, unsparing, unsympathetic ~*adv.* **5.** energetically, fiercely, forcefully, forcibly, heavily, intensely, powerfully, severely, sharply, strongly, vigorously, violently, with all one's might, with might and main **6.** assiduously, determinedly, diligently, doggedly, earnestly, industriously, intently, persistently, steadily, strenuously, untiringly **7.** agonizingly, badly, distressingly, harshly, laboriously, painfully, roughly, severely, with difficulty **8.** bitterly, hardly, keenly, rancorously, reluctantly, resentfully, slowly, sorely

Antonyms *adj.* clear, direct, easy, flexible, gentle, good, humane, kind, lenient, light, malleable, merciful, mild, pleasant, pliable, simple, soft, straightforward, uncomplicated, weak ~*adv.* calmly, easily, gently, lazily, lightly, loosely, mildly, serenely, softly, weakly

harden 1. anneal, bake, cake, freeze, set, solidify, stiffen **2.** brace, buttress, fortify, gird, indurate, nerve, reinforce, steel, strengthen, toughen

hardened 1. chronic, fixed, habitual, incorrigible, inveterate, irredeemable, reprobate, set, shameless **2.** accustomed, habituated, inured, seasoned, toughened

hard-headed astute, cool, hard-boiled (*Inf.*), level-headed, practical, pragmatic, realistic, sensible, shrewd, tough, unsentimental

hardhearted callous, cold, cruel, hard, heartless, indifferent, inhuman, insensitive, intolerant, merciless, pitiless, stony, uncaring, unfeeling, unkind, unsympathetic

Antonyms compassionate, forgiving, gentle, humane, kind, loving, merciful, sensitive, softhearted, sympathetic, understanding, warm, warm-hearted

hard-hitting critical, no holds barred, pulling no punches, strongly worded, tough, uncompromising, unsparing, vigorous

hardly almost not, barely, by no means, faintly, infrequently, just, not at all, not quite, no way, only, only just, scarcely, with difficulty

Antonyms abundantly, amply, by all means, certainly, completely, easily, fully, indubitably, more than, really, truly, undoubtedly, well over

hardship adversity, affliction, austerity, burden, calamity, destitution, difficulty, fatigue, grievance, labour, misery, misfortune, need, oppression, persecution, privation, suffering, toil, torment, trial, tribulation, trouble, want

Antonyms aid, blessing, boon, comfort, ease, good fortune, happiness, help, prosperity, relief

hard up bankrupt, broke (*Inf.*), bust (*Inf.*), cleaned out (*Sl.*), impecunious, impoverished, in the red (*Inf.*), on one's uppers (*Inf.*), out of pocket, penniless, poor, short, short of cash *or* funds, skint (*Brit. sl.*)

Antonyms affluent, comfortable (*Inf.*), fortunate, loaded (*Sl.*), rich, wealthy, well-heeled (*Inf.*), well-off

hard-wearing durable, resilient, rugged, stout, strong, tough, well-made

hard-working assiduous, busy, conscientious, diligent, energetic, indefatigable, industrious, sedulous, zealous

Antonyms careless, dilatory, inconstant, indifferent, lazy

hardy firm, fit, hale, healthy, hearty, in fine fettle, lusty, robust, rugged, sound, stalwart, stout, strong, sturdy, tough, vigorous

Antonyms delicate, fainthearted, feeble, fragile, frail, sickly, soft, weak, weedy (*Inf.*), wimpish *or* wimpy (*Inf.*)

harm 1. *n.* abuse, damage, detriment, disservice, hurt, ill, impairment, injury, loss, mischief, misfortune 2. *v.* abuse, blemish, damage, hurt, ill-treat, ill-use, impair, injure, maltreat, mar, molest, ruin, spoil, wound

Antonyms *n.* aid, assistance, benefit, blessing, boon, gain, good, help, improvement, reparation ~ *v.* aid, alleviate, ameliorate, assist, benefit, better, cure, heal, help, improve, repair

harmful baleful, baneful, damaging, deleterious, destructive, detrimental, disadvantageous, evil, hurtful, injurious, noxious, pernicious

Antonyms beneficial, good, harmless, healthy, helpful, innocuous, safe, wholesome

harmless gentle, innocent, innocuous, innoxious, inoffensive, nontoxic, not dangerous, safe, unobjectionable

Antonyms dangerous, destructive, harmful, unhealthy, unsafe, unwholesome

harmonious agreeable, compatible, concordant, congruous, consonant, coordinated, correspondent, dulcet, euphonious, harmonic, harmonizing, matching, mellifluous, melodious, musical, sweet-sounding, symphonious (*Literary*), tuneful

Antonyms cacophonous, contrasting, discordant, grating, harsh, incompatible, inconsistent, unlike, unmelodious

harmony 1. accord, agreement, amicability, amity, compatibility, concord, conformity, consensus, cooperation, friendship, good will, like-mindedness, peace, rapport, sympathy, unanimity, understanding, unity **2.** euphony, melodiousness, melody, tune, tunefulness
Antonyms antagonism, cacophony, conflict, contention, disagreement, dissension, hostility, opposition

harness n. **1.** equipment, gear, tack, tackle, trappings ~v. **2.** couple, hitch up, put in harness, saddle, yoke **3.** apply, channel, control, employ, exploit, make productive, mobilize, render useful, turn to account, utilize

harsh 1. coarse, croaking, crude, discordant, dissonant, glaring, grating, guttural, jarring, rasping, raucous, rough, strident, unmelodious **2.** abusive, austere, bitter, bleak, brutal, comfortless, cruel, dour, Draconian, grim, hard, pitiless, punitive, relentless, ruthless, severe, sharp, Spartan, stern, stringent, unfeeling, unkind, unpleasant, unrelenting
Antonyms agreeable, gentle, harmonious, kind, loving, mellifluous, merciful, mild, pleasant, smooth, soft, soothing, sweet

harshness acerbity, acrimony, asperity, austerity, bitterness, brutality, churlishness, coarseness, crudity, hardness, illtemper, rigour, roughness, severity, sourness, sternness

harvest n. **1.** harvesting, harvesttime, ingathering, reaping **2.** crop, produce, yield

hash confusion, hotchpotch, jumble, mess, mishmash, mix-up, muddle, shambles

haste 1. alacrity, briskness, celerity, dispatch, expedition, fleetness, nimbleness, promptitude, quickness, rapidity, rapidness, speed, swiftness, urgency, velocity **2.** bustle, hastiness, helterskelter, hurry, hustle, impetuos-

ity, precipitateness, rashness, recklessness, rush
Antonyms calmness, care, delay, deliberation, leisureliness, slowness, sluggishness, sureness

hasten bolt, dash, fly, haste, hurry (up), make haste, race, run, rush, scurry, scuttle, speed, sprint, step on it (Inf.), tear (along)
Antonyms crawl, creep, dawdle, move slowly

hastily 1. apace, double-quick, fast, posthaste, promptly, quickly, rapidly, speedily, straightaway **2.** heedlessly, hurriedly, impetuously, impulsively, on the spur of the moment, precipitately, rashly, recklessly, too quickly

hasty 1. brisk, eager, expeditious, fast, fleet, hurried, prompt, rapid, speedy, swift, urgent **2.** foolhardy, headlong, heedless, impetuous, impulsive, indiscreet, precipitate, rash, reckless, thoughtless, unduly quick
Antonyms careful, cautious, leisurely, protracted, slow, thoughtful

hatch 1. breed, bring forth, brood, incubate **2.** Fig. conceive, concoct, contrive, cook up (Inf.), design, devise, dream up (Inf.), plan, plot, project, scheme, think up

hate 1. v. abhor, abominate, be hostile to, be repelled by, be sick of, despise, detest, dislike, execrate, have an aversion to, loathe, recoil from **2.** n. abhorrence, abomination, animosity, animus, antagonism, antipathy, aversion, detestation, dislike, enmity, execration, hatred, hostility, loathing, odium
Antonyms v. be fond of, cherish, dote on, enjoy, esteem, fancy, like, love, relish, treasure, wish ~n. affection, amity, devotion, fondness, good will, liking, love

hateful abhorrent, abominable, despicable, detestable, disgusting, execrable, forbidding, foul, heinous, horrible, loathsome, obnoxious, odious, offensive, repel-

lent, repugnant, repulsive, revolting, vile

hatred abomination, animosity,
animus, antagonism, antipathy,
aversion, detestation, dislike, enmity, execration, hate, ill will,
odium, repugnance, revulsion
Antonyms affection, amity, attachment, devotion, fondness,
friendliness, good will, liking,
love

haughty arrogant, assuming,
conceited, contemptuous, disdainful, high, high and mighty
(*Inf.*), hoity-toity (*Inf.*), imperious, lofty, overweening, proud,
scornful, snobbish, snooty (*Inf.*),
stuck-up (*Inf.*), supercilious, uppish (*Brit. inf.*)
Antonyms humble, meek, mild,
modest, self-effacing, subservient, wimpish *or* wimpy (*Inf.*)

haul 1. *v.* drag, draw, hale, heave,
lug, pull, tow, trail, tug 2. *n.* booty,
catch, find, gain, harvest, loot,
spoils, takings, yield

haunt *v.* 1. visit, walk 2. beset,
come back, obsess, plague, possess, prey on, recur, stay with,
torment, trouble, weigh on 3.
frequent, hang around *or* about,
repair, resort, visit ~*n.* 4. den,
gathering place, hangout (*Inf.*),
meeting place, rendezvous, resort, stamping ground

haunting disturbing, eerie,
evocative, indelible, nostalgic,
persistent, poignant, recurrent,
recurring, unforgettable

have 1. hold, keep, obtain, occupy,
own, possess, retain 2. endure,
enjoy, experience, feel, meet
with, suffer, sustain, undergo 3.
Usually **have to** be bound, be
compelled, be forced, be obliged,
have got to, must, ought, should

haven 1. anchorage, harbour,
port, roads (*Nautical*) 2. *Fig.*
asylum, refuge, retreat, sanctuary, sanctum, shelter

havoc 1. carnage, damage, desolation, despoliation, destruction,
devastation, rack and ruin, ravages, ruin, slaughter, waste,
wreck 2. *Inf.* chaos, confusion,

disorder, disruption, mayhem,
shambles

hazardous dangerous, dicey (*Sl.*,
chiefly Brit.), difficult, fraught
with danger, hairy (*Sl.*), insecure,
perilous, precarious, risky,
unsafe
Antonyms safe, secure, sound,
stable, sure

haze cloud, dimness, film, fog,
mist, obscurity, smog, smokiness,
steam, vapour

hazy 1. blurry, cloudy, dim, dull,
faint, foggy, misty, nebulous, obscure, overcast, smoky, veiled 2.
Fig. fuzzy, ill-defined, indefinite,
indistinct, loose, muddled, muzzy,
nebulous, uncertain, unclear,
vague
Antonyms bright, certain, clear,
detailed, light, sunny, well-
defined

head *n.* 1. conk (*Sl.*), cranium,
crown, loaf (*Sl.*), noddle (*Inf.*,
chiefly Brit.), nut (*Sl.*), pate, skull
2. boss (*Inf.*), captain, chief,
chieftain, commander, director,
headmaster, headmistress, head
teacher, leader, manager, master, principal, superintendent,
supervisor 3. apex, crest, crown,
height, peak, pitch, summit, tip,
top, vertex 4. ability, aptitude,
brain, brains (*Inf.*), capacity,
faculty, flair, intellect, intelligence, mentality, mind, talent,
thought, understanding 5. branch,
category, class, department, division, heading, section, subject,
topic ~*adj.* 6. arch, chief, first,
foremost, front, highest, leading,
main, pre-eminent, premier,
prime, principal, supreme, topmost ~*v.* 7. be *or* go first, cap,
crown, lead, lead the way, precede, top 8. be in charge of,
command, control, direct, govern, guide, lead, manage, rule,
run, supervise

heading 1. caption, headline,
name, rubric, title 2. category,
class, division, section

headlong 1. *adj.* breakneck, dangerous, hasty, impetuous, impulsive, inconsiderate, precipitate,

reckless, thoughtless 2. *adv.* hastily, heedlessly, helter-skelter, hurriedly, pell-mell, precipitately, rashly, thoughtlessly, wildly

headstrong contrary, foolhardy, froward, heedless, imprudent, impulsive, intractable, mulish, obstinate, perverse, pig-headed, rash, reckless, self-willed, stubborn, ungovernable, unruly, wilful

Antonyms cautious, impressionable, manageable, pliant, subservient, tractable

headway advance, improvement, progress, progression, way

heal 1. cure, make well, mend, regenerate, remedy, restore, treat 2. alleviate, ameliorate, compose, conciliate, harmonize, patch up, reconcile, settle, soothe

Antonyms aggravate, exacerbate, harm, hurt, inflame, injure, make worse, reopen, wound

health fitness, good condition, haleness, healthiness, robustness, salubrity, soundness, strength, vigour, wellbeing

Antonyms debility, disease, frailty, illness, sickness, weakness

healthy active, blooming, fit, flourishing, hale, hale and hearty, hardy, hearty, in fine feather, in fine fettle, in fine form, in good condition, in good shape (*Inf.*), in the pink, physically fit, robust, sound, strong, sturdy, vigorous, well

Antonyms ailing, debilitated, delicate, diseased, feeble, fragile, frail, ill, infirm, poorly (*Inf.*), sick, sickly, unfit, unhealthy, unsound, unwell, weak, weedy (*Inf.*)

heap 1. *n.* accumulation, aggregation, collection, hoard, lot, mass, mound, mountain, pile, stack, stockpile, store 2. *v.* accumulate, amass, augment, bank, collect, gather, hoard, increase, mound, pile, stack, stockpile, store

hear 1. attend, be all ears (*Inf.*), catch, eavesdrop, give attention, hark, hearken (*Archaic*), heed,

listen in, listen to, overhear 2. ascertain, be informed, be told of, discover, find out, gather, get wind of (*Inf.*), hear tell (*Dialect*), learn, pick up, understand 3. *Law* examine, investigate, judge, try

hearing 1. audition, auditory (*Archaic*), ear, perception 2. audience, audition, chance to speak, interview 3. auditory range, earshot, hearing distance, range, reach, sound 4. inquiry, investigation, review, trial

hearsay buzz, gossip, grapevine (*Inf.*), idle talk, mere talk, *on dit*, report, rumour, scuttlebutt (*Sl.*, *chiefly U.S.*), talk, talk of the town, tittle-tattle, word of mouth

heart 1. affection, benevolence, compassion, concern, humanity, love, pity, tenderness, understanding 2. balls (*Sl.*), boldness, bravery, courage, fortitude, guts (*Inf.*), mettle, mind, nerve, pluck, purpose, resolution, spirit, spunk (*Inf.*) 3. central part, centre, core, crux, essence, hub, kernel, marrow, middle, nucleus, pith, quintessence, root 4. by heart by memory, by rote, off pat, parrot-fashion (*Inf.*), pat, word for word

heartbreaking agonizing, bitter, desolating, disappointing, distressing, grievous, heart-rending, pitiful, poignant, sad, tragic

heartbroken brokenhearted, crestfallen, crushed, dejected, desolate, despondent, disappointed, disconsolate, disheartened, dispirited, downcast, grieved, heartsick, miserable

Antonyms cheerful, elated, exuberant, happy, in seventh heaven, joyful, joyous, on cloud nine

heartfelt ardent, cordial, deep, devout, earnest, fervent, genuine, hearty, honest, profound, sincere, unfeigned, warm, wholehearted

Antonyms false, feigned, flippant, fraudulent, frivolous, half-hearted, hypocritical, insincere, phoney (*Inf.*), pretended, put on, reserved, unenthusiastic, unimpassioned

heartless brutal, callous, cold,

cold-blooded, cold-hearted, cruel, hard, hardhearted, harsh, inhuman, merciless, pitiless, uncaring, unfeeling, unkind
Antonyms compassionate, generous, humane, kind, merciful, sensitive, sympathetic, warm-hearted

hearty 1. affable, ardent, back-slapping, cordial, eager, ebullient, effusive, enthusiastic, friendly, generous, genial, jovial, unreserved, warm **2.** active, energetic, hale, hardy, healthy, robust, sound, strong, vigorous, well **Antonyms** cold, cool, delicate, feeble, frail, half-hearted, mild, sickly, unhealthy, weak

heat n. **1.** calefaction, fever, fieriness, high temperature, hotness, hot spell, sultriness, swelter, torridity, warmness, warmth **2.** Fig. agitation, ardour, earnestness, excitement, fervour, fever, fury, impetuosity, intensity, passion, vehemence, violence, warmth, zeal ~v. **3.** become warm, chafe, flush, glow, grow hot, make hot, reheat, warm up **4.** animate, excite, impassion, inflame, inspirit, rouse, stimulate, stir, warm
Antonyms n. calmness, cold, coldness, composure, coolness ~v. chill, cool, cool off, freeze

heated angry, bitter, excited, fierce, fiery, frenzied, furious, impassioned, intense, passionate, raging, stormy, tempestuous, vehement, violent
Antonyms calm, civilized, dispassionate, friendly, half-hearted, mellow, mild, peaceful, quiet, rational, reasoned, serene, subdued, unemotional, unruffled

heathen n. **1.** idolater, idolatress, infidel, pagan, unbeliever **2.** barbarian, philistine, savage ~adj. **3.** godless, heathenish, idolatrous, infidel, irreligious, pagan **4.** barbaric, philistine, savage, uncivilized, unenlightened

heave 1. drag (up), elevate, haul (up), heft (Inf.), hoist, lever, lift, pull (up), raise, tug **2.** cast, fling,

hurl, pitch, send, sling, throw, toss

heaven Fig. bliss, dreamland, ecstasy, enchantment, felicity, happiness, paradise, rapture, seventh heaven, sheer bliss, transport, utopia

heavenly Inf. alluring, beautiful, blissful, delightful, divine (Inf.), entrancing, exquisite, glorious, lovely, rapturous, ravishing, sublime, wonderful
Antonyms abominable, appalling, awful, bad, depressing, dire, disagreeable, dreadful, dreary, dull, frightful, gloomy, grim, horrible, lousy (Sl.), miserable, rotten (Inf.), terrible, unpleasant, vile

heaviness 1. gravity, heftiness, ponderousness, weight **2.** arduousness, burdensomeness, grievousness, onerousness, oppressiveness, severity, weightiness **3.** deadness, dullness, languor, lassitude, numbness, sluggishness, torpor

heavy 1. bulky, hefty, massive, ponderous, portly, weighty **2.** burdensome, difficult, grievous, hard, harsh, intolerable, laborious, onerous, oppressive, severe, tedious, vexatious, wearisome **3.** apathetic, drowsy, dull, inactive, indolent, inert, listless, slow, sluggish, stupid, torpid, wooden **4.** burdened, encumbered, laden, loaded, oppressed, weighted
Antonyms agile, alert, bearable, brisk, compact, easy, exciting, gentle, handy, light, quick, slight, small, soft, sparse, weak

heckle bait, barrack (Inf.), disrupt, interrupt, jeer, pester, shout down, taunt

hectic animated, boisterous, chaotic, excited, fevered, feverish, flurrying, flustering, frantic, frenetic, frenzied, furious, heated, riotous, rumbustious, tumultuous, turbulent, wild
Antonyms calm, peaceful, relaxing, tranquil

hedge n. **1.** hedgerow, quickset **2.**

barrier, boundary, screen, wind~break ~v. **3.** border, edge, en~close, fence, surround **4.** block, confine, hem in (about, around), hinder, obstruct, restrict **5.** beg the question, be noncommittal, dodge, duck, equivocate, evade, prevaricate, pussyfoot (*Inf.*), quibble, sidestep, temporize, waffle (*Inf.*)

heed 1. *n.* attention, care, caution, consideration, ear, heedfulness, mind, note, notice, regard, re~spect, thought, watchfulness **2.** *v.* attend, bear in mind, be guided by, consider, follow, give ear to, listen to, mark, mind, note, obey, observe, pay attention to, regard, take notice of, take to heart
Antonyms *n.* carelessness, disre~gard, inattention, neglect, thoughtlessness ~v. be inatten~tive to, disobey, disregard, flout, ignore, neglect, overlook, reject, shun, turn a deaf ear to

heedless careless, foolhardy, imprudent, inattentive, incau~tious, neglectful, negligent, oblivious, precipitate, rash, reck~less, thoughtless, unmindful, un~observant, unthinking
Antonyms attentive, aware, careful, cautious, concerned, heedful, mindful, observant, thoughtful, vigilant, wary, watchful

heel[1] *n.* **1.** crust, end, remainder, rump, stub, stump **2.** down at heel dowdy, impoverished, out at elbows, run-down, seedy, shabby, slipshod, slovenly, worn

height 1. altitude, elevation, highness, loftiness, stature, tall~ness **2.** apex, apogee, crest, crown, elevation, hill, mountain, peak, pinnacle, summit, top, ver~tex, zenith **3.** acme, dignity, emi~nence, exaltation, grandeur, loftiness, prominence
Antonyms abyss, base, bottom, canyon, chasm, depth, lowland, lowness, low point, minimum, moderation, nadir, ravine, short~ness, smallness, tininess, trivial~ity, valley

heighten add to, aggravate, am~plify, augment, enhance, im~prove, increase, intensify, mag~nify, sharpen, strengthen

hell 1. Abaddon, abode of the damned, abyss, Acheron (*Greek myth*), bottomless pit, fire and brimstone, Gehenna (*New Tes~tament, Judaism*), Hades (*Greek myth*), hellfire, infernal regions, inferno, lower world, nether world, Tartarus (*Greek myth*), underworld **2.** affliction, agony, anguish, martyrdom, misery, nightmare, ordeal, suffering, tor~ment, trial, wretchedness

hellish damnable, damned, de~moniacal, devilish, diabolical, fiendish, infernal

help *v.* **1.** abet, aid, assist, back, befriend, cooperate, lend a hand, promote, relieve, save, second, serve, stand by, succour, support **2.** alleviate, ameliorate, cure, ease, facilitate, heal, improve, mitigate, relieve, remedy, re~store ~n. **3.** advice, aid, assis~tance, avail, benefit, cooperation, guidance, helping hand, service, support, use, utility
Antonyms *v.* aggravate, bar, block, discourage, fight, foil, frustrate, harm, hinder, hurt, im~pede, injure, irritate, make worse, obstruct, oppose ~n. block, discouragement, hin~drance, obstruction, opposition

helper abettor, adjutant, aide, aider, ally, assistant, attendant, auxiliary, coadjutor, collabora~tor, colleague, deputy, helpmate, mate, partner, right-hand man, second, subsidiary, supporter

helpful 1. advantageous, benefi~cial, constructive, favourable, fortunate, practical, productive, profitable, serviceable, timely, useful **2.** accommodating, benefi~cent, benevolent, caring, consid~erate, cooperative, friendly, kind, neighbourly, supportive, sympa~thetic

helping *n.* dollop, piece (*Inf.*), plateful, portion, ration, serving

helpless 1. abandoned, defence~

less, dependent, destitute, exposed, forlorn, unprotected, vulnerable 2. debilitated, disabled, feeble, impotent, incapable, incompetent, infirm, paralysed, powerless, unfit, weak
Antonyms able, capable, competent, equipped, fit, hardy, healthy, hearty, invulnerable, mighty, powerful, robust, safe, secure, solid, strong, sturdy, thriving, tough, well-protected

hem n. border, edge, fringe, margin, trimming

herald n. 1. bearer of tidings, crier, messenger 2. forerunner, harbinger, indication, omen, precursor, sign, signal, token

herd 1. n. assemblage, collection, crowd, crush, drove, flock, horde, mass, mob, multitude, press, swarm, throng 2. v. assemble, associate, collect, congregate, flock, gather, huddle, muster, rally

hereafter adv. after this, from now on, hence, henceforth, henceforward, in future

hereditary family, genetic, inborn, inbred, inheritable, transmissible

heresy apostasy, dissidence, error, heterodoxy, iconoclasm, impiety, revisionism, schism, unorthodoxy

heretic apostate, dissenter, dissident, nonconformist, renegade, revisionist, schismatic, sectarian, separatist

heritage bequest, birthright, endowment, estate, inheritance, legacy, lot, patrimony, portion, share, tradition

hermit anchoret, anchorite, eremite, monk, recluse, solitary, stylite

hero 1. celeb (Inf.), celebrity, champion, conqueror, exemplar, great man, heart-throb (Brit.), idol, man of the hour, popular figure, star, superstar, victor 2. lead actor, leading man, male lead, principal male character, protagonist

heroic bold, brave, courageous,

daring, dauntless, doughty, fearless, gallant, intrepid, lionhearted, stouthearted, undaunted, valiant, valorous
Antonyms base, chicken (Sl.), cowardly, craven, faint-hearted, ignoble, irresolute, mean, timid

heroine 1. celeb (Inf.), celebrity, goddess, ideal, woman of the hour 2. diva, female lead, lead actress, leading lady, prima donna, principal female character, protagonist

heroism boldness, bravery, courage, courageousness, daring, fearlessness, fortitude, gallantry, intrepidity, prowess, spirit, valour

hesitant diffident, doubtful, half-hearted, halting, hanging back, hesitating, irresolute, lacking confidence, reluctant, sceptical, shy, timid, uncertain, unsure, vacillating, wavering
Antonyms arrogant, avid, clear, confident, definite, determined, dogmatic, eager, enthusiastic, firm, forceful, keen, positive, resolute, self-assured, spirited, sure, unhesitating, unwavering

hesitate be uncertain, delay, dither, doubt, haver (Brit.), pause, shillyshally (Inf.), swither (Scot. dialect), vacillate, wait, waver
Antonyms be confident, be decisive, be firm, continue, decide

hesitation delay, doubt, dubiety, hesitancy, indecision, irresolution, uncertainty, vacillation

hew 1. axe, chop, cut, hack, lop, split 2. carve, fashion, form, make, model, sculpt, sculpture, shape, smooth

heyday bloom, flowering, pink, prime, prime of life, salad days

hidden abstruse, clandestine, close, concealed, covered, covert, cryptic, dark, hermetic, hermetical, masked, mysterious, mystic, mystical, obscure, occult, recondite, secret, shrouded, ulterior, unrevealed, unseen, veiled

hide 1. cache, conceal, go into hiding, go to ground, go underground, hole up, lie low, secrete, take cover 2. blot out, bury, camouflage, cloak, conceal, cover, disguise, eclipse, mask, obscure, screen, shelter, shroud, veil

Antonyms bare, display, exhibit, expose, find, flaunt, reveal, show, uncover, unveil

hidebound brassbound, conventional, narrow, narrow-minded, rigid, set in one's ways, straitlaced, ultraconservative

hideous ghastly, grim, grisly, grotesque, gruesome, monstrous, repulsive, revolting, ugly, unsightly

Antonyms appealing, beautiful, captivating, charming, entrancing, lovely, pleasant, pleasing

hiding n. beating, caning, drubbing, flogging, larruping (*Brit. dialect*), lathering (*Inf.*), licking (*Inf.*), spanking, tanning (*Sl.*), thrashing, walloping (*Inf.*), whaling, whipping

high adj. **1.** elevated, lofty, soaring, steep, tall, towering **2.** excessive, extraordinary, extreme, great, intensified, sharp, strong **3.** arch, chief, consequential, distinguished, eminent, exalted, important, influential, leading, powerful, prominent, ruling, significant, superior **4.** costly, dear, exorbitant, expensive, high-priced, steep (*Inf.*), stiff **5.** acute, high-pitched, penetrating, piercing, piping, sharp, shrill, soprano, strident, treble ~adv. **6.** aloft, at great height, far up, way up

Antonyms adj. (*sense 1*) dwarfed, low, short, stunted (*sense 2*) average, low, mild, moderate, reduced, restrained, routine, suppressed (*sense 3*) average, common, degraded, ignoble, inconsequential, insignificant, low, lowly, low-ranking, menial, routine, secondary, undistinguished, unimportant (*sense 5*) alto, bass, deep, gruff, low, low-pitched

highbrow 1. n. aesthete, Brahmin (*U.S.*), brain (*Inf.*), brainbox (*Sl.*), egghead (*Inf.*), intellectual,

mastermind, savant, scholar **2.** adj. bookish, brainy (*Inf.*), cultivated, cultured, deep, highbrowed, intellectual, sophisticated

Antonyms n. idiot, ignoramus, illiterate, imbecile (*Inf.*), lowbrow, moron, philistine ~adj. ignorant, lowbrow, philistine, shallow, uncultivated, uninformed, unintellectual, unlearned, unsophisticated

high-handed arbitrary, autocratic, bossy (*Inf.*), despotic, dictatorial, domineering, imperious, inconsiderate, oppressive, overbearing, peremptory, self-willed, tyrannical, wilful

highlight 1. n. best part, climax, feature, focal point, focus, high point, high spot, main feature, memorable part, peak **2.** v. accent, accentuate, bring to the fore, emphasize, feature, focus attention on, give prominence to, play up, set off, show up, spotlight, stress, underline

Antonyms n. disappointment, low point ~v. de-emphasize, gloss over, neglect, overlook, play down

highly decidedly, eminently, exceptionally, extraordinarily, extremely, greatly, immensely, supremely, tremendously, vastly, very, very much

high-powered aggressive, driving, dynamic, effective, energetic, enterprising, fast-track, forceful, go-ahead, go-getting (*Inf.*), highly capable, vigorous

high-speed brisk, express, fast, hotted-up (*Inf.*), quick, rapid, souped-up (*Inf.*), streamlined, swift

high-spirited animated, boisterous, bold, bouncy, daring, dashing, ebullient, effervescent, energetic, exuberant, frolicsome, full of life, fun-loving, gallant, lively, mettlesome, sparky, spirited, spunky (*Inf.*), vibrant, vital, vivacious

high spirits abandon, boisterousness, exhilaration, exuberance, good cheer, hilarity, *joie de vivre*, rare good humour

hijack commandeer, expropriate, seize, skyjack, take over

hike 1. *v.* back-pack, hoof it (*Sl.*), leg it (*Inf.*), ramble, tramp, walk 2. *n.* journey on foot, march, ramble, tramp, trek, walk

hilarious amusing, comical, convivial, entertaining, exhilarated, funny, gay, happy, humorous, jolly, jovial, joyful, joyous, merry, mirthful, noisy, rollicking, side-splitting, uproarious
Antonyms dull, gloomy, quiet, sad, sedate, serious

hilarity amusement, boisterousness, cheerfulness, conviviality, exhilaration, exuberance, gaiety, glee, high spirits, jollification, jollity, joviality, joyousness, laughter, levity, merriment, mirth

hill brae (*Scot.*), down (*Archaic*), elevation, eminence, fell, height, hillock, hilltop, knoll, mound, mount, prominence, tor

hinder arrest, check, debar, delay, deter, encumber, frustrate, hamper, hamstring, handicap, hold up *or* back, impede, interrupt, obstruct, oppose, prevent, retard, slow down, stop, stymie, thwart, trammel
Antonyms accelerate, advance, aid, benefit, encourage, expedite, facilitate, further, help, hurry, promote, quicken, speed, support

hindrance bar, barrier, check, deterrent, difficulty, drag, drawback, encumbrance, handicap, hitch, impediment, interruption, limitation, obstacle, obstruction, restraint, restriction, snag, stoppage, stumbling block, trammel
Antonyms advancement, advantage, aid, asset, assistance, benefit, boon, boost, encouragement, furtherance, help, support

hinge *v.* be contingent, be subject to, depend, hang, pivot, rest, revolve around, turn

hint *n.* 1. allusion, clue, implication, indication, inkling, innuendo, insinuation, intimation, men-

tion, reminder, suggestion, tip-off, word to the wise 2. advice, help, pointer, suggestion, tip, wrinkle (*Inf.*) 3. breath, dash, soupçon, speck, suggestion, suspicion, taste, tinge, touch, trace, undertone, whiff, whisper ~*v.* 4. allude, cue, imply, indicate, insinuate, intimate, let it be known, mention, prompt, suggest, tip off

hire *v.* 1. appoint, commission, employ, engage, sign up, take on 2. charter, engage, lease, let, rent ~*n.* 3. charge, cost, fee, price, rent, rental

hiss *n.* 1. buzz, hissing, sibilance, sibilation 2. boo, catcall, contempt, derision, jeer, raspberry ~*v.* 3. rasp, shrill, sibilate, wheeze, whirr, whistle, whiz 4. blow a raspberry, boo, catcall, condemn, damn, decry, deride, hoot, jeer, mock, revile, ridicule

historic celebrated, consequential, epoch-making, extraordinary, famous, momentous, notable, outstanding, red-letter, remarkable, significant

history account, annals, autobiography, biography, chronicle, memoirs, narration, narrative, recapitulation, recital, record, relation, saga, story

hit *v.* 1. bang, bash (*Inf.*), batter, beat, belt (*Sl.*), clip (*Sl.*), clobber (*Sl.*), clout (*Inf.*), cuff, flog, knock, lob, punch, slap, smack, smite (*Archaic*), sock (*Sl.*), strike, swat, thump, wallop (*Inf.*), whack 2. bang into, bump, clash with, collide with, crash against, meet head-on, run into, smash into ~*n.* 3. blow, bump, clash, clout (*Inf.*), collision, cuff, impact, knock, rap, shot, slap, smack, stroke, swipe (*Inf.*), wallop (*Inf.*) 4. *Inf.* sellout, sensation, smash (*Inf.*), success, triumph, winner

hitch 1. *v.* attach, connect, couple, fasten, harness, join, make fast, tether, tie, unite, yoke 2. *n.* catch, check, delay, difficulty, drawback, hindrance, hold-up, impediment, mishap, problem, snag, stoppage, trouble

hitherto heretofore, previously, so far, thus far, till now, until now, up to now

hit on or **upon** arrive at, chance upon, come upon, discover, guess, invent, light upon, realize, strike upon, stumble on, think up

hit or miss aimless, casual, cursory, disorganized, haphazard, indiscriminate, perfunctory, random, undirected, uneven
Antonyms arranged, deliberate, organized, planned, systematic

hit out (at) assail, attack, castigate, condemn, denounce, inveigh against, lash out, rail against, strike out at

hoard 1. n. accumulation, cache, fund, heap, mass, pile, reserve, stockpile, store, supply, treasure-trove **2.** v. accumulate, amass, buy up, cache, collect, deposit, garner, gather, hive, lay up, put away, put by, save, stash away (Inf.), stockpile, store, treasure

hoarse croaky, discordant, grating, gravelly, growling, gruff, guttural, harsh, husky, rasping, raucous, rough, throaty
Antonyms harmonious, mellifluous, mellow, melodious, smooth

hoax n. cheat, con (Sl.), deception, fast one (Inf.), fraud, imposture, joke, practical joke, prank, ruse, spoof (Inf.), swindle, trick

hobby diversion, favourite occupation, (leisure) activity, leisure pursuit, pastime, relaxation, sideline

hoist 1. v. elevate, erect, heave, lift, raise, rear, upraise **2.** n. crane, elevator, lift, tackle, winch

hold v. 1. have, keep, maintain, occupy, own, possess, retain **2.** adhere, clasp, cleave, clinch, cling, clutch, cradle, embrace, enfold, grasp, grip, stick **3.** arrest, bind, check, confine, curb, detain, imprison, restrain, stay, stop, suspend **4.** assume, believe, consider, deem, entertain, esteem, judge, maintain, presume, reckon, regard, think, view **5.** continue, endure, last, persevere,

persist, remain, resist, stay, wear **6.** assemble, call, carry on, celebrate, conduct, convene, have, officiate at, preside over, run, solemnize **7.** bear, brace, carry, prop, shoulder, support, sustain, take **8.** accommodate, comprise, contain, have a capacity for, seat, take ~n. **9.** clasp, clutch, grasp, grip **10.** anchorage, foothold, footing, leverage, prop, purchase, stay, support, vantage
Antonyms bestow, break, call off, cancel, come undone, deny, disavow, disclaim, free, give, give up, give way, hand over, let go, let loose, loosen, offer, postpone, put down, refute, reject, release, turn over

hold back check, control, curb, inhibit, repress, restrain, suppress

holder bearer, custodian, incumbent, keeper, occupant, owner, possessor, proprietor, purchaser

hold forth declaim, descant, discourse, go on (Inf.), harangue, lecture, orate, preach, speak, speechify, spiel (Inf.), spout (Inf.)

hold off 1. avoid, defer, delay, keep from, postpone, put off, refrain **2.** fend off, keep off, rebuff, repel, repulse, stave off

hold out 1. extend, give, offer, present, proffer **2.** carry on, continue, endure, hang on, last, persevere, persist, stand fast, withstand

hold-up bottleneck, delay, difficulty, hitch, obstruction, setback, snag, stoppage, traffic jam, trouble, wait

hold up 1. delay, detain, hinder, impede, retard, set back, slow down, stop **2.** brace, buttress, jack up, prop, shore up, support, sustain

hole 1. aperture, breach, break, crack, fissure, gap, opening, orifice, outlet, perforation, puncture, rent, split, tear, vent **2.** defect, discrepancy, error, fallacy, fault, flaw, inconsistency, loophole

holiday 1. break, leave, recess,

time off, vacation **2.** anniversary, bank holiday, celebration, feast, festival, festivity, fête, gala, public holiday, saint's day

hollow *adj.* **1.** empty, not solid, unfilled, vacant, void **2.** cavernous, concave, deep-set, depressed, indented, sunken **3.** deep, dull, expressionless, flat, low, muffled, muted, reverberant, rumbling, sepulchral, toneless **4.** empty, fruitless, futile, meaningless, pointless, Pyrrhic, specious, unavailing, useless, vain, worthless ~*n.* **5.** basin, bowl, cave, cavern, cavity, concavity, crater, cup, den, dent, depression, dimple, excavation, hole, indentation, pit, trough **6.** bottom, dale, dell, dingle, glen, valley
Antonyms *adj.* (*sense 1*) full, occupied, solid (*sense 2*) convex, rounded (*sense 4*) expressive, vibrant (*sense 4*) gratifying, meaningful, pleasing, satisfying, valuable, worthwhile ~*n.* (*sense 5*) bump, mound, projection (*sense 6*) bluff, height, hill, knoll, mountain, rise

holy devout, divine, faithful, godfearing, godly, hallowed, pious, pure, religious, righteous, saintly, sublime, virtuous
Antonyms blasphemous, corrupt, desecrated, evil, immoral, impious, irreligious, sacrilegious, sinful, unholy, wicked,

home *n.* **1.** abode, domicile, dwelling, dwelling place, habitation, house, residence **2.** birthplace, family, fireside, hearth, homestead, home town, household **3.** abode, element, environment, habitat, habitation, haunt, home ground, range, stamping ground, territory **4. at home a.** available, in, present **b.** at ease, comfortable, familiar, relaxed **c.** entertaining, giving a party, having guests, receiving **d.** *As a noun* party, reception, soirée **5. at home in, on,** *or* **with** conversant with, familiar with, knowledge-

able, proficient, skilled, well-versed

homeland country of origin, fatherland, mother country, motherland, native land

homespun artless, coarse, homely, home-made, inelegant, plain, rough, rude, rustic, unpolished, unsophisticated

homicidal deadly, death-dealing, lethal, maniacal, mortal, murderous

homicide bloodshed, killing, manslaughter, murder, slaying

homogeneous akin, alike, analogous, cognate, comparable, consistent, identical, kindred, similar, uniform, unvarying
Antonyms different, disparate, dissimilar, divergent, diverse, heterogeneous, mixed, unlike, unrelated, varied, various, varying

honest 1. conscientious, decent, ethical, high-minded, honourable, law-abiding, reliable, reputable, scrupulous, trustworthy, trusty, truthful, upright, veracious, virtuous **2.** equitable, fair, fair and square, impartial, just **3.** candid, direct, forthright, frank, ingenuous, open, outright, plain, sincere, straightforward, undisguised, unfeigned
Antonyms bad, corrupt, disguised, guilty, immoral, insincere, secretive, treacherous, unfair, unfaithful, unprincipled, unreliable, unrighteous, unscrupulous, untrustworthy, untruthful

honestly 1. by fair means, cleanly, ethically, honourably, in good faith, lawfully, legally, legitimately, on the level (*Inf.*), with clean hands **2.** candidly, frankly, in all sincerity, in plain English, plainly, straight (out), to one's face, truthfully

honesty faithfulness, fidelity, honour, incorruptibility, integrity, morality, probity, rectitude, reputability, scrupulousness, straightness, trustworthiness, truthfulness, uprightness, veracity, virtue

honour n. 1. credit, dignity, distinction, elevation, esteem, fame, glory, high standing, prestige, rank, renown, reputation, repute 2. acclaim, accolade, adoration, commendation, deference, homage, kudos, praise, recognition, regard, respect, reverence, tribute, veneration 3. decency, fairness, goodness, honesty, integrity, morality, principles, probity, rectitude, righteousness, trustworthiness, uprightness 4. compliment, credit, favour, pleasure, privilege, source of pride or satisfaction 5. chastity, innocence, modesty, purity, virginity, virtue ~v. 6. admire, adore, appreciate, esteem, exalt, glorify, hallow, prize, respect, revere, reverence, value, venerate, worship

Antonyms n. condemnation, contempt, degradation, disfavour, disgrace, dishonesty, dishonour, disrepute, disrespect, infamy, insincerity, insult, lowness, meanness, scorn, shame, slight, unscrupulousness ~v. condemn, defame, degrade, dishonour, disobey, insult, offend, refuse, scorn, slight

honourable 1. ethical, fair, high-minded, honest, just, moral, principled, true, trustworthy, trusty, upright, upstanding, virtuous 2. distinguished, eminent, great, illustrious, noble, notable, noted, prestigious, renowned, venerable

honours adornments, awards, decorations, dignities, distinctions, laurels, titles

hoodwink bamboozle (*Inf.*), befool, cheat, con (*Inf.*), cozen, deceive, delude, dupe, fool, gull (*Archaic*), hoax, impose, lead up the garden path (*Inf.*), mislead, pull a fast one on (*Inf.*), rook (*Sl.*), swindle, trick

hook n. 1. catch, clasp, fastener, hasp, holder, link, lock, peg 2. noose, snare, springe, trap ~v. 3. catch, clasp, fasten, fix, hasp, secure 4. catch, enmesh, ensnare, entrap, snare, trap

hooligan casual, delinquent, hoodlum (*Chiefly U.S.*), lager lout, ned (*Sl.*), rowdy, ruffian, tough, vandal, yob or yobbo (*Brit. sl.*)

hoop band, circlet, girdle, loop, ring, wheel

hoot n. 1. call, cry, toot 2. boo, catcall, hiss, jeer, yell ~v. 3. boo, catcall, condemn, decry, denounce, execrate, hiss, howl down, jeer, yell at 4. cry, scream, shout, shriek, toot, whoop, yell

hop 1. v. bound, caper, dance, jump, leap, skip, spring, vault 2. n. bounce, bound, jump, leap, skip, spring, step, vault

hope 1. n. ambition, anticipation, assumption, belief, confidence, desire, dream, expectancy, expectation, faith, longing 2. v. anticipate, aspire, await, believe, contemplate, count on, desire, expect, foresee, long, look forward to, rely, trust

Antonyms despair, distrust, doubt, dread, hopelessness

hopeful 1. anticipating, assured, buoyant, confident, expectant, looking forward to, optimistic, sanguine 2. auspicious, bright, cheerful, encouraging, heartening, promising, propitious, reassuring, rosy

Antonyms (*sense 1*) cheerless, dejected, despairing, hopeless, pessimistic (*sense 2*) depressing, discouraging, disheartening, unpromising

hopefully 1. confidently, expectantly, optimistically, sanguinely 2. *Inf.* all being well, conceivably, expectedly, feasibly, probably

hopeless 1. defeatist, dejected, demoralized, despairing, desperate, despondent, disconsolate, downhearted, forlorn, in despair, pessimistic, woebegone 2. helpless, incurable, irremediable, irreparable, irreversible, lost, past remedy, remediless 3. forlorn, futile, impossible, impracticable, pointless, unachievable, unattainable, useless, vain

Antonyms (*sense 1*) assured,

cheerful, confident, expectant, happy, heartened, hopeful, optimistic, uplifted (*sense 2*) curable, encouraging, favourable, heartening, promising, reassuring, remediable

horde band, crew, crowd, drove, gang, host, mob, multitude, pack, press, swarm, throng, troop

horizon 1. field of vision, skyline, vista 2. compass, ken, perspective, prospect, purview, range, realm, scope, sphere, stretch

horrible 1. abhorrent, abominable, appalling, awful, dreadful, fearful, frightful, ghastly, grim, grisly, gruesome, heinous, hideous, horrid, loathsome, repulsive, revolting, shameful, shocking, terrible, terrifying 2. *Inf.* awful, beastly (*Inf.*), cruel, disagreeable, dreadful, ghastly (*Inf.*), mean, nasty, terrible, unkind, unpleasant

Antonyms agreeable, appealing, attractive, charming, delightful, enchanting, fetching, lovely, pleasant, wonderful

horrid 1. awful, disagreeable, disgusting, dreadful, horrible, nasty, offensive, terrible, unpleasant 2. abominable, alarming, appalling, formidable, frightening, hair-raising, harrowing, hideous, horrific, odious, repulsive, revolting, shocking, terrifying, terrorizing

horrify 1. affright, alarm, frighten, intimidate, petrify, scare, terrify, terrorize 2. appal, disgust, dismay, outrage, shock, sicken

horror 1. alarm, apprehension, awe, consternation, dismay, dread, fear, fright, panic, terror 2. abhorrence, abomination, antipathy, aversion, detestation, disgust, hatred, loathing, repugnance, revulsion

Antonyms affinity, approval, attraction, delight, liking, love

horseplay buffoonery, clowning, fooling around, high jinks, pranks, romping, rough-and-tumble, roughhousing (*Sl.*), skylarking (*Inf.*)

hospitable amicable, bountiful,

cordial, friendly, generous, genial, gracious, kind, liberal, sociable, welcoming

Antonyms inhospitable, parsimonious

hospitality cheer, conviviality, cordiality, friendliness, heartiness, hospitableness, neighbourliness, sociability, warmth, welcome

host[1] *n.* entertainer, innkeeper, landlord, master of ceremonies, proprietor

host[2] army, array, drove, horde, legion, multitude, myriad, swarm, throng

hostage captive, gage, pawn, pledge, prisoner, security, surety

hostile 1. antagonistic, anti (*Inf.*), bellicose, belligerent, contrary, ill-disposed, inimical, malevolent, opposed, opposite, rancorous, unkind, warlike 2. adverse, alien, inhospitable, unfriendly, unpropitious, unsympathetic, unwelcoming

Antonyms agreeable, amiable, approving, congenial, cordial, friendly, kind, peaceful, sympathetic, warm

hostilities conflict, fighting, state of war, war, warfare

Antonyms alliance, peace, treaty, truce

hostility abhorrence, animosity, animus, antagonism, antipathy, aversion, detestation, enmity, hatred, ill will, malevolence, malice, opposition, resentment, unfriendliness

Antonyms agreement, amity, approval, congeniality, cordiality, friendliness, good will, sympathy

hot 1. blistering, boiling, burning, fiery, flaming, heated, piping hot, roasting, scalding, scorching, searing, steaming, sultry, sweltering, torrid, warm 2. acrid, biting, peppery, piquant, pungent, sharp, spicy

Antonyms (*sense 1*) chilly, cold, cool, freezing, frigid, frosty, icy (*sense 2*) mild

hot air blather, blether, bombast,

bosh (*Inf.*), bunkum, claptrap (*Inf.*), empty talk, gas (*Sl.*), guff (*Sl.*), rant, tall talk (*Inf.*), verbiage, wind

hotchpotch conglomeration, farrago, gallimaufry, hash, jumble, medley, *mélange*, mess, miscellany, mishmash, mixture, olio, olla podrida, potpourri

hothead daredevil, desperado, hotspur, madcap, tearaway

hot-headed fiery, foolhardy, hasty, hot-tempered, impetuous, precipitate, quick-tempered, rash, reckless, unruly, volatile

hound v. chase, drive, give chase, hunt, hunt down, pursue

house n. 1. abode, building, domicile, dwelling, edifice, habitation, home, homestead, residence 2. family, household, ménage 3. ancestry, clan, dynasty, family tree, kindred, line, lineage, race, tribe 4. business, company, concern, establishment, firm, organization, outfit (*Inf.*), partnership 5. hotel, inn, public house, tavern ~v. 6. accommodate, billet, board, domicile, harbour, lodge, put up, quarter, take in

household n. family, home, house, ménage

housing accommodation, dwellings, homes, houses

hovel cabin, den, hole, hut, shack, shanty, shed

hover 1. be suspended, drift, float, flutter, fly, hang, poise 2. hang about, linger, wait nearby

however after all, anyhow, be that as it may, but, nevertheless, nonetheless, notwithstanding, on the other hand, still, though, yet

howl 1. n. bay, bellow, clamour, cry, groan, hoot, outcry, roar, scream, shriek, ululation, wail, yelp, yowl 2. v. bellow, cry, cry out, lament, quest (*used of hounds*), roar, scream, shout, shriek, ululate, wail, weep, yell, yelp

howler bloomer (*Brit. inf.*), blunder, boner (*Sl.*), boob (*Brit. Sl.*), booboo (*Inf.*), bull (*Sl.*), clanger (*Inf.*), error, malapropism, mistake, schoolboy howler

huddle n. 1. confusion, crowd, disorder, heap, jumble, mass, mess, muddle 2. *Inf.* confab (*Inf.*), conference, discussion, meeting, powwow ~v. 3. cluster, converge, crowd, flock, gather, press, throng 4. crouch, cuddle, curl up, hunch up, make oneself small, nestle, snuggle

hue colour, dye, shade, tincture, tinge, tint, tone

hug v. 1. clasp, cuddle, embrace, enfold, hold close, squeeze, take in one's arms 2. cling to, follow closely, keep close, stay near ~n. 3. bear hug, clasp, clinch (*Sl.*), embrace, squeeze

huge Brobdingnagian, bulky, colossal, enormous, extensive, gargantuan, giant, gigantic, ginormous (*Inf.*), great, immense, jumbo (*Inf.*), mammoth, massive, mega (*Sl.*), monumental, mountainous, prodigious, stupendous, titanic, tremendous, vast
Antonyms insignificant, little, microscopic, minute, petty, puny, small, tiny

hulk derelict, frame, hull, shell, shipwreck, wreck

hull n. 1. body, casing, covering, frame, framework, skeleton 2. husk, peel, pod, rind, shell, shuck, skin

hum 1. bombinate *or* bombilate (*Literary*), buzz, croon, drone, mumble, murmur, purr, sing, throb, thrum, vibrate, whir 2. be active, be busy, bustle, buzz, move, pulsate, pulse, stir, vibrate

human adj. 1. anthropoid, fleshly, manlike, mortal 2. approachable, compassionate, considerate, fallible, forgivable, humane, kind, kindly, natural, understandable, understanding, vulnerable

humane benevolent, benign, charitable, clement, compassionate, forbearing, forgiving, gentle, good, good-natured, kind, kind-hearted, kindly, lenient,

merciful, mild, sympathetic, tender, understanding
Antonyms barbarous, brutal, cruel, inhuman, inhumane, ruthless, uncivilized, unkind, unmerciful, unsympathetic

humanity flesh, Homo sapiens, humankind, human race, man, mankind, men, mortality, people

humble adj. 1. meek, modest, self-effacing, submissive, unassuming, unostentatious, unpretentious 2. common, commonplace, insignificant, low, low-born, lowly, mean, modest, obscure, ordinary, plebeian, poor, simple, undistinguished, unimportant, unpretentious
Antonyms adj. (sense 1) arrogant, assuming, conceited, haughty, immodest, lordly, ostentatious, overbearing, pompous, presumptuous, pretentious, proud, snobbish, superior, vain (sense 2) aristocratic, distinguished, elegant, famous, glorious, high, important, rich, significant, superior, wealthy

humbug n. 1. bluff, cheat, deceit, deception, dodge, feint, fraud, hoax, imposition, imposture, ruse, sham, swindle, trick, trickery, wile 2. charlatan, cheat, con man (Sl.), faker, fraud, impostor, phoney (Sl.), quack, swindler, trickster

humdrum boring, commonplace, dreary, dull, monotonous, mundane, ordinary, repetitious, routine, tedious, tiresome, uneventful, uninteresting, unvaried, wearisome
Antonyms entertaining, exciting, extraordinary, interesting, lively, sexy (Inf.), stimulating

humid clammy, damp, dank, moist, muggy, steamy, sticky, sultry, watery, wet
Antonyms arid, dry, sunny, torrid

humiliate abase, abash, bring low, chagrin, chasten, crush, debase, degrade, discomfit, disgrace, embarrass, humble, make (someone) eat humble pie, mortify, put down (Sl.), shame, subdue, take down a peg (Inf.)
Antonyms elevate, honour, magnify, make proud

humility diffidence, humbleness, lack of pride, lowliness, meekness, modesty, self-abasement, servility, submissiveness, unpretentiousness
Antonyms arrogance, conceit, disdain, haughtiness, pomposity, presumption, pretentiousness, pride, snobbishness, superciliousness, superiority, vanity

humorist comedian, comic, droll, eccentric, funny man, jester, joker, wag, wit

humorous amusing, comic, comical, entertaining, facetious, farcical, funny, hilarious, jocose, jocular, laughable, ludicrous, merry, playful, pleasant, side-splitting, waggish, whimsical, witty
Antonyms earnest, grave, sad, serious, sober, solemn

humour n. 1. amusement, comedy, drollery, facetiousness, fun, funniness, jocularity, ludicrousness, wit 2. comedy, farce, gags (Sl.), jesting, jests, jokes, joking, pleasantry, wisecracks (Inf.), wit, witticisms, wittiness 3. disposition, frame of mind, mood, spirits, temper 4. bent, bias, fancy, freak, mood, propensity, quirk, vagary, whim ~v. 5. accommodate, cosset, favour, flatter, go along with, gratify, indulge, mollify, pamper, spoil
Antonyms n. gravity, grief, melancholy, sadness, seriousness, sobriety, solemnity, sorrow ~v. aggravate, excite, oppose, rouse, stand up to

hump n. bulge, bump, hunch, knob, lump, mound, projection, protrusion, protuberance, swelling

hunch n. feeling, idea, impression, inkling, intuition, premonition, presentiment, suspicion

hunger n. 1. appetite, emptiness, esurience, famine, hungriness, ravenousness, starvation, voracity **2.** appetence, appetite, craving, desire, greediness, itch, lust, yearning, yen (*Inf.*) ~*v.* **3.** crave, desire, hanker, itch, long, pine, starve, thirst, want, wish, yearn

hungry 1. empty, famished, famishing, hollow, peckish (*Inf., chiefly Brit.*), ravenous, sharpset, starved, starving, voracious **2.** athirst, avid, covetous, craving, desirous, eager, greedy, keen, yearning

hunk block, chunk, gobbet, lump, mass, piece, slab, wedge, wodge (*Brit. inf.*)

hunt *v.* **1.** chase, gun for, hound, pursue, stalk, track, trail **2.** ferret about, forage, go in quest of, look, look high and low, rummage through, scour, search, seek, try to find ~*n.* **3.** chase, hunting, investigation, pursuit, quest, search

hurdle *n.* **1.** barricade, barrier, fence, hedge, wall **2.** barrier, complication, difficulty, handicap, hindrance, impediment, obstacle, obstruction, snag, stumbling block

hurl cast, chuck (*Inf.*), fire, fling, heave, launch, let fly, pitch, project, propel, send, shy, sling, throw, toss

hurricane cyclone, gale, storm, tempest, tornado, twister (*U.S. inf.*), typhoon, willy-willy (*Aust.*), windstorm

hurried breakneck, brief, cursory, hasty, hectic, perfunctory, precipitate, quick, rushed, short, slapdash, speedy, superficial, swift

hurry *v.* **1.** dash, fly, get a move on (*Inf.*), lose no time, make haste, rush, scoot, scurry, step on it (*Inf.*) **2.** accelerate, expedite, goad, hasten, hustle, push on, quicken, speed (up), urge ~*n.* **3.** bustle, celerity, commotion, dispatch, expedition, flurry, haste, precipitation, promptitude, quickness, rush, speed, urgency
Antonyms *v.* crawl, creep, dawdle, delay, move slowly, retard, slow, slow down ~*n.* calmness, slowness

hurt *v.* **1.** bruise, damage, disable, harm, impair, injure, mar, spoil, wound **2.** ache, be sore, be tender, burn, pain, smart, sting, throb **3.** afflict, aggrieve, annoy, cut to the quick, distress, grieve, pain, sadden, sting, upset, wound ~*n.* **4.** discomfort, distress, pain, pang, soreness, suffering **5.** bruise, sore, wound
Antonyms *v.* aid, alleviate, benefit, calm, compensate, compliment, console, cure, forward, heal, heighten, help, increase, please, relieve, repair, restore, soothe ~*n.* delight, happiness, joy, pleasure, pride, satisfaction

hush *v.* **1.** mute, muzzle, quieten, shush, silence, still, suppress **2.** allay, appease, calm, compose, mollify, soothe ~*n.* **3.** calm, peace, peacefulness, quiet, silence, still (*Poetic*), stillness, tranquillity

husky croaking, croaky, gruff, guttural, harsh, hoarse, rasping, raucous, rough, throaty

hustle bustle, crowd, elbow, force, hasten, hasten, hurry, impel, jog, jostle, push, rush, shove, thrust

hut cabin, den, hovel, lean-to, refuge, shanty, shed, shelter

hygiene cleanliness, hygienics, sanitary measures, sanitation

hygienic aseptic, clean, disinfected, germ-free, healthy, pure, salutary, sanitary, sterile
Antonyms dirty, filthy, germ-ridden, harmful, insanitary, polluted, unhealthy, unhygienic, unwholesome

hypnotize 1. mesmerize, put in a trance, put to sleep **2.** entrance, fascinate, magnetize, spellbind

hypocrisy cant, deceit, deceitfulness, deception, dissembling, duplicity, falsity, imposture, insincerity, pharisaism, phariseeism, phoneyness (*Sl.*), pretence, sanctimoniousness, speciousness, two-facedness

Antonyms honesty, sincerity, truthfulness

hypocrite charlatan, deceiver, dissembler, fraud, Holy Willie, impostor, Pecksniff, pharisee, phoney (*Sl.*), pretender, Tartuffe, whited sepulchre

hypocritical canting, deceitful, deceptive, dissembling, duplicitous, false, fraudulent, hollow, insincere, Janus-faced, pharisaical, phoney (*Sl.*), sanctimonious, specious, spurious, two-faced

hypothesis assumption, postulate, premise, premiss, proposition, supposition, theory, thesis

hypothetical academic, assumed, conjectural, imaginary, putative, speculative, supposed, theoretical

Antonyms actual, confirmed, established, known, proven, real, true

hysteria agitation, delirium, frenzy, hysterics, madness, panic, unreason

hysterical berserk, beside oneself, convulsive, crazed, distracted, distraught, frantic, frenzied, mad, overwrought, raving, uncontrollable

Antonyms calm, composed, poised, self-possessed

I

icy 1. arctic, biting, bitter, chill, chilling, chilly, cold, freezing, frost-bound, frosty, frozen over, ice-cold, raw **2.** *Fig.* aloof, cold, distant, forbidding, frigid, frosty, glacial, hostile, indifferent, steely, stony, unfriendly, unwelcoming
Antonyms (*sense 1*) blistering, boiling, hot, sizzling, warm (*sense 2*) cordial, friendly, gracious, warm

idea 1. abstraction, concept, conception, conclusion, fancy, impression, judgment, perception, thought, understanding **2.** belief, conviction, doctrine, interpretation, notion, opinion, teaching, view, viewpoint

ideal *n.* **1.** archetype, criterion, epitome, example, exemplar, last word, model, nonpareil, paradigm, paragon, pattern, perfection, prototype, standard, standard of perfection ~*adj.* **2.** archetypal, classic, complete, consummate, model, optimal, perfect, quintessential, supreme **3.** abstract, conceptual, hypothetical, intellectual, mental, theoretical, transcendental
Antonyms *adj.* (*sense 2*) deficient, flawed, impaired, imperfect, unsuitable

idealist *n.* dreamer, romantic, Utopian, visionary

identical alike, corresponding, duplicate, equal, equivalent, indistinguishable, interchangeable, like, matching, selfsame, the same, twin
Antonyms different, disparate, distinct, diverse, separate, unlike

identification 1. cataloguing, classifying, establishment of identity, labelling, naming, pinpointing, recognition **2.** credentials, ID, letters of introduction, papers

identify catalogue, classify, diagnose, label, make out, name, pick out, pinpoint, place, put one's finger on (*Inf.*), recognize, single out, spot, tag

identity distinctiveness, existence, individuality, oneness, particularity, personality, self, selfhood, singularity, uniqueness

idiocy abject stupidity, asininity, cretinism, fatuity, fatuousness, foolishness, imbecility, inanity, insanity, lunacy, senselessness, tomfoolery
Antonyms acumen, sagacity, sanity, sense, soundness, wisdom

idiom 1. expression, locution, phrase, set phrase, turn of phrase **2.** jargon, language, mode of expression, parlance, style, talk, usage, vernacular

idiosyncrasy affectation, characteristic, eccentricity, habit, mannerism, oddity, peculiarity, personal trait, quirk, singularity, trick

idiot airhead (*Sl.*), ass, blockhead, booby, cretin, dimwit (*Inf.*), dunderhead, fool, halfwit, imbecile, mooncalf, moron, nincompoop, nitwit, pillock (*Sl.*), plonker (*Sl.*), simpleton, wally (*Sl.*)

idiotic asinine, crazy, daft (*Inf.*), dumb (*Inf.*), fatuous, foolhardy, foolish, halfwitted, harebrained, imbecile, imbecilic, inane, insane, lunatic, moronic, senseless, stupid, unintelligent
Antonyms brilliant, commonsensical, intelligent, sensible, thoughtful, wise

idle *adj.* **1.** dead, empty, gathering dust, inactive, jobless, mothballed, out of action *or* operation, out of work, redundant, station-

ary, ticking over, unemployed, unoccupied, unused, vacant **2.** indolent, lackadaisical, lazy, shiftless, slothful, sluggish **3.** frivolous, insignificant, irrelevant, nugatory, superficial, trivial, unhelpful, unnecessary ~v. **4.** coast, drift, mark time, shirk, sit back and do nothing, skive (*Brit. sl.*), slack, slow down, take it easy (*Inf.*), vegetate, veg out (*Sl.*)
Antonyms (*senses 1 & 2*) active, busy, employed, energetic, functional, industrious, occupied, operative, working (*sense 3*) important, meaningful

idleness 1. inaction, inactivity, leisure, time on one's hands, unemployment **2.** hibernation, inertia, laziness, shiftlessness, sloth, sluggishness, torpor, vegetating **3.** dilly-dallying (*Inf.*), lazing, loafing, pottering, skiving (*Brit. sl.*), time-wasting, trifling

idol deity, god, graven image, image, pagan symbol

idolize admire, adore, apotheosize, bow down before, deify, dote upon, exalt, glorify, hero-worship, look up to, love, revere, reverence, venerate, worship, worship to excess

ignite burn, burst into flames, catch fire, fire, flare up, inflame, kindle, light, put a match to (*Inf.*), set alight, set fire to, take fire, touch off

ignominious abject, despicable, discreditable, disgraceful, dishonourable, disreputable, humiliating, indecorous, inglorious, mortifying, scandalous, shameful, sorry, undignified
Antonyms creditable, honourable, reputable, worthy

ignorance benightedness, blindness, illiteracy, lack of education, mental darkness, unenlightenment, unintelligence
Antonyms comprehension, enlightenment, insight, intelligence, knowledge, understanding, wisdom

ignorant 1. benighted, blind to, inexperienced, innocent, in the dark about, oblivious, unaware, unconscious, unenlightened, uninformed, uninitiated, unknowing, unschooled, unwitting **2.** green, illiterate, naive, unaware, uncultivated, uneducated, unknowledgeable, unlearned, unlettered, unread, untaught, untrained, untutored
Antonyms astute, aware, brilliant, conscious, cultured, educated, informed, knowledgeable, learned, literate, sagacious, wise

ignore be oblivious to, bury one's head in the sand, cold-shoulder, cut (*Inf.*), disregard, give the cold shoulder to, neglect, overlook, pass over, pay no attention to, reject, send (someone) to Coventry, shut one's eyes to, take no notice of, turn a blind eye to, turn a deaf ear to, turn one's back on
Antonyms acknowledge, heed, note, pay attention to, recognize, regard

ill *adj.* **1.** ailing, dicky (*Sl.*), diseased, funny (*Inf.*), indisposed, infirm, laid up (*Inf.*), not up to snuff (*Inf.*), off-colour, on the sick list (*Inf.*), out of sorts (*Inf.*), poorly (*Inf.*), queasy, queer, seedy (*Inf.*), sick, under the weather (*Inf.*), unhealthy, unwell, valetudinarian **2.** bad, damaging, deleterious, detrimental, evil, foul, harmful, iniquitous, injurious, ruinous, unfortunate, unlucky, vile, wicked, wrong **3.** disturbing, foreboding, inauspicious, ominous, sinister, threatening, unfavourable, unhealthy, unlucky, unpromising, unpropitious, unwholesome ~n. **4.** affliction, harm, hurt, injury, misery, misfortune, pain, trial, tribulation, trouble, unpleasantness, woe **5.** ailment, complaint, disease, disorder, illness, indisposition, infirmity, malady, malaise, sickness **6.** abuse, badness, cruelty, damage, depravity, destruction, evil, ill usage, malice, mischief, suffering, wickedness ~adv. **7.** badly, hard, inauspiciously, poorly, unfavourably, unfortunately, unluckily

Antonyms adj. (sense 1) hale, healthy, strong, well (sense 2) favourable, good ~n. good, honour, kindness ~adv. easily, well

ill-advised foolhardy, foolish, ill-considered, ill-judged, impolitic, imprudent, inappropriate, incautious, indiscreet, injudicious, misguided, overhasty, rash, reckless, short-sighted, thoughtless, unseemly, unwise, wrong-headed

Antonyms appropriate, cautious, discreet, judicious, politic, prudent, seemly, sensible, wise

illegal actionable (Law), banned, black-market, bootleg, criminal, felonious, forbidden, illicit, lawless, outlawed, prohibited, proscribed, unauthorized, unconstitutional, under the counter, unlawful, unlicensed, unofficial, wrongful

Antonyms lawful, legal, licit, permissible

illegality crime, criminality, felony, illegitimacy, illicitness, lawlessness, unlawfulness, wrong, wrongness

illegible crabbed, faint, hard to make out, hieroglyphic, indecipherable, obscure, scrawled, undecipherable, unreadable

Antonyms clear, decipherable, legible, plain, readable

illegitimate 1. illegal, illicit, improper, unauthorized, unconstitutional, unlawful, unsanctioned 2. baseborn (Archaic), bastard, born on the wrong side of the blanket, born out of wedlock, fatherless, misbegotten (Literary), natural, spurious (Rare)

Antonyms (sense 1) authorized, constitutional, lawful, legal, legitimate, proper, sanctioned

ill-fated blighted, doomed, hapless, ill-omened, ill-starred, luckless, star-crossed, unfortunate, unhappy, unlucky

ill feeling animosity, animus, antagonism, bad blood, bitterness, disgruntlement, dissatisfaction, dudgeon (Archaic), enmity, frustration, hard feelings, hostility, ill will, indignation, offence, rancour, resentment

Antonyms amity, benevolence, favour, friendship, good will, satisfaction

ill-founded baseless, empty, groundless, idle, unjustified, unproven, unreliable, unsubstantiated, unsupported

illicit 1. black-market, bootleg, contraband, criminal, felonious, illegal, illegitimate, prohibited, unauthorized, unlawful, unlicensed 2. clandestine, forbidden, furtive, guilty, immoral, improper, wrong

Antonyms above-board, lawful, legal, legitimate, licit, permissible, proper

illiterate benighted, ignorant, uncultured, uneducated, unlettered, untaught, untutored

Antonyms cultured, educated, lettered, literate, taught, tutored

ill-mannered badly behaved, boorish, churlish, coarse, discourteous, ill-behaved, ill-bred, impolite, insolent, loutish, rude, uncivil, uncouth, unmannerly

Antonyms civil, courteous, cultivated, mannerly, polished, polite, refined, well-mannered

illness affliction, ailment, attack, complaint, disability, disease, disorder, ill health, indisposition, infirmity, malady, malaise, poor health, sickness

illogical absurd, fallacious, faulty, inconclusive, inconsistent, incorrect, invalid, irrational, meaningless, senseless, sophistical, specious, spurious, unreasonable, unscientific, unsound

Antonyms coherent, consistent, correct, logical, rational, reasonable, scientific, sound, valid

ill-treat abuse, damage, handle roughly, harass, harm, harry, illuse, injure, knock about, maltreat, mishandle, misuse, oppress, wrong

illuminate 1. brighten, illumine (Literary), irradiate, light, light up **2.** clarify, clear up, elucidate, enlighten, explain, give insight into, instruct, make clear, shed light on

Antonyms (*sense 1*) black out, darken, dim, obscure, overshadow (*sense 2*) befog, cloud, dull, obfuscate, overcast, shade, veil

illuminating enlightening, explanatory, helpful, informative, instructive, revealing

illumination awareness, clarification, edification, enlightenment, insight, inspiration, instruction, perception, revelation, understanding

illusion 1. chimera, daydream, fantasy, figment of the imagination, hallucination, ignis fatuus, mirage, mockery, phantasm, semblance, will-o'-the-wisp **2.** deception, delusion, error, fallacy, false impression, fancy, misapprehension, misconception

Antonyms actuality, reality, truth

illusory *or* **illusive** apparent, Barmecide, beguiling, chimerical, deceitful, deceptive, delusive, fallacious, false, hallucinatory, misleading, mistaken, seeming, sham, unreal, untrue

Antonyms authentic, down-to-earth, factual, genuine, real, reliable, solid, true

illustrate 1. bring home, clarify, demonstrate, elucidate, emphasize, exemplify, exhibit, explain, instance, interpret, make clear, make plain, point up, show **2.** adorn, decorate, depict, draw, ornament, picture, sketch

illustration 1. analogy, case, case in point, clarification, demonstration, elucidation, example, exemplification, explanation, instance, interpretation, specimen **2.** adornment, decoration, figure, picture, plate, sketch

illustrious brilliant, celebrated, distinguished, eminent, exalted, famed, famous, glorious, great, noble, notable, noted, prominent,

remarkable, renowned, resplendent, signal, splendid

ill will acrimony, animosity, animus, antagonism, antipathy, aversion, bad blood, dislike, enmity, envy, grudge, hard feelings, hatred, hostility, malevolence, malice, no love lost, rancour, resentment, spite, unfriendliness, venom

Antonyms amiability, amity, charity, congeniality, cordiality, friendship, good will

image 1. appearance, effigy, figure, icon, idol, likeness, picture, portrait, reflection, representation, statue **2.** conceit, concept, conception, figure, idea, impression, mental picture, perception, trope

imaginable believable, comprehensible, conceivable, credible, likely, plausible, possible, supposable, thinkable, under the sun, within the bounds of possibility

Antonyms impossible, incomprehensible, inconceivable, incredible, unbelievable, unimaginable, unlikely, unthinkable

imaginary assumed, chimerical, dreamlike, fancied, fanciful, fictional, fictitious, hallucinatory, hypothetical, ideal, illusive, illusory, imagined, invented, legendary, made-up, mythological, nonexistent, phantasmal, shadowy, supposed, supposititious, unreal, unsubstantial, visionary

Antonyms actual, factual, genuine, known, proven, real, substantial, tangible, true

imagination creativity, enterprise, fancy, ingenuity, insight, inspiration, invention, inventiveness, originality, resourcefulness, vision, wit, wittiness

imaginative clever, creative, dreamy, enterprising, fanciful, fantastic, ingenious, inspired, inventive, original, poetical, visionary, vivid, whimsical

Antonyms literal, mundane, ordinary, uncreative, unimaginative, uninspired, unoriginal, unpoetical, unromantic

imagine conceive, conceptualize, conjure up, create, devise, dream up (*Inf.*), envisage, fantasize, form a mental picture of, frame, invent, picture, plan, project, scheme, see in the mind's eye, think of, think up, visualize

imbecile 1. *n.* bungler, cretin, dolt, dotard, fool, halfwit, idiot, moron, pillock (*Sl.*), plonker (*Sl.*), thickhead, tosser (*Sl.*), wally (*Sl.*) **2.** *adj.* asinine, fatuous, feeble-minded, foolish, idiotic, imbecilic, inane, ludicrous, moronic, simple, stupid, thick, witless

imitate affect, ape, burlesque, caricature, copy, counterfeit, do (*Inf.*), do an impression of, duplicate, echo, emulate, follow, follow in the footsteps of, follow suit, impersonate, mimic, mirror, mock, parody, personate, repeat, send up (*Brit. inf.*), simulate, spoof (*Inf.*), take a leaf out of (someone's) book, take off (*Inf.*), travesty

imitation *n.* **1.** aping, copy, counterfeit, counterfeiting, duplication, echoing, likeness, mimicry, resemblance, simulation **2.** fake, forgery, impersonation, impression, mockery, parody, reflection, replica, reproduction, sham, substitution, takeoff (*Inf.*), travesty ~*adj.* **3.** artificial, dummy, ersatz, man-made, mock, phoney (*Inf.*), pseudo (*Inf.*), repro, reproduction, sham, simulated, synthetic

Antonyms *adj.* authentic, genuine, original, real, true, valid

imitator aper, copier, copycat (*Inf.*), echo, epigone (*Rare*), follower, impersonator, impressionist, mimic, parrot, shadow

immaculate 1. clean, impeccable, neat, neat as a new pin, spick-and-span, spruce, trim, unexceptionable **2.** above reproach, faultless, flawless, guiltless, incorrupt, innocent, perfect, pure, sinless, spotless, stainless, unblemished, uncontaminated, un-

defiled, unpolluted, unsullied, untarnished, virtuous

Antonyms contaminated, corrupt, dirty, filthy, impeachable, impure, polluted, stained, tainted, unclean

immaterial a matter of indifference, extraneous, impertinent, inapposite, inconsequential, inconsiderable, inessential, insignificant, irrelevant, of little account, of no consequence, of no importance, trifling, trivial, unimportant, unnecessary

immature 1. adolescent, crude, green, imperfect, premature, raw, undeveloped, unfinished, unfledged, unformed, unripe, unseasonable, untimely, young **2.** babyish, callow, childish, inexperienced, infantile, jejune, juvenile, puerile, wet behind the ears (*Inf.*)

Antonyms adult, developed, fully-fledged, mature, mellow, responsible, ripe

immediate 1. instant, instantaneous **2.** adjacent, close, contiguous, direct, near, nearest, next, primary, proximate, recent

Antonyms delayed, distant, far, late, later, postponed, remote, slow

immediately at once, before you could say Jack Robinson (*Inf.*), directly, forthwith, instantly, now, promptly, pronto (*Inf.*), right away, right now, straight away, this instant, this very minute, *tout de suite*, unhesitatingly, without delay, without hesitation

immense Brobdingnagian, colossal, elephantine, enormous, extensive, giant, gigantic, ginormous (*Inf.*), great, huge, illimitable, immeasurable, infinite, interminable, jumbo (*Inf.*), large, mammoth, massive, mega (*Inf.*), monstrous, monumental, prodigious, stupendous, titanic, tremendous, vast

immigrant incomer, newcomer, settler

imminent at hand, brewing, close, coming, fast-approaching, forth-

coming, gathering, impending, in the air, in the offing, looming, menacing, near, nigh (*Archaic*), on the horizon, on the way, threatening
Antonyms delayed, distant, far-off, remote

immobile at a standstill, at rest, fixed, frozen, immobilized, immotile, immovable, like a statue, motionless, rigid, riveted, rooted, stable, static, stationary, stiff, still, stock-still, stolid, unmoving
Antonyms active, mobile, movable, on the move, pliant, portable, vigorous

immobilize bring to a standstill, cripple, disable, freeze, halt, lay up (*Inf.*), paralyse, put out of action, render inoperative, stop, transfix

immoderate egregious, enormous, exaggerated, excessive, exorbitant, extravagant, extreme, inordinate, intemperate, over the odds (*Inf.*), profligate, steep (*Inf.*), uncalled-for, unconscionable, uncontrolled, undue, unjustified, unreasonable, unrestrained, unwarranted, wanton
Antonyms controlled, judicious, mild, moderate, reasonable, restrained, temperate

immoral abandoned, bad, corrupt, debauched, degenerate, depraved, dishonest, dissolute, evil, impure, indecent, iniquitous, lewd, licentious, nefarious, obscene, of easy virtue, pornographic, profligate, reprobate, sinful, unchaste, unethical, unprincipled, vicious, vile, wicked, wrong
Antonyms conscientious, good, honourable, inoffensive, law-abiding, moral, pure, upright, virtuous

immortal *adj.* **1.** abiding, constant, death-defying, deathless, endless, enduring, eternal, everlasting, imperishable, incorruptible, indestructible, lasting, perennial, perpetual, sempiternal (*Literary*), timeless, undying, unfading ~*n.* **2.** god, goddess, Olympian **3.**

genius, great (*Usually plural*), hero, paragon
Antonyms *adj.* ephemeral, fading, fleeting, mortal, passing, perishable, temporary, transitory

immovable 1. fast, firm, fixed, immutable, jammed, rooted, secure, set, stable, stationary, stuck, unbudgeable **2.** adamant, constant, impassive, inflexible, obdurate, resolute, steadfast, stony-hearted, unchangeable, unimpressionable, unshakable, unshaken, unwavering, unyielding
Antonyms (*sense 2*) changeable, flexible, impressionable, movable, shakable, wavering, yielding

immune clear, exempt, free, insusceptible, invulnerable, let off (*Inf.*), not affected, not liable, not subject, proof (against), protected, resistant, safe, unaffected
Antonyms exposed, liable, prone, susceptible, unprotected, vulnerable

immunity amnesty, charter, exemption, exoneration, franchise, freedom, indemnity, invulnerability, liberty, licence, prerogative, privilege, release, right
Antonyms exposure, liability, openness, proneness, susceptibility, vulnerability

impact *n.* bang, blow, bump, collision, concussion, contact, crash, force, jolt, knock, shock, smash, stroke, thump

impair blunt, damage, debilitate, decrease, deteriorate, diminish, enervate, enfeeble, harm, hinder, injure, lessen, mar, reduce, spoil, undermine, vitiate, weaken, worsen
Antonyms ameliorate, amend, better, enhance, facilitate, improve, strengthen

impart communicate, convey, disclose, discover, divulge, make known, pass on, relate, reveal, tell

impartial detached, disinterested, equal, equitable, even-handed, fair, just, neutral, nondiscriminating, nonpartisan, objective, open-minded, unbiased, unprejudiced, without fear or favour **Antonyms** biased, bigoted, influenced, partial, prejudiced, swayed, unfair, unjust

impasse blind alley (*Inf.*), dead end, deadlock, stalemate, stand-off, standstill

impassioned animated, ardent, blazing, excited, fervent, fervid, fiery, furious, glowing, heated, inflamed, inspired, intense, passionate, rousing, stirring, vehement, violent, vivid, warm, worked up

impatience haste, hastiness, heat, impetuosity, intolerance, irritability, irritableness, quick temper, rashness, shortness, snappiness, vehemence, violence

impatient 1. abrupt, brusque, curt, demanding, edgy, hasty, hot-tempered, indignant, intolerant, irritable, quick-tempered, snappy, sudden, testy, vehement, violent **2.** agog, athirst, chafing, eager, fretful, headlong, impetuous, like a cat on hot bricks (*Inf.*), restless, straining at the leash **Antonyms** (*sense 1*) calm, composed, cool, easy-going, imperturbable, patient, quiet, serene, tolerant

impeach accuse, arraign, blame, censure, charge, criminate (*Rare*), denounce, indict, tax

impeccable above suspicion, blameless, exact, exquisite, faultless, flawless, immaculate, incorrupt, innocent, irreproachable, perfect, precise, pure, sinless, stainless, unblemished, unerring, unimpeachable **Antonyms** blameworthy, corrupt, cursory, defective, deficient, faulty, flawed, shallow, sinful, superficial

impede bar, block, brake, check, clog, curb, delay, disrupt, hamper, hinder, hold up, obstruct, restrain, retard, slow (down), stop, throw a spanner in the works (*Inf.*), thwart

Antonyms advance, aid, assist, further, help, promote

impediment bar, barrier, block, check, clog, curb, defect, difficulty, encumbrance, hindrance, obstacle, obstruction, snag, stumbling block **Antonyms** advantage, aid, assistance, benefit, encouragement, relief, support

impel actuate, chivy, compel, constrain, drive, force, goad, incite, induce, influence, inspire, instigate, motivate, move, oblige, power, prod, prompt, propel, push, require, spur, stimulate, urge **Antonyms** check, discourage, dissuade, rebuff, repulse, restrain

impending approaching, brewing, coming, forthcoming, gathering, hovering, imminent, in the offing, looming, menacing, near, nearing, on the horizon, threatening

imperative compulsory, crucial, essential, exigent, indispensable, insistent, obligatory, pressing, urgent, vital **Antonyms** avoidable, discretional, nonessential, optional, unimportant, unnecessary

imperceptible faint, fine, gradual, impalpable, inappreciable, inaudible, indiscernible, indistinguishable, infinitesimal, insensible, invisible, microscopic, minute, shadowy, slight, small, subtle, tiny, undetectable, unnoticeable **Antonyms** audible, detectable, discernible, distinguishable, noticeable, perceptible, visible

imperfect broken, damaged, defective, deficient, faulty, flawed, immature, impaired, incomplete, inexact, limited, partial, patchy, rudimentary, sketchy, undeveloped, unfinished **Antonyms** complete, developed, exact, finished, flawless, perfect

imperfection blemish, defect, deficiency, failing, fallibility, fault, flaw, foible, frailty, inadequacy, incompleteness, infirmity, insufficiency, peccadillo, shortcoming, stain, taint, weakness, weak point

Antonyms adequacy, completeness, consummation, excellence, faultlessness, flawlessness, perfection, sufficiency

imperial 1. kingly, majestic, princely, queenly, regal, royal, sovereign 2. august, exalted, grand, great, high, imperious, lofty, magnificent, noble, superior, supreme

imperil endanger, expose, hazard, jeopardize, risk

Antonyms care for, guard, protect, safeguard, secure

impersonal aloof, bureaucratic, businesslike, cold, detached, dispassionate, formal, inhuman, neutral, remote

Antonyms friendly, intimate, outgoing, personal, warm

impersonate act, ape, caricature, do (*Inf.*), do an impression of, enact, imitate, masquerade as, mimic, parody, pass oneself off as, personate, pose as (*Inf.*), take off (*Inf.*)

impertinence assurance, audacity, backchat (*Inf.*), boldness, brass neck (*Sl.*), brazenness, cheek (*Inf.*), disrespect, effrontery, forwardness, impudence, incivility, insolence, nerve (*Inf.*), pertness, presumption, rudeness, sauce (*Inf.*)

impertinent bold, brazen, cheeky (*Inf.*), discourteous, disrespectful, flip (*Inf.*), forward, fresh (*Inf.*), impolite, impudent, insolent, interfering, pert, presumptuous, rude, saucy (*Inf.*), uncivil, unmannerly

Antonyms mannerly, polite, respectful

impetuous ardent, eager, fierce, furious, hasty, headlong, impassioned, impulsive, passionate, precipitate, rash, spontaneous, spur-of-the-moment, unbridled, unplanned, unpremeditated, unreflecting, unrestrained, unthinking, vehement, violent

Antonyms cautious, leisurely, mild, slow, wary

impetus 1. catalyst, goad, impulse, impulsion, incentive, motivation, push, spur, stimulus 2. energy, force, momentum, power

impish devilish, elfin, mischievous, prankish, puckish, rascally, roguish, sportive, waggish

implant inculcate, infix, infuse, inseminate, instil, sow

implement 1. *n.* agent, apparatus, appliance, device, gadget, instrument, tool, utensil 2. *v.* bring about, carry out, complete, effect, enforce, execute, fulfil, perform, put into action *or* effect, realize

Antonyms *v.* delay, hamper, hinder, impede, weaken

implicate associate, compromise, concern, embroil, entangle, imply, include, incriminate, inculpate, involve, mire, tie up with

Antonyms acquit, disentangle, dissociate, eliminate, exclude, exculpate, rule out

implication 1. association, connection, entanglement, incrimination, involvement 2. conclusion, inference, innuendo, meaning, overtone, presumption, ramification, significance, signification, suggestion

implicit contained, implied, inferred, inherent, latent, tacit, taken for granted, undeclared, understood, unspoken

Antonyms declared, explicit, expressed, obvious, patent, spoken, stated

implied hinted at, implicit, indirect, inherent, insinuated, suggested, tacit, undeclared, unexpressed, unspoken, unstated

implore beg, beseech, conjure, crave, entreat, go on bended knee to, importune, plead with, pray, solicit, supplicate

imply 1. connote, give (someone) to understand, hint, insinuate, intimate, signify, suggest 2. betoken, denote, entail, evidence, import, include, indicate, involve, mean, point to, presuppose

impolite bad-mannered, boorish, churlish, discourteous, disrespectful, ill-bred, ill-mannered, indecorous, indelicate, insolent, loutish, rough, rude, uncivil, ungallant, ungentlemanly, ungracious, unladylike, unmannerly, unrefined
Antonyms courteous, decorous, gallant, gracious, mannerly, polite, refined, respectful, well-bred

importance 1. concern, consequence, import, interest, moment, momentousness, significance, substance, value, weight 2. distinction, eminence, esteem, influence, mark, pre-eminence, prestige, prominence, standing, status, usefulness, worth

important 1. far-reaching, grave, large, material, meaningful, momentous, of substance, primary, salient, serious, signal, significant, substantial, urgent, weighty 2. eminent, foremost, high-level, high-ranking, influential, leading, notable, noteworthy, of note, outstanding, powerful, pre-eminent, prominent, seminal
Antonyms inconsequential, insignificant, minor, needless, negligible, secondary, trivial, undistinctive, unimportant, unnecessary

impose decree, establish, exact, fix, institute, introduce, lay, levy, ordain, place, promulgate, put, set

imposing august, commanding, dignified, effective, grand, impressive, majestic, stately, striking
Antonyms insignificant, mean, modest, ordinary, petty, poor, unimposing

imposition 1. application, decree, introduction, laying on, levying, promulgation 2. cheek (*Inf.*), encroachment, intrusion, liberty, presumption

impossible beyond one, beyond the bounds of possibility, hopeless, impracticable, inconceivable, not to be thought of, out of the question, unachievable, unattainable, unobtainable, unthinkable
Antonyms conceivable, imaginable, likely, plausible, possible, reasonable

impostor charlatan, cheat, deceiver, fake, fraud, hypocrite, impersonator, knave (*Archaic*), phoney (*Sl.*), pretender, quack, rogue, sham, trickster

impotence disability, enervation, feebleness, frailty, helplessness, inability, inadequacy, incapacity, incompetence, ineffectiveness, inefficacy, inefficiency, infirmity, paralysis, powerlessness, uselessness, weakness
Antonyms ability, adequacy, competence, effectiveness, efficacy, efficiency, powerfulness, strength, usefulness

impotent disabled, emasculate, enervated, feeble, frail, helpless, incapable, incapacitated, incompetent, ineffective, infirm, nerveless, paralysed, powerless, unable, unmanned, weak
Antonyms able, capable, competent, effective, manned, potent, powerful, strong

impoverished bankrupt, destitute, distressed, impecunious, indigent, in reduced *or* straitened circumstances, necessitous, needy, on one's uppers, penurious, poverty-stricken, ruined, straitened
Antonyms affluent, rich, wealthy, well-off

impracticable 1. impossible, out of the question, unachievable, unattainable, unfeasible, unworkable 2. awkward, impractical, inapplicable, inconvenient, unserviceable, unsuitable, useless
Antonyms feasible, possible, practicable, practical, serviceable, suitable

impractical 1. impossible, impracticable, inoperable, nonviable, unrealistic, unserviceable, unworkable, visionary, wild 2. idealistic, romantic, starry-eyed, unbusinesslike, unrealistic, visionary

Antonyms (*sense 1*) possible, practical, serviceable, viable, workable (*sense 2*) down-to-earth, realistic, sensible

imprecise ambiguous, blurred round the edges, careless, equivocal, estimated, fluctuating, hazy, ill-defined, inaccurate, indefinite, indeterminate, inexact, inexplicit, loose, rough, sloppy (*Inf.*), vague, wide of the mark, woolly

Antonyms accurate, careful, definite, determinate, exact, explicit, precise

impress affect, excite, grab (*Sl.*), influence, inspire, make an impression, move, stir, strike, sway, touch

impression 1. effect, feeling, impact, influence, reaction, sway **2.** belief, concept, conviction, fancy, feeling, funny feeling (*Inf.*), hunch, idea, memory, notion, opinion, recollection, sense, suspicion **3.** imitation, impersonation, parody, send-up (*Brit. inf.*), takeoff (*Inf.*)

impressive affecting, exciting, forcible, moving, powerful, stirring, touching

Antonyms ordinary, unimposing, unimpressive, uninspiring, unmemorable, weak

imprint 1. *n.* impression, indentation, mark, print, sign, stamp **2.** *v.* engrave, establish, etch, fix, impress, print, stamp

imprison confine, constrain, detain, immure, incarcerate, intern, jail, lock up, put away, put under lock and key, send down (*Inf.*), send to prison

Antonyms discharge, emancipate, free, liberate, release

imprisonment confinement, custody, detention, durance (*Archaic*), duress, incarceration, internment, porridge (*Sl.*)

improbability doubt, doubtfulness, dubiety, uncertainty, unlikelihood

improbable doubtful, dubious,

fanciful, far-fetched, implausible, questionable, unbelievable, uncertain, unconvincing, unlikely, weak

Antonyms certain, convincing, doubtless, likely, plausible, probable, reasonable

impromptu *adj.* ad-lib, extemporaneous, extempore, extemporized, improvised, offhand, off the cuff (*Inf.*), spontaneous, unpremeditated, unprepared, unrehearsed, unscripted, unstudied

Antonyms considered, planned, premeditated, prepared, rehearsed

improper 1. impolite, indecent, indecorous, indelicate, off-colour, risqué, smutty, suggestive, unbecoming, unfitting, unseemly, untoward, vulgar **2.** abnormal, erroneous, false, inaccurate, incorrect, irregular, wrong

Antonyms (*sense 1*) becoming, decent, decorous, delicate, fitting, proper, seemly

impropriety 1. bad taste, immodesty, incongruity, indecency, indecorum, unsuitability, vulgarity **2.** blunder, faux pas, gaffe, gaucherie, mistake, slip, solecism

Antonyms (*sense 1*) decency, decorum, delicacy, modesty, propriety, suitability

improve advance, ameliorate, amend, augment, better, correct, face-lift, help, mend, polish, rectify, touch up, upgrade **2.** develop, enhance, gain strength, increase, look up, make strides, perk up, pick up, progress, rally, reform, rise, take a turn for the better (*Inf.*), take on a new lease of life (*Inf.*)

Antonyms damage, harm, impair, injure, mar, worsen

improvement 1. advancement, amelioration, amendment, augmentation, betterment, correction, face-lift, gain, rectification **2.** advance, development, enhancement, furtherance, increase, progress, rally, recovery, reformation, rise, upswing

improvise 1. ad-lib, coin, extemporize, invent, play it by ear (*Inf.*), speak off the cuff (*Inf.*) 2. concoct, contrive, devise, make do, throw together

imprudent careless, foolhardy, foolish, heedless, ill-advised, ill-considered, ill-judged, impolitic, improvident, incautious, inconsiderate, indiscreet, injudicious, irresponsible, overhasty, rash, reckless, temerarious, unthinking, unwise
Antonyms careful, cautious, considerate, discreet, judicious, politic, provident, prudent, responsible, wise

impudence assurance, audacity, backchat (*Inf.*), boldness, brass neck (*Sl.*), brazenness, bumptiousness, cheek (*Inf.*), effrontery, face (*Inf.*), impertinence, insolence, lip (*Sl.*), nerve (*Inf.*), pertness, presumption, rudeness, sauciness (*Inf.*), shamelessness

impudent audacious, bold, bold-faced, brazen, bumptious, cheeky (*Inf.*), cocky (*Inf.*), forward, fresh (*Inf.*), immodest, impertinent, insolent, pert, presumptuous, rude, saucy (*Inf.*), shameless
Antonyms courteous, modest, polite, respectful, retiring, self-effacing, timid, well-behaved

impulse catalyst, force, impetus, momentum, movement, pressure, push, stimulus, surge, thrust

impulsive devil-may-care, emotional, hasty, headlong, impetuous, instinctive, intuitive, passionate, precipitate, quick, rash, spontaneous, unconsidered, unpredictable, unpremeditated
Antonyms arresting, calculating, cautious, considered, cool, deliberate, halting, planned, premeditated, rehearsed, restrained

impure 1. admixed, adulterated, alloyed, debased, mixed, unrefined 2. contaminated, defiled, dirty, filthy, foul, infected, polluted, sullied, tainted, unclean, unwholesome, vitiated
Antonyms (*sense 2*) clean, immaculate, spotless, undefiled, unsullied

impurity 1. admixture, adulteration, mixture 2. befoulment, contamination, defilement, dirtiness, filth, foulness, infection, pollution, taint, uncleanness

imputation accusation, ascription, aspersion, attribution, blame, censure, charge, insinuation, reproach, slander, slur

inability disability, disqualification, impotence, inadequacy, incapability, incapacity, incompetence, ineptitude, powerlessness
Antonyms ability, adequacy, capability, capacity, competence, potential, power, talent

inaccessible impassable, out of reach, out of the way, remote, unapproachable, unattainable, un-get-at-able (*Inf.*), unreachable
Antonyms accessible, approachable, attainable, reachable

inaccurate careless, defective, discrepant, erroneous, faulty, imprecise, incorrect, in error, inexact, mistaken, out, unfaithful, unreliable, unsound, wide of the mark, wild, wrong
Antonyms accurate, correct, exact, precise, reliable, sound

inactive abeyant, dormant, idle, immobile, inert, inoperative, jobless, kicking one's heels, latent, mothballed, out of service, out of work, unemployed, unoccupied, unused
Antonyms employed, mobile, occupied, operative, running, used, working

inactivity 1. dormancy, hibernation, immobility, inaction, passivity, unemployment 2. dilatoriness, *dolce far niente*, dullness, heaviness, indolence, inertia, inertness, lassitude, laziness, lethargy, quiescence, sloth, sluggishness, stagnation, torpor, vegetation
Antonyms action, activeness, bustle, employment, exertion, mobility, movement

inadequate 1. defective, deficient, faulty, imperfect, incommensurate, incomplete, insubstantial, insufficient, meagre, niggardly, scanty, short, sketchy, skimpy, sparse **2.** found wanting, inapt, incapable, incompetent, not up to scratch (*Inf.*), unequal, unfitted, unqualified

Antonyms (*sense 1*) adequate, ample, complete, perfect, satisfactory, substantial, sufficient (*sense 2*) apt, capable, competent, equal, fit, qualified

inadmissible immaterial, improper, inappropriate, incompetent, irrelevant, unacceptable, unallowable, unqualified, unreasonable

inadvisable ill-advised, impolitic, imprudent, inexpedient, injudicious, unwise

inane asinine, daft (*Inf.*), devoid of intelligence, empty, fatuous, frivolous, futile, idiotic, imbecilic, mindless, puerile, senseless, silly, stupid, trifling, unintelligent, vacuous, vain, vapid, worthless

inanimate cold, dead, defunct, extinct, inactive, inert, insensate, insentient, lifeless, quiescent, soulless, spiritless

Antonyms active, alive, animate, lively, living, moving

inapplicable inapposite, inappropriate, inapt, irrelevant, unsuitable, unsuited

Antonyms applicable, apposite, appropriate, apt, pertinent, relevant, suitable

inappropriate disproportionate, ill-fitted, ill-suited, ill-timed, improper, incongruous, malapropos, out of place, tasteless, unbecoming, unbefitting, unfit, unfitting, unseemly, unsuitable, untimely

Antonyms appropriate, becoming, congruous, fitting, proper, seemly, suitable, timely

inapt 1. ill-fitted, ill-suited, inapposite, inappropriate, infelicitous, unsuitable, unsuited **2.** awkward, clumsy, dull, gauche, incompetent, inept, inexpert, maladroit, slow, stupid

Antonyms (*sense 1*) apposite, appropriate, apt, felicitous, suitable, suited

inarticulate 1. blurred, incoherent, incomprehensible, indistinct, muffled, mumbled, unclear, unintelligible **2.** dumb, mute, silent, speechless, tongue-tied, unspoken, unuttered, unvoiced, voiceless, wordless **3.** faltering, halting, hesitant, poorly spoken

Antonyms (*senses 1 & 3*) articulate, clear, coherent, comprehensible, intelligible, well-spoken

inattentive absent-minded, careless, distracted, distrait, dreamy, heedless, inadvertent, neglectful, negligent, preoccupied, regardless, remiss, thoughtless, unheeding, unmindful, unobservant, vague

Antonyms attentive, aware, careful, considerate, heeding, mindful, observant, thoughtful

inaudible indistinct, low, mumbling, out of earshot, stifled, unheard

Antonyms audible, clear, discernible, distinct, perceptible

inaugurate 1. begin, commence, get under way, initiate, institute, introduce, kick off (*Inf.*), launch, originate, set in motion, set up, usher in **2.** induct, install, instate, invest

inauguration initiation, institution, launch, launching, opening, setting up

incalculable boundless, countless, enormous, immense, incomputable, inestimable, infinite, innumerable, limitless, measureless, numberless, uncountable, untold, vast, without number

incapable feeble, inadequate, incompetent, ineffective, inept, inexpert, insufficient, not equal to, not up to, unfit, unfitted, unqualified, weak

Antonyms adequate, capable, competent, efficient, expert, fit, qualified, sufficient

incapacitate cripple, disable, disqualify, immobilize, lay up (*Inf.*), paralyse, prostrate, put out of action (*Inf.*), scupper (*Brit. sl.*), unfit (*Rare*)

incapacity disqualification, feebleness, impotence, inability, inadequacy, incapability, incompetency, ineffectiveness, powerlessness, unfitness, weakness

incautious careless, hasty, heedless, ill-advised, ill-judged, improvident, imprudent, impulsive, inconsiderate, indiscreet, injudicious, negligent, precipitate, rash, reckless, thoughtless, unguarded, unthinking, unwary
Antonyms careful, cautious, considerate, discreet, guarded, heedful, judicious, prudent, thoughtful, wary

incentive bait, carrot (*Inf.*), encouragement, enticement, goad, impetus, impulse, inducement, lure, motivation, motive, spur, stimulant, stimulus
Antonyms deterrent, discouragement, disincentive, dissuasion, warning

incessant ceaseless, constant, continual, continuous, endless, eternal, everlasting, interminable, never-ending, nonstop, perpetual, persistent, relentless, unbroken, unceasing, unending, unrelenting, unremitting
Antonyms infrequent, intermittent, occasional, periodic, rare, sporadic

incident 1. adventure, circumstance, episode, event, fact, happening, matter, occasion, occurrence 2. brush, clash, commotion, confrontation, contretemps, disturbance, mishap, scene, skirmish

incidental accidental, casual, chance, fortuitous, odd, random

incipient beginning, commencing, developing, embryonic, inceptive, inchoate, nascent, originating, starting

incision cut, gash, notch, opening, slash, slit

incisive 1. acute, keen, penetrating, perspicacious, piercing, trenchant 2. acid, biting, caustic, cutting, mordant, sarcastic, sardonic, satirical, severe, sharp
Antonyms (*sense 1*) dense, dull, superficial, vague, woolly

incite agitate for *or* against, animate, drive, egg on, encourage, excite, foment, goad, impel, inflame, instigate, prompt, provoke, put up to, rouse, set on, spur, stimulate, stir up, urge, whip up
Antonyms dampen, deter, discourage, dishearten, dissuade, restrain

incitement agitation, encouragement, goad, impetus, impulse, inducement, instigation, motivation, motive, prompting, provocation, spur, stimulus

incivility bad manners, boorishness, discourteousness, discourtesy, disrespect, ill-breeding, impoliteness, rudeness, unmannerliness
Antonyms civility, courteousness, courtesy, good manners, mannerliness, politeness, respect

inclement bitter, boisterous, foul, harsh, intemperate, rigorous, rough, severe, stormy, tempestuous
Antonyms balmy, calm, clement, fine, mild, pleasant, temperate

inclination affection, aptitude, bent, bias, desire, disposition, fancy, fondness, leaning, liking, partiality, penchant, predilection, predisposition, prejudice, proclivity, proneness, propensity, stomach, taste, tendency, turn, turn of mind, wish
Antonyms antipathy, aversion, disinclination, dislike, revulsion

incline v. 1. be disposed *or* predisposed, bias, influence, persuade, predispose, prejudice, sway, tend, turn 2. bend, bevel, cant, deviate, diverge, lean, slant, slope, tend, tilt, tip, veer ~n. 3. acclivity, ascent, declivity, descent, dip, grade, gradient, ramp, rise, slope

inclined apt, disposed, given, liable, likely, minded, of a mind (*Inf.*), predisposed, prone, willing

include comprehend, comprise, contain, cover, embody, embrace, encompass, incorporate, involve, subsume, take in, take into account

Antonyms eliminate, exclude, leave out, omit, rule out

inclusion addition, incorporation, insertion

Antonyms exception, exclusion, omission, rejection

inclusive across-the-board, all-embracing, all in, all together, blanket, catch-all (*Chiefly U.S.*), comprehensive, full, general, global, *in toto*, overall, sweeping, umbrella, without exception

Antonyms confined, exclusive, limited, narrow, restricted, unique

incoherent confused, disconnected, disjointed, disordered, inarticulate, inconsistent, jumbled, loose, muddled, rambling, stammering, stuttering, unconnected, uncoordinated, unintelligible, wandering, wild

Antonyms coherent, connected, intelligible, logical, rational

income earnings, gains, interest, means, pay, proceeds, profits, receipts, revenue, salary, takings, wages

incomparable beyond compare, inimitable, matchless, paramount, peerless, superlative, supreme, transcendent, unequalled, unmatched, unparalleled, unrivalled

incompatible antagonistic, antipathetic, conflicting, contradictory, discordant, discrepant, disparate, ill-assorted, incongruous, inconsistent, inconsonant, irreconcilable, mismatched, uncongenial, unsuitable, unsuited

Antonyms alike, appropriate, compatible, congenial, consistent, harmonious, reconcilable, suitable, suited

incompetent bungling, floundering, incapable, incapacitated, ineffectual, inept, inexpert, insufficient, skill-less, unable, unfit, unfitted, unskilful, useless

Antonyms able, capable, competent, expert, fit, proficient, skilful

incomplete broken, defective, deficient, fragmentary, imperfect, insufficient, lacking, partial, short, unaccomplished, undeveloped, undone, unexecuted, unfinished, wanting

Antonyms accomplished, complete, developed, finished, perfect, unified, whole

incomprehensible above one's head, all Greek to (*Inf.*), baffling, beyond comprehension, beyond one's grasp, enigmatic, impenetrable, inconceivable, inscrutable, mysterious, obscure, opaque, perplexing, puzzling, unfathomable, unimaginable, unintelligible, unthinkable

inconceivable beyond belief, impossible, incomprehensible, incredible, mind-boggling (*Sl.*), not to be thought of, out of the question, staggering (*Inf.*), unbelievable, unheard-of, unimaginable, unknowable, unthinkable

Antonyms believable, comprehensible, conceivable, credible, imaginable, likely, plausible, possible, reasonable

inconclusive ambiguous, indecisive, indeterminate, open, uncertain, unconvincing, undecided, unsettled, up in the air (*Inf.*), vague

incongruous absurd, conflicting, contradictory, contrary, dissonant, discordant, extraneous, improper, inappropriate, inapt, incoherent, incompatible, inconsistent, out of keeping, out of place, unbecoming, unsuitable, unsuited

inconsiderate careless, indelicate, insensitive, intolerant, rude, self-centred, selfish, tactless, thoughtless, uncharitable, ungracious, unkind, unthinking

Antonyms attentive, careful, considerate, gracious, kind, sensitive, tactful, thoughtful, tolerant

inconsistency contrariety, disagreement, discrepancy, disparity, divergence, incompatibility, incongruity, inconsonance, paradox, variance

inconsistent 1. at odds, at variance, conflicting, contradictory, contrary, discordant, discrepant, incoherent, incompatible, in conflict, incongruous, irreconcilable, out of step **2.** capricious, changeable, erratic, fickle, inconstant, irregular, unpredictable, unstable, unsteady, vagarious (*Rare*), variable

Antonyms (*sense 1*) coherent, compatible, homogeneous, orderly, reconcilable, uniform (*sense 2*) consistent, constant, predictable, reliable, stable, steady, unchanging

inconspicuous camouflaged, hidden, insignificant, modest, muted, ordinary, plain, quiet, retiring, unassuming, unnoticeable, unobtrusive, unostentatious

Antonyms conspicuous, noticeable, obtrusive, obvious, significant, visible

inconvenience *n.* annoyance, awkwardness, bother, difficulty, disadvantage, disruption, disturbance, drawback, fuss, hindrance, nuisance, trouble, uneasiness, upset, vexation

inconvenient annoying, awkward, bothersome, disadvantageous, disturbing, embarrassing, inopportune, tiresome, troublesome, unseasonable, unsuitable, untimely, vexatious

Antonyms convenient, handy, opportune, seasonable, suitable, timely

incorporate absorb, amalgamate, assimilate, blend, coalesce, combine, consolidate, embody, fuse, include, integrate, merge, mix, subsume, unite

incorrect erroneous, false, faulty, flawed, improper, inaccurate, inappropriate, inexact, mistaken, out, specious, unfitting, unsuitable, untrue, wide of the mark (*Inf.*), wrong

Antonyms accurate, correct, exact, faultless, fitting, flawless, right, suitable, true

incorrigible hardened, hopeless, incurable, intractable, inveterate, irredeemable, unreformed

increase 1. *v.* add to, advance, aggrandize, amplify, augment, boost, build up, develop, dilate, enhance, enlarge, escalate, expand, extend, grow, heighten, inflate, intensify, magnify, mount, multiply, proliferate, prolong, raise, snowball, spread, step up (*Inf.*), strengthen, swell, wax **2.** *n.* addition, augmentation, boost, development, enlargement, escalation, expansion, extension, gain, growth, increment, intensification, rise, upsurge, upturn

Antonyms *v.* abate, abbreviate, abridge, condense, curtail, decline, decrease, deflate, diminish, dwindle, lessen, reduce, shorten, shrink

incredible absurd, beyond belief, far-fetched, implausible, impossible, improbable, inconceivable, preposterous, unbelievable, unimaginable, unthinkable

incredulous disbelieving, distrustful, doubtful, doubting, dubious, mistrustful, sceptical, suspicious, unbelieving, unconvinced

Antonyms believing, credulous, gullible, naive, trusting, unsuspecting

incriminate accuse, arraign, blacken the name of, blame, charge, impeach, implicate, inculpate, indict, involve, point the finger at (*Inf.*), stigmatize

incur arouse, bring (upon oneself), contract, draw, earn, expose oneself to, gain, induce, lay oneself open to, meet with, provoke

incurable *adj.* **1.** dyed-in-the-wool, hopeless, incorrigible, inveterate **2.** fatal, inoperable, irrecoverable, irremediable, remediless, terminal

indebted beholden, grateful, in debt, obligated, obliged, under an obligation

indecency bawdiness, coarseness, crudity, foulness, grossness, immodesty, impropriety, impurity, indecorum, indelicacy, lewdness, licentiousness, obscenity, outrageousness, pornog-

raphy, smut, smuttiness, un~
seemliness, vileness, vulgarity
Antonyms decency, decorum,
delicacy, modesty, propriety, pu~
rity, seemliness

indecent blue, coarse, crude,
dirty, filthy, foul, gross, immod~
est, improper, impure, indelicate,
lewd, licentious, pornographic,
salacious, scatological, smutty,
vile
Antonyms decent, delicate,
modest, pure, respectable, taste~
ful

indecision ambivalence, doubt,
hesitancy, hesitation, indecisive~
ness, irresolution, shilly-shallying
(*Inf.*), uncertainty, vacillation,
wavering

indecisive doubtful, faltering,
hesitating, in two minds (*Inf.*),
irresolute, pussyfooting (*Inf.*),
tentative, uncertain, undecided,
undetermined, vacillating,
wavering
Antonyms certain, decided, de~
termined, positive, resolute, un~
hesitating

indeed actually, certainly, doubt~
lessly, in point of fact, in truth,
positively, really, strictly, to be
sure, truly, undeniably, undoubt~
edly, verily (*Archaic*), veritably

indefensible faulty, inexcusable,
insupportable, unforgivable, un~
justifiable, unpardonable, unten~
able, unwarrantable, wrong
Antonyms defensible, excusable,
forgivable, justifiable, legitimate,
pardonable, supportable, tenable,
warrantable

indelible enduring, indestructible,
ineffaceable, ineradicable, inex~

pungible, inextirpable, ingrained,
lasting, permanent
Antonyms eradicable, erasable,
impermanent, removable, short-
lived, temporary, washable

indelicate blue, coarse, crude,
embarrassing, gross, immodest,
improper, indecent, indecorous,
low, near the knuckle (*Inf.*), ob~
scene, off-colour, offensive, ris~
qué, rude, suggestive, tasteless,
unbecoming, unseemly, unto~
ward, vulgar
Antonyms becoming, decent,
decorous, delicate, modest,
proper, refined, seemly

independence autarchy,
autonomy, freedom, home rule,
liberty, self-determination, self-
government, self-reliance, self-
rule, self-sufficiency, separation,
sovereignty
Antonyms bondage, dependence,
subjection, subjugation, subor~
dination, subservience

independent absolute, free, lib~
erated, separate, unconnected,
unconstrained, uncontrolled, un~
related

independently alone, autono~
mously, by oneself, individually,
on one's own, separately, solo,
unaided

indescribable beggaring de~
scription, beyond description,
beyond words, incommunicable,
indefinable, ineffable, inexpress~
ible, unutterable

indestructible abiding, durable,
enduring, everlasting, immortal,
imperishable, incorruptible, in~
delible, indissoluble, lasting, non-
perishable, permanent, unbreak~
able, unfading
Antonyms breakable, corrup~
tible, destructible, fading, imper~
manent, mortal, perishable

indeterminate imprecise, incon~
clusive, indefinite, inexact, un~
certain, undefined, undeter~
mined, unfixed, unspecified, un~
stipulated, vague

index 1. clue, guide, indication,
mark, sign, symptom, token 2.

indefinite ambiguous, confused,
doubtful, equivocal, evasive,
general, ill-defined, imprecise,
indeterminate, indistinct, inex~
act, loose, obscure, uncertain,
unclear, undefined, undeter~
mined, unfixed, unknown, unlim~
ited, unsettled, vague
Antonyms certain, clear, defi~
nite, determinate, distinct, exact,
fixed, settled, specific

director, forefinger, hand, indicator, needle, pointer

indicate add up to (*Inf.*), bespeak, be symptomatic of, betoken, denote, evince, imply, manifest, point to, reveal, show, signify, suggest

indication clue, evidence, explanation, forewarning, hint, index, inkling, intimation, manifestation, mark, note, omen, portent, sign, signal, suggestion, symptom, warning

indicator display, gauge, guide, index, mark, marker, meter, pointer, sign, signal, signpost, symbol

indictment accusation, allegation, charge, impeachment, prosecution, summons

indifference absence of feeling, aloofness, apathy, callousness, carelessness, coldness, coolness, detachment, disregard, heedlessness, inattention, lack of interest, negligence, stoicalness, unconcern
Antonyms attention, care, commitment, concern, enthusiasm, heed, regard

indifferent 1. aloof, apathetic, callous, careless, cold, cool, detached, distant, heedless, impervious, inattentive, regardless, uncaring, unconcerned, unimpressed, uninterested, unmoved, unresponsive, unsympathetic 2. average, fair, mediocre, middling, moderate, ordinary, passable, perfunctory, so-so (*Inf.*), undistinguished, uninspired
Antonyms (*sense 1*) avid, compassionate, concerned, eager, enthusiastic, interested, keen, responsive, sensitive, susceptible, sympathetic (*sense 2*) excellent, exceptional, fine, first-class, notable, remarkable

indignant angry, annoyed, disgruntled, exasperated, fuming (*Inf.*), furious, heated, huffy (*Inf.*), in a huff, incensed, in high dudgeon, irate, livid, mad (*Inf.*), miffed (*Inf.*), narked (*Sl.*), peeved (*Inf.*), provoked, resentful, riled,

scornful, seeing red (*Inf.*), sore (*Inf.*), up in arms (*Inf.*), wrathful

indignation anger, exasperation, fury, ire (*Literary*), pique, rage, resentment, righteous anger, scorn, umbrage, wrath

indirect backhanded, circuitous, circumlocutory, crooked, devious, long-drawn-out, meandering, oblique, periphrastic, rambling, roundabout, tortuous, wandering, winding, zigzag
Antonyms clear-cut, direct, straight, straightforward, undeviating, uninterrupted

indiscreet foolish, hasty, heedless, ill-advised, ill-considered, illjudged, impolitic, imprudent, incautious, injudicious, naive, rash, reckless, tactless, undiplomatic, unthinking, unwise
Antonyms cautious, diplomatic, discreet, judicious, politic, prudent, tactful, wise

indiscriminate aimless, careless, desultory, general, hit or miss (*Inf.*), random, sweeping, uncritical, undiscriminating, unmethodical, unselective, unsystematic, wholesale
Antonyms deliberate, discriminating, exclusive, methodical, selective, systematic

indispensable crucial, essential, imperative, key, necessary, needed, needful, requisite, vital
Antonyms dispensable, disposable, nonessential, superfluous, unimportant, unnecessary

indisposed ailing, confined to bed, ill, laid up (*Inf.*), on the sick list (*Inf.*), poorly (*Inf.*), sick, unwell
Antonyms fine, fit, hardy, healthy, sound, well

indisputable absolute, beyond doubt, certain, evident, incontestable, incontrovertible, indubitable, irrefutable, positive, sure, unassailable, undeniable, unquestionable
Antonyms assailable, disputable, doubtful, indefinite, questionable, refutable, uncertain, vague

indistinct ambiguous, bleary,

blurred, confused, dim, doubtful, faint, fuzzy, hazy, ill-defined, indefinite, indeterminate, indiscernible, indistinguishable, misty, muffled, obscure, out of focus, shadowy, unclear, undefined, unintelligible, vague, weak
Antonyms clear, defined, determinate, discernible, distinct, distinguishable, evident, intelligible

indistinguishable alike, identical, like as two peas in a pod (*Inf.*), (the) same, twin

individual 1. *adj.* characteristic, discrete, distinct, distinctive, exclusive, identical, idiosyncratic, own, particular, peculiar, personal, personalized, proper, respective, separate, several, single, singular, special, specific, unique **2.** *n.* being, body (*Inf.*), character, creature, mortal, party, person, personage, soul, type, unit
Antonyms *adj.* collective, common, conventional, general, indistinct, ordinary, universal

individuality character, discreteness, distinction, distinctiveness, originality, peculiarity, personality, separateness, singularity, uniqueness

indomitable bold, invincible, resolute, staunch, steadfast, unbeatable, unconquerable, unflinching, untameable, unyielding

indubitable certain, evident, incontestable, incontrovertible, indisputable, irrefutable, obvious, sure, unarguable, undeniable, undoubted, unquestionable, veritable

induce actuate, convince, draw, encourage, get, impel, incite, influence, instigate, move, persuade, press, prevail upon, prompt, talk into
Antonyms curb, deter, discourage, dissuade, hinder, prevent, restrain, stop, suppress

inducement attraction, bait, carrot (*Inf.*), cause, come-on (*Inf.*), consideration, encouragement, impulse, incentive, incitement,

influence, lure, motive, reward, spur, stimulus, urge

indulge 1. cater to, give way to, gratify, pander to, regale, satiate, satisfy, treat oneself to, yield to **2.** *With* **in** bask in, give free rein to, give oneself up to, luxuriate in, revel in, wallow in

indulgence 1. excess, fondness, immoderation, intemperance, intemperateness, kindness, leniency, pampering, partiality, permissiveness, profligacy, profligateness, spoiling **2.** courtesy, forbearance, good will, patience, tolerance, understanding
Antonyms (*sense 1*) moderation, strictness, temperance, temperateness

indulgent compliant, easy-going, favourable, fond, forbearing, gentle, gratifying, kind, kindly, lenient, liberal, mild, permissive, tender, tolerant, understanding
Antonyms austere, demanding, harsh, intolerant, rigorous, stern, strict, stringent, unmerciful

industrious active, assiduous, busy, conscientious, diligent, energetic, hard-working, laborious, persevering, persistent, productive, purposeful, sedulous, steady, tireless, zealous
Antonyms idle, indolent, lackadaisical, lazy, shiftless, slothful

industry 1. business, commerce, commercial enterprise, manufacturing, production, trade **2.** activity, application, assiduity, determination, diligence, effort, labour, perseverance, persistence, tirelessness, toil, vigour, zeal

ineffective barren, bootless, feeble, fruitless, futile, idle, impotent, inadequate, ineffectual, inefficacious, inefficient, unavailing, unproductive, useless, vain, weak, worthless
Antonyms effective, efficacious, efficient, fruitful, potent, productive, useful, worthwhile

ineffectual abortive, bootless, emasculate, feeble, fruitless, futile, idle, impotent, inadequate, incompetent, ineffective, inefficacious, inefficient, inept, lame, powerless, unavailing, useless, vain, weak

inefficient disorganized, feeble, incapable, incompetent, ineffectual, inefficacious, inept, inexpert, slipshod, sloppy, wasteful, weak

Antonyms able, capable, competent, effective, efficient, expert, organized, skilled

ineligible disqualified, incompetent (*Law*), objectionable, ruled out, unacceptable, undesirable, unequipped, unfit, unfitted, unqualified, unsuitable

inept awkward, bumbling, bungling, cack-handed (*Inf.*), clumsy, gauche, incompetent, inexpert, maladroit, unhandy, unskilful, unworkmanlike

Antonyms able, adroit, competent, dexterous, efficient, effectual, germane, qualified, sensible, skilful, talented

ineptitude clumsiness, gaucheness, incapacity, incompetence, inexpertness, unfitness, unhandiness

inequality bias, difference, disparity, disproportion, diversity, imparity, irregularity, lack of balance, preferentiality, prejudice, unevenness

inert dead, dormant, dull, idle, immobile, inactive, inanimate, indolent, lazy, leaden, lifeless, motionless, passive, quiescent, slack, slothful, sluggish, slumberous (*Chiefly poetic*), static, still, torpid, unmoving, unreactive, unresponsive

inertia apathy, deadness, disinclination to move, drowsiness, dullness, idleness, immobility, inactivity, indolence, languor, lassitude, laziness, lethargy, listlessness, passivity, sloth, sluggishness, stillness, stupor, torpor, unresponsiveness

inescapable certain, destined, fated, ineluctable, ineludible (*Rare*), inevitable, inexorable, sure, unavoidable

inevitable assured, certain, decreed, destined, fixed, ineluctable, inescapable, inexorable, necessary, ordained, settled, sure, unavoidable, unpreventable

Antonyms avoidable, escapable, evadable, preventable, uncertain

inexcusable indefensible, inexpiable, outrageous, unforgivable, unjustifiable, unpardonable, unwarrantable

Antonyms defensible, excusable, forgivable, justifiable, pardonable

inexpensive bargain, budget, cheap, economical, low-cost, low-priced, modest, reasonable

Antonyms costly, dear, exorbitant, expensive, high-priced, pricey, uneconomical

inexperienced amateur, callow, fresh, green, immature, new, raw, unaccustomed, unacquainted, unfamiliar, unfledged, unpractised, unschooled, unseasoned, unskilled, untrained, untried, unused, unversed, wet behind the ears (*Inf.*)

Antonyms experienced, familiar, knowledgeable, practised, seasoned, skilled, trained, versed

inexpert amateurish, awkward, bungling, cack-handed (*Inf.*), clumsy, inept, maladroit, skilless, unhandy, unpractised, unprofessional, unskilful, unskilled, unworkmanlike

inexplicable baffling, beyond comprehension, enigmatic, incomprehensible, inscrutable, insoluble, mysterious, mystifying, strange, unaccountable, unfathomable, unintelligible

Antonyms comprehensible, explainable, explicable, fathomable, intelligible, soluble, understandable

infallible 1. faultless, impeccable, omniscient, perfect, unerring, unimpeachable 2. certain, dependable, foolproof, reliable, sure, sure-fire (*Inf.*), trustworthy, unbeatable, unfailing

Antonyms (*sense 1*) errant, fallible, human, imperfect, mortal (sense 2) doubtful, dubious, uncertain, undependable, unreliable, unsure

infamous abominable, atrocious, base, detestable, disgraceful, dishonourable, disreputable, egregious, flagitious, hateful, heinous, ignominious, ill-famed, iniquitous, loathsome, monstrous, nefarious, notorious, odious, opprobrious, outrageous, scandalous, scurvy, shameful, shocking, vile, villainous, wicked
Antonyms esteemed, glorious, honourable, noble, reputable, virtuous

infancy 1. babyhood, early childhood 2. beginnings, cradle, dawn, early stages, emergence, inception, origins, outset, start
Antonyms (sense 2) close, conclusion, death, end, expiration, finish, termination

infant n. babe, baby, bairn (Scot.), child, little one, neonate, newborn child, suckling, toddler, tot, wean (Scot.)

infantile babyish, childish, immature, puerile, tender, weak, young
Antonyms adult, developed, mature

infatuated beguiled, besotted, bewitched, captivated, carried away, crazy about (Inf.), enamoured, enraptured, fascinated, head over heels in love with, inflamed, intoxicated, obsessed, possessed, smitten (Inf.), spellbound, swept off one's feet, under the spell of

infect affect, blight, contaminate, corrupt, defile, influence, poison, pollute, spread to or among, taint, touch, vitiate

infection contagion, contamination, corruption, defilement, poison, pollution, septicity, virus

infectious catching, communicable, contagious, contaminating, corrupting, defiling, infective, pestilential, poisoning, polluting, spreading, transmittable, virulent, vitiating

infer conclude, conjecture, de-

duce, derive, gather, presume, read between the lines, surmise, understand

inference assumption, conclusion, conjecture, consequence, corollary, deduction, illation (Rare), presumption, reading, surmise

inferior adj. junior, lesser, lower, menial, minor, secondary, subordinate, subsidiary, under, underneath
Antonyms greater, higher, senior, superior, top

inferiority badness, deficiency, imperfection, inadequacy, insignificance, meanness, mediocrity, shoddiness, unimportance, worthlessness
Antonyms advantage, ascendancy, dominance, eminence, excellence, superiority

infertile barren, infecund, nonproductive, sterile, unfruitful, unproductive
Antonyms fecund, fertile, fruitful, generative, productive

infest beset, flood, invade, overrun, penetrate, permeate, ravage, swarm, throng

infiltrate creep in, filter through, insinuate oneself, penetrate, percolate, permeate, pervade, sneak in (Inf.), work or worm one's way into

infinite absolute, all-embracing, bottomless, boundless, enormous, eternal, everlasting, illimitable, immeasurable, immense, inestimable, inexhaustible, interminable, limitless, measureless, never-ending, numberless, perpetual, stupendous, total, unbounded, uncounted, untold, vast, wide, without end, without number
Antonyms bounded, circumscribed, finite, limited, measurable, restricted

infinity boundlessness, endlessness, eternity, immensity, infinitude, perpetuity, vastness

infirm ailing, debilitated, decrepit, doddering, doddery, enfeebled, failing, feeble, frail, lame, weak

Antonyms healthy, hearty, robust, sound, strong, sturdy, vigorous

inflame agitate, anger, arouse, embitter, enrage, exasperate, excite, fire, foment, heat, ignite, impassion, incense, infuriate, intoxicate, kindle, madden, provoke, rile, rouse, stimulate

inflamed angry, chafing, festering, fevered, heated, hot, infected, red, septic, sore, swollen

inflammable combustible, flammable, incendiary

inflate aerate, aggrandize, amplify, balloon, bloat, blow up, boost, dilate, distend, enlarge, escalate, exaggerate, expand, increase, puff up *or* out, pump up, swell
Antonyms collapse, compress, contract, deflate, diminish, lessen, shrink

inflated bombastic, exaggerated, grandiloquent, ostentatious, overblown, swollen

inflation aggrandizement, blowing up, distension, enhancement, enlargement, escalation, expansion, extension, increase, intensification, puffiness, rise, spread, swelling, tumefaction

inflection 1. accentuation, bend, bow, crook, curvature, intonation, modulation 2. *Gram.* conjugation, declension

inflexible adamant, brassbound, dyed-in-the-wool, firm, fixed, hard and fast, immovable, immutable, implacable, inexorable, intractable, iron, obdurate, obstinate, relentless, resolute, rigorous, set, set in one's ways, steadfast, steely, strict, stringent, stubborn, unadaptable, unbending, unchangeable, uncompromising, unyielding
Antonyms flexible, irresolute, movable, pliant, variable, yielding

inflict administer, apply, deliver, exact, impose, levy, mete *or* deal out, visit, wreak

influence *n.* 1. agency, ascendancy, authority, control, credit, direction, domination, effect, guidance, magnetism, mastery, power, pressure, rule, spell, sway, weight 2. clout (*Inf.*), connections, good offices, hold, importance, leverage, power, prestige, pull (*Inf.*), weight ~ *v.* 3. act *or* work upon, affect, arouse, bias, control, count, direct, dispose, guide, impel, impress, incite, incline, induce, instigate, lead to believe, manipulate, modify, move, persuade, predispose, prompt, rouse, sway

inform acquaint, advise, apprise, communicate, enlighten, give (someone) to understand, instruct, leak to, let know, make conversant (with), notify, put (someone) in the picture (*Inf.*), send word to, teach, tell, tip off

informal casual, colloquial, cosy, easy, familiar, natural, relaxed, simple, unceremonious, unconstrained, unofficial
Antonyms ceremonious, constrained, conventional, formal, official, stiff

information advice, blurb, counsel, data, dope (*Sl.*), facts, gen (*Brit. inf.*), info (*Inf.*), inside story, instruction, intelligence, knowledge, lowdown (*Inf.*), material, message, news, notice, report, tidings, word

informed abreast, acquainted, *au courant*, *au fait*, briefed, conversant, enlightened, erudite, expert, familiar, genned up (*Brit. inf.*), in the know (*Inf.*), knowledgeable, learned, posted, primed, reliable, up, up to date, versed, well-read

informer accuser, betrayer, grass (*Brit. sl.*), Judas, nark (*Brit. sl.*), sneak, squealer (*Sl.*), stool pigeon

infrequent few and far between, occasional, rare, sporadic, uncommon, unusual
Antonyms common, customary, frequent, habitual, often, regular, usual

infringe break, contravene, disobey, transgress, violate

infuriate anger, be like a red rag to a bull, enrage, exasperate, get one's back up (*Inf.*), get one's

goat (*Sl.*), incense, irritate, madden, make one's blood boil, make one see red (*Inf.*), make one's hackles rise, provoke, raise one's hackles, rile
Antonyms appease, calm, mollify, pacify, placate, propitiate, soothe

infuriating aggravating (*Inf.*), annoying, exasperating, galling, irritating, maddening, mortifying, pestilential, provoking, vexatious

ingenious adroit, bright, brilliant, clever, crafty, creative, dexterous, fertile, inventive, masterly, original, ready, resourceful, shrewd, skilful, subtle
Antonyms artless, clumsy, unimaginative, uninventive, unoriginal, unresourceful, unskilful

ingenuous artless, candid, childlike, frank, guileless, honest, innocent, naive, open, plain, simple, sincere, trustful, trusting, unreserved, unsophisticated, unstudied

ingratitude thanklessness, unappreciativeness, ungratefulness
Antonyms appreciation, gratefulness, gratitude, thankfulness, thanks, thanksgiving

ingredient component, constituent, element, part

inhabit abide, dwell, live, lodge, make one's home, occupy, people, populate, possess, reside, take up residence in, tenant

inhabitant aborigine, citizen, denizen, dweller, indigene, indweller, inmate, native, occupant, occupier, resident, tenant

inhabited colonized, developed, held, occupied, peopled, populated, settled, tenanted

inherit accede to, be bequeathed, be left, come into, fall heir to, succeed to

inheritance bequest, birthright, heritage, legacy, patrimony

inhibit arrest, bar, bridle, check, constrain, cramp (someone's) style (*Inf.*), curb, debar, discourage, forbid, frustrate, hinder,

hold back *or* in, impede, obstruct, prevent, prohibit, restrain, stop
Antonyms abet, allow, encourage, further, let, permit, support

inhibition bar, check, embargo, hang-up (*Sl.*), hindrance, interdict, mental blockage, obstacle, prohibition, reserve, restraint, restriction, reticence, self-consciousness, shyness

inhospitable 1. cool, uncongenial, unfriendly, ungenerous, unkind, unreceptive, unwelcoming, xenophobic **2.** bare, barren, bleak, desolate, empty, forbidding, hostile, lonely, sterile, unfavourable, uninhabitable
Antonyms (*sense 1*) amicable, friendly, generous, genial, gracious, hospitable, sociable, welcoming

inhuman animal, barbaric, barbarous, bestial, brutal, cold-blooded, cruel, diabolical, fiendish, heartless, merciless, pitiless, remorseless, ruthless, savage, unfeeling, vicious
Antonyms charitable, compassionate, feeling, humane, merciful, sensitive, tender, warm-hearted

inhumane brutal, cruel, heartless, pitiless, uncompassionate, unfeeling, unkind, unsympathetic

initial *adj.* beginning, commencing, early, first, inaugural, inceptive, inchoate, incipient, introductory, opening, primary
Antonyms closing, concluding, ending, final, last, terminal, ultimate

initially at *or* in the beginning, at first, at the outset, at the start, first, firstly, in the early stages, originally, primarily, to begin with

initiate *v.* **1.** begin, break the ice, commence, get under way, inaugurate, institute, kick off (*Inf.*), launch, lay the foundations of, open, originate, pioneer, set going, set in motion, set the ball rolling, start **2.** coach, familiarize with, indoctrinate, induct, instate, instruct, introduce, invest, teach, train

initiative advantage, beginning, commencement, first move, first step, lead

inject 1. inoculate, jab (*Inf.*), shoot (*Inf.*), vaccinate **2.** bring in, infuse, insert, instil, interject, introduce

injunction admonition, command, dictate, exhortation, instruction, mandate, order, precept, ruling

injure abuse, blemish, blight, break, damage, deface, disable, harm, hurt, impair, maltreat, mar, ruin, spoil, tarnish, undermine, vitiate, weaken, wound, wrong

injury abuse, damage, detriment, disservice, evil, grievance, harm, hurt, ill, injustice, mischief, ruin, wound, wrong

injustice bias, discrimination, favouritism, inequality, inequity, iniquity, one-sidedness, oppression, partiality, partisanship, prejudice, unfairness, unjustness, unlawfulness, wrong
   Antonyms equality, equity, fairness, impartiality, justice, lawfulness, rectitude, right

inland *adj.* domestic, interior, internal, upcountry

inlet arm (of the sea), bay, bight, cove, creek, entrance, firth or frith (*Scot.*), ingress, passage, sea loch (*Scot.*)

inmost or **innermost** basic, buried, central, deep, deepest, essential, intimate, personal, private, secret

innate congenital, connate, constitutional, essential, inborn, inbred, indigenous, ingrained, inherent, inherited, instinctive, intrinsic, intuitive, native, natural
   Antonyms accidental, acquired, affected, assumed, cultivated, fostered, incidental, learned, nurtured, unnatural

inner central, essential, inside, interior, internal, intestinal, inward, middle

   Antonyms exterior, external, outer, outside, outward

innocence 1. blamelessness, chastity, clean hands, guiltlessness, incorruptibility, probity, purity, righteousness, sinlessness, stainlessness, uprightness, virginity, virtue **2.** artlessness, credulousness, freshness, guilelessness, gullibility, inexperience, ingenuousness, naiveté, simplicity, unsophistication, unworldliness
   Antonyms (*sense 1*) corruption, guilt, impurity, offensiveness, sinfulness, wrongness (*sense 2*) artfulness, cunning, disingenuousness, guile, wiliness, worldliness

innocent *adj.* **1.** blameless, clear, faultless, guiltless, honest, in the clear, not guilty, uninvolved, unoffending **2.** chaste, immaculate, impeccable, incorrupt, pristine, pure, righteous, sinless, spotless, stainless, unblemished, unsullied, upright, virgin, virginal **3.** artless, childlike, credulous, frank, guileless, gullible, ingenuous, naive, open, simple, unsuspicious, unworldly, wet behind the ears (*Inf.*)
   Antonyms (*sense 1*) blameworthy, culpable, dishonest, guilty, responsible (*sense 2*) corrupt, immoral, impure, sinful, wrong (*sense 3*) artful, disingenuous, sophisticated, worldly

innovation alteration, change, departure, introduction, modernism, modernization, newness, novelty, variation

innuendo aspersion, hint, implication, imputation, insinuation, intimation, overtone, suggestion, whisper

innumerable beyond number, countless, incalculable, infinite, many, multitudinous, myriad, numberless, numerous, unnumbered, untold
   Antonyms calculable, computable, finite, limited, measurable, numbered

inoffensive harmless, humble,

innocent, innocuous, innoxious, mild, neutral, nonprovocative, peaceable, quiet, retiring, unobjectionable, unobtrusive, unoffending

Antonyms abrasive, harmful, irksome, irritating, malicious, objectionable, offensive, provocative

inopportune ill-chosen, ill-timed, inappropriate, inauspicious, inconvenient, malapropos, mistimed, unfavourable, unfortunate, unpropitious, unseasonable, unsuitable, untimely

Antonyms appropriate, auspicious, convenient, favourable, fortunate, opportune, seasonable, suitable, timely, well-timed

inordinate disproportionate, excessive, exorbitant, extravagant, immoderate, intemperate, preposterous, unconscionable, undue, unreasonable, unrestrained, unwarranted

inquest inquiry, inquisition, investigation, probe

inquire examine, explore, inspect, investigate, look into, make inquiries, probe, scrutinize, search

inquiry examination, exploration, inquest, interrogation, investigation, probe, research, scrutiny, search, study, survey

inquisition cross-examination, examination, grilling (*Inf.*), inquest, inquiry, investigation, question, quizzing, third degree (*Inf.*)

inquisitive curious, inquiring, intrusive, nosy (*Inf.*), nosy-parkering (*Inf.*), peering, probing, prying, questioning, scrutinizing, snooping (*Inf.*), snoopy (*Inf.*)

Antonyms apathetic, incurious, indifferent, unconcerned, uninterested, unquestioning

insane crazed, crazy, demented, deranged, mad, mentally disordered, mentally ill, *non compos mentis*, of unsound mind, out of one's mind, unhinged

Antonyms logical, lucid, normal,

practical, rational, reasonable, reasoned, sane, sensible, sound

insanitary contaminated, dirtied, dirty, disease-ridden, feculent, filthy, impure, infected, infested, insalubrious, noxious, polluted, unclean, unhealthy, unhygienic

Antonyms clean, healthy, hygienic, pure, salubrious, unpolluted

insanity aberration, craziness, delirium, dementia, frenzy, madness, mental derangement, mental disorder, mental illness

Antonyms logic, lucidity, normality, rationality, reason, sanity, soundness

insatiable gluttonous, greedy, insatiate, intemperate, quenchless, rapacious, ravenous, unappeasable, unquenchable, voracious

Antonyms appeasable, limited, quenchable, satiable, temperate

inscribe 1. carve, cut, engrave, etch, impress, imprint 2. address, dedicate

inscription dedication, engraving, label, legend, lettering, saying, words

inscrutable 1. blank, deadpan, enigmatic, impenetrable, poker-faced (*Inf.*), sphinxlike, unreadable 2. hidden, incomprehensible, inexplicable, mysterious, undiscoverable, unexplainable, unfathomable, unintelligible

Antonyms clear, comprehensible, evident, explainable, explicable, intelligible, lucid, manifest, obvious, open, palpable, patent, penetrable, plain, readable, revealing, transparent, understandable

insecure 1. afraid, anxious, uncertain, unconfident, unsure 2. built upon sand, flimsy, frail, insubstantial, loose, on thin ice, precarious, rickety, rocky, shaky, unreliable, unsound, unstable, unsteady, weak, wobbly

Antonyms (*sense 1*) assured, certain, confident, decisive, secure (*sense 2*) firm, reliable, safe, secure, sound, stable, steady, substantial, sure

insensible anaesthetized, benumbed, dull, inert, insensate, numbed, senseless, stupid, torpid

insensitive callous, crass, hardened, imperceptive, indifferent, obtuse, tactless, thick-skinned, tough, uncaring, unconcerned, unfeeling, unresponsive, unsusceptible
Antonyms caring, concerned, perceptive, responsive, sensitive, sentient, susceptible, tactful, tender

inseparable 1. conjoined, inalienable, indissoluble, indivisible, inseverable 2. bosom, close, devoted, intimate

insert embed, enter, implant, infix, interject, interpolate, interpose, introduce, place, pop in (*Inf.*), put, set, stick in, tuck in, work in
Antonyms delete, extract, pull out, remove, take out, withdraw

insertion addition, implant, inclusion, insert, inset, interpolation, introduction, supplement

inside *n.* 1. contents, inner part, interior 2. *Often plural. Inf.* belly, bowels, entrails, gut, guts, innards (*Inf.*), internal organs, stomach, viscera, vitals ~*adv.* 3. indoors, under cover, within ~*adj.* 4. inner, innermost, interior, internal, intramural, inward
Antonyms (*sense 4*) exterior, external, extramural, outer, outermost, outside, outward

insidious artful, crafty, crooked, cunning, deceitful, deceptive, designing, disingenuous, duplicitous, guileful, intriguing, Machiavellian, slick, sly, smooth, sneaking, stealthy, subtle, surreptitious, treacherous, tricky, wily

insight acumen, awareness, comprehension, discernment, intuition, intuitiveness, judgment, observation, penetration, perception, perspicacity, understanding, vision

insignia badge, crest, decoration, distinguishing mark, earmark, emblem, ensign, symbol

insignificant flimsy, immaterial, inconsequential, inconsiderable, irrelevant, meagre, meaningless, minor, negligible, nondescript, nonessential, not worth mentioning, nugatory, of no account (consequence, moment), paltry, petty, scanty, trifling, trivial, unimportant, unsubstantial
Antonyms consequential, considerable, essential, important, meaningful, momentous, relevant, significant, substantial, vital, weighty

insincere deceitful, deceptive, devious, dishonest, disingenuous, dissembling, dissimulating, double-dealing, duplicitous, evasive, faithless, false, hollow, hypocritical, Janus-faced, lying, mendacious, perfidious, pretended, two-faced, unfaithful, untrue, untruthful
Antonyms direct, earnest, faithful, genuine, honest, sincere, straightforward, true, truthful

insinuate 1. allude, hint, imply, indicate, intimate, suggest 2. infiltrate, infuse, inject, instil, introduce

insinuation allusion, aspersion, hint, implication, innuendo, slur, suggestion

insipid 1. anaemic, banal, bland, characterless, colourless, drab, dry, dull, flat, jejune, lifeless, limp, pointless, prosaic, prosy, spiritless, stale, stupid, tame, tedious, trite, unimaginative, uninteresting, vapid, weak, wearisome, wishy-washy (*Inf.*) 2. bland, flavourless, savourless, tasteless, unappetizing, watered down, watery, wishy-washy (*Inf.*)
Antonyms (*sense 1*) colourful, engaging, exciting, interesting, lively, provocative, spirited, stimulating (*sense 2*) appetizing, fiery, palatable, piquant, pungent, savoury, tasteful

insist 1. be firm, brook no refusal, demand, lay down the law, not take no for an answer, persist, press (someone), require, stand firm, stand one's ground, take *or* make a stand, urge 2. assert, asseverate, aver, claim, contend, hold, maintain, reiterate, repeat, swear, urge, vow

insistent demanding, dogged, emphatic, exigent, forceful, importunate, incessant, peremptory, persevering, persistent, pressing, unrelenting, urgent

insolence abuse, audacity, backchat (*Inf.*), boldness, cheek (*Inf.*), chutzpah (*U.S. inf.*), contemptuousness, contumely, disrespect, effrontery, gall (*Inf.*), impertinence, impudence, incivility, insubordination, offensiveness, pertness, rudeness, sauce (*Inf.*), uncivility
Antonyms civility, courtesy, deference, esteem, mannerliness, politeness, respect, submission

insolent abusive, bold, brazenfaced, contemptuous, fresh (*Inf.*), impertinent, impudent, insubordinate, insulting, pert, rude, saucy, uncivil
Antonyms civil, courteous, deferential, mannerly, polite, respectful, submissive

insoluble baffling, impenetrable, indecipherable, inexplicable, mysterious, mystifying, obscure, unaccountable, unfathomable, unsolvable
Antonyms accountable, comprehensible, explicable, fathomable, penetrable, soluble, solvable

insolvent bankrupt, broke (*Inf.*), failed, gone bust (*Inf.*), gone to the wall (*Inf.*), in queer street (*Inf.*), in receivership, in the hands of the receivers, on the rocks (*Inf.*), ruined

insomnia sleeplessness, wakefulness

inspect audit, check, examine, give (something or someone) the once-over (*Inf.*), go over or through, investigate, look over, oversee, scan, scrutinize, search, superintend, supervise, survey, vet

inspection check, checkup, examination, investigation, lookover, once-over (*Inf.*), review, scan, scrutiny, search, superin-

tendence, supervision, surveillance, survey

inspector censor, checker, critic, examiner, investigator, overseer, scrutineer, scrutinizer, superintendent, supervisor

inspiration arousal, awakening, encouragement, influence, muse, spur, stimulus

inspire animate, be responsible for, encourage, enliven, fire or touch the imagination of, galvanize, hearten, imbue, influence, infuse, inspirit, instil, spark off, spur, stimulate
Antonyms daunt, deflate, depress, discourage, disenchant, dishearten, dispirit

inspired brilliant, dazzling, enthralling, exciting, impressive, memorable, of genius, outstanding, superlative, thrilling, wonderful

inspiring affecting, encouraging, exciting, exhilarating, heartening, moving, rousing, stimulating, stirring, uplifting

instability capriciousness, changeableness, disequilibrium, fickleness, fitfulness, fluctuation, fluidity, frailty, imbalance, impermanence, inconstancy, insecurity, irresolution, mutability, oscillation, precariousness, restlessness, shakiness, transience, unpredictability, unsteadiness, vacillation, variability, volatility, wavering, weakness
Antonyms balance, constancy, equilibrium, permanence, predictability, resolution, security, stability, steadiness, strength

install, instal 1. fix, lay, lodge, place, position, put in, set up, station 2. establish, inaugurate, induct, instate, institute, introduce, invest, set up

installation 1. inauguration, induction, instatement, investiture 2. equipment, machinery, plant, system

instalment chapter, division, episode, part, portion, repayment, section

instance 1. *n.* case, case in point,

example, illustration, occasion, occurrence, precedent, situation, time **2.** *v.* adduce, cite, mention, name, quote, specify

instant 1. *n.* flash, jiffy (*Inf.*), moment, second, shake (*Inf.*), split second, tick (*Brit. inf.*), trice, twinkling, twinkling of an eye (*Inf.*), two shakes of a lamb's tail (*Inf.*) **2.** *adj.* direct, immediate, instantaneous, on-the-spot, prompt, quick, split-second, urgent

instantaneous direct, immediate, instant, on-the-spot

instantly at once, directly, forthwith, immediately, instantaneously, instanter (*Law*), now, on the spot, pronto (*Inf.*), right away, right now, straight away, there and then, this minute, *tout de suite*, without delay

instead alternatively, in lieu, in preference, on second thoughts, preferably, rather

instigate actuate, bring about, encourage, foment, impel, incite, influence, initiate, kindle, move, persuade, prompt, provoke, rouse, set on, spur, start, stimulate, stir up, urge, whip up
Antonyms discourage, repress, restrain, stop, suppress

instil, instill engender, engraft, imbue, implant, impress, inculcate, infix, infuse, insinuate, introduce

instinct aptitude, faculty, feeling, gift, gut feeling (*Inf.*), gut reaction (*Inf.*), impulse, intuition, knack, natural inclination, predisposition, proclivity, sixth sense, talent, tendency, urge

instinctive automatic, inborn, inherent, innate, instinctual, intuitional, intuitive, involuntary, mechanical, native, natural, reflex, spontaneous, unlearned, unpremeditated, unthinking, visceral
Antonyms acquired, calculated, considered, learned, mindful, premeditated, thinking, voluntary, willed

institute[1] *v.* appoint, begin, bring into being, commence, consti-

tute, enact, establish, fix, found, induct, initiate, install, introduce, invest, launch, ordain, organize, originate, pioneer, put into operation, set in motion, settle, set up, start
Antonyms abandon, abolish, cancel, cease, discontinue, end, stop, suspend, terminate

institute[2] *n.* academy, association, college, conservatory, foundation, guild, institution, school, seat of learning, seminary, society

institution 1. constitution, creation, enactment, establishment, formation, foundation, initiation, introduction, investiture, investment, organization **2.** academy, college, establishment, foundation, hospital, institute, school, seminary, society, university **3.** convention, custom, fixture, law, practice, ritual, rule, tradition

instruct 1. bid, charge, command, direct, enjoin, order, tell **2.** coach, discipline, drill, educate, enlighten, ground, guide, inform, school, teach, train, tutor

instruction apprenticeship, coaching, discipline, drilling, education, enlightenment, grounding, guidance, information, lesson(s), preparation, schooling, teaching, training, tuition, tutelage

instructions advice, directions, guidance, information, key, orders, recommendations, rules

instructor adviser, coach, demonstrator, exponent, guide, master, mentor, mistress, pedagogue, preceptor (*Rare*), schoolmaster, schoolmistress, teacher, trainer, tutor

instrument apparatus, appliance, contraption (*Inf.*), contrivance, device, gadget, implement, mechanism, tool, utensil

instrumental active, assisting, auxiliary, conducive, contributory, helpful, helping, influential, involved, of help *or* service, subsidiary, useful

insubordinate contumacious,

defiant, disobedient, disorderly, fractious, insurgent, mutinous, rebellious, recalcitrant, refractory, riotous, seditious, turbulent, undisciplined, ungovernable, unruly

Antonyms compliant, deferential, disciplined, docile, obedient, orderly, submissive, subservient

insubordination defiance, disobedience, indiscipline, insurrection, mutinousness, mutiny, rebellion, recalcitrance, revolt, riotousness, sedition, ungovernability

Antonyms acquiescence, compliance, deference, discipline, docility, obedience, submission, subordination

insufferable detestable, dreadful, enough to test the patience of a saint, enough to try the patience of Job, impossible, insupportable, intolerable, more than flesh and blood can stand, outrageous, past bearing, too much, unbearable, unendurable, unspeakable

Antonyms appealing, attractive, bearable, charming, disarming, pleasant

insufficient deficient, inadequate, incapable, incommensurate, incompetent, lacking, short, unfitted, unqualified

Antonyms adequate, ample, commensurate, competent, enough, plentiful, qualified, sufficient

insular *Fig.* blinkered, circumscribed, closed, contracted, cut off, illiberal, inward-looking, isolated, limited, narrow, narrow-minded, parish-pump, parochial, petty, prejudiced, provincial

Antonyms broad-minded, cosmopolitan, experienced, liberal, open-minded, tolerant, worldly

insulate *Fig.* close off, cocoon, cushion, cut off, isolate, protect, sequester, shield, wrap up in cotton wool

insult 1. *n.* abuse, affront, aspersion, contumely, indignity, insolence, offence, outrage, rudeness, slap in the face (*Inf.*), slight, snub

2. *v.* abuse, affront, call names, give offence to, injure, miscall (*Dialect*), offend, outrage, revile, slag (*Sl.*), slander, slight, snub

Antonyms *n.* compliment, flattery, honour ~*v.* flatter, please, praise

insurance assurance, cover, coverage, guarantee, indemnification, indemnity, protection, provision, safeguard, security, something to fall back on (*Inf.*), warranty

insure assure, cover, guarantee, indemnify, underwrite, warrant

intact all in one piece, complete, entire, perfect, scatheless, sound, together, unbroken, undamaged, undefiled, unharmed, unhurt, unimpaired, uninjured, unscathed, untouched, unviolated, virgin, whole

Antonyms broken, damaged, harmed, impaired, injured

integral 1. basic, component, constituent, elemental, essential, fundamental, indispensable, intrinsic, necessary, requisite 2. complete, entire, full, intact, undivided, whole

Antonyms fractional, inessential, unimportant, unnecessary

integrate accommodate, amalgamate, assimilate, blend, coalesce, combine, fuse, harmonize, incorporate, intermix, join, knit, merge, mesh, unite

Antonyms disperse, divide, segregate, separate

integrity candour, goodness, honesty, honour, incorruptibility, principle, probity, purity, rectitude, righteousness, uprightness, virtue

Antonyms corruption, deceit, dishonesty, disrepute, duplicity, faultiness, flimsiness, fragility, immorality, uncertainty, unsoundness

intellect brains (*Inf.*), intelligence, judgment, mind, reason, sense, understanding

intellectual 1. *adj.* bookish, cerebral, highbrow, intelligent, mental, rational, scholarly, studious, thoughtful 2. *n.* academic, egghead (*Inf.*), highbrow, thinker **Antonyms** *adj.* ignorant, illiterate, material, physical, stupid, unintellectual, unlearned ~*n.* idiot, moron

intelligence 1. acumen, alertness, aptitude, brain power, brains (*Inf.*), brightness, capacity, cleverness, comprehension, discernment, grey matter (*Inf.*), intellect, mind, nous (*Brit. sl.*), penetration, perception, quickness, reason, understanding 2. advice, data, disclosure, facts, findings, gen (*Inf.*), information, knowledge, low-down (*Inf.*), news, notice, notification, report, rumour, tidings, tip-off, word **Antonyms** (*sense 1*) dullness, ignorance, stupidity (*sense 2*) concealment, misinformation

intelligent acute, alert, apt, brainy (*Inf.*), bright, clever, discerning, enlightened, instructed, knowing, penetrating, perspicacious, quick, quick-witted, rational, sharp, smart, thinking, well-informed **Antonyms** dim-witted, dull, foolish, ignorant, obtuse, stupid, unintelligent

intelligible clear, comprehensible, distinct, lucid, open, plain, understandable **Antonyms** confused, garbled, incomprehensible, puzzling, unclear, unintelligible

intend aim, be resolved *or* determined, contemplate, determine, have in mind *or* view, mean, meditate, plan, propose, purpose, scheme

intense 1. acute, agonizing, close, concentrated, deep, excessive, exquisite, extreme, fierce, forceful, great, harsh, intensive, powerful, profound, protracted, severe, strained 2. ardent, burning, consuming, eager, earnest, energetic, fanatical, fervent, fervid, fierce, forcible, heightened, impassioned, keen, passionate, speaking, vehement **Antonyms** (*sense 1*) easy, gentle,

mild, moderate, relaxed, slight (*sense 2*) casual, cool, indifferent, subdued, weak

intensify add fuel to the flames (*Inf.*), add to, aggravate, boost, concentrate, deepen, emphasize, enhance, escalate, exacerbate, heighten, increase, magnify, quicken, redouble, reinforce, set off, sharpen, step up (*Inf.*), strengthen, whet **Antonyms** damp down, decrease, dilute, diminish, dull, lessen, minimize, weaken

intensity ardour, concentration, depth, earnestness, emotion, energy, excess, extremity, fanaticism, fervency, fervour, fierceness, fire, force, intenseness, keenness, passion, potency, power, severity, strain, strength, tension, vehemence, vigour

intensive all-out, comprehensive, concentrated, demanding, exhaustive, in-depth, thorough, thoroughgoing **Antonyms** apathetic, careless, feeble, hit-or-miss, superficial, weakened

intent *adj.* absorbed, alert, attentive, committed, concentrated, determined, eager, earnest, engrossed, fixed, industrious, intense, occupied, piercing, preoccupied, rapt, resolute, resolved, steadfast, steady, watchful, wrapped up **Antonyms** casual, indifferent, irresolute, unsteady, wavering

intention aim, design, end, end in view, goal, idea, intent, meaning, object, objective, point, purpose, scope, target, view

intentional calculated, deliberate, designed, done on purpose, intended, meant, planned, prearranged, preconcerted, premeditated, purposed, studied, wilful **Antonyms** accidental, inadvertent, unintentional, unplanned

intercept arrest, block, catch, check, cut off, deflect, head off, interrupt, obstruct, seize, stop, take

interchangeable commutable,

equivalent, exchangeable, identical, reciprocal, synonymous, the same, transposable

intercourse 1. association, commerce, communication, communion, connection, contact, converse, correspondence, dealings, intercommunication, trade, traffic, truck 2. carnal knowledge, coition, coitus, congress, copulation, intimacy, sex (*Inf.*), sexual act, sexual intercourse, sexual relations

interest *n.* 1. affection, attention, attentiveness, attraction, concern, curiosity, notice, regard, suspicion, sympathy 2. concern, consequence, importance, moment, note, relevance, significance, weight 3. activity, diversion, hobby, leisure activity, pastime, preoccupation, pursuit, relaxation 4. advantage, benefit, gain, good, profit ~*v.* 5. amuse, arouse one's curiosity, attract, divert, engross, fascinate, hold the attention of, intrigue, move, touch 6. affect, concern, engage, involve
Antonyms (*sense 1*) boredom, coolness, disinterest, dispassion, disregard, unconcern (*sense 2*) inconsequence, insignificance, irrelevance, worthlessness ~*v.* bore, burden, irk, repel, tire, weary

interested 1. affected, attentive, attracted, curious, drawn, excited, fascinated, intent, keen, moved, responsive, stimulated 2. biased, concerned, implicated, involved, partial, partisan, predisposed, prejudiced
Antonyms (*sense 1*) apathetic, bored, detached, inattentive, indifferent, unconcerned, uninterested, wearied

interesting absorbing, amusing, appealing, attractive, compelling, curious, engaging, engrossing, entertaining, gripping, intriguing, pleasing, provocative, stimulating, suspicious, thought-provoking, unusual

Antonyms boring, dull, tedious, uninteresting

interfere butt in, get involved, intermeddle, intervene, intrude, meddle, poke one's nose in (*Inf.*), stick one's oar in (*Inf.*), tamper

interference 1. intermeddling, intervention, intrusion, meddlesomeness, meddling, prying 2. clashing, collision, conflict, impedance, obstruction, opposition

interior *adj.* 1. inner, inside, internal, inward 2. *Geog.* central, inland, remote, upcountry 3. hidden, inner, intimate, mental, personal, private, secret, spiritual ~*n.* 4. *Geog.* centre, heartland, upcountry
Antonyms (*sense 1*) exposed, exterior, external, outer, outside, outward

interlude break, breathing space, delay, episode, halt, hiatus, intermission, interval, pause, respite, rest, spell, stop, stoppage, wait

intermediate halfway, in-between (*Inf.*), intermediary, interposed, intervening, mean, mid, middle, midway, transitional

intermittent broken, discontinuous, fitful, irregular, occasional, periodic, punctuated, recurrent, recurring, spasmodic, sporadic, stop-go (*Inf.*)
Antonyms continuous, steady, unceasing

internal inner, inside, interior, intimate, private, subjective
Antonyms exposed, exterior, external, outer, outermost, outside, revealed, unconcealed

international cosmopolitan, ecumenical (*Rare*), global, intercontinental, universal, worldwide

interpose 1. come *or* place between, intercede, interfere, intermediate, intervene, intrude, mediate, step in 2. insert, interject, interrupt (with), introduce, put forth

interpret adapt, clarify, construe, decipher, decode, define, elucidate, explain, explicate, expound, make sense of, paraphrase, read, render, solve, spell out, take, throw light on, translate, understand

interpretation analysis, clarification, construction, diagnosis, elucidation, exegesis, explanation, explication, exposition, meaning, performance, portrayal, reading, rendering, rendition, sense, signification, translation, understanding, version

interpreter annotator, commentator, exponent, scholiast, translator

interrogate ask, catechize, cross-examine, cross-question, enquire, examine, give (someone) the third degree (*Inf.*), grill (*Inf.*), inquire, investigate, pump, put the screws on (*Inf.*), question, quiz

interrogation cross-examination, cross-questioning, enquiry, examination, grilling (*Inf.*), inquiry, inquisition, probing, questioning, third degree (*Inf.*)

interrupt barge in (*Inf.*), break, break in, break off, break (someone's) train of thought, butt in, check, cut, cut off, cut short, delay, disconnect, discontinue, disjoin, disturb, disunite, divide, heckle, hinder, hold up, interfere (with), intrude, lay aside, obstruct, punctuate, separate, sever, stay, stop, suspend

interruption break, cessation, disconnection, discontinuance, disruption, dissolution, disturbance, disuniting, division, halt, hiatus, hindrance, hitch, impediment, intrusion, obstacle, obstruction, pause, separation, severance, stop, stoppage, suspension

intersection crossing, crossroads, interchange, junction

interval break, delay, distance, gap, hiatus, interim, interlude, intermission, meantime, meanwhile, opening, pause, period, playtime, rest, season, space, spell, term, time, wait

intervene arbitrate, intercede, interfere, interpose oneself, intrude, involve oneself, mediate, step in (*Inf.*), take a hand (*Inf.*)

intervention agency, intercession, interference, interposition, intrusion, mediation

interview 1. *n.* audience, conference, consultation, dialogue, evaluation, meeting, oral (examination), press conference, talk 2. *v.* examine, interrogate, question, sound out, talk to

intimacy closeness, confidence, confidentiality, familiarity, fraternization, understanding
Antonyms alienation, aloofness, coldness, detachment, distance, estrangement, remoteness, separation

intimate¹ *adj.* 1. bosom, cherished, close, confidential, dear, friendly, near, nearest and dearest, thick (*Inf.*), warm 2. confidential, personal, private, privy, secret 3. comfy (*Inf.*), cosy, friendly, informal, snug, tête-à-tête, warm ~ *n.* 4. bosom friend, buddy (*Inf.*), china (*Brit. sl.*), chum (*Inf.*), close friend, comrade, confidant, confidante, (constant) companion, crony, familiar, friend, mate (*Inf.*), mucker (*Brit. sl.*), pal
Antonyms (*sense 1*) distant, remote, superficial (*sense 2*) known, open, public ~ *n.* enemy, foe, stranger

intimate² *v.* allude, announce, communicate, declare, drop a hint, give (someone) to understand, hint, impart, imply, indicate, insinuate, let it be known, make known, remind, state, suggest, tip (someone) the wink (*Brit. inf.*), warn

intimately 1. affectionately, closely, confidentially, confidingly, familiarly, personally, tenderly, very well, warmly 2. fully, in detail, inside out, thoroughly, through and through, to the core, very well

intimidate affright (*Archaic*), alarm, appal, browbeat, bully, coerce, cow, daunt, dishearten, dismay, dispirit, frighten, lean on

(*Inf.*), overawe, scare, scare off (*Inf.*), subdue, terrify, terrorize, threaten, twist someone's arm (*Inf.*)

intimidation arm-twisting (*Inf.*), browbeating, bullying, coercion, fear, menaces, pressure, terror, terrorization, threat(s)

intolerable beyond bearing, excruciating, impossible, insufferable, insupportable, more than flesh and blood can stand, not to be borne, painful, unbearable, unendurable
Antonyms bearable, endurable, painless, possible, sufferable, supportable, tolerable

intolerant bigoted, chauvinistic, dictatorial, dogmatic, fanatical, illiberal, impatient, narrow, narrow-minded, one-sided, prejudiced, racialist, racist, small-minded, uncharitable, xenophobic
Antonyms broad-minded, charitable, lenient, liberal, open-minded, patient, tolerant, understanding

intoxicated blotto (*Sl.*), canned (*Sl.*), cut (*Brit. sl.*), drunk, drunken, fuddled, half seas over (*Brit. inf.*), high (*Inf.*), inebriated, in one's cups (*Inf.*), lit up (*Sl.*), plastered (*Sl.*), smashed (*Sl.*), sozzled (*Inf.*), stewed (*Sl.*), stiff (*Sl.*), stoned (*Sl.*), the worse for drink, three sheets in the wind (*Inf.*), tight (*Inf.*), tipsy, under the influence

intoxication drunkenness, inebriation, inebriety, insobriety, tipsiness

intrepid audacious, bold, brave, courageous, daring, dauntless, doughty, fearless, gallant, game (*Inf.*), heroic, lion-hearted, nerveless, plucky, resolute, stalwart, stouthearted, unafraid, undaunted, unflinching, valiant, valorous

intricate baroque, Byzantine, complex, complicated, convoluted, daedal (*Literary*), difficult, elaborate, fancy, involved, knotty, labyrinthine, obscure, per-plexing, rococo, sophisticated, tangled, tortuous
Antonyms clear, easy, obvious, plain, simple, straightforward

intrigue v. 1. arouse the curiosity of, attract, charm, fascinate, interest, pique, rivet, tickle one's fancy, titillate 2. connive, conspire, machinate, manoeuvre, plot, scheme ~*n*. 3. cabal, chicanery, collusion, conspiracy, double-dealing, knavery, machination, manipulation, manoeuvre, plot, ruse, scheme, sharp practice, stratagem, trickery, wile 4. affair, amour, intimacy, liaison, romance

intriguing beguiling, compelling, diverting, exciting, fascinating, interesting, tantalizing, titillating

intrinsic basic, built-in, central, congenital, constitutional, elemental, essential, fundamental, genuine, inborn, inbred, inherent, native, natural, real, true, underlying

introduce 1. acquaint, do the honours, familiarize, make known, make the introduction, present 2. begin, bring in, commence, establish, found, inaugurate, initiate, institute, launch, organize, pioneer, set up, start, usher in 3. announce, lead into, lead off, open, preface

introduction 1. baptism, debut, establishment, first acquaintance, inauguration, induction, initiation, institution, launch, pioneering, presentation 2. commencement, exordium, foreword, intro (*Inf.*), lead-in, opening, opening passage, opening remarks, overture, preamble, preface, preliminaries, prelude, proem, prolegomena, prolegomenon, prologue
Antonyms (*sense 1*) completion, elimination, termination (*sense 2*) afterward, conclusion, end, epilogue

introductory early, elementary, first, inaugural, initial, initiatory, opening, precursory, prefatory, preliminary, preparatory, starting

Antonyms closing, concluding, final, last, terminating

intrude butt in, encroach, infringe, interfere, interrupt, meddle, obtrude, push in, thrust oneself in or forward, trespass, violate

intruder burglar, gate-crasher (Inf.), infiltrator, interloper, invader, prowler, raider, snooper (Inf.), squatter, thief, trespasser

intrusion encroachment, infringement, interference, interruption, invasion, trespass, violation

intuition discernment, hunch, insight, instinct, perception, presentiment, sixth sense

invade assail, assault, attack, burst in, descend upon, encroach, infringe, make inroads, occupy, raid, violate

invader aggressor, alien, attacker, looter, plunderer, raider, trespasser

invalid[1] adj. ailing, bedridden, disabled, feeble, frail, ill, infirm, poorly (Inf.), sick, sickly, valetudinarian, weak

invalid[2] adj. baseless, fallacious, false, ill-founded, illogical, inoperative, irrational, not binding, nugatory, null, null and void, unfounded, unscientific, unsound, untrue, void, worthless

Antonyms logical, operative, rational, solid, sound, true, valid, viable

invaluable beyond price, costly, inestimable, precious, priceless, valuable

Antonyms cheap, rubbishy, valueless, worthless

invariable changeless, consistent, constant, fixed, immutable, inflexible, regular, rigid, set, unalterable, unchangeable, unchanging, unfailing, uniform, unvarying, unwavering

Antonyms alterable, changeable, changing, differing, flexible, inconsistent, irregular, variable, varying

invasion aggression, assault, attack, foray, incursion, inroad, irruption, offensive, onslaught, raid

invent coin, come up with (Inf.), conceive, contrive, create, design, devise, discover, dream up (Inf.), formulate, imagine, improvise, originate, think up

invention 1. brainchild (Inf.), contraption, contrivance, creation, design, development, device, discovery, gadget 2. deceit, fabrication, fake, falsehood, fantasy, fib (Inf.), fiction, figment or product of (someone's) imagination, forgery, lie, prevarication, sham, story, tall story (Inf.), untruth, yarn

inventive creative, fertile, gifted, imaginative, ingenious, innovative, inspired, original, resourceful

Antonyms imitative, pedestrian, trite, unimaginative, uninspired, uninventive

inventor architect, author, coiner, creator, designer, father, framer, maker, originator

inventory n. account, catalogue, file, list, record, register, roll, roster, schedule, stock book

inverse adj. contrary, converse, inverted, opposite, reverse, reversed, transposed

invert capsize, introvert, intussuscept (Pathol.), invaginate (Pathol.), overset, overturn, reverse, transpose, turn inside out, turn turtle, turn upside down, upset, upturn

invest 1. advance, devote, lay out, put in, sink, spend 2. endow, endue, provide, supply 3. Mil. beleaguer, beset, besiege, enclose, lay siege to, surround

investigate consider, enquire into, examine, explore, go into, inquire into, inspect, look into, make enquiries, probe, put to the test, scrutinize, search, sift, study

investigation analysis, enquiry, examination, exploration, fact finding, hearing, inquest, inquiry, inspection, probe, research, review, scrutiny, search, study, survey

investigator dick (*Sl.*), examiner, gumshoe (*U.S. sl.*), inquirer, (private) detective, private eye (*Inf.*), researcher, reviewer, sleuth *or* sleuthhound (*Inf.*)

investment asset, investing, speculation, transaction, venture

inveterate chronic, confirmed, deep-dyed, deep-rooted, deep-seated, dyed-in-the-wool, entrenched, established, habitual, hard-core, hardened, incorrigible, incurable, ineradicable, ingrained, long-standing, obstinate

invigorate animate, brace, buck up (*Inf.*), energize, enliven, exhilarate, fortify, freshen (up), galvanize, harden, liven up, nerve, pep up, perk up, put new heart into, quicken, refresh, rejuvenate, revitalize, stimulate, strengthen

invincible impregnable, indestructible, indomitable, inseparable, insuperable, invulnerable, unassailable, unbeatable, unconquerable, unsurmountable, unyielding
Antonyms assailable, beatable, conquerable, defenceless, fallible, powerless, unprotected, vulnerable, weak, yielding

invisible imperceptible, indiscernible, out of sight, unperceivable, unseen 2. concealed, disguised, hidden, inappreciable, inconspicuous, infinitesimal, microscopic
Antonyms (*sense 1*) discernible, distinct, obvious, perceptible, seen, visible

invitation 1. asking, begging, bidding, call, invite (*Inf.*), request, solicitation, summons, supplication 2. allurement, challenge, come-on (*Inf.*), coquetry, enticement, glad eye (*Inf.*), incitement, inducement, open door, overture, provocation, temptation

invite 1. ask, beg, bid, call, request, request the pleasure of (someone's) company, solicit, summon 2. allure, ask for (*Inf.*),

attract, bring on, court, draw, encourage, entice, lead, leave the door open to, provoke, solicit, tempt, welcome

inviting alluring, appealing, attractive, beguiling, captivating, delightful, engaging, enticing, fascinating, intriguing, magnetic, mouthwatering, pleasing, seductive, tempting, warm, welcoming, winning

invoke adjure, appeal to, beg, beseech, call upon, conjure, entreat, implore, petition, pray, solicit, supplicate

involuntary compulsory, forced, obligatory, reluctant, unwilling

involve 1. entail, imply, mean, necessitate, presuppose, require 2. affect, associate, compromise, concern, connect, draw in, implicate, incriminate, inculpate, mix up (*Inf.*), touch 3. absorb, bind, commit, engage, engross, grip, hold, preoccupy, rivet, wrap up

involvement association, commitment, concern, connection, dedication, interest, participation, responsibility

inward *adj.* 1. entering, inbound, incoming, inflowing, ingoing, inpouring, penetrating 2. confidential, hidden, inmost, inner, innermost, inside, interior, internal, personal, private, privy, secret
Antonyms (*sense 2*) exterior, external, open, outer, outermost, outside, outward, public

irksome aggravating, annoying, boring, bothersome, burdensome, disagreeable, exasperating, irritating, tedious, tiresome, troublesome, uninteresting, unwelcome, vexatious, vexing, wearisome
Antonyms agreeable, enjoyable, gratifying, interesting, pleasant, pleasing, welcome

iron *adj. Fig.* adamant, cruel, hard, heavy, immovable, implacable, indomitable, inflexible, obdurate, rigid, robust, steel, steely, strong, tough, unbending, unyielding

Antonyms bending, easy, flex~ible, light, malleable, pliable, soft, weak, yielding

ironic, ironical 1. double-edged, mocking, sarcastic, sardonic, satirical, scoffing, sneering, wry 2. incongruous, paradoxical

iron out clear up, eliminate, eradicate, erase, expedite, get rid of, harmonize, put right, reconcile, resolve, settle, simplify, smooth over, sort out, straighten out, unravel

irony 1. mockery, sarcasm, satire 2. contrariness, incongruity, paradox

irrational absurd, crazy, foolish, illogical, injudicious, nonsensical, preposterous, silly, unreasonable, unreasoning, unsound, unthinking, unwise
Antonyms circumspect, judicious, logical, rational, reasonable, sensible, sound, wise

irregular adj. 1. desultory, disconnected, eccentric, erratic, fitful, fluctuating, fragmentary, haphazard, intermittent, nonuniform, occasional, out of order, patchy, random, shifting, spasmodic, sporadic, uncertain, unmethodical, unpunctual, unsteady, unsystematic, variable, wavering 2. asymmetrical, broken, bumpy, craggy, crooked, elliptic, elliptical, holey, jagged, lopsided, lumpy, pitted, ragged, rough, serrated, unequal, uneven, unsymmetrical ~n. 3. guerrilla, partisan, volunteer
Antonyms (sense 1) certain, invariable, methodical, punctual, reliable, steady, systematic (sense 2) balanced, equal, even, regular, smooth, symmetrical

irregularity 1. asymmetry, bumpiness, crookedness, jaggedness, lack of symmetry, lopsidedness, lumpiness, patchiness, raggedness, roughness, unevenness 2. aberration, abnormality, anomaly, breach, deviation, eccentricity, freak, malfunction, malpractice, oddity, peculiarity,

singularity, unconventionality, unorthodoxy

irrelevant beside the point, extraneous, immaterial, impertinent, inapplicable, inapposite, inappropriate, inapt, inconsequent, neither here nor there, unconnected, unrelated
Antonyms applicable, apposite, appropriate, apt, connected, pertinent, related, relevant, suitable

irreparable beyond repair, incurable, irrecoverable, irremediable, irreplaceable, irretrievable, irreversible

irrepressible boisterous, bubbling over, buoyant, ebullient, effervescent, insuppressible, uncontainable, uncontrollable, unmanageable, unquenchable, unrestrainable, unstoppable

irreproachable beyond reproach, blameless, faultless, guiltless, impeccable, inculpable, innocent, irreprehensible, irreprovable, perfect, pure, unblemished, unimpeachable

irresistible 1. compelling, imperative, overmastering, overpowering, overwhelming, potent, urgent 2. alluring, beckoning, enchanting, fascinating, ravishing, seductive, tempting

irresponsible careless, featherbrained, flighty, giddy, harebrained, harum-scarum, ill-considered, immature, reckless, scatter-brained, shiftless, thoughtless, undependable, unreliable, untrustworthy, wild
Antonyms careful, dependable, level-headed, mature, reliable, responsible, sensible, trustworthy

irreverent cheeky (Inf.), contemptuous, derisive, disrespectful, flip (Inf.), flippant, iconoclastic, impertinent, impious, impudent, mocking, saucy, tongue-in-cheek
Antonyms awed, deferential, meek, pious, respectful, reverent, submissive

irreversible final, incurable, irreparable, irrevocable, unalterable

irrevocable changeless, fated, fixed, immutable, invariable, irremediable, irretrievable, irreversible, predestined, predetermined, settled, unalterable, unchangeable, unreversible

irrigate flood, inundate, moisten, water, wet

irritable bad-tempered, cantankerous, choleric, crabbed, crabby, cross, crotchety (*Inf.*), dyspeptic, exasperated, fiery, fretful, hasty, hot, ill-humoured, ill-tempered, irascible, narky (*Inf.*), out of humour, oversensitive, peevish, petulant, prickly, snappish, snappy, snarling, tense, testy, touchy
Antonyms agreeable, calm, cheerful, complacent, composed, even-tempered, good-natured, imperturbable, patient, unexcitable

irritate 1. aggravate (*Inf.*), anger, annoy, bother, drive one up the wall (*Inf.*), enrage, exasperate, fret, get in one's hair (*Inf.*), get one's back up (*Inf.*), get one's hackles up, get on one's nerves (*Inf.*), harass, incense, inflame, infuriate, needle (*Inf.*), nettle, offend, pester, provoke, raise one's hackles, rankle with, rub up the wrong way (*Inf.*), ruffle, try one's patience, vex 2. aggravate, chafe, fret, inflame, intensify, pain, rub
Antonyms (*sense 1*) calm, comfort, gratify, mollify, placate, please, soothe

irritated angry, annoyed, bothered, cross, displeased, exasperated, flustered, harassed, impatient, irritable, nettled, out of humour, peeved (*Inf.*), piqued, put out, ruffled, vexed

irritating aggravating (*Inf.*), annoying, displeasing, disquieting, disturbing, galling, infuriating, irksome, maddening, nagging, pestilential, provoking, thorny, troublesome, trying, upsetting, vexatious, worrisome
Antonyms agreeable, assuaging, calming, comforting, mollifying,

pleasant, pleasing, quieting, soothing

irritation anger, annoyance, crossness, displeasure, exasperation, ill humour, ill temper, impatience, indignation, irritability, resentment, shortness, snappiness, testiness, vexation, wrath
Antonyms calm, composure, ease, pleasure, quietude, satisfaction, serenity, tranquillity

isolate cut off, detach, disconnect, divorce, insulate, quarantine, segregate, separate, sequester, set apart

isolated backwoods, hidden, incommunicado, lonely, off the beaten track, outlying, out-of-the-way, remote, retired, secluded, unfrequented

isolation aloofness, detachment, disconnection, exile, insularity, insulation, loneliness, quarantine, remoteness, retirement, seclusion, segregation, self-sufficiency, separation, solitude, withdrawal

issue *n.* 1. affair, argument, concern, controversy, matter, matter of contention, point, point in question, problem, question, subject, topic 2. copy, edition, impression, instalment, number, printing 3. children, descendants, heirs, offspring, progeny, scions, seed (*Biblical*) ~*v.* 4. announce, broadcast, circulate, deliver, distribute, emit, give out, promulgate, publish, put in circulation, put out, release 5. arise, be a consequence of, come forth, emanate, emerge, flow, originate, proceed, rise, spring, stem
Antonyms *n.* (*sense 3*) parent, sire ~*v.* cause, revoke, withdraw

itch *v.* 1. crawl, irritate, prickle, tickle, tingle 2. ache, burn, crave, hanker, hunger, long, lust, pant, pine, yearn ~*n.* 3. irritation, itchiness, prickling, tingling 4. craving, desire, hankering, hunger, longing, lust, passion, restlessness, yearning, yen (*Inf.*)

item 1. article, aspect, component, consideration, detail, entry, matter, particular, point, thing **2.** paragraph, piece, report account, article, bulletin, dis~ patch, feature, note, notice,

itinerary circuit, journey, line, programme, route, schedule, tour

J

jab *v./n.* dig, lunge, nudge, poke, prod, punch, stab, tap, thrust

jacket case, casing, coat, covering, envelope, folder, sheath, skin, wrapper, wrapping

jackpot award, bonanza, kitty, pool, pot, prize, reward, winnings

jaded 1. exhausted, fagged (out) (*Inf.*), fatigued, spent, tired, tired-out, weary 2. bored, cloyed, dulled, glutted, gorged, sated, satiated, surfeited, tired
Antonyms eager, enthusiastic, fresh, keen, life-loving, naive, refreshed

jagged barbed, broken, cleft, craggy, denticulate, indented, notched, pointed, ragged, ridged, rough, serrated, snaggy, spiked, toothed, uneven
Antonyms glassy, level, regular, rounded, smooth

jail, gaol 1. *n.* borstal, brig (*Chiefly U.S.*), clink (*Sl.*), cooler (*Sl.*), inside (*Sl.*), jailhouse (*Southern U.S.*), jug (*Sl.*), lockup, nick (*Sl.*), penitentiary (*U.S.*), prison, quod (*Sl.*), reformatory, stir (*Sl.*) 2. *v.* confine, detain, immure, impound, imprison, incarcerate, lock up, send down

jailer, gaoler captor, guard, keeper, screw (*Sl.*), turnkey (*Archaic*), warden, warder

jam *v.* 1. cram, crowd, crush, force, pack, press, ram, squeeze, stuff, throng, wedge 2. block, cease, clog, congest, halt, obstruct, stall, stick ~ *n.* 3. crowd, crush, horde, mass, mob, multitude, pack, press, swarm, throng 4. bind, dilemma, fix (*Inf.*), hole (*Sl.*), pickle (*Inf.*), plight, predicament, quandary, scrape (*Inf.*), spot (*Inf.*), strait, trouble

jangle 1. *v.* chime, clank, clash, clatter, jingle, rattle, vibrate 2. *n.*

cacophony, clang, clangour, clash, din, dissonance, jar, racket, rattle, reverberation
Antonyms (*sense 2*) harmoniousness, mellifluousness, quiet, silence

janitor caretaker, concierge, custodian, doorkeeper, porter

jar[1] amphora, carafe, container, crock, flagon, jug, pitcher, pot, receptacle, urn, vase, vessel

jar[2] *v.* 1. bicker, clash, contend, disagree, interfere, oppose, quarrel, wrangle 2. agitate, convulse, disturb, grate, irritate, jolt, offend, rasp, rattle (*Inf.*), rock, shake, vibrate 3. annoy, clash, discompose, grate, grind, irk, irritate, nettle

jargon argot, cant, dialect, idiom, lingo (*Inf.*), parlance, patois, slang, tongue, usage

jaunt airing, excursion, expedition, outing, promenade, ramble, stroll, tour, trip

jaunty airy, breezy, buoyant, carefree, dapper, gay, high-spirited, lively, perky, self-confident, showy, smart, sparky, sprightly, spruce, trim
Antonyms dignified, dull, lifeless, sedate, serious, staid

jealous covetous, desirous, emulous, envious, green, green-eyed, grudging, intolerant, invidious, resentful, rival
Antonyms indifferent, satisfied

jealousy covetousness, distrust, envy, heart-burning, ill will, mistrust, possessiveness, resentment, spite, suspicion

jeer *v.* banter, barrack, cock a snook at (*Brit.*), contemn, deride, flout, gibe, heckle, hector, knock (*Sl.*), mock, ridicule, scoff, sneer, taunt

Antonyms acclaim, applaud, cheer, clap, praise

jeopardize chance, endanger, expose, gamble, hazard, imperil, risk, stake, venture

jeopardy danger, endangerment, exposure, hazard, insecurity, liability, peril, precariousness, risk, venture, vulnerability

jerk v./n. jolt, lurch, pull, throw, thrust, tug, tweak, twitch, wrench, yank

jest 1. n. banter, bon mot, crack (Sl.), fun, gag (Sl.), hoax, jape, joke, play, pleasantry, prank, quip, sally, sport, wisecrack (Inf.), witticism 2. v. banter, chaff, deride, gibe, jeer, joke, kid (Inf.), mock, quip, scoff, sneer, tease

jester 1. comedian, comic, humorist, joker, quipster, wag, wit 2. buffoon, clown, fool, harlequin, madcap, mummer, pantaloon, prankster, zany

jet 1. n. flow, fountain, gush, spout, spray, spring, stream 2. atomizer, nose, nozzle, rose, spout, sprayer, sprinkler ~v. 3. flow, gush, issue, rush, shoot, spew, spout, squirt, stream, surge

jettison abandon, discard, dump, eject, expel, heave, scrap, throw overboard, unload

jetty breakwater, dock, groyne, mole, pier, quay, wharf

jewel 1. brilliant, gemstone, ornament, precious stone, rock (Sl.), sparkler (Inf.), trinket 2. charm, find, gem, humdinger (Sl.), masterpiece, paragon, pearl, prize, rarity, treasure (Fig.), wonder

jig v. bob, bounce, caper, jiggle, jounce, prance, shake, skip, twitch, wiggle, wobble

jingle v. 1. chime, clatter, clink, jangle, rattle, ring, tinkle, tintinnabulate ~n. 2. clang, clangour, clink, rattle, reverberation, ringing, tinkle 3. chorus, ditty, doggerel, limerick, melody, song, tune

jinx 1. n. black magic, curse, evil eye, hex (U.S.), nemesis, plague,

voodoo 2. v. bewitch, curse, hex (U.S.)

job 1. affair, assignment, charge, chore, concern, contribution, duty, enterprise, errand, function, pursuit, responsibility, role, stint, task, undertaking, venture, work 2. activity, business, calling, capacity, career, craft, employment, function, livelihood, métier, occupation, office, position, post, profession, situation, trade, vocation

jocular amusing, comical, droll, facetious, frolicsome, funny, humorous, jesting, jocose, jocund, joking, jolly, jovial, playful, roguish, sportive, teasing, waggish, whimsical, witty

Antonyms earnest, humourless, serious, solemn

jog 1. activate, arouse, nudge, prod, prompt, push, remind, shake, stimulate, stir, suggest 2. canter, dogtrot, lope, run, trot 3. lumber, plod, traipse (Inf.), tramp, trudge

join 1. accompany, add, adhere, annex, append, attach, cement, combine, connect, couple, fasten, knit, link, marry, splice, tie, unite, yoke 2. affiliate with, associate with, enlist, enrol, enter, sign up

Antonyms detach, disconnect, disengage, disentangle, divide, leave, part, quit, resign, separate, sever, unfasten

joint n. 1. articulation, connection, hinge, intersection, junction, juncture, knot, nexus, node, seam, union ~adj. 2. collective, combined, communal, concerted, consolidated, cooperative, joined, mutual, shared, united

jointly as one, collectively, in common, in conjunction, in league, in partnership, mutually, together, unitedly

Antonyms individually, separately, singly

joke 1. n. frolic, fun, gag (Sl.), jape, jest, lark, play, pun, quip, quirk, sally, sport, whimsy, wisecrack (Inf.), witticism, yarn 2. v.

banter, chaff, deride, frolic, gambol, jest, kid (*Inf.*), mock, quip, ridicule, taunt, tease

jolly blithesome, carefree, cheerful, convivial, festive, frolicsome, funny, gay, gladsome, hilarious, jocund, jovial, joyful, joyous, jubilant, merry, mirthful, playful, sportive, sprightly
Antonyms doleful, gaunt, grave, lugubrious, miserable, morose, saturnine, serious, solemn

jolt *v.* **1.** jar, jerk, jog, jostle, knock, push, shake, shove **2.** astonish, discompose, disturb, perturb, stagger, startle, stun, surprise, upset ~*n.* **3.** bump, jar, jerk, jog, jump, lurch, quiver, shake, start **4.** blow, bolt from the blue, bombshell, reversal, setback, shock, surprise, thunderbolt

jostle bump, butt, crowd, elbow, hustle, jog, joggle, jolt, press, push, scramble, shake, shove, squeeze, throng, thrust

journal 1. chronicle, daily, gazette, magazine, monthly, newspaper, paper, periodical, record, register, review, tabloid, weekly **2.** chronicle, commonplace book, daybook, diary, log, record

journalist broadcaster, columnist, commentator, contributor, correspondent, hack, newsman, newspaperman, pressman, reporter, scribe (*Inf.*), stringer

journey *n.* excursion, expedition, jaunt, odyssey, outing, passage, peregrination, pilgrimage, progress, ramble, tour, travel, trek, trip, voyage

jovial airy, animated, blithe, buoyant, cheery, convivial, cordial, gay, glad, happy, hilarious, jocose, jocund, jolly, jubilant, merry, mirthful
Antonyms antisocial, doleful, grumpy, morose, solemn, unfriendly

joy bliss, delight, ecstasy, elation, exaltation, exultation, felicity, festivity, gaiety, gladness, glee, hilarity, pleasure, rapture, ravishment, satisfaction, transport

Antonyms bane, despair, grief, misery, sorrow, tribulation, unhappiness

joyful blithesome, delighted, elated, enraptured, glad, gladsome, gratified, happy, jocund, jolly, jovial, jubilant, light-hearted, merry, pleased, satisfied

joyless cheerless, dejected, depressed, dismal, dispirited, downcast, dreary, gloomy, miserable, sad, unhappy

jubilant elated, enraptured, euphoric, excited, exuberant, exultant, glad, joyous, overjoyed, rejoicing, rhapsodic, thrilled, triumphal, triumphant

judge *n.* **1.** adjudicator, arbiter, arbitrator, moderator, referee, umpire **2.** appraiser, arbiter, assessor, authority, connoisseur, critic, evaluator, expert **3.** beak (*Brit. sl.*), justice, magistrate ~*v.* **4.** adjudge, adjudicate, arbitrate, ascertain, conclude, decide, determine, discern, distinguish, mediate, referee, umpire **5.** appraise, appreciate, assess, consider, criticize, esteem, estimate, evaluate, examine, rate, review, value

judgment 1. acumen, common sense, discernment, discrimination, intelligence, penetration, percipience, perspicacity, prudence, sagacity, sense, shrewdness, taste, understanding, wisdom **2.** arbitration, award, conclusion, decision, decree, determination, finding, order, result, ruling, sentence, verdict **3.** appraisal, assessment, belief, conviction, deduction, diagnosis, estimate, finding, opinion, valuation, view

judicial judiciary, juridical, legal, official

judicious acute, astute, careful, cautious, circumspect, considered, diplomatic, discerning, discreet, discriminating, enlightened, expedient, informed, politic, prudent, rational, reasonable, sagacious, sage, sane, sapient, sensible, shrewd, skilful, sober,

jug carafe, container, crock, ewer, jar, pitcher, urn, vessel

juice extract, fluid, liquid, liquor, nectar, sap, secretion, serum

juicy 1. lush, moist, sappy, succulent, watery **2.** colourful, interesting, provocative, racy, risqué, sensational, spicy, suggestive, vivid

jumble 1. v. confound, confuse, disarrange, dishevel, disorder, disorganize, entangle, mistake, mix, muddle, shuffle, tangle **2.** n. chaos, clutter, confusion, disarrangement, disarray, disorder, farrago, gallimaufry, hodgepodge, hotchpotch, litter, medley, *mélange*, mess, miscellany, mishmash, mixture, muddle

jump v. **1.** bounce, bound, caper, clear, gambol, hop, hurdle, leap, skip, spring, vault **2.** avoid, digress, evade, miss, omit, overshoot, skip, switch ~n. **3.** bound, buck, caper, hop, leap, skip, spring, vault **4.** advance, augmentation, boost, increase, increment, rise, upsurge, upturn

jumpy agitated, anxious, apprehensive, fidgety, hyper (*Inf.*), jittery (*Inf.*), nervous, on edge, restless, shaky, tense, timorous
Antonyms calm, composed, laidback (*Inf.*), nerveless, together (*Sl.*), unflustered

junction alliance, combination, connection, coupling, joint, juncture, linking, seam, union

junior inferior, lesser, lower, minor, secondary, subordinate, younger
Antonyms elder, higher-ranking, older, senior, superior

junk clutter, debris, leavings, litter, oddments, odds and ends, refuse, rubbish, rummage, scrap, trash, waste

jurisdiction authority, command, control, dominion, influence, power, prerogative, rule, say, sway

just adj. **1.** blameless, conscientious, decent, equitable, fair, fair-minded, good, honest, honourable, impartial, lawful, pure, right, righteous, unbiased, upright, virtuous **2.** appropriate, apt, condign, deserved, due, fitting, justified, legitimate, merited, proper, reasonable, rightful, suitable, well-deserved ~adv. **3.** absolutely, completely, entirely, exactly, perfectly, precisely **4.** hardly, lately, only now, recently, scarcely
Antonyms adj. corrupt, devious, dishonest, inappropriate, inequitable, prejudiced, undeserved, unfair, unfit, unjust, unlawful, unreasonable, untrue

justice 1. equity, fairness, honesty, impartiality, integrity, justness, law, legality, legitimacy, reasonableness, rectitude, right **2.** amends, compensation, correction, penalty, recompense, redress, reparation
Antonyms dishonesty, favouritism, inequity, injustice, partiality, unfairness, unlawfulness, unreasonableness, untruth, wrong

justifiable acceptable, defensible, excusable, fit, lawful, legitimate, proper, reasonable, right, sound, tenable, understandable, valid, vindicable, warrantable, well-founded
Antonyms arbitrary, capricious, indefensible, inexcusable, unreasonable, unwarranted

justification absolution, apology, approval, defence, exculpation, excuse, exoneration, explanation, extenuation, plea, rationalization, vindication

justify absolve, acquit, approve, confirm, defend, establish, exculpate, excuse, exonerate, explain, legalize, legitimatize, maintain, substantiate, support, sustain, uphold, validate, vindicate, warrant

juvenile n. adolescent, boy, child, girl, infant, minor, youth
Antonyms adult, grown-up ~adj. adult, grown-up, mature, responsible

K

keen 1. ardent, avid, devoted to, eager, earnest, ebullient, enthusiastic, fervid, fierce, fond of, impassioned, intense, zealous 2. acid, acute, biting, caustic, cutting, edged, finely honed, incisive, penetrating, piercing, pointed, razorlike, sardonic, satirical, sharp, tart, trenchant **Antonyms** (*sense 1*) apathetic, half-hearted, indifferent, laodicean, lukewarm, unenthusiastic, uninterested (*Sense 2*) blunt, dull

keenness ardour, avidity, avidness, diligence, eagerness, earnestness, ebullience, enthusiasm, fervour, impatience, intensity, passion, zeal, zest

keep *v.* 1. conserve, control, hold, maintain, possess, preserve, retain 2. accumulate, amass, carry, deal in, deposit, furnish, garner, heap, hold, pile, place, stack, store, trade in 3. care for, defend, guard, look after, maintain, manage, mind, operate, protect, safeguard, shelter, shield, tend, watch over 4. board, feed, foster, maintain, nourish, nurture, provide for, provision, subsidize, support, sustain, victual 5. adhere to, celebrate, commemorate, comply with, fulfil, hold, honour, obey, observe, perform, respect, ritualize, solemnize ~*n.* 6. board, food, livelihood, living, maintenance, means, nourishment, subsistence, support 7. castle, citadel, donjon, dungeon, fastness, stronghold, tower **Antonyms** abandon, discard, disregard, expedite, free, give up, ignore, liberate, lose, release, speed

keep back check, constrain, control, curb, delay, hold back, limit, prohibit, restrain, restrict, retard, withhold

keeper attendant, caretaker, curator, custodian, defender, gaoler, governor, guard, guardian, jailer, overseer, preserver, steward, superintendent, warden, warder

keeping aegis, auspices, care, charge, custody, guardianship, keep, maintenance, patronage, possession, protection, safekeeping, trust

keepsake emblem, favour, memento, relic, remembrance, reminder, souvenir, symbol, token

keep up balance, compete, contend, continue, emulate, keep pace, maintain, match, persevere, preserve, rival, sustain, vie

key *n.* 1. latchkey, opener 2. *Fig.* answer, clue, cue, explanation, guide, indicator, interpretation, lead, means, pointer, sign, solution, translation ~*adj.* 3. basic, chief, crucial, decisive, essential, fundamental, important, leading, main, major, pivotal, principal **Antonyms** (*sense 3*) minor, secondary, subsidiary, superficial

keynote centre, core, essence, gist, heart, kernel, marrow, pith, substance, theme

kick 1. *v.* boot, punt 2. *n.* force, intensity, pep, power, punch, pungency, snap (*Inf.*), sparkle, strength, tang, verve, vitality, zest

kid 1. *n.* baby, bairn, boy, child, girl, infant, lad, little one, stripling, teenager, tot, youngster, youth 2. *v.* bamboozle, beguile, cozen, delude, fool, gull (*Archaic*), hoax, hoodwink, jest, joke, mock, plague, pretend, rag (*Sl.*), ridicule, tease, trick

kidnap abduct, capture, hijack, hold to ransom, remove, seize, steal

kill 1. annihilate, assassinate, blow away (*Sl. chiefly U.S.*), bump off (*Sl.*), butcher, destroy, dispatch, do away with, do in (*Sl.*), eradicate, execute, exterminate, extirpate, knock off (*Sl.*), liquidate, massacre, murder, neutralize, obliterate, slaughter, slay, take (someone's) life, waste (*Sl.*) **2.** *Fig.* cancel, cease, deaden, defeat, extinguish, halt, quash, quell, ruin, scotch, smother, stifle, still, stop, suppress, veto

killer assassin, butcher, cutthroat, destroyer, executioner, exterminator, gunman, hit man (*Sl.*), liquidator, murderer, slaughterer, slayer

killing *n.* bloodshed, carnage, execution, extermination, fatality, homicide, manslaughter, massacre, murder, slaughter, slaying

kin *n.* affinity, blood, connection, consanguinity, extraction, kinship, lineage, relationship, stock

kind¹ *n.* brand, breed, class, family, genus, ilk, race, set, sort, species, variety

kind² *adj.* affectionate, amiable, amicable, beneficent, benevolent, benign, bounteous, charitable, clement, compassionate, congenial, considerate, cordial, courteous, friendly, generous, gentle, good, gracious, humane, indulgent, kind-hearted, kindly, lenient, loving, mild, neighbourly, obliging, philanthropic, propitious, sympathetic, tenderhearted, thoughtful, understanding

Antonyms cruel, hard-hearted, harsh, heartless, merciless, severe, unkind, unsympathetic, vicious

kindle fire, ignite, inflame, light, set fire to

Antonyms douse, extinguish, quell, quench

kindliness amiability, beneficence, benevolence, benignity, charity, compassion, friendliness, gentleness, humanity, kind-heartedness, kindness, sympathy

kindly 1. *adj.* beneficial, benevolent, benign, compassionate, cordial, favourable, genial, gentle, good-natured, hearty, helpful, kind, mild, pleasant, polite, sympathetic, warm **2.** *adv.* agreeably, cordially, graciously, politely, tenderly, thoughtfully

Antonyms *adj.* cruel, harsh, malevolent, malicious, mean, severe, spiteful, unkindly, unsympathetic ~*adv.* cruelly, harshly, malevolently, maliciously, meanly, spitefully, unkindly, unsympathetically

kindness 1. affection, amiability, beneficence, benevolence, charity, clemency, compassion, decency, fellow feeling, generosity, gentleness, goodness, good will, grace, hospitality, humanity, indulgence, kindliness, magnanimity, patience, philanthropy, tenderness, tolerance, understanding **2.** aid, assistance, benefaction, bounty, favour, generosity, good deed, help, service

Antonyms (*sense 1*) animosity, callousness, cold-heartedness, cruelty, hard-heartedness, heartlessness, ill will, inhumanity, malevolence, malice, misanthropy, viciousness

king crowned head, emperor, majesty, monarch, overlord, prince, ruler, sovereign

kingdom 1. dominion, dynasty, empire, monarchy, realm, reign, sovereignty **2.** commonwealth, county, division, nation, province, state, territory, tract

kink 1. bend, coil, corkscrew, crimp, entanglement, frizz, knot, tangle, twist, wrinkle **2.** crotchet, eccentricity, fetish, foible, idiosyncrasy, quirk, singularity, vagary, whim

kiosk bookstall, booth, counter, newsstand, stall, stand

kiss *v.* buss (*Archaic*), canoodle (*Inf.*), greet, neck (*Inf.*), osculate, peck (*Inf.*), salute, smooch (*Inf.*)

kit accoutrements, apparatus, effects, equipment, gear, impedi~ menta, implements, instruments, outfit, paraphernalia, provisions, rig, supplies, tackle, tools, trap~ pings, utensils

knack ability, adroitness, apti~ tude, bent, capacity, dexterity, expertise, expertness, facility, flair, forte, genius, gift, handi~ ness, ingenuity, propensity, quickness, skilfulness, skill, tal~ ent, trick

Antonyms awkwardness, clum~ siness, disability, ineptitude

kneel bow, bow down, curtsy, genuflect, get down on one's knees, kowtow, make obeisance, stoop

knell 1. *v.* announce, chime, her~ ald, peal, resound, ring, sound, toll 2. *n.* chime, peal, ringing, sound, toll

knickers bloomers, briefs, draw~ ers, panties, smalls, underwear

knick-knack bagatelle, bauble, bibelot, bric-a-brac, gewgaw, gimcrack, kickshaw, plaything, trifle, trinket

knife *n.* blade, cutter, cutting tool

knit affix, ally, bind, connect, contract, fasten, heal, interlace, intertwine, join, link, loop, mend, secure, tie, unite, weave

knob boss, bulk, bump, bunch, door-handle, knot, knurl, lump, nub, projection, protrusion, pro~ tuberance, snag, stud, swell, swelling, tumour

knock 1. *v.* buffet, clap, cuff, hit, punch, rap, slap, smack, smite (*Archaic*), strike, thump, thwack 2. *n.* blow, box, clip, clout, cuff, hammering, rap, slap, smack, thump

knot 1. *v.* bind, complicate, en~ tangle, knit, loop, secure, tether, tie, weave 2. *n.* bond, bow, braid,

connection, joint, ligature, loop, rosette, tie

know 1. apprehend, comprehend, experience, fathom, feel certain, ken (*Scot.*), learn, notice, per~ ceive, realize, recognize, see, undergo, understand 2. associate with, be acquainted with, be fa~ miliar with, fraternize with, have dealings with, have knowledge of, recognize 3. differentiate, dis~ cern, distinguish, identify, make out, perceive, recognize, see, tell

Antonyms be ignorant, be unfa~ miliar with, misunderstand

knowing astute, clever, compe~ tent, discerning, experienced, expert, intelligent, qualified, skilful, well-informed

Antonyms ignorant, naive, ob~ tuse

knowledge 1. education, enlight~ enment, erudition, instruction, intelligence, learning, scholar~ ship, schooling, science, tuition, wisdom 2. ability, apprehension, cognition, comprehension, con~ sciousness, discernment, grasp, judgment, recognition, under~ standing

Antonyms ignorance, illiteracy, misunderstanding, unawareness

knowledgeable acquainted, *au courant*, *au fait*, aware, cogni~ zant, conscious, conversant, ex~ perienced, familiar, in the know (*Inf.*), understanding, well~ informed

known acknowledged, admitted, avowed, celebrated, common, confessed, familiar, famous, manifest, noted, obvious, patent, plain, popular, published, recog~ nized, well-known

Antonyms closet (*Inf.*), con~ cealed, hidden, secret, unfamil~ iar, unknown, unrecognized, un~ revealed

L

label *n.* **1.** docket (*Chiefly Brit.*), marker, sticker, tag, tally, ticket **2.** brand, company, mark, trademark ~*v.* **3.** docket (*Chiefly Brit.*), mark, stamp, sticker, tag, tally **4.** brand, call, characterize, class, classify, define, describe, designate, identify, name

labour *n.* **1.** industry, toil, work **2.** employees, hands, labourers, workers, work force, workmen **3.** donkey-work, drudgery, effort, exertion, grind (*Inf.*), industry, pains, painstaking, sweat (*Inf.*), toil, travail **4.** childbirth, contractions, delivery, labour pains, pains, parturition, throes, travail ~*v.* **5.** dwell on, elaborate, overdo, overemphasize, strain

Antonyms *n.* ease, idleness, leisure, relaxation, repose, respite, rest

laboured awkward, difficult, forced, heavy, stiff, strained

labourer blue-collar worker, drudge, hand, labouring man, manual worker, navvy (*Brit. inf.*), unskilled worker, worker, working man, workman

lacerate claw, cut, gash, jag, maim, mangle, rend, rip, slash, tear, wound

lack 1. *n.* absence, dearth, deficiency, deprivation, destitution, insufficiency, need, privation, scantiness, scarcity, shortage, shortcoming, shortness, want **2.** *v.* be deficient in, be short of, be without, miss, need, require, want

Antonyms *n.* abundance, adequacy, excess, plentifulness, sufficiency, surplus ~*v.* enjoy, have, own, possess

lackadaisical apathetic, dull, enervated, half-hearted, indifferent, languid, languorous, lethargic, limp, listless, spiritless

Antonyms ambitious, diligent, excited, inspired, spirited

lacking defective, deficient, flawed, impaired, inadequate, minus (*Inf.*), missing, needing, sans (*Archaic*), wanting, without

lacklustre boring, dim, drab, dry, dull, flat, leaden, lifeless, lustreless, muted, prosaic, sombre, unimaginative, uninspired, vapid

lad boy, chap (*Inf.*), fellow, guy (*Inf.*), juvenile, kid, laddie (*Scot.*), schoolboy, shaver (*Inf.*), stripling, youngster, youth

laden burdened, charged, encumbered, fraught, full, hampered, loaded, oppressed, taxed, weighed down, weighted

ladylike courtly, cultured, decorous, elegant, genteel, modest, polite, proper, refined, respectable, well-bred

Antonyms discourteous, ill-bred, ill-mannered, impolite, rude, uncultured, unladylike, unmannerly, unrefined

lag be behind, dawdle, delay, drag (behind), drag one's feet, hang back, idle, linger, loiter, saunter, straggle, tarry, trail

laid-back at ease, casual, easygoing, free and easy, relaxed, together (*Sl., chiefly U.S.*), unflappable (*Inf.*), unhurried

Antonyms edgy, jittery (*Inf.*), jumpy, keyed-up, nervous, on edge, tense, uptight (*Inf.*), wound-up (*Inf.*)

lame 1. crippled, defective, disabled, game, halt (*Archaic*), handicapped, hobbling, limping **2.** *Fig.* feeble, flimsy, inadequate, insufficient, poor, thin, unconvincing, unsatisfactory, weak

lament 1. *v.* bemoan, bewail, complain, deplore, grieve, mourn, regret, sorrow, wail, weep 2. *n.* complaint, keening, lamentation, moan, moaning, plaint, ululation, wail, wailing

lamentable 1. deplorable, distressing, grievous, mournful, regrettable, sorrowful, tragic, unfortunate, woeful 2. low, meagre, mean, miserable, pitiful, poor, unsatisfactory, wretched

lampoon 1. *n.* burlesque, caricature, parody, pasquinade, satire, send-up (*Brit. inf.*), skit, squib, takeoff (*Inf.*) 2. *v.* burlesque, caricature, make fun of, mock, parody, pasquinade, ridicule, satirize, send up (*Brit. inf.*), squib, take off (*Inf.*)

land *n.* 1. dry land, earth, ground, terra firma 2. dirt, ground, loam, soil 3. acres, estate, grounds, property, real property, realty 4. country, district, fatherland, motherland, nation, province, region, territory, tract ~*v.* 5. alight, arrive, berth, come to rest, debark, disembark, dock, touch down

landlord host, hotelier, hotelkeeper, innkeeper

landmark 1. feature, monument 2. crisis, milestone, turning point, watershed

landscape countryside, outlook, panorama, prospect, scene, scenery, view, vista

language 1. communication, conversation, discourse, expression, interchange, parlance, speech, talk, utterance, verbalization, vocalization 2. argot, cant, dialect, idiom, jargon, lingo (*Inf.*), lingua franca, patois, speech, terminology, tongue, vernacular, vocabulary 3. diction, expression, phraseology, phrasing, style, wording

languid 1. drooping, faint, feeble, languorous, limp, pining, sickly, weak, weary 2. indifferent, lackadaisical, languorous, lazy, listless, spiritless, unenthusiastic, uninterested 3. dull, heavy, inactive, inert, lethargic, sluggish, torpid

Antonyms active, energetic, strong, tireless, vigorous

languish decline, droop, fade, fail, faint, flag, sicken, waste, weaken, wilt, wither

lank 1. dull, lifeless, limp, long, lustreless, straggling 2. attenuated, emaciated, gaunt, lanky, lean, rawboned, scraggy, scrawny, skinny, slender, slim, spare, thin

lanky angular, bony, gangling, gaunt, loose-jointed, rangy, rawboned, scraggy, scrawny, spare, tall, thin, weedy (*Inf.*)

Antonyms brawny, burly, chubby, fat, muscular, plump, portly, rotund, rounded, short, sinewy, stocky, stout

lap 1. *n.* circle, circuit, course, distance, loop, orbit, round, tour 2. *v.* cover, enfold, envelop, fold, swaddle, swathe, turn, twist, wrap

lapse *n.* 1. error, failing, fault, indiscretion, mistake, negligence, omission, oversight, slip ~*v.* 2. decline, degenerate, deteriorate, drop, fail, fall, sink, slide, slip 3. become obsolete, become void, end, expire, run out, stop, terminate

large 1. big, bulky, colossal, considerable, enormous, giant, gigantic, ginormous (*Inf.*), goodly, great, huge, immense, jumbo (*Inf.*), king-size, man-size, massive, mega (*Inf.*), monumental, sizable, substantial, tidy (*Inf.*), vast 2. abundant, ample, broad, capacious, comprehensive, copious, extensive, full, generous, grand, grandiose, liberal, plentiful, roomy, spacious, sweeping, wide

Antonyms brief, inconsiderable, infinitesimal, little, minute, narrow, petty, scanty, scarce, short, slender, slight, slim, small, sparse, thin, tiny, trivial

largely as a rule, by and large, chiefly, considerably, extensively, generally, mainly, mostly, predominantly, primarily, principally, to a great extent, widely

lark *n.* antic, caper, escapade,

fling, frolic, fun, gambol, game, jape, mischief, prank, revel, rollick, romp, skylark, spree

lash[1] *n.* **1.** blow, hit, stripe, stroke, swipe (*Inf.*) ~*v.* **2.** beat, birch, chastise, flagellate, flog, horsewhip, lam (*Sl.*), scourge, thrash, whip **3.** beat, buffet, dash, drum, hammer, hit, knock, larrup (*Dialect*), pound, smack, strike

lash[2] bind, fasten, join, make fast, rope, secure, strap, tie

lass bird (*Sl.*), chick (*Sl.*), colleen (*Irish*), damsel, girl, lassie (*Scot.*), maid, maiden, miss, schoolgirl, young woman

last[1] *adj.* **1.** aftermost, at the end, hindmost, rearmost **2.** latest, most recent **3.** closing, concluding, extreme, final, furthest, remotest, terminal, ultimate, utmost ~*adv.* **4.** after, behind, bringing up the rear, in *or* at the end, in the rear
Antonyms (*sense 1*) first, foremost, leading (*sense 3*) earliest, first, initial, introductory, opening

last[2] *v.* abide, carry on, continue, endure, hold on, hold out, keep, keep on, persist, remain, stand up, survive, wear
Antonyms cease, depart, die, end, expire, fade, fail, stop, terminate

lasting abiding, continuing, deep-rooted, durable, enduring, indelible, lifelong, long-standing, long-term, perennial, permanent, perpetual, unceasing, undying, unending
Antonyms ephemeral, fleeting, momentary, passing, short-lived, transient, transitory

latch *n.* bar, bolt, catch, clamp, fastening, hasp, hook, lock, sneck (*Dialect*)

late *adj.* **1.** behind, behindhand, belated, delayed, last-minute, overdue, slow, tardy, unpunctual **2.** advanced, fresh, modern, new, recent **3.** dead, deceased, defunct, departed, ex-, former, old, past, preceding, previous
Antonyms *adj.* (*sense 1*) before-

hand, early, prompt, punctual, seasoned, timely (*sense 2*) old (*sense 3*) alive, existing

lately in recent times, just now, latterly, not long ago, of late, recently

lateness advanced hour, belatedness, delay, late date, retardation, tardiness, unpunctuality

later *adv.* after, afterwards, by and by, in a while, in time, later on, next, subsequently, thereafter

latest *adj.* current, fashionable, in, modern, most recent, newest, now, up-to-date, up-to-the-minute, with it (*Inf.*)

lather *n.* bubbles, foam, froth, soap, soapsuds, suds

latitude 1. breadth, compass, extent, range, reach, room, scope, space, span, spread, sweep, width **2.** elbowroom, freedom, indulgence, laxity, leeway, liberty, licence, play, unrestrictedness

latter closing, concluding, last, last-mentioned, later, latest, modern, recent, second
Antonyms antecedent, earlier, foregoing, former, preceding, previous, prior

lattice fretwork, grating, grid, grille, latticework, mesh, network, openwork, reticulation, tracery, trellis, web

laudable admirable, commendable, creditable, estimable, excellent, meritorious, of note, praiseworthy, worthy
Antonyms base, blameworthy, contemptible, ignoble, lowly, unworthy

laugh *v.* **1.** be convulsed (*Inf.*), be in stitches, chortle, chuckle, crease up (*Inf.*), giggle, guffaw, roar with laughter, snigger, split one's sides, titter **2.** **laugh at** belittle, deride, jeer, lampoon, make a mock of, make fun of, mock, ridicule, scoff at, take the mickey (out of) (*Inf.*), taunt ~*n.* **3.** belly laugh (*Inf.*), chortle, chuckle, giggle, guffaw, roar *or* shriek of laughter, snigger, titter

laughable absurd, derisive, derisory, ludicrous, nonsensical, preposterous, ridiculous, worthy of scorn

laughter amusement, glee, hilarity, merriment, mirth

launch 1. cast, discharge, dispatch, fire, project, propel, send off, set afloat, set in motion, throw **2.** begin, commence, embark upon, inaugurate, initiate, instigate, introduce, open, start

lavatory bathroom, bog (*Brit. sl.*), can (*U.S. sl.*), cloakroom (*Brit.*), Gents, head(s) (*Nautical sl.*), john (*U.S. sl.*), Ladies, latrine, loo (*Brit. inf.*), powder room, (public) convenience, toilet, washroom, water closet, W.C.

lavish *adj.* **1.** abundant, copious, exuberant, lush, luxuriant, opulent, plentiful, profuse, prolific, sumptuous **2.** bountiful, effusive, free, generous, liberal, munificent, open-handed, unstinting
Antonyms *adj.* cheap, frugal, meagre, miserly, parsimonious, scanty, sparing, stingy, thrifty, tight-fisted

law 1. charter, code, constitution, jurisprudence **2.** act, code, command, commandment, covenant, decree, edict, enactment, order, ordinance, rule, statute

law-abiding compliant, dutiful, good, honest, honourable, lawful, obedient, orderly, peaceable, peaceful

lawful allowable, authorized, constitutional, just, legal, legalized, legitimate, licit, permissible, proper, rightful, valid, warranted
Antonyms banned, forbidden, illegal, illegitimate, illicit, prohibited, unauthorized, unlawful

lawless anarchic, chaotic, disorderly, insubordinate, insurgent, mutinous, rebellious, reckless, riotous, seditious, ungoverned, unrestrained, unruly, wild
Antonyms civilized, compliant, disciplined, law-abiding, lawful, legitimate, licit, obedient, orderly, regimented, restrained, well-governed

lawsuit action, argument, case, cause, contest, dispute, litigation, proceedings, prosecution, suit, trial

lawyer advocate, attorney, barrister, counsel, counsellor, legal adviser, solicitor

lax careless, casual, easy-going, lenient, neglectful, negligent, overindulgent, remiss, slack, slipshod
Antonyms conscientious, disciplined, firm, heedful, moral, rigid, scrupulous, severe, stern, strict, stringent

lay¹ 1. deposit, establish, leave, place, plant, posit, put, set, set down, settle, spread **2.** arrange, dispose, locate, organize, position, set out **3.** bear, deposit, produce **4.** allocate, allot, ascribe, assign, attribute, charge, impute **5.** concoct, contrive, design, devise, hatch, plan, plot, prepare, work out **6.** bet, gamble, give odds, hazard, risk, stake, wager

lay² 1. laic, laical, nonclerical, secular **2.** amateur, inexpert, nonprofessional, nonspecialist

layabout beachcomber, couch potato (*Sl.*), good-for-nothing, idler, laggard, loafer, lounger, ne'er-do-well, shirker, skiver (*Brit. sl.*), slubberdegullion (*Archaic*), vagrant, wastrel

layer bed, ply, row, seam, stratum, thickness, tier

layman amateur, lay person, nonprofessional, outsider

lay-off discharge, dismissal, unemployment

lay off discharge, dismiss, drop, let go, make redundant, oust, pay off

lay on cater (for), furnish, give, provide, supply

layout arrangement, design, draft, formation, geography, outline, plan

lay out arrange, design, display, exhibit, plan, spread out

laziness dilatoriness, do-nothingness, faineance, faineancy, idleness, inactivity, indolence, lackadaisicalness, slackness, sloth, slothfulness, slowness, sluggishness, tardiness

lazy 1. idle, inactive, indolent, inert, remiss, shiftless, slack, slothful, slow, workshy **2.** drowsy, languid, languorous, lethargic, sleepy, slow-moving, sluggish, somnolent, torpid
Antonyms active, assiduous, diligent, energetic, industrious, quick, stimulated

lead v. **1.** conduct, escort, guide, pilot, precede, show the way, steer, usher **2.** cause, dispose, draw, incline, induce, influence, persuade, prevail, prompt **3.** command, direct, govern, head, manage, preside over, supervise **4.** be ahead (of), blaze a trail, come first, exceed, excel, outdo, outstrip, surpass, transcend **5.** experience, have, live, pass, spend, undergo ~n. **6.** advance, advantage, cutting edge, edge, first place, margin, precedence, primacy, priority, start, supremacy, van, vanguard **7.** direction, example, guidance, leadership, model **8.** clue, guide, hint, indication, suggestion, tip, trace **9.** leading role, principal, protagonist, star part, title role

leader bellwether, boss (*Inf.*), captain, chief, chieftain, commander, conductor, counsellor, director, guide, head, number one, principal, ringleader, ruler, superior
Antonyms adherent, disciple, follower, hanger-on, henchman, sidekick (*Sl.*), supporter

leadership 1. administration, direction, directorship, domination, guidance, management, running, superintendency **2.** authority, command, control, influence, initiative, pre-eminence, supremacy, sway

leading chief, dominant, first, foremost, governing, greatest, highest, main, number one, outstanding, pre-eminent, primary, principal, ruling, superior
Antonyms following, hindmost, incidental, inferior, lesser, minor,

secondary, subordinate, superficial

leaf n. **1.** blade, bract, flag, foliole, frond, needle, pad **2.** folio, page, sheet

leaflet advert (*Brit. inf.*), bill, booklet, brochure, circular, handbill, mailshot, pamphlet

league n. alliance, association, band, coalition, combination, combine, compact, confederacy, confederation, consortium, federation, fellowship, fraternity, group, guild, partnership, union

leak n. **1.** aperture, chink, crack, crevice, fissure, hole, opening, puncture **2.** drip, leakage, leaking, oozing, percolation, seepage **3.** disclosure, divulgence ~v. **4.** discharge, drip, escape, exude, ooze, pass, percolate, seep, spill, trickle **5.** disclose, divulge, give away, let slip, let the cat out of the bag, make known, make public, pass on, reveal, spill the beans (*Inf.*), tell

lean[1] v. **1.** be supported, prop, recline, repose, rest **2.** bend, incline, slant, slope, tilt, tip

lean[2] adj. **1.** angular, bony, emaciated, gaunt, lank, rangy, scraggy, scrawny, skinny, slender, slim, spare, thin, unfatty, wiry **2.** bare, barren, inadequate, infertile, meagre, pitiful, poor, scanty, sparse, unfruitful, unproductive
Antonyms abundant, ample, brawny, burly, fat, fertile, full, obese, plentiful, plump, portly, profuse, rich

leaning aptitude, bent, bias, disposition, inclination, liking, partiality, penchant, predilection, proclivity, proneness, propensity, taste, tendency

leap 1. v. bounce, bound, caper, cavort, frisk, gambol, hop, jump, skip, spring **2.** n. bound, caper, frisk, hop, jump, skip, spring, vault

learn 1. acquire, attain, become able, grasp, imbibe, master, pick up **2.** commit to memory, con (*Archaic*), get off pat, get (something) word-perfect, learn by heart, memorize **3.** ascertain, detect, determine, discern, discover, find out, gain, gather, hear, understand

learned academic, cultured, erudite, experienced, expert, highbrow, intellectual, lettered, literate, scholarly, skilled, versed, well-informed, well-read
Antonyms ignorant, illiterate, uneducated, unlearned

learner 1. apprentice, beginner, neophyte, novice, tyro **2.** disciple, pupil, scholar, student
Antonyms (*sense 1*) adept, expert, grandmaster, master, maven, pastmaster, virtuoso, wizard (*sense 2*) coach, instructor, mentor, teacher, tutor

learning acquirements, attainments, culture, education, erudition, information, knowledge, letters, literature, lore, research, scholarship, schooling, study, tuition, wisdom

lease *v.* charter, hire, let, loan, rent

least feeblest, fewest, last, lowest, meanest, minimum, minutest, poorest, slightest, smallest, tiniest

leave[1] *v.* **1.** abandon, decamp, depart, desert, disappear, do a bunk (*Brit. sl.*), exit, flit (*Inf.*), forsake, go, go away, move, pull out, quit, relinquish, retire, set out, take off (*Inf.*), withdraw **2.** abandon, cease, desert, desist, drop, evacuate, forbear, give up, refrain, relinquish, renounce, stop, surrender **3.** allot, assign, cede, commit, consign, entrust, give over, refer **4.** bequeath, demise, devise (*Law*), hand down, transmit, will
Antonyms appear, arrive, assume, come, continue, emerge, hold, persist, remove, retain, stay

leave[2] *n.* **1.** allowance, authorization, concession, consent, dispensation, freedom, liberty, permission, sanction **2.** furlough, holiday, leave of absence, sabbatical, time off, vacation

leave out bar, cast aside, count out, disregard, except, exclude, ignore, neglect, omit, overlook, reject

lecture *n.* **1.** address, discourse, disquisition, harangue, instruction, lesson, speech, talk ~*v.* **2.** address, discourse, expound, give a talk, harangue, hold forth, speak, talk, teach ~*n.* **3.** castigation, censure, chiding, dressing-down (*Inf.*), going-over (*Inf.*), heat (*Inf.*), rebuke, reprimand, reproof, scolding, talking-to (*Inf.*), telling-off (*Inf.*), wigging (*Brit. sl.*) ~*v.* **4.** admonish, berate, carpet (*Inf.*), castigate, censure, chide, rate, reprimand, reprove, scold, tell off (*Inf.*)

leeway elbowroom, latitude, margin, play, room, scope, space

left-handed awkward, cack-handed (*Inf.*), careless, clumsy, fumbling, gauche, maladroit

leg *n.* **1.** limb, lower limb, member, pin (*Inf.*), stump (*Inf.*) **2.** brace, prop, support, upright **3.** lap, part, portion, section, segment, stage, stretch

legacy 1. bequest, devise (*Law*), estate, gift, heirloom, inheritance **2.** birthright, endowment, heritage, inheritance, patrimony, throwback, tradition

legal allowable, allowed, authorized, constitutional, lawful, legalized, legitimate, licit, permissible, proper, rightful, sanctioned, valid

legalize allow, approve, authorize, decriminalize, legitimate, legitimatize, license, permit, sanction, validate

legend 1. fable, fiction, folk tale, myth, narrative, saga, story, tale **2.** caption, device, inscription, motto

legendary apocryphal, fabled, fabulous, fanciful, fictitious, mythical, romantic, storied, traditional
Antonyms factual, genuine, historical

legible clear, decipherable, distinct, easily read, easy to read, neat, plain, readable

legion *n.* **1.** army, brigade, company, division, force, troop **2.** drove, horde, host, mass, multitude, myriad, number, throng ~*adj.* **3.** countless, multitudinous, myriad, numberless, numerous, very many

legislate codify, constitute, enact, establish, make laws, ordain, pass laws, prescribe, put in force

legislation 1. codification, enactment, lawmaking, prescription, regulation **2.** act, bill, charter, law, measure, regulation, ruling, statute

legislative *adj.* congressional, judicial, juridical, jurisdictive, lawgiving, lawmaking, ordaining, parliamentary

legitimate *adj.* acknowledged, authentic, authorized, genuine, lawful, legal, legit (*Sl.*), licit, proper, real, rightful, sanctioned, statutory, true
Antonyms false, fraudulent, illegal, illegitimate, unlawful

leisure breathing space, ease, freedom, free time, holiday, liberty, opportunity, pause, quiet, recreation, relaxation, respite, rest, retirement, spare moments, spare time, time off, vacation
Antonyms business, duty, employment, labour, obligation, occupation, work

leisurely *adj.* comfortable, easy, gentle, laid-back (*Inf.*), lazy, relaxed, restful, slow, unhurried
Antonyms brisk, fast, hasty, hectic, hurried, quick, rapid, rushed

lend 1. accommodate one with, advance, loan **2.** add, afford, bestow, confer, contribute, furnish, give, grant, impart, present, provide, supply

length 1. *Of linear extent* distance, extent, longitude, measure, reach, span **2.** *Of time* duration, period, space, span, stretch, term

lengthen continue, draw out, elongate, expand, extend, increase, make longer, prolong, protract, spin out, stretch
Antonyms abbreviate, abridge,

curtail, cut, cut down, diminish, shorten, trim

lengthy diffuse, drawn-out, extended, interminable, lengthened, long, long-drawn-out, long-winded, overlong, prolix, prolonged, protracted, tedious, verbose, very long
Antonyms brief, concise, condensed, limited, short, succinct, terse, to the point

leniency, lenience clemency, compassion, forbearance, gentleness, indulgence, lenity, mercy, mildness, moderation, tenderness, tolerance

lenient clement, compassionate, forbearing, forgiving, gentle, indulgent, kind, merciful, mild, sparing, tender, tolerant
Antonyms harsh, merciless, rigid, rigorous, severe, stern, strict, stringent

less *adj.* **1.** shorter, slighter, smaller **2.** inferior, minor, secondary, subordinate ~*adv.* **3.** barely, little, meagrely, to a smaller extent

lessen abate, abridge, contract, curtail, decrease, de-escalate, degrade, die down, diminish, dwindle, ease, erode, grow less, impair, lighten, lower, minimize, moderate, narrow, reduce, shrink, slacken, slow down, weaken, wind down
Antonyms add to, augment, boost, enhance, enlarge, expand, increase, magnify, multiply, raise

lesser inferior, less important, lower, minor, secondary, slighter, subordinate, under-
Antonyms greater, higher, major, primary, superior

lesson 1. class, coaching, instruction, period, schooling, teaching, tutoring **2.** deterrent, example, exemplar, message, model, moral, precept

let *v.* **1.** allow, authorize, give leave, give permission, give the go-ahead (green light, O.K.) (*Inf.*), grant, permit, sanction, suffer (*Archaic*), tolerate, warrant **2.** hire, lease, rent

let down disappoint, disenchant, disillusion, dissatisfy, fail, fall short, leave in the lurch, leave stranded

lethal baneful, dangerous, deadly, deathly, destructive, devastating, fatal, mortal, murderous, noxious, pernicious, poisonous, virulent
Antonyms harmless, healthy, innocuous, safe, wholesome

lethargic apathetic, comatose, debilitated, drowsy, dull, enervated, heavy, inactive, indifferent, inert, languid, lazy, listless, sleepy, slothful, slow, sluggish, somnolent, stupefied, torpid
Antonyms active, alert, animated, energetic, responsive, spirited, stimulated, vigorous

lethargy apathy, drowsiness, dullness, hebetude (*Rare*), inaction, indifference, inertia, languor, lassitude, listlessness, sleepiness, sloth, slowness, sluggishness, stupor, torpidity, torpor
Antonyms animation, energy, life, liveliness, spirit, verve, vigour, vim, vitality, vivacity, zeal, zest

let in admit, allow to enter, give access to, greet, include, incorporate, receive, take in, welcome

let off 1. detonate, discharge, emit, explode, exude, fire, give off, leak, release **2.** absolve, discharge, dispense, excuse, exempt, exonerate, forgive, pardon, release, spare

let out 1. emit, give vent to, produce **2.** discharge, free, let go, liberate, release **3.** betray, disclose, leak, let fall, let slip, make known, reveal

letter 1. character, sign, symbol **2.** acknowledgment, answer, billet (*Archaic*), communication, dispatch, epistle, line, message, missive, note, reply

let-up abatement, break, cessation, interval, lessening, lull, pause, recess, remission, respite, slackening

let up abate, decrease, diminish, ease (up), moderate, slacken, stop, subside

level *adj.* **1.** consistent, even, flat, horizontal, plain, plane, smooth, uniform **2.** aligned, balanced, commensurate, comparable, equivalent, even, flush, in line, neck and neck, on a line, on a par, proportionate **3.** calm, equable, even, even-tempered, stable, steady ~*v.* **4.** even off or out, flatten, make flat, plane, smooth **5.** bulldoze, demolish, destroy, devastate, equalize, flatten, knock down, lay low, pull down, raze, smooth, tear down, wreck ~*n.* **6.** altitude, elevation, height, vertical position **7.** bed, floor, layer, storey, stratum, zone
Antonyms *adj.* (*sense 1*) bumpy, hilly, slanted, tilted, uneven, vertical, warped (*sense 2*) above, below, even ~*v.* (*sense 5*) build, erect, raise, roughen

level-headed balanced, calm, collected, composed, cool, dependable, even-tempered, reasonable, sane, self-possessed, sensible, steady, together (*Sl., chiefly U.S.*), unflappable (*Inf.*)

lever 1. *n.* bar, crowbar, handle, handspike, jemmy **2.** *v.* force, jemmy, move, prise, pry (*U.S.*), purchase

levy 1. *v.* charge, collect, demand, exact, gather, impose, tax **2.** *n.* assessment, collection, exaction, gathering, imposition

lewd bawdy, blue, dirty, impure, indecent, lascivious, libidinous, licentious, loose, lustful, obscene, pornographic, profligate, salacious, smutty, unchaste, vile, vulgar, wanton, wicked

liability 1. accountability, answerability, culpability, duty, obligation, onus, responsibility **2.** arrear, debit, debt, indebtedness, obligation **3.** burden, disadvantage, drag, drawback, encumbrance, handicap, hindrance, impediment, inconvenience, millstone, minus (*Inf.*), nuisance

liable 1. accountable, amenable, answerable, bound, chargeable, obligated, responsible **2.** exposed, open, subject, susceptible, vulnerable

liaison 1. communication, connection, contact, go-between, hook-up, interchange, intermediary **2.** affair, amour, entanglement, illicit romance, intrigue, love affair, romance

liar fabricator, falsifier, fibber, perjurer, prevaricator, storyteller (*Inf.*)

libel 1. *n.* aspersion, calumny, defamation, denigration, obloquy, slander, smear, vituperation **2.** *v.* blacken, calumniate, defame, derogate, drag (someone's) name through the mud, malign, revile, slander, slur, smear, traduce, vilify

libellous aspersive, calumniatory, calumnious, defamatory, derogatory, false, injurious, malicious, maligning, scurrilous, slanderous, traducing, untrue, vilifying, vituperative

liberal 1. advanced, humanistic, latitudinarian, libertarian, progressive, radical, reformist, right-on (*Inf.*) **2.** altruistic, beneficent, bounteous, bountiful, charitable, free-handed, generous, kind, open-handed, open-hearted, unstinting **3.** abundant, ample, bountiful, copious, handsome, lavish, munificent, plentiful, profuse, rich
Antonyms cheap, conservative, fixed, inadequate, left-wing, literal, reactionary, right-wing, skimpy, small, stingy, strict

liberality 1. altruism, beneficence, benevolence, bounty, charity, free-handedness, generosity, kindness, largess, munificence, open-handedness, philanthropy **2.** breadth, broadmindedness, candour, catholicity, impartiality, latitude, liberalism, libertarianism, magnanimity, permissiveness, progressivism, toleration

liberate deliver, discharge, disenthral, emancipate, free, let loose, let out, manumit, redeem, release, rescue, set free
Antonyms confine, detain, immure, imprison, incarcerate, intern, jail, lock up, put away

liberation deliverance, emancipation, enfranchisement, freedom, freeing, liberating, liberty, manumission, redemption, release, unfettering, unshackling

libertine *n.* debauchee, lecher, loose liver, profligate, rake, reprobate, roué, seducer, sensualist, voluptuary, womanizer

liberty 1. autonomy, emancipation, freedom, immunity, independence, liberation, release, self-determination, sovereignty **2.** authorization, carte blanche, dispensation, exemption, franchise, freedom, leave, licence, permission, prerogative, privilege, right, sanction
Antonyms captivity, compulsion, constraint, duress, enslavement, imprisonment, restraint, restriction, slavery, tyranny

licence *n.* **1.** authority, authorization, carte blanche, certificate, charter, dispensation, entitlement, exemption, immunity, leave, liberty, permission, permit, privilege, right, warrant **2.** abandon, anarchy, disorder, excess, immoderation, impropriety, indulgence, irresponsibility, lawlessness, laxity, profligacy, unruliness
Antonyms constraint, denial, moderation, prohibition, restraint, restriction, strictness

license *v.* accredit, allow, authorize, certify, commission, empower, permit, sanction, warrant
Antonyms ban, debar, disallow, forbid, outlaw, prohibit, proscribe, rule out, veto

licentious abandoned, debauched, disorderly, dissolute, immoral, impure, lascivious, lax, lewd, libertine, libidinous, lubricious, lustful, profligate, promiscuous, sensual, uncontrollable, uncontrolled, uncurbed, unruly, wanton

Antonyms chaste, law-abiding, lawful, moral, principled, proper, scrupulous, virtuous

lick v. brush, lap, taste, tongue, touch, wash

lie¹ **1.** v. dissimulate, equivocate, fabricate, falsify, fib, forswear oneself, invent, misrepresent, perjure, prevaricate, tell a lie, tell untruths **2.** n. deceit, fabrication, falsehood, falsification, falsity, fib, fiction, invention, mendacity, prevarication, untruth, white lie

lie² v. **1.** be prone, be prostrate, be recumbent, be supine, couch, loll, lounge, recline, repose, rest, sprawl, stretch out **2.** be buried, be found, be interred, be located, belong, be placed, be situated, exist, extend, remain

life 1. animation, being, breath, entity, growth, sentience, viability, vitality **2.** being, career, continuance, course, duration, existence, lifetime, span, time **3.** human, human being, individual, mortal, person, soul **4.** autobiography, biography, career, confessions, history, life story, memoirs, story **5.** behaviour, conduct, lifestyle, way of life **6.** activity, animation, brio, energy, get-up-and-go (*Inf.*), go (*Inf.*), high spirits, liveliness, oomph (*Inf.*), sparkle, spirit, verve, vigour, vitality, vivacity, zest

lifeless 1. cold, dead, deceased, defunct, extinct, inanimate, inert **2.** comatose, dead to the world, in a faint, inert, insensate, insensible, out cold, out for six, unconscious

Antonyms active, alive, animate, animated, live, lively, living, spirited, vital

lifelike authentic, exact, faithful, graphic, natural, photographic, real, realistic, true-to-life, undistorted, vivid

lifelong constant, deep-rooted, enduring, for all one's life, for life, lasting, lifetime, long-lasting,

long-standing, perennial, permanent, persistent

lift v. **1.** bear aloft, buoy up, draw up, elevate, heft (*Inf.*), hoist, pick up, raise, raise high, rear, upheave, uplift, upraise **2.** annul, cancel, countermand, end, relax, remove, rescind, revoke, stop, terminate **3.** ascend, be dispelled, climb, disappear, disperse, dissipate, mount, rise, vanish ~n. **4.** car ride, drive, ride, run, transport **5.** boost, encouragement, fillip, pick-me-up, reassurance, shot in the arm (*Inf.*), uplift

Antonyms v. (*sense 1*) dash, depress, drop, drop, hang, lower (*sense 2*) establish, impose (*sense 3*) descend, drop, fall, lower ~n. (*sense 5*) blow, letdown

light¹ n. **1.** blaze, brightness, brilliance, effulgence, flash, glare, gleam, glint, glow, illumination, incandescence, lambency, luminescence, luminosity, lustre, phosphorescence, radiance, ray, refulgence, scintillation, shine, sparkle **2.** beacon, bulb, candle, flare, lamp, lantern, lighthouse, star, taper, torch, windowpane **3.** broad day, cockcrow, dawn, daybreak, daylight, daytime, morn (*Poetic*), morning, sun, sunbeam, sunrise, sunshine **4.** example, exemplar, guiding light, model, paragon, shining example **5.** flame, lighter, match **6. bring to light** disclose, discover, expose, reveal, show, uncover, unearth, unveil **7. come to light** appear, be disclosed, be discovered, be revealed, come out, transpire, turn up **8. in (the) light of** bearing in mind, because of, considering, in view of, taking into account, with knowledge of ~adj. **9.** aglow, bright, brilliant, glowing, illuminated, luminous, lustrous, shining, sunny, well-lighted, well-lit **10.** bleached, blond, faded, fair, light-hued, light-toned, pale, pastel ~v. **11.** fire, ignite, inflame, kindle, set a match to **12.** brighten, clarify, floodlight, flood with light, illuminate, illumine, irradiate, lighten, light up, put on, switch on, turn on **13.** animate, brighten, cheer, irradiate, lighten **Antonyms** *n.* cloud, dark, darkness, dusk, mystery, obscurity, shade, shadow ~*adj.* dark, deep, dim, dusky, gloomy ~*v.* cloud, darken, douse, dull, extinguish, put out, quench

light² *adj.* **1.** airy, buoyant, delicate, easy, flimsy, imponderous, insubstantial, lightsome, lightweight, portable, slight, underweight **2.** faint, gentle, indistinct, mild, moderate, slight, soft, weak **3.** inconsequential, inconsiderable, insignificant, minute, scanty, slight, small, thin, tiny, trifling, trivial, unsubstantial, wee **4.** cushy (*Sl.*), easy, effortless, manageable, moderate, simple, undemanding, unexacting, untaxing **5.** agile, airy, graceful, light-footed, lithe, nimble, sprightly, sylphlike **6.** amusing, diverting, entertaining, frivolous, funny, gay, humorous, light-hearted, pleasing, superficial, trifling, trivial, witty **7.** airy, animated, blithe, cheerful, cheery, fickle, frivolous, gay, lively, merry, sunny **8.** digestible, frugal, modest, not heavy, not rich, restricted, small ~*v.* **9.** alight, land, perch, settle **Antonyms** *adj.* burdensome, clumsy, deep, forceful, hard, heavy, intense, profound, rich, serious, sombre, strenuous, strong, substantial, weighty

lighten¹ become light, brighten, flash, gleam, illuminate, irradiate, light up, make bright, shine

lighten² **1.** disburden, ease, make lighter, reduce in weight, unload **2.** alleviate, ameliorate, assuage, ease, facilitate, lessen, mitigate, reduce, relieve **Antonyms** (*sense 1*) burden, encumber, handicap (*sense 2*) aggravate, heighten, increase, intensify, make worse, worsen

light-headed bird-brained (*Inf.*), featherbrained, fickle, flighty, flippant, foolish, frivolous, giddy, inane, rattlebrained (*Inf.*), shallow, silly, superficial, trifling

light-hearted blithe, blithesome (*Literary*), bright, carefree, cheerful, effervescent, frolicsome, gay, glad, gleeful, happy-go-lucky, insouciant, jocund, jolly, jovial, joyful, joyous, merry, playful, sunny, untroubled, upbeat (*Inf.*) **Antonyms** cheerless, dejected, depressed, despondent, gloomy, heavy-hearted, melancholy, morose, sad

lightweight *adj.* inconsequential, insignificant, of no account, paltry, petty, slight, trifling, trivial, unimportant, worthless

likable, likeable agreeable, amiable, appealing, attractive, charming, engaging, friendly, genial, nice, pleasant, pleasing, sympathetic, winning, winsome

like¹ *adj.* akin, alike, allied, analogous, approximating, cognate, corresponding, equivalent, identical, parallel, relating, resembling, same, similar **Antonyms** contrasted, different, dissimilar, divergent, diverse, opposite, unlike

like² *v.* **1.** adore (*Inf.*), be fond of, be keen on, be partial to, delight in, dig (*Sl.*), enjoy, go for (*Sl.*), love, relish, revel in **2.** admire, appreciate, approve, cherish, esteem, hold dear, prize, take a shine to (*Inf.*), take to **Antonyms** *v.* abominate, despise, detest, dislike, hate, loathe

likelihood chance, good chance, liability, likeliness, possibility, probability, prospect, reasonableness, strong possibility

likely 1. *adj.* anticipated, apt, disposed, expected, in a fair way, inclined, liable, on the cards, possible, probable, prone, tending, to be expected **2.** *adv.* doubtlessly, in all probability, like as not (*Inf.*), like enough (*Inf.*), no doubt, presumably, probably

liken compare, equate, juxtapose, match, parallel, relate, set beside

likeness 1. affinity, correspondence, resemblance, similarity, similitude **2.** copy, counterpart, delineation, depiction, effigy, facsimile, image, model, photograph, picture, portrait, replica, representation, reproduction, study

liking affection, affinity, appreciation, attraction, bent, bias, desire, fondness, inclination, love, partiality, penchant, predilection, preference, proneness, propensity, soft spot, stomach, taste, tendency, weakness

Antonyms abhorrence, aversion, dislike, hatred, loathing, repugnance

limb appendage, arm, extension, extremity, leg, member, part, wing

limelight attention, celebrity, fame, glare of publicity, prominence, public eye, publicity, public notice, recognition, stardom, the spotlight

limit n. **1.** bound, breaking point, cutoff point, deadline, end, end point, furthest bound, greatest extent, termination, the bitter end, ultimate, utmost **2.** Often plural border, boundary, confines, edge, end, extent, frontier, perimeter, periphery, precinct **3.** ceiling, check, curb, limitation, maximum, obstruction, restraint, restriction ~v. **4.** bound, check, circumscribe, confine, curb, delimit, demarcate, fix, hem in, hinder, ration, restrain, restrict, specify

limitation block, check, condition, constraint, control, curb, disadvantage, drawback, impediment, obstruction, qualification, reservation, restraint, restriction, snag

limited bounded, checked, circumscribed, confined, constrained, controlled, curbed, defined, finite, fixed, hampered, hemmed in, restricted

Antonyms boundless, limitless, unlimited, unrestricted

limitless boundless, countless, endless, illimitable, immeasurable, immense, inexhaustible, infinite, measureless, never-ending, numberless, unbounded, uncalculable, undefined, unending, unlimited, untold, vast

limp¹ v. falter, halt (Archaic), hobble, hop, shamble, shuffle

limp² adj. drooping, flabby, flaccid, flexible, floppy, lax, limber, loose, pliable, relaxed, slack, soft

Antonyms firm, hard, rigid, solid, stiff, taut, tense, unyielding

line¹ n. **1.** band, bar, channel, dash, groove, mark, rule, score, scratch, streak, stripe, stroke, underline **2.** crease, crow's-foot, furrow, mark, wrinkle **3.** border, borderline, boundary, demarcation, edge, frontier, limit, mark **4.** configuration, contour, features, figure, outline, profile, silhouette **5.** cable, cord, filament, rope, strand, string, thread, wire **6.** axis, course, direction, path, route, track, trajectory **7.** approach, avenue, belief, course, course of action, ideology, method, policy, position, practice, procedure, scheme, system **8.** activity, area, bag (Sl.), business, calling, department, employment, field, forte, interest, job, occupation, profession, province, pursuit, specialization, trade, vocation **9.** column, crocodile (Brit.), file, procession, queue, rank, row, sequence, series **10.** ancestry, breed, family, lineage, race, stock, strain, succession **11.** card, letter, message, note, postcard, report, word **12.** draw the line lay down the law, object, prohibit, put one's foot down, restrict, set a limit ~v. **13.** crease, cut, draw, furrow, inscribe, mark, rule, score, trace, underline **14.** border, bound, edge, fringe, rank, rim, skirt, verge

line-up arrangement, array, row, selection, team

line up 1. fall in, form ranks, queue up **2.** assemble, come up with, lay on, obtain, organize, prepare, procure, produce, secure

linger 1. hang around, loiter, remain, stay, stop, tarry, wait **2.** abide, continue, endure, persist, remain, stay

lingering dragging, long-drawn-out, persistent, protracted, remaining, slow

link *n.* **1.** component, constituent, division, element, member, part, piece **2.** association, attachment, bond, connection, joint, knot, relationship, tie, tie-up, vinculum ~*v.* **3.** attach, bind, connect, couple, fasten, join, tie, unite, yoke **4.** associate, bracket, connect, identify, relate
Antonyms *v.* detach, disconnect, divide, separate, sever, split, sunder

liquid *n.* **1.** fluid, juice, liquor, solution ~*adj.* **2.** aqueous, flowing, fluid, liquefied, melted, molten, running, runny, thawed, wet **3.** bright, brilliant, clear, limpid, shining, translucent, transparent **4.** dulcet, fluent, mellifluent, mellifluous, melting, smooth, soft, sweet **5.** *Of assets* convertible, negotiable

liquidate 1. clear, discharge, honour, pay, pay off, settle, square **2.** abolish, annul, cancel, dissolve, terminate **3.** cash, convert to cash, realize, sell off, sell up **4.** annihilate, blow away (*Sl., chiefly U.S.*), bump off (*Sl.*), destroy, dispatch, do away with, do in (*Sl.*), eliminate, exterminate, finish off, get rid of, kill, murder, remove, rub out (*U.S. sl.*), silence, wipe out (*Inf.*)

liquor alcohol, booze (*Inf.*), drink, grog, hard stuff (*Inf.*), hooch (*Sl., chiefly U.S.*), intoxicant, juice (*Inf.*), spirits, strong drink

list¹ 1. *n.* catalogue, directory, file, index, inventory, invoice, leet (*Scot.*), listing, record, register, roll, schedule, series, syllabus, tabulation, tally **2.** *v.* bill, book, catalogue, enrol, enter, enumerate, file, index, itemize, note,

record, register, schedule, set down, tabulate, write down

list² 1. *v.* cant, careen, heel, heel over, incline, lean, tilt, tip **2.** *n.* cant, leaning, slant, tilt

listen 1. attend, be all ears, be attentive, give ear, hang on (someone's) words, hark, hear, hearken (*Archaic*), keep one's ears open, lend an ear, pin back one's ears (*Inf.*), prick up one's ears **2.** concentrate, do as one is told, give heed to, heed, mind, obey, observe, pay attention, take notice

listless apathetic, enervated, heavy, impassive, inattentive, indifferent, indolent, inert, languid, languishing, lethargic, lifeless, limp, lymphatic, mopish, sluggish, spiritless, supine, torpid, vacant
Antonyms active, alert, attentive, energetic, lively, sparky, spirited, wide-awake

literal 1. accurate, close, exact, faithful, strict, verbatim, word for word **2.** actual, bona fide, genuine, gospel, plain, real, simple, true, unexaggerated, unvarnished

literally actually, exactly, faithfully, plainly, precisely, really, simply, strictly, to the letter, truly, verbatim, word for word

literary bookish, erudite, formal, learned, lettered, literate, scholarly, well-read

literate cultivated, cultured, educated, erudite, informed, knowledgeable, learned, lettered, scholarly, well-informed, well-read

literature belles-lettres, letters, lore, writings, written works

lithe flexible, limber, lissom, loose-jointed, loose-limbed, pliable, pliant, supple

litigation action, case, contending, disputing, lawsuit, process, prosecution

litter *n.* **1.** debris, detritus, fragments, garbage (*Chiefly U.S.*), grot (*Sl.*), muck, refuse, rubbish, shreds **2.** clutter, confusion, disarray, disorder, jumble, mess, scatter, untidiness **3.** brood, family, offspring, progeny, young **4.** bedding, couch, floor cover, mulch, straw bed **5.** palanquin, stretcher ~*v.* **6.** clutter, derange, disarrange, disorder, mess up, scatter, strew

little *adj.* **1.** diminutive, dwarf, elfin, infinitesimal, Lilliputian, mini, miniature, minute, petite, pygmy, short, slender, small, tiny, wee **2.** babyish, immature, infant, junior, undeveloped, young **3.** hardly any, insufficient, meagre, scant, skimpy, small, sparse **4.** brief, fleeting, hasty, passing, short, short-lived **5.** inconsiderable, insignificant, minor, negligible, paltry, trifling, trivial, unimportant **6.** base, cheap, illiberal, mean, narrow-minded, petty, small-minded ~*adv.* **7.** barely, hardly, not much, not quite, only just **8.** hardly ever, not often, rarely, scarcely, seldom
Antonyms *adj.* abundant, ample, big, colossal, considerable, enormous, giant, ginormous (*Inf.*), grave, great, huge, immense, important, large, long, major, mega (*Inf.*), momentous, much, plentiful, serious, significant ~*adv.* always, certainly, much, surely

live[1] *v.* **1.** be, be alive, breathe, draw breath, exist, have life **2.** be permanent, be remembered, last, persist, prevail, remain alive **3.** *Sometimes with* **in** abide, dwell, hang out (*Inf.*), inhabit, lodge, occupy, reside, settle, stay (*Chiefly Scot.*) **4.** abide, continue, earn a living, endure, fare, feed, get along, lead, make ends meet, pass, remain, subsist, support oneself, survive

live[2] *adj.* **1.** alive, animate, breathing, existent, living, quick (*Archaic*), vital **2.** active, burning, controversial, current, hot, pertinent, pressing, provocative, topical, unsettled, vital **3.** *Inf.* active, alert, brisk, dynamic, ear-

nest, energetic, lively, sparky, vigorous, vivid, wide-awake

livelihood employment, job, living, maintenance, means, (means of) support, occupation, (source of) income, subsistence, sustenance, work

liveliness activity, animation, boisterousness, briskness, dynamism, energy, gaiety, quickness, smartness, spirit, sprightliness, vitality, vivacity

lively 1. active, agile, alert, brisk, chipper (*Inf.*), chirpy, energetic, full of pep (*Inf.*), keen, nimble, perky, quick, sprightly, spry, vigorous **2.** animated, blithe, blithesome, cheerful, frisky, frolicsome, gay, merry, sparkling, sparky, spirited, vivacious **3.** astir, bustling, busy, buzzing, crowded, eventful, moving, stirring **4.** bright, colourful, exciting, forceful, invigorating, racy, refreshing, stimulating, vivid
Antonyms apathetic, debilitated, disabled, dull, inactive, lifeless, listless, slow, sluggish, torpid

liven animate, brighten, buck up (*Inf.*), enliven, hot up (*Inf.*), pep up, perk up, put life into, rouse, stir, vitalize, vivify

livid 1. angry, black-and-blue, bruised, contused, discoloured, purple **2.** ashen, blanched, bloodless, doughy, greyish, leaden, pale, pallid, pasty, wan, waxen **3.** *Inf.* angry, beside oneself, boiling, enraged, exasperated, fuming, furious, incensed, indignant, infuriated, mad (*Inf.*), outraged
Antonyms (*sense 3*) assuaged, blissful, content, delighted, enchanted, forgiving, happy, mollified, overjoyed, pleased

living *adj.* **1.** active, alive, animated, breathing, existing, in the land of the living (*Inf.*), lively, quick (*Archaic*), strong, vigorous, vital ~*n.* **2.** animation, being, existence, existing, life, subsistence **3.** job, livelihood, maintenance, (means of) support, occupation, (source of) income, subsistence, sustenance, work

Antonyms adj. (sense 1) dead, deceased, defunct, departed, expired, late, lifeless, perished

load n. **1.** bale, cargo, consignment, freight, lading, shipment **2.** affliction, burden, encumbrance, incubus, millstone, onus, oppression, pressure, trouble, weight, worry ~v. **3.** cram, fill, freight, heap, lade, pack, pile, stack, stuff **4.** burden, encumber, hamper, oppress, saddle with, trouble, weigh down, worry **5.** Of firearms charge, make ready, prepare to fire, prime

loaded 1. burdened, charged, freighted, full, laden, weighted **2.** biased, distorted, weighted **3.** at the ready, charged, primed, ready to shoot or fire **4.** Sl. affluent, flush (Inf.), moneyed, rich, rolling (Sl.), wealthy, well-heeled (Sl.), well-off, well-to-do

loan n. accommodation, advance, allowance, credit, mortgage, touch (Sl.)

loathing abhorrence, abomination, antipathy, aversion, detestation, disgust, execration, hatred, horror, odium, repugnance, repulsion, revulsion

loathsome abhorrent, abominable, detestable, disgusting, execrable, hateful, horrible, nasty, nauseating, obnoxious, odious, offensive, repugnant, repulsive, revolting, vile
Antonyms adorable, attractive, charming, delightful, enchanting, engaging, fetching, likable, lovable, lovely

lobby n. **1.** corridor, entrance hall, foyer, hall, hallway, passage, passageway, porch, vestibule **2.** pressure group ~v. **3.** bring pressure to bear, campaign for, exert influence, influence, persuade, press for, pressure, promote, pull strings (Brit. inf.), push for, solicit votes, urge

local adj. **1.** community, district, neighbourhood, parish, provincial, regional **2.** confined, limited, narrow, parish pump, parochial, provincial, restricted, small-town ~n. **3.** character (Inf.), inhabitant, local yokel (Disparaging), native, resident

locality area, district, neck of the woods (Inf.), neighbourhood, region, vicinity

locate come across, detect, discover, find, lay one's hands on, pin down, pinpoint, run to earth, track down, unearth

location bearings, locale, locus, place, point, position, site, situation, spot, venue, whereabouts

lock 1. n. bolt, clasp, fastening, padlock **2.** v. bolt, close, fasten, latch, seal, secure, shut, sneck (Dialect)

lodge n. **1.** cabin, chalet, cottage, gatehouse, house, hunting lodge, hut, shelter **2.** assemblage, association, branch, chapter, club, group, society ~v. **3.** accommodate, billet, board, entertain, harbour, put up, quarter, room, shelter, sojourn, stay, stop **4.** become fixed, catch, come to rest, imbed, implant, stick

lodger boarder, guest, paying guest, P.G., resident, roomer, tenant

lodging Often plural abode, accommodation, apartments, boarding, digs (Brit. inf.), dwelling, habitation, quarters, residence, rooms, shelter

lofty 1. elevated, high, raised, sky-high, soaring, tall, towering **2.** dignified, distinguished, elevated, exalted, grand, illustrious, imposing, majestic, noble, renowned, stately, sublime, superior **3.** arrogant, condescending, disdainful, haughty, high and mighty (Inf.), lordly, patronizing, proud, snooty (Inf.), supercilious, toffee-nosed (Brit. sl.)
Antonyms debased, degraded, dwarfed, friendly, humble, low, lowly, mean, modest, short, stunted, unassuming, warm

log n. **1.** block, bole, chunk, piece of timber, stump, trunk **2.** account, chart, daybook, journal, listing, logbook, record, tally ~v. **3.** book, chart, make a note of, note, record, register, report, set down, tally

logic 1. good reason, good sense, reason, sense, sound judgment 2. chain of thought, coherence, connection, link, rationale, relationship

logical clear, cogent, coherent, consistent, deducible, pertinent, rational, reasonable, relevant, sound, valid, well-organized
Antonyms illogical, implausible, instinctive, irrational, unorganized, unreasonable

loiter dally, dawdle, delay, dilly-dally (*Inf.*), hang about *or* around, idle, lag, linger, loaf, loll, saunter, skulk, stroll

lone by oneself, deserted, isolated, lonesome, one, only, separate, separated, single, sole, solitary, unaccompanied

loneliness aloneness, desertedness, desolation, dreariness, forlornness, isolation, lonesomeness, seclusion, solitariness, solitude

lonely 1. abandoned, destitute, estranged, forlorn, forsaken, friendless, lonesome, outcast 2. alone, apart, by oneself, companionless, isolated, lone, single, solitary, withdrawn 3. deserted, desolate, isolated, off the beaten track (*Inf.*), out-of-the-way, remote, secluded, sequestered, solitary, unfrequented, uninhabited
Antonyms (*sense 1*) accompanied, befriended, popular, together (*sense 2*) bustling, crowded, frequented, populous, teeming

long¹ *adj.* elongated, expanded, extended, extensive, far-reaching, lengthy, spread out, stretched
Antonyms abbreviated, abridged, brief, compressed, contracted, little, momentary, quick, short, short-lived, small

long² *v.* covet, crave, desire, dream of, hanker, hunger, itch, lust, pine, want, wish, yearn

longing *n.* ambition, aspiration, coveting, craving, desire, hankering, hungering, itch, thirst, urge, wish, yearning, yen (*Inf.*)
Antonyms abhorrence, antipathy, apathy, disgust, indifference, loathing, revulsion, unconcern

long-standing abiding, enduring, established, fixed, hallowed by time, long-established, long-lasting, long-lived, time-honoured

long-suffering easy-going, forbearing, forgiving, patient, resigned, stoical, tolerant, uncomplaining

long-winded diffuse, discursive, garrulous, lengthy, long-drawn-out, overlong, prolix, prolonged, rambling, repetitious, tedious, verbose, wordy
Antonyms brief, concise, crisp, curt, laconic, pithy, sententious, short, succinct, terse, to the point

look *v.* 1. behold (*Archaic*), check out (*Inf.*), consider, contemplate, examine, eye, feast one's eyes upon, gaze, glance, inspect, observe, peep, regard, scan, scrutinize, see, study, survey, take a gander at (*Inf.*), view, watch 2. appear, display, evidence, exhibit, look like, make clear, manifest, present, seem, seem to be, show, strike one as 3. forage, hunt, search, seek ~ *n.* 4. examination, eyeful (*Inf.*), gaze, glance, glimpse, inspection, look-see (*Sl.*), observation, once-over (*Inf.*), peek, review, sight, squint (*Inf.*), survey, view 5. air, appearance, aspect, bearing, cast, complexion, countenance, demeanour, effect, expression, face, fashion, guise, manner, mien (*Literary*), semblance

look after attend to, care for, guard, keep an eye on, mind, nurse, protect, sit with, supervise, take care of, take charge of, tend, watch

look down on *or* **upon** contemn, despise, disdain, hold in contempt, look down one's nose at (*Inf.*), misprize, scorn, sneer, spurn, treat with contempt, turn one's nose up (at) (*Inf.*)

look forward to anticipate, await, count on, count the days until, expect, hope for, long for, look for, wait for

look into check out, delve into, examine, explore, follow up, go into, inquire about, inspect, investigate, look over, make inquiries, probe, research, scrutinize, study

lookout 1. guard, qui vive, readiness, vigil, watch **2.** guard, sentinel, sentry, vedette (*Military*), watchman **3.** beacon, citadel, observation post, post, tower, watchtower

look out be alert, be careful, be on guard, be on the qui vive, be vigilant, beware, keep an eye out, keep one's eyes open (peeled, skinned), pay attention, watch out

look over cast an eye over, check, examine, flick through, inspect, look through, monitor, peruse, scan, view

loom appear, become visible, be imminent, bulk, emerge, hover, impend, menace, take shape, threaten

loop 1. *n.* bend, circle, coil, convolution, curl, curve, eyelet, hoop, kink, loophole, noose, ring, spiral, twirl, twist, whorl **2.** *v.* bend, braid, circle, coil, connect, curl, curve round, encircle, fold, join, knot, roll, spiral, turn, twist, wind round

loophole 1. aperture, knothole, opening, slot **2.** *Fig.* avoidance, escape, evasion, excuse, let-out, means of escape, plea, pretence, pretext, subterfuge

loose *adj.* **1.** floating, free, insecure, movable, released, unattached, unbound, unconfined, unfastened, unfettered, unrestricted, unsecured, untied, wobbly **2.** baggy, easy, hanging, loosened, not fitting, not tight, relaxed, slack, slackened, sloppy **3.** diffuse, disconnected, disordered, ill-defined, imprecise, inaccurate, indefinite, indistinct, inexact, rambling, random, vague **4.**

abandoned, debauched, disreputable, dissipated, dissolute, fast, immoral, lewd, libertine, licentious, profligate, promiscuous, unchaste, wanton ~ *v.* **5.** detach, disconnect, disengage, ease, free, let go, liberate, loosen, release, set free, slacken, unbind, undo, unfasten, unleash, unloose, untie **Antonyms** *adj.* (*sense 1*) bound, curbed, fastened, fettered, restrained, secured, tethered, tied (*sense 2*) tight (*sense 3*) accurate, clear, concise, exact, precise (*sense 4*) chaste, disciplined, moral, virtuous ~ *v.* bind, cage, capture, fasten, fetter, imprison, tether

loosen 1. detach, let out, separate, slacken, unbind, undo, unloose, unstick, untie, work free, work loose **2.** deliver, free, let go, liberate, release, set free

loot *n.* booty, goods, haul, plunder, prize, spoils, swag (*Sl.*)

lopsided askew, asymmetrical, awry, cockeyed, crooked, disproportionate, off balance, onesided, out of shape, out of true, squint, tilting, unbalanced, unequal, uneven, warped

lord 1. commander, governor, king, leader, liege, master, monarch, overlord, potentate, prince, ruler, seigneur, sovereign, superior **2.** earl, noble, nobleman, peer, viscount

lore beliefs, doctrine, experience, folk-wisdom, mythos, saws, sayings, teaching, traditional wisdom, traditions, wisdom

lose 1. be deprived of, displace, drop, fail to keep, forget, mislay, misplace, miss, suffer loss **2.** capitulate, default, fail, fall short, forfeit, lose out on (*Inf.*), miss, pass up (*Inf.*), yield **3.** be defeated, be the loser, be worsted, come a cropper (*Inf.*), come to grief, get the worst of, lose out, suffer defeat, take a licking (*Inf.*)

loser also-ran, dud (*Inf.*), failure, flop (*Inf.*), lemon (*Sl.*), no-hoper (*Inf.*), underdog, washout (*Inf.*)

loss 1. bereavement, deprivation,

disappearance, failure, forfeiture, losing, misfortune, mislaying, privation, squandering, waste 2. cost, damage, defeat, destruction, detriment, disadvantage, harm, hurt, impairment, injury, ruin

Antonyms acquisition, advantage, finding, gain, preservation, recovery, reimbursement, restoration, saving, winning

lost 1. disappeared, forfeited, mislaid, misplaced, missed, missing, strayed, vanished, wayward 2. adrift, astray, at sea, disoriented, off-course, off-track 3. baffled, bewildered, clueless (*Sl.*), confused, helpless, ignorant, mystified, perplexed, puzzled 4. absent, absorbed, abstracted, distracted, dreamy, engrossed, entranced, preoccupied, rapt, spellbound, taken up 5. bygone, dead, extinct, forgotten, gone, lapsed, obsolete, out-of-date, past, unremembered 6. abandoned, corrupt, damned, depraved, dissolute, fallen, irreclaimable, licentious, profligate, unchaste, wanton

lot 1. assortment, batch, bunch (*Inf.*), collection, consignment, crowd, group, quantity, set 2. accident, chance, destiny, doom, fate, fortune, hazard, plight, portion 3. allowance, cut (*Inf.*), parcel, part, percentage, piece, portion, quota, ration, share 4. a lot *or* lots abundance, a great deal, heap(s), large amount, load(s) (*Inf.*), masses (*Inf.*), numbers, ocean(s), oodles (*Inf.*), piles, plenty, quantities, reams (*Inf.*), scores, stack(s)

lotion balm, cream, embrocation, liniment, salve, solution

lottery 1. draw, raffle, sweepstake 2. chance, gamble, hazard, risk, toss-up (*Inf.*), venture

loud 1. blaring, blatant, boisterous, booming, clamorous, deafening, ear-piercing, ear-splitting, forte (*Music*), high-sounding, noisy, obstreperous, piercing, resounding, rowdy, sonorous, stentorian, strident, strong, thunder-

ing, tumultuous, turbulent, vehement, vociferous 2. *Fig.* brassy, flamboyant, flashy, garish, gaudy, glaring, lurid, ostentatious, showy, tasteless, tawdry, vulgar 3. brash, brazen, coarse, crass, crude, loud-mouthed (*Inf.*), offensive, raucous, vulgar

Antonyms (*sense 1*) gentle, inaudible, low, low-pitched, quiet, silent, soft, soundless, subdued (*sense 2*) conservative, dull, sober, sombre (*sense 3*) quiet, reserved, retiring, shy, unassuming

lounge *v.* laze, lie about, loaf, loiter, loll, recline, relax, saunter, sprawl, take it easy (*Inf.*)

lout bear, boor, bumpkin, churl, clod, clumsy idiot, dolt, gawk, lubber, lummox (*Inf.*), ned (*Sl.*), oaf, yahoo, yob *or* yobbo (*Brit. sl.*)

lovable adorable, amiable, attractive, captivating, charming, cuddly, delightful, enchanting, endearing, engaging, fetching (*Inf.*), likable, lovely, pleasing, sweet, winning, winsome

Antonyms abhorrent, abominable, detestable, hateful, loathsome, obnoxious, odious, offensive, revolting

love *v.* 1. adore, adulate, be attached to, be in love with, cherish, dote on, have affection for, hold dear, idolize, prize, think the world of, treasure, worship 2. appreciate, delight in, desire, enjoy, fancy, have a weakness for, like, relish, savour, take pleasure in 3. canoodle (*Sl.*), caress, cuddle, embrace, fondle, kiss, neck (*Inf.*), pet ~*n.* 4. adoration, adulation, affection, amity, ardour, attachment, devotion, fondness, friendship, infatuation, liking, passion, rapture, regard, tenderness, warmth

Antonyms *v.* (*senses 1 & 2*) abhor, abominate, detest, dislike, hate, scorn ~*n.* (*sense 4*) abhorrence, abomination, animosity, antagonism, antipathy, aversion, bitterness, detestation, disgust, dislike, hate, hatred, hostility, ill will, incompatibility, loathing, malice, repugnance, resentment, scorn

lovely 1. admirable, adorable, amiable, attractive, beautiful, charming, comely, exquisite, graceful, handsome, pretty, sweet, winning **2.** agreeable, captivating, delightful, enchanting, engaging, enjoyable, gratifying, nice, pleasant, pleasing
Antonyms abhorrent, detestable, hateful, hideous, loathsome, odious, repellent, repugnant, revolting, ugly, unattractive

lover admirer, beau, beloved, boyfriend, fancy man (*Sl.*), fancy woman (*Sl.*), fiancé, fiancée, flame (*Inf.*), girlfriend, inamorata, inamorato, mistress, paramour, suitor, swain (*Archaic*), sweetheart, toy boy

loving affectionate, amorous, ardent, cordial, dear, demonstrative, devoted, doting, fond, friendly, kind, solicitous, tender, warm, warm-hearted
Antonyms aloof, cold, contemptuous, cruel, detached, distasteful, hateful, hostile, indifferent, mean, scornful, unconcerned, unloving

low 1. little, short, small, squat, stunted **2.** deep, depressed, ground-level, low-lying, shallow, subsided, sunken **3.** depleted, insignificant, little, meagre, paltry, reduced, scant, small, sparse, trifling **4.** deficient, inadequate, inferior, low-grade, mediocre, poor, puny, second-rate, shoddy, substandard, worthless **5.** coarse, common, crude, disgraceful, dishonourable, disreputable, gross, ill-bred, obscene, rough, rude, unbecoming, undignified, unrefined, vulgar **6.** humble, lowborn, lowly, meek, obscure, plain, plebeian, poor, simple, unpretentious **7.** blue, brassed off (*Inf.*), dejected, depressed, despondent, disheartened, down, downcast, down in the dumps (*Inf.*), fed up (*Inf.*), forlorn, gloomy, glum, miserable, morose, sad, unhappy

8. gentle, hushed, muffled, muted, quiet, soft, subdued, whispered **9.** cheap, economical, inexpensive, moderate, modest, reasonable **10.** abject, base, contemptible, dastardly, degraded, depraved, despicable, ignoble, mean, menial, nasty, scurvy, servile, sordid, unworthy, vile, vulgar
Antonyms admirable, alert, brave, cheerful, elated, elevated, eminent, energetic, enthusiastic, exalted, fine, grand, happy, high, high-ranking, honourable, important, laudable, lofty, loud, noisy, praiseworthy, significant, strong, superior, tall, towering, worthy

lower *adj.* **1.** inferior, junior, lesser, low-level, minor, secondary, second-class, smaller, subordinate, under ~ *v.* **2.** depress, drop, fall, let down, make lower, sink, submerge, take down **3.** abase, belittle, condescend, debase, degrade, deign, demean, devalue, disgrace, downgrade, humble, humiliate, stoop
Antonyms *adj.* higher ~ *v.* boost, elevate, hoist, lift, magnify, raise

loyal attached, constant, dependable, devoted, dutiful, faithful, patriotic, staunch, steadfast, tried and true, true, true-blue, truehearted, trustworthy, trusty, unswerving, unwavering
Antonyms disloyal, false, perfidious, traitorous, treacherous, unfaithful, untrustworthy

loyalty allegiance, constancy, dependability, devotion, faithfulness, fealty, fidelity, patriotism, reliability, staunchness, steadfastness, true-heartedness, trueness, trustiness, trustworthiness

lubricate grease, make slippery, make smooth, oil, oil the wheels, smear, smooth the way

lucid 1. clear, clear-cut, comprehensible, crystal-clear, distinct, evident, explicit, intelligible, limpid, obvious, pellucid, plain, transparent **2.** beaming, bright, brilliant, effulgent, gleaming, luminous, radiant, resplendent, shining **3.** clear, crystalline, diaphanous, glassy, limpid, pellucid, pure, translucent, transparent

Antonyms (*sense 1*) ambiguous, confused, equivocal, incomprehensible, indistinct, muddled, unclear, unintelligible, vague (*sense 2*) dull (*sense 3*) unclear

luck **1.** accident, chance, destiny, fate, fortuity, fortune, hap (*Archaic*), hazard **2.** advantage, blessing, break (*Inf.*), fluke, godsend, good fortune, good luck, prosperity, serendipity, stroke, success, windfall

luckily favourably, fortunately, happily, opportunely, propitiously, providentially

lucky advantageous, blessed, charmed, favoured, fortunate, prosperous, serendipitous, successful

Antonyms bad, detrimental, ominous, unfavourable, unfortunate, unhappy, unlucky, unpromising

lucrative advantageous, fat, fruitful, gainful, high-income, money-making, paying, productive, profitable, remunerative, well-paid

ludicrous absurd, burlesque, comic, comical, crazy, droll, farcical, funny, incongruous, laughable, nonsensical, odd, outlandish, preposterous, ridiculous, silly, zany

Antonyms grave, logical, sad, sensible, serious, solemn

luggage baggage, bags, cases, gear, impedimenta, paraphernalia, suitcases, things, trunks

lukewarm *Fig.* apathetic, cold, cool, half-hearted, indifferent, laodicean, phlegmatic, unconcerned, unenthusiastic, uninterested, unresponsive

lull **1.** *v.* allay, calm, compose, hush, lullaby, pacify, quell, quiet, rock to sleep, soothe, still, subdue, tranquillize **2.** *n.* calm, calmness, hush, let-up (*Inf.*), pause, quiet, respite, silence, stillness, tranquillity

lumber *n.* castoffs, clutter, discards, jumble, junk, refuse, rubbish, trash, trumpery, white elephants

lumbering awkward, blundering, bovine, bumbling, clumsy, elephantine, heavy, heavy-footed, hulking, lubberly, overgrown, ponderous, ungainly, unwieldy

luminous bright, brilliant, glowing, illuminated, lighted, lit, luminescent, lustrous, radiant, resplendent, shining, vivid

lump *n.* **1.** ball, bunch, cake, chunk, clod, cluster, dab, gob, gobbet, group, hunk, mass, nugget, piece, spot, wedge **2.** bulge, bump, growth, protrusion, protuberance, swelling, tumescence, tumour ~*v.* **3.** agglutinate, aggregate, batch, bunch, coalesce, collect, combine, conglomerate, consolidate, group, mass, pool, unite

lunacy **1.** dementia, derangement, idiocy, insanity, madness, mania, psychosis **2.** aberration, absurdity, craziness, folly, foolhardiness, foolishness, idiocy, imbecility, madness, senselessness, stupidity, tomfoolery

Antonyms prudence, reason, sanity, sense

lunatic **1.** *adj.* barmy (*Sl.*), bonkers (*Sl.*), crackbrained, crazy, daft, demented, deranged, insane, irrational, mad, maniacal, nuts (*Sl.*), psychotic, unhinged **2.** *n.* loony (*Sl.*), madman, maniac, nut (*Sl.*), nutcase (*Sl.*), nutter (*Sl.*), psychopath

lunge **1.** *n.* charge, cut, jab, pass, pounce, spring, stab, swing, swipe, thrust **2.** *v.* bound, charge, cut, dash, dive, fall upon, hit at, jab, leap, pitch into, plunge, poke, pounce, set upon, stab, strike at, thrust

lure **1.** *v.* allure, attract, beckon, decoy, draw, ensnare, entice, inveigle, invite, lead on, seduce, tempt **2.** *n.* allurement, attraction, bait, carrot (*Inf.*), come-on (*Inf.*), decoy, enticement, inducement, magnet, siren song, temptation

lurid 1. exaggerated, graphic, melodramatic, sensational, shocking, startling, unrestrained, vivid, yellow (*Of journalism*) 2. disgusting, ghastly, gory, grim, grisly, gruesome, macabre, revolting, savage, violent

lurk conceal oneself, crouch, go furtively, hide, lie in wait, move with stealth, prowl, skulk, slink, sneak, snoop

luscious appetizing, delectable, delicious, honeyed, juicy, mouthwatering, palatable, rich, savoury, scrumptious (*Inf.*), succulent, sweet, toothsome, yummy (*Sl.*)

lush abundant, dense, flourishing, green, lavish, overgrown, prolific, rank, teeming, verdant

lust *n.* 1. carnality, concupiscence, lasciviousness, lechery, lewdness, libido, licentiousness, prurience, randiness (*Sl., chiefly Brit.*), salaciousness, sensuality, the hots (*Sl.*), wantonness 2. appetence, appetite, avidity, covetousness, craving, cupidity, desire, greed, longing, passion, thirst ~*v.* 3. be consumed with desire for, covet, crave, desire, hunger for *or* after, lech after (*Inf.*), need, slaver over, want, yearn

lustre 1. burnish, gleam, glint, glitter, gloss, glow, sheen, shimmer, shine, sparkle 2. brightness, brilliance, dazzle, lambency, luminousness, radiance, resplendence 3. distinction, fame, glory, honour, illustriousness, prestige, renown

lusty brawny, energetic, hale, healthy, hearty, in fine fettle, powerful, Rabelaisian, redblooded (*Inf.*), robust, rugged, stalwart, stout, strapping, strong, sturdy, vigorous, virile

luxurious comfortable, costly, de luxe, expensive, lavish, magnificent, opulent, plush (*Inf.*), rich, ritzy (*Sl.*), splendid, sumptuous, well-appointed
Antonyms ascetic, austere, deprived, economical, plain, poor, sparing, Spartan, squalid, thrifty

luxury 1. affluence, hedonism, opulence, richness, splendour, sumptuousness, voluptuousness 2. bliss, comfort, delight, enjoyment, gratification, indulgence, pleasure, satisfaction, wellbeing 3. extra, extravagance, frill, indulgence, nonessential, treat
Antonyms austerity, burden, deprivation, destitution, difficulty, discomfort, hardship, infliction, misery, necessity, need, poverty, privation, want

lying 1. *n.* deceit, dishonesty, dissimulation, double-dealing, duplicity, fabrication, falsity, fibbing, guile, mendacity, perjury, prevarication, untruthfulness 2. *adj.* deceitful, dishonest, dissembling, double-dealing, false, guileful, mendacious, perfidious, treacherous, two-faced, untruthful
Antonyms *adj.* candid, forthright, frank, honest, reliable, sincere, straight, straightforward, truthful, veracious

M

machine 1. apparatus, appliance, contraption, contrivance, device, engine, instrument, mechanism, tool 2. agency, machinery, organization, party, setup (*Inf.*), structure, system

machinery 1. apparatus, equipment, gear, instruments, mechanism, tackle, tools, works 2. agency, channels, machine, organization, procedure, structure, system

mad 1. aberrant, bananas (*Sl.*), barmy (*Sl.*), batty (*Sl.*), bonkers (*Sl.*), crackers (*Sl.*), crazed, crazy (*Inf.*), cuckoo (*Inf.*), delirious, demented, deranged, distracted, flaky (*U.S. sl.*), frantic, frenzied, insane, loony (*Sl.*), loopy (*Inf.*), lunatic, mental (*Sl.*), *non compos mentis*, nuts (*Sl.*), nutty (*Sl.*), off one's chump (*Sl.*), off one's head, off one's nut (*Sl.*), off one's rocker (*Sl.*), off one's trolley (*Sl.*), of unsound mind, out of one's mind, psychotic, rabid, raving, round the bend (*Brit. sl.*), round the twist (*Brit. sl.*), screwy (*Inf.*), unbalanced, unhinged, unstable 2. absurd, daft (*Inf.*), foolhardy, foolish, imprudent, irrational, ludicrous, nonsensical, preposterous, senseless, unreasonable, unsafe, unsound, wild
Antonyms calm, composed, cool, rational, sane, sensible, sound

madden annoy, craze, derange, drive one crazy (*Inf.*), drive one out of one's mind, round the bend (*Brit. sl.*), round the twist (*Brit. sl.*), to distraction), enrage, exasperate, get one's hackles up, incense, inflame, infuriate, irritate, make one's blood boil, make one see red (*Inf.*), make one's hackles rise, provoke, raise one's hackles, unhinge, upset, vex

Antonyms appease, calm, mollify, pacify, soothe

made-up fabricated, false, fictional, imaginary, invented, make-believe, mythical, specious, trumped-up, unreal, untrue

madly 1. crazily, deliriously, dementedly, distractedly, frantically, frenziedly, hysterically, insanely, rabidly 2. absurdly, foolishly, irrationally, ludicrously, nonsensically, senselessly, unreasonably, wildly 3. energetically, excitedly, furiously, hastily, hurriedly, like mad (*Inf.*), quickly, rapidly, recklessly, speedily, violently, wildly

madness 1. aberration, craziness, delusion, dementia, derangement, distraction, insanity, lunacy, mania, mental illness, psychopathy, psychosis 2. absurdity, daftness (*Inf.*), folly, foolhardiness, foolishness, nonsense, preposterousness, wildness 3. anger, exasperation, frenzy, fury, ire, rage, raving, wildness, wrath 4. ardour, craze, enthusiasm, fanaticism, fondness, infatuation, keenness, passion, rage, zeal 5. abandon, agitation, excitement, frenzy, furore, intoxication, riot, unrestraint, uproar

magazine 1. journal, pamphlet, paper, periodical 2. ammunition dump, arsenal, depot, powder room (*Obsolete*), store, storehouse, warehouse

magic *n.* 1. black art, enchantment, necromancy, occultism, sorcery, sortilege, spell, theurgy, witchcraft, wizardry 2. conjuring, hocus-pocus, illusion, jiggery-pokery (*Inf., chiefly Brit.*), jugglery, legerdemain, prestidigitation, sleight of hand, trickery 3. allurement, charm, enchantment, fascination, glamour, magnetism, power ~*adj.* 4. *Also* **magical** bewitching, charismatic, charming, enchanting, entrancing, fascinating, magnetic, marvellous, miraculous, sorcerous, spellbinding

magistrate bailie (*Scot.*), J.P., judge, justice, justice of the peace, provost (*Scot.*)

magnanimous beneficent, big, big-hearted, bountiful, charitable, free, generous, great-hearted, handsome, high-minded, kind, kindly, munificent, noble, open-handed, selfless, ungrudging, unselfish, unstinting

magnate 1. baron, big cheese (*Sl.*), big noise (*Sl.*), big shot (*Sl.*), big wheel (*Sl.*), bigwig (*Sl.*), captain of industry, chief, fat cat (*Sl.*), leader, mogul, Mr. Big (*Sl.*), nabob (*Inf.*), notable, plutocrat, tycoon, V.I.P. 2. aristo (*Inf.*), aristocrat, baron, bashaw, grandee, magnifico, merchant, noble, notable, personage, prince

magnetic alluring, attractive, captivating, charismatic, charming, enchanting, entrancing, fascinating, hypnotic, irresistible, mesmerizing, seductive

magnetism allure, appeal, attraction, attractiveness, captivatingness, charisma, charm, draw, drawing power, enchantment, fascination, hypnotism, magic, mesmerism, power, pull, seductiveness, spell

magnificence brilliance, glory, gorgeousness, grandeur, luxuriousness, luxury, majesty, nobility, opulence, pomp, resplendence, splendour, stateliness, sublimity, sumptuousness

magnificent august, brilliant, elegant, elevated, exalted, excellent, fine, glorious, gorgeous, grand, grandiose, imposing, impressive, lavish, luxurious, majestic, noble, opulent, outstanding, princely, regal, resplendent, rich, splendid, stately, sublime, sumptuous, superb, superior, transcendent
Antonyms bad, humble, ignoble,

lowly, mean, modest, ordinary, petty, poor, trivial, undistinguished, unimposing

magnify 1. aggrandize, amplify, augment, blow up (*Inf.*), boost, build up, deepen, dilate, enlarge, expand, heighten, increase, intensify 2. aggravate, blow up, blow up out of all proportion, dramatize, enhance, exaggerate, inflate, make a mountain out of a molehill, overdo, overemphasize, overestimate, overplay, overrate, overstate
Antonyms belittle, decrease, deflate, deprecate, diminish, disparage, lessen, lower, minimize, reduce, shrink, understate

magnitude 1. consequence, eminence, grandeur, greatness, importance, mark, moment, note, significance, weight 2. amount, amplitude, bigness, bulk, capacity, dimensions, enormity, expanse, extent, hugeness, immensity, intensity, largeness, mass, measure, proportions, quantity, size, space, strength, vastness, volume

maid 1. damsel, girl, lass, lassie (*Inf.*), maiden, miss, nymph (*Poetic*), wench 2. abigail (*Archaic*), handmaiden (*Archaic*), housemaid, maidservant, servant, serving-maid

maiden *n.* 1. damsel, girl, lass, lassie (*Inf.*), maid, miss, nymph (*Poetic*), virgin, wench ~*adj.* 2. chaste, intact, pure, undefiled, unmarried, unwed, virgin, virginal 3. first, inaugural, initial, initiatory, introductory 4. fresh, new, unbroached, untapped, untried, unused

mail *n.* 1. correspondence, letters, packages, parcels, post 2. post, postal service, postal system ~*v.* 3. dispatch, forward, post, send, send by mail *or* post

maim cripple, disable, hamstring, hurt, impair, incapacitate, injure, lame, mangle, mar, mutilate, put out of action, wound

main 1. *adj.* capital, cardinal, central, chief, critical, crucial, essential, foremost, head, leading, necessary, outstanding, paramount, particular, predominant, pre-eminent, premier, primary, prime, principal, special, supreme, vital 2. *n.* cable, channel, conduit, duct, line, pipe

Antonyms *adj.* auxiliary, dependent, insignificant, least, lesser, minor, secondary, subordinate, trivial, unimportant

mainly above all, chiefly, first and foremost, for the most part, generally, in general, in the main, largely, mostly, most of all, on the whole, overall, predominantly, primarily, principally, substantially, to the greatest extent, usually

mainstay anchor, backbone, bulwark, buttress, chief support, linchpin, pillar, prop

maintain 1. care for, carry on, conserve, continue, finance, keep, keep up, look after, nurture, perpetuate, preserve, prolong, provide, retain, supply, support, sustain, take care of, uphold 2. affirm, allege, assert, asseverate, aver, avow, claim, contend, declare, hold, insist, profess, state 3. advocate, argue for, back, champion, defend, fight for, justify, plead for, stand by, take up the cudgels for, uphold, vindicate

Antonyms (*sense 1*) abolish, break off, conclude, discontinue, drop, end, finish, give up, relinquish, suspend, terminate (*sense 2*) disavow (*sense 3*) abandon, desert

maintenance 1. care, carrying-on, conservation, continuance, continuation, keeping, nurture, perpetuation, preservation, prolongation, provision, repairs, retainment, supply, support, sustainment, sustention, upkeep 2. aliment, alimony, allowance, food, keep, livelihood, living, subsistence, support, sustenance, upkeep

majestic august, awesome, dignified, elevated, exalted, grand,

grandiose, imperial, imposing, impressive, kingly, lofty, magnificent, monumental, noble, pompous, princely, regal, royal, splendid, stately, sublime, superb

Antonyms humble, ignoble, lowly, mean, modest, ordinary, unassuming, undistinguished, unimposing

majesty augustness, awesomeness, dignity, exaltedness, glory, grandeur, imposingness, impressiveness, kingliness, loftiness, magnificence, nobility, pomp, queenliness, royalty, splendour, state, stateliness, sublimity

major better, bigger, chief, elder, greater, higher, larger, leading, main, most, senior, superior, supreme, uppermost

majority 1. best part, bulk, greater number, mass, more, most, plurality, preponderance, superiority 2. adulthood, manhood, maturity, seniority, womanhood

make *v.* 1. assemble, build, compose, constitute, construct, create, fabricate, fashion, forge, form, frame, manufacture, mould, originate, produce, put together, shape, synthesize 2. accomplish, beget, bring about, cause, create, effect, engender, generate, give rise to, lead to, occasion, produce 3. cause, coerce, compel, constrain, dragoon, drive, force, impel, induce, oblige, press, pressurize, prevail upon, require 4. appoint, assign, create, designate, elect, install, invest, nominate, ordain 5. draw up, enact, establish, fix, form, frame, pass 6. add up to, amount to, compose, constitute, embody, form, represent 7. calculate, estimate, gauge, judge, reckon, suppose, think 8. acquire, clear, earn, gain, get, net, obtain, realize, secure, take in, win ~*n.* 9. brand, build, character, composition, constitution, construction, cut, designation, form, kind, make-up, mark, model, shape, sort, structure, style, type, variety

make-believe *n.* charade, dream, fantasy, imagination, play-acting, pretence, unreality
Antonyms actuality, fact, reality, truthfulness

make believe act as if *or* though, dream, enact, fantasize, imagine, play, play-act, pretend

make do cope, get along *or* by, improvise, manage, muddle through, scrape along *or* by

make off abscond, beat a hasty retreat, bolt, clear out (*Inf.*), cut and run (*Inf.*), decamp, flee, fly, make away, run away *or* off, run for it (*Inf.*), take to one's heels

make out 1. descry, detect, discern, discover, distinguish, espy, perceive, recognize, see **2.** comprehend, decipher, fathom, follow, grasp, perceive, realize, see, understand, work out **3.** complete, draw up, fill in *or* out, inscribe, write (out)

maker author, builder, constructor, director, fabricator, framer, manufacturer, producer

makeshift 1. *adj.* expedient, jury (*Chiefly nautical*), make-do, provisional, rough and ready, stopgap, substitute, temporary **2.** *n.* expedient, shift, stopgap, substitute

make-up 1. cosmetics, face (*Inf.*), greasepaint (*Theatre*), maquillage, paint (*Inf.*), powder, war paint (*Inf., humorous*) **2.** arrangement, assembly, composition, configuration, constitution, construction, form, format, formation, organization, structure

make up 1. compose, comprise, constitute, form **2.** coin, compose, concoct, construct, cook up (*Inf.*), create, devise, dream up, fabricate, formulate, frame, hatch, invent, originate, trump up, write **3.** complete, fill, meet, supply

maladjusted alienated, disturbed, estranged, hung-up (*Sl.*), neurotic, unstable

malady affliction, ailment, complaint, disease, disorder, ill, illness, indisposition, infirmity, sickness

male manful, manlike, manly, masculine, virile
Antonyms effeminate, female, feminine, unmanly, wimpish *or* wimpy (*Inf.*), womanish, womanly

malevolence hate, hatred, ill will, malice, maliciousness, malignity, rancour, spite, spitefulness, vengefulness, vindictiveness

malevolent baleful, evil-minded, hateful (*Archaic*), hostile, ill-natured, malicious, malign, malignant, pernicious, rancorous, spiteful, vengeful, vicious, vindictive
Antonyms amiable, benevolent, benign, friendly, gracious, kind, warm-hearted

malfunction 1. *v.* break down, develop a fault, fail, go wrong **2.** *n.* breakdown, defect, failure, fault, flaw, glitch, impairment

malice animosity, animus, bad blood, bitterness, enmity, evil intent, hate, hatred, ill will, malevolence, maliciousness, malignity, rancour, spite, spitefulness, spleen, vengefulness, venom, vindictiveness

malicious baleful, bitchy (*Sl.*), bitter, catty (*Inf.*), evil-minded, hateful, ill-disposed, ill-natured, injurious, malevolent, malignant, mischievous, pernicious, rancorous, resentful, spiteful, vengeful, vicious
Antonyms amiable, benevolent, friendly, kind, warm-hearted

malign 1. *adj.* bad, baleful, baneful, deleterious, destructive, evil, harmful, hostile, hurtful, injurious, malevolent, malignant, pernicious, vicious, wicked **2.** *v.* abuse, blacken (someone's name), calumniate, defame, denigrate, derogate, disparage, do a hatchet job on (*Inf.*), harm, injure, libel, revile, run down, slander, smear, speak ill of, traduce, vilify
Antonyms *adj.* agreeable, amiable, beneficial, benevolent, benign, friendly, good, harmless,

honourable, innocuous, kind, moral, virtuous, warm-hearted, wholesome ~ v. commend, compliment, extol, praise

malignant baleful, bitter, destructive, harmful, hostile, hurtful, inimical, injurious, malevolent, malicious, malign, of evil intent, pernicious, spiteful, vicious

Antonyms amicable, benign, friendly, kind, warm-hearted

malpractice abuse, dereliction, misbehaviour, misconduct, mismanagement, negligence

maltreat abuse, bully, damage, handle roughly, harm, hurt, ill-treat, injure, mistreat

man n. 1. bloke (*Brit. inf.*), chap (*Inf.*), gentleman, guy (*Inf.*), male 2. adult, being, body, human, human being, individual, one, person, personage, somebody, soul 3. Homo sapiens, humanity, humankind, human race, mankind, mortals, people 4. attendant, employee, follower, hand, hireling, manservant, retainer, servant, soldier, subject, subordinate, valet, vassal, worker, workman ~ v. 5. crew, fill, furnish with men, garrison, occupy, people, staff

manage 1. administer, be in charge (of), command, concert, conduct, direct, govern, manipulate, oversee, preside over, rule, run, superintend, supervise 2. accomplish, arrange, bring about *or* off, contrive, cope with, deal with, effect, engineer, succeed 3. control, dominate, govern, guide, handle, influence, manipulate, operate, pilot, ply, steer, train, use, wield

Antonyms botch, fail, follow, make a mess of, mismanage, muff, spoil, starve

manageable amenable, compliant, controllable, convenient, docile, easy, governable, handy, submissive, tamable, tractable, user-friendly, wieldy

Antonyms demanding, difficult, disobedient, hard, headstrong,

obstinate, refractory, stubborn, ungovernable, unruly, unyielding, wild

management administration, board, bosses (*Inf.*), directorate, directors, employers, executive(s)

manager administrator, boss (*Inf.*), comptroller, conductor, controller, director, executive, gaffer (*Inf.*), governor, head, organizer, overseer, proprietor, superintendent, supervisor

mandatory binding, compulsory, obligatory, required, requisite

mangle butcher, cripple, crush, cut, deform, destroy, disfigure, distort, hack, lacerate, maim, mar, maul, mutilate, rend, ruin, spoil, tear, wreck

mangy dirty, grungy (*Sl., chiefly U.S.*), mean, moth-eaten, scabby (*Inf.*), scruffy, scuzzy (*Sl., chiefly U.S.*), seedy, shabby, shoddy, squalid

Antonyms attractive, choice, clean, de luxe, fine, splendid, spotless, superb, tidy, well-dressed, well-kempt, well-kept

manhandle 1. handle roughly, knock about, maul, paw (*Inf.*), pull, push, rough up 2. carry, haul, heave, hump (*Brit. sl.*), lift, manoeuvre, pull, push, shove, tug

manhood bravery, courage, determination, firmness, fortitude, hardihood, manfulness, manliness, masculinity, maturity, mettle, resolution, spirit, strength, valour, virility

mania aberration, craziness, delirium, dementia, derangement, disorder, frenzy, insanity, lunacy, madness

maniac loony (*Sl.*), lunatic, madman, madwoman, nutcase (*Sl.*), nutter (*Brit. sl.*), psycho (*Sl.*), psychopath

manifest adj. apparent, clear, conspicuous, distinct, evident, glaring, noticeable, obvious, open, palpable, patent, plain, unmistakable, visible

manifestation appearance, demonstration, disclosure, display, exhibition, exposure, expression, indication, instance, mark, materialization, revelation, show, sign, symptom, token

manifold abundant, assorted, copious, diverse, diversified, many, multifarious, multifold, multiple, multiplied, multitudinous, numerous, varied, various

manipulate 1. employ, handle, operate, ply, use, wield, work **2.** conduct, control, direct, engineer, guide, influence, manoeuvre, negotiate, steer

mankind Homo sapiens, humanity, humankind, human race, man, people

manly bold, brave, butch (*Sl.*), courageous, daring, dauntless, fearless, gallant, hardy, heroic, macho, male, manful, masculine, muscular, noble, powerful, Ramboesque, red-blooded (*Inf.*), resolute, robust, stout-hearted, strapping, strong, valiant, valorous, vigorous, virile, well-built

Antonyms cowardly, craven, delicate, effeminate, faint-hearted, feeble, feminine, frail, ignoble, irresolute, sickly, soft, timid, unmanly, weak, wimpish *or* wimpy (*Inf.*), womanish

man-made artificial, ersatz, manufactured, plastic (*Sl.*), synthetic

manner 1. air, appearance, aspect, bearing, behaviour, comportment, conduct, demeanour, deportment, look, mien (*Literary*), presence, tone **2.** approach, custom, fashion, form, genre, habit, line, means, method, mode, practice, procedure, process, routine, style, tack, tenor, usage, way, wont

mannerism characteristic, foible, habit, idiosyncrasy, peculiarity, quirk, trait, trick

mannerly civil, civilized, courteous, decorous, genteel, gentlemanly, gracious, ladylike, polished, polite, refined, respectful, well-behaved, well-bred, well-mannered

Antonyms boorish, discourteous,

disrespectful, ill-mannered, impertinent, impolite, impudent, insolent, rude, unmannerly

manners 1. bearing, behaviour, breeding, carriage, comportment, conduct, demeanour, deportment **2.** ceremony, courtesy, decorum, etiquette, formalities, good form, polish, politeness, politesse, proprieties, protocol, refinement, social graces, the done thing

manoeuvre *n.* **1.** action, artifice, dodge, intrigue, machination, move, movement, plan, plot, ploy, ruse, scheme, stratagem, subterfuge, tactic, trick ~*v.* **2.** contrive, devise, engineer, intrigue, machinate, manage, manipulate, plan, plot, pull strings, scheme, wangle (*Inf.*) **3.** direct, drive, guide, handle, navigate, negotiate, pilot, steer

mansion abode, dwelling, habitation, hall, manor, residence, seat, villa

manual 1. *adj.* done by hand, hand-operated, human, physical **2.** *n.* bible, enchiridion (*Rare*), guide, guidebook, handbook, instructions, workbook

manufacture 1. *v.* assemble, build, compose, construct, create, fabricate, forge, form, make, mass-produce, mould, process, produce, put together, shape, turn out **2.** *n.* assembly, construction, creation, fabrication, making, mass-production, produce, production

manure compost, droppings, dung, excrement, fertilizer, muck, ordure

many *adj.* abundant, copious, countless, divers (*Archaic*), frequent, innumerable, manifold, multifarious, multifold, multitudinous, myriad, numerous, profuse, sundry, umpteen (*Inf.*), varied, various

mar blemish, blight, blot, damage, deface, detract from, disfigure, harm, hurt, impair, injure, maim, mangle, mutilate, ruin, scar, spoil, stain, sully, taint, tarnish, vitiate

Antonyms adorn, ameliorate, better, embellish, improve, or~ nament

march v. **1.** file, footslog, pace, parade, stalk, stride, strut, tramp, tread, walk ~n. **2.** hike, route~ march, tramp, trek, walk **3.** demo (Inf.), demonstration, parade, procession

margin 1. border, bound, bounda~ ry, brim, brink, confine, edge, limit, perimeter, periphery, rim, side, verge **2.** allowance, com~ pass, elbowroom, extra, latitude, leeway, play, room, scope, space, surplus

marginal bordering, borderline, on the edge, peripheral

marine maritime, nautical, naval, ocean-going, oceanic, pelagic, saltwater, sea, seafaring, sea~ going, thalassic

mariner bluejacket, gob (Inf.), hand, Jack Tar, matelot (Brit. sl.), navigator, sailor, salt, sea dog, seafarer, seafaring man, seaman, tar

marital conjugal, connubial, mar~ ried, matrimonial, nuptial, spousal, wedded

maritime marine, nautical, naval, oceanic, sea, seafaring

mark n. **1.** blemish, blot, blotch, bruise, dent, impression, line, nick, pock, scar, scratch, smudge, splotch, spot, stain, streak **2.** badge, blaze, brand, characteristic, device, earmark, emblem, evidence, feature, hall~ mark, impression, incision, in~ dex, indication, label, note, print, proof, seal, sign, stamp, symbol, symptom, token **3.** aim, end, goal, object, objective, purpose, target **4.** footmark, footprint, sign, trace, track, trail, vestige ~v. **5.** blem~ ish, blot, blotch, brand, bruise, dent, impress, imprint, nick, scar, scratch, smudge, splotch, stain, streak **6.** brand, characterize, identify, label, stamp **7.** attend, hearken (Archaic), mind, note,

notice, observe, pay attention, pay heed, regard, remark, watch

marked apparent, clear, consid~ erable, conspicuous, decided, distinct, evident, manifest, no~ table, noted, noticeable, obvious, outstanding, patent, prominent, pronounced, remarkable, salient, signal, striking

market 1. n. bazaar, fair, mart **2.** v. offer for sale, retail, sell, vend

maroon abandon, cast ashore, cast away, desert, leave, leave high and dry (Inf.), strand

marriage 1. espousal, match, matrimony, nuptial rites, nup~ tials, wedding, wedding ceremo~ ny, wedlock **2.** alliance, amal~ gamation, association, confed~ eration, coupling, link, merger, union

married 1. hitched (Inf.), joined, one, spliced (Inf.), united, wed, wedded **2.** conjugal, connubial, husbandly, marital, matrimonial, nuptial, spousal, wifely

marrow core, cream, essence, gist, heart, kernel, pith, quick, quintessence, soul, spirit, sub~ stance

marry 1. become man and wife, espouse, get hitched (Inf.), get spliced (Inf.), take the plunge (Inf.), take to wife, tie the knot (Inf.), walk down the aisle (Inf.), wed, wive (Archaic) **2.** ally, bond, join, knit, link, match, merge, splice, tie, unify, unite, yoke

marsh bog, fen, morass, moss (Scot. & northern English dia~ lect), quagmire, slough, swamp

marshal align, arrange, array, assemble, collect, deploy, dis~ pose, draw up, gather, group, line up, muster, order, organize, rank

marshy boggy, fenny, miry, quaggy, spongy, swampy, water~ logged, wet

marvel 1. v. be amazed, be awed, be filled with surprise, gape, gaze, goggle, wonder **2.** n. genius, miracle, phenomenon, portent, prodigy, whiz (Inf.), wonder

marvellous amazing, astonishing, astounding, breathtaking,

extraordinary, miraculous, phenomenal, prodigious, remarkable, singular, spectacular, stupendous, wondrous
Antonyms commonplace, everyday, ordinary

masculine 1. male, manful, manlike, manly, mannish, virile **2.** bold, brave, butch (*Sl.*), gallant, hardy, macho, muscular, powerful, Ramboesque, red-blooded (*Inf.*), resolute, robust, stouthearted, strapping, strong, vigorous, well-built

mass *n.* **1.** block, chunk, concretion, hunk, lump, piece **2.** aggregate, body, collection, entirety, sum, sum total, totality, whole **3.** accumulation, aggregation, assemblage, batch, bunch, collection, combination, conglomeration, heap, load, lot, pile, quantity, stack **4.** assemblage, band, body, bunch (*Inf.*), crowd, group, horde, host, lot, mob, number, throng, troop **5.** bulk, bulk, greater part, lion's share, majority, preponderance **6.** bulk, dimension, greatness, magnitude, size ~*adj.* **7.** extensive, general, indiscriminate, large-scale, pandemic, popular, wholesale, widespread ~*v.* **8.** accumulate, amass, assemble, collect, congregate, forgather, gather, mob, muster, rally, swarm, throng

massacre 1. *n.* annihilation, blood bath, butchery, carnage, extermination, holocaust, killing, mass slaughter, murder, slaughter **2.** *v.* annihilate, blow away (*Sl., chiefly U.S.*), butcher, cut to pieces, exterminate, kill, mow down, murder, slaughter, slay, wipe out

massage 1. *n.* acupressure, kneading, manipulation, reflexology, rubbing, rub-down, shiatsu **2.** *v.* knead, manipulate, rub, rub down

massive big, bulky, colossal, enormous, extensive, gargantuan, gigantic, ginormous (*Inf.*), great, heavy, hefty, huge, hulking, immense, imposing, impressive, mammoth, mega (*Inf.*), monster, monumental, ponderous, solid, substantial, titanic, vast, weighty, whacking (*Inf.*), whopping (*Inf.*)
Antonyms frail, light, little, minute, petty, slight, small, thin, tiny, trivial

master *n.* **1.** boss (*Inf.*), captain, chief, commander, controller, director, employer, governor, head, lord, manager, overlord, overseer, owner, principal, ruler, skipper (*Inf.*), superintendent **2.** ace (*Inf.*), adept, dab hand (*Brit. inf.*), doyen, expert, genius, grandmaster, maestro, maven (*U.S.*), past master, pro (*Inf.*), virtuoso, wizard ~*adj.* **3.** adept, crack (*Inf.*), expert, masterly, proficient, skilful, skilled ~*v.* **4.** acquire, become proficient in, get the hang of (*Inf.*), grasp, learn **5.** bridle, check, conquer, curb, defeat, overcome, overpower, quash, quell, subdue, subjugate, suppress, tame, triumph over, vanquish
Antonyms *n.* (*sense 1*) crew, servant, slave, subject (*sense 2*) amateur, novice ~*adj.* (*sense 3*) amateurish, clumsy, incompetent, inept, novice, unaccomplished, unskilled, untalented ~*v.* (*sense 5*) give in, surrender, yield

masterful 1. adept, adroit, clever, consummate, crack (*Inf.*), deft, dexterous, excellent, expert, exquisite, fine, finished, first-rate, masterly, skilful, skilled, superior, superlative, supreme **2.** arrogant, authoritative, bossy (*Inf.*), despotic, dictatorial, domineering, high-handed, imperious, magisterial, overbearing, overweening, peremptory, self-willed, tyrannical
Antonyms (*sense 1*) amateurish, clumsy, incompetent, inept, unaccomplished, untalented (*sense 2*) irresolute, meek, spineless, weak, wimpish or wimpy (*Inf.*)

masterly adept, adroit, clever,

consummate, crack (*Inf.*), dexterous, excellent, expert, exquisite, fine, finished, first-rate, masterful, skilful, skilled, superior, superlative, supreme

masterpiece *chef d'oeuvre*, classic, jewel, magnum opus, master work, *pièce de résistance*, tour de force

mastery 1. command, comprehension, familiarity, grasp, knowledge, understanding **2.** ability, acquirement, attainment, cleverness, deftness, dexterity, expertise, finesse, know-how (*Inf.*), proficiency, prowess, skill, virtuosity

match *n.* **1.** bout, competition, contest, game, test, trial **2.** competitor, counterpart, equal, equivalent, peer, rival **3.** copy, dead ringer (*Sl.*), double, duplicate, equal, lookalike, replica, ringer (*Sl.*), spit (*Inf.*), spit and image (*Inf.*), spitting image (*Inf.*), twin **4.** affiliation, alliance, combination, couple, duet, item (*Inf.*), marriage, pair, pairing, partnership, union ~*v.* **5.** ally, combine, couple, join, link, marry, mate, pair, unite, yoke **6.** accompany, accord, adapt, agree, blend, coordinate, correspond, fit, go with, harmonize, suit, tally, tone with **7.** compare, compete, contend, emulate, equal, measure up to, oppose, pit against, rival, vie

matching analogous, comparable, coordinating, corresponding, double, duplicate, equal, equivalent, identical, like, paired, parallel, same, toning, twin
Antonyms different, disparate, dissimilar, distinct, divergent, diverse, nonparallel, other, unequal, unlike

matchless consummate, exquisite, incomparable, inimitable, peerless, perfect, superlative, supreme, unequalled, unique, unmatched, unparalleled, unrivalled, unsurpassed

mate *n.* **1.** better half (*Humorous*), husband, partner, spouse, wife **2.** *Inf.* buddy (*Inf.*), china (*Brit. sl.*),

chum (*Inf.*), comrade, crony, friend, pal (*Inf.*) **3.** assistant, helper, subordinate ~*v.* **4.** breed, copulate, couple, pair **5.** marry, match, wed **6.** couple, join, match, pair, yoke

material *n.* **1.** body, constituents, element, matter, stuff, substance **2.** data, evidence, facts, information, notes, work **3.** cloth, fabric, stuff ~*adj.* **4.** bodily, concrete, corporeal, fleshly, nonspiritual, palpable, physical, substantial, tangible, worldly **5.** consequential, essential, grave, important, indispensable, key, meaningful, momentous, serious, significant, vital, weighty

materialize appear, come about, come into being, come to pass, happen, occur, take place, take shape, turn up

matrimonial conjugal, connubial, hymeneal, marital, married, nuptial, spousal, wedded, wedding

matrimony marital rites, marriage, nuptials, wedding ceremony, wedlock

matter *n.* **1.** body, material, stuff, substance **2.** affair, business, concern, episode, event, incident, issue, occurrence, proceeding, question, situation, subject, thing, topic, transaction **3.** consequence, import, importance, moment, note, significance, weight ~*v.* **4.** be important, be of consequence, carry weight, count, have influence, make a difference, mean something, signify

matter-of-fact deadpan, down-to-earth, dry, dull, emotionless, flat, lifeless, mundane, plain, prosaic, sober, unembellished, unimaginative, unsentimental, unvarnished

mature 1. *adj.* adult, complete, fit, full-blown, full-grown, fully-fledged, grown, grown-up, matured, mellow, of age, perfect, prepared, ready, ripe, ripened, seasoned **2.** *v.* age, become adult, bloom, come of age, develop, grow up, maturate, mellow, perfect, reach adulthood, ripen, season

Antonyms adolescent, childish, green, immature, incomplete, juvenile, puerile, undeveloped, unfinished, unperfected, unripe, young, youthful

maturity adulthood, completion, experience, full bloom, full growth, fullness, majority, manhood, maturation, matureness, perfection, ripeness, wisdom, womanhood

Antonyms childishness, excitability, immaturity, imperfection, incompletion, irresponsibility, juvenility, puerility, youthfulness

maul 1. abuse, handle roughly, ill-treat, manhandle, molest, paw 2. batter, beat, beat up (Inf.), claw, knock about, lacerate, mangle, pummel, rough up, thrash

maxim adage, aphorism, apophthegm, axiom, byword, gnome, motto, proverb, rule, saw, saying

maximum 1. n. apogee, ceiling, crest, extremity, height, most, peak, pinnacle, summit, top, upper limit, utmost, uttermost, zenith 2. adj. greatest, highest, maximal, most, paramount, supreme, topmost, utmost

Antonyms bottom, least, lowest, minimum

maybe it could be, mayhap (Archaic), peradventure (Archaic), perchance (Archaic), perhaps, possibly

mayhem chaos, commotion, confusion, destruction, disorder, fracas, havoc, trouble, violence

maze 1. convolutions, intricacy, labyrinth, meander 2. Fig. bewilderment, confusion, imbroglio, mesh, perplexity, puzzle, snarl, tangle, uncertainty, web

meadow field, grassland, lea (Poetic), ley, pasture

meagre deficient, exiguous, inadequate, insubstantial, little, paltry, poor, puny, scanty, scrimpy, short, skimpy, slender, slight, small, spare, sparse

mean[1] v. 1. betoken, connote, convey, denote, drive at, express, hint at, imply, indicate, purport, represent, say, signify, spell, stand for, suggest, symbolize 2. aim, aspire, contemplate, design, desire, have in mind, intend, plan, propose, purpose, set out, want, wish

mean[2] adj. 1. beggarly, close, mercenary, mingy (Brit. inf.), miserly, near (Inf.), niggardly, parsimonious, penny-pinching, penurious, selfish, stingy, tight, tight-fisted, ungenerous 2. abject, base, callous, contemptible, degenerate, degraded, despicable, disgraceful, dishonourable, hard-hearted, ignoble, low-minded, narrow-minded, petty, scurvy, shabby, shameful, sordid, vile, wretched 3. beggarly, contemptible, down-at-heel, grungy (Sl., chiefly U.S.), insignificant, miserable, paltry, petty, poor, run-down, scruffy, scuzzy (Sl., chiefly U.S.), seedy, shabby, sordid, squalid, tawdry, wretched

Antonyms altruistic, big, bountiful, choice, consequential, de luxe, excellent, first-rate, generous, gentle, good, honourable, humane, important, kind, liberal, munificent, noble, praiseworthy, significant, superb, superior, sympathetic, unselfish, warm-hearted

mean[3] 1. n. average, balance, compromise, happy medium, median, middle, middle course or way, mid-point, norm 2. adj. average, intermediate, medial, median, medium, middle, middling, normal, standard

meander 1. v. ramble, snake, stravaig (Scot.), stray, stroll, turn, wander, wind, zigzag 2. n. bend, coil, curve, loop, turn, twist, zigzag

meaning n. 1. connotation, denotation, drift, explanation, gist, implication, import, interpretation, message, purport, sense, significance, signification, substance, upshot, value 2. aim, design, end, goal, idea, intention, object, plan, point, purpose, trend

3. effect, efficacy, force, point, thrust, use, usefulness, validity, value, worth

meaningful 1. important, material, purposeful, relevant, serious, significant, useful, valid, worthwhile **2.** eloquent, expressive, meaning, pointed, pregnant, speaking, suggestive

Antonyms inconsequential, insignificant, meaningless, senseless, superficial, trivial, unimportant, useless, worthless

meaningless aimless, empty, futile, hollow, inane, inconsequential, insignificant, insubstantial, nonsensical, nugatory, pointless, purposeless, senseless, trifling, trivial, useless, vain, valueless, worthless

Antonyms clear, coherent, comprehensible, consequential, decipherable, deep, evident, important, intelligible, legible, meaningful, obvious, purposeful, sensible, significant, understandable, useful, valuable, worthwhile

means 1. agency, avenue, channel, course, expedient, instrument, measure, medium, method, mode, process, way **2.** affluence, capital, estate, fortune, funds, income, money, property, resources, riches, substance, wealth, wherewithal

measurable assessable, computable, determinable, gaugeable, material, mensurable, perceptible, quantifiable, quantitative, significant

measure *n.* **1.** allotment, allowance, amount, amplitude, capacity, degree, extent, magnitude, portion, proportion, quantity, quota, range, ration, reach, scope, share, size **2.** gauge, metre, rule, scale, yardstick **3.** method, standard, system **4.** criterion, example, model, norm, standard, test, touchstone, yardstick **5.** act, action, course, deed, expedient, manoeuvre, means, procedure, proceeding, step **6.** act, bill, enactment, law, resolution, statute **7.** beat, cadence,

foot, metre, rhythm, verse ~ *v.* **8.** appraise, assess, calculate, calibrate, compute, determine, estimate, evaluate, gauge, judge, mark out, quantify, rate, size, sound, survey, value, weigh

measurement appraisal, assessment, calculation, calibration, computation, estimation, evaluation, judgment, mensuration, metage, survey, valuation

measure up (to) be adequate, be capable, be equal to, be fit, be suitable, be suited, come up to scratch (*Inf.*), come up to standard, compare, cut the mustard (*U.S. sl.*), equal, fit *or* fill the bill, fulfil the expectations, make the grade (*Inf.*), match, meet, rival

mechanical 1. automated, automatic, machine-driven **2.** automatic, cold, cursory, dead, emotionless, habitual, impersonal, instinctive, involuntary, lacklustre, lifeless, machine-like, matter-of-fact, perfunctory, routine, spiritless, unconscious, unfeeling, unthinking

Antonyms (*sense 1*) manual (*sense 2*) conscious, genuine, sincere, thinking, voluntary, warm, wholehearted

mechanism 1. apparatus, appliance, contrivance, device, instrument, machine, structure, system, tool **2.** agency, execution, functioning, means, medium, method, operation, performance, procedure, process, system, technique, workings

meddle butt in, interfere, intermeddle, interpose, intervene, intrude, pry, put one's oar in, stick one's nose in (*Inf.*), tamper

mediate act as middleman, arbitrate, bring to an agreement, bring to terms, conciliate, intercede, interpose, intervene, make peace between, moderate, reconcile, referee, resolve, restore harmony, settle, step in (*Inf.*), umpire

medicine cure, drug, medicament, medication, physic, remedy

medieval *Inf.* antediluvian, antiquated, antique, archaic, old-fashioned, primitive, unenlightened

mediocre average, commonplace, fair to middling (*Inf.*), indifferent, inferior, insignificant, mean, medium, middling, ordinary, passable, pedestrian, run-of-the-mill, second-rate, so-so (*Inf.*), tolerable, undistinguished, uninspired
Antonyms distinctive, distinguished, excellent, extraordinary, fine, incomparable, superb, superior, unexcelled, unique, unrivalled, unsurpassed

meditate be in a brown study, cogitate, consider, contemplate, deliberate, muse, ponder, reflect, ruminate, study, think

medium *adj.* **1.** average, fair, intermediate, mean, medial, median, mediocre, middle, middling, midway ~*n.* **2.** average, centre, compromise, mean, middle, middle course (ground, path, way), midpoint **3.** agency, avenue, channel, form, instrument, instrumentality, means, mode, organ, vehicle, way

medley assortment, confusion, farrago, gallimaufry, hodgepodge, hotchpotch, jumble, *mélange*, miscellany, mishmash, mixed bag (*Inf.*), mixture, olio, omnium-gatherum, pastiche, patchwork, potpourri, salmagundi

meek **1.** deferential, docile, forbearing, gentle, humble, long-suffering, mild, modest, patient, peaceful, soft, submissive, unassuming, unpretentious, yielding **2.** acquiescent, compliant, resigned, spineless, spiritless, tame, timid, unresisting, weak, weak-kneed (*Inf.*), wimpish *or* wimpy (*Inf.*)
Antonyms arrogant, bold, bossy, domineering, forward, immodest, overbearing, presumptuous, pretentious, proud, self-assertive, spirited, wilful

meet **1.** bump into, chance on, come across, confront, contact, encounter, find, happen on, run across, run into **2.** abut, adjoin, come together, connect, converge, cross, intersect, join, link up, touch, unite **3.** answer, carry out, come up to, comply, cope with, discharge, equal, fulfil, gratify, handle, match, measure up, perform, satisfy **4.** assemble, collect, come together, congregate, convene, forgather, gather, muster, rally
Antonyms (*sense 1*) avoid, elude, escape, miss (*sense 2*) diverge (*sense 3*) fail, fall short, renege (*sense 4*) adjourn, disperse, scatter

meeting **1.** assignation, confrontation, encounter, engagement, introduction, rendezvous, tryst (*Archaic*) **2.** assembly, audience, company, conclave, conference, congregation, convention, convocation, gathering, get-together (*Inf.*), meet, powwow, rally, reunion, session **3.** concourse, confluence, conjunction, convergence, crossing, intersection, junction, union

melancholy **1.** *n.* blues, dejection, depression, despondency, gloom, gloominess, low spirits, misery, pensiveness, sadness, sorrow, unhappiness, woe **2.** *adj.* blue, dejected, depressed, despondent, disconsolate, dismal, dispirited, doleful, down, downcast, down-hearted, down in the dumps (*Inf.*), down in the mouth, gloomy, glum, heavy-hearted, joyless, low, low-spirited, lugubrious, melancholic, miserable, moody, mournful, pensive, sad, sombre, sorrowful, unhappy, woebegone, woeful
Antonyms *n.* delight, gladness, happiness, joy, pleasure ~*adj.* blithe, bright, cheerful, gay, glad, happy, jolly, joyful, joyous, light-hearted, lively, merry, sunny

mellow *adj.* **1.** delicate, full-flavoured, juicy, mature, perfect, rich, ripe, soft, sweet, well-matured **2.** dulcet, full, mellifluous, melodious, rich, rounded, smooth, sweet, tuneful, well-tuned **3.** cheerful, cordial, elevated, expansive, genial, half-tipsy, happy, jolly, jovial, merry (*Brit. inf.*), relaxed ~ *v.* **4.** develop, improve, mature, perfect, ripen, season, soften, sweeten

melodious concordant, dulcet, euphonious, harmonious, melodic, musical, silvery, sweet-sounding, sweet-toned, tuneful
Antonyms cacophonous, discordant, grating, harsh, unharmonious, unmelodic, unmelodious, unmusical, untuneful

melodramatic blood-and-thunder, extravagant, hammy (*Inf.*), histrionic, overdramatic, overemotional, sensational, stagy, theatrical

melody air, descant, music, refrain, song, strain, theme, tune

melt 1. deliquesce, diffuse, dissolve, flux, fuse, liquefy, soften, thaw **2.** disarm, mollify, relax, soften, touch

member 1. associate, fellow, representative **2.** appendage, arm, component, constituent, element, extremity, leg, limb, organ, part, portion

memoir account, biography, essay, journal, life, monograph, narrative, record, register

memoirs autobiography, diary, experiences, journals, life, life story, memories, recollections, reminiscences

memorable catchy, celebrated, distinguished, extraordinary, famous, historic, illustrious, important, impressive, momentous, notable, noteworthy, remarkable, signal, significant, striking, unforgettable
Antonyms commonplace, forgettable, insignificant, ordinary, trivial, undistinguished, unimportant, unimpressive, unmemorable

memorial 1. *adj.* commemorative, monumental **2.** *n.* cairn, memento, monument, plaque, record, remembrance, souvenir

memorize commit to memory,

con (*Archaic*), get by heart, learn, learn by heart, learn by rote, remember

memory 1. recall, recollection, remembrance, reminiscence, retention **2.** commemoration, honour, remembrance

menace *v.* **1.** alarm, bode ill, browbeat, bully, frighten, impend, intimidate, loom, lour, lower, terrorize, threaten, utter threats to ~ *n.* **2.** commination, intimidation, scare, threat, warning **3.** danger, hazard, jeopardy, peril

menacing alarming, dangerous, frightening, intimidating, intimidatory, looming, louring, lowering, minacious, minatory, ominous, threatening

mend *v.* **1.** cure, darn, fix, heal, patch, rectify, refit, reform, remedy, renew, renovate, repair, restore, retouch **2.** ameliorate, amend, better, correct, emend, improve, rectify, reform, revise ~ *n.* **3.** darn, patch, repair, stitch

menial *adj.* boring, dull, humdrum, low-status, routine, unskilled

mental cerebral, intellectual

mentality 1. brainpower, brains, comprehension, grey matter (*Inf.*), intellect, intelligence quotient, I.Q., mental age, mind, rationality, understanding, wit **2.** attitude, cast of mind, character, disposition, frame of mind, make-up, outlook, personality, psychology, turn of mind, way of thinking

mentally in one's head, intellectually, in the mind, inwardly, psychologically, rationally, subjectively

mention *v.* **1.** acknowledge, adduce, allude to, bring up, broach, call attention to, cite, communicate, declare, disclose, divulge, hint at, impart, intimate, make known, name, point out, recount, refer to, report, reveal, speak about *or* of, state, tell, touch upon ~ *n.* **2.** acknowledgment, citation, recognition, tribute **3.** allusion, announcement, indication, notification, observation, reference, remark

mercenary *adj.* **1.** acquisitive, avaricious, bribable, covetous, grasping, greedy, money-grubbing (*Inf.*), sordid, venal **2.** bought, hired, paid, venal ~*n.* **3.** condottiere (*Hist.*), free companion (*Hist.*), freelance (*Hist.*), hireling, soldier of fortune
Antonyms altruistic, benevolent, generous, idealistic, liberal, munificent, philanthropic, unselfish

merchandise *n.* commodities, goods, produce, products, staples, stock, stock in trade, truck, vendibles, wares

merchant broker, dealer, retailer, salesman, seller, shopkeeper, trader, tradesman, trafficker, vendor, wholesaler

merciful beneficent, benignant, clement, compassionate, forbearing, forgiving, generous, gracious, humane, kind, lenient, liberal, mild, pitying, soft, sparing, sympathetic, tender-hearted
Antonyms cruel, hard-hearted, inhumane, merciless, pitiless, uncompassionate, unfeeling

merciless barbarous, callous, cruel, fell (*Archaic*), hard, hard-hearted, harsh, heartless, implacable, inexorable, inhumane, pitiless, relentless, ruthless, severe, unappeasable, unfeeling, unforgiving, unmerciful, unpitying, unsparing, unsympathetic

mercy **1.** benevolence, charity, clemency, compassion, favour, forbearance, forgiveness, grace, kindness, leniency, pity, quarter **2.** benison (*Archaic*), blessing, boon, godsend, piece of luck, relief
Antonyms brutality, cruelty, harshness, inhumanity, pitilessness, severity

mere *adj.* absolute, bare, common, complete, entire, nothing more than, plain, pure, pure and simple, sheer, simple, stark, unadulterated, unmitigated, unmixed, utter

merge amalgamate, be swallowed up by, become lost in, blend, coalesce, combine, consolidate, converge, fuse, incorporate, intermix, join, meet, meld, melt into, mingle, mix, tone with, unite
Antonyms detach, diverge, divide, part, separate, sever

merger amalgamation, coalition, combination, consolidation, fusion, incorporation, union

merit *n.* **1.** advantage, asset, excellence, good, goodness, integrity, quality, strong point, talent, value, virtue, worth, worthiness **2.** claim, credit, desert, due, right ~*v.* **3.** be entitled to, be worthy of, deserve, earn, have a claim to, have a right to, have coming to one, incur, rate, warrant

merriment amusement, conviviality, festivity, frolic, fun, gaiety, glee, hilarity, jocularity, jollity, joviality, laughter, levity, liveliness, merrymaking, mirth, revelry, sport

merry **1.** blithe, blithesome, carefree, cheerful, convivial, festive, frolicsome, fun-loving, gay, glad, gleeful, happy, jocund, jolly, joyful, joyous, light-hearted, mirthful, rollicking, sportive, vivacious **2.** amusing, comic, comical, facetious, funny, hilarious, humorous, jocular, mirthful
Antonyms dejected, dismal, gloomy, miserable, sad, unhappy

mesh *n.* **1.** net, netting, network, plexus, reticulation, tracery, web **2.** entanglement, snare, tangle, toils, trap, web ~*v.* **3.** catch, enmesh, ensnare, entangle, net, snare, tangle, trap **4.** combine, come together, connect, coordinate, dovetail, engage, fit together, harmonize, interlock, knit

mess *n.* **1.** botch, chaos, clutter, confusion, dirtiness, disarray, disorder, disorganization, grot (*Sl.*), hash (*Inf.*), jumble, litter, mishmash, shambles, turmoil, untidiness **2.** difficulty, dilemma, fine kettle of fish (*Inf.*), fix (*Inf.*), imbroglio, jam (*Inf.*), mix-up, muddle, perplexity, pickle (*Inf.*), plight, predicament, stew (*Inf.*) ~*v.* **3.** *Often with* **up** befoul, besmirch, botch, bungle, clutter, dirty, disarrange, dishevel, foul, litter, make a hash of (*Inf.*), muck up (*Brit. sl.*), muddle, pollute, scramble

message 1. bulletin, communication, communiqué, dispatch, intimation, letter, memorandum, missive, note, notice, tidings, word **2.** idea, import, meaning, moral, point, purport, theme

messenger agent, bearer, carrier, courier, delivery boy, emissary, envoy, errand-boy, go-between, harbinger, herald, runner

messy chaotic, cluttered, confused, dirty, dishevelled, disordered, disorganized, grubby, littered, muddled, scuzzy (*Sl., chiefly U.S.*), shambolic (*Inf.*), sloppy (*Inf.*), slovenly, unkempt, untidy
Antonyms clean, meticulous, neat, ordered, orderly, shipshape, smart, squeaky-clean, tidy

metaphor allegory, analogy, emblem, figure of speech, image, symbol, trope

method 1. approach, arrangement, course, fashion, form, manner, mode, modus operandi, plan, practice, procedure, process, programme, routine, rule, scheme, style, system, technique, way **2.** design, form, order, orderliness, organization, pattern, planning, purpose, regularity, structure, system

methodical businesslike, deliberate, disciplined, efficient, meticulous, neat, ordered, orderly, organized, painstaking, planned, precise, regular, structured, systematic, tidy, well-regulated
Antonyms casual, chaotic, confused, disordered, disorderly, haphazard, irregular, random, unmethodical

meticulous detailed, exact, fastidious, fussy, microscopic, painstaking, particular, perfec~

tionist, precise, punctilious, scrupulous, strict, thorough
Antonyms careless, haphazard, imprecise, inexact, loose, negligent, slapdash, sloppy

microscopic imperceptible, infinitesimal, invisible, minuscule, minute, negligible, tiny

midday noon, noonday, noontide, noontime, twelve noon, twelve o'clock

middle 1. *adj.* central, halfway, inner, inside, intermediate, intervening, mean, medial, median, medium, mid **2.** *n.* centre, focus, halfway point, heart, inside, mean, midpoint, midsection, midst, thick

middling adequate, all right, average, fair, indifferent, mediocre, medium, moderate, modest, O.K. (*Inf.*), okay (*Inf.*), ordinary, passable, run-of-the-mill, so-so (*Inf.*), tolerable, unexceptional, unremarkable

midget *n.* dwarf, gnome, homunculus, homunculus, manikin, pygmy, shrimp (*Inf.*), Tom Thumb

midst bosom, centre, core, depths, heart, hub, interior, middle, thick

might ability, capability, capacity, clout (*Sl.*), efficacy, efficiency, energy, force, potency, power, prowess, puissance, strength, sway, valour, vigour

mighty doughty, forceful, hardy, indomitable, lusty, manful, potent, powerful, puissant, Ramboesque, robust, stalwart, stout, strapping, strong, sturdy, vigorous
Antonyms feeble, impotent, unimposing, unimpressive, weak, weedy (*Inf.*), wimpish *or* wimpy (*Inf.*)

migrant *n.* drifter, emigrant, gypsy, immigrant, itinerant, nomad, rover, tinker, transient, traveller, vagrant, wanderer

migrate drift, emigrate, journey, move, roam, rove, shift, travel, trek, voyage, wander

migration emigration, journey,

movement, roving, shift, travel, trek, voyage, wandering

migratory gypsy, itinerant, migrant, nomadic, peripatetic, roving, shifting, transient, travelling, unsettled, vagrant, wandering

mild amiable, balmy, bland, calm, clement, compassionate, docile, easy, easy-going, equable, forbearing, forgiving, gentle, indulgent, kind, meek, mellow, merciful, moderate, pacific, peaceable, placid, pleasant, serene, temperate, soft, temperate, tender, tranquil, warm
Antonyms bitter, cold, fierce, harsh, rough, stormy, unkind, unpleasant, violent, wild

mildness blandness, calmness, clemency, docility, forbearance, gentleness, indulgence, kindness, leniency, lenity, meekness, mellowness, moderation, placidity, smoothness, softness, temperateness, tenderness, tranquillity, warmth

militant adj. 1. active, aggressive, assertive, combative, Rambo-esque, vigorous 2. belligerent, combating, contending, embattled, fighting, in arms, warring
Antonyms concessive, pacific, pacifist, peaceful

military 1. adj. armed, martial, soldierlike, soldierly, warlike 2. n. armed forces, army, forces, services

mill n. 1. factory, foundry, plant, shop, works 2. crusher, grinder

mime 1. n. dumb show, gesture, mummery, pantomime 2. v. act out, gesture, pantomime, represent, simulate

mimic 1. v. ape, caricature, do (Inf.), imitate, impersonate, parody, take off (Inf.) 2. n. caricaturist, copycat (Inf.), imitator, impersonator, impressionist, parodist, parrot

mind n. 1. brain(s) (Inf.), grey matter (Inf.), intellect, intelligence, mentality, ratiocination, reason, sense, spirit, understanding, wits 2. memory, recollection, remembrance 3. brain, head, im-

agination, psyche 4. bent, desire, disposition, fancy, inclination, intention, leaning, notion, purpose, tendency, urge, will, wish 5. attention, concentration, thinking, thoughts 6. **make up one's mind** choose, come to a decision, decide, determine, reach a decision, resolve 7. **bear** or **keep in mind** be cognizant of, be mindful of, remember, take note of ~v. 8. be affronted, be bothered, care, disapprove, dislike, look askance at, object, resent, take offence 9. adhere to, attend, comply with, follow, heed, listen to, mark, note, notice, obey, observe, pay attention, pay heed to, regard, respect, take heed, watch 10. be sure, ensure, make certain 11. attend to, guard, have charge of, keep an eye on, look after, take care of, tend, watch

mindful alert, alive to, attentive, aware, careful, chary, cognizant, conscious, heedful, regardful, respectful, sensible, thoughtful, wary, watchful
Antonyms heedless, inattentive, incautious, mindless, oblivious, thoughtless, unaware

mine n. 1. coalfield, colliery, deposit, excavation, lode, pit, shaft, vein 2. abundance, fund, hoard, reserve, source, stock, store, supply, treasury, wealth ~v. 3. delve, dig for, dig up, excavate, extract, hew, quarry, unearth

mingle 1. alloy, blend, coalesce, combine, commingle, compound, intermingle, intermix, interweave, join, marry, merge, mix, unite 2. associate, circulate, consort, fraternize, hang about or around, hang out (Inf.), hobnob, rub shoulders (Inf.), socialize
Antonyms avoid, detach, dissociate, dissolve, divide, estrange, part, separate

miniature adj. baby, diminutive, dwarf, Lilliputian, little, midget, mini, minuscule, minute, pocket, pygmy, reduced, scaled-down, small, tiny, toy, wee
Antonyms big, enlarged, enor-

mous, giant, gigantic, ginormous (*Inf.*), great, huge, immense, large, mega (*Inf.*), oversize

minimal least, least possible, littlest, minimum, nominal, slightest, smallest, token

minimize 1. abbreviate, attenuate, curtail, decrease, diminish, miniaturize, prune, reduce, shrink **2.** belittle, decry, deprecate, depreciate, discount, disparage, make light or little of, play down, underestimate, underrate

Antonyms augment, boast about, elevate, enhance, enlarge, exalt, expand, extend, heighten, increase, magnify, vaunt

minimum 1. *n.* bottom, depth, least, lowest, nadir, slightest **2.** *adj.* least, least possible, littlest, lowest, minimal, slightest, smallest

Antonyms greatest, highest, largest, maximum, most

minister *n.* **1.** chaplain, churchman, clergyman, cleric, divine, ecclesiastic, padre (*Inf.*), parson, pastor, preacher, priest, rector, vicar **2.** administrator, ambassador, cabinet member, delegate, diplomat, envoy, executive, office-holder, official, plenipotentiary ~*v.* **3.** accommodate, administer, answer, attend, be solicitous of, cater to, pander to, serve, take care of, tend

ministry administration, cabinet, council, government, holy orders, the church, the priesthood, the pulpit

minor inconsequential, inconsiderable, inferior, insignificant, junior, lesser, light, negligible, paltry, petty, secondary, slight, small, smaller, subordinate, trifling, trivial, unimportant, younger

Antonyms appreciable, consequential, considerable, essential, grand, great, heavy, important, major, profound, serious, significant, substantial, superior, vital, weighty

mint 1. *adj.* brand-new, excellent,

first-class, fresh, perfect, unblemished, undamaged, untarnished **2.** *v.* cast, coin, make, produce, punch, stamp, strike

minute[1] *n.* flash, instant, jiffy (*Inf.*), moment, second, shake (*Inf.*), tick (*Inf.*), trice

minute[2] *adj.* diminutive, fine, infinitesimal, Lilliputian, little, microscopic, miniature, minuscule, slender, small, tiny

Antonyms (*sense 1*) enormous, gigantic, ginormous (*Inf.*), grand, great, huge, immense, monstrous

minutes memorandum, notes, proceedings, record(s), transactions, transcript

minx baggage (*Inf.*), coquette, flirt, hoyden, hussy, jade, tomboy, wanton

miracle marvel, phenomenon, prodigy, thaumaturgy, wonder

miraculous amazing, astonishing, astounding, extraordinary, incredible, inexplicable, magical, marvellous, phenomenal, preternatural, prodigious, superhuman, supernatural, thaumaturgic, unaccountable, unbelievable, wonderful, wondrous

Antonyms awful, bad, common, commonplace, everyday, normal, ordinary, run-of-the-mill, terrible, unexceptional, unremarkable, usual

mirage hallucination, illusion, optical illusion, phantasm

mire *n.* bog, marsh, morass, quagmire, swamp

mirror *n.* **1.** glass, looking-glass, reflector, speculum **2.** copy, double, image, likeness, reflection, replica, representation, twin ~*v.* **3.** copy, depict, echo, emulate, follow, reflect, represent, show

mirth amusement, cheerfulness, festivity, frolic, fun, gaiety, gladness, glee, hilarity, jocularity, jollity, joviality, joyousness, laughter, levity, merriment, merrymaking, pleasure, rejoicing, revelry, sport

misappropriate defalcate (*Law*), embezzle, misapply, misspend, misuse, peculate, pocket, steal, swindle

misbehaviour acting up (*Inf.*), bad behaviour, impropriety, incivility, indiscipline, insubordination, mischief, misconduct, misdeeds, misdemeanour, monkey business (*Inf.*), naughtiness, rudeness, shenanigans (*Inf.*)

miscalculate blunder, calculate wrongly, err, get (it) wrong (*Inf.*), go wrong, make a mistake, misjudge, overestimate, overrate, slip up, underestimate, underrate

miscellaneous assorted, confused, diverse, diversified, farraginous, heterogeneous, indiscriminate, jumbled, many, mingled, mixed, motley, multifarious, multiform, promiscuous, sundry, varied, various

mischance accident, bad break (*Inf.*), bad luck, calamity, contretemps, disaster, ill chance, ill fortune, ill luck, infelicity, misadventure, misfortune, mishap

mischief 1. devilment, impishness, misbehaviour, monkey business (*Inf.*), naughtiness, pranks, roguery, roguishness, shenanigans (*Inf.*), trouble, waywardness **2.** damage, detriment, disadvantage, disruption, evil, harm, hurt, injury, misfortune, trouble

mischievous 1. arch, bad, badly behaved, exasperating, frolicsome, impish, naughty, playful, puckish, rascally, roguish, sportive, teasing, troublesome, vexatious, wayward **2.** bad, damaging, deleterious, destructive, detrimental, evil, harmful, hurtful, injurious, malicious, malignant, pernicious, sinful, spiteful, troublesome, vicious, wicked

misconception delusion, error, fallacy, misapprehension, misconstruction, mistaken belief, misunderstanding, wrong end of the stick (*Inf.*), wrong idea

misconduct *n.* delinquency, dereliction, immorality, impropriety, malfeasance (*Law*), malpractice, malversation (*Rare*),

misbehaviour, misdemeanour, mismanagement, naughtiness, rudeness, transgression, unethical behaviour, wrongdoing

misdemeanour fault, infringement, misbehaviour, misconduct, misdeed, offence, peccadillo, transgression, trespass

miser cheapskate (*Inf.*), churl, curmudgeon, hunks (*Rare*), niggard, penny-pincher (*Inf.*), screw (*Sl.*), Scrooge, skinflint, tightwad (*U.S. sl.*)

miserable 1. afflicted, brokenhearted, crestfallen, dejected, depressed, desolate, despondent, disconsolate, distressed, doleful, down, downcast, down in the mouth (*Inf.*), forlorn, gloomy, heartbroken, melancholy, mournful, sorrowful, unhappy, woebegone, wretched **2.** destitute, impoverished, indigent, meagre, needy, penniless, poor, poverty-stricken, scanty **3.** abject, bad, contemptible, deplorable, despicable, detestable, disgraceful, lamentable, low, mean, pathetic, piteous, pitiable, scurvy, shabby, shameful, sordid, sorry, squalid, vile, worthless, wretched **Antonyms** admirable, cheerful, comfortable, good, happy, respectable, rich

miserly avaricious, beggarly, close, close-fisted, covetous, grasping, illiberal, mean, mingy (*Brit. inf.*), near, niggardly, parsimonious, penny-pinching (*Inf.*), penurious, sordid, stingy, tightfisted, ungenerous **Antonyms** charitable, extravagant, generous, prodigal, unselfish

misery 1. agony, anguish, depression, desolation, despair, discomfort, distress, gloom, grief, hardship, melancholy, sadness, sorrow, suffering, torment, torture, unhappiness, woe, wretchedness **2.** affliction, bitter pill (*Inf.*), burden, calamity, catastrophe, curse, disaster, load, misfortune, ordeal, sorrow, trial, tribulation, trouble, woe

Antonyms contentment, enjoyment, happiness, joy, pleasure

misfire fail, fail to go off, fall through, go phut (*Inf.*), go wrong, miscarry

misfit eccentric, fish out of water (*Inf.*), nonconformist, oddball (*Inf.*), square peg (in a round hole) (*Inf.*)

misfortune 1. bad luck, evil fortune, hard luck, ill luck, infelicity **2.** accident, adversity, affliction, blow, calamity, disaster, evil chance, failure, hardship, harm, loss, misadventure, mischance, misery, mishap, reverse, setback, stroke of bad luck, tragedy, trial, tribulation, trouble

Antonyms fortune, good luck, relief

misgiving anxiety, apprehension, distrust, doubt, hesitation, qualm, reservation, scruple, suspicion, uncertainty, unease, worry

misguided deluded, erroneous, foolish, ill-advised, imprudent, injudicious, labouring under a delusion *or* misapprehension, misled, misplaced, mistaken, uncalled-for, unreasonable, unwarranted, unwise

mishandle botch, bungle, make a hash of (*Inf.*), make a mess of, mess up (*Inf.*), mismanage, muff, screw (up) (*Inf.*)

mishap accident, adversity, bad luck, calamity, contretemps, disaster, evil chance, evil fortune, hard luck, ill fortune, ill luck, infelicity, misadventure, mischance, misfortune

misinform deceive, give (someone) a bum steer (*Sl.*), give (someone) duff gen (*Brit. inf.*), misdirect, misguide, mislead

misinterpret distort, falsify, get wrong, misapprehend, misconceive, misconstrue, misjudge, misread, misrepresent, mistake, misunderstand, pervert

mislead beguile, bluff, deceive, delude, fool, give (someone) a bum steer (*Sl.*), hoodwink, lead astray, misdirect, misguide, misinform, pull the wool over

(someone's) eyes (*Inf.*), take in (*Inf.*)

misleading ambiguous, casuistical, confusing, deceitful, deceptive, delusive, delusory, disingenuous, evasive, false, sophistical, specious, spurious, tricky (*Inf.*), unstraightforward

Antonyms candid, clear, correct, direct, explicit, frank, genuine, honest, obvious, open, plain, simple, sincere, straightforward, true, truthful

mismanage be incompetent, be inefficient, botch, bungle, make a hash of (*Inf.*), make a mess of, maladminister, mess up, misconduct, misdirect, misgovern, mishandle

misquote distort, falsify, garble, mangle, misreport, misrepresent, misstate, muddle, pervert, quote *or* take out of context, twist

misrepresent belie, disguise, distort, falsify, garble, misinterpret, misstate, pervert, twist

misrule 1. bad government, maladministration, misgovernment, mismanagement **2.** anarchy, chaos, confusion, disorder, lawlessness, tumult, turmoil

miss[1] *v.* **1.** avoid, be late for, blunder, err, escape, evade, fail, fail to grasp, fail to notice, forego, lack, leave out, let go, let slip, lose, miscarry, mistake, omit, overlook, pass over, pass up, skip, slip, trip **2.** feel the loss of, hunger for, long for, need, pine for, want, wish, yearn for ~*n.* **3.** blunder, error, failure, fault, loss, mistake, omission, oversight, want

miss[2] damsel, girl, lass, lassie (*Inf.*), maid, maiden, schoolgirl, spinster, young lady

misshapen contorted, crippled, crooked, deformed, distorted, grotesque, ill-made, ill-proportioned, malformed, twisted, ugly, ungainly, unshapely, unsightly, warped, wry

missile projectile, rocket, weapon

missing absent, astray, gone, lacking, left behind, left out, lost, mislaid, misplaced, not present,

nowhere to be found, unaccounted-for, wanting
Antonyms accounted for, at hand, available, here, in attendance, on hand, present, there, to hand

mission 1. n. aim, assignment, business, calling, charge, commission, duty, errand, goal, job, office, operation, purpose, pursuit, quest, task, trust, undertaking, vocation, work **2.** commission, delegation, deputation, embassy, legation, ministry, task force

missionary apostle, converter, evangelist, preacher, propagandist, proselytizer

mist n. cloud, condensation, dew, drizzle, film, fog, haar (*Eastern Brit.*), haze, smog, smur *or* smir (*Scot.*), spray, steam, vapour

mistake 1. n. bloomer (*Brit. inf.*), blunder, boob (*Brit. sl.*), boo-boo (*Inf.*), clanger (*Inf.*), erratum, error, error of judgment, false move, fault, faux pas, gaffe, goof (*Inf.*), howler (*Inf.*), inaccuracy, miscalculation, misconception, misstep, misunderstanding, oversight, slip, slip-up (*Inf.*), solecism **2.** v. get wrong, misapprehend, misconceive, misconstrue, misinterpret, misjudge, misread, misunderstand

mistaken barking up the wrong tree (*Inf.*), erroneous, fallacious, false, faulty, inaccurate, inappropriate, incorrect, in the wrong, labouring under a misapprehension, misguided, misinformed, misled, off target, off the mark, unfounded, unsound, wide of the mark, wrong
Antonyms accurate, correct, logical, right, sound, true

mistress concubine, doxy (*Archaic*), fancy woman (*Sl.*), floozy (*Sl.*), girlfriend, inamorata, kept woman, ladylove (*Rare*), lover, paramour

mistrust 1. v. apprehend, beware, be wary of, distrust, doubt, fear, have doubts about, suspect **2.** n. apprehension, distrust, doubt, dubiety, fear, misgiving, scepti-cism, suspicion, uncertainty, wariness

misty bleary, blurred, cloudy, dark, dim, foggy, fuzzy, hazy, indistinct, murky, nebulous, obscure, opaque, overcast, unclear, vague
Antonyms bright, clear, distinct, lucid, obvious, plain, sunny, well-defined

misunderstand get (it) wrong, get the wrong end of the stick (*Inf.*), get the wrong idea (about), misapprehend, misconceive, misconstrue, mishear, misinterpret, misjudge, misread, miss the point (of), mistake

misunderstanding error, false impression, misapprehension, misconception, misconstruction, misinterpretation, misjudgment, misreading, mistake, mix-up, wrong idea

misuse 1. n. abuse, barbarism, catachresis, corruption, desecration, dissipation, malapropism, misapplication, misemployment, misusage, perversion, profanation, solecism, squandering, waste **2.** v. abuse, corrupt, desecrate, dissipate, misapply, misemploy, pervert, profane, prostitute, squander, waste
Antonyms v. appreciate, cherish, honour, prize, respect, treasure, use

mitigate abate, allay, appease, assuage, blunt, calm, check, diminish, dull, ease, extenuate, lessen, lighten, moderate, modify, mollify, pacify, palliate, placate, quiet, reduce the force of, remit, soften, soothe, subdue, take the edge off, temper, tone down, tranquillize, weaken

mix v. **1.** alloy, amalgamate, associate, blend, coalesce, combine, commingle, commix, compound, cross, fuse, incorporate, intermingle, interweave, join, jumble, merge, mingle, put together, unite **2.** associate, come together, consort, fraternize, hang out (*Inf.*), hobnob, join, mingle, socialize

mixed 1. alloyed, amalgamated, blended, combined, composite, compound, fused, incorporated, joint, mingled, united **2.** assorted, cosmopolitan, diverse, diversified, heterogeneous, miscellaneous, motley, varied **3.** ambivalent, equivocal, indecisive, uncertain
Antonyms homogeneous, isolated, pure, straight, unmixed

mixture admixture, alloy, amalgam, amalgamation, association, assortment, blend, brew, combine, composite, compound, concoction, conglomeration, cross, fusion, hotchpotch, jumble, medley, *mélange*, miscellany, mix, potpourri, salmagundi, union, variety

mix-up confusion, disorder, fankle (*Scot.*), jumble, mess, mistake, misunderstanding, muddle, snarl-up (*Brit. inf.*), tangle

moan 1. *n.* groan, lament, lamentation, sigh, sob, sough, wail, whine **2.** *v.* bemoan, bewail, deplore, grieve, groan, keen, lament, mourn, sigh, sob, sough, whine

mob 1. *n.* assemblage, body, collection, crowd, drove, flock, gang, gathering, herd, horde, host, mass, multitude, pack, press, swarm, throng **2.** *v.* crowd around, jostle, overrun, set upon, surround, swarm around

mobile 1. ambulatory, itinerant, locomotive, migrant, motile, movable, moving, peripatetic, portable, travelling, wandering **2.** animated, changeable, ever-changing, expressive

mobilize activate, animate, call to arms, call up, get *or* make ready, marshal, muster, organize, prepare, put in motion, rally, ready

mock *v.* **1.** chaff, deride, flout, insult, jeer, laugh at, laugh to scorn, make fun of, poke fun at, ridicule, scoff, scorn, show contempt for, sneer, take the mickey (out of) (*Inf.*), taunt, tease ~*n.* **2.** banter, derision, gibe, jeering,

mockery, ridicule, scorn, sneer, sneering **3.** counterfeit, fake, forgery, fraud, imitation, phoney (*Sl.*), sham ~*adj.* **4.** artificial, bogus, counterfeit, dummy, ersatz, fake, faked, false, feigned, forged, fraudulent, imitation, phoney (*Sl.*), pretended, pseudo (*Inf.*), sham, spurious
Antonyms *v.* encourage, praise, respect, revere ~*adj.* authentic, genuine, natural, real, sincere, true, unfeigned

mockery 1. contempt, contumely, derision, disdain, disrespect, gibes, insults, jeering, ridicule, scoffing, scorn **2.** burlesque, caricature, deception, farce, imitation, lampoon, laughing stock, mimicry, parody, pretence, send-up (*Brit. sl.*), sham, spoof (*Inf.*), take-off (*Inf.*), travesty

mocking contemptuous, contumelious, derisive, derisory, disdainful, disrespectful, insulting, irreverent, sarcastic, sardonic, satiric, satirical, scoffing, scornful, taunting

model *n.* **1.** copy, dummy, facsimile, image, imitation, miniature, mock-up, replica, representation **2.** archetype, design, epitome, example, exemplar, gauge, ideal, lodestar, mould, original, paradigm, paragon, pattern, prototype, standard, type **3.** poser, sitter, subject **4.** mannequin ~*v.* **5.** base, carve, cast, design, fashion, form, mould, pattern, plan, sculpt, shape **6.** display, show off, sport (*Inf.*) ~*adj.* **7.** copy, dummy, facsimile, imitation, miniature **8.** archetypal, exemplary, ideal, illustrative, paradigmatic, perfect, standard, typical

moderate 1. *adj.* calm, controlled, cool, deliberate, equable, gentle, judicious, limited, middle-of-the-road, mild, modest, peaceable, reasonable, restrained, sober, steady, temperate **2.** *v.* abate, allay, appease, assuage, calm, control, curb, decrease, diminish, lessen, mitigate, modulate, pacify, play down, quiet, regulate, repress, restrain, soften, soft-pedal (*Inf.*), subdue, tame, temper, tone down

Antonyms *adj.* (*sense 1*) extreme, intemperate, ruffled, unreasonable, wild ~*v.* heighten, increase, intensify

moderately fairly, gently, in moderation, passably, quite, rather, reasonably, slightly, somewhat, to a degree, tolerably, to some extent, within limits, within reason

moderation calmness, composure, coolness, equanimity, fairness, judiciousness, justice, justness, mildness, moderateness, reasonableness, restraint, sedateness, temperance

modern contemporary, current, fresh, late, latest, neoteric (*Rare*), new, newfangled, novel, present, present-day, recent, twentieth-century, up-to-date, up-to-the-minute, with-it (*Inf.*)

Antonyms ancient, antiquated, archaic, former, obsolete, old, old-fashioned, old hat, outmoded, passé, past, square (*Inf.*), uncool (*Sl.*)

modernize bring into the twentieth century, bring up to date, face-lift, make over, rejuvenate, remake, remodel, renew, renovate, revamp, update

modest 1. bashful, blushing, coy, demure, diffident, discreet, humble, meek, quiet, reserved, reticent, retiring, self-conscious, self-effacing, shy, simple, unassuming, unpretentious **2.** fair, limited, middling, moderate, ordinary, small, unexceptional

modesty bashfulness, coyness, decency, demureness, diffidence, discreetness, humbleness, humility, lack of pretension, meekness, propriety, quietness, reserve, reticence, self-effacement, shyness, simplicity, timidity, unobtrusiveness, unpretentiousness

Antonyms arrogance, assurance, boastfulness, boldness, conceit, confidence, egotism, extrava-

gance, forwardness, haughtiness, immodesty, indecency, ostentation, presumption, pretentiousness, pride, showiness, vanity

modification adjustment, alteration, change, modulation, mutation, qualification, refinement, reformation, restriction, revision, variation

modify adapt, adjust, alter, change, convert, recast, redo, refashion, reform, remodel, reorganize, reshape, revise, rework, transform, vary

moist clammy, damp, dampish, dank, dewy, dripping, drizzly, humid, not dry, rainy, soggy, wet, wettish

moisten bedew, damp, dampen, humidify, lick, moisturize, soak, water, wet

moisture damp, dampness, dankness, dew, humidity, liquid, perspiration, sweat, water, wateriness, wetness

molest abuse, afflict, annoy, badger, beset, bother, bug (*Inf.*), disturb, harass, harry, hector, irritate, persecute, pester, plague, tease, torment, upset, vex, worry

moment 1. flash, instant, jiffy (*Inf.*), minute, no time, second, shake (*Inf.*), split second, tick (*Brit. inf.*), trice, twinkling, two shakes (*Inf.*), two shakes of a lamb's tail (*Inf.*) **2.** hour, instant, juncture, point, point in time, stage, time

momentous consequential, critical, crucial, decisive, earthshaking (*Inf.*), fateful, grave, historic, important, of moment, pivotal, serious, significant, vital, weighty

Antonyms inconsequential, insignificant, trifling, trivial, unimportant

momentum drive, energy, force, impetus, power, propulsion, push, strength, thrust

monarch crowned head, emperor, empress, king, potentate, prince, princess, queen, ruler, sovereign

monastery abbey, cloister, convent, friary, house, nunnery, priory, religious community

monastic ascetic, austere, celibate, cenobitic, cloistered, cloistral, coenobitic, contemplative, conventual, eremitic, hermit-like, monachal, monkish, recluse, reclusive, secluded, sequestered, withdrawn

monetary budgetary, capital, cash, financial, fiscal, pecuniary

money banknotes, bread (*Sl.*), capital, cash, coin, currency, dosh (*Brit. sl.*), dough (*Sl.*), filthy lucre (*Facetious*), funds, gelt (*Sl.*), green (*Sl.*), hard cash, legal tender, lolly (*Brit. sl.*), loot (*Inf.*), mazuma (*Sl., chiefly U.S.*), moolah (*Sl.*), pelf (*Contemptuous*), readies (*Inf.*), riches, specie, spondulix (*Sl.*), the ready (*Inf.*), the wherewithal, wealth

mongrel 1. *n.* bigener (*Biol.*), cross, crossbreed, half-breed, hybrid, mixed breed **2.** *adj.* bastard, crossbred, half-breed, hybrid, or mixed breed

monitor 1. *n.* guide, invigilator, overseer, prefect (*Brit.*), supervisor, watchdog **2.** *v.* check, follow, keep an eye on, keep track of, observe, oversee, record, scan, supervise, survey, watch

monk brother, friar (*loosely*), monastic, religious

monkey *n.* **1.** primate, simian **2.** devil, imp, mischief maker, rascal, rogue, scamp ~*v.* **3.** fiddle, fool, interfere, meddle, mess, play, tamper, tinker, trifle

monologue harangue, lecture, sermon, soliloquy, speech

monopolize control, corner, corner the market in, dominate, engross, exercise *or* have a monopoly of, hog (*Sl.*), keep to oneself, take over, take up

monotonous all the same, boring, colourless, droning, dull, flat, humdrum, plodding, repetitious, repetitive, samey (*Inf.*), soporific, tedious, tiresome, toneless, unchanging, uniform, uninflected, unvaried, wearisome

Antonyms animated, enjoyable, entertaining, enthralling, exciting, exhilarating, interesting, lively, sexy (*Inf.*), stimulating

monster 1. *n.* barbarian, beast, bogeyman, brute, demon, devil, fiend, ogre, savage, villain **2.** *adj.* Brobdingnagian, colossal, enormous, gargantuan, giant, gigantic, ginormous (*Inf.*), huge, immense, jumbo (*Inf.*), mammoth, massive, mega (*Inf.*), monstrous, stupendous, titanic, tremendous

monstrous 1. abnormal, dreadful, enormous, fiendish, freakish, frightful, grotesque, gruesome, hellish, hideous, horrendous, horrible, miscreated, obscene, teratoid, terrible, unnatural **2.** atrocious, cruel, devilish, diabolical, disgraceful, egregious, evil, fiendish, foul, heinous, horrifying, infamous, inhuman, intolerable, loathsome, odious, outrageous, satanic, scandalous, shocking, vicious, villainous **3.** colossal, elephantine, enormous, gargantuan, giant, gigantic, ginormous (*Inf.*), great, huge, immense, mammoth, massive, mega (*Inf.*), prodigious, stupendous, titanic, towering, tremendous, vast

Antonyms (*sense 1*) appealing, attractive, beautiful, delightful, lovely, natural, normal, ordinary, pleasant (*sense 2*) admirable, decent, fine, good, honourable, humane, kind, merciful, mild (*sense 3*) diminutive, insignificant, little, meagre, miniature, minute, puny, slight, small, tiny

monument cairn, cenotaph, commemoration, gravestone, headstone, marker, mausoleum, memorial, obelisk, pillar, shrine, statue, tombstone

monumental awe-inspiring, awesome, classic, enduring, enormous, epoch-making, historic, immortal, important, lasting, majestic, memorable, outstanding, prodigious, significant, stupendous, unforgettable

Antonyms ephemeral, inconsequential, insignificant, modest, negligible, ordinary, trivial, un-distinguished, unimportant, un-impressive, unremarkable

mood 1. disposition, frame of mind, humour, spirit, state of mind, temper, tenor, vein **2.** bad temper, blues, depression, dol-drums, dumps (*Inf.*), fit of pique, grumps (*Inf.*), low spirits, melan-choly, sulk, the sulks

moody angry, broody, cantan-kerous, crabbed, crabby, crest-fallen, cross, crotchety (*Inf.*), crusty, curt, dismal, doleful, dour, downcast, down in the dumps (*Inf.*), down in the mouth (*Inf.*), frowning, gloomy, glum, huffish, huffy, ill-humoured, ill-tempered, in a huff, in the doldrums, intro-spective, irascible, irritable, lu-gubrious, melancholy, miserable, mopish, moping, morose, offended, out of sorts (*Inf.*), pensive, petu-lant, piqued, sad, saturnine, short-tempered, splenetic, sulky, sul-len, temperamental, testy, touchy, waspish, wounded **Antonyms** amiable, cheerful, compatible, gay, happy, optimis-tic

moon 1. *n.* satellite **2.** *v.* day-dream, idle, languish, mooch (*Sl.*), mope, waste time

moor¹ fell (*Brit.*), heath, moor-land, muir (*Scot.*)

moor² anchor, berth, dock, fasten, fix, lash, make fast, secure, tie up

mop up clean up, mop, soak up, sponge, swab, wash, wipe

moral *adj.* **1.** ethical **2.** blameless, chaste, decent, ethical, good, high-minded, honest, honourable, incorruptible, innocent, just, meritorious, noble, principled, proper, pure, right, righteous, upright, upstanding, virtuous ~*n.* **3.** lesson, meaning, message, point, significance **Antonyms** amoral, dishonest, dishonourable, immoral, im-proper, sinful, unethical, unfair, unjust, wrong

morale confidence, esprit de corps, heart, mettle, self-esteem, spirit, temper

morality chastity, decency, ethi-cality, ethicalness, goodness, honesty, integrity, justice, prin-ciple, rectitude, righteousness, rightness, uprightness, virtue

morals behaviour, conduct, eth-ics, habits, integrity, manners, morality, mores, principles, scruples, standards

morbid 1. brooding, ghoulish, gloomy, grim, melancholy, pes-simistic, sick, sombre, unhealthy, unwholesome **2.** dreadful, ghast-ly, grisly, gruesome, hideous, horrid, macabre **Antonyms** bright, cheerful, hap-py, healthy, salubrious, whole-some

more 1. *adj.* added, additional, extra, fresh, further, new, other, spare, supplementary **2.** *adv.* better, further, longer, to a greater extent

moreover additionally, also, as well, besides, further, further-more, in addition, into the bar-gain, likewise, to boot, too, what is more, withal (*Literary*)

morning a.m., break of day, dawn, daybreak, forenoon, morn (*Poetic*), morrow (*Archaic*), sun-rise

moron airhead (*Sl.*), ass, block-head, bonehead (*Sl.*), cretin, dickhead (*Sl.*), dimwit (*Inf.*), dolt, dope (*Sl.*), dummy (*Sl.*), dunce, dunderhead, fool, halfwit, idiot, imbecile, mental defective, muttonhead (*Sl.*), numskull, nurd (*Sl.*), pillock (*Brit. sl.*), plonker (*Sl.*), simpleton, thickhead, tosser (*Brit. sl.*)

morose blue, churlish, crabbed, crabby, cross, crusty, depressed, dour, down, down in the dumps (*Inf.*), gloomy, glum, grouchy (*Inf.*), gruff, ill-humoured, ill-natured, ill-tempered, in a bad mood, low, melancholy, miser-able, moody, mournful, perverse, pessimistic, saturnine, sour, sulky, sullen, surly, taciturn **Antonyms** amiable, blithe, cheerful, friendly, gay, genial, good-humoured, good-natured, happy, pleasant, sweet

morsel bit, bite, crumb, fraction, fragment, grain, mouthful, nibble, part, piece, scrap, segment, slice, snack, soupçon, tad (*Inf. chiefly U.S.*), taste, titbit

mortal *adj.* 1. corporeal, earthly, ephemeral, human, impermanent, passing, sublunary, temporal, transient, worldly 2. deadly, death-dealing, destructive, fatal, killing, lethal, murderous, terminal ~*n.* 3. being, body, earthling, human, human being, individual, man, person, woman

mortality 1. ephemerality, humanity, impermanence, temporality, transience 2. bloodshed, carnage, death, destruction, fatality, killing, loss of life

mortified abashed, affronted, annoyed, ashamed, chagrined, chastened, confounded, crushed, deflated, discomfited, displeased, embarrassed, given a showing-up (*Inf.*), humbled, humiliated, made to eat humble pie (*Inf.*), put down, put out (*Inf.*), put to shame, rendered speechless, shamed, vexed

mostly above all, almost entirely, as a rule, chiefly, customarily, for the most part, generally, largely, mainly, most often, on the whole, particularly, predominantly, primarily, principally, usually

mother *n.* 1. dam, ma (*Inf.*), mater, mom (*U.S. inf.*), mum (*Brit. inf.*), mummy (*Brit. inf.*), old lady (*Inf.*), old woman (*Inf.*) ~*adj.* 2. connate, inborn, innate, native, natural ~*v.* 3. bear, bring forth, drop, give birth to, produce 4. care for, cherish, nurse, nurture, protect, raise, rear, tend

motherly affectionate, caring, comforting, fond, gentle, kind, loving, maternal, protective, sheltering, tender, warm

motion *n.* 1. action, change, flow, kinesics, locomotion, mobility, motility, move, movement, passage, passing, progress, travel 2. proposal, proposition, recommendation, submission, suggestion ~*v.* 3. beckon, direct, gesticulate, gesture, nod, signal, wave

motionless at a standstill, at rest, calm, fixed, frozen, halted, immobile, inanimate, inert, lifeless, paralysed, standing, static, stationary, still, stock-still, transfixed, unmoved, unmoving

Antonyms active, agitated, animated, frantic, lively, mobile, moving, restless, travelling

motivate actuate, arouse, bring, cause, draw, drive, give incentive to, impel, induce, inspire, inspirit, instigate, lead, move, persuade, prompt, provoke, set on, stimulate, stir, trigger

motivation ambition, desire, drive, hunger, inspiration, interest, wish

motive *n.* cause, design, ground(s), incentive, incitement, inducement, influence, inspiration, intention, mainspring, motivation, object, occasion, purpose, rationale, reason, spur, stimulus, thinking

motley assorted, disparate, dissimilar, diversified, heterogeneous, mingled, miscellaneous, mixed, unlike, varied

Antonyms homogeneous, similar, uniform

mottled blotchy, brindled, chequered, dappled, flecked, freckled, marbled, piebald, pied, speckled, spotted, stippled, streaked, tabby, variegated

motto adage, byword, cry, formula, gnome, maxim, precept, proverb, rule, saw, saying, slogan, watchword

mould *n.* 1. cast, die, form, matrix, pattern, shape 2. brand, build, configuration, construction, cut, design, fashion, form, format, frame, kind, line, make, pattern, shape, structure, style ~*v.* 3. carve, cast, construct, create, fashion, forge, form, make, model, sculpt, shape, stamp, work

mouldy bad, blighted, decaying,

fusty, mildewed, musty, rotten, rotting, spoiled, stale

mound 1. bing (*Scot.*), drift, heap, pile, stack **2.** bank, dune, embankment, hill, hillock, knoll, rise

mount v. **1.** ascend, clamber up, climb, escalade, go up, make one's way up, scale **2.** bestride, climb onto, climb up on, get astride, get (up) on, jump on **3.** arise, ascend, rise, soar, tower **4.** accumulate, build, escalate, grow, increase, intensify, multiply, pile up, swell **5.** display, frame, set, set off **6.** exhibit, get up (*Inf.*), prepare, produce, put on, stage ~n. **7.** backing, base, fixture, foil, frame, mounting, setting, stand, support **8.** horse, steed (*Literary*)

Antonyms (*sense 1*) descend, drop, go down, make one's way down (*sense 2*) climb down from, climb off, dismount, get down from, get off, jump off (*sense 4*) contract, decline, decrease, diminish, dwindle, fall, lessen, lower, reduce, shrink, wane

mountain alp, ben (*Scot.*), elevation, eminence, fell (*Brit.*), height, mount, Munro, peak

mountainous alpine, high, highland, rocky, soaring, steep, towering, upland

mourn bemoan, bewail, deplore, grieve, keen, lament, miss, rue, sorrow, wail, wear black, weep

mournful afflicting, calamitous, deplorable, distressing, grievous, lamentable, melancholy, painful, piteous, plaintive, sad, sorrowful, tragic, unhappy, woeful

Antonyms agreeable, cheerful, fortunate, happy, lucky, pleasant, satisfying

mourning bereavement, grief, grieving, keening, lamentation, weeping, woe

mouth n. **1.** chops (*Sl.*), gob (*Sl.*), jaws, lips, maw, trap (*Sl.*), yap (*Sl.*) **2.** aperture, cavity, crevice, door, entrance, gateway, inlet, lips, opening, orifice, rim **3. down in or at the mouth** blue, crestfallen, dejected, depressed, dis-

heartened, dispirited, down, downcast, down in the dumps (*Inf.*), in low spirits, melancholy, miserable, sad, unhappy

move v. **1.** advance, budge, change position, drift, go, march, proceed, progress, shift, stir, walk **2.** carry, change, shift, switch, transfer, transport, transpose **3.** change residence, flit (*Scot., & northern English dialect*), go away, leave, migrate, move house, quit, relocate, remove **4.** activate, drive, impel, motivate, operate, propel, push, set going, shift, shove, start, turn **5.** actuate, affect, agitate, cause, excite, give rise to, impel, impress, incite, induce, influence, inspire, instigate, lead, make an impression on, motivate, persuade, prompt, rouse, stimulate, touch, urge **6.** advocate, propose, put forward, recommend, suggest, urge ~n. **7.** act, action, deed, manoeuvre, measure, motion, movement, ploy, shift, step, stratagem, stroke, turn

Antonyms (*sense 5*) deter, discourage, dissuade, prevent, stop

movement 1. act, action, activity, advance, agitation, change, development, displacement, exercise, flow, gesture, manoeuvre, motion, move, moving, operation, progress, progression, shift, steps, stir, stirring, transfer **2.** campaign, crusade, drive, faction, front, group, grouping, organization, party **3.** Music division, part, passage, section **4.** beat, cadence, measure, metre, pace, rhythm, swing, tempo

moving affecting, arousing, emotional, emotive, exciting, impelling, impressive, inspiring, pathetic, persuasive, poignant, stirring, touching

Antonyms unemotional, unexciting, unimpressive, uninspiring

mow crop, cut, scythe, shear, trim

much 1. adj. abundant, a lot of, ample, considerable, copious, great, plenteous, plenty of, sizeable, substantial **2.** adv. a great

deal, a lot, considerably, decid~
edly, exceedingly, frequently,
greatly, indeed, often, regularly
Antonyms adj. inadequate, in~
sufficient, little, scant ~adv.
barely, hardly, infrequently, ir~
regularly, not a lot, not much,
occasionally, only just, rarely,
scarcely, seldom, slightly
mud clay, dirt, mire, ooze, silt,
sludge
muddle v. 1. confuse, disarrange,
disorder, disorganize, jumble,
make a mess of, mess, mix up,
scramble, spoil, tangle 2. befud~
dle, bewilder, confound, confuse,
daze, disorient, perplex, stupefy
~n. 3. chaos, clutter, confusion,
daze, disarray, disorder, disor~
ganization, fankle (Scot.), jumble,
mess, mix-up, perplexity, plight,
predicament, tangle
muddy adj. bespattered, boggy,
clarty (Scot. & northern English
dialect), dirty, grimy, marshy,
miry, mucky, mud-caked, quag~
gy, soiled, swampy
muffle cloak, conceal, cover, dis~
guise, envelop, hood, mask,
shroud, swaddle, swathe, wrap up
muffled dim, dull, faint, indistinct,
muted, stifled, strangled, sub~
dued, suppressed
mug beaker, cup, flagon, jug, pot,
tankard, toby jug
muggy clammy, close, damp, hu~
mid, moist, oppressive, sticky,
stuffy, sultry
multiple collective, manifold,
many, multitudinous, numerous,
several, sundry, various
multiply accumulate, augment,
breed, build up, expand, extend,
increase, proliferate, propagate,
reproduce, spread
Antonyms abate, decline, de~
crease, diminish, lessen, reduce
multitude army, assemblage, as~
sembly, collection, concourse,
congregation, crowd, great num~
ber, horde, host, legion, lot, lots
(Inf.), mass, mob, myriad, sea,
swarm, throng
mundane banal, commonplace,
day-to-day, everyday, humdrum,

ordinary, prosaic, routine,
workaday
Antonyms exciting, extraordi~
nary, imaginative, interesting,
novel, original, special, uncom~
mon, unusual
municipal borough, city, civic,
community, public, town, urban
murder 1. n. assassination, blood~
shed, butchery, carnage, homi~
cide, killing, manslaughter, mas~
sacre, slaying 2. v. assassinate,
blow away (Sl., chiefly U.S.),
bump off (Inf.), butcher, destroy,
dispatch, do in (Inf.), do to death,
eliminate (Sl.), hit (U.S. sl.), kill,
massacre, rub out (U.S. sl.),
slaughter, slay, take the life of,
waste (U.S. sl.)
murderer assassin, butcher, cut~
throat, hit man (Sl.), homicide,
killer, slaughterer, slayer
murderous barbarous, blood~
thirsty, bloody, brutal, cruel,
deadly, death-dealing, destruc~
tive, devastating, fatal, fell (Ar~
chaic), ferocious, internecine, le~
thal, sanguinary, savage, slaugh~
terous, withering
murky cheerless, cloudy, dark,
dim, dismal, dreary, dull, dusky,
foggy, gloomy, grey, impen~
etrable, misty, nebulous, obscure,
overcast
Antonyms bright, cheerful, clear,
distinct, sunny
murmur 1. n. babble, buzzing,
drone, humming, mumble, mut~
tering, purr, rumble, susurrus
(Literary), undertone, whisper,
whispering 2. v. babble, buzz,
drone, hum, mumble, mutter,
purr, rumble, speak in an under~
tone, whisper
muscle n. 1. muscle tissue, sinew,
tendon, thew 2. brawn, clout (Sl.),
force, forcefulness, might, po~
tency, power, stamina, strength,
sturdiness, weight
muscular athletic, beefy (Inf.),
brawny, husky (Inf.), lusty, pow~
erful, powerfully built,
Ramboesque, robust, sinewy,
stalwart, strapping, strong, stur~
dy, vigorous, well-knit

muse be in a brown study, be lost in thought, brood, cogitate, consider, contemplate, deliberate, dream, meditate, mull over, ponder, reflect, ruminate, speculate, think, think over, weigh

musical dulcet, euphonious, harmonious, lilting, lyrical, melodic, melodious, sweet-sounding, tuneful

Antonyms discordant, grating, harsh, unmelodious, unmusical

must *n.* duty, essential, fundamental, imperative, necessary thing, necessity, obligation, prerequisite, requirement, requisite, *sine qua non*

muster 1. *v.* assemble, call together, call up, collect, come together, congregate, convene, convoke, enrol, gather, group, marshal, meet, mobilize, rally, round up, summon **2.** *n.* assemblage, assembly, collection, concourse, congregation, convention, convocation, gathering, meeting, mobilization, rally, roundup

musty airless, dank, decayed, frowsty, fusty, mildewed, mildewy, mouldy, old, smelly, stale, stuffy

mute 1. *adj.* aphasiac, aphasic, aphonic, dumb, mum, silent, speechless, unexpressed, unspeaking, unspoken, voiceless, wordless **2.** *v.* dampen, deaden, lower, moderate, muffle, soften, soft-pedal, subdue, tone down, turn down

mutilate amputate, butcher, cripple, cut to pieces, cut up, damage, disable, disfigure, dismember, hack, injure, lacerate, lame, maim, mangle

mutinous bolshie (*Brit. inf.*), contumacious, disobedient, insubordinate, insurgent, rebellious, refractory, revolutionary, riotous, seditious, subversive, turbulent, ungovernable, unmanageable, unruly

mutiny 1. *n.* defiance, disobedi-

ence, insubordination, insurrection, rebellion, refusal to obey orders, resistance, revolt, revolution, riot, rising, strike, uprising **2.** *v.* be insubordinate, defy authority, disobey, rebel, refuse to obey orders, resist, revolt, rise up, strike

mutter complain, grouch, grouse, grumble, mumble, murmur, rumble

mutual common, communal, correlative, interactive, interchangeable, interchanged, joint, reciprocal, reciprocated, requited, returned, shared

muzzle censor, choke, curb, gag (*Inf.*), restrain, silence, stifle, suppress

mysterious abstruse, arcane, baffling, concealed, covert, cryptic, curious, dark, enigmatic, furtive, hidden, impenetrable, incomprehensible, inexplicable, inscrutable, insoluble, mystical, mystifying, obscure, perplexing, puzzling, recondite, secret, secretive, sphinxlike, strange, uncanny, unfathomable, unknown, veiled, weird

Antonyms apparent, clear, intelligible, manifest, open, plain

mystery conundrum, enigma, problem, puzzle, question, riddle, secrecy, secret

mystify baffle, bamboozle (*Inf.*), beat (*Sl.*), befog, bewilder, confound, confuse, elude, escape, perplex, puzzle, stump

myth allegory, fable, fairy story, fiction, folk tale, legend, parable, saga, story, tradition

mythical 1. allegorical, chimerical, fabled, fabulous, fairy-tale, legendary, mythological, storied **2.** fabricated, fanciful, fantasy, fictitious, imaginary, invented, made-up, make-believe, nonexistent, pretended, unreal, untrue

mythology folklore, folk tales, legend, lore, mythos, myths, stories, tradition

N

nadir bottom, depths, lowest point, minimum, rock bottom, zero

Antonyms acme, apex, climax, height, high point, peak, pinnacle, summit, top, vertex, zenith

nag 1. *v.* annoy, badger, berate, chivvy, goad, harass, harry, henpeck, irritate, pester, plague, provoke, scold, torment, upbraid, vex, worry 2. *n.* harpy, scold, shrew, tartar, termagant, virago

nail *v.* attach, beat, fasten, fix, hammer, join, pin, secure, tack

naive artless, candid, childlike, confiding, frank, guileless, ingenuous, innocent, jejune, natural, open, simple, trusting, unaffected, unpretentious, unsophisticated, unworldly

Antonyms artful, disingenuous, experienced, sly, sophisticated, urbane, worldly, worldly-wise

naivety artlessness, candour, frankness, guilelessness, inexperience, ingenuousness, innocence, naturalness, openness, simplicity

naked 1. bare, denuded, disrobed, divested, exposed, in one's birthday suit (*Inf.*), in the altogether (*Inf.*), in the buff (*Inf.*), nude, starkers (*Inf.*), stripped, unclothed, unconcealed, uncovered, undraped, undressed 2. defenceless, helpless, insecure, unarmed, unguarded, unprotected, vulnerable

Antonyms clothed, covered, dressed, wrapped up

name *n.* 1. appellation, cognomen, denomination, designation, epithet, handle (*Sl.*), moniker (*Sl.*), nickname, sobriquet, term, title 2. distinction, eminence, esteem, fame, honour, note, praise, renown, repute 3. character, credit, reputation ~ *v.* 4. baptize, call,

christen, denominate, dub, entitle, label, style, term 5. appoint, choose, cite, classify, commission, designate, identify, mention, nominate, select, specify

named baptized, called, christened, denominated, dubbed, entitled, known as, labelled, styled, termed

nameless 1. anonymous, innominate, undesignated, unnamed, untitled 2. incognito, obscure, undistinguished, unheard-of, unknown, unsung 3. abominable, horrible, indescribable, ineffable, inexpressible, unmentionable, unspeakable, unutterable

namely i.e., specifically, that is to say, to wit, viz.

narrate chronicle, describe, detail, recite, recount, rehearse, relate, repeat, report, set forth, tell, unfold

narration description, explanation, reading, recital, rehearsal, relation, storytelling, telling, voice-over (*in film*)

narrative account, chronicle, detail, history, report, statement, story, tale

narrator annalist, author, bard, chronicler, commentator, raconteur, reciter, relater, reporter, storyteller, writer

narrow *adj.* 1. circumscribed, close, confined, constricted, contracted, cramped, incapacious, limited, meagre, near, pinched, restricted, scanty, straitened, tight 2. biased, bigoted, dogmatic, illiberal, intolerant, narrow-minded, partial, prejudiced, reactionary, small-minded ~ *v.* 3. circumscribe, constrict, diminish, limit, reduce, simplify, straiten, tighten

Antonyms broad-minded, liberal,

open, receptive, spacious, tolerant, wide

narrowly barely, by a whisker *or* hair's-breadth, just, only just, scarcely

narrow-minded biased, bigoted, conservative, hidebound, illiberal, insular, intolerant, opinionated, parochial, petty, prejudiced, provincial, reactionary, short-sighted, small-minded, straitlaced

Antonyms broad-minded, catholic, cosmopolitan, freethinking, indulgent, open-minded, permissive, tolerant, unprejudiced

nastiness 1. defilement, dirtiness, filth, filthiness, foulness, impurity, pollution, squalor, uncleanliness **2.** indecency, licentiousness, obscenity, pollution, porn (*Inf.*), pornography, ribaldry, smuttiness **3.** disagreeableness, malice, meanness, offensiveness, spitefulness, unpleasantness

nasty 1. dirty, disagreeable, disgusting, filthy, foul, grotty (*Sl.*), horrible, loathsome, malodorous, mephitic, nauseating, noisome, objectionable, obnoxious, odious, offensive, polluted, repellent, repugnant, sickening, unappetizing, unpleasant, vile **2.** blue, foul, gross, impure, indecent, lascivious, lewd, licentious, obscene, pornographic, ribald, smutty **3.** abusive, annoying, bad-tempered, despicable, disagreeable, distasteful, malicious, mean, spiteful, unpleasant, vicious, vile

Antonyms admirable, agreeable, clean, decent, enjoyable, kind, nice, pleasant, sweet

nation commonwealth, community, country, people, population, race, realm, society, state, tribe

national *adj.* **1.** civil, countrywide, governmental, nationwide, public, state, widespread **2.** domestic, internal, social

nationalism allegiance, chauvinism, fealty, jingoism, loyalty, nationality, patriotism

nationality birth, ethnic group, nation, race

native *adj.* **1.** built-in, congenital, endemic, hereditary, inborn, inbred, indigenous, ingrained, inherent, inherited, innate, instinctive, intrinsic, inveterate, natal, natural **2.** genuine, original, real **3.** domestic, home, home-grown, home-made, indigenous, local, mother, vernacular ~*n.* **4.** aborigine, autochthon, citizen, countryman, dweller, inhabitant, national, resident

natural 1. common, everyday, legitimate, logical, normal, ordinary, regular, typical, usual **2.** characteristic, congenital, essential, inborn, indigenous, inherent, innate, instinctive, intuitive, natal, native **3.** artless, candid, frank, genuine, ingenuous, open, real, simple, spontaneous, unaffected, unpretentious, unsophisticated, unstudied

Antonyms (*sense 1*) abnormal, irregular, out of the ordinary, strange, untypical (*sense 3*) affected, artificial, assumed, counterfeit, feigned, phoney (*Inf.*), unnatural

nature 1. attributes, character, complexion, constitution, essence, features, make-up, quality, traits **2.** category, description, kind, sort, species, style, type, variety **3.** cosmos, creation, earth, environment, universe, world **4.** disposition, humour, mood, outlook, temper, temperament **5.** country, countryside, landscape, natural history, scenery

naughty annoying, bad, disobedient, exasperating, fractious, impish, misbehaved, mischievous, perverse, playful, refractory, roguish, sinful, teasing, wayward, wicked, worthless

Antonyms good, obedient, polite, proper, seemly, well-behaved, well-mannered

nausea 1. biliousness, qualm(s), queasiness, retching, sickness, squeamishness, vomiting **2.** abhorrence, aversion, disgust, loathing, repugnance, revulsion

nauseate disgust, gross out (*U.S. sl.*), horrify, offend, repel, repulse, revolt, sicken, turn one's stomach

nautical marine, maritime, naval, oceanic, seafaring, seagoing, yachting

naval marine, maritime, nautical, oceanic

navigable clear, negotiable, passable, traversable, unobstructed

navigate con (*Nautical*), cross, cruise, direct, drive, guide, handle, journey, manoeuvre, pilot, plan, plot, sail, skipper, steer, voyage

navigation cruising, helmsmanship, pilotage, sailing, seamanship, steering, voyaging

navy argosy (*Archaic*), armada, fleet, flotilla, warships

near *adj.* **1.** adjacent, adjoining, alongside, at close quarters, beside, bordering, close, close by, contiguous, nearby, neighbouring, nigh, touching **2.** approaching, forthcoming, imminent, impending, in the offing, looming, near-at-hand, next, on the cards (*Inf.*) **3.** akin, allied, attached, connected, dear, familiar, intimate, related
Antonyms distant, far, faraway, far-flung, far-off, far-removed, long, outlying, out-of-the-way, remote, removed

nearby *adj.* adjacent, adjoining, convenient, handy, neighbouring

nearly *adv.* about, all but, almost, approaching, approximately, as good as, closely, just about, not quite, practically, roughly, virtually, well-nigh

nearness 1. accessibility, availability, closeness, contiguity, handiness, juxtaposition, propinquity, proximity, vicinity **2.** immediacy, imminence

neat 1. accurate, dainty, fastidious, methodical, nice, orderly, shipshape, smart, spick-and-span, spruce, straight, systematic, tidy, trim, uncluttered **2.** adept, adroit, agile, apt, clever, deft, dexterous,

efficient, effortless, elegant, expert, graceful, handy, nimble, practised, precise, skilful, stylish, well-judged **3.** *Of alcoholic drinks* pure, straight, undiluted, unmixed
Antonyms (*senses 1 & 2*) awful, bad, clumsy, cluttered, disorderly, disorganized, incompetent, inefficient, inelegant, messy, slobby (*Inf.*), sloppy (*Inf.*), terrible, untidy

neatness 1. accuracy, daintiness, fastidiousness, methodicalness, niceness, nicety, orderliness, smartness, spruceness, straightness, tidiness, trimness **2.** adeptness, adroitness, agility, aptness, cleverness, deftness, dexterity, efficiency, effortlessness, elegance, expertness, grace, gracefulness, handiness, nimbleness, preciseness, precision, skilfulness, skill, style, stylishness

necessarily accordingly, automatically, axiomatically, by definition, certainly, compulsorily, consequently, incontrovertibly, ineluctably, inevitably, inexorably, irresistibly, naturally, *nolens volens*, of course, of necessity, perforce, undoubtedly, willy-nilly

necessary compulsory, *de rigueur*, essential, imperative, indispensable, mandatory, needed, needful, obligatory, required, requisite, vital
Antonyms dispensable, expendable, inessential, nonessential, superfluous, unnecessary

necessitate call for, coerce, compel, constrain, demand, force, impel, make necessary, oblige, require

necessity 1. demand, exigency, indispensability, need, needfulness, requirement **2.** desideratum, essential, fundamental, necessary, need, prerequisite, requirement, requisite, *sine qua non*, want

need *v.* **1.** call for, demand, have occasion to *or* for, lack, miss, necessitate, require, want ~*n.* **2.**

longing, requisite, want, wish **3.** deprivation, destitution, distress, extremity, impecuniousness, inadequacy, indigence, insufficiency, lack, neediness, paucity, penury, poverty, privation, shortage **4.** emergency, exigency, necessity, obligation, urgency, want **5.** demand, desideratum, essential, requirement, requisite

needless causeless, dispensable, excessive, expendable, gratuitous, groundless, nonessential, pointless, redundant, superfluous, uncalled-for, undesired, unnecessary, unwanted, useless
Antonyms beneficial, essential, obligatory, required, useful

needy deprived, destitute, disadvantaged, impecunious, impoverished, indigent, on the breadline (*Inf.*), penniless, poor, poverty-stricken, underprivileged
Antonyms affluent, comfortable, moneyed, prosperous, rich, wealthy, well-off, well-to-do

negate abrogate, annul, cancel, countermand, invalidate, neutralize, nullify, repeal, rescind, retract, reverse, revoke, void, wipe out
Antonyms affirm, assert, attest, avouch, avow, certify, confirm, maintain, ratify, swear, testify

negation antithesis, antonym, contradiction, contrary, converse, counterpart, denial, disavowal, disclaimer, inverse, opposite, rejection, renunciation, reverse

negative *adj.* **1.** contradictory, contrary, denying, dissenting, opposing, recusant, refusing, rejecting, resisting **2.** annulling, counteractive, invalidating, neutralizing, nullifying **3.** antagonistic, colourless, contrary, cynical, gloomy, jaundiced, neutral, pessimistic, uncooperative, unenthusiastic, uninterested, unwilling, weak ~*n.* **4.** contradiction, denial, refusal
Antonyms *adj.* affirmative, approving, assenting, cheerful,

concurring, enthusiastic, optimistic, positive

neglect *v.* **1.** contemn, disdain, disregard, ignore, leave alone, overlook, pass by, rebuff, scorn, slight, spurn **2.** be remiss, evade, forget, let slide, omit, pass over, procrastinate, shirk, skimp ~*n.* **3.** disdain, disregard, disrespect, heedlessness, inattention, indifference, slight, unconcern **4.** carelessness, default, dereliction, failure, forgetfulness, laxity, laxness, neglectfulness, negligence, oversight, remissness, slackness, slovenliness
Antonyms *v.* appreciate, attend to, notice, observe, regard, remember, value ~*n.* attention, care, consideration, notice, regard, respect

neglected abandoned, derelict, overgrown

negligent careless, cursory, disregardful, forgetful, heedless, inadvertent, inattentive, indifferent, neglectful, nonchalant, offhand, regardless, remiss, slack, thoughtless, unmindful, unthinking
Antonyms attentive, careful, considerate, mindful, painstaking, rigorous, thorough, thoughtful

negligible imperceptible, inconsequential, insignificant, minor, minute, petty, small, trifling, trivial, unimportant
Antonyms important, noteworthy, significant, vital

negotiate adjudicate, arbitrate, arrange, bargain, conciliate, confer, consult, contract, deal, debate, discuss, handle, manage, mediate, parley, settle, transact, work out

negotiation arbitration, bargaining, debate, diplomacy, discussion, mediation, transaction, wheeling and dealing (*Inf.*)

neighbourhood community, confines, district, environs, locale, locality, precincts, proximity, purlieus, quarter, region, surroundings, vicinity

neighbouring abutting, adjacent, adjoining, bordering, connecting, contiguous, near, nearby, nearest, next, surrounding

nerve n. 1. balls (Sl.), bottle (Brit. sl.), bravery, coolness, courage, daring, determination, endurance, energy, fearlessness, firmness, force, fortitude, gameness, grit (Inf.), guts (Inf.), hardihood, intrepidity, mettle, might, pluck, resolution, spirit, spunk (Inf.), steadfastness, vigour, will 2. Inf. audacity, boldness, brass (Inf.), brass neck (Brit. inf.), brazenness, cheek (Inf.), effrontery, gall, impertinence, impudence, insolence, sauce (Inf.), temerity

nerves anxiety, fretfulness, imbalance, nervousness, strain, stress, tension, worry

nervous agitated, anxious, apprehensive, edgy, excitable, fearful, fidgety, flustered, hesitant, highly strung, hyper (Inf.), hysterical, jittery (Inf.), jumpy, nervy (Inf.), neurotic, on edge, ruffled, shaky, tense, timid, timorous, uneasy, uptight (Inf.), weak, worried
Antonyms bold, calm, cool, confident, constant, equable, even, laid-back (Inf.), peaceful, relaxed, steady, together (Sl.)

nest 1. den, haunt, hideaway, refuge, resort, retreat, snuggery 2. breeding ground, den, hotbed

nestle cuddle, curl up, huddle, nuzzle, snuggle

net[1] 1. n. lacework, lattice, mesh, netting, network, openwork, reticulum, tracery, web 2. v. bag, capture, catch, enmesh, ensnare, entangle, nab (Inf.), trap

net[2], **nett** adj. 1. after taxes, clear, final, take-home 2. closing, conclusive, final ~ v. 3. accumulate, bring in, clear, earn, gain, make, realize, reap

network arrangement, channels, circuitry, complex, convolution, grid, grill, interconnections, labyrinth, maze, mesh, net, nexus, organization, plexus, structure, system, tracks, web

neurosis abnormality, affliction, derangement, deviation, instability, maladjustment, mental disturbance, mental illness, obsession, phobia, psychological or emotional disorder

neurotic abnormal, anxious, compulsive, deviant, disordered, distraught, disturbed, hyper (Inf.), maladjusted, manic, nervous, obsessive, overwrought, unhealthy, unstable
Antonyms calm, laid-back (Inf.), level-headed, normal, rational, sane, stable, together (Sl.), well-adjusted, well-balanced

neuter v. castrate, doctor (Inf.), dress, emasculate, fix (Inf.), geld, spay

neutral disinterested, dispassionate, even-handed, impartial, indifferent, nonaligned, nonbelligerent, noncombatant, noncommittal, nonpartisan, sitting on the fence, unaligned, unbiased, uncommitted, undecided, uninvolved, unprejudiced
Antonyms active, belligerent, biased, decided, interested, interfering, partial, participating, positive, prejudiced

neutralize cancel, compensate for, counteract, counterbalance, frustrate, invalidate, negate, nullify, offset, undo

never-ending boundless, ceaseless, constant, continual, continuous, eternal, everlasting, incessant, interminable, nonstop, perpetual, persistent, relentless, unbroken, unceasing, unchanging, uninterrupted, unremitting

nevertheless but, even so, however, nonetheless, notwithstanding, regardless, still, yet

new 1. advanced, contemporary, current, different, fresh, latest, modern, modernistic, modish, newfangled, novel, original, recent, state-of-the-art, topical, ultramodern, unfamiliar, unknown, unused, unusual, up-to-date, virgin 2. added, extra, more, supplementary 3. altered,

changed, improved, modernized, redesigned, renewed, restored
Antonyms aged, ancient, antiquated, antique, experienced, hackneyed, old, old-fashioned, outmoded, passé, stale, trite

newcomer alien, arrival, beginner, foreigner, immigrant, incomer, Johnny-come-lately (*Inf.*), novice, outsider, parvenu, settler, stranger

newly anew, freshly, just, lately, latterly, recently

news account, advice, bulletin, communiqué, disclosure, dispatch, exposé, gossip, hearsay, information, intelligence, leak, news-flash, release, report, revelation, rumour, scandal, statement, story, tidings, word

next *adj.* 1. consequent, ensuing, following, later, subsequent, succeeding 2. adjacent, adjoining, closest, nearest, neighbouring ~*adv.* 3. afterwards, closely, following, later, subsequently, thereafter

nice 1. agreeable, amiable, attractive, charming, commendable, courteous, delightful, friendly, good, kind, likable, pleasant, pleasurable, polite, prepossessing, refined, well-mannered 2. dainty, fine, neat, tidy, trim 3. accurate, careful, critical, delicate, discriminating, exact, exacting, fastidious, fine, meticulous, precise, rigorous, scrupulous, strict, subtle
Antonyms awful, careless, disagreeable, dreadful, mean, miserable, rough, shabby, sloppy (*Inf.*), unfriendly, unkind, unpleasant, vague

niche alcove, corner, hollow, nook, opening, recess

nick chip, cut, damage, dent, mark, notch, scar, score, scratch, snick

nickname diminutive, epithet, familiar name, handle (*Sl.*), label, pet name, moniker (*Sl.*), sobriquet

niggardly avaricious, close, covetous, frugal, grudging, mean,

mercenary, miserly, near (*Inf.*), parsimonious, penurious, Scroogelike, sordid, sparing, stinging, stingy, tightfisted, ungenerous
Antonyms bountiful, generous, liberal, munificent

niggle 1. carp, cavil, criticize, find fault, fuss 2. annoy, irritate, rankle, worry

niggling 1. cavilling, finicky, fussy, insignificant, minor, nit-picking (*Inf.*), pettifogging, petty, piddling (*Inf.*), quibbling, trifling, unimportant 2. gnawing, irritating, persistent, troubling, worrying

night dark, darkness, dead of night, hours of darkness, nighttime, night watches

nightfall crepuscule, dusk, eve (*Archaic*), evening, eventide, gloaming, sundown, sunset, twilight, vespers
Antonyms aurora (*Literary*), cockcrow, dawn, dawning, daybreak, daylight, morning, sunrise

nightmare 1. bad dream, hallucination, incubus, succubus 2. horror, ordeal, torment, trial, tribulation

nil duck, love, naught, *nihil*, none, nothing, zero, zilch (*Sl.*)

nimble active, agile, alert, brisk, deft, dexterous, lively, nippy (*Brit. inf.*), proficient, prompt, quick, quick-witted, ready, smart, sprightly, spry, swift
Antonyms awkward, clumsy, dull, heavy, inactive, indolent, lethargic, slow

nip[1] *v.* bite, catch, clip, compress, grip, nibble, pinch, snag, snap, snip, squeeze, tweak, twitch

nip[2] *n.* dram, draught, drop, finger, mouthful, peg (*Brit.*), portion, shot (*Inf.*), sip, snifter (*Inf.*), soupçon, sup, swallow, taste

nippy biting, chilly, nipping, sharp, stinging

nitty-gritty basics, brass tacks (*Inf.*), core, crux, essence, essentials, facts, fundamentals, gist, heart of the matter, reality, substance

nobility 1. aristocracy, elite, high society, lords, nobles, patricians, peerage, ruling class, upper class **2.** dignity, eminence, excellence, grandeur, greatness, illustriousness, loftiness, magnificence, majesty, nobleness, stateliness, sublimity, superiority, worthiness **3.** honour, incorruptibility, integrity, uprightness, virtue

noble *n.* **1.** aristocrat, lord, nobleman, peer ~*adj.* **2.** aristocratic, blue-blooded, gentle (*Archaic*), highborn, lordly, patrician, titled **3.** august, dignified, distinguished, elevated, eminent, excellent, grand, great, imposing, impressive, lofty, splendid, stately **4.** generous, honourable, magnanimous, upright, virtuous, worthy
Antonyms *n.* commoner, peasant, serf ~*adj.* base, contemptible, despicable, dishonest, humble, ignoble, insignificant, lowborn, lowly, mean, modest, peasant, plain, plebeian, selfish, vulgar

nobody 1. no-one **2.** cipher, lightweight (*Inf.*), menial, nonentity, nothing (*Inf.*)
Antonyms big noise (*Brit. sl.*), big shot (*Sl.*), celeb (*Inf.*), celebrity, personage, star, superstar, V.I.P.

nocturnal night, nightly, nighttime, of the night

nod *v.* **1.** acknowledge, bob, bow, dip, duck, gesture, indicate, salute, signal **2.** agree, assent, concur, show agreement **3.** be sleepy, doze, droop, drowse, nap, sleep, slump ~*n.* **4.** acknowledgment, beck, gesture, greeting, indication, salute, sign, signal

noise *n.* babble, blare, clamour, clatter, commotion, cry, din, fracas, hubbub, outcry, pandemonium, racket, row, sound, talk, tumult, uproar

noisy boisterous, cacophonous, chattering, clamorous, deafening, ear-splitting, loud, obstreperous, piercing, riotous, strident, tumultuous, turbulent, uproarious, vociferous

Antonyms hushed, quiet, silent, still, subdued, tranquil, tuneful

nomad drifter, itinerant, migrant, rambler, rover, vagabond, wanderer

nomadic itinerant, migrant, migratory, pastoral, peripatetic, roaming, roving, travelling, vagrant, wandering

nominal formal, ostensible, pretended, professed, puppet, purported, self-styled, so-called, *soi-disant*, supposed, theoretical, titular

nominate appoint, assign, choose, commission, designate, elect, elevate, empower, name, present, propose, recommend, select, submit, suggest, term

nomination appointment, choice, designation, election, proposal, recommendation, selection, suggestion

nominee aspirant, candidate, contestant, entrant, favourite, protégé, runner

nonchalant airy, apathetic, blasé, calm, careless, casual, collected, cool, detached, dispassionate, indifferent, insouciant, laid-back (*Inf.*), offhand, unconcerned, unemotional, unperturbed
Antonyms anxious, caring, concerned, involved, worried

noncommittal ambiguous, careful, cautious, circumspect, discreet, equivocal, evasive, guarded, indefinite, neutral, politic, reserved, tactful, temporizing, tentative, unrevealing, vague, wary

nonconformist dissenter, dissentient, eccentric, heretic, iconoclast, individualist, maverick, protester, radical, rebel
Antonyms Babbitt (*U.S.*), conventionalist, stick-in-the-mud (*Inf.*), traditionalist, yes man

nondescript characterless, common or garden (*Inf.*), commonplace, dull, featureless, indeterminate, mousy, ordinary, unclassifiable, unclassified, undistinguished, unexceptional, uninspiring, uninteresting, unmemorable, unremarkable, vague

none nil, nobody, no-one, no part, not a bit, not any, nothing, not one, zero

nonentity cipher, lightweight (*Inf.*), mediocrity, nobody, small fry, unimportant person

nonessential dispensable, excessive, expendable, extraneous, inessential, peripheral, superfluous, unimportant, unnecessary
Antonyms appropriate, essential, important, indispensable, significant, vital

nonetheless despite that, even so, however, in spite of that, nevertheless, yet

nonexistent chimerical, fancied, fictional, hallucinatory, hypothetical, illusory, imaginary, imagined, insubstantial, legendary, missing, mythical, unreal
Antonyms actual, existent, existing, genuine, real, true, veritable

nonsense absurdity, balderdash, blather, bombast, bunk (*Inf.*), claptrap (*Inf.*), crap (*Sl.*), double Dutch (*Brit. inf.*), drivel, fatuity, folly, foolishness, gibberish, inanity, jest, ludicrousness, ridiculousness, rot, rubbish, senselessness, silliness, stuff, stupidity, trash, twaddle, waffle (*Brit. inf.*)

nonstop 1. *adj.* ceaseless, constant, continuous, direct, endless, incessant, interminable, relentless, steady, unbroken, unending, unfaltering, uninterrupted, unremitting 2. *adv.* ceaselessly, constantly, continuously, directly, endlessly, incessantly, interminably, relentlessly, steadily, unbrokenly, unendingly, unfalteringly, uninterruptedly, unremittingly, without stopping
Antonyms *adj.* broken, discontinuous, fitful, intermittent, irregular, occasional, periodic, punctuated, recurrent, spasmodic, sporadic, stop-go (*Inf.*)

nook alcove, cavity, corner, cranny, crevice, cubbyhole, hide-

out, inglenook (*Brit.*), niche, opening, recess, retreat

norm average, benchmark, criterion, mean, measure, model, pattern, rule, standard, type, yardstick

normal accustomed, acknowledged, average, common, conventional, habitual, natural, ordinary, popular, regular, routine, run-of-the-mill, typical, usual
Antonyms abnormal, exceptional, irregular, peculiar, rare, remarkable, singular, uncommon, unnatural, unusual

nostalgia homesickness, longing, pining, regret, regretfulness, remembrance, reminiscence, wistfulness, yearning

nostalgic emotional, homesick, longing, maudlin, regretful, sentimental, wistful

notable 1. *adj.* celebrated, conspicuous, distinguished, eminent, evident, extraordinary, famous, manifest, marked, memorable, noteworthy, noticeable, notorious, outstanding, pre-eminent, pronounced, rare, remarkable, renowned, striking, uncommon, unusual, well-known 2. *n.* celeb (*Inf.*), celebrity, dignitary, notability, personage, V.I.P., worthy
Antonyms anonymous, concealed, hidden, imperceptible, obscure, unknown, vague

notation characters, code, script, signs, symbols, system

notch *n.* cleft, cut, incision, indentation, mark, nick, score

note *n.* 1. annotation, comment, communication, epistle, gloss, jotting, letter, memo, memorandum, message, minute, record, remark, reminder 2. indication, mark, sign, symbol, token 3. heed, notice, observation, regard ~4. denote, designate, indicate, mark, mention, notice, observe, perceive, record, register, remark, see

noted acclaimed, celebrated, conspicuous, distinguished, eminent, famous, illustrious, notable,

notorious, prominent, recognized, renowned, well-known
Antonyms infamous, obscure, undistinguished, unknown

noteworthy exceptional, extraordinary, important, notable, outstanding, remarkable, significant, unusual
Antonyms commonplace, insignificant, normal, ordinary, pedestrian, run-of-the-mill, unexceptional, unremarkable

nothing bagatelle, cipher, emptiness, naught, nobody, nonentity, nonexistence, nothingness, nought, nullity, trifle, void, zero

notice v. 1. detect, discern, distinguish, heed, mark, mind, note, observe, perceive, remark, see, spot ~n. 2. cognizance, consideration, heed, note, observation, regard 3. advice, announcement, communication, instruction, intelligence, intimation, news, notification, order, warning 4. advertisement, comment, criticism, poster, review, sign
Antonyms v. disregard, ignore, neglect, over-look ~n. disregard, ignorance, neglect, omission, oversight

noticeable appreciable, clear, conspicuous, distinct, evident, manifest, observable, obvious, perceptible, plain, striking, unmistakable

notification advice, alert, announcement, declaration, information, intelligence, message, notice, notifying, publication, statement, telling, warning

notify acquaint, advise, alert, announce, apprise, declare, inform, publish, tell, warn

notion 1. apprehension, belief, concept, conception, idea, impression, inkling, judgment, knowledge, opinion, sentiment, understanding, view 2. caprice, desire, fancy, impulse, inclination, whim, wish

notoriety dishonour, disrepute, infamy, obloquy, opprobrium, scandal

notorious 1. dishonourable, disreputable, infamous, opprobrious, scandalous 2. blatant, flagrant, glaring, obvious, open, overt, patent, undisputed

notwithstanding although, despite, however, nevertheless, nonetheless, though, yet

nought naught, nil, nothing, nothingness, zero

nourish attend, feed, furnish, nurse, nurture, supply, sustain, tend

nourishing alimentative, beneficial, healthful, health-giving, nutritious, nutritive, wholesome

nourishment aliment, diet, food, nutriment, nutrition, sustenance, viands, victuals

novel 1. adj. different, fresh, innovative, new, original, rare, singular, strange, uncommon, unfamiliar, unusual 2. n. fiction, narrative, romance, story, tale
Antonyms adj. ancient, common, customary, familiar, habitual, old-fashioned, ordinary, run-of-the-mill, traditional, usual

novelty 1. freshness, innovation, newness, oddity, originality, strangeness, surprise, unfamiliarity, uniqueness 2. bagatelle, bauble, curiosity, gadget, gewgaw, gimcrack, gimmick, knick-knack, memento, souvenir, trifle, trinket

novice amateur, apprentice, beginner, convert, learner, neophyte, newcomer, novitiate, probationer, proselyte, pupil, tyro
Antonyms ace, doyen, expert, grandmaster, master, maven, old hand, professional, teacher

now at once, immediately, instanter (Law), instantly, presently (Scot. & U.S.), promptly, straightaway

nucleus basis, centre, core, focus, heart, kernel, nub, pivot

nude au naturel, bare, disrobed, exposed, in one's birthday suit (Inf.), in the altogether (Inf.), in the buff (Inf.), naked, starkers (Inf.), stark-naked, stripped, unclad, unclothed, uncovered, undraped, undressed

Antonyms attired, clothed, covered, dressed

nudge v. bump, dig, elbow, jog, poke, prod, push, shove, touch

nudity bareness, dishabille, nakedness, nudism, undress

nugget chunk, clump, hunk, lump, mass, piece

nuisance annoyance, bore, bother, inconvenience, infliction, irritation, offence, pest, plague, problem, trouble, vexation
Antonyms benefit, blessing, delight, happiness, joy, pleasure, satisfaction

numb 1. adj. benumbed, dead, deadened, frozen, immobilized, insensible, insensitive, paralysed, stupefied, torpid, unfeeling **2.** v. benumb, deaden, dull, freeze, immobilize, paralyse, stun, stupefy
Antonyms adj. feeling, responsive, sensitive, sentient

number n. **1.** character, count, digit, figure, integer, numeral, sum, total, unit **2.** aggregate, amount, collection, company, crowd, horde, many, multitude, quantity, throng **3.** copy, edition, imprint, issue, printing ~v. **4.** account, add, calculate, compute, count, enumerate, include, reckon, tell, total
Antonyms n. insufficiency, lack, scantiness, scarcity, shortage,

want ~v. conjecture, guess, theorize

numbness deadness, dullness, insensibility, insensitivity, paralysis, stupefaction, torpor, unfeelingness

numeral character, cipher, digit, figure, integer, number, symbol

numerous abundant, copious, many, plentiful, profuse, several
Antonyms few, not many, scarcely any

nunnery abbey, cloister, convent, house, monastery

nurse v. **1.** care for, look after, minister to, tend, treat **2.** breast-feed, feed, nourish, nurture, suckle, wet-nurse **3.** Fig. cherish, cultivate, encourage, foster, harbour, keep alive, preserve, promote, succour, support

nurture n. **1.** diet, food, nourishment ~v. **2.** feed, nourish, nurse, support, sustain, tend **3.** bring up, cultivate, develop, discipline, educate, instruct, rear, school, train
Antonyms v. deprive, disregard, ignore, neglect, overlook

nutrition food, nourishment, nutriment, sustenance

nutritious alimental, alimentative, beneficial, healthful, health-giving, invigorating, nourishing, nutritive, strengthening, wholesome

O

oasis *Fig.* haven, island, refuge, resting place, retreat, sanctuary, sanctum

oath 1. affirmation, avowal, bond, pledge, promise, sworn statement, vow, word 2. blasphemy, curse, cuss (*Inf.*), expletive, imprecation, malediction, profanity, strong language, swearword

obedience accordance, acquiescence, agreement, compliance, conformability, deference, docility, dutifulness, duty, observance, respect, reverence, submission, submissiveness, subservience, tractability
Antonyms defiance, disobedience, insubordination, obstinacy, recalcitrance, stubbornness, wilfulness

obedient acquiescent, amenable, biddable, compliant, deferential, docile, duteous, dutiful, law-abiding, observant, regardful, respectful, submissive, subservient, tractable, under control, well-trained, yielding
Antonyms arrogant, contrary, disobedient, disrespectful, intractable, obdurate, obstinate, rebellious, stubborn, undutiful, ungovernable, unmanageable, unruly, wayward

obese corpulent, Falstaffian, fat, fleshy, gross, heavy, outsize, overweight, paunchy, plump, podgy, portly, roly-poly, rotund, stout, tubby, well-upholstered (*Inf.*)

obey 1. abide by, act upon, adhere to, be ruled by, carry out, comply, conform, discharge, do what is expected, embrace, execute, follow, fulfil, heed, keep, mind, observe, perform, respond, serve 2. bow to, come to heel, do what one is told, get into line, give in, give way, knuckle under (*Inf.*), submit, surrender (to), take orders from, toe the line, yield
Antonyms contravene, defy, disobey, disregard, ignore, rebel, transgress, violate

object[1] *n.* 1. article, body, entity, fact, item, phenomenon, reality, thing 2. aim, butt, focus, recipient, target, victim 3. design, end, end in view, end purpose, goal, idea, intent, intention, motive, objective, point, purpose, reason

object[2] *v.* argue against, demur, expostulate, oppose, protest, raise objections, take exception
Antonyms accept, acquiesce, admire, agree, approve, assent, compliment, comply, concur, consent, like, relish, welcome

objection cavil, censure, counter-argument, demur, doubt, exception, niggle (*Inf.*), opposition, protest, remonstrance, scruple
Antonyms acceptance, affirmation, agreement, approbation, assent, concession, endorsement, support

objectionable abhorrent, deplorable, disagreeable, dislikable, displeasing, distasteful, exceptionable, indecorous, insufferable, intolerable, noxious, obnoxious, offensive, regrettable, repugnant, unacceptable, undesirable, unpleasant, unseemly, unsociable
Antonyms acceptable, agreeable, desirable, likable, pleasant, pleasing, welcome

objective 1. *adj.* detached, disinterested, dispassionate, equitable, even-handed, fair, impartial, impersonal, judicial, just, open-minded, unbiased, uncoloured, unemotional, uninvolved, unprejudiced 2. *n.* aim, ambition, aspiration, design, end, end in

view, goal, intention, mark, object, purpose, target
Antonyms (*sense 1*) abstract, biased, personal, prejudiced, subjective, theoretical, unfair, unjust
obligation accountability, accountableness, burden, charge, compulsion, duty, liability, must, onus, requirement, responsibility, trust
obligatory binding, coercive, compulsory, *de rigueur*, enforced, essential, imperative, mandatory, necessary, required, requisite, unavoidable
Antonyms discretionary, elective, noncompulsory, optional, voluntary
oblige 1. bind, coerce, compel, constrain, force, impel, make, necessitate, obligate, require 2. accommodate, benefit, do (someone) a favour *or* a kindness, favour, gratify, indulge, please, put oneself out for, serve
Antonyms (*sense 2*) bother, discommode, disoblige, disrupt, inconvenience, put out, trouble
obliging accommodating, agreeable, amiable, civil, complaisant, considerate, cooperative, courteous, eager to please, friendly, good-natured, helpful, kind, polite, willing
Antonyms discourteous, disobliging, inconsiderate, rude, sullen, surly, unaccommodating, uncooperative, unhelpful, unobliging
oblique angled, aslant, at an angle, inclined, slanted, slanting, sloped, sloping, tilted
obliterate annihilate, blot out, cancel, delete, destroy, destroy root and branch, efface, eradicate, erase, expunge, extirpate, root out, wipe off the face of the earth, wipe out
oblivion 1. abeyance, disregard, forgetfulness, insensibility, neglect, obliviousness, unawareness, unconsciousness, (waters of) Lethe 2. blackness, darkness, eclipse, extinction, limbo, nothingness, obscurity, void

Antonyms (*sense 1*) awareness, consciousness, perception, realization, recognition, sensibility
oblivious blind, careless, deaf, disregardful, forgetful, heedless, ignorant, inattentive, insensible, neglectful, negligent, regardless, unaware, unconcerned, unconscious, unmindful, unobservant
Antonyms alert, attentive, aware, conscious, heedful, mindful, observant, watchful
obnoxious abhorrent, abominable, detestable, disagreeable, disgusting, dislikable, foul, hateable, hateful, horrid, insufferable, loathsome, nasty, nauseating, objectionable, odious, offensive, repellent, reprehensible, repugnant, repulsive, revolting, sickening, unpleasant
obscene bawdy, blue, coarse, dirty, disgusting, Fescennine (*Rare*), filthy, foul, gross, immodest, immoral, improper, impure, indecent, lewd, licentious, loose, offensive, pornographic, prurient, ribald, salacious, scabrous, shameless, smutty, suggestive, unchaste, unwholesome
Antonyms chaste, decent, decorous, inoffensive, modest, proper, pure, refined, respectable, seemly
obscenity 1. bawdiness, blueness, coarseness, dirtiness, filthiness, foulness, grossness, immodesty, impurity, lewdness, licentiousness, pornography, prurience, salacity, smuttiness, suggestiveness, vileness 2. four-letter word, impropriety, indecency, indelicacy, profanity, smut, swearword, vulgarism
obscure adj. 1. abstruse, ambiguous, arcane, concealed, confusing, cryptic, deep, doubtful, enigmatic, esoteric, hazy, hidden, incomprehensible, indefinite, intricate, involved, mysterious, occult, opaque, recondite, unclear, vague 2. blurred, clouded, cloudy, dim, dusky, faint, gloomy, indistinct, murky, obfuscated, shadowy, shady, sombre, tenebrous,

unlit, veiled ~ v. **3.** conceal, cover, disguise, hide, muddy, obfuscate, screen, throw a veil over, veil **4.** adumbrate, bedim, befog, block, block out, blur, cloak, cloud, darken, dim, dull, eclipse, mask, overshadow, shade, shroud **Antonyms** (senses 1 & 2) apparent, bright, clear, conspicuous, definite, distinct, evident, explicit, intelligible, lucid, manifest, obvious, plain, prominent, sharp, significant, straightforward, transparent, unmistakable, well-defined ~ v. brighten, clarify, disclose, explain, expose, reveal, show, uncover, unmask, unveil

obscurity 1. abstruseness, ambiguity, complexity, impenetrableness, incomprehensibility, intricacy, reconditeness, vagueness **2.** darkness, dimness, dusk, duskiness, gloom, haze, haziness, indistinctness, murkiness, shadowiness, shadows **3.** inconspicuousness, ingloriousness, insignificance, lowliness, namelessness, nonrecognition, unimportance

observance 1. adherence to, attention, carrying out, celebration, compliance, discharge, fulfilment, heeding, honouring, notice, observation, performance **2.** ceremonial, ceremony, custom, fashion, form, formality, practice, rite, ritual, service, tradition **Antonyms** (sense 1) disdain, disregard, evasion, heedlessness, inattention, neglect, nonobservance, omission, oversight

observant alert, attentive, eagle-eyed, heedful, mindful, obedient, perceptive, quick, sharp-eyed, submissive, vigilant, watchful, wide-awake **Antonyms** distracted, dreamy, heedless, inattentive, indifferent, negligent, preoccupied, unobservant

observation attention, cognition, consideration, examination, experience, information, inspection, knowledge, monitoring, notice, review, scrutiny, study, surveillance, watching

observe 1. detect, discern, discover, espy, note, notice, perceive, see, spot, witness **2.** contemplate, keep an eye on (Inf.), keep under observation, look at, monitor, pay attention to, regard, scrutinize, study, survey, view, watch **3.** animadvert, comment, declare, mention, note, opine, remark, say, state **4.** abide by, adhere to, comply, conform to, follow, fulfil, heed, honour, keep, mind, obey, perform, respect **5.** celebrate, commemorate, keep, remember, solemnize **Antonyms** (sense 4) disregard, ignore, miss, neglect, omit, overlook, violate

observer beholder, bystander, commentator, eyewitness, looker-on, onlooker, spectator, spotter, viewer, watcher, witness

obsessive besetting, compulsive, consuming, fixed, gripping, haunting, tormenting, unforgettable

obsolescent ageing, declining, dying out, not with it (Inf.), on the decline, on the wane, on the way out, past its prime, waning

obsolete anachronistic, ancient, antediluvian, antiquated, antique, archaic, bygone, dated, démodé, discarded, disused, extinct, musty, old, old-fashioned, old hat, out, outmoded, out of date, out of fashion, out of the ark (Inf.), outworn, passé, superannuated, vieux jeu **Antonyms** à la mode, contemporary, current, fashionable, in, in vogue, modern, new, present day, trendy (Inf.), up-to-date

obstacle bar, barrier, check, difficulty, hindrance, hitch, hurdle, impediment, interference, interruption, obstruction, snag, stumbling block **Antonyms** advantage, aid, asset, assistance, benefit, crutch, help, support

obstinate contumacious, determined, dogged, firm, headstrong, immovable, inflexible, intractable, intransigent, mulish, opin-

ionated, persistent, pertinacious, perverse, pig-headed, recalcitrant, refractory, self-willed, steadfast, strong-minded, stubborn, tenacious, unyielding, wilful
Antonyms amenable, biddable, complaisant, compliant, docile, flexible, irresolute, manageable, obedient, submissive, tractable, undecided, wavering

obstruct arrest, bar, barricade, block, bring to a standstill, check, choke, clog, cumber, curb, cut off, frustrate, get in the way of, hamper, hamstring, hide, hinder, hold up, impede, inhibit, interfere with, interrupt, mask, obscure, prevent, restrict, retard, shield, shut off, slow down, stop, thwart, trammel
Antonyms abet, advance, aid, assist, encourage, favour, further, help, promote, support

obstruction bar, barricade, barrier, blockage, barrier, difficulty, hindrance, impediment, snag, stop, stoppage, trammel
Antonyms aid, assistance, cooperation, encouragement, favour, furtherance, help, support

obstructive awkward, blocking, delaying, hindering, inhibiting, preventative, restrictive, stalling, uncooperative, unhelpful
Antonyms cooperative, encouraging, favourable, helpful, obliging, supportive

obtain achieve, acquire, attain, come by, earn, gain, get, get hold of, get one's hands on, procure, secure
Antonyms forfeit, forgo, give up, hand over, lose, relinquish, renounce, surrender

obtrusive forward, importunate, interfering, intrusive, meddling, nosy, officious, prying, pushy (*Inf.*)

obvious apparent, clear, clear as a bell, conspicuous, distinct, evident, indisputable, manifest, much in evidence, noticeable, open, overt, palpable, patent, perceptible, plain, plain as the

nose on your face (*Inf.*), pronounced, recognizable, right under one's nose (*Inf.*), self-evident, self-explanatory, staring one in the face (*Inf.*), sticking out a mile (*Inf.*), straightforward, transparent, unconcealed, undeniable, undisguised, unmistakable, unsubtle, visible
Antonyms ambiguous, concealed, dark, hidden, imperceptible, inconspicuous, indistinct, invisible, obscure, unapparent, unclear, vague

occasion *n.* **1.** chance, convenience, incident, moment, occurrence, opening, opportunity, time **2.** affair, celebration, event, experience, happening, occurrence **3.** call, cause, excuse, ground(s), inducement, influence, justification, motive, prompting, provocation, reason

occasional casual, desultory, incidental, infrequent, intermittent, irregular, odd, rare, sporadic, uncommon
Antonyms customary, constant, continual, frequent, habitual, incessant, regular, routine, usual

occasionally at intervals, at times, (every) now and then, every so often, from time to time, irregularly, now and again, off and on, on and off, once in a while, on occasion, periodically, sometimes
Antonyms constantly, continually, continuously, frequently, habitually, often, regularly, routinely

occupant addressee, denizen, holder, incumbent, indweller, inhabitant, inmate, lessee, occupier, resident, tenant, user

occupation 1. activity, business, calling, craft, employment, job, line (of work), post, profession, pursuit, trade, vocation, walk of life, work **2.** control, holding, occupancy, possession, residence, tenancy, tenure, use **3.** conquest, foreign rule, invasion, seizure, subjugation

occupied 1. busy, employed, engaged, hard at it (*Inf.*), tied up (*Inf.*), working 2. engaged, full, in use, taken, unavailable

occupy 1. *Often passive* absorb, amuse, busy, divert, employ, engage, engross, entertain, hold the attention of, immerse, interest, involve, keep busy *or* occupied, monopolize, preoccupy, take up, tie up 2. capture, garrison, hold, invade, keep, overrun, seize, take over, take possession of
Antonyms abandon, desert, quit, retreat, vacate, withdraw

occur arise, befall, betide, chance, come about, come (*Inf.*), come to pass (*Archaic*), crop up (*Inf.*), eventuate, happen, materialize, result, take place, turn up (*Inf.*)

occurrence adventure, affair, circumstance, episode, event, happening, incident, instance, proceeding, transaction

odd 1. abnormal, atypical, bizarre, curious, deviant, different, eccentric, exceptional, extraordinary, fantastic, freak, freakish, freaky (*Sl.*), funny, irregular, kinky (*Sl.*), outlandish, out of the ordinary, peculiar, quaint, queer, rare, remarkable, singular, strange, uncanny, uncommon, unconventional, unusual, weird, whimsical 2. leftover, lone, remaining, single, solitary, spare, surplus, unconsumed, uneven, unmatched, unpaired
Antonyms common, customary, even, familiar, habitual, matched, natural, normal, ordinary, paired, permanent, regular, steady, typical, unexceptional, unremarkable, usual

oddity abnormality, anomaly, eccentricity, freak, idiosyncrasy, irregularity, kink (*Sl.*), peculiarity, phenomenon, quirk, rarity

odds 1. advantage, allowance, edge, lead, superiority 2. balance, chances, likelihood, probability 3. *Brit.* difference, disparity, dissimilarity, distinction

odious abhorrent, abominable, detestable, disgusting, execrable, foul, hateful, horrible, horrid, loathsome, obnoxious, offensive, repellent, repugnant, repulsive, revolting, unpleasant, vile

odour aroma, bouquet, essence, fragrance, perfume, redolence, scent, smell, stench, stink

off *adj.* 1. absent, cancelled, finished, gone, inoperative, postponed, unavailable 2. bad, below par, disappointing, disheartening, displeasing, low-quality, mortifying, poor, quiet, slack, substandard, unrewarding, unsatisfactory 3. bad, decomposed, high, mouldy, rancid, rotten, sour, turned

off and on (every) now and again, every once in a while, from time to time, intermittently, now and then, occasionally, on and off, sometimes, sporadically

offbeat bizarre, Bohemian, eccentric, far-out (*Sl.*), freaky (*Sl.*), idiosyncratic, kinky (*Sl.*), novel, oddball (*Chiefly U.S. inf.*), outré, strange, uncommon, unconventional, unorthodox, unusual, way-out (*Inf.*), weird

offence 1. breach of conduct, crime, delinquency, fault, lapse, misdeed, misdemeanour, peccadillo, sin, transgression, trespass, wrong, wrongdoing 2. anger, annoyance, displeasure, hard feelings, huff, indignation, ire (*Literary*), needle (*Sl.*), pique, resentment, umbrage, wounded feelings, wrath

offend 1. affront, annoy, disgruntle, displease, fret, gall, give offence, hurt (someone's) feelings, insult, irritate, miff (*Inf.*), outrage, pain, pique, provoke, put (someone's) back up (*Inf.*), rile, slight, snub, tread on (someone's) toes (*Inf.*), upset, vex, wound 2. be disagreeable to, disgust, make (someone) sick, nauseate, repel, repulse, sicken, turn (someone) off (*Sl.*)
Antonyms (*sense 1*) appease, assuage, conciliate, delight, mollify, placate, please, soothe

offender criminal, crook, culprit, delinquent, lawbreaker, malefactor, miscreant, sinner, transgressor, wrongdoer

offensive adj. 1. abusive, annoying, detestable, discourteous, displeasing, disrespectful, embarrassing, impertinent, insolent, insulting, irritating, objectionable, rude, uncivil, unmannerly 2. abominable, detestable, disagreeable, disgusting, grisly, loathsome, nasty, nauseating, noisome, obnoxious, odious, repellent, revolting, sickening, unpalatable, unpleasant, unsavoury, vile 3. aggressive, attacking, invading ~n. 4. attack, drive, onslaught, push (Inf.)
Antonyms adj. agreeable, attractive, captivating, charming, civil, conciliatory, courteous, defensive, deferential, delightful, pleasant, polite, respectful ~n. defensive

offer v. 1. bid, extend, give, hold out, proffer, put on the market, put under the hammer, put up for sale, tender 2. afford, furnish, make available, place at (someone's) disposal, present, provide, show 3. advance, extend, move, propose, put forth, put forward, submit, suggest 4. be at (someone's) service, come forward, offer one's services, volunteer ~n. 5. attempt, bid, endeavour, essay, overture, proposal, proposition, submission, suggestion, tender
Antonyms (sense 1) recant, refuse, retract, revoke, take back, withdraw, withhold

offering contribution, donation, gift, oblation (in religious contexts), present, sacrifice, subscription, widow's mite

offhand adj. abrupt, aloof, brusque, careless, casual, cavalier, couldn't-care-less, curt, glib, informal, offhanded, perfunctory, take-it-or-leave-it (Inf.), unceremonious, unconcerned, uninterested
Antonyms attentive, careful, grave, intent, planned, premeditated, prepared, responsible, serious, thoughtful

office appointment, business, capacity, charge, commission, duty, employment, function, obligation, occupation, place, post, responsibility, role, service, situation, station, trust, work

officer agent, appointee, bureaucrat, dignitary, executive, functionary, office-holder, official, public servant, representative

official 1. adj. accredited, authentic, authoritative, authorized, bona fide, certified, endorsed, ex cathedra, ex officio, formal, legitimate, licensed, proper, sanctioned, straight from the horse's mouth (Inf.) **2.** n. agent, bureaucrat, executive, functionary, office bearer, officer, representative

officiate chair, conduct, emcee (Inf.), manage, oversee, preside, serve, superintend

officious bustling, dictatorial, forward, impertinent, inquisitive, interfering, intrusive, meddlesome, meddling, mischievous, obtrusive, opinionated, overbusy, overzealous, pragmatical (Rare), pushy (Inf.), self-important

off-load disburden, discharge, dump, get rid of, jettison, shift, take off, transfer, unburden, unload, unship

off-putting daunting, discomfiting, disconcerting, discouraging, dismaying, dispiriting, disturbing, formidable, frustrating, intimidating, unnerving, unsettling, upsetting

offset v. balance out, cancel out, compensate for, counteract, counterbalance, counterpoise, countervail, make up for, neutralize

offshoot adjunct, appendage, branch, by-product, development, limb, outgrowth, spin-off, sprout

often again and again, frequently, generally, many a time, much, oft (Poetic), oftentimes (Archaic), ofttimes (Archaic), over and over again, repeatedly, time after time, time and again

Antonyms hardly ever, infrequently, irregularly, never, now and then, occasionally, rarely, scarely, seldom

oil *v.* grease, lubricate

old 1. advanced in years, aged, ancient, decrepit, elderly, full of years, getting on (*Inf.*), grey, grey-haired, grizzled, hoary, mature, over the hill (*Inf.*), past one's prime, patriarchal, senescent, senile, venerable **2.** antediluvian, antiquated, antique, cast-off, crumbling, dated, decayed, done, hackneyed, obsolete, old-fashioned, outdated, outmoded, out of date, passé, stale, superannuated, timeworn, unfashionable, unoriginal, worn-out **3.** aboriginal, antique, archaic, bygone, early, immemorial, of old, of yore, olden (*Archaic*), original, primeval, primitive, primordial, pristine, remote **4.** age-old, experienced, familiar, hardened, long-established, of long standing, practised, skilled, time-honoured, traditional, versed, veteran, vintage

Antonyms current, fashionable, immature, juvenile, modern, modish, new, novel, recent, up-to-date, young, youthful

old-fashioned ancient, antiquated, archaic, behind the times, corny (*Sl.*), dated, dead, démodé, fusty, musty, not with it (*Inf.*), obsolescent, obsolete, oldfangled, (old-)fogyish, old hat, old-time, outdated, outmoded, out of date, out of style, out of the ark (*Inf.*), passé, past, square (*Inf.*), superannuated, unfashionable

Antonyms chic, contemporary, current, fashionable, modern, modish, trendy (*Inf.*), up-to-date, voguish, with-it (*Sl.*)

omen augury, foreboding, foretoken, indication, portent, premonition, presage, prognostic, prognostication, sign, straw in the wind, warning, writing on the wall

ominous baleful, dark, fateful, foreboding, inauspicious, menacing, minatory, portentous, premonitory, sinister, threatening, unpromising, unpropitious

Antonyms auspicious, encouraging, favourable, promising, propitious

omission default, exclusion, failure, forgetfulness, gap, lack, leaving out, neglect, noninclusion, oversight

Antonyms addition, inclusion, incorporation, insertion

omit disregard, drop, eliminate, exclude, fail, forget, give (something) a miss (*Inf.*), leave out, leave (something) undone, let (something) slide, miss (out), neglect, overlook, pass over, skip

Antonyms add, enter, include, incorporate, insert, put in

omnipotent all-powerful, almighty, supreme

Antonyms feeble, frail, impotent, incapable, inferior, powerless, vulnerable, weak

once 1. at one time, formerly, in the old days, in the past, in times gone by, in times past, long ago, once upon a time, previously **2. at once a.** directly, forthwith, immediately, instantly, now, right away, straight away, straightway (*Archaic*), this (very) minute, without delay, without hesitation **b.** at *or* in one go (*Inf.*), at the same time, simultaneously, together

one-sided biased, coloured, discriminatory, inequitable, lop-sided, partial, partisan, prejudiced, unequal, unfair, unjust

Antonyms equal, equitable, fair, impartial, just, unbiased, uncoloured, unprejudiced

onlooker bystander, eyewitness, looker-on, observer, spectator, viewer, watcher, witness

only 1. *adv.* at most, barely, exclusively, just, merely, purely, simply **2.** *adj.* exclusive, individual, lone, one and only, single, sole, solitary, unique

onslaught assault, attack, blitz, charge, offensive, onrush, onset

ooze v. bleed, discharge, drain, dribble, drip, drop, emit, escape, exude, filter, leach, leak, overflow with, percolate, seep, strain, sweat, weep

opaque clouded, cloudy, dim, dull, filmy, hazy, impenetrable, lustreless, muddied, muddy, murky, obfuscated, turbid
Antonyms bright, clear, crystal clear, limpid, lucid, pellucid, transparent, transpicuous

open adj. **1.** agape, ajar, expanded, extended, gaping, revealed, spread out, unbarred, unclosed, uncovered, unfastened, unfolded, unfurled, unlocked, unobstructed, unsealed, yawning **2.** airy, bare, clear, exposed, extensive, free, navigable, not built-up, passable, rolling, spacious, sweeping, uncluttered, uncrowded, unenclosed, unfenced, unsheltered, wide, wide-open **3.** accessible, available, free, general, nondiscriminatory, public, unconditional, unengaged, unoccupied, unqualified, unrestricted, vacant **4.** apparent, avowed, barefaced, blatant, clear, conspicuous, downright, evident, flagrant, frank, manifest, noticeable, obvious, overt, plain, unconcealed, undisguised, visible **5.** arguable, debatable, moot, undecided, unresolved, unsettled, up in the air, yet to be decided **6.** artless, candid, fair, frank, guileless, honest, ingenuous, innocent, natural, sincere, transparent, unreserved **7.** exposed, undefended, unfortified, unprotected ~v. **8.** begin, begin business, commence, get or start the ball rolling, inaugurate, initiate, kick off (Inf.), launch, put up one's plate, set in motion, set up shop, start **9.** clear, crack, throw wide, unbar, unblock, unclose, uncork, uncover, undo, unfasten, unlock, unseal, untie, unwrap **10.** expand, spread (out), unfold, unfurl, unroll
Antonyms adj. (senses 1 & 2)

bounded, closed, concealed, confined, covered, crowded, enclosed, fastened, limited, locked, obstructed, restricted, sealed, shut (senses 3 & 4) covert, disguised, hidden, inaccessible, private, protected, restricted, secret, veiled (sense 6) artful, cunning, introverted, reserved, secretive, sly, withdrawn (sense 7) defended, protected ~v. (sense 8) close, conclude, end, finish, terminate (sense 9) block, close, fasten, lock, obstruct, seal, shut (sense 10) fold

open-air alfresco, outdoor

opening n. **1.** aperture, breach, break, chink, cleft, crack, fissure, gap, hole, interstice, orifice, perforation, rent, rupture, slot, space, split, vent **2.** break (Inf.), chance, look-in (Inf.), occasion, opportunity, vacancy **3.** beginning, birth, commencement, dawn, inauguration, inception, initiation, kickoff (Inf.), launch, launching, onset, outset, start ~adj. **4.** beginning, commencing, early, first, inaugural, initial, initiatory, introductory, maiden, primary
Antonyms (sense 1) blockage, cessation, closing, closure, obstruction, plug, seal, stoppage (sense 3) close, completion, conclusion, culmination, ending, finale, finish, termination, winding up (Inf.)

open-minded broad, broadminded, catholic, dispassionate, enlightened, free, impartial, liberal, reasonable, receptive, tolerant, unbiased, undogmatic, unprejudiced
Antonyms assertive, biased, bigoted, dogmatic, intolerant, narrow-minded, opinionated, pigheaded, prejudiced, uncompromising

operate act, be in action, function, go, perform, run, work
Antonyms break down, conk out (Inf.), cut out (Inf.), fail, falter, halt, seize up, stall, stop

operation **1.** action, affair,

course, exercise, motion, move~
ment, performance, procedure,
process, use, working **2. in op~
eration** effective, functioning,
going, in action, in force, opera~
tive **3.** activity, agency, effect,
effort, force, influence, instru~
mentality, manipulation **4.** affair,
business, deal, enterprise, pro~
ceeding, transaction, undertak~
ing **5.** assault, campaign, exer~
cise, manoeuvre

operational functional, going, in
working order, operative, pre~
pared, ready, usable, viable,
workable, working
Antonyms broken, ineffective,
inoperative, kaput (*Inf.*), non~
functional, on the blink (*Inf.*), out
of order

operator conductor, driver, han~
dler, mechanic, operative, prac~
titioner, skilled employee, tech~
nician, worker

opinion assessment, belief, con~
ception, conjecture, estimation,
feeling, idea, impression, judg~
ment, mind, notion, persuasion,
point of view, sentiment, theory,
view

opinionated adamant, biased,
bigoted, bull-headed, cocksure,
dictatorial, doctrinaire, dogmat~
ic, inflexible, obdurate, obstinate,
overbearing, pig-headed, preju~
diced, self-assertive, single-
minded, stubborn, uncompro~
mising
Antonyms broad-minded, com~
pliant, compromising, dispas~
sionate, flexible, open-minded,
receptive, tolerant, unbiased, un~
bigoted, unprejudiced

opponent adversary, antagonist,
challenger, competitor, contest~
ant, disputant, dissentient, en~
emy, foe, opposer, rival, the
opposition
Antonyms accomplice, ally, as~
sociate, colleague, friend, helper,
mate, supporter

opportune advantageous, appro~
priate, apt, auspicious, conveni~
ent, favourable, felicitous, fit, fit~
ting, fortunate, happy, lucky,

proper, propitious, seasonable,
suitable, timely, well-timed
Antonyms inappropriate, incon~
venient, inopportune, unfavour~
able, unfortunate, unsuitable, un~
timely

opportunity break (*Inf.*), chance,
convenience, hour, look-in (*Inf.*),
moment, occasion, opening,
scope, time

oppose bar, check, combat, con~
front, contradict, counter,
counterattack, defy, face, fight,
fly in the face of, hinder, ob~
struct, prevent, resist, speak
against, stand up to, take a stand
against, take issue with, take on,
thwart, withstand
Antonyms advance, advocate,
aid, back, defend, help, promote,
support

opposed against, antagonistic,
anti (*Inf.*), antipathetic, anti~
thetical, at daggers drawn,
clashing, conflicting, contrary,
dissentient, hostile, incompatible,
inimical, in opposition, opposing,
opposite

opposite *adj.* **1.** corresponding,
facing, fronting **2.** adverse, an~
tagonistic, antithetical, conflict~
ing, contradictory, contrary,
contrasted, diametrically op~
posed, different, differing, di~
verse, hostile, inconsistent, in~
imical, irreconcilable, opposed,
reverse, unlike ~ *n.* **3.** antithesis,
contradiction, contrary, con~
verse, inverse, reverse, the other
extreme, the other side of the
coin (*Inf.*)
Antonyms (*sense 2*) alike, con~
sistent, corresponding, identical,
like, matching, same, similar,
uniform

opposition 1. antagonism, com~
petition, contrariety, counterac~
tion, disapproval, hostility, ob~
struction, obstructiveness, pre~
vention, resistance, unfriendli~
ness **2.** antagonist, competition,
foe, opponent, other side, rival
Antonyms (*sense 1*) agreement,
approval, collaboration, concur~
rence, cooperation, correspond~

ence, friendliness, responsiveness

oppress 1. afflict, burden, depress, dispirit, harass, lie *or*
weigh heavy upon, sadden, take
the heart out of, torment, vex 2.
abuse, crush, harry, maltreat,
overpower, overwhelm, persecute, rule with an iron hand,
subdue, subjugate, suppress,
trample underfoot, tyrannize
over, wrong
Antonyms deliver, emancipate,
free, liberate, loose, release, set
free, unburden

oppression abuse, brutality, calamity, cruelty, hardship, harshness, injury, injustice, iron hand,
maltreatment, misery, persecution, severity, subjection, suffering, tyranny
Antonyms benevolence, clemency, compassion, goodness, humaneness, justice, kindness,
mercy, sympathy, tenderness

oppressive 1. brutal, burdensome, cruel, despotic, grinding,
harsh, heavy, inhuman, onerous,
overbearing, overwhelming, repressive, severe, tyrannical, unjust 2. airless, close, heavy, muggy, overpowering, stifling, stuffy,
suffocating, sultry, torrid
Antonyms (*sense 1*) encouraging, gentle, humane, just, lenient,
merciful, propitious, soft

oppressor autocrat, bully, despot, harrier, intimidator, iron
hand, persecutor, scourge, slave-
driver, taskmaster, tormentor,
tyrant

opt (for) choose, decide (on),
elect, exercise one's discretion
(in favour of), go for (*Inf.*), make
a selection, plump for, prefer
Antonyms decide against, dismiss, eliminate, exclude, preclude, reject, rule out, turn down

optimistic assured, bright, buoyant, buoyed up, cheerful, confident, encouraged, expectant,
hopeful, positive, sanguine
Antonyms despairing, despondent, downhearted, gloomy, glum,
hopeless

optimum *adj.* A1 (*Inf.*), best,
choicest, flawless, highest, ideal,
most favourable *or* advantageous, optimal, peak, perfect,
superlative
Antonyms inferior, least, lowest,
minimal, poorest, worst

option alternative, choice, election, preference, selection

optional discretionary, elective,
extra, noncompulsory, open,
possible, up to the individual,
voluntary
Antonyms compulsory, de
rigueur, mandatory, obligatory,
required

oracle 1. augur, Cassandra,
prophet, seer, sibyl, soothsayer 2.
answer, augury, divination, divine utterance, prediction, prognostication, prophecy, revelation,
vision

oral spoken, verbal, viva voce,
vocal

orator Cicero, declaimer, lecturer, public speaker, rhetorician,
speaker, spellbinder, spieler
(*Inf.*)

oratory declamation, elocution,
eloquence, grandiloquence, public speaking, rhetoric, speechify-
ing, speech-making, spieling
(*Inf.*)

orbit *n.* 1. circle, circumgyration,
course, cycle, ellipse, path, revolution, rotation, track, trajectory
2. *Fig.* ambit, compass, course,
domain, influence, range, reach,
scope, sphere, sphere of influence, sweep ~*v.* 3. circle, circumnavigate, encircle, revolve
around

ordain 1. anoint, appoint, call,
consecrate, destine, elect, frock,
invest, nominate 2. fate, foreordain, intend, predestine, prede-
termine 3. decree, dictate, enact,
enjoin, fix, lay down, legislate,
order, prescribe, pronounce,
rule, set, will

ordeal affliction, agony, anguish,
nightmare, suffering, test, torture, trial, tribulation(s), trou-
ble(s)

order *n.* 1. arrangement, harmo-

ny, method, neatness, orderli~
ness, organization, pattern, plan,
propriety, regularity, symmetry,
system, tidiness **2.** arrangement,
array, categorization, classifica~
tion, codification, disposal, dispo~
sition, grouping, layout, line, line-
up, ordering, placement, pro~
gression, sequence, series, setup
(*Inf.*), structure, succession **3.**
calm, control, discipline, law, law
and order, peace, quiet, tranquil~
lity **4.** caste, class, degree, grade,
hierarchy, pecking order (*Inf.*),
position, rank, status **5.** breed,
cast, class, family, genre, genus,
ilk, kind, sort, species, subclass,
taxonomic group, tribe, type **6.**
behest, command, decree, dic~
tate, direction, directive, injunc~
tion, instruction, law, mandate,
ordinance, precept, regulation,
rule, say-so (*Inf.*), stipulation **7.**
application, booking, commis~
sion, request, requisition, reser~
vation **8.** association, brother~
hood, community, company, fra~
ternity, guild, league, lodge, or~
ganization, sect, sisterhood, soci~
ety, sodality, union ~*v.* **9.** adjure,
bid, charge, command, decree,
direct, enact, enjoin, instruct, or~
dain, prescribe, require **10.** apply
for, authorize, book, call for,
contract for, engage, prescribe,
request, reserve, send away for
11. adjust, align, arrange, cata~
logue, class, classify, conduct,
control, dispose, group, lay out,
manage, marshal, neaten, or~
ganize, put to rights, regulate, set
in order, sort out, systematize,
tabulate, tidy
Antonyms (*senses 1 & 2*) chaos,
clutter, confusion, disarray, dis~
order, jumble, mess, muddle,
pandemonium, shambles ~*v.*
(*sense 11*) clutter, confuse, disar~
range, disorder, disturb, jumble
up, mess up, mix up, muddle,
scramble

orderly *adj.* **1.** businesslike, in
apple-pie order (*Inf.*), in order,
methodical, regular, scien~
tific, shipshape, systematic, sys~
tematized, tidy, trim, well-

organized, well-regulated **2.** con~
trolled, decorous, disciplined,
law-abiding, nonviolent, peace~
able, quiet, restrained, well-
behaved
Antonyms chaotic, disorderly,
disorganized, higgledy-piggledy
(*Inf.*), messy, riotous, sloppy, un~
controlled, undisciplined, unsys~
tematic

ordinary 1. accustomed, common,
customary, established, every~
day, habitual, humdrum, normal,
prevailing, quotidian, regular,
routine, settled, standard, stock,
typical, usual, wonted **2.** common
or garden (*Inf.*), conventional,
familiar, homespun, household,
humble, modest, plain, prosaic,
run-of-the-mill, simple, un~
memorable, unpretentious, un~
remarkable, workaday **3.** aver~
age, commonplace, fair, indiffer~
ent, inferior, mean, mediocre,
pedestrian, second-rate, stereo~
typed, undistinguished, unexcep~
tional, uninspired, unremarkable
Antonyms consequential, distin~
guished, exceptional, extraordi~
nary, important, impressive, in~
spired, novel, outstanding, rare,
significant, superior, uncommon,
unconventional, unique, unusual

organ 1. device, implement, in~
strument, tool **2.** element, mem~
ber, part, process, structure, unit
3. agency, channel, forum, jour~
nal, means, medium, mouth~
piece, newspaper, paper, peri~
odical, publication, vehicle, voice
organism animal, being, body,
creature, entity, living thing,
structure
organization 1. assembling, as~
sembly, construction, coordina~
tion, disposal, formation, form~
ing, formulation, making, man~
agement, methodology, organiz~
ing, planning, regulation, run~
ning, standardization, structuring
2. arrangement, chemistry, com~
position, configuration, confor~
mation, constitution, design, for~
mat, framework, grouping,
make-up, method, organism, pat~

tern, plan, structure, system, unity, whole **3.** association, body, combine, company, concern, confederation, consortium, corporation, federation, group, institution, league, outfit (*Inf.*), syndicate

organize arrange, be responsible for, catalogue, classify, codify, constitute, construct, coordinate, dispose, establish, form, frame, get going (*Inf.*), get together (*Sl.*), group, lay the foundations of, lick into shape, look after, marshal, pigeonhole, put in order, put together, run, see to (*Inf.*), set up, shape, straighten out, systematize, tabulate, take care of
Antonyms confuse, derange, disorganize, disrupt, jumble, mix up, muddle, scramble, upset

orgy 1. bacchanal, bacchanalia, debauch, revel, revelry, Saturnalia **2.** binge (*Inf.*), bout, excess, indulgence, overindulgence, splurge, spree, surfeit

origin 1. base, basis, cause, derivation, *fons et origo*, font (*Poetic*), fountain, fountainhead, occasion, provenance, root, roots, source, spring, wellspring **2.** beginning, birth, commencement, creation, dawning, early stages, emergence, foundation, genesis, inauguration, inception, launch, origination, outset, start
Antonyms conclusion, culmination, death, end, expiry, finale, finish, outcome, termination

original *adj.* **1.** aboriginal, autochthonous, commencing, earliest, early, embryonic, first, infant, initial, introductory, opening, primary, primitive, primordial, pristine, rudimentary, starting **2.** creative, fertile, fresh, imaginative, ingenious, innovative, innovatory, inventive, new, novel, resourceful, seminal, unconventional, unprecedented, untried, unusual **3.** archetypal, authentic, first, first-hand, genuine, master, primary, prototypical ~*n.* **4.** archetype, master,

model, paradigm, pattern, precedent, prototype, standard, type
Antonyms *adj.* antiquated, banal, borrowed, commonplace, conventional, copied, familiar, final, last, latest, normal, old, old-fashioned, ordinary, secondary, stale, standard, stock, traditional, typical, unimaginative, unoriginal, usual ~*n.* copy, imitation, replica, reproduction

originality boldness, break with tradition, cleverness, creativeness, creative spirit, creativity, daring, freshness, imagination, imaginativeness, individuality, ingenuity, innovation, innovativeness, inventiveness, new ideas, newness, novelty, resourcefulness, unconventionality, unorthodoxy
Antonyms conformity, conventionality, imitativeness, normality, orthodoxy, regularity, staleness, traditionalism

originate 1. arise, be born, begin, come, derive, emanate, emerge, flow, issue, proceed, result, rise, spring, start, stem **2.** bring about, conceive, create, develop, discover, evolve, form, formulate, generate, give birth to, inaugurate, initiate, institute, introduce, invent, launch, pioneer, produce, set in motion, set up
Antonyms cease, conclude, culminate, end, expire, finish, terminate, wind up (*Inf.*)

ornament *n.* **1.** accessory, adornment, bauble, decoration, embellishment, frill, furbelow, garnish, gewgaw, knick-knack, trimming, trinket **2.** flower, honour, jewel, leading light, pride, treasure

ornamental attractive, beautifying, decorative, embellishing, for show, showy

ornate aureate, baroque, beautiful, bedecked, busy, convoluted, decorated, elaborate, elegant, fancy, florid, flowery, fussy, high-wrought, ornamented, overelaborate, rococo
Antonyms austere, bare, basic, ordinary, plain, severe, simple,

stark, subdued, unadorned, unfussy

orthodox accepted, approved, conformist, conventional, correct, customary, doctrinal, established, kosher (*Inf.*), official, received, sound, traditional, true, well-established

Antonyms eccentric, heretical, liberal, nonconformist, novel, original, radical, unconventional, unorthodox, unusual

ostensible alleged, apparent, avowed, exhibited, manifest, outward, plausible, pretended, professed, purported, seeming, so-called, specious, superficial, supposed

ostentation affectation, display, exhibitionism, flamboyance, flashiness, flaunting, flourish, pageantry, parade, pomp, pretension, pretentiousness, show, showiness, showing off (*Inf.*), swank (*Inf.*), vaunting, window-dressing

Antonyms humility, inconspicuousness, modesty, plainness, reserve, simplicity, unpretentiousness

ostentatious boastful, conspicuous, crass, dashing, extravagant, flamboyant, flash (*Inf.*), flashy, flaunted, gaudy, loud, obtrusive, pompous, pretentious, showy, swanky (*Inf.*), vain, vulgar

Antonyms conservative, inconspicuous, low-key, modest, plain, reserved, simple, sombre

other *adj.* 1. added, additional, alternative, auxiliary, extra, further, more, spare, supplementary 2. contrasting, different, dissimilar, distinct, diverse, remaining, separate, unrelated, variant

otherwise *adv.* if not, or else, or then

out *adj.* 1. impossible, not allowed, not on (*Inf.*), ruled out, unacceptable 2. abroad, absent, away, elsewhere, gone, not at home, outside

outbreak burst, epidemic, eruption, explosion, flare-up, flash, outburst, rash, spasm, upsurge

outcast *n.* castaway, derelict, displaced person, exile, leper, pariah, *persona non grata*, refugee, reprobate, untouchable, vagabond, wretch

outcome aftereffect, aftermath, conclusion, consequence, end, end result, issue, payoff (*Inf.*), result, upshot

outcry clamour, commotion, complaint, cry, exclamation, howl, hue and cry, hullaballoo, noise, outburst, protest, scream, screech, uproar, yell

outdated antiquated, antique, archaic, behind the times (*Inf.*), démodé, obsolete, old-fashioned, outmoded, out of date, out of style, passé, unfashionable

Antonyms à la mode, all the rage, contemporary, current, fashionable, in vogue, modern, modish, stylish, trendy (*Inf.*), up-to-date, with it (*Inf.*)

outdoor alfresco, open-air, out-of-door(s), outside

Antonyms indoor, inside, interior, within

outer exposed, exterior, external, outlying, outside, outward, peripheral, remote, superficial, surface

Antonyms central, closer, inner, inside, interior, internal, inward, nearer

outfit 1. *n.* accoutrements, clothes, costume, ensemble, garb, gear, get-up (*Inf.*), kit, rig-out (*Inf.*), suit, togs (*Inf.*), trappings 2. *v.* accoutre, appoint, equip, fit out, furnish, kit out, provision, stock, supply, turn out

outgoing departing, ex-, former, last, leaving, past, retiring, withdrawing

Antonyms arriving, entering, incoming

outgoings costs, expenditure, expenses, outlay, overheads

outing excursion, expedition, jaunt, pleasure trip, spin (*Inf.*), trip

outlandish alien, barbarous, bizarre, eccentric, exotic, fantastic, far-out (*Sl.*), foreign, freakish, grotesque, outré, preposterous, queer, strange, unheard-of, weird

outlaw 1. *n.* bandit, brigand, desperado, fugitive, highwayman, marauder, outcast, pariah, robber 2. *v.* ban, banish, bar, condemn, disallow, embargo, exclude, forbid, interdict, make illegal, prohibit, proscribe, put a price on (someone's) head

outlay *n.* cost, disbursement, expenditure, expenses, investment, outgoings, spending

outlet avenue, channel, duct, egress, exit, means of expression, opening, orifice, release, safety valve, vent, way out

outline *n.* 1. draft, drawing, frame, framework, layout, lineament(s), plan, rough, skeleton, sketch, tracing 2. bare facts, main features, recapitulation, résumé, rough idea, rundown, summary, synopsis, thumbnail sketch 3. configuration, contour, delineation, figure, form, profile, shape, silhouette ~*v.* 4. adumbrate, delineate, draft, plan, rough out, sketch (in), summarize, trace

outlook 1. angle, attitude, frame of mind, perspective, point of view, slant, standpoint, viewpoint, views 2. expectations, forecast, future, prospect

output achievement, manufacture, outturn (*Rare*), product, production, productivity, yield

outrage *n.* 1. atrocity, barbarism, enormity, evil, inhumanity 2. abuse, affront, desecration, indignity, injury, insult, offence, profanation, rape, ravishing, shock, violation, violence 3. anger, fury, hurt, indignation, resentment, shock, wrath ~*v.* 4. affront, incense, infuriate, madden, make one's blood boil, offend, scandalize, shock

outrageous 1. abominable, atrocious, barbaric, beastly, egregious, flagrant, heinous, horrible, infamous, inhuman, iniquitous, nefarious, scandalous, shocking, unspeakable, villainous, violent,

wicked 2. disgraceful, excessive, exorbitant, extravagant, immoderate, offensive, preposterous, scandalous, shocking, steep (*Inf.*), unreasonable

outright *adj.* 1. absolute, arrant, complete, consummate, downright, out-and-out, perfect, pure, thorough, thoroughgoing, total, unconditional, undeniable, unmitigated, unqualified, utter, wholesale 2. definite, direct, flat, straightforward, unequivocal, unqualified ~*adv.* 3. absolutely, completely, explicitly, openly, overtly, straightforwardly, thoroughly, to the full, without hesitation, without restraint 4. at once, cleanly, immediately, instantaneously, instantly, on the spot, straight away, there and then, without more ado

outset beginning, commencement, early days, inauguration, inception, kickoff (*Inf.*), onset, opening, start, starting point

outside *adj.* 1. exterior, external, extramural, extraneous, extreme, out, outdoor, outer, outermost, outward, surface 2. distant, faint, marginal, negligible, remote, slight, slim, small, unlikely ~*n.* 3. exterior, façade, face, front, skin, surface, topside **Antonyms** (*sense 1*) in, indoor, inner, innermost, inside, interior, internal, intramural, inward

outskirts borders, boundary, edge, environs, faubourgs, periphery, purlieus, suburbia, suburbs, vicinity

outspoken abrupt, blunt, candid, direct, explicit, forthright, frank, free, free-spoken, open, plainspoken, round, unceremonious, undissembling, unequivocal, unreserved **Antonyms** diplomatic, gracious, judicious, reserved, reticent, tactful

outstanding 1. celebrated, distinguished, eminent, excellent, exceptional, great, important, impressive, meritorious, preeminent, special, superior,

superlative, well-known **2.** arresting, conspicuous, eye-catching, marked, memorable, notable, noteworthy, prominent, salient, signal, striking **3.** due, ongoing, open, owing, payable, pending, remaining, uncollected, unpaid, unresolved, unsettled
Antonyms (*senses 1 & 2*) dull, inferior, insignificant, mediocre, ordinary, pedestrian, run-of-the-mill, unexceptional, unimpressive

outward *adj.* apparent, evident, exterior, external, noticeable, observable, obvious, ostensible, outer, outside, perceptible, superficial, surface, visible
Antonyms inner, inside, interior, internal, invisible, inward, obscure, unnoticeable

outweigh cancel (out), compensate for, eclipse, make up for, outbalance, overcome, override, predominate, preponderate, prevail over, take precedence over, tip the scales

outwit cheat, circumvent, deceive, defraud, dupe, get the better of, gull (*Archaic*), make a fool or monkey of, outfox, outjockey, outmanoeuvre, outsmart (*Inf.*), outthink, put one over on (*Inf.*), run rings round (*Inf.*), swindle, take in (*Inf.*)

ovation acclaim, acclamation, applause, cheering, cheers, clapping, laudation, plaudits, tribute
Antonyms abuse, booing, catcalls, derision, heckling, jeers, jibes, mockery, ridicule

over *adj.* **1.** accomplished, ancient history (*Inf.*), at an end, by-gone, closed, completed, concluded, done (with), ended, finished, gone, past, settled, up (*Inf.*) ~*adj./adv.* **2.** beyond, extra, in addition, in excess, left over, remaining, superfluous, surplus, unused ~*prep.* **3.** above, on, on top of, superior to, upon **4.** above, exceeding, in excess of, more than ~*adv.* **5.** above, aloft, on high, overhead

overall *adj.* all-embracing, blanket, complete, comprehensive, general, global, inclusive, long-range, long-term, total, umbrella

overbalance capsize, keel over, lose one's balance, lose one's footing, overset, overturn, slip, take a tumble, tip over, topple over, tumble, turn turtle, upset

overbearing arrogant, autocratic, bossy (*Inf.*), cavalier, despotic, dictatorial, dogmatic, domineering, haughty, high-handed, imperious, lordly, magisterial, officious, oppressive, overweening, peremptory, supercilious, superior, tyrannical
Antonyms deferential, humble, modest, self-effacing, submissive, unassertive, unassuming

overcast clouded, clouded over, cloudy, darkened, dismal, dreary, dull, grey, hazy, leaden, lowering, murky, sombre, sunless, threatening
Antonyms bright, brilliant, clear, cloudless, fine, sunny, unclouded

overcharge cheat, clip (*Sl.*), diddle (*Inf.*), do (*Sl.*), fleece, rip off (*Sl.*), short-change, sting (*Inf.*), surcharge

overcome *v.* beat, best, be victorious, come out on top (*Inf.*), conquer, crush, defeat, get the better of, lick (*Inf.*), master, overpower, overthrow, overwhelm, prevail, render incapable (helpless, powerless), rise above, subdue, subjugate, surmount, survive, triumph over, vanquish, weather, worst

overcrowded choked, congested, crammed full, hoatching (*Scot.*), jam-packed, like the Black Hole of Calcutta, overloaded, over-populated, packed (out), swarming

overdo be intemperate, belabour, carry too far, do to death (*Inf.*), exaggerate, gild the lily, go overboard (*Inf.*), go to extremes, lay it on thick (*Inf.*), not know when to stop, overindulge, overplay, overreach, overstate, overuse, overwork, run riot
Antonyms belittle, disparage,

minimize, play down, underplay, underrate, understate, underuse, undervalue

overdone 1. beyond all bounds, exaggerated, excessive, fulsome, immoderate, inordinate, over~ elaborate, preposterous, too much, undue, unnecessary **2.** burnt, burnt to a cinder, charred, dried up, overcooked, spoiled
Antonyms (*sense 1*) belittled, minimized, moderated, played down, underdone, underplayed, understated

overdue behindhand, behind schedule, behind time, belated, late, long delayed, not before time (*Inf.*), owing, tardy, un~ punctual
Antonyms ahead of time, beforehand, early, in advance, in good time, punctual

overemphasize belabour, blow up out of all proportion, lay too much stress on, make a big thing of (*Inf.*), make a mountain out of a molehill (*Inf.*), make something out of nothing, make too much of, overdramatize, overstress

overflow 1. *v.* cover, deluge, drown, flood, inundate, soak, submerge, swamp **2.** *n.* dis~ charge, flash flood, flood, flood~ ing, inundation, overabundance, spill, spilling over, surplus

overflowing abounding, bounti~ ful, brimful, copious, plentiful, profuse, rife, superabundant, swarming, teeming, thronged

overhaul *v.* **1.** check, do up (*Inf.*), examine, inspect, recondition, re~ examine, repair, restore, service, survey ~*n.* **2.** check, checkup, examination, going-over (*Inf.*), inspection, reconditioning, ser~ vice ~*v.* **3.** catch up with, draw level with, get ahead of, over~ take, pass

overhead 1. *adv.* above, aloft, atop, in the sky, on high, sky~ ward, up above, upward **2.** *adj.* aerial, overhanging, roof, upper
Antonyms (*sense 1*) below, be~ neath, downward, underfoot, underneath

overheads burden, oncosts, op~ erating cost(s), running cost(s)

overindulgence excess, immod~ eration, intemperance, overeat~ ing, surfeit

overjoyed delighted, deliriously happy, elated, euphoric, happy as a lark, in raptures, joyful, jubi~ lant, on cloud nine (*Inf.*), only too happy, over the moon (*Inf.*), rap~ turous, thrilled, tickled pink, transported
Antonyms crestfallen, dejected, disappointed, downcast, heart~ broken, miserable, sad, unhappy, woebegone

overload burden, encumber, op~ press, overburden, overcharge, overtax, saddle (with), strain, weigh down

overlook 1. disregard, fail to no~ tice, forget, ignore, leave out of consideration, leave undone, miss, neglect, omit, pass, slight, slip up on **2.** blink at, condone, disregard, excuse, forgive, let bygones be bygones, let one off with, let pass, let ride, make allowances for, pardon, turn a blind eye to, wink at
Antonyms (*sense 1*) discern, heed, mark, note, notice, ob~ serve, perceive, regard, spot

overpower beat, conquer, crush, defeat, get the upper hand over, immobilize, knock out, master, overcome, overthrow, over~ whelm, quell, subdue, subjugate, vanquish

overrate assess too highly, exag~ gerate, make too much of, over~ estimate, overpraise, overprize, oversell, overvalue, rate too highly, think *or* expect too much of, think too highly of

overriding cardinal, compelling, determining, dominant, final, major, number one, overruling, paramount, pivotal, predomi~ nant, prevailing, primary, prime, ruling, supreme, ultimate

overrule alter, annul, cancel, countermand, disallow, invali~ date, make null and void, out~ vote, override, overturn, recall,

repeal, rescind, reverse, revoke, rule against, set aside, veto
Antonyms allow, approve, consent to, endorse, pass, permit, sanction

overseer boss (*Inf.*), chief, foreman, gaffer (*Inf.*), manager, master, super (*Inf.*), superintendent, superior, supervisor

overshadow 1. dominate, dwarf, eclipse, excel, leave *or* put in the shade, outshine, outweigh, render insignificant by comparison, rise above, steal the limelight from, surpass, take precedence over, throw into the shade, tower above **2.** adumbrate, becloud, bedim, cloud, darken, dim, obfuscate, obscure, veil

oversight 1. blunder, carelessness, delinquency, error, fault, inattention, lapse, laxity, mistake, neglect, omission, slip **2.** administration, care, charge, control, custody, direction, handling, inspection, keeping, management, superintendence, supervision, surveillance

overtake catch up with, do better than, draw level with, get past, leave behind, outdistance, outdo, outstrip, overhaul, pass

overthrow *v.* **1.** abolish, beat, bring down, conquer, crush, defeat, depose, dethrone, do away with, master, oust, overcome, overpower, overwhelm, subdue, subjugate, topple, unseat, vanquish **2.** bring to ruin, demolish, destroy, knock down, level, overturn, put an end to, raze, ruin, subvert, upend, upset ~*n.* **3.** defeat, deposition, destruction, dethronement, discomfiture, disestablishment, displacement, dispossession, downfall, end, fall, ousting, prostration, rout, ruin, subjugation, subversion, suppression, undoing, unseating

overture *Often plural* advance, approach, conciliatory move, invitation, offer, opening move, proposal, proposition, signal, tender

overturn 1. capsize, keel over, knock over *or* down, overbalance, reverse, spill, tip over, topple, tumble, upend, upset, upturn **2.** abolish, annul, bring down, countermand, depose, destroy, invalidate, overthrow, repeal, rescind, reverse, set aside, unseat

overwhelm 1. bury, crush, deluge, engulf, flood, inundate, snow under, submerge, swamp **2.** bowl over (*Inf.*), confuse, devastate, knock (someone) for six (*Inf.*), overcome, overpower, prostrate, render speechless, stagger

overwhelming breathtaking, crushing, devastating, invincible, irresistible, overpowering, shattering, stunning, towering, uncontrollable, vast, vastly superior

overwork be a slave-driver *or* hard taskmaster, to burden, burn the midnight oil, drive into the ground, exhaust, exploit, fatigue, oppress, overstrain, overtax, overuse, prostrate, strain, sweat (*Inf.*), wear out, weary, work one's fingers to the bone

overwrought agitated, beside oneself, distracted, excited, frantic, in a state (tizzy, twitter) (*Inf.*), keyed up, on edge, overexcited, overworked, stirred, strung up (*Inf.*), tense, uptight (*Inf.*), worked up (*Inf.*), wound up (*Inf.*)
Antonyms calm, collected, controlled, cool, dispassionate, emotionless, impassive, self-contained, unmoved

owing *adj.* due, outstanding, overdue, owed, payable, unpaid, unsettled

own *adj.* **1.** individual, particular, personal, private ~*pron.* **2. on one's own** alone, by oneself, by one's own efforts, independently, isolated, left to one's own devices, off one's own bat, on one's tod (*Brit. sl.*), singly, (standing) on one's own two feet, unaided, unassisted **3. hold one's own** compete, keep going, keep one's end up, keep one's head above water, maintain one's position ~*v.* **4.** be in possession of, be responsible for, enjoy, have, hold, keep, possess, retain **5. own up (to)** admit, come clean (about) (*Inf.*), confess, make a clean breast of, tell the truth (about) **6.** acknowledge, admit, allow, allow to be valid, avow, concede, con~ fess, disclose, go along with (*Inf.*), grant, recognize

owner holder, landlord, lord, master, mistress, possessor, pro~ prietor, proprietress, proprietrix

ownership dominion, possession, proprietary rights, proprietor~ ship, right of possession, title

P

pace n. **1.** gait, measure, step, stride, tread, walk **2.** clip (Inf.), lick (Inf.), momentum, motion, movement, progress, rate, speed, tempo, time, velocity ~v. **3.** march, patrol, pound, stride, walk back and forth, walk up and down **4.** count, determine, mark out, measure, step

pack n. **1.** back pack, bale, bundle, burden, fardel (Archaic), kit, kit-bag, knapsack, load, package, packet, parcel, rucksack, truss **2.** assemblage, band, bunch, collection, company, crew, crowd, deck, drove, flock, gang, group, herd, lot, mob, set, troop ~v. **3.** batch, bundle, burden, load, package, packet, store, stow **4.** charge, compact, compress, cram, fill, jam, mob, press, ram, stuff, tamp, throng, wedge

package n. **1.** box, carton, container, packet, parcel **2.** amalgamation, combination, entity, unit, whole ~v. **3.** batch, box, pack, packet, parcel (up), wrap, wrap up

packed brimful, chock-a-block, chock-full, congested, cram-full, crammed, crowded, filled, full, hoatching (Scot.), jammed, jam-packed, loaded or full to the gunwales, overflowing, over-loaded, packed like sardines, seething, swarming
Antonyms deserted, empty, uncongested, uncrowded

packet bag, carton, container, package, parcel, poke (Dialect), wrapper, wrapping

pact agreement, alliance, arrangement, bargain, bond, compact, concord, concordat, contract, convention, covenant, deal, league, protocol, treaty, understanding

pad n. **1.** buffer, cushion, protection, stiffening, stuffing, wad **2.** block, jotter, notepad, tablet, writing pad **3.** foot, paw, sole ~v. **4.** cushion, fill, line, pack, protect, shape, stuff **5.** Often with out amplify, augment, eke, elaborate, fill out, flesh out, inflate, lengthen, protract, spin out, stretch

padding filling, packing, stuffing, wadding

paddle¹ **1.** n. oar, scull, sweep **2.** v. oar, propel, pull, row, scull

paddle² dabble, plash, slop, splash (about), stir, wade

pagan 1. n. Gentile, heathen, idolater, infidel, polytheist, unbeliever **2.** adj. Gentile, heathen, heathenish, idolatrous, infidel, irreligious, polytheistic

page¹ **1.** n. folio, leaf, sheet, side

page² **1.** n. attendant, bellboy (U.S.), footboy, pageboy, servant, squire **2.** v. announce, call, call out, preconize, seek, send for, summon

pageant display, extravaganza, parade, procession, ritual, show, spectacle, tableau

pain n. **1.** ache, cramp, discomfort, hurt, irritation, pang, smarting, soreness, spasm, suffering, tenderness, throb, throe (Rare), trouble, twinge **2.** affliction, agony, anguish, bitterness, distress, grief, heartache, misery, suffering, torment, torture, tribulation, woe, wretchedness ~v. **3.** ail, chafe, discomfort, harm, hurt, inflame, injure, smart, sting, throb **4.** afflict, aggrieve, agonize, cut to the quick, disquiet, distress, grieve, hurt, sadden, torment, torture, vex, worry, wound

pained aggrieved, anguished, distressed, hurt, injured, miffed

(*Inf.*), offended, reproachful, stung, unhappy, upset, worried, wounded

painful 1. afflictive, disagreeable, distasteful, distressing, grievous, saddening, unpleasant **2.** aching, agonizing, excruciating, harrowing, hurting, inflamed, raw, smarting, sore, tender, throbbing **3.** arduous, difficult, hard, laborious, severe, tedious, troublesome, trying, vexatious **Antonyms** (*sense 1*) agreeable, enjoyable, pleasant, satisfying (*sense 2*) comforting, painless, relieving, soothing (*sense 3*) a piece of cake (*Inf.*), easy, effortless, interesting, short, simple, straightforward, undemanding

painkiller anaesthetic, analgesic, anodyne, drug, palliative, remedy, sedative

painless easy, effortless, fast, no trouble, pain-free, quick, simple, trouble-free

pains assiduousness, bother, care, diligence, effort, industry, labour, special attention, trouble

painstaking assiduous, careful, conscientious, diligent, earnest, exacting, hard-working, industrious, meticulous, persevering, punctilious, scrupulous, sedulous, strenuous, thorough, thoroughgoing **Antonyms** careless, half-hearted, haphazard, heedless, lazy, negligent, slapdash, slipshod, thoughtless

paint *n.* **1.** colour, colouring, dye, emulsion, pigment, stain, tint ~*v.* **2.** catch a likeness, delineate, depict, draw, figure, picture, portray, represent, sketch **3.** apply, coat, colour, cover, daub, decorate, slap on (*Inf.*)

pair 1. *n.* brace, combination, couple, doublet, duo, match, matched set, span, twins, two of a kind, twosome, yoke **2.** *v.* bracket, couple, join, marry, match, match up, mate, pair off, put together, team, twin, wed, yoke

palatial de luxe, grand, grandiose, illustrious, imposing, luxurious, magnificent, majestic, opulent, plush (*Inf.*), regal, spacious, splendid, stately, sumptuous

pale *adj.* **1.** anaemic, ashen, ashy, bleached, bloodless, colourless, faded, light, pallid, pasty, sallow, wan, washed-out, white, whitish **2.** dim, faint, feeble, inadequate, poor, thin, weak **Antonyms** (*sense 1*) blooming, florid, flushed, glowing, rosy-cheeked, rubicund, ruddy, sanguine

paltry base, beggarly, contemptible, derisory, despicable, inconsiderable, insignificant, low, meagre, mean, Mickey Mouse (*Sl.*), minor, miserable, petty, picayune (*U.S.*), piddling (*Inf.*), pitiful, poor, puny, slight, small, sorry, trifling, trivial, twopenny-halfpenny (*Brit. inf.*), unimportant, worthless, wretched **Antonyms** consequential, considerable, essential, grand, important, major, mega (*Sl.*), significant, valuable

pamper baby, cater to one's every whim, coddle, cosset, fondle, gratify, humour, indulge, mollycoddle, pet, spoil

pamphlet booklet, brochure, circular, folder, leaflet, tract

pan 1. *n.* container, pot, saucepan, vessel **2.** *v. Inf.* censure, criticize, flay, hammer (*Brit.*), knock (*Inf.*), roast (*Inf.*), rubbish (*Inf.*), slag (*Sl.*), slam (*Sl.*), slate (*Inf.*), throw brickbats at (*Inf.*)

panacea catholicon, cure-all, elixir, nostrum, sovereign remedy, universal cure

panache a flourish, brio, dash, élan, flair, flamboyance, spirit, style, swagger, verve

pandemonium babel, bedlam, chaos, clamour, commotion, confusion, din, hubbub, hue and cry, hullabaloo, racket, ruckus (*Inf.*), ruction (*Inf.*), rumpus, tumult, turmoil, uproar **Antonyms** arrangement, calm, hush, order, peace, peacefulness, quietude, repose, stillness, tranquillity

pang ache, agony, anguish, discomfort, distress, gripe, pain, prick, spasm, stab, sting, stitch, throe (*Rare*), twinge, wrench

panic *n.* agitation, alarm, consternation, dismay, fear, fright, horror, hysteria, scare, terror

panorama 1. bird's-eye view, prospect, scenery, scenic view, view, vista **2.** overall picture, overview, perspective, survey

pant *v.* blow, breathe, gasp, heave, huff, palpitate, puff, throb, wheeze

paper *n.* **1.** *Often plural* certificate, deed, documents, instrument, record **2.** *Plural* archive, diaries, documents, dossier, file, letters, records **3.** daily, gazette, journal, news, newspaper, organ, rag (*Inf.*) ~*v.* **4.** cover with paper, hang, line, paste up, wallpaper

par *n.* average, level, mean, median, norm, standard, usual

parable allegory, exemplum, fable, lesson, moral tale, story

parade *n.* **1.** array, cavalcade, ceremony, column, march, pageant, procession, review, spectacle, train **2.** array, display, exhibition, flaunting, ostentation, pomp, show, spectacle, vaunting ~*v.* **3.** defile, march, process **4.** air, brandish, display, exhibit, flaunt, make a show of, show, show off (*Inf.*), strut, swagger, vaunt

paradise bliss, delight, felicity, heaven, seventh heaven, utopia

paradox absurdity, ambiguity, anomaly, contradiction, enigma, inconsistency, mystery, oddity, puzzle

paragon apotheosis, archetype, criterion, cynosure, epitome, exemplar, ideal, jewel, masterpiece, model, nonesuch (*Archaic*), nonpareil, paradigm, pattern, prototype, quintessence, standard

paragraph clause, item, notice, part, passage, portion, section, subdivision

parallel *adj.* **1.** aligned, alongside, coextensive, equidistant, side by side **2.** akin, analogous, complementary, correspondent, corresponding, like, matching, resembling, similar, uniform ~*n.* **3.** analogue, complement, corollary, counterpart, duplicate, equal, equivalent, likeness, match, twin **4.** analogy, comparison, correlation, correspondence, likeness, parallelism, resemblance, similarity

Antonyms *adj.* different, dissimilar, divergent, non-parallel, unlike ~*n.* difference, dissimilarity, divergence, opposite, reverse

paralyse 1. cripple, debilitate, disable, incapacitate, lame **2.** anaesthetize, arrest, benumb, freeze, halt, immobilize, numb, petrify, stop dead, stun, stupefy, transfix

paralysis 1. immobility, palsy, paresis (*Pathol.*) **2.** arrest, breakdown, halt, shutdown, stagnation, standstill, stoppage

paramount capital, cardinal, chief, dominant, eminent, first, foremost, main, outstanding, predominant, pre-eminent, primary, prime, principal, superior, supreme

paraphernalia accoutrements, apparatus, appurtenances, baggage, belongings, clobber (*Brit. sl.*), effects, equipage, equipment, gear, impedimenta, material, stuff, tackle, things, trappings

parasite bloodsucker (*Inf.*), cadger, drone (*Brit.*), hanger-on, leech, scrounger (*Inf.*), sponge (*Inf.*), sponger (*Inf.*)

parcel 1. *n.* bundle, carton, pack, package, packet **2.** *Often with* up do up, pack, package, tie up, wrap

parched arid, dehydrated, dried out *or* up, drouthy (*Scot.*), dry, scorched, shrivelled, thirsty, waterless, withered

pardon 1. *v.* absolve, acquit, amnesty, condone, exculpate, excuse, exonerate, forgive, free, let off (*Inf.*), liberate, overlook, release, remit, reprieve **2.** *n.* abso-

lution, acquittal, allowance, amnesty, condonation, discharge, excuse, exoneration, forgiveness, grace, indulgence, mercy, release, remission, reprieve
Antonyms v. admonish, blame, castigate, censure, chasten, chastise, condemn, discipline, fine, penalize, punish, rebuke ~n. condemnation, guilt, penalty, punishment, redress, retaliation, retribution, revenge, vengeance

pardonable allowable, condonable, excusable, forgivable, minor, not serious, permissible, understandable, venial

parent begetter, father, guardian, mother, procreator, progenitor, sire

parentage ancestry, birth, derivation, descent, extraction, family, line, lineage, origin, paternity, pedigree, race, stirps, stock

parish church, churchgoers, community, congregation, flock, fold, parishioners

park n. estate, garden, grounds, parkland, pleasure garden, recreation ground, woodland

parliament assembly, congress, convocation, council, diet, legislature, senate, talking shop (*Inf.*)

parliamentary congressional, deliberative, governmental, lawgiving, lawmaking, legislative

parlour best room, drawing room, front room, lounge, reception room, sitting room

parody 1. n. burlesque, caricature, imitation, lampoon, satire, send-up (*Brit. inf.*), skit, spoof (*Inf.*), takeoff (*Inf.*) 2. v. burlesque, caricature, do a take-off of (*Inf.*), lampoon, mimic, poke fun at, satirize, send up (*Brit. inf.*), spoof (*Inf.*), take off (*Inf.*), take the piss out of (*Sl.*), travesty

parry 1. block, deflect, fend off, hold at bay, rebuff, repel, repulse, stave off, ward off 2. avoid, circumvent, dodge, duck (*Inf.*),

evade, fence, fight shy of, shun, sidestep

part n. 1. bit, fraction, fragment, lot, particle, piece, portion, scrap, section, sector, segment, share, slice 2. branch, component, constituent, department, division, element, ingredient, limb, member, module, organ, piece, unit 3. behalf, cause, concern, faction, interest, party, side 4. bit, business, capacity, charge, duty, function, involvement, office, place, responsibility, role, say, share, task, work 5. *Theat.* character, lines, role 6. in good part cheerfully, cordially, goodnaturedly, well, without offence 7. in part a little, in some measure, partially, partly, slightly, somewhat, to a certain extent, to some degree ~v. 8. break, cleave, come apart, detach, disconnect, disjoin, dismantle, disunite, divide, rend, separate, sever, split, tear 9. break up, depart, go, go away, go (their) separate ways, leave, part company, quit, say goodbye, separate, split up, take one's leave, withdraw
Antonyms (senses 1 & 2) n. bulk, entirety, mass, totality, whole ~v. (sense 8) adhere, close, combine, hold, join, stick, unite (sense 9) appear, arrive, come, gather, remain, show up (*Inf.*), stay, turn up

partake With in engage, enter into, participate, share, take part

partial 1. fragmentary, imperfect, incomplete, limited, uncompleted, unfinished 2. biased, discriminatory, influenced, interested, one-sided, partisan, predisposed, prejudiced, tendentious, unfair, unjust
Antonyms (sense 1) complete, entire, finished, full, total, whole (sense 2) impartial, objective, unbiased, unprejudiced

partiality 1. bias, favouritism, partisanship, predisposition, preference, prejudice 2. affinity, fondness, inclination, liking, love, penchant, predilection, predis-

position, preference, proclivity, taste, weakness
Antonyms (*sense 1*) disinterest, equity, fairness, impartiality, objectivity(*sense 2*) abhorrence, antipathy, aversion, disgust, disinclination, dislike, distaste, loathing, revulsion
participant associate, contributor, member, partaker, participator, party, shareholder
participate be a participant, be a party to, engage in, enter into, get in on the act, have a hand in, join in, partake, perform, share, take part
Antonyms abstain, boycott, forgo, forsake, forswear, opt out, pass up, refrain from, take no part of
particle atom, bit, crumb, grain, iota, jot, mite, molecule, mote, piece, scrap, shred, speck, tittle, whit
particular *adj.* 1. distinct, exact, express, peculiar, precise, special, specific 2. especial, exceptional, marked, notable, noteworthy, remarkable, singular, uncommon, unusual 3. choosy (*Inf.*), critical, dainty, demanding, discriminating, exacting, fastidious, finicky, fussy, meticulous, nice (*Rare*), overnice, pernickety (*Inf.*), picky (*Inf.*) ~ *n.* 4. Usually plural circumstance, detail, fact, feature, item, specification
Antonyms (*sense 1*) general, imprecise, indefinite, indistinct, inexact, unspecified, vague (*sense 3*) casual, easy, easy to please, indiscriminate, negligent, slack, sloppy, uncritical
particularly decidedly, especially, exceptionally, markedly, notably, outstandingly, peculiarly, singularly, surprisingly, uncommonly, unusually
parting *n.* 1. adieu, departure, farewell, going, goodbye, leave-taking, valediction 2. breaking, detachment, divergence, division, partition, rift, rupture, separation, split

partisan *n.* 1. adherent, backer, champion, devotee, disciple, follower, stalwart, supporter, upholder, votary ~*adj.* 2. biased, factional, interested, one-sided, partial, prejudiced, sectarian, tendentious ~*n.* 3. guerrilla, irregular, resistance fighter, underground fighter
Antonyms *n.* adversary, contender, critic, detractor, foe, knocker, leader, opponent, rival ~*adj.* broad-minded, disinterested, impartial, non-partisan, unbiased, unprejudiced
partition *n.* 1. dividing, division, segregation, separation, severance, splitting 2. barrier, divider, room divider, screen, wall 3. allotment, apportionment, distribution, portion, rationing out, share ~ *v.* 4. apportion, cut up, divide, parcel out, portion, section, segment, separate, share, split up, subdivide
partly halfway, incompletely, in part, in some measure, not fully, partially, relatively, slightly, somewhat, to a certain degree *or* extent, up to a certain point
Antonyms completely, entirely, fully, in full, totally, wholly
partner 1. accomplice, ally, associate, bedfellow, collaborator, colleague, companion, comrade, confederate, copartner, helper, mate, participant, team-mate 2. bedfellow, consort, helpmate, husband, mate, spouse, wife
partnership alliance, association, combine, company, conglomerate, cooperative, corporation, firm, house, society, union
party 1. at-home, bash (*Inf.*), celebration, do (*Inf.*), festivity, function, gathering, get-together (*Inf.*), knees-up (*Brit. inf.*), rave-up (*Brit. sl.*), reception, shindig (*Sl.*), social, social gathering, soirée 2. band, body, bunch (*Inf.*), company, crew, detachment (*Military*), gang, gathering, group, squad, team, unit 3. alliance, association, cabal, clique, coalition, combination, confed~

...n, grouping, ... individual, ...meone ... lapse, flow, ...apse, leave, ...ls, proceed, ...ed, excel, go beyond, outdistance, outdo, outstrip, surmount, surpass, transcend **3.** answer, come up to scratch (*Inf.*), do, get through, graduate, pass muster, qualify, succeed, suffice, suit **4.** befall, come up, develop, fall out, happen, occur, take place **5.** convey, deliver, exchange, give, hand, kick, let have, reach, send, throw, transfer, transmit **6.** accept, adopt, approve, authorize, decree, enact, establish, legislate, ordain, ratify, sanction, validate

Antonyms (*sense 1*) bring *or* come to a standstill, cease, halt, pause, stop (*senses 2 & 3*) be inadequate, be inferior to, be unsuccessful, come a cropper (*Inf.*), fail, lose, suffer defeat (*sense 6*) ban, disallow, invalidate, overrule, prohibit, refuse, reject, veto

pass[2] *n.* **1.** canyon, col, defile, gap, gorge, ravine **2.** authorization, identification, licence, passport, permission, permit, safe-conduct, ticket, warrant

passable acceptable, adequate, admissible, allowable, all right, average, fair, fair enough, mediocre, middling, moderate, not too bad, ordinary, presentable, so-so (*Inf.*), tolerable, unexceptional

Antonyms A-one (*Inf.*), exceptional, extraordinary, first-class, inadequate, inadmissible, marvellous, outstanding, superb, tops (*Sl.*), unacceptable, unsatisfactory

passage **1.** avenue, channel, course, lane, opening, path, road, route, thoroughfare, way **2.** corridor, doorway, entrance, entrance hall, exit, hall, hallway, lobby, passageway, vestibule **3.** clause, excerpt, extract, paragraph, piece, quotation, reading, section, sentence, text, verse **4.** crossing, journey, tour, trek, trip, voyage **5.** allowance, authorization, freedom, permission, right, safe-conduct, visa, warrant

passenger fare, hitchhiker, pillion rider, traveller

passing *adj.* **1.** brief, ephemeral, fleeting, momentary, short, short-lived, temporary, transient, transitory **2.** casual, cursory, glancing, hasty, quick, shallow, short, slight, superficial

passion **1.** animation, ardour, eagerness, emotion, excitement, feeling, fervour, fire, heat, intensity, joy, rapture, spirit, transport, warmth, zeal, zest **2.** adoration, affection, ardour, attachment, concupiscence, desire, fondness, infatuation, itch, keenness, love, lust, the hots (*Sl.*) **3.** bug (*Inf.*), craving, craze, enthusiasm, fancy, fascination, idol, infatuation, mania, obsession **4.** anger, fit, flare-up (*Inf.*), frenzy, fury, indignation, ire, outburst, paroxysm, rage, resentment, storm, vehemence, wrath

Antonyms apathy, calmness, coldness, coolness, frigidity, hate, indifference, unconcern

passionate **1.** amorous, ardent, aroused, desirous, erotic, hot, loving, lustful, sensual, sexy (*Inf.*), wanton **2.** animated, ardent, eager, emotional, enthusiastic, excited, fervent, fervid, fierce, frenzied, heartfelt, impassioned, impetuous, impulsive, intense, strong, vehement, warm, wild, zealous

Antonyms (*sense 1*) cold, frigid, passionless, unloving, unresponsive (*sense 2*) apathetic, calm, cold, half-hearted, indifferent, languorous, nonchalant, subdued, unemotional, unenthusiastic

passive acquiescent, compliant, docile, enduring, inactive, inert, lifeless, long-suffering, nonviolent, patient, quiescent, receptive, resigned, submissive, unassertive, uninvolved, unresisting

Antonyms active, alive, assertive, bossy (*Inf.*), defiant, domineering, energetic, impatient,
involved, lively, spirited, spirited, violent, zippy (*Inf.*)

pass over disregard, forget, ignore, not dwell on, omit, overlook, pass by, take no notice of

past *adj.* 1. accomplished, completed, done, elapsed, ended, extinct, finished, forgotten, gone,
over, over and done with, spent 2.
ancient, bygone, early, erstwhile,
foregoing, former, late, long-ago,
olden, preceding, previous, prior,
quondam, recent ~*n.* 3. background, experience, history, life,
past life ~*adv.* 4. across, beyond,
by, on, over

Antonyms arrived, begun,
coming, future, now, present

pastel *adj.* delicate, light, muted,
pale, soft, soft-hued

pastime activity, amusement,
distraction, diversion, entertainment, game, hobby, leisure, play,
recreation, relaxation, sport

pastoral *adj.* 1. Arcadian, bucolic,
country, georgic (*Literary*), idyl-
lic, rural, rustic, simple 2. cleri-
cal, ecclesiastical, ministerial,
priestly

pasture grass, grassland, grazing,
grazing land, lea (*Poetic*), meadow, pasturage, shieling (*Scot.*)

pat 1. *v.* caress, dab, fondle, pet,
slap, stroke, tap, touch 2. *n.* clap,
dab, light blow, slap, stroke, tap

patch *n.* 1. piece of material,
reinforcement 2. bit, scrap,
shred, small piece, spot, stretch
3. area, ground, land, plot, tract
~*v.* 4. cover, fix, mend, reinforce, repair, sew up

patchy bitty, erratic, fitful, irregular, random, sketchy, spotty,
uneven, variable, varying
Antonyms constant, even, regular, unbroken, unvarying

patent 1. *adj.* apparent, blatant,
clear, conspicuous, downright,
evident, flagrant, glaring, indisputable, manifest, obvious, open,
palpable, transparent, unconcealed, unequivocal, unmistak-

able 2. *n.* copyright,
licence

path 1. footpath, footway,
way, towpath, track, trail, wal
way (*Chiefly U.S.*) 2. avenue,
course, direction, passage, procedure, road, route, track, walk,
way

pathetic affecting, distressing,
heartbreaking, heart-rending,
melting, moving, pitiable, plaintive, poignant, sad, tender,
touching
Antonyms amusing, comical,
droll, entertaining, funny, laughable, ludicrous, ridiculous

pathos pitiableness, pitifulness,
plaintiveness, poignancy, sadness

patience 1. calmness, composure, cool (*Sl.*), equanimity, even
temper, forbearance, imperturbability, restraint, serenity, sufferance, tolerance, toleration 2.
constancy, diligence, endurance,
fortitude, long-suffering, perseverance, persistence, resignation, stoicism, submission
Antonyms (*sense 1*) agitation,
exasperation, excitement, impatience, irritation, nervousness,
passion, restlessness (*sense 2*) irresolution, vacillation

patient *adj.* 1. calm, composed,
enduring, long-suffering, persevering, persistent, philosophical,
quiet, resigned, self-possessed,
serene, stoical, submissive, uncomplaining, untiring 2. accommodating, even-tempered, forbearing, forgiving, indulgent, lenient, mild, tolerant, understanding ~*n.* 3. case, invalid, sick
person, sufferer

patriot chauvinist, flag-waver
(*Inf.*), jingo, lover of one's country, loyalist, nationalist

patriotic chauvinistic, flag-
waving (*Inf.*), jingoistic, loyal,
nationalistic

patrol *n.* 1. guarding, policing,
protecting, rounds, safeguarding,
vigilance, watching 2. garrison,
guard, patrolman, sentinel,
watch, watchman ~*v.* 3. cruise,
guard, inspect, keep guard, keep

watch, make the rounds, police, pound, range, safeguard, walk the beat

patron 1. advocate, angel (Inf.), backer, benefactor, champion, defender, friend, guardian, helper, philanthropist, protector, sponsor, supporter **2.** buyer, client, customer, frequenter, habitué, shopper

patronage 1. aid, assistance, backing, benefaction, championship, encouragement, help, promotion, sponsorship, support **2.** business, clientele, commerce, custom, trade, trading, traffic

patronize 1. be lofty with, look down on, talk down to, treat as inferior, treat condescendingly, treat like a child **2.** assist, back, befriend, foster, fund, help, maintain, promote, sponsor, subscribe to, support **3.** be a customer or client of, buy from, deal with, do business with, frequent, shop at, trade with

patronizing condescending, contemptuous, disdainful, gracious, haughty, lofty, snobbish, stooping, supercilious, superior, toffee-nosed (Sl.)

pattern n. **1.** arrangement, decoration, decorative design, design, device, figure, motif, ornament **2.** arrangement, method, order, orderliness, plan, sequence, system **3.** kind, shape, sort, style, type, variety **4.** design, diagram, guide, instructions, original, plan, stencil, template **5.** archetype, criterion, cynosure, example, exemplar, guide, model, norm, original, paradigm, paragon, prototype, sample, specimen, standard ~v. **6.** copy, emulate, follow, form, imitate, model, mould, order, shape, style

pauper bankrupt, beggar, down-and-out, have-not, indigent, insolvent, mendicant, poor person

pause 1. v. break, cease, delay, deliberate, desist, discontinue, halt, have a breather (Inf.), hesitate, interrupt, rest, stop briefly, take a break, wait, waver **2.** n.

break, breather (Inf.), caesura, cessation, delay, discontinuance, gap, halt, hesitation, interlude, intermission, interruption, interval, let-up (Inf.), lull, respite, rest, stay, stoppage, wait

Antonyms v. advance, continue, proceed, progress ~n. advancement, continuance, progression

pawn v. deposit, gage (Archaic), hazard, hock (Inf., chiefly U.S.), mortgage, pledge, pop (Inf.), stake, wager

pay v. **1.** clear, compensate, cough up (Inf.), discharge, foot, give, honour, liquidate, meet, offer, recompense, reimburse, remit, remunerate, render, requite, reward, settle, square up **2.** be advantageous, benefit, be worthwhile, repay, serve **3.** bestow, extend, give, grant, present, proffer, render **4.** bring in, produce, profit, return, yield ~n. **5.** allowance, compensation, earnings, emoluments, fee, hire, income, payment, recompense, reimbursement, remuneration, reward, salary, stipend, takings, wages

payable due, mature, obligatory, outstanding, owed, owing, receivable, to be paid

pay back get even with (Inf.), get one's own back, reciprocate, recompense, retaliate, settle a score

payment 1. defrayal, discharge, outlay, paying, remittance, settlement **2.** fee, hire, remuneration, reward, wage

pay off 1. discharge, dismiss, fire, lay off, let go, sack (Inf.) **2.** clear, discharge, liquidate, pay in full, settle, square **3.** be effective (profitable, successful), succeed, work

pay out cough up (Inf.), disburse, expend, fork out or over or up (Sl.), lay out (Inf.), shell out (Inf.), spend

peace 1. accord, agreement, amity, concord, harmony **2.** armistice, cessation of hostilities, conciliation, pacification, treaty, truce 3. calm, composure, contentment, placidity, relaxation, repose, serenity 4. calm, calmness, hush, peacefulness, quiet, quietude, repose, rest, silence, stillness, tranquility

peaceable 1. amiable, amicable, conciliatory, dovish, friendly, gentle, inoffensive, mild, nonbelligerent, pacific, peaceful, peace-loving, placid, unwarlike 2. balmy, calm, peaceful, quiet, restful, serene, still, tranquil, undisturbed

peaceful 1. amicable, at peace, free from strife, friendly, harmonious, nonviolent, on friendly or good terms, without hostility 2. calm, gentle, placid, quiet, restful, serene, still, tranquil, undisturbed, unruffled, untroubled 3. conciliatory, irenic, pacific, peaceable, peace-loving, placatory, unwarlike

Antonyms agitated, antagonistic, belligerent, bitter, disquieted, disturbed, hostile, loud, nervous, noisy, Ramboesque, raucous, restless, unfriendly, upset, violent, warlike, wartime

peak n. **1.** aiguille, apex, brow, crest, pinnacle, point, summit, tip, top 2. acme, apogee, climax, crown, culmination, high point, maximum point, ne plus ultra, zenith ~v. 3. be at its height, climax, come to a head, culminate, reach its highest point, reach the zenith

peal 1. n. blast, carillon, chime, clamour, clang, clap, crash, resounding, reverberation, ring, ringing, roar, rumble, sound, tintinnabulation 2. v. chime, crack, crash, resonate, resound, reverberate, ring, roar, roll, rumble, sound, tintinnabulate, toll

peasant 1. churl (Archaic), countryman, hind (Archaic), rustic, son of the soil, swain (Archaic) 2. Inf. boor, churl, country bumpkin, lout, provincial, yokel

peculiar abnormal, bizarre, curious, eccentric, exceptional, extraordinary, far-out (Sl.),

freakish, funny, odd, offbeat, outlandish, out-of-the-way, quaint, queer, singular, strange, uncommon, unconventional, unusual, weird

Antonyms commonplace, conventional, expected, familiar, ordinary, usual

peculiarity abnormality, bizarreness, eccentricity, foible, freakishness, idiosyncrasy, mannerism, oddity, odd trait, queerness, quirk

pedantic abstruse, academic, bookish, didactic, donnish, erudite, formal, fussy, hairsplitting, nit-picking (Inf.), overnice, particular, pedagogic, pompous, precise, priggish, punctilious, scholastic, schoolmasterly, sententious, stilted

pedestal base, dado (Architect.), foot, foundation, mounting, pier, plinth, socle, stand, support

pedestrian 1. n. footslogger, foot-traveller, walker 2. adj. banal, boring, commonplace, dull, flat, humdrum, mediocre, mundane, ordinary, plodding, prosaic, run-of-the-mill, unimaginative, uninspired, uninteresting

Antonyms n. driver ~adj. exciting, fascinating, imaginative, important, interesting, noteworthy, outstanding, remarkable, significant

pedigree n. ancestry, blood, breed, derivation, descent, extraction, family, family tree, genealogy, heritage, line, lineage, race, stemma, stirps, stock

peek v. glance, keek (Scot.), look, peep, peer, snatch a glimpse, sneak a look, spy, squinny, take or have a gander (Inf.), take a look

peel v. decorticate, desquamate, flake off, pare, scale, skin, strip of

peer n. **1.** aristo (Inf.), aristocrat, baron, count, duke, earl, lord, marquess, marquis, noble, nobleman, viscount 2. coequal, compeer, equal, fellow, like, match

peerless beyond compare, excellent, incomparable, matchless, nonpareil, outstanding, second to none, superlative, unequalled, unique, unmatched, unparalleled, unrivalled, unsurpassed

Antonyms commonplace, inferior, mediocre, ordinary, poor, second-rate

peevish acrimonious, cantankerous, captious, childish, churlish, crabbed, cross, crotchety (*Inf.*), crusty, fractious, fretful, grumpy, ill-natured, ill-tempered, irritable, pettish, petulant, querulous, ratty (*Brit. sl.*), short-tempered, snappy, splenetic, sulky, sullen, surly, testy, touchy, waspish, whingeing (*Inf.*)

Antonyms affable, agreeable, cheerful, cheery, easy-going, even-tempered, genial, good-natured, happy, merry, pleasant, sweet

pelt v. assail, batter, beat, belabour, bombard, cast, hurl, pepper, pummel, shower, sling, strike, thrash, throw, wallop (*Inf.*)

pen[1] v. commit to paper, compose, draft, draw up, jot down, write

pen[2] **1.** n. cage, coop, enclosure, fold, hutch, sty **2.** v. cage, confine, coop up, enclose, fence in, hedge, hem in, hurdle, mew (up), shut up or in

penal corrective, disciplinary, penalizing, punitive, retributive

penalize award a penalty against (*Sport*), correct, discipline, handicap, impose a penalty on, inflict a handicap on, punish, put at a disadvantage

penalty disadvantage, fine, forfeit, forfeiture, handicap, mulct, price, punishment, retribution

penance atonement, mortification, penalty, punishment, reparation, sackcloth and ashes

penchant affinity, bent, bias, disposition, fondness, inclination, leaning, liking, partiality, predilection, proclivity,

proneness, propensity, taste, tendency, turn

pending awaiting, forthcoming, hanging fire, imminent, impending, in the balance, in the offing, undecided, undetermined, unsettled, up in the air

penetrate **1.** bore, enter, go through, perforate, pierce, prick, probe, stab **2.** diffuse, enter, get in, infiltrate, permeate, pervade, seep, suffuse

penetration **1.** entrance, entry, incision, inroad, invasion, perforation, piercing, puncturing **2.** acuteness, astuteness, discernment, insight, keenness, perception, perspicacity, sharpness, shrewdness, wit

penniless bankrupt, broke (*Inf.*), cleaned out (*Sl.*), destitute, impecunious, impoverished, indigent, moneyless, necessitous, needy, on one's uppers, penurious, poor, poverty-stricken, ruined, skint (*Brit. sl.*), stony-broke (*Brit. sl.*), strapped (*U.S. sl.*), without a penny to one's name

Antonyms affluent, filthy rich, loaded (*Sl.*), rich, rolling (*Sl.*), wealthy, well-heeled (*Inf.*)

pension allowance, annuity, benefit, superannuation

pensive blue (*Inf.*), cogitative, contemplative, dreamy, grave, in a brown study (*Inf.*), meditative, melancholy, mournful, musing, preoccupied, reflective, ruminative, sad, serious, sober, solemn, sorrowful, thoughtful, wistful

people n. **1.** human beings, humanity, humans, mankind, men and women, mortals, persons **2.** citizens, clan, community, family, folk, inhabitants, nation, population, public, race, tribe **3.** commonalty, crowd, general public, grass roots, hoi polloi, masses, mob, multitude, plebs (*Brit. sl.*), populace, rabble, rank and file, the herd ~v. **4.** colonize, inhabit, occupy, populate, settle

perceive be aware of, behold, descry, discern, discover, distinguish, espy, make out, note, notice, observe, recognize, remark, see, spot

perceptible apparent, appreciable, clear, conspicuous, detectable, discernible, distinct, evident, noticeable, observable, obvious, palpable, perceivable, recognizable, tangible, visible

perception apprehension, awareness, conception, consciousness, discernment, feeling, grasp, idea, impression, insight, notion, observation, recognition, sensation, sense, taste, understanding

perceptive acute, alert, astute, aware, discerning, insightful, intuitive, observant, penetrating, percipient, perspicacious, quick, responsive, sensitive, sharp
Antonyms dull, indifferent, insensitive, obtuse, slow-witted, stupid, thick

perch 1. *n.* branch, pole, post, resting place, roost **2.** *v.* alight, balance, land, rest, roost, settle, sit on

perennial abiding, chronic, constant, continual, continuing, enduring, incessant, inveterate, lasting, lifelong, persistent, recurrent, unchanging

perfect *adj.* **1.** absolute, complete, completed, consummate, entire, finished, full, out-and-out, sheer, unadulterated, unalloyed, unmitigated, utter, whole **2.** blameless, excellent, faultless, flawless, ideal, immaculate, impeccable, pure, splendid, spotless, sublime, superb, superlative, supreme, unblemished, unmarred, untarnished ~*v.* **3.** accomplish, achieve, carry out, complete, consummate, effect, finish, fulfil, perform, realize
Antonyms *adj.* bad, damaged, defective, deficient, faulty, flawed, impaired, imperfect, impure, incomplete, inferior, partial, poor, ruined, spoiled, worthless

perfection 1. accomplishment, achievement, achieving, completion, consummation, evolution, fulfilment, realization **2.** completeness, exactness, excellence, exquisiteness, faultlessness, integrity, maturity, perfectness, precision, purity, sublimity, superiority, wholeness **3.** acme, crown, ideal, paragon

perform 1. accomplish, achieve, act, bring about, carry out, complete, comply with, discharge, do, effect, execute, fulfil, function, observe, pull off, satisfy, transact, work **2.** act, appear as, depict, enact, play, present, produce, put on, render, represent, stage

performance 1. accomplishment, achievement, act, carrying out, completion, conduct, consummation, discharge, execution, exploit, feat, fulfilment, work **2.** acting, appearance, exhibition, gig (*Inf.*), interpretation, play, portrayal, presentation, production, representation, show

performer actor, actress, artiste, play-actor, player, Thespian, trouper

perfume aroma, attar, balminess, bouquet, cologne, essence, fragrance, incense, odour, redolence, scent, smell, sweetness

perfunctory automatic, careless, cursory, heedless, inattentive, indifferent, mechanical, negligent, offhand, routine, sketchy, slipshod, slovenly, stereotyped, superficial, unconcerned, unthinking, wooden

perhaps as the case may be, conceivably, feasibly, for all one knows, it may be, maybe, perchance (*Archaic*), possibly

peril danger, exposure, hazard, insecurity, jeopardy, menace, pitfall, risk, uncertainty, vulnerability
Antonyms certainty, impregnability, invulnerability, safety, security, surety

perimeter ambit, border, borderline, boundary, bounds, circumference, confines, edge, limit, margin, periphery

period interval, season, space,

span, spell, stretch, term, time, while

periodical n. journal, magazine, monthly, organ, paper, publication, quarterly, review, serial, weekly

perish 1. be killed, be lost, decease, die, expire, lose one's life, pass away **2.** be destroyed, collapse, decline, disappear, fall, go under, vanish **3.** decay, decompose, disintegrate, moulder, rot, waste, wither

perishable decaying, decomposable, destructible, easily spoilt, liable to rot, short-lived, unstable **Antonyms** durable, lasting, long-life, long-lived, non-perishable

perjury bearing false witness, false oath, false statement, false swearing, forswearing, giving false testimony, lying under oath, oath breaking, violation of an oath, wilful falsehood

permanence constancy, continuance, continuity, dependability, durability, duration, endurance, finality, fixedness, fixity, immortality, indestructibility, lastingness, perdurability (Rare), permanency, perpetuity, stability, survival

permanent abiding, constant, durable, enduring, everlasting, fixed, immutable, imperishable, indestructible, invariable, lasting, long-lasting, perennial, perpetual, persistent, stable, steadfast, unchanging, unfading **Antonyms** brief, changing, ephemeral, finite, fleeting, impermanent, inconstant, momentary, mortal, passing, short-lived, temporary, transitory, variable

permeate charge, diffuse throughout, fill, filter through, imbue, impregnate, infiltrate, pass through, penetrate, percolate, pervade, saturate, seep through, soak through, spread throughout

permissible acceptable, admissible, allowable, all right, authorized, kosher (Inf.), lawful, legal, legit (Sl.), legitimate, licit, O.K.

(Inf.), permitted, proper, sanctioned **Antonyms** banned, forbidden, illegal, illicit, prohibited, unauthorized, unlawful

permission allowance, approval, assent, authorization, consent, dispensation, freedom, go-ahead (Inf.), green light, leave, liberty, licence, permit, sanction, sufferance, tolerance

permissive acquiescent, easygoing, forbearing, free, indulgent, latitudinarian, lax, lenient, liberal, open-minded, tolerant **Antonyms** authoritarian, denying, domineering, forbidding, grudging, rigid, strict

permit 1. v. admit, agree, allow, authorize, consent, empower, enable, endorse, endure, give leave or permission, grant, let, license, sanction, suffer, tolerate, warrant **2.** n. authorization, liberty, licence, pass, passport, permission, sanction, warrant

perpendicular at right angles to, on end, plumb, straight, upright, vertical

perpetrate be responsible for, bring about, carry out, commit, do, effect, enact, execute, inflict, perform, wreak

perpetual abiding, endless, enduring, eternal, everlasting, immortal, infinite, lasting, never-ending, perennial, permanent, sempiternal (Literary), unchanging, undying, unending **Antonyms** brief, ephemeral, fleeting, impermanent, momentary, passing, short-lived, temporary, transitory

perpetuate continue, eternalize, immortalize, keep alive, keep going, keep up, maintain, preserve, sustain **Antonyms** abolish, destroy, end, forget, ignore, put an end to, stamp out, suppress

perplex 1. baffle, befuddle, beset, bewilder, confound, confuse, dumbfound, mix up, muddle, mystify, nonplus, puzzle, stump **2.** complicate, encumber, entangle, involve, jumble, mix up, snarl up, tangle, thicken

persecute 1. afflict, distress, dragoon, harass, hound, hunt, illtreat, injure, maltreat, martyr, molest, oppress, pursue, torment, torture, victimize **2.** annoy, badger, bait, bother, pester, tease, vex, worry
Antonyms accommodate, back, calm, coddle, comfort, console, cosset, humour, indulge, leave alone, let alone, mollycoddle, pamper, pet, spoil, support

perseverance constancy, dedication, determination, diligence, doggedness, endurance, indefatigability, persistence, pertinacity, purposefulness, resolution, sedulity, stamina, steadfastness, tenacity

persevere be determined *or* resolved, carry on, continue, endure, go on, hang on, hold fast, hold on (*Inf.*), keep going, keep on *or* at, maintain, persist, plug away (*Inf.*), pursue, remain, stand firm, stick at *or* to
Antonyms be irresolute, dither, end, falter, give in, give up, hesitate, quit, shillyshally (*Inf.*), swither (*Scot.*), throw in the towel, vacillate, waver

persist 1. be resolute, continue, hold on (*Inf.*), insist, persevere, stand firm **2.** abide, carry on, continue, endure, keep up, last, linger, remain

persistence constancy, determination, diligence, doggedness, endurance, grit, indefatigability, perseverance, pertinacity, pluck, resolution, stamina, steadfastness, tenacity, tirelessness

persistent assiduous, determined, dogged, enduring, fixed, immovable, indefatigable, obdurate, obstinate, persevering, pertinacious, resolute, steadfast, steady, stubborn, tenacious, tireless, unflagging
Antonyms changeable, flexible, irresolute, tractable, yielding

person being, body, human, human being, individual, living soul, soul

personal exclusive, individual, intimate, own, particular, peculiar, private, privy, special

personality 1. character, disposition, identity, individuality, make-up, nature, psyche, temperament, traits **2.** celebrity, famous name, household name, notable, personage, star, well-known face, well-known person

personally 1. alone, by oneself, independently, in person, in the flesh, on one's own, solely **2.** individualistically, individually, privately, specially, subjectively

personification embodiment, image, incarnation, likeness, portrayal, recreation, representation, semblance

personify body forth, embody, epitomize, exemplify, express, image (*Rare*), incarnate, mirror, represent, symbolize, typify

personnel employees, helpers, human resources, liveware, members, men and women, people, staff, workers, work force

perspective 1. angle, attitude, broad view, context, frame of reference, objectivity, outlook, overview, proportion, relation, relative importance, relativity, way of looking **2.** outlook, panorama, prospect, scene, view, vista

perspire be damp, be wet, drip, exude, glow, pour with sweat, secrete, sweat, swelter

persuade actuate, advise, allure, bring round (*Inf.*), coax, counsel, entice, impel, incite, induce, influence, inveigle, prevail upon, prompt, sway, talk into, urge, win over
Antonyms deter, discourage, dissuade, forbid, prohibit

persuasion 1. blandishment, cajolery, conversion, enticement, exhortation, inducement, influencing, inveiglement, wheedling **2.** cogency, force, persuasiveness, potency, power, pull (*Inf.*) **3.** belief, certitude, conviction, credo, creed, faith, firm belief, fixed opinion, opinion, tenet, views

persuasive cogent, compelling, convincing, credible, effective, eloquent, forceful, impelling, impressive, inducing, influential, logical, moving, plausible, sound, telling, touching, valid, weighty, winning
Antonyms feeble, flimsy, illogical, implausible, incredible, ineffective, invalid, unconvincing, unimpressive, weak

pertain appertain, apply, be appropriate, bear on, befit, belong, be part of, be relevant, concern, refer, regard, relate

pertinent admissible, *ad rem*, applicable, apposite, appropriate, apropos, apt, fit, fitting, germane, material, pat, proper, relevant, suitable, to the point, to the purpose
Antonyms discordant, foreign, immaterial, inappropriate, incongruous, irrelevant, unfitting, unrelated, unsuitable

perturb agitate, alarm, bother, discompose, disconcert, discountenance, disquiet, disturb, fluster, ruffle, trouble, unsettle, upset, vex, worry

peruse browse, check, examine, inspect, look through, read, run one's eye over, scan, scrutinize, study

pervade affect, charge, diffuse, extend, fill, imbue, infuse, overspread, penetrate, percolate, permeate, spread through, suffuse

pervasive common, extensive, general, inescapable, omnipresent, permeating, pervading, prevalent, rife, ubiquitous, universal, widespread

perverse 1. abnormal, contradictory, contrary, delinquent, depraved, deviant, disobedient, froward, improper, incorrect, miscreant, rebellious, refractory, troublesome, unhealthy, unmanageable, unreasonable **2.** contrary, contumacious, cross-grained, dogged, headstrong, intractable,

intransigent, obdurate, wilful, wrong-headed **3.** contrary, mulish, obstinate, pig-headed, stubborn, unyielding, wayward
Antonyms accommodating, agreeable, amiable, complaisant, cooperative, flexible, good-natured, malleable, obedient, obliging

pervert *v.* **1.** abuse, distort, falsify, garble, misconstrue, misinterpret, misrepresent, misuse, twist, warp **2.** corrupt, debase, debauch, degrade, deprave, desecrate, initiate, lead astray, subvert ~ *n.* **3.** debauchee, degenerate, deviant, weirdo (*Sl.*)

perverted aberrant, abnormal, corrupt, debased, debauched, depraved, deviant, distorted, evil, immoral, impaired, kinky (*Sl.*), misguided, sick, twisted, unhealthy, unnatural, vicious, vitiated, warped, wicked

pessimism cynicism, dejection, depression, despair, despondency, distrust, gloom, gloominess, gloomy outlook, glumness, hopelessness, melancholy

pessimist cynic, defeatist, doomster, gloom merchant (*Inf.*), killjoy, melancholic, misanthrope, prophet of doom, wet blanket (*Inf.*), worrier

pessimistic bleak, cynical, dark, dejected, depressed, despairing, despondent, distrustful, downhearted, fatalistic, foreboding, gloomy, glum, hopeless, melancholy, misanthropic, morose, resigned, sad
Antonyms assured, bright, buoyant, cheerful, cheery, encouraged, exhilarated, hopeful, in good heart, optimistic, sanguine

pest 1. annoyance, bane, bore, bother, irritation, nuisance, pain (*Inf.*), pain in the neck (*Inf.*), thorn in one's flesh, trial, vexation **2.** bane, blight, bug, curse, epidemic, infection, pestilence, plague, scourge

pester annoy, badger, bedevil, bother, bug (*Inf.*), chivvy, disturb, drive one up the wall (*Sl.*), fret,

pet get at, get on someone's nerves, harass, harry, hassle (*Inf.*), irk, nag, pick on, plague, ride (*Inf.*), torment, worry

pet n. 1. apple of one's eye, blue-eyed boy (*Inf.*), darling, favourite, idol, jewel, treasure ~adj. 2. cherished, dearest, dear to one's heart, favoured, favourite, particular, preferred, special ~v. 3. baby, coddle, cosset, mollycoddle, pamper, spoil 4. caress, fondle, pat, stroke

peter out come to nothing, die out, dwindle, ebb, evaporate, fade, fail, give out, run dry, run out, stop, taper off, wane

petition 1. n. address, appeal, application, entreaty, invocation, memorial, plea, prayer, request, round robin, solicitation, suit, supplication 2. v. adjure, appeal, ask, beg, beseech, call upon, crave, entreat, plead, pray, press, solicit, sue, supplicate, urge

petty 1. contemptible, inconsiderable, inessential, inferior, insignificant, little, measly (*Inf.*), negligible, paltry, piddling (*Inf.*), slight, small, trifling, trivial, unimportant 2. cheap, grudging, mean, mean-minded, shabby, small-minded, spiteful, stingy, ungenerous
Antonyms (*sense 1*) consequential, considerable, essential, important, major, momentous, significant (*sense 2*) broad-minded, generous, liberal, magnanimous, open-minded, tolerant

petulant bad-tempered, captious, cavilling, crabbed, cross, crusty, fault-finding, fretful, ill-humoured, impatient, irritable, moody, peevish, perverse, pouting, querulous, snappish, sour, sulky, sullen, ungracious, waspish
Antonyms affable, cheerful, congenial, easy-going, even-tempered, good-humoured, good-natured, happy, patient, smiling

phantom apparition, eidolon, ghost, phantasm, revenant, shade (*Literary*), spectre, spook (*Inf.*), wraith

phase aspect, chapter, condition, development, juncture, period, point, position, stage, state, step, time

phase out close, deactivate, dispose of gradually, ease off, eliminate, pull out, remove, replace, run down, taper off, terminate, wind down, wind up (*Inf.*), withdraw
Antonyms activate, begin, create, establish, form, initiate, open, set up, start

phenomenal exceptional, extraordinary, fantastic, marvellous, miraculous, outstanding, prodigious, remarkable, sensational, singular, uncommon, unique, unparalleled, unusual, wondrous
Antonyms average, common, mediocre, ordinary, poor, run-of-the-mill, second-rate, unexceptional, unremarkable, usual

phenomenon 1. circumstance, episode, event, fact, happening, incident, occurrence 2. exception, marvel, miracle, nonpareil, prodigy, rarity, sensation, sight, spectacle, wonder

philanthropist alms-giver, altruist, benefactor, contributor, donor, giver, humanitarian, patron

philistine 1. n. barbarian, boor, bourgeois, Goth, ignoramus, lout, lowbrow, vulgarian, yahoo 2. adj. anti-intellectual, boorish, bourgeois, crass, ignorant, lowbrow, tasteless, uncultivated, uncultured, uneducated, unrefined

philosopher dialectician, logician, metaphysician, sage, seeker after truth, theorist, thinker, wise man

philosophical, philosophic 1. abstract, erudite, learned, logical, rational, sagacious, theoretical, thoughtful, wise 2. calm, collected, composed, cool, impassive, imperturbable, patient, resigned, serene, stoical, tranquil, unruffled
Antonyms (*sense 1*) factual, illogical, irrational, practical, pragmatic, scientific (*sense 2*)

emotional, hot-headed, impulsive, perturbed, rash, restless, upset

philosophy 1. aesthetics, knowledge, logic, metaphysics, rationalism, reason, reasoning, thinking, thought, wisdom 2. attitude to life, basic idea, beliefs, convictions, doctrine, ideology, principle, tenets, thinking, values, viewpoint, *Weltanschauung*, world-view

phobia aversion, detestation, dislike, distaste, dread, fear, hatred, horror, irrational fear, loathing, obsession, overwhelming anxiety, repulsion, revulsion, terror, thing (*Inf.*)
Antonyms bent, fancy, fondness, inclination, liking, love, partiality, passion, penchant, soft spot

phone n. 1. blower (*Inf.*), telephone 2. bell (*Brit. sl.*), buzz (*Inf.*), call, ring, tinkle (*Brit. inf.*) ~v. 3. buzz (*Inf.*), call, get on the blower (*Inf.*), give someone a bell (*Brit. sl.*), give someone a buzz (*Inf.*), give someone a call, give someone a ring, give someone a tinkle (*Brit. inf.*), make a call, ring, ring up, telephone

phoney 1. adj. affected, assumed, bogus, counterfeit, fake, false, forged, imitation, pseudo (*Inf.*), put-on, sham, spurious, trick 2. n. counterfeit, fake, faker, forgery, fraud, humbug, impostor, pretender, pseud (*Sl.*), sham
Antonyms authentic, bona fide, genuine, original, real, sincere, unaffected, unassumed, unfeigned

photograph 1. n. image, likeness, photo (*Inf.*), picture, print, shot, slide, snap (*Inf.*), snapshot, transparency 2. v. capture on film, film, get a shot of, record, shoot, snap (*Inf.*), take, take a picture of, take (someone's) picture

phrase 1. n. expression, group of words, idiom, locution, motto, remark, saying, tag, utterance, way of speaking 2. v. couch, express, formulate, frame, present, put,

put into words, say, term, utter, voice, word

physical 1. bodily, carnal, corporal, corporeal, earthly, fleshly, incarnate, mortal, somatic, unspiritual 2. material, natural, palpable, real, sensible, solid, substantial, tangible, visible

physique body, build, constitution, figure, form, frame, make-up, shape, structure

pick v. 1. choose, decide upon, elect, fix upon, hand-pick, mark out, opt for, select, settle upon, sift out, single out, sort out 2. collect, cull, cut, gather, harvest, pluck, pull ~n. 3. choice, choosing, decision, option, preference, selection 4. choicest, crème de la crème, elect, elite, flower, pride, prize, the best, the cream, the tops (*Sl.*)
Antonyms (sense 1) cast aside, decline, discard, dismiss, reject, spurn, turn down

pick up v. 1. gather, grasp, hoist, lift, raise, take up, uplift 2. buy, come across, find, garner, happen upon, obtain, purchase, score (*Sl.*) 3. gain, gain ground, get better, improve, make a comeback (*Inf.*), mend, perk up, rally, recover, take a turn for the better 4. call for, collect, get, give someone a lift, go to get, uplift (*Scot.*) 5. acquire, get the hang of (*Inf.*), learn, master

picnic excursion, fête champêtre, outdoor meal, outing

pictorial expressive, graphic, illustrated, picturesque, representational, scenic, striking, vivid

picture n. 1. delineation, drawing, effigy, engraving, illustration, image, likeness, painting, photograph, portrait, portrayal, print, representation, similitude, sketch 2. account, depiction, description, image, impression, re-creation, report 3. carbon copy, copy, dead ringer (*Sl.*), double, duplicate, image, likeness, living image, lookalike, replica, ringer (*Sl.*), spit (*Inf.*), spit and image (*Inf.*), spitting image (*Inf.*), twin 4. film, flick (*Sl.*), motion picture, movie (*U.S. inf.*) ~*v.* **5.** conceive of, envision, image, see, see in the mind's eye, visualize

picturesque attractive, beautiful, charming, colourful, graphic, pretty, quaint, scenic, striking, vivid

Antonyms commonplace, drab, dull, everyday, inartistic, unattractive, uninteresting

piece *n.* **1.** allotment, bit, chunk, division, fraction, fragment, length, morsel, mouthful, part, portion, quantity, scrap, section, segment, share, shred, slice **2.** article, bit (*Sl.*), composition, creation, item, production, study, work, work of art

pier *n.* **1.** jetty, landing place, promenade, quay, wharf **2.** buttress, column, pile, piling, pillar, post, support, upright

pierce bore, drill, enter, penetrate, perforate, prick, probe, puncture, run through, spike, stab, stick into, transfix

piety devotion, devoutness, dutifulness, duty, faith, godliness, grace, holiness, piousness, religion, reverence, sanctity, veneration

pig boar, grunter, hog, piggy, piglet, porker, shoat, sow, swine

pigeonhole **1.** *n.* compartment, cubbyhole, cubicle, locker, niche, place, section **2.** *v.* defer, file, postpone, put off, shelve

pig-headed bull-headed, contrary, cross-grained, dense, froward, inflexible, mulish, obstinate, perverse, self-willed, stiff-necked, stubborn, stupid, unyielding, wilful, wrong-headed

Antonyms agreeable, amiable, complaisant, cooperative, flexible, obliging, open-minded, tractable

pile *n.* **1.** accumulation, assemblage, assortment, collection, heap, hoard, mass, mound, mountain, stack, stockpile **2.** building, edifice, erection, structure ~*v.* **3.** accumulate, amass,

assemble, collect, gather, heap, hoard, load up, mass, stack, store

pile-up accident, collision, crash, multiple collision, smash, smash-up (*Inf.*)

pilgrim crusader, hajji, palmer, traveller, wanderer, wayfarer

pilgrimage crusade, excursion, expedition, hajj, journey, mission, tour, trip

pillage **1.** *v.* depredate (*Rare*), despoil, freeboot, loot, maraud, plunder, raid, ransack, ravage, reive (*Dialect*), rifle, rob, sack, spoil (*Archaic*), spoliate, strip **2.** *n.* depredation, devastation, marauding, plunder, rapine, robbery, sack, spoliation

pillar **1.** column, pier, pilaster, piling, post, prop, shaft, stanchion, support, upright **2.** leader, leading light (*Inf.*), mainstay, rock, supporter, tower of strength, upholder, worthy

pilot **1.** *n.* airman, aviator, captain, conductor, coxswain, director, flier, guide, helmsman, leader, navigator, steersman **2.** *v.* conduct, control, direct, drive, fly, guide, handle, lead, manage, navigate, operate, shepherd, steer **3.** *adj.* experimental, model, test, trial

pin *v.* **1.** affix, attach, fasten, fix, join, secure **2.** fix, hold down, hold fast, immobilize, pinion, press, restrain

pinch *v.* **1.** compress, grasp, nip, press, squeeze, tweak **2.** chafe, confine, cramp, crush, hurt, pain ~*n.* **3.** nip, squeeze, tweak **4.** bit, dash, jot, mite, small quantity, soupçon, speck, taste **5.** crisis, difficulty, emergency, exigency, hardship, necessity, oppression, pass, plight, predicament, pressure, strait, stress

pin down **1.** compel, constrain, force, make, press, pressurize **2.** bind, confine, constrain, fix, hold, hold down, immobilize, nail down, tie down

pink *adj.* flesh, flushed, reddish, rose, roseate, rosy, salmon

pinnacle acme, apex, apogee,

crest, crown, eminence, height, meridian, peak, summit, top, vertex, zenith

pinpoint define, distinguish, get a fix on, home in on, identify, locate, spot

pioneer *n.* **1.** colonist, colonizer, explorer, frontiersman, settler **2.** developer, founder, founding father, innovator, leader, trailblazer ~*v.* **3.** create, develop, discover, establish, initiate, instigate, institute, invent, launch, lay the groundwork, map out, open up, originate, prepare, show the way, start, take the lead

pious 1. dedicated, devoted, devout, God-fearing, godly, holy, religious, reverent, righteous, saintly, spiritual **2.** goody-goody, holier-than-thou, hypocritical, pietistic, religiose, sanctimonious, self-righteous, unctuous

Antonyms (*sense 1*) impious, irreligious, irreverent, ungodly, unholy (*sense 2*) humble, meek, sincere

pipe *n.* **1.** conduit, conveyor, duct, hose, line, main, passage, pipeline, tube **2.** briar, clay, meerschaum **3.** fife, horn, tooter, whistle, wind instrument ~*v.* **4.** cheep, peep, play, sing, sound, tootle, trill, tweet, twitter, warble, whistle

piquant biting, highly-seasoned, peppery, pungent, savoury, sharp, spicy, stinging, tangy, tart, with a kick (*Inf.*), zesty

Antonyms bland, insipid, mild

pique 1. *n.* annoyance, displeasure, grudge, huff, hurt feelings, irritation, miff (*Inf.*), offence, resentment, umbrage, vexation, wounded pride **2.** *v.* affront, annoy, displease, gall, get (*Inf.*), incense, irk, irritate, miff (*Inf.*), mortify, nettle, offend, peeve (*Inf.*), provoke, put out, put someone's nose out of joint (*Inf.*), rile, sting, vex, wound

piracy buccaneering, freebooting, hijacking, infringement, plagiarism, rapine, robbery at sea, stealing, theft

pirate *n.* **1.** buccaneer, corsair, filibuster, freebooter, marauder, raider, rover, sea robber, sea rover, sea wolf **2.** cribber (*Inf.*), infringer, plagiarist, plagiarizer ~*v.* **3.** appropriate, borrow, copy, crib (*Inf.*), lift (*Inf.*), plagiarize, poach, reproduce, steal

pit *n.* abyss, cavity, chasm, coal mine, crater, dent, depression, dimple, excavation, gulf, hole, hollow, indentation, mine, pockmark, pothole, trench

pitch *v.* **1.** bung (*Brit. sl.*), cast, chuck (*Inf.*), fling, heave, hurl, launch, lob (*Inf.*), sling, throw, toss **2.** erect, fix, locate, place, plant, put up, raise, settle, set up, station ~*n.* **3.** angle, cant, dip, gradient, incline, slope, steepness, tilt **4.** degree, height, highest point, level, point, summit **5.** harmonic, modulation, sound, timbre, tone **6.** line, patter, sales talk, spiel (*Inf.*) **7.** field of play, ground, park (*Brit. inf.*), sports field

piteous affecting, deplorable, distressing, doleful, grievous, heartbreaking, heart-rending, lamentable, miserable, mournful, moving, pathetic, pitiable, pitiful, plaintive, poignant, sad, sorrowful, woeful, wretched

pitfall catch, danger, difficulty, drawback, hazard, peril, snag, trap

pith 1. core, crux, essence, gist, heart, heart of the matter, kernel, marrow, meat, nub, point, quintessence, salient point, the long and the short of it **2.** consequence, depth, force, import, importance, matter, moment, power, significance, strength, substance, value, weight

pitiful 1. deplorable, distressing, grievous, heartbreaking, heart-rending, lamentable, miserable, pathetic, piteous, pitiable, sad, woeful, wretched **2.** abject, base, beggarly, contemptible, despicable, inadequate, insignificant, low, mean, miserable, paltry, scurvy, shabby, sorry, vile, worthless

Antonyms (*sense 1*) amusing, cheerful, cheering, comical, funny, happy, heartening, laughable, merry (*sense 2*) adequate, admirable, honourable, laudable, praiseworthy, significant, valuable

pitiless brutal, callous, cold-blooded, cold-hearted, cruel, hardhearted, harsh, heartless, implacable, inexorable, inhuman, merciless, relentless, ruthless, uncaring, unfeeling, unmerciful, unsympathetic

Antonyms caring, compassionate, kind, merciful, relenting, responsive, soft-hearted, sparing

pittance allowance, chicken feed (*Sl.*), drop, mite, modicum, peanuts (*Sl.*), portion, ration, slave wages, trifle

pity 1. *n.* charity, clemency, commiseration, compassion, condolence, fellow feeling, forbearance, kindness, mercy, sympathy, tenderness, understanding **2.** *v.* bleed for, commiserate with, condole with, feel for, feel sorry for, grieve for, have compassion for, sympathize with, weep for

Antonyms (*sense 1*) anger, apathy, brutality, cruelty, disdain, fury, hard-heartedness, indifference, inhumanity, mercilessness, pitilessness, ruthlessness, scorn, severity, unconcern, wrath

pivot *n.* **1.** axis, axle, fulcrum, spindle, swivel **2.** centre, focal point, heart, hinge, hub, kingpin ~*v.* **3.** revolve, rotate, spin, swivel, turn, twirl **4.** be contingent, depend, hang, hinge, rely, revolve round, turn

placard advertisement, *affiche*, bill, poster, public notice, sticker

placate appease, assuage, calm, conciliate, humour, mollify, pacify, propitiate, satisfy, soothe, win over

place *n.* **1.** area, location, locus, point, position, site, situation, spot, station, venue, whereabouts **2.** city, district, hamlet, locale,

locality, neighbourhood, quarter, region, town, vicinity, village **3.** grade, position, rank, station, status **4.** appointment, berth (*Inf.*), billet (*Inf.*), employment, job, position, post **5.** accommodation, room, space, stead **6.** affair, charge, concern, duty, function, prerogative, responsibility, right, role **7.** *take place* befall, betide, come about, come to pass (*Archaic*), go on, happen, occur, transpire (*Inf.*) ~*v.* **8.** bung (*Inf.*), deposit, dispose, establish, fix, install, lay, locate, plant, position, put, rest, set, settle, situate, stand, station, stick (*Inf.*) **9.** arrange, class, classify, grade, group, order, rank, sort **10.** allocate, appoint, assign, charge, commission, entrust, give

placid calm, collected, composed, cool, equable, even, even-tempered, gentle, halcyon, imperturbable, mild, peaceful, quiet, self-possessed, serene, still, tranquil, undisturbed, unexcitable, unmoved, unruffled, untroubled

Antonyms agitated, disturbed, emotional, excitable, impulsive, passionate, rough, temperamental, tempestuous

plague *n.* **1.** contagion, disease, epidemic, infection, pandemic, pestilence **2.** *Fig.* affliction, bane, blight, calamity, cancer, curse, evil, scourge, torment, trial **3.** *Inf.* aggravation (*Inf.*), annoyance, bother, irritant, nuisance, pain (*Inf.*), pest, problem, thorn in one's flesh, vexation ~*v.* **4.** afflict, annoy, badger, bedevil, bother, disturb, fret, harass, harry, hassle (*Inf.*), haunt, molest, pain, persecute, pester, tease, torment, torture, trouble, vex

plain *adj.* **1.** apparent, clear, comprehensible, distinct, evident, legible, lucid, manifest, obvious, patent, unambiguous, understandable, unmistakable, visible **2.** artless, blunt, candid, direct, downright, forthright, frank, guileless, honest, ingenu-

ous, open, outspoken, sincere, straightforward 3. common, commonplace, everyday, frugal, homely, lowly, modest, ordinary, simple, unaffected, unpretentious, workaday 4. austere, bare, basic, discreet, modest, muted, pure, restrained, severe, simple, Spartan, stark, unadorned, unembellished, unornamented, unpatterned, unvarnished 5. ill-favoured, not beautiful, not striking, ordinary, ugly, unalluring, unattractive, unlovely, unprepossessing 6. even, flat, level, plane, smooth ~n. 7. flatland, grassland, lowland, open country, plateau, prairie, steppe, tableland
Antonyms (sense 1) ambiguous, complex, concealed, deceptive, difficult, disguised, hidden, illegible, incomprehensible, inconspicuous, indiscernible, indistinct, obscure, vague, veiled (sense 2) circuitous, indirect, meandering, rambling, roundabout (sense 3) affected, distinguished, egotistic, ostentatious, pretentious, sophisticated, worldly (sense 4) adorned, decorated, fancy, ornate (sense 5) attractive, beautiful, comely, good-looking, gorgeous, handsome (sense 6) bumpy, not level, uneven

plain-spoken blunt, candid, direct, downright, explicit, forthright, frank, open, outright, outspoken, straightforward, unequivocal
Antonyms diplomatic, discreet, evasive, guarded, indirect, reticent, subtle, tactful, thoughtful

plaintive disconsolate, doleful, grief-stricken, grievous, heart-rending, melancholy, mournful, pathetic, piteous, pitiful, rueful, sad, sorrowful, wistful, woebegone, woeful

plan n. 1. contrivance, design, device, idea, method, plot, procedure, programme, project, proposal, proposition, scenario, scheme, strategy, suggestion, system 2. blueprint, chart, delin-

eation, diagram, drawing, illustration, layout, map, representation, scale drawing, sketch ~v. 3. arrange, concoct, contrive, design, devise, draft, formulate, frame, invent, organize, outline, plot, prepare, represent, scheme, think out 4. aim, contemplate, envisage, foresee, intend, mean, propose, purpose

plane n. 1. flat surface, level surface 2. condition, degree, footing, level, position, stratum ~adj. 3. even, flat, flush, horizontal, level, plain, regular, smooth, uniform

plant n. 1. bush, flower, herb, shrub, vegetable, weed 2. factory, foundry, mill, shop, works, yard 3. apparatus, equipment, gear, machinery ~v. 4. implant, put in the ground, scatter, seed, set out, sow, transplant

plaster n. 1. gypsum, mortar, plaster of Paris, stucco 2. adhesive plaster, bandage, dressing, Elastoplast (*Trademark*), sticking plaster ~v. 3. bedaub, besmear, coat, cover, daub, overlay, smear, spread

plastic adj. 1. ductile, fictile, flexible, mouldable, pliable, pliant, soft, supple
Antonyms brittle, hard, inflexible, rigid, stiff, unbending, unyielding

plate n. 1. dish, platter, trencher (*Archaic*) 2. course, dish, helping, portion, serving 3. layer, panel, sheet, slab

plateau highland, mesa, table, tableland, upland

platform dais, podium, rostrum, stage, stand

platitude banality, bromide, cliché, commonplace, hackneyed saying, inanity, stereotype, trite remark, truism

plausible believable, colourable, conceivable, credible, fair-spoken, glib, likely, persuasive, possible, probable, reasonable, smooth, smooth-talking, smooth-tongued, specious, tenable
Antonyms genuine, illogical, implausible, impossible, improb-

able, inconceivable, incredible, real, unbelievable, unlikely

play v. **1.** amuse oneself, caper, engage in games, entertain oneself, frisk, frolic, gambol, have fun, revel, romp, sport, trifle **2.** be in a team, challenge, compete, contend against, participate, rival, take on, take part, vie with **3.** act, act the part of, execute, impersonate, perform, personate, portray, represent, take the part of **4.** play by ear ad lib, extemporize, improvise, rise to the occasion, take it as it comes **5. play for time** delay, drag one's feet (*Inf.*), filibuster, hang fire, procrastinate, stall, temporize ~n. **6.** comedy, drama, dramatic piece, entertainment, farce, masque, performance, piece, radio play, show, soap opera, stage show, television drama, tragedy **7.** amusement, caper, diversion, entertainment, frolic, fun, gambol, game, jest, pastime, prank, recreation, romp, sport **8.** foolery, fun, humour, jest, joking, lark (*Inf.*), prank, sport, teasing

playboy gay dog, ladies' man, lady-killer (*Inf.*), lover boy (*Sl.*), man about town, philanderer, pleasure seeker, rake, roué, socialite, womanizer

player 1. competitor, contestant, participant, sportsman, sportswoman, team member **2.** actor, actress, entertainer, performer, Thespian, trouper **3.** artist, instrumentalist, musician, music maker, performer, virtuoso

playful cheerful, coltish, frisky, frolicsome, gay, impish, joyous, kittenish, larkish (*Inf.*), lively, merry, mischievous, puckish, rollicking, spirited, sportive, sprightly, vivacious
Antonyms despondent, gloomy, grave, morose, sedate, serious

playmate chum (*Inf.*), companion, comrade, friend, neighbour, pal (*Inf.*), playfellow

plaything amusement, bauble, game, gewgaw, gimcrack, pastime, toy, trifle, trinket

plea appeal, begging, entreaty, intercession, overture, petition, prayer, request, suit, supplication

plead 1. appeal (to), ask, beg, beseech, crave, entreat, implore, importune, petition, request, solicit, supplicate **2.** adduce, allege, argue, assert, maintain, put forward, use as an excuse

pleasant 1. acceptable, agreeable, amusing, delectable, delightful, enjoyable, fine, gratifying, lovely, nice, pleasing, pleasurable, refreshing, satisfying, welcome **2.** affable, agreeable, amiable, charming, cheerful, cheery, congenial, engaging, friendly, genial, good-humoured, likable, nice
Antonyms awful, cold, disagreeable, distasteful, horrible, impolite, miserable, offensive, repulsive, rude, unfriendly, unlikeable, unpleasant

please amuse, charm, cheer, content, delight, entertain, give pleasure to, gladden, gratify, humour, indulge, rejoice, satisfy, suit, tickle, tickle pink
Antonyms anger, annoy, depress, disgust, displease, dissatisfy, grieve, incense, offend, provoke, sadden, vex

pleased chuffed (*Brit. sl.*), contented, delighted, euphoric, glad, gratified, happy, in high spirits, over the moon (*Inf.*), pleased as punch (*Inf.*), satisfied, thrilled, tickled, tickled pink

pleasing agreeable, amiable, amusing, attractive, charming, delightful, engaging, enjoyable, entertaining, gratifying, likable, pleasurable, polite, satisfying, winning
Antonyms boring, disagreeable, dull, monotonous, rude, unattractive, unlikeable, unpleasant

pleasure amusement, bliss, comfort, contentment, delectation, delight, diversion, ease, enjoyment, gladness, gratification, happiness, joy, recreation, satisfaction, solace
Antonyms abstinence, anger,

disinclination, displeasure, duty, labour, misery, necessity, obligation, pain, sadness, sorrow, suffering, unhappiness

pledge n. **1.** assurance, covenant, oath, promise, undertaking, vow, warrant, word, word of honour **2.** bail, bond, collateral, deposit, earnest, gage, guarantee, pawn, security, surety **3.** health, toast ~v. **4.** contract, engage, give one's oath (word, word of honour), promise, swear, undertake, vouch, vow

plentiful abundant, ample, bounteous (*Literary*), bountiful, complete, copious, generous, inexhaustible, infinite, lavish, liberal, overflowing, plenteous, profuse
Antonyms deficient, inadequate, insufficient, scant, scarce, skimpy, small, sparing, sparse

plenty 1. abundance, enough, fund, good deal, great deal, heap(s) (*Inf.*), lots (*Inf.*), mass, masses, mine, mountain(s), oodles (*Inf.*), pile(s) (*Inf.*), plethora, quantities, quantity, stack(s), store, sufficiency, volume **2.** abundance, affluence, copiousness, fertility, fruitfulness, luxury, opulence, plenitude, plenteousness, plentifulness, profusion, prosperity, wealth

pliable 1. bendable, bendy, ductile, flexible, limber, lithe, malleable, plastic, pliant, supple **2.** adaptable, compliant, docile, easily led, impressionable, influenceable, manageable, persuadable, pliant, receptive, responsive, susceptible, tractable, yielding
Antonyms headstrong, inflexible, intractable, obdurate, obstinate, rigid, stiff, stubborn, unadaptable, unbending, unyielding, wilful

plight n. case, circumstances, condition, difficulty, dilemma, extremity, hole (*Sl.*), jam (*Inf.*), perplexity, pickle (*Inf.*), predicament, scrape (*Inf.*), situation, spot (*Inf.*), state, straits, trouble

plod clump, drag, lumber, slog, stomp (*Inf.*), tramp, tread, trudge

plot¹ n. **1.** cabal, conspiracy, covin (*Law*), intrigue, machination, plan, scheme, stratagem **2.** action, narrative, outline, scenario, story, story line, subject, theme, thread ~v. **3.** cabal, collude, conspire, contrive, hatch, intrigue, machinate, manoeuvre, plan, scheme **4.** calculate, chart, compute, draft, draw, locate, map, mark, outline **5.** brew, conceive, concoct, contrive, cook up (*Inf.*), design, devise, frame, hatch, imagine, lay, project

plot² n. allotment, area, ground, lot, parcel, patch, tract

plough v. break ground, cultivate, dig, furrow, ridge, till, turn over

pluck v. **1.** collect, draw, gather, harvest, pick, pull out *or* off **2.** finger, pick, plunk, strum, thrum, twang

plucky bold, brave, courageous, daring, doughty, game, gritty, gutsy (*Sl.*), hardy, heroic, intrepid, mettlesome, spirited, spunky (*Inf.*), undaunted, unflinching, valiant
Antonyms afraid, chicken (*Sl.*), cowardly, dastardly, dispirited, lifeless, scared, spineless, spiritless, timid, yellow (*Inf.*), weary

plug n. **1.** bung, cork, spigot, stopper, stopple **2.** *Inf.* advert (*Brit. inf.*), advertisement, good word, hype (*Sl.*), mention, publicity, puff, push ~v. **3.** block, bung, choke, close, cork, cover, fill, pack, seal, stop, stopper, stopple, stop up, stuff **4.** *Inf.* advertise, build up, hype (*Sl.*), mention, promote, publicize, puff, push, write up

plumb n. **1.** lead, plumb bob, plummet, weight ~adv. **2.** perpendicularly, up and down, vertically **3.** bang, exactly, precisely, slap, spot-on (*Brit. inf.*) ~v. **4.** delve, explore, fathom, gauge, go into, measure, penetrate, probe, search, sound, unravel

plump adj. beefy (*Inf.*), burly, buxom, chubby, corpulent, dumpy, fat, fleshy, full, obese, podgy, portly, roly-poly, rotund, round, stout, tubby, well-covered, well-upholstered (*Inf.*)

Antonyms anorexic, bony, emaciated, lanky, lean, scrawny, skinny, slender, slim, sylphlike, thin

plunder 1. *v.* despoil, devastate, loot, pillage, raid, ransack, ravage, rifle, rob, sack, spoil, steal, strip **2.** *n.* booty, ill-gotten gains, loot, pillage, prey, prize, rapine, spoils, swag (*Sl.*)

plunge 1. *v.* cast, descend, dip, dive, douse, drop, fall, go down, immerse, jump, nose-dive, pitch, plummet, sink, submerge, swoop, throw, tumble **2.** *n.* descent, dive, drop, fall, immersion, jump, submersion, swoop

plus 1. *prep.* added to, and, coupled with, with, with the addition of **2.** *adj.* added, additional, extra, positive, supplementary

poach appropriate, encroach, hunt *or* fish illegally, infringe, intrude, plunder, rob, steal, steal game, trespass

pocket 1. *n.* bag, compartment, hollow, pouch, receptacle, sack **2.** *adj.* abridged, compact, concise, little, miniature, pint-size(d) (*Inf.*), portable, potted (*Inf.*), small

poem lyric, ode, rhyme, song, sonnet, verse

poet bard, lyricist, maker (*Archaic*), rhymer, versifier

poetic elegiac, lyric, lyrical, metrical, rhythmical, songlike

poetry metrical composition, poems, poesy (*Archaic*), rhyme, rhyming, verse

poignant 1. affecting, agonizing, bitter, distressing, heartbreaking, heart-rending, intense, moving, painful, pathetic, sad, touching, upsetting **2.** acute, biting, caustic, keen, penetrating, piercing, pointed, sarcastic, severe

point *n.* **1.** dot, full stop, mark, period, speck, stop **2.** location, place, position, site, spot, stage, station **3.** apex, end, nib, prong, sharp end, spike, spur, summit, tine, tip, top **4.** bill, cape, fore-

land, head, headland, ness (*Archaic*), promontory **5.** circumstance, condition, degree, extent, position, stage **6.** instant, juncture, moment, time, very minute **7.** aim, design, end, goal, intent, intention, motive, object, objective, purpose, reason, use, usefulness, utility **8.** burden, core, crux, drift, essence, gist, heart, import, main idea, marrow, matter, meaning, nub, pith, proposition, question, subject, text, theme, thrust **9.** aspect, attribute, characteristic, peculiarity, property, quality, respect, side, trait **10.** score, tally, unit **11. beside the point** immaterial, incidental, inconsequential, irrelevant, not to the purpose, off the subject, out of the way, pointless, unimportant, without connection **12. to the point** applicable, appropriate, apropos, apt, brief, fitting, germane, pertinent, pithy, pointed, relevant, short, suitable, terse ~ *v.* **13.** bespeak, call attention to, denote, designate, direct, indicate, show, signify

point-blank 1. *adj.* abrupt, blunt, categorical, direct, downright, explicit, express, plain, straight-from-the-shoulder, unreserved **2.** *adv.* bluntly, brusquely, candidly, directly, explicitly, forthrightly, frankly, openly, plainly, straight, straightforwardly

pointer 1. guide, hand, indicator, needle **2.** advice, caution, hint, information, recommendation, suggestion, tip, warning

pointless absurd, aimless, fruitless, futile, inane, ineffectual, irrelevant, meaningless, nonsensical, senseless, silly, stupid, unavailing, unproductive, unprofitable, useless, vague, vain, worthless

Antonyms appropriate, beneficial, desirable, fitting, fruitful, logical, meaningful, productive, profitable, proper, sensible, to the point, useful, worthwhile

point out allude to, bring up, call attention to, identify, indicate, mention, remind, reveal, show, specify

poise 1. *n.* aplomb, assurance, calmness, composure, cool (*Sl.*), coolness, dignity, elegance, equanimity, equilibrium, grace, presence, presence of mind, sang-froid, savoir-faire, self-possession, serenity **2.** *v.* balance, float, hang, hang in midair, hang suspended, hold, hover, position, support, suspend

poised 1. calm, collected, composed, dignified, graceful, nonchalant, self-confident, self-possessed, serene, suave, together (*Inf.*), unruffled, urbane **2.** all set, in the wings, on the brink, prepared, ready, standing by, waiting

poison *n.* **1.** bane, toxin, venom **2.** bane, blight, cancer, canker, contagion, contamination, corruption, malignancy, miasma, virus ~*v.* **3.** adulterate, contaminate, envenom, give (someone) poison, infect, kill, murder, pollute

poisonous 1. baneful (*Archaic*), deadly, fatal, lethal, mephitic, mortal, noxious, toxic, venomous, virulent **2.** baleful, baneful (*Archaic*), corruptive, evil, malicious, noxious, pernicious, pestiferous, pestilential, vicious

poke *v.* **1.** butt, dig, elbow, hit, jab, nudge, prod, punch, push, shove, stab, stick, thrust **2. poke fun at** chaff, jeer, make a mock of, make fun of, mock, rib (*Inf.*), ridicule, send up (*Brit. inf.*), take the mickey (*Inf.*), take the piss (*Inf.*), tease ~*n.* **3.** butt, dig, hit, jab, nudge, prod, punch, thrust

pole bar, mast, post, rod, shaft, spar, staff, standard, stick

police 1. *n.* boys in blue (*Inf.*), constabulary, fuzz (*Sl.*), law enforcement agency, police force, the law (*Inf.*), the Old Bill (*Sl.*) **2.** *v.* control, guard, keep in order, keep the peace, patrol, protect, regulate, watch

policeman bobby (*Inf.*), bogey (*Sl.*), constable, cop (*Sl.*), copper

(*Sl.*), flatfoot (*Sl.*), fuzz (*Sl.*), gendarme (*Sl.*), officer, peeler (*Obsolete Brit. sl.*), pig (*Sl.*), rozzer (*Sl.*)

policy action, approach, code, course, custom, guideline, line, plan, practice, procedure, programme, protocol, rule, scheme, stratagem, theory

polish *v.* **1.** brighten, buff, burnish, clean, furbish, rub, shine, smooth, wax **2.** brush up, correct, cultivate, emend, enhance, finish, improve, perfect, refine, touch up ~*n.* **3.** brightness, brilliance, finish, glaze, gloss, lustre, sheen, smoothness, sparkle, veneer **4.** varnish, wax **5.** *Fig.* class (*Inf.*), elegance, finesse, finish, grace, politesse, refinement, style, suavity, urbanity

polished 1. bright, burnished, furbished, glassy, gleaming, glossy, shining, slippery, smooth **2.** *Fig.* civilized, courtly, cultivated, elegant, finished, genteel, polite, refined, sophisticated, urbane, well-bred **3.** accomplished, adept, expert, faultless, fine, flawless, impeccable, masterly, outstanding, professional, skilful, superlative
Antonyms (*sense 1*) dark, dull, matt, rough (*sense 2*) inelegant, uncivilized, uncultivated, unrefined, unsophisticated (*sense 3*) amateurish, inept, inexpert, unaccomplished, unskilled

polite affable, civil, complaisant, courteous, deferential, gracious, mannerly, obliging, respectful, well-behaved, well-mannered
Antonyms discourteous, ill-mannered, impertinent, impolite, impudent, insulting, rude

politician legislator, Member of Parliament, M.P., office bearer, politico (*Inf., chiefly U.S.*), public servant, statesman

politics affairs of state, civics, government, government policy, political science, polity, statecraft, statesmanship

poll *n.* **1.** figures, returns, tally, vote, voting **2.** ballot, canvass, census, count, Gallup Poll, (public) opinion poll, sampling, survey

pollute 1. adulterate, befoul, contaminate, dirty, foul, infect, make filthy, mar, poison, soil, spoil, stain, taint 2. besmirch, corrupt, debase, debauch, defile, deprave, desecrate, dishonour, profane, sully, violate
Antonyms (sense 1) clean, cleanse, decontaminate, disinfect, purge, sanitize, sterilize (sense 2) esteem, honour

pompous 1. affected, arrogant, bloated, grandiose, imperious, magisterial, ostentatious, overbearing, pontifical, portentous, pretentious, puffed up, self-important, showy, supercilious, vainglorious 2. boastful, bombastic, flatulent, fustian, grandiloquent, high-flown, inflated, magniloquent, orotund, overblown, turgid, windy
Antonyms direct, humble, modest, natural, plain-spoken, self-effacing, simple, succinct, unaffected, unpretentious

ponder brood, cerebrate, cogitate, consider, contemplate, deliberate, examine, excogitate, give thought to, meditate, mull over, muse, puzzle over, reflect, ruminate, study, think, weigh

pool¹ 1. lake, mere, pond, puddle, splash, tarn 2. swimming bath, swimming pool

pool² n. 1. collective, combine, consortium, group, syndicate, team, trust 2. bank, funds, jackpot, kitty, pot, stakes ~v. 3. amalgamate, combine, join forces, league, merge, put together, share

poor 1. badly off, broke (Inf.), destitute, hard up (Inf.), impecunious, impoverished, indigent, in need, in want, necessitous, needy, on one's beam-ends, on one's uppers, on the rocks, penniless, penurious, poverty-stricken, skint (Brit. sl.), stony-broke (Brit. sl.) 2. deficient, exiguous, inadequate, incomplete, insufficient, lacking,

meagre, miserable, niggardly, pitiable, reduced, scanty, skimpy, slight, sparse, straitened 3. below par, faulty, feeble, inferior, low-grade, mediocre, rotten (Inf.), rubbishy, second-rate, shabby, shoddy, sorry, substandard, unsatisfactory, valueless, weak, worthless 4. bad, bare, barren, depleted, exhausted, fruitless, impoverished, infertile, sterile, unfruitful, unproductive 5. hapless, ill-fated, luckless, miserable, pathetic, pitiable, unfortunate, unhappy, unlucky, wretched 6. humble, insignificant, lowly, mean, modest, paltry, plain, trivial
Antonyms (sense 1) affluent, comfortable (Inf.), prosperous, rich, wealthy, well-heeled (Inf.), well-off (sense 2) abundant, adequate, ample, complete, dense, plentiful, satisfactory, sufficient, thick (sense 3) excellent, exceptional, first-class, first-rate, satisfactory, superior, valuable (sense 4) fertile, fruitful, productive, teeming, yielding (sense 5) fortunate, happy, lucky, successful

pop v. 1. bang, burst, crack, explode, go off, report, snap 2. insert, push, put, shove, slip, stick, thrust, tuck ~n. 3. bang, burst, crack, explosion, noise, report

populace commonalty, crowd, general public, hoi polloi, inhabitants, masses, mob, multitude, people, rabble, throng

popular 1. accepted, approved, celebrated, famous, fashionable, favoured, favourite, in, in demand, in favour, liked, sought-after, well-liked 2. common, conventional, current, general, prevailing, prevalent, public, standard, stock, ubiquitous, universal, widespread
Antonyms (sense 1) despised, detested, disliked, hated, loathed, unaccepted, unpopular (sense 2) infrequent, rare, uncommon, unusual

popularity acceptance, acclaim, adoration, approval, celebrity, currency, esteem, fame, favour, idolization, lionization, recognition, regard, renown, reputation, repute, vogue

populate colonize, inhabit, live in, occupy, people, settle

population citizenry, community, denizens, folk, inhabitants, natives, people, populace, residents, society

pore v. brood, contemplate, dwell on, examine, go over, peruse, ponder, read, scrutinize, study

port Nautical anchorage, harbour, haven, roads, roadstead, seaport

portable compact, convenient, easily carried, handy, light, lightweight, manageable, movable, portative

portend adumbrate, augur, bespeak, betoken, bode, foreshadow, foretell, foretoken, forewarn, harbinger, herald, indicate, omen, point to, predict, presage, prognosticate, promise, threaten, warn of

porter[1] baggage attendant, bearer, carrier

porter[2] caretaker, concierge, doorman, gatekeeper, janitor

portion n. 1. bit, fraction, fragment, morsel, part, piece, scrap, section, segment 2. allocation, allotment, allowance, division, lot, measure, parcel, quantity, quota, ration, share 3. helping, piece, serving 4. cup, destiny, fate, fortune, lot, luck

portrait image, likeness, painting, photograph, picture, portraiture, representation, sketch

portray 1. delineate, depict, draw, figure, illustrate, limn, paint, picture, render, represent, sketch 2. characterize, depict, describe, paint a mental picture of, put in words

pose v. 1. arrange, model, position, sit, sit for 2. Often with as feign, impersonate, masquerade as, pass oneself off as, pretend to be, profess to be, sham 3. affect, attitudinize, posture, put on airs, show off (Inf.), strike an attitude

4. advance, posit, present, propound, put, put forward, set, state, submit ~n. 5. attitude, bearing, mien (Literary), position, posture, stance 6. act, affectation, air, attitudinizing, façade, front, mannerism, masquerade, posturing, pretence, role

poser brain-teaser (Inf.), conundrum, enigma, knotty point, problem, puzzle, question, riddle, tough one, vexed question

position n. 1. area, bearings, locale, locality, location, place, point, post, reference, site, situation, spot, station, whereabouts 2. arrangement, attitude, disposition, pose, posture, stance 3. angle, attitude, belief, opinion, outlook, point of view, slant, stance, stand, standpoint, view, viewpoint 4. circumstances, condition, pass, plight, predicament, situation, state, strait(s) 5. caste, class, consequence, importance, place, prestige, rank, reputation, standing, station, stature, status 6. berth (Inf.), billet (Inf.), capacity, duty, employment, function, job, occupation, office, place, post, role, situation ~v. 7. arrange, array, dispose, fix, lay out, locate, place, put, set, settle, stand, stick (Inf.)

positive 1. absolute, actual, affirmative, categorical, certain, clear, clear-cut, conclusive, concrete, decisive, definite, direct, explicit, express, firm, incontrovertible, indisputable, real, unequivocal, unmistakable 2. assured, certain, confident, convinced, sure 3. assertive, cocksure, decided, dogmatic, emphatic, firm, forceful, opinionated, peremptory, resolute, stubborn 4. beneficial, constructive, effective, efficacious, forward-looking, helpful, practical, productive, progressive, useful 5. Inf. absolute, complete, consummate, out-and-out, perfect, rank, thorough, thoroughgoing, unmitigated, utter

Antonyms (sense 1) contestable,

possess

disputable, doubtful, inconclusive, indecisive, indefinite, uncertain (*sense 2*) not confident, unassured, uncertain, unconvinced, unsure (*sense 3*) diffident, open-minded, receptive, retiring, timid, unassertive, unobtrusive (*sense 4*) conservative, detrimental, harmful, impractical, reactionary, unhelpful, useless

possess 1. be blessed with, be born with, be endowed with, enjoy, have, have to one's name, hold, own **2.** acquire, control, dominate, hold, occupy, seize, take over, take possession of

possessed bedevilled, berserk, bewitched, consumed, crazed, cursed, demented, enchanted, frenetic, frenzied, hag-ridden, haunted, maddened, obsessed, raving, under a spell

possession 1. control, custody, hold, occupancy, occupation, ownership, proprietorship, tenure, title **2.** *Plural* assets, belongings, chattels, effects, estate, goods and chattels, property, things, wealth

possibility 1. feasibility, likelihood, plausibility, potentiality, practicability, workableness **2.** chance, hazard, hope, liability, likelihood, odds, probability, prospect, risk

possible 1. conceivable, credible, hypothetical, imaginable, likely, potential **2.** attainable, doable, feasible, on (*Inf.*), practicable, realizable, viable, within reach, workable **3.** hopeful, likely, potential, probable, promising
Antonyms impossible, impracticable, improbable, inconceivable, incredible, unfeasible, unimaginable, unlikely, unobtainable, unreasonable, unthinkable

post¹ 1. *n.* column, newel, pale, palisade, picket, pillar, pole, shaft, stake, standard, stock, support, upright **2.** *v.* advertise, affix, announce, display, make known, pin up, proclaim, promulgate, publicize, publish, put up, stick up

post² 1. *n.* appointment, assignment, berth (*Inf.*), billet (*Inf.*), employment, job, office, place, position, situation **2.** *v.* assign, establish, locate, place, position, put, situate, station

post³ 1. *n.* collection, delivery, mail, postal service **2.** *v.* dispatch, mail, send, transmit

poster advertisement, affiche, announcement, bill, notice, placard, public notice, sticker

posterity 1. children, descendants, family, heirs, issue, offspring, progeny, scions, seed **2.** future, future generations, succeeding generations

postpone adjourn, defer, delay, hold over, put back, put off, shelve, suspend, table
Antonyms advance, bring forward, call to order, carry out, go ahead with

postscript addition, afterthought, afterword, appendix, P.S., supplement

postulate advance, assume, hypothesize, posit, predicate, presuppose, propose, put forward, suppose, take for granted, theorize

posture 1. *n.* attitude, bearing, carriage, disposition, mien (*Literary*), pose, position, set, stance **2.** *v.* affect, attitudinize, do for effect, make a show, pose, put on airs, show off (*Inf.*), try to attract attention

potent efficacious, forceful, mighty, powerful, puissant, strong, vigorous
Antonyms impotent, ineffective, weak

potential 1. *adj.* budding, dormant, embryonic, future, hidden, inherent, latent, likely, possible, promising, undeveloped, unrealized **2.** *n.* ability, aptitude, capability, capacity, possibility, potentiality, power, the makings, what it takes (*Inf.*), wherewithal

potter dabble, fiddle (*Inf.*), footle (*Inf.*), fribble, fritter, mess about, poke along, tinker

pouch bag, container, pocket, poke (*Dialect*), purse, sack

pounce 1. *v.* ambush, attack, bound onto, dash at, drop, fall upon, jump, leap at, snatch, spring, strike, swoop, take by surprise, take unawares 2. *n.* assault, attack, bound, jump, leap, spring, swoop

pound 1. batter, beat, belabour, clobber (*Sl.*), hammer, pelt, pummel, strike, thrash, thump 2. bray (*Dialect*), bruise, comminute, crush, powder, pulverize, triturate

pour 1. decant, let flow, spill, splash 2. course, emit, flow, gush, run, rush, spew, spout, stream 3. bucket down (*Inf.*), come down in torrents, rain, rain cats and dogs (*Inf.*), rain hard *or* heavily, sheet, teem

pout *v.* glower, look petulant, look sullen, lower, make a *moue*, mope, pull a long face, purse one's lips, sulk, turn down the corners of one's mouth

poverty 1. beggary, destitution, distress, hand-to-mouth existence, hardship, indigence, insolvency, necessitousness, necessity, need, pauperism, pennilessness, penury, privation, want 2. dearth, deficiency, insufficiency, lack, paucity, scarcity, shortage 3. aridity, bareness, barrenness, deficiency, infertility, meagreness, poorness, sterility, unfruitfulness

Antonyms (*sense 1*) affluence, comfort, luxury, opulence, richness, wealth (*sense 2*) abundance, plethora, sufficiency (*sense 3*) fecundity, fertility, fruitfulness, productiveness

powder *n.* 1. dust, fine grains, loose particles, pounce, talc ~*v.* 2. crush, granulate, grind, pestle, pound, pulverize 3. cover, dredge, dust, scatter, sprinkle, strew

power 1. ability, capability, capacity, competence, competency, faculty, potential 2. brawn, energy, force, forcefulness, intensity, might, muscle, potency, strength, vigour, weight 3. ascendancy, authority, command,

control, dominance, domination, dominion, influence, mastery, rule, sovereignty, supremacy, sway 4. authority, authorization, licence, prerogative, privilege, right, warrant

Antonyms (*sense 1*) inability, incapability, incapacity, incompetence (*sense 2*) enervation, feebleness, impotence, listlessness, weakness

powerful 1. energetic, mighty, potent, robust, stalwart, strapping, strong, sturdy, vigorous 2. authoritative, commanding, controlling, dominant, influential, prevailing, puissant, sovereign, supreme 3. cogent, compelling, convincing, effective, effectual, forceful, forcible, impressive, persuasive, telling, weighty

powerless 1. debilitated, disabled, etiolated, feeble, frail, helpless, impotent, incapable, incapacitated, ineffectual, infirm, paralysed, prostrate, weak 2. defenceless, dependent, disenfranchised, disfranchised, ineffective, subject, tied, unarmed, vulnerable

Antonyms (*sense 1*) able-bodied, fit, healthy, lusty, powerful, robust, strong, sturdy

practicability advantage, feasibility, operability, possibility, practicality, use, usefulness, value, viability, workability

practicable achievable, attainable, doable, feasible, performable, possible, viable, within the realm of possibility, workable

Antonyms beyond the bounds of possibility, impossible, out of the question, unachievable, unattainable, unfeasible, unworkable

practical 1. applied, efficient, empirical, experimental, factual, functional, pragmatic, realistic, utilitarian 2. businesslike, down-to-earth, everyday, hard-headed, matter-of-fact, mundane, ordinary, realistic, sensible, workaday 3. accomplished, efficient, experienced, proficient, quali fied, seasoned, skilled, trained, veteran, working

Antonyms (*senses 1 & 2*) impractical, inefficient, speculative, theoretical, unpractical, unrealistic (*sense 3*) inefficient, inexperienced, unaccomplished, unqualified, unskilled, untrained

practically 1. all but, almost, basically, close to, essentially, fundamentally, in effect, just about, nearly, to all intents and purposes, very nearly, virtually, well-nigh **2.** clearly, matter-of-factly, rationally, realistically, reasonably, sensibly, unsentimentally, with common sense

practice 1. custom, habit, method, mode, praxis, routine, rule, system, tradition, usage, use, usual procedure, way, wont **2.** discipline, drill, exercise, preparation, rehearsal, repetition, study, training, work-out **3.** business, career, profession, vocation, work

practise 1. discipline, drill, exercise, go over, go through, polish, prepare, rehearse, repeat, study, train, warm up, work out **2.** apply, carry out, do, follow, live up to, observe, perform, put into practice **3.** carry on, engage in, ply, pursue, specialize in, undertake, work at

praise *n.* **1.** acclaim, acclamation, accolade, applause, approbation, approval, cheering, commendation, compliment, congratulation, encomium, eulogy, good word, kudos, laudation, ovation, panegyric, plaudit, tribute **2.** adoration, devotion, glory, homage, thanks, worship ~*v.* **3.** acclaim, admire, applaud, approve, cheer, compliment, congratulate, cry up, eulogize, extol, honour, laud, pay tribute to, sing the praises of **4.** adore, bless, exalt, give thanks to, glorify, magnify (*Archaic*), pay homage to, worship

pray adjure, ask, beg, beseech, call upon, crave, cry for, entreat, implore, importune, invoke, pe-

tition, plead, request, solicit, sue, supplicate, urge

prayer 1. communion, devotion, invocation, litany, orison, supplication **2.** appeal, entreaty, petition, plea, request, suit, supplication

preach 1. address, deliver a sermon, evangelize, exhort, orate **2.** admonish, advocate, exhort, harangue, lecture, moralize, sermonize, urge

preacher clergyman, evangelist, minister, missionary, parson, revivalist

precarious chancy (*Inf.*), dangerous, dicey (*Sl.*), dodgy (*Brit. inf.*), doubtful, dubious, hairy (*Sl.*), hazardous, insecure, perilous, risky, shaky, slippery, touch and go, tricky, uncertain, unreliable, unsafe, unsettled, unstable, unsteady, unsure

Antonyms certain, dependable, reliable, safe, secure, stable, steady

precaution 1. insurance, preventative measure, protection, provision, safeguard, safety measure **2.** anticipation, care, caution, circumspection, foresight, forethought, providence, prudence, wariness

precede antecede, antedate, come first, forerun, go ahead of, go before, head, herald, introduce, lead, pave the way, preface, take precedence, usher

precedent *n.* antecedent, authority, criterion, example, exemplar, instance, model, paradigm, pattern, previous example, prototype, standard

precinct 1. bound, boundary, confine, enclosure, limit **2.** area, district, quarter, section, sector, zone

precious 1. adored, beloved, cherished, darling, dear, dearest, favourite, idolized, loved, prized, treasured, valued **2.** choice, costly, dear, expensive, exquisite, fine, high-priced, inestimable, invaluable, priceless, prized, rare, recherché, valuable

precipice bluff, brink, cliff, cliff face, crag, height, rock face, sheer drop, steep

precipitate v. 1. accelerate, advance, bring on, dispatch, expedite, further, hasten, hurry, press, push forward, quicken, speed up, trigger ~adj. 2. breakneck, headlong, plunging, rapid, rushing, swift, violent 3. abrupt, brief, quick, sudden, unexpected, without warning

precise absolute, accurate, actual, clear-cut, correct, definite, exact, explicit, express, fixed, literal, particular, specific, strict, unequivocal
Antonyms ambiguous, careless, equivocal, incorrect, indefinite, indistinct, inexact, loose, vague

precisely absolutely, accurately, bang, correctly, exactly, just, just so, literally, neither more nor less, plumb (Inf.), slap (Inf.), smack (Inf.), square, squarely, strictly

precision accuracy, care, correctness, definiteness, exactitude, exactness, fidelity, meticulousness, nicety, particularity, preciseness, rigour

preclude check, debar, exclude, forestall, hinder, inhibit, make impossible, make impracticable, obviate, prevent, prohibit, put a stop to, restrain, rule out, stop

precocious advanced, ahead, bright, developed, forward, quick, smart
Antonyms backward, dense, dull, retarded, slow, underdeveloped, unresponsive

precursor forerunner, harbinger, herald, messenger, usher, vanguard

predatory carnivorous, hunting, predacious, rapacious, raptorial, ravening

predecessor antecedent, forerunner, precursor, previous (former, prior) job holder

predetermined agreed, arranged in advance, cut and dried (Inf.), decided beforehand, fixed, prearranged, preplanned, set, settled, set up

predicament corner, dilemma, emergency, fix (Inf.), hole (Sl.), jam (Inf.), mess, pickle (Inf.), pinch, plight, quandary, scrape (Inf.), situation, spot (Inf.), state

predict augur, divine, forebode, forecast, foresee, foretell, portend, presage, prognosticate, prophesy, soothsay

predictable anticipated, calculable, certain, expected, foreseeable, foreseen, likely, reliable, sure, sure-fire (Inf.)
Antonyms out of the blue, surprising, unexpected, unforeseen, unlikely, unpredictable

prediction augury, divination, forecast, prognosis, prognostication, prophecy, soothsaying

predisposed agreeable, amenable, given to, inclined, liable, minded, prone, ready, subject, susceptible, willing

predominant ascendant, capital, chief, controlling, dominant, important, leading, main, paramount, preponderant, prevailing, prevalent, primary, prime, principal, prominent, ruling, sovereign, superior, supreme, top-priority

preface 1. n. exordium, foreword, introduction, preamble, preliminary, prelude, proem, prolegomenon, prologue 2. v. begin, introduce, launch, lead up to, open, precede, prefix

prefer adopt, be partial to, choose, desire, elect, fancy, favour, go for, incline towards, like better, opt for, pick, plump for, select, single out, wish, would rather, would sooner

preferable best, better, choice, chosen, favoured, more desirable, more eligible, superior, worthier

preferably as a matter of choice, by choice, first, in or for preference, much rather, much sooner, rather, sooner, willingly

preference 1. choice, desire, election, favourite, first choice,

option, partiality, pick, predilec~
tion, selection, top of the list 2.
advantage, favoured treatment,
favouritism, first place, prec~
edence, pride of place, priority

prejudge anticipate, forejudge,
jump to conclusions, make a
hasty assessment, presume, pre~
suppose

prejudice n. 1. bias, jaundiced
eye, partiality, preconceived no~
tion, preconception, prejudg~
ment, warp 2. bigotry, chauvin~
ism, discrimination, injustice, in~
tolerance, narrow-mindedness,
racism, sexism, unfairness 3.
damage, detriment, disadvant~
age, harm, hurt, impairment,
loss, mischief ~v. 4. bias, colour,
distort, influence, jaundice, poi~
son, predispose, prepossess,
slant, sway, warp 5. damage,
harm, hinder, hurt, impair, in~
jure, mar, spoil, undermine

preliminary 1. adj. exploratory,
first, initial, initiatory, introduc~
tory, opening, pilot, precursory,
prefatory, preparatory, prior,
qualifying, test, trial 2. n. begin~
ning, first round, foundation,
groundwork, initiation, introduc~
tion, opening, preamble, preface,
prelims, prelude, preparation,
start

prelude beginning, commence~
ment, curtain-raiser, exordium,
foreword, intro (Inf.), introduc~
tion, overture, preamble, pref~
ace, preliminary, preparation,
proem, prolegomenon, prologue,
start

premature 1. abortive, early,
embryonic, forward, green, im~
mature, incomplete, predevel~
oped, raw, undeveloped, un~
fledged, unripe, unseasonable,
untimely 2. Fig. hasty, ill-
considered, ill-timed, impulsive,
inopportune, overhasty, precipi~
tate, previous (Inf.), rash, too
soon, untimely

premeditated aforethought, cal~
culated, conscious, considered,
contrived, deliberate, intended,

intentional, planned, prepense,
studied, wilful
Antonyms accidental, inadvert~
ent, unintentional, unplanned,
unpremeditated, unwitting

premier n. 1. chancellor, head of
government, P.M., prime minis~
ter ~adj. 2. arch, chief, first,
foremost, head, highest, leading,
main, primary, prime, principal,
top 3. earliest, first, inaugural,
initial, original

premiere debut, first night, first
performance, first showing,
opening

premises building, establish~
ment, place, property, site

premiss, premise argument, as~
sertion, assumption, ground, hy~
pothesis, postulate, postulation,
presupposition, proposition, sup~
position, thesis

premium 1. bonus, boon, bounty,
fee, percentage (Inf.), perk (Brit.
inf.), perquisite, prize, recom~
pense, remuneration, reward 2.
appreciation, regard, stock,
store, value

premonition apprehension, feel~
ing, feeling in one's bones, fore~
boding, forewarning, funny feel~
ing (Inf.), hunch, idea, intuition,
misgiving, omen, portent, pres~
age, presentiment, sign, suspi~
cion, warning

preoccupation absence of mind,
absent-mindedness, absorption,
abstraction, brown study, day~
dreaming, engrossment, immer~
sion, inattentiveness, musing,
oblivion, pensiveness, prepossess~
sion, reverie, woolgathering

preoccupied absent-minded, ab~
sorbed, abstracted, caught up in,
distracted, distrait, engrossed,
faraway, heedless, immersed, in
a brown study, intent, lost in, lost
in thought, oblivious, rapt, taken
up, unaware, wrapped up

preparation 1. development, get~
ting ready, groundwork, prepar~
ing, putting in order 2. alertness,
anticipation, expectation, fore~
sight, precaution, preparedness,
provision, readiness, safeguard 3.

composition, compound, concoction, medicine, mixture, tincture **4.** homework, prep (*Inf.*), revision, schoolwork, study, swotting (*Inf.*)

preparatory basic, elementary, introductory, opening, prefatory, preliminary, preparative, primary

prepare 1. adapt, adjust, anticipate, arrange, coach, dispose, form, groom, make provision, make ready, plan, practise, prime, put in order, train, warm up **2.** brace, fortify, gird, ready, steel, strengthen **3.** assemble, concoct, construct, contrive, draw up, fashion, fix up, get up (*Inf.*), make, produce, put together, turn out

prepared 1. all set, arranged, fit, in order, in readiness, planned, primed, ready, set **2.** able, disposed, inclined, minded, of a mind, predisposed, willing

preposterous absurd, asinine, bizarre, crazy, excessive, exorbitant, extravagant, extreme, foolish, impossible, incredible, insane, irrational, laughable, ludicrous, monstrous, nonsensical, out of the question, outrageous, ridiculous, senseless, shocking, unreasonable, unthinkable

prerequisite 1. *adj.* called for, essential, imperative, indispensable, mandatory, necessary, needful, obligatory, of the essence, required, requisite, vital **2.** *n.* condition, essential, imperative, must, necessity, precondition, qualification, requirement, requisite, *sine qua non*

prescribe appoint, assign, command, decree, define, dictate, direct, enjoin, fix, impose, lay down, ordain, order, require, rule, set, specify, stipulate

prescription drug, medicine, mixture, preparation, remedy

presence 1. attendance, being, companionship, company, existence, habitation, inhabitance, occupancy, residence **2.** closeness, immediate circle, nearness, neighbourhood, propinquity, proximity, vicinity **3.** air, appearance, aspect, aura, bearing, carriage, comportment, demeanour, ease, mien (*Literary*), personality, poise, self-assurance

present[1] *adj.* **1.** contemporary, current, existent, existing, extant, immediate, instant, present-day **2.** accounted for, at hand, available, here, in attendance, near, nearby, ready, there, to hand ~*n.* **3.** here and now, now, present moment, the time being, this day and age, today

present[2] *v.* **1.** acquaint with, introduce, make known **2.** demonstrate, display, exhibit, give, mount, put before the public, put on, show, stage **3.** adduce, advance, declare, expound, extend, hold out, introduce, offer, pose, produce, proffer, put forward, raise, recount, relate, state, submit, suggest, tender ~*n.* **4.** benefaction, boon, bounty, donation, endowment, favour, gift, grant, gratuity, largess, offering, prezzie (*Inf.*)

presentation 1. award, bestowal, conferral, donation, giving, investiture, offering **2.** appearance, arrangement, delivery, exposition, production, rendition, staging, submission **3.** demonstration, display, exhibition, performance, production, representation, show

presently anon (*Archaic*), before long, by and by, in a minute, in a moment, in a short while, pretty soon (*Inf.*), shortly, soon

preservation conservation, defence, keeping, maintenance, perpetuation, protection, safeguarding, safekeeping, safety, salvation, security, storage, support, upholding

preserve 1. *v.* care for, conserve, defend, guard, keep, protect, safeguard, save, secure, shelter, shield **2.** *n.* area, domain, field, realm, specialism, sphere
Antonyms (*sense 1*) assail, assault, attack, leave unprotected, turn out

preside administer, be at the head of, be in authority, chair, conduct, control, direct, govern, head, lead, manage, officiate, run, supervise

press v. **1.** bear down on, compress, condense, crush, depress, force down, jam, mash, push, reduce, squeeze, stuff **2.** calender, finish, flatten, iron, mangle, put the creases in, smooth, steam **3.** clasp, crush, embrace, encircle, enfold, fold in one's arms, hold close, hug, squeeze **4.** compel, constrain, demand, enforce, enjoin, force, insist on **5.** beg, entreat, exhort, implore, importune, petition, plead, pressurize, sue, supplicate, urge **6.** cluster, crowd, flock, gather, hasten, herd, hurry, mill, push, rush, seethe, surge, swarm, throng ~n. **7.** the press **a.** Fleet Street, fourth estate, journalism, news media, newspapers, the papers **b.** columnists, correspondents, gentlemen of the press, journalists, newsmen, photographers, pressmen, reporters

pressure 1. compressing, compression, crushing, force, heaviness, squeezing, weight **2.** coercion, compulsion, constraint, force, influence, obligation, power, sway

prestige authority, cachet, celebrity, credit, distinction, eminence, esteem, fame, honour, importance, influence, kudos, regard, renown, reputation, standing, stature, status, weight

presume assume, believe, conjecture, infer, posit, postulate, presuppose, suppose, surmise, take for granted, take it, think

presumption assurance, audacity, boldness, brass (*Inf.*), brass neck (*Inf.*), cheek (*Inf.*), effrontery, forwardness, gall (*Inf.*), impudence, insolence, nerve (*Inf.*), presumptuousness, temerity

pretence 1. acting, charade, deceit, deception, fabrication, fakery, faking, falsehood, feigning, invention, make-believe, sham,

simulation, subterfuge, trickery **2.** affectation, appearance, artifice, display, façade, posing, posturing, pretentiousness, show, veneer

Antonyms (*sense 1*) actuality, fact, reality (*sense 2*) candour, frankness, honesty, ingenuousness, openness

pretend 1. affect, allege, assume, counterfeit, dissemble, dissimulate, fake, falsify, feign, impersonate, make out, pass oneself off as, profess, put on, sham, simulate **2.** act, imagine, make believe, make up, play, play the part of, suppose

pretension 1. aspiration, assertion, assumption, claim, demand, pretence, profession **2.** affectation, airs, conceit, hypocrisy, ostentation, pomposity, pretentiousness, self-importance, show, showiness, snobbery, snobbishness, vainglory, vanity

pretentious affected, assuming, bombastic, conceited, exaggerated, extravagant, flaunting, grandiloquent, grandiose, highfalutin (*Inf.*), high-flown, high-sounding, hollow, inflated, magniloquent, mannered, ostentatious, overambitious, pompous, puffed up, showy, snobbish, specious, vainglorious

Antonyms modest, natural, plain, simple, unaffected, unassuming, unpretentious

pretext affectation, alleged reason, appearance, cloak, cover, device, excuse, guise, mask, ploy, pretence, red herring, ruse, semblance, show, simulation, veil

pretty 1. *adj.* appealing, attractive, beautiful, bonny, charming, comely, cute, fair, good-looking, graceful, lovely, personable **2.** *adv. Inf.* fairly, kind of (*Inf.*), moderately, quite, rather, reasonably, somewhat

Antonyms plain, ugly, unattractive, unshapely, unsightly

prevail 1. be victorious, carry the day, gain mastery, overcome, overrule, prove superior, succeed, triumph, win **2.** abound, be current (prevalent, widespread), exist generally, obtain, predominate, preponderate **3.** *Often with* **on** *or* **upon** bring round, convince, dispose, incline, induce, influence, persuade, prompt, sway, talk into, win over

prevailing common, current, customary, established, fashionable, general, in style, in vogue, ordinary, popular, prevalent, set, usual, widespread

prevaricate beat about the bush, beg the question, cavil, deceive, dodge, equivocate, evade, give a false colour to, hedge, lie, palter, quibble, shift, shuffle, stretch the truth, tergiversate
Antonyms be blunt, be direct, be frank, be straightforward, come straight to the point, not beat about the bush

prevent anticipate, avert, avoid, balk, bar, block, check, counteract, defend against, foil, forestall, frustrate, hamper, head off, hinder, impede, inhibit, intercept, nip in the bud, obstruct, obviate, preclude, restrain, stave off, stop, thwart, ward off
Antonyms allow, encourage, help, incite, permit, support, urge

prevention 1. anticipation, avoidance, deterrence, elimination, forestalling, obviation, precaution, preclusion, prophylaxis, safeguard, thwarting **2.** bar, check, deterrence, frustration, hindrance, impediment, interruption, obstacle, obstruction, stoppage

preventive, preventative 1. *adj.* hampering, hindering, impeding, obstructive **2.** *n.* block, hindrance, impediment, obstacle, obstruction

previous antecedent, anterior, earlier, erstwhile, ex-, foregoing, former, one-time, past, preceding, prior, quondam, sometime
Antonyms consequent, following, later, subsequent, succeeding

previously at one time, a while ago, before, beforehand, earlier,

formerly, heretofore, hitherto, in advance, in anticipation, in days *or* years gone by, in the past, once, then, until now

prey *n.* **1.** game, kill, quarry **2.** dupe, fall guy (*Inf.*), mark, mug (*Sl.*), target, victim

price *n.* **1.** amount, asking price, assessment, bill, charge, cost, damage (*Inf.*), estimate, expenditure, expense, face value, fee, figure, outlay, payment, rate, valuation, value, worth **2.** consequences, cost, penalty, sacrifice, toll ~*v.* **3.** assess, cost, estimate, evaluate, put a price on, rate, value

priceless beyond price, cherished, costly, dear, expensive, incalculable, incomparable, inestimable, invaluable, irreplaceable, precious, prized, rare, rich, treasured, worth a king's ransom
Antonyms cheap, cheapo (*Inf.*), common, inexpensive, worthless

prick *v.* **1.** bore, jab, lance, perforate, pierce, pink, punch, puncture, stab **2.** bite, itch, prickle, smart, sting, tingle ~*n.* **3.** cut, gash, hole, perforation, pinhole, puncture, wound

prickly 1. barbed, brambly, briery, bristly, spiny, thorny **2.** crawling, itchy, pricking, prickling, scratchy, sharp, smarting, stinging, tingling

pride *n.* **1.** *amour-propre,* dignity, honour, self-esteem, self-respect, self-worth **2.** arrogance, bigheadedness (*Inf.*), conceit, egotism, haughtiness, hauteur, hubris, loftiness, *morgue,* presumption, pretension, pretentiousness, self-importance, self-love, smugness, snobbery, superciliousness, vainglory, vanity **3.** boast, gem, jewel, pride and joy, prize, treasure **4.** best, choice, cream, elite, flower, glory, pick ~*v.* **5.** be proud of, boast, brag, congratulate oneself, crow, exult, flatter oneself, glory in, pique, plume, preen, revel in, take pride, vaunt
Antonyms (*sense 1*) humility, meekness, modesty

priest churchman, clergyman, cleric, curate, divine, ecclesiastic, father, father confessor, holy man, man of God, man of the cloth, minister, padre (*Inf.*), vicar

prim demure, fastidious, formal, fussy, old-maidish (*Inf.*), particular, precise, priggish, prissy (*Inf.*), proper, prudish, puritanical, schoolmarmish (*Brit. inf.*), starchy (*Inf.*), stiff, strait-laced

primarily above all, basically, chiefly, especially, essentially, for the most part, fundamentally, generally, mainly, mostly, on the whole, principally

primary 1. best, capital, cardinal, chief, dominant, first, greatest, highest, leading, main, paramount, prime, principal, top **2.** basic, beginning, elemental, essential, fundamental, radical, ultimate, underlying
Antonyms (*sense 1*) inferior, lesser, lowest, subordinate, supplementary, unimportant

prime *adj.* **1.** best, capital, choice, excellent, first-class, first-rate, grade A, highest, quality, select, selected, superior, top **2.** basic, earliest, fundamental, original, primary, underlying **3.** chief, leading, main, predominant, pre-eminent, primary, principal, ruling, senior ~*n.* **4.** best days, bloom, flower, full flowering, height, heyday, maturity, peak, perfection, zenith ~*v.* **5.** break in, coach, fit, get ready, groom, make ready, prepare, train **6.** brief, clue up, fill in (*Inf.*), gen up (*Brit. inf.*), give someone the lowdown (*Inf.*), inform, notify, tell

primitive 1. earliest, early, elementary, first, original, primary, primeval, primordial, pristine **2.** barbarian, barbaric, crude, rough, rude, rudimentary, savage, simple, uncivilized, uncultivated, undeveloped, unrefined
Antonyms (*sense 1*) advanced, later, modern (*sense 2*) civilized, comfortable, developed, elaborate, refined

prince lord, monarch, potentate, ruler, sovereign

principal *adj.* **1.** capital, cardinal, chief, controlling, dominant, essential, first, foremost, highest, key, leading, main, most important, paramount, pre-eminent, primary, prime, strongest ~*n.* **2.** boss (*Inf.*), chief, director, head, leader, master, ruler, superintendent **3.** dean, director, head (*Inf.*), headmaster, headmistress, head teacher, master, rector **4.** assets, capital, capital funds, money
Antonyms auxiliary, inferior, minor, subordinate, subsidiary, supplementary, weakest

principally above all, chiefly, especially, first and foremost, for the most part, in the main, mainly, mostly, particularly, predominantly, primarily

principle 1. assumption, axiom, canon, criterion, dictum, doctrine, dogma, ethic, formula, fundamental, golden rule, law, maxim, moral law, precept, proposition, rule, standard, truth, verity **2.** attitude, belief, code, credo, ethic, morality, opinion, tenet **3.** conscience, integrity, morals, probity, rectitude, scruples, sense of duty, sense of honour, uprightness

print *v.* **1.** engrave, go to press, impress, imprint, issue, mark, publish, put to bed (*Inf.*), run off, stamp ~*n.* **2.** book, magazine, newspaper, newsprint, periodical, printed matter, publication, typescript **3.** copy, engraving, photo (*Inf.*), photograph, picture, reproduction

priority first concern, greater importance, precedence, pre-eminence, preference, prerogative, rank, right of way, seniority, superiority, supremacy, the lead

prison can (*Sl.*), choky (*Sl.*), clink (*Sl.*), confinement, cooler (*Sl.*), dungeon, gaol, glasshouse (*Military inf.*), jail, jug (*Sl.*), lockup, penal institution, penitentiary

(*U.S.*), quod (*Sl.*), slammer (*Sl.*), stir (*Sl.*)

prisoner 1. con (*Sl.*), convict, jailbird, lag (*Sl.*) **2.** captive, detainee, hostage, internee

privacy isolation, privateness, retirement, retreat, seclusion, separateness, sequestration, solitude

private *adj.* **1.** clandestine, closet, confidential, hush-hush (*Inf.*), in camera, inside, off the record, privy (*Archaic*), secret, unofficial **2.** exclusive, individual, intimate, own, particular, personal, reserved, special **3.** concealed, isolated, not overlooked, retired, secluded, secret, separate, sequestered, solitary, withdrawn
Antonyms (*sense 1*) disclosed, known, official, open, public, revealed (*sense 2*) common, general, open, public, unlimited, unrestricted

privilege advantage, benefit, birthright, claim, concession, due, entitlement, franchise, freedom, immunity, liberty, prerogative, right, sanction

prize¹ *n.* **1.** accolade, award, honour, premium, reward, trophy **2.** haul, jackpot, purse, stakes, windfall, winnings **3.** aim, ambition, conquest, desire, gain, goal, hope **4.** booty, capture, loot, pickings, pillage, plunder, spoil(s), trophy ~*adj.* **5.** award-winning, best, champion, first-rate, outstanding, top, topnotch (*Inf.*), winning

prize² *v.* appreciate, cherish, esteem, hold dear, regard highly, set store by, treasure, value

probability chance(s), expectation, liability, likelihood, likeliness, odds, presumption, prospect

probable apparent, credible, feasible, likely, most likely, odds-on, on the cards, ostensible, plausible, possible, presumable, presumed, reasonable, seeming
Antonyms doubtful, improbable, not likely, unlikely

probably as likely as not, doubt-

less, in all likelihood, in all probability, likely, maybe, most likely, perchance (*Archaic*), perhaps, possibly, presumably

probe *v.* **1.** examine, explore, go into, investigate, look into, query, scrutinize, search, sift, sound, test, verify **2.** explore, feel around, poke, prod ~*n.* **3.** detection, examination, exploration, inquest, inquiry, investigation, research, scrutiny, study

problem *n.* **1.** can of worms (*Inf.*), complication, difficulty, dilemma, disagreement, dispute, disputed point, doubt, hard nut to crack (*Inf.*), point at issue, predicament, quandary, trouble **2.** brain-teaser (*Inf.*), conundrum, enigma, poser, puzzle, question, riddle ~*adj.* **3.** delinquent, difficult, intractable, uncontrollable, unmanageable, unruly

procedure action, conduct, course, custom, form, formula, method, modus operandi, operation, performance, plan of action, policy, practice, process, routine, scheme, step, strategy, system, transaction

proceed 1. advance, carry on, continue, get going, get on with, get under way with, go ahead, go on, make a start, move on, press on, progress, set in motion **2.** arise, come, derive, emanate, ensue, flow, follow, issue, originate, result, spring, stem
Antonyms (*sense 1*) break off, cease, discontinue, end, get behind, halt, leave off, pack in (*Brit. inf.*), retreat, stop

proceeding 1. act, action, course of action, deed, measure, move, occurrence, procedure, process, step, undertaking, venture **2.** *Plural* account, affairs, annals, archives, business, dealings, doings, matters, minutes, records, report, transactions

proceeds earnings, gain, income, produce, products, profit, receipts, returns, revenue, takings, yield

process *n.* **1.** action, course,

course of action, manner, means, measure, method, mode, operation, performance, practice, procedure, proceeding, system, transaction 2. advance, course, development, evolution, formation, growth, movement, progress, progression, stage, step, unfolding ~v. 3. deal with, dispose of, fulfil, handle, take care of 4. alter, convert, prepare, refine, transform, treat

procession cavalcade, column, cortege, file, march, motorcade, parade, train

proclaim advertise, affirm, announce, blaze (abroad), blazon (abroad), circulate, declare, enunciate, give out, herald, indicate, make known, profess, promulgate, publish, shout from the housetops (Inf.), show, trumpet
Antonyms conceal, hush up, keep back, keep secret, suppress, withhold

proclamation announcement, declaration, decree, edict, manifesto, notice, notification, promulgation, pronouncement, pronunciamento, publication

procrastinate adjourn, be dilatory, dally, defer, delay, drag one's feet (Inf.), gain time, play a waiting game, play for time, postpone, prolong, protract, put off, retard, stall, temporize
Antonyms advance, expedite, get on with, hasten, hurry (up), proceed, speed up

procure acquire, appropriate, buy, come by, earn, effect, find, gain, get, get hold of, lay hands on, manage to get, obtain, pick up, purchase, secure, win

prod v. 1. dig, drive, elbow, jab, nudge, poke, prick, propel, push, shove 2. egg on, goad, impel, incite, motivate, move, prompt, rouse, spur, stimulate, stir up, urge ~n. 3. boost, dig, elbow, jab, nudge, poke, push, shove 4. goad, poker, spur, stick 5. boost, cue, prompt, reminder, signal, stimulus

prodigal 1. adj. excessive, extravagant, immoderate, improvident, intemperate, profligate, reckless, spendthrift, squandering, wanton, wasteful 2. n. big spender, profligate, spendthrift, squanderer, wastrel
Antonyms (sense 1) economical, frugal, miserly, parsimonious, sparing, stingy, thrifty, tight

prodigy 1. child genius, genius, mastermind, talent, whiz (Inf.), whiz kid (Inf.), wizard, wonder child, wunderkind 2. marvel, miracle, one in a million, phenomenon, rare bird (Inf.), sensation, wonder

produce v. 1. compose, construct, create, develop, fabricate, invent, make, manufacture, originate, put together, turn out 2. afford, bear, beget, breed, bring forth, deliver, engender, furnish, give, render, supply, yield 3. bring about, cause, effect, generate, give rise to, make for, occasion, provoke, set off 4. advance, bring forward, bring to light, demonstrate, exhibit, offer, present, put forward, set forth, show 5. direct, do, exhibit, mount, present, put before the public, put on, show, stage 6. Geometry extend, lengthen, prolong, protract ~n. 7. crop, fruit and vegetables, greengrocery, harvest, product, yield

producer 1. director, impresario, régisseur 2. farmer, grower, maker, manufacturer

product 1. artefact, commodity, concoction, creation, goods, invention, merchandise, produce, production, work 2. consequence, effect, fruit, issue, legacy, offshoot, outcome, result, returns, spin-off, upshot, yield

production 1. assembly, construction, creation, fabrication, formation, making, manufacture, manufacturing, origination, preparation, producing 2. direction, management, presentation, staging

productive creative, dynamic,

energetic, fecund, fertile, fruitful, generative, inventive, plentiful, producing, prolific, rich, teeming, vigorous

Antonyms barren, poor, sterile, unfertile, unfruitful, unproductive

productivity abundance, mass production, output, production, productive capacity, productiveness, work rate, yield

profane adj. 1. disrespectful, godless, heathen, idolatrous, impious, impure, irreligious, irreverent, pagan, sacrilegious, sinful, ungodly, wicked 2. lay, secular, temporal, unconsecrated, unhallowed, unholy, unsanctified, worldly 3. abusive, blasphemous, coarse, crude, filthy, foul, obscene, vulgar ~ v. 4. abuse, commit sacrilege, contaminate, debase, defile, desecrate, misuse, pervert, pollute, prostitute, violate, vitiate

profanity abuse, blasphemy, curse, cursing, execration, foul language, four-letter word, impiety, imprecation, irreverence, malediction, obscenity, profaneness, sacrilege, swearing, swearword

profess acknowledge, admit, affirm, announce, assert, asseverate, aver, avow, certify, confess, confirm, declare, maintain, own, proclaim, state, vouch

professed 1. avowed, certified, confirmed, declared, proclaimed, self-acknowledged, self-confessed 2. alleged, apparent, ostensible, pretended, purported, self-styled, so-called, *soi-disant*, supposed, would-be

profession 1. business, calling, career, employment, line, line of work, métier, occupation, office, position, sphere, vocation, walk of life 2. acknowledgment, affirmation, assertion, attestation, avowal, claim, confession, declaration, statement, testimony, vow

professional 1. adj. ace (*Inf.*), adept, competent, crack (*Sl.*), efficient, experienced, expert, finished, masterly, polished, prac-

tised, proficient, qualified, skilled, slick, trained 2. n. adept, authority, dab hand (*Brit. inf.*), expert, maestro, master, past master, pro (*Inf.*), specialist, virtuoso, wizard

Antonyms amateurish, incapable, incompetent, inefficient, inept, inexperienced, unpolished, unqualified, unskilled, untrained

professor don (*Brit.*), fellow (*Brit.*), head of faculty, prof (*Inf.*)

proficiency ability, accomplishment, aptitude, competence, dexterity, expertise, expertness, facility, knack, know-how (*Inf.*), mastery, skilfulness, skill, talent

proficient able, accomplished, adept, apt, capable, clever, competent, conversant, efficient, experienced, expert, gifted, masterly, qualified, skilful, skilled, talented, trained, versed

Antonyms bad, incapable, incompetent, inept, unaccomplished, unskilled

profile n. 1. contour, drawing, figure, form, outline, portrait, shape, side view, silhouette, sketch 2. biography, characterization, character sketch, sketch, thumbnail sketch, vignette 3. analysis, chart, diagram, examination, graph, review, study, survey, table

profit n. 1. Often plural bottom line, earnings, emoluments, gain, percentage (*Inf.*), proceeds, receipts, return, revenue, surplus, takings, winnings, yield 2. advancement, advantage, avail, benefit, gain, good, interest, use, value ~ v. 3. aid, avail, benefit, be of advantage to, better, contribute, gain, help, improve, promote, serve, stand in good stead 4. capitalize on, cash in on (*Sl.*), exploit, learn from, make capital of, make good use of, make the most of, put to good use, reap the benefit of, take advantage of, turn to advantage or account, use, utilize 5. clean up (*Inf.*), clear, earn, gain, make a good thing of (*Inf.*), make a killing (*Inf.*), make money

profitable 1. commercial, cost-effective, fruitful, gainful, lucrative, money-making, paying, remunerative, rewarding, worthwhile **2.** advantageous, beneficial, fruitful, productive, rewarding, serviceable, useful, valuable, worthwhile
Antonyms disadvantageous, fruitless, unremunerative, unrewarding, useless, vain, worthless

profound 1. abstruse, deep, discerning, erudite, learned, penetrating, philosophical, recondite, sagacious, sage, serious, skilled, subtle, thoughtful, weighty, wise **2.** abysmal, bottomless, cavernous, deep, fathomless, yawning **3.** abject, acute, deeply felt, extreme, great, heartfelt, heartrending, hearty, intense, keen, sincere
Antonyms imprudent, insincere, shallow, slight, stupid, superficial, thoughtless, uneducated, uninformed, unknowledgeable, unwise

profuse 1. abundant, ample, bountiful, copious, luxuriant, overflowing, plentiful, prolific, teeming **2.** excessive, extravagant, exuberant, fulsome, generous, immoderate, lavish, liberal, open-handed, prodigal, unstinting
Antonyms (*sense 1*) deficient, inadequate, meagre, scanty, scarce, skimpy, sparse (*sense 2*) frugal, illiberal, moderate, provident, thrifty

profusion abundance, bounty, copiousness, cornucopia, excess, extravagance, exuberance, glut, lavishness, luxuriance, multitude, oversupply, plenitude, plethora, prodigality, quantity, riot, superabundance, superfluity, surplus, wealth

programme *n.* **1.** agenda, curriculum, line-up, list, listing, list of players, order of events, order of the day, plan, schedule, syllabus **2.** broadcast, performance, presentation, production, show **3.**

design, order of the day, plan, plan of action, procedure, project, scheme ~ *v.* **4.** arrange, bill, book, design, engage, formulate, itemize, lay on, line up, list, map out, plan, prearrange, schedule, work out

progress *n.* **1.** advance, course, movement, onward course, passage, progression, way **2.** advance, advancement, amelioration, betterment, breakthrough, development, gain, gaining ground, growth, headway, improvement, increase, progression, promotion, step forward ~ *v.* **3.** advance, come on, continue, cover ground, forge ahead, gain ground, gather way, get on, go forward, make headway, make one's way, make strides, move on, proceed, travel **4.** advance, ameliorate, better, blossom, develop, gain, grow, improve, increase, mature
Antonyms *n.* decline, failure, recession, regression, relapse, retrogression ~ *v.* decrease, get behind, lose, lose ground, recede, regress, retrogress

progressive 1. accelerating, advancing, continuous, developing, escalating, growing, increasing, intensifying, ongoing **2.** advanced, avant-garde, dynamic, enlightened, enterprising, forward-looking, go-ahead, liberal, modern, radical, reformist, revolutionary, up-and-coming

prohibit 1. ban, debar, disallow, forbid, interdict, outlaw, proscribe, veto **2.** constrain, hamper, hinder, impede, make impossible, obstruct, preclude, prevent, restrict, rule out, stop
Antonyms allow, authorize, command, consent to, endure, further, give leave, let, license, order, permit, suffer, tolerate

prohibition 1. constraint, exclusion, forbiddance, interdiction, negation, obstruction, prevention, restriction **2.** ban, bar, disallowance, embargo, injunction, interdict, proscription, veto

project n. 1. activity, assignment, design, enterprise, job, occupation, plan, programme, proposal, scheme, task, undertaking, venture, work ~v. 2. contemplate, contrive, design, devise, draft, frame, map out, outline, plan, propose, purpose, scheme 3. cast, discharge, fling, hurl, launch, make carry, propel, shoot, throw, transmit 4. beetle, bulge, extend, jut, overhang, protrude, stand out, stick out

projectile bullet, missile, rocket, shell

prolific abundant, bountiful, copious, fecund, fertile, fruitful, generative, luxuriant, productive, profuse, rank, rich, teeming
Antonyms barren, fruitless, infertile, sterile, unfruitful, unproductive, unprolific

prologue exordium, foreword, introduction, preamble, preface, preliminary, prelude, proem

prolong carry on, continue, delay, drag out, draw out, extend, lengthen, make longer, perpetuate, protract, spin out, stretch
Antonyms abbreviate, abridge, curtail, cut, cut down, shorten, summarize

promenade n. 1. boulevard, esplanade, parade, prom, public walk, walkway 2. airing, constitutional, saunter, stroll, turn, walk ~v. 3. perambulate, saunter, stretch one's legs, stroll, take a walk, walk

prominence 1. cliff, crag, crest, elevation, headland, height, high point, hummock, mound, pinnacle, projection, promontory, rise, rising ground, spur 2. bulge, jutting, projection, protrusion, protuberance, swelling 3. conspicuousness, markedness, outstandingness, precedence, salience, specialness, top billing, weight 4. celebrity, distinction, eminence, fame, greatness, importance, name, notability, pre-eminence, prestige, rank, reputation, standing

prominent 1. bulging, jutting, projecting, protruding, protrusive, protuberant, standing out 2. conspicuous, easily seen, eye-catching, in the foreground, noticeable, obtrusive, obvious, outstanding, pronounced, remarkable, salient, striking, to the fore, unmistakable 3. celebrated, chief, distinguished, eminent, famous, foremost, important, leading, main, noted, outstanding, popular, pre-eminent, renowned, respected, top, well-known, well-thought-of
Antonyms (sense 1) concave, indented, receding (sense 2) inconspicuous, indistinct, insignificant, unnoticeable (sense 3) insignificant, minor, secondary, undistinguished, unimportant, unknown, unnotable

promiscuous 1. abandoned, debauched, dissipated, dissolute, fast, immoral, lax, libertine, licentious, loose, of easy virtue, profligate, unbridled, unchaste, wanton, wild 2. careless, casual, haphazard, heedless, indifferent, indiscriminate, irregular, irresponsible, random, slovenly, uncontrolled, uncritical, undiscriminating, unfastidious, unselective
Antonyms (sense 1) chaste, decent, innocent, modest, moral, pure, undefiled, unsullied, vestal, virginal, virtuous (sense 2) careful, critical, discriminating, fastidious, responsible, selective

promise v. 1. assure, contract, cross one's heart, engage, give an undertaking, give one's word, guarantee, pledge, plight, stipulate, swear, take an oath, undertake, vouch, vow, warrant 2. augur, bespeak, betoken, bid fair, denote, give hope of, hint at, hold a probability, hold out hopes of, indicate, lead one to expect, look like, seem likely to, show signs of, suggest ~n. 3. assurance, bond, commitment, compact, covenant, engagement, guarantee, oath, pledge, undertaking, vow, word, word of honour 4.

ability, aptitude, capability, capacity, flair, potential, talent

promising 1. auspicious, bright, encouraging, favourable, full of promise, hopeful, likely, propitious, reassuring, rosy 2. able, gifted, likely, rising, talented, up-and-coming

Antonyms (*sense 1*) discouraging, unauspicious, unfavourable, unpromising

promote 1. advance, aid, assist, back, boost, contribute to, develop, encourage, forward, foster, further, help, nurture, stimulate, support 2. aggrandize, dignify, elevate, exalt, honour, kick upstairs (*Inf.*), prefer, raise, upgrade 3. advocate, call attention to, champion, endorse, espouse, popularize, push for, recommend, speak for, sponsor, support, urge, work for 4. advertise, beat the drum for (*Inf.*), hype (*Sl.*), plug (*Inf.*), publicize, puff, push, sell

Antonyms (*sense 1*) discourage, hinder, hold back, impede, obstruct, oppose, prevent (*sense 2*) demote, downgrade, lower or reduce in rank

promotion 1. advancement, aggrandizement, elevation, ennoblement, exaltation, honour, move up, preferment, rise, upgrading 2. advancement, advocacy, backing, boosting, cultivation, development, encouragement, espousal, furtherance, progress, support 3. advertising, advertising campaign, ballyhoo (*Inf.*), hard sell, hype (*Sl.*), media hype (*Sl.*), plugging (*Inf.*), propaganda, publicity, puffery (*Inf.*), pushing

prompt *adj.* 1. early, immediate, instant, instantaneous, on time, punctual, quick, rapid, speedy, swift, timely, unhesitating 2. alert, brisk, eager, efficient, expeditious, quick, ready, responsive, smart, willing ~*adv.* 3. exactly, on the dot, promptly, punctually, sharp ~*v.* 4. cause, impel, incite, induce, inspire, in-

stigate, motivate, move, provoke, spur, stimulate, urge 5. assist, cue, help out, jog the memory, prod, refresh the memory, remind 6. call forth, cause, elicit, evoke, give rise to, occasion, provoke ~*n.* 7. cue, help, hint, jog, jolt, prod, reminder, spur, stimulus

Antonyms *adj.* hesitating, inactive, inattentive, inefficient, late, remiss, slack, slow, tardy, unresponsive ~*v.* deter, discourage, prevent, restrain, talk out of

prone 1. face down, flat, horizontal, lying down, procumbent, prostrate, recumbent, supine 2. apt, bent, disposed, given, inclined, liable, likely, predisposed, subject, susceptible, tending

pronounce 1. accent, articulate, enunciate, say, sound, speak, stress, utter, vocalize, voice 2. affirm, announce, assert, declare, decree, deliver, judge, proclaim

pronouncement announcement, declaration, decree, dictum, edict, judgment, manifesto, notification, proclamation, promulgation, pronunciamento, statement

pronunciation accent, accentuation, articulation, diction, elocution, enunciation, inflection, intonation, speech, stress

proof *n.* 1. attestation, authentication, certification, confirmation, corroboration, demonstration, evidence, substantiation, testimony, verification 2. *Printing* galley, galley proof, page proof, pull, slip, trial impression, trial print ~*adj.* 3. impenetrable, impervious, repellent, resistant, strong, tight, treated

prop *v.* 1. bolster, brace, buttress, hold up, maintain, shore, stay, support, sustain, truss, uphold 2. lean, rest, set, stand ~*n.* 3. brace, buttress, mainstay, stanchion, stay, support, truss

propaganda advertising, agit-prop, ballyhoo (*Inf.*), brainwashing, disinformation, hype (*Sl.*), information, newspeak, promotion, publicity

propagate 1. beget, breed, engender, generate, increase, multiply, procreate, produce, proliferate, reproduce **2.** broadcast, circulate, diffuse, disseminate, make known, proclaim, promote, promulgate, publicize, publish, spread, transmit

propel drive, force, impel, launch, push, send, set in motion, shoot, shove, start, thrust

proper 1. appropriate, apt, becoming, befitting, fit, fitting, legitimate, meet (*Archaic*), right, suitable, suited **2.** *comme il faut*, decent, decorous, *de rigueur*, genteel, gentlemanly, ladylike, mannerly, polite, punctilious, refined, respectable, seemly **3.** accepted, accurate, conventional, correct, established, exact, formal, orthodox, precise, right

Antonyms coarse, common, crude, discourteous, impolite, improper, inappropriate, indecent, rude, unbecoming, unconventional, ungentlemanly, unladylike, unorthodox, unrefined, unseemly, unsuitable, wrong

property 1. assets, belongings, building(s), capital, chattels, effects, estate, goods, holdings, house(s), means, possessions, resources, riches, wealth **2.** acres, estate, freehold, holding, land, real estate, real property, realty, title **3.** ability, attribute, characteristic, feature, hallmark, idiosyncrasy, mark, peculiarity, quality, trait, virtue

prophecy augury, divination, forecast, foretelling, prediction, prognosis, prognostication, revelation, second sight, soothsaying, vaticination (*Rare*)

prophesy augur, divine, forecast, foresee, foretell, forewarn, predict, presage, prognosticate, soothsay, vaticinate (*Rare*)

prophet augur, Cassandra, clairvoyant, diviner, forecaster, oracle, prognosticator, prophesier, seer, sibyl, soothsayer

prophetic augural, divinatory, fatidic (*Rare*), foreshadowing, mantic, oracular, predictive, presaging, prescient, prognostic, sibylline, vatic (*Rare*)

proportion 1. distribution, ratio, relationship, relative amount **2.** agreement, balance, congruity, correspondence, harmony, symmetry **3.** amount, cut (*Inf.*), division, fraction, measure, part, percentage, quota, segment, share **4.** *Plural* amplitude, breadth, bulk, capacity, dimensions, expanse, extent, magnitude, measurements, range, scope, size, volume

proportional, proportionate balanced, commensurate, comparable, compatible, consistent, correspondent, corresponding, equitable, equivalent, even, in proportion, just

proposal bid, design, motion, offer, overture, plan, presentation, proffer, programme, project, proposition, recommendation, scheme, suggestion, tender, terms

propose 1. advance, come up with, present, proffer, propound, put forward, submit, suggest, tender **2.** introduce, invite, name, nominate, present, put up, recommend **3.** aim, design, have every intention, have in mind, intend, mean, plan, purpose, scheme **4.** ask for someone's hand (in marriage), offer marriage, pay suit, pop the question (*Inf.*)

proposition *n.* motion, plan, programme, project, proposal, recommendation, scheme, suggestion

proprietor, proprietress deed holder, freeholder, landlady, landlord, landowner, owner, possessor, titleholder

propriety 1. appropriateness, aptness, becomingness, correctness, fitness, rightness, seemliness, suitableness **2.** breeding, courtesy, decency, decorum, delicacy, etiquette, good form,

good manners, manners, modes~
ty, politeness, protocol, punctilio,
rectitude, refinement, respect~
ability, seemliness
Antonyms (*sense 2*) bad form,
bad manners, immodesty, impo~
liteness, indecency, indecorum,
indelicacy, vulgarity

prosecute 1. *Law* arraign, bring
action against, bring suit against,
bring to trial, do (*Sl.*), indict,
litigate, prefer charges, put in
the dock, put on trial, seek re~
dress, sue, summon, take to
court, try **2.** carry on, conduct,
direct, discharge, engage in,
manage, perform, practise, work
at

prospect *n.* **1.** anticipation, cal~
culation, contemplation, expec~
tation, future, hope, odds, open~
ing, outlook, plan, presumption,
probability, promise, proposal,
thought **2.** landscape, outlook,
panorama, perspective, scene,
sight, spectacle, view, vision, vis~
ta **3.** *Sometimes plural* chance,
likelihood, possibility ~*v.* **4.** ex~
plore, go after, look for, search,
seek, survey

prospective about to be, antici~
pated, approaching, awaited,
coming, destined, eventual, ex~
pected, forthcoming, future,
hoped-for, imminent, intended,
likely, looked-for, possible, po~
tential, soon-to-be, to-be, to come

prospectus announcement,
catalogue, conspectus, list, out~
line, plan, programme, scheme,
syllabus, synopsis

prosper advance, be fortunate,
bloom, do well, fare well, flour~
ish, flower, get on, grow rich,
make good, make it (*Inf.*), pro~
gress, succeed, thrive

prosperity affluence, boom, ease,
fortune, good fortune, good
times, life of luxury, life of Riley
(*Inf.*), luxury, plenty, prosper~
ousness, riches, success, the good
life, wealth, well-being
Antonyms adversity, depression,
destitution, failure, indigence,

misfortune, poverty, shortage,
want

prosperous 1. blooming, boom~
ing, doing well, flourishing, for~
tunate, lucky, on the up and up
(*Brit.*), palmy, prospering, suc~
cessful, thriving **2.** affluent, in
clover (*Inf.*), in the money (*Inf.*),
moneyed, opulent, rich, wealthy,
well-heeled (*Sl.*), well-off, well-to-
do
Antonyms defeated, failing, im~
poverished, poor, unfortunate,
unlucky, unsuccessful

prostitute 1. *n.* bawd (*Archaic*),
brass (*Sl.*), call girl, camp follow~
er, cocotte, courtesan, fallen
woman, *fille de joie*, harlot,
hooker (*U.S. sl.*), hustler (*Sl.*),
loose woman, moll (*Sl.*), pro (*Sl.*),
streetwalker, strumpet, tart
(*Inf.*), trollop, white slave, whore
2. *v.* cheapen, debase, degrade,
demean, devalue, misapply, per~
vert, profane

prostrate *adj.* **1.** abject, bowed
low, flat, horizontal, kowtowing,
procumbent, prone **2.** at a low
ebb, dejected, depressed, deso~
late, drained, exhausted, fagged
out (*Inf.*), fallen, inconsolable,
overcome, spent, worn out **3.**
brought to one's knees, defence~
less, disarmed, helpless, impo~
tent, overwhelmed, paralysed,
powerless, reduced ~*v.* **4.** *Of
oneself* abase, bend the knee to,
bow before, bow down to, cast
oneself before, cringe, fall at
(someone's) feet, fall on one's
knees before, grovel, kneel,
kowtow, submit **5.** bring low,
crush, depress, disarm, lay low,
overcome, overthrow, overturn,
overwhelm, paralyse, reduce,
ruin

protagonist central character,
hero, heroine, lead, leading
character, principal

protect care for, chaperon, cov~
er, cover up for, defend, foster,
give sanctuary, guard, harbour,
keep, keep safe, look after,
mount *or* stand guard over, pre~
serve, safeguard, save, screen,

secure, shelter, shield, support, take under one's wing, watch over

Antonyms assail, assault, attack, betray, endanger, expose, expose to danger, threaten

protection 1. aegis, care, charge, custody, defence, guardianship, guarding, preservation, protecting, safeguard, safekeeping, safety, security 2. armour, barrier, buffer, bulwark, cover, guard, refuge, safeguard, screen, shelter, shield

protective careful, covering, defensive, fatherly, insulating, jealous, maternal, motherly, paternal, possessive, protecting, safeguarding, sheltering, shielding, vigilant, warm, watchful

protector advocate, benefactor, bodyguard, champion, counsel, defender, guard, guardian, guardian angel, knight in shining armour, patron, safeguard, tower of strength

protégé, protégée charge, dependant, discovery, pupil, student, ward

protest 1. *n.* complaint, declaration, demur, demurral, disapproval, dissent, formal complaint, objection, outcry, protestation, remonstrance 2. *v.* complain, cry out, demonstrate, demur, disagree, disapprove, expostulate, express disapproval, kick (against) (*Inf.*), object, oppose, remonstrate, say no to, take exception

protester agitator, demonstrator, dissenter, dissident, protest marcher, rebel

protocol 1. code of behaviour, conventions, courtesies, customs, decorum, etiquette, formalities, good form, manners, politesse, propriety, rules of conduct 2. agreement, compact, concordat, contract, convention, covenant, pact, treaty

prototype archetype, example, first, mock-up, model, norm, original, paradigm, pattern, precedent, standard, type

proud 1. appreciative, content, contented, glad, gratified, honoured, pleased, satisfied, self-respecting, well-pleased 2. arrogant, boastful, conceited, disdainful, egotistical, haughty, high and mighty (*Inf.*), imperious, lordly, narcissistic, orgulous (*Archaic*), overbearing, presumptuous, self-important, self-satisfied, snobbish, snooty (*Inf.*), stuck-up (*Inf.*), supercilious, toffee-nosed (*Sl.*), vain

Antonyms abject, ashamed, base, deferential, discontented, displeased, dissatisfied, humble, ignoble, ignominious, lowly, meek, modest, submissive, unassuming, undignified, unobtrusive

prove 1. ascertain, attest, authenticate, bear out, confirm, corroborate, demonstrate, determine, establish, evidence, evince, justify, show, show clearly, substantiate, verify 2. analyse, assay, check, examine, experiment, put to the test, put to trial, test, try 3. be found to be, come out, end up, result, turn out

Antonyms (*sense 1*) discredit, disprove, give the lie to, refute, rule out

proverb adage, aphorism, apophthegm, byword, dictum, gnome, maxim, saw, saying

provide 1. accommodate, cater, contribute, equip, furnish, outfit, provision, stock up, supply 2. add, afford, bring, give, impart, lend, present, produce, render, serve, yield 3. *With for or against* anticipate, arrange for, forearm, get ready, make arrangements, make plans, plan ahead, plan for, prepare for, take measures, take precautions 4. *With for* care for, keep, look after, maintain, support, sustain, take care of

Antonyms (*sense 1*) deprive, keep back, refuse, withhold (*sense 3*) disregard, fail to notice, miss, neglect, overlook (*sense 4*) neglect

providence 1. destiny, divine intervention, fate, fortune, God's will, predestination 2. care, caution, discretion, far-sightedness, foresight, forethought, perspicacity, presence of mind, prudence

provident canny, careful, cautious, discreet, economical, equipped, far-seeing, far-sighted, forearmed, foresighted, frugal, prudent, sagacious, shrewd, thrifty, vigilant, well-prepared, wise
Antonyms careless, heedless, improvident, imprudent, negligent, prodigal, profligate, reckless, short-sighted, spendthrift, thoughtless, thriftless, uneconomical, unthrifty, wasteful

providing, provided conj. as long as, contingent upon, given, if and only if, in case, in the event, on condition, on the assumption, subject to, upon these terms, with the proviso, with the understanding

province 1. colony, county, department, dependency, district, division, domain, region, section, territory, tract, zone 2. Fig. area, business, capacity, charge, concern, duty, employment, field, function, line, orbit, part, pigeon (Brit. inf.), post, responsibility, role, sphere

provision 1. accoutrement, catering, equipping, fitting out, furnishing, providing, supplying, victualling 2. arrangement, plan, prearrangement, precaution, preparation 3. Fig. agreement, clause, condition, demand, proviso, requirement, specification, stipulation, term

provisional conditional, contingent, interim, limited, pro tem, provisory, qualified, stopgap, temporary, tentative, transitional
Antonyms definite, fixed, permanent

provisions comestibles, eatables, eats (Sl.), edibles, fare, food, foodstuff, groceries, grub (Sl.), provender, rations, stores, supplies, sustenance, viands, victuals

provocation 1. casus belli, cause,

grounds, incitement, inducement, instigation, justification, motivation, reason, stimulus 2. affront, annoyance, challenge, dare, grievance, indignity, injury, insult, offence, red rag, taunt, vexation

provocative aggravating (Inf.), annoying, challenging, disturbing, galling, goading, incensing, insulting, offensive, outrageous, provoking, stimulating

provoke 1. affront, aggravate (Inf.), anger, annoy, chafe, enrage, exasperate, gall, get on one's nerves, incense, infuriate, insult, irk, irritate, madden, make one's blood boil, offend, pique, put out, rile, try one's patience, vex 2. bring about, bring on or down, call forth, cause, draw forth, elicit, evoke, excite, fire, generate, give rise to, incite, induce, inflame, inspire, instigate, kindle, lead to, motivate, move, occasion, precipitate, produce, promote, prompt, rouse, stimulate, stir
Antonyms (sense 1) appease, calm, conciliate, mollify, pacify, placate, propitiate, quiet, soothe, sweeten (sense 2) abate, allay, assuage, blunt, curb, ease, lessen, lull, mitigate, moderate, modify, relieve, temper

prowess ability, accomplishment, adeptness, adroitness, aptitude, attainment, command, dexterity, excellence, expertise, expertness, facility, genius, mastery, skill, talent

proximity adjacency, closeness, contiguity, juxtaposition, nearness, neighbourhood, propinquity, vicinity

prudent 1. canny, careful, cautious, circumspect, discerning, discreet, judicious, politic, sagacious, sage, sensible, shrewd, vigilant, wary, wise 2. canny, careful, economical, far-sighted, frugal, provident, sparing, thrifty
Antonyms careless, extravagant, heedless, improvident, imprudent, inconsiderate, indiscreet,

irrational, rash, thoughtless, un~
wise, wasteful

prune clip, cut, cut back, dock,
lop, pare down, reduce, shape,
shorten, snip, trim

pry be a busybody, be inquisitive,
be nosy (*Inf.*), ferret about,
interfere, intrude, meddle, nose
into, peep, peer, poke, poke one's
nose in *or* into (*Inf.*), snoop (*Inf.*)

pseudo *adj.* artificial, bogus,
counterfeit, ersatz, fake, false,
imitation, mock, not genuine,
phoney (*Sl.*), pretended, quasi-,
sham, spurious
    Antonyms actual, authentic,
bona fide, genuine, heartfelt,
honest, real, sincere, true, un~
feigned

pseudonym alias, assumed
name, false name, incognito,
nom de guerre, nom de plume,
pen name, professional name,
stage name

psychic clairvoyant, extrasenso~
ry, mystic, occult, preternatural,
supernatural, telekinetic, tele~
pathic

psychopath insane person, luna~
tic, madman, maniac, mental
case, nutcase (*Sl.*), nutter (*Brit.
sl.*), psychotic, sociopath

pub *or* **public house** alehouse
(*Archaic*), bar, boozer (*Inf.*), inn,
local (*Brit. inf.*), roadhouse, tav~
ern

puberty adolescence, awkward
age, juvenescence, pubescence,
teenage, teens, young adulthood

public *adj.* **1.** civic, civil, common,
general, national, popular, social,
state, universal, widespread **2.**
accessible, communal, commu~
nity, free to all, not private, open,
open to the public, unrestricted **3.**
acknowledged, exposed, in cir~
culation, known, notorious, obvi~
ous, open, overt, patent, plain,
published, recognized **4.** impor~
tant, prominent, respected, well-
known ~ *n.* **5.** citizens, common~
alty, community, country, elec~
torate, everyone, hoi polloi,
masses, multitude, nation, peo~
ple, populace, population, soci~

ety, voters **6.** audience, buyers,
clientele, followers, following,
patrons, supporters, those inter~
ested, trade **7. in public** *coram
populo*, for all to see, in full view,
openly, publicly
    Antonyms (*sense 2*) barred,
closed, exclusive, inaccessible,
personal, private, restricted, un~
available (*sense 3*) hidden, se~
cluded, secret, unknown, unre~
vealed

publication book, booklet, bro~
chure, handbill, issue, leaflet,
magazine, newspaper, pamphlet,
periodical

publicity advertising, attention,
ballyhoo (*Sl.*), boost, build-up,
hype (*Sl.*), plug (*Inf.*), press, pro~
motion, public notice, puff, puff~
ery (*Inf.*)

publicize advertise, beat the
drum for (*Inf.*), bring to public
notice, broadcast, give publicity
to, hype (*Sl.*), make known, play
up, plug (*Inf.*), promote, puff,
push, spotlight, spread about,
write up
    Antonyms conceal, contain, cov~
er up, keep dark, keep secret,
smother, stifle, suppress, with~
hold

publish 1. bring out, issue, print,
produce, put out **2.** advertise,
announce, broadcast, circulate,
communicate, declare, disclose,
distribute, divulge, impart, leak,
proclaim, promulgate, publicize,
reveal, spread

puerile babyish, childish, foolish,
immature, inane, infantile, irre~
sponsible, jejune, juvenile, naive,
petty, ridiculous, silly, trivial,
weak
    Antonyms adult, grown-up, ma~
ture, responsible, sensible

puff *n.* **1.** blast, breath, draught,
emanation, flurry, gust, whiff **2.**
drag (*Inf.*), pull, smoke **3.** adver~
tisement, commendation, fa~
vourable mention, good word,
plug (*Inf.*), sales talk ~ *v.* **4.** blow,
breathe, exhale, gasp, gulp, pant,
wheeze **5.** drag (*Sl.*), draw, inhale,
pull at *or* on, smoke, suck **6.**

Usually with **up** bloat, dilate, distend, expand, inflate, swell

pull v. **1.** drag, draw, haul, jerk, tow, trail, tug, yank **2.** cull, draw out, extract, gather, pick, pluck, remove, take out, uproot, weed **3.** dislocate, rend, rip, sprain, strain, stretch, tear, wrench **4.** *Inf.* attract, draw, entice, lure, magnetize **5. pull strings** *Brit. inf.* influence, pull wires (*U.S.*), use one's influence ~n. **6.** jerk, tug, twitch, yank **7.** attraction, drawing power, effort, exertion, force, forcefulness, influence, lure, magnetism, power **8.** *Inf.* advantage, clout (*Inf.*), influence, leverage, muscle, weight

Antonyms v. (*sense 1*) drive, nudge, push, ram, shove, thrust (*sense 2*) implant, insert, plant (*sense 4*) deter, discourage, put one off, repel ~n. (*sense 6*) nudge, push, shove, thrust

pull out abandon, depart, evacuate, leave, quit, rat on, retreat, stop participating, withdraw

pull through come through, get better, get over, pull round, rally, recover, survive, weather

pull up 1. brake, come to a halt, halt, reach a standstill, stop **2.** admonish, carpet (*Inf.*), castigate, dress down (*Inf.*), rebuke, reprimand, reprove, take to task, tell off (*Inf.*), tick off (*Inf.*)

pulp n. **1.** flesh, marrow, soft part **2.** mash, mush, pap, paste, pomace, semiliquid, semisolid, triturate ~v. **3.** crush, mash, pulverize, squash, triturate ~adj. **4.** cheap, lurid, mushy (*Inf.*), rubbishy, sensational, trashy

pulse 1. n. beat, beating, oscillation, pulsation, rhythm, stroke, throb, throbbing, vibration **2.** v. beat, pulsate, throb, tick, vibrate

pump v. **1.** drive, force, inject, pour, push, send, supply **2.** cross-examine, give (someone) the third degree, grill (*Inf.*), interrogate, probe, question closely, quiz, worm out of

pun double entendre, equivoque,

paronomasia (*Rhetoric*), play on words, quip, witticism

punch[1] v. **1.** bash (*Inf.*), biff (*Sl.*), bop (*Inf.*), box, clout (*Inf.*), hit, plug (*Sl.*), pummel, slam, slug, smash, sock (*Sl.*), strike, wallop (*Inf.*) ~n. **2.** bash (*Inf.*), biff (*Sl.*), blow, bop (*Inf.*), clout (*Inf.*), hit, jab, knock, plug (*Sl.*), sock (*Sl.*), thump, wallop (*Inf.*) **3.** *Inf.* bite, drive, effectiveness, force, forcefulness, impact, point, verve, vigour

punch[2] v. bore, cut, drill, perforate, pierce, pink, prick, puncture, stamp

punctual early, exact, in good time, on the dot, on time, precise, prompt, punctilious, seasonable, strict, timely

Antonyms behind, behindhand, belated, delayed, late, overdue, tardy, unpunctual

punctuate 1. break, interject, interrupt, intersperse, pepper, sprinkle **2.** accentuate, emphasize, lay stress on, mark, point up, stress, underline

puncture n. **1.** break, cut, damage, hole, leak, nick, opening, perforation, rupture, slit **2.** flat, flat tyre ~v. **3.** bore, cut, nick, penetrate, perforate, pierce, prick, rupture **4.** deflate, go down, go flat

pungent 1. acid, acrid, aromatic, bitter, highly flavoured, hot, peppery, piquant, seasoned, sharp, sour, spicy, stinging, strong, tangy, tart **2.** acrimonious, acute, barbed, biting, caustic, cutting, incisive, keen, mordant, penetrating, piercing, poignant, pointed, sarcastic, scathing, sharp, stinging, stringent, telling, trenchant

Antonyms bland, dull, inane, mild, moderate, tasteless, unsavoury, unstimulating, weak

punish 1. beat, castigate, chasten, chastise, correct, discipline, flog, give a lesson to, give (someone) the works (*Sl.*), lash, penalize, rap someone's knuckles, scourge, sentence, slap someone's wrist, whip **2.** abuse, batter, give (someone) a going over (*Inf.*), harm, hurt, injure, knock about, maltreat, manhandle, misuse, oppress, rough up

punishment 1. chastening, chastisement, comeuppance (*Sl.*), correction, discipline, just deserts, penalty, penance, punitive measures, retribution, sanction, what for (*Inf.*) **2.** *Inf.* abuse, beating, hard work, maltreatment, manhandling, pain, rough treatment, slave labour, torture, victimization

puny diminutive, dwarfish, feeble, frail, little, pint-sized (*Inf.*), pygmy, sickly, stunted, tiny, underfed, undersized, undeveloped, weak, weakly

pupil beginner, catechumen, disciple, learner, neophyte, novice, scholar, schoolboy, schoolgirl, student, tyro
Antonyms coach, instructor, master, mistress, schoolmaster, schoolmistress, schoolteacher, teacher, trainer, tutor

purchase *v.* **1.** acquire, buy, come by, gain, get, get hold of, invest in, make a purchase, obtain, pay for, pick up, procure, secure, shop for **2.** achieve, attain, earn, gain, realize, win ~*n.* **3.** acquisition, asset, buy, gain, investment, possession, property
Antonyms *v.* (*sense 1*) hawk, market, merchandise, peddle, retail, sell, trade in, vend ~*n.* marketing, sale, selling, vending

pure 1. authentic, clear, flawless, genuine, natural, neat, perfect, real, simple, straight, true, unalloyed, unmixed **2.** clean, disinfected, germ-free, immaculate, pasteurized, sanitary, spotless, sterile, sterilized, unadulterated, unblemished, uncontaminated, unpolluted, untainted, wholesome **3.** blameless, chaste, guileless, honest, immaculate, innocent, maidenly, modest, true, uncorrupted, undefiled, unspotted, unstained, unsullied, upright, virgin, virginal, virtuous

Antonyms (*senses 1 & 2*) adulterated, contaminated, dirty, filthy, flawed, imperfect, impure, infected, insincere, mixed, polluted, tainted (*sense 3*) contaminated, corrupt, defiled, guilty, immodest, immoral, impure, indecent, obscene, sinful, spoiled, unchaste, unclean, untrue

purge *v.* **1.** clean out, dismiss, do away with, eject, eradicate, expel, exterminate, get rid of, kill, liquidate, oust, remove, rid of, rout out, sweep out, wipe out **2.** absolve, cleanse, clear, exonerate, expiate, forgive, pardon, purify, wash ~*n.* **3.** cleanup, crushing, ejection, elimination, eradication, expulsion, liquidation, reign of terror, removal, suppression, witch hunt

purify 1. clarify, clean, cleanse, decontaminate, disinfect, filter, fumigate, refine, sanitize, wash **2.** absolve, cleanse, exculpate, exonerate, lustrate, redeem, sanctify, shrive
Antonyms adulterate, befoul, contaminate, corrupt, defile, foul, infect, pollute, soil, stain, sully, taint, tarnish, vitiate

puritan 1. *n.* fanatic, moralist, pietist, prude, rigorist, zealot **2.** *adj.* ascetic, austere, hidebound, intolerant, moralistic, narrow, narrow-minded, prudish, puritanical, severe, strait-laced, strict

purpose *n.* **1.** aim, design, function, idea, intention, object, point, principle, reason **2.** aim, ambition, aspiration, design, desire, end, goal, hope, intention, object, objective, plan, project, scheme, target, view, wish **3.** constancy, determination, firmness, persistence, resolution, resolve, singlemindedness, steadfastness, tenacity, will **4. on purpose** by design, deliberately, designedly, intentionally, knowingly, purposely, wilfully, wittingly ~*v.* **5.** aim, aspire, commit oneself, contemplate, decide, design, determine, have a mind to, intend, make up one's mind, mean, meditate, plan, propose, resolve, set one's sights on, think to, work towards

purposely by design, calculatedly, consciously, deliberately, designedly, expressly, intentionally, knowingly, on purpose, wilfully, with intent

Antonyms accidentally, by accident, by chance, by mistake, inadvertently, unconsciously, unintentionally, unknowingly, unwittingly

purse n. **1.** money-bag, pouch, wallet **2.** coffers, exchequer, funds, means, money, resources, treasury, wealth, wherewithal **3.** award, gift, present, prize, reward

pursue 1. accompany, attend, chase, dog, follow, give chase to, go after, harass, harry, haunt, hound, hunt, hunt down, plague, run after, shadow, stalk, tail, track **2.** aim for, aspire to, desire, have as one's goal, purpose, seek, strive for, try for, work towards **3.** adhere to, carry on, continue, cultivate, hold to, keep on, maintain, persevere in, persist in, proceed, see through **4.** chase after, court, make up to (*Inf.*), pay attention to, pay court to, set one's cap at, woo

Antonyms avoid, eschew, fight shy of, flee, give (someone or something) a wide berth, keep away from, run away from, shun, steer clear of

pursuit 1. chase, hunt, hunting, inquiry, quest, search, seeking, tracking, trail, trailing **2.** activity, hobby, interest, line, occupation, pastime, pleasure, vocation

push v. **1.** depress, drive, poke, press, propel, ram, shove, thrust **2.** elbow, jostle, make or force one's way, move, shoulder, shove, squeeze, thrust **3.** egg on, encourage, expedite, hurry, impel, incite, persuade, press, prod, speed (up), spur, urge **4.** advertise, boost, cry up, hype (*Sl.*), make known, plug (*Inf.*), promote, propagandize, publicize,

puff ~n. **5.** butt, jolt, nudge, poke, prod, shove, thrust **6.** *Inf.* ambition, determination, drive, dynamism, energy, enterprise, get-up-and-go (*Inf.*), go (*Inf.*), gumption (*Inf.*), initiative, vigour, vitality **7.** *Inf.* advance, assault, attack, charge, effort, offensive, onset, thrust

Antonyms v. (*sense 1*) drag, draw, haul, jerk, pull, tow, trail, tug, yank (*sense 2*) discourage, dissuade, put off ~n. (*sense 5*) jerk, pull, tug, yank

pushy 1. ambitious, determined, driving, dynamic, enterprising, go-ahead, on the go, purposeful, resourceful **2.** assertive, bold, brash, bumptious, forward, impertinent, intrusive, presumptuous, pushy (*Inf.*), self-assertive

put 1. bring, deposit, establish, fix, lay, place, position, rest, set, settle, situate **2.** assign, constrain, employ, force, induce, make, oblige, require, set, subject to **3.** advance, bring forward, forward, offer, posit, present, propose, set before, submit, tender **4.** cast, fling, heave, hurl, lob, pitch, throw, toss

put across or **over** communicate, convey, explain, get across, get through, make clear, make oneself understood, spell out

put aside or **by** cache, deposit, keep in reserve, lay by, salt away, save, squirrel away, stockpile, store, stow away

put away 1. put back, replace, return to (its) place, tidy away **2.** deposit, keep, lay in, put by, save, set aside, store away

put down 1. enter, inscribe, log, record, set down, take down, transcribe, write down **2.** crush, quash, quell, repress, silence, stamp out, suppress **3.** *With to* ascribe, attribute, impute, set down **4.** destroy, do away with, put away, put out of its misery, put to sleep **5.** *Sl.* condemn, crush, deflate, dismiss, disparage, humiliate, mortify, reject, shame, slight, snub

put forward advance, introduce, move, nominate, present, press, proffer, propose, recommend, submit, suggest, tender

put off 1. defer, delay, hold over, postpone, put back, reschedule **2.** abash, confuse, discomfit, disconcert, dismay, distress, nonplus, perturb, rattle (*Inf.*), throw (*Inf.*), unsettle **3.** discourage, dishearten, dissuade
Antonyms (*sense 3*) egg on, encourage, incite, persuade, prompt, push, spur, urge

put on 1. do, mount, present, produce, show, stage **2.** add, gain, increase by

put out 1. anger, annoy, confound, disturb, exasperate, harass, irk, irritate, nettle, perturb, provoke, vex **2.** blow out, douse, extinguish, quench, smother, snuff out, stamp out **3.** bother, discomfit, discommode, discompose, disconcert, discountenance, disturb, embarrass, impose upon, incommode, inconvenience, put on the spot, trouble, upset

put up 1. build, construct, erect, fabricate, raise **2.** accommodate, board, entertain, give one lodging, house, lodge, take in **3.** float, nominate, offer, present, propose, put forward, recommend, submit **4.** advance, give, invest, pay, pledge, provide, supply **5. put up with** *Inf.* abide, bear, brook, endure, lump (*Inf.*), pocket, stand, stand for, stomach, suffer, swallow, take, tolerate

Antonyms (*sense 1*) demolish, destroy, flatten, knock down, level, pull down, raze, tear down (*sense 5*) not stand for, object to, oppose, protest against, reject, take exception to

puzzle *v.* **1.** baffle, beat (*Sl.*), bewilder, confound, confuse, flummox, mystify, nonplus, perplex, stump **2.** ask oneself, brood, cudgel or rack one's brains, mull over, muse, ponder, study, think about, think hard, wonder **3.** *Usually with* **out** clear up, crack, crack the code, decipher, figure out, find the key, get it, get the answer, resolve, see, solve, sort out, think through, unravel, work out ~*n.* **4.** brain-teaser (*Inf.*), conundrum, enigma, labyrinth, maze, mystery, paradox, poser, problem, question, question mark, riddle **5.** bafflement, bewilderment, confusion, difficulty, dilemma, perplexity, quandary, uncertainty

puzzling abstruse, ambiguous, baffling, bewildering, beyond one, enigmatic, full of surprises, hard, incomprehensible, inexplicable, involved, knotty, labyrinthine, misleading, mystifying, perplexing, unaccountable, unclear, unfathomable
Antonyms clear, comprehensible, easy, evident, intelligible, lucid, manifest, obvious, patent, plain, simple, unambiguous, unequivocal, unmistakable

Q

quagmire 1. bog, fen, marsh, mire, morass, quicksand, slough, swamp 2. difficulty, dilemma, entanglement, fix (*Inf.*), imbroglio, impasse, jam (*Inf.*), muddle, pass, pickle (*Inf.*), pinch, plight, predicament, quandary, scrape (*Inf.*)

quaint bizarre, curious, droll, eccentric, fanciful, fantastic, odd, old-fashioned, original, peculiar, queer, singular, strange, unusual, whimsical

quake convulse, move, pulsate, quail, quiver, rock, shake, shiver, shudder, throb, totter, tremble, vibrate, waver, wobble

qualification 1. ability, accomplishment, aptitude, attribute, capability, capacity, eligibility, endowment(s), fitness, quality, skill, suitability, suitableness 2. allowance, caveat, condition, criterion, exception, exemption, limitation, modification, objection, prerequisite, proviso, requirement, reservation, restriction, stipulation

qualified 1. able, accomplished, adept, capable, certificated, competent, efficient, equipped, experienced, expert, fit, knowledgeable, licensed, practised, proficient, skilful, talented, trained 2. bounded, circumscribed, conditional, confined, contingent, equivocal, guarded, limited, modified, provisional, reserved, restricted

Antonyms (*sense 1*) amateur, apprentice, self-styled, self-taught, trainee, uncertificated, unqualified, untrained (*sense 2*) categorical, outright, unconditional, unequivocal, wholehearted

qualify 1. capacitate, certify, commission, condition, empower, endow, equip, fit, ground, permit, prepare, ready, sanction, train 2. abate, adapt, assuage, circumscribe, diminish, ease, lessen, limit, mitigate, moderate, modify, modulate, reduce, regulate, restrain, restrict, soften, temper, vary

Antonyms (*sense 1*) ban, debar, disqualify, forbid, preclude, prevent

quality 1. aspect, attribute, characteristic, condition, feature, mark, peculiarity, property, trait 2. character, constitution, description, essence, kind, make, nature, sort 3. calibre, distinction, excellence, grade, merit, position, pre-eminence, rank, standing, status, superiority, value, worth

quandary bewilderment, cleft stick, delicate situation, difficulty, dilemma, doubt, embarrassment, impasse, perplexity, plight, predicament, puzzle, strait, uncertainty

quantity aggregate, allotment, amount, lot, number, part, portion, quota, sum, total

quarrel 1. *n.* affray, altercation, argument, brawl, breach, broil, commotion, contention, controversy, difference (of opinion), disagreement, discord, disputation, dispute, dissension, dissidence, disturbance, feud, fight, fracas, fray, misunderstanding, row, scrap (*Inf.*), spat, squabble, strife, tiff, tumult, vendetta, wrangle 2. *v.* altercate, argue, bicker, brawl, clash, differ, disagree, dispute, fall out (*Inf.*), fight, row, spar, squabble, wrangle

Antonyms (*sense 1*) accord, agreement, concord (*sense 2*) agree, get on *or* along (with)

quarrelsome argumentative, belligerent, cat-and-dog (Inf.), choleric, combative, contentious, cross, disputatious, fractious, ill-tempered, irascible, irritable, peevish, petulant, pugnacious, querulous
Antonyms easy-going, equable, even-tempered, placid

quarry aim, game, goal, objective, prey, prize, victim

quarter 1. n. area, direction, district, locality, location, neighbourhood, part, place, point, position, province, region, side, spot, station, territory, zone **2.** v. accommodate, billet, board, house, install, lodge, place, post, put up, station

quarters abode, accommodation, barracks, billet, cantonment (Military), chambers, digs (Inf.), domicile, dwelling, habitation, lodging, lodgings, post, residence, rooms, shelter, station

quash annul, cancel, declare null and void, invalidate, nullify, overrule, overthrow, rescind, reverse, revoke, set aside, void

queen consort, monarch, ruler, sovereign

queer adj. **1.** abnormal, anomalous, atypical, curious, disquieting, droll, eerie, erratic, extraordinary, funny, odd, outlandish, outré, peculiar, remarkable, singular, strange, uncanny, uncommon, unconventional, unnatural, unorthodox, unusual, weird **2.** doubtful, dubious, fishy (Inf.), irregular, mysterious, puzzling, questionable, shady (Inf.), suspicious **3.** crazy, demented, eccentric, idiosyncratic, irrational, mad, odd, touched, unbalanced, unhinged ~v. **4.** botch, endanger, harm, impair, imperil, injure, jeopardize, mar, ruin, spoil, thwart, wreck
Antonyms adj. believable, common, conventional, customary, natural, normal, ordinary, orthodox, rational, regular, straight, unexceptional, unoriginal

quench check, crush, destroy, douse, end, extinguish, put out, smother, snuff out, squelch, stifle, suppress

query v. **1.** ask, enquire, question **2.** challenge, disbelieve, dispute, distrust, doubt, mistrust, suspect ~n. **3.** demand, doubt, hesitation, inquiry, objection, problem, question, reservation, scepticism, suspicion

question v. **1.** ask, catechize, cross-examine, enquire, examine, grill (Inf.), interrogate, interview, investigate, probe, pump (Inf.), quiz, sound out **2.** call into question, cast doubt upon, challenge, controvert, disbelieve, dispute, distrust, doubt, impugn, mistrust, oppose, query, suspect ~n. **3.** examination, inquiry, interrogation, investigation **4.** argument, confusion, contention, controversy, debate, difficulty, dispute, doubt, dubiety, misgiving, problem, query, uncertainty **5.** issue, motion, point, point at issue, proposal, proposition, subject, theme, topic
Antonyms (senses 1 & 3) answer, reply (sense 2) accept, believe, take on trust

questionable arguable, controversial, controvertible, debatable, disputable, doubtful, dubious, dubitable, equivocal, fishy (Inf.), moot, paradoxical, problematical, shady (Inf.), suspect, suspicious, uncertain, unproven, unreliable
Antonyms authoritative, certain, incontrovertible, indisputable, straightforward, unequivocal

queue chain, concatenation, file, line, order, progression, sequence, series, string, succession, train

quibble 1. v. carp, cavil, equivocate, evade, pretend, prevaricate, shift, split hairs **2.** n. artifice, cavil, complaint, criticism, duplicity, equivocation, evasion, nicety, niggle, objection, pretence, prevarication, protest, quirk, shift, sophism, subterfuge, subtlety

quick 1. active, brief, brisk, cursory, expeditious, express, fast, fleet, hasty, headlong, hurried, perfunctory, prompt, rapid, speedy, sudden, swift 2. agile, alert, animated, energetic, flying, keen, lively, nimble, spirited, sprightly, spry, vivacious, winged 3. able, acute, adept, adroit, all there (*Inf.*), apt, astute, bright, clever, deft, dexterous, discerning, intelligent, nimble-witted, perceptive, quick on the uptake (*Inf.*), quick-witted, receptive, sharp, shrewd, skilful, smart
Antonyms deliberate, dull, gradual, heavy, inactive, inexpert, lazy, lethargic, long, maladroit, patient, restrained, slow, sluggish, stupid, unintelligent, unresponsive, unskilful

quicken 1. accelerate, dispatch, expedite, hasten, hurry, impel, precipitate, speed 2. activate, animate, arouse, energize, excite, galvanize, incite, inspire, invigorate, kindle, refresh, reinvigorate, resuscitate, revitalize, revive, rouse, stimulate, strengthen, vitalize, vivify

quiet *adj.* 1. dumb, hushed, inaudible, low, low-pitched, noiseless, peaceful, silent, soft, soundless 2. calm, contented, gentle, mild, motionless, pacific, peaceful, placid, restful, serene, smooth, tranquil, untroubled 3. isolated, private, retired, secluded, secret, sequestered, undisturbed, unfrequented 4. conservative, modest, plain, restrained, simple, sober, subdued, unassuming, unobtrusive, unpretentious 5. collected, docile, even-tempered, gentle, imperturbable, meek, mild, phlegmatic, reserved, retiring, sedate, shy, unexcitable ~*n.* 6. calmness, ease, peace, quietness, repose, rest, serenity, silence, stillness, tranquillity
Antonyms *adj.* (*sense 1*) deafening, ear-splitting, high-decibel, high-volume, loud, noisy, stentorian (*sense 2*) agitated, alert, excitable, exciting, frenetic, troubled, turbulent, violent (*sense 3*) bustling, busy, crowded, exciting, fashionable, lively, popular, vibrant (*sense 4*) blatant, bright, conspicuous, glaring, loud, obtrusive, ostentatious, pretentious, showy (*sense 5*) agitated, excited, high-spirited, impatient, loquacious, passionate, restless, talkative, verbose, violent ~*n.* (*sense 6*) activity, bustle, commotion, din, disturbance, noise, racket

quieten *v.* allay, alleviate, appease, assuage, blunt, calm, compose, deaden, dull, hush, lull, mitigate, mollify, muffle, mute, palliate, quell, quiet, shush (*Inf.*), silence, soothe, stifle, still, stop, subdue, tranquillize
Antonyms aggravate, exacerbate, intensify, provoke, upset, worsen

quietness calm, calmness, hush, peace, placidity, quiescence, quiet, quietude, repose, rest, serenity, silence, still, stillness, tranquillity

quip *n.* badinage, *bon mot*, gibe, jest, joke, pleasantry, repartee, retort, riposte, sally, wisecrack (*Inf.*), witticism

quit *v.* 1. abandon, abdicate, decamp, depart, desert, exit, forsake, go, leave, pull out, relinquish, renounce, resign, retire, surrender, take off (*Inf.*), withdraw 2. abandon, cease, conclude, discontinue, drop, end, give up, halt, stop, suspend
Antonyms (*sense 2*) complete, continue, finish, go on with, see through

quite 1. absolutely, completely, considerably, entirely, fully, in all respects, largely, perfectly, precisely, totally, wholly, without reservation 2. fairly, moderately, rather, reasonably, relatively, somewhat, to a certain extent, to some degree

quiver *v.* agitate, convulse, oscillate, palpitate, pulsate, quake, quaver, shake, shiver, shudder, tremble, vibrate

quiz 1. *n.* examination, investigation, questioning, test **2.** *v.* ask, catechize, examine, grill (*Inf.*), interrogate, investigate, pump (*Inf.*), question

quota allocation, allowance, assignment, cut (*Inf.*), part, portion, proportion, ration, share, slice, whack (*Inf.*)

quotation 1. citation, cutting, excerpt, extract, passage, quote (*Inf.*), reference, selection **2.** *Commerce* bid price, charge, cost, estimate, figure, price, quote (*Inf.*), rate, tender

quote adduce, attest, cite, detail, extract, instance, name, paraphrase, proclaim, recall, recite, recollect, refer to, repeat, retell

R

rabble canaille, crowd, herd, horde, mob, swarm, throng

race[1] 1. *n.* chase, competition, contention, contest, dash, pursuit, rivalry 2. *v.* career, compete, contest, dart, dash, fly, gallop, hare (*Brit. inf.*), hasten, hurry, run, run like mad (*Inf.*), speed, tear, zoom

race[2] blood, breed, clan, ethnic group, family, folk, house, issue, kin, kindred, line, lineage, nation, offspring, people, progeny, seed (*Archaic*), stock, tribe, type

rack *n.* 1. frame, framework, stand, structure 2. affliction, agony, anguish, misery, pain, pang, persecution, suffering, torment, torture ~ *v.* 3. afflict, agonize, crucify, distress, excruciate, harass, harrow, oppress, pain, torment, torture

racket 1. babel, ballyhoo (*Inf.*), clamour, commotion, din, disturbance, fuss, hubbub, hullaballoo, noise, outcry, pandemonium, row, shouting, tumult, uproar 2. criminal activity, fraud, illegal enterprise, scheme

racy animated, buoyant, energetic, entertaining, exciting, exhilarating, heady, lively, sparkling, spirited, stimulating, vigorous, zestful

radiant beaming, bright, brilliant, effulgent, gleaming, glittering, glorious, glowing, incandescent, luminous, lustrous, resplendent, shining, sparkling, sunny

radiate 1. diffuse, disseminate, emanate, emit, give off *or* out, gleam, glitter, pour, scatter, send out, shed, shine, spread 2. branch out, diverge, issue, spread out

radical *adj.* 1. basic, constitutional, deep-seated, essential, fundamental, innate, native, natural, organic, profound, thoroughgoing 2. complete, entire, excessive, extreme, extremist, fanatical, revolutionary, severe, sweeping, thorough, violent ~ *n.* 3. extremist, fanatic, militant, revolutionary

Antonyms *adj.* insignificant, minor, superficial, token, trivial ~ *n.* conservative, moderate, reactionary

rage 1. *n.* agitation, anger, frenzy, fury, high dudgeon, ire, madness, mania, obsession, passion, rampage, raving, vehemence, violence, wrath 2. *v.* be beside oneself, be furious, blow one's top, blow up (*Inf.*), chafe, foam at the mouth, fret, fume, rant and rave, rave, seethe, storm, throw a fit (*Inf.*)

Antonyms *n.* acceptance, calmness, equanimity, gladness, good humour, joy, pleasure, resignation ~ *v.* accept, keep one's cool, remain unruffled, resign oneself to, stay calm

ragged contemptible, down at heel, frayed, in holes, in rags, in tatters, mean, poor, rent, scraggy, shabby, shaggy, tattered, tatty, threadbare, torn, unkempt, worn-out

raid 1. *n.* attack, break-in, descent, foray, hit-and-run attack, incursion, inroad, invasion, irruption, onset, sally, seizure, sortie, surprise attack 2. *v.* assault, attack, break into, descend on, fall upon, forage (*Military*), foray, invade, pillage, plunder, reive (*Dialect*), rifle, sack, sally forth, swoop down upon

raider attacker, forager (*Military*), invader, marauder, plunderer, reiver (*Dialect*), robber, thief

rain *n.* 1. cloudburst, deluge,

downpour, drizzle, fall, precipita~
tion, raindrops, rainfall, showers
2. deluge, flood, hail, shower,
spate, stream, torrent, volley ~v.
3. bucket down (*Inf.*), come down
in buckets (*Inf.*), drizzle, fall,
pour, rain cats and dogs (*Inf.*),
shower, teem

raise 1. build, construct, elevate,
erect, exalt, heave, hoist, lift,
move up, promote, put up, rear,
set upright, uplift **2.** advance,
aggravate, amplify, augment,
boost, enhance, enlarge, esca~
late, exaggerate, heighten, hike
(up) (*Inf.*), increase, inflate, in~
tensify, jack up, magnify, put on,
reinforce, strengthen **3.** advance,
aggrandize, elevate, exalt, pre~
fer, promote, upgrade **4.** bring
about, cause, create, engender,
give rise to, occasion, originate,
produce, provoke, start **5.** ad~
vance, bring up, broach, intro~
duce, moot, put forward, suggest
6. assemble, collect, form, gath~
er, get, levy, mass, mobilize,
muster, obtain, rally, recruit **7.**
breed, bring up, cultivate, devel~
op, grow, nurture, produce,
propagate, rear
Antonyms calm, cut, decrease,
demolish, depress, destroy, di~
minish, drop, lessen, let down,
level, lower, quash, quell, reduce,
ruin, sink, soothe, suppress,
wreck

rake[1] *v.* **1.** collect, gather, re~
move, scrape up **2.** break up,
harrow, hoe, scour, scrape,
scratch

rake[2] *n.* debauchee, dissolute
man, lecher, libertine, playboy,
profligate, rakehell (*Archaic*),
roué, sensualist, voluptuary
Antonyms ascetic, celibate,
monk, puritan

rally *v.* **1.** bring *or* come to order,
reassemble, re-form, regroup,
reorganize, unite ~*n.* **2.** re~
grouping, reorganization, reu~
nion, stand ~*v.* **3.** assemble, bond
together, bring *or* come together,
collect, convene, gather, get to~
gether, marshal, mobilize, mus~

ter, organize, round up, summon,
unite ~*n.* **4.** assembly, confer~
ence, congregation, convention,
convocation, gathering, mass
meeting, meeting, muster ~*v.* **5.**
come round, get better, get one's
second wind, improve, perk up,
pick up, pull through, recover,
recuperate, regain one's
strength, revive, take a turn for
the better ~*n.* **6.** comeback
(*Inf.*), improvement, recovery,
recuperation, renewal, resur~
gence, revival, turn for the better

ram *v.* butt, collide with, crash,
dash, drive, force, hit, impact,
run into, slam, smash, strike

ramble *v.* **1.** amble, drift, peram~
bulate, peregrinate, range, roam,
rove, saunter, straggle, stravaig
(*Scot.*), stray, stroll, traipse (*Inf.*),
walk, wander **2.** babble, chatter,
digress, expatiate, maunder,
rabbit on (*Brit. sl.*), rattle on,
wander, witter on (*Inf.*) ~*n.* **3.**
excursion, hike, perambulation,
peregrination, roaming, roving,
saunter, stroll, tour, traipse (*Inf.*),
trip, walk

ramification 1. branch, develop~
ment, divarication, division, ex~
crescence, extension, forking,
offshoot, outgrowth, subdivision
2. complication, consequence,
development, result, sequel, up~
shot

rampage 1. *v.* go berserk, rage,
run amuck, run riot, run wild,
storm, tear **2.** *n.* destruction,
frenzy, fury, rage, storm, tem~
pest, tumult, uproar, violence

rampant aggressive, dominant,
excessive, flagrant, on the ram~
page, out of control, out of hand,
outrageous, raging, rampaging,
riotous, unbridled, uncontrol~
lable, ungovernable, unre~
strained, vehement, violent,
wanton, wild

rampart barricade, bastion,
breastwork, bulwark, defence,
earthwork, embankment, fence,
fort, fortification, guard, parapet,
security, stronghold, wall

ramshackle broken-down, crum~

bling, decrepit, derelict, dilapi-dated, flimsy, jerry-built, rickety, shaky, tottering, tumbledown, unsafe, unsteady

random 1. accidental, adventitious, aimless, arbitrary, casual, chance, desultory, fortuitous, haphazard, hit or miss, inciden-tal, indiscriminate, purposeless, spot, stray, unplanned, unpre-meditated

Antonyms definite, deliberate, intended, planned, premeditated, specific

range n. 1. amplitude, area, bounds, compass, confines, dis-tance, domain, extent, field, lati-tude, limits, orbit, parameters (Inf.), province, purview, radius, reach, scope, span, sphere, sweep ~v. 2. align, arrange, ar-ray, dispose, draw up, line up, order 3. cruise, explore, ramble, roam, rove, straggle, stray, stroll, sweep, traverse, wander

rank[1] n. 1. caste, class, classifica-tion, degree, dignity, division, echelon, grade, level, nobility, order, position, quality, sort, standing, station, status, stratum, type 2. column, file, formation, group, line, range, row, series, tier ~v. 3. align, arrange, array, class, classify, dispose, grade, line up, locate, marshal, order, position, range, sort

rank[2] 1. abundant, dense, exuber-ant, flourishing, lush, luxuriant, productive, profuse, strong-growing, vigorous 2. bad, dis-agreeable, disgusting, fetid, foul, fusty, gamy, mephitic, musty, noisome, noxious, off, offensive, pungent, putrid, rancid, revolting, stale, stinking, strong-smelling

ransack 1. comb, explore, go through, rake, rummage, scour, search, turn inside out 2. despoil, gut, loot, pillage, plunder, raid, ravage, rifle, sack, strip

ransom n. 1. deliverance, libera-tion, redemption, release, rescue 2. money, payment, payoff, price ~v. 3. buy (someone) out (Inf.), buy the freedom of, deliver, lib-

erate, obtain or pay for the re-lease of, redeem, release, rescue, set free

rant v. bellow, bluster, cry, de-claim, rave, roar, shout, spout (Inf.), vociferate, yell

rape n. 1. outrage, ravishment, sexual assault, violation 2. dep-redation, despoilment, despolia-tion, pillage, plundering, rapine, sack, spoliation 3. abuse, defile-ment, desecration, maltreat-ment, perversion, violation ~v. 4. outrage, ravish, sexually as-sault, violate 5. despoil, loot, pil-lage, plunder, ransack, sack, spoliate

rapid brisk, expeditious, express, fast, fleet, flying, hasty, hurried, precipitate, prompt, quick, speedy, swift

rapt absorbed, carried away, en-grossed, enthralled, entranced, fascinated, gripped, held, intent, preoccupied, spellbound

rapture beatitude, bliss, cloud nine (Inf.), delectation, delight, ecstasy, enthusiasm, euphoria, exaltation, felicity, happiness, joy, ravishment, rhapsody, sev-enth heaven, spell, transport

rare 1. exceptional, few, infre-quent, out of the ordinary, re-cherché, scarce, singular, sparse, sporadic, strange, thin on the ground, uncommon, unusual 2. admirable, choice, excellent, ex-quisite, extreme, fine, great, in-comparable, peerless, superb, superlative

Antonyms abundant, bountiful, common, frequent, habitual, manifold, many, plentiful, pro-fuse, regular

rarely almost never, hardly, hardly ever, infrequently, little, once in a blue moon, once in a while, only now and then, on rare occasions, scarcely ever, seldom

Antonyms frequently, often, regularly

rarity 1. curio, curiosity, find, gem, one-off, pearl, treasure 2. infrequency, scarcity, shortage, singularity, sparseness, strange-

ness, uncommonness, unusual~
ness

rascal blackguard, caitiff (*Archa~
ic*), devil, disgrace, good-for-
nothing, imp, knave (*Archaic*),
miscreant, ne'er-do-well, rake,
rapscallion, reprobate, rogue,
scallywag (*Inf.*), scamp, scoun~
drel, varmint (*Inf.*), villain, wast~
rel, wretch

rash[1] adventurous, audacious,
brash, careless, foolhardy, harebrained, harum-scarum, hasty,
headlong, headstrong, heedless,
helter-skelter, hot-headed, ill-
advised, ill-considered, impetu~
ous, imprudent, impulsive, incautious, indiscreet, injudicious,
madcap, precipitate, premature,
reckless, thoughtless, unguarded,
unthinking, unwary, venture~
some
Antonyms canny, careful, cau~
tious, considered, premeditated,
prudent, well thought out

rash[2] 1. eruption, outbreak 2. epidemic, flood, outbreak, plague,
series, spate, succession, wave

rate *n.* 1. degree, percentage,
proportion, ratio, relation, scale,
standard 2. charge, cost, dues,
duty, fee, figure, hire, price, tar~
iff, tax, toll 3. gait, measure, pace,
speed, tempo, time, velocity 4.
class, classification, degree,
grade, position, quality, rank,
rating, status, value, worth 5. at
any rate anyhow, anyway, at all
events, in any case, nevertheless
~*v.* 6. adjudge, appraise, assess,
class, classify, consider, count,
esteem, estimate, evaluate,
grade, measure, rank, reckon,
regard, value, weigh

rather 1. a bit, a little, fairly, kind
of (*Inf.*), moderately, pretty
(*Inf.*), quite, relatively, slightly,
somewhat, sort of (*Inf.*), to some
degree, to some extent 2. a good
bit, noticeably, significantly, very
3. instead, more readily, more
willingly, preferably, sooner

ratify affirm, approve, authenti~
cate, authorize, bear out, bind,
certify, confirm, consent to, cor-

roborate, endorse, establish,
sanction, sign, uphold, validate

ratio arrangement, correlation,
correspondence, equation, frac~
tion, percentage, proportion,
rate, relation, relationship

ration *n.* 1. allotment, allowance,
dole, helping, measure, part,
portion, provision, quota, share 2.
Plural commons (*Brit.*), food,
provender, provisions, stores,
supplies ~*v.* 3. With out allocate,
allot, apportion, deal, distribute,
dole, give out, issue, measure out,
mete, parcel out 4. budget, con~
serve, control, limit, restrict,
save

rational enlightened, intelligent,
judicious, logical, lucid, realistic,
reasonable, sagacious, sane, sen~
sible, sound, wise
Antonyms irrational, unreason~
able, unsound

rationalize 1. account for, excuse,
explain away, extenuate, justify,
make allowance for, make ex~
cuses for, vindicate 2. apply logic
to, elucidate, reason out, resolve,
think through

rattle *v.* 1. bang, clatter, jangle 2.
bounce, jar, jiggle, jolt, jounce,
shake, vibrate 3. *Inf.* discomfit,
discompose, disconcert, discoun~
tenance, disturb, faze (*U.S. inf.*),
frighten, perturb, put (someone)
off his stride, put (someone) out
of countenance, scare, shake,
upset

raucous grating, harsh, hoarse,
husky, loud, noisy, rasping,
rough, strident

ravage *v.* demolish, desolate, de~
spoil, destroy, devastate, gut, lay
waste, leave in ruins, loot, pillage, plunder, ransack, raze, ruin,
sack, shatter, spoil, wreak havoc
on, wreck

rave *v.* babble, be delirious, fume,
go mad, rage, rant, roar, run
amuck, splutter, storm, talk
wildly, thunder

ravenous famished, starved,
starving, very hungry
Antonyms full, glutted, sated, sa~
tiated

ravine canyon, clough (*Dialect*), defile, flume, gap (*U.S.*), gorge, gulch (*U.S.*), gully, linn (*Scot.*), pass

raw 1. bloody (*of meat*), fresh, natural, uncooked, undressed, unprepared **2.** basic, coarse, crude, green, natural, organic, rough, unfinished, unprocessed, unrefined, unripe, untreated **3.** abraded, chafed, grazed, open, scratched, sensitive, skinned, sore, tender **4.** callow, green, ignorant, immature, inexperienced, new, undisciplined, unpractised, unseasoned, unskilled, untrained, untried **5.** biting, bitter, bleak, chill, chilly, cold, damp, freezing, harsh, piercing, unpleasant, wet
Antonyms (*sense 1*) baked, cooked, done (*sense 2*) finished, prepared, refined (*sense 4*) experienced, practised, professional, skilled, trained

ray 1. bar, beam, flash, gleam, shaft **2.** flicker, glimmer, hint, indication, scintilla, spark, trace

reach *v.* **1.** arrive at, attain, get as far as, get to, land at, make **2.** contact, extend to, get (a) hold of, go as far as, grasp, stretch to, touch **3.** amount to, arrive at, attain, climb to, come to, drop, fall, move, rise, sink ~*n.* **4.** ambit, capacity, command, compass, distance, extension, extent, grasp, influence, jurisdiction, mastery, power, range, scope, spread, stretch, sweep

react 1. acknowledge, answer, reply, respond **2.** act, behave, conduct oneself, function, operate, proceed, work

reaction 1. acknowledgment, answer, feedback, reply, response **2.** compensation, counteraction, counterbalance, counterpoise, recoil **3.** conservatism, counter-revolution, obscurantism, the right

reactionary 1. *adj.* blimpish, conservative, counter-revolutionary, obscurantist, rightist **2.** *n.* Colonel Blimp, conservative, counter-

revolutionary, die-hard, obscurantist, rightist, right-winger
Antonyms (*senses 1 & 2*) leftist, progressive, radical, reformist, revolutionary, socialist

read 1. glance at, look at, peruse, pore over, refer to, run one's eye over, scan, study **2.** announce, declaim, deliver, recite, speak, utter **3.** comprehend, construe, decipher, discover, interpret, perceive the meaning of, see, understand **4.** display, indicate, record, register, show

readily 1. cheerfully, eagerly, freely, gladly, promptly, quickly, voluntarily, willingly, with good grace, with pleasure **2.** at once, easily, effortlessly, in no time, quickly, right away, smoothly, speedily, straight away, unhesitatingly, without delay, without demur, without difficulty, without hesitation
Antonyms hesitatingly, reluctantly, slowly, unwillingly, with difficulty

reading 1. examination, inspection, perusal, review, scrutiny, study **2.** homily, lecture, lesson, performance, recital, rendering, rendition, sermon **3.** conception, construction, grasp, impression, interpretation, treatment, understanding, version **4.** book-learning, edification, education, erudition, knowledge, learning, scholarship

ready *adj.* **1.** all set, arranged, completed, fit, in readiness, organized, prepared, primed, ripe, set **2.** agreeable, apt, disposed, eager, game (*Inf.*), glad, happy, inclined, keen, minded, predisposed, prone, willing **3.** acute, adroit, alert, apt, astute, bright, clever, deft, dexterous, expert, handy, intelligent, keen, perceptive, prompt, quick, quick-witted, rapid, resourceful, sharp, skilful, smart **4.** accessible, at *or* on hand, at one's fingertips, at the ready, available, close to hand, convenient, handy, near, on call, on tap (*Inf.*), present

Antonyms *adj.* disinclined, distant, hesitant, immature, inaccessible, inexpert, late, loath, reluctant, slow, unavailable, unequipped, unfit, unhandy, unprepared, unwilling

real absolute, actual, authentic, bona fide, certain, essential, existent, factual, genuine, heartfelt, honest, intrinsic, legitimate, positive, right, rightful, sincere, true, unaffected, unfeigned, valid, veritable

Antonyms affected, counterfeit, fake, faked, false, feigned, imaginary, imitation, insincere

realistic 1. businesslike, commonsense, down-to-earth, hardheaded, level-headed, matter-of-fact, practical, pragmatic, rational, real, sensible, sober, unromantic, unsentimental 2. authentic, faithful, genuine, graphic, lifelike, natural, naturalistic, representational, true, true to life, truthful

Antonyms fanciful, idealistic, impractical, unrealistic

reality actuality, authenticity, certainty, corporeality, fact, genuineness, materiality, realism, truth, validity, verisimilitude, verity

realization 1. appreciation, apprehension, awareness, cognizance, comprehension, conception, consciousness, grasp, imagination, perception, recognition, understanding 2. accomplishment, achievement, carrying-out, completion, consummation, effectuation, fulfilment

realize 1. appreciate, apprehend, be cognizant of, become aware of, become conscious of, catch on (*Inf.*), comprehend, conceive, grasp, imagine, recognize, take in, twig (*Brit. inf.*), understand 2. accomplish, actualize, bring about, bring off, bring to fruition, carry out *or* through, complete, consummate, do, effect, effectuate, fulfil, make concrete, make happen, perform, reify 3. ac-

quire, bring *or* take in, clear, earn, gain, get, go for, make, net, obtain, produce, sell for

reap acquire, bring in, collect, cut, derive, gain, garner, gather, get, harvest, obtain, win

rear[1] 1. *n.* back, back end, end, rearguard, stern, tail, tail end 2. *adj.* aft, after (*Nautical*), back, following, hind, hindmost, last, trailing

Antonyms *n.* bow, forward end, front, nose, stem, vanguard ~*adj.* foremost, forward, front, leading

rear[2] *v.* 1. breed, bring up, care for, cultivate, educate, foster, grow, nurse, nurture, raise, train 2. build, construct, erect, fabricate, put up

reason *n.* 1. apprehension, brains, comprehension, intellect, judgment, logic, mentality, mind, ratiocination, rationality, reasoning, sanity, sense(s), sound mind, soundness, understanding 2. aim, basis, cause, design, end, goal, grounds, impetus, incentive, inducement, intention, motive, object, occasion, purpose, target, warrant, why and wherefore (*Inf.*) 3. bounds, limits, moderation, propriety, reasonableness, sense, sensibleness, wisdom ~*v.* 4. conclude, deduce, draw conclusions, infer, make out, ratiocinate, resolve, solve, syllogize, think, work out

reasonable 1. advisable, arguable, believable, credible, intelligent, judicious, justifiable, logical, plausible, practical, rational, reasoned, sane, sensible, sober, sound, tenable, well-advised, well thought-out, wise 2. acceptable, average, equitable, fair, fit, honest, inexpensive, just, moderate, modest, O.K. (*Inf.*), proper, right, tolerable, within reason

Antonyms impossible, irrational, unfair, unintelligent, unreasonable, unsound

reasoning 1. analysis, cogitation, deduction, logic, ratiocination, reason, thinking, thought 2. argument, case, exposition, hypothesis, interpretation, proof, train of thought

reassure bolster, buoy up, cheer up, comfort, encourage, hearten, inspirit, put *or* set one's mind at rest, relieve (someone) of anxiety, restore confidence to

rebel *v.* 1. man the barricades, mutiny, resist, revolt, rise up, take to the streets, take up arms 2. come out against, defy, disobey, dissent, refuse to obey 3. flinch, recoil, show repugnance, shrink, shy away ~*n.* 4. insurgent, insurrectionary, mutineer, resistance fighter, revolutionary, revolutionist, secessionist 5. apostate, dissenter, heretic, nonconformist, schismatic ~*adj.* 6. insubordinate, insurgent, insurrectionary, mutinous, rebellious, revolutionary

rebellion 1. insurgence, insurgency, insurrection, mutiny, resistance, revolt, revolution, rising, uprising 2. apostasy, defiance, disobedience, dissent, heresy, insubordination, nonconformity, schism

rebellious 1. contumacious, defiant, disaffected, disloyal, disobedient, disorderly, insubordinate, insurgent, insurrectionary, intractable, mutinous, rebel, recalcitrant, revolutionary, seditious, turbulent, ungovernable, unruly 2. difficult, incorrigible, obstinate, recalcitrant, refractory, resistant, unmanageable **Antonyms** dutiful, loyal, obedient, patriotic, subordinate, subservient

rebound *v.* 1. bounce, recoil, resound, return, ricochet, spring back 2. backfire, boomerang, misfire, recoil ~*n.* 3. bounce, comeback, kickback, repercussion, return, ricochet

rebuff 1. *v.* brush off (*Sl.*), check, cold-shoulder, cut, decline, deny, discourage, put off, refuse, reject, repulse, resist, slight, snub, spurn, turn down 2. *n.* brushoff (*Sl.*), check, cold shoulder, defeat, de-

nial, discouragement, opposition, refusal, rejection, repulse, slight, snub, thumbs down

rebuke 1. *v.* admonish, bawl out (*Inf.*), berate, blame, carpet (*Inf.*), castigate, censure, chide, dress down (*Inf.*), haul (someone) over the coals (*Inf.*), lecture, reprehend, reprimand, reproach, reprove, scold, take to task, tear (someone) off a strip (*Inf.*), tell off (*Inf.*), tick off (*Inf.*), upbraid 2. *n.* admonition, blame, castigation, censure, dressing down (*Inf.*), lecture, reprimand, reproach, reproof, reproval, row, telling-off (*Inf.*), ticking-off (*Inf.*), tongue-lashing, wigging (*Brit. sl.*) **Antonyms** *v.* applaud, approve, commend, compliment, congratulate, laud, praise ~*n.* commendation, compliment, laudation, praise

recall *v.* 1. bring *or* call to mind, call *or* summon up, evoke, look *or* think back to, mind (*Dialect*), recollect, remember, reminisce about 2. abjure, annul, call back, call in, cancel, countermand, nullify, repeal, rescind, retract, revoke, take back, withdraw ~*n.* 3. annulment, cancellation, nullification, recision, repeal, rescindment, rescission, retraction, revocation, withdrawal 4. memory, recollection, remembrance

recede 1. abate, draw back, ebb, fall back, go back, regress, retire, retreat, retrogress, return, subside, withdraw 2. decline, diminish, dwindle, fade, lessen, shrink, sink, wane

receipt 1. acknowledgment, counterfoil, proof of purchase, sales slip, stub, voucher 2. acceptance, delivery, receiving, reception, recipience

receive 1. accept, accept delivery of, acquire, be given, be in receipt of, collect, derive, get, obtain, pick up, take 2. apprehend, be informed of, be told, gather, hear, perceive 3. bear, be subjected to, encounter, experience, go through, meet with, suffer, sustain, undergo 4. accommodate, admit, be at home to, entertain, greet, meet, take in, welcome

recent contemporary, current, fresh, late, latter, latter-day, modern, new, novel, present-day, up-to-date, young

Antonyms ancient, antique, earlier, early, historical, old

reception 1. acceptance, admission, receipt, receiving, recipience 2. acknowledgment, greeting, reaction, recognition, response, treatment, welcome 3. do (Inf.), entertainment, function, levee, party, soirée

receptive alert, bright, perceptive, quick on the uptake (Inf.), responsive, sensitive

Antonyms unreceptive, unresponsive

recess 1. alcove, bay, cavity, corner, depression, hollow, indentation, niche, nook, oriel 2. break, cessation of business, closure, holiday, intermission, interval, respite, rest, vacation

recession decline, depression, downturn, slump

Antonyms boom, upturn

recipe 1. directions, ingredients, instructions, receipt (Obsolete) 2. formula, method, modus operandi, prescription, procedure, process, programme, technique

reciprocate barter, exchange, feel in return, interchange, reply, requite, respond, return, return the compliment, swap, trade

recital account, description, detailing, enumeration, narration, narrative, performance, reading, recapitulation, recitation, rehearsal, relation, rendering, repetition, statement, story, tale, telling

recite declaim, deliver, describe, detail, do one's party piece (Inf.), enumerate, itemize, narrate, perform, recapitulate, recount, rehearse, relate, repeat, speak, tell

reckless careless, daredevil, devil-may-care, foolhardy, harebrained, harum-scarum, hasty, headlong, heedless, ill-advised, imprudent, inattentive, incautious, indiscreet, irresponsible, madcap, mindless, negligent, overventuresome, precipitate, rash, regardless, thoughtless, wild

Antonyms careful, cautious, heedful, mindful, observant, responsible, thoughtful, wary

reckon 1. add up, calculate, compute, count, enumerate, figure, number, tally, total 2. account, appraise, consider, count, deem, esteem, estimate, evaluate, gauge, hold, judge, look upon, rate, regard, think of 3. assume, believe, be of the opinion, conjecture, expect, fancy, guess (Inf.), imagine, suppose, surmise, think

reckoning 1. adding, addition, calculation, computation, count, counting, estimate, summation, working 2. account, bill, charge, due, score, settlement

reclaim get or take back, recapture, recover, redeem, reform, regain, regenerate, reinstate, rescue, restore, retrieve, salvage

recline be recumbent, lay (something) down, lean, lie (down), loll, lounge, repose, rest, sprawl, stretch out

recluse anchoress, anchorite, ascetic, eremite, hermit, monk, solitary

recognition 1. detection, discovery, identification, recall, recollection, remembrance 2. acceptance, acknowledgment, admission, allowance, appreciation, avowal, awareness, cognizance, concession, confession, notice, perception, realization, respect, understanding

recognize 1. identify, know, know again, make out, notice, place, recall, recollect, remember, spot 2. accept, acknowledge, admit, allow, appreciate, avow, be aware of, concede, confess,

grant, own, perceive, realize, respect, see, understand
Antonyms (*sense 2*) be unaware of, forget, ignore, overlook

recoil *v.* **1.** jerk back, kick, react, rebound, resile, spring back **2.** balk at, draw back, falter, flinch, quail, shrink, shy away **3.** backfire, boomerang, go wrong, misfire, rebound ~*n.* **4.** backlash, kick, reaction, rebound, repercussion

recollect call to mind, mind (*Dialect*), place, recall, remember, reminisce, summon up

recollection impression, memory, mental image, recall, remembrance, reminiscence

recommend advance, advise, advocate, counsel, enjoin, exhort, propose, put forward, suggest, urge

recommendation 1. advice, counsel, proposal, suggestion, urging **2.** advocacy, approbation, approval, blessing, commendation, endorsement, favourable mention, good word, plug (*Inf.*), praise, reference, sanction, testimonial

reconcile 1. accept, accommodate, get used, make the best of, put up with (*Inf.*), resign, submit, yield **2.** appease, bring to terms, conciliate, make peace between, pacify, placate, propitiate, re-establish friendly relations between, restore harmony between, reunite **3.** adjust, compose, harmonize, patch up, put to rights, rectify, resolve, settle, square

reconnaissance exploration, inspection, investigation, observation, patrol, recce (*Sl.*), reconnoitring, scan, scouting, scrutiny, survey

reconnoitre explore, get the lie of the land, inspect, investigate, make a reconnaissance (of), observe, patrol, recce (*Sl.*), scan, scout, scrutinize, see how the land lies, spy out, survey

reconsider change one's mind, have second thoughts, reassess,

re-evaluate, re-examine, rethink, review, revise, take another look at, think again, think better of, think over, think twice

reconstruct 1. reassemble, rebuild, recreate, re-establish, reform, regenerate, remake, remodel, renovate, reorganize, restore **2.** build up, build up a picture of, deduce, piece together

record *n.* **1.** account, annals, archives, chronicle, diary, document, entry, file, journal, log, memoir, memorandum, memorial, minute, register, report **2.** documentation, evidence, memorial, remembrance, testimony, trace, witness **3.** background, career, curriculum vitae, history, performance, track record (*Inf.*) **4.** album, black disc, disc, EP, forty-five, gramophone record, LP, platter (*U.S. sl.*), recording, release, single, vinyl **5. off the record** confidential, confidentially, in confidence, in private, not for publication, private, sub rosa, under the rose, unofficial, unofficially ~*v.* **6.** chalk up (*Inf.*), chronicle, document, enrol, enter, inscribe, log, minute, note, preserve, put down, put on file, put on record, register, report, set down, take down, transcribe, write down

recount delineate, depict, describe, detail, enumerate, give an account of, narrate, portray, recite, rehearse, relate, repeat, report, tell, tell the story of

recover 1. find again, get back, make good, recapture, reclaim, recoup, redeem, regain, repair, repossess, restore, retake, retrieve, take back, win back **2.** bounce back, come round, convalesce, feel oneself again, get back on one's feet, get better, get well, heal, improve, mend, pick up, pull through, rally, recuperate, regain one's health *or* strength, revive, take a turn for the better
Antonyms (*sense 1*) abandon, forfeit, lose (*sense 2*) deteriorate,

go downhill, relapse, take a turn for the worse, weaken, worsen

recovery 1. convalescence, healing, improvement, mending, rally, recuperation, return to health, revival, turn for the better **2.** amelioration, betterment, improvement, rally, rehabilitation, restoration, revival, upturn

recreation amusement, distraction, diversion, enjoyment, entertainment, exercise, fun, hobby, leisure activity, pastime, play, pleasure, refreshment, relaxation, relief, sport

recruit *v.* **1.** draft, enlist, enrol, impress, levy, mobilize, muster, raise, strengthen **2.** engage, enrol, gather, obtain, procure, proselytize, round up, take on, win (over) **3.** augment, build up, refresh, reinforce, renew, replenish, restore, strengthen, supply ~*n.* **4.** apprentice, beginner, convert, greenhorn (*Inf.*), helper, initiate, learner, neophyte, novice, proselyte, rookie (*Inf.*), trainee, tyro

rectify adjust, amend, correct, emend, fix, improve, make good, mend, put right, redress, reform, remedy, repair, right, square

recuperate convalesce, get back on one's feet, get better, improve, mend, pick up, recover, regain one's health

recur come again, come and go, come back, happen again, persist, reappear, repeat, return, revert

recurrent continued, cyclical, frequent, habitual, periodic, recurring, regular, repeated, repetitive

Antonyms isolated, one-off

red *adj.* **1.** cardinal, carmine, cherry, coral, crimson, gules (*Heraldry*), maroon, pink, rose, ruby, scarlet, vermeil, vermilion, wine **2.** bay, carroty, chestnut, flame-coloured, flaming, foxy, reddish, sandy, titian **3.** blushing, embarrassed, florid, flushed, rubicund, shamefaced, suffused **4.**

bloodstained, bloody, ensanguined (*Literary*), gory, sanguine

redeem 1. buy back, reclaim, recover, recover possession of, regain, repossess, repurchase, retrieve, win back **2.** cash (in), change, exchange, trade in **3.** abide by, acquit, adhere to, be faithful to, carry out, discharge, fulfil, hold to, keep, keep faith with, make good, meet, perform, satisfy **4.** buy the freedom of, deliver, emancipate, extricate, free, liberate, pay the ransom of, ransom, rescue, save, set free

redress *v.* **1.** compensate for, make amends (reparation, restitution) for, make up for, pay for, put right, recompense for **2.** adjust, amend, balance, correct, ease, even up, mend, put right, rectify, reform, regulate, relieve, remedy, repair, restore the balance, square

reduce 1. abate, abridge, contract, curtail, cut down, debase, decrease, depress, dilute, diminish, impair, lessen, lower, moderate, shorten, slow down, tone down, truncate, turn down, weaken, wind down **2.** bring, bring to the point of, conquer, drive, force, master, overpower, subdue, vanquish **3.** bring down the price of, cheapen, cut, discount, lower, mark down, slash **4.** break, bring low, degrade, demote, downgrade, humble, humiliate, lower in rank, lower the status of, take down a peg (*Inf.*)

Antonyms augment, defend, elevate, enhance, enlarge, exalt, extend, heighten, increase, promote

redundant 1. de trop, excessive, extra, inessential, inordinate, supererogatory, superfluous, supernumerary, surplus, unnecessary, unwanted **2.** diffuse, padded, periphrastic, pleonastic, prolix, repetitious, tautological, verbose, wordy

Antonyms essential, necessary, needed, vital

reek 1. *v.* hum (*Sl.*), pong (*Brit.*

inf.), smell, smell to high heaven, stink **2.** *n.* effluvium, fetor, mephitis, odour, pong (*Brit. inf.*), smell, stench, stink

reel 1. falter, lurch, pitch, rock, roll, stagger, stumble, sway, totter, waver, wobble **2.** go round and round, revolve, spin, swim, swirl, twirl, whirl

refer 1. advert, allude, bring up, cite, hint, invoke, make mention of, make reference, mention, speak of, touch on **2.** direct, guide, point, recommend, send **3.** apply, consult, go, have recourse to, look up, seek information from, turn to **4.** apply, be directed to, belong, be relevant to, concern, pertain, relate

referee 1. *n.* adjudicator, arbiter, arbitrator, judge, ref (*Inf.*), umpire **2.** *v.* adjudicate, arbitrate, judge, umpire

reference 1. allusion, citation, mention, note, quotation, remark **2.** applicability, bearing, concern, connection, consideration, regard, relation, respect **3.** certification, character, credentials, endorsement, good word, recommendation, testimonial

refine 1. clarify, cleanse, distil, filter, process, purify, rarefy **2.** civilize, cultivate, elevate, hone, improve, perfect, polish, temper

refined 1. civil, civilized, courtly, cultivated, cultured, elegant, genteel, gentlemanly, gracious, ladylike, polished, polite, sophisticated, urbane, well-bred, well-mannered **2.** cultured, delicate, discerning, discriminating, exact, fastidious, fine, nice, precise, punctilious, sensitive, sublime, subtle

Antonyms boorish, coarse, common, ill-bred, inelegant, uncultured, ungentlemanly, unladylike, unmannerly, unrefined

refinement 1. clarification, cleansing, distillation, filtering, processing, purification, rarefaction, rectification **2.** fine point, fine tuning, nicety, nuance, subtlety **3.** civility, civilization, courtesy, courtliness, cultivation, culture, delicacy, discrimination, elegance, fastidiousness, fineness, finesse, finish, gentility, good breeding, good manners, grace, graciousness, polish, politeness, politesse, precision, sophistication, style, taste, urbanity

reflect 1. echo, give back, imitate, mirror, reproduce, return, throw back **2.** cogitate, consider, contemplate, deliberate, meditate, mull over, muse, ponder, ruminate, think, wonder

reflection 1. counterpart, echo, image, mirror image **2.** cerebration, cogitation, consideration, contemplation, deliberation, idea, impression, meditation, musing, observation, opinion, pondering, rumination, study, thinking, thought, view

reform 1. *v.* ameliorate, amend, better, correct, improve, mend, rebuild, reclaim, reconstitute, reconstruct, rectify, regenerate, rehabilitate, remodel, renovate, reorganize, repair, restore, revolutionize **2.** *n.* amelioration, amendment, betterment, correction, improvement, rectification, rehabilitation, renovation

refrain *v.* abstain, avoid, cease, desist, do without, eschew, forbear, give up, leave off, renounce, stop

refresh 1. brace, breathe new life into, cheer, cool, enliven, freshen, inspirit, reanimate, reinvigorate, rejuvenate, revitalize, revive, revivify, stimulate **2.** brush up (*Inf.*), jog, prod, prompt, renew, stimulate

refreshing bracing, cooling, different, fresh, inspiriting, invigorating, new, novel, original, revivifying, stimulating, thirst-quenching

Antonyms enervating, exhausting, soporific, tiring, wearisome

refreshment 1. enlivenment, freshening, reanimation, renewal, renovation, repair, restoration, revival, stimulation **2.** *Plural* drinks, food and drink, snacks, titbits

refuge asylum, bolt hole, harbour, haven, hide-out, protection, re~ sort, retreat, sanctuary, security, shelter

refugee displaced person, émi~ gré, escapee, exile, fugitive, run~ away

refund 1. *v.* give back, make good, pay back, reimburse, repay, re~ store, return 2. *n.* reimburse~ ment, repayment, return

refusal 1. defiance, denial, knockback (*Sl.*), negation, no, re~ buff, rejection, repudiation, thumbs down 2. choice, consid~ eration, opportunity, option

refuse *v.* decline, deny, reject, repel, repudiate, say no, spurn, turn down, withhold
Antonyms accept, agree, allow, approve, consent, give, permit

regain get back, recapture, re~ coup, recover, redeem, repos~ sess, retake, retrieve, take back, win back

regard *v.* 1. behold, eye, gaze at, look closely at, mark, notice, ob~ serve, remark, scrutinize, view, watch 2. account, adjudge, be~ lieve, consider, deem, esteem, estimate, hold, imagine, judge, look upon, rate, see, suppose, think, treat, value, view 3. attend, heed, listen to, mind, note, pay attention to, respect, take into consideration, take notice of ~*n.* 4. attention, heed, mind, notice 5. account, affection, attachment, care, concern, consideration, deference, esteem, honour, love, note, reputation, repute, respect, store, sympathy, thought

regardless 1. *adj.* disregarding, heedless, inattentive, inconsider~ ate, indifferent, neglectful, negli~ gent, rash, reckless, remiss, un~ concerned, unmindful 2. *adv.* anyway, come what may, despite everything, for all that, in any case, in spite of everything, nevertheless, no matter what, nonetheless

Antonyms *adj.* heedful, mindful, regardful

regime administration, establish~ ment, government, leadership, management, reign, rule, system

region area, country, district, di~ vision, expanse, land, locality, part, place, province, quarter, section, sector, territory, tract, zone

regional district, local, parochial, provincial, sectional, zonal

register *n.* 1. annals, archives, catalogue, chronicle, diary, file, ledger, list, log, memorandum, record, roll, roster, schedule ~ *v.* 2. catalogue, check in, chronicle, enlist, enrol, enter, inscribe, list, note, record, set down, sign on *or* up, take down 3. be shown, be~ speak, betray, display, exhibit, express, indicate, manifest, mark, read, record, reflect, re~ veal, say, show

regret 1. *v.* bemoan, be upset, bewail, deplore, feel remorse for, feel sorry for, grieve, lament, miss, mourn, repent, rue, weep over 2. *n.* bitterness, compunc~ tion, contrition, disappointment, grief, lamentation, pang of con~ science, penitence, remorse, re~ pentance, ruefulness, self~ reproach, sorrow
Antonyms *v.* be happy, be satis~ fied, feel satisfaction, rejoice ~ *n.* callousness, contentment, im~ penitence, lack of compassion, pleasure, satisfaction

regrettable deplorable, disap~ pointing, distressing, ill-advised, lamentable, pitiable, sad, shame~ ful, unfortunate, unhappy, woeful, wrong

regular 1. common, common~ place, customary, daily, every~ day, habitual, normal, ordinary, routine, typical, unvarying, usual 2. consistent, constant, estab~ lished, even, fixed, ordered, peri~ odic, rhythmic, set, stated, steady, systematic, uniform 3. balanced, even, flat, level, smooth, straight, symmetrical, uniform

Antonyms abnormal, exceptional, inconsistent, inconstant, irregular, occasional, uncommon, unconventional, uneven, unmethodical, unusual, varied

regulate adjust, administer, arrange, balance, conduct, control, direct, fit, govern, guide, handle, manage, moderate, modulate, monitor, order, organize, oversee, rule, run, settle, superintend, supervise, systematize, tune

regulation n. 1. adjustment, administration, arrangement, control, direction, governance, government, management, modulation, supervision, tuning 2. commandment, decree, dictate, direction, edict, law, order, ordinance, precept, procedure, requirement, rule, standing order, statute

rehearsal drill, going-over, practice, practice session, preparation, reading, rehearsing, run-through

rehearse act, drill, go over, practise, prepare, ready, recite, repeat, run through, study, train, try out

reign 1. n. ascendancy, command, control, dominion, empire, hegemony, influence, monarchy, power, rule, sovereignty, supremacy, sway 2. v. administer, be in power, command, govern, hold sway, influence, occupy or sit on the throne, rule, wear the crown, wield the sceptre

reinforce augment, bolster, buttress, emphasize, fortify, harden, increase, prop, shore up, stiffen, strengthen, stress, supplement, support, toughen, underline
Antonyms contradict, undermine, weaken

reinforcement 1. addition, amplification, augmentation, enlargement, fortification, increase, strengthening, supplement 2. brace, buttress, prop, shore, stay, support 3. Plural additional or fresh troops, auxiliaries, reserves, support

reinstate bring back, recall, re-

establish, rehabilitate, replace, restore, return

reject 1. v. bin, cast aside, decline, deny, despise, disallow, discard, eliminate, exclude, jettison, jilt, rebuff, refuse, renounce, repel, repudiate, repulse, say no to, scrap, spurn, throw away or out, turn down, veto 2. n. castoff, discard, failure, flotsam, second
Antonyms v. accept, agree, allow, approve, permit, receive, select ∼n. prize, treasure

rejection brushoff (Sl.), denial, dismissal, elimination, exclusion, rebuff, refusal, renunciation, repudiation, thumbs down, veto
Antonyms acceptance, affirmation, approval, selection

rejoice be glad (happy, overjoyed), celebrate, delight, exult, glory, joy, jump for joy, make merry, revel, triumph
Antonyms be sad (unhappy, upset), grieve, lament, mourn

relapse v. 1. backslide, degenerate, fail, fall back, lapse, regress, retrogress, revert, slip back, weaken 2. deteriorate, fade, fail, sicken, sink, weaken, worsen ∼n. 3. backsliding, fall from grace, lapse, recidivism, regression, retrogression, reversion 4. deterioration, recurrence, setback, turn for the worse, weakening, worsening
Antonyms v. (sense 2) get better, improve, rally, recover ∼n. (sense 4) improvement, rally, recovery, turn for the better

relate 1. chronicle, describe, detail, give an account of, impart, narrate, present, recite, recount, rehearse, report, set forth, tell 2. ally, associate, connect, coordinate, correlate, couple, join, link 3. appertain, apply, bear upon, be relevant to, concern, have reference to, have to do with, pertain, refer

related 1. accompanying, affiliated, agnate, akin, allied, associated, cognate, concomitant, connected, correlated, interconnected, joint, linked 2. agnate, akin, cognate, consanguineous, kin, kindred

Antonyms separate, unconnected, unrelated

relation 1. affiliation, affinity, consanguinity, kindred, kinship, propinquity, relationship **2.** kin, kinsman, kinswoman, relative **3.** application, bearing, bond, comparison, connection, correlation, interdependence, link, pertinence, reference, regard, similarity, tie-in

relations 1. affairs, associations, communications, connections, contact, dealings, interaction, intercourse, liaison, meetings, rapport, relationship, terms **2.** clan, family, kin, kindred, kinsmen, relatives, tribe

relationship affair, association, bond, communications, conjunction, connection, correlation, exchange, kinship, liaison, link, parallel, proportion, rapport, ratio, similarity, tie-up

relative adj. **1.** allied, associated, comparative, connected, contingent, corresponding, dependent, proportionate, reciprocal, related, respective **2.** applicable, apposite, appropriate, appurtenant, apropos, germane, pertinent, relevant ~n. **3.** connection, kinsman, kinswoman, member of one's or the family, relation

relatively comparatively, in or by comparison, rather, somewhat, to some extent

relax 1. abate, diminish, ease, ebb, lessen, let up, loosen, lower, mitigate, moderate, reduce, relieve, slacken, weaken **2.** be or feel at ease, calm, laze, let oneself go (Inf.), let one's hair down (Inf.), loosen up, put one's feet up, rest, soften, take it easy (Inf.), take one's ease, tranquillize, unbend, unwind

Antonyms alarm, alert, heighten, increase, intensify, tense, tighten, work

relaxation amusement, enjoyment, entertainment, fun, leisure,

pleasure, recreation, refreshment, rest

relay n. **1.** relief, shift, turn **2.** communication, dispatch, message, transmission ~v. **3.** broadcast, carry, communicate, hand on, pass on, send, spread, transmit

release v. **1.** deliver, discharge, disengage, drop, emancipate, extricate, free, let go, let out, liberate, loose, manumit, set free, turn loose, unchain, undo, unfasten, unfetter, unloose, unshackle, untie **2.** absolve, acquit, dispense, excuse, exempt, exonerate, let go, let off **3.** break, circulate, disseminate, distribute, issue, launch, make known, make public, present, publish, put out, unveil ~n. **4.** acquittal, deliverance, delivery, discharge, emancipation, freedom, liberation, liberty, manumission, relief

Antonyms v. detain, engage, fasten, hold, imprison, incarcerate, keep, suppress, withhold ~n. detention, imprisonment, incarceration, internment

relent acquiesce, be merciful, capitulate, change one's mind, come round, forbear, give in, give quarter, give way, have pity, melt, show mercy, soften, unbend, yield

Antonyms be unyielding, give no quarter, remain firm, show no mercy

relentless cruel, fierce, grim, hard, harsh, implacable, inexorable, inflexible, merciless, pitiless, remorseless, ruthless, uncompromising, undeviating, unforgiving, unrelenting, unstoppable, unyielding

Antonyms compassionate, forgiving, merciful, submissive, yielding

relevant admissible, ad rem, applicable, apposite, appropriate, appurtenant, apt, fitting, germane, material, pertinent, proper, related, relative, significant, suited, to the point, to the purpose

Antonyms beside the point, extraneous, extrinsic, immaterial, inapplicable, inappropriate, irrelevant, unconnected, unrelated

reliable certain, dependable, faithful, honest, predictable, regular, responsible, safe, sound, stable, sure, tried and true, true, trustworthy, trusty, unfailing, upright
Antonyms irresponsible, undependable, unreliable, untrustworthy

relic fragment, keepsake, memento, remembrance, remnant, scrap, souvenir, survival, token, trace, vestige

relief 1. abatement, alleviation, assuagement, balm, comfort, cure, deliverance, ease, easement, mitigation, palliation, release, remedy, solace 2. aid, assistance, help, succour, support, sustenance 3. break, breather (Inf.), diversion, let-up (Inf.), refreshment, relaxation, remission, respite, rest

relieve 1. abate, alleviate, appease, assuage, calm, comfort, console, cure, diminish, dull, ease, mitigate, mollify, palliate, relax, salve, soften, solace, soothe 2. aid, assist, bring aid to, help, succour, support, sustain 3. give (someone) a break or rest, stand in for, substitute for, take over from, take the place of
Antonyms (sense 1) aggravate, exacerbate, heighten, intensify, worsen

religious churchgoing, devotional, devout, divine, doctrinal, faithful, god-fearing, godly, holy, pious, pure, reverent, righteous, sacred, scriptural, sectarian, spiritual, theological
Antonyms godless, infidel, irreligious, rational, secular, unbelieving

relish v. 1. appreciate, delight in, enjoy, fancy, like, look forward to, luxuriate in, prefer, revel in, savour, taste ~n. 2. appetite, appreciation, enjoyment, fancy,

fondness, gusto, liking, love, partiality, penchant, predilection, stomach, taste, zest 3. appetizer, condiment, sauce, seasoning 4. flavour, piquancy, savour, smack, spice, tang, taste, trace
Antonyms v. be unenthusiastic about, dislike, loathe ~n. (sense 2) dislike, distaste, loathing

reluctant averse, backward, disinclined, grudging, hesitant, indisposed, loath, recalcitrant, slow, unenthusiastic, unwilling
Antonyms eager, enthusiastic, inclined, keen, willing

rely bank, be confident of, be sure of, bet, count, depend, have confidence in, lean, reckon, repose trust in, swear by, trust

remain abide, be left, cling, continue, delay, dwell, endure, go on, last, linger, persist, prevail, rest, stand, stay, stay behind, stay put (Inf.), survive, tarry, wait
Antonyms depart, go, leave

remainder balance, dregs, excess, leavings, relic, remains, remnant, residue, residuum, rest, surplus, trace, vestige(s)

remains balance, crumbs, debris, detritus, dregs, fragments, leavings, leftovers, oddments, odds and ends, pieces, relics, remainder, remnants, residue, rest, scraps, traces, vestiges

remark v. 1. animadvert, comment, declare, mention, observe, pass comment, reflect, say, state 2. espy, heed, make out, mark, note, notice, observe, perceive, regard, see, take note or notice of ~n. 3. assertion, comment, declaration, observation, opinion, reflection, statement, thought, utterance, word

remarkable conspicuous, distinguished, extraordinary, famous, impressive, miraculous, notable, noteworthy, odd, outstanding, phenomenal, pre-eminent, prominent, rare, signal, singular, strange, striking, surprising, uncommon, unusual, wonderful
Antonyms common, commonplace, everyday, insignificant,

mundane, ordinary, unexceptional, unimpressive, unsurprising, usual

remedy 1. *n.* antidote, counteractive, cure, medicament, medicine, nostrum, panacea, physic (*Rare*), relief, restorative, specific, therapy, treatment **2.** *v.* alleviate, assuage, control, cure, ease, heal, help, mitigate, palliate, relieve, restore, soothe, treat

remember bear in mind, call to mind, call up, commemorate, keep in mind, look back (on), recall, recognize, recollect, reminisce, retain, summon up, think back
Antonyms disregard, forget, ignore, neglect, overlook

remind awaken memories of, bring back to, bring to mind, call to mind, call up, jog one's memory, make (someone) remember, prompt, put in mind, refresh one's memory

reminiscence anecdote, memoir, memory, recall, recollection, reflection, remembrance, retrospection, review

reminiscent evocative, redolent, remindful, similar, suggestive

remission 1. absolution, acquittal, amnesty, discharge, excuse, exemption, exoneration, forgiveness, indulgence, pardon, release, reprieve **2.** abatement, abeyance, alleviation, amelioration, decrease, diminution, ebb, lessening, let-up (*Inf.*), lull, moderation, reduction, relaxation, respite, suspension

remit *v.* **1.** dispatch, forward, mail, post, send, transmit **2.** cancel, desist, forbear, halt, repeal, rescind, stop ~*n.* **3.** authorization, brief, guidelines, instructions, orders, terms of reference

remorse anguish, bad *or* guilty conscience, compassion, compunction, contrition, grief, guilt, pangs of conscience, penitence, pity, regret, repentance, ruefulness, self-reproach, shame, sorrow

remorseless 1. inexorable, relentless, unrelenting, unremitting, unstoppable **2.** callous, cruel, hard, hardhearted, harsh, implacable, inhumane, merciless, pitiless, ruthless, savage, uncompassionate, unforgiving, unmerciful

remote 1. backwoods, distant, far, faraway, far-off, godforsaken, inaccessible, isolated, lonely, off the beaten track, outlying, out-of-the-way, secluded **2.** alien, extraneous, extrinsic, foreign, immaterial, irrelevant, outside, removed, unconnected, unrelated **3.** abstracted, aloof, cold, detached, distant, faraway, indifferent, introspective, introverted, removed, reserved, standoffish, unapproachable, uncommunicative
Antonyms (*sense 1*) adjacent, central, close, near, nearby, neighbouring (*sense 2*) intrinsic, related, relevant (*sense 3*) alert, attentive, aware, gregarious, interested, involved, outgoing, sociable

removal 1. abstraction, dislodgment, dismissal, displacement, dispossession, ejection, elimination, eradication, erasure, expulsion, expunction, extraction, purging, stripping, subtraction, taking off, uprooting, withdrawal **2.** departure, flitting (*Scot. & northern English dialect*), move, relocation, transfer

remove 1. abolish, abstract, amputate, carry off *or* away, delete, depose, detach, dethrone, discharge, dislodge, dismiss, displace, do away with, doff, efface, eject, eliminate, erase, expel, expunge, extract, get rid of, move, oust, purge, relegate, shed, strike out, take away, take off, take out, throw out, transfer, transport, unseat, wipe out, withdraw **2.** depart, flit (*Scot. & northern English dialect*), move, move away, quit, relocate, shift, transfer, transport, vacate
Antonyms (*sense 1*) appoint, don, insert, install, join, link, place,

put, put back, put in, put on, replace, set

render 1. contribute, deliver, furnish, give, make available, pay, present, provide, show, submit, supply, tender, turn over, yield 2. display, evince, exhibit, manifest, show 3. exchange, give, return, swap, trade 4. cause to become, leave, make 5. act, depict, do, give, interpret, perform, play, portray, present, represent 6. construe, explain, interpret, put, reproduce, restate, transcribe, translate 7. give back, make restitution, pay back, repay, restore, return

renew begin again, breathe new life into, bring up to date, continue, extend, fix up (*Inf., chiefly U.S.*), mend, modernize, overhaul, prolong, reaffirm, recommence, recreate, re-establish, refit, refresh, refurbish, regenerate, rejuvenate, renovate, reopen, repair, repeat, replace, replenish, restate, restock, restore, resume, revitalize, transform

renounce abandon, abdicate, abjure, abnegate, abstain from, cast off, decline, deny, discard, disclaim, disown, eschew, forgo, forsake, forswear, give up, leave off, quit, recant, reject, relinquish, repudiate, resign, spurn, swear off, throw off, waive, wash one's hands of

renovate do up (*Inf.*), fix up (*Inf., chiefly U.S.*), modernize, overhaul, recondition, reconstruct, recreate, refit, reform, refurbish, rehabilitate, remodel, renew, repair, restore, revamp

renowned acclaimed, celebrated, distinguished, eminent, esteemed, famed, famous, illustrious, notable, noted, well-known
Antonyms forgotten, little-known, neglected, obscure, unknown

rent 1. *n.* fee, hire, lease, payment, rental, tariff 2. *v.* charter, hire, lease, let

repair 1. *v.* compensate for, fix, heal, make good, make up for,

mend, patch, patch up, put back together, put right, recover, rectify, redress, renew, renovate, restore, restore to working order, retrieve, square 2. *n.* adjustment, darn, mend, overhaul, patch, restoration
Antonyms *v.* damage, destroy, harm, ruin, wreck

repay 1. compensate, make restitution, pay back, recompense, refund, reimburse, remunerate, requite, restore, return, reward, settle up with, square 2. avenge, even *or* settle the score with, get back at (*Inf.*), get even with (*Inf.*), get one's own back on (*Inf.*), make reprisal, reciprocate, retaliate, return the compliment, revenge

repeal 1. *v.* abolish, abrogate, annul, cancel, countermand, declare null and void, invalidate, nullify, recall, rescind, reverse, revoke, set aside, withdraw 2. *n.* abolition, abrogation, annulment, cancellation, invalidation, nullification, rescinding, rescindment, rescission, revocation, withdrawal
Antonyms *v.* confirm, enact, introduce, pass, ratify, reaffirm, validate ~*n.* confirmation, enactment, introduction, passing, ratification, reaffirmation, validation

repeat 1. *v.* duplicate, echo, iterate, quote, recapitulate, recite, redo, rehearse, reiterate, relate, renew, replay, reproduce, rerun, reshow, restate, retell 2. *n.* duplicate, echo, recapitulation, reiteration, repetition, replay, reproduction, rerun, reshowing

repeatedly again and again, frequently, many a time and oft, many times, often, over and over, time after time, time and (time) again

repel 1. beat off, check, confront, decline, drive off, fight, hold off, keep at arm's length, oppose, parry, put to flight, rebuff, refuse, reject, repulse, resist, ward off 2. disgust, give one the creeps

(*Inf.*), make one shudder, make one sick, nauseate, offend, put one off, revolt, sicken, turn one off (*Inf.*), turn one's stomach
Antonyms attract, delight, draw, entrance, fascinate, invite, please, submit

repent atone, be ashamed, be contrite, be sorry, deplore, feel remorse, lament, regret, relent, reproach oneself, rue, see the error of one's ways, show penitence, sorrow

repentant apologetic, ashamed, chastened, contrite, penitent, regretful, remorseful, rueful, self-reproachful, sorry

repercussion backlash, consequence, echo, rebound, recoil, result, reverberation, side effect

repetition duplication, echo, iteration, reappearance, recapitulation, recital, recurrence, redundancy, rehearsal, reiteration, relation, renewal, repeat, repetitiousness, replication, restatement, return, tautology

replace follow, oust, put back, re-establish, reinstate, restore, stand in lieu of, substitute, succeed, supersede, supplant, supply, take over from, take the place of

replacement double, fill-in, proxy, stand-in, substitute, successor, surrogate, understudy

replenish fill, furnish, make up, provide, refill, reload, renew, replace, restock, restore, stock, supply, top up
Antonyms consume, drain, empty, exhaust, use up

replica carbon copy, copy, duplicate, facsimile, imitation, model, reproduction

reply 1. *v.* acknowledge, answer, come back, counter, echo, make answer, react, reciprocate, rejoin, respond, retaliate, retort, return, riposte, write back 2. *n.* acknowledgment, answer, comeback (*Inf.*), counter, echo, reaction, reciprocation, rejoinder, response, retaliation, retort, return, riposte

report *n.* 1. account, announcement, article, communication, communiqué, declaration, description, detail, dispatch, information, message, narrative, news, note, paper, piece, recital, record, relation, statement, story, summary, tale, tidings, version, word, write-up 2. gossip, hearsay, rumour, talk 3. bang, blast, boom, crack, crash, detonation, discharge, explosion, noise, reverberation, sound ~ *v.* 4. air, announce, bring word, broadcast, circulate, communicate, cover, declare, describe, detail, document, give an account of, inform of, mention, narrate, note, notify, pass on, proclaim, publish, recite, record, recount, relate, relay, state, tell, write up 5. appear, arrive, be present, clock in *or* on, come, present oneself, show up (*Inf.*), turn up

reporter announcer, correspondent, hack (*Derogatory*), journalist, newscaster, newshound (*Inf.*), newspaperman, newspaperwoman, pressman, writer

reprehensible bad, blameworthy, censurable, condemnable, culpable, delinquent, discreditable, disgraceful, errant, erring, ignoble, objectionable, opprobrious, remiss, shameful, unworthy

represent 1. act for, be, betoken, correspond to, equal, equate with, express, mean, serve as, speak for, stand for, substitute for, symbolize 2. embody, epitomize, exemplify, personify, symbolize, typify 3. delineate, denote, depict, describe, designate, evoke, express, illustrate, outline, picture, portray, render, reproduce, show, sketch 4. act, appear as, assume the role of, enact, exhibit, perform, play the part of, produce, put on, show, stage

representation 1. account, delineation, depiction, description, illustration, image, likeness, model, narration, narrative, picture, portrait, portrayal, relation, resemblance, sketch 2. *Often plural* account, argument, explanation, exposition, expostulation, remonstrance, statement

representative *n.* 1. agent, commercial traveller, rep, salesman, traveller 2. archetype, embodiment, epitome, exemplar, personification, type, typical example 3. agent, commissioner, councillor, delegate, depute (*Scot.*), deputy, member, member of parliament, M.P., proxy, spokesman, spokeswoman ~*adj.* 4. archetypal, characteristic, emblematic, evocative, exemplary, illustrative, symbolic, typical 5. chosen, delegated, elected, elective

Antonyms (*sense 4*) atypical, extraordinary, uncharacteristic

repress bottle up, chasten, check, control, crush, curb, hold back, hold in, inhibit, keep in check, master, muffle, overcome, overpower, quash, quell, restrain, silence, smother, stifle, subdue, subjugate, suppress, swallow

reprieve 1. *v.* abate, allay, alleviate, mitigate, palliate, relieve, respite 2. *n.* abeyance, amnesty, deferment, pardon, postponement, remission, stay of execution, suspension

reprimand 1. *n.* admonition, blame, castigation, censure, dressing-down (*Inf.*), flea in one's ear (*Inf.*), lecture, rebuke, reprehension, reproach, reproof, row, talking-to (*Inf.*), telling-off (*Inf.*), ticking-off (*Inf.*), tongue-lashing, wigging (*Brit. sl.*) 2. *v.* admonish, blame, castigate, censure, check, chide, dress down (*Inf.*), give (someone) a row (*Inf.*), haul over the coals (*Inf.*), lecture, rap over the knuckles (*Inf.*), rebuke, reprehend, reproach, reprove, scold, send one away with a flea in one's ear (*Inf.*), take to task, tell off (*Inf.*), tick off (*Inf.*), tongue-lash, upbraid

Antonyms *n.* commendation, compliment, congratulations,

praise ~*v.* applaud, commend, compliment, congratulate, praise

reproach 1. *v.* abuse, blame, censure, chide, condemn, criticize, defame, discredit, disparage, find fault with, rebuke, reprehend, reprimand, reprove, scold, take to task, upbraid 2. *n.* abuse, blame, blemish, censure, condemnation, contempt, disapproval, discredit, disgrace, dishonour, disrepute, ignominy, indignity, obloquy, odium, opprobrium, scorn, shame, slight, slur, stain, stigma

reproduce 1. copy, duplicate, echo, emulate, imitate, match, mirror, parallel, print, recreate, repeat, replicate, represent, transcribe 2. breed, generate, multiply, procreate, produce young, proliferate, propagate, spawn

reproduction 1. breeding, generation, increase, multiplication, procreation, proliferation, propagation 2. copy, duplicate, facsimile, imitation, picture, print, replica

Antonyms (*sense 2*) original

repulsive abhorrent, abominable, disagreeable, disgusting, distasteful, forbidding, foul, hateful, hideous, horrid, loathsome, nauseating, objectionable, obnoxious, odious, offensive, repellent, revolting, sickening, ugly, unpleasant, vile

Antonyms appealing, attractive, delightful, enticing, lovely, pleasant

reputable creditable, estimable, excellent, good, honourable, honoured, legitimate, of good repute, reliable, respectable, trustworthy, upright, well-thought-of, worthy

Antonyms cowboy (*Inf.*), disreputable, fly-by-night, shady (*Inf.*), unreliable, untrustworthy

reputation character, credit, distinction, esteem, estimation, fame, honour, name, opinion, renown, repute, standing, stature

reputed accounted, alleged, believed, considered, deemed, estimated, held, ostensible, putative, reckoned, regarded, rumoured, said, seeming, supposed, thought

request 1. *v.* appeal for, apply for, ask (for), beg, beseech, call for, demand, desire, entreat, petition, pray, put in for, requisition, seek, solicit, sue for, supplicate 2. *n.* appeal, application, asking, begging, call, demand, desire, entreaty, petition, prayer, requisition, solicitation, suit, supplication

require 1. crave, depend upon, desire, have need of, lack, miss, need, stand in need of, want, wish 2. ask, beg, beseech, bid, call upon, command, compel, constrain, demand, direct, enjoin, exact, insist upon, instruct, oblige, order, request

requirement demand, desideratum, essential, lack, must, necessity, need, precondition, prerequisite, qualification, requisite, *sine qua non*, specification, stipulation, want

rescue 1. *v.* deliver, extricate, free, get out, liberate, recover, redeem, release, salvage, save, save the life of, set free 2. *n.* deliverance, extrication, liberation, recovery, redemption, release, relief, salvage, salvation, saving

research 1. *n.* analysis, delving, examination, experimentation, exploration, fact-finding, groundwork, inquiry, investigation, probe, scrutiny, study 2. *v.* analyse, consult the archives, do tests, examine, experiment, explore, investigate, look into, make inquiries, probe, scrutinize, study

resemblance affinity, analogy, closeness, comparability, comparison, conformity, correspondence, counterpart, facsimile, image, kinship, likeness, parallel, parity, sameness, semblance, similarity, similitude

Antonyms difference, disparity, dissimilarity, heterogeneity, unlikeness, variation

resemble bear a resemblance to, be like, be similar to, duplicate, echo, favour (*Inf.*), look like, mirror, parallel, put one in mind of, remind one of, take after

resent be angry about, bear a grudge about, begrudge, be in a huff about, be offended by, dislike, feel bitter about, grudge, harbour a grudge against, have hard feelings about, object to, take amiss, take as an insult, take exception to, take offence at, take umbrage at

resentful aggrieved, angry, bitter, embittered, exasperated, grudging, huffish, huffy, hurt, in a huff, incensed, indignant, in high dudgeon, irate, jealous, miffed (*Inf.*), offended, peeved (*Inf.*), piqued, put out, revengeful, unforgiving, wounded

resentment anger, animosity, bitterness, displeasure, fury, grudge, huff, hurt, ill feeling, ill will, indignation, ire, irritation, malice, pique, rage, rancour, umbrage, vexation, wrath

reservation 1. condition, demur, doubt, hesitancy, proviso, qualification, scepticism, scruple, stipulation 2. enclave, homeland, preserve, reserve, sanctuary, territory, tract

reserve *v.* 1. conserve, hang on to, hoard, hold, husband, keep, keep back, lay up, preserve, put by, retain, save, set aside, stockpile, store, withhold 2. bespeak, book, engage, prearrange, preengage, retain, secure 3. defer, delay, keep back, postpone, put off, withhold ~*n.* 4. backlog, cache, capital, fund, hoard, reservoir, savings, stock, stockpile, store, supply 5. park, preserve, reservation, sanctuary, tract 6. aloofness, constraint, coolness, formality, modesty, reluctance, reservation, restraint, reticence, secretiveness, shyness, silence, taciturnity ~*adj.* 7. alternate, auxiliary, extra, secondary, spare, substitute

reserved aloof, cautious, close-mouthed, cold, cool, demure, formal, modest, prim, restrained, reticent, retiring, secretive, shy, silent, standoffish, taciturn, unapproachable, uncommunicative, undemonstrative, unforthcoming, unresponsive, unsociable
Antonyms ardent, demonstrative, forward, open, sociable, uninhibited, unreserved, warm

reside abide, dwell, hang out (*Inf.*), have one's home, inhabit, live, lodge, remain, settle, sojourn, stay
Antonyms holiday in, visit

residence 1. abode, domicile, dwelling, habitation, home, house, household, lodging, pad (*Sl.*), place, quarters 2. hall, manor, mansion, palace, seat, villa

resident *n.* citizen, denizen, indweller, inhabitant, local, lodger, occupant, tenant
Antonyms nonresident, visitor

resign abandon, abdicate, cede, forgo, forsake, give in one's notice, give up, hand over, leave, quit, relinquish, renounce, surrender, turn over, vacate, yield

resignation 1. abandonment, abdication, departure, leaving, notice, relinquishment, renunciation, retirement, surrender 2. acceptance, acquiescence, compliance, endurance, forbearing, fortitude, nonresistance, passivity, patience, submission, sufferance

resigned acquiescent, compliant, long-suffering, patient, stoical, subdued, submissive, unprotesting, unresisting

resist battle, be proof against, check, combat, confront, contend with, counteract, countervail, curb, defy, dispute, fight back, hinder, hold out against, oppose, put up a fight (against), refuse, repel, stand up to, struggle against, thwart, weather, withstand

Antonyms accept, acquiesce, give in, submit, succumb, surrender, welcome, yield

resolute bold, constant, determined, dogged, firm, fixed, inflexible, obstinate, persevering, purposeful, relentless, set, staunch, steadfast, strong-willed, stubborn, tenacious, unbending, undaunted, unflinching, unshakable, unshaken, unwavering
Antonyms doubtful, irresolute, undecided, undetermined, unresolved, unsteady, weak

resolution 1. boldness, constancy, courage, dedication, determination, doggedness, earnestness, energy, firmness, fortitude, obstinacy, perseverance, purpose, relentlessness, resoluteness, resolve, sincerity, staunchness, staying power, steadfastness, stubbornness, tenacity, willpower 2. aim, decision, declaration, determination, intent, intention, judgment, motion, purpose, resolve, verdict

resolve *v.* 1. agree, conclude, decide, design, determine, fix, intend, make up one's mind, purpose, settle, undertake 2. answer, clear up, crack, elucidate, fathom, find the solution to, work out 3. analyse, anatomize, break down, clear, disentangle, disintegrate, dissect, dissolve, liquefy, melt, reduce, separate, solve, split up, unravel ~ *n.* 4. conclusion, decision, design, intention, objective, project, purpose, resolution, undertaking 5. boldness, courage, determination, earnestness, firmness, resoluteness, resolution, steadfastness, willpower
Antonyms (*sense 5*) cowardice, half-heartedness, indecision, vacillation, wavering

resort *v.* 1. avail oneself of, bring into play, employ, exercise, fall back on, have recourse to, look to, make use of, turn to, use, utilize 2. frequent, go, haunt, head for, repair, visit ~ *n.* 3. haunt, holiday centre, refuge, retreat, spot, tourist centre, watering place (*Brit.*)

resound echo, fill the air, re-echo, resonate, reverberate, ring

resourceful able, bright, capable, clever, creative, imaginative, ingenious, inventive, quick-witted, sharp, talented

resources assets, capital, funds, holdings, materials, means, money, property, reserves, riches, supplies, wealth, wherewithal

respect *n.* 1. admiration, appreciation, approbation, consideration, deference, esteem, estimation, honour, recognition, regard, reverence, veneration 2. aspect, characteristic, detail, facet, feature, matter, particular, point, sense, way 3. bearing, connection, reference, regard, relation ~*v.* 4. admire, adore, appreciate, defer to, esteem, have a good *or* high opinion of, honour, look up to, recognize, regard, revere, reverence, set store by, show consideration for, think highly of, value, venerate 5. abide by, adhere to, attend, comply with, follow, heed, honour, notice, obey, observe, pay attention to, regard, show consideration for
Antonyms *n.* (*sense 1*) contempt, disdain, disregard, disrespect, irreverence, scorn ~*v.* abuse, disregard, disrespect, ignore, neglect, scorn

respectable 1. admirable, decent, decorous, dignified, estimable, good, honest, honourable, proper, reputable, respected, upright, venerable, worthy 2. ample, appreciable, considerable, decent, fair, fairly good, goodly, presentable, reasonable, sizable, substantial, tidy (*Inf.*), tolerable
Antonyms (*sense 1*) dishonourable, disreputable, ignoble, impolite, improper, indecent, unrefined, unworthy (*sense 2*) paltry, poor, small

respective corresponding, individual, own, particular, personal,

relevant, separate, several, specific, various

respite break, breather (*Inf.*), breathing space, cessation, halt, hiatus, intermission, interruption, interval, let-up (*Inf.*), lull, pause, recess, relaxation, relief, rest

respond acknowledge, act in response, answer, come back, counter, react, reciprocate, rejoin, reply, retort, return
Antonyms ignore, remain silent, turn a blind eye

response acknowledgment, answer, comeback (*Inf.*), counterblast, feedback, reaction, rejoinder, reply, retort, return, riposte

responsibility 1. accountability, amenability, answerability, care, charge, duty, liability, obligation, onus, trust 2. authority, importance, power 3. blame, burden, culpability, fault, guilt

responsible 1. at the helm, carrying the can (*Inf.*), in authority, in charge, in control 2. accountable, amenable, answerable, bound, chargeable, duty-bound, liable, subject, under obligation 3. authoritative, decision-making, executive, high, important 4. at fault, culpable, guilty, to blame
Antonyms irresponsible, unaccountable, unconscientious, undependable, unreliable, untrustworthy

rest[1] *n.* 1. calm, doze, forty winks (*Inf.*), idleness, inactivity, leisure, lie-down, motionlessness, nap, refreshment, relaxation, relief, repose, siesta, sleep, slumber, snooze (*Inf.*), somnolence, standstill, stillness, tranquillity 2. break, breather (*Inf.*), breathing space, cessation, halt, holiday, interlude, intermission, interval, lull, pause, stop, time off, vacation 3. base, holder, prop, shelf, stand, support, trestle ~*v.* 4. be at ease, be calm, doze, have a snooze (*Inf.*), have forty winks (*Inf.*), idle, laze, lie down, lie still, nap, put one's feet up, refresh oneself, relax, sit down, sleep, slumber, snooze (*Inf.*), take a nap, take it easy (*Inf.*), take one's ease **5.** be supported, lay, lean, lie, prop, recline, repose, sit, stand, stretch out

Antonyms *v.* keep going, slog away (*Inf.*), work ~*n.* activity, bustle, work

rest² *n.* balance, excess, leftovers, others, remainder, remains, remnants, residue, residuum, rump, surplus

restful calm, calming, comfortable, languid, pacific, peaceful, placid, quiet, relaxed, relaxing, serene, sleepy, soothing, tranquil, tranquillizing, undisturbed, unhurried

Antonyms agitated, busy, disturbing, restless, uncomfortable, unrelaxed

restless 1. active, bustling, changeable, footloose, hurried, inconstant, irresolute, moving, nomadic, roving, transient, turbulent, unsettled, unstable, unsteady, wandering **2.** agitated, anxious, disturbed, edgy, fidgeting, fidgety, fitful, fretful, ill at ease, jumpy, nervous, on edge, restive, sleepless, tossing and turning, troubled, uneasy, unquiet, unruly, unsettled, worried

Antonyms comfortable, composed, easy, quiet, relaxed, restful, steady, undisturbed

restore 1. fix, mend, rebuild, recondition, reconstruct, recover, refurbish, rehabilitate, renew, renovate, repair, retouch, set to rights, touch up **2.** bring back to health, build up, reanimate, refresh, rejuvenate, revitalize, revive, revivify, strengthen **3.** bring back, give back, hand back, recover, re-establish, reinstate, replace, return, send back

Antonyms (*sense 1*) demolish, scrap, wreck (*sense 2*) make worse, sicken, weaken

restrain bridle, check, confine, constrain, contain, control, curb, curtail, debar, govern, hamper, handicap, harness, hinder, hold, hold back, inhibit, keep, keep under control, limit, muzzle, prevent, repress, restrict, subdue, suppress

Antonyms assist, encourage, help, incite, urge on

restrained 1. calm, controlled, mild, moderate, muted, reasonable, reticent, self-controlled, soft, steady, temperate, undemonstrative **2.** discreet, quiet, subdued, tasteful, unobtrusive

Antonyms (*sense 1*) fiery, hotheaded, intemperate, unrestrained, wild (*sense 2*) garish, loud, over-the-top, self-indulgent, tasteless

restraint 1. coercion, command, compulsion, confines, constraint, control, curtailment, grip, hindrance, hold, inhibition, limitation, moderation, prevention, restriction, self-control, self-discipline, self-possession, self-restraint, suppression **2.** arrest, bondage, bonds, captivity, chains, confinement, detention, fetters, imprisonment, manacles, pinions, straitjacket **3.** ban, bridle, check, curb, embargo, interdict, limit, limitation, rein, taboo

Antonyms (*sense 1*) excess, immoderation, intemperance, licence, self-indulgence (*sense 2*) freedom, liberty

restrict bound, circumscribe, confine, contain, cramp, demarcate, hamper, handicap, hem in, impede, inhibit, keep within bounds *or* limits, limit, regulate, restrain

Antonyms broaden, encourage, foster, free, promote, widen

restriction check, condition, confinement, constraint, containment, control, curb, demarcation, handicap, inhibition, limitation, regulation, restraint, rule, stipulation

result *n.* **1.** conclusion, consequence, decision, development, effect, end, event, fruit, issue, outcome, product, reaction, sequel, termination, upshot ~*v.* **2.** appear, arise, derive, develop, emanate, ensue, eventuate, flow, follow, happen, issue, spring,

stem, turn out 3. With in culmi~
nate, end, finish, terminate, wind
up (Inf.)
Antonyms (sense 1) beginning,
cause, germ, origin, outset, root,
source

resume begin again, carry on,
continue, go on, proceed, recom~
mence, reinstitute, reopen, re~
start, take up or pick up where
one left off
Antonyms cease, discontinue,
stop

resurrect breathe new life into,
bring back, raise from the dead,
reintroduce, renew, restore to
life, revive

resurrection comeback (Inf.),
raising or rising from the dead,
reappearance, rebirth, renais~
sance, renascence, renewal, res~
toration, resurgence, resuscita~
tion, return, return from the
dead, revival

retain 1. absorb, contain, detain,
grasp, grip, hang or hold onto,
hold, hold back, hold fast, keep,
keep possession of, maintain,
preserve, reserve, restrain, save
2. bear in mind, impress on the
memory, keep in mind, memo~
rize, recall, recollect, remember
3. commission, employ, engage,
hire, pay, reserve

retainer 1. attendant, dependant,
domestic, flunky, footman, lack~
ey, servant, supporter, valet,
vassal 2. advance, deposit, fee

retaliate even the score, exact
retribution, get back at (Inf.), get
even with (Inf.), get one's own
back (Inf.), give as good as one
gets (Inf.), give one a taste of
one's own medicine, give tit for
tat, make reprisal, pay one back
in one's own coin, reciprocate,
return like for like, strike back,
take an eye for an eye, take
revenge, wreak vengeance
Antonyms accept, submit, turn
the other cheek

retaliation an eye for an eye, a
taste of one's own medicine,
counterblow, counterstroke, re~
ciprocation, repayment, reprisal,

requital, retribution, revenge, tit
for tat, vengeance

reticent close-mouthed, mum,
quiet, reserved, restrained, se~
cretive, silent, taciturn, tight-
lipped, uncommunicative, un~
forthcoming, unspeaking

retire 1. be pensioned off, (be) put
out to grass (Inf.), give up work,
stop working 2. absent oneself,
betake oneself, depart, exit, go
away, leave, remove, withdraw 3.
go to bed, go to one's room, go to
sleep, hit the sack (Sl.), kip down
(Brit. sl.), turn in (Inf.)

retiring bashful, coy, demure, dif~
fident, humble, meek, modest,
quiet, reclusive, reserved, reti~
cent, self-effacing, shrinking, shy,
timid, timorous, unassertive, un~
assuming
Antonyms audacious, bold,
brassy, forward, gregarious, out~
going, sociable

retract 1. draw in, pull back, pull
in, reel in, sheathe 2. abjure,
cancel, deny, disavow, disclaim,
disown, recall, recant, renounce,
repeal, repudiate, rescind, re~
verse, revoke, take back, unsay,
withdraw

retreat v. 1. back away, depart,
draw back, ebb, fall back, give
ground, go back, leave, pull back,
recede, recoil, retire, shrink, turn
tail, withdraw ~n. 2. departure,
ebb, evacuation, flight, retire~
ment, withdrawal 3. asylum, den,
haunt, haven, hideaway, privacy,
refuge, resort, retirement, sanc~
tuary, seclusion, shelter
Antonyms v. advance, engage,
move forward ~n. (sense 2) ad~
vance, charge, entrance

retribution an eye for an eye,
compensation, justice, Nemesis,
punishment, reckoning, recom~
pense, redress, repayment, re~
prisal, requital, retaliation, re~
venge, reward, satisfaction,
vengeance

retrieve fetch back, get back,
recall, recapture, recoup, reco~
ver, redeem, regain, repair, re~

possess, rescue, restore, salvage, save, win back

return v. 1. come back, come round again, go back, reappear, rebound, recoil, recur, repair, retreat, revert, turn back 2. carry back, convey, give back, put back, re-establish, reinstate, remit, render, replace, restore, send, send back, take back, transmit 3. give back, pay back, reciprocate, recompense, refund, reimburse, repay, requite 4. bring in, earn, make, net, repay, yield 5. choose, elect, pick, vote in ~n. 6. homecoming, reappearance, rebound, recoil, recrudescence, recurrence, retreat, reversion 7. re-establishment, reinstatement, replacement, restoration 8. advantage, benefit, gain, income, interest, proceeds, profit, revenue, takings, yield 9. compensation, reciprocation, recompense, reimbursement, reparation, repayment, requital, retaliation, reward 10. account, form, list, report, statement, summary 11. answer, comeback (*Inf.*), rejoinder, reply, response, retort, riposte
Antonyms v. (*sense 1*) depart, disappear, go away, leave (*senses 2 & 3*) hold, keep, leave, remove, retain (*sense 4*) lose ~n. (*sense 6*) departure, leaving (*sense 7*) removal

reveal 1. announce, betray, broadcast, communicate, disclose, divulge, give away, give out, impart, leak, let on, let out, let slip, make known, make public, proclaim, publish, tell 2. bare, bring to light, display, exhibit, expose to view, lay bare, manifest, open, show, uncover, unearth, unmask, unveil
Antonyms conceal, cover up, hide, keep quiet about

revel v. 1. *With* in bask, crow, delight, gloat, indulge, joy, lap up, luxuriate, rejoice, relish, savour, take pleasure, thrive on, wallow 2. carouse, celebrate, go on a

spree, live it up (*Inf.*), make merry, paint the town red (*Inf.*), push the boat out (*Brit. inf.*), rave (*Brit. sl.*), roister, whoop it up (*Inf.*) ~n. 3. *Often plural* bacchanal, carousal, carouse, celebration, debauch, festivity, gala, jollification, merrymaking, party, saturnalia, spree

revelation announcement, betrayal, broadcasting, communication, disclosure, discovery, display, exhibition, exposé, exposition, exposure, giveaway, leak, manifestation, news, proclamation, publication, telling, uncovering, unearthing, unveiling

revenge 1. *n.* an eye for an eye, reprisal, requital, retaliation, retribution, satisfaction, vengeance, vindictiveness 2. *v.* avenge, even the score for, get one's own back for (*Inf.*), make reprisal for, repay, requite, retaliate, take an eye for an eye for, take revenge for, vindicate

revenue gain, income, interest, proceeds, profits, receipts, returns, rewards, takings, yield
Antonyms expenditure, expenses, outgoings

reverberate echo, rebound, recoil, re-echo, resound, ring, vibrate

revere adore, be in awe of, defer to, exalt, have a high opinion of, honour, look up to, put on a pedestal, respect, reverence, think highly of, venerate, worship
Antonyms deride, despise, hold in contempt, scorn, sneer at

reverence *n.* admiration, adoration, awe, deference, devotion, high esteem, homage, honour, respect, veneration, worship
Antonyms contempt, contumely, derision, disdain, scorn

reverent adoring, awed, decorous, deferential, devout, humble, loving, meek, pious, respectful, reverential, solemn, submissive
Antonyms cheeky, disrespectful, flippant, impious, irreverent, mocking, sacrilegious

reverse v. 1. invert, transpose, turn back, turn over, turn round, turn upside down, upend 2. alter, annul, cancel, change, countermand, declare null and void, invalidate, negate, overrule, overset, overthrow, overturn, quash, repeal, rescind, retract, revoke, set aside, undo, upset 3. back, backtrack, back up, go backwards, move backwards, retreat ~n. 4. antithesis, contradiction, contrary, converse, inverse, opposite 5. adversity, affliction, blow, check, defeat, disappointment, failure, hardship, misadventure, misfortune, mishap, repulse, reversal, setback, trial, vicissitude ~adj. 6. back to front, backward, contrary, converse, inverse, inverted, opposite
Antonyms v. (sense 2) carry out, enforce, implement, validate (sense 3) advance, go forward, move forward

review v. 1. go over again, look at again, reassess, recapitulate, reconsider, re-evaluate, re-examine, rethink, revise, run over, take another look at, think over 2. call to mind, look back on, recall, recollect, reflect on, remember, summon up 3. assess, criticize, discuss, evaluate, examine, give one's opinion of, inspect, judge, read through, scrutinize, study, weigh, write a critique of ~n. 4. analysis, examination, report, scrutiny, study, survey 5. commentary, critical assessment, criticism, critique, evaluation, judgment, notice, study 6. journal, magazine, periodical 7. another look, fresh look, reassessment, recapitulation, reconsideration, re-evaluation, re-examination, rethink, retrospect, revision, second look 8. Military display, inspection, march past, parade, procession

revise alter, amend, change, correct, edit, emend, modify, reconsider, redo, re-examine, revamp, review, rework, rewrite, update

revision 1. alteration, amendment, change, correction, editing, emendation, modification, re-examination, review, rewriting, updating 2. homework, memorizing, rereading, studying, swotting (Brit. inf.)

revival awakening, quickening, reanimation, reawakening, rebirth, recrudescence, renaissance, renascence, renewal, restoration, resurgence, resurrection, resuscitation, revitalization, revivification

revive animate, awaken, breathe new life into, bring back to life, bring round, cheer, come round, comfort, invigorate, quicken, rally, reanimate, recover, refresh, rekindle, renew, renovate, restore, resuscitate, revitalize, rouse, spring up again
Antonyms die out, disappear, enervate, exhaust, tire out, weary

revoke abolish, abrogate, annul, call back, cancel, countermand, declare null and void, disclaim, invalidate, negate, nullify, quash, recall, recant, renounce, repeal, repudiate, rescind, retract, reverse, set aside, take back, withdraw

revolt n. 1. defection, insurgency, insurrection, mutiny, putsch, rebellion, revolution, rising, sedition, uprising ~v. 2. defect, mutiny, rebel, resist, rise, rise to the streets, take up arms (against) 3. disgust, give one the creeps (Sl.), make one's flesh creep, nauseate, offend, repel, repulse, shock, sicken, turn off (Inf.), turn one's stomach

revolting abhorrent, abominable, appalling, disgusting, distasteful, foul, horrible, horrid, loathsome, nasty, nauseating, nauseous, noisome, obnoxious, obscene, offensive, repellent, repugnant, repulsive, shocking, sickening
Antonyms agreeable, attractive, delightful, fragrant, palatable, pleasant

revolution n. 1. coup, coup d'état, insurgency, mutiny, putsch, rebellion, revolt, rising, uprising **2.** drastic *or* radical change, innovation, metamorphosis, reformation, sea change, shift, transformation, upheaval **3.** circle, circuit, cycle, gyration, lap, orbit, rotation, round, spin, turn, wheel, whirl

revolutionary *n.* **1.** insurgent, insurrectionary, insurrectionist, mutineer, rebel, revolutionist ~*adj.* **2.** extremist, insurgent, insurrectionary, mutinous, radical, rebel, seditious, subversive **3.** avant-garde, different, drastic, experimental, fundamental, innovative, new, novel, progressive, radical, thoroughgoing
Antonyms (*senses 1 & 2*) counter-revolutionary, loyalist, reactionary (*sense 3*) conservative, conventional, mainstream, minor, traditional, trivial

revolve circle, go round, gyrate, orbit, rotate, spin, turn, twist, wheel, whirl

revulsion abhorrence, abomination, aversion, detestation, disgust, distaste, loathing, recoil, repugnance, repulsion
Antonyms attraction, desire, fascination, liking, pleasure

reward *n.* **1.** benefit, bonus, bounty, compensation, gain, honour, merit, payment, premium, prize, profit, recompense, remuneration, repayment, requital, return, wages **2.** comeuppance (*Sl.*), desert, just deserts, punishment, requital, retribution ~*v.* **3.** compensate, honour, make it worth one's while, pay, recompense, remunerate, repay, requite
Antonyms *n.* (*sense 1*) fine, penalty, punishment ~*v.* (*sense 3*) fine, penalize, punish

rewarding advantageous, beneficial, edifying, enriching, fruitful, fulfilling, gainful, gratifying, pleasing, productive, profitable, remunerative, satisfying, valuable, worthwhile
Antonyms barren, boring, fruitless, unproductive, unprofitable, unrewarding, vain

rhyme 1. *n.* ode, poem, poetry, song, verse **2.** *v.* chime, harmonize, sound like

rhythm accent, beat, cadence, flow, lilt, measure (*Prosody*), metre, movement, pattern, periodicity, pulse, swing, tempo, time

rich 1. affluent, filthy rich (*Inf.*), flush (*Inf.*), loaded (*Sl.*), made of money (*Inf.*), moneyed, opulent, propertied, prosperous, rolling (*Sl.*), stinking rich (*Inf.*), wealthy, well-heeled (*Sl.*), well-off, well-to-do **2.** abounding, full, productive, well-endowed, well-provided, well-stocked, well-supplied **3.** abounding, abundant, ample, copious, exuberant, fecund, fertile, fruitful, full, lush, luxurious, plenteous, plentiful, productive, prolific **4.** beyond price, costly, elaborate, elegant, expensive, exquisite, fine, gorgeous, lavish, palatial, precious, priceless, splendid, sumptuous, superb, valuable **5.** creamy, delicious, fatty, flavoursome, full-bodied, heavy, highly-flavoured, juicy, luscious, savoury, spicy, succulent, sweet, tasty
Antonyms (*sense 1*) destitute, impoverished, needy, penniless, poor (*sense 2*) lacking, poor, scarce, wanting (*sense 3*) barren, poor, unfertile, unfruitful, unproductive (*sense 4*) cheap, cheapo (*Inf.*), inexpensive, valueless, worthless (*sense 5*) bland, dull

riches abundance, affluence, assets, fortune, gold, money, opulence, plenty, property, resources, richness, substance, treasure, wealth
Antonyms dearth, indigence, lack, need, paucity, poverty, scantiness, scarcity, want

rid 1. clear, deliver, disabuse, disburden, disembarrass, disencumber, free, make free, purge, relieve, unburden **2. get rid of** dispense with, dispose of, do away with, dump, eject, eliminate, expel, jettison, remove, shake off, throw away *or* out, unload, weed out

riddle brain-teaser (*Inf.*), Chinese puzzle, conundrum, enigma, mystery, poser, problem, puzzle, rebus

ride v. 1. control, handle, manage, sit on 2. be borne (carried, supported), float, go, journey, move, progress, sit, travel ~ n. 3. drive, jaunt, journey, lift, outing, spin (*Inf.*), trip, whirl (*Inf.*)

ridicule 1. *n.* banter, chaff, derision, gibe, irony, jeer, laughter, mockery, raillery, sarcasm, satire, scorn, sneer, taunting 2. *v.* banter, caricature, chaff, deride, humiliate, jeer, lampoon, laugh at, laugh out of court, laugh to scorn, make a fool of, make fun of, make one a laughing stock, mock, parody, poke fun at, poohpooh, satirize, scoff, send up (*Brit. inf.*), sneer, take the mickey out of (*Inf.*), taunt

ridiculous absurd, comical, contemptible, derisory, farcical, foolish, funny, hilarious, incredible, laughable, ludicrous, nonsensical, outrageous, preposterous, risible, silly, stupid, unbelievable

Antonyms bright, clever, intelligent, logical, prudent, rational, reasonable, sagacious, sane, sensible, serious, smart, solemn, well-thought-out, wise

rift 1. breach, break, chink, cleavage, cleft, crack, cranny, crevice, fault, fissure, flaw, fracture, gap, opening, space, split 2. alienation, breach, difference, disagreement, division, estrangement, falling out (*Inf.*), quarrel, schism, separation, split

rig v. 1. accoutre, equip, fit out, furnish, kit out, outfit, provision, supply, turn out 2. arrange, doctor, engineer, fake, falsify, fiddle with (*Inf.*), fix (*Inf.*), gerrymander, juggle, manipulate, tamper with, trump up ~ n. 3. accoutrements, apparatus, equipage, equipment, fitments, fittings, fix-

tures, gear, machinery, outfit, tackle

right *adj.* 1. equitable, ethical, fair, good, honest, honourable, just, lawful, moral, proper, righteous, true, upright, virtuous 2. accurate, admissible, authentic, correct, exact, factual, genuine, precise, satisfactory, sound, spoton (*Brit. inf.*), true, unerring, valid, veracious 3. advantageous, appropriate, becoming, *comme il faut*, convenient, deserved, desirable, done, due, favourable, fit, fitting, ideal, opportune, proper, propitious, rightful, seemly, suitable 4. all there (*Inf.*), balanced, *compos mentis*, fine, fit, healthy, in good health, in the pink, lucid, normal, rational, reasonable, sane, sound, unimpaired, up to par, well 5. conservative, reactionary, Tory 6. absolute, complete, out-and-out, pure, real, thorough, thoroughgoing, utter ~*adv.* 7. accurately, aright, correctly, exactly, factually, genuinely, precisely, truly 8. appropriately, aptly, befittingly, fittingly, properly, satisfactorily, suitably 9. directly, immediately, instantly, promptly, quickly, straight, straightaway, without delay 10. bang, exactly, precisely, slap-bang (*Inf.*), squarely 11. absolutely, all the way, altogether, completely, entirely, perfectly, quite, thoroughly, totally, utterly, wholly 12. ethically, fairly, honestly, honourably, justly, morally, properly, righteously, virtuously 13. advantageously, beneficially, favourably, for the better, fortunately, to advantage, well ~*n.* 14. authority, business, claim, due, freedom, interest, liberty, licence, permission, power, prerogative, privilege, title 15. equity, good, goodness, honour, integrity, justice, lawfulness, legality, morality, propriety, reason, rectitude, righteousness, truth, uprightness, virtue 16. **by rights** equitably, in fairness, justly, properly ~*v.* 17. compensate for, correct, fix, put right, rectify, redress, repair, settle, set up-right, sort out, straighten, vindicate

Antonyms *adj.* (*sense 1*) bad, dishonest, immoral, improper, indecent, unethical, unfair, un-just, wrong (*sense 2*) counterfeit, erroneous, fake, false, fraudulent, illegal, illicit, inaccurate, incor-rect, inexact, invalid, mistaken, questionable, uncertain, unlaw-ful, untruthful, wrong (*sense 3*) disadvantageous, inappropriate, inconvenient, undesirable, unfit-ting, unseemly, unsuitable, wrong (*sense 4*) abnormal, unsound (*sense 5*) left, leftist, left-wing, liberal, radical, right-on (*Inf.*), socialist ~*adv.* (*sense 7*) inaccu-rately, incorrectly (*sense 8*) im-properly (*sense 9*) incompletely, indirectly, slowly (*sense 13*) bad-ly, poorly, unfavourably ~*n.* (*sense 15*) badness, dishonour, evil, immorality, impropriety ~*v.* (*sense 17*) make crooked, topple

rigid adamant, austere, exact, fixed, harsh, inflexible, intransi-gent, invariable, rigorous, set, severe, stern, stiff, strict, strin-gent, unalterable, unbending, un-compromising, undeviating, un-relenting, unyielding

Antonyms bending, elastic, flex-ible, indulgent, lax, lenient, lim-ber, merciful, mobile, pliable, pliant, soft, supple, tolerant, yielding

rigorous 1. austere, challenging, demanding, exacting, firm, hard, harsh, inflexible, rigid, severe, stern, strict, stringent, tough 2. bad, bleak, extreme, harsh, in-clement, inhospitable, severe

Antonyms (*sense 1*) easy, flex-ible, friendly, genial, gentle, hu-mane, indulgent, kind, lax, leni-ent, loose, merciful, mild, per-missive, relaxed, soft, sympa-thetic, tolerant, weak (*sense 2*) agreeable, mild, pleasant

rigour asperity, austerity, firm-ness, hardness, hardship, harsh-ness, inflexibility, ordeal, priva-

tion, rigidity, sternness, strict-ness, stringency, suffering, trial

rim border, brim, brink, circum-ference, edge, lip, margin, verge

ring[1] *n.* 1. band, circle, circuit, halo, hoop, loop, round 2. arena, circus, enclosure, rink 3. asso-ciation, band, cabal, cartel, cell, circle, clique, combine, coterie, crew (*Inf.*), gang, group, junta, knot, mob, organization, syndi-cate ~*v.* 4. circumscribe, encir-cle, enclose, encompass, gird, girdle, hem in, seal off, surround

ring[2] *v.* 1. chime, clang, peal, resonate, resound, reverberate, sound, toll 2. buzz (*Inf.*), call, phone, telephone ~*n.* 3. chime, knell, peal 4. buzz (*Inf.*), call, phone call

riot *n.* 1. anarchy, commotion, confusion, disorder, disturbance, donnybrook, fray, lawlessness, mob violence, quarrel, row, street fighting, strife, tumult, turbulence, turmoil, uproar 2. boisterousness, carousal, excess, festivity, frolic, high jinks, jollifi-cation, merrymaking, revelry, romp 3. display, extravaganza, flourish, show, splash 4. **run riot a.** be out of control, break *or* cut loose, go wild, let oneself go, raise hell, rampage, throw off all restraint **b.** grow like weeds, grow profusely, luxuriate, spread like wildfire ~*v.* 5. carouse, cut loose, frolic, go on a binge *or* spree, make merry, paint the town red (*Inf.*), revel, roister, romp

riotous 1. anarchic, disorderly, insubordinate, lawless, mutinous, rampageous, rebellious, refrac-tory, rowdy, tumultuous, ungov-ernable, unruly, uproarious, vio-lent 2. boisterous, loud, luxurious, noisy, orgiastic, rambunctious (*Inf.*), roisterous, rollicking, sat-urnalian, side-splitting, unre-strained, uproarious, wanton, wild

ripe 1. fully developed, fully grown, mature, mellow, ready, ripened, seasoned 2. auspicious,

favourable, ideal, opportune, right, suitable, timely
Antonyms (*sense 1*) green, immature, undeveloped, unripe (*sense 2*) disadvantageous, inappropriate, inconvenient, inopportune, unfavourable, unfitting, unseemly, unsuitable, untimely

ripen burgeon, come of age, come to fruition, develop, get ready, grow ripe, make ripe, mature, prepare, season

rise *v.* **1.** arise, get out of bed, get to one's feet, get up, rise and shine, stand up, surface **2.** arise, ascend, climb, enlarge, go up, grow, improve, increase, intensify, levitate, lift, mount, move up, soar, swell, wax **3.** advance, be promoted, climb the ladder, get on, get somewhere, go places (*Inf.*), progress, prosper, work one's way up **4.** appear, become apparent, crop up, emanate, emerge, eventuate, flow, happen, issue, occur, originate, spring, turn up **5.** mount the barricades, mutiny, rebel, resist, revolt, take up arms **6.** ascend, climb, get steeper, go uphill, mount, slope upwards ~*n.* **7.** advance, ascent, climb, improvement, increase, upsurge, upswing, upturn, upward turn **8.** advancement, aggrandizement, climb, progress, promotion **9.** acclivity, ascent, elevation, hillock, incline, rising ground, upward slope **10.** increment, pay increase, raise (*U.S.*)
Antonyms *v.* abate, abbreviate, abridge, condense, curtail, decline, decrease, descend, diminish, drop, dwindle, fall, lessen, plunge, reduce, shrink, sink, wane ~*n.* blip, decline, decrease, downswing, downturn, drop, fall

risk 1. *n.* chance, danger, gamble, hazard, jeopardy, peril, possibility, speculation, uncertainty, venture **2.** *v.* chance, dare, endanger, expose to danger, gamble, hazard, imperil, jeopardize, put in jeopardy, take a chance on, venture

rival 1. *n.* adversary, antagonist,

challenger, competitor, contender, contestant, emulator, opponent **2.** *adj.* competing, competitive, conflicting, emulating, opposed, opposing **3.** *v.* be a match for, bear comparison with, come up to, compare with, compete, contend, emulate, equal, match, measure up to, oppose, seek to displace, vie with

rivalry antagonism, competition, competitiveness, conflict, contention, contest, duel, emulation, opposition, struggle, vying

road avenue, course, direction, highway, lane, motorway, path, pathway, roadway, route, street, thoroughfare, track, way

roam drift, meander, peregrinate, prowl, ramble, range, rove, stravaig (*Scot.*), stray, stroll, travel, walk, wander

roar *v.* **1.** bawl, bay, bellow, clamour, crash, cry, howl, rumble, shout, thunder, vociferate, yell **2.** guffaw, hoot, laugh heartily, split one's sides (*Inf.*) ~*n.* **3.** bellow, clamour, crash, cry, howl, outcry, rumble, shout, thunder, yell

rob bereave, burgle, cheat, con (*Sl.*), defraud, deprive, despoil, dispossess, do out of (*Inf.*), gyp (*Sl.*), hold up, loot, mug (*Inf.*), pillage, plunder, raid, ransack, rifle, rip off (*Inf.*), sack, steam (*Inf.*), strip, swindle

robber bandit, brigand, burglar, cheat, con man (*Inf.*), fraud, highwayman, looter, mugger (*Inf.*), pirate, plunderer, raider, stealer, swindler, thief

robbery burglary, depredation, embezzlement, filching, fraud, hold-up, larceny, mugging (*Inf.*), pillage, plunder, raid, rapine, rip-off (*Inf.*), spoliation, stealing, steaming (*Inf.*), stick-up (*U.S. sl.*), swindle, theft, thievery

robe 1. *n.* costume, gown, habit, vestment **2.** *v.* apparel (*Archaic*), attire, clothe, drape, dress, garb

robust 1. able-bodied, athletic, brawny, fit, hale, hardy, healthy, hearty, husky (*Inf.*), in fine fettle, in good health, lusty, muscular, powerful, Ramboesque, rude, rugged, sinewy, sound, staunch, stout, strapping, strong, sturdy, tough, vigorous, well 2. boisterous, coarse, earthy, indecorous, raw, roisterous, rollicking, rough, rude, unsubtle

Antonyms delicate, feeble, frail, hothouse (*Inf., often disparaging*), infirm, refined, sickly, slender, unfit, unhealthy, unsound, weak, weedy (*Inf.*), wimpish *or* wimpy (*Inf.*)

rock 1. lurch, pitch, reel, roll, sway, swing, toss, wobble **2.** astonish, astound, daze, dumbfound, jar, set one back on one's heels (*Inf.*), shake, shock, stagger, stun, surprise

rod bar, baton, birch, cane, dowel, mace, pole, sceptre, shaft, staff, stick, switch, wand

rogue blackguard, charlatan, cheat, con man (*Inf.*), crook (*Inf.*), deceiver, devil, fraud, knave (*Archaic*), mountebank, ne'er-do-well, rapscallion, rascal, reprobate, scamp, scoundrel, sharper, swindler, villain

role 1. character, impersonation, part, portrayal, representation **2.** capacity, duty, function, job, part, position, post, task

roll *v.* **1.** elapse, flow, go past, go round, gyrate, pass, pivot, reel, revolve, rock, rotate, run, spin, swivel, trundle, turn, twirl, undulate, wheel, whirl **2.** bind, coil, curl, enfold, entwine, envelop, furl, swathe, twist, wind, wrap **3.** even, flatten, level, press, smooth, spread **4.** boom, drum, echo, grumble, resound, reverberate, roar, rumble, thunder **5.** billow, lurch, reel, rock, sway, swing, toss, tumble, wallow, welter **6.** lumber, lurch, reel, stagger, swagger, sway, waddle ~*n.* **7.** cycle, gyration, reel, revolution, rotation, run, spin, turn, twirl, undulation, wheel, whirl **8.** annals, catalogue, census, chronicle, directory, index, inventory, list, record, register, roster, schedule, scroll, table **9.** boom,

drumming, growl, grumble, resonance, reverberation, roar, rumble, thunder

romance *n.* **1.** affair, *affaire* (*du coeur*), affair of the heart, amour, attachment, intrigue, liaison, love affair, passion, relationship **2.** adventure, charm, colour, excitement, exoticness, fascination, glamour, mystery, nostalgia, sentiment **3.** fairy tale, fantasy, fiction, idyll, legend, love story, melodrama, novel, story, tale, tear-jerker (*Inf.*)

romantic *adj.* **1.** amorous, fond, lovey-dovey, loving, mushy (*Inf.*), passionate, sentimental, sloppy (*Inf.*), soppy (*Brit. inf.*), tender **2.** charming, colourful, exciting, exotic, fascinating, glamorous, mysterious, nostalgic, picturesque **3.** dreamy, high-flown, idealistic, impractical, quixotic, starry-eyed, unrealistic, utopian, visionary, whimsical ~*n.* **4.** Don Quixote, dreamer, idealist, romancer, sentimentalist, utopian, visionary

Antonyms *adj.* cold-hearted, insensitive, practical, realistic, unaffectionate, unimpassioned, uninspiring, unloving, unromantic, unsentimental

room 1. allowance, area, capacity, compass, elbowroom, expanse, extent, latitude, leeway, margin, play, range, scope, space, territory, volume **2.** apartment, chamber, office **3.** chance, occasion, opportunity, scope

root *n.* **1.** radicle, radix, rhizome, stem, tuber **2.** base, beginnings, bottom, cause, core, crux, derivation, essence, foundation, fountainhead, fundamental, germ, heart, mainspring, nub, nucleus, occasion, origin, seat, seed, source, starting point **3.** *Plural* birthplace, cradle, family, heritage, home, origins, sense of belonging **4. root and branch** completely, entirely, finally, radically, thoroughly, totally, to the last man, utterly, wholly, without exception ~*v.* **5.** anchor, become established, become settled, embed, entrench, establish, fasten, fix, ground, implant, moor, set, stick, take root

rope 1. *n.* cable, cord, hawser, line, strand **2.** *v.* bind, fasten, hitch, lash, lasso, moor, pinion, tether, tie

roster agenda, catalogue, inventory, list, listing, register, roll, rota, schedule, scroll, table

rosy 1. pink, red, roseate, rose-coloured **2.** blooming, blushing, flushed, fresh, glowing, healthy-looking, reddish, roseate, rubicund, ruddy **3.** auspicious, bright, cheerful, encouraging, favourable, hopeful, optimistic, promising, reassuring, roseate, rose-coloured, sunny

Antonyms (*sense 2*) ashen, colourless, grey, pale, pallid, sickly, wan, white (*sense 3*) cheerless, depressing, discouraging, dismal, dull, gloomy, hopeless, miserable, pessimistic, unhappy, unpromising

rot *v.* **1.** corrode, corrupt, crumble, decay, decompose, degenerate, deteriorate, disintegrate, fester, go bad, moulder, perish, putrefy, spoil, taint **2.** decline, degenerate, deteriorate, languish, waste away, wither away ~*n.* **3.** blight, canker, corrosion, corruption, decay, decomposition, deterioration, disintegration, mould, putrefaction, putrescence

rotate 1. go round, gyrate, pirouette, pivot, reel, revolve, spin, swivel, turn, wheel **2.** alternate, follow in sequence, interchange, switch, take turns

rotation 1. gyration, orbit, pirouette, reel, revolution, spin, spinning, turn, turning, wheel **2.** alternation, cycle, interchanging, sequence, succession, switching

rotten 1. bad, corroded, corrupt, crumbling, decayed, decaying, decomposed, decomposing, disintegrating, festering, fetid, foul, mouldering, mouldy, perished, putrescent, putrid, rank, sour,

stinking, tainted, unsound **2.** bent (*Sl.*), corrupt, crooked (*Inf.*), deceitful, degenerate, dishonest, dishonourable, disloyal, faithless, immoral, mercenary, perfidious, treacherous, untrustworthy, venal, vicious **3.** *Inf.* bad, deplorable, disappointing, regrettable, unfortunate, unlucky

Antonyms (*sense 1*) fresh, good, pure, wholesome (*sense 2*) decent, honest, honourable, moral, scrupulous, trustworthy

rotter bad lot, blackguard, blighter (*Brit. inf.*), bounder (*Brit. inf.*), cad (*Brit. inf.*), cur, louse (*Sl.*), rat (*Sl.*), scumbag (*Sl.*), stinker (*Sl.*), swine

rough *adj.* **1.** broken, bumpy, craggy, irregular, jagged, rocky, rugged, stony, uneven **2.** bristly, bushy, coarse, dishevelled, disordered, fuzzy, hairy, shaggy, tangled, tousled, uncut, unshaven, unshorn **3.** agitated, boisterous, choppy, inclement, squally, stormy, tempestuous, turbulent, wild **4.** bearish, bluff, blunt, brusque, churlish, coarse, curt, discourteous, ill-bred, ill-mannered, impolite, inconsiderate, indelicate, loutish, rude, unceremonious, uncivil, uncouth, uncultured, ungracious, unmannerly, unpolished, unrefined, untutored **5.** boisterous, cruel, curt, drastic, extreme, hard, harsh, nasty, rowdy, severe, sharp, tough, unfeeling, unjust, unpleasant, violent **6.** cacophonous, discordant, grating, gruff, harsh, husky, inharmonious, jarring, rasping, raucous, unmusical **7.** arduous, austere, hard, rugged, spartan, tough, uncomfortable, unpleasant, unrefined **8.** basic, crude, cursory, formless, hasty, imperfect, incomplete, quick, raw, rough-and-ready, roughhewn, rudimentary, shapeless, sketchy, unfinished, unpolished, unrefined, untutored **9.** amorphous, approximate, estimated, foggy, general, hazy, imprecise, inexact, sketchy, vague ~*n.* **10.**

Inf. bruiser, bully boy, casual, lager lout, ned (*Sl.*), roughneck (*Sl.*), rowdy, ruffian, thug, tough **Antonyms** (*sense 1*) even, level, regular, smooth, unbroken (*sense 2*) smooth, soft (*sense 3*) calm, gentle, quiet, smooth, tranquil (*sense 4*) civil, considerate, courteous, courtly, delicate, elegant, graceful, gracious, pleasant, polite, refined, smooth, sophisticated, urbane, well-bred, well-mannered (*sense 5*) gentle, just, kind, mild, pleasant, quiet, soft (*sense 6*) harmonious, smooth (*sense 7*) comfortable, cushy, easy, pleasant, soft (*sense 8*) complete, detailed, finished, perfected, polished, refined, specific (*sense 9*) exact, perfected, specific

round *adj.* 1. annular, ball-shaped, bowed, bulbous, circular, curved, curvilinear, cylindrical, discoid, disc-shaped, globular, orbicular, ring-shaped, rotund, rounded, spherical 2. ample, fleshy, full, full-fleshed, plump, roly-poly, rotund, rounded 3. full, mellifluous, orotund, resonant, rich, rotund, sonorous ~*n.* 4. ball, band, circle, disc, globe, orb, ring, sphere 5. bout, cycle, sequence, series, session, succession 6. division, lap, level, period, session, stage, turn 7. ambit, beat, circuit, compass, course, routine, schedule, series, tour, turn 8. bullet, cartridge, discharge, shell, shot ~*v.* 9. bypass, circle, circumnavigate, encircle, flank, go round, skirt, turn

round off bring to a close, cap, close, complete, conclude, crown, finish off, put the finishing touch to, settle

rouse 1. arouse, awaken, call, get up, rise, wake, wake up 2. agitate, anger, animate, arouse, bestir, disturb, excite, exhilarate, galvanize, get going, incite, inflame, instigate, move, provoke, startle, stimulate, stir, whip up

rout 1. *n.* beating, debacle, defeat, disorderly retreat, drubbing,

headlong flight, hiding (*Inf.*), licking (*Inf.*), overthrow, overwhelming defeat, ruin, shambles, thrashing 2. *v.* beat, chase, conquer, crush, cut to pieces, defeat, destroy, dispel, drive off, drub, lick (*Inf.*), overpower, overthrow, put to flight, put to rout, scatter, thrash, throw back in confusion, worst

route *n.* avenue, beat, circuit, course, direction, itinerary, journey, passage, path, road, round, run, way

routine *n.* 1. custom, formula, grind (*Inf.*), groove, method, order, pattern, practice, procedure, programme, usage, way, wont ~*adj.* 2. conventional, customary, everyday, familiar, habitual, normal, ordinary, standard, typical, usual, wonted, workaday 3. boring, clichéd, dull, hackneyed, humdrum, predictable, run-of-the-mill, tedious, tiresome, unimaginative, uninspired, unoriginal **Antonyms** *adj.* abnormal, different, exceptional, irregular, special, unusual

row[1] bank, column, file, line, queue, range, rank, sequence, series, string, tier

row[2] 1. *n.* altercation, brawl, commotion, controversy, dispute, disturbance, falling-out (*Inf.*), fracas, fray, fuss, noise, quarrel, racket, ruckus (*Inf.*), ruction (*Inf.*), rumpus, scrap (*Inf.*), shouting match (*Inf.*), slanging match (*Brit.*), squabble, tiff, trouble, tumult, uproar 2. *v.* argue, brawl, dispute, fight, scrap (*Inf.*), squabble, wrangle

rowdy *adj.* boisterous, brawling, loud, loutish, noisy, obstreperous, rough, unruly, uproarious, wild **Antonyms** decorous, gentle, law-abiding, mannerly, orderly, peaceful, refined

royal 1. imperial, kinglike, kingly, monarchical, princely, queenly, regal, sovereign 2. august, grand, impressive, magnificent, majestic, splendid, stately, superb, superior

rub v. 1. abrade, caress, chafe, clean, fray, grate, knead, massage, polish, scour, scrape, shine, smooth, stroke, wipe 2. apply, put, smear, spread ~n. 3. caress, kneading, massage, polish, shine, stroke, wipe

rubbish 1. crap (*Sl.*), debris, dregs, dross, flotsam and jetsam, garbage (*Chiefly U.S.*), grit (*Inf.*), junk, litter, lumber, offal, offscourings, refuse, scrap, trash, waste 2. balderdash, bosh (*Inf.*), bunkum, claptrap (*Inf.*), codswallop (*Brit. sl.*), crap (*Sl.*), drivel, flapdoodle (*Sl.*), garbage (*Chiefly U.S.*), gibberish, guff (*Sl.*), havers (*Scot.*), hogwash, moonshine, nonsense, piffle (*Inf.*), poppycock (*Inf.*), rot, stuff and nonsense, tommyrot, twaddle (*Inf.*), twaddle

rub out cancel, delete, efface, erase, expunge, obliterate, remove, wipe out

rude 1. abrupt, abusive, blunt, brusque, cheeky, churlish, curt, discourteous, disrespectful, ill-mannered, impertinent, impolite, impudent, inconsiderate, insolent, insulting, offhand, peremptory, short, uncivil, unmannerly 2. barbarous, boorish, brutish, coarse, crude, graceless, gross, ignorant, illiterate, loutish, low, oafish, obscene, rough, savage, scurrilous, uncivilized, uncouth, uncultured, uneducated, ungracious, unpolished, unrefined, untutored, vulgar 3. artless, crude, inartistic, inelegant, makeshift, primitive, raw, rough, rough-hewn, roughly-made, simple 4. abrupt, harsh, sharp, startling, sudden, unpleasant, violent

Antonyms (*sense 1*) civil, considerate, cordial, courteous, courtly, decent, gentlemanly, gracious, ladylike, mannerly, polite, respectful, sociable, urbane, well-bred (*sense 2*) artful, civilized, cultured, educated, elegant, learned, polished, refined, urbane (*sense 3*) even, finished, shapely, smooth, well-made

rudiments basics, beginnings, elements, essentials, first principles, foundation, fundamentals

ruffle 1. derange, disarrange, discompose, dishevel, disorder, mess up, rumple, tousle, wrinkle 2. agitate, annoy, confuse, disconcert, disquiet, disturb, fluster, harass, irritate, nettle, peeve (*Inf.*), perturb, put out, rattle (*Inf.*), shake up (*Inf.*), stir, torment, trouble, unsettle, upset, vex, worry

rugged 1. broken, bumpy, craggy, difficult, irregular, jagged, ragged, rocky, rough, stark, uneven 2. furrowed, leathery, lined, rough-hewn, strong-featured, weather-beaten, weathered, worn, wrinkled

Antonyms (*sense 1*) even, gentle, level, regular, smooth, unbroken (*sense 2*) delicate, pretty, refined, smooth, unmarked, youthful

ruin 1. n. bankruptcy, breakdown, collapse, crackup (*Inf.*), crash, damage, decay, defeat, destitution, destruction, devastation, disintegration, disrepair, dissolution, downfall, failure, fall, havoc, insolvency, nemesis, overthrow, ruination, subversion, the end, undoing, Waterloo, wreck, wreckage 2. v. bankrupt, break, bring down, bring to nothing, bring to ruin, crush, defeat, demolish, destroy, devastate, impoverish, lay in ruins, lay waste, overthrow, overturn, overwhelm, pauperize, raze, shatter, smash, wreak havoc upon, wreck

Antonyms n. creation, preservation, success, triumph, victory ~v. build, construct, create, enhance, enrich, improve, keep, mend, preserve, repair, restore, save, start, strengthen, submit to, succumb to, support, surrender to, yield to

rule n. 1. axiom, canon, criterion, decree, direction, guide, guideline, law, maxim, order, ordinance, precept, principle, regulation, ruling, standard, tenet 2. administration, ascendancy, authority, command, control, direction, domination, dominion, empire, government, influence, jurisdiction, leadership, mastery, power, regime, reign, supremacy, sway **3.** condition, convention, custom, form, habit, order *or* way of things, practice, procedure, routine, wont **4.** course, formula, method, policy, procedure, way ~*v.* **5.** administer, be in authority, be in power, be number one (*Inf.*), command, control, direct, dominate, govern, guide, hold sway, lead, manage, preside over, regulate, reign, wear the crown **6.** adjudicate, decide, decree, determine, establish, find, judge, lay down, pronounce, resolve, settle

ruler 1. commander, controller, crowned head, emperor, empress, governor, head of state, king, leader, lord, monarch, potentate, prince, princess, queen, sovereign **2.** measure, rule, straight edge, yardstick

ruling *n.* **1.** adjudication, decision, decree, finding, judgment, pronouncement, resolution, verdict ~*adj.* **2.** commanding, controlling, dominant, governing, leading, regnant, reigning, upper **3.** chief, current, dominant, main, predominant, pre-eminent, preponderant, prevailing, prevalent, principal, regnant, supreme

Antonyms (*sense 3*) auxiliary, inferior, least, minor, secondary, subordinate, subsidiary, unimportant

rumour *n.* bruit (*Archaic or U.S.*), buzz, canard, gossip, hearsay, news, report, story, talk, tidings, whisper, word

run *v.* **1.** bolt, career, dart, dash, gallop, hare (*Brit. inf.*), hasten, hie, hotfoot, hurry, jog, leg it (*Inf.*), lope, race, rush, scamper, scramble, scud, scurry, speed, sprint **2.** abscond, beat a retreat, beat it (*Sl.*), bolt, clear out, cut and run (*Inf.*), decamp, depart, escape, flee, leg it (*Inf.*), make a run for it, make off, scarper

(*Brit. sl.*), show a clean pair of heels, skedaddle (*Inf.*), take flight, take off (*Inf.*), take to one's heels **3.** go, operate, ply **4.** function, go, operate, perform, tick, work **5.** administer, be in charge of, boss (*Inf.*), carry on, conduct, control, coordinate, direct, head, lead, look after, manage, mastermind, operate, oversee, own, regulate, superintend, supervise, take care of **6.** continue, extend, go, last, lie, proceed, range, reach, stretch **7.** cascade, discharge, flow, go, gush, issue, leak, move, pour, proceed, spill, spout, stream **8.** dissolve, fuse, go soft, liquefy, melt, turn to liquid **9.** come apart, come undone, ladder, tear, unravel **10.** be current, circulate, climb, creep, go round, spread, trail **11.** display, feature, print, publish **12.** be a candidate, challenge, compete, contend, put oneself up for, stand, take part **13.** bootleg, deal in, ship, smuggle, sneak, traffic in ~*n.* **14.** dash, gallop, jog, race, rush, sprint, spurt **15.** drive, excursion, jaunt, journey, joy ride (*Inf.*), lift, outing, ride, round, spin (*Inf.*), trip **16.** chain, course, cycle, passage, period, round, season, sequence, series, spell, streak, stretch, string **17.** ladder, rip, snag, tear **18.** coop, enclosure, pen **19. in the long run** at the end of the day, eventually, in the end, in the final analysis, in time, ultimately, when all is said and done **20. on the run a.** at liberty, escaping, fugitive, in flight, on the lam (*U.S. sl.*), on the loose **b.** defeated, falling back, fleeing, in flight, in retreat, retreating, running away **c.** at speed, hastily, hurriedly, hurrying, in a hurry, in a rush, in haste

Antonyms (*sense 1*) crawl, creep, dawdle, walk (*sense 2*) remain, stay (*sense 6*) cease, stop

runaway *n.* **1.** absconder, deserter, escapee, escaper, fugitive, refugee, truant ~*adj.* **2.** escaped, fleeing, fugitive, loose, out of control, uncontrolled, wild **3.** easily won, easy, effortless

run away abscond, beat it (*Sl.*), bolt, clear out, cut and run (*Inf.*), decamp, do a bunk (*Brit. inf.*), escape, flee, make a run for it, run off, scarper (*Brit. sl.*), scram (*Inf.*), show a clean pair of heels, skedaddle (*Inf.*), take flight, take off, take to one's heels

run-down 1. below par, debilitated, drained, enervated, exhausted, fatigued, out of condition, peaky, tried, under the weather (*Inf.*), unhealthy, weak, weary, worn-out **2.** broken-down, decrepit, dilapidated, dingy, ramshackle, seedy, shabby, tumbledown, worn-out

Antonyms (*sense 1*) fighting fit, fine, fit as a fiddle, full of beans (*Inf.*), healthy, well

run into 1. bump into, collide with, crash into, dash against, hit, ram, strike **2.** be beset by, be confronted by, bump into, chance upon, come across, come upon, encounter, meet, meet with, run across

running *adj.* **1.** constant, continuous, incessant, in succession, on the trot (*Inf.*), perpetual, together, unbroken, unceasing, uninterrupted **2.** flowing, moving, streaming ~*n.* **3.** administration, charge, conduct, control, coordination, direction, leadership, management, organization, regulation, superintendency, supervision **4.** functioning, maintenance, operation, performance, working **5.** competition, contention, contest

run-of-the-mill average, common, commonplace, fair, mediocre, middling, modest, ordinary, passable, tolerable, undistinguished, unexceptional, unexciting, unimpressive

run over 1. hit, knock down, knock over, run down, strike **2.** brim over, overflow, spill, spill over **3.** check, examine, go over, go through, rehearse, reiterate, review, run through, survey

rupture *n.* **1.** breach, break, burst, cleavage, cleft, crack, fissure, fracture, rent, split, tear **2.** altercation, breach, break, bust-up (*Inf.*), contention, disagreement, disruption, dissolution, estrangement, falling-out (*Inf.*), feud, hostility, quarrel, rift, schism, split ~*v.* **3.** break, burst, cleave, crack, fracture, puncture, rend, separate, sever, split, tear **4.** break off, cause a breach, come between, disrupt, dissever, divide, split

rural agrarian, agricultural, Arcadian, bucolic, countrified, country, pastoral, rustic, sylvan, upcountry

Antonyms city, cosmopolitan, town, urban

rush 1. *v.* accelerate, bolt, career, dart, dash, dispatch, expedite, fly, hasten, hotfoot, hurry, hustle, lose no time, make haste, make short work of, press, push, quicken, race, run, scramble, scurry, shoot, speed, speed up, sprint, tear **2.** *n.* charge, dash, dispatch, expedition, haste, hurry, race, scramble, speed, surge, swiftness, urgency

Antonyms (*sense 1*) dally, dawdle, delay, procrastinate, slow down, tarry, wait

rust *n.* **1.** corrosion, oxidation ~*v.* **2.** corrode, oxidize ~*n.* **3.** blight, mildew, mould, must, rot

rustic *adj.* **1.** Arcadian, bucolic, countrified, country, pastoral, rural, sylvan, upcountry **2.** artless, homely, homespun, plain, simple, unaffected, unpolished, unrefined, unsophisticated **3.** awkward, boorish, churlish, cloddish, clodhopping (*Inf.*), clownish, coarse, crude, graceless, loutish, lumpish, maladroit, rough, uncouth, uncultured, unmannerly ~*n.* **4.** boor, bumpkin, clod, clodhopper (*Inf.*), clown, country boy, country cousin, countryman, countrywoman, hillbilly, Hodge, peasant, son of the soil, swain (*Archaic*), yokel

Antonyms *adj.* cosmopolitan,

courtly, elegant, grand, polished, refined, sophisticated, urban, urbane ~*n.* city slicker, cosmopolitan, courtier, sophisticate, townee, townsman

rustle 1. *v.* crackle, crepitate, crinkle, susurrate (*Literary*), swish, whish, whisper, whoosh **2.** *n.* crackle, crepitation, crinkling, susurration *or* susurrus (*Literary*), rustling, whisper

rut *n.* **1.** furrow, gouge, groove, indentation, pothole, score, track, trough, wheelmark **2.** dead end,

groove, habit, humdrum existence, pattern, routine, system

ruthless adamant, barbarous, brutal, callous, cruel, ferocious, fierce, hard, hard-hearted, harsh, heartless, inexorable, inhuman, merciless, pitiless, relentless, remorseless, savage, severe, stern, unfeeling, unmerciful, unpitying, unrelenting, without pity

Antonyms compassionate, forgiving, gentle, humane, kind, lenient, merciful, pitying, sparing

S

sabotage 1. *v.* cripple, damage, destroy, disable, disrupt, incapacitate, sap the foundations of, subvert, throw a spanner in the works (*Inf.*), undermine, vandalize, wreck 2. *n.* damage, destruction, disruption, subversion, treachery, treason, wrecking

sack *v.* axe (*Inf.*), discharge, dismiss, fire (*Inf.*), give (someone) his books (*Inf.*), give (someone) his cards, give (someone) his marching orders, give (someone) the boot (*Sl.*), give (someone) the elbow (*Inf.*), kick out (*Inf.*)

sacred 1. blessed, consecrated, divine, hallowed, holy, revered, sanctified, venerable 2. inviolable, inviolate, invulnerable, protected, sacrosanct, secure 3. ecclesiastical, holy, religious, solemn

Antonyms lay, nonspiritual, profane, secular, temporal, unconsecrated, worldly

sacrifice 1. *v.* forego, forfeit, give up, immolate, let go, lose, offer, offer up, surrender 2. *n.* burnt offering, destruction, hecatomb, holocaust (*Rare*), immolation, loss, oblation, renunciation, surrender, votive offering

sacrilege blasphemy, desecration, heresy, impiety, irreverence, mockery, profanation, profaneness, profanity, violation

sad 1. blue, cheerless, dejected, depressed, disconsolate, dismal, doleful, down, downcast, down in the dumps (*Inf.*), down in the mouth (*Inf.*), gloomy, glum, griefstricken, grieved, heavy-hearted, low, low-spirited, lugubrious, melancholy, mournful, pensive, sick at heart, sombre, triste (*Archaic*), unhappy, wistful, woebegone 2. calamitous, dark, depressing, disastrous, dismal, grievous, heart-rending, lachrymose, moving, pathetic, pitiable, pitiful, poignant, sorry, tearful, tragic, upsetting 3. bad, deplorable, dismal, distressing, grave, lamentable, miserable, regrettable, serious, shabby, sorry, to be deplored, unfortunate, unhappy, unsatisfactory, wretched

Antonyms blithe, cheerful, cheery, fortunate, glad, good, happy, in good spirits, jolly, joyful, joyous, light-hearted, merry, pleased

sadden aggrieve, bring tears to one's eyes, cast a gloom upon, cast down, dash, deject, depress, desolate, dispirit, distress, grieve, make blue, make one's heart bleed, upset

sadistic barbarous, beastly, brutal, cruel, fiendish, inhuman, perverse, perverted, ruthless, savage, vicious

sadness bleakness, cheerlessness, dejection, depression, despondency, dolefulness, dolour (*Poetic*), gloominess, grief, heavy heart, melancholy, misery, mournfulness, poignancy, sorrow, sorrowfulness, the blues, the dumps (*Inf.*), tragedy, unhappiness, wretchedness

safe *adj.* 1. all right, free from harm, guarded, impregnable, in safety, intact, O.K. *or* okay (*Inf.*), out of danger, out of harm's way, protected, safe and sound, secure, undamaged, unharmed, unhurt, unscathed 2. harmless, innocuous, nonpoisonous, nontoxic, pure, tame, unpolluted, wholesome 3. cautious, circumspect, conservative, dependable, discreet, on the safe side, prudent, realistic, reliable, sure, tried and true, trustworthy, unadventurous ~*n.* 4. coffer, de~

posit box, repository, safe-deposit box, strongbox, vault
Antonyms (*sense 1*) at risk, damaged, endangered, imperilled, insecure, jeopardied, put at risk, (*sense 2*) baneful, dangerous, harmful, hazardous, hurtful, injurious, noxious, pernicious, unsafe (*sense 3*) imprudent, incautious, reckless, risky, unsafe

safeguard 1. v. defend, guard, look after, preserve, protect, screen, shield, watch over **2.** n. aegis, armour, bulwark, convoy, defence, escort, guard, protection, security, shield, surety

safety assurance, cover, immunity, impregnability, protection, refuge, sanctuary, security, shelter

sail v. **1.** cast or weigh anchor, embark, get under way, hoist the blue peter, put to sea, set sail **2.** captain, cruise, go by water, navigate, pilot, ride the waves, skipper, steer, voyage **3.** drift, float, fly, glide, scud, shoot, skim, skirr, soar, sweep, wing **4.** *Inf.* With in or into assault, attack, begin, belabour, fall upon, get going, get to work on, lambaste, set about, tear into (*Inf.*)

sailor hearty (*Inf.*), Jack Tar, lascar, leatherneck (*Sl.*), marine, mariner, matelot (*Sl.*), navigator, salt, sea dog, seafarer, seafaring man, seaman, tar (*Inf.*)

sake account, advantage, behalf, benefit, consideration, gain, good, interest, profit, regard, respect, welfare, wellbeing

salary earnings, emolument, income, pay, remuneration, stipend, wage, wages

sale 1. auction, deal, disposal, marketing, selling, transaction, vending **2.** buyers, consumers, customers, demand, market, outlet, purchasers **3. for sale** available, in stock, obtainable, on offer, on sale, on the market

salt 1. n. flavour, relish, savour, seasoning, taste **2.** adj. brackish, briny, saline, salted, salty

salute v. **1.** accost, acknowledge, address, doff one's cap to, greet, hail, kiss, pay one's respects to, salaam, welcome **2.** acknowledge, honour, pay tribute or homage to, present arms, recognize, take one's hat off to (*Inf.*) ~n. **3.** address, greeting, kiss, obeisance, recognition, salaam, salutation, tribute

salvage v. glean, recover, redeem, rescue, restore, retrieve, save

salvation deliverance, escape, lifeline, preservation, redemption, rescue, restoration, saving
Antonyms condemnation, damnation, doom, downfall, hell, loss, perdition, ruin

same adj. **1.** aforementioned, aforesaid, selfsame, very **2.** alike, corresponding, duplicate, equal, equivalent, identical, indistinguishable, interchangeable, synonymous, twin
Antonyms altered, different, dissimilar, diverse, miscellaneous, other

sample 1. n. cross section, example, exemplification, illustration, indication, instance, model, pattern, representative, sign, specimen **2.** v. experience, inspect, partake of, taste, test, try **3.** adj. illustrative, pilot, representative, specimen, test, trial

sanctimonious canting, false, goody-goody (*Inf.*), holier-than-thou, hypocritical, pharisaical, pi (*Brit. sl.*), pietistic, pious, priggish, self-righteous, self-satisfied, smug, Tartuffian or Tartufian, too good to be true, unctuous

sanction n. **1.** allowance, approbation, approval, authority, authorization, backing, confirmation, countenance, endorsement, O.K. or okay (*Inf.*), ratification, stamp or seal of approval, support **2.** Often plural ban, boycott, coercive measures, embargo, penalty ~v. **3.** allow, approve, authorize, back, countenance, endorse, lend one's name to, permit, support, vouch for

sanctuary 1. altar, church, Holy of Holies, sanctum, shrine, temple **2.** asylum, haven, protection, refuge, retreat, shelter

sane 1. all there (*Inf.*), *compos mentis*, in one's right mind, in possession of all one's faculties, lucid, mentally sound, normal, of sound mind, rational **2.** balanced, judicious, level-headed, moderate, reasonable, sensible, sober, sound
Antonyms bonkers (*Sl.*), crazy, daft (*Inf.*), foolish, insane, loony (*Sl.*), mad, mentally ill, *non compos mentis*, nuts (*Sl.*), off one's head (*Sl.*), round the bend *or* twist (*Sl.*), stupid, unreasonable, unsound

sanitary clean, germ-free, healthy, hygienic, salubrious, unpolluted, wholesome

sanity 1. mental health, normality, rationality, reason, right mind (*Inf.*), saneness, stability **2.** common sense, good sense, judiciousness, level-headedness, rationality, sense, soundness of judgment
Antonyms craziness, dementia, folly, insanity, lunacy, madness, mental derangement, mental illness, senselessness, stupidity

sap *n.* **1.** animating force, essence, lifeblood, vital fluid **2.** *Inf.* charlie (*Brit. inf.*), chump (*Inf.*), drip (*Inf.*), fool, gull (*Archaic*), idiot, jerk (*Sl.*), muggins (*Brit. sl.*), nincompoop, ninny, nitwit, noddy, noodle, nurd (*Sl.*), plonker (*Sl.*), prat (*Sl.*), Simple Simon, simpleton, twit (*Inf.*), wally (*Sl.*), weakling, wet (*Inf.*)

sarcasm bitterness, causticness, contempt, cynicism, derision, irony, mockery, mordancy, satire, scorn, sneering, venom, vitriol

sarcastic acerbic, acid, acrimonious, backhanded, bitchy, biting, caustic, contemptuous, cutting, cynical, derisive, disparaging, ironical, mocking, mordant, sardonic, sarky (*Brit. inf.*), satirical, sharp, sneering, taunting

satanic accursed, black, demoniac, demoniacal, demonic, devilish, diabolic, evil, fiendish, hellish, infernal, inhuman, iniquitous, malevolent, malignant, wicked

satiate 1. cloy, glut, gorge, jade, nauseate, overfill, stuff **2.** sate, satisfy, slake, surfeit

satire burlesque, caricature, irony, lampoon, parody, pasquinade, raillery, ridicule, sarcasm, send-up (*Brit. inf.*), skit, spoof (*Inf.*), takeoff (*Inf.*), travesty, wit

satirical, satiric biting, bitter, burlesque, caustic, censorious, cutting, cynical, incisive, ironical, mocking, mordant, pungent, Rabelaisian, sarcastic, sardonic, taunting

satisfaction 1. comfort, complacency, content, contentedness, contentment, ease, enjoyment, gratification, happiness, peace of mind, pleasure, pride, repletion, satiety, well-being **2.** achievement, appeasing, assuaging, fulfilment, gratification, resolution, settlement **3.** amends, atonement, compensation, damages, indemnification, justice, recompense, redress, reimbursement, remuneration, reparation, requital, restitution, settlement, vindication
Antonyms (*senses 1 & 2*) annoyance, discontent, displeasure, dissatisfaction, frustration, grief, injury, misgivings, pain, shame, unhappiness

satisfactory acceptable, adequate, all right, average, competent, fair, good enough, passable, sufficient, suitable, up to standard, up to the mark
Antonyms bad, below par, inadequate, insufficient, leaving a lot to be desired, mediocre, not up to scratch (*Inf.*), poor, sub-standard, unacceptable, unsatisfactory, unsuitable

satisfy 1. appease, assuage, content, fill, gratify, indulge, mollify, pacify, please, quench, sate, satiate, slake, surfeit **2.** answer, be enough (adequate, sufficient),

come up to expectations, do, fill the bill (*Inf.*), fulfil, meet, qualify, serve, serve the purpose, suffice **3.** assure, convince, dispel (someone's) doubts, persuade, put (someone's) mind at rest, quiet, reassure **4.** answer, comply with, discharge, fulfil, meet, pay (off), settle, square up **5.** atone, compensate, indemnify, make good, make reparation for, recompense, remunerate, requite, reward
Antonyms (*senses 1, 2, 3 & 4*) annoy, displease, dissatisfy, dissuade, exasperate, fail to meet, fail to persuade, frustrate, give cause for complaint

saturate douse, drench, drouk (*Scot.*), imbue, impregnate, ret (*used of flax, etc.*), soak, souse, steep, suffuse, waterlog, wet through

saunter 1. *v.* amble, dally, linger, loiter, meander, mosey (*Inf.*), ramble, roam, rove, stravaig (*Scot. & Northern English dialect*), stroll, take a stroll, tarry, wander **2.** *n.* airing, amble, breather, constitutional, perambulation, promenade, ramble, stroll, turn, walk

savage *adj.* **1.** feral, rough, rugged, uncivilized, uncultivated, undomesticated, untamed, wild **2.** barbarous, beastly, bestial, bloodthirsty, bloody, brutal, brutish, cruel, devilish, diabolical, ferocious, fierce, harsh, inhuman, merciless, murderous, pitiless, ravening, ruthless, sadistic, vicious **3.** in a state of nature, nonliterate, primitive, rude, unspoilt ~*n.* **4.** aboriginal, aborigine, autochthon, barbarian, heathen, indigene, native, primitive **5.** barbarian, bear, boor, roughneck (*Sl.*), yahoo, yobbo (*Brit. sl.*) **6.** beast, brute, fiend, monster ~*v.* **7.** attack, lacerate, mangle, maul, tear into (*Inf.*)
Antonyms *adj.* balmy, civilized, cultivated, domesticated, gentle, humane, kind, merciful, mild, refined, restrained, tame ~*v.* ac-

claim, celebrate, praise, rave about (*Inf.*)

save 1. bail (someone) out, come to (someone's) rescue, deliver, free, liberate, recover, redeem, rescue, salvage, set free **2.** be frugal, be thrifty, collect, economize, gather, hide away, hoard, hold, husband, keep, keep up one's sleeve (*Inf.*), lay by, put aside for a rainy day, put by, reserve, retrench, salt away, set aside, store, tighten one's belt (*Inf.*), treasure up **3.** conserve, guard, keep safe, look after, preserve, protect, safeguard, screen, shield, take care of
Antonyms (*senses 1 & 3*) abandon, condemn, discard, endanger, expose, imperil, risk, threaten (*sense 2*) be extravagant, blow (*Inf.*), consume, fritter away, spend, splurge, squander, use, use up, waste

saving 1. *adj.* compensatory, extenuating, qualifying, redeeming **2.** *n.* bargain, discount, economy, reduction

saviour defender, deliverer, friend in need, Good Samaritan, guardian, knight in shining armour, liberator, preserver, protector, redeemer, rescuer, salvation

savour *n.* **1.** flavour, piquancy, relish, smack, smell, tang, taste, zest **2.** distinctive, quality, excitement, flavour, interest, salt, spice, zest ~*v.* **3.** appreciate, delight in, enjoy, enjoy to the full, gloat over, like, luxuriate in, partake, relish, revel in, smack one's lips over

savoury 1. agreeable, appetizing, dainty, delectable, delicious, full-flavoured, good, luscious, mouthwatering, palatable, piquant, rich, scrumptious (*Inf.*), spicy, tangy, tasty, toothsome **2.** decent, edifying, honest, reputable, respectable, wholesome

say *v.* **1.** add, affirm, announce, assert, come out with (*Inf.*), declare, give voice *or* utterance to, maintain, mention, pronounce, put into words, remark, speak, state, utter, voice **2.** answer, disclose, divulge, give as one's opinion, make known, reply, respond, reveal, tell **3.** allege, bruit (*Archaic or U.S.*), claim, noise abroad, put about, report, rumour, suggest **4.** deliver, do, orate, perform, read, recite, rehearse, render, repeat **5.** assume, conjecture, dare say, estimate, guess, hazard a guess, imagine, judge, presume, suppose, surmise **6.** communicate, convey, express, give the impression that, imply ~*n.* **7.** authority, clout (*Inf.*), influence, power, sway, weight

saying adage, aphorism, apophthegm, axiom, byword, dictum, gnome, maxim, proverb, saw, slogan

scale *n.* **1.** calibration, degrees, gamut, gradation, graduated system, graduation, hierarchy, ladder, pecking order (*Inf.*), progression, ranking, register, seniority system, sequence, series, spectrum, spread, steps **2.** proportion, ratio **3.** degree, extent, range, reach, scope, way ~*v.* **4.** ascend, clamber, climb, escalade, mount, surmount

scamper dart, dash, fly, hasten, hie (*Archaic*), hurry, romp, run, scoot, scurry, scuttle, sprint

scan check, con (*Archaic*), examine, glance over, investigate, look one up and down, look through, run one's eye over, run over, scour, scrutinize, search, size up (*Inf.*), skim, survey, sweep, take stock of

scandal 1. crime, crying shame (*Inf.*), disgrace, embarrassment, offence, sin, wrongdoing **2.** calumny, defamation, detraction, discredit, disgrace, dishonour, ignominy, infamy, obloquy, offence, opprobrium, reproach, shame, stigma **3.** abuse, aspersion, backbiting, dirt, dirty linen (*Inf.*), gossip, rumours, skeleton in the cupboard, slander, talk, tattle

scandalous 1. atrocious, disgraceful, disreputable, highly improper, infamous, monstrous, odious, opprobrious, outrageous, shameful, shocking, unseemly **2.** defamatory, gossiping, libellous, scurrilous, slanderous, untrue
Antonyms decent, kind, laudatory, proper, reputable, respectable, seemly, unimpeachable, upright

scanty bare, deficient, exiguous, inadequate, insufficient, meagre, narrow, poor, restricted, scant, short, skimpy, slender, sparing, sparse, thin

scar 1. *n.* blemish, cicatrix, injury, mark, wound **2.** *v.* brand, damage, disfigure, mark, traumatize

scarce at a premium, deficient, few, few and far between, infrequent, in short supply, insufficient, rare, seldom met with, uncommon, unusual, wanting
Antonyms abundant, ample, common, commonplace, frequent, numerous, plenteous, plentiful, sufficient

scarcely 1. barely, hardly, only just, scarce (*Archaic*) **2.** by no means, definitely not, hardly, not at all, on no account, under no circumstances

scarcity dearth, deficiency, infrequency, insufficiency, lack, paucity, poverty, rareness, shortage, undersupply, want
Antonyms abundance, excess, glut, superfluity, surfeit, surplus

scare 1. *v.* affright (*Archaic*), alarm, daunt, dismay, frighten, give (someone) a fright, give (someone) a turn (*Inf.*), intimidate, panic, put the wind up (someone) (*Inf.*), shock, startle, terrify, terrorize **2.** *n.* alarm, alert, fright, panic, shock, start, terror

scathing belittling, biting, brutal, caustic, critical, cutting, harsh, mordant, sarcastic, savage, scornful, searing, trenchant, vitriolic, withering

scatter 1. broadcast, diffuse, disseminate, fling, litter, shower, sow, spread, sprinkle, strew **2.** disband, dispel, disperse, dissipate, disunite, put to flight, separate

Antonyms assemble, cluster, collect, congregate, converge, rally, unite

scene 1. display, drama, exhibition, pageant, picture, representation, show, sight, spectacle, tableau **2.** area, locality, place, position, setting, site, situation, spot, whereabouts **3.** backdrop, background, location, *mise en scène*, set, setting **4.** act, division, episode, incident, part, stage **5.** carry-on (*Brit. inf.*), commotion, confrontation, display of emotion, drama, exhibition, fuss, performance, row, tantrum, to-do, upset **6.** landscape, panorama, prospect, view, vista

scenery 1. landscape, surroundings, terrain, view, vista **2.** *Theatre* backdrop, décor, flats, *mise en scène*, set, setting, stage set

scent *n.* **1.** aroma, bouquet, fragrance, odour, perfume, redolence, smell **2.** spoor, track, trail ~*v.* **3.** be on the track *or* trail of, detect, discern, get wind of, nose out, recognize, sense, smell, sniff, sniff out

sceptic agnostic, cynic, disbeliever, doubter, doubting Thomas, Pyrrhonist, scoffer, unbeliever

sceptical cynical, disbelieving, doubtful, doubting, dubious, hesitating, incredulous, mistrustful, questioning, quizzical, scoffing, unbelieving, unconvinced

Antonyms believing, certain, convinced, credulous, dogmatic, free from doubt, of fixed mind, sure, trusting, undoubting, unquestioning

schedule 1. *n.* agenda, calendar, catalogue, inventory, itinerary, list, list of appointments, plan, programme, timetable **2.** *v.* appoint, arrange, be due, book, organize, plan, programme, slot, time

scheme *n.* **1.** contrivance, course

of action, design, device, plan, programme, project, proposal, strategy, system, tactics, theory **2.** arrangement, blueprint, chart, codification, diagram, disposition, draft, layout, outline, pattern, schedule, schema, system **3.** conspiracy, dodge, game (*Inf.*), intrigue, machinations, manoeuvre, plot, ploy, ruse, shift, stratagem, subterfuge ~*v.* **4.** contrive, design, devise, frame, imagine, lay plans, plan, project, work out **5.** collude, conspire, intrigue, machinate, manoeuvre, plot, wheel and deal (*Inf.*)

scholar 1. academic, bookworm, egghead (*Inf.*), intellectual, man of letters, savant **2.** disciple, learner, pupil, schoolboy, schoolgirl, student

scholarship 1. accomplishments, attainments, book-learning, education, erudition, knowledge, learning, lore **2.** bursary, exhibition, fellowship

school *n.* **1.** academy, alma mater, college, department, discipline, faculty, institute, institution, seminary **2.** adherents, circle, class, clique, denomination, devotees, disciples, faction, followers, following, group, pupils, sect, set **3.** creed, faith, outlook, persuasion, school of thought, stamp, way of life ~*v.* **4.** coach, discipline, drill, educate, indoctrinate, instruct, prepare, prime, train, tutor, verse

schooling 1. book-learning, education, formal education, teaching, tuition **2.** coaching, drill, grounding, guidance, instruction, preparation, training

science 1. body of knowledge, branch of knowledge, discipline **2.** art, skill, technique

scientific accurate, controlled, exact, mathematical, precise, systematic

scoff belittle, deride, despise, flout, gibe, jeer, knock (*Inf.*), laugh at, make light of, make sport of, mock, poke fun at, poohpooh, revile, ridicule, scorn, scout (*Archaic*), slag (*Sl.*), sneer, taunt, twit

scold v. bawl out (*Inf.*), berate, blame, bring (someone) to book, castigate, censure, chide, find fault with, give (someone) a dressing-down (row, talking-to) (*Inf.*), go on at (*Inf.*), haul (someone) over the coals (*Inf.*), have (someone) on the carpet (*Inf.*), lecture, nag, rate, rebuke, remonstrate with, reprimand, reproach, reprove, take (someone) to task, tell off (*Inf.*), tick off (*Inf.*), upbraid, vituperate

scoop n. 1. dipper, ladle, spoon 2. coup, exclusive, exposé, inside story, revelation, sensation ∼ v. 3. bail, dig, dip, empty, excavate, gouge, hollow, ladle, scrape, shovel

scope area, capacity, compass, confines, elbowroom, extent, field of reference, freedom, latitude, liberty, opportunity, orbit, outlook, purview, range, reach, room, space, span, sphere

scorch blacken, blister, burn, char, parch, roast, sear, shrivel, singe, wither

score n. 1. grade, mark, outcome, points, record, result, total 2. account, basis, cause, ground, grounds, reason 3. a bone to pick, grievance, grudge, injury, injustice, wrong 4. account, amount due, bill, charge, debt, obligation, reckoning, tab (*U.S. inf.*), tally, total ∼ v. 5. achieve, amass, chalk up (*Inf.*), gain, make, notch up (*Inf.*), win 6. count, keep a tally of, keep count, record, register, tally 7. crosshatch, cut, deface, gouge, graze, indent, mar, mark, nick, notch, scrape, scratch, slash 8. *With* out *or* through cancel, cross out, delete, obliterate, put a line through, strike out 9. *Music* adapt, arrange, orchestrate, set 10. gain an advantage, go down well with (someone), impress, make a hit (*Inf.*), make an impact or impression, make a point, put oneself across, triumph

scorn 1. n. contempt, contemptuousness, contumely, derision, despite, disdain, disparagement, mockery, sarcasm, scornfulness, slight, sneer 2. v. be above, consider beneath one, contemn, curl one's lip at, deride, disdain, flout, hold in contempt, look down on, make fun of, reject, scoff at, scout (*Archaic*), slight, sneer at, spurn, turn up one's nose at (*Inf.*) **Antonyms** n. acceptance, admiration, affection, esteem, high regard, respect, tolerance, toleration, veneration, worship ∼ v. accept, admire, esteem, look favourably on, respect, revere, tolerate, venerate, worship

scornful contemptuous, contumelious, defiant, derisive, disdainful, haughty, insolent, insulting, jeering, mocking, sarcastic, sardonic, scathing, scoffing, slighting, sneering, supercilious, withering

scoundrel blackguard, caitiff (*Archaic*), cheat, dastard (*Archaic*), good-for-nothing, heel (*Sl.*), incorrigible, knave (*Archaic*), miscreant, ne'er-do-well, rascal, reprobate, rogue, rotter (*Sl.*), scamp, scapegrace, swine (*Sl.*), vagabond, villain, wretch

scour[1] abrade, buff, burnish, clean, cleanse, flush, furbish, polish, purge, rub, scrub, wash, whiten

scour[2] beat, comb, forage, go over with a fine-tooth comb, hunt, look high and low, rake, ransack, search

scourge n. 1. affliction, bane, curse, infliction, misfortune, penalty, pest, plague, punishment, terror, torment, visitation 2. cat, cat-o'-nine-tails, lash, strap, switch, thong, whip ∼ v. 3. beat, belt, cane, castigate, chastise, discipline, flog, horsewhip, lash, lather (*Inf.*), leather, punish, take a strap to, tan (someone's) hide (*Sl.*), thrash, trounce, wallop (*Inf.*), whale, whip

scout v. 1. case (*Sl.*), check out, investigate, make a reconnais-

scowl 1. *v.* frown, glower, grimace, look daggers at, lower **2.** *n.* black look, dirty look, frown, glower, grimace

scramble *v.* **1.** clamber, climb, crawl, move with difficulty, push, scrabble, struggle, swarm **2.** contend, hasten, jockey for position, jostle, look lively *or* snappy (*Inf.*), make haste, push, run, rush, strive, vie ~*n.* **3.** climb, trek **4.** commotion, competition, confusion, free-for-all (*Inf.*), hassle (*Inf.*), hustle, melee, muddle, race, rat race, rush, struggle, tussle

scrap *n.* **1.** atom, bit, bite, crumb, fragment, grain, iota, mite, modicum, morsel, mouthful, part, particle, piece, portion, sliver, snatch, snippet, trace **2.** junk, off cuts, waste **3.** *Plural* bits, leavings, leftovers, remains, scrapings ~*v.* **4.** abandon, break up, demolish, discard, dispense with, ditch (*Sl.*), drop, get rid of, jettison, junk (*Inf.*), shed, throw away *or* out, throw on the scrapheap, toss out, trash (*Sl.*), write off

scrape *v.* **1.** abrade, bark, graze, rub, scratch, scuff, skin **2.** grate, grind, rasp, scratch, screech, set one's teeth on edge, squeak **3.** clean, erase, file, remove, rub, scour **4.** pinch, save, scrimp, skimp, stint

scratch *v.* **1.** claw, cut, damage, etch, grate, graze, incise, lacerate, make a mark on, mark, rub, score, scrape **2.** annul, cancel, delete, eliminate, erase, pull out, stand down, strike off, withdraw ~*n.* **3.** blemish, claw mark, gash, graze, laceration, mark, scrape ~*adj.* **4.** haphazard, hastily prepared, impromptu, improvised, rough, rough-and-ready

scream *v.* **1.** bawl, cry, holler (*Inf.*), screech, shriek, shrill, sing out, squeal, yell **2.** *Fig.* be conspicuous, clash, jar, shriek ~*n.* **3.** howl, outcry, screech, shriek, wail, yell, yelp

screen *v.* **1.** cloak, conceal, cover, hide, mask, shade, shroud, shut out, veil **2.** defend, guard, protect, safeguard, shelter, shield **3.** cull, evaluate, examine, filter, gauge, grade, process, riddle, scan, sieve, sift, sort, vet **4.** broadcast, present, put on, show ~*n.* **5.** awning, canopy, cloak, concealment, cover, guard, hedge, mantle, shade, shelter, shield, shroud **6.** mesh, net, partition, room divider

screw *v.* **1.** tighten, turn, twist, work in **2.** *Inf.* bring pressure to bear on, coerce, constrain, force, hold a knife to (someone's) throat, oppress, pressurize, put the screws on (*Inf.*), squeeze

script 1. calligraphy, hand, handwriting, letters, longhand, penmanship, writing **2.** book, copy, dialogue, libretto, lines, manuscript, text, words

scrounge beg, bum (*Inf., chiefly U.S.*), cadge, forage for, freeload (*U.S. sl.*), hunt around (for), sorn (*Scot.*), sponge (*Inf.*), wheedle

scrounger bum (*Sl.*), cadger, freeloader (*U.S. sl.*), parasite, sorner (*Scot.*), sponger (*Inf.*)

scrub *v.* **1.** clean, cleanse, rub, scour **2.** *Inf.* abandon, abolish, call off, cancel, delete, discontinue, do away with, drop, forget about, give up

scruffy disreputable, draggle-tailed (*Archaic*), frowzy, ill-groomed, mangy, messy, ragged, run-down, scrubby (*Brit. inf.*), seedy, shabby, slatternly, sloppy (*Inf.*), slovenly, sluttish, squalid, tattered, tatty, ungroomed, unkempt, untidy
Antonyms chic, dapper, natty, neat, spruce, tidy, well-dressed, well-groomed, well-turned-out

scrupulous careful, conscientious, exact, fastidious, honourable, meticulous, minute, moral,

---

sance, observe, probe, reconnoitre, see how the land lies, spy, spy out, survey, watch ~*n.* **2.** advance guard, escort, lookout, outrider, precursor, reconnoitrer, vanguard **3.** recruiter, talent scout

nice, painstaking, precise, prin~
cipled, punctilious, rigorous,
strict, upright

Antonyms amoral, careless, dis~
honest, inexact, reckless, slap~
dash, superficial, uncaring, un~
conscientious, unprincipled, un~
scrupulous, without scruples

scrutinize analyse, dissect, ex~
amine, explore, inquire into, in~
spect, investigate, peruse, pore
over, probe, scan, search, sift,
study

scrutiny analysis, close study,
examination, exploration, in~
quiry, inspection, investigation,
perusal, search, sifting, study

scuffle 1. v. clash, come to blows,
contend, exchange blows, fight,
grapple, jostle, struggle, tussle **2.**
n. affray (*Law*), barney (*Inf.*),
brawl, commotion, disturbance,
fight, fray, ruck (*Sl.*), ruckus
(*Inf.*), ruction (*Inf.*), rumpus,
scrap (*Inf.*), set-to (*Inf.*), tussle

scum 1. algae, crust, dross, film,
froth, impurities, offscourings,
scruff **2.** *Fig.* canaille, dregs of
society, dross, lowest of the low,
rabble, ragtag and bobtail, riff~
raff, rubbish, trash (*Chiefly U.S.*)

scurrilous abusive, coarse, de~
famatory, foul, foul-mouthed,
gross, indecent, infamous, insult~
ing, low, obscene, offensive,
Rabelaisian, ribald, salacious,
scabrous, scandalous, slanderous,
vituperative, vulgar

sea n. **1.** main, ocean, the briny
(*Inf.*), the deep, the drink (*Inf.*),
the waves **2.** *Fig.* abundance, ex~
panse, mass, multitude, plethora,
profusion, sheet, vast number
~adj. **3.** aquatic, briny, marine,
maritime, ocean, ocean-going,
oceanic, pelagic, salt, saltwater,
seagoing

seal v. **1.** close, cork, enclose,
fasten, make airtight, plug, se~
cure, shut, stop, stopper, stop up,
waterproof **2.** assure, attest,
authenticate, confirm, establish,
ratify, stamp, validate **3.** clinch,
conclude, consummate, finalize,
settle, shake hands on (*Inf.*) **4.**

With off board up, fence off,
isolate, put out of bounds, quar~
antine, segregate ~n. **5.** assur~
ance, attestation, authentication,
confirmation, imprimatur, insig~
nia, notification, ratification,
stamp

search v. **1.** cast around, check,
comb, examine, explore, ferret,
frisk (*Inf.*), go over with a fine-
tooth comb, inquire, inspect, in~
vestigate, leave no stone un~
turned, look, look high and low,
probe, pry, ransack, rifle
through, rummage through,
scour, scrutinize, seek, sift, turn
inside out, turn upside down ~n.
2. examination, exploration,
going-over (*Inf.*), hunt, inquiry,
inspection, investigation, pursuit,
quest, researches, rummage,
scrutiny **3. in search of** hunting
for, in need of, in pursuit of,
looking for, making enquiries
concerning, on the lookout for,
on the track of, seeking

season n. **1.** division, interval,
juncture, occasion, opportunity,
period, spell, term, time, time of
year ~v. **2.** colour, enliven, fla~
vour, lace, leaven, pep up, salt,
salt and pepper, spice **3.** accli~
matize, accustom, anneal, disci~
pline, habituate, harden, inure,
mature, prepare, toughen, train

seasoned battle-scarred, experi~
enced, hardened, long-serving,
mature, old, practised, time-
served, veteran, weathered, well-
versed

Antonyms callow, green, inex~
perienced, new, novice, unprac~
tised, unseasoned, unskilled

seat n. **1.** bench, chair, pew, set~
tle, stall, stool, throne **2.** axis,
capital, centre, cradle, head~
quarters, heart, hub, location,
place, site, situation, source, sta~
tion **3.** base, bed, bottom, cause,
footing, foundation, ground,
groundwork **4.** abode, ancestral
hall, house, mansion, residence **5.**
chair, constituency, incumbency,
membership, place ~v. **6.** ac~
commodate, cater for, contain,

have room *or* capacity for, hold, sit, take **7.** deposit, fix, install, locate, place, set, settle, sit

secluded cloistered, cut off, isolated, lonely, off the beaten track, out-of-the-way, private, reclusive, remote, retired, sequestered, sheltered, solitary, tucked away, unfrequented
Antonyms accessible, busy, frequented, open, public, sociable

second¹ *adj.* **1.** following, next, subsequent, succeeding **2.** additional, alternative, extra, further, other, repeated **3.** inferior, lesser, lower, secondary, subordinate, supporting **4.** double, duplicate, reproduction, twin ∼*n.* **5.** assistant, backer, helper, supporter ∼*v.* **6.** advance, aid, approve, assist, back, encourage, endorse, forward, further, give moral support to, go along with, help, promote, support

second² *n.* flash, instant, jiffy (*Inf.*), minute, moment, sec (*Inf.*), split second, tick (*Brit. inf.*), trice, twinkling, twinkling of an eye, two shakes of a lamb's tail (*Inf.*)

secondary 1. derivative, derived, indirect, resultant, resulting, second-hand **2.** consequential, contingent, inferior, lesser, lower, minor, second-rate, subordinate, unimportant **3.** alternate, auxiliary, backup, extra, relief, reserve, second, subsidiary, supporting
Antonyms cardinal, chief, head, larger, main, major, more important, only, original, preceding, primary, prime, principal, superior

second-hand 1. *adj.* handed down, hand-me-down (*Inf.*), nearly new, reach-me-down (*Inf.*), used **2.** *adv.* at second-hand, indirectly, on the grapevine (*Inf.*)

second-rate cheap, cheap and nasty (*Inf.*), commonplace, inferior, low-grade, low-quality, mediocre, poor, rubbishy, shoddy, substandard, tacky (*Inf.*), tawdry
Antonyms a cut above (*Inf.*),

choice, de luxe, excellent, fine, first-class, first-rate, good quality, high-class, quality, superior

secret *adj.* **1.** backstairs, camouflaged, cloak-and-dagger, close, closet (*Inf.*), concealed, conspiratorial, covered, covert, disguised, furtive, hidden, hole-and-corner (*Inf.*), hush-hush (*Inf.*), reticent, shrouded, undercover, underground, under wraps, undisclosed, unknown, unpublished, unrevealed, unseen **2.** abstruse, arcane, cabbalistic, clandestine, classified, cryptic, esoteric, mysterious, occult, recondite **3.** hidden, out-of-the-way, private, retired, secluded, unfrequented, unknown **4.** close, deep, discreet, reticent, secretive, sly, stealthy, underhand ∼*n.* **5.** code, confidence, enigma, formula, key, mystery, recipe, skeleton in the cupboard
Antonyms *adj.* apparent, candid, disclosed, exoteric, frank, manifest, obvious, open, overt, public, straightforward, unconcealed, visible, well-known

secretive cagey (*Inf.*), clamlike, close, cryptic, deep, enigmatic, playing one's cards close to one's chest, reserved, reticent, tight-lipped, uncommunicative, unforthcoming, withdrawn
Antonyms candid, communicative, expansive, forthcoming, frank, open, unreserved

secretly behind closed doors, behind (someone's) back, clandestinely, confidentially, covertly, furtively, in camera, in confidence, in one's heart, in one's inmost thoughts, in secret, on the q.t. (*Inf.*), on the sly, privately, quietly, stealthily, surreptitiously, unobserved

sectarian *adj.* bigoted, clannish, cliquish, doctrinaire, dogmatic, exclusive, factional, fanatic, fanatical, hidebound, insular, limited, narrow-minded, parochial, partisan, rigid

section *n.* component, cross section, division, fraction, fragment, instalment, part, passage, piece, portion, sample, segment, slice, subdivision

secular civil, earthly, laic, laical, lay, nonspiritual, profane, state, temporal, worldly
Antonyms divine, holy, religious, sacred, spiritual, theological

secure adj. 1. immune, impregnable, out of harm's way, protected, safe, sheltered, shielded, unassailable, undamaged, unharmed 2. dependable, fast, fastened, firm, fixed, fortified, immovable, stable, steady, tight 3. assured, certain, confident, easy, reassured, sure 4. absolute, conclusive, definite, in the bag (*Inf.*), reliable, solid, steadfast, tried and true, well-founded ~v. 5. acquire, come by, gain, get, get hold of (*Inf.*), make sure of, obtain, pick up, procure, win possession of 6. attach, batten down, bolt, chain, fasten, fix, lash, lock, lock up, make fast, moor, padlock, rivet, tie up
Antonyms adj. endangered, ill-at-ease, insecure, loose, not fastened, precarious, unassured, uncertain, uneasy, unfixed, unprotected, unsafe, unsound, unsure ~v. endanger, give up, imperil, leave unguaranteed, let (something) slip through (one's) fingers, loose, lose, unloose, untie

security 1. asylum, care, cover, custody, immunity, preservation, protection, refuge, retreat, safekeeping, safety, sanctuary 2. defence, guards, precautions, protection, safeguards, safety measures, surveillance 3. assurance, certainty, confidence, conviction, ease of mind, freedom from doubt, positiveness, reliance, sureness 4. collateral, gage, guarantee, hostage, insurance, pawn, pledge, surety
Antonyms (senses 1, 2 & 3) exposure, insecurity, jeopardy, uncertainty, vulnerability

sedate calm, collected, composed, cool, decorous, deliberate, demure, dignified, earnest, grave, imperturbable, middle-aged, placid, proper, quiet, seemly, serene, serious, slow-moving, sober, solemn, staid, tranquil, unflappable (*Inf.*), unruffled

sedative 1. adj. allaying, anodyne, calmative, calming, lenitive, relaxing, sleep-inducing, soothing, soporific, tranquillizing 2. n. anodyne, calmative, downer or down (*Sl.*), narcotic, opiate, sleeping pill, tranquillizer

seduce 1. betray, corrupt, debauch, deflower, deprave, dishonour, ruin (*Archaic*) 2. allure, attract, beguile, deceive, decoy, ensnare, entice, inveigle, lead astray, lure, mislead, tempt

seductive alluring, attractive, beguiling, bewitching, captivating, come-hither (*Inf.*), come-to-bed (*Inf.*), enticing, flirtatious, inviting, irresistible, provocative, ravishing, sexy (*Inf.*), siren, specious, tempting

see v. 1. behold, catch a glimpse of, catch sight of, descry, discern, distinguish, espy, get a load of (*Sl.*), glimpse, heed, identify, lay or clap eyes on (*Inf.*), look, make out, mark, note, notice, observe, perceive, recognize, regard, sight, spot, view, witness 2. appreciate, catch on (*Inf.*), comprehend, fathom, feel, follow, get, get the drift of, get the hang of (*Inf.*), grasp, know, make out, realize, take in, understand 3. ascertain, determine, discover, find out, investigate, learn, make enquiries, refer to 4. ensure, guarantee, make certain, make sure, mind, see to it, take care 5. consider, decide, deliberate, give some thought to, judge, make up one's mind, mull over, reflect, think over 6. confer with, consult, encounter, interview, meet, receive, run into, speak to, visit 7. accompany, attend, escort, lead, show, usher, walk 8. anticipate, divine, envisage, foresee, foretell, imagine, picture, visualize

seed 1. egg, egg cell, embryo,

germ, grain, kernel, ovule, ovum, spore 2. beginning, germ, inkling, nucleus, source, start, suspicion

seedy crummy (*Sl.*), decaying, dilapidated, down at heel, faded, grotty (*Sl.*), grubby, mangy, manky (*Scot. dialect*), old, run-down, scruffy (*Brit. inf.*), shabby, sleazy, slovenly, squalid, tatty, unkempt, worn
Antonyms classy, elegant, fashionable, posh, ritzy (*Sl.*), smart, swanky (*Inf.*), swish (*Inf.*), up-market

seek 1. be after, follow, go gunning for, go in pursuit (quest, search) of, hunt, inquire, look for, pursue, search for 2. aim, aspire to, attempt, endeavour, essay, have a go (*Inf.*), strive, try 3. ask, beg, entreat, inquire, invite, petition, request, solicit

seem appear, assume, give the impression, have the or every appearance of, look, look as if, look like, look to be, pretend, sound like, strike one as being

seemly appropriate, becoming, befitting, *comme il faut*, decent, decorous, fit, fitting, in good taste, meet (*Archaic*), nice, proper, suitable, suited, the done thing
Antonyms improper, inappropriate, indecorous, in poor taste, out of keeping, out of place, unbecoming, unbefitting, unseemly, unsuitable

seethe 1. boil, bubble, churn, ferment, fizz, foam, froth 2. be in a state (*Inf.*), be livid (furious, incensed), breathe fire and slaughter, foam at the mouth, fume, get hot under the collar (*Inf.*), rage, simmer, storm 3. be alive with, swarm, teem

see through v. be undeceived by, be wise to, fathom, get to the bottom of, have (someone's) number (*Inf.*), not fall for, penetrate

segregate discriminate against, dissociate, isolate, separate, set apart, single out

seize 1. clutch, collar (*Inf.*), fasten, grab, grasp, grip, lay hands on, snatch, take 2. apprehend, catch, get, grasp 3. abduct, annex, appropriate, arrest, capture, commandeer, confiscate, hijack, impound, take by storm, take captive, take possession of
Antonyms hand back, free, let go, let pass, loose, release, relinquish, set free, turn loose

seizure 1. abduction, annexation, apprehension, arrest, capture, commandeering, confiscation, grabbing, taking 2. attack, convulsion, fit, paroxysm, spasm

seldom hardly ever, infrequently, not often, occasionally, once in a blue moon (*Inf.*), rarely, scarcely ever
Antonyms again and again, frequently, many a time, much, often, over and over again, time after time, time and again

select v. 1. choose, opt for, pick, prefer, single out, sort out ~adj. 2. choice, excellent, first-class, first-rate, hand-picked, picked, posh (*Inf.*), preferable, prime, rare, recherché, selected, special, superior, topnotch (*Inf.*)
Antonyms v. eliminate, reject, turn down ~adj. cheap, indifferent, indiscriminate, inferior, ordinary, random, run-of-the-mill, second-rate, shoddy, substandard, unremarkable

selection 1. choice, choosing, option, pick, preference 2. anthology, assortment, choice, collection, line-up, medley, miscellany, potpourri, range, variety

selective careful, discerning, discriminating, discriminatory, eclectic, particular
Antonyms all-embracing, careless, desultory, indiscriminate, unselective

self-centred egotistic, inward looking, narcissistic, self-absorbed, selfish, self-seeking, wrapped up in oneself

self-confidence aplomb, confidence, high morale, nerve, poise, self-assurance, self-reliance, self-respect

self-confident assured, confident, fearless, poised, secure, self-assured, self-reliant, sure of oneself

self-conscious affected, awkward, bashful, diffident, embarrassed, ill at ease, insecure, nervous, out of countenance, shamefaced, sheepish, uncomfortable

self-control calmness, cool, coolness, restraint, self-discipline, self-mastery, self-restraint, strength of mind *or* will, willpower

self-evident axiomatic, clear, incontrovertible, inescapable, manifestly *or* patently true, obvious, undeniable, written all over (something)

self-indulgence dissipation, excess, extravagance, incontinence, intemperance, self-gratification, sensualism

selfish egoistic, egoistical, egotistic, egotistical, greedy, looking out for number one (*Inf.*), mean, mercenary, narrow, self-centred, self-interested, self-seeking, ungenerous
Antonyms altruistic, benevolent, considerate, generous, magnanimous, philanthropic, self-denying, selfless, self-sacrificing, ungrudging, unselfish

self-possessed collected, confident, cool, cool as a cucumber (*Inf.*), poised, self-assured, sure of oneself, together (*Sl.*), unruffled

self-respect amour-propre, dignity, faith in oneself, morale, one's own image, pride, self-esteem

self-righteous complacent, goody-goody (*Inf.*), holier-than-thou, hypocritical, pharisaic, pi (*Brit. sl.*), pietistic, pious, priggish, sanctimonious, self-satisfied, smug, superior, too good to be true

self-sacrifice altruism, generosity, self-abnegation, self-denial, selflessness

self-satisfied complacent, flushed with success, like a cat that has swallowed the cream *or* the canary, pleased with oneself, proud of oneself, puffed up, self-congratulatory, smug, well-pleased

sell 1. barter, dispose of, exchange, put up for sale, trade **2.** be in the business of, deal in, handle, hawk, market, merchandise, peddle, retail, stock, trade in, traffic in, vend
Antonyms acquire, get, invest in, obtain, pay for, procure, purchase, shop for

seller agent, dealer, merchant, rep, representative, retailer, salesman, saleswoman, shopkeeper, tradesman, traveller, vendor

send 1. communicate, consign, convey, direct, dispatch, forward, remit, transmit **2.** cast, deliver, fire, fling, hurl, let fly, propel, shoot

send for call for, order, request, summon

sendoff departure, farewell, going-away party, leave-taking, start, valediction

senile decrepit, doddering, doting, failing, imbecile, in one's dotage, in one's second childhood

senior adj. elder, higher ranking, major (*Brit.*), older, superior
Antonyms inferior, junior, lesser, lower, minor, subordinate, younger

seniority eldership, longer service, precedence, priority, rank, superiority

sensation 1. awareness, consciousness, feeling, impression, perception, sense, tingle, vibes (*Inf.*) **2.** agitation, commotion, crowd puller (*Inf.*), excitement, furore, hit (*Inf.*), scandal, stir, surprise, thrill, wow (*Sl.*, chiefly U.S.*)

sensational amazing, astounding, breathtaking, dramatic, electrifying, exciting, hair-raising, horrifying, lurid, melodramatic, revealing, scandalous, sensationalistic, shocking, spectacular, staggering, startling, thrilling, yellow (*of the press*)

Antonyms boring, commonplace, dull, humdrum, in good taste, mediocre, ordinary, prosaic, run-of-the-mill, understated, undramatic, unexaggerated, unexciting

sense *n.* 1. faculty, feeling, sensation, sensibility 2. appreciation, atmosphere, aura, awareness, consciousness, feel, impression, intuition, perception, premonition, presentiment, sentiment 3. definition, denotation, drift, gist, implication, import, interpretation, meaning, message, nuance, purport, significance, signification, substance 4. *Sometimes plural* brains (*Inf.*), clear-headedness, cleverness, common sense, discernment, discrimination, gumption (*Brit. inf.*), intelligence, judgment, mother wit, nous (*Brit. sl.*), quickness, reason, sagacity, sanity, sharpness, tact, understanding, wisdom, wit(s) ~*v.* 5. appreciate, apprehend, be aware of, discern, divine, feel, get the impression, grasp, have a feeling in one's bones (*Inf.*), have a hunch, just know, notice, observe, perceive, pick up, realize, suspect, understand

Antonyms *n.* (*sense 4*) folly, foolishness, nonsense, silliness, stupidity ~*v.* be unaware of, fail to grasp or notice, miss, misunderstand, overlook

senseless 1. absurd, asinine, crazy, daft (*Inf.*), fatuous, foolish, halfwitted, idiotic, illogical, imbecilic, inane, incongruous, inconsistent, irrational, ludicrous, mad, meaningless, mindless, moronic, nonsensical, pointless, ridiculous, silly, simple, stupid, unintelligent, unreasonable, unwise 2. anaesthetized, cold, deadened, insensate, insensible, numb, numbed, out, out cold, stunned, unconscious, unfeeling

sensible canny, discreet, discriminating, down-to-earth, far-sighted, intelligent, judicious,

matter-of-fact, practical, prudent, rational, realistic, reasonable, sagacious, sage, sane, shrewd, sober, sound, well-reasoned, well-thought-out, wise

Antonyms blind, daft, foolish, idiotic, ignorant, injudicious, insensible, insensitive, irrational, senseless, silly, stupid, unaware, unmindful, unreasonable, unwise

sensitive 1. acute, delicate, easily affected, fine, impressionable, keen, perceptive, precise, reactive, responsive, sentient, susceptible 2. delicate, easily upset (hurt, offended), irritable, temperamental, tender, thin-skinned, touchy, umbrageous (*Rare*)

Antonyms callous, hard, hardened, insensitive, obtuse, thick-skinned, tough, uncaring, unfeeling, unperceptive

sensual 1. animal, bodily, carnal, epicurean, fleshly, luxurious, physical, unspiritual, voluptuous 2. erotic, lascivious, lecherous, lewd, libidinous, licentious, lustful, randy (*Sl.*), raunchy (*U.S. sl.*), sexual, sexy (*Inf.*), unchaste

sensuous epicurean, gratifying, hedonistic, lush, pleasurable, rich, sensory, sumptuous, sybaritic

sentence 1. *n.* condemnation, decision, decree, doom, judgment, order, pronouncement, ruling, verdict 2. *v.* condemn, doom, mete out justice to, pass judgment on, penalize

sentiment 1. emotion, sensibility, soft-heartedness, tender feeling, tenderness 2. *Often plural* attitude, belief, feeling, idea, judgment, opinion, persuasion, saying, thought, view, way of thinking 3. emotionalism, mawkishness, overemotionalism, romanticism, sentimentality, slush (*Inf.*)

sentimental corny (*Sl.*), dewy-eyed, drippy (*Inf.*), emotional, gushy (*Inf.*), impressionable, maudlin, mawkish, mushy (*Inf.*), nostalgic, overemotional, pathetic, romantic, schmaltzy (*Sl.*), simpering, sloppy (*Inf.*), slushy

(*Inf.*), soft-hearted, tearful, tear~
jerking (*Inf.*), tender, touching,
weepy (*Inf.*)

Antonyms commonsensical, dis~
passionate, down-to-earth,
earthy, hard-headed, practical,
realistic, undemonstrative, un~
emotional, unfeeling, unroman~
tic, unsentimental

sentimentality bathos, corniness
(*Sl.*), emotionalism, gush (*Inf.*),
mawkishness, mush (*Inf.*), nos~
talgia, play on the emotions, ro~
manticism, schmaltz (*Sl.*), slop~
piness (*Inf.*), slush (*Inf.*), sob stuff
(*Inf.*), tenderness

separate *v.* 1. break off, cleave,
come apart, come away, come
between, detach, disconnect, dis~
entangle, disjoin, divide, keep
apart, remove, sever, split, sun~
der, uncouple 2. discriminate be~
tween, isolate, put on one side,
segregate, single out, sort out 3.
bifurcate, break up, disunite, di~
verge, divorce, estrange, go dif~
ferent ways, part, part company,
set at variance *or* at odds, split
up ~*adj.* 4. detached, discon~
nected, discrete, disjointed, di~
vided, divorced, isolated, unat~
tached, unconnected 5. alone,
apart, autonomous, distinct, in~
dependent, individual, particular,
single, solitary

Antonyms *v.* amalgamate, com~
bine, connect, join, link, merge,
mix, unite ~*adj.* affiliated, alike,
connected, interdependent,
joined, similar, unified, united

separately alone, apart, inde~
pendently, individually, one at a
time, one by one, personally,
severally, singly

Antonyms as a group, as one,
collectively, in a body, in con~
cert, in unison, jointly, together

separation 1. break, detachment,
disconnection, disengagement,
disjunction, dissociation, disun~
ion, division, gap, segregation,
severance 2. break-up, divorce,
estrangement, farewell, leave-
taking, parting, rift, split, split-up

sequel conclusion, consequence,

continuation, development, end,
follow-up, issue, outcome, payoff
(*Inf.*), result, upshot

sequence arrangement, chain,
course, cycle, order, procession,
progression, series, succession

serene 1. calm, composed, im~
perturbable, peaceful, placid,
tranquil, undisturbed, unruffled,
untroubled 2. bright, clear,
cloudless, fair, halcyon, uncloud~
ed

series arrangement, chain,
course, line, order, progression,
run, sequence, set, string, suc~
cession, train

serious 1. grave, humourless,
long-faced, pensive, sedate, so~
ber, solemn, stern, thoughtful,
unsmiling 2. deliberate, deter~
mined, earnest, genuine, honest,
in earnest, resolute, resolved,
sincere 3. crucial, deep, difficult,
far-reaching, fateful, grim, im~
portant, momentous, no laughing
matter, of moment *or* conse~
quence, pressing, significant, ur~
gent, weighty, worrying 4. acute,
alarming, critical, dangerous,
grave, severe

Antonyms capricious, carefree,
flighty, flippant, frivolous, insig~
nificant, insincere, jolly, joyful,
light-hearted, minor, slight, smil~
ing, trivial, uncommitted, unde~
cided, unimportant

seriously 1. all joking aside, ear~
nestly, gravely, in all conscience,
in earnest, no joking (*Inf.*), sin~
cerely, solemnly, thoughtfully,
with a straight face 2. acutely,
badly, critically, dangerously,
distressingly, gravely, grievously,
severely, sorely

sermon 1. address, exhortation,
homily 2. dressing-down (*Inf.*),
harangue, lecture, talking-to
(*Inf.*)

servant attendant, domestic,
drudge, help, helper, lackey,
maid, menial, retainer, servitor
(*Archaic*), skivvy, slave, vassal

serve 1. aid, assist, attend to, be
in the service of, be of assistance,
be of use, help, minister to,

oblige, succour, wait on, work for 2. act, attend, complete, discharge, do, fulfil, go through, observe, officiate, pass, perform 3. answer, answer the purpose, be acceptable, be adequate, be enough, content, do, do duty as, do the work of, fill the bill (*Inf.*), function as, satisfy, suffice, suit 4. arrange, deal, deliver, dish up, distribute, handle, present, provide, set out, supply

service *n.* 1. advantage, assistance, avail, benefit, help, ministrations, supply, use, usefulness, utility 2. check, maintenance, overhaul, servicing 3. business, duty, employ, employment, labour, office, work 4. ceremony, function, observance, rite, worship ~*v.* 5. check, fine tune, go over, maintain, overhaul, recondition, repair, tune (up)

session assembly, conference, discussion, get-together (*Inf.*), hearing, meeting, period, sitting, term

set¹ *v.* 1. aim, apply, deposit, direct, embed, fasten, fix, install, lay, locate, lodge, mount, park, place, plant, plonk, plump, position, put, rest, seat, situate, station, stick, turn 2. agree upon, allocate, appoint, arrange, assign, conclude, decide (upon), designate, determine, establish, fix, fix up, name, ordain, regulate, resolve, schedule, settle, specify 3. arrange, lay, make ready, prepare, spread 4. adjust, coordinate, rectify, regulate, synchronize 5. cake, condense, congeal, crystallize, gelatinize, harden, jell, solidify, stiffen, thicken 6. allot, decree, impose, lay down, ordain, prescribe, specify 7. decline, dip, disappear, go down, sink, subside, vanish ~*n.* 8. attitude, bearing, carriage, fit, hang, position, posture, turn 9. *mise-en-scène*, scene, scenery, setting, stage set, stage setting ~*adj.* 10. agreed, appointed, arranged, customary, decided, definite, established,

firm, fixed, prearranged, predetermined, prescribed, regular, scheduled, settled, usual 11. entrenched, firm, hard and fast, hardened, hidebound, immovable, inflexible, rigid, strict, stubborn

Antonyms (*sense 11*) flexible, free, open, open-minded, undecided

set² *n.* 1. band, circle, class, clique, company, coterie, crew (*Inf.*), crowd, faction, gang, group, outfit (*Inf.*), sect 2. assemblage, assortment, batch, collection, compendium, coordinated group, kit, outfit, series

setback bit of trouble, blow, check, defeat, disappointment, hitch, hold-up, misfortune, rebuff, reverse, upset

set off 1. depart, embark, leave, sally forth, set out, start out 2. detonate, explode, ignite, light, set in motion, touch off, trigger off

setting backdrop, background, context, frame, locale, location, *mise en scène*, mounting, perspective, scene, scenery, set, site, surround, surroundings

settle 1. adjust, dispose, order, put into order, regulate, set to rights, straighten out, work out 2. choose, clear up, complete, conclude, decide, dispose of, put an end to, reconcile, resolve 3. calm, compose, lull, pacify, quell, quiet, quieten, reassure, relax, relieve, sedate, soothe, tranquillize 4. alight, bed down, come to rest, descend, land, light, make oneself comfortable 5. dwell, inhabit, live, make one's home, move to, put down roots, reside, set up home, take up residence 6. colonize, found, people, pioneer, plant, populate 7. acquit oneself of, clear, discharge, liquidate, pay, quit, square (up) 8. decline, fall, sink, subside

Antonyms (*sense 3*) agitate, bother, discompose, disquieten, disturb, rattle, trouble, unsettle, upset

settlement 1. adjustment, agree~
ment, arrangement, completion,
conclusion, confirmation, dispo~
sition, establishment, resolution,
termination, working out **2.**
clearance, clearing, defrayal,
discharge, liquidation, payment,
satisfaction **3.** colonization, colo~
ny, community, encampment,
hamlet, outpost, peopling

settler colonist, colonizer, fron~
tiersman, immigrant, pioneer,
planter

set up 1. arrange, begin, com~
pose, establish, found, initiate,
install, institute, make provision
for, organize, prearrange, pre~
pare **2.** assemble, build, con~
struct, elevate, erect, put togeth~
er, put up, raise

several adj. assorted, different,
disparate, distinct, divers (Ar~
chaic), diverse, indefinite, indi~
vidual, many, particular, respec~
tive, single, some, sundry, vari~
ous

severe 1. austere, cruel, Draco~
nian, hard, harsh, inexorable,
iron-handed, oppressive, pitiless,
relentless, rigid, strict, unbend~
ing, unrelenting **2.** cold, disap~
proving, dour, flinty, forbidding,
grave, grim, serious, sober, stern,
strait-laced, tight-lipped, un~
smiling **3.** acute, bitter, critical,
dangerous, distressing, extreme,
fierce, grinding, inclement, in~
tense, violent **4.** ascetic, austere,
chaste, classic, forbidding, func~
tional, plain, restrained, simple,
Spartan, unadorned, unembel~
lished, unfussy **5.** arduous, de~
manding, difficult, exacting,
fierce, hard, punishing, rigorous,
stringent, taxing, tough,
unrelenting

Antonyms (senses 1, 2, 3 & 5)
affable, clement, compassionate,
easy, genial, gentle, kind, lax,
lenient, manageable, mild, mi~
nor, moderate, relaxed, temper~
ate, tractable (sense 4) embel~
lished, fancy, ornamental, ornate

sex 1. gender **2.** Inf. coition, coi~
tus, copulation, fornication, going

to bed (with someone), intimacy,
lovemaking, (sexual) inter~
course, sexual relations **3.** desire,
facts of life, libido, reproduction,
sexuality, the birds and the bees
(Inf.)

shabby 1. dilapidated, down at
heel, faded, frayed, having seen
better days, mean, neglected,
poor, ragged, run-down, scruffy,
seedy, tattered, tatty, the worse
for wear, threadbare, worn,
worn-out **2.** cheap, contemptible,
despicable, dirty, dishonourable,
ignoble, low, low-down (Inf.),
mean, rotten (Inf.), scurvy,
shameful, shoddy, ungentleman~
ly, unworthy

shade n. **1.** coolness, dimness,
dusk, gloom, gloominess, obscu~
rity, screen, semidarkness,
shadiness, shadow, shadows **2.**
blind, canopy, cover, covering,
curtain, screen, shield, veil **3.**
colour, hue, stain, tinge, tint, tone
4. apparition, ghost, manes,
phantom, shadow, spectre, spirit
~v. **5.** cast a shadow over, cloud,
conceal, cover, darken, dim,
hide, mute, obscure, protect,
screen, shadow, shield, shut out
the light, veil

shadow n. **1.** cover, darkness,
dimness, dusk, gathering dark~
ness, gloaming, gloom, obscurity,
protection, shade, shelter **2.** hint,
suggestion, suspicion, trace **3.**
ghost, image, phantom, remnant,
representation, spectre, vestige
4. blight, cloud, gloom, sadness
~v. **5.** cast a shadow over, dark~
en, overhang, screen, shade,
shield **6.** dog, follow, spy on, stalk,
tail (Inf.), trail

shadowy 1. crepuscular, dark,
dim, dusky, gloomy, indistinct,
murky, obscure, shaded, shady,
tenebrious, tenebrous **2.** dim,
dreamlike, faint, ghostly, illusory,
imaginary, impalpable, intan~
gible, nebulous, obscure, phan~
tom, spectral, undefined, unreal,
insubstantial, vague, wraithlike

shady 1. bosky (Literary), bow~
ery, cool, dim, leafy, shaded,

shadowy, umbrageous **2.** *Inf.* crooked, disreputable, dubious, fishy (*Inf.*), questionable, shifty, slippery, suspect, suspicious, un~ ethical, unscrupulous, untrust~ worthy

Antonyms (*sense 1*) bright, ex~ posed, open, out in the open, sunlit, sunny, unshaded (*sense 2*) above-board, ethical, honest, honourable, respectable, straight, trustworthy, upright

shaft 1. handle, pole, rod, shank, stem, upright **2.** beam, gleam, ray, streak **3.** barb, cut, dart, gibe, sting, thrust

shake *v.* **1.** bump, fluctuate, jar, joggle, jolt, jounce, oscillate, quake, quiver, rock, shiver, shudder, sway, totter, tremble, vibrate, waver, wobble **2.** bran~ dish, flourish, wave **3.** discom~ pose, distress, disturb, frighten, intimidate, move, rattle (*Inf.*), shock, unnerve, upset ~*n.* **4.** agi~ tation, convulsion, disturbance, jar, jerk, jolt, jounce, pulsation, quaking, shiver, shock, shudder, trembling, tremor, vibration

shaky 1. all of a quiver (*Inf.*), faltering, insecure, precarious, quivery, rickety, tottering, trem~ bling, tremulous, unstable, un~ steady, weak, wobbly **2.** dubious, questionable, suspect, uncertain, undependable, unreliable, un~ sound, unsupported

shallow *adj. Fig.* empty, flimsy, foolish, frivolous, idle, ignorant, meaningless, puerile, simple, skin-deep, slight, superficial, sur~ face, trivial, unintelligent

Antonyms analytical, compre~ hensive, deep, in-depth, mean~ ingful, penetrating, perceptive, profound, searching, serious, thoughtful, weighty

sham 1. *n.* counterfeit, feint, for~ gery, fraud, hoax, humbug, imi~ tation, impostor, imposture, pho~ ney (*Sl.*), pretence, pretender, pseud (*Sl.*), wolf in sheep's cloth~ ing **2.** *adj.* artificial, bogus, counterfeit, ersatz, false, feigned, imitation, mock, phoney (*Sl.*),

pretended, pseud (*Sl.*), pseudo (*Inf.*), simulated, spurious, syn~ thetic **3.** *v.* affect, assume, counterfeit, fake, feign, imitate, play possum, pretend, put on, simulate

shame *n.* **1.** blot, contempt, deg~ radation, derision, discredit, dis~ grace, dishonour, disrepute, ill repute, infamy, obloquy, odium, opprobrium, reproach, scandal, skeleton in the cupboard, smear **2.** abashment, chagrin, com~ punction, embarrassment, hu~ miliation, ignominy, loss of face, mortification, shamefacedness ~*v.* **3.** abash, confound, discon~ cert, disgrace, embarrass, hum~ ble, humiliate, mortify, reproach, ridicule, take (someone) down a peg (*Inf.*) **4.** blot, debase, defile, degrade, discredit, dishonour, smear, stain

Antonyms *n.* (*sense 1*) credit, distinction, esteem, glory, hon~ our, pride, renown, self-respect (*sense 2*) brass-neck, brazenness, cheek, shamelessness, un~ abashedness ~*v.* acclaim, credit, do credit to, enhance the reputation of, honour, make proud

shameful 1. atrocious, base, das~ tardly, degrading, disgraceful, dishonourable, ignominious, in~ decent, infamous, low, mean, outrageous, reprehensible, scan~ dalous, unbecoming, unworthy, vile, wicked **2.** blush-making (*Inf.*), degrading, embarrassing, humiliating, mortifying, shaming **Antonyms** admirable, creditable, estimable, exemplary, honour~ able, laudable, right, worthy

shameless abandoned, auda~ cious, barefaced, brash, brazen, corrupt, depraved, dissolute, fla~ grant, hardened, immodest, im~ proper, impudent, incorrigible, indecent, insolent, profligate, reprobate, unabashed, un~ ashamed, unblushing, unprinci~ pled, wanton

shape *n.* **1.** build, configuration, contours, cut, figure, form, lines, make, outline, profile, silhouette **2.** frame, model, mould, pattern **3.** appearance, aspect, form, guise, likeness, semblance **4.** condition, fettle, health, kilter, state, trim ~*v.* **5.** create, fashion, form, make, model, mould, produce **6.** accommodate, adapt, define, develop, devise, frame, guide, modify, plan, prepare, regulate, remodel

share 1. *v.* apportion, assign, distribute, divide, go Dutch (*Inf.*), go fifty-fifty (*Inf.*), go halves, parcel out, partake, participate, receive, split, use in common **2.** *n.* allotment, allowance, contribution, cut (*Inf.*), division, due, lot, part, portion, proportion, quota, ration, whack (*Inf.*)

sharp *adj.* **1.** acute, cutting, honed, jagged, keen, knife-edged, knife-like, pointed, razor-sharp, serrated, sharpened, spiky **2.** abrupt, distinct, extreme, marked, sudden **3.** alert, apt, astute, bright, clever, discerning, knowing, long-headed, observant, penetrating, perceptive, quick, quick-witted, ready, subtle **4.** acute, distressing, excruciating, fierce, intense, painful, piercing, severe, shooting, sore, stabbing, stinging, violent **5.** clear, clear-cut, crisp, distinct, well-defined **6.** acrimonious, barbed, biting, bitter, caustic, cutting, harsh, hurtful, sarcastic, sardonic, scathing, severe, trenchant, vitriolic **7.** acerbic, acid, acrid, burning, hot, piquant, pungent, sour, tart, vinegary ~*adv.* **8.** exactly, on the dot, on time, precisely, promptly, punctually

Antonyms *adj.* (*sense 1*) blunt, dull, edgeless, pointed, rounded, unsharpened (*sense 2*) even, gentle, gradual, moderate, progressive (*sense 3*) dim, dull-witted, dumb (*Inf.*), slow, slow-on-the-uptake, stupid (*sense 5*) blurred, fuzzy, ill-defined, indistinct, unclear (*sense 6*) amicable, courteous, friendly, gentle, kindly, mild (*sense 7*) bland, mild,

tasteless ~*adv.* (*sense 8*) approximately, more or less, roughly, round about, vaguely

sharpen edge, grind, hone, put an edge on, strop, whet

shatter 1. break, burst, crack, crush, crush to smithereens, demolish, explode, implode, pulverize, shiver, smash, split **2.** blast, blight, bring to nought, demolish, destroy, disable, exhaust, impair, overturn, ruin, torpedo, wreck **3.** break (someone's) heart, crush, devastate, dumbfound, knock the stuffing out of (someone) (*Inf.*), upset

sheer 1. abrupt, headlong (*Archaic*), perpendicular, precipitous, steep **2.** absolute, arrant, complete, downright, out-and-out, pure, rank, thoroughgoing, total, unadulterated, unalloyed, unmitigated, unqualified, utter

sheet 1. coat, film, folio, lamina, layer, leaf, membrane, overlay, pane, panel, piece, plate, slab, stratum, surface, veneer **2.** area, blanket, covering, expanse, stretch, sweep

shell *n.* **1.** carapace, case, husk, pod ~*v.* **2.** husk, shuck **3.** attack, barrage, blitz, bomb, bombard, strafe, strike ~*n.* **4.** chassis, frame, framework, hull, skeleton, structure

shelter 1. *v.* cover, defend, guard, harbour, hide, protect, safeguard, seek refuge, shield, take in, take shelter **2.** *n.* asylum, cover, covert, defence, guard, haven, protection, refuge, retreat, roof over one's head, safety, sanctuary, screen, security, shiel (*Scot.*), umbrella

sheltered cloistered, conventual, ensconced, hermitic, isolated, protected, quiet, reclusive, retired, screened, secluded, shaded, shielded, withdrawn

Antonyms exposed, laid bare, made public, open, public, unconcealed, unprotected, unsheltered

shelve defer, dismiss, freeze, hold in abeyance, hold over, lay aside, mothball, pigeonhole, postpone, put aside, put off, put on ice, suspend, table (*U.S.*)

shield *n.* 1. buckler, escutcheon (*Heraldry*), targe (*Archaic*) 2. aegis, bulwark, cover, defence, guard, protection, rampart, safeguard, screen, shelter, ward (*Archaic*) ~*v.* 3. cover, defend, guard, protect, safeguard, screen, shelter, ward off

shift *v.* 1. alter, budge, change, displace, fluctuate, move, move around, rearrange, relocate, remove, reposition, swerve, switch, transfer, transpose, vary, veer ~*n.* 2. about-turn, alteration, change, displacement, fluctuation, modification, move, permutation, rearrangement, removal, shifting, switch, transfer, veering 3. artifice, contrivance, craft, device, dodge, equivocation, evasion, expedient, move, resource, ruse, stratagem, subterfuge, trick, wile

shimmer *v.* dance, gleam, glisten, phosphoresce, scintillate, twinkle

shine *v.* 1. beam, emit light, flash, give off light, glare, gleam, glimmer, glisten, glitter, glow, radiate, scintillate, shimmer, sparkle, twinkle 2. be conspicuous (distinguished, outstanding, pre-eminent), excel, stand out, stand out in a crowd, star ~*n.* 3. brightness, glare, gleam, lambency, light, luminosity, radiance, shimmer, sparkle

shining 1. beaming, bright, brilliant, effulgent, gleaming, glistening, glittering, luminous, radiant, resplendent, shimmering, sparkling 2. *Fig.* brilliant, celebrated, conspicuous, distinguished, eminent, glorious, illustrious, leading, outstanding, splendid

shirk avoid, dodge, duck (out of) (*Inf.*), evade, get out of, scrimshank (*Brit. military sl.*), shun, sidestep, skive (*Brit. sl.*), slack

shock 1. *v.* agitate, appal, astound, disgust, disquiet, give (someone) a turn (*Inf.*), horrify,

jar, jolt, nauseate, numb, offend, outrage, paralyse, revolt, scandalize, shake, shake out of one's complacency, shake up (*Inf.*), sicken, stagger, stun, stupefy, traumatize, unsettle 2. *n.* blow, bolt from the blue, bombshell, breakdown, collapse, consternation, distress, disturbance, prostration, state of shock, stupefaction, stupor, trauma, turn (*Inf.*), upset

shocking abominable, appalling, atrocious, detestable, disgraceful, disgusting, disquieting, distressing, dreadful, foul, frightful, ghastly, hideous, horrible, horrifying, loathsome, monstrous, nauseating, odious, offensive, outrageous, repulsive, revolting, scandalous, sickening, stupefying, unspeakable

shoddy cheap-jack (*Inf.*), cheapo (*Inf.*), inferior, junky, poor, rubbishy, second-rate, slipshod, tacky (*Inf.*), tatty, tawdry, trashy **Antonyms** accurate, careful, considerate, craftsman-like, excellent, fastidious, fine, first-rate, meticulous, noble, quality, superlative, well-made

shoot[1] *v.* 1. bag, blast (*Sl.*), bring down, hit, kill, open fire, pick off, plug (*Sl.*), pump full of lead (*Sl.*), zap (*Sl.*) 2. discharge, emit, fire, fling, hurl, launch, let fly, project, propel 3. bolt, charge, dart, dash, flash, fly, hurtle, race, rush, scoot, speed, spring, streak, tear, whisk, whiz (*Inf.*)

shoot[2] 1. *n.* branch, bud, offshoot, scion, slip, sprig, sprout, twig 2. *v.* bud, burgeon, germinate, put forth new growth, sprout

shore *n.* beach, coast, foreshore, lakeside, sands, seaboard (*Chiefly U.S.*), seashore, strand (*Poetic*), waterside

short *adj.* 1. abridged, brief, compendious, compressed, concise, curtailed, laconic, pithy, sententious, succinct, summary, terse 2. diminutive, dumpy, little, low, petite, small, squat, wee 3. brief, fleeting, momentary, short-lived, short-term **4.** *Often with of* defi~ cient, inadequate, insufficient, lacking, limited, low (on), mea~ gre, poor, scant, scanty, scarce, short-handed, slender, slim, sparse, tight, wanting ~*adv.* **5.** abruptly, by surprise, suddenly, unaware, without warning

Antonyms *adj.* (*sense 1*) diffuse, lengthy, long, long-drawn-out, long-winded, prolonged, ram~ bling, unabridged, verbose, wordy (*sense 2*) big, high, lanky, lofty, tall (*sense 3*) extended, long, long-term (*sense 4*) abun~ dant, adequate, ample, bountiful, copious, inexhaustible, plentiful, sufficient, well-stocked ~*adv.* (*sense 5*) bit by bit, gently, gradually, little by little, slowly

shortage dearth, deficiency, deficit, failure, inadequacy, in~ sufficiency, lack, leanness, pau~ city, poverty, scarcity, shortfall, want

Antonyms abundance, adequate amount, excess, overabundance, plethora, profusion, sufficiency, surfeit, surplus

shortcoming defect, drawback, failing, fault, flaw, foible, frailty, imperfection, weakness, weak point

shorten abbreviate, abridge, cur~ tail, cut, cut back, cut down, decrease, diminish, dock, lessen, prune, reduce, trim, truncate, turn up

Antonyms draw out, elongate, expand, extend, increase, lengthen, make longer, prolong, protract, spin out, stretch

shot *n.* **1.** discharge, lob, pot shot, throw **2.** ball, bullet, lead, pellet, projectile, slug **3.** marksman, shooter **4.** *Inf.* attempt, chance, conjecture, crack (*Inf.*), effort, endeavour, essay, go, guess, op~ portunity, stab, surmise, try, turn **5. have a shot** *Inf.* attempt, have a go (bash (*Inf.*), crack (*Inf.*), stab), tackle, try, try one's luck **6. like a shot** at once, eagerly, immediately, like a flash, quick~ ly, unhesitatingly

shoulder *v.* **1.** accept, assume, bear, be responsible for, carry, take on, take upon oneself **2.** elbow, jostle, press, push, shove, thrust

shout 1. *n.* bellow, call, cry, roar, scream, yell **2.** *v.* bawl, bay, bel~ low, call (out), cry (out), holler (*Inf.*), hollo, raise one's voice, roar, scream, yell

shove *v.* crowd, drive, elbow, im~ pel, jostle, press, propel, push, shoulder, thrust

show *v.* **1.** appear, be visible, disclose, display, divulge, evi~ dence, evince, exhibit, indicate, make known, manifest, present, register, reveal, testify to **2.** as~ sert, clarify, demonstrate, eluci~ date, evince, explain, instruct, point out, present, prove, teach **3.** accompany, attend, conduct, es~ cort, guide, lead ~*n.* **4.** array, demonstration, display, exhibi~ tion, expo (*Inf.*), exposition, fair, manifestation, pageant, pageant~ ry, parade, representation, sight, spectacle, view **5.** affectation, air, appearance, display, illusion, likeness, ostentation, parade, pose, pretence, pretext, profes~ sion, semblance

Antonyms (*senses 1 & 2*) be invisible, conceal, deny, disprove, gainsay, hide, keep secret, mask, obscure, refute, suppress, veil, withhold

showdown breaking point, clash, climax, confrontation, crisis, cul~ mination, *dénouement*, exposé, moment of truth

shower 1. *n. Fig.* barrage, deluge, fusillade, plethora, rain, stream, torrent, volley **2.** *v.* deluge, heap, inundate, lavish, load, pour, rain, spray, sprinkle

show off 1. advertise, demon~ strate, display, exhibit, flaunt, parade, spread out **2.** boast, brag, make a spectacle of oneself, shoot a line (*Inf.*), swagger

show up 1. expose, highlight, lay bare, pinpoint, put the spotlight on, reveal, unmask **2.** appear, be conspicuous, be visible, catch the

shrewd eye, leap to the eye, stand out **3.** *Inf.* embarrass, let down, mortify, put to shame, shame, show in a bad light **4.** *Inf.* appear, arrive, come, make an appearance, put in an appearance, turn up

shrewd acute, artful, astute, calculated, calculating, canny, clever, crafty, cunning, discerning, discriminating, far-seeing, farsighted, fly (*Sl.*), intelligent, keen, knowing, long-headed, perceptive, perspicacious, sagacious, sharp, sly, smart, wily

Antonyms artless, dull, gullible, imprudent, ingenuous, innocent, naive, obtuse, slow-witted, stupid, trusting, undiscerning, unsophisticated, unworldly

shrill acute, ear-piercing, ear-splitting, high, high-pitched, penetrating, piercing, piping, screeching, sharp

Antonyms deep, dulcet, mellifluous, silver-toned, soft, soothing, sweet-sounding, velvety, well-modulated

shrink 1. contract, decrease, deflate, diminish, drop off, dwindle, fall off, grow smaller, lessen, narrow, shorten, shrivel, wither, wrinkle **2.** cower, cringe, draw back, flinch, hang back, quail, recoil, retire, shy away, wince, withdraw

Antonyms (*sense 1*) balloon, dilate, distend, enlarge, expand, increase, inflate, mushroom, stretch, swell (*sense 2*) attack, challenge, confront, embrace, face, receive, welcome

shrivel 1. burn, dry (up), parch, scorch, sear **2.** dehydrate, desiccate, dwindle, shrink, wilt, wither, wizen, wrinkle

shudder 1. *v.* convulse, quake, quiver, shake, shiver, tremble **2.** *n.* convulsion, quake, spasm, trembling, tremor

shuffle 1. drag, scrape, scuff, scuffle, shamble **2.** confuse, disarrange, disorder, intermix, jumble, mix, rearrange, shift

shun avoid, cold-shoulder, elude, eschew, evade, fight shy of, give

(someone *or* something) a wide berth, have no part in, keep away from, shy away from, steer clear of

shut bar, close, draw to, fasten, push to, seal, secure, slam

Antonyms open, throw wide, unbar, unclose, undo, unfasten, unlock

shut out debar, exclude, keep out, lock out, ostracize

shut up 1. bottle up, box in, cage, confine, coop up, immure, imprison, incarcerate, intern, keep in **2.** *Inf.* be quiet, fall silent, gag, hold one's tongue, hush, keep one's trap shut (*Sl.*), muzzle, pipe down (*Sl.*), silence

shy *adj.* backward, bashful, cautious, chary, coy, diffident, distrustful, hesitant, modest, mousy, nervous, reserved, reticent, retiring, self-conscious, self-effacing, shrinking, suspicious, timid, wary

Antonyms assured, bold, brash, cheeky, confident, fearless, forward, pushy, rash, reckless, self-assured, self-confident, unsuspecting, unwary

sick 1. green around the gills (*Inf.*), ill, nauseated, nauseous, puking (*Sl.*), qualmish, queasy **2.** ailing, diseased, feeble, indisposed, laid up (*Inf.*), on the sick list (*Inf.*), poorly (*Inf.*), under par, under the weather (*Inf.*), unwell, weak **3.** *Inf.* black, ghoulish, macabre, morbid, sadistic

Antonyms (*senses 1 & 2*) able-bodied, fine, fit, fit and well, fit as a fiddle, hale and hearty, healthy, robust, tranquil, untroubled, unworried, up to par, well

sicken 1. disgust, make one's gorge rise, nauseate, repel, revolt, turn one's stomach **2.** be stricken by, contract, fall ill, go down with (*Brit.*), show symptoms of, take sick

sickly 1. ailing, bilious, bloodless, delicate, faint, feeble, indisposed, infirm, in poor health, lacklustre, languid, pallid, peaky, pining, unhealthy, wan, weak **2.** bilious

(*Inf.*), cloying, mawkish, nauseating, revolting (*Inf.*), syrupy (*Inf.*)

sickness 1. barfing (*Sl.*), nausea, queasiness, (the) collywobbles (*Sl.*), puking (*Sl.*), vomiting **2.** affliction, ailment, bug (*Inf.*), complaint, disease, disorder, illness, indisposition, infirmity, malady

side n. **1.** border, boundary, division, edge, limit, margin, part, perimeter, periphery, rim, sector, verge **2.** aspect, face, facet, flank, hand, part, surface, view **3.** angle, light, opinion, point of view, position, slant, stand, standpoint, viewpoint **4.** camp, cause, faction, party, sect, team **5.** *Brit. sl.* airs, arrogance, insolence, pretentiousness ~*adj.* **6.** flanking, lateral **7.** ancillary, incidental, indirect, lesser, marginal, minor, oblique, roundabout, secondary, subordinate, subsidiary

sidetrack deflect, distract, divert, lead off the subject

sideways 1. *adv.* crabwise, edgeways, laterally, obliquely, sidelong, sidewards, to the side **2.** *adj.* oblique, side, sidelong, slanted

sift 1. bolt, filter, pan, part, riddle, separate, sieve **2.** analyse, examine, fathom, go through, investigate, pore over, probe, screen, scrutinize

sight n. **1.** eye, eyes, eyesight, seeing, vision **2.** appearance, apprehension, eyeshot, field of vision, ken, perception, range of vision, view, viewing, visibility **3.** display, exhibition, pageant, scene, show, spectacle, vista **4.** **catch sight of** descry, espy, glimpse, recognize, spot, view ~*v.* **5.** behold, discern, distinguish, make out, observe, perceive, see, spot

sign n. **1.** clue, evidence, gesture, giveaway, hint, indication, manifestation, mark, note, proof, signal, spoor, suggestion, symptom, token, trace, vestige **2.** board, badge, character, cipher, device,

emblem, ensign, figure, logo, mark, representation, symbol **4.** augury, auspice, foreboding, forewarning, omen, portent, presage, warning, writing on the wall ~*v.* **5.** autograph, endorse, initial, inscribe, set one's hand to, subscribe **6.** beckon, gesticulate, gesture, indicate, signal, use sign language, wave

signal 1. *n.* beacon, cue, flare, gesture, go-ahead (*Inf.*), green light, indication, indicator, mark, sign, token **2.** *v.* beckon, communicate, gesticulate, gesture, give a sign to, indicate, motion, nod, sign, wave

significance 1. force, implication(s), import, meaning, message, point, purport, sense, signification **2.** consequence, consideration, importance, impressiveness, matter, moment, relevance, weight

significant 1. denoting, eloquent, expressing, expressive, indicative, knowing, meaning, meaningful, pregnant, suggestive **2.** critical, important, material, momentous, noteworthy, serious, vital, weighty

Antonyms immaterial, inconsequential, insignificant, irrelevant, meaningless, nit-picking, nugatory, of no consequence, paltry, petty, trivial, unimportant, worthless

silence n. **1.** calm, hush, lull, noiselessness, peace, quiescence, quiet, stillness **2.** dumbness, muteness, reticence, speechlessness, taciturnity, uncommunicativeness ~*v.* **3.** cut off, cut short, deaden, extinguish, gag, muffle, quell, quiet, quieten, stifle, still, strike dumb, subdue, suppress

Antonyms *n.* babble, bawling, cacophony, chatter, clamour, din, garrulousness, hubbub, loquaciousness, murmuring, noise, prattle, racket, shouting, sound, speech, talk, talking, tumult, uproar, verbosity, whispering, yelling ~*v.* amplify, broadcast, champion, disseminate, encourage, foster, make louder, promote, promulgate, publicize, rouse, spread, support, ungag

silent 1. hushed, muted, noiseless, quiet, soundless, still, stilly (*Poetic*) **2.** dumb, mum, mute, nonvocal, not talkative, speechless, struck dumb (*Inf.*), taciturn, tongue-tied, uncommunicative, unspeaking, voiceless, wordless **3.** aphonic (*Phonetics*), implicit, implied, tacit, understood, unexpressed, unpronounced, unspoken

silhouette 1. *n.* delineation, form, outline, profile, shape **2.** *v.* delineate, etch, outline, stand out

silly *adj.* **1.** absurd, asinine, brainless, childish, dopy (*Sl.*), dozy (*Inf.*), fatuous, foolhardy, foolish, frivolous, giddy, idiotic, immature, imprudent, inane, inappropriate, irresponsible, meaningless, pointless, preposterous, puerile, ridiculous, senseless, stupid, unwise, witless **2.** *Inf.* benumbed, dazed, groggy (*Inf.*), in a daze, muzzy, stunned, stupefied
Antonyms acute, aware, bright, clever, intelligent, mature, perceptive, profound, prudent, reasonable, sane, sensible, serious, smart, thoughtful, well thought-out, wise

similar alike, analogous, close, comparable, congruous, corresponding, homogenous, homogeneous, in agreement, much the same, resembling, uniform
Antonyms antithetical, clashing, contradictory, contrary, different, disparate, dissimilar, diverse, heterogeneous, irreconcilable, opposite, unlike, unrelated, various, varying

similarity affinity, agreement, analogy, closeness, comparability, concordance, congruence, correspondence, likeness, point of comparison, relation, resemblance, sameness, similitude
Antonyms antithesis, contradictoriness, difference, disagreement, discordance, discrepancy, disparity, dissimilarity, diversity,

heterogeneity, incomparability, irreconcilability, unalikeness, variation, variety

simple 1. clear, easy, elementary, intelligible, lucid, manageable, plain, straightforward, uncomplicated, understandable, uninvolved **2.** classic, clean, natural, plain, Spartan, unadorned, uncluttered, unembellished, unfussy **3.** elementary, pure, single, unalloyed, unblended, uncombined, undivided, unmixed **4.** artless, childlike, frank, green, guileless, ingenuous, innocent, naive, natural, simplistic, sincere, unaffected, unpretentious, unsophisticated **5.** bald, basic, direct, frank, honest, naked, plain, sincere, stark, undeniable, unvarnished **6.** homely, humble, lowly, modest, rustic, unpretentious **7.** brainless, credulous, dense, dumb (*Inf.*), feeble, feeble-minded, foolish, half-witted, moronic, obtuse, shallow, silly, slow, stupid, thick
Antonyms (*senses 1 & 3*) advanced, complex, complicated, convoluted, difficult, elaborate, highly developed, intricate, involved, refined, sophisticated (*senses 2, 4 & 6*) artful, contrived, elaborate, extravagant, fancy, flashy, fussy, intricate, ornate, smart, sophisticated, worldly, worldly-wise (*sense 7*) astute, bright, clever, intelligent, knowing, on the ball, quick, quick on the uptake, quick-witted, sharp, smart, wise

simplicity 1. absence of complications, clarity, clearness, ease, easiness, elementariness, obviousness, straightforwardness **2.** clean lines, lack of adornment, modesty, naturalness, plainness, purity, restraint **3.** artlessness, candour, directness, guilelessness, innocence, lack of sophistication, naivety, openness
Antonyms (*sense 1*) complexity, complicatedness, difficulty, intricacy, lack of clarity (*sense 2*) decoration, elaborateness, embellishment, fanciness, fussiness,

ornateness, ostentation (*sense 3*) brains, craftiness, cunning, deviousness, guile, insincerity, knowingness, sharpness, slyness, smartness, sophistication, wariness, wisdom, worldliness

simplify abridge, decipher, disentangle, facilitate, make intelligible, reduce to essentials, streamline

sin 1. *n.* crime, damnation, error, evil, guilt, iniquity, misdeed, offence, sinfulness, transgression, trespass, ungodliness, unrighteousness, wickedness, wrong, wrongdoing **2.** *v.* err, fall, fall from grace, go astray, lapse, offend, transgress, trespass (*Archaic*)

sincere artless, bona fide, candid, earnest, frank, genuine, guileless, heartfelt, honest, natural, nononsense, open, real, serious, straightforward, true, unaffected, unfeigned, wholehearted
Antonyms affected, artificial, deceitful, deceptive, dishonest, false, feigned, hollow, insincere, phoney, pretended, put on, synthetic, token, two-faced

sincerity artlessness, bona fides, candour, frankness, genuineness, good faith, guilelessness, honesty, probity, seriousness, straightforwardness, truth, wholeheartedness

sinful bad, corrupt, criminal, depraved, erring, guilty, immoral, iniquitous, irreligious, morally wrong, ungodly, unholy, unrighteous, wicked
Antonyms beatified, blessed, chaste, decent, free from sin, godly, holy, honest, honourable, immaculate, moral, pure, righteous, sinless, spotless, unblemished, upright, virtuous, without sin

sing carol, chant, chirp, croon, make melody, pipe, trill, vocalize, warble, yodel

single *adj.* **1.** distinct, individual, lone, one, only, particular, separate, singular, sole, solitary, unique **2.** free, unattached, un-

married, unwed **3.** exclusive, individual, separate, simple, unblended, uncompounded, undivided, unmixed, unshared

single-minded dedicated, determined, dogged, fixed, hellbent (*Inf.*), monomaniacal, steadfast, stubborn, tireless, undeviating, unswerving, unwavering

singular 1. conspicuous, eminent, exceptional, noteworthy, outstanding, prodigious, rare, remarkable, uncommon, unique, unparalleled **2.** atypical, curious, eccentric, extraordinary, odd, out-of-the-way, peculiar, puzzling, queer, strange, unusual **3.** individual, separate, single, sole

sinister dire, disquieting, evil, injurious, malevolent, malign, malignant, menacing, ominous, threatening

sink *v.* **1.** cave in, decline, descend, dip, disappear, droop, drop, drown, ebb, engulf, fall, founder, go down, go under, lower, merge, plummet, plunge, sag, slope, submerge, subside **2.** abate, collapse, drop, fall, lapse, relapse, retrogress, slip, slump, subside **3.** decay, decline, decrease, degenerate, depreciate, deteriorate, die, diminish, dwindle, fade, fail, flag, go downhill (*Inf.*), lessen, weaken, worsen **4.** bore, dig, drill, drive, excavate, lay, put down **5.** be the ruin of, defeat, destroy, finish, overwhelm, ruin, scupper (*Brit. sl.*), seal the doom of **6.** be reduced to, debase oneself, lower oneself, stoop, succumb
Antonyms (*senses 1, 2 & 3*) arise, ascend, climb, enlarge, go up, grow, improve, increase, intensify, move up, rise, rise up, swell, wax

sip 1. *v.* sample, sup, taste **2.** *n.* drop, swallow, taste, thimbleful

sit 1. be seated, perch, rest, settle, take a seat, take the weight off one's feet **2.** assemble, be in session, convene, deliberate, meet, officiate, preside

site 1. *n.* ground, location, place,

plot, position, setting, spot **2.** v. install, locate, place, position, set, situate

situation 1. locale, locality, location, place, position, seat, setting, site, spot **2.** ball game (Inf.), case, circumstances, condition, kettle of fish (Inf.), plight, scenario, state, state of affairs, status quo, the picture (Inf.) **3.** rank, sphere, station, status **4.** berth (Inf.), employment, job, office, place, position, post

size amount, bigness, bulk, dimensions, extent, greatness, hugeness, immensity, largeness, magnitude, mass, measurement(s), proportions, range, vastness, volume

sketch 1. v. block out, delineate, depict, draft, draw, outline, paint, plot, portray, represent, rough out **2.** n. delineation, design, draft, drawing, outline, plan, skeleton

sketchy bitty, cobbled together, crude, cursory, inadequate, incomplete, outline, perfunctory, rough, scrappy, skimpy, slight, superficial, unfinished, vague

skilful able, accomplished, adept, adroit, apt, clever, competent, dexterous, experienced, expert, handy, masterly, practised, professional, proficient, quick, ready, skilled, trained

Antonyms amateurish, awkward, bungling, cack-handed, clumsy, ham-fisted, incompetent, inept, inexperienced, maladroit, slapdash, unaccomplished, unqualified, unskilful, unskilled

skill ability, accomplishment, adroitness, aptitude, art, cleverness, competence, dexterity, expertise, expertness, facility, finesse, handiness, ingenuity, intelligence, knack, proficiency, quickness, readiness, skilfulness, talent, technique

skilled able, accomplished, a dab hand at (Brit. inf.), experienced, expert, masterly, practised, professional, proficient, skilful, trained

Antonyms amateurish, inexperi-

enced, inexpert, uneducated, unprofessional, unqualified, unskilled, untalented, untrained

skin n. **1.** fell, hide, integument, pelt, tegument **2.** casing, coating, crust, film, husk, membrane, outside, peel, rind

skinny emaciated, lean, scraggy, skeletal, skin-and-bone (Inf.), thin, twiggy, undernourished

Antonyms beefy (Inf.), broad in the beam (Inf.), fat, fleshy, heavy, obese, plump, podgy, portly, stout, tubby

skip v. **1.** bob, bounce, caper, cavort, dance, flit, frisk, gambol, hop, prance, trip **2.** eschew, give (something) a miss, leave out, miss out, omit, pass over, skim over

skirmish 1. n. affair, affray (Law), battle, brush, clash, combat, conflict, contest, dust-up (Inf.), encounter, engagement, fracas, incident, scrap (Inf.), scrimmage, set-to (Inf.), spat, tussle **2.** v. clash, collide, come to blows, scrap (Inf.), tussle

skirt v. border, edge, flank, lie alongside

slack adj. **1.** baggy, easy, flaccid, flexible, lax, limp, loose, not taut, relaxed **2.** asleep on the job (Inf.), easy-going, idle, inactive, inattentive, lax, lazy, neglectful, negligent, permissive, remiss, tardy **3.** dull, inactive, quiet, slow, slow-moving, sluggish ~n. **4.** excess, give (Inf.), leeway, looseness, play, room ~v. **5.** dodge, flag, idle, neglect, relax, shirk, skive (Brit. sl.), slacken

slacken (off) abate, decrease, diminish, drop off, ease (off), lessen, let up, loosen, moderate, reduce, relax, release, slack off, slow down, tire

slacker dodger, do-nothing, gold brick (U.S. sl.), good-for-nothing, idler, layabout, loafer, passenger, scrimshanker (Brit. military sl.), shirker, skiver (Brit. sl.)

slam bang, crash, dash, fling, hurl, smash, throw, thump

slander 1. n. aspersion, backbiting, calumny, defamation, detraction, libel, misrepresentation, muckraking, obloquy, scandal, smear **2.** *v.* backbite, blacken (someone's) name, calumniate, decry, defame, detract, disparage, libel, malign, muckrake, slur, smear, traduce, vilify

Antonyms *n.* acclaim, acclamation, approval, laudation, praise, tribute ~*v.* acclaim, applaud, approve, compliment, eulogize, laud, praise, sing the praises of

slant *v.* **1.** angle off, bend, bevel, cant, incline, lean, list, shelve, skew, slope, tilt ~*n.* **2.** camber, declination, diagonal, gradient, incline, pitch, rake, ramp, slope, tilt ~*v.* **3.** angle, bias, colour, distort, twist, weight ~*n.* **4.** angle, attitude, bias, emphasis, leaning, one-sidedness, point of view, prejudice, viewpoint

slanting angled, aslant, asymmetrical, at an angle, bent, canted, cater-cornered (*U.S. inf.*), diagonal, inclined, oblique, on the bias, sideways, slanted, slantwise, sloping, tilted, tilting

slap 1. *n.* bang, blow, clout (*Inf.*), cuff, smack, spank, wallop (*Inf.*), whack **2.** *v.* bang, clap, clout (*Inf.*), cuff, hit, spank, strike, whack

slapdash careless, clumsy, disorderly, haphazard, hasty, hurried, last-minute, messy, negligent, perfunctory, slipshod, sloppy (*Inf.*), slovenly, thoughtless, thrown-together, untidy

slash 1. *v.* cut, gash, hack, lacerate, rend, rip, score, slit **2.** *n.* cut, gash, incision, laceration, rent, rip, slit

slate *v.* berate, blame, castigate, censure, criticize, haul over the coals (*Inf.*), lambaste, lay into (*Inf.*), pan (*Inf.*), pitch into, rail against, rap (someone's) knuckles (*Inf.*), rebuke, roast (*Inf.*), scold, slam (*Sl.*), slang, take to task, tear (someone) off a strip (*Inf.*)

slaughter 1. *n.* blood bath, bloodshed, butchery, carnage, extermination, holocaust, killing, liquidation, massacre, murder, slaying **2.** *v.* butcher, destroy, do to death, exterminate, kill, liquidate, massacre, murder, put to the sword, slay

slave 1. *n.* bondservant, bondsman, drudge, scullion (*Archaic*), serf, servant, skivvy, slavey (*Brit. inf.*), vassal, villein **2.** *v.* drudge, grind (*Inf.*), skivvy (*Brit.*), slog, sweat, toil, work one's fingers to the bone

slavery bondage, captivity, enslavement, serfdom, servitude, subjugation, thraldom, thrall, vassalage

Antonyms emancipation, freedom, liberty, manumission, release

sleep 1. *v.* be in the land of Nod, catnap, doze, drop off (*Inf.*), drowse, hibernate, nod off (*Inf.*), rest in the arms of Morpheus, slumber, snooze (*Inf.*), snore, take a nap, take forty winks (*Inf.*) **2.** *n.* beauty sleep (*Inf.*), dormancy, doze, forty winks (*Inf.*), hibernation, nap, repose, rest, shuteye (*Sl.*), siesta, slumber(s), snooze (*Inf.*)

sleepless disturbed, insomniac, restless, unsleeping, wakeful

sleepy 1. drowsy, dull, heavy, inactive, lethargic, sluggish, slumbersome, somnolent, torpid **2.** dull, hypnotic, inactive, quiet, sleep-inducing, slow, slumberous, somnolent, soporific

Antonyms active, alert, animated, attentive, awake, boisterous, bustling, busy, energetic, lively, restless, thriving, wakeful, wide-awake

slender 1. lean, narrow, slight, slim, svelte, sylphlike, willowy **2.** inadequate, inconsiderable, insufficient, little, meagre, scanty, small, spare **3.** faint, feeble, flimsy, fragile, remote, slight, slim, tenuous, thin, weak

slice 1. *n.* cut, helping, piece, portion, segment, share, sliver, wedge **2.** *v.* carve, cut, divide, sever

slick adj. 1. glib, meretricious, plausible, polished, smooth, sophistical, specious 2. adroit, deft, dexterous, polished, professional, sharp, skilful

slide v. coast, glide, glissade, skim, slip, slither, toboggan, veer

slight adj. 1. feeble, inconsiderable, insignificant, insubstantial, meagre, minor, modest, negligible, paltry, scanty, small, superficial, trifling, trivial, unimportant, weak 2. delicate, feeble, fragile, lightly-built, slim, small, spare ~v. 3. affront, cold-shoulder, despise, disdain, disparage, give offence or umbrage to, ignore, insult, neglect, scorn, show disrespect for, snub, treat with contempt ~n. 4. affront, contempt, discourtesy, disdain, disregard, disrespect, inattention, indifference, insult, neglect, rebuff, slap in the face (Inf.), snub, (the) cold shoulder

Antonyms adj. appreciable, considerable, great, heavy, important, large, muscular, noticeable, obvious, significant, solid, strong, sturdy, substantial, well-built ~v. compliment, flatter, praise, speak well of, treat considerately ~n. compliment, flattery, praise

slightly a little, marginally, on a small scale, somewhat, to some extent or degree

slim adj. 1. lean, narrow, slender, slight, svelte, sylphlike, thin, trim 2. faint, poor, remote, slender, slight ~v. 3. diet, lose weight, reduce, slenderize (Chiefly U.S.)

Antonyms adj. broad, bulky, chubby, fat, good, heavy, muscular, obese, overweight, strong, sturdy, tubby, well-built, wide ~v. build oneself up, put on weight

slimy 1. clammy, glutinous, miry, mucous, muddy, oozy, viscous 2. creeping, grovelling, obsequious, oily, servile, smarmy (Brit. inf.), soapy (Sl.), sycophantic, toadying, unctuous

slip v. 1. glide, skate, slide, slither 2. fall, lose one's balance, miss or

lose one's footing, skid, trip (over) 3. conceal, creep, hide, insinuate oneself, sneak, steal 4. Sometimes with up blunder, boob (Brit. sl.), err, go wrong, make a mistake, miscalculate, misjudge, mistake ~n. 5. bloomer (Brit. inf.), blunder, boob (Brit. sl.), error, failure, fault, faux pas, imprudence, indiscretion, mistake, omission, oversight, slip of the tongue, slip-up (Inf.)

slippery 1. glassy, greasy, icy, lubricious (Rare), perilous, skiddy (Inf.), slippy (Inf.), smooth, unsafe, unstable, unsteady 2. crafty, cunning, devious, dishonest, duplicitous, evasive, false, foxy, shifty, sneaky, treacherous, tricky, two-faced, unpredictable, unreliable, untrustworthy

slit 1. v. cut (open), gash, knife, lance, pierce, rip, slash, split open 2. n. cut, fissure, gash, incision, opening, rent, split, tear

slogan catch-phrase, catchword, jingle, motto, rallying cry

slope v. 1. drop away, fall, incline, lean, pitch, rise, slant, tilt n. 2. brae (Scot.), declination, declivity, descent, downgrade (Chiefly U.S.), gradient, inclination, incline, ramp, rise, scarp, slant, tilt

sloppy 1. sludgy, slushy, splashy, watery, wet 2. Inf. amateurish, careless, clumsy, hit-or-miss (Inf.), inattentive, messy, slipshod, slovenly, unkempt, untidy, weak

slot n. 1. aperture, channel, groove, hole, slit 2. Inf. niche, opening, place, position, space, time, vacancy

slovenly careless, disorderly, heedless, loose, negligent, slack, slapdash, slatternly, slipshod, sloppy (Inf.), unkempt, untidy

slow adj. 1. creeping, dawdling, deliberate, easy, lackadaisical, laggard, lagging, lazy, leaden, leisurely, loitering, measured, plodding, ponderous, slow-moving, sluggardly, sluggish, tortoise-like, unhurried 2. backward, behind, behindhand, de~

layed, dilatory, late, long-delayed, tardy, unpunctual **3.** gradual, lingering, long-drawn-out, prolonged, protracted, time-consuming **4.** behind the times, boring, conservative, dead, dead-and-alive (*Brit.*), dull, inactive, one-horse (*Inf.*), quiet, slack, sleepy, sluggish, stagnant, tame, tedious, uneventful, uninteresting, unproductive, unprogressive, wearisome **5.** blockish, bovine, dense, dim, dull, dull-witted, dumb (*Inf.*), obtuse, retarded, slow on the uptake (*Inf.*), slow-witted, stupid, thick, unresponsive

Antonyms *adj.* (*senses 1, 2, 3 & 4*) action-packed, animated, brisk, eager, exciting, fast, hectic, hurried, interesting, lively, precipitate, prompt, quick, quick-moving, sharp, speedy, stimulating, swift (*sense 5*) bright, clever, intelligent, perceptive, quick, quick-witted, sharp, smart

slowly at a snail's pace, at one's leisure, by degrees, gradually, inchmeal, in one's own (good) time, leisurely, ploddingly, steadily, taking one's time, unhurriedly, with leaden steps

sluggish dull, heavy, inactive, indolent, inert, lethargic, lifeless, listless, phlegmatic, slothful, slow, slow-moving, torpid, unresponsive

slump 1. *v.* collapse, crash, decline, deteriorate, fall, fall off, go downhill (*Inf.*), plummet, plunge, reach a new low, sink, slip **2.** *n.* collapse, crash, decline, depreciation, depression, downturn, failure, fall, falling-off, low, recession, reverse, stagnation, trough

Antonyms *v.* advance, boom, develop, expand, flourish, grow, increase, prosper, thrive ~*n.* advance, boom, boost, development, expansion, gain, growth, improvement, increase, upsurge, upswing, upturn

slur *n.* affront, aspersion, blot, brand, calumny, discredit, disgrace, innuendo, insinuation, insult, reproach, smear, stain, stigma

sly 1. *adj.* artful, astute, clever, conniving, covert, crafty, cunning, devious, foxy, furtive, guileful, insidious, scheming, secret, shifty, stealthy, subtle, underhand, wily **2.** *n.* on the sly behind (someone's) back, covertly, like a thief in the night, on the q.t. (*Inf.*), on the quiet, privately, secretly, surreptitiously, underhandedly, under the counter (*Inf.*)

Antonyms *adj.* above-board, artless, direct, frank, honest, guileless, ingenuous, open, straightforward, trustworthy ~*n.* above-board, candidly, forthrightly, on the level, openly, overtly, publicly

small 1. diminutive, immature, Lilliputian, little, mini, miniature, minute, petite, pint-sized (*Inf.*), pocket-sized, puny, slight, teeny, teensy-weensy, tiny, undersized, wee, young **2.** insignificant, lesser, minor, negligible, paltry, petty, trifling, trivial, unimportant **3.** inadequate, inconsiderable, insufficient, limited, meagre, scanty **4.** humble, modest, small-scale, unpretentious **5.** base, grudging, illiberal, mean, narrow, petty, selfish

Antonyms (*sense 1*) ample, big, colossal, enormous, great, huge, immense, massive, mega (*Sl.*), sizable, vast (*senses 2, 3 & 4*) appreciable, considerable, generous, grand, important, large-scale, major, powerful, serious, significant, substantial, urgent, vital, weighty

small-minded bigoted, envious, grudging, hidebound, intolerant, mean, narrow-minded, petty, rigid, ungenerous

smart[1] *adj.* **1.** acute, adept, agile, apt, astute, bright, brisk, canny, clever, ingenious, intelligent, keen, nimble, quick, quick-witted, ready, sharp, shrewd **2.** chic, elegant, fashionable, fine, modish, natty (*Inf.*), neat, snappy, spruce, stylish, trendy (*Inf.*), trim, well turned-out **3.** effective, impertinent, nimble-witted, pointed, ready, saucy, smart-alecky (*Inf.*), witty

Antonyms (*sense 1*) daft, dim-witted (*Inf.*), dull, dumb, foolish, idiotic, moronic, slow, stupid, thick, unintelligent (*sense 2*) dowdy, dull, fogeyish, old-fashioned, out-moded, out-of-date, passé, scruffy, sloppy, uncool, unfashionable, untrendy (*Inf.*) (*sense 3*) modest, polite, respectful, restrained, unobtrusive

smart² *v.* burn, hurt, pain, sting, throb, tingle

smash *v.* **1.** break, collide, crash, crush, demolish, disintegrate, pulverize, shatter ∼*n.* **2.** accident, collision, crash, pile-up (*Inf.*), smash-up (*Inf.*) ∼*v.* **3.** defeat, destroy, lay waste, overthrow, ruin, wreck ∼*n.* **4.** collapse, defeat, destruction, disaster, downfall, failure, ruin, shattering

smear *v.* **1.** bedaub, bedim, besmirch, blur, coat, cover, daub, dirty, patch, plaster, rub on, smudge, soil, spread over, stain, sully ∼*n.* blot, blotch, daub, smudge, splotch, streak ∼*v.* **3.** asperse, besmirch, blacken, calumniate, drag (someone's) name through the mud (*Inf.*), malign, sully, tarnish, traduce, vilify ∼*n.* calumny, defamation, libel, mudslinging, slander, vilification, whispering campaign

smell *n.* **1.** aroma, bouquet, fragrance, odour, perfume, redolence, scent, whiff ∼*v.* **2.** get a whiff of (*Brit. sl.*), nose, scent, sniff **3.** be malodorous, hum (*Sl.*), niff (*Sl.*), pong (*Brit. inf.*), reek, stink, stink to high heaven (*Inf.*), whiff (*Brit. sl.*)

smooth *adj.* **1.** even, flat, flush, horizontal, level, plain, plane, unwrinkled **2.** glossy, polished, shiny, silky, sleek, soft, velvety **3.** calm, equable, glassy, mirror-like, peaceful, serene, tranquil,

undisturbed, unruffled **4.** agreeable, bland, mellow, mild, pleasant, soothing **5.** facile, glib, ingratiating, persuasive, silky, slick, smarmy (*Brit. inf.*), suave, unctuous, urbane **6.** easy, effortless, flowing, fluent, frictionless, regular, rhythmic, steady, unbroken, uneventful, uniform, uninterrupted, untroubled, well-ordered ∼*v.* **7.** flatten, iron, level, plane, polish, press **8.** allay, alleviate, appease, assuage, calm, ease, extenuate, facilitate, iron out the difficulties of, mitigate, mollify, palliate, pave the way, soften

Antonyms *adj.* (*senses 1 & 2*) abrasive, bumpy, coarse, irregular, jagged, lumpy, rough, sharp, uneven (*sense 3*) agitated, edgy, excitable, disturbed, nervous, ruffled, troubled, troublesome, turbulent, uneasy ∼*v.* aggravate, exacerbate, hamper, hinder, intensify, make worse, roughen

smother *v.* **1.** choke, extinguish, snuff, stifle, strangle, suffocate **2.** conceal, hide, keep back, muffle, repress, stifle, suppress

smug complacent, conceited, holier-than-thou, priggish, self-opinionated, self-righteous, self-satisfied, superior

smuggler bootlegger, contrabandist, gentleman, moonshiner (*U.S.*), rum-runner, runner, trafficker, wrecker

snack bite, bite to eat, break, elevenses (*Brit. inf.*), light meal, nibble, refreshment(s), titbit

snap *v.* **1.** break, come apart, crack, give way, separate **2.** bite, bite at, catch, grip, nip, seize, snatch **3.** bark, flare out, flash, fly off the handle at (*Inf.*), growl, jump down (someone's) throat (*Inf.*), lash out at, retort, snarl, speak sharply **4.** click, crackle, pop ∼*adj.* **5.** abrupt, immediate, instant, on-the-spot, sudden, unpremeditated

snare 1. *v.* catch, entrap, net, seize, springe, trap, trepan (*Ar-*

chaic), wire 2. *n.* catch, gin, net, noose, pitfall, springe, trap, wire

snatch 1. *v.* clutch, gain, grab, grasp, grip, make off with, pluck, pull, rescue, seize, take, win, wrench, wrest 2. *n.* bit, fragment, part, piece, smattering, snippet, spell

sneak *v.* 1. cower, lurk, pad, sidle, skulk, slink, slip, smuggle, spirit, steal 2. *Inf.* grass on (*Brit. inf.*), inform on, peach (*Sl.*), tell on (*Inf.*), tell tales ~*n.* 3. informer, snake in the grass, telltale

sneaking 1. hidden, private, secret, suppressed, unavowed, unconfessed, undivulged, unexpressed, unvoiced 2. intuitive, nagging, niggling, persistent, uncomfortable, worrying

sneer 1. *v.* curl one's lip, deride, disdain, gibe, hold in contempt, hold up to ridicule, jeer, laugh, look down on, mock, ridicule, scoff, scorn, sniff at, snigger, turn up one's nose (*Inf.*) 2. *n.* derision, disdain, gibe, jeer, mockery, ridicule, scorn, snidery, snigger

sniff *v.* breathe, inhale, smell, snuff, snuffle

snigger giggle, laugh, smirk, sneer, snicker, titter

snip *v.* 1. clip, crop, cut, nick, nip off, notch, shave, trim ~*n.* 2. bit, clipping, fragment, piece, scrap, shred, snippet 3. *Inf.* bargain, giveaway, good buy

snobbish arrogant, condescending, high and mighty (*Inf.*), hifalutin (*Inf., chiefly U.S.*), hoity-toity (*Inf.*), patronizing, pretentious, snooty (*Inf.*), stuck-up (*Inf.*), superior, toffee-nosed (*Sl.*), uppish (*Brit. inf.*), uppity

snooze 1. *v.* catnap, doze, drop off (*Inf.*), drowse, kip (*Brit. sl.*), nap, nod off (*Inf.*), take forty winks (*Inf.*) 2. *n.* catnap, doze, forty winks (*Inf.*), kip (*Brit. sl.*), nap, siesta

snub 1. *v.* cold-shoulder, cut (*Inf.*), cut dead (*Inf.*), give (someone) the brush-off (*Sl.*), give (someone) the cold shoulder, humble, humiliate, mortify, rebuff,

shame, slight 2. *n.* affront, brush-off (*Sl.*), humiliation, insult, put-down, slap in the face

snug comfortable, comfy (*Inf.*), cosy, homely, intimate, sheltered, warm

soak *v.* bathe, damp, drench, immerse, infuse, marinate (*Cookery*), moisten, penetrate, permeate, saturate, steep, wet

soaking drenched, dripping, drookit (*Scot.*), saturated, soaked, soaked to the skin, sodden, sopping, streaming, waterlogged, wet through, wringing wet

sob *v.* bawl, blubber, boohoo, cry, greet (*Dialect*), howl, shed tears, snivel, weep

sober *adj.* 1. abstemious, abstinent, moderate, on the wagon (*Inf.*), temperate 2. calm, clear-headed, cold, composed, cool, dispassionate, grave, level-headed, lucid, peaceful, practical, rational, realistic, reasonable, sedate, serene, serious, solemn, sound, staid, steady, unexcited, unruffled 3. dark, drab, plain, quiet, severe, sombre, subdued
Antonyms *adj.* (*sense 1*) drunk, fu' (*Scot.*), guttered (*Sl.*), neon too many, inebriated, intoxicated, merry (*Brit. inf.*), pie-eyed (*Sl.*), pissed (*Sl.*), plastered, sloshed (*Sl.*), tiddly (*Sl.*), tight (*Sl.*), tipsy, tired and emotional (*Euphemistic*) (*senses 2 & 3*) bright, excessive, flamboyant, flashy, frivolous, garish, gaudy, giddy, happy, immoderate, imprudent, injudicious, irrational, light, light-hearted, lively, sensational, unrealistic

sociable accessible, affable, approachable, companionable, conversable, convivial, cordial, familiar, friendly, genial, gregarious, neighbourly, outgoing, social, warm
Antonyms antisocial, boorish, businesslike, cold, distant, formal, introverted, reclusive, standoffish, stiff, tense, uncommunicative, unfriendly, unsociable, withdrawn

social 1. *adj.* collective, common, communal, community, general, group, organized, public, societal **2.** *n.* do (*Inf.*), gathering, get-together (*Inf.*), party

society 1. civilization, culture, humanity, mankind, people, population, social order, the community, the general public, the public, the world at large **2.** camaraderie, companionship, company, fellowship, friendship **3.** association, brotherhood, circle, club, corporation, fellowship, fraternity, group, guild, institute, league, organization, sisterhood, union **4.** beau monde, elite, gentry, *haut monde*, high society, polite society, the country set, the nobs (*Sl.*), the smart set, the swells (*Inf.*), the toffs (*Brit. sl.*), the top drawer, upper classes, upper crust (*Inf.*)

soft 1. creamy, cushioned, cushiony, doughy, elastic, gelatinous, pulpy, quaggy, spongy, squashy, swampy, yielding **2.** bendable, ductile (*of metals*), elastic, flexible, impressible, malleable, mouldable, plastic, pliable, supple **3.** downy, feathery, fleecy, flowing, fluid, furry, like a baby's bottom (*Inf.*), rounded, silky, smooth, velvety **4.** balmy, bland, caressing, delicate, diffuse, dim, dimmed, dulcet, faint, gentle, light, low, mellifluous, mellow, melodious, mild, murmured, muted, pale, pastel, pleasing, quiet, restful, shaded, soft-toned, soothing, subdued, sweet, temperate, twilight, understated, whispered **5.** compassionate, gentle, kind, pitying, sensitive, sentimental, sympathetic, tender, tenderhearted **6.** effeminate, flabby, flaccid, limp, namby-pamby, out of condition, out of training, overindulged, pampered, podgy, weak
Antonyms (*senses 1, 2 & 3*) abrasive, coarse, firm, grating, hard, inflexible, irritating, rigid, rough, solid, stiff, tough, unyielding (*sense 4*) bright, garish, gaudy,

glaring, hard, harsh, loud, noisy, strident, unpleasant

soften abate, allay, alleviate, appease, assuage, calm, cushion, diminish, ease, lessen, lighten, lower, melt, mitigate, moderate, modify, mollify, muffle, palliate, quell, relax, soothe, still, subdue, temper, tone down, turn down

soil[1] *n.* clay, dirt, dust, earth, ground, loam

soil[2] *v.* bedraggle, befoul, begrime, besmirch, defile, dirty, foul, maculate (*Literary*), muddy, pollute, smear, spatter, spot, stain, sully, tarnish

soldier enlisted man (*U.S.*), fighter, GI (*U.S. inf.*), man-at-arms, military man, redcoat, serviceman, squaddy (*Brit. inf.*), Tommy (*Brit.*), trooper, warrior

sole alone, exclusive, individual, one, one and only, only, single, singular, solitary

solemn 1. earnest, glum, grave, portentous, sedate, serious, sober, staid, thoughtful **2.** august, awe-inspiring, ceremonial, ceremonious, dignified, formal, grand, grave, imposing, impressive, majestic, momentous, stately
Antonyms bright, cheerful, comical, frivolous, happy, informal, jovial, light-hearted, merry, relaxed, unceremonious

solid *adj.* **1.** compact, concrete, dense, firm, hard, massed, stable, strong, sturdy, substantial, unshakable **2.** genuine, good, pure, real, reliable, sound **3.** constant, decent, dependable, estimable, law-abiding, level-headed, reliable, sensible, serious, sober, trusty, upright, upstanding, worthy
Antonyms (*sense 1*) broken, crumbling, decaying, flimsy, gaseous, hollow, liquid, permeable, precarious, shaky, unstable, unsteady, unsubstantial (*sense 2*) impure, unreliable, unsound (*sense 3*) flighty, irresponsible, unreliable, unsound, unstable, unsteady

solidarity accord, camaraderie, cohesion, community of interest, concordance, esprit de corps, harmony, like-mindedness, singleness of purpose, soundness, stability, team spirit, unanimity, unification, unity

solidify cake, coagulate, cohere, congeal, harden, jell, set

solitary adj. **1.** desolate, hidden, isolated, lonely, out-of-the-way, remote, retired, secluded, sequestered, unfrequented, unvisited **2.** alone, lone, single, sole **3.** cloistered, companionless, friendless, hermitical, lonely, lonesome, reclusive, unsociable, unsocial

Antonyms adj. (sense 1) bustling, busy, frequented, public, well-frequented (senses 2 & 3) companionable, convivial, cordial, gregarious, one of a group, outgoing, sociable, social

solitude isolation, loneliness, privacy, reclusiveness, retirement, seclusion

solution 1. answer, clarification, elucidation, explanation, explication, key, resolution, result, solving, unfolding, unravelling **2.** blend, compound, emulsion, mix, mixture, solvent, suspension (Chem.)

solve answer, clarify, clear up, crack, decipher, disentangle, elucidate, explain, expound, get to the bottom of, interpret, resolve, unfold, unravel, work out

sombre dark, dim, dismal, doleful, drab, dull, dusky, funereal, gloomy, grave, joyless, lugubrious, melancholy, mournful, obscure, sad, sepulchral, shadowy, shady, sober

somebody n. big noise (Brit. sl.), big shot (Sl.), big wheel (Sl.), bigwig (Sl.), celeb (Inf.), celebrity, dignitary, heavyweight (Inf.), household name, luminary, name, notable, personage, person of note, public figure, star, superstar, V.I.P.

Antonyms also-ran, cipher,

lightweight (Inf.), menial, nobody, nonentity, nothing (Inf.)

sometimes at times, every now and then, every so often, from time to time, now and again, now and then, occasionally, off and on, once in a while, on occasion

Antonyms always, consistently, constantly, continually, eternally, ever, everlastingly, evermore, forever, invariably, perpetually, unceasingly, without exception

soon anon (Archaic), any minute now, before long, betimes (Archaic), in a little while, in a minute, in a short time, in the near future, shortly

soothe allay, alleviate, appease, assuage, calm, calm down, compose, ease, hush, lull, mitigate, mollify, pacify, quiet, relieve, settle, smooth down, soften, still, tranquillize

Antonyms aggravate, agitate, annoy, disquiet, disturb, exacerbate, excite, increase, inflame, irritate, rouse, stimulate, upset, vex, worry

sophisticated 1. blasé, citified, cosmopolitan, cultivated, cultured, jet-set, refined, seasoned, urbane, worldly, worldly-wise, world-weary **2.** advanced, complex, complicated, delicate, elaborate, highly-developed, intricate, multifaceted, refined, subtle

Antonyms basic, naive, old-fashioned, plain, primitive, simple, uncomplicated, unrefined, unsophisticated, unsubtle, unworldly

soporific 1. adj. hypnotic, sedative, sleep-inducing, sleepy, somniferous (Rare), somnolent, tranquillizing **2.** n. anaesthetic, hypnotic, narcotic, opiate, sedative, tranquillizer

sorcerer enchanter, mage (Archaic), magician, magus, necromancer, sorceress, warlock, witch, wizard

sordid 1. dirty, filthy, foul, mean, seamy, seedy, sleazy, slovenly, slummy, squalid, unclean, wretched 2. backstreet, base, debauched, degenerate, degraded, despicable, disreputable, low, shabby, shameful, vicious, vile 3. avaricious, corrupt, covetous, grasping, mercenary, miserly, niggardly, selfish, self-seeking, ungenerous, venal

Antonyms blameless, clean, decent, fresh, honourable, noble, pure, spotless, unblemished, undefiled, unsullied, upright

sore adj. 1. angry, burning, chafed, inflamed, irritated, painful, raw, reddened, sensitive, smarting, tender 2. annoying, distressing, grievous, harrowing, severe, sharp, troublesome 3. acute, critical, desperate, dire, extreme, pressing, urgent 4. afflicted, aggrieved, angry, annoyed, grieved, hurt, irked, irritated, pained, peeved (Inf.), resentful, stung, upset, vexed

sorrow 1. n. affliction, anguish, distress, grief, heartache, heartbreak, misery, mourning, regret, sadness, unhappiness, woe 2. v. agonize, bemoan, be sad, bewail, grieve, lament, moan, mourn, weep

Antonyms n. bliss, delight, elation, exaltation, exultation, gladness, happiness, joy, pleasure ~v. celebrate, delight, exult, jump for joy, rejoice, revel

sorrowful affecting, afflicted, dejected, depressed, disconsolate, distressing, doleful, grievous, heartbroken, heart-rending, heavy-hearted, lamentable, lugubrious, melancholy, miserable, mournful, painful, piteous, rueful, sad, sick at heart, sorry, tearful, unhappy, woebegone, woeful, wretched

sorry 1. apologetic, conscience-stricken, contrite, guilt-ridden, in sackcloth and ashes, penitent, regretful, remorseful, repentant, self-reproachful, shamefaced 2. disconsolate, distressed, grieved, melancholy, mournful, sad, sorrowful, unhappy 3. commiserative, compassionate, full of pity,

moved, pitying, sympathetic 4. abject, base, deplorable, dismal, distressing, mean, miserable, paltry, pathetic, piteous, pitiable, pitiful, poor, sad, shabby, vile, wretched

Antonyms (sense 1) impenitent, not contrite, shameless, unapologetic, unashamed, unremorseful, unrepentant (sense 2) cheerful, delighted, elated, happy, joyful (sense 3) compassionless (Rare), heartless, indifferent, uncompassionate, unconcerned, unmoved, unpitying, unsympathetic

sort 1. n. brand, breed, category, character, class, denomination, description, family, genus, group, ilk, kind, make, nature, order, quality, race, species, stamp, style, type, variety 2. v. arrange, assort, catalogue, categorize, choose, class, classify, distribute, divide, file, grade, group, order, put in order, rank, select, separate, systematize

sort out 1. clarify, clear up, organize, put or get straight, resolve, tidy up 2. pick out, put on one side, segregate, select, separate, sift

soul 1. animating principle, essence, intellect, life, mind, psyche, reason, spirit, vital force 2. being, body, creature, individual, man, mortal, person, woman 3. embodiment, essence, incarnation, personification, quintessence, type

sound¹ n. 1. din, noise, report, resonance, reverberation, tone, voice 2. drift, idea, implication(s), impression, look, tenor 3. earshot, hearing, range ~v. 4. echo, resonate, resound, reverberate 5. appear, give the impression of, look, seem, strike one as being 6. announce, articulate, declare, enunciate, express, pronounce, signal, utter

sound² adj. 1. complete, entire, firm, fit, hale, hale and hearty, healthy, intact, perfect, robust, solid, sturdy, substantial, undamaged, unhurt, unimpaired, unin-

jured, vigorous, well-constructed, whole **2.** correct, fair, just, level-headed, logical, orthodox, proper, prudent, rational, reasonable, reliable, responsible, right, right-thinking, sensible, true, trustworthy, valid, well-founded, well-grounded, wise **3.** established, orthodox, proven, recognized, reliable, reputable, safe, secure, solid, solvent, stable, tried-and-true **4.** deep, peaceful, unbroken, undisturbed, untroubled
Antonyms (*sense 1*) ailing, damaged, flimsy, frail, light, shaky, sketchy, superficial, unbalanced, unstable, weak (*senses 2 & 3*) fallacious, faulty, flawed, incompetent, irrational, irresponsible, specious, unreliable, unsound, unstable (*sense 4*) broken, fitful, shallow, troubled

sound³ *v.* fathom, plumb, probe

sour *adj.* **1.** acetic, acid, acidulated, bitter, pungent, sharp, tart, unpleasant **2.** acrid, acrimonious, churlish, crabbed, cynical, disagreeable, discontented, embittered, grouchy (*Inf.*), grudging, ill-natured, ill-tempered, jaundiced, peevish, tart, ungenerous, waspish
Antonyms *adj.* (*sense 1*) agreeable, bland, mild, pleasant, savoury, sugary, sweet (*sense 2*) affable, amiable, friendly, genial, good-humoured, good-natured, good-tempered, pleasant, warm-hearted

source 1. author, begetter, beginning, cause, commencement, derivation, fountainhead, origin, originator, rise, spring, wellspring **2.** authority, informant

souvenir keepsake, memento, relic, remembrancer (*Archaic*), reminder, token

sovereign 1. *n.* chief, emperor, empress, king, monarch, potentate, prince, queen, ruler, shah, supreme ruler, tsar **2.** *adj.* absolute, chief, dominant, imperial, kingly, monarchal, paramount, predominant, principal, queenly, regal, royal, ruling, supreme, unlimited

sow broadcast, disseminate, implant, inseminate, lodge, plant, scatter, seed

space 1. amplitude, capacity, elbowroom, expanse, extension, extent, leeway, margin, play, room, scope, spaciousness, volume **2.** blank, distance, gap, interval, lacuna, omission **3.** duration, interval, period, span, time, while

spacious ample, broad, capacious, comfortable, commodious, expansive, extensive, huge, large, roomy, sizable, uncrowded, vast
Antonyms close, confined, cramped, crowded, limited, narrow, poky, restricted, small

span *n.* **1.** amount, distance, extent, length, reach, spread, stretch **2.** duration, period, spell, term ~ *v.* **3.** arch across, bridge, cover, cross, extend across, link, range over, traverse, vault

spank *v.* belt (*Sl.*), cuff, give (someone) a hiding (*Inf.*), put (someone) over one's knee, slap, slipper (*Inf.*), smack, tan (*Sl.*), wallop (*Inf.*), whack (*Inf.*)

spare *adj.* **1.** additional, emergency, extra, free, going begging (*Inf.*), in excess, in reserve, leftover, odd, over, superfluous, supernumerary, surplus, unoccupied, unused, unwanted **2.** gaunt, lank, lean, meagre, slender, slight, slim, wiry **3.** economical, frugal, meagre, modest, scanty, sparing ~ *v.* **4.** afford, allow, bestow, dispense with, do without, give, grant, let (someone) have, manage without, part with, relinquish **5.** be merciful to, deal leniently with, go easy on (*Inf.*), have mercy on, leave, let off (*Inf.*), pardon, refrain from, release, relieve from, save from
Antonyms *adj.* (*sense 1*) allocated, designated, earmarked, in use, necessary, needed, set aside, spoken for (*sense 2*) corpulent, fat, flabby, fleshy, generous,

heavy, large, plump ~v. (*sense* 5) afflict, condemn, damn, destroy, hurt, punish, show no mercy to

sparing careful, chary, cost-conscious, economical, frugal, money-conscious, prudent, saving, thrifty

spark n. 1. flare, flash, flicker, gleam, glint, scintillation, spit 2. atom, hint, jot, scintilla, scrap, trace, vestige

sparkle v. 1. beam, coruscate, dance, flash, gleam, glint, glisten, glister (*Archaic*), glitter, glow, scintillate, shimmer, shine, spark, twinkle, wink 2. bubble, effervesce, fizz, fizzle ~n. 3. brilliance, coruscation, dazzle, flash, flicker, gleam, glint, radiance, spark, twinkle 4. animation, dash, élan, gaiety, life, panache, spirit, vim (*Sl.*), vitality, vivacity, zip (*Inf.*)

spasm 1. contraction, convulsion, paroxysm, throe (*Rare*), twitch 2. access, burst, eruption, fit, frenzy, outburst, seizure

speak 1. articulate, communicate, converse, discourse, enunciate, express, make known, pronounce, say, state, talk, tell, utter, voice 2. address, argue, declaim, deliver an address, descant, discourse, harangue, hold forth, lecture, plead, speechify, spiel (*Inf.*)

speaker lecturer, mouthpiece, orator, public speaker, spieler (*Inf.*), spokesman, spokesperson, spokeswoman, word-spinner

special 1. distinguished, especial, exceptional, extraordinary, festive, gala, important, memorable, momentous, out of the ordinary, red-letter, significant, uncommon, unique, unusual 2. appropriate, certain, characteristic, distinctive, especial, individual, particular, peculiar, precise, specialized, specific 3. chief, main, major, particular, primary **Antonyms** common, everyday, general, humdrum, mediocre, multi-purpose, normal, ordinary, routine, run-of-the-mill, undistinctive, undistinguished, unexceptional, unspecialized, usual

species breed, category, class, collection, description, genus, group, kind, sort, type, variety

specific adj. 1. clear-cut, definite, exact, explicit, express, limited, particular, precise, unambiguous, unequivocal 2. characteristic, distinguishing, especial, peculiar, special **Antonyms** approximate, common, general, hazy, imprecise, non-specific, uncertain, unclear, vague, woolly

specify be specific about, cite, define, designate, detail, enumerate, indicate, individualize, itemize, mention, name, particularize, spell out, stipulate

specimen copy, embodiment, example, exemplar, exemplification, exhibit, individual, instance, model, pattern, proof, representative, sample, type

speckled brindled, dappled, dotted, flecked, freckled, mottled, speckledy, spotted, spotty, sprinkled, stippled

spectacle 1. display, event, exhibition, extravaganza, pageant, parade, performance, show, sight 2. curiosity, laughing stock, marvel, phenomenon, scene, sight, wonder

spectacular adj. breathtaking, daring, dazzling, dramatic, eyecatching, fantastic (*Inf.*), grand, impressive, magnificent, marked, remarkable, sensational, splendid, staggering, striking, stunning (*Inf.*)

spectator beholder, bystander, eyewitness, looker-on, observer, onlooker, viewer, watcher, witness **Antonyms** contestant, contributor, partaker, participant, participator, party, player

speculate 1. cogitate, conjecture, consider, contemplate, deliberate, hypothesize, meditate, muse, scheme, suppose, surmise, theorize, wonder 2. gamble, have a flutter (*Inf.*), hazard, play the market, risk, take a chance with, venture

speech 1. communication, conversation, dialogue, discussion, intercourse, talk **2.** address, discourse, disquisition, harangue, homily, lecture, oration, spiel (*Inf.*)

speechless 1. dumb, inarticulate, mum, mute, silent, tongue-tied, unable to get a word out (*Inf.*), wordless **2.** *Fig.* aghast, amazed, astounded, dazed, dumbfounded, dumbstruck, shocked, thunderstruck

speed *n.* **1.** acceleration, celerity, expedition, fleetness, haste, hurry, momentum, pace, precipitation, quickness, rapidity, rush, swiftness, velocity ~*v.* **2.** belt (along) (*Sl.*), bomb (along), bowl along, career, dispatch, exceed the speed limit, expedite, flash, gallop, get a move on (*Inf.*), go hell for leather (*Inf.*), go like a bat out of hell (*Inf.*), go like the wind, hasten, hurry, lose no time, make haste, press on, put one's foot down (*Inf.*), quicken, race, rush, sprint, step on it (*Inf.*), tear, urge, zoom **3.** advance, aid, assist, boost, expedite, facilitate, further, help, impel, promote
Antonyms *n.* delay, slowness, sluggishness, tardiness ~*v.* crawl, creep, dawdle, delay, hamper, hinder, hold up, retard, slow, take one's time, tarry

speedy expeditious, express, fast, fleet, fleet of foot, hasty, headlong, hurried, immediate, nimble, precipitate, prompt, quick, rapid, summary, swift, winged
Antonyms dead slow and stop, delayed, dilatory, late, leisurely, lingering, long-drawn-out, plodding, slow, sluggish, tardy, unhurried, unrushed

spell¹ *n.* bout, course, interval, patch, period, season, stint, stretch, term, time, tour of duty, turn

spell² *n.* abracadabra, charm, conjuration, exorcism, incantation, sorcery, witchery

spend 1. disburse, expend, fork out (*Inf.*), lay out, pay out, shell out (*Inf.*), splash out (*Brit. inf.*) **2.** blow (*Sl.*), consume, deplete, dispense, dissipate, drain, empty, exhaust, fritter away, run through, squander, use up, waste **3.** fill, occupy, pass, while away
Antonyms (*senses 1 & 2*) hoard, invest, keep, put aside, put by, save, store

sphere 1. ball, circle, globe, globule, orb **2.** capacity, compass, department, domain, employment, field, function, pale, province, range, rank, realm, scope, station, stratum, territory, walk of life

spherical globe-shaped, globular, orbicular, rotund, round

spice *n.* **1.** relish, savour, seasoning **2.** colour, excitement, gusto, kick (*Inf.*), pep, piquancy, tang, zap (*Sl.*), zest, zip (*Inf.*)

spike 1. *n.* barb, point, prong, spine **2.** *v.* impale, spear, spit, stick

spill *v.* discharge, disgorge, overflow, overturn, scatter, shed, slop over, spill *or* run over, throw off, upset

spin *v.* **1.** birl (*Scot.*), gyrate, pirouette, reel, revolve, rotate, turn, twirl, twist, wheel, whirl **2.** be giddy, be in a whirl, grow dizzy, reel, swim, whirl ~ *n.* **3.** gyration, revolution, roll, twist, whirl

spiral 1. *adj.* circular, cochlear, cochleate (*Biol.*), coiled, corkscrew, helical, scrolled, voluted, whorled, winding **2.** *n.* coil, corkscrew, curlicue, gyre (*Literary*), helix, screw, volute, whorl

spirit *n.* **1.** air, breath, life, life force, psyche, soul, vital spark **2.** attitude, character, complexion, disposition, essence, humour, outlook, quality, temper, temperament **3.** animation, ardour, backbone, courage, dauntlessness, earnestness, energy, enterprise, enthusiasm, fire, force, gameness, grit, guts (*Inf.*), life, liveliness, mettle, resolution, sparkle, spunk (*Inf.*), stout~ heartedness, vigour, warmth, zest **4.** motivation, resolution, re~ solve, will, willpower **5.** atmos~ phere, feeling, gist, humour, te~ nor, tone **6.** essence, intent, in~ tention, meaning, purport, pur~ pose, sense, substance **7.** *Plural* feelings, frame of mind, humour, mood, morale **8.** apparition, ghost, phantom, shade (*Literary*), shadow, spectre, spook (*Inf.*), sprite, vision

spiritual devotional, divine, ethe~ real, ghostly, holy, immaterial, incorporeal, nonmaterial, other~ worldly, pure, religious, sacred **Antonyms** concrete, corporeal, material, nonspiritual, palpable, physical, substantial, tangible

spit 1. *v.* discharge, eject, expec~ torate, hiss, spew, splutter, sput~ ter, throw out **2.** *n.* dribble, drool, saliva, slaver, spittle, sputum

spite *n.* **1.** animosity, bitchiness (*Sl.*), gall, grudge, hate, hatred, ill will, malevolence, malice, ma~ lignity, pique, rancour, spiteful~ ness, spleen, venom **2. in spite of** despite, in defiance of, notwith~ standing, regardless of

spiteful barbed, bitchy (*Inf.*), catty (*Inf.*), cruel, ill-disposed, ill-natured, malevolent, malicious, malignant, nasty, rancorous, snide, splenetic, venomous, vin~ dictive

splash *v.* **1.** bespatter, shower, slop, slosh (*Inf.*), spatter, splodge, spray, spread, sprinkle, squirt, strew, wet **2.** bathe, dabble, pad~ dle, plunge, wade, wallow **3.** bat~ ter, break, buffet, dash, plash, plop, smack, strike, surge, wash **4.** blazon, broadcast, flaunt, headline, plaster, publicize, tout, trumpet ~*n.* **5.** burst, dash, patch, spattering, splodge, touch **6.** *Inf.* display, effect, impact, sensation, splurge, stir

splendid 1. admirable, brilliant, exceptional, glorious, grand, he~ roic, illustrious, magnificent, outstanding, rare, remarkable, renowned, resplendent, sterling, su~ perb, supreme **2.** costly, dazzling, gorgeous, imposing, impressive, lavish, luxurious, magnificent, ornate, resplendent, rich, sump~ tuous, superb **3.** excellent, fan~ tastic (*Inf.*), fine, first-class, glo~ rious, great (*Inf.*), marvellous, wonderful **4.** beaming, bright, brilliant, glittering, glowing, lus~ trous, radiant, refulgent **Antonyms** beggarly, depressing, disgusting, distressed, drab, dull, ignoble, ignominious, lacklustre, low, mean, mediocre, miserable, ordinary, pathetic, plain, poor, poverty-stricken, rotten, run-of-the-mill, sombre, sordid, squalid, tarnished, tawdry, undistin~ guished, unexceptional

splendour brightness, brilliance, ceremony, dazzle, display, efful~ gence, glory, gorgeousness, grandeur, lustre, magnificence, majesty, pomp, radiance, reful~ gence, renown, resplendence, richness, show, solemnity, spec~ tacle, stateliness, sumptuousness

splinter 1. *n.* chip, flake, frag~ ment, needle, paring, shaving, sliver **2.** *v.* break into smither~ eens, disintegrate, fracture, shatter, shiver, split

split *v.* **1.** bifurcate, branch, break, break up, burst, cleave, come apart, come undone, crack, disband, disunite, diverge, fork, gape, give way, go separate ways, open, part, pull apart, rend, rip, separate, slash, slit, snap, splinter **2.** allocate, allot, appor~ tion, carve up, distribute, divide, divvy up (*Inf.*), dole out, halve, parcel out, partition, share out, slice up ~*n.* **3.** breach, crack, damage, division, fissure, gap, rent, rip, separation, slash, slit, tear **4.** breach, break, break-up, difference, discord, disruption, dissension, disunion, divergence, division, estrangement, partition, rift, rupture, schism ~*adj.* **5.** ambivalent, bisected, broken, cleft, cracked, divided, dual, fractured, ruptured, twofold

split up break up, disband, divorce, go separate ways, part, part company, separate

spoil v. 1. blemish, damage, debase, deface, destroy, disfigure, harm, impair, injure, mar, mess up, ruin, upset, wreck 2. baby, cocker (*Rare*), coddle, cosset, indulge, kill with kindness, mollycoddle, overindulge, pamper, spoon-feed 3. addle, become tainted, curdle, decay, decompose, go bad, go off (*Brit. inf.*), mildew, putrefy, rot, turn
Antonyms (*sense 1*) augment, conserve, enhance, improve, keep, preserve, save (*sense 2*) be strict with, deprive, ignore, pay no attention to, treat harshly

spoken expressed, oral, phonetic, put into words, said, told, unwritten, uttered, verbal, viva voce, voiced, by word of mouth

sponsor 1. n. angel (*Inf.*), backer, godparent, guarantor, patron, promoter 2. v. back, finance, fund, guarantee, lend one's name to, patronize, promote, put up the money for, subsidize

spontaneous extempore, free, impromptu, impulsive, instinctive, natural, unbidden, uncompelled, unconstrained, unforced, unpremeditated, unprompted, voluntary, willing
Antonyms arranged, calculated, contrived, deliberate, forced, mannered, orchestrated, planned, prearranged, premeditated, preplanned, stage-managed, studied

sport n. 1. amusement, diversion, entertainment, exercise, game, pastime, physical activity, play, recreation 2. badinage, banter, frolic, fun, jest, joking, kidding (*Inf.*), merriment, mirth, raillery, teasing 3. buffoon, butt, derision, fair game, game, laughing stock, mockery, plaything, ridicule ~v. 4. *Inf.* display, exhibit, show off, wear

spot n. 1. blemish, blot, blotch,

daub, discoloration, flaw, mark, pimple, plook (*Scot.*), pustule, smudge, speck, stain, taint, zit (*U.S. sl.*) 2. locality, location, place, point, position, scene, site, situation 3. *Inf.* difficulty, mess, plight, predicament, quandary, trouble ~v. 4. catch sight of, descry, detect, discern, espy, identify, make out, observe, pick out, recognize, see, sight 5. besmirch, blot, dirty, dot, fleck, mark, mottle, soil, spatter, speckle, splodge, splotch, stain, sully, taint, tarnish

spotted dappled, dotted, flecked, mottled, pied, polka-dot, specked, speckled

spouse better half (*Inf.*), companion, consort, helpmate, husband, mate, partner, wife

spout v. discharge, emit, erupt, gush, jet, shoot, spray, spurt, squirt, stream, surge

sprawl v. flop, loll, lounge, ramble, slouch, slump, spread, straggle, trail

spray v. 1. atomize, diffuse, scatter, shower, sprinkle ~n. 2. drizzle, droplets, fine mist, moisture, spindrift, spoondrift 3. aerosol, atomizer, sprinkler

spread v. 1. be displayed, bloat, broaden, dilate, expand, extend, fan out, open, open out, sprawl, stretch, swell, unfold, unfurl, unroll, widen 2. escalate, multiply, mushroom, proliferate ~n. 3. advance, advancement, development, diffusion, dispersion, dissemination, escalation, expansion, increase, proliferation, spreading, suffusion, transmission 4. compass, extent, period, reach, span, stretch, sweep, term

spree bacchanalia, bender (*Inf.*), binge (*Inf.*), carouse, debauch, fling, jag (*Sl.*), junketing, orgy, revel, splurge

sprightly active, agile, airy, alert, animated, blithe, brisk, cheerful, energetic, frolicsome, gay, jaunty, joyous, lively, nimble, perky, playful, spirited, sportive, spry, vivacious

spring v. 1. bounce, bound, hop, jump, leap, rebound, recoil, vault 2. *Often with* **from** arise, be derived, be descended, come, derive, descend, emanate, emerge, grow, issue, originate, proceed, start, stem 3. *With* **up** appear, burgeon, come into existence *or* being, develop, mushroom, shoot up ~n. 4. bound, buck, hop, jump, leap, saltation, vault 5. bounce, bounciness, buoyancy, elasticity, flexibility, give (*Inf.*), recoil, resilience, springiness 6. beginning, cause, fountainhead, origin, root, source, well, wellspring

sprinkle v. dredge, dust, pepper, powder, scatter, shower, spray, strew

sprout v. bud, develop, germinate, grow, push, shoot, spring, vegetate

spur v. 1. animate, drive, goad, impel, incite, press, prick, prod, prompt, stimulate, urge ~n. 2. goad, prick, rowel 3. impetus, impulse, incentive, incitement, inducement, motive, stimulus

spurious artificial, bogus, contrived, counterfeit, deceitful, fake, false, feigned, forged, imitation, mock, phoney (*Sl.*), pretended, pseudo (*Inf.*), sham, simulated, specious, unauthentic

spurn cold-shoulder, contemn, despise, disdain, disregard, rebuff, reject, repulse, scorn, slight, snub, turn one's nose up at (*Inf.*)
Antonyms embrace, grasp, seize, take up, welcome

spy 1. *n.* double agent, fifth columnist, foreign agent, mole, secret agent, secret service agent, undercover agent 2. *v.* catch sight of, descry, espy, glimpse, notice, observe, set eyes on, spot

squabble 1. *v.* argue, bicker, brawl, clash, dispute, fall out (*Inf.*), fight, have words, quarrel, row, scrap (*Inf.*), wrangle 2. *n.* argument, barney (*Inf.*), difference of opinion, disagreement, dispute, fight, row, scrap (*Inf.*), set-to (*Inf.*), spat, tiff

squad band, company, crew, force, gang, group, team, troop

squalid broken-down, decayed, dirty, disgusting, fetid, filthy, foul, low, nasty, poverty-stricken, repulsive, run-down, seedy, sleazy, slovenly, slummy, sordid, unclean

squalor decay, filth, foulness, meanness, sleaziness, slumminess, squalidness, wretchedness

squander be prodigal with, blow (*Sl.*), consume, dissipate, expend, fritter away, frivol away, lavish, misspend, misuse, run through, scatter, spend, spend like water, throw away, waste
Antonyms be frugal, be thrifty, economize, keep, put aside for a rainy day, save, store

square adj. 1. aboveboard, decent, equitable, ethical, fair, fair and square, genuine, honest, just, on the level (*Inf.*), straight, straightforward, upright 2. *Inf.* behind the times (*Inf.*), bourgeois, conservative, conventional, old-fashioned, out of date, straight (*Sl.*), strait-laced, stuffy ~n. 3. *Inf.* antediluvian, back number (*Inf.*), conservative, diehard, fuddy-duddy (*Inf.*), old buffer (*Brit. inf.*), (old) fogy, stick-in-the-mud (*Inf.*), traditionalist

squash v. 1. compress, crush, distort, flatten, mash, pound, press, pulp, smash, stamp on, trample down 2. annihilate, crush, humiliate, put down (*Sl.*), put (someone) in his (*or* her) place, quash, quell, silence, sit on (*Inf.*), suppress

squeak v. peep, pipe, shrill, squeal, whine, yelp

squeal 1. *n.* scream, screech, shriek, wail, yell, yelp, yowl 2. *v.* scream, screech, shout, shriek, shrill, wail, yelp

squeamish 1. delicate, fastidious, finicky, nice (*Rare*), particular, prissy (*Inf.*), prudish, punctilious, scrupulous, strait-laced 2. nauseous, qualmish, queasy, queer, sick, sickish

squeeze v. 1. clutch, compress,

crush, grip, nip, pinch, press, squash, wring **2.** cram, crowd, force, jam, jostle, pack, press, ram, stuff, thrust, wedge **3.** clasp, cuddle, embrace, enfold, hold tight, hug **4.** bleed (*Inf.*), bring pressure to bear on, extort, lean on (*Inf.*), milk, oppress, pressurize, put the screws on (*Inf.*), put the squeeze on (*Inf.*), wrest ~*n.* **5.** clasp, embrace, handclasp, hold, hug **6.** congestion, crowd, crush, jam, press, squash

stab *v.* **1.** bayonet, cut, gore, injure, jab, knife, pierce, puncture, run through, spear, stick, thrust, transfix, wound ~*n.* **2.** gash, incision, jab, puncture, rent, thrust, wound **3.** ache, pang, prick, twinge

stable abiding, constant, deep-rooted, durable, enduring, established, fast, firm, fixed, immutable, invariable, lasting, permanent, reliable, secure, sound, steadfast, steady, strong, sturdy, sure, unalterable, unchangeable, unwavering, well-founded

Antonyms changeable, deteriorating, erratic, excitable, fickle, frail, inconstant, insecure, irresolute, mercurial, mutable, over-emotional, shaky, shifting, uncertain, unpredictable, unreliable, unstable, unsteady, variable, volatile, wavering

stack 1. *n.* clamp (*Brit. agriculture*), cock, heap, hoard, load, mass, mound, mountain, pile **2.** *v.* accumulate, amass, assemble, bank up, heap up, load, pile, stockpile

staff *n.* **1.** employees, lecturers, officers, organization, personnel, teachers, team, · workers, work force **2.** cane, pole, prop, rod, stave, wand

stage *n.* division, juncture, lap, leg, length, level, period, phase, point, step

stagger *v.* **1.** falter, hesitate, lurch, reel, sway, teeter, totter, vacillate, waver, wobble **2.** amaze, astonish, astound, bowl over (*Inf.*), confound, dumbfound,

flabbergast, give (someone) a shock, nonplus, overwhelm, shake, shock, strike (someone) dumb (*Inf.*), stun, stupefy, surprise, take (someone) aback, take (someone's) breath away, throw off balance **3.** alternate, overlap, step, zigzag

stagnant brackish, motionless, quiet, sluggish, stale, standing, still

Antonyms active, clear, flowing, fresh, lively, moving, pure, running, thriving, unpolluted

stagnate decay, decline, deteriorate, fester, go to seed, idle, languish, lie fallow, rot, rust, stand still, vegetate

staid calm, composed, decorous, demure, grave, quiet, sedate, self-restrained, serious, sober, solemn, steady

Antonyms adventurous, capricious, demonstrative, exuberant, flighty, giddy, indecorous, lively, rowdy, sportive, wild

stain *v.* **1.** blemish, blot, colour, dirty, discolour, dye, mark, soil, spot, tarnish, tinge **2.** besmirch, blacken, contaminate, corrupt, defile, deprave, disgrace, drag through the mud, sully, taint ~*n.* **3.** blemish, blot, discoloration, dye, spot, tint **4.** blemish, blot on the escutcheon, disgrace, dishonour, infamy, reproach, shame, slur, stigma

stale decayed, dry, faded, fetid, flat, fusty, hard, insipid, musty, old, sour, stagnant, tasteless

Antonyms crisp, fresh, new, refreshing

stalk *v.* creep up on, follow, haunt, hunt, pursue, shadow, tail (*Inf.*), track

stamina energy, force, grit (*Inf.*), indefatigability, lustiness, power, power of endurance, resilience, resistance, staying power, strength, vigour

stammer *v.* falter, hem and haw, hesitate, pause, splutter, stumble, stutter

stamp *v.* **1.** beat, crush, trample **2.** engrave, fix, impress, imprint,

inscribe, mark, mould, print ~n.
3. brand, cast, earmark, hallmark, imprint, mark, mould, signature 4. breed, cast, character, cut, description, fashion, form, kind, sort, type

stampede n. charge, flight, rout, rush, scattering

stamp out crush, destroy, eliminate, eradicate, extinguish, extirpate, put down, put out, quell, quench, scotch, suppress

stance 1. bearing, carriage, deportment, posture 2. attitude, position, stand, standpoint, viewpoint

stand v. 1. be erect, be upright, be vertical, rise 2. erect, mount, place, position, put, rank, set 3. be in force, belong, be situated or located, be valid, continue, exist, halt, hold, obtain, pause, prevail, remain, rest, stay, stop 4. abide, allow, bear, brook, cope with, countenance, endure, experience, handle, put up with (Inf.), stomach, submit to, suffer, support, sustain, take, thole (Dialect), tolerate, undergo, wear (Brit. sl.), weather, withstand ~n. 5. halt, rest, standstill, stay, stop, stopover 6. attitude, determination, firm stand, opinion, position, stance, standpoint

standard 1. n. average, benchmark, canon, criterion, example, gauge, grade, guide, guideline, measure, model, norm, pattern, principle, requirement, rule, sample, specification, touchstone, type, yardstick 2. adj. accepted, average, basic, customary, normal, orthodox, popular, prevailing, regular, set, staple, stock, typical, usual

Antonyms adj. abnormal, atypical, exceptional, extraordinary, irregular, singular, strange, uncommon, unconventional, unusual

standardize assimilate, bring into line, institutionalize, massproduce, regiment, stereotype

stand out attract attention, be highlighted, be prominent (conspicuous, distinct, obvious, striking), be thrown into relief, bulk large, catch the eye, leap to the eye, project, stare one in the face (Inf.), stick out a mile (Inf.)

standpoint angle, point of view, position, post, stance, station, vantage point, viewpoint

stand up for champion, come to the defence of, defend, side with, stick up for (Inf.), support, uphold

star 1. n. celeb (Inf.), celebrity, draw (Inf.), idol, lead, leading man or lady, luminary, main attraction, name 2. adj. brilliant, celebrated, illustrious, leading, major, paramount, principal, prominent, talented, well-known

stare v. gape, gawk, gawp (Brit. sl.), goggle, look, ogle, rubberneck (Sl.), watch

start v. 1. appear, arise, begin, come into being, come into existence, commence, depart, first see the light of day, get on the road, get under way, go ahead (Inf.), hit the road (Inf.), issue, leave, originate, pitch in (Inf.), sally forth, set off, set out 2. activate, embark upon, engender, enter upon, get going, initiate, instigate, kick off (Inf.), make a beginning, open, originate, put one's hand to the plough (Inf.), set about, set in motion, start the ball rolling, take the first step, take the plunge (Inf.), turn on 3. begin, create, establish, father, found, inaugurate, initiate, institute, introduce, launch, lay the foundations of, pioneer, set up 4. blench, flinch, jerk, jump, recoil, shy, twitch ~n. 5. beginning, birth, commencement, dawn, first step(s), foundation, inauguration, inception, initiation, kick-off (Inf.), onset, opening, outset 6. advantage, edge, head start, lead 7. convulsion, jar, jump, spasm, twitch

Antonyms v. (senses 1, 2 & 3) abandon, bring to an end, call it a day (Inf.), cease, conclude, delay, desist, end, finish, give up, put aside, put off, quit, stop, switch off, terminate, turn off, wind up ~*n.* (*sense 5*) cessation, conclusion, dénouement, end, finale, finish, outcome, result, stop, termination, turning off, wind-up

startle agitate, alarm, amaze, astonish, alarm, frighten, give (someone) a turn (*Inf.*), make (someone) jump, scare, shock, surprise, take (someone) aback

starving faint from lack of food, famished, hungering, hungry, ravenous, ready to eat a horse (*Inf.*), sharp-set, starved

state[1] *v.* 1. affirm, articulate, assert, asseverate, aver, declare, enumerate, explain, expound, express, present, propound, put, report, say, specify, voice ~*n.* 2. case, category, circumstances, condition, mode, pass, plight, position, predicament, shape, situation, state of affairs 3. attitude, frame of mind, humour, mood, spirits 4. ceremony, dignity, display, glory, grandeur, majesty, pomp, splendour, style

state[2] *n.* body politic, commonwealth, country, federation, government, kingdom, land, nation, republic, territory

stately august, ceremonious, deliberate, dignified, elegant, grand, imperial, imposing, impressive, lofty, majestic, measured, noble, pompous, regal, royal, solemn

statement account, announcement, communication, communiqué, declaration, explanation, proclamation, recital, relation, report, testimony, utterance

station *n.* 1. base, depot, headquarters, location, place, position, post, seat, situation 2. appointment, business, calling, employment, grade, occupation, position, post, rank, situation, sphere, standing, status ~*v.* 3. assign, establish, fix, garrison, install, locate, post, set

stationary at a standstill, fixed, inert, moored, motionless,

parked, standing, static, stock-still, unmoving

Antonyms changeable, changing, inconstant, mobile, moving, shifting, travelling, unstable, variable, varying, volatile

status condition, consequence, degree, distinction, eminence, grade, position, prestige, rank, standing

stay *v.* 1. abide, continue, delay, establish oneself, halt, hang around (*Inf.*), hover, linger, loiter, pause, put down roots, remain, reside, settle, sojourn, stand, stay put, stop, tarry, wait 2. adjourn, defer, discontinue, hold in abeyance, hold over, prorogue, put off, suspend ~*n.* 3. holiday, sojourn, stop, stopover, visit

Antonyms *v.* (*sense 1*) abandon, depart, exit, go, leave, move on, pass through, quit, withdraw

steadfast constant, dedicated, dependable, established, faithful, fast, firm, fixed, intent, loyal, persevering, reliable, resolute, single-minded, stable, staunch, steady, unfaltering, unflinching, unswerving, unwavering

steady *v.* 1. firm, fixed, immovable, safe, stable, substantial, unchangeable, uniform 2. balanced, calm, dependable, equable, having both feet on the ground, imperturbable, level-headed, reliable, sedate, sensible, serene, serious-minded, settled, sober, staid, steadfast 3. ceaseless, confirmed, consistent, constant, continuous, even, faithful, habitual, incessant, nonstop, persistent, regular, rhythmic, unbroken, unfaltering, unfluctuating, uninterrupted, unremitting, unvarying, unwavering ~*v.* 4. balance, brace, secure, stabilize, support

Antonyms *adj.* careless, changeable, faltering, fickle, fluctuating, half-hearted, inconsistent, infrequent, insecure, intermittent, in two minds, irregular, occasional, sporadic, uncommitted, unconscientious, undependable, unpredictable, unreliable, unsettled, unstable, unsteady, vacillating, wavering ~*v.* agitate, shake, tilt, upset, worry

steal 1. appropriate, be light-fingered, embezzle, filch, half-inch (*Inf.*), heist (*U.S. sl.*), lift (*Inf.*), misappropriate, nick (*Sl.*), peculate, pilfer, pinch (*Inf.*), pirate, plagiarize, poach, prig (*Brit. sl.*), purloin, shoplift, snitch (*Sl.*), swipe (*Sl.*), take, thieve, walk or make off with 2. creep, flit, insinuate oneself, slink, slip, sneak, tiptoe

stealth furtiveness, secrecy, slyness, sneakiness, stealthiness, surreptitiousness, unobtrusiveness

stealthy clandestine, covert, furtive, secret, secretive, skulking, sly, sneaking, sneaky, surreptitious, underhand

steep *adj.* 1. abrupt, headlong, precipitous, sheer 2. *Inf.* excessive, exorbitant, extortionate, extreme, high, overpriced, stiff, uncalled-for, unreasonable

Antonyms (*sense 1*) easy, gentle, gradual, moderate, slight (*sense 2*) fair, moderate, reasonable

steer 1. be in the driver's seat, conduct, control, direct, govern, guide, pilot 2. **steer clear of** avoid, circumvent, eschew, evade, give a wide berth to, sheer off, shun

stem[1] *n.* axis, branch, peduncle, shoot, stalk, stock, trunk

stem[2] *v.* bring to a standstill, check, contain, curb, dam, hold back, oppose, resist, restrain, stanch, stay (*Archaic*), stop, withstand

step *n.* 1. footfall, footprint, footstep, gait, impression, pace, print, stride, trace, track, walk 2. act, action, deed, expedient, manoeuvre, means, measure, move, procedure, proceeding 3. **take steps** act, intervene, move in, prepare, take action, take measures, take the initiative 4. advance, advancement, move, phase, point, process, progres-

sion, stage 5. degree, level, rank, remove 6. **in step** coinciding, conforming, in harmony (agreement, conformity, unison), in line 7. **out of step** erratic, incongruous, in disagreement, out of harmony, out of line, out of phase, pulling different ways ~*v.* 8. move, pace, tread, walk

stereotype 1. *n.* formula, mould, pattern, received idea 2. *v.* categorize, conventionalize, dub, pigeonhole, standardize, take to be, typecast

sterile 1. abortive, bare, barren, dry, empty, fruitless, infecund, unfruitful, unproductive, unprofitable, unprolific 2. antiseptic, aseptic, disinfected, germ-free, sterilized

Antonyms (*sense 1*) fecund, fertile, fruitful, productive, prolific (*sense 2*) contaminated, dirty, germ-ridden, infected, insanitary, unhygenic, unsterile

stern austere, authoritarian, bitter, cruel, flinty, forbidding, frowning, grim, hard, harsh, inflexible, relentless, rigid, rigorous, serious, severe, steely, strict, unrelenting, unsparing, unyielding

Antonyms amused, approachable, compassionate, flexible, friendly, gentle, kind, lenient, liberal, permissive, soft, sympathetic, tolerant, warm

stick[1] *v.* 1. adhere, affix, attach, bind, bond, cement, cleave, cling, fasten, fix, fuse, glue, hold, hold on, join, paste, weld 2. dig, gore, insert, jab, penetrate, pierce, pin, poke, prod, puncture, spear, stab, thrust, transfix 3. **With out, up** *etc.* bulge, extend, jut, obtrude, poke, project, protrude, show 4. be bogged down, become immobilized, be embedded, catch, clog, come to a standstill, jam, lodge, snag, stop 5. linger, persist, remain, stay 6. **stick up for** *Inf.* champion, defend, stand up for, support, take the part or side of, uphold

stick[2] *n.* baton, birch, cane, pole,

rod, staff, stake, switch, twig, wand

sticky 1. adhesive, claggy (*Dialect*), clinging, gluey, glutinous, gooey (*Inf.*), gummy, syrupy, tacky, tenacious, viscid, viscous **2.** *Inf.* awkward, delicate, difficult, discomforting, embarrassing, hairy (*Sl.*), nasty, painful, thorny, tricky, unpleasant

stiff 1. brittle, firm, hard, hardened, inelastic, inflexible, rigid, solid, solidified, taut, tense, tight, unbending, unyielding **2.** artificial, austere, ceremonious, chilly, cold, constrained, forced, formal, laboured, mannered, pompous, priggish, prim, punctilious, standoffish, starchy (*Inf.*), stilted, uneasy, unnatural, unrelaxed, wooden **3.** arthritic, awkward, clumsy, creaky (*Inf.*), crude, graceless, inelegant, jerky, rheumaticky (*Inf.*), ungainly, ungraceful, unsupple
Antonyms (*senses 1 & 3*) bendable, ductile, elastic, flexible, limber, lithe, pliable, pliant, supple, yielding (*sense 2*) casual, easy, informal, laid-back, natural, relaxed, spontaneous, unceremonious, unofficial

stiffen brace, coagulate, congeal, crystallize, harden, jell, reinforce, set, solidify, starch, tauten, tense, thicken

stifle 1. asphyxiate, choke, smother, strangle, suffocate **2.** check, choke back, cover up, curb, extinguish, hush, muffle, prevent, repress, restrain, silence, smother, stop, suppress

still 1. *adj.* at rest, calm, hushed, inert, lifeless, motionless, noiseless, pacific, peaceful, placid, quiet, restful, serene, silent, smooth, stationary, stilly (*Poetic*), tranquil, undisturbed, unruffled, unstirring **2.** *v.* allay, alleviate, appease, calm, hush, lull, pacify, quiet, quieten, settle, silence, smooth, smooth over, soothe, subdue, tranquillize **3.** *conj.* but, for all that, however,

nevertheless, notwithstanding, yet
Antonyms *adj.* active, agitated, astir, bustling, busy, humming, lively, moving, noisy, restless, turbulent ~*v.* aggravate, agitate, exacerbate, increase, inflame, rouse, stir up

stimulant analeptic, bracer (*Inf.*), energizer, excitant, pep pill (*Inf.*), pick-me-up (*Inf.*), restorative, reviver, tonic, upper (*Sl.*)
Antonyms calmant, depressant, downer (*Sl.*), sedative, tranquilliser

stimulate animate, arouse, encourage, fan, fire, foment, goad, impel, incite, inflame, instigate, prompt, provoke, quicken, rouse, spur, turn on (*Inf.*), urge, whet

sting *v.* burn, hurt, pain, smart, tingle, wound

stint *n.* assignment, bit, period, quota, share, shift, spell, stretch, term, time, tour, turn

stipulate agree, contract, covenant, engage, guarantee, insist upon, lay down, lay down *or* impose conditions, make a point of, pledge, postulate, promise, require, settle, specify

stipulation agreement, clause, condition, contract, engagement, precondition, prerequisite, provision, proviso, qualification, requirement, restriction, settlement, *sine qua non*, specification, term

stir *v.* **1.** agitate, beat, disturb, flutter, mix, move, quiver, rustle, shake, tremble **2.** *Often with* up animate, arouse, awaken, excite, incite, inflame, instigate, kindle, prompt, provoke, quicken, raise, spur, stimulate, urge **3.** except: be up and about (*Inf.*), budge, exert oneself, get a move on (*Inf.*), get moving (*Inf.*), hasten, look lively (*Inf.*), make an effort, mill about, move, shake a leg (*Inf.*) ~*n.* **4.** activity, ado, agitation, bustle, commotion, disorder, disturbance, excitement, ferment, flurry, fuss, movement, to-do, tumult, uproar

stock *n.* **1.** array, assets, assort~
ment, cache, choice, commod~
ities, fund, goods, hoard, inven~
tory, merchandise, range, re~
serve, reservoir, selection,
stockpile, store, supply, variety,
wares **2.** *Animals* beasts, cattle,
domestic animals, flocks, herds,
horses, livestock, sheep **3.** *Money*
capital, funds, investment, prop~
erty **4. take stock** appraise, esti~
mate, review the situation, see
how the land lies, size up (*Inf.*),
weigh up ~*adj.* **5.** banal, basic,
commonplace, conventional,
customary, formal, hackneyed,
ordinary, overused, regular, rou~
tine, run-of-the-mill, set, standard,
staple, stereotyped, traditional,
trite, usual, worn-out ~*v.* **6.** deal
in, handle, keep, sell, supply,
trade in **7.** *With* **up** accumulate,
amass, buy up, gather, hoard, lay
in, put away, replenish, save,
store (up), supply

stomach *n.* **1.** abdomen, belly,
breadbasket (*Sl.*), gut (*Inf.*), in~
side(s) (*Inf.*), paunch, pot, pot~
belly, spare tyre (*Inf.*), tummy
(*Inf.*) **2.** appetite, desire, inclina~
tion, mind, relish, taste ~*v.* **3.**
abide, bear, endure, put up with
(*Inf.*), reconcile or resign oneself
to, submit to, suffer, swallow,
take, tolerate

stony *Fig.* adamant, blank, cal~
lous, chilly, expressionless, frigid,
hard, heartless, hostile, icy, in~
different, inexorable, merciless,
obdurate, pitiless, unfeeling, un~
forgiving, unresponsive

stoop *v.* be bowed *or* round-
shouldered, bend, bow, crouch,
descend, duck, hunch, incline,
kneel, lean, squat

stop *v.* **1.** be over, break off, bring
or come to a halt, bring *or* come
to a standstill, call it a day (*Inf.*),
cease, come to an end, conclude,
cut out (*Inf.*), cut short, desist,
discontinue, draw up, end, finish,
halt, leave off, pack in (*Brit. inf.*),
pause, peter out, pull up, put an
end to, quit, refrain, run down,
run its course, shut down, stall,

terminate **2.** arrest, bar, block,
break, check, close, forestall,
frustrate, hinder, hold back, im~
pede, intercept, interrupt, ob~
struct, plug, prevent, rein in, re~
press, restrain, seal, silence,
staunch, stem, suspend **3.** break
one's journey, lodge, put up, rest,
sojourn, stay, tarry ~*n.* **4.** cessa~
tion, conclusion, discontinuation,
end, finish, halt, standstill **5.**
break, rest, sojourn, stay, stop~
over, visit **6.** bar, block, break,
check, control, hindrance, im~
pediment, plug, stoppage **7.** de~
pot, destination, halt, stage, sta~
tion, termination, terminus

Antonyms *v.* (*senses 1 & 3*) ad~
vance, begin, commence, con~
tinue, get going, get under way,
give the go ahead, go, institute,
keep going, kick off (*Inf.*), keep
on, proceed, set in motion, set off,
start (*sense 2*) assist, boost, en~
courage, expedite, facilitate, fur~
ther, hasten, promote, push ~*n.*
(*sense 4*) beginning, commence~
ment, kick-off (*Inf.*), start (*sense
6*) boost, encouragement, incite~
ment

stoppage abeyance, arrest,
close, closure, cutoff, deduction,
discontinuance, halt, hindrance,
lay-off, shutdown, standstill,
stopping

store *v.* **1.** accumulate, deposit,
garner, hoard, husband, keep,
keep in reserve, lay by *or* in, lock
away, put aside, put aside for a
rainy day, put by, put in storage,
reserve, salt away, save, stash
(*Inf.*), stock, stockpile ~*n.* **2.**
abundance, accumulation, cache,
fund, hoard, lot, mine, plenty,
plethora, provision, quantity, re~
serve, reservoir, stock, stockpile,
supply, wealth **3.** chain store,
department store, emporium,
market, mart, outlet, shop,
supermarket **4.** depository, re~
pository, storehouse, storeroom,
warehouse

storm *n.* **1.** blast, blizzard, cy~
clone, gale, gust, hurricane,
squall, tempest, tornado, whirl~

wind **2.** *Fig.* agitation, anger, clamour, commotion, disturbance, furore, hubbub, outbreak, outburst, outcry, passion, roar, row, rumpus, stir, strife, tumult, turmoil, violence ~*v.* **3.** assail, assault, beset, charge, rush, take by storm ~*n.* **4.** assault, attack, blitz, blitzkrieg, offensive, onset, onslaught, rush ~*v.* **5.** bluster, complain, fly off the handle (*Inf.*), fume, rage, rant, rave, scold, thunder **6.** flounce, fly, rush, stalk, stamp, stomp (*Inf.*)

stormy blustering, blustery, boisterous, dirty, foul, gusty, raging, rough, squally, tempestuous, turbulent, wild, windy

story 1. account, anecdote, chronicle, fictional account, history, legend, narration, narrative, novel, recital, record, relation, romance, tale, version, yarn **2.** article, feature, news, news item, report, scoop

stout 1. big, bulky, burly, corpulent, fat, fleshy, heavy, obese, on the large *or* heavy side, overweight, plump, portly, rotund, substantial, tubby **2.** able-bodied, athletic, beefy (*Inf.*), brawny, hardy, hulking, husky (*Inf.*), lusty, muscular, robust, stalwart, strapping, strong, sturdy, substantial, tough, vigorous **3.** bold, brave, courageous, dauntless, doughty, fearless, gallant, intrepid, lion-hearted, manly, plucky, resolute, valiant, valorous
Antonyms (*senses 1 & 2*) feeble, flimsy, frail, insubstantial, lanky, lean, puny, skin-and-bones, skinny, slender, slight, slim (*sense 3*) cowardly, faint-hearted, fearful, irresolute, shrinking, soft, spineless, timid, weak

straight *adj.* **1.** direct, near, short, undeviating, unswerving **2.** aligned, erect, even, horizontal, in line, level, perpendicular, plumb, right, smooth, square, true, upright, vertical **3.** above board, accurate, authentic, decent, equitable, fair, fair and square, honest, honourable, just,

law-abiding, reliable, respectable, trustworthy, upright **4.** arranged, in order, neat, orderly, organized, put to rights, shipshape, sorted out, tidy **5.** consecutive, continuous, nonstop, running, solid, successive, sustained, through, uninterrupted, unrelieved **6.** neat, pure, unadulterated, undiluted, unmixed ~*adv.* **7.** as the crow flies, at once, directly, immediately, instantly
Antonyms *adj.* (*sense 1*) circuitous, indirect, roundabout, winding, zigzag (*sense 2*) askew, bent, crooked, curved, twisted, uneven (*sense 3*) bent (*Sl.*), crooked (*Inf.*), dishonest, dishonourable, shady (*Inf.*), unlawful (*sense 4*) confused, disorderly, disorganized, in disarray, messy, untidy (*sense 5*) broken, discontinuous, interrupted, non-consecutive

straightaway at once, directly, immediately, instantly, now, on the spot, right away, straightway (*Archaic*), there and then, this minute, without any delay, without more ado

straightforward 1. above board, candid, direct, forthright, genuine, guileless, honest, open, sincere, truthful **2.** clear-cut, easy, elementary, routine, simple, uncomplicated, undemanding
Antonyms complex, complicated, confused, convoluted, devious, disingenuous, roundabout, shady, sharp, unclear, unscrupulous

strain *v.* **1.** distend, draw tight, extend, stretch, tauten, tighten **2.** drive, exert, fatigue, injure, overexert, overtax, overwork, pull, push to the limit, sprain, tax, tear, tire, twist, weaken, wrench **3.** endeavour, go all out for (*Inf.*), labour, make a supreme effort, strive, struggle **4.** filter, percolate, purify, riddle, screen, seep, separate, sieve, sift ~*n.* **5.** effort, exertion, force, injury, pull, sprain, struggle, tautness, tension, tensity (*Rare*), wrench **6.**

anxiety, burden, pressure, stress, tension

Antonyms v. (senses 2 & 3) idle, loose, pamper, relax, rest, slacken, take it easy (Inf.), yield ~n. (senses 5 & 6) ease, effortlessness, lack of tension, relaxation

strained artificial, awkward, constrained, difficult, embarrassed, false, forced, laboured, put on, self-conscious, stiff, tense, uncomfortable, uneasy, unnatural, unrelaxed

Antonyms comfortable, natural, relaxed

strait-laced moralistic, narrow, narrow-minded, of the old school, old-maidish (Inf.), overscrupulous, prim, proper, prudish, puritanical, strict, Victorian

Antonyms broad-minded, earthy, immoral, loose, relaxed, uninhibited, unreserved

strand n. fibre, filament, length, lock, rope, string, thread, tress, twist

stranded aground, ashore, beached, cast away, grounded, marooned, wrecked

strange 1. abnormal, astonishing, bizarre, curious, eccentric, exceptional, extraordinary, fantastic, funny, irregular, marvellous, mystifying, odd, out-of-the-way, peculiar, perplexing, queer, rare, remarkable, singular, unaccountable, uncanny, uncommon, unheard of, weird, wonderful **2.** alien, exotic, foreign, new, novel, outside one's experience, remote, unexplored, unfamiliar, unknown, untried

Antonyms accustomed, common, commonplace, conventional, familiar, habitual, ordinary, regular, routine, run-of-the-mill, standard, typical, unexceptional, usual, well-known

stranger alien, foreigner, guest, incomer, new arrival, newcomer, outlander, unknown, visitor

strangle 1. asphyxiate, choke, garrotte, smother, strangulate, suffocate, throttle **2.** gag (Inf.), inhibit, repress, stifle, suppress

strap 1. n. belt, leash, thong, tie **2.** v. bind, buckle, fasten, lash, secure, tie, truss

strategy approach, grand design, manoeuvring, plan, planning, policy, procedure, programme, scheme

stray v. **1.** deviate, digress, diverge, get off the point, get sidetracked, go off at a tangent, ramble **2.** be abandoned or lost, drift, err, go astray, lose one's way, meander, range, roam, rove, straggle, wander ~adj. **3.** abandoned, homeless, lost, roaming, vagrant

streak n. **1.** band, layer, line, slash, smear, strip, stripe, stroke, vein **2.** dash, element, strain, touch, trace, vein ~v. **3.** dart, flash, fly, hurtle, move like greased lightning (Inf.), speed, sprint, sweep, tear, whistle, whiz (Inf.), zoom

stream **1.** n. beck, brook, burn, course, creek (U.S.), current, drift, flow, freshet, outpouring, rill, river, rivulet, run, rush, surge, tide, torrent, tributary **2.** v. cascade, course, emit, flood, flow, glide, gush, issue, pour, run, shed, spill, spout

street avenue, boulevard, lane, road, roadway, row, terrace, thoroughfare

strength 1. backbone, brawn, brawniness, courage, firmness, fortitude, health, lustiness, might, muscle, robustness, sinew, stamina, stoutness, sturdiness, toughness **2.** cogency, concentration, effectiveness, efficacy, energy, force, intensity, potency, power, resolution, spirit, vehemence, vigour, virtue (Archaic) **3.** advantage, anchor, asset, mainstay, security, strong point, succour, tower of strength

Antonyms (senses 1 & 2) debility, feebleness, frailty, impotence, infirmity, powerlessness, weakness (sense 3) Achilles heel, chink in one's armour, defect, failing, flaw, shortcoming, weakness

strengthen 1. animate, brace up, consolidate, encourage, fortify, give new energy to, harden, hearten, invigorate, nerve, nourish, rejuvenate, restore, stiffen, toughen 2. bolster, brace, build up, buttress, confirm, corroborate, enhance, establish, give a boost to, harden, heighten, increase, intensify, justify, reinforce, steel, substantiate, support
Antonyms crush, debilitate, destroy, dilute, enervate, render impotent, sap, subvert, undermine, weaken

strenuous 1. arduous, demanding, exhausting, hard, Herculean, laborious, taxing, toilsome, tough, tough going, unrelaxing, uphill 2. active, bold, determined, eager, earnest, energetic, persistent, resolute, spirited, strong, tireless, vigorous, zealous
Antonyms easy, effortless, relaxed, relaxing, undemanding, unenergetic, untaxing

stress n. 1. emphasis, force, importance, significance, urgency, weight 2. anxiety, burden, hassle (Inf.), nervous tension, oppression, pressure, strain, tautness, tension, trauma, worry 3. accent, accentuation, beat, emphasis ~v. 4. accentuate, belabour, dwell on, emphasize, harp on, lay emphasis upon, point up, repeat, rub in, underline, underscore

stretch v. 1. cover, extend, put forth, reach, spread, unfold, unroll 2. distend, draw out, elongate, expand, inflate, lengthen, pull, pull out of shape, rack, strain, swell, tighten ~n. 3. area, distance, expanse, extent, spread, sweep, tract

strict 1. austere, authoritarian, firm, harsh, no-nonsense, rigid, rigorous, severe, stern, stringent 2. accurate, close, exact, faithful, meticulous, particular, precise, religious, scrupulous, true 3. absolute, complete, perfect, total, utter
Antonyms (sense 1) easy-going, flexible, laid-back (Inf.), lax, mild, moderate, soft, tolerant

strike v. 1. bang, beat, box, buffet, chastise, clobber (Sl.), clout (Inf.), clump (Sl.), cuff, hammer, hit, knock, lay a finger on (Inf.), pound, punish, slap, smack, smite, sock (Sl.), thump, wallop (Inf.) 2. be in collision with, bump into, clash, collide with, come into contact with, dash, hit, knock into, run into, smash into, touch 3. drive, force, hit, impel, thrust 4. affect, come to, come to the mind of, dawn on or upon, hit, impress, make an impact on, occur to, reach, register (Inf.), seem 5. affect, assail, assault, attack, deal a blow to, devastate, fall upon, hit, invade, set upon, smite 6. achieve, arrange, arrive at, attain, effect, reach 7. down tools, mutiny, revolt, walk out

striking astonishing, conspicuous, dazzling, extraordinary, forcible, impressive, memorable, noticeable, out of the ordinary, outstanding, stunning (Inf.), wonderful
Antonyms average, dull, indifferent, undistinguished, unexceptional, unextraordinary, unimpressive, uninteresting

string n. 1. cord, fibre, twine 2. chain, file, line, procession, queue, row, sequence, series, strand, succession

strip[1] v. 1. bare, denude, deprive, despoil, dismantle, divest, empty, gut, lay bare, loot, peel, pillage, plunder, ransack, rob, sack, skin, spoil 2. disrobe, unclothe, uncover, undress

strip[2] n. band, belt, bit, fillet, piece, ribbon, shred, slip, swathe, tongue

strive attempt, compete, contend, do all one can, do one's best, do one's utmost, endeavour, exert oneself, fight, go all out (Inf.), labour, leave no stone unturned, make every effort, strain, struggle, toil, try, try hard

stroke n. 1. accomplishment, achievement, blow, feat, flourish,

stroll 1. *v.* amble, make one's way, mooch (*Inf.*), mosey (*Inf.*), promenade, ramble, saunter, stooge (*Inf.*), stretch one's legs, take a turn, toddle, wander 2. *n.* airing, breath of air, constitutional, excursion, promenade, ramble, turn, walk

strong 1. athletic, beefy (*Inf.*), brawny, burly, capable, hale, hardy, healthy, Herculean, lusty, muscular, powerful, robust, sinewy, sound, stalwart, stout, strapping, sturdy, tough, virile 2. aggressive, brave, courageous, determined, firm in spirit, forceful, hard as nails, hard-nosed (*Inf.*), high-powered, plucky, resilient, resolute, resourceful, self-assertive, steadfast, stouthearted, tenacious, tough, unyielding 3. acute, dedicated, deep, deep-rooted, eager, fervent, fervid, fierce, firm, intense, keen, severe, staunch, vehement, violent, zealous 4. clear, clear-cut, cogent, compelling, convincing, distinct, effective, formidable, great, marked, overpowering, persuasive, potent, redoubtable, sound, telling, trenchant, unmistakable, urgent, weighty, well-established, well-founded 5. Draconian, drastic, extreme, forceful, severe 6. durable, hard-wearing, heavy-duty, on a firm foundation, reinforced, sturdy, substantial, well-armed, well-built, well-protected 7. biting, concentrated, heady, highly-flavoured, highly-seasoned, hot, intoxicating, piquant, pungent, pure, sharp, spicy, undiluted
Antonyms (*senses 1, 2, 3, 4, 5 & 6*) characterless, delicate, faint-hearted, feeble, frail, ineffectual, lacking drive, namby-pamby, puny, slight, spineless, timid, un-assertive, uncommitted, unimpassioned, weak (*sense 7*) bland, mild, tasteless, vapid, weak

structure *n.* 1. arrangement, configuration, conformation, construction, design, fabric, form, formation, interrelation of parts, make, make-up, organization 2. building, construction, edifice, erection, pile ~*v.* 3. arrange, assemble, build up, design, organize, put together, shape

struggle *v.* 1. exert oneself, go all out (*Inf.*), labour, make every effort, strain, strive, toil, work, work like a Trojan ~*n.* 2. effort, exertion, grind (*Inf.*), labour, long haul, pains, scramble, toil, work ~*v.* 3. battle, compete, contend, fight, grapple, lock horns, scuffle, wrestle ~*n.* 4. battle, brush, clash, combat, conflict, contest, encounter, hostilities, skirmish, strife, tussle

stubborn bull-headed, contumacious, cross-grained, dogged, dour, fixed, headstrong, inflexible, intractable, mulish, obdurate, obstinate, opinionated, persistent, pig-headed, recalcitrant, refractory, self-willed, stiff-necked, tenacious, unbending, unmanageable, unshakable, unyielding, wilful
Antonyms biddable, compliant, docile, flexible, half-hearted, irresolute, malleable, manageable, pliable, pliant, tractable, vacillating, wavering, yielding

stuck 1. cemented, fast, fastened, firm, fixed, glued, joined 2. *Inf.* at a loss, at a standstill, at one's wits' end, baffled, beaten, bereft of ideas, nonplussed, stumped, up against a brick wall (*Inf.*)
student apprentice, disciple, learner, observer, pupil, scholar, undergraduate
studied calculated, conscious, deliberate, intentional, planned, premeditated, purposeful, well-considered, wilful
studious academic, assiduous, attentive, bookish, careful, diligent, eager, earnest, hard-working, intellectual, meditative, reflective, scholarly, sedulous, serious, thoughtful

study v. 1. apply oneself (to), bone up (on) (*Inf.*), burn the midnight oil, cogitate, con (*Archaic*), consider, contemplate, cram (*Inf.*), examine, go into, hammer away at, learn, lucubrate (*Rare*), meditate, mug up (*Brit. sl.*), ponder, pore over, read, read up, swot (up) (*Brit. inf.*) 2. analyse, deliberate, examine, investigate, look into, peruse, research, scrutinize, survey ~n. 3. academic work, application, book work, cramming (*Inf.*), learning, lessons, reading, research, school work, swotting (*Brit. inf.*), thought 4. analysis, attention, cogitation, consideration, contemplation, examination, inquiry, inspection, investigation, review, scrutiny, survey

stuff v. 1. compress, cram, crowd, fill, force, jam, load, pack, pad, push, ram, shove, squeeze, stow, wedge 2. gobble, gorge, gormandize, guzzle, make a pig of oneself (*Inf.*), overindulge, sate, satiate ~n. 3. belongings, bits and pieces, clobber (*Brit. sl.*), effects, equipment, gear, goods and chattels, impedimenta, junk, kit, luggage, materials, objects, paraphernalia, possessions, tackle, things, trappings 4. cloth, fabric, material, raw material, textile 5. essence, matter, pith, quintessence, staple, substance

stuffy 1. airless, close, fetid, frowsty, fuggy, heavy, muggy, oppressive, stale, stifling, suffocating, sultry, unventilated 2. conventional, deadly, dreary, dull, fusty, humourless, musty, old-fashioned, old-fogyish, pompous, priggish, prim, prim and proper, staid, stilted, stodgy, strait-laced, uninteresting

Antonyms (*sense 1*) airy, breezy, cool, draughty, fresh, gusty, pleasant, well-ventilated

stumble 1. blunder about, come a cropper (*Inf.*), fall, falter, flounder, hesitate, lose one's balance, lurch, reel, slip, stagger, trip 2. With on or upon blunder upon,

chance upon, come across, discover, encounter, find, happen upon, light upon, run across, turn up

stun *Fig.* amaze, astonish, astound, bewilder, confound, confuse, daze, dumbfound, flabbergast (*Inf.*), hit (someone) like a ton of bricks (*Inf.*), knock out, knock (someone) for six (*Inf.*), overcome, overpower, shock, stagger, strike (someone) dumb (*Inf.*), stupefy, take (someone's) breath away

stunning beautiful, brilliant, dazzling, devastating (*Inf.*), gorgeous, great (*Inf.*), heavenly, impressive, lovely, marvellous, out of this world (*Inf.*), ravishing, remarkable, sensational, smashing (*Inf.*), spectacular, striking, wonderful

stunt n. act, deed, exploit, feat, feature, gest (*Archaic*), tour de force, trick

stupendous amazing, astounding, breathtaking, colossal, enormous, fabulous (*Inf.*), fantastic (*Inf.*), gigantic, huge, marvellous, mega (*Sl.*), mind-blowing (*Sl.*), mind-boggling (*Inf.*), out of this world (*Inf.*), overwhelming, phenomenal, prodigious, staggering, stunning (*Inf.*), superb, surpassing belief, surprising, tremendous (*Inf.*), vast, wonderful

stupid 1. Boeotian, brainless, cretinous, deficient, dense, dim, doltish, dopey (*Sl.*), dozy (*Brit. inf.*), dull, dumb (*Inf.*, *chiefly U.S.*), foolish, gullible, half-witted, moronic, naive, obtuse, simple, simple-minded, slow, slow on the uptake (*Inf.*), slow-witted, sluggish, stolid, thick, thickheaded, unintelligent, witless, woodenheaded (*Inf.*) 2. crackbrained, daft, futile, half-baked (*Inf.*), idiotic, ill-advised, imbecilic, inane, indiscreet, irrelevant, irresponsible, laughable, ludicrous, meaningless, mindless, nonsensical, pointless, puerile, rash, senseless, short-sighted, trivial, unintelligent, unthinking 3 dazed, groggy, in a daze, insensate, punch-drunk, semiconscious, senseless, stunned, stupefied

Antonyms astute, brainy, bright, brilliant, clear-headed, clever, intelligent, lucid, on the ball (*Inf.*), prudent, quick, quick on the uptake, quick-witted, realistic, reasonable, sensible, sharp, shrewd, smart, thoughtful, well thought-out, wise

stupidity 1. asininity, brainlessness, denseness, dimness, dopiness (*Sl.*), doziness (*Brit. inf.*), dullness, dumbness (*Inf., chiefly U.S.*), feeble-mindedness, imbecility, lack of brain, lack of intelligence, naivety, obtuseness, puerility, simplicity, slowness, thickheadedness, thickness **2.** absurdity, fatuity, fatuousness, folly, foolhardiness, foolishness, futility, idiocy, impracticality, inanity, indiscretion, ineptitude, irresponsibility, ludicrousness, lunacy, madness, pointlessness, rashness, senselessness, silliness

sturdy athletic, brawny, built to last, determined, durable, firm, flourishing, hardy, hearty, lusty, muscular, powerful, resolute, robust, secure, solid, stalwart, staunch, steadfast, stouthearted, substantial, vigorous, well-built, well-made

Antonyms feeble, flimsy, frail, infirm, irresolute, puny, rickety, skinny, uncertain, unsubstantial, weak, weakly

style *n.* **1.** cut, design, form, hand, manner, technique **2.** fashion, mode, rage, trend, vogue **3.** approach, custom, manner, method, mode, way **4.** *bon ton*, chic, cosmopolitanism, dash, dressiness (*Inf.*), élan, elegance, fashionableness, flair, grace, panache, polish, refinement, savoir-faire, smartness, sophistication, stylishness, taste, urbanity **5.** affluence, comfort, ease, elegance, gracious living, grandeur, luxury **6.** appearance, category, characteristic, genre, kind, pattern, sort,

spirit, strain, tenor, tone, type, variety ~*v.* **7.** adapt, arrange, cut, design, dress, fashion, shape, tailor **8.** address, call, christen, denominate, designate, dub, entitle, label, name, term

stylish à la mode, chic, classy (*Sl.*), dapper, dressy (*Inf.*), fashionable, in fashion, in vogue, modish, natty (*Inf.*), polished, smart, snappy, snazzy (*Inf.*), trendy (*Brit. inf.*), urbane, voguish, well turned-out

Antonyms badly-tailored, old-fashioned, out-moded, out-of-date, passé, scruffy, shabby, slovenly, tacky, tawdry, unfashionable, unstylish, untrendy (*Brit. inf.*)

subconscious *adj.* hidden, inner, innermost, intuitive, latent, repressed, subliminal, suppressed

subdue 1. beat down, break, conquer, control, crush, defeat, discipline, gain ascendancy over, get the better of, get the upper hand over, get under control, humble, master, overcome, overpower, overrun, put down, quell, tame, trample, triumph over, vanquish **2.** check, control, mellow, moderate, quieten down, repress, soften, suppress, tone down

Antonyms (*sense 2*) agitate, arouse, awaken, incite, provoke, stir up, waken, whip up

subject *n.* **1.** affair, business, field of enquiry *or* reference, issue, matter, object, point, question, subject matter, substance, theme, topic **2.** case, client, guinea pig (*Inf.*), participant, patient, victim **3.** citizen, dependant, liegeman, national, subordinate, vassal ~*adj.* **4.** at the mercy of, disposed, exposed, in danger of, liable, open, prone, susceptible, vulnerable **5.** conditional, contingent, dependent **6.** answerable, bound by, captive, dependent, enslaved, inferior, obedient, satellite, subjugated, submissive, subordinate, subservient ~*v.* **7.** expose, lay open, make liable, put through, submit, treat

subjective biased, emotional, idiosyncratic, instinctive, intuitive, nonobjective, personal, prejudiced
Antonyms concrete, detached, disinterested, dispassionate, impartial, impersonal, objective, open-minded, unbiased

submerge deluge, dip, drown, duck, dunk, engulf, flood, immerse, inundate, overflow, overwhelm, plunge, sink, swamp

submission 1. acquiescence, assent, capitulation, giving in, surrender, yielding 2. compliance, deference, docility, meekness, obedience, passivity, resignation, submissiveness, tractability, unassertiveness 3. argument, contention, proposal 4. entry, handing in, presentation, submitting, tendering

submit 1. accede, acquiesce, agree, bend, bow, capitulate, comply, defer, endure, give in, hoist the white flag, knuckle under, lay down arms, put up with (Inf.), resign oneself, stoop, succumb, surrender, throw in the sponge, toe the line, tolerate, yield 2. commit, hand in, present, proffer, put forward, refer, table, tender

subordinate adj. 1. dependent, inferior, junior, lesser, lower, minor, secondary, subject, subservient 2. ancillary, auxiliary, subsidiary, supplementary ~n. 3. aide, assistant, attendant, dependant, inferior, junior, second, subaltern, underling
Antonyms adj. central, essential, greater, higher, key, main, necessary, predominant, senior, superior, vital ~n. boss (Inf.), captain, chief, commander, head, leader, master, principal, senior, superior

subscribe chip in (Inf.), contribute, donate, give, offer, pledge, promise

subscription annual payment,

contribution, donation, dues, gift, membership fee, offering

subsequent after, consequent, consequential, ensuing, following, later, succeeding, successive
Antonyms antecedent, earlier, erstwhile, former, on-time, past, preceding, previous, prior

subside abate, decrease, de-escalate, diminish, dwindle, ease, ebb, lessen, let up, level off, melt away, moderate, peter out, quieten, recede, slacken, wane
Antonyms grow, escalate, heighten, increase, inflate, intensify, mount, rise, soar, swell, tumefy, wax

subsidiary aiding, ancillary, assistant, auxiliary, contributory, cooperative, helpful, lesser, minor, secondary, serviceable, subordinate, subservient, supplemental, supplementary, useful
Antonyms central, chief, head, key, leading, main, major, primary, principal, vital

subsidize finance, fund, promote, put up the money for, sponsor, support, underwrite

subsidy aid, allowance, assistance, contribution, financial aid, grant, help, subvention, support

substance 1. body, element, fabric, material, stuff, texture 2. burden, essence, gist, gravamen (Law), import, main point, matter, meaning, pith, significance, subject, sum and substance, theme 3. actuality, concreteness, entity, force, reality 4. affluence, assets, estate, means, property, resources, wealth

substantial ample, big, considerable, generous, goodly, important, large, significant, sizable, tidy (Inf.), worthwhile

substantiate affirm, attest to, authenticate, bear out, confirm, corroborate, establish, prove, support, validate, verify

substitute 1. v. change, commute, exchange, interchange, replace, swap (Inf.), switch 2. n. agent, depute (Chiefly Scot.), deputy, equivalent, expedient, locum, locum tenens, makeshift, proxy, relief, replacement, representative, reserve, stand-by, stopgap, sub, supply, surrogate, temp (*Inf.*), temporary **3.** *adj.* acting, additional, alternative, proxy, replacement, reserve, second, surrogate, temporary

subtle 1. deep, delicate, discriminating, ingenious, nice, penetrating, profound, refined, sophisticated **2.** delicate, faint, implied, indirect, insinuated, slight, understated **3.** artful, astute, crafty, cunning, designing, devious, intriguing, keen, Machiavellian, scheming, shrewd, sly, wily
Antonyms artless, blunt, crass, direct, guileless, heavy-handed, lacking finesse, obvious, overwhelming, simple, straightforward, strong, tactless, unsophisticated, unsubtle

subtlety 1. acumen, acuteness, cleverness, delicacy, discernment, fine point, intricacy, nicety, refinement, sagacity, skill, sophistication **2.** artfulness, astuteness, craftiness, cunning, deviousness, guile, slyness, wiliness

subtract deduct, detract, diminish, remove, take away, take from, take off, withdraw
Antonyms add, add to, append, increase by, supplement

suburbs dormitory area (*Brit.*), environs, faubourgs, neighbourhood, outskirts, precincts, purlieus, residential areas, suburbia

subversive *adj.* destructive, incendiary, inflammatory, insurrectionary, overthrowing, perversive, riotous, seditious, treasonous, underground, undermining

succeed 1. arrive (*Inf.*), be successful, come off (*Inf.*), do all right for oneself (*Inf.*), do the trick (*Inf.*), flourish, gain one's end, get to the top (*Inf.*), make good, make it (*Inf.*), prosper, thrive, triumph, turn out well, work **2.** be subsequent, come next, ensue, follow, result, supervene

Antonyms (*sense 1*) be unsuccessful, collapse, come a cropper (*Inf.*), fail, fall flat, fall short, flop, not make the grade, not manage to (*sense 2*) be a precursor of, come before, go ahead of, go before, pave the way, precede

success 1. ascendancy, eminence, fame, favourable outcome, fortune, happiness, hit (*Inf.*), luck, prosperity, triumph **2.** best seller, big name, celebrity, hit (*Inf.*), market leader, sensation, smash hit (*Inf.*), somebody, star, V.I.P., winner
Antonyms collapse, dead duck (*Inf.*), disaster, downfall, failure, fiasco, flop, loser, misfortune, nobody, no-hoper, washout

successful acknowledged, at the top of the tree, best-selling, booming, efficacious, favourable, flourishing, fortunate, fruitful, lucky, lucrative, moneymaking, out in front (*Inf.*), paying, profitable, prosperous, rewarding, thriving, top, unbeaten, victorious, wealthy
Antonyms defeated, failed, ineffective, losing, luckless, uneconomic, unprofitable, unsuccessful, useless

succession 1. chain, continuation, course, cycle, flow, order, procession, progression, run, sequence, series, train **2.** accession, assumption, elevation, entering upon, inheritance, taking over

successive consecutive, following, in a row, in succession, sequent, succeeding

succinct brief, compact, compendious, concise, condensed, gnomic, in a few well-chosen words, laconic, pithy, summary, terse, to the point

succulent juicy, luscious, lush, mellow, moist, mouthwatering, rich

succumb capitulate, die, fall, fall victim to, give in, give way, go under, knuckle under, submit, surrender, yield

sudden abrupt, hasty, hurried, impulsive, quick, rapid, rash, swift, unexpected, unforeseen, unusual

Antonyms anticipated, deliberate, expected, foreseen, gentle, gradual, slow, unhasty

sue 1. *Law* bring an action against (someone), charge, have the law on (someone) (*Inf.*), indict, institute legal proceedings against (someone), prefer charges against (someone), prosecute, summon, take (someone) to court 2. appeal for, beg, beseech, entreat, petition, plead, solicit, supplicate

suffer 1. ache, agonize, be affected, be in pain, be racked, feel wretched, go through a lot (*Inf.*), grieve, have a thin *or* bad time, hurt 2. bear, endure, experience, feel, go through, put up with (*Inf.*), support, sustain, tolerate, undergo 3. appear in a poor light, be handicapped, be impaired, deteriorate, fall off, show to disadvantage

suffering *n.* affliction, agony, anguish, discomfort, distress, hardship, martyrdom, misery, ordeal, pain, torment, torture

sufficient adequate, competent, enough, enow (*Archaic*), satisfactory

Antonyms deficient, inadequate, insufficient, meagre, not enough, poor, scant, short, sparse

suggest 1. advise, advocate, move, offer a suggestion, propose, put forward, recommend 2. bring to mind, connote, evoke, put one in mind of 3. hint, imply, indicate, insinuate, intimate, lead one to believe

suggestion 1. motion, plan, proposal, proposition, recommendation 2. breath, hint, indication, insinuation, intimation, suspicion, trace, whisper

suit *v.* 1. agree, agree with, answer, be acceptable to, become, befit, be seemly, conform to, correspond, do, go with, gratify, harmonize, match, please, satisfy, tally 2. accommodate, adapt, adjust, fashion, fit, modify, proportion, tailor ~*n.* 3. *Law* action, case, cause, lawsuit, proceeding, prosecution, trial 4. clothing, costume, dress, ensemble, habit, outfit 5. **follow suit** accord with, copy, emulate, run with the herd, take one's cue from

suitable acceptable, applicable, apposite, appropriate, apt, becoming, befitting, convenient, cut out for, due, fit, fitting, in character, in keeping, opportune, pertinent, proper, relevant, right, satisfactory, seemly, suited

Antonyms discordant, inapposite, inappropriate, incorrect, inopportune, jarring, out of character, out of keeping, unbecoming, unfitting, unseemly, unsuitable, unsuited

sulk be in a huff, be put out, brood, have the hump (*Brit. inf.*), look sullen, pout

sulky aloof, churlish, cross, disgruntled, ill-humoured, in the sulks, moody, morose, perverse, petulant, put out, querulous, resentful, sullen, vexed

sullen brooding, cheerless, cross, dismal, dull, gloomy, glowering, heavy, moody, morose, obstinate, out of humour, perverse, silent, sombre, sour, stubborn, surly, unsociable

Antonyms amiable, bright, cheerful, cheery, good-humoured, good-natured, pleasant, sociable, sunny, warm, warm-hearted

sultry close, hot, humid, muggy, oppressive, sticky, stifling, stuffy, sweltering

Antonyms cool, fresh, invigorating, refreshing

sum aggregate, amount, entirety, quantity, reckoning, score, sum total, tally, total, totality, whole

summarize abridge, condense, encapsulate, epitomize, give a rundown of, give the main points of, outline, précis, put in a nutshell, review, sum up

summary *n.* abridgment, abstract, compendium, digest, epitome, essence, extract, out-

line, précis, recapitulation, ré~
sumé, review, rundown,
summing-up, synopsis

summit acme, apex, crown,
crowning point, culmination,
head, height, peak, pinnacle, top,
zenith
Antonyms base, bottom, depths,
foot, lowest point, nadir

summon arouse, assemble, bid,
call, call together, cite, convene,
convoke, invite, rally, rouse, send
for

sumptuous costly, dear, de luxe,
expensive, extravagant, gor~
geous, grand, lavish, luxurious,
magnificent, opulent, plush (*Inf.*),
posh (*Inf.*), rich, ritzy (*Sl.*), splen~
did, superb
Antonyms austere, basic, cheap,
frugal, inexpensive, meagre,
mean, miserly, plain, shabby,
wretched

sum up 1. close, conclude, put in a
nutshell, recapitulate, review,
summarize **2.** estimate, form an
opinion of, get the measure of,
size up (*Inf.*)

sundry assorted, different, divers
(*Archaic*), miscellaneous, sever~
al, some, varied, various

sunny 1. bright, brilliant, clear,
fine, luminous, radiant, sum~
mery, sunlit, sunshiny, uncloud~
ed, without a cloud in the sky **2.**
Fig. beaming, blithe, buoyant,
cheerful, cheery, genial, happy,
joyful, light-hearted, optimistic,
pleasant, smiling
Antonyms cloudy, depressing,
doleful, down in the dumps,
dreary, dreich (*Scot.*), dull,
gloomy, miserable, morbid,
murky, overcast, rainy, shaded,
shadowy, sunless, unsmiling, wet,
wintry

superb admirable, breathtaking,
choice, excellent, exquisite, fine,
first-rate, gorgeous, grand, mag~
nificent, marvellous, mega (*Sl.*),
of the first water, splendid, su~
perior, unrivalled
Antonyms awful, bad, disap~
pointing, dreadful, inferior, me~
diocre, pathetic, poor quality,

run-of-the-mill, terrible, third-
rate, uninspired, woeful

superficial 1. exterior, external,
on the surface, peripheral, shal~
low, skin-deep, slight, surface **2.**
casual, cosmetic, cursory, desul~
tory, hasty, hurried, inattentive,
nodding, passing, perfunctory,
sketchy, slapdash
Antonyms complete, compre~
hensive, deep, detailed, earnest,
exhaustive, in depth, major, pen~
etrating, probing, profound, sub~
stantial, thorough

superfluous excess, excessive,
extra, in excess, left over, need~
less, on one's hands, pleonastic
(*Rhetoric*), redundant, remain~
ing, residuary, spare, superabun~
dant, supererogatory, supernu~
merary, surplus, surplus to re~
quirements, uncalled-for, unnec~
essary, unneeded, unrequired
Antonyms called for, essential,
imperative, indispensable, nec~
essary, needed, requisite, vital,
wanted

superhuman 1. herculean, hero~
ic, phenomenal, prodigious, stu~
pendous, valiant **2.** divine, para~
normal, preternatural, super~
natural

superintendent administrator,
chief, conductor, controller, di~
rector, governor, inspector,
manager, overseer, supervisor

superior *adj.* **1.** better, grander,
greater, higher, more advanced
(expert, extensive, skilful), para~
mount, predominant, preferred,
prevailing, surpassing, unrivalled
2. a cut above (*Inf.*), admirable,
choice, de luxe, distinguished,
excellent, exceptional, exclusive,
fine, first-class, first-rate, good,
good quality, high calibre, high-
class, of the first order **3.** airy,
condescending, disdainful,
haughty, lofty, lordly, patroniz~
ing, pretentious, snobbish, stuck-
up (*Inf.*), supercilious ~*n.* **4.** boss
(*Inf.*), chief, director, manager,
principal, senior, supervisor
Antonyms *adj.* (senses 1 & 2)
average, inferior, less, lesser,

lower, mediocre, not as good, ordinary, poorer, second-class, second-rate, substandard, unremarkable, worse ~n. 2. assistant, dogsbody, inferior, junior, lackey, minion, subordinate, underling

superiority advantage, ascendancy, excellence, lead, predominance, pre-eminence, preponderance, prevalence, supremacy

supernatural abnormal, dark, ghostly, hidden, miraculous, mysterious, mystic, occult, paranormal, phantom, preternatural, psychic, spectral, supranatural, uncanny, unearthly, unnatural

supervise administer, be on duty at, be responsible for, conduct, control, direct, handle, have or be in charge of, inspect, keep an eye on, look after, manage, oversee, preside over, run, superintend

supervision administration, auspices, care, charge, control, direction, guidance, instruction, management, oversight, stewardship, superintendence, surveillance

supervisor administrator, boss (*Inf.*), chief, foreman, gaffer (*Inf.*), inspector, manager, overseer, steward, superintendent

supple bending, elastic, flexible, limber, lithe, loose-limbed, plastic, pliable, pliant
Antonyms awkward, creaky (*Inf.*), firm, inelastic, inflexible, rigid, stiff, taut, unbending, unsupple, unyielding

supplement 1. n. added feature, addendum, addition, appendix, codicil, complement, extra, insert, postscript, pull-out, sequel **2.** v. add, augment, complement, extend, fill out, reinforce, supply, top up

supplementary accompanying, additional, ancillary, auxiliary, complementary, extra, secondary, supplemental

supply v. **1.** afford, cater to or for, come up with, contribute, endow, fill, furnish, give, grant, minister, outfit, produce, provide, purvey,
replenish, satisfy, stock, store, victual, yield ~n. **2.** cache, fund, hoard, quantity, reserve, reservoir, source, stock, stockpile, store **3.** *Usually plural* equipment, food, foodstuff, items, materials, necessities, provender, provisions, rations, stores

support v. **1.** bear, bolster, brace, buttress, carry, hold, hold up, prop, reinforce, shore up, sustain, underpin, uphold **2.** be a source of strength to, buoy up, cherish, finance, foster, fund, keep, look after, maintain, nourish, provide for, strengthen, subsidize, succour, sustain, take care of, underwrite **3.** advocate, aid, assist, back, boost (someone's) morale, champion, defend, forward, go along with, help, promote, second, side with, stand behind, stand up for, stick up for (*Inf.*), take (someone's) part, take up the cudgels for, uphold **4.** bear, brook, countenance, endure, put up with (*Inf.*), stand (for), stomach, submit, suffer, thole (*Dialect*), tolerate, undergo ~n. **5.** abutment, back, brace, foundation, lining, pillar, post, prop, shore, stanchion, stay, stiffener, underpinning **6.** aid, approval, assistance, backing, blessing, championship, comfort, encouragement, friendship, furtherance, help, loyalty, moral support, patronage, protection, relief, succour, sustenance **7.** keep, livelihood, maintenance, subsistence, sustenance, upkeep **8.** backbone, backer, comforter, mainstay, prop, second, stay, supporter, tower of strength
Antonyms v. (*sense 2*) live off, sponge off (*senses 3 & 5*) challenge, contradict, deny, go against, hinder, hold out against, oppose, refute, reject, stab in the back, turn one's back on, undermine, walk away from ~n. (*senses 7 & 9*) antagonist, burden, denial, encumbrance, hindrance, impediment, opposition, refutation, rejection, undermining

supporter adherent, advocate, ally, apologist, champion, co-worker, defender, fan, follower, friend, helper, patron, sponsor, upholder, well-wisher
Antonyms adversary, antagonist, challenger, competitor, foe, opponent, rival

suppose 1. assume, calculate (*U.S. dialect*), conjecture, dare say, expect, guess (*Inf.*), infer, judge, opine, presume, presuppose, surmise, take as read, take for granted, think 2. believe, conceive, conclude, conjecture, consider, fancy, hypothesize, imagine, postulate, pretend

supposition conjecture, doubt, guess, guesswork, hypothesis, idea, notion, postulate, presumption, speculation, surmise, theory

suppress 1. beat down, check, clamp down on, conquer, crack down on, crush, drive underground, extinguish, overpower, overthrow, put an end to, quash, quell, quench, snuff out, stamp out, stop, subdue, trample on 2. censor, conceal, contain, cover up, curb, hold in *or* back, hold in check, keep secret, muffle, muzzle, repress, restrain, silence, smother, stifle, withhold
Antonyms encourage, foster, further, incite, inflame, promote, rouse, spread, stimulate, stir up, whip up

supremacy absolute rule, ascendancy, dominance, domination, dominion, lordship, mastery, paramountcy, predominance, pre-eminence, primacy, sovereignty, supreme authority, sway

supreme cardinal, chief, crowning, culminating, extreme, final, first, foremost, greatest, head, highest, incomparable, leading, matchless, paramount, peerless, predominant, pre-eminent, prevailing, prime, principal, sovereign, superlative, surpassing, top, ultimate, unsurpassed, utmost

sure 1. assured, certain, clear, confident, convinced, decided, definite, free from doubt, per-

suaded, positive, satisfied 2. accurate, dependable, effective, foolproof, honest, indisputable, infallible, never-failing, precise, reliable, sure-fire (*Inf.*), tried and true, trustworthy, trusty, undeniable, undoubted, unerring, unfailing, unmistakable, well-proven 3. assured, bound, guaranteed, ineluctable, inescapable, inevitable, irrevocable
Antonyms distrustful, dodgy, doubtful, dubious, fallible, insecure, sceptical, touch-and-go, unassured, uncertain, unconvinced, undependable, uneasy, unreliable, unsure, untrustworthy, vague

surface 1. *n.* covering, exterior, façade, face, facet, outside, plane, side, skin, superficies (*Rare*), top, veneer 2. *v.* appear, come to light, come up, crop up (*Inf.*), emerge, materialize, rise, transpire

surfeit 1. *n.* excess, glut, overindulgence, plethora, satiety, superabundance, superfluity 2. *v.* cram, fill, glut, gorge, overfeed, overfill, satiate, stuff
Antonyms *n.* dearth, deficiency, insufficiency, lack, scarcity, shortage, shortness, want

surge *v.* billow, eddy, gush, heave, rise, roll, rush, swell, swirl, tower, undulate, well forth

surly bearish, brusque, churlish, crabbed, cross, crusty, curmudgeonly, grouchy (*Inf.*), gruff, ill-natured, morose, perverse, sulky, sullen, testy, uncivil, ungracious

surpass beat, best, eclipse, exceed, excel, go one better than (*Inf.*), outdo, outshine, outstrip, override, overshadow, top, tower above, transcend

surplus 1. *n.* balance, excess, remainder, residue, superabundance, superfluity, surfeit 2. *adj.* excess, extra, in excess, left over, odd, remaining, spare, superfluous, unused
Antonyms *n.* dearth, deficiency, deficit, insufficiency, lack, paucity, shortage, shortfall ~*adj.*

deficient, falling short, inadequate, insufficient, lacking, limited, scant, scanty, scarce

surprise v. 1. amaze, astonish, astound, bewilder, bowl over (Inf.), confuse, disconcert, flabbergast (Inf.), leave open-mouthed, nonplus, stagger, stun, take aback 2. burst in on, catch in the act or red-handed, catch napping, catch unawares or off-guard, come down on like a bolt from the blue, discover, spring upon, startle ~n. 3. amazement, astonishment, bewilderment, incredulity, stupefaction, wonder 4. bolt from the blue, bombshell, eye-opener (Inf.), jolt, revelation, shock, start (Inf.)

surprised amazed, astonished, at a loss, caught on the hop (Brit. inf.), caught on the wrong foot (Inf.), disconcerted, incredulous, nonplussed, open-mouthed, speechless, startled, taken aback, taken by surprise, thunderstruck, unable to believe one's eyes

surprising amazing, astonishing, astounding, extraordinary, incredible, marvellous, remarkable, staggering, startling, unexpected, unlooked-for, unusual, wonderful

surrender v. 1. abandon, cede, concede, deliver up, forego, give up, part with, relinquish, renounce, resign, waive, yield 2. capitulate, give in, give oneself up, give way, lay down arms, quit, show the white flag, submit, succumb, throw in the towel, yield ~n. 3. capitulation, delivery, relinquishment, renunciation, resignation, submission, yielding
Antonyms v. defy, fight (on), make a stand against, oppose, resist, stand up to, withstand

surreptitious clandestine, covert, fraudulent, furtive, secret, sly, sneaking, stealthy, unauthorized, underhand, veiled
Antonyms blatant, conspicuous, frank, honest, manifest, obvious,

open, overt, unconcealed, undisguised

surround close in on, encircle, enclose, encompass, envelop, environ, fence in, girdle, hem in, ring

surroundings background, environment, environs, location, milieu, neighbourhood, setting

surveillance care, control, direction, inspection, observation, scrutiny, superintendence, supervision, vigilance, watch

survey v. 1. contemplate, examine, inspect, look over, observe, reconnoitre, research, review, scan, scrutinize, study, supervise, view 2. appraise, assess, estimate, measure, plan, plot, prospect, size up, take stock of, triangulate ~n. 3. examination, inquiry, inspection, overview, perusal, random sample, review, scrutiny, study

survive be extant, endure, exist, hold out, keep body and soul together (Inf.), last, live, live on, outlast, outlive, pull through, remain alive, subsist

suspect v. 1. distrust, doubt, harbour suspicions about, have one's doubts about, mistrust, smell a rat (Inf.) 2. believe, conclude, conjecture, consider, fancy, feel, guess, have a sneaking suspicion, hazard a guess, speculate, suppose, surmise, think probable ~adj. 3. doubtful, dubious, fishy (Inf.), open to suspicion, questionable
Antonyms v. accept, be certain, be confident of, believe, have faith in, know, think innocent, trust ~adj. above suspicion, innocent, reliable, straightforward, trustworthy, trusty

suspend 1. append, attach, dangle, hang, swing 2. adjourn, arrest, cease, cut short, debar, defer, delay, discontinue, hold off, interrupt, lay aside, pigeonhole, postpone, put off, shelve, stay, withhold

suspense anticipation, anxiety, apprehension, doubt, expectancy, expectation, indecision, insecurity, irresolution, tension, uncertainty, wavering

suspicion 1. bad vibes (*Inf.*), chariness, distrust, doubt, funny feeling (*Inf.*), jealousy, lack of confidence, misgiving, mistrust, qualm, scepticism, wariness **2.** conjecture, guess, gut feeling (*Inf.*), hunch, idea, impression, notion, supposition, surmise **3.** glimmer, hint, shade, shadow, soupçon (*Inf.*), strain, streak, suggestion, tinge, touch, trace

suspicious 1. apprehensive, distrustful, doubtful, jealous, mistrustful, sceptical, suspecting, unbelieving, wary **2.** doubtful, dubious, fishy (*Inf.*), funny, irregular, of doubtful honesty, open to doubt or misconstruction, queer, questionable, shady (*Inf.*), suspect

Antonyms (*sense 1*) believing, credulous, gullible, open, trustful, trusting, unsuspecting, unsuspicious (*sense 2*) above board, beyond suspicion, not open to question, open, straight, straightforward, unquestionable, upright

sustain 1. bear, carry, keep from falling, keep up, support, uphold **2.** bear, bear up under, endure, experience, feel, suffer, undergo, withstand **3.** aid, assist, comfort, foster, help, keep alive, nourish, nurture, provide for, relieve **4.** approve, confirm, continue, keep alive, keep going, keep up, maintain, prolong, protract, ratify **5.** endorse, uphold, validate, verify

swallow *v.* absorb, consume, devour, down (*Inf.*), drink, eat, gulp, ingest, swig (*Inf.*), swill, wash down

swamp 1. *n.* bog, everglade(s) (*U.S.*), fen, marsh, mire, morass, moss (*Scot., & northern English dialect*), quagmire, slough **2.** *v.* capsize, drench, engulf, flood, inundate, overwhelm, sink, submerge, swallow up, upset, wash over, waterlog

swap, swop *v.* bandy, barter, exchange, interchange, switch, trade, traffic

swarm *n.* **1.** army, bevy, concourse, crowd, drove, flock, herd, horde, host, mass, multitude, myriad, shoal, throng ~*v.* **2.** congregate, crowd, flock, mass, stream, throng **3.** *With* with abound, be alive (infested, overrun), bristle, crawl, teem

sway *v.* **1.** bend, fluctuate, incline, lean, lurch, oscillate, rock, roll, swing, wave **2.** affect, control, direct, dominate, govern, guide, induce, influence, persuade, prevail on, win over ~*n.* **3.** ascendency, authority, clout (*Inf.*), command, control, dominion, government, influence, jurisdiction, power, predominance, rule, sovereignty

swear 1. affirm, assert, attest, avow, declare, depose, give one's word, pledge oneself, promise, state under oath, take an oath, testify, vow, warrant **2.** be foulmouthed, blaspheme, curse, cuss (*Inf.*), imprecate, take the Lord's name in vain, turn the air blue, utter profanities

sweat *n.* **1.** diaphoresis (*Medical*), exudation, perspiration, sudor (*Medical*) **2.** *Inf.* agitation, anxiety, distress, flap (*Inf.*), panic, strain, worry **3.** *Inf.* backbreaking task, chore, drudgery, effort, labour, toil ~*v.* **4.** break out in a sweat, exude moisture, glow, perspire **5.** *Inf.* agonize, be on pins and needles (*Inf.*), be on tenterhooks, chafe, fret, lose sleep over, suffer, torture oneself, worry

sweep *v.* **1.** brush, clean, clear, remove **2.** career, flounce, fly, glance, glide, hurtle, pass, sail, scud, skim, tear, zoom ~*n.* **3.** arc, bend, curve, gesture, move, movement, stroke, swing **4.** compass, extent, range, scope, span, stretch, vista

sweet *adj.* **1.** cloying, honeyed, luscious, melting, saccharine, sugary, sweetened, syrupy, toothsome **2.** affectionate, agree~

able, amiable, appealing, attractive, beautiful, charming, delightful, engaging, fair, gentle, kind, lovable, sweet-tempered, taking, tender, unselfish, winning, winsome **3.** beloved, cherished, darling, dear, dearest, pet, precious, treasured **4.** aromatic, balmy, clean, fragrant, fresh, new, perfumed, pure, redolent, sweet-smelling, wholesome ~*n.* **5.** *Usually plural* bonbon, candy (*U.S.*), confectionery, sweetie, sweetmeats

Antonyms *adj.* (*sense 1*) acerbic, acid, bitter, savoury, sharp, sour, tart (*senses 2, 3 & 4*) bad-tempered, disagreeable, fetid, foul, grouchy, grumpy, hated, illtempered, loathsome, nasty, noisome, objectionable, obnoxious, rank, stinking, unappealing, unattractive, unlovable, unpleasant, unwanted

sweeten 1. honey, sugar, sugarcoat **2.** alleviate, appease, mollify, pacify, soften up, soothe, sugar the pill

sweetheart admirer, beau, beloved, boyfriend, darling, dear, flame (*Inf.*), follower (*Obsolete*), girlfriend, inamorata, inamorato, love, lover, steady (*Inf.*), suitor, swain (*Archaic*), sweetie (*Inf.*), truelove, valentine

swell *v.* **1.** balloon, become bloated *or* distended, become larger, be inflated, belly, billow, bloat, bulge, dilate, distend, enlarge, expand, extend, fatten, grow, increase, protrude, puff up, rise, round out, tumefy, well up **2.** add to, aggravate, augment, enhance, heighten, intensify, mount, surge ~*n.* **3.** billow, rise, surge, undulation, wave

Antonyms *v.* become smaller, contract, decrease, deflate, diminish, ebb, fall, go down, lessen, reduce, shrink, wane

swelling *n.* blister, bruise, bulge, bump, dilation, distension, enlargement, inflammation, lump, protuberance, puffiness, tumescence

swerve *v.* bend, deflect, depart from, deviate, diverge, incline, sheer off, shift, skew, stray, swing, turn, turn aside, veer, wander, wind

swift abrupt, expeditious, express, fast, fleet, fleet-footed, flying, hurried, nimble, nippy (*Brit. inf.*), prompt, quick, rapid, ready, short, short-lived, spanking, speedy, sudden, winged

Antonyms lead-footed, lingering, plodding, ponderous, slow, sluggish, tardy, tortoise-like, unhurried

swindle 1. *v.* bamboozle (*Inf.*), bilk (of), cheat, con (*Sl.*), deceive, defraud, diddle (*Inf.*), do (*Sl.*), dupe, fleece, hornswoggle (*Sl.*), overcharge, pull a fast one (on someone) (*Inf.*), put one over on (someone) (*Inf.*), rip (someone) off (*Sl.*), rook (*Sl.*), take (someone) for a ride (*Inf.*), take to the cleaners (*Inf.*), trick **2.** *n.* con trick (*Inf.*), deceit, deception, double-dealing, fiddle (*Brit. inf.*), fraud, imposition, knavery, racket, rip-off (*Sl.*), roguery, sharp practice, swizz (*Brit. inf.*), swizzle (*Brit. inf.*), trickery

swindler charlatan, cheat, confidence man, con man (*Sl.*), fraud, impostor, knave (*Archaic*), mountebank, rascal, rogue, rook (*Sl.*), shark, sharper, trickster

swing *v.* **1.** be pendent, be suspended, dangle, hang, move back and forth, suspend **2.** fluctuate, oscillate, rock, sway, vary, veer, vibrate, wave ~*n.* **3.** fluctuation, oscillation, stroke, sway, swaying, vibration

swirl *v.* agitate, boil, churn, eddy, spin, surge, twirl, twist, whirl

switch 1. *v.* change, change course, deflect, deviate, divert, exchange, interchange, rearrange, replace by, shift, substitute, swap (*Inf.*), trade, turn aside **2.** *n.* about-turn, alteration, change, change of direction, exchange, reversal, shift, substitution, swap (*Inf.*)

swollen bloated, distended, drop-

sical, edematous, enlarged, in~
flamed, oedematous, puffed up,
puffy, tumescent, tumid

swoop 1. *v.* descend, dive,
pounce, rush, stoop, sweep 2. *n.*
descent, drop, lunge, plunge,
pounce, rush, stoop, sweep

syllabus course of study, cur~
riculum

symbol badge, emblem, figure,
image, logo, mark, representa~
tion, sign, token, type

symmetrical balanced, in pro~
portion, proportional, regular,
well-proportioned
Antonyms asymmetrical, disor~
derly, irregular, lopsided, unbal~
anced, unequal, unsymmetrical

symmetry agreement, balance,
correspondence, evenness, form,
harmony, order, proportion,
regularity

sympathetic 1. affectionate, car~
ing, commiserating, compas~
sionate, concerned, condoling,
feeling, interested, kind, kindly,
pitying, responsive, supportive,
tender, understanding, warm,
warm-hearted 2. agreeable, ap~
preciative, companionable, com~
patible, congenial, friendly, like-
minded, responsive, well-
intentioned
Antonyms apathetic, callous,
cold, cold-hearted, disdainful,
disinterested, indifferent, inhu~
mane, insensitive, scornful,
steely, uncaring, uncompassion~
ate, uncongenial, unfeeling, un~
interested, unmoved, unrespon~
sive, unsympathetic

sympathize 1. bleed for, com~
miserate, condole, empathize,
feel for, feel one's heart go out to,
grieve with, have compassion,
offer consolation, pity, share an~
other's sorrow 2. agree, be in
accord, be in sympathy, go along
with, identify with, side with,
understand
Antonyms disagree, disregard,

fail to understand, have no feel~
ings for, misunderstand, mock,
oppose, reject, scorn

sympathizer condoler, fellow
traveller, partisan, supporter,
well-wisher

sympathy 1. commiseration,
compassion, condolence(s), em~
pathy, pity, tenderness, thought~
fulness, understanding 2. affinity,
agreement, congeniality, corre~
spondence, fellow feeling, har~
mony, rapport, union, warmth
Antonyms (*sense 1*) callousness,
coldness, disdain, hard-
heartedness, indifference, insen~
sitivity, lack of feeling *or* under~
standing *or* sympathy, pitiless~
ness, scorn (*sense 2*) antagonism,
disapproval, hostility, opposition,
resistance, unfriendliness

symptom expression, indication,
mark, note, sign, syndrome, to~
ken, warning

synthetic artificial, ersatz, fake,
man-made, manufactured, mock,
pseudo, sham, simulated
Antonyms authentic, genuine,
kosher (*Inf.*), natural, real

system 1. arrangement, classifi~
cation, combination, coordina~
tion, organization, scheme, setup
(*Sl.*), structure 2. fixed order,
frame of reference, method,
methodology, modus operandi,
practice, procedure, routine,
technique, theory, usage 3. defi~
nite plan, logical process, meth~
od, methodicalness, orderliness,
regularity, systematization

systematic businesslike, effi~
cient, methodical, orderly, or~
ganized, precise, standardized,
systematized, well-ordered
Antonyms arbitrary, cursory,
disorderly, disorganized, haphaz~
ard, indiscriminate, random,
slapdash, unbusinesslike, unme~
thodical, unpremeditated, unsys~
tematic

T

table *n.* 1. bench, board, counter, slab, stand 2. board, diet, fare, food, spread (*Inf.*), victuals 3. agenda, catalogue, chart, diagram, digest, graph, index, inventory, list, plan, record, register, roll, schedule, synopsis, tabulation ~*v.* 4. enter, move, propose, put forward, submit, suggest

taboo 1. *adj.* anathema, banned, beyond the pale, disapproved of, forbidden, frowned on, not allowed, not permitted, outlawed, prohibited, proscribed, ruled out, unacceptable, unmentionable, unthinkable 2. *n.* anathema, ban, disapproval, interdict, prohibition, proscription, restriction
Antonyms *adj.* acceptable, allowed, permitted, sanctioned

tacit implicit, implied, inferred, silent, taken for granted, undeclared, understood, unexpressed, unspoken, unstated, wordless

taciturn aloof, antisocial, closelipped, cold, distant, dumb, mute, quiet, reserved, reticent, silent, tight-lipped, uncommunicative, unforthcoming, withdrawn

tack *n.* 1. drawing pin, nail, pin, staple, thumbtack (*U.S.*), tintack 2. approach, bearing, course, direction, heading, line, method, path, plan, procedure, tactic, way ~*v.* 3. affix, attach, fasten, fix, nail, pin, staple 4. baste, stitch

tackle *n.* 1. accoutrements, apparatus, equipment, gear, implements, outfit, paraphernalia, rig, rigging, tools, trappings 2. block, challenge, stop ~*v.* 3. apply oneself to, attempt, begin, come or get to grips with, deal with, embark upon, engage in, essay, get stuck into (*Inf.*), have a go at (*Inf.*), set about, take on, try, turn one's hand to, undertake, wade

into 4. block, bring down, challenge, clutch, confront, grab, grasp, halt, intercept, seize, stop, take hold of, throw

tact address, adroitness, consideration, delicacy, diplomacy, discretion, finesse, judgment, perception, savoir-faire, sensitivity, skill, thoughtfulness, understanding
Antonyms awkwardness, clumsiness, gaucherie, heavy-handedness, indiscretion, insensitivity, lack of consideration, lack of discretion, tactlessness

tactful careful, considerate, delicate, diplomatic, discreet, judicious, perceptive, polished, polite, politic, prudent, sensitive, subtle, thoughtful, understanding
Antonyms awkward, clumsy, gauche, inconsiderate, indiscreet, insensitive, tactless, tasteless, thoughtless, undiplomatic, unsubtle, untoward

tactic 1. approach, course, device, line, manoeuvre, means, method, move, ploy, policy, scheme, stratagem, tack, trick, way 2. *Plural* campaign, generalship, manoeuvres, plans, strategy

tactical adroit, artful, clever, cunning, diplomatic, foxy, politic, shrewd, skilful, smart, strategic

tactless blundering, boorish, careless, clumsy, discourteous, gauche, harsh, impolite, impolitic, imprudent, inconsiderate, indelicate, indiscreet, inept, injudicious, insensitive, maladroit, rough, rude, sharp, thoughtless, uncivil, undiplomatic, unfeeling, unkind, unsubtle

tail *n.* 1. appendage, conclusion, empennage, end, extremity, rear end, tailpiece, train 2. file, line, queue, tailback, train ~*v.* 3. *Inf.* dog the footsteps of, follow, keep an eye on, shadow, stalk, track, trail

taint 1. *v.* adulterate, blight, contaminate, corrupt, dirty, foul, infect, poison, pollute, soil, spoil **2.** *n.* black mark, blemish, blot, blot on one's escutcheon, defect, disgrace, dishonour, fault, flaw, shame, smear, spot, stain, stigma **Antonyms** *v.* clean, cleanse, decontaminate, disinfect, purify

take *v.* **1.** abduct, acquire, arrest, capture, carry off, catch, clutch, ensnare, entrap, gain possession of, get, get hold of, grasp, grip, have, help oneself to, lay hold of, obtain, receive, secure, seize, win **2.** abstract, appropriate, carry off, filch, misappropriate, nick (*Brit. sl.*), pinch (*Inf.*), purloin, run off with, steal, swipe (*Sl.*), walk off with **3.** book, buy, engage, hire, lease, pay for, pick, purchase, rent, reserve, select **4.** abide, bear, brave, brook, endure, go through, pocket, put up with (*Inf.*), stand, stomach, submit to, suffer, swallow, thole (*Scot.*), tolerate, undergo, weather, withstand **5.** consume, drink, eat, imbibe, ingest, inhale, swallow **6.** accept, adopt, assume, enter upon, undertake **7.** assume, believe, consider, deem, hold, interpret as, perceive, presume, receive, regard, see as, think of as, understand **8.** bear, bring, carry, cart, convey, ferry, fetch, haul, tote (*Inf.*), transport **9.** accompany, bring, conduct, convoy, escort, guide, lead, usher **10.** deduct, eliminate, remove, subtract **11.** accept, accommodate, contain, have room for, hold **Antonyms** add, avoid, buckle, crack, decline, dismiss, dodge, eschew, fail, flop, free, give, give back, give in, give way, hand over, ignore, let go, put, refuse, reject, release, restore, return, scorn, send, spurn, surrender, yield

take back disavow, disclaim, recant, renounce, retract, unsay, withdraw

take down make a note of, minute, note, put on record, record, set down, transcribe, write down

take in 1. absorb, assimilate, comprehend, digest, grasp, understand **2.** comprise, contain, cover, embrace, encompass, include **3.** accommodate, admit, let in, receive **4.** *Inf.* bilk, cheat, con (*Inf.*), deceive, do (*Sl.*), dupe, fool, gull (*Archaic*), hoodwink, mislead, pull the wool over (someone's) eyes (*Inf.*), swindle, trick

takeoff 1. departure, launch, liftoff **2.** *Inf.* caricature, imitation, lampoon, mocking, parody, satire, send-up (*Brit. inf.*), spoof (*Inf.*), travesty

take off 1. discard, divest oneself of, doff, drop, peel off, remove, strip off **2.** become airborne, leave the ground, lift off, take to the air **3.** *Inf.* beat it (*Sl.*), decamp, depart, disappear, go, hit the road (*Sl.*), leave, set out, split (*Sl.*), strike out **4.** *Inf.* caricature, hit off, imitate, lampoon, mimic, mock, parody, satirize, send up (*Brit. inf.*), spoof (*Inf.*), travesty

take on 1. employ, engage, enlist, enrol, hire, retain **2.** accept, address oneself to, agree to do, have a go at (*Inf.*), tackle, undertake **3.** compete against, contend with, enter the lists against, face, fight, match oneself against, oppose, pit oneself against, vie with

take up 1. adopt, assume, become involved in, engage in, start **2.** begin again, carry on, continue, follow on, go on, pick up, proceed, recommence, restart, resume **3.** absorb, consume, cover, extend over, fill, occupy, use up

taking 1. *adj.* attractive, beguiling, captivating, charming, compelling, delightful, enchanting, engaging, fascinating, fetching (*Inf.*), intriguing, pleasing, prepossessing, winning **2.** *n. Plural* earnings, gain, gate, income, pickings, proceeds, profits, receipts, returns, revenue, take, yield

tale 1. account, anecdote, *conte*,

fable, fiction, legend, narration, narrative, novel, relation, report, romance, saga, short story, spiel, story, yarn (*Inf.*) 2. cock-and-bull story (*Inf.*), fabrication, falsehood, fib, lie, rigmarole, rumour, spiel (*Inf.*), tall story (*Inf.*), untruth

talent ability, aptitude, bent, capacity, endowment, faculty, flair, forte, genius, gift, knack, parts, power

talented able, artistic, brilliant, gifted, well-endowed

talk v. 1. articulate, chat, chatter, communicate, converse, crack (*Scot.*), express oneself, gab (*Inf.*), give voice to, gossip, natter, prate, prattle, rap (*Sl.*), say, speak, utter, verbalize, witter (*Inf.*) 2. chew the rag (*Inf.*), confabulate, confer, have a confab (*Inf.*), hold discussions, negotiate, palaver, parley 3. blab, crack, give the game away, grass (*Sl.*), inform, reveal information, sing (*Inf.*), spill the beans (*Inf.*), squeak (*Inf.*), squeal (*Sl.*) ~n. 4. address, discourse, disquisition, dissertation, harangue, lecture, oration, sermon, speech 5. blather, blether, chat, chatter, chit-chat, conversation, crack (*Scot.*), gab (*Inf.*), gossip, hearsay, jaw (*Sl.*), natter, rap (*Sl.*), rumour, tittle-tattle 6. colloquy, conclave, confab (*Inf.*), confabulation, conference, consultation, dialogue, discussion, meeting, negotiation, palaver, parley, seminar, symposium 7. argot, dialect, jargon, language, lingo (*Inf.*), patois, slang, speech, words

talking-to criticism, dressing-down (*Inf.*), lecture, rap on the knuckles (*Inf.*), rebuke, reprimand, reproach, reproof, row, scolding, slating (*Inf.*), telling-off (*Inf.*), ticking-off (*Inf.*), wigging (*Brit. sl.*)

tall 1. big, elevated, giant, high, lanky, lofty, soaring, towering 2. *Inf.* demanding, difficult, exorbitant, hard, unreasonable, well-nigh impossible

Antonyms easy, reasonable, short, small, squat, stumpy, tiny, wee

tally v. 1. accord, agree, coincide, concur, conform, correspond, fit, harmonize, jibe (*Inf.*), match, parallel, square, suit 2. compute, count up, keep score, mark, reckon, record, register, total ~n. 3. count, mark, reckoning, record, running total, score, total

Antonyms (*sense 1*) clash, conflict, contradict, differ, disagree

tame adj. 1. amenable, broken, cultivated, disciplined, docile, domesticated, gentle, obedient, tractable 2. compliant, docile, manageable, meek, obedient, spiritless, subdued, submissive, unresisting 3. bland, boring, dull, flat, humdrum, insipid, lifeless, prosaic, tedious, unexciting, uninspiring, uninteresting, vapid, wearisome ~v. 4. break in, domesticate, gentle, house-train, make tame, pacify, train 5. break the spirit of, bridle, bring to heel, conquer, curb, discipline, enslave, humble, master, repress, subdue, subjugate, suppress

Antonyms adj. aggressive, argumentative, exciting, feral, ferocious, frenzied, hot, interesting, lively, obdurate, savage, stimulating, strong-willed, stubborn, undomesticated, unmanageable, untamed, wild ~v. arouse, incite, intensify, make fiercer

tamper 1. alter, damage, fiddle (*Inf.*), fool about (*Inf.*), interfere, intrude, meddle, mess about, monkey around, muck about (*Brit. sl.*), poke one's nose into (*Inf.*), tinker 2. bribe, corrupt, fix (*Inf.*), get at, influence, manipulate, rig

tangle n. 1. coil, confusion, entanglement, jam, jungle, knot, mass, mat, mesh, snarl, twist, web 2. complication, entanglement, fix (*Inf.*), imbroglio, labyrinth, maze, mess, mix-up ~v. 3. coil, confuse, entangle, interlace, interlock, intertwist, interweave, jam, kink, knot, mat, mesh, snarl, twist

Antonyms (*sense 3*) disentangle, extricate, free, straighten out, unravel, untangle

tangled 1. entangled, jumbled, knotted, knotty, matted, messy, scrambled, snarled, tousled, twisted **2.** complex, complicated, confused, convoluted, involved, knotty, messy, mixed-up

tantalize baffle, balk, disappoint, entice, frustrate, keep (someone) hanging on, lead on, make (someone's) mouth water, provoke, taunt, tease, thwart, titillate, torment, torture

tantrum fit, flare-up, hysterics, ill humour, outburst, paddy (*Brit. inf.*), paroxysm, storm, temper, wax (*Inf.*)

tap¹ 1. *v.* beat, drum, knock, pat, rap, strike, touch **2.** *n.* beat, knock, light blow, pat, rap, touch

tap² 1. faucet (*U.S.*), spigot, spout, stopcock, valve **2.** bung, plug, spile, stopper ~*v.* **3.** bleed, broach, drain, draw off, open, pierce, siphon off, unplug **4.** draw on, exploit, make use of, milk, mine, put to use, turn to account, use, utilize

tape *n.* **1.** band, ribbon, strip ~*v.* **2.** bind, seal, secure, stick, wrap **3.** record, tape-record, video

taper come to a point, narrow, thin

target 1. aim, ambition, bull's-eye, end, goal, intention, mark, object, objective **2.** butt, quarry, scapegoat, victim

tariff 1. assessment, duty, excise, impost, levy, rate, tax, toll **2.** bill of fare, charges, menu, price list, schedule

tarnish *v.* befoul, blacken, blemish, blot, darken, dim, discolour, drag through the mud, dull, lose lustre *or* shine, rust, soil, spot, stain, sully, taint

tart¹ 1. pastry, pie, tartlet **2.** call girl, fallen woman, *fille de joie*, floozy (*Sl.*), harlot, hooker (*U.S. sl.*), loose woman, prostitute, slut,

streetwalker, strumpet, trollop, whore, woman of easy virtue

tart² 1. acid, acidulous, astringent, bitter, piquant, pungent, sharp, sour, tangy, vinegary **2.** acrimonious, astringent, barbed, biting, caustic, crusty, cutting, harsh, nasty, scathing, sharp, short, snappish, testy, trenchant, wounding

task *n.* assignment, business, charge, chore, duty, employment, enterprise, exercise, job, labour, mission, occupation, toil, undertaking, work

taste *n.* **1.** flavour, relish, savour, smack, tang **2.** bit, bite, dash, drop, morsel, mouthful, nip, sample, sip, *soupçon*, spoonful, swallow, titbit, touch **3.** appetite, bent, desire, fancy, fondness, inclination, leaning, liking, palate, partiality, penchant, predilection, preference, relish **4.** appreciation, cultivation, culture, discernment, discrimination, elegance, grace, judgment, perception, polish, refinement, style ~*v.* **5.** differentiate, discern, distinguish, perceive **6.** assay, nibble, relish, sample, savour, sip, test, try **7.** come up against, encounter, experience, feel, have knowledge of, know, meet with, partake of, undergo

Antonyms *n.* bawdiness, blandness, blueness, coarseness, crudeness, disinclination, dislike, distaste, hatred, impropriety, indelicacy, insipidity, lack of discernment, lack of judgment, loathing, mawkishness, obscenity, tackiness, tactlessness, tastelessness, unsubtlety ~*v.* fail to achieve, fail to discern, miss, remain ignorant of

tasteful aesthetically pleasing, artistic, beautiful, charming, cultivated, cultured, delicate, discriminating, elegant, exquisite, fastidious, graceful, handsome, harmonious, in good taste, polished, refined, restrained, smart, stylish

Antonyms flashy, garish, gaudy,

inelegant, loud, objectionable, offensive, showy, sick, tacky, tasteless, tawdry, tense, uncultured, unrefined, vulgar

tasteless 1. bland, boring, dull, flat, flavourless, insipid, mild, stale, tame, thin, uninspired, uninteresting, vapid, watered-down, weak **2.** cheap, coarse, crass, crude, flashy, garish, gaudy, graceless, gross, impolite, improper, indecorous, indelicate, indiscreet, inelegant, low, rude, tactless, tawdry, uncouth, unseemly, vulgar

Antonyms (*sense 1*) appetizing, delectable, delicious, flavoursome, savoury, scrumptious (*Inf.*), tasty (*sense 2*) elegant, graceful, refined, tasteful

tasty appetizing, delectable, delicious, flavourful, flavoursome, full-flavoured, good-tasting, luscious, palatable, sapid, savoury, scrumptious (*Inf.*), toothsome, yummy (*Sl.*)

Antonyms bland, flavourless, insipid, tasteless, unappetizing, unsavoury

taunt 1. *v.* deride, flout, gibe, guy (*Inf.*), insult, jeer, mock, provoke, reproach, revile, ridicule, sneer, tease, torment, twit, upbraid **2.** *n.* barb, censure, cut, derision, dig, gibe, insult, jeer, provocation, reproach, ridicule, sarcasm, teasing

taut flexed, rigid, strained, stressed, stretched, tense, tight

Antonyms loose, relaxed, slack

tawdry brummagem, cheap, cheap-jack (*Inf.*), flashy, gaudy, gimcrack, glittering, meretricious, plastic (*Sl.*), raffish, showy, tacky, tasteless, tatty, tinsel, tinselly, vulgar

tax *n.* **1.** assessment, charge, contribution, customs, duty, excise, imposition, impost, levy, rate, tariff, tithe, toll, tribute **2.** burden, demand, drain, load, pressure, strain, weight ~*v.* **3.** assess, charge, demand, exact, extract, impose, levy a tax on, rate, tithe **4.** burden, drain, enervate, exhaust, load, make heavy demands on, overburden, push, put pressure on, sap, strain, stretch, task, try, weaken, wear out, weary, weigh heavily on **5.** accuse, arraign, blame, charge, impeach, impugn, incriminate, lay at one's door

teach advise, coach, demonstrate, direct, discipline, drill, edify, educate, enlighten, give lessons in, guide, impart, implant, inculcate, inform, instil, instruct, school, show, train, tutor

teacher coach, dominie (*Scot.*), don, educator, guide, guru, instructor, lecturer, master, mentor, mistress, pedagogue, professor, schoolmaster, schoolmistress, schoolteacher, trainer, tutor

team 1. *n.* band, body, bunch, company, crew, gang, group, line-up, set, side, squad, troupe **2.** *v.* Often with **up** band together, cooperate, couple, get together, join, link, unite, work together, yoke

tear *v.* **1.** claw, divide, lacerate, mangle, mutilate, pull apart, rend, rip, rive, run, rupture, scratch, sever, shred, split, sunder **2.** belt (*Sl.*), bolt, career, charge, dart, dash, fly, gallop, hurry, race, run, rush, shoot, speed, sprint, zoom **3.** grab, pluck, pull, rip, seize, snatch, wrench, wrest, yank ~*n.* **4.** hole, laceration, mutilation, rent, rip, run, rupture, scratch, split

tearful blubbering, crying, in tears, lachrymose, sobbing, weeping, weepy (*Inf.*), whimpering

tease aggravate (*Inf.*), annoy, badger, bait, bedevil, chaff, gibe, goad, guy (*Inf.*), lead on, mock, needle, pester, plague (*Inf.*), provoke, rag, rib (*Inf.*), ridicule, tantalize, taunt, torment, twit, vex, worry

technique 1. approach, course, fashion, manner, means, method, mode, modus operandi, procedure, style, system, way **2.** ad~

dress, adroitness, art, artistry, craft, craftsmanship, delivery, execution, facility, knack, know-how (*Inf.*), performance, proficiency, skill, touch

tedious annoying, banal, boring, deadly dull, drab, dreary, dreich (*Scot.*), dull, fatiguing, humdrum, irksome, laborious, lifeless, long-drawn-out, monotonous, prosaic, prosy, soporific, tiring, unexciting, uninteresting, vapid, wearisome

Antonyms enjoyable, enthralling, exciting, exhilarating, imaginative, inspiring, interesting, quickly finished, short, stimulating

tedium banality, boredom, deadness, drabness, dreariness, dullness, ennui, lifelessness, monotony, routine, sameness, tediousness, the doldrums

Antonyms challenge, excitement, exhilaration, fascination, interest, liveliness, stimulation

teem abound, be abundant, bear, be crawling with, be full of, be prolific, brim, bristle, burst at the seams, overflow, produce, pullulate, swarm

teeming abundant, alive, brimful, brimming, bristling, bursting, chock-a-block, chock-full, crawling, fruitful, full, numerous, overflowing, packed, replete, swarming, thick

telepathy mind-reading, sixth sense, thought transference

telephone 1. *n.* blower (*Inf.*), handset, line, phone **2.** *v.* buzz (*Inf.*), call, call up, dial, get on the blower (*Inf.*), give (someone) a buzz (*Inf.*), give (someone) a call, give (someone) a ring (*Brit.*), give someone a tinkle (*Brit. inf.*), phone, put a call through to, ring (*Brit.*)

telescope *n.* **1.** glass, spyglass ~*v.* **2.** concertina, crush, squash **3.** abbreviate, abridge, capsulize, compress, condense, consolidate, contract, curtail, cut, shorten, shrink, tighten, trim, truncate

tell *v.* **1.** acquaint, announce, apprise, communicate, confess, disclose, divulge, express, impart, inform, let know, make known, mention, notify, proclaim, reveal, say, speak, state, utter **2.** authorize, bid, call upon, command, direct, enjoin, instruct, order, require, summon **3.** chronicle, depict, describe, give an account of, narrate, portray, recount, rehearse, relate, report **4.** comprehend, discern, discover, make out, see, understand **5.** differentiate, discern, discriminate, distinguish, identify **6.** carry weight, count, have or take effect, have force, make its presence felt, register, take its toll, weigh **7.** calculate, compute, count, enumerate, number, reckon, tally

temper *n.* **1.** attitude, character, constitution, disposition, frame of mind, humour, mind, mood, nature, temperament, tenor, vein **2.** bad mood, fit of pique, fury, paddy (*Brit. inf.*), passion, rage, tantrum, wax (*Inf.*) **3.** anger, annoyance, heat, hot-headedness, ill humour, irascibility, irritability, irritation, passion, peevishness, petulance, resentment, surliness **4.** calm, calmness, composure, cool (*Sl.*), coolness, equanimity, good humour, moderation, self-control, tranquillity ~*v.* **5.** abate, admix, allay, assuage, calm, lessen, mitigate, moderate, mollify, palliate, restrain, soften, soft-pedal (*Inf.*), soothe, tone down

temperament bent, cast of mind, character, complexion, constitution, disposition, frame of mind, humour, make-up, mettle, nature, outlook, personality, quality, soul, spirit, stamp, temper, tendencies, tendency

temperamental 1. capricious, easily upset, emotional, erratic, excitable, explosive, fiery, highly strung, hot-headed, hypersensitive, impatient, irritable, mercurial, moody, neurotic, passionate, petulant, sensitive, touchy, volatile **2.** erratic, inconsistent, undependable, unpredictable, unreliable

Antonyms calm, constant, coolheaded, dependable, easy-going, even-tempered, level-headed, phlegmatic, reliable, stable, steady, unexcitable, unflappable, unperturbable

temperance 1. continence, discretion, forbearance, moderation, restraint, self-control, self-discipline, self-restraint **2.** abstemiousness, abstinence, prohibition, sobriety, teetotalism

Antonyms crapulence, excess, immoderation, intemperance, overindulgence, prodigality

temperate 1. agreeable, balmy, calm, clement, cool, fair, gentle, mild, moderate, pleasant, soft **2.** calm, composed, dispassionate, equable, even-tempered, mild, moderate, reasonable, self-controlled, self-restrained, sensible, stable **3.** abstemious, abstinent, continent, moderate, sober

Antonyms excessive, extreme, harsh, immoderate, inclement, inordinate, intemperate, prodigal, severe, torrid, uncontrolled, undisciplined, unreasonable, unrestrained, wild

temple church, holy place, place of worship, sanctuary, shrine

temporarily briefly, fleetingly, for a little while, for a moment, for a short time, for a short while, for the moment, for the time being, momentarily, pro tem

temporary brief, ephemeral, evanescent, fleeting, fugacious, fugitive, here today and gone tomorrow, impermanent, interim, momentary, passing, pro tem, *pro tempore*, provisional, short-lived, transient, transitory

Antonyms durable, enduring, everlasting, long-lasting, long-term, permanent

tempt 1. allure, appeal to, attract, coax, decoy, draw, entice, inveigle, invite, lead on, lure, make one's mouth water, seduce, tantalize, whet the appetite of, woo

2. bait, dare, fly in the face of, provoke, risk, test, try

Antonyms (*sense 1*) deter, discourage, dissuade, hinder, inhibit, put off

temptation allurement, appeal, attraction, attractiveness, bait, blandishments, coaxing, come-on (*Inf.*), decoy, draw, enticement, inducement, invitation, lure, pull, seduction, snare, tantalization

tempting alluring, appetizing, attractive, enticing, inviting, mouthwatering, seductive, tantalizing

Antonyms off-putting, unappetizing, unattractive, undesirable, uninviting, untempting

tenacious 1. clinging, fast, firm, forceful, iron, strong, tight, unshakable **2.** retentive, unforgetful **3.** adamant, determined, dogged, firm, inflexible, intransigent, obdurate, obstinate, persistent, pertinacious, resolute, staunch, steadfast, strong-willed, stubborn, sure, unswerving, unyielding

Antonyms (*sense 3*) changeable, flexible, irresolute, vacillating, wavering, yielding

tenancy holding, lease, occupancy, occupation, possession, renting, residence

tenant holder, inhabitant, leaseholder, lessee, occupant, occupier, renter, resident

tend[1] be apt, be biased, be disposed, be inclined, be liable, be likely, gravitate, have a leaning, have an inclination, have a tendency, incline, lean, trend

tend[2] attend, care for, cater to, control, cultivate, feed, guard, handle, keep, keep an eye on, look after, maintain, manage, minister to, nurse, nurture, protect, see to, serve, take care of, wait on, watch, watch over

Antonyms disregard, ignore, neglect, overlook, shirk

tendency bent, disposition, inclination, leaning, liability, partiality, penchant, predilection, predisposition, proclivity, proneness, propensity, readiness, susceptibility

tender 1. breakable, delicate, feeble, fragile, frail, soft, weak **2.** callow, green, immature, impressionable, inexperienced, new, raw, sensitive, unripe, vulnerable, wet behind the ears (*Inf.*), young, youthful **3.** affectionate, amorous, benevolent, caring, compassionate, considerate, fond, gentle, humane, kind, loving, merciful, pitiful, sentimental, softhearted, sympathetic, tenderhearted, warm, warm-hearted **4.** complicated, dangerous, difficult, risky, sensitive, ticklish, touchy, tricky **5.** aching, acute, bruised, inflamed, irritated, painful, raw, sensitive, smarting, sore
Antonyms advanced, brutal, cold-hearted, cruel, elderly, experienced, grown-up, hard, hard-hearted, inhuman, insensitive, leathery, mature, pitiless, seasoned, sophisticated, strong, tough, uncaring, unkind, unsympathetic, worldly, worldly-wise

tenderness 1. delicateness, feebleness, fragility, frailness, sensitiveness, sensitivity, softness, vulnerability, weakness **2.** callowness, greenness, immaturity, impressionableness, inexperience, newness, rawness, sensitivity, vulnerability, youth, youthfulness **3.** affection, amorousness, attachment, benevolence, care, compassion, consideration, devotion, fondness, gentleness, humaneness, humanity, kindness, liking, love, mercy, pity, sentimentality, softheartedness, sympathy, tenderheartedness, warm-heartedness, warmth **4.** ache, aching, bruising, inflammation, irritation, pain, painfulness, rawness, sensitiveness, sensitivity, smart, soreness
Antonyms (*sense 3*) cruelty, hardness, harshness, indifference, insensitivity, unkindness

tense *adj.* **1.** rigid, strained, stretched, taut, tight **2.** anxious,

apprehensive, edgy, fidgety, jittery (*Inf.*), jumpy, keyed up, nervous, on edge, overwrought, restless, strained, strung up (*Inf.*), under pressure, uptight (*Sl.*), wound up (*Inf.*), wrought up **3.** exciting, moving, nerve-racking, stressful, worrying
Antonyms adj. boring, calm, collected, cool-headed, dull, easy-going, flaccid, flexible, limp, loose, pliant, relaxed, self-possessed, serene, unconcerned, uninteresting, unruffled, unworried

tension 1. pressure, rigidity, stiffness, straining, stress, stretching, tautness, tightness **2.** anxiety, apprehension, edginess, hostility, ill feeling, nervousness, pressure, restlessness, strain, stress, suspense, the jitters (*Inf.*), unease
Antonyms (*sense 2*) calmness, peacefulness, relaxation, restfulness, serenity, tranquillity

tentative 1. conjectural, experimental, indefinite, provisional, speculative, unconfirmed, unsettled **2.** backward, cautious, diffident, doubtful, faltering, hesitant, timid, uncertain, undecided, unsure
Antonyms (*sense 1*) conclusive, decisive, definite, final, fixed, resolved, settled (*sense 2*) assured, bold, certain, confident, unhesitating

tepid 1. lukewarm, slightly warm, warmish **2.** apathetic, cool, half-hearted, indifferent, lukewarm, unenthusiastic

term *n.* **1.** appellation, denomination, designation, expression, locution, name, phrase, title, word **2.** duration, interval, period, season, space, span, spell, time, while **3.** course, session **4.** bound, boundary, close, conclusion, confine, culmination, end, finish, fruition, limit, terminus ~*v.* **5.** call, denominate, designate, dub, entitle, label, name, style

terminate abort, bring *or* come to an end, cease, close, complete, conclude, cut off, discontinue,

end, expire, finish, issue, lapse, put an end to, result, run out, stop, wind up
Antonyms begin, commence, inaugurate, initiate, instigate, introduce, open, start

termination abortion, cessation, close, completion, conclusion, consequence, cut-off point, discontinuation, effect, end, ending, expiry, finale, finis, finish, issue, result, wind-up (*Inf.*)
Antonyms beginning, commencement, inauguration, initiation, opening, start

terms 1. language, manner of speaking, phraseology, terminology **2.** conditions, particulars, premises (*Law*), provisions, provisos, qualifications, specifications, stipulations **3.** charges, fee, payment, price, rates

terrible 1. bad, dangerous, desperate, extreme, serious, severe **2.** *Inf.* abhorrent, awful, bad, beastly (*Inf.*), dire, dreadful, duff (*Brit. sl.*), foul, frightful, hateful, hideous, loathsome, obnoxious, odious, offensive, poor, repulsive, revolting, rotten (*Inf.*), unpleasant, vile **3.** appalling, awful, dread, dreaded, dreadful, fearful, frightful, gruesome, harrowing, horrendous, horrible, horrid, horrifying, monstrous, shocking, terrifying, unspeakable
Antonyms (*sense 1*) harmless, insignificant, mild, moderate, paltry, small (*sense 2*) admirable, brilliant, delightful, excellent, fine, great, magic, noteworthy, pleasant, remarkable, super, superb, terrific, very good, wonderful (*sense 3*) calming, comforting, encouraging, reassuring, settling, soothing

terrific 1. awesome, awful, dreadful, enormous, excessive, extreme, fearful, fierce, gigantic, great, harsh, horrific, huge, intense, monstrous, severe, terrible, tremendous **2.** *Inf.* ace (*Inf.*), amazing, breathtaking, excellent, fabulous (*Inf.*), fantastic (*Inf.*), fine, great (*Inf.*), magnificent,

marvellous, outstanding, sensational (*Inf.*), smashing (*Inf.*), stupendous, super (*Inf.*), superb, very good, wonderful
Antonyms appalling, awful, bad, calming, comforting, dreadful, encouraging, harmless, hideous, insignificant, lousy, mediocre, mild, moderate, paltry, reassuring, rotten, settling, shocking, soothing, terrible, uninspired, unpleasant

terrify alarm, appal, awe, dismay, fill with terror, frighten, frighten out of one's wits, horrify, intimidate, make one's blood run cold, make one's flesh creep, make one's hair stand on end, petrify, put the fear of God into, scare, scare to death, shock, terrorize

territory area, bailiwick, country, district, domain, land, province, region, sector, state, terrain, tract, zone

terror alarm, anxiety, awe, consternation, dismay, dread, fear, fear and trembling, fright, horror, intimidation, panic, shock

terrorize 1. browbeat, bully, coerce, intimidate, menace, oppress, strong-arm (*Inf.*), threaten **2.** alarm, appal, awe, dismay, fill with terror, frighten, frighten out of one's wits, horrify, inspire panic in, intimidate, make one's blood run cold, make one's flesh creep, make one's hair stand on end, petrify, put the fear of God into, scare, scare to death, shock, strike terror into, terrify

terse 1. aphoristic, brief, clipped, compact, concise, condensed, crisp, elliptical, epigrammatic, gnomic, incisive, laconic, neat, pithy, sententious, short, succinct, summary, to the point **2.** abrupt, brusque, curt, short, snappy

test 1. *v.* analyse, assay, assess, check, examine, experiment, investigate, prove, put to the proof, put to the test, try, try out, verify **2.** *n.* analysis, assessment, attempt, catechism, check, evaluation, examination, investigation, ordeal, probation, proof, trial

testify affirm, assert, attest, bear witness, certify, corroborate, declare, depone (*Scots Law*), depose (*Law*), evince, give testimony, show, state, swear, vouch, witness

Antonyms belie, contradict, controvert, disprove, dispute, gainsay, oppose

testimonial certificate, character, commendation, credential, endorsement, recommendation, reference, tribute

testimony affidavit, affirmation, attestation, avowal, confirmation, corroboration, declaration, deposition, evidence, information, profession, statement, submission, witness

text 1. body, contents, main body, matter 2. wording, words 3. argument, matter, motif, subject, theme, topic

texture character, composition, consistency, constitution, fabric, feel, grain, make, quality, structure, surface, tissue, weave

thanks acknowledgment, appreciation, credit, gratefulness, gratitude, recognition, thanksgiving

thaw defrost, dissolve, liquefy, melt, soften, unfreeze, warm

Antonyms chill, congeal, freeze, harden, solidify, stiffen

theatrical affected, artificial, ceremonious, dramatic, exaggerated, hammy (*Inf.*), histrionic, mannered, ostentatious, overdone, pompous, showy, stagy, stilted, unreal

theft embezzlement, fraud, larceny, pilfering, purloining, rip-off (*Sl.*), robbery, stealing, swindling, thievery, thieving

theme 1. argument, burden, idea, keynote, matter, subject, subject matter, text, thesis, topic 2. leitmotiv, motif, recurrent image, unifying idea 3. composition, dissertation, essay, exercise, paper

theoretical abstract, academic,

conjectural, hypothetical, ideal, impractical, pure, speculative

Antonyms applied, experiential, factual, practical, realistic

theorize conjecture, formulate, guess, hypothesize, project, propound, speculate, suppose

theory 1. assumption, conjecture, guess, hypothesis, presumption, speculation, supposition, surmise, thesis 2. philosophy, plan, proposal, scheme, system

Antonyms certainty, experience, fact, practice, reality

therapeutic ameliorative, analeptic, beneficial, corrective, curative, good, healing, remedial, restorative, salubrious, salutary, sanative

therefore accordingly, as a result, consequently, ergo, for that reason, hence, so, then, thence, thus, whence

thick *adj.* 1. broad, bulky, deep, fat, solid, substantial, wide 2. close, clotted, coagulated, compact, concentrated, condensed, crowded, deep, dense, heavy, impenetrable, opaque 3. abundant, brimming, bristling, bursting, chock-a-block, chock-full, covered, crawling, frequent, full, numerous, packed, replete, swarming, teeming 4. blockheaded, brainless, dense, dimwitted (*Inf.*), dopey (*Sl.*), dull, insensitive, moronic, obtuse, slow, slow-witted, stupid, thickheaded 5. dense, heavy, impenetrable, soupy 6. distorted, guttural, hoarse, husky, inarticulate, indistinct, throaty 7. broad, decided, distinct, marked, pronounced, rich, strong 8. *Inf.* chummy (*Inf.*), close, confidential, devoted, familiar, friendly, hand in glove, inseparable, intimate, matey (*Brit. inf.*), on good terms, pally (*Inf.*), thick (in *Inf.*)

Antonyms (*sense 1*) narrow, slight, slim, thin (*sense 2*) clear, diluted, runny, thin, watery, weak (*sense 3*) bare, clear, devoid of, empty, free from, sparse, thin (*sense 4*) articulate, brainy, bright, clever, intellectual, intelligent, quick-witted, sharp, smart (*sense 5*) clear, thin (*sense 6*) articulate, clear, distinct, sharp, shrill, thin (*sense 7*) faint, slight, vague, weak (*sense 8*) antagonistic, distant, hostile, unfriendly

thicken cake, clot, coagulate, condense, congeal, deepen, gel, inspissate (*Archaic*), jell, set
Antonyms dilute, thin, water down, weaken

thief bandit, burglar, cheat, cracksman (*Sl.*), crook (*Inf.*), embezzler, housebreaker, larcenist, mugger (*Inf.*), pickpocket, pilferer, plunderer, purloiner, robber, shoplifter, stealer, swindler

thin *adj.* 1. attenuate, attenuated, fine, narrow, threadlike 2. delicate, diaphanous, filmy, fine, flimsy, gossamer, seethrough, sheer, translucent, transparent, unsubstantial 3. bony, emaciated, lank, lanky, lean, light, meagre, scraggy, scrawny, skeletal, skinny, slender, slight, slim, spare, spindly, thin as a rake, undernourished, underweight 4. deficient, meagre, scanty, scarce, scattered, skimpy, sparse, wispy 5. dilute, diluted, rarefied, runny, watery, weak, wishy-washy (*Inf.*) 6. feeble, flimsy, inadequate, insufficient, lame, poor, scant, scanty, shallow, slight, superficial, unconvincing, unsubstantial, weak
Antonyms (*sense 1*) heavy, thick (*sense 2*) bulky, dense, heavy, strong, substantial, thick (*sense 3*) bulky, corpulent, fat, heavy, obese, stout (*sense 4*) abundant, adequate, plentiful, profuse (*sense 5*) concentrated, dense, strong, thick, viscous (*sense 6*) adequate, convincing, strong, substantial

thing 1. affair, article, being, body, circumstance, concept, entity, fact, matter, object, part, portion, something, substance 2. act, deed, event, eventuality, feat, happening, incident, occurrence, phenomenon, proceeding 3. apparatus, contrivance, device, gadget, implement, instrument, machine, means, mechanism, tool 4. aspect, detail, facet, factor, feature, item, particular, point, statement, thought 5. *Plural* baggage, belongings, bits and pieces, clobber (*Brit. sl.*), clothes, effects, equipment, gear (*Inf.*), goods, impedimenta, luggage, odds and ends, paraphernalia, possessions, stuff

think *v.* 1. believe, conceive, conclude, consider, deem, determine, esteem, estimate, hold, imagine, judge, reckon, regard, suppose, surmise 2. brood, cerebrate, chew over (*Inf.*), cogitate, consider, contemplate, deliberate, have in mind, meditate, mull over, muse, ponder, reason, reflect, revolve, ruminate, turn over in one's mind, weigh up 3. call to mind, recall, recollect, remember 4. anticipate, envisage, expect, foresee, imagine, plan for, presume, suppose 5. **think better of** change one's mind about, decide against, go back on, have second thoughts about, reconsider, repent, think again, think twice about

thinking *adj.* contemplative, cultured, intelligent, meditative, philosophical, ratiocinative, rational, reasoning, reflective, sophisticated, thoughtful

think over chew over (*Inf.*), consider, consider the pros and cons of, contemplate, give thought to, mull over, ponder, reflect upon, turn over in one's mind, weigh up

third-rate bad, cheap-jack, duff (*Brit. sl.*), indifferent, inferior, low-grade, mediocre, poor, poor-quality, ropy (*Brit. inf.*), shoddy

thirst *n.* 1. craving to drink, drought, dryness, thirstiness 2. appetite, craving, desire, eagerness, hankering, hunger, keenness, longing, lust, passion, yearning, yen (*Inf.*)

thirsty arid, dehydrated, dry, parched

thorny 1. barbed, bristling with thorns, bristly, pointed, prickly, sharp, spiky, spinous, spiny 2. awkward, difficult, harassing, hard, irksome, problematic, sticky (*Inf.*), ticklish, tough, troublesome, trying, unpleasant, upsetting, vexatious, worrying

thorough *or* **thoroughgoing** 1. all-embracing, all-inclusive, assiduous, careful, complete, comprehensive, conscientious, efficient, exhaustive, full, in-depth, intensive, leaving no stone unturned, meticulous, painstaking, scrupulous, sweeping 2. absolute, arrant, complete, downright, entire, out-and-out, perfect, pure, sheer, total, unmitigated, unqualified, utter
   Antonyms careless, cursory, half-hearted, haphazard, imperfect, incomplete, lackadaisical, partial, sloppy, superficial

though *conj.* albeit, allowing, although, despite the fact that, even if, even supposing, granted, notwithstanding, while

thought 1. brainwork, cerebration, cogitation, consideration, contemplation, deliberation, introspection, meditation, musing, reflection, regard, rumination, thinking 2. assessment, belief, concept, conception, conclusion, conjecture, conviction, estimation, idea, judgment, notion, opinion, thinking, view 3. attention, consideration, heed, regard, scrutiny, study 4. aim, design, idea, intention, notion, object, plan, purpose 5. anticipation, aspiration, dream, expectation, hope, prospect 6. anxiety, attentiveness, care, compassion, concern, kindness, regard, solicitude, sympathy, thoughtfulness

thoughtful 1. attentive, caring, considerate, helpful, kind, kindly, solicitous, unselfish 2. contemplative, deliberative, in a brown study, introspective, lost in thought, meditative, musing, pensive, rapt, reflective, ruminative, serious, studious, thinking, wistful
   Antonyms cold-hearted, extrovert, flippant, heedless, impolite, inconsiderate, insensitive, irresponsible, neglectful, rash, selfish, shallow, superficial, thoughtless, uncaring, unthinking

thoughtless 1. impolite, inconsiderate, indiscreet, insensitive, rude, selfish, tactless, uncaring, undiplomatic, unkind 2. absent-minded, careless, foolish, heedless, ill-considered, imprudent, inadvertent, inattentive, injudicious, mindless, neglectful, negligent, rash, reckless, regardless, remiss, silly, stupid, unmindful, unobservant, unthinking
   Antonyms attentive, considerate, considered, diplomatic, intelligent, prudent, smart, tactful, thoughtful, unselfish, well-advised, well thought-out, wise

thrash 1. beat, belt, birch, cane, chastise, drub, flagellate, flog, give (someone) a (good) hiding (*Inf.*), hide (*Inf.*), horsewhip, lambaste, leather, paste (*Sl.*), punish, scourge, spank, take a stick to, tan (*Sl.*), whip 2. beat, beat (someone) hollow (*Brit. inf.*), clobber (*Brit. sl.*), crush, defeat, drub, hammer (*Inf.*), maul, overwhelm, paste (*Sl.*), rout, slaughter (*Inf.*), trounce, wipe the floor with (*Inf.*)

threat 1. commination, intimidatory remark, menace, threatening remark, warning 2. foreboding, foreshadowing, omen, portent, presage, warning, writing on the wall

threaten 1. endanger, imperil, jeopardize, put at risk, put in jeopardy 2. be imminent, be in the air, be in the offing, forebode, foreshadow, hang over, impend, loom over, portend, presage, warn 3. browbeat, bully, cow, intimidate, lean on (*Sl.*), make threats to, menace, pressurize, terrorize, warn
   Antonyms defend, guard, protect, safeguard, shelter, shield

threshold 1. door, doorsill, door~ step, doorway, entrance, sill 2. beginning, brink, dawn, inception, opening, outset, start, starting point, verge
Antonyms (*sense 2*) close, decline, end, finish, twilight

thrift carefulness, economy, frugality, good husbandry, parsimony, prudence, saving, thriftiness
Antonyms carelessness, extravagance, prodigality, profligacy, recklessness, squandering, waste

thrill *n.* 1. adventure, buzz (*Sl.*), charge (*Sl.*), flush of excitement, glow, kick (*Inf.*), pleasure, sensation, stimulation, tingle, titillation 2. flutter, fluttering, quiver, shudder, throb, tremble, tremor, vibration ~*v.* 3. arouse, excite, flush, get a charge (*Sl.*), get a kick (*Inf.*), glow, move, send (*Sl.*), stimulate, stir, tingle, titillate 4. flutter, quake, quiver, shake, shudder, throb, tremble, vibrate

thrilling 1. electrifying, exciting, gripping, hair-raising, rip-roaring (*Inf.*), riveting, rousing, sensational, stimulating, stirring 2. quaking, shaking, shivering, shuddering, trembling, vibrating
Antonyms boring, dreary, dull, monotonous, quiet, staid, tedious, uninteresting, unmoving

thrive advance, bloom, boom, burgeon, develop, do well, flourish, get on, grow, grow rich, increase, prosper, succeed, wax
Antonyms decline, droop, fail, languish, perish, shrivel, stagnate, wane, wilt, wither

throb 1. *v.* beat, palpitate, pound, pulsate, pulse, thump, vibrate 2. *n.* beat, palpitation, pounding, pulsating, pulse, thump, thumping, vibration

throng 1. *n.* assemblage, concourse, congregation, crowd, crush, horde, host, jam, mass, mob, multitude, pack, press, swarm 2. *v.* bunch, congregate, converge, cram, crowd, fill, flock,

hem in, herd, jam, mill around, pack, press, swarm around, troop
Antonyms (*sense 2*) break up, disband, dispel, disperse, scatter, separate, spread out

throttle *v.* 1. choke, garrotte, strangle, strangulate 2. control, gag (*Inf.*), inhibit, silence, stifle, suppress

through *prep.* 1. between, by, from end to end of, from one side to the other of, in and out of, past 2. as a consequence *or* result of, because of, by means of, by virtue of, by way of, using, via, with the help of 3. during, in, in the middle of, throughout ~*adj.* 4. completed, done, ended, finished, terminated, washed up (*Inf.*)

throughout all over, all the time, all through, during the whole of, everywhere, for the duration of, from beginning to end, from end to end, from start to finish, from the start, over the length and breadth of, right through, the whole time, through the whole of

throw 1. *v.* cast, chuck (*Inf.*), fling, heave, hurl, launch, lob (*Inf.*), pitch, project, propel, put, send, shy, sling, toss 2. *n.* cast, fling, heave, lob (*Inf.*), pitch, projection, put, shy, sling, toss

throw away 1. cast off, discard, dispense with, dispose of, ditch (*Sl.*), dump (*Inf.*), get rid of, jettison, reject, scrap, throw out 2. blow (*Sl.*), fail to exploit, fritter away, lose, make poor use of, squander, waste
Antonyms (*sense 1*) conserve, keep, preserve, rescue, retain, retrieve, salvage, save

throw off 1. abandon, cast off, discard, drop, free oneself of, rid oneself of, shake off 2. elude, escape from, evade, get away from, give (someone) the slip, leave behind, lose, outdistance, outrun, shake off, show a clean pair of heels to 3. confuse, disconcert, disturb, put one off one's stroke, throw (*Inf.*), throw one off one's stride, unsettle, upset

throw out 1. cast off, discard,

dismiss, dispense with, ditch (*Sl.*), dump (*Inf.*), eject, evict, expel, get rid of, jettison, kick out (*Inf.*), reject, scrap, show the door to, throw away, turf out (*Brit. inf.*), turn down **2.** confuse, disconcert, disturb, put one off one's stroke, throw (*Inf.*), throw one off one's stride, unsettle, upset

thrust v. **1.** butt, drive, elbow *or* shoulder one's way, force, impel, jam, plunge, poke, press, prod, propel, push, ram, shove, urge **2.** jab, lunge, pierce, stab, stick ~n. **3.** drive, lunge, poke, prod, push, shove, stab **4.** impetus, momentum, motive force, motive power, propulsive force

thud n./v. clonk, clump, clunk, crash, knock, smack, thump, wallop (*Inf.*)

thug assassin, bandit, bruiser (*Inf.*), bully boy, cutthroat, gangster, hooligan, killer, mugger (*Inf.*), murderer, robber, ruffian, tough

thump **1.** n. bang, blow, clout (*Inf.*), clunk, crash, knock, rap, smack, thud, thwack, wallop (*Inf.*), whack **2.** v. bang, batter, beat, belabour, clout (*Inf.*), crash, hit, knock, lambaste (*Sl.*), pound, rap, smack, strike, thrash, throb, thud, thwack, wallop (*Inf.*), whack

thunder **1.** n. boom, booming, cracking, crash, crashing, detonation, explosion, pealing, rumble, rumbling **2.** v. blast, boom, clap, crack, crash, detonate, explode, peal, resound, reverberate, roar, rumble

thunderstruck aghast, amazed, astonished, astounded, bowled over (*Inf.*), dazed, dumbfounded, flabbergasted (*Inf.*), floored (*Inf.*), flummoxed, knocked for six (*Inf.*), left speechless, nonplussed, open-mouthed, paralysed, petrified, rooted to the spot, shocked, staggered, struck dumb, stunned, taken aback

thus **1.** as follows, in this fashion (manner, way), like so, like this, so, to such a degree **2.** accord-

ingly, consequently, ergo, for this reason, hence, on that account, so, then, therefore

tick n. **1.** clack, click, clicking, tap, tapping, ticktock **2.** dash, mark, stroke ~v. **3.** clack, click, tap, ticktock **4.** check off, choose, indicate, mark, mark off, select

tide course, current, ebb, flow, stream

tidy **1.** adj. businesslike, clean, cleanly, methodical, neat, ordered, orderly, shipshape, spick-and-span, spruce, systematic, trim, well-groomed, well-kept, well-ordered **2.** v. clean, groom, neaten, order, put in order, put in trim, put to rights, spruce up, straighten
Antonyms adj. careless, dirty, dishevelled, disordered, disorderly, filthy, in disarray, messy, scruffy, sloppy, slovenly, unbusinesslike, unkempt, unmethodical, unsystematic, untidy ~v. dirty, dishevel, disorder, mess, mess up

tie v. **1.** attach, bind, connect, fasten, interlace, join, knot, lash, link, make fast, moor, rope, secure, tether, truss, unite **2.** bind, confine, hamper, hinder, hold, limit, restrain, restrict **3.** be even, be neck and neck, draw, equal, match ~n. **4.** band, bond, connection, cord, fastening, fetter, joint, knot, ligature, link, rope, string **5.** affiliation, allegiance, bond, commitment, connection, duty, kinship, liaison, obligation, relationship **6.** dead heat, deadlock, draw, stalemate **7.** *Brit.* contest, fixture, game, match
Antonyms free, loose, release, separate, undo, unfasten, unhitch, unknot, untie

tier bank, echelon, file, layer, level, line, order, rank, row, series, storey, stratum

tight **1.** close, close-fitting, compact, constricted, cramped, fast, firm, fixed, narrow, rigid, secure, snug, stiff, stretched, taut, tense **2.** hermetic, impervious, proof, sealed, sound, watertight **3.** close, grasping, mean, miserly, niggardly, parsimonious, penurious, sparing, stingy, tightfisted **4.** close, even, evenly-balanced, near, well-matched **5.** *Inf.* drunk, half cut (*Brit. sl.*), half seas over (*Brit. inf.*), inebriated, in one's cups, intoxicated, pickled (*Inf.*), pie-eyed (*Sl.*), plastered (*Sl.*), smashed (*Sl.*), sozzled (*Inf.*), stewed (*Sl.*), stoned (*Sl.*), three sheets in the wind (*Sl.*), tiddly (*Brit. sl.*), tipsy, under the influence (*Inf.*)

Antonyms (*sense 1*) lax, loose, relaxed, slack, spacious (*sense 2*) loose, open, porous (*sense 3*) abundant, extravagant, generous, lavish, munificent, open, prodigal, profuse, spendthrift (*sense 4*) easy, landslide, overwhelming, runaway, uneven (*sense 5*) sober

tighten close, constrict, cramp, fasten, fix, narrow, rigidify, screw, secure, squeeze, stiffen, stretch, tauten, tense

Antonyms ease off, let out, loosen, relax, slacken, unbind, weaken

till[1] cultivate, dig, plough, turn over, work

till[2] cash box, cash drawer, cash register

tilt *v.* **1.** cant, incline, lean, list, slant, slope, tip **2.** attack, break a lance, clash, contend, cross swords, duel, encounter, fight, joust, overthrow, spar ~ *n.* **3.** angle, cant, inclination, incline, list, pitch, slant, slope

timber beams, boards, forest, logs, planks, trees, wood

time *n.* **1.** age, chronology, date, duration, epoch, era, generation, hour, interval, period, season, space, span, spell, stretch, term, while **2.** allotted span, day, duration, life, life span, lifetime, season **3.** heyday, hour, peak, period **4.** *Mus.* beat, measure, metre, rhythm, tempo **5. in time a.** at the ap-

pointed time, early, in good time, on schedule, on time, with time to spare **b.** by and by, eventually, one day, someday, sooner or later, ultimately ~ *v.* **6.** clock, control, count, judge, measure, regulate, schedule, set

timely appropriate, at the right time, convenient, judicious, opportune, prompt, propitious, punctual, seasonable, suitable, well-timed

Antonyms ill-timed, inconvenient, inopportune, late, tardy, unseasonable, untimely

timetable agenda, calendar, curriculum, diary, list, order of the day, programme, schedule

timid afraid, apprehensive, bashful, cowardly, coy, diffident, faint-hearted, fearful, irresolute, modest, mousy, nervous, pusillanimous, retiring, shrinking, shy, timorous

Antonyms aggressive, arrogant, bold, brave, confident, daring, fearless, fierce, forceful, forward, presumptuous, self-assured, self-confident, shameless, unabashed

tinker *v.* dabble, fiddle (*Inf.*), meddle, mess about, monkey, muck about (*Brit. sl.*), play, potter, toy

tint *n.* **1.** cast, colour, hue, shade, tone **2.** dye, rinse, stain, tincture, tinge, wash ~ *v.* **3.** colour, dye, rinse, stain, tincture, tinge **4.** affect, colour, influence, taint, tinge

tiny diminutive, dwarfish, infinitesimal, insignificant, Lilliputian, little, microscopic, mini, miniature, minute, negligible, petite, pint-sized (*Inf.*), puny, pygmy, slight, small, trifling, wee

Antonyms colossal, enormous, extra-large, gargantuan, giant, gigantic, great, huge, immense, mammoth, massive, monstrous, titanic, vast

tip[1] *n.* apex, cap, crown, end, extremity, head, peak, point, summit, top

tip[2] *v.* **1.** cant, capsize, incline, lean, list, overturn, slant, spill, tilt, topple over, upend, upset **2.** *Brit.* ditch (*Sl.*), dump, empty, pour out, unload ~*n.* **3.** *Brit.* dump, midden (*Dialect*), refuse heap, rubbish heap

tip³ *n.* **1.** baksheesh, gift, gratuity, perquisite, *pourboire* **2.** *Also* **tip-off** clue, forecast, gen (*Brit. inf.*), hint, information, inside information, pointer, suggestion, warning, word, word of advice ~*v.* **3.** remunerate, reward **4.** *Also* **tip off** advise, caution, forewarn, give a clue, give a hint, suggest, tip (someone) the wink (*Brit. inf.*), warn

tire 1. drain, droop, enervate, exhaust, fag (*Inf.*), fail, fatigue, flag, jade, knacker (*Sl.*), sink, take it out of (*Inf.*), wear down, wear out, weary, whack (*Brit. inf.*) **2.** annoy, bore, exasperate, harass, irk, irritate, weary
Antonyms (*sense 1*) energize, enliven, exhilarate, invigorate, liven up, pep up, refresh, restore, revive

tired all in (*Sl.*), asleep *or* dead on one's feet, dead beat (*Inf.*), dogtired (*Inf.*), done in (*Inf.*), drained, drooping, drowsy, enervated, exhausted, fagged (*Inf.*), fatigued, flagging, jaded, knackered (*Sl.*), ready to drop, sleepy, spent, weary, whacked (*Brit. inf.*), worn out
Antonyms energetic, fresh, full of beans, lively, refreshed, rested, wide-awake

tireless determined, energetic, indefatigable, industrious, resolute, unflagging, untiring, unwearied, vigorous
Antonyms drained, exhausted, fatigued, flagging, tired, weak, weary, worn out

tiresome annoying, boring, dull, exasperating, flat, irksome, irritating, laborious, monotonous, tedious, trying, uninteresting, vexatious, wearing, wearisome
Antonyms exhilarating, inspiring, interesting, refreshing, rousing, stimulating

tiring arduous, demanding, enervative, exacting, exhausting, fatiguing, laborious, strenuous, tough, wearing, wearying

title *n.* **1.** caption, heading, inscription, label, legend, name, style **2.** appellation, denomination, designation, epithet, handle (*Sl.*), moniker (*Inf.*), name, nickname, nom de plume, pseudonym, sobriquet, term **3.** championship, crown, laurels **4.** claim, entitlement, ownership, prerogative, privilege, right ~*v.* **5.** call, designate, label, name, style, term

toady 1. *n.* apple polisher (*U.S. sl.*), bootlicker (*Inf.*), crawler (*Sl.*), creep (*Sl.*), fawner, flatterer, flunkey, groveller, hanger-on, jackal, lackey, lickspittle, minion, parasite, spaniel, sycophant, truckler, yes man **2.** *v.* be obsequious to, bow and scrape, butter up, crawl, creep, cringe, curry favour with, fawn on, flatter, grovel, kiss the feet of, kowtow to, lick the boots of (*Inf.*), suck up to (*Inf.*)

together *adv.* **1.** as a group, as one, cheek by jowl, closely, collectively, hand in glove, hand in hand, in a body, in concert, in cooperation, in unison, jointly, mutually, shoulder to shoulder, side by side **2.** all at once, as one, at one fell swoop, at the same time, concurrently, contemporaneously, en masse, in unison, simultaneously, with one accord **3.** consecutively, continuously, in a row, in succession, one after the other, on end, successively, without a break, without interruption
Antonyms (*sense 1*) alone, apart, independently, individually, one at a time, one by one, separately, singly

toil 1. *n.* application, donkey-work, drudgery, effort, elbow grease (*Inf.*), exertion, graft (*Inf.*), hard work, industry, labour, pains, slog, sweat, travail **2.** *v.* drag oneself, drudge, graft (*Inf.*), grind (*Inf.*), grub, knock oneself out, labour, push oneself, slave, slog, strive, struggle, sweat (*Inf.*), work, work like a dog, work like a Trojan, work one's fingers to the bone

toilet 1. ablutions (*Military inf.*), bathroom, bog (*Brit. sl.*), closet, convenience, gents (*Brit. inf.*), ladies' room, latrine, lavatory, loo (*Brit. inf.*), outhouse, powder room, privy, urinal, washroom, water closet, W.C. **2.** ablutions, bathing, dressing, grooming, toilette

token *n.* **1.** badge, clue, demonstration, earnest, evidence, expression, index, indication, manifestation, mark, note, proof, representation, sign, symbol, warning **2.** keepsake, memento, memorial, remembrance, reminder, souvenir ~*adj.* **3.** hollow, minimal, nominal, perfunctory, superficial, symbolic

tolerable 1. acceptable, allowable, bearable, endurable, sufferable, supportable **2.** acceptable, adequate, all right, average, fair, fairly good, fair to middling, good enough, indifferent, mediocre, middling, not bad (*Inf.*), O.K. (*Inf.*), ordinary, passable, run-of-the-mill, so-so (*Inf.*), unexceptional

tolerance 1. broad-mindedness, charity, forbearance, indulgence, lenity, magnanimity, openmindedness, patience, permissiveness, sufferance, sympathy **2.** endurance, fortitude, hardiness, hardness, resilience, resistance, stamina, staying power, toughness **3.** fluctuation, play, swing, variation
Antonyms (*sense 1*) bigotry, discrimination, intolerance, narrowmindedness, prejudice, sectarianism

tolerant 1. broad-minded, catholic, charitable, fair, forbearing, latitudinarian, liberal, long-suffering, magnanimous, open-minded, patient, sympathetic, unbigoted, understanding, unprejudiced **2.** complaisant, easy-going, free and easy, indulgent, kind-hearted, lax, lenient, permissive, soft
Antonyms authoritarian, biased, bigoted, despotic, dictatorial, dogmatic, illiberal, intolerant, narrow-minded, prejudiced, repressive, rigid, sectarian, stern, strict, tyrannical, uncharitable

tolerate abide, accept, admit, allow, bear, brook, condone, countenance, endure, indulge, permit, pocket, put up with (*Inf.*), receive, sanction, stand, stomach, submit to, suffer, swallow, take, thole (*Scot.*), turn a blind eye to, undergo, wink at
Antonyms ban, disallow, disapprove, forbid, outlaw, preclude, prohibit, veto

toll[1] *v.* **1.** chime, clang, knell, peal, ring, sound, strike **2.** announce, call, signal, summon, warn ~*n.* **3.** chime, clang, knell, peal, ring, ringing, tolling

toll[2] **1.** assessment, charge, customs, demand, duty, fee, impost, levy, payment, rate, tariff, tax, tribute **2.** cost, damage, inroad, loss, penalty

tomb burial chamber, catacomb, crypt, grave, mausoleum, sepulchre, vault

tombstone gravestone, headstone, marker, memorial, monument

tone *n.* **1.** accent, emphasis, force, inflection, intonation, modulation, pitch, strength, stress, timbre, tonality, volume **2.** air, approach, aspect, attitude, character, drift, effect, feel, frame, grain, manner, mood, note, quality, spirit, style, temper, tenor, vein **3.** cast, colour, hue, shade, tinge, tint ~*v.* **4.** blend, go well with, harmonize, match, suit

tongue 1. argot, dialect, idiom, language, lingo (*Inf.*), parlance, patois, speech, talk, vernacular **2.** articulation, speech, utterance, verbal expression, voice

tonic analeptic, boost, bracer (*Inf.*), cordial, fillip, livener, pick-me-up (*Inf.*), refresher, restorative, roborant, shot in the arm (*Inf.*), stimulant

too 1. also, as well, besides, further, in addition, into the bargain, likewise, moreover, to boot **2.** excessively, exorbitantly, extremely, immoderately, inordinately, over-, overly, unduly, unreasonably, very

tool *n.* **1.** apparatus, appliance, contraption, contrivance, device, gadget, implement, instrument, machine, utensil **2.** agency, agent, intermediary, means, medium, vehicle, wherewithal **3.** cat's-paw, creature, dupe, flunkey, hireling, jackal, lackey, minion, pawn, puppet, stooge (*Sl.*)

top *n.* **1.** acme, apex, apogee, crest, crown, culmination, head, height, high point, meridian, peak, pinnacle, summit, vertex, zenith **2.** cap, cork, cover, lid, stopper **3.** first place, head, highest rank, lead **4. over the top** a bit much (*Inf.*), excessive, going too far, immoderate, inordinate, over the limit, too much, uncalled-for ~*adj.* **5.** best, chief, crack (*Inf.*), crowning, culminating, dominant, elite, finest, first, foremost, greatest, head, highest, lead, leading, pre-eminent, prime, principal, ruling, sovereign, superior, topmost, upper, uppermost ~*v.* **6.** be first, be in charge of, command, head, lead, rule **7.** beat, best, better, eclipse, exceed, excel, go beyond, outdo, outshine, outstrip, surpass, transcend

Antonyms *n.* base, bottom, foot, nadir, underneath, underside ~*adj.* amateurish, bottom, incompetent, inept, inferior, least, lower, lowest, second-rate, unknown, unranked, worst ~*v.* be at the bottom of, fail to equal, fall short of, not be as good as

topic issue, matter, point, question, subject, subject matter, text, theme, thesis

topical contemporary, current, newsworthy, popular, up-to-date, up-to-the-minute

topsy-turvy chaotic, confused, disarranged, disorderly, disorganized, inside-out, jumbled, messy, mixed-up, untidy, upside-down

Antonyms neat, ordered, orderly, organized, shipshape, systematic, tidy

torment *v.* **1.** afflict, agonize, crucify, distress, excruciate, harrow, pain, rack, torture **2.** annoy, bedevil, bother, chivvy, devil (*Inf.*), harass, harry, hound, irritate, nag, persecute, pester, plague, provoke, tease, trouble, vex, worry ~*n.* **3.** agony, anguish, distress, hell, misery, pain, suffering, torture **4.** affliction, annoyance, bane, bother, harassment, irritation, nag, nagging, nuisance, pain in the neck (*Inf.*), persecution, pest, plague, provocation, scourge, thorn in one's flesh, trouble, vexation, worry

Antonyms *v.* comfort, delight, ease, encourage, make happy, put at ease, reassure, soothe ~*n.* bliss, comfort, ease, ecstasy, encouragement, happiness, joy, reassurance, rest

tornado cyclone, gale, hurricane, squall, storm, tempest, twister (*U.S. inf.*), typhoon, whirlwind, windstorm

torrent cascade, deluge, downpour, effusion, flood, flow, gush, outburst, rush, spate, stream, tide

torture 1. afflict, agonize, crucify, distress, excruciate, harrow, lacerate, martyr, pain, persecute, put on the rack, rack, torment **2.** *n.* affliction, agony, anguish, distress, hell, laceration, martyrdom, misery, pain, pang(s), persecution, rack, suffering, torment

Antonyms (*sense 1*) alleviate, comfort, console, ease, mollify, relieve, salve, solace, soothe (*sense 2*) amusement, bliss, delight, enjoyment, happiness, joy, pleasure, well-being

toss *v.* **1.** cast, chuck (*Inf.*), fling, flip, hurl, launch, lob (*Inf.*), pitch, project, propel, shy, sling, throw **2.** agitate, disturb, jiggle, joggle, jolt, rock, roll, shake, thrash, tumble, wriggle, writhe ~*n.* **3.** cast, fling, lob (*Inf.*), pitch, shy, throw

total 1. *n.* aggregate, all, amount, entirety, full amount, mass, sum, totality, whole **2.** *adj.* absolute, all-out, complete, comprehensive, consummate, downright, entire, full, gross, integral, out-and-out, outright, perfect, sheer, sweeping, thorough, thoroughgoing, unconditional, undisputed, undivided, unmitigated, unqualified, utter, whole **3.** *v.* add up, amount to, come to, mount up to, reach, reckon, sum up, tot up
Antonyms *n.* individual amount, part, subtotal ~*adj.* conditional, fragmentary, incomplete, limited, mixed, part, partial, qualified, restricted, uncombined ~*v.* deduct, subtract

touch *n.* **1.** feel, feeling, handling, palpation, physical contact, tactility **2.** blow, brush, caress, contact, fondling, hit, pat, push, stroke, tap **3.** bit, dash, detail, drop, hint, intimation, jot, pinch, smack, small amount, smattering, *soupçon*, speck, spot, suggestion, suspicion, taste, tincture, tinge, trace, whiff **4.** approach, characteristic, handiwork, manner, method, style, technique, trademark, way **5.** ability, adroitness, art, artistry, command, deftness, facility, flair, knack, mastery, skill, virtuosity ~*v.* **6.** brush, caress, contact, feel, finger, fondle, graze, handle, hit, lay a finger on, palpate, pat, push, strike, stroke, tap **7.** abut, adjoin, be in contact, border, brush, come together, contact, converge, graze, impinge upon, meet **8.** affect, disturb, get through to, get to (*Inf.*), have an effect on, impress, influence, inspire, make an impression on, mark, melt, move, soften, stir, strike, upset **9.** be a match for, be in the same league as, be on a par with, come near, come up to, compare with,

equal, hold a candle to (*Inf.*), match, parallel, rival

touching affecting, emotive, heartbreaking, melting, moving, pathetic, piteous, pitiable, pitiful, poignant, sad, stirring, tender

tough *adj.* **1.** cohesive, durable, firm, hard, inflexible, leathery, resilient, resistant, rigid, rugged, solid, stiff, strong, sturdy, tenacious **2.** brawny, fit, hard as nails, hardened, hardy, resilient, seasoned, stalwart, stout, strapping, strong, sturdy, vigorous **3.** hard-bitten, pugnacious, rough, ruffianly, ruthless, vicious, violent **4.** adamant, callous, exacting, firm, hard, hard-boiled (*Inf.*), hard-nosed (*Sl.*), inflexible, intractable, merciless, obdurate, obstinate, refractory, resolute, severe, stern, strict, stubborn, unbending, unforgiving, unyielding **5.** arduous, baffling, difficult, exacting, exhausting, hard, intractable, irksome, knotty, laborious, perplexing, puzzling, strenuous, thorny, troublesome, uphill **6.** *Inf.* bad, hard cheese (*Brit. sl.*), hard lines (*Brit. inf.*), hard luck, lamentable, regrettable, too bad (*Inf.*), unfortunate, unlucky ~*n.* **7.** bravo, bruiser (*Inf.*), brute, bully, bully boy, hooligan, rough (*Inf.*), roughneck (*Sl.*), rowdy, ruffian, thug
Antonyms accommodating, benign, civilized, compassionate, considerate, delicate, easy, flexible, flimsy, fragile, gentle, humane, indulgent, kind, lenient, merciful, mild, simple, soft, sympathetic, tender, unexacting, weak

tour *n.* **1.** excursion, expedition, jaunt, journey, outing, peregrination, progress, trip **2.** circuit, course, round ~*v.* **3.** explore, go on the road, go round, holiday in, journey, sightsee, travel round, travel through, visit

tourist excursionist, globetrotter, holiday-maker, journeyer, sightseer, traveller, tripper, voyager

tow v. drag, draw, haul, lug, pull, trail, trawl, tug

towards 1. en route for, for, in the direction of, in the vicinity of, on the road to, on the way to, to **2.** about, concerning, for, regarding, with regard to, with respect to **3.** almost, close to, coming up to, getting on for, just before, nearing, nearly, not quite, shortly before

tower n. **1.** belfry, column, obelisk, pillar, skyscraper, steeple, turret **2.** castle, citadel, fort, fortification, fortress, keep, refuge, stronghold ~v. **3.** ascend, be head and shoulders above, dominate, exceed, loom, mount, overlook, overtop, rear, rise, soar, surpass, top, transcend

toy 1. n. doll, game, plaything **2.** v. amuse oneself, dally, fiddle (*Inf.*), flirt, play, sport, trifle, wanton

trace n. **1.** evidence, indication, mark, record, relic, remains, remnant, sign, survival, token, vestige **2.** bit, dash, drop, hint, iota, jot, shadow, *soupçon*, suggestion, suspicion, tincture, tinge, touch, trifle, whiff ~v. **3.** ascertain, detect, determine, discover, ferret out, find, follow, hunt down, pursue, search for, seek, shadow, stalk, track, trail, unearth **4.** chart, copy, delineate, depict, draw, map, mark out, outline, record, show, sketch

track n. **1.** footmark, footprint, footstep, mark, path, scent, slot, spoor, trace, trail, wake **2.** course, flight path, line, orbit, path, pathway, road, track, trajectory, way **3.** line, permanent way, rail, rails **4. keep track of** follow, keep an eye on, keep in sight, keep in touch with, keep up to date with, keep up with, monitor, oversee, watch **5. lose track of** lose, lose sight of, misplace ~v. **6.** chase, dog, follow, follow the trail of, hunt down, pursue, shadow, stalk, tail (*Inf.*), trace, trail

tracks footprints, impressions,

imprints, tyremarks, tyreprints, wheelmarks

trade n. **1.** barter, business, buying and selling, commerce, dealing, exchange, traffic, transactions, truck **2.** avocation, business, calling, craft, employment, job, line, line of work, métier, occupation, profession, pursuit, skill **3.** deal, exchange, interchange, swap **4.** clientele, custom, customers, market, patrons, public ~v. **5.** bargain, barter, buy and sell, deal, do business, exchange, have dealings, peddle, traffic, transact, truck **6.** barter, exchange, swap, switch

tradesman 1. dealer, merchant, retailer, seller, shopkeeper, vendor **2.** artisan, craftsman, journeyman, skilled worker, workman

tradition convention, custom, customs, established practice, folklore, habit, institution, lore, praxis, ritual, unwritten law, usage

traditional accustomed, ancestral, conventional, customary, established, fixed, folk, historic, long-established, old, oral, time-honoured, transmitted, unwritten, usual

    Antonyms avant-garde, contemporary, innovative, modern, new, novel, original, revolutionary, unconventional, unusual

traffic n. **1.** coming and going, freight, movement, passengers, transport, transportation, vehicles **2.** barter, business, buying and selling, commerce, communication, dealing, dealings, doings, exchange, intercourse, peddling, relations, trade, truck ~v. **3.** bargain, barter, buy and sell, deal, do business, exchange, have dealings, have transactions, market, peddle, trade, truck

tragedy adversity, affliction, calamity, catastrophe, disaster, grievous blow, misfortune

tragic anguished, appalling, awful, calamitous, catastrophic, deadly, dire, disastrous, doleful,

dreadful, fatal, grievous, heart-breaking, heart-rending, ill-fated, ill-starred, lamentable, miserable, mournful, pathetic, pitiable, ruinous, sad, shocking, sorrowful, unfortunate, woeful, wretched
Antonyms agreeable, beneficial, cheerful, comic, fortunate, glorious, happy, joyful, lucky, satisfying, worthwhile

trail v. 1. dangle, drag, draw, hang down, haul, pull, stream, tow 2. chase, follow, hunt, pursue, shadow, stalk, tail (*Inf.*), trace, track 3. bring up the rear, dawdle, drag oneself, fall behind, follow, hang back, lag, linger, loiter, straggle, traipse (*Inf.*) ~n. 4. footprints, footsteps, mark, marks, path, scent, spoor, trace, track, wake 5. beaten track, footpath, path, road, route, track, way

train v. 1. coach, discipline, drill, educate, guide, improve, instruct, prepare, rear, rehearse, school, teach, tutor 2. aim, bring to bear, direct, focus, level, line up, point ~n. 3. chain, concatenation, course, order, progression, sequence, series, set, string, succession 4. caravan, column, convoy, file, procession 5. appendage, tail, trail 6. attendants, cortege, court, entourage, followers, following, household, retinue, staff, suite

training 1. coaching, discipline, education, grounding, guidance, instruction, schooling, teaching, tuition, tutelage, upbringing 2. body building, exercise, practice, preparation, working-out

trait attribute, characteristic, feature, idiosyncrasy, lineament, mannerism, peculiarity, quality, quirk

traitor apostate, back-stabber, betrayer, deceiver, defector, deserter, double-crosser (*Inf.*), fifth columnist, informer, Judas, miscreant, quisling, rebel, renegade, snake in the grass (*Inf.*), turncoat
Antonyms defender, loyalist, patriot, supporter

tramp v. 1. footslog, hike, march,

ramble, range, roam, rove, slog, trek, walk, yomp 2. march, plod, stamp, stump, toil, traipse (*Inf.*), trudge, walk heavily 3. crush, stamp, stomp (*Inf.*), trample, tread, walk over ~n. 4. derelict, dosser (*Brit. sl.*), down-and-out, drifter, hobo (*Chiefly U.S.*), vagabond, vagrant 5. hike, march, ramble, slog, trek

trample 1. crush, flatten, run over, squash, stamp, tread, walk over 2. do violence to, encroach upon, hurt, infringe, ride roughshod over, show no consideration for, violate

trance abstraction, daze, dream, ecstasy, hypnotic state, muse, rapture, reverie, spell, stupor, unconsciousness

tranquil at peace, calm, composed, cool, pacific, peaceful, placid, quiet, restful, sedate, serene, still, undisturbed, unexcited, unperturbed, unruffled, untroubled
Antonyms agitated, busy, confused, disturbed, excited, hectic, restless, troubled

tranquillizer barbiturate, bromide, downer (*Sl.*), opiate, red (*Sl.*), sedative

transaction action, affair, bargain, business, coup, deal, deed, enterprise, event, matter, negotiation, occurrence, proceeding, undertaking

transcribe 1. copy out, engross, note, reproduce, rewrite, set out, take down, transfer, write out 2. interpret, render, translate, transliterate 3. record, tape, tape-record

transfer 1. v. carry, change, consign, convey, displace, hand over, make over, move, pass on, relocate, remove, shift, translate, transmit, transplant, transport, transpose, turn over 2. n. change, displacement, handover, move, relocation, removal, shift, transference, translation, transmission, transposition

transform alter, change, convert, make over, metamorphose, reconstruct, remodel, renew, revolutionize, transfigure, translate, transmogrify (*Jocular*), transmute

transformation alteration, change, conversion, metamorphosis, radical change, renewal, revolution, revolutionary change, sea change, transfiguration, transmogrification (*Jocular*), transmutation

transgress break, break the law, contravene, defy, disobey, do *or* go wrong, encroach, err, exceed, fall from grace, go astray, go beyond, infringe, lapse, misbehave, offend, overstep, sin, trespass, violate

transient brief, ephemeral, evanescent, fleeting, flying, fugacious, fugitive, here today and gone tomorrow, impermanent, momentary, passing, short, short-lived, short-term, temporary, transitory
Antonyms abiding, constant, durable, enduring, imperishable, long-lasting, long-term, permanent, perpetual, persistent, undying

transit *n.* 1. carriage, conveyance, crossing, motion, movement, passage, portage, shipment, transfer, transport, transportation, travel, traverse 2. alteration, change, changeover, conversion, shift, transition 3. **in transit** during passage, en route, on the journey, on the move, on the road, on the way, while travelling ~*v.* 4. cross, journey, move, pass, travel, traverse

transition alteration, change, changeover, conversion, development, evolution, flux, metamorphosis, metastasis, passage, passing, progression, shift, transit, transmutation, upheaval

transitional changing, developmental, fluid, intermediate, passing, provisional, temporary, transitionary, unsettled

transitory brief, ephemeral, evanescent, fleeting, flying, fugacious, here today and gone to-

morrow, impermanent, momentary, passing, short, short-lived, short-term, temporary, transient
Antonyms abiding, enduring, eternal, everlasting, lasting, long-lived, long-term, permanent, perpetual, persistent, undying

translate 1. construe, convert, decipher, decode, interpret, paraphrase, render, transcribe, transliterate 2. elucidate, explain, make clear, paraphrase, put in plain English, simplify, spell out, state in layman's language 3. alter, change, convert, metamorphose, transfigure, transform, transmute, turn 4. carry, convey, move, remove, send, transfer, transplant, transport, transpose

translation 1. construction, decoding, gloss, interpretation, paraphrase, rendering, rendition, transcription, transliteration, version 2. elucidation, explanation, paraphrase, rephrasing, rewording, simplification 3. alteration, change, conversion, metamorphosis, transfiguration, transformation, transmutation 4. conveyance, move, removal, transference, transposition

transmission 1. carriage, communication, conveyance, diffusion, dispatch, dissemination, remission, sending, shipment, spread, transfer, transference, transport 2. broadcasting, dissemination, putting out, relaying, sending, showing 3. broadcast, programme, show

transmit 1. bear, carry, communicate, convey, diffuse, dispatch, disseminate, forward, hand down, hand on, impart, pass on, remit, send, spread, take, transfer, transport 2. broadcast, disseminate, put on the air, radio, relay, send, send out

transparent 1. clear, crystal clear, crystalline, diaphanous, filmy, gauzy, limpid, lucent, lucid, pellucid, seethrough, sheer, translucent, transpicuous 2. apparent, as plain as the nose on one's face (*Inf.*), distinct, easy, evident, explicit, manifest, obvious, patent, perspicuous, plain, plain, recognizable, unambiguous, understandable, undisguised, visible **3.** candid, direct, forthright, frank, open, plain-spoken, straight, straightforward, unambiguous, unequivocal

Antonyms ambiguous, cloudy, deceptive, disingenuous, hidden, muddy, mysterious, opaque, thick, turbid, uncertain, unclear, vague

transpire 1. *Inf.* arise, befall, chance, come about, come to pass (*Archaic*), happen, occur, take place, turn up **2.** become known, be disclosed, be discovered, be made public, come out, come to light, emerge

transport *v.* **1.** bear, bring, carry, convey, fetch, haul, move, remove, run, ship, take, transfer **2.** banish, deport, exile, sentence to transportation **3.** captivate, carry away, delight, electrify, enchant, enrapture, entrance, move, ravish, spellbind ~*n.* **4.** conveyance, transportation, vehicle **5.** carriage, conveyance, removal, shipment, shipping, transference, transportation **6.** cloud nine (*Inf.*), enchantment, euphoria, heaven, rapture, seventh heaven **7.** bliss, delight, ecstasy, happiness, ravishment

transpose alter, change, exchange, interchange, move, rearrange, relocate, reorder, shift, substitute, swap (*Inf.*), switch, transfer

trap *n.* **1.** ambush, gin, net, noose, pitfall, snare, springe, toils **2.** ambush, artifice, deception, device, ruse, stratagem, subterfuge, trick, wile ~*v.* **3.** catch, corner, enmesh, ensnare, entrap, snare, take **4.** ambush, beguile, deceive, dupe, ensnare, inveigle, trick

trappings accoutrements, adornments, decorations, dress, equipment, finery, fittings, fixtures, fripperies, furnishings, gear, livery, ornaments, panoply,

paraphernalia, raiment (*Archaic*), things, trimmings

trash 1. balderdash, drivel, foolish talk, hogwash, inanity, nonsense, rot, rubbish, tripe (*Inf.*), trumpery, twaddle **2.** dregs, dross, garbage, junk, litter, offscourings, refuse, rubbish, sweepings, waste

trashy brummagem, catchpenny, cheap, cheap-jack (*Inf.*), flimsy, inferior, meretricious, rubbishy, shabby, shoddy, tawdry, thrown together, tinsel, worthless

Antonyms A-1 (*Inf.*), excellent, exceptional, first-class, first rate, outstanding, superlative

travel *v.* cross, go, journey, make a journey, make one's way, move, proceed, progress, ramble, roam, rove, take a trip, tour, traverse, trek, voyage, walk, wander, wend

traveller excursionist, explorer, globetrotter, gypsy, hiker, holiday-maker, journeyer, migrant, nomad, passenger, tourist, tripper, voyager, wanderer, wayfarer

travelling *adj.* itinerant, migrant, migratory, mobile, moving, nomadic, peripatetic, restless, roaming, roving, touring, unsettled, wandering, wayfaring

travesty 1. *n.* burlesque, caricature, distortion, lampoon, mockery, parody, perversion, send-up (*Brit. inf.*), sham, spoof (*Inf.*), takeoff (*Inf.*) **2.** *v.* burlesque, caricature, deride, distort, lampoon, make a mockery of, make fun of, mock, parody, pervert, ridicule, send up (*Brit. inf.*), sham, spoof (*Inf.*), take off (*Inf.*)

treacherous 1. deceitful, disloyal, double-crossing (*Inf.*), double-dealing, duplicitous, faithless, false, perfidious, recreant (*Archaic*), traitorous, treasonable, unfaithful, unreliable, untrue, untrustworthy **2.** dangerous, deceptive, hazardous, icy, perilous, precarious, risky, slippery, slippy (*Inf.*), tricky, unreliable, unsafe, unstable

Antonyms dependable, faithful,

treachery betrayal, disloyalty, double-cross (*Inf.*), double-dealing, duplicity, faithlessness, infidelity, perfidiousness, perfidy, stab in the back, treason
Antonyms allegiance, dependability, faithfulness, fealty, fidelity, loyalty, reliability

tread *v.* 1. hike, march, pace, plod, stamp, step, stride, tramp, trudge, walk 2. crush underfoot, squash, trample 3. bear down, crush, oppress, quell, repress, ride roughshod over, subdue, subjugate, suppress ~*n.* 4. footfall, footstep, gait, pace, step, stride, walk

treason disaffection, disloyalty, duplicity, lese-majesty, mutiny, perfidy, sedition, subversion, traitorousness, treachery
Antonyms allegiance, faithfulness, fealty, fidelity, loyalty, patriotism

treasure *n.* 1. cash, fortune, funds, gold, jewels, money, riches, valuables, wealth 2. apple of one's eye, darling, gem, jewel, nonpareil, paragon, pearl, precious, pride and joy, prize ~*v.* 3. adore, cherish, dote upon, esteem, hold dear, idolize, love, prize, revere, value, venerate, worship

treasury 1. bank, cache, hoard, repository, store, storehouse, vault 2. assets, capital, coffers, exchequer, finances, funds, money, resources, revenues

treat *n.* 1. banquet, celebration, entertainment, feast, gift, party, refreshment 2. delight, enjoyment, fun, gratification, joy, pleasure, satisfaction, surprise, thrill ~*v.* 3. act towards, behave towards, consider, deal with, handle, look upon, manage, regard, use 4. apply treatment to, attend to, care for, doctor, medicate, nurse 5. buy for, entertain, feast, foot *or* pay the bill, give, lay on, pay for, provide, regale, stand (*Inf.*), take out, wine and dine 6. be concerned with, contain, deal with, discourse upon, discuss, go into, touch upon

treatise disquisition, dissertation, essay, exposition, monograph, pamphlet, paper, study, thesis, tract, work, writing

treatment 1. care, cure, healing, medication, medicine, remedy, surgery, therapy 2. action towards, behaviour towards, conduct, dealing, handling, management, manipulation, reception, usage

treaty agreement, alliance, bargain, bond, compact, concordat, contract, convention, covenant, entente, pact

trek 1. *n.* expedition, footslog, hike, journey, long haul, march, odyssey, safari, slog, tramp 2. *v.* footslog, hike, journey, march, plod, range, roam, rove, slog, traipse (*Inf.*), tramp, trudge, yomp

tremble 1. *v.* oscillate, quake, quiver, rock, shake, shake in one's shoes, shiver, shudder, teeter, totter, vibrate, wobble 2. *n.* oscillation, quake, quiver, shake, shiver, shudder, tremor, vibration, wobble

tremendous 1. appalling, awesome, awful, colossal, deafening, dreadful, enormous, fearful, formidable, frightful, gargantuan, gigantic, great, huge, immense, mammoth, monstrous, prodigious, stupendous, terrible, terrific, titanic, towering, vast, whopping (*Inf.*) 2. *Inf.* ace (*Inf.*), amazing, excellent, exceptional, extraordinary, fabulous (*Inf.*), fantastic (*Inf.*), great, incredible, marvellous, super (*Inf.*), terrific (*Inf.*), wonderful
Antonyms appalling, average, awful, diminutive, dreadful, little, mediocre, minuscule, minute, ordinary, rotten, run-of-the-mill, small, so-so, terrible, tiny

trench channel, cut, ditch, drain, earthwork, entrenchment, excavation, fosse, furrow, gutter, pit, trough, waterway

trend *n.* **1.** bias, course, current, direction, drift, flow, inclination, leaning, tendency **2.** craze, fad (*Inf.*), fashion, look, mode, rage, style, thing, vogue

trespass 1. *v.* encroach, infringe, intrude, invade, obtrude, poach **2.** *n.* encroachment, infringement, intrusion, invasion, poaching, unlawful entry, wrongful entry

trial *n.* **1.** assay, audition, check, dry run (*Inf.*), examination, experience, experiment, probation, proof, test, testing, test-run **2.** contest, hearing, judicial examination, litigation, tribunal **3.** attempt, crack (*Inf.*), effort, endeavour, go, shot (*Inf.*), stab, try, venture, whack (*Inf.*) **4.** adversity, affliction, burden, cross to bear, distress, grief, hardship, hard times, load, misery, ordeal, pain, suffering, tribulation, trouble, unhappiness, vexation, woe, wretchedness **5.** bane, bother, hassle (*Inf.*), irritation, nuisance, pain in the neck (*Inf.*), pest, plague (*Inf.*), thorn in one's flesh, vexation ~*adj.* **6.** experimental, exploratory, pilot, probationary, provisional, testing

tribe *n.* blood, caste, clan, class, division, dynasty, ethnic group, family, gens, house, people, race, seed, sept, stock

tribute accolade, acknowledgment, applause, commendation, compliment, encomium, esteem, eulogy, gift, gratitude, honour, laudation, panegyric, praise, recognition, respect, testimonial **2.** charge, contribution, customs, duty, excise, homage, impost, offering, payment, ransom, subsidy, tax, toll

Antonyms (*sense 1*) blame, complaint, condemnation, criticism, disapproval, reproach, reproof

trick *n.* **1.** artifice, con (*Sl.*), deceit, deception, device, dodge, feint, fraud, gimmick, hoax, imposition, imposture, manoeuvre, ploy, ruse, stratagem, subterfuge, swindle, trap, wile **2.** antic, can-

trip (*Scot.*), caper, device, feat, frolic, gag (*Sl.*), gambol, jape, joke, juggle, legerdemain, leg-pull (*Brit. inf.*), practical joke, prank, put-on (*Sl.*), sleight of hand, turn **3.** art, command, craft, device, expertise, gift, hang (*Inf.*), knack, know-how (*Inf.*), secret, skill, technique ~*v.* **4.** bamboozle (*Inf.*), cheat, con (*Sl.*), deceive, defraud, delude, dupe, fool, gull (*Archaic*), have (someone) on, hoax, hoodwink, impose upon, mislead, pull the wool over (someone's) eyes, put one over on (someone) (*Inf.*), swindle, take in (*Inf.*), trap

trickle 1. *v.* crawl, creep, dribble, drip, drop, exude, ooze, percolate, run, seep, stream **2.** *n.* dribble, drip, seepage

tricky complicated, delicate, difficult, knotty, problematic, risky, sticky (*Inf.*), thorny, ticklish, touch-and-go

Antonyms clear, easy, obvious, simple, straightforward, uncomplicated

trifle *n.* **1.** bagatelle, bauble, child's play, gewgaw, knick-knack, nothing, plaything, toy, triviality **2.** bit, dash, drop, jot, little, pinch, spot, touch, trace ~*v.* **3.** amuse oneself, coquet, dally, dawdle, flirt, fritter, idle, mess about, palter, play, toy, wanton, waste, waste time

trim *adj.* **1.** compact, dapper, natty (*Inf.*), neat, nice, orderly, shipshape, smart, soigné, soignée, spick-and-span, spruce, tidy, well-groomed, well-ordered, well turned-out **2.** fit, shapely, sleek, slender, slim, streamlined, svelte, willowy ~*v.* **3.** barber, clip, crop, curtail, cut, cut back, dock, even up, lop, pare, prune, shave, shear, tidy **4.** adorn, array, beautify, bedeck, deck out, decorate, dress, embellish, embroider, garnish, ornament, trick out **5.** adjust, arrange, balance, distribute, order, prepare, settle

Antonyms (*sense 1*) disorderly,

messy, scruffy, shabby, sloppy, ungroomed, unkempt, untidy

trimming 1. adornment, border, braid, decoration, edging, embellishment, frill, fringe, garnish, ornamentation, piping **2.** *Plural* accessories, accompaniments, appurtenances, extras, frills, garnish, ornaments, paraphernalia, trappings

trinket bagatelle, bauble, bibelot, gewgaw, gimcrack, kickshaw, knick-knack, nothing, ornament, piece of bric-a-brac, toy, trifle

trio threesome, triad, trilogy, trine, trinity, triple, triplet, triptych, triumvirate, triune

trip *n.* **1.** errand, excursion, expedition, foray, jaunt, journey, outing, ramble, run, tour, travel, voyage **2.** blunder, boob (*Brit. sl.*), error, fall, false move, false step, faux pas, indiscretion, lapse, misstep, slip, stumble ~*v.* **3.** blunder, boob (*Brit. sl.*), err, fall, go wrong, lapse, lose one's balance, lose one's footing, make a false move, make a faux pas, miscalculate, misstep, slip, slip up (*Inf.*), stumble, tumble **4.** catch out, confuse, disconcert, put off one's stride, throw off, trap, unsettle

triple 1. *adj.* threefold, three times as much, three-way, tripartite **2.** *n.* threesome, triad, trilogy, trine, trinity, trio, triplet, triumvirate, triune

trite banal, bromidic, clichéd, common, commonplace, corny (*Sl.*), dull, hack, hackneyed, ordinary, pedestrian, routine, run-of-the-mill, stale, stereotyped, stock, threadbare, tired, uninspired, unoriginal, worn
Antonyms exciting, fresh, interesting, new, novel, original, out-of-the-ordinary, uncommon, unexpected, unfamiliar

triumph *n.* **1.** elation, exultation, happiness, joy, jubilation, pride, rejoicing **2.** accomplishment, achievement, ascendancy, attainment, conquest, coup, feat, hit (*Inf.*), mastery, sensation,

smash (*Inf.*), smash-hit (*Inf.*), success, *tour de force*, victory, walkover (*Inf.*) ~*v.* **3.** celebrate, crow, exult, gloat, glory, jubilate, rejoice, revel, swagger
Antonyms *n.* (*sense 2*) catastrophe, defeat, disaster, failure, fiasco, flop, washout (*Inf.*)

triumphant boastful, celebratory, cock-a-hoop, conquering, dominant, elated, exultant, glorious, jubilant, proud, rejoicing, successful, swaggering, triumphal, undefeated, victorious, winning
Antonyms beaten, defeated, embarrassed, humbled, humiliated, shamed, unsuccessful

trivial commonplace, everyday, frivolous, incidental, inconsequential, inconsiderable, insignificant, little, meaningless, minor, negligible, paltry, petty, puny, slight, small, trifling, trite, unimportant, valueless, worthless
Antonyms considerable, crucial, essential, important, profound, serious, significant, uncommon, unusual, vital, weighty, worthwhile

troop *n.* **1.** assemblage, band, body, bunch (*Inf.*), company, contingent, crew (*Inf.*), crowd, drove, flock, gang, gathering, group, herd, horde, multitude, pack, squad, swarm, team, throng, unit **2.** *Plural* armed forces, army, fighting men, men, military, servicemen, soldiers, soldiery ~*v.* **3.** crowd, flock, march, parade, stream, swarm, throng, traipse (*Inf.*)

trophy award, bays, booty, cup, laurels, memento, prize, souvenir, spoils

tropical hot, humid, lush, steamy, stifling, sultry, sweltering, torrid
Antonyms arctic, chilly, cold, cool, freezing, frosty, frozen

trot 1. *v.* canter, go briskly, jog, lope, run, scamper **2.** *n.* brisk pace, canter, jog, lope, run

trouble *n.* **1.** agitation, annoyance, anxiety, disquiet, distress, grief, hassle (*Inf.*), heartache, irritation, misfortune, pain, sorrow, suffering, torment, tribulation, vexation, woe, worry **2.** agitation, bother (*Inf.*), commotion, discontent, discord, disorder, dissatisfaction, disturbance, row, strife, tumult, unrest **3.** ailment, complaint, defect, disability, disease, disorder, failure, illness, malfunction, upset **4.** bother, concern, danger, difficulty, dilemma, dire straits, hot water (*Inf.*), mess, nuisance, pest, pickle (*Inf.*), predicament, problem, scrape (*Inf.*), spot (*Inf.*) **5.** attention, bother, care, effort, exertion, inconvenience, labour, pains, struggle, thought, work ~*v.* **6.** afflict, agitate, annoy, bother, discompose, disconcert, disquiet, distress, disturb, fret, grieve, harass, inconvenience, pain, perplex, perturb, pester, plague, sadden, torment, upset, vex, worry **7.** be concerned, bother, burden, discomfort, discommode, disturb, impose upon, incommode, inconvenience, put out **8.** exert oneself, go to the effort of, make an effort, take pains, take the time

Antonyms *n.* agreement, comfort, contentment, convenience, ease, facility, good fortune, happiness, harmony, peace, pleasure, tranquillity, unity ~*v.* appease, avoid, be unharassed, calm, dodge, ease, mollify, please, relieve, soothe

troublesome 1. annoying, arduous, bothersome, burdensome, demanding, difficult, harassing, hard, importunate, inconvenient, irksome, irritating, laborious, oppressive, pestilential, plaguy (*Inf.*), taxing, tiresome, tricky, trying, upsetting, vexatious, wearisome, worrisome, worrying **2.** disorderly, insubordinate, rebellious, recalcitrant, refractory, rowdy, turbulent, uncooperative, undisciplined, unruly, violent

Antonyms agreeable, calming, congenial, disciplined, eager-to-please, easy, obedient, simple, soothing, pleasant, undemanding, well-behaved

truant *n.* absentee, delinquent, deserter, dodger, malingerer, runaway, shirker, skiver (*Brit. sl.*), straggler

truce armistice, break, ceasefire, cessation, cessation of hostilities, intermission, interval, let-up (*Inf.*), lull, moratorium, peace, respite, rest, stay, treaty

trudge 1. *v.* clump, drag oneself, footslog, hike, lumber, march, plod, slog, stump, traipse (*Inf.*), tramp, trek, walk heavily, yomp **2.** *n.* footslog, haul, hike, march, slog, traipse (*Inf.*), tramp, trek, yomp

true *adj.* **1.** accurate, actual, authentic, bona fide, correct, exact, factual, genuine, legitimate, natural, precise, pure, real, right, truthful, valid, veracious, veritable **2.** confirmed, constant, dedicated, devoted, dutiful, faithful, fast, firm, honest, honourable, loyal, pure, reliable, sincere, staunch, steady, true-blue, trustworthy, trusty, unswerving, upright **3.** accurate, correct, exact, on target, perfect, precise, proper, spot-on (*Brit. inf.*), unerring ~*adv.* **4.** honestly, rightly, truthfully, veraciously, veritably **5.** accurately, correctly, on target, perfectly, precisely, properly, unerringly

Antonyms (*sense 1*) abnormal, artificial, atypical, bogus, counterfeit, erroneous, fake, false, fictional, fictitious, illegitimate, imaginary, inaccurate, incorrect, made-up, make-believe, phoney, pretended, self-styled, spurious, unofficial, untrue, untruthful (*sense 2*) deceitful, disloyal, faithless, false, treacherous, unreliable, untrue, untrustworthy (*sense 3*) askew, awry, erroneous, inaccurate, incorrect, untrue

truly 1. accurately, authentically, beyond doubt, beyond question, correctly, exactly, factually, genuinely, in actuality, in fact, in reality, in truth, legitimately, precisely, really, rightly, truth-

fully, veraciously, veritably, without a doubt 2. confirmedly, constantly, devotedly, dutifully, faithfully, firmly, honestly, honourably, loyally, sincerely, staunchly, steadily, with all one's heart, with dedication, with devotion 3. exceptionally, extremely, greatly, indeed, of course, really, to be sure, verily, very
Antonyms (*sense 1*) doubtfully, falsely, fraudulently, inaccurately, incorrectly, mistakenly

trunk 1. bole, stalk, stem, stock **2.** body, torso **3.** proboscis, snout **4.** bin, box, case, chest, coffer, crate, kist (*Scot.*), locker, portmanteau

trust *n.* **1.** assurance, belief, certainty, certitude, confidence, conviction, credence, credit, expectation, faith, hope, reliance **2.** duty, obligation, responsibility **3.** care, charge, custody, guard, guardianship, protection, safekeeping, trusteeship ~*v.* **4.** assume, believe, expect, hope, presume, suppose, surmise, think likely **5.** bank on, believe, count on, depend on, have faith in, lean on, pin one's faith on, place confidence in, place one's trust in, place reliance on, rely upon, swear by, take at face value **6.** assign, command, commit, confide, consign, delegate, entrust, give, put into the hands of, sign over, turn over
Antonyms *n.* distrust, doubt, fear, incredulity, lack of faith, mistrust, scepticism, suspicion, uncertainty, wariness ~*v.* be sceptical of, beware, disbelieve, discredit, distrust, doubt, lack confidence in, lack faith in, mistrust, suspect

trustworthy dependable, ethical, honest, honourable, level-headed, mature, principled, reliable, responsible, righteous, sensible, steadfast, to be trusted, true, trusty, truthful, upright
Antonyms deceitful, dishonest, disloyal, irresponsible, treacherous, undependable, unethical,

unprincipled, unreliable, untrustworthy

truth 1. accuracy, actuality, exactness, fact, factuality, factualness, genuineness, legitimacy, precision, reality, truthfulness, validity, veracity, verity **2.** candour, constancy, dedication, devotion, dutifulness, faith, faithfulness, fidelity, frankness, honesty, integrity, loyalty, naturalism, realism, uprightness **3.** axiom, certainty, fact, law, maxim, proven principle, reality, truism, verity
Antonyms deceit, deception, delusion, dishonesty, error, fabrication, falsehood, falsity, fiction, inaccuracy, invention, legend, lie, make-believe, myth, old wives' tale, untruth

truthful accurate, candid, correct, exact, faithful, forthright, frank, honest, literal, naturalistic, plainspoken, precise, realistic, reliable, sincere, straight, straightforward, true, trustworthy, veracious, veritable
Antonyms deceptive, dishonest, fabricated, false, fictional, fictitious, inaccurate, incorrect, insincere, lying, made-up, untrue, untruthful

try *v.* **1.** aim, attempt, do one's best, do one's damnedest (*Inf.*), endeavour, essay, exert oneself, have a go (crack, shot, stab, whack), make an attempt, make an effort, seek, strive, struggle, undertake **2.** appraise, check out, evaluate, examine, experiment, inspect, investigate, prove, put to the test, sample, taste, test **3.** afflict, annoy, inconvenience, irk, irritate, pain, plague, strain, stress, tax, tire, trouble, upset, vex, weary **4.** adjudge, adjudicate, examine, hear ~*n.* **5.** attempt, crack (*Inf.*), effort, endeavour, essay, go, shot (*Inf.*), stab, whack (*Inf.*)

try out appraise, check out, evaluate, experiment with, inspect, put into practice, put to the test, sample, taste, test

tuck *v.* **1.** fold, gather, insert, push

~*n.* **2.** fold, gather, pinch, pleat **3.** *Inf.* comestibles, eats (*Sl.*), food, grub (*Sl.*), nosh (*Sl.*), scoff (*Sl.*), victuals

tuck in 1. bed down, enfold, fold under, make snug, put to bed, swaddle, wrap up **2.** eat heartily, get stuck in (*Sl.*)

tug 1. *v.* drag, draw, haul, heave, jerk, lug, pull, tow, wrench, yank **2.** *n.* drag, haul, heave, jerk, pull, tow, traction, wrench, yank

tuition education, instruction, lessons, schooling, teaching, training, tutelage, tutoring

tumble 1. *v.* drop, fall, fall end over end, fall headlong, fall head over heels, flop, lose one's footing, pitch, plummet, roll, stumble, topple, toss, trip up **2.** *n.* collapse, drop, fall, flop, headlong fall, plunge, roll, spill, stumble, toss, trip

tumult ado, affray (*Law*), agitation, altercation, bedlam, brawl, brouhaha, clamour, commotion, din, disorder, disturbance, excitement, fracas, hubbub, hullabaloo, outbreak, pandemonium, quarrel, racket, riot, row, ruction (*Inf.*), stir, stramash (*Scot.*), strife, turmoil, unrest, upheaval, uproar
Antonyms calm, hush, peace, quiet, repose, serenity, silence, stillness

tune *n.* **1.** air, melody, melody line, motif, song, strain, theme **2.** agreement, concert, concord, consonance, euphony, harmony, pitch, sympathy, unison ~*v.* **3.** adapt, adjust, attune, bring into harmony, harmonize, pitch, regulate

tunnel 1. *n.* burrow, channel, hole, passage, passageway, shaft, subway, underpass **2.** *v.* burrow, dig, dig one's way, excavate, mine, penetrate, scoop out, undermine

turbulence agitation, boiling, commotion, confusion, disorder, instability, pandemonium, roughness, storm, tumult, turmoil, unrest, upheaval

Antonyms calm, peace, quiet, repose, rest, stillness

turbulent 1. agitated, blustery, boiling, choppy, confused, disordered, foaming, furious, raging, rough, tempestuous, tumultuous, unsettled, unstable **2.** agitated, anarchic, boisterous, disorderly, insubordinate, lawless, mutinous, obstreperous, rebellious, refractory, riotous, rowdy, seditious, tumultuous, unbridled, undisciplined, ungovernable, unruly, uproarious, violent, wild
Antonyms (*sense 1*) calm, glassy, peaceful, quiet, smooth, still, unruffled

turf clod, divot, grass, green, sod, sward

turmoil agitation, bedlam, brouhaha, bustle, chaos, commotion, confusion, disorder, disturbance, ferment, flurry, hubbub, noise, pandemonium, row, stir, strife, trouble, tumult, turbulence, uproar, violence
Antonyms calm, peace, quiet, repose, rest, serenity, stillness, tranquillity

turn *v.* **1.** circle, go round, gyrate, move in a circle, pivot, revolve, roll, rotate, spin, swivel, twirl, twist, wheel, whirl **2.** change course, change position, go back, move, return, reverse, shift, swerve, switch, veer, wheel **3.** arc, come round, corner, go round, negotiate, pass, pass around, take a bend **4.** adapt, alter, become, change, convert, divert, fashion, fit, form, metamorphose, mould, mutate, remodel, shape, transfigure, transform, transmute **5.** become rancid, curdle, go bad, go off (*Brit. inf.*), go sour, make rancid, sour, spoil, taint **6.** appeal, apply, approach, go, have recourse, look, resort **7.** nauseate, sicken, upset **8.** apostatize, bring round (*Inf.*), change one's mind, change sides, defect, desert, go over, influence, persuade, prejudice, prevail upon, renege, retract, talk into **9.** construct, deliver, execute, fash~

ion, frame, make, mould, perform, shape, write **10. turn tail** beat a hasty retreat, bolt, cut and run (*Inf.*), flee, run away, run off, show a clean pair of heels, take off (*Inf.*), take to one's heels. ~ *n.* **11.** bend, change, circle, curve, cycle, gyration, pivot, reversal, revolution, rotation, spin, swing, turning, twist, whirl **12.** bias, direction, drift, heading, tendency, trend **13.** bend, change of course, change of direction, curve, departure, deviation, shift **14.** chance, crack (*Inf.*), fling, go, opportunity, period, round, shift, shot (*Inf.*), spell, stint, succession, time, try, whack (*Inf.*) **15.** affinity, aptitude, bent, bias, flair, gift, inclination, knack, leaning, propensity, talent **16.** act, action, deed, favour, gesture, service **17.** bend, distortion, twist, warp **18. by turns** alternately, in succession, one after another, reciprocally, turn and turn about

turning point change, climacteric, crisis, critical moment, crossroads, crux, decisive moment, moment of decision, moment of truth

turn off 1. branch off, change direction, depart from, deviate, leave, quit, take another road, take a side road **2.** cut out, kill, put out, shut down, stop, switch off, turn out, unplug

turn on 1. activate, energize, ignite, put on, set in motion, start, start up, switch on **2.** balance, be contingent on, be decided by, depend, hang, hinge, pivot, rest **3.** assail, assault, attack, fall on, lose one's temper with, round on

Antonyms (*sense 1*) cut out, put out, shut off, stop, switch off, turn off

turn up 1. appear, arrive, attend, come, put in an appearance, show (*Sl.*), show one's face, show up (*Inf.*) **2.** appear, become known, be found, bring to light, come to light, come to pass, come up with, crop up (*Inf.*), dig up, disclose, discover, expose,

find, pop up, reveal, transpire, unearth

Antonyms (*sense 2*) disappear, evaporate, fade, hide, vanish

tutor 1. *n.* coach, educator, governor, guardian, guide, guru, instructor, lecturer, master, mentor, preceptor, schoolmaster, teacher **2.** *v.* coach, direct, discipline, drill, edify, educate, guide, instruct, lecture, school, teach, train

twilight *n.* **1.** dimness, dusk, evening, gloaming (*Scot.*), half-light, sundown, sunset **2.** decline, ebb, last phase ~ *adj.* **3.** crepuscular, darkening, dim, evening

Antonyms climax, crowning moment, dawn, daybreak, height, morning, peak, sunrise, sunup

twin 1. *n.* clone, corollary, counterpart, double, duplicate, fellow, likeness, lookalike, match, mate, ringer (*Sl.*) **2.** *adj.* corresponding, double, dual, duplicate, geminate, identical, matched, matching, paired, parallel, twofold

twine *n.* **1.** cord, string, yarn **2.** coil, convolution, interlacing, twist, whorl **3.** knot, snarl, tangle ~ *v.* **4.** braid, entwine, interlace, interweave, knit, plait, splice, twist, twist together, weave **5.** bend, coil, curl, encircle, loop, meander, spiral, surround, twist, wind, wrap, wreathe

twinkling *n.* **1.** blink, coruscation, flash, flashing, flicker, gleam, glimmer, glistening, glittering, scintillation, shimmer, shining, sparkle, twinkle, wink **2.** flash, instant, jiffy (*Inf.*), moment, second, shake (*Inf.*), split second, tick (*Inf.*), trice, twinkle, two shakes of a lamb's tail (*Inf.*)

twirl 1. *v.* gyrate, pirouette, pivot, revolve, rotate, spin, turn, turn on one's heel, twiddle, twist, wheel, whirl, wind **2.** *n.* gyration, pirouette, revolution, rotation, spin, turn, twist, wheel, whirl

twist *v.* **1.** coil, corkscrew, curl, encircle, entwine, intertwine, screw, spin, swivel, twine, weave, wind, wrap, wreathe, wring **2.** contort, distort, screw up **3.** rick, sprain, turn, wrench **4.** alter, change, distort, falsify, garble, misquote, misrepresent, pervert, warp ~*n.* **5.** coil, curl, spin, swivel, twine, wind **6.** braid, coil, curl, hank, plug, quid, roll **7.** change, development, revelation, slant, surprise, turn, variation **8.** arc, bend, convolution, curve, meander, turn, undulation, zigzag **9.** defect, deformation, distortion, flaw, imperfection, kink, warp **10.** jerk, pull, sprain, turn, wrench **11.** aberration, bent, characteristic, crotchet, eccentricity, fault, foible, idiosyncrasy, oddity, peculiarity, proclivity, quirk, trait **12.** confusion, entanglement, kink, knot, mess, mix-up, snarl, tangle

twitch 1. *v.* blink, flutter, jerk, jump, pluck, pull, snatch, squirm, tug, yank **2.** *n.* blink, flutter, jerk, jump, pull, spasm, tic, tremor, twinge

tycoon baron, big cheese (*Sl.*), big noise (*Sl.*), capitalist, captain of industry, fat cat (*Sl.*), financier, industrialist, magnate, merchant prince, mogul, plutocrat, potentate, wealthy businessman

type 1. breed, category, class, classification, form, genre, group, ilk, kidney, kind, order, sort, species, strain, subdivision, variety **2.** case, characters, face, fount, print, printing **3.** archetype, epitome, essence, example, exemplar, model, original, paradigm, pattern, personification, prototype, quintessence, specimen, standard

typical archetypal, average, characteristic, classic, conventional, essential, illustrative, in character, indicative, in keeping, model, normal, orthodox, representative, standard, stock, true to type, usual

Antonyms atypical, exceptional, out of keeping, out of the ordinary, singular, uncharacteristic, unconventional, unexpected, unique, unrepresentative, unusual

typify characterize, embody, epitomize, exemplify, illustrate, incarnate, personify, represent, sum up, symbolize

tyrannical absolute, arbitrary, authoritarian, autocratic, coercive, cruel, despotic, dictatorial, domineering, high-handed, imperious, inhuman, magisterial, oppressive, overbearing, overweening, peremptory, severe, tyrannous, unjust, unreasonable

Antonyms democratic, easygoing, lax, lenient, liberal, reasonable, tolerant, understanding

tyranny absolutism, authoritarianism, autocracy, coercion, cruelty, despotism, dictatorship, harsh discipline, high-handedness, imperiousness, oppression, peremptoriness, reign of terror, unreasonableness

Antonyms democracy, ease, laxity, leniency, liberality, mercy, relaxation, tolerance, understanding

tyrant absolutist, authoritarian, autocrat, bully, despot, dictator, Hitler, martinet, oppressor, slave-driver

U

ugly 1. hard-favoured, hard-featured, homely (*Chiefly U.S.*), ill-favoured, misshapen, not much to look at, plain, unattractive, unlovely, unprepossessing, unsightly **2.** disagreeable, disgusting, distasteful, frightful, hideous, horrid, monstrous, objectionable, offensive, repugnant, repulsive, revolting, shocking, terrible, unpleasant, vile **3.** dangerous, forbidding, menacing, ominous, sinister, threatening **4.** angry, bad-tempered, dark, evil, malevolent, nasty, spiteful, sullen, surly
Antonyms agreeable, attractive, auspicious, beautiful, friendly, good-humoured, good-looking, good-natured, gorgeous, handsome, likable, lovely, peaceful, pleasant, pretty, promising

ulterior concealed, covert, hidden, personal, secondary, secret, selfish, undisclosed, unexpressed

ultimate *adj.* **1.** conclusive, decisive, end, eventual, extreme, final, furthest, last, terminal **2.** extreme, greatest, highest, maximum, most significant, paramount, superlative, supreme, topmost, utmost

umpire 1. *n.* adjudicator, arbiter, arbitrator, judge, moderator, ref (*Inf.*), referee **2.** *v.* adjudicate, arbitrate, call (*Sport*), judge, moderate, referee

unabashed blatant, bold, brazen, confident, unawed, unblushing, unconcerned, undaunted, undismayed, unembarrassed
Antonyms abashed, embarrassed, humbled, mortified, shame-faced, sheepish

unable impotent, inadequate, incapable, ineffectual, no good, not able, not equal to, not up to, powerless, unfit, unfitted, unqualified
Antonyms able, adept, adequate, capable, competent, effective, potent, powerful

unabridged complete, full-length, uncondensed, uncut, unexpurgated, unshortened, whole

unacceptable disagreeable, displeasing, distasteful, improper, inadmissible, insupportable, objectionable, offensive, undesirable, unpleasant, unsatisfactory, unwelcome
Antonyms acceptable, agreeable, delightful, desirable, pleasant, pleasing, welcome

unaccompanied a cappella (*Music*), alone, by oneself, lone, on one's own, solo, unescorted

unaccustomed *With* to a newcomer to, a novice at, green, inexperienced, not given to, not used to, unfamiliar with, unpractised, unused to, unversed in
Antonyms experienced, given to, habituated, practised, seasoned, used to, well-versed

unaffected artless, genuine, honest, ingenuous, naive, natural, plain, simple, sincere, straightforward, unassuming, unpretentious, unsophisticated, unspoilt, unstudied, without airs
Antonyms affected, assumed, designing, devious, insincere, mannered, pretentious, put-on, snobbish, sophisticated

unalterable fixed, fixed as the laws of the Medes and the Persians, immutable, invariable, permanent, steadfast, unchangeable, unchanging
Antonyms alterable, changeable, changing, flexible, mutable, variable

unanimous agreed, agreeing, at one, common, concerted, con-

cordant, harmonious, in agreement, in complete accord, likeminded, of one mind, united
Antonyms differing, discordant, dissident, disunited, divided, schismatic, split

unanimously by common consent, nem. con., unitedly, unopposed, with one accord, without exception, without opposition

unanswerable absolute, conclusive, incontestable, incontrovertible, indisputable, irrefutable, unarguable, undeniable

unanswered disputed, ignored, in doubt, open, undecided, undenied, unnoticed, unrefuted, unresolved, unsettled, up in the air, vexed

unapproachable 1. aloof, chilly, cool, distant, frigid, offish (*Inf.*), remote, reserved, standoffish, unfriendly, unsociable, withdrawn **2.** inaccessible, out of reach, out-of-the-way, remote, unget-at-able (*Inf.*), unreachable
Antonyms (*sense 1*) affable, approachable, congenial, cordial, friendly, sociable

unarmed assailable, defenceless, exposed, helpless, open, open to attack, unarmoured, unprotected, weak, weaponless, without arms
Antonyms armed, equipped, fortified, protected, ready, strengthened

unassailable impregnable, invincible, invulnerable, secure, well-defended

unassuming diffident, humble, meek, modest, quiet, reserved, retiring, self-effacing, simple, unassertive, unobtrusive, unostentatious, unpretentious
Antonyms assuming, audacious, conceited, ostentatious, overconfident, presumptuous, pretentious

unattached 1. autonomous, free, independent, nonaligned, unaffiliated, uncommitted **2.** a free agent, available, by oneself, footloose and fancy-free, not spoken for, on one's own, single, unengaged, unmarried

Antonyms (*sense 1*) affiliated, aligned, attached, committed, dependent, implicated, involved

unattended 1. abandoned, disregarded, ignored, left alone, not cared for, unguarded, unwatched **2.** alone, on one's own, unaccompanied, unescorted

unauthorized illegal, unapproved, unconstitutional, unlawful, unofficial, unsanctioned, unwarranted
Antonyms authorized, constitutional, lawful, legal, official, sanctioned, warranted

unavoidable bound to happen, certain, compulsory, fated, ineluctable, inescapable, inevitable, inexorable, necessary, obligatory, sure

unaware heedless, ignorant, incognizant, oblivious, unconscious, unenlightened, uninformed, unknowing, unmindful, unsuspecting
Antonyms attentive, aware, conscious, informed, knowing, mindful

unawares 1. aback, abruptly, by surprise, off guard, on the hop (*Brit. inf.*), suddenly, unexpectedly, unprepared, without warning **2.** accidentally, by accident, by mistake, inadvertently, mistakenly, unconsciously, unintentionally, unknowingly, unwittingly
Antonyms deliberately, forewarned, knowingly, on purpose, on the look-out, prepared, wittingly

unbalanced 1. asymmetrical, irregular, lopsided, not balanced, shaky, unequal, uneven, unstable, unsymmetrical, wobbly **2.** crazy, demented, deranged, disturbed, eccentric, erratic, insane, irrational, lunatic, mad, non compos mentis, not all there, touched, unhinged, unsound, unstable
Antonyms (*sense 1*) balanced, equal, even, stable, symmetrical

unbearable insufferable, insupportable, intolerable, oppressive, too much (*Inf.*), unacceptable, unendurable

Antonyms acceptable, bearable, endurable, supportable, tolerable

unbeatable indomitable, invincible, more than a match for, unconquerable, unstoppable, unsurpassable

unbeaten triumphant, unbowed, undefeated, unsubdued, unsurpassed, unvanquished, victorious, winning

unbecoming 1. ill-suited, inappropriate, incongruous, unattractive, unbefitting, unfit, unflattering, unsightly, unsuitable, unsuited **2.** discreditable, improper, indecorous, indelicate, offensive, tasteless, unseemly

Antonyms (*sense 2*) becoming, decent, decorous, delicate, proper, seemly

unbelievable astonishing, beyond belief, far-fetched, implausible, impossible, improbable, inconceivable, incredible, outlandish, preposterous, questionable, staggering, unconvincing, unimaginable, unthinkable

Antonyms authentic, believable, credible, likely, plausible, possible, probable, trustworthy

unbending 1. aloof, distant, formal, inflexible, reserved, rigid, stiff, uptight (*Sl.*) **2.** firm, hardline, intractable, resolute, severe, strict, stubborn, tough, uncompromising, unyielding

Antonyms approachable, at ease, flexible, friendly, outgoing, relaxed, sociable

unbiased disinterested, dispassionate, equitable, even-handed, fair, impartial, just, neutral, objective, open-minded, unprejudiced

Antonyms biased, bigoted, partial, prejudiced, slanted, swayed, unfair, unjust

unblemished flawless, immaculate, perfect, pure, spotless, unflawed, unspotted, unstained, unsullied, untarnished

Antonyms blemished, flawed,

imperfect, impure, stained, sullied, tarnished

unborn 1. awaited, embryonic, expected, *in utero* **2.** coming, future, hereafter, latter, subsequent, to come

unbreakable armoured, durable, indestructible, infrangible, lasting, nonbreakable, resistant, rugged, shatterproof, solid, strong, toughened

Antonyms breakable, brittle, delicate, flimsy, fragile, frangible

unbridled excessive, intemperate, licentious, rampant, riotous, unchecked, unconstrained, uncontrolled, uncurbed, ungovernable, ungoverned, unrestrained, unruly, violent, wanton

unbroken complete, entire, intact, solid, total, unimpaired, whole

Antonyms broken, cracked, damaged, fragmented, in pieces, shattered

unburden 1. disburden, discharge, disencumber, ease the load, empty, lighten, relieve, unload **2.** come clean (*Inf.*), confess, confide, disclose, get (something) off one's chest (*Inf.*), lay bare, make a clean breast of, reveal, tell all, unbosom

uncalled-for gratuitous, inappropriate, needless, undeserved, unjust, unjustified, unnecessary, unprovoked, unwarranted, unwelcome

Antonyms appropriate, deserved, just, justified, necessary, needed, provoked, warranted

uncanny 1. creepy (*Inf.*), eerie, eldritch (*Poetic*), mysterious, preternatural, queer, spooky (*Inf.*), strange, supernatural, unearthly, unnatural, weird **2.** astonishing, astounding, exceptional, extraordinary, fantastic, incredible, inspired, miraculous, prodigious, remarkable, singular, unheard-of, unusual

unceasing ceaseless, constant, continual, continuing, continuous, endless, incessant, never-ending,

nonstop, perpetual, persistent, unending, unfailing, unremitting
Antonyms fitful, intermittent, irregular, occasional, periodic, spasmodic, sporadic

uncertain 1. ambiguous, chancy, conjectural, doubtful, iffy, incalculable, indefinite, indeterminate, indistinct, questionable, risky, speculative, undetermined, unforeseeable, unpredictable **2.** ambivalent, doubtful, dubious, hazy, in two minds, irresolute, unclear, unconfirmed, undecided, undetermined, unfixed, unresolved, unsettled, unsure, up in the air, vacillating, vague
Antonyms certain, clear, clear-cut, decided, definite, firm, fixed, known, positive, resolute, settled, sure, unambiguous

uncertainty ambiguity, bewilderment, confusion, dilemma, doubt, hesitancy, hesitation, inconclusiveness, indecision, irresolution, lack of confidence, misgiving, mystification, perplexity, puzzlement, qualm, quandary, scepticism, state of suspense, unpredictability, vagueness
Antonyms assurance, certainty, confidence, decision, predictability, resolution, sureness, trust

unchangeable changeless, constant, fixed, immutable, inevitable, invariable, irreversible, permanent, stable, steadfast, strong, unalterable
Antonyms changeable, inconstant, irregular, mutable, shifting, unstable, variable, wavering

uncivil bad-mannered, bearish, boorish, brusque, churlish, discourteous, disrespectful, gruff, ill-bred, ill-mannered, impolite, rude, surly, uncouth, unmannerly
Antonyms civil, courteous, mannerly, polished, polite, refined, respectful, well-bred, well-mannered

uncivilized 1. barbarian, barbaric, barbarous, illiterate, primitive, savage, wild **2.** beyond the pale, boorish, brutish, churlish,

coarse, gross, philistine, uncouth, uncultivated, uncultured, uneducated, unmannered, unpolished, unsophisticated, vulgar

unclean contaminated, corrupt, defiled, dirty, evil, filthy, foul, impure, nasty, polluted, soiled, spotted, stained, sullied, tainted
Antonyms clean, faultless, flawless, pure, spotless, unblemished, unstained, unsullied

uncomfortable 1. awkward, causing discomfort, cramped, disagreeable, hard, ill-fitting, incommodious, irritating, painful, rough, troublesome **2.** awkward, confused, discomfited, disquieted, distressed, disturbed, embarrassed, ill at ease, out of place, self-conscious, troubled, uneasy
Antonyms (*sense 2*) at ease, comfortable, easy, relaxed, serene, untroubled

uncommon 1. bizarre, curious, few and far between, infrequent, novel, odd, out of the ordinary, peculiar, queer, rare, scarce, singular, strange, unfamiliar, unusual **2.** distinctive, exceptional, extraordinary, incomparable, inimitable, notable, noteworthy, outstanding, rare, remarkable, singular, special, superior, unparalleled, unprecedented
Antonyms (*sense 1*) common, familiar, frequent, regular, routine, usual (*sense 2*) average, banal, commonplace, everyday, humdrum, ordinary, run-of-the-mill

uncommonly 1. hardly ever, infrequently, not often, occasionally, only now and then, rarely, scarcely ever, seldom **2.** exceptionally, extremely, particularly, peculiarly, remarkably, strangely, unusually, very

uncommunicative close, curt, guarded, reserved, reticent, retiring, secretive, short, shy, silent, taciturn, tight-lipped, unforthcoming, unresponsive, unsociable, withdrawn
Antonyms chatty, communicative, forthcoming, garrulous, lo-

quacious, responsive, talkative, voluble

uncompromising decided, diehard, firm, hard-line, inexorable, inflexible, intransigent, obdurate, obstinate, rigid, steadfast, strict, stubborn, tough, unbending, unyielding

unconcerned aloof, apathetic, callous, cool, detached, dispassionate, distant, incurious, indifferent, oblivious, uninterested, uninvolved, unmoved, unsympathetic
Antonyms avid, curious, eager, interested, involved

unconditional absolute, categorical, complete, downright, entire, explicit, full, out-and-out, outright, plenary, positive, thoroughgoing, total, unlimited, unqualified, unreserved, unrestricted, utter
Antonyms conditional, limited, partial, qualified, reserved, restricted

unconnected 1. detached, disconnected, divided, independent, separate 2. disconnected, disjointed, illogical, incoherent, irrelevant, meaningless, nonsensical, not related, unrelated
Antonyms (*sense 2*) coherent, connected, intelligible, logical, meaningful, related, relevant

unconscious 1. blacked out (*Inf.*), comatose, dead to the world, insensible, knocked out, numb, out cold, senseless, stunned 2. blind to, deaf to, heedless, ignorant, in ignorance, lost to, oblivious, unaware, unknowing, unmindful, unsuspecting 3. accidental, inadvertent, unintended, unintentional, unpremeditated, unwitting 4. automatic, gut (*Inf.*), inherent, innate, instinctive, involuntary, latent, reflex, repressed, subconscious, subliminal, suppressed, unrealized
Antonyms (*sense 1*) alert, awake, aware, conscious, responsive, sensible (*sense 3*) calculated,

conscious, deliberate, intentional, planned, studied, wilful

uncontrollable beside oneself, carried away, frantic, furious, irrepressible, irresistible, like one possessed, mad, strong, ungovernable, unmanageable, unruly, violent, wild

uncontrolled boisterous, furious, lacking self-control, out of control, out of hand, rampant, riotous, running wild, unbridled, unchecked, uncurbed, undisciplined, ungoverned, unrestrained, unruly, unsubmissive, untrammelled, violent
Antonyms contained, controlled, disciplined, restrained, subdued, submissive

unconventional atypical, bizarre, bohemian, different, eccentric, far-out (*Sl.*), freakish (*Inf.*), idiosyncratic, individual, individualistic, informal, irregular, nonconformist, odd, offbeat, original, out of the ordinary, uncustomary, unorthodox, unusual, way-out (*Inf.*)
Antonyms conventional, normal, ordinary, orthodox, proper, regular, typical, usual

uncouth awkward, barbaric, boorish, clownish, clumsy, coarse, crude, gawky, graceless, gross, ill-mannered, loutish, lubberly, oafish, rough, rude, rustic, uncivilized, uncultivated, ungainly, unrefined, unseemly, vulgar
Antonyms civilized, courteous, cultivated, elegant, graceful, refined, seemly, well-mannered

uncover 1. bare, lay open, lift the lid, open, show, strip, take the wraps off, unwrap 2. bring to light, disclose, discover, divulge, expose, lay bare, make known, reveal, unearth, unmask
Antonyms clothe, conceal, cover, cover up, drape, dress, hide, keep under wraps, suppress

uncritical easily pleased, indiscriminate, undiscerning, undiscriminating, unexacting, unfussy, unperceptive, unselective, unthinking

Antonyms critical, discerning, discriminating, fastidious, fussy, perceptive, selective

undecided 1. ambivalent, dithering, doubtful, dubious, hesitant, in two minds, irresolute, swithering (*Scot.*), torn, uncertain, uncommitted, unsure, wavering 2. debatable, indefinite, in the balance, moot, open, pending, tentative, unconcluded, undetermined, unsettled, up in the air, vague

Antonyms certain, committed, decided, definite, determined, resolute, resolved, settled, sure

undefined 1. formless, hazy, indefinite, indistinct, shadowy, tenuous, vague 2. imprecise, indeterminate, inexact, unclear, unexplained, unspecified

Antonyms (*sense 2*) clear, defined, definite, determinate, exact, explicit, precise, specified

undeniable beyond (a) doubt, beyond question, certain, clear, evident, incontestable, incontrovertible, indisputable, indubitable, irrefutable, manifest, obvious, patent, proven, sound, sure, unassailable, undoubted, unquestionable

Antonyms debatable, deniable, doubtful, dubious, questionable, uncertain, unproven

under *prep.* 1. below, beneath, on the bottom of, underneath 2. directed by, governed by, inferior to, junior to, reporting to, secondary to, subject to, subordinate to, subservient to 3. belonging to, comprised in, included in, subsumed under ~*adv.* 4. below, beneath, down, downward, lower, to the bottom

Antonyms (*senses 1 & 4*) above, over, up, upper, upward

underclothes lingerie, smalls (*Inf.*), underclothing, undergarments, underlinen, underthings (*Inf.*), underwear, undies (*Inf.*)

undercover clandestine, concealed, confidential, covert, hidden, hush-hush (*Inf.*), intelli-gence, private, secret, spy, surreptitious, underground

Antonyms manifest, open, overt, plain, unconcealed, visible

undercurrent 1. crosscurrent, rip, rip current, riptide, underflow, undertow 2. atmosphere, aura, drift, feeling, flavour, hidden feeling, hint, murmur, overtone, sense, suggestion, tendency, tenor, tinge, trend, undertone, vibes (*Inf.*), vibrations

underestimate belittle, hold cheap, minimize, miscalculate, misprize, not do justice to, rate too low, sell short (*Inf.*), set no store by, think too little of, underrate, undervalue

Antonyms exaggerate, inflate, overdo, overestimate, overrate, overstate

undergo bear, be subjected to, endure, experience, go through, stand, submit to, suffer, sustain, weather, withstand

underground *adj.* 1. below ground, below the surface, buried, covered, subterranean 2. clandestine, concealed, covert, hidden, secret, surreptitious, undercover ~*n.* 3. **the underground** the metro, the subway, the tube (*Brit.*)

undergrowth bracken, brambles, briars, brush, brushwood, scrub, underbrush, underbush, underwood

underhand clandestine, crafty, crooked (*Inf.*), deceitful, deceptive, devious, dishonest, dishonourable, fraudulent, furtive, secret, secretive, sly, sneaky, stealthy, surreptitious, treacherous, underhanded, unethical, unscrupulous

Antonyms above board, frank, honest, honourable, legal, open, outright, principled, scrupulous

underline 1. italicize, mark, rule a line under, underscore 2. accentuate, bring home, call *or* draw attention to, emphasize, give emphasis to, highlight, point up, stress

Antonyms (*sense 2*) gloss over,

make light of, minimize, play down, soft-pedal (*Inf.*), underrate

underlying 1. concealed, hidden, latent, lurking, veiled **2.** basal, basic, elementary, essential, fundamental, intrinsic, primary, prime, root

undermine 1. dig out, eat away at, erode, excavate, mine, tunnel, undercut, wear away **2.** debilitate, disable, impair, sabotage, sap, subvert, threaten, weaken
Antonyms (*sense 2*) buttress, fortify, promote, reinforce, strengthen, sustain

underprivileged badly off, deprived, destitute, disadvantaged, impoverished, in need, in want, needy, poor

underrate belittle, discount, disparage, fail to appreciate, misprize, not do justice to, set (too) little store by, underestimate, undervalue
Antonyms exaggerate, overestimate, overprize, overrate, overvalue

undersized atrophied, dwarfish, miniature, pygmy, runtish, runty, small, squat, stunted, tiny, underdeveloped, underweight

understand 1. appreciate, apprehend, be aware, catch on (*Inf.*), comprehend, conceive, cotton on (*Inf.*), discern, fathom, follow, get, get the hang of (*Inf.*), get to the bottom of, grasp, know, make head or tail of (*Inf.*), make out, penetrate, perceive, realize, recognize, savvy (*Sl.*), see, take in, tumble to (*Inf.*), twig (*Brit. inf.*) **2.** assume, be informed, believe, conclude, gather, hear, learn, presume, suppose, take it, think **3.** accept, appreciate, be able to see, commiserate, show compassion for, sympathize with, tolerate

understanding n. **1.** appreciation, awareness, comprehension, discernment, grasp, insight, intelligence, judgment, knowledge, penetration, perception, sense **2.** belief, conclusion, estimation, idea, interpretation, judgment,

notion, opinion, perception, view, viewpoint **3.** accord, agreement, common view, gentlemen's agreement, meeting of minds, pact ~*adj.* **4.** accepting, compassionate, considerate, discerning, forbearing, forgiving, kind, kindly, patient, perceptive, responsive, sensitive, sympathetic, tolerant
Antonyms n. (*sense 1*) ignorance, incomprehension, insensitivity, misapprehension, misunderstanding, obtuseness (*sense 3*) aloofness, coldness, disagreement, dispute ~*adj.* inconsiderate, insensitive, intolerant, obtuse, rigid, strict, unfeeling, unsympathetic

understood 1. implicit, implied, inferred, tacit, unspoken, unstated **2.** accepted, assumed, axiomatic, presumed, taken for granted

understudy n. double, fill-in, replacement, reserve, stand-in, sub, substitute

undertake 1. agree, bargain, commit oneself, contract, covenant, engage, guarantee, pledge, promise, stipulate, take upon oneself **2.** attempt, begin, commence, embark on, endeavour, enter upon, set about, tackle, take on, try

undertaking 1. affair, attempt, business, effort, endeavour, enterprise, game, operation, project, task, venture **2.** assurance, commitment, pledge, promise, solemn word, vow, word, word of honour

undertone 1. low tone, murmur, subdued voice, whisper **2.** atmosphere, feeling, flavour, hint, suggestion, tinge, touch, trace, undercurrent

underwater submarine, submerged, sunken, undersea

under way afoot, begun, going on, in motion, in operation, in progress, started

underwear lingerie, smalls (*Inf.*), underclothes, underclothing,

undergarments, underlinen, un~
dies (*Inf.*), unmentionables

underworld 1. criminal element,
criminals, gangland (*Inf.*), gang~
sters, organized crime **2.** abode
of the dead, Hades, hell, infernal
region, nether regions, nether
world, the inferno

underwrite 1. back, finance, fund,
guarantee, insure, provide secu~
rity, sponsor, subsidize **2.**
countersign, endorse, initial, sign,
subscribe **3.** agree to, approve,
consent, okay (*Inf.*), sanction

undesirable disagreeable, dis~
liked, distasteful, dreaded, objec~
tionable, obnoxious, offensive,
out of place, repugnant, (to be)
avoided, unacceptable, unattrac~
tive, unpleasing, unpopular, un~
savoury, unsuitable, unwanted,
unwelcome, unwished-for
Antonyms acceptable, agree~
able, appealing, attractive, de~
sirable, inviting, pleasing, popu~
lar, welcome

undeveloped embryonic, imma~
ture, inchoate, in embryo, latent,
potential, primordial (*Biol.*)

undignified beneath one, be~
neath one's dignity, improper,
inappropriate, indecorous, inel~
egant, infra dig (*Inf.*), lacking
dignity, unbecoming, ungentle~
manly, unladylike, unrefined,
unseemly, unsuitable
Antonyms appropriate, becom~
ing, decorous, dignified, elegant,
proper, refined, seemly, suitable

undisciplined disobedient, errat~
ic, fitful, obstreperous, uncon~
trolled, unpredictable, unreliable,
unrestrained, unruly, unschooled,
unsteady, unsystematic, un~
trained, wayward, wild, wilful
Antonyms controlled, disci~
plined, obedient, predictable, re~
liable, restrained, steady, trained

undisguised complete, evident,
explicit, genuine, manifest, obvi~
ous, open, out-and-out, overt, pa~
tent, thoroughgoing, transparent,
unconcealed, unfeigned, unmis~
takable, utter, wholehearted

Antonyms concealed, covert,
disguised, feigned, hidden, secret

undisputed accepted, acknowl~
edged, beyond question, certain,
conclusive, freely admitted, in~
contestable, incontrovertible, in~
disputable, irrefutable, not dis~
puted, recognized, sure, unchal~
lenged, uncontested, undeniable,
undoubted, unquestioned
Antonyms deniable, disputed,
doubtful, dubious, inconclusive,
questioned, uncertain

undistinguished commonplace,
everyday, indifferent, mediocre,
no great shakes (*Inf.*), nothing to
write home about (*Inf.*), ordi~
nary, pedestrian, prosaic, run-of-
the-mill, so-so (*Inf.*), unexcep~
tional, unexciting, unimpressive,
unremarkable
Antonyms distinguished, excep~
tional, exciting, extraordinary,
impressive, outstanding, re~
markable, striking

undisturbed 1. not moved, quiet,
uninterrupted, untouched, with~
out interruption **2.** calm, collect~
ed, composed, equable, even,
motionless, placid, serene, tran~
quil, unagitated, unbothered, un~
perturbed, unruffled, untroubled
Antonyms (*sense 1*) confused,
disordered, interfered with, in~
terrupted, moved, muddled
(*sense 2*) agitated, bothered,
busy, disturbed, excited, flus~
tered, nervous, perturbed, trou~
bled, upset

undivided combined, complete,
concentrated, concerted, entire,
exclusive, full, solid, thorough,
unanimous, undistracted, united,
whole, wholehearted

undo 1. disengage, disentangle,
loose, loosen, open, unbutton, un~
fasten, unlock, untie, unwrap **2.**
annul, cancel, invalidate, neu~
tralize, nullify, offset, reverse,
wipe out **3.** bring to naught, de~
feat, destroy, impoverish, invali~
date, mar, overturn, quash, ruin,
shatter, subvert, undermine, up~
set, wreck

undoing 1. collapse, defeat, de~

struction, disgrace, downfall, humiliation, overthrow, overturn, reversal, ruin, ruination, shame **2.** affliction, blight, curse, fatal flaw, misfortune, the last straw, trial, trouble, weakness

undone incomplete, left, neglected, not completed, not done, omitted, outstanding, passed over, unattended to, unfinished, unfulfilled, unperformed
Antonyms accomplished, attended to, complete, done, finished, fulfilled, performed

undoubtedly assuredly, beyond a shadow of (a) doubt, beyond question, certainly, definitely, doubtless, of course, surely, undeniably, unmistakably, unquestionably, without doubt

undress 1. v. disrobe, divest oneself of, peel off (*Sl.*), shed, strip, take off one's clothes **2.** n. disarray, dishabille, nakedness, nudity

undue disproportionate, excessive, extravagant, extreme, immoderate, improper, inordinate, intemperate, needless, overmuch, too great, too much, uncalled-for, undeserved, unnecessary, unseemly, unwarranted
Antonyms appropriate, due, fitting, justified, necessary, proper, suitable, well-considered

unduly disproportionately, excessively, extravagantly, immoderately, improperly, inordinately, out of all proportion, overly, overmuch, unjustifiably, unnecessarily, unreasonably
Antonyms duly, justifiably, moderately, ordinately, properly, proportionately, reasonably

unearth 1. dig up, disinter, dredge up, excavate, exhume **2.** bring to light, discover, expose, ferret out, find, reveal, root up, turn up, uncover

unearthly 1. eerie, eldritch (*Poetic*), ghostly, haunted, nightmarish, phantom, spectral, spooky (*Inf.*), strange, uncanny, weird **2.** ethereal, heavenly, not of this world, preternatural, sublime, supernatural **3.** abnormal,

absurd, extraordinary, ridiculous, strange, ungodly (*Inf.*), unholy (*Inf.*), unreasonable

uneasiness agitation, alarm, anxiety, apprehension, apprehensiveness, disquiet, doubt, misgiving, nervousness, perturbation, qualms, suspicion, worry
Antonyms calm, composure, cool, ease, peace, quiet, serenity

uneasy 1. agitated, anxious, apprehensive, discomposed, disturbed, edgy, ill at ease, impatient, jittery (*Inf.*), nervous, on edge, perturbed, restive, restless, troubled, uncomfortable, unsettled, upset, worried **2.** awkward, constrained, insecure, precarious, shaky, strained, tense, uncomfortable, unstable
Antonyms at ease, calm, comfortable, relaxed, tranquil, unflustered, unperturbed, unruffled

uneconomic loss-making, non-paying, non-profit-making, non-viable, unprofitable
Antonyms economic, money-making, productive, profitable, remunerative, viable

uneducated 1. ignorant, illiterate, unlettered, unread, unschooled, untaught **2.** benighted, lowbrow, uncultivated, uncultured
Antonyms (*sense 1*) educated, informed, instructed, literate, schooled, taught, tutored

unemotional apathetic, cold, cool, impassive, indifferent, listless, passionless, phlegmatic, reserved, undemonstrative, unexcitable, unfeeling, unimpressionable, unresponsive
Antonyms demonstrative, emotional, excitable, feeling, passionate, responsive, sensitive

unemployed idle, jobless, laid off, on the dole (*Brit. inf.*), out of a job, out of work, redundant, resting (*of an actor*), workless

unending ceaseless, constant, continual, endless, eternal, everlasting, incessant, interminable, never-ending, perpetual, unceasing, unremitting

unenthusiastic apathetic, blasé, bored, half-hearted, indifferent, lukewarm, neutral, nonchalant, unimpressed, uninterested, un~ moved, unresponsive

Antonyms ardent, eager, en~ thusiastic, excited, interested, keen, passionate

unenviable disagreeable, painful, thankless, uncomfortable, unde~ sirable, unpleasant

Antonyms agreeable, attractive, desirable, enviable, pleasant

unequalled beyond compare, in~ comparable, inimitable, match~ less, nonpareil, paramount, peerless, pre-eminent, second to none, supreme, transcendent, unmatched, unparalleled, unri~ valled, unsurpassed, without equal

unethical dirty, dishonest, dis~ honourable, disreputable, illegal, immoral, improper, shady (*Inf.*), underhand, unfair, unprincipled, unprofessional, unscrupulous, wrong

Antonyms ethical, honest, hon~ ourable, legal, moral, proper, scrupulous, upright

uneven 1. bumpy, not flat, not level, not smooth, rough **2.** bro~ ken, changeable, fitful, fluctuat~ ing, intermittent, irregular, jerky, patchy, spasmodic, unsteady, variable **3.** asymmetrical, lop~ sided, not parallel, odd, out of true, unbalanced **4.** disparate, ill-matched, one-sided, unequal, unfair

Antonyms (*sense 1*) even, flat, level, plane, smooth

uneventful boring, common~ place, dull, humdrum, monoto~ nous, ordinary, quiet, routine, te~ dious, unexceptional, unexciting, uninteresting, unmemorable, un~ remarkable, unvaried

Antonyms eventful, exceptional, exciting, interesting, memorable, momentous, remarkable

unexpected abrupt, accidental, astonishing, chance, fortuitous, not bargained for, out of the blue, startling, sudden, surprising, unanticipated, unforeseen, un~ looked-for, unpredictable

Antonyms anticipated, awaited, expected, foreseen, normal, planned, predictable

unfailing 1. bottomless, bound~ less, ceaseless, continual, con~ tinuous, endless, inexhaustible, never-failing, persistent, unflag~ ging, unlimited **2.** certain, con~ stant, dependable, faithful, infal~ lible, loyal, reliable, staunch, steadfast, sure, tried and true, true

Antonyms (*sense 2*) disloyal, fal~ lible, inconstant, uncertain, un~ faithful, unreliable, unsure, un~ trustworthy

unfair 1. arbitrary, biased, bigot~ ed, discriminatory, inequitable, one-sided, partial, partisan, prejudiced, unjust **2.** crooked (*Inf.*), dishonest, dishonourable, uncalled-for, unethical, unprinci~ pled, unscrupulous, unsporting, unwarranted, wrongful

Antonyms (*sense 2*) ethical, fair, honest, just, principled, scrupu~ lous

unfaithful 1. deceitful, disloyal, faithless, false, false-hearted, perfidious, recreant (*Archaic*), traitorous, treacherous, treason~ able, unreliable, untrustworthy **2.** adulterous, faithless, fickle, in~ constant, two-timing (*Inf.*), un~ chaste, untrue

Antonyms (*sense 1*) constant, faithful, loyal, steadfast, true, trustworthy

unfamiliar alien, curious, differ~ ent, little known, new, novel, out-of-the-way, strange, unaccus~ tomed, uncommon, unknown, unusual

Antonyms accustomed, ac~ quainted, average, common, commonplace, everyday, ex~ perienced, familiar, knowledge~ able, normal, unexceptional, well-known

unfashionable antiquated, be~ hind the times, dated, obsolete, old-fashioned, old hat, out, out~

moded, out of date, out of fashion, passé, square, unpopular
Antonyms à la mode, fashionable, modern, popular, stylish, trendy (*Inf.*)

unfasten detach, disconnect, let go, loosen, open, separate, uncouple, undo, unlace, unlock, untie

unfavourable 1. adverse, bad, contrary, disadvantageous, hostile, ill-suited, infelicitous, inimical, low, negative, poor, unfortunate, unfriendly, unsuited **2.** inauspicious, inopportune, ominous, threatening, unlucky, unpromising, unpropitious, unseasonable, untimely, untoward
Antonyms (*sense 1*) amicable, approving, favourable, friendly, positive, warm, well-disposed

unfinished 1. deficient, half-done, imperfect, incomplete, in the making, lacking, unaccomplished, uncompleted, undone, unfulfilled, wanting **2.** bare, crude, natural, raw, rough, sketchy, unpolished, unrefined, unvarnished
Antonyms (*sense 2*) finished, flawless, perfected, polished, refined, smooth, varnished

unfit 1. ill-equipped, inadequate, incapable, incompetent, ineligible, no good, not cut out for, not equal to, not up to, unprepared, unqualified, untrained, useless **2.** ill-adapted, inadequate, inappropriate, ineffective, not designed, not fit, unsuitable, unsuited, useless **3.** debilitated, decrepit, feeble, flabby, in poor condition, out of kelter, out of shape, out of trim, unhealthy
Antonyms (*senses 1 & 2*) able, acceptable, capable, competent, equipped, qualified, ready, suitable (*sense 3*) fit, healthy, in good condition, strong, sturdy, well

unflattering 1. blunt, candid, critical, honest, uncomplimentary, warts and all **2.** not shown in the best light, not shown to advantage, plain, unattractive, unbecoming, unprepossessing

unfold 1. disentangle, expand, flatten, open, spread out, straighten, stretch out, undo, unfurl, unravel, unroll, unwrap **2.** *Fig.* clarify, disclose, divulge, explain, illustrate, make known, present, reveal, show, uncover

unforeseen abrupt, accidental, out of the blue, startling, sudden, surprise, surprising, unanticipated, unexpected, unlooked-for, unpredicted
Antonyms anticipated, envisaged, expected, foreseen, intended, predicted

unforgettable exceptional, extraordinary, fixed in the mind, impressive, memorable, never to be forgotten, notable

unforgivable deplorable, disgraceful, indefensible, inexcusable, shameful, unjustifiable, unpardonable, unwarrantable
Antonyms allowable, excusable, forgivable, justifiable, pardonable, venial

unfortunate 1. adverse, calamitous, disastrous, ill-fated, ill-starred, inopportune, ruinous, unfavourable, untoward **2.** cursed, doomed, hapless, hopeless, luckless, out of luck, poor, star-crossed, unhappy, unlucky, unprosperous, unsuccessful, wretched **3.** deplorable, ill-advised, inappropriate, infelicitous, lamentable, regrettable, unbecoming, unsuitable
Antonyms (*senses 1 & 3*) appropriate, opportune, suitable, tactful, timely (*sense 2*) auspicious, felicitous, fortuitous, fortunate, happy, lucky, successful

unfounded baseless, fabricated, false, groundless, idle, spurious, trumped up, unjustified, unproven, unsubstantiated, vain, without basis, without foundation
Antonyms attested, confirmed, factual, justified, proven, substantiated, verified

unfriendly 1. aloof, antagonistic, chilly, cold, disagreeable, distant, hostile, ill-disposed, inhospitable,

not on speaking terms, quarrel-some, sour, surly, uncongenial, unneighbourly, unsociable **2.** alien, hostile, inauspicious, inhospitable, inimical, unfavourable, unpropitious
Antonyms affable, amiable, auspicious, congenial, convivial, friendly, hospitable, propitious, sociable, warm

ungainly awkward, clumsy, gangling, gawky, inelegant, loutish, lubberly, lumbering, slouching, uncoordinated, uncouth, ungraceful
Antonyms attractive, comely, elegant, graceful, pleasing

ungodly blasphemous, corrupt, depraved, godless, immoral, impious, irreligious, profane, sinful, vile, wicked

ungracious bad-mannered, churlish, discourteous, ill-bred, impolite, offhand, rude, uncivil, unmannerly
Antonyms affable, civil, courteous, gracious, mannerly, polite, well-mannered

ungrateful heedless, ingrate (*Archaic*), selfish, thankless, unappreciative, unmindful, unthankful
Antonyms appreciative, aware, grateful, mindful, thankful

unguarded 1. careless, foolhardy, heedless, ill-considered, impolitic, imprudent, incautious, indiscreet, rash, thoughtless, uncircumspect, undiplomatic, unthinking, unwary **2.** defenceless, open to attack, undefended, unpatrolled, unprotected, vulnerable
Antonyms (*sense 1*) cagey (*Inf.*), careful, cautious, diplomatic, discreet, guarded, prudent, wary

unhappy 1. blue, crestfallen, dejected, depressed, despondent, disconsolate, dispirited, down, downcast, gloomy, long- faced, melancholy, miserable, mournful, sad, sorrowful **2.** cursed, hapless, ill-fated, ill-omened, luckless, unfortunate, unlucky, wretched **3.** awkward, clumsy, gauche, ill-advised, ill-timed, in-

appropriate, inept, infelicitous, injudicious, malapropos, tactless, unsuitable, untactful
Antonyms (*sense 1*) cheerful, content, exuberant, good-humoured, happy, joyful, light-hearted, over the moon (*Inf.*), overjoyed, satisfied (*senses 2 & 3*) apt, becoming, fortunate, lucky, prudent, suitable, tactful

unharmed in one piece (*Inf.*), intact, safe, safe and sound, sound, undamaged, unhurt, uninjured, unscarred, unscathed, untouched, whole, without a scratch
Antonyms damaged, harmed, hurt, impaired, injured, scarred, scathed

unhealthy 1. ailing, delicate, feeble, frail, infirm, in poor health, invalid, poorly (*Inf.*), sick, sickly, unsound, unwell, weak **2.** deleterious, detrimental, harmful, insalubrious, insanitary, noisome, noxious, unwholesome
Antonyms beneficial, fit, good, healthy, robust, salubrious, salutary, well, wholesome

unheard-of 1. little known, obscure, undiscovered, unfamiliar, unknown, unregarded, unremarked, unsung **2.** inconceivable, never before encountered, new, novel, singular, unbelievable, undreamed of, unexampled, unique, unprecedented, unusual **3.** disgraceful, extreme, offensive, outlandish, outrageous, preposterous, shocking, unacceptable, unthinkable

unhesitating 1. implicit, resolute, steadfast, unfaltering, unquestioning, unreserved, unswerving, unwavering, wholehearted **2.** immediate, instant, instantaneous, prompt, ready, without delay
Antonyms (*sense 1*) diffident, hesitant, irresolute, questioning, tentative, uncertain, unsure, wavering

unholy base, corrupt, depraved, dishonest, evil, heinous, immoral, iniquitous, irreligious, profane, sinful, ungodly, vile, wicked

Antonyms devout, faithful, godly, holy, pious, religious, saintly, virtuous

unhurried calm, deliberate, easy, easy-going, leisurely, sedate, slow, slow and steady, slow-paced
Antonyms brief, cursory, hasty, hectic, hurried, quick, rushed, speedy, swift

unidentified anonymous, mysterious, nameless, unclassified, unfamiliar, unknown, unmarked, unnamed, unrecognized, unrevealed
Antonyms classified, familiar, identified, known, marked, named, recognized

uniform n. 1. costume, dress, garb, habit, livery, outfit, regalia, regimentals, suit ~adj. 2. consistent, constant, equable, even, regular, smooth, unbroken, unchanging, undeviating, unvarying 3. alike, equal, identical, like, same, selfsame, similar
Antonyms adj. (sense 2) changeable, changing, deviating, inconsistent, irregular, uneven, variable

unimaginable beyond one's wildest dreams, fantastic, impossible, inconceivable, incredible, indescribable, ineffable, mind-boggling (Inf.), unbelievable, unheard-of, unthinkable

unimaginative barren, commonplace, derivative, dry, dull, hackneyed, lifeless, matter-of-fact, ordinary, pedestrian, predictable, prosaic, routine, tame, uncreative, uninspired, unoriginal, unromantic, usual
Antonyms creative, different, exciting, fresh, imaginative, innovative, inventive, original, unhackneyed, unusual

unimportant immaterial, inconsequential, insignificant, irrelevant, low-ranking, minor, not worth mentioning, nugatory, of no account, of no consequence, of no moment, paltry, petty, slight, trifling, trivial, worthless
Antonyms essential, grave, important, major, significant, urgent, vital, weighty

uninhabited abandoned, barren, desert, deserted, desolate, empty, unoccupied, unpopulated, unsettled, untenanted, vacant, waste

uninspired commonplace, dull, humdrum, indifferent, ordinary, prosaic, stale, stock, unexciting, unimaginative, uninspiring, uninteresting, unoriginal
Antonyms brilliant, different, exciting, imaginative, inspired, interesting, original, outstanding

unintelligent brainless, dense, dull, empty-headed, foolish, gormless (Brit. inf.), obtuse, slow, stupid, thick, unreasoning, unthinking
Antonyms bright, clever, intelligent, sharp, smart, thinking

unintelligible double Dutch (Brit. inf.), illegible, inarticulate, incoherent, incomprehensible, indecipherable, indistinct, jumbled, meaningless, muddled, unfathomable
Antonyms clear, coherent, comprehensible, intelligible, legible, lucid, understandable

unintentional accidental, casual, fortuitous, inadvertent, involuntary, unconscious, undesigned, unintended, unpremeditated, unthinking, unwitting
Antonyms conscious, deliberate, designed, intended, intentional, premeditated, voluntary, wilful

uninterested apathetic, blasé, bored, distant, impassive, incurious, listless, unconcerned, uninvolved, unresponsive
Antonyms alert, concerned, curious, enthusiastic, interested, involved, keen, responsive

uninteresting boring, commonplace, drab, dreary, dry, dull, flat, humdrum, monotonous, tedious, tiresome, unenjoyable, uneventful, unexciting, uninspiring, wearisome
Antonyms absorbing, compelling, enjoyable, exciting, gripping, inspiring, interesting, intriguing, stimulating

uninterrupted constant, continual, continuous, nonstop, peaceful, steady, sustained, unbroken, undisturbed, unending

union 1. amalgam, amalgamation, blend, combination, conjunction, fusion, junction, mixture, synthesis, uniting **2.** alliance, association, Bund, coalition, confederacy, confederation, federation, league **3.** accord, agreement, concord, concurrence, harmony, unanimity, unison, unity

unique 1. lone, one and only, only, single, solitary, sui generis **2.** incomparable, inimitable, matchless, nonpareil, peerless, unequalled, unexampled, unmatched, unparalleled, unrivalled, without equal

unison accord, accordance, agreement, concert, concord, cooperation, harmony, unanimity, unity
Antonyms disagreement, discord, disharmony, dissension, dissidence, dissonance

unit 1. assembly, detachment, entity, group, section, system, whole **2.** component, constituent, element, item, member, module, part, piece, portion, section, segment

unite 1. amalgamate, blend, coalesce, combine, confederate, consolidate, couple, fuse, incorporate, join, link, marry, merge, unify, wed **2.** ally, associate, band, close ranks, club together, cooperate, join forces, join together, league, pool, pull together
Antonyms break, detach, disunite, divide, divorce, part, separate, sever, split

united 1. affiliated, allied, banded together, collective, combined, concerted, in partnership, leagued, pooled, unified **2.** agreed, in accord, in agreement, like-minded, of like mind, of one mind, of the same opinion, one, unanimous

unity 1. entity, integrity, oneness, singleness, undividedness, unification, union, wholeness **2.** accord, agreement, concord, concurrence, consensus, harmony, peace, solidarity, unanimity
Antonyms disagreement, discord, disunity, division, factionalism, heterogeneity, ill will, independence, individuality, infighting, separation, strife

universal all-embracing, catholic, common, ecumenical, entire, general, omnipresent, total, unlimited, whole, widespread, worldwide

universally always, everywhere, in all cases, in every instance, invariably, uniformly, without exception

universe cosmos, creation, everything, macrocosm, nature, the natural world

unjust biased, inequitable, one-sided, partial, partisan, prejudiced, undeserved, unfair, unjustified, unmerited, wrong, wrongful
Antonyms equitable, ethical, fair, impartial, just, justified, right, unbiased

unkind cruel, hardhearted, harsh, inconsiderate, inhuman, insensitive, malicious, mean, nasty, spiteful, thoughtless, uncaring, uncharitable, unchristian, unfeeling, unfriendly, unsympathetic
Antonyms benevolent, caring, charitable, considerate, generous, kind, softhearted, sympathetic, thoughtful

unknown 1. alien, concealed, dark, hidden, mysterious, new, secret, strange, unrecognized, unrevealed, untold **2.** anonymous, nameless, uncharted, undiscovered, unexplored, unidentified, unnamed **3.** humble, little known, obscure, undistinguished, unfamiliar, unheard-of, unrenowned, unsung
Antonyms (sense 3) celebrated, distinguished, familiar, known, recognized, renowned, well-known

unlawful actionable, against the

law, banned, criminal, forbidden, illegal, illegitimate, illicit, outlawed, prohibited, unauthorized, unlicensed

unlike contrasted, different, dissimilar, distinct, divergent, diverse, ill-matched, incompatible, not alike, opposite, unequal, unrelated
Antonyms compatible, equal, like, matched, related, similar

unlikely 1. doubtful, faint, improbable, not likely, remote, slight, unimaginable **2.** implausible, incredible, questionable, unbelievable, unconvincing

unlimited 1. boundless, countless, endless, extensive, great, illimitable, immeasurable, immense, incalculable, infinite, limitless, unbounded, vast **2.** absolute, all-encompassing, complete, full, total, unconditional, unconstrained, unfettered, unqualified, unrestricted
Antonyms (sense 1) bounded, circumscribed, confined, constrained, finite, limited, restricted

unload disburden, discharge, dump, empty, off-load, relieve, unburden, unlade, unpack

unloved disliked, forsaken, loveless, neglected, rejected, spurned, uncared-for, uncherished, unpopular, unwanted
Antonyms adored, beloved, cherished, liked, loved, popular, precious, wanted

unlucky 1. cursed, disastrous, hapless, luckless, miserable, unfortunate, unhappy, unsuccessful, wretched **2.** doomed, ill-fated, ill-omened, ill-starred, inauspicious, ominous, unfavourable, untimely
Antonyms (sense 1) blessed, favoured, fortunate, happy, lucky, prosperous

unmarried bachelor, celibate, maiden, single, unattached, unwed, unwedded, virgin

unmentionable disgraceful, disreputable, forbidden, frowned on, immodest, indecent, scandalous, shameful, shocking, taboo, unspeakable, unutterable

unmerciful brutal, cruel, hard, heartless, implacable, merciless, pitiless, relentless, remorseless, ruthless, uncaring, unfeeling, unsparing
Antonyms beneficent, caring, feeling, humane, merciful, pitying, sparing, tender-hearted

unmistakable certain, clear, conspicuous, decided, distinct, evident, glaring, indisputable, manifest, obvious, palpable, patent, plain, positive, pronounced, sure, unambiguous, unequivocal
Antonyms ambiguous, dim, doubtful, equivocal, hidden, mistakable, obscure, uncertain, unclear, unsure

unmitigated 1. grim, harsh, intense, oppressive, persistent, relentless, unabated, unalleviated, unbroken, undiminished, unmodified, unqualified, unredeemed, unrelieved **2.** absolute, arrant, complete, consummate, downright, out-and-out, outright, perfect, rank, sheer, thorough, thoroughgoing, utter

unmoved 1. fast, firm, in place, in position, steady, unchanged, untouched **2.** cold, dry-eyed, impassive, indifferent, unaffected, unfeeling, unimpressed, unresponsive, unstirred, untouched **3.** determined, firm, inflexible, resolute, resolved, steadfast, undeviating, unshaken, unwavering
Antonyms (sense 1) shifted, touched, transferred (sense 2) affected, concerned, impressed, moved, persuaded, stirred, swayed, touched (sense 3) adaptable, flexible, shaken, wavering

unnatural 1. aberrant, abnormal, anomalous, irregular, odd, perverse, perverted, unusual **2.** bizarre, extraordinary, freakish, outlandish, queer, strange, supernatural, unaccountable, uncanny **3.** affected, artificial, assumed, contrived, factitious, false, feigned, forced, insincere, laboured, mannered, phoney

(*Sl.*), self-conscious, stagy, stiff, stilted, strained, studied, theatrical
Antonyms (*senses 1 & 2*) normal, ordinary, typical (*sense 3*) genuine, honest, natural, sincere, unaffected, unfeigned, unpretentious

unnecessary dispensable, expendable, inessential, needless, nonessential, redundant, supererogatory, superfluous, surplus to requirements, uncalled-for, unneeded, unrequired, useless
Antonyms essential, indispensable, necessary, needed, required, vital

unnerve confound, daunt, demoralize, disarm, disconcert, discourage, dishearten, dismay, dispirit, fluster, frighten, intimidate, rattle (*Inf.*), shake, throw off balance, unhinge, unman, upset
Antonyms arm, brace, encourage, hearten, nerve, steel, strengthen, support

unobtrusive humble, inconspicuous, keeping a low profile, low-key, meek, modest, quiet, restrained, retiring, self-effacing, subdued, unassuming, unnoticeable, unostentatious, unpretentious
Antonyms assertive, blatant, bold, conspicuous, eccentric, eye-catching, getting in the way, high-profile, noticeable, obtrusive, outgoing, prominent

unoccupied empty, tenantless, uninhabited, untenanted, vacant

unofficial informal, personal, private, unauthorized, unconfirmed, wildcat

unorthodox abnormal, heterodox, irregular, unconventional, uncustomary, unusual, unwonted
Antonyms conventional, customary, established, orthodox, sound, traditional, usual

unpaid 1. due, not discharged, outstanding, overdue, owing, payable, unsettled **2.** honorary, unsalaried, voluntary

unpalatable bitter, disagreeable,

displeasing, distasteful, offensive, repugnant, unappetizing, unattractive, uneatable, unpleasant, unsavoury
Antonyms agreeable, appetizing, attractive, eatable, palatable, pleasant, pleasing, savoury, tasteful

unpardonable deplorable, disgraceful, indefensible, inexcusable, outrageous, scandalous, shameful, unforgivable, unjustifiable

unperturbed calm, collected, composed, cool, placid, poised, self-possessed, tranquil, undismayed, unflustered, unruffled, untroubled, unworried
Antonyms anxious, dismayed, flustered, perturbed, ruffled, troubled, worried

unpleasant abhorrent, bad, disagreeable, displeasing, distasteful, ill-natured, irksome, nasty, objectionable, obnoxious, repulsive, troublesome, unattractive, unlikable, unlovely, unpalatable
Antonyms agreeable, congenial, delicious, good-natured, likable, lovely, nice, pleasant

unpopular avoided, detested, disliked, not sought out, out in the cold, out of favour, rejected, shunned, unattractive, undesirable, unloved, unwanted, unwelcome
Antonyms desirable, favoured, liked, loved, popular, wanted, welcome

unprecedented abnormal, exceptional, extraordinary, freakish, new, novel, original, remarkable, singular, unexampled, unheard-of, unparalleled, unrivalled, unusual

unpredictable chance, changeable, doubtful, erratic, fickle, fluky (*Inf.*), iffy, inconstant, random, unforeseeable, unreliable, unstable, variable
Antonyms certain, constant, dependable, foreseeable, predictable, reliable, stable, steady, unchanging

unprejudiced balanced, even-handed, fair, fair-minded, impartial, just, nonpartisan, objective, open-minded, unbiased, uninfluenced

Antonyms biased, bigoted, influenced, narrow-minded, partial, prejudiced, unfair, unjust

unpremeditated extempore, impromptu, impulsive, offhand, off the cuff (*Inf.*), spontaneous, spur-of-the-moment, unplanned, unprepared

unprepared 1. half-baked (*Inf.*), ill-considered, incomplete, not thought out, unfinished, unplanned **2.** caught napping, caught on the hop (*Brit. inf.*), surprised, taken aback, taken off guard, unaware, unready, unsuspecting **3.** ad-lib, extemporaneous, improvised, off the cuff (*Inf.*), spontaneous

unpretentious homely, honest, humble, modest, plain, simple, straightforward, unaffected, unassuming, unimposing, unobtrusive, unostentatious, unspoiled

Antonyms affected, assuming, conceited, flaunting, inflated, obtrusive, ostentatious, pretentious, showy

unprincipled amoral, corrupt, crooked, deceitful, devious, dishonest, immoral, tricky, unconscionable, underhand, unethical, unprofessional, unscrupulous

Antonyms decent, ethical, honest, honourable, moral, righteous, scrupulous, upright, virtuous

unproductive 1. bootless, fruitless, futile, idle, ineffective, inefficacious, otiose, unavailing, unprofitable, unremunerative, unrewarding, useless, vain, valueless, worthless **2.** barren, dry, fruitless, sterile, unprolific

Antonyms (*sense 1*) effective, fruitful, profitable, remunerative, rewarding, useful, worthwhile (*sense 2*) abundant, fertile, fruitful, productive, prolific

unprofessional 1. improper, lax, negligent, unethical, unfitting, unprincipled, unseemly, unworthy **2.** amateur, amateurish, in-

competent, inefficient, inexperienced, inexpert, untrained

Antonyms (*sense 2*) adept, competent, efficient, experienced, expert, professional, skilful

unprotected defenceless, exposed, helpless, naked, open, open to attack, pregnable, unarmed, undefended, unguarded, unsheltered, unshielded, vulnerable

Antonyms defended, guarded, immune, protected, safe, secure, shielded

unqualified 1. ill-equipped, incapable, incompetent, ineligible, not equal to, unfit, unprepared **2.** categorical, downright, outright, unconditional, unmitigated, unreserved, unrestricted, without reservation **3.** absolute, complete, consummate, downright, out-and-out, thorough, thoroughgoing, total, utter

unquestionable absolute, beyond a shadow of doubt, certain, clear, conclusive, definite, faultless, flawless, incontestable, incontrovertible, indisputable, indubitable, irrefutable, manifest, patent, perfect, self-evident, sure, undeniable, unequivocal, unmistakable

Antonyms ambiguous, doubtful, dubious, inconclusive, questionable, uncertain, unclear

unravel disentangle, extricate, free, separate, straighten out, undo, unknot, untangle, unwind

unreal 1. chimerical, dreamlike, fabulous, fanciful, fictitious, illusory, imaginary, make-believe, phantasmagoric, storybook, visionary **2.** hypothetical, immaterial, impalpable, insubstantial, intangible, mythical, nebulous **3.** artificial, fake, false, insincere, mock, ostensible, pretended, seeming, sham

Antonyms authentic, bona fide, genuine, real, realistic, sincere, true, veritable

unrealistic half-baked (*Inf.*), impracticable, impractical, improbable, quixotic, romantic, starry-eyed, theoretical, unworkable

Antonyms practical, pragmatic, probable, realistic, sensible, unromantic, workable

unreasonable 1. excessive, exorbitant, extortionate, extravagant, immoderate, steep (*Brit. inf.*), too great, uncalled-for, undue, unfair, unjust, unwarranted 2. arbitrary, biased, blinkered, capricious, erratic, headstrong, inconsistent, opinionated, quirky

Antonyms (*sense 1*) fair, just, justified, moderate, reasonable, temperate, warranted (*sense 2*) fair-minded, flexible, open-minded

unrelated 1. different, dissimilar, not kin, not kindred, not related, unconnected, unlike 2. beside the point, extraneous, inapplicable, inappropriate, irrelevant, not germane, unassociated, unconnected

unreliable 1. disreputable, irresponsible, not conscientious, treacherous, undependable, unstable, untrustworthy 2. deceptive, delusive, erroneous, fake, fallible, false, implausible, inaccurate, mistaken, specious, uncertain, unconvincing, unsound

Antonyms (*sense 1*) conscientious, dependable, regular, reliable, responsible, stable, trustworthy (*sense 2*) accurate, infallible

unreserved 1. demonstrative, extrovert, forthright, frank, free, open, open-hearted, outgoing, outspoken, uninhibited, unrestrained, unreticent 2. absolute, complete, entire, full, total, unconditional, unlimited, unqualified, wholehearted, without reservation

Antonyms demure, inhibited, modest, reserved, restrained, reticent, shy, undemonstrative

unresolved doubtful, moot, open to question, pending, problematical, unanswered, undecided, undetermined, unsettled, unsolved, up in the air, vague, yet to be decided

unrest 1. agitation, disaffection, discontent, discord, dissatisfaction, dissension, protest, rebellion, sedition, strife, tumult, turmoil 2. agitation, anxiety, disquiet, distress, perturbation, restlessness, uneasiness, worry

Antonyms calm, contentment, peace, relaxation, repose, rest, stillness, tranquillity

unrestrained abandoned, boisterous, free, immoderate, inordinate, intemperate, natural, unbounded, unbridled, unchecked, unconstrained, uncontrolled, unhindered, uninhibited, unrepressed

Antonyms checked, constrained, frustrated, hindered, inhibited, repressed, restrained

unrestricted 1. absolute, free, free-for-all (*Inf.*), freewheeling (*Inf.*), open, unbounded, uncircumscribed, unhindered, unlimited, unregulated 2. clear, open, public, unobstructed, unopposed

unrivalled beyond compare, incomparable, matchless, nonpareil, peerless, supreme, unequalled, unexcelled, unmatched, unparalleled, unsurpassed, without equal

unruly disobedient, disorderly, fractious, headstrong, insubordinate, intractable, lawless, mutinous, obstreperous, rebellious, refractory, riotous, rowdy, turbulent, uncontrollable, ungovernable, unmanageable, wayward, wild, wilful

Antonyms amenable, biddable, docile, governable, manageable, obedient, orderly, tractable

unsafe dangerous, hazardous, insecure, perilous, precarious, risky, threatening, treacherous, uncertain, unreliable, unsound, unstable

Antonyms certain, harmless, reliable, safe, secure, sound, stable, sure

unsatisfactory deficient, disappointing, displeasing, inadequate,

insufficient, mediocre, not good enough, not up to par, not up to scratch (*Inf.*), poor, unacceptable, unsuitable, unworthy, weak
Antonyms acceptable, adequate, passable, pleasing, satisfactory, sufficient, suitable

unsavoury 1. distasteful, nasty, objectionable, obnoxious, offensive, repellent, repugnant, repulsive, revolting, unpleasant **2.** disagreeable, distasteful, nauseating, sickening, unappetizing, unpalatable
Antonyms appetizing, palatable, pleasant, savoury, tasteful, tasty, toothsome

unscrupulous conscienceless, corrupt, crooked (*Inf.*), dishonest, dishonourable, exploitative, immoral, improper, knavish, roguish, ruthless, unconscientious, unconscionable, unethical, unprincipled
Antonyms ethical, honest, honourable, moral, principled, proper, scrupulous, upright

unseemly discreditable, disreputable, improper, inappropriate, indecorous, indelicate, in poor taste, out of keeping, out of place, unbecoming, unbefitting, undignified, unrefined, unsuitable
Antonyms acceptable, appropriate, becoming, decorous, fitting, proper, refined, seemly, suitable

unseen concealed, hidden, invisible, lurking, obscure, undetected, unnoticed, unobserved, unobtrusive, unperceived, veiled

unselfish altruistic, charitable, devoted, disinterested, generous, humanitarian, kind, liberal, magnanimous, noble, self-denying, selfless, self-sacrificing

unsettle agitate, bother, confuse, discompose, disconcert, disorder, disturb, fluster, perturb, rattle (*Inf.*), ruffle, throw (*Inf.*), throw into confusion (disorder, uproar), throw off balance, trouble, unbalance, upset

unsettled 1. disorderly, insecure, shaky, unstable, unsteady **2.** changeable, changing, incon-

stant, uncertain, unpredictable, variable **3.** agitated, anxious, confused, disturbed, flustered, on edge, perturbed, restive, restless, shaken, tense, troubled, uneasy, unnerved **4.** debatable, doubtful, moot, open, undecided, undetermined, unresolved **5.** due, in arrears, outstanding, owing, payable, pending

unsightly disagreeable, hideous, horrid, repulsive, revolting (*Inf.*), ugly, unattractive, unpleasant, unprepossessing
Antonyms agreeable, attractive, beautiful, comely, handsome, pleasing, prepossessing, pretty

unskilled amateurish, inexperienced, uneducated, unprofessional, unqualified, untalented, untrained
Antonyms adept, expert, masterly, professional, qualified, skilled, talented

unsociable chilly, cold, distant, hostile, inhospitable, introverted, reclusive, retiring, standoffish, uncongenial, unforthcoming, unfriendly, unneighbourly, unsocial, withdrawn
Antonyms congenial, convivial, friendly, gregarious, hospitable, neighbourly, outgoing, sociable

unsolicited free-will, gratuitous, spontaneous, unasked for, uncalled-for, unforced, uninvited, unrequested, unsought, unwelcome, voluntary, volunteered

unsophisticated 1. artless, childlike, guileless, inexperienced, ingenuous, innocent, naive, natural, unaffected, untutored, unworldly **2.** plain, simple, straightforward, uncomplex, uncomplicated, uninvolved, unrefined, unspecialized
Antonyms (*sense 2*) advanced, complex, complicated, elegant, esoteric, intricate, sophisticated

unsound 1. ailing, defective, delicate, deranged, diseased, frail, ill, in poor health, unbalanced, unhealthy, unhinged, unstable, unwell, weak **2.** defective, erroneous, fallacious, false, faulty, flawed, ill-founded, illogical, invalid, shaky, specious, unreliable, weak

unspeakable 1. beyond description, beyond words, inconceivable, indescribable, ineffable, inexpressible, overwhelming, unbelievable, unimaginable, unutterable, wonderful **2.** abominable, appalling, awful, bad, dreadful, evil, execrable, frightful, heinous, horrible, loathsome, monstrous, odious, repellent, shocking, too horrible for words

unspoiled, unspoilt 1. intact, perfect, preserved, unaffected, unblemished, unchanged, undamaged, unharmed, unimpaired, untouched **2.** artless, innocent, natural, unaffected, unassuming, unstudied, wholesome
Antonyms (*sense 1*) affected, blemished, changed, damaged, harmed, impaired, imperfect, spoilt, touched

unspoken assumed, implicit, implied, left to the imagination, not put into words, not spelt out, tacit, taken for granted, undeclared, understood, unexpressed, unspoken, unstated
Antonyms clear, declared, explicit, expressed, spoken, stated

unsteady 1. infirm, insecure, precarious, reeling, rickety, shaky, tottering, treacherous, unsafe, unstable, wobbly **2.** changeable, erratic, flickering, flighty, fluctuating, inconstant, irregular, unreliable, unsettled, vacillating, variable, volatile, wavering

unsuccessful 1. abortive, bootless, failed, fruitless, futile, ineffective, unavailing, unproductive, useless, vain **2.** balked, defeated, foiled, frustrated, hapless, ill-starred, losing, luckless, unfortunate, unlucky
Antonyms (*sense 1*) flourishing, fruitful, productive, prosperous, remunerative, successful, thriving, useful, worthwhile (*sense 2*) fortunate, lucky, triumphant, victorious, winning

unsuitable improper, inapposite, inappropriate, inapt, incompatible, incongruous, ineligible, infelicitous, out of character, out of keeping, out of place, unacceptable, unbecoming, unbefitting, unfitting, unseasonable, unseemly, unsuited
Antonyms acceptable, apposite, appropriate, apt, compatible, eligible, fitting, apt, proper, suitable

unsure 1. insecure, lacking in confidence, unassured, unconfident **2.** distrustful, doubtful, dubious, hesitant, in a quandary, irresolute, mistrustful, sceptical, suspicious, unconvinced, undecided
Antonyms assured, certain, confident, convinced, decided, persuaded, resolute, sure

unsuspecting confiding, credulous, gullible, inexperienced, ingenuous, innocent, naive, off guard, trustful, trusting, unconscious, unsuspicious, unwarned, unwary

unsympathetic apathetic, callous, cold, compassionless (*Rare*), cruel, hard, harsh, heartless, indifferent, insensitive, soulless, stony-hearted, uncompassionate, unconcerned, unfeeling, unkind, unmoved, unpitying, unresponsive
Antonyms caring, compassionate, concerned, kind, pitying, sensitive, supportive, sympathetic, understanding

untangle clear up, disentangle, explain, extricate, solve, straighten out, unravel, unsnarl
Antonyms complicate, confuse, enmesh, entangle, jumble, muddle, puzzle, snarl, tangle

unthinkable 1. absurd, illogical, impossible, improbable, not on (*Inf.*), out of the question, preposterous, unlikely, unreasonable **2.** beyond belief, beyond the bounds of possibility, implausible, inconceivable, incredible, insupportable, unbelievable, unimaginable

untidy bedraggled, chaotic, cluttered, disorderly, higgledy-piggledy (*Inf.*), jumbled, shambolic, messy, muddled, muddly, mussy (*U.S. inf.*), rumpled, shambolic, slatternly, slipshod, sloppy (*Inf.*), slovenly, topsy-turvy, unkempt

Antonyms methodical, neat, orderly, presentable, ship-shape, spruce, systematic, tidy, well-kept

untie free, loosen, release, unbind, undo, unfasten, unknot, unlace

untimely awkward, badly timed, early, ill-timed, inappropriate, inauspicious, inconvenient, inopportune, mistimed, premature, unfortunate, unseasonable, unsuitable

Antonyms appropriate, auspicious, convenient, fortunate, opportune, seasonable, suitable, timely, welcome, well-timed

untiring constant, dedicated, determined, devoted, dogged, incessant, indefatigable, patient, persevering, persistent, staunch, steady, tireless, unfaltering, unflagging, unremitting, unwearied

untouched 1. intact, safe and sound, undamaged, unharmed, unhurt, uninjured, unscathed, without a scratch **2.** dry-eyed, indifferent, unaffected, unconcerned, unimpressed, unmoved, unstirred

Antonyms (*sense 2*) affected, concerned, impressed, melted, moved, softened, stirred, touched

untoward 1. annoying, awkward, disastrous, ill-timed, inconvenient, inimical, irritating, troublesome, unfortunate, vexatious **2.** adverse, contrary, inauspicious, inopportune, unfavourable, unlucky, untimely **3.** improper, inappropriate, indecorous, out of place, unbecoming, unfitting, unseemly, unsuitable

untrained amateur, green, inexperienced, raw, uneducated, unpractised, unqualified, unschooled, unskilled, untaught, untutored

Antonyms educated, experi-

enced, expert, qualified, schooled, skilled, taught, trained

untroubled calm, composed, cool, peaceful, placid, serene, steady, tranquil, unagitated, unconcerned, undisturbed, unflappable (*Inf.*), unflustered, unperturbed, unruffled, unstirred, unworried

Antonyms agitated, anxious, concerned, disturbed, flustered, perturbed, ruffled, troubled, worried

untrue 1. deceptive, dishonest, erroneous, fallacious, false, inaccurate, incorrect, lying, misleading, mistaken, sham, spurious, untruthful, wrong **2.** deceitful, disloyal, faithless, false, forsworn, inconstant, perfidious, traitorous, treacherous, two-faced, unfaithful, untrustworthy **3.** deviant, distorted, inaccurate, off, out of line, out of true, wide

Antonyms (*sense 1*) accurate, correct, factual, right, true (*sense 2*) constant, dependable, faithful, honest, honourable, loyal, truthful, virtuous

untrustworthy capricious, deceitful, devious, dishonest, disloyal, fair-weather, faithless, false, fickle, fly-by-night (*Inf.*), not to be depended on, slippery, treacherous, tricky, two-faced, undependable, unfaithful, unreliable, untrue, untrusty

Antonyms dependable, faithful, honest, loyal, reliable, steadfast, true, trustworthy, trusty

untruth deceit, fabrication, falsehood, falsification, fib, fiction, lie, prevarication, story, tale, trick, whopper (*Inf.*)

untruthful crooked (*Inf.*), deceitful, deceptive, dishonest, dissembling, false, fibbing, hypocritical, lying, mendacious

Antonyms candid, honest, sincere, true, truthful, veracious

unusual abnormal, atypical, bizarre, curious, different, exceptional, extraordinary, odd, out of the ordinary, phenomenal, queer, rare, remarkable, singular,

strange, surprising, uncommon, unconventional, unexpected, unfamiliar, unwonted
Antonyms average, commonplace, conventional, everyday, familiar, normal, routine, traditional, typical, unremarkable, usual

unveil bare, bring to light, disclose, divulge, expose, lay bare, lay open, make known, make public, reveal, uncover
Antonyms cloak, conceal, cover, disguise, hide, mask, obscure, veil

unwanted *de trop*, going begging, outcast, rejected, superfluous, surplus to requirements, unasked, undesired, uninvited, unneeded, unsolicited, unwelcome, useless
Antonyms desired, necessary, needed, useful, wanted, welcome

unwavering consistent, dedicated, determined, resolute, single-minded, staunch, steadfast, steady, undeviating, unfaltering, unflagging, unshakable, unshaken, unswerving, untiring

unwelcome 1. excluded, rejected, unacceptable, undesirable, uninvited, unpopular, unwanted, unwished for **2.** disagreeable, displeasing, distasteful, thankless, undesirable, unpleasant
Antonyms acceptable, agreeable, desirable, pleasant, pleasing, popular, wanted, welcome

unwell ailing, ill, indisposed, in poor health, off colour, out of sorts, poorly (*Inf.*), sick, sickly, under the weather (*Inf.*), unhealthy
Antonyms fine, healthy, robust, sound, well

unwholesome 1. deleterious, harmful, insalubrious, junk (*Inf.*), noxious, poisonous, tainted, unhealthy, unnourishing **2.** bad, corrupting, degrading, demoralizing, depraving, evil, immoral, perverting, wicked
Antonyms (*sense 1*) beneficial, germ-free, healthy, hygienic, sa-

lubrious, sanitary, wholesome (*sense 2*) edifying, moral

unwieldy 1. awkward, burdensome, cumbersome, inconvenient, unhandy, unmanageable **2.** bulky, clumsy, hefty, massive, ponderous, ungainly, weighty

unwilling averse, demurring, disinclined, grudging, indisposed, laggard (*Rare*), loath, not in the mood, opposed, reluctant, resistant, unenthusiastic
Antonyms amenable, compliant, disposed, eager, enthusiastic, inclined, voluntary, willing

unwind 1. disentangle, slacken, uncoil, undo, unravel, unreel, unroll, untwine, untwist **2.** calm down, let oneself go, loosen up, quieten down, relax, sit back, slow down, take a break, take it easy (*Inf.*), wind down

unwise foolhardy, foolish, ill-advised, ill-considered, ill-judged, impolitic, improvident, imprudent, inadvisable, indiscreet, injudicious, irresponsible, rash, reckless, senseless, short-sighted, silly, stupid
Antonyms discreet, judicious, politic, prudent, responsible, sensible, shrewd, wise

unwitting 1. ignorant, innocent, unaware, unconscious, unknowing, unsuspecting **2.** accidental, chance, inadvertent, involuntary, undesigned, unintended, unintentional, unmeant, unplanned
Antonyms (*sense 2*) conscious, deliberate, designed, intended, intentional, knowing, meant, planned, witting

unworldly 1. abstract, celestial, metaphysical, nonmaterialistic, religious, spiritual, transcendental **2.** green, idealistic, inexperienced, innocent, naive, raw, trusting, unsophisticated **3.** ethereal, extraterrestrial, otherworldly, unearthly

unworthy 1. base, contemptible, degrading, discreditable, disgraceful, dishonourable, disreputable, ignoble, shameful **2.** ineligible, not deserving of, not fit for, not good enough, not worth, undeserving

Antonyms (*sense 2*) commendable, creditable, deserving, eligible, fit, honourable, meritorious, worthy

unwritten 1. oral, unrecorded, vocal, word-of-mouth **2.** accepted, conventional, customary, tacit, traditional, understood, unformulated

unyielding adamant, determined, firm, hardline, immovable, inexorable, inflexible, intractable, obdurate, obstinate, relentless, resolute, rigid, staunch, steadfast, stubborn, tough, unbending, uncompromising, unwavering

Antonyms adaptable, compliant, compromising, cooperative, flexible, movable, tractable, yielding

upbringing breeding, bringing-up, care, cultivation, education, nurture, raising, rearing, tending, training

upgrade advance, ameliorate, better, elevate, enhance, improve, promote, raise

Antonyms decry, degrade, demote, denigrate, downgrade, lower

upheaval cataclysm, disorder, disruption, disturbance, eruption, overthrow, revolution, turmoil, violent change

uphill *adj.* **1.** ascending, climbing, mounting, rising **2.** arduous, difficult, exhausting, gruelling, hard, laborious, punishing, Sisyphean, strenuous, taxing, tough, wearisome

Antonyms (*sense 1*) descending, downhill, lowering

uphold advocate, aid, back, champion, defend, encourage, endorse, hold to, justify, maintain, promote, stand by, support, sustain, vindicate

upkeep 1. conservation, keep, maintenance, preservation, repair, running, subsistence, support, sustenance **2.** expenditure, expenses, oncosts (*Brit.*), operat-

ing costs, outlay, overheads, running costs

uplift *v.* **1.** elevate, heave, hoist, lift up, raise **2.** advance, ameliorate, better, civilize, cultivate, edify, improve, inspire, raise, refine, upgrade ~*n.* **3.** advancement, betterment, cultivation, edification, enhancement, enlightenment, enrichment, improvement, refinement

upper 1. high, higher, loftier, top, topmost **2.** elevated, eminent, greater, important, superior

Antonyms bottom, inferior, junior, low, lower

upper hand advantage, ascendancy, control, dominion, edge, mastery, superiority, supremacy, sway, whip hand

uppermost 1. highest, loftiest, most elevated, top, topmost, upmost **2.** chief, dominant, foremost, greatest, leading, main, paramount, predominant, preeminent, primary, principal, supreme

Antonyms bottom, bottommost, humblest, least, lowermost, lowest, lowliest, slightest

upright 1. erect, on end, perpendicular, straight, vertical **2.** *Fig.* above board, conscientious, ethical, faithful, good, high-minded, honest, honourable, incorruptible, just, principled, righteous, straightforward, true, trustworthy, unimpeachable, virtuous

Antonyms (*sense 1*) flat, horizontal, lying, prone, prostrate, supine (*sense 2*) corrupt, devious, dishonest, dishonourable, unethical, unjust, untrustworthy, wicked

uproar brawl, brouhaha, clamour, commotion, confusion, din, furore, hubbub, hullabaloo, hurly-burly, mayhem, noise, outcry, pandemonium, racket, riot, ruckus (*Inf.*), ruction (*Inf.*), rumpus, turbulence, turmoil

upset *v.* **1.** capsize, knock over, overturn, spill, tip over, topple over **2.** change, disorder, disorganize, disturb, mess up, mix up, put out of order, spoil, turn topsy-turvy 3. agitate, bother, discompose, disconcert, disturb, disquiet, distress, disturb, fluster, grieve, perturb, ruffle, throw (someone) off balance, trouble 4. be victorious over, conquer, defeat, get the better of, overcome, overthrow, triumph over, win against the odds ~n. 5. clear, reverse, shake-up (*Inf.*), sudden change, surprise 6. bug (*Inf.*), complaint, disorder, disturbance, illness, indisposition, malady, queasiness, sickness 7. agitation, bother, discomposure, disquiet, distress, disturbance, shock, trouble, worry ~adj. 8. capsized, overturned, spilled, tipped over, toppled, tumbled, upside down 9. disordered, disturbed, gippy (*Sl.*), ill, poorly (*Inf.*), queasy, sick 10. agitated, bothered, confused, disconcerted, dismayed, disquieted, distressed, disturbed, frantic, grieved, hurt, overwrought, put out, ruffled, troubled, worried 11. at sixes and sevens, chaotic, confused, disordered, in disarray *or* disorder, messed up, muddled, topsy-turvy 12. beaten, conquered, defeated, overcome, overthrown, vanquished

upshot conclusion, consequence, culmination, end, end result, event, finale, issue, outcome, payoff (*Inf.*), result

upside down 1. bottom up, inverted, on its head, overturned, upturned, wrong side up 2. *Inf.* chaotic, confused, disordered, higgledy-piggledy (*Inf.*), in confusion (chaos, disarray, disorder), jumbled, muddled, topsy-turvy

upstart arriviste, nobody, *nouveau riche*, parvenu, social climber, status seeker

urban city, civic, inner-city, metropolitan, municipal, oppidan (*Rare*), town

urchin brat, gamin, guttersnipe, mudlark (*Sl.*), ragamuffin, street Arab (*Offens.*), waif, young rogue

urge v. 1. appeal to, beg, beseech, entreat, exhort, implore, plead, press, solicit 2. advise, advocate, champion, counsel, insist on, push for, recommend, support 3. compel, constrain, drive, egg on, encourage, force, goad, hasten, impel, incite, instigate, press, propel, push, spur, stimulate ~n. 4. compulsion, desire, drive, fancy, impulse, itch, longing, wish, yearning, yen (*Inf.*)
Antonyms v. (*senses 1 & 2*) caution, deter, discourage, dissuade, remonstrate, warn ~n. aversion, disinclination, distaste, indisposition, reluctance, repugnance

urgency exigency, extremity, gravity, hurry, imperativeness, importance, importunity, necessity, need, pressure, seriousness, stress

urgent 1. compelling, critical, crucial, immediate, imperative, important, instant, not to be delayed, pressing, top-priority 2. clamorous, earnest, importunate, insistent, intense, persistent, persuasive
Antonyms apathetic, casual, feeble, half-hearted, lackadaisical, low-priority, minor, perfunctory, trivial, unimportant, weak

usable at one's disposal, available, current, fit for use, functional, in running order, practical, ready for use, serviceable, utilizable, valid, working

usage 1. control, employment, handling, management, operation, regulation, running, treatment, use 2. convention, custom, form, habit, matter of course, method, mode, practice, procedure, regime, routine, rule, tradition, wont

use v. 1. apply, avail oneself of, bring into play, employ, exercise, find a use for, make use of, operate, ply, practise, profit by, put to use, turn to account, utilize, wield, work 2. act towards, behave towards, deal with, exploit, handle, manipulate, misuse, take advantage of, treat 3. consume, exhaust, expend, run through, spend, waste ~n. 4. application, employment, exercise, handling, operation, practice, service, treatment, usage, wear and tear **5.** advantage, application, avail, benefit, good, help, mileage (*Inf.*), point, profit, service, usefulness, utility, value, worth **6.** custom, habit, practice, usage, way, wont

used cast-off, hand-me-down (*Inf.*), nearly new, not new, reach-me-down (*Inf.*), second-hand, shopsoiled, worn

Antonyms brand-new, fresh, intact, new, pristine, unused

useful advantageous, all-purpose, beneficial, effective, fruitful, general-purpose, helpful, of help, of service, of use, practical, profitable, salutary, serviceable, valuable, worthwhile

Antonyms inadequate, ineffective, unbeneficial, unhelpful, unproductive, useless, vain, worthless

useless 1. bootless, disadvantageous, fruitless, futile, hopeless, idle, impractical, ineffective, ineffectual, of no use, pointless, profitless, unavailing, unproductive, unworkable, vain, valueless, worthless **2.** *Inf.* hopeless, incompetent, ineffectual, inept, no good, stupid, weak

Antonyms (*sense 1*) advantageous, effective, fruitful, practical, productive, profitable, useful, valuable, workable, worthwhile

use up absorb, burn up, consume, deplete, devour, drain, exhaust, finish, fritter away, run through, squander, swallow up, waste

usher 1. *n.* attendant, doorkeeper, escort, guide, usherette **2.** *v.* conduct, direct, escort, guide, lead, pilot, show in *or* out, steer

usual accustomed, common, constant, customary, everyday, expected, familiar, fixed, general, habitual, normal, ordinary, regular, routine, standard, stock, typical, wonted

Antonyms exceptional, extraordinary, new, novel, off-beat, out of the ordinary, peculiar, rare, singular, strange, uncommon, unexpected, unhackneyed, unique, unorthodox, unusual

usually as a rule, as is the custom, as is usual, by and large, commonly, for the most part, generally, habitually, in the main, mainly, mostly, most often, normally, on the whole, ordinarily, regularly, routinely

utility advantageousness, avail, benefit, convenience, efficacy, fitness, point, practicality, profit, service, serviceableness, use, usefulness

utmost *adj.* **1.** chief, extreme, greatest, highest, maximum, paramount, pre-eminent, supreme **2.** extreme, farthest, final, last, most distant, outermost, remotest, uttermost $\sim n.$ **3.** best, greatest, hardest, highest, most

utter[1] *v.* **1.** articulate, enunciate, express, pronounce, put into words, say, speak, verbalize, vocalize, voice **2.** declare, divulge, give expression to, make known, proclaim, promulgate, publish, reveal, state

utter[2] *adj.* absolute, arrant, complete, consummate, downright, entire, out-and-out, perfect, sheer, stark, thorough, thoroughgoing, total, unmitigated, unqualified

utterly absolutely, completely, entirely, extremely, fully, perfectly, thoroughly, totally, to the core, wholly

V

vacancy 1. job, opening, opportunity, position, post, room, situation 2. absent-mindedness, abstraction, blankness, inanity, inattentiveness, incomprehension, incuriousness, lack of interest, vacuousness

vacant 1. available, disengaged, empty, free, idle, not in use, to let, unemployed, unengaged, unfilled, unoccupied, untenanted, void 2. absent-minded, abstracted, blank, dreaming, dreamy, expressionless, idle, inane, incurious, thoughtless, unthinking, vacuous

Antonyms (sense 1) busy, engaged, full, inhabited, in use, occupied, taken (sense 2) animated, engrossed, expressive, lively, reflective, thoughtful

vacuum emptiness, free space, gap, nothingness, space, vacuity, void

vague amorphous, blurred, dim, doubtful, fuzzy, generalized, hazy, ill-defined, imprecise, indefinite, indeterminate, indistinct, lax, loose, nebulous, obscure, shadowy, uncertain, unclear, unknown, unspecified, woolly

Antonyms clear, clear-cut, definite, distinct, exact, explicit, lucid, precise, specific, well-defined

vain 1. arrogant, bigheaded (Inf.), cocky, conceited, egotistical, inflated, narcissistic, ostentatious, overweening, peacockish, pleased with oneself, proud, self-important, stuck-up (Inf.), swaggering, swanky (Inf.), swollen-headed (Inf.), vainglorious 2. abortive, empty, fruitless, futile, hollow, idle, nugatory, pointless, senseless, time-wasting, trifling, trivial, unavailing, unimportant, unproductive, unprofitable, useless, worthless 3. **in vain** bootless,

fruitless(ly), ineffectual(ly), to no avail, to no purpose, unsuccessful(ly), useless(ly), vain(ly), wasted, without success

Antonyms (sense 1) bashful, humble, meek, modest, self-deprecating (sense 2) fruitful, profitable, serious, successful, useful, valid, worthwhile, worthy

valiant bold, brave, courageous, dauntless, doughty, fearless, gallant, heroic, indomitable, intrepid, lion-hearted, plucky, redoubtable, stouthearted, valorous, worthy

valid authentic, bona fide, genuine, in force, lawful, legal, legally binding, legitimate, official

Antonyms illegal, inoperative, invalid, unlawful, unofficial

valley coomb, cwm (Welsh), dale, dell, depression, dingle, glen, hollow, strath (Scot.), vale

valuable adj. 1. costly, dear, expensive, high-priced, precious 2. beneficial, cherished, esteemed, estimable, held dear, helpful, important, prized, profitable, serviceable, treasured, useful, valued, worthwhile, worthy

Antonyms (sense 1) cheap, cheapo (Inf.), inexpensive, worthless (sense 2) insignificant, pointless, silly, trifling, trivial, unimportant, useless, worthless

value n. 1. cost, equivalent, market price, monetary worth, rate 2. advantage, benefit, desirability, help, importance, merit, profit, serviceableness, significance, use, usefulness, utility, worth 3. Plural code of behaviour, ethics, (moral) standards, principles ~v. 4. account, appraise, assess, compute, estimate, evaluate, price, put a price on, rate, set at, survey 5. appreciate, cherish, esteem, hold dear,

hold in high regard *or* esteem, prize, regard highly, respect, set store by, treasure
Antonyms *n.* (*sense 2*) insignificance, unimportance, uselessness, worthlessness ~*v.* disregard, have no time for, hold a low opinion of, underestimate, undervalue

vanguard advance guard, cutting edge, forefront, forerunners, front, front line, front rank, leaders, spearhead, trailblazers, trendsetters, van
Antonyms back, rear, rearguard, stern, tail, tail end

vanish become invisible, be lost to sight, die out, disappear, disappear from sight *or* from the face of the earth, dissolve, evanesce, evaporate, exit, fade (away), melt (away)
Antonyms appear, arrive, become visible, come into view, materialize, pop up

vanity 1. affected ways, airs, arrogance, bigheadedness (*Inf.*), conceit, conceitedness, egotism, narcissism, ostentation, pretension, pride, self-admiration, self-love, showing off (*Inf.*), swollen-headedness (*Inf.*), vainglory **2.** emptiness, frivolity, fruitlessness, futility, hollowness, inanity, pointlessness, profitlessness, triviality, unproductiveness, unreality, unsubstantiality, uselessness, worthlessness

vapour breath, dampness, exhalation, fog, fumes, haze, miasma, mist, smoke, steam

variable capricious, chameleonic, changeable, fickle, fitful, flexible, fluctuating, inconstant, mercurial, mutable, protean, shifting, temperamental, unstable, unsteady, vacillating, wavering
Antonyms constant, firm, fixed, settled, stable, steady, unalterable, unchanging

variance difference, difference of opinion, disagreement, discord, discrepancy, dissension, dissent, divergence, inconsistency, lack of harmony, strife, variation

Antonyms accord, agreement, congruity, correspondence, harmony, similarity, unison

variation alteration, break in routine, change, departure, departure from the norm, deviation, difference, discrepancy, diversification, diversity, innovation, modification, novelty, variety
Antonyms dullness, monotony, sameness, tedium, uniformity

varied assorted, different, diverse, heterogeneous, miscellaneous, mixed, motley, sundry, various
Antonyms homogeneous, repetitive, similar, standardized, uniform, unvarying

variety 1. change, difference, discrepancy, diversification, diversity, many-sidedness, multifariousness, variation **2.** array, assortment, collection, cross section, intermixture, medley, miscellany, mixture, multiplicity, range **3.** brand, breed, category, class, kind, make, order, sort, species, strain, type
Antonyms (*sense 1*) homogeneity, invariability, monotony, similarity, similitude, uniformity

various assorted, different, differing, disparate, distinct, divers (*Archaic*), diverse, diversified, heterogeneous, many, many-sided, miscellaneous, several, sundry, varied, variegated
Antonyms alike, equivalent, matching, same, similar, uniform

varnish *v.* adorn, decorate, embellish, gild, glaze, gloss, japan, lacquer, polish, shellac

vary alter, alternate, be unlike, change, depart, differ, disagree, diverge, diversify, fluctuate, intermix, modify, permutate, reorder, transform

vast astronomical, boundless, colossal, enormous, extensive, gigantic, ginormous (*Inf.*), great, huge, illimitable, immeasurable, immense, limitless, mammoth, massive, measureless, mega (*Inf.*), monstrous, monumental, never-ending, prodigious, sweeping, tremendous, unbounded, unlimited, vasty (*Archaic*), voluminous, wide

Antonyms bounded, limited, microscopic, narrow, negligible, paltry, puny, small, tiny, trifling

vault[1] *v.* bound, clear, hurdle, jump, leap, spring

vault[2] *n.* **1.** arch, ceiling, roof, span **2.** catacomb, cellar, crypt, mausoleum, tomb, undercroft **3.** depository, repository, strongroom ~*v.* **4.** arch, bend, bow, curve, overarch, span

veer be deflected, change, change course, change direction, sheer, shift, swerve, tack, turn

vegetate be inert, deteriorate, exist, go to seed, idle, languish, loaf, moulder, stagnate, veg out (*Sl., chiefly U.S.*)

Antonyms accomplish, develop, grow, participate, perform, react, respond

vehemence ardour, eagerness, earnestness, emphasis, energy, enthusiasm, fervency, fervour, fire, force, forcefulness, heat, impetuosity, intensity, keenness, passion, verve, vigour, violence, warmth, zeal

Antonyms apathy, coolness, indifference, lethargy, listlessness, passivity, stoicism, torpor

vehement ardent, eager, earnest, emphatic, enthusiastic, fervent, fervid, fierce, forceful, forcible, impassioned, impetuous, intense, passionate, powerful, strong, violent, zealous

Antonyms apathetic, calm, cool, dispassionate, half-hearted, impassive, lukewarm, moderate

veil **1.** *v.* cloak, conceal, cover, dim, disguise, hide, mantle, mask, obscure, screen, shield **2.** *n.* blind, cloak, cover, curtain, disguise, film, mask, screen, shade, shroud

Antonyms *v.* disclose, display, divulge, expose, lay bare, reveal, uncover, unveil

vein 1. blood vessel, course, current, lode, seam, stratum, streak, stripe **2.** dash, hint, strain, streak,

thread, trait **3.** attitude, bent, character, faculty, humour, mode, mood, note, style, temper, tenor, tone, turn

vendetta bad blood, blood feud, feud, quarrel

veneer *n. Fig.* appearance, façade, false front, finish, front, gloss, guise, mask, pretence, semblance, show

venerable august, esteemed, grave, honoured, respected, revered, reverenced, sage, sedate, wise, worshipped

vengeance an eye for an eye, avenging, lex talionis, reprisal, requital, retaliation, retribution, revenge, settling of scores

Antonyms absolution, acquittal, exoneration, forbearance, forgiveness, mercy, pardon, remission

venom 1. bane, poison, toxin **2.** acidity, acrimony, bitterness, gall, grudge, hate, ill will, malevolence, malice, maliciousness, malignity, rancour, spite, spitefulness, spleen, virulence

Antonyms (*sense 2*) benevolence, charity, compassion, favour, good will, kindness, love, mercy

vent 1. *n.* aperture, duct, hole, opening, orifice, outlet, split **2.** *v.* air, come out with, discharge, emit, empty, express, give expression to, give vent to, pour out, release, utter, voice

Antonyms *vb.* bottle up, curb, hold back, inhibit, quash, quell, repress, stifle, subdue

ventilate *Fig.* air, bring out into the open, broadcast, debate, discuss, examine, make known, scrutinize, sift, talk about

venture *v.* **1.** chance, endanger, hazard, imperil, jeopardize, put in jeopardy, risk, speculate, stake, wager **2.** advance, dare, dare say, hazard, make bold, presume, stick one's neck out (*Inf.*), take the liberty, volunteer ~*n.* **3.** adventure, chance, endeavour, enterprise, fling, gamble, hazard, jeopardy, project, risk, speculation, undertaking

verbal literal, oral, spoken, unwritten, verbatim, word-of-mouth

verbatim exactly, precisely, to the letter, word for word

verdict adjudication, conclusion, decision, finding, judgment, opinion, sentence

verge 1. *n.* border, boundary, brim, brink, edge, extreme, limit, lip, margin, roadside, threshold 2. *v.* approach, border, come near

verification authentication, confirmation, corroboration, proof, substantiation, validation

verify attest, attest to, authenticate, bear out, check, confirm, corroborate, prove, substantiate, support, validate
Antonyms deny, discount, discredit, dispute, invalidate, nullify, undermine, weaken

vernacular 1. *adj.* colloquial, common, indigenous, informal, local, mother, native, popular, vulgar 2. *n.* argot, cant, dialect, idiom, jargon, native language, parlance, patois, speech, vulgar tongue

versatile adaptable, adjustable, all-purpose, all-round, flexible, functional, handy, many-sided, multifaceted, protean, resourceful, variable
Antonyms fixed, inflexible, invariable, limited, one-sided, unadaptable

version account, adaptation, exercise, interpretation, portrayal, reading, rendering, side, translation

vertical erect, on end, perpendicular, upright
Antonyms flat, horizontal, level, plane, prone

vertigo dizziness, giddiness, lightheadedness, loss of equilibrium, swimming of the head

very *adv.* absolutely, acutely, awfully (*Inf.*), decidedly, deeply, eminently, exceedingly, excessively, extremely, greatly, highly, jolly (*Brit.*), noticeably, particularly, profoundly, really, remarkably, superlatively, surpassingly, terribly, truly, uncommonly, unusually, wonderfully

vessel 1. barque (*Poetic*), boat, craft, ship 2. container, pot, receptacle, utensil

vest *v. With in or with* authorize, be devolved upon, bestow, confer, consign, empower, endow, entrust, furnish, invest, lodge, place, put in the hands of, settle

vet *v.* appraise, check, check out, examine, give (someone *or* something) the once-over (*Inf.*), investigate, look over, pass under review, review, scan, scrutinize, size up (*Inf.*)

veteran 1. *n.* master, old hand, old stager, old-timer, past master, past mistress, pro (*Inf.*), trouper, warhorse (*Inf.*) 2. *adj.* adept, battle-scarred, expert, long-serving, old, proficient, seasoned
Antonyms *n.* apprentice, beginner, freshman, initiate, neophyte, novice, recruit, tyro

veto 1. *v.* ban, disallow, forbid, give the thumbs down to, interdict, kill (*Inf.*), negative, prohibit, put the kibosh on (*Sl.*), refuse permission, reject, rule out, turn down 2. *n.* ban, embargo, interdict, nonconsent, prohibition
Antonyms *v.* approve, endorse, okay, pass, ratify ~*n.* approval, endorsement, go-ahead, ratification

vex afflict, aggravate (*Inf.*), agitate, annoy, bother, bug (*Inf.*), displease, distress, disturb, exasperate, fret, gall, grate on, harass, irritate, molest, needle (*Inf.*), nettle, offend, peeve (*Inf.*), perplex, pester, pique, plague, provoke, put out, rile, tease, torment, trouble, upset, worry
Antonyms allay, appease, comfort, console, gratify, hush, mollify, please, quiet, soothe

vexed afflicted, aggravated (*Inf.*), agitated, annoyed, bothered, confused, displeased, distressed, disturbed, exasperated, fed up, harassed, irritated, miffed (*Inf.*), nettled, out of countenance, peeved (*Inf.*), perplexed, provoked, put out, riled, ruffled, tormented, troubled, upset, worried

vibrant 1. aquiver, oscillating, palpitating, pulsating, quivering, trembling **2.** alive, animated, colourful, dynamic, electrifying, full of pep (*Inf.*), responsive, sensitive, sparkling, spirited, vivacious, vivid

vibrate fluctuate, judder (*Inf.*), oscillate, pulsate, pulse, quiver, resonate, reverberate, shake, shiver, sway, swing, throb, tremble, undulate

vibration juddering (*Inf.*), oscillation, pulsation, pulse, quiver, resonance, reverberation, shaking, throb, throbbing, trembling, tremor

vice corruption, degeneracy, depravity, evil, evildoing, immorality, iniquity, profligacy, sin, venality, wickedness
Antonyms honour, morality, virtue

vicious 1. abandoned, abhorrent, atrocious, bad, barbarous, corrupt, cruel, dangerous, debased, degenerate, degraded, depraved, diabolical, ferocious, fiendish, foul, heinous, immoral, infamous, monstrous, profligate, savage, sinful, unprincipled, vile, violent, wicked, worthless, wrong **2.** backbiting, bitchy (*Sl.*), defamatory, malicious, mean, rancorous, slanderous, spiteful, venomous, vindictive
Antonyms complimentary, docile, friendly, gentle, good, honourable, kind, playful, tame, upright, virtuous

victim 1. casualty, fatality, injured party, martyr, sacrifice, scapegoat, sufferer **2.** dupe, easy prey, fall guy (*Inf.*), gull (*Archaic*), innocent, patsy (*Sl., chiefly U.S.*), sitting duck (*Inf.*), sitting target, sucker (*Sl.*)
Antonyms (*sense 1*) survivor (*sense 2*) assailant, attacker, culprit, guilty party, offender

victimize 1. discriminate against,

have a down on (someone) (*Inf.*), have it in for (someone) (*Inf.*), have one's knife into (someone), persecute, pick on **2.** cheat, deceive, defraud, dupe, exploit, fool, gull (*Archaic*), hoodwink, prey on, swindle, take advantage of, use

victor champ (*Inf.*), champion, conquering hero, conqueror, first, prizewinner, top dog (*Inf.*), vanquisher, winner
Antonyms also-ran, dud (*Inf.*), failure, flop (*Inf.*), loser, vanquished

victorious champion, conquering, first, prizewinning, successful, triumphant, vanquishing, winning
Antonyms beaten, conquered, defeated, failed, losing, overcome, unsuccessful, vanquished

victory conquest, laurels, mastery, success, superiority, the palm, the prize, triumph, win
Antonyms defeat, failure, loss

view *n.* **1.** aspect, landscape, outlook, panorama, perspective, picture, prospect, scene, spectacle, vista **2.** range *or* field of vision, sight, vision **3.** *Sometimes plural* attitude, belief, conviction, feeling, impression, judgment, notion, opinion, point of view, sentiment, thought, way of thinking ~*v.* **4.** behold, contemplate, examine, explore, eye, gaze at, inspect, look at, observe, regard, scan, spectate, stare at, survey, watch, witness **5.** consider, deem, judge, look on, regard, think about

viewer observer, one of an audience, onlooker, spectator, TV watcher, watcher

viewpoint angle, frame of reference, perspective, point of view, position, slant, stance, standpoint, vantage point, way of thinking

vigilant alert, Argus-eyed, attentive, careful, cautious, circumspect, keeping one's eyes peeled *or* skinned (*Inf.*), on one's guard, on one's toes, on the alert, on the lookout, on the qui vive, on the

watch, sleepless, unsleeping, wakeful, watchful, wide awake
Antonyms careless, inattentive, lax, neglectful, negligent, remiss, slack

vigorous active, brisk, dynamic, effective, efficient, energetic, enterprising, flourishing, forceful, forcible, full of energy, hale, hale and hearty, hardy, healthy, intense, lively, lusty, powerful, Ramboesque, red-blooded, robust, sound, spanking, spirited, strenuous, strong, virile, vital, zippy (*Inf.*)
Antonyms apathetic, effete, enervated, feeble, frail, inactive, indolent, lethargic, lifeless, spiritless, torpid, weak, weedy (*Inf.*), wimpish *or* wimpy (*Inf.*), wishy-washy

vigour activity, animation, balls (*Sl.*), dash, dynamism, energy, force, forcefulness, gusto, health, liveliness, might, oomph (*Inf.*), pep, power, punch (*Inf.*), robustness, snap (*Inf.*), soundness, spirit, strength, verve, vim (*Sl.*), virility, vitality, zip (*Inf.*)
Antonyms apathy, feebleness, fragility, frailty, impotence, inactivity, infirmity, lethargy, sluggishness, weakness

vile 1. abandoned, abject, appalling, bad, base, coarse, contemptible, corrupt, debased, degenerate, degrading, depraved, despicable, disgraceful, evil, humiliating, ignoble, impure, loathsome, low, mean, miserable, nefarious, perverted, shocking, sinful, ugly, vicious, vulgar, wicked, worthless, wretched **2.** disgusting, foul, horrid, loathsome, nasty, nauseating, noxious, offensive, repellent, repugnant, repulsive, revolting, sickening
Antonyms agreeable, chaste, cultured, delicate, genteel, honourable, lovely, marvellous, noble, pleasant, polite, pure, refined, righteous, splendid, sublime, upright, worthy

villain blackguard, caitiff (*Archaic*), criminal, evildoer, knave

(*Archaic*), libertine, malefactor, miscreant, profligate, rapscallion, reprobate, rogue, scoundrel, wretch

villainous atrocious, bad, base, blackguardly, criminal, cruel, debased, degenerate, depraved, detestable, diabolical, evil, fiendish, hateful, heinous, ignoble, infamous, inhuman, mean, nefarious, outrageous, ruffianly, scoundrelly, sinful, terrible, thievish, vicious, vile, wicked
Antonyms angelic, good, heroic, humane, moral, noble, righteous, saintly, virtuous

vindicate absolve, acquit, clear, defend, do justice to, exculpate, excuse, exonerate, free from blame, justify, rehabilitate
Antonyms accuse, blame, condemn, convict, incriminate, punish, reproach

vindication apology, assertion, defence, exculpating, exculpation, excuse, exoneration, justification, maintenance, plea, rehabilitation, substantiation, support

vindictive full of spleen, implacable, malicious, malignant, rancorous, relentless, resentful, revengeful, spiteful, unforgiving, unrelenting, vengeful, venomous
Antonyms forgiving, generous, magnanimous, merciful, relenting, unvindictive

vintage 1. *n.* collection, crop, epoch, era, generation, harvest, origin, year **2.** *adj.* best, choice, classic, mature, prime, rare, ripe, select, superior, venerable

violate 1. break, contravene, disobey, disregard, encroach upon, infract, infringe, transgress **2.** abuse, assault, befoul, debauch, defile, desecrate, dishonour, invade, outrage, pollute, profane, rape, ravish
Antonyms (*sense 1*) honour, obey, respect, uphold (*sense 2*) defend, honour, protect, respect, revere, set on a pedestal

violence bestiality, bloodshed, bloodthirstiness, brutality, brute force, cruelty, destructiveness, ferocity, fierceness, fighting, force, frenzy, fury, murderousness, passion, rough handling, savagery, strong-arm tactics (*Inf.*), terrorism, thuggery, vehemence, wildness

violent 1. *n.* berserk, bloodthirsty, brutal, cruel, destructive, fiery, forcible, furious, headstrong, homicidal, hot-headed, impetuous, intemperate, maddened, maniacal, murderous, passionate, powerful, raging, Ramboesque, riotous, rough, savage, strong, tempestuous, uncontrollable, ungovernable, unrestrained, vehement, vicious, wild **2.** blustery, boisterous, devastating, full of force, gale force, powerful, raging, ruinous, strong, tempestuous, tumultuous, turbulent, wild
Antonyms calm, composed, gentle, mild, peaceful, quiet, rational, sane, serene, unruffled, well-behaved

virgin 1. *n.* damsel (*Archaic*), girl, maid (*Archaic*), maiden (*Archaic*), vestal, virgo intacta **2.** *adj.* chaste, fresh, immaculate, maidenly, modest, new, pristine, pure, snowy, uncorrupted, undefiled, unsullied, untouched, unused, vestal, virginal
Antonyms *adj.* contaminated, corrupted, defiled, dirty, impure, polluted, spoiled, used

virtually as good as, effectually, for all practical purposes, in all but name, in effect, in essence, nearly, practically, to all intents and purposes

virtue 1. ethicalness, excellence, goodness, high-mindedness, incorruptibility, integrity, justice, morality, probity, quality, rectitude, righteousness, uprightness, worth, worthiness **2.** advantage, asset, attribute, credit, good point, good quality, merit, plus (*Inf.*), strength **3.** chastity, honour, innocence, morality, purity, virginity
Antonyms (*sense 1*) corruption, debauchery, depravity, dishonesty, dishonour, evil, immorality,

sin, sinfulness, vice (*sense 2*) drawback, failing, frailty, shortcoming, weak point (*sense 3*) promiscuity, unchastity

virtuoso 1. *n.* artist, genius, grandmaster, maestro, magician, master, master hand, maven (*U.S.*) **2.** *adj.* bravura (*Music*), brilliant, dazzling, masterly

virtuous 1. blameless, ethical, excellent, exemplary, good, high-principled, honest, honourable, incorruptible, moral, praiseworthy, pure, righteous, upright, worthy **2.** celibate, chaste, clean-living, innocent, pure, spotless, virginal
Antonyms (*sense 1*) corrupt, debauched, depraved, dishonest, evil, immoral, sinful, unrighteous, vicious, wicked (*sense 2*) impure, loose, promiscuous, unchaste

virulent 1. baneful (*Archaic*), deadly, infective, injurious, lethal, malignant, pernicious, poisonous, septic, toxic, venomous **2.** acrimonious, bitter, envenomed, hostile, malevolent, malicious, rancorous, resentful, spiteful, splenetic, venomous, vicious, vindictive

visible anywhere to be seen, apparent, clear, conspicuous, detectable, discernible, discoverable, distinguishable, evident, in sight, in view, manifest, not hidden, noticeable, observable, obvious, palpable, patent, perceivable, perceptible, plain, to be seen, unconcealed, unmistakable
Antonyms concealed, hidden, imperceptible, invisible, obscured, unnoticeable, unseen

vision 1. eyes, eyesight, perception, seeing, sight, view **2.** breadth of view, discernment, farsightedness, foresight, imagination, insight, intuition, penetration, prescience **3.** castle in the air, concept, conception, daydream, dream, fantasy, idea, ideal, image, mental picture, pipe dream **4.** apparition, chimera, delusion, ghost, hallucination, illusion, mirage, phantasm, phantom, revelation, spectre, wraith

visionary 1. *adj.* dreaming, dreamy, idealistic, quixotic, romantic, starry-eyed, with one's head in the clouds **2.** *n.* daydreamer, Don Quixote, dreamer, enthusiast (*Archaic*), idealist, mystic, prophet, romantic, seer, theorist, utopian, zealot
Antonyms *adj.* mundane, pragmatic, realistic ~*n.* cynic, pessimist, pragmatist, realist

visit *v.* **1.** be the guest of, call in, call on, drop in on (*Inf.*), go to see, inspect, look (someone) up, pay a call on, pop in (*Inf.*), stay at, stay with, stop by, take in (*Inf.*) **2.** afflict, assail, attack, befall, descend upon, haunt, smite, trouble ~*n.* **3.** call, sojourn, stay, stop

visitation 1. examination, inspection, visit **2.** bane, blight, calamity, cataclysm, catastrophe, disaster, infliction, ordeal, punishment, scourge, trial

visitor caller, company, guest, visitant

visual 1. ocular, optic, optical **2.** discernible, observable, perceptible, visible
Antonyms (*sense 2*) imperceptible, indiscernible, invisible, out of sight, unnoticeable, unperceivable

visualize conceive of, conjure up a mental picture of, envisage, imagine, picture, see in the mind's eye

vital 1. basic, cardinal, essential, fundamental, imperative, indispensable, necessary, requisite **2.** critical, crucial, decisive, important, key, life-or-death, significant, urgent **3.** animated, dynamic, energetic, forceful, full of the joy of living, lively, sparky, spirited, vibrant, vigorous, vivacious, zestful **4.** alive, animate, generative, invigorative, lifegiving, live, living, quickening
Antonyms (*sense 1*) dispensable, inessential, nonessential, unnecessary (*sense 2*) minor, trivial,

unimportant (*sense 3*) apathetic, lethargic, listless, uninvolved (*sense 4*) dead, dying, inanimate, moribund

vitality animation, energy, exuberance, go (*Inf.*), life, liveliness, lustiness, pep, robustness, sparkle, stamina, strength, vigour, vim (*Sl.*), vivaciousness, vivacity
Antonyms apathy, inertia, lethargy, listlessness, sluggishness, weakness

vivacious animated, bubbling, cheerful, ebullient, effervescent, frolicsome, gay, full of life, gayspirited, jolly, light-hearted, lively, merry, scintillating, sparkling, sparky, spirited, sportive, sprightly, vital
Antonyms boring, dull, languid, lifeless, listless, melancholy, spiritless, unenthusiastic

vivid 1. bright, brilliant, clear, colourful, glowing, intense, rich **2.** distinct, dramatic, graphic, highly-coloured, lifelike, memorable, powerful, realistic, sharp, sharply-etched, stirring, strong, telling, true to life
Antonyms colourless, cool, drab, dull, lifeless, nondescript, ordinary, pale, pastel, quiet, routine, run-of-the-mill, sombre, unclear, unmemorable, unremarkable, vague

vocabulary dictionary, glossary, language, lexicon, wordbook, word hoard, words, word stock

vocal *adj.* **1.** articulate, articulated, oral, put into words, said, spoken, uttered, voiced **2.** articulate, blunt, clamorous, eloquent, expressive, forthright, frank, free-spoken, noisy, outspoken, plain-spoken, strident, vociferous
Antonyms (*sense 2*) inarticulate, quiet, reserved, reticent, retiring, shy, silent, uncommunicative

vocation business, calling, career, employment, job, life's work, life work, métier, mission, office, post, profession, pursuit, role, trade

vociferous clamant, clamorous, loud, loudmouthed (*Inf.*), noisy, obstreperous, outspoken, ranting, shouting, strident, uproarious, vehement, vocal

Antonyms hushed, muted, noise~ less, quiet, silent, still

vogue n. **1.** craze, custom, *dernier cri*, fashion, last word, mode, style, the latest, the rage, the thing (*Inf.*), trend, way **2.** accept~ ance, currency, fashionableness, favour, popularity, prevalence, usage, use

voice n. **1.** articulation, language, power of speech, sound, tone, utterance, words **2.** decision, ex~ pression, part, say, view, vote, will, wish **3.** agency, instrument, medium, mouthpiece, organ, spokesman, spokesperson, spokeswoman, vehicle ~v. **4.** air, articulate, assert, come out with (*Inf.*), declare, divulge, enunci~ ate, express, give expression or utterance to, put into words, say, utter, ventilate

void adj. **1.** bare, clear, drained, emptied, empty, free, tenantless, unfilled, unoccupied, vacant **2.** *With of* destitute, devoid, lacking, without **3.** dead, ineffective, inef~ fectual, inoperative, invalid, nonviable, nugatory, null and void, unenforceable, useless, vain, worthless ~n. **4.** blank, blankness, emptiness, gap, lack, opening, space, vacuity, vacuum, want ~v. **5.** discharge, drain, eject, eliminate (*Physiol.*), emit, empty, evacuate

Antonyms adj. (*sense 1*) abound~ ing, complete, filled, full, occu~ pied, replete, tenanted

volatile airy, changeable, erratic, explosive, fickle, flighty, gay, giddy, inconstant, lively, mercu~ rial, sprightly, unsettled, unsta~ ble, unsteady, up and down (*Inf.*), variable, whimsical

Antonyms calm, consistent, con~ stant, cool-headed, dependable, inert, reliable, self-controlled, settled, sober, stable, steady

volley n. barrage, blast, bom~ bardment, burst, cannonade, dis~

charge, explosion, fusillade, hail, salvo, shower

volume 1. aggregate, amount, body, bulk, capacity, compass, cubic content, dimensions, mass, quantity, total **2.** book, publica~ tion, tome, treatise

voluntarily by choice, freely, of one's own accord, of one's own free will, on one's own initiative, willingly, without being asked, without prompting

voluntary discretionary, free, gratuitous, honorary, intended, intentional, optional, sponta~ neous, uncompelled, uncon~ strained, unforced, unpaid, vol~ unteer, willing

Antonyms automatic, conscript~ ed, forced, instinctive, involun~ tary, obligatory, unintentional

volunteer v. advance, let oneself in for (*Inf.*), need no invitation, offer, offer one's services, pres~ ent, proffer, propose, put for~ ward, put oneself at (someone's) disposal, step forward, suggest, tender

Antonyms begrudge, deny, keep, refuse, retain, withdraw, with~ hold

vomit v. barf (*Sl.*), belch forth, be sick, bring up, disgorge, eject, emit, heave, puke (*Sl.*), regurgi~ tate, retch, sick up (*Inf.*), spew out or up, throw up (*Inf.*)

voracious avid, devouring, glut~ tonous, greedy, hungry, insa~ tiable, omnivorous, prodigious, rapacious, ravening, ravenous, uncontrolled, unquenchable

Antonyms moderate, sated, sat~ isfied, self-controlled, temperate

vote 1. n. ballot, franchise, plebi~ scite, poll, referendum, right to vote, show of hands, suffrage **2.** v. ballot, cast one's vote, elect, go to the polls, opt, return

vouch Usually with for affirm, answer for, assert, asseverate, attest to, back, certify, confirm, give assurance of, go bail for, guarantee, stand witness, sup~ port, swear to, uphold

vow 1. v. affirm, consecrate,

dedicate, devote, pledge, promise, swear, undertake solemnly **2.** *n.* oath, pledge, promise, troth (*Archaic*)

voyage *n.* crossing, cruise, journey, passage, travels, trip

vulgar 1. blue, boorish, cheap and nasty, coarse, common, crude, dirty, flashy, gaudy, gross, ill-bred, impolite, improper, indecent, indecorous, indelicate, low, nasty, naughty, off colour, ribald, risqué, rude, suggestive, tasteless, tawdry, uncouth, unmannerly, unrefined **2.** general, native, ordinary, unrefined, vernacular
Antonyms aristocratic, classical, decorous, elegant, genteel, highbrow, polite, refined, sophisticated, tasteful, upper-class, well-mannered

vulgarity bad taste, coarseness, crudeness, crudity, gaudiness, grossness, indecorum, indelicacy, lack of refinement, ribaldry, rudeness, suggestiveness, tastelessness, tawdriness
Antonyms decorum, gentility, good breeding, good manners, good taste, refinement, sensitivity, sophistication, tastefulness

vulnerable accessible, assailable, defenceless, exposed, open to attack, sensitive, susceptible, tender, thin-skinned, unprotected, weak, wide open
Antonyms guarded, immune, impervious, insensitive, invulnerable, thick-skinned, unassailable, well-protected

W

wade 1. ford, paddle, splash, walk through 2. *With in or into* assail, attack, get stuck in (*Sl.*), go for, launch oneself at, light into (*Inf.*), set about, tackle, tear into (*Inf.*)

waft *v.* bear, be carried, carry, convey, drift, float, ride, transmit, transport

wag 1. *v.* bob, flutter, nod, oscillate, quiver, rock, shake, stir, vibrate, waggle, wave, wiggle 2. *n.* bob, flutter, nod, oscillation, quiver, shake, toss, vibration, waggle, wave, wiggle

wage *n. Also* **wages** allowance, compensation, earnings, emolument, fee, hire, pay, payment, recompense, remuneration, reward, stipend

wager 1. *n.* bet, flutter (*Brit. inf.*), gamble, pledge, punt, stake, venture 2. *v.* bet, chance, gamble, hazard, lay, pledge, punt, put on, risk, speculate, stake, venture

waif foundling, orphan, stray

wail 1. *v.* bemoan, bewail, cry, deplore, grieve, howl, keen, lament, ululate, weep, yowl 2. *n.* complaint, cry, grief, howl, keen, lament, lamentation, moan, ululation, weeping, yowl

wait 1. *v.* abide, bide one's time, cool one's heels, dally, delay, hang fire, hold back, hold on (*Inf.*), linger, mark time, pause, remain, rest, stand by, stay, tarry 2. *n.* delay, halt, hold-up, interval, pause, rest, stay
Antonyms (*sense 1*) depart, go, go away, leave, move off, quit, set off, take off (*Inf.*)

waiter, waitress attendant, server, steward, stewardess

wait on or upon attend, minister to, serve, tend

waive abandon, defer, dispense with, forgo, give up, postpone, put off, refrain from, relinquish, remit, renounce, resign, set aside, surrender
Antonyms claim, demand, insist, maintain, press, profess, pursue, uphold

wake¹ *v.* 1. arise, awake, awaken, bestir, come to, get up, rouse, rouse from sleep, stir 2. activate, animate, arouse, awaken, enliven, excite, fire, galvanize, kindle, provoke, quicken, stimulate, stir up
Antonyms (*sense 1*) catnap, doze, drop off (*Inf.*), hibernate, nod off (*Inf.*), sleep, snooze (*Inf.*), take a nap

wake² aftermath, backwash, path, track, trail, train, wash, waves

wakeful 1. insomniac, restless, sleepless, unsleeping 2. alert, alive, attentive, heedful, observant, on guard, on the alert, on the lookout, on the qui vive, unsleeping, vigilant, wary, watchful
Antonyms (*sense 2*) asleep, dormant, dozing, dreamy, drowsy, heedless, inattentive, off guard, sleepy

waken activate, animate, arouse, awake, awaken, be roused, come awake, come to, enliven, fire, galvanize, get up, kindle, quicken, rouse, stimulate, stir
Antonyms be inactive, doze, lie dormant, nap, repose, sleep, slumber, snooze (*Inf.*)

walk *v.* 1. advance, amble, foot it, go, go by shanks's pony (*Inf.*), go on foot, hike, hoof it (*Sl.*), march, move, pace, perambulate, promenade, saunter, step, stride, stroll, traipse (*Inf.*), tramp, travel on foot, trek, trudge 2. accompany, convoy, escort, take ~*n.* 3. constitutional, hike, march, perambulation, promenade, ramble, saunter, stroll, traipse (Inf.), tramp, trek, trudge, turn 4. carriage, gait, manner of walking, pace, step, stride 5. aisle, alley, avenue, esplanade, footpath, lane, path, pathway, pavement, promenade, sidewalk, trail 6. area, arena, calling, career, course, field, line, métier, profession, sphere, trade, vocation

walker footslogger, hiker, pedestrian, rambler, wayfarer

walkout industrial action, protest, stoppage, strike

wall 1. divider, enclosure, panel, partition, screen 2. barricade, breastwork, bulwark, embankment, fortification, palisade, parapet, rampart, stockade 3. barrier, block, fence, hedge, impediment, obstacle, obstruction 4. **go to the wall** Inf. be ruined, collapse, fail, fall, go bust (Inf.), go under

wallet case, holder, notecase, pocketbook, pouch, purse

wallow 1. lie, roll about, splash around, tumble, welter 2. flounder, lurch, stagger, stumble, wade 3. bask, delight, glory, indulge oneself, luxuriate, relish, revel, take pleasure
Antonyms (sense 3) abstain, avoid, do without, eschew, forgo, give up, refrain

wand baton, rod, sprig, stick, twig, withe, withy

wander v. 1. cruise, drift, knock about, knock around, meander, mooch around (Sl.), peregrinate, ramble, range, roam, rove, straggle, stravaig (Scot.), stray, stroll, traipse (Inf.) 2. depart, deviate, digress, divagate (Rare), diverge, err, get lost, go astray, go off at a tangent, go off course, lapse, lose concentration, lose one's train of thought, lose one's way, swerve, veer 3. babble, be delirious, be incoherent, ramble, rave, speak incoherently, talk nonsense ~n. 4. cruise, excursion, meander, peregrination, ramble, traipse (Inf.)
Antonyms (sense 2) comply,

conform, fall in with, follow, run with the pack, toe the line

wanderer bird of passage, drifter, gypsy, itinerant, nomad, rambler, ranger, rolling stone, rover, stroller, traveller, vagabond, vagrant, voyager

wandering drifting, homeless, itinerant, migratory, nomadic, peripatetic, rambling, rootless, roving, strolling, travelling, vagabond, vagrant, voyaging, wayfaring

wane 1. v. abate, atrophy, decline, decrease, die out, dim, diminish, draw to a close, drop, dwindle, ebb, fade, fade away, fail, lessen, sink, subside, taper off, weaken, wind down, wither 2. n. **on the wane** at its lowest ebb, declining, dropping, dwindling, dying out, ebbing, fading, lessening, obsolescent, on its last legs, on the decline, on the way out, subsiding, tapering off, weakening, withering
Antonyms v. blossom, brighten, develop, expand, grow, improve, increase, rise, strengthen, wax ~n. strengthening, waxing

want v. 1. covet, crave, desire, feel a need for, hanker after, have a fancy for, have a yen for (Inf.), hunger for, long for, need, pine for, require, thirst for, wish, yearn for 2. be able to do with, be deficient in, be short of, be without, call for, demand, fall short in, have need of, lack, miss, need, require, stand in need of ~n. 3. appetite, craving, demand, desire, fancy, hankering, hunger, longing, necessity, need, requirement, thirst, wish, yearning, yen (Inf.) 4. absence, dearth, default, deficiency, famine, insufficiency, lack, paucity, scantiness, scarcity, shortage 5. destitution, indigence, need, neediness, pauperism, penury, poverty, privation
Antonyms v. be sated, detest, dislike, enjoy, hate, have, loathe, own, possess, reject, spurn, surfeit ~n. abundance, adequacy,

comfort, ease, excess, luxury, plenty, surplus, sufficiency, wealth

wanting 1. absent, incomplete, lacking, less, missing, short, shy **2.** defective, deficient, disappointing, faulty, imperfect, inadequate, inferior, leaving much to be desired, not good enough, not up to expectations, not up to par, patchy, poor, sketchy, substandard, unsound
Antonyms adequate, complete, enough, full, replete, satisfactory, saturated, sufficient

wanton adj. **1.** abandoned, dissipated, dissolute, fast, immoral, lecherous, lewd, libertine, libidinous, licentious, loose, lustful, of easy virtue, promiscuous, rakish, shameless, unchaste **2.** arbitrary, cruel, evil, gratuitous, groundless, malevolent, malicious, motiveless, needless, senseless, spiteful, uncalled-for, unjustifiable, unjustified, unprovoked, vicious, wicked, wilful ~n. **3.** Casanova, debauchee, Don Juan, gigolo, harlot, lecher, libertine, loose woman, profligate, prostitute, rake, roué, slut, strumpet, tart (*Inf.*), trollop, voluptuary, whore, woman of easy virtue ~v. **4.** debauch, dissipate, revel, riot, sleep around (*Inf.*), wench (*Archaic*), whore **5.** fritter away, misspend, squander, throw away, waste
Antonyms (*sense 1*) overmodest, priggish, prim, prudish, puritanical, rigid, strait-laced, stuffy, Victorian (*sense 2*) called-for, excusable, justified, legitimate, motivated, provoked, warranted

war 1. n. armed conflict, battle, bloodshed, combat, conflict, contention, contest, enmity, fighting, hostilities, hostility, strife, struggle, warfare **2.** v. battle, campaign against, carry on hostilities, clash, combat, conduct a war, contend, contest, fight, make war, strive, struggle, take up arms, wage war
Antonyms n. accord, armistice,

cease-fire, co-existence, compliance, co-operation, harmony, peace, peace-time, treaty, truce ~v. call a ceasefire, co-exist, co-operate, make peace

ward 1. area, district, division, precinct, quarter, zone **2.** charge, dependant, minor, protégé, pupil **3.** care, charge, custody, guardianship, keeping, protection, safekeeping

warden administrator, caretaker, curator, custodian, guardian, janitor, keeper, ranger, steward, superintendent, warder, watchman

warder, wardress custodian, gaoler, guard, jailer, keeper, prison officer, screw (*Sl.*), turnkey (*Archaic*)

ward off avert, avoid, beat off, block, deflect, fend off, forestall, keep at arm's length, keep at bay, parry, repel, stave off, thwart, turn aside, turn away

wardrobe 1. closet, clothes cupboard, clothes-press **2.** apparel, attire, clothes, collection of clothes, outfit

warehouse depository, depot, stockroom, store, storehouse

wares commodities, goods, lines, manufactures, merchandise, produce, products, stock, stuff

warfare armed conflict, armed struggle, arms, battle, blows, campaigning, clash of arms, combat, conflict, contest, discord, fighting, hostilities, passage of arms, strategy, strife, struggle, war
Antonyms accord, amity, armistice, cessation of hostilities, conciliation, harmony, peace, treaty, truce

warily cagily (*Inf.*), carefully, cautiously, charily, circumspectly, distrustfully, gingerly, guardedly, suspiciously, vigilantly, watchfully, with care
Antonyms carelessly, hastily, heedlessly, irresponsibly, rashly, recklessly, thoughtlessly, unwarily

warlike aggressive, bellicose,

belligerent, bloodthirsty, combative, hawkish, hostile, inimical, jingoistic, martial, militaristic, military, pugnacious, sabre-rattling, unfriendly, warmongering

Antonyms amicable, conciliatory, friendly, nonbelligerent, pacific, peaceable, peaceful, placid, unwarlike

warm *adj.* 1. balmy, heated, lukewarm, moderately hot, pleasant, sunny, tepid, thermal 2. affable, affectionate, amiable, amorous, cheerful, cordial, friendly, genial, happy, hearty, hospitable, kindly, loving, pleasant, tender 3. animated, ardent, cordial, earnest, effusive, emotional, enthusiastic, excited, fervent, glowing, heated, intense, keen, lively, passionate, spirited, stormy, vehement, vigorous, violent, zealous 4. irascible, irritable, passionate, quick, sensitive, short, touchy ~*v.* 5. heat, heat up, melt, thaw, warm up 6. animate, awaken, excite, get going (*Inf.*), interest, make enthusiastic, put some life into, rouse, stimulate, stir, turn on (*Sl.*)

Antonyms *adj.* aloof, apathetic, chilly, cold, cool, distant, freezing, half-hearted, hostile, icy, phlegmatic, remote, stand-offish, uncaring, unenthusiastic, unfriendly, unwelcoming ~*v.* alienate, chill, cool, cool down, depress, freeze, sadden

warmonger belligerent, hawk, jingo, militarist, sabre-rattler

warmth 1. heat, hotness, warmness 2. animation, ardour, eagerness, earnestness, effusiveness, enthusiasm, excitement, fervency, fervour, fire, heat, intensity, passion, spirit, transport, vehemence, vigour, violence, zeal, zest 3. affability, affection, amorousness, cheerfulness, cordiality, happiness, heartiness, hospitableness, kindliness, love, tenderness

Antonyms aloofness, apathy, austerity, chill, chilliness, cold, cold-heartedness, coldness, cool-

ness, hard-heartedness, hostility, iciness, indifference, insincerity, lack of enthusiasm, sternness, remoteness

warn admonish, advise, alert, apprise, caution, forewarn, give fair warning, give notice, inform, make (someone) aware, notify, put one on one's guard, summon, tip off

warning *n.* admonition, advice, alarm, alert, augury, caution, caveat, foretoken, hint, notice, notification, omen, premonition, presage, sign, signal, threat, tip, tip-off, token, word, word to the wise

warrant *n.* 1. assurance, authority, authorization, carte blanche, commission, guarantee, licence, permission, permit, pledge, sanction, security, warranty ~*v.* 2. affirm, answer for, assure, attest, avouch, certify, declare, guarantee, pledge, secure, stand behind, underwrite, uphold, vouch for 3. approve, authorize, call for, commission, demand, empower, entitle, excuse, give ground for, justify, license, necessitate, permit, require, sanction

warrior champion, combatant, fighter, fighting man, man-at-arms, soldier

wary alert, attentive, cagey (*Inf.*), careful, cautious, chary, circumspect, distrustful, guarded, heedful, leery (*Sl.*), on one's guard, on the lookout, on the qui vive, prudent, suspicious, vigilant, watchful, wide-awake

Antonyms careless, foolhardy, imprudent, negligent, rash, reckless, remiss, unguarded, unsuspecting, unwary

wash *v.* 1. bath, bathe, clean, cleanse, launder, moisten, rinse, scrub, shampoo, shower, wet 2. *With away* bear away, carry off, erode, move, sweep away, wash off 3. *Inf.* bear scrutiny, be convincing, be plausible, carry weight, hold up, hold water, stand up, stick 4. **wash one's hands of**

abandon, accept no responsibility for, give up on, have nothing to do with, leave to one's own devices ~n. **5.** ablution, bath, bathe, cleaning, cleansing, laundering, rinse, scrub, shampoo, shower, washing **6.** ebb and flow, flow, roll, surge, sweep, swell, wave

washout disappointment, disaster, dud (*Inf.*), failure, fiasco, flop (*Inf.*), mess
Antonyms conquest, feat, success, triumph, victory, winner

waste v. **1.** blow (*Sl.*), dissipate, fritter away, frivol away (*Inf.*), lavish, misuse, run through, squander, throw away **2.** atrophy, consume, corrode, crumble, debilitate, decay, decline, deplete, disable, drain, dwindle, eat away, ebb, emaciate, enfeeble, exhaust, fade, gnaw, perish, sap the strength of, sink, undermine, wane, wear out, wither **3.** despoil, destroy, devastate, lay waste, pillage, rape, ravage, raze, ruin, sack, spoil, wreak havoc upon ~n. **4.** dissipation, expenditure, extravagance, frittering away, loss, lost opportunity, misapplication, misuse, prodigality, squandering, unthriftiness, wastefulness **5.** desolation, destruction, devastation, havoc, ravage, ruin **6.** debris, dregs, dross, garbage, leavings, leftovers, litter, offal, offscourings, refuse, rubbish, scrap, sweepings, trash **7.** desert, solitude, void, wasteland, wild, wilderness ~adj. **8.** leftover, superfluous, supernumerary, unused, unwanted, useless, worthless **9.** bare, barren, desolate, devastated, dismal, dreary, empty, uncultivated, uninhabited, unproductive, wild
Antonyms v. build, conserve, defend, develop, economize, husband, increase, preserve, protect, rally, restore, save, strengthen ~n. economy, frugality, good housekeeping, saving, thrift ~adj. arable, developed, fruitful, habitable, in use, necessary,

needed, productive, utilized, verdant

wasteful extravagant, improvident, lavish, prodigal, profligate, ruinous, spendthrift, thriftless, uneconomical, unthrifty
Antonyms economical, frugal, money-saving, parsimonious, penny-wise, provident, sparing, thrifty

watch v. **1.** contemplate, eye, gaze at, look, look at, look on, mark, note, observe, pay attention, peer at, regard, see, stare at, view **2.** attend, be on the alert, be on the lookout, be vigilant, be wary, be watchful, keep an eye open (*Inf.*), look out, take heed, wait **3.** guard, keep, look after, mind, protect, superintend, take care of, tend ~n. **4.** chronometer, clock, pocket watch, timepiece, wristwatch **5.** alertness, attention, eye, heed, inspection, lookout, notice, observation, supervision, surveillance, vigil, vigilance, watchfulness

watchdog 1. guard dog **2.** custodian, guardian, inspector, monitor, protector, scrutineer

watchful alert, attentive, circumspect, guarded, heedful, observant, on one's guard, on the lookout, on the qui vive, on the watch, suspicious, vigilant, wary, wide awake
Antonyms careless, inattentive, reckless, thoughtless, unaware, unguarded, unmindful, unobservant, unwary

watchman caretaker, custodian, guard, security guard, security man

watch over defend, guard, keep safe, look after, preserve, protect, shelter, shield, stand guard over

water n. **1.** Adam's ale *or* wine, aqua, H_2O ~v. **2.** damp, dampen, douse, drench, flood, hose, irrigate, moisten, soak, souse, spray, sprinkle **3.** add water to, adulterate, dilute, put water in, thin, water down, weaken

waterfall cascade, cataract,

chute, fall, force (*Northern Brit.*), linn (*Scot.*)

watertight 1. sound, waterproof 2. airtight, firm, flawless, foolproof, impregnable, incontrovertible, sound, unassailable

watery 1. aqueous, damp, fluid, humid, liquid, marshy, moist, soggy, squelchy, wet 2. adulterated, dilute, diluted, flavourless, insipid, runny, tasteless, thin, washy, watered-down, waterish, weak, wishy-washy (*Inf.*)
Antonyms concentrated, condensed, dense, fortified, solid, strong, thick

wave v. 1. brandish, flap, flourish, flutter, move to and fro, oscillate, quiver, ripple, shake, stir, sway, swing, undulate, wag, waver, wield 2. beckon, direct, gesticulate, gesture, indicate, sign, signal ~n. 3. billow, breaker, comber, ridge, ripple, roller, sea surf, swell, undulation, unevenness 4. current, drift, flood, ground swell, movement, outbreak, rash, rush, stream, surge, sweep, tendency, trend, upsurge

waver 1. be indecisive, be irresolute, be unable to decide, be unable to make up one's mind, blow hot and cold (*Inf.*), dither, falter, fluctuate, hesitate, hum and haw, seesaw, shillyshally (*Inf.*), swither (*Scot.*), vacillate 2. flicker, fluctuate, quiver, reel, shake, sway, totter, tremble, undulate, vary, wave, weave, wobble
Antonyms be decisive, be determined, be of fixed opinion, be resolute, determine, resolve, stand firm

wax v. become fuller, become larger, develop, dilate, enlarge, expand, fill out, get bigger, grow, increase, magnify, mount, rise, swell
Antonyms contract, decline, decrease, diminish, dwindle, fade, lessen, narrow, shrink, wane

way 1. approach, course of action, fashion, manner, means, method, mode, plan, practice, procedure, process, scheme, system, technique 2. access, avenue, channel, course, direction, highway, lane, path, pathway, road, route, street, thoroughfare, track, trail 3. elbowroom, opening, room, space 4. distance, journey, length, stretch, trail 5. advance, approach, journey, march, passage, progress 6. characteristic, conduct, custom, habit, idiosyncrasy, manner, nature, personality, practice, style, trait, usage, wont 7. aspect, detail, feature, particular, point, respect, sense 8. by the way by the bye, en passant, incidentally, in parenthesis, in passing 9. give way a. break down, cave in, collapse, crack, crumple, fall, fall to pieces, give, go to pieces, subside b. accede, acknowledge defeat, acquiesce, back down, concede, make concessions, withdraw, yield 10. under way afoot, begun, going, in motion, in progress, moving, on the go (*Inf.*), on the move, started

wayfarer bird of passage, globetrotter, Gypsy, itinerant, journeyer, nomad, rover, traveller, trekker, voyager, walker, wanderer

wayward capricious, changeable, contrary, contumacious, crossgrained, disobedient, erratic, fickle, flighty, froward, headstrong, inconstant, incorrigible, insubordinate, intractable, mulish, obdurate, obstinate, perverse, rebellious, refractory, selfwilled, stubborn, undependable, ungovernable, unmanageable, unpredictable, unruly, wilful
Antonyms complaisant, compliant, dependable, good-natured, malleable, manageable, obedient, obliging, predictable, reliable, submissive, tractable

weak 1. anaemic, debilitated, decrepit, delicate, effete, enervated, exhausted, faint, feeble, fragile, frail, infirm, languid, puny, shaky, sickly, spent, tender, unsound, unsteady, wasted, weakly

2. cowardly, impotent, indecisive, ineffectual, infirm, irresolute, namby-pamby, powerless, soft, spineless, timorous, weak-kneed (*Inf.*) **3.** distant, dull, faint, imperceptible, low, muffled, poor, quiet, slight, small, soft **4.** deficient, faulty, inadequate, lacking, poor, substandard, understrength, wanting **5.** feeble, flimsy, hollow, inconclusive, invalid, lame, pathetic, shallow, slight, unconvincing, unsatisfactory **6.** defenceless, exposed, helpless, unguarded, unprotected, unsafe, untenable, vulnerable, wide open **7.** diluted, insipid, milk-and-water, runny, tasteless, thin, understrength, waterish, watery, wishy-washy (*Inf.*)
Antonyms able, capable, conclusive, convincing, effective, energetic, firm, flavoursome, forceful, hardy, healthy, hefty, intoxicating, invulnerable, mighty, obvious, potent, powerful, safe, secure, solid, strong, substantial, tasty, tough, trustworthy, uncontrovertible, valid, well-defended

weaken 1. abate, debilitate, depress, diminish, droop, dwindle, ease up, enervate, fade, fail, flag, give way, impair, invalidate, lessen, lower, mitigate, moderate, reduce, sap, sap the strength of, soften up, temper, tire, undermine, wane **2.** adulterate, cut, debase, dilute, thin, thin out, water down
Antonyms boost, enhance, grow, improve, increase, invigorate, revitalize, strengthen

weakness 1. debility, decrepitude, enervation, faintness, feebleness, fragility, frailty, impotence, infirmity, irresolution, powerlessness, vulnerability **2.** Achilles heel, blemish, chink in one's armour, defect, deficiency, failing, fault, flaw, imperfection, lack, shortcoming **3.** fondness, inclination, liking, passion, penchant, predilection, proclivity, proneness, soft spot

Antonyms advantage, aversion, dislike, forte, hardiness, hatred, health, impregnability, loathing, potency, power, stamina, strength, strong point, sturdiness, validity, vigour, virtue, vitality

wealth 1. affluence, assets, capital, cash, estate, fortune, funds, goods, lucre, means, money, opulence, pelf, possessions, property, prosperity, resources, riches, substance **2.** abundance, bounty, copiousness, cornucopia, fullness, plenitude, plenty, profusion, richness, store
Antonyms dearth, deprivation, destitution, indigence, lack, need, paucity, penury, poverty, scarcity, shortage, want, wretchedness

wealthy affluent, comfortable, filthy rich (*Sl.*), flush (*Inf.*), in the money (*Inf.*), loaded (*Sl.*), made of money (*Inf.*), moneyed, on easy street (*Sl.*), opulent, prosperous, quids in (*Sl.*), rich, rolling in it (*Sl.*), stinking rich (*Sl.*), well-heeled (*Sl.*), well-off, well-to-do
Antonyms broke (*Inf.*), deprived, destitute, impoverished, indigent, needy, penniless, poor, poverty-stricken, skint (*Sl.*)

wear *v.* **1.** bear, be clothed in, be dressed in, carry, clothe oneself, don, dress in, have on, put on, sport **2.** display, exhibit, fly, show **3.** abrade, consume, corrode, deteriorate, erode, fray, grind, impair, rub, use, wash away, waste **4.** bear up, be durable, endure, hold up, last, stand up to **5.** annoy, drain, enervate, exasperate, fatigue, harass, irk, pester, tax, undermine, vex, weaken, weary ~*n.* **6.** employment, mileage (*Inf.*), service, use, usefulness, utility **7.** apparel, attire, clothes, costume, dress, garb, garments, gear, habit, outfit, things **8.** abrasion, attrition, corrosion, damage, depreciation, deterioration, erosion, friction, use, wear and tear
Antonyms (*sense 8*) conserva-

tion, maintenance, preservation, repair, upkeep

weariness drowsiness, enervation, exhaustion, fatigue, languor, lassitude, lethargy, listlessness, prostration, tiredness

Antonyms drive, energy, freshness, get-up-and-go (*Inf.*), liveliness, stamina, vigour, vitality, zeal, zest

wearisome annoying, boring, bothersome, burdensome, dull, exasperating, exhausting, fatiguing, humdrum, irksome, monotonous, oppressive, pestilential, prosaic, tedious, troublesome, trying, uninteresting, vexatious, wearing

Antonyms agreeable, delightful, enjoyable, exhilarating, interesting, invigorating, pleasurable, refreshing, stimulating

wear off abate, decrease, diminish, disappear, dwindle, ebb, fade, lose effect, lose strength, peter out, subside, wane, weaken

Antonyms grow, increase, intensify, magnify, persist, reinforce, step up, strengthen, wax

wear out 1. become useless, become worn, consume, deteriorate, erode, fray, impair, use up, wear through **2.** enervate, exhaust, fag out (*Inf.*), fatigue, frazzle (*Inf.*), knacker (*Brit. sl.*), prostrate, sap, tire, weary

Antonyms (*sense 2*) buck up (*Inf.*), energize, invigorate, pep up, perk up, refresh, revitalize, stimulate, strengthen

weary adj. **1.** all in (*Sl.*), asleep or dead on one's feet (*Inf.*), dead beat (*Inf.*), dog-tired (*Inf.*), done in (*Inf.*), drained, drooping, drowsy, enervated, exhausted, fagged (*Inf.*), fatigued, flagging, jaded, knackered (*Sl.*), ready to drop, sleepy, spent, tired, wearied, whacked (*Brit. inf.*), worn out **2.** arduous, enervative, irksome, laborious, taxing, tiresome, tiring, wearing, wearisome ~ v. **3.** burden, debilitate, drain, droop, enervate, fade, fag (*Inf.*), fail, fatigue, grow tired, sap, take

it out of (*Inf.*), tax, tire, tire out, wear out **4.** annoy, become bored, bore, exasperate, have had enough, irk, jade, make discontented, plague, sicken, try the patience of, vex

Antonyms adj. energetic, excited, exciting, forebearing, fresh, full of beans (*Inf.*), full of get-up-and-go (*Inf.*), invigorated, invigorating, lively, original, patient, refreshed, refreshing ~ v. amuse, enliven, excite, interest, invigorate, refresh, revive, stimulate

weather n. **1.** climate, conditions **2. under the weather a.** ailing, below par, ill, indisposed, nauseous, not well, off-colour, out of sorts, poorly (*Inf.*), seedy (*Inf.*), sick **b.** crapulent, crapulous, drunk, groggy (*Inf.*), hung over (*Inf.*), inebriated, intoxicated, one over the eight (*Sl.*), the worse for drink, three sheets in the wind (*Inf.*), under the influence (*Inf.*) ~ v. **3.** expose, harden, season, toughen **4.** bear up against, brave, come through, endure, get through, live through, make it (*Inf.*), overcome, pull through, resist, ride out, rise above, stand, stick it out (*Inf.*), suffer, surmount, survive, withstand

Antonyms (*sense 4*) cave in, collapse, fail, fall, give in, go under, succumb, surrender, yield

weave 1. blend, braid, entwine, fuse, incorporate, interlace, intermingle, intertwine, introduce, knit, mat, merge, plait, twist, unite **2.** build, construct, contrive, create, fabricate, make, make up, put together, spin **3.** crisscross, move in and out, weave one's way, wind, zigzag

web 1. cobweb, spider's web **2.** interlacing, lattice, mesh, net, netting, network, screen, tangle, toils, weave, webbing

wed become man and wife, be married to, espouse, get hitched (*Inf.*), get married, join, make one, marry, splice (*Inf.*), take as one's husband, take as one's wife, take to wife, tie the knot (*Inf.*), unite

wedding espousals, marriage, marriage ceremony, nuptial rite, nuptials, wedlock

wedge 1. *n.* block, chock, chunk, lump, wodge (*Brit. inf.*) **2.** *v.* block, cram, crowd, force, jam, lodge, pack, ram, split, squeeze, stuff, thrust

weep bemoan, bewail, blub (*Sl.*), blubber, boohoo, complain, cry, greet (*Dialect*), keen, lament, moan, mourn, shed tears, snivel, sob, ululate, whimper, whinge (*Inf.*)
Antonyms be glad, celebrate, delight, exult, joy, rejoice, revel, triumph

weigh 1. consider, contemplate, deliberate upon, evaluate, examine, give thought to, meditate upon, mull over, ponder, reflect upon, study, think over **2.** be influential, carry weight, count, cut any ice (*Inf.*), have influence, impress, matter, tell **3.** bear down, burden, oppress, prey

weight *n.* **1.** avoirdupois, burden, gravity, heaviness, heft (*Inf.*), load, mass, poundage, pressure, tonnage **2.** ballast, heavy object, load, mass **3.** burden, load, millstone, oppression, pressure, strain **4.** greatest force, main force, onus, preponderance **5.** authority, clout (*Inf.*), consequence, consideration, efficacy, emphasis, impact, import, importance, influence, moment, persuasiveness, power, significance, substance, value ~*v.* **6.** add weight to, ballast, charge, freight, increase the load on, increase the weight of, load, make heavier **7.** burden, encumber, handicap, impede, oppress, overburden, weigh down **8.** bias, load, unbalance

weighty 1. burdensome, cumbersome, dense, heavy, hefty (*Inf.*), massive, ponderous **2.** consequential, considerable, critical, crucial, forcible, grave, important, momentous, portentous, serious, significant, solemn, substantial **3.** backbreaking, burdensome, crushing, demanding, difficult, exacting, onerous, oppressive, taxing, worrisome, worrying
Antonyms (*sense 2*) frivolous, immaterial, incidental, inconsequential, insignificant, minor, petty, trivial, unimportant

weird bizarre, creepy (*Inf.*), eerie, eldritch (*Poetic*), far-out (*Sl.*), freakish, ghostly, grotesque, mysterious, odd, outlandish, queer, spooky (*Inf.*), strange, supernatural, uncanny, unearthly, unnatural
Antonyms common, mundane, natural, normal, ordinary, regular, typical, usual

welcome *adj.* **1.** acceptable, accepted, agreeable, appreciated, delightful, desirable, gladly received, gratifying, pleasant, pleasing, pleasurable, refreshing, wanted **2.** at home, free, invited, under no obligation ~*n.* **3.** acceptance, entertainment, greeting, hospitality, reception, salutation ~*v.* **4.** accept gladly, bid welcome, embrace, greet, hail, meet, offer hospitality to, receive, receive with open arms, roll out the red carpet for, usher in
Antonyms (*sense 1*) disagreeable, excluded, rebuffed, rejected, unacceptable, undesirable, unpleasant, unwanted, unwelcome (*sense 3*) cold shoulder, exclusion, ostracism, rebuff, rejection, slight, snub (*sense 4*) exclude, rebuff, refuse, reject, slight, snub, spurn, turn away

welfare advantage, benefit, good, happiness, health, interest, profit, prosperity, success, wellbeing

well[1] *adv.* **1.** agreeably, capitally, famously (*Inf.*), happily, in a satisfactory manner, nicely, pleasantly, satisfactorily, smoothly, splendidly, successfully **2.** ably, adeptly, adequately, admirably, conscientiously, correctly, effectively, efficiently, expertly, proficiently, properly, skilfully, with skill 3. accurately, attentively, carefully, closely 4. comfortably, flourishingly, prosperously 5. correctly, easily, fairly, fittingly, in all fairness, justly, properly, readily, rightly, suitably 6. closely, completely, deeply, fully, intimately, personally, profoundly, thoroughly 7. approvingly, favourably, glowingly, graciously, highly, kindly, warmly 8. abundantly, amply, completely, considerably, fully, greatly, heartily, highly, substantially, sufficiently, thoroughly, very much ~*adj.* 9. able-bodied, fit, hale, healthy, hearty, in fine fettle, in good health, robust, sound, strong, up to par

Antonyms *adv.* badly, coldly, disapprovingly, gracelessly, hamfistedly, inadequately, incompetently, incorrectly, ineptly, inexpertly, poorly, slightly, sloppily, somewhat, unfairly, unjustly, unkindly, unskilfully, unsympathetically, vaguely, wrongly ~*adj.* ailing, below par, feeble, frail, ill, infirm, poorly, run-down, sick, sickly, under-the-weather, unwell, weak

well² 1. *n.* fountain, pool, source, spring, waterhole 2. bore, hole, pit, shaft ~*v.* 3. flow, gush, jet, ooze, pour, rise, run, seep, spout, spring, spurt, stream, surge, trickle

well-balanced graceful, harmonious, proportional, symmetrical, well-proportioned

well-known celebrated, familiar, famous, illustrious, notable, noted, popular, renowned, widely known

well-off comfortable, flourishing, fortunate, lucky, successful, thriving

wet *adj.* 1. aqueous, damp, dank, drenched, dripping, humid, moist, moistened, saturated, soaked, soaking, sodden, soggy, sopping, waterlogged, watery, wringing wet 2. clammy, dank, drizzling, humid, misty, pouring,

raining, rainy, showery, teeming ~*n.* 3. clamminess, condensation, damp, dampness, humidity, liquid, moisture, water, wetness ~*v.* 4. damp, dampen, dip, douse, drench, humidify, irrigate, moisten, saturate, soak, splash, spray, sprinkle, steep, water

Antonyms *adj.* arid, bone-dry, dried, dry, fine, hardened, parched, set, sunny ~*n.* dryness ~*v.* dehydrate, desiccate, dry, parch

wharf dock, jetty, landing stage, pier, quay

wheel 1. *n.* circle, gyration, pivot, revolution, roll, rotation, spin, turn, twirl, whirl 2. *v.* circle, gyrate, orbit, pirouette, revolve, roll, rotate, spin, swing, swivel, turn, twirl, whirl

wheeze *v.* 1. breathe roughly, catch one's breath, cough, gasp, hiss, rasp, whistle ~*n.* 2. cough, gasp, hiss, rasp, whistle 3. *Brit. sl.* expedient, idea, plan, ploy, ruse, scheme, stunt, trick, wrinkle (*Inf.*)

whereabouts location, position, site, situation

whet edge, file, grind, hone, sharpen, strop

whiff 1. *n.* aroma, blast, breath, draught, gust, hint, odour, puff, scent, smell, sniff 2. *v.* breathe, inhale, puff, smell, smoke, sniff, waft

whim caprice, conceit, craze, crotchet, fad (*Inf.*), fancy, freak, humour, impulse, notion, passing thought, quirk, sport, sudden notion, urge, vagary, whimsy

whimper 1. *v.* blub (*Sl.*), blubber, cry, grizzle (*Inf.*), mewl, moan, pule, snivel, sob, weep, whine, whinge (*Inf.*) 2. *n.* moan, snivel, sob, whine

whine *n.* 1. cry, moan, plaintive cry, sob, wail, whimper 2. beef (*Sl.*), complaint, gripe (*Inf.*), grouse, grumble, moan ~*v.* 3. beef (*Sl.*), bellyache (*Sl.*), carp, complain, cry, gripe (*Inf.*), grizzle (*Inf.*), grouse, grumble, moan, sob, wail, whimper, whinge (*Inf.*)

whip v. **1.** beat, birch, cane, casti~
gate, flagellate, flog, give a hid~
ing (*Inf.*), lash, leather, punish,
scourge, spank, strap, switch, tan
(*Sl.*), thrash **2.** exhibit, flash, jerk,
produce, pull, remove, seize,
show, snatch, whisk **3.** beat,
whisk ~*n.* **4.** birch, bullwhip,
cane, cat-o'-nine-tails, crop,
horsewhip, knout, lash, rawhide,
riding crop, scourge, switch,
thong

whirl v. **1.** circle, gyrate, pirou~
ette, pivot, reel, revolve, roll,
rotate, spin, swirl, turn, twirl,
twist, wheel **2.** feel dizzy, reel,
spin ~*n.* **3.** birl (*Scot.*), circle,
gyration, pirouette, reel, revolu~
tion, roll, rotation, spin, swirl,
turn, twirl, twist, wheel **4.** confu~
sion, daze, dither, flurry, giddi~
ness, spin

whirlwind 1. *n.* dust devil, torna~
do, waterspout **2.** *adj.* hasty,
headlong, impetuous, impulsive,
lightning, quick, rapid, rash,
short, speedy, swift
Antonyms (*sense 2*) calculated,
cautious, considered, deliberate,
measured, prudent, slow, unhur~
ried

whisper v. **1.** breathe, murmur,
say softly, speak in hushed tones,
utter under the breath **2.** gossip,
hint, insinuate, intimate, mur~
mur, spread rumours **3.** hiss,
murmur, rustle, sigh, sough, su~
surrate (*Literary*), swish ~*n.* **4.**
hushed tone, low voice, murmur,
soft voice, undertone **5.** hiss,
murmur, rustle, sigh, sighing,
soughing, susurration or susurrus
(*Literary*), swish **6.** breath, frac~
tion, hint, shadow, suggestion,
suspicion, tinge, trace, whiff **7.**
Inf. buzz, gossip, innuendo, insin~
uation, report, rumour, word
Antonyms (*sense 1*) bawl, bel~
low, clamour, roar, shout, thun~
der, yell

white 1. ashen, bloodless, ghastly,
grey, pale, pallid, pasty, wan,
waxen, wheyfaced **2.** grey, griz~
zled, hoary, silver, snowy **3.**
clean, immaculate, innocent,

pure, spotless, stainless, unblem~
ished, unsullied
Antonyms (*senses 2 & 3*) black,
blackish, blemished, dark, dirty,
impure, soiled, stained, tarnished

whiten blanch, bleach, blench,
etiolate, fade, go white, pale, turn
pale
Antonyms blacken, colour,
darken

whitewash 1. *n.* camouflage,
concealment, cover-up, decep~
tion, extenuation **2.** *v.* camou~
flage, conceal, cover up, extenu~
ate, gloss over, make light of,
suppress
Antonyms *v.* disclose, expose, lay
bare, reveal, uncover, unmask,
unveil

whole *adj.* **1.** complete, entire,
full, in one piece, integral, total,
unabridged, uncut, undivided **2.**
faultless, flawless, good, in one
piece, intact, inviolate, mint,
perfect, sound, unbroken, un~
damaged, unharmed, unhurt, un~
impaired, uninjured, unmutilated,
unscathed, untouched **3.** able-
bodied, better, cured, fit, hale,
healed, healthy, in fine fettle, in
good health, recovered, robust,
sound, strong, well ~*n.* **4.** aggre~
gate, all, everything, lot, sum
total, the entire amount, total **5.**
ensemble, entirety, entity, full~
ness, piece, totality, unit, unity
Antonyms *adj.* ailing, broken,
cut, damaged, diseased, divided,
fragmented, ill, incomplete, in
pieces, partial, sick, sickly,
under-the-weather, unwell ~*n.*
bit, component, constituent, divi~
sion, element, fragment, part,
piece, portion

wholehearted committed, com~
plete, dedicated, determined, de~
voted, earnest, emphatic, enthu~
siastic, genuine, heartfelt, hearty,
real, sincere, true, unfeigned,
unqualified, unreserved, unstint~
ing, warm, zealous
Antonyms cool, grudging, half-
hearted, insincere, qualified, re~
served, unreal

wholesale 1. *adj.* all-inclusive,

broad, comprehensive, extensive, far-reaching, indiscriminate, mass, sweeping, wide-ranging **2.** *adv.* all at once, comprehensively, extensively, indiscriminately, on a large scale, without exception
Antonyms *adj.* confined, discriminate, limited, partial, restricted, selective

wicked 1. abandoned, abominable, amoral, atrocious, bad, black-hearted, corrupt, debased, depraved, devilish, dissolute, egregious, evil, fiendish, flagitious, foul, guilty, heinous, immoral, impious, iniquitous, irreligious, nefarious, scandalous, shameful, sinful, unprincipled, unrighteous, vicious, vile, villainous, worthless **2.** arch, impish, incorrigible, mischievous, naughty, rascally, roguish **3.** bothersome, difficult, distressing, galling, offensive, troublesome, trying, unpleasant
Antonyms benevolent, ethical, good, honourable, mannerly, mild, moral, noble, obedient, pleasant, principled, virtuous, well-behaved

wide *adj.* **1.** ample, broad, catholic, comprehensive, distended, encyclopedic, expanded, expansive, extensive, far-reaching, general, immense, inclusive, large, sweeping, vast **2.** away, distant, off, off course, off target, remote **3.** dilated, distended, expanded, fully open, outspread, outstretched **4.** ample, baggy, capacious, commodious, full, loose, roomy, spacious ~*adv.* **5.** as far as possible, completely, fully, right out, to the furthest extent **6.** astray, nowhere near, off course, off target, off the mark, out
Antonyms *adj.* closed, confined, constricted, cramped, limited, narrow, restricted, shut, strict, tight ~*adv.* barely, narrowly, partially, partly

widen broaden, dilate, enlarge,

expand, extend, open out *or* up, open wide, spread, stretch
Antonyms compress, constrict, contract, cramp, diminish, narrow, reduce, shrink, tighten

widespread broad, common, epidemic, extensive, far-flung, far-reaching, general, pervasive, popular, prevalent, rife, sweeping, universal, wholesale
Antonyms confined, exclusive, limited, local, narrow, rare, sporadic, uncommon

width breadth, compass, diameter, extent, girth, measure, range, reach, scope, span, thickness, wideness

wield 1. brandish, employ, flourish, handle, manage, manipulate, ply, swing, use **2.** apply, be possessed of, command, control, exercise, exert, have, have at one's disposal, hold, maintain, make use of, manage, possess, put to use, utilize

wife better half (*Humorous*), bride, helpmate, helpmeet, little woman (*Inf.*), mate, old lady (*Inf.*), old woman (*Inf.*), partner, spouse, (the) missis *or* missus (*Inf.*), woman (*Inf.*)

wild *adj.* **1.** feral, ferocious, fierce, savage, unbroken, undomesticated, untamed **2.** free, indigenous, native, natural, uncultivated **3.** desert, deserted, desolate, empty, godforsaken, trackless, uncivilized, uncultivated, uninhabited, unpopulated, virgin **4.** barbaric, barbarous, brutish, ferocious, fierce, primitive, rude, savage, uncivilized **5.** boisterous, chaotic, disorderly, impetuous, lawless, noisy, riotous, rough, rowdy, self-willed, turbulent, unbridled, uncontrolled, undisciplined, unfettered, ungovernable, unmanageable, unrestrained, unruly, uproarious, violent, wayward **6.** at one's wits' end, berserk, beside oneself, crazed, crazy, delirious, demented, excited, frantic, frenzied, hysterical, irrational, mad, maniacal, rabid, raving

Antonyms *adj.* advanced, broken, calm, careful, controlled, disciplined, domesticated, friendly, genteel, gentle, lawful, logical, mild, ordered, peaceful, polite, quiet, restrained, self-controlled, tame, thoughtful, well-behaved (*senses 2 & 3*) civilized, cultivated, farmed, inhabited, planted, populated, urban

wilderness desert, jungle, waste, wasteland, wild

wile artfulness, artifice, cheating, chicanery, craft, craftiness, cunning, fraud, guile, slyness, trickery

wilful 1. adamant, bull-headed, determined, dogged, froward, headstrong, inflexible, intractable, intransigent, mulish, obdurate, obstinate, persistent, perverse, pig-headed, refractory, self-willed, stubborn, uncompromising, unyielding 2. conscious, deliberate, intended, intentional, purposeful, volitional, voluntary, willed

Antonyms (*sense 1*) biddable, complaisant, compromising, docile, flexible, good-natured, obedient, pliant, tractable, yielding (*sense 2*) accidental, involuntary, uncalculated, unconscious, unintentional, unplanned, unwitting

will *n.* 1. choice, decision, determination, discretion, option, prerogative, volition 2. declaration, last wishes, testament 3. choice, decision, decree, desire, fancy, inclination, mind, pleasure, preference, wish 4. aim, determination, intention, purpose, resolution, resolve, willpower 5. attitude, disposition, feeling ∼*v.* 6. bid, bring about, cause, command, decree, determine, direct, effect, ordain, order, resolve 7. choose, desire, elect, opt, prefer, see fit, want, wish 8. bequeath, confer, give, leave, pass on, transfer

willing agreeable, amenable, compliant, consenting, content, desirous, disposed, eager, enthusiastic, favourable, game (*Inf.*), happy, inclined, in favour, in the mood, nothing loath, pleased, prepared, ready, so-minded

Antonyms averse, disinclined, grudging, loath, indisposed, not keen, reluctant, unenthusiastic, unwilling

willingly by choice, cheerfully, eagerly, freely, gladly, happily, of one's own accord, of one's own free will, readily, voluntarily, with all one's heart, without hesitation, with pleasure

Antonyms grudgingly, hesitantly, involuntarily, reluctantly, unwillingly

willingness agreeableness, agreement, consent, desire, disposition, enthusiasm, favour, good will, inclination, volition, will, wish

Antonyms aversion, disagreement, disinclination, hesitation, loathing, reluctance, unwillingness

willpower determination, drive, firmness of purpose *or* will, fixity of purpose, force *or* strength of will, grit, resolution, resolve, self-control, self-discipline, single-mindedness

Antonyms apathy, hesitancy, indecision, irresolution, languor, lethargy, shilly-shallying (*Inf.*), torpor, uncertainty, weakness

win *v.* 1. achieve first place, achieve mastery, be victorious, carry all before one, carry the day, come first, conquer, finish first, gain victory, overcome, prevail, succeed, take the prize, triumph 2. accomplish, achieve, acquire, attain, bag (*Inf.*), catch, collect, come away with, earn, gain, get, net, obtain, pick up, procure, receive, secure ∼*v.* 3. *Inf.* conquest, success, triumph, victory

Antonyms *v.* fail, fall, forfeit, lose, miss, suffer defeat, suffer loss ∼*n.* beating, defeat, downfall, failure, loss, washout (*Inf.*)

wind[1] 1. *n.* air, air-current, blast, breath, breeze, current of air, draught, gust, zephyr **2.** babble, blather, bluster, boasting, empty talk, gab (*Inf.*), hot air, humbug, idle talk, talk, verbalizing **3.** breath, puff, respiration **4. in the wind** about to happen, approaching, close at hand, coming, imminent, impending, in the offing, near, on the cards (*Inf.*), on the way

wind[2] *v.* **1.** coil, curl, encircle, furl, loop, reel, roll, spiral, turn around, twine, twist, wreathe **2.** bend, curve, deviate, meander, ramble, snake, turn, twist, zigzag ~*n.* **3.** bend, curve, meander, turn, twist, zigzag

windfall bonanza, find, godsend, jackpot, manna from heaven, stroke of luck

Antonyms bad luck, disaster, infelicity, misadventure, mischance, misfortune, mishap

winding 1. *n.* bend, convolution, curve, meander, turn, twist, undulation **2.** *adj.* anfractuous, bending, circuitous, convoluted, crooked, curving, flexuous, indirect, meandering, roundabout, serpentine, sinuous, spiral, tortuous, turning, twisting

Antonyms *adj.* direct, even, level, plumb, smooth, straight, undeviating, unswerving

wind up bring to a close, close, close down, conclude, end, finalize, finish, liquidate, settle, terminate, tie up the loose ends (*Inf.*), wrap up

Antonyms begin, commence, embark on, initiate, instigate, institute, open, start

windy blowy, blustering, blustery, boisterous, breezy, gusty, squally, stormy, tempestuous, wild, windswept

Antonyms becalmed, calm, motionless, smooth, still, windless

wing *n.* **1.** organ of flight, pennon (*Poetic*), pinion (*Poetic*) **2.** arm, branch, circle, clique, coterie, faction, group, grouping, section, segment, set, side **3.** adjunct, annexe, ell, extension ~*v.* **4.** fly, glide, soar **5.** fleet, fly, hasten,

hurry, race, speed, zoom **6.** clip, hit, nick, wound

wink *v.* **1.** bat, blink, flutter, nictate, nictitate **2.** flash, gleam, glimmer, sparkle, twinkle ~*n.* **3.** blink, flutter, nictation **4.** flash, gleam, glimmering, sparkle, twinkle **5.** instant, jiffy (*Inf.*), moment, second, split second, twinkling

winner champ (*Inf.*), champion, conquering hero, conqueror, first, master, vanquisher, victor

winning alluring, amiable, attractive, bewitching, captivating, charming, delectable, delightful, disarming, enchanting, endearing, engaging, fascinating, fetching, lovely, pleasing, prepossessing, sweet, taking, winsome

Antonyms disagreeable, irksome, offensive, repellent, tiresome, unappealing, unattractive, uninteresting, unpleasant

winnow comb, cull, divide, fan, part, screen, select, separate, separate the wheat from the chaff, sift, sort out

wintry 1. brumal, chilly, cold, freezing, frosty, frozen, harsh, hibernal, hiemal, icy, snowy **2.** bleak, cheerless, cold, desolate, dismal

Antonyms balmy, bright, mild, pleasant, summery, sunny, tepid, warm

wipe *v.* **1.** brush, clean, dry, dust, mop, rub, sponge, swab **2.** clean off, erase, get rid of, remove, rub off, take away, take off ~*n.* **3.** brush, lick, rub, swab

wipe out annihilate, blot out, destroy, efface, eradicate, erase, expunge, exterminate, extirpate, kill to the last man, massacre, obliterate

wisdom astuteness, circumspection, comprehension, discernment, enlightenment, erudition, foresight, insight, intelligence, judgment, judiciousness, knowledge, learning, penetration, prudence, reason, sagacity, sapience, sense, sound judgment, understanding

Antonyms absurdity, daftness, folly, foolishness, idiocy, injudiciousness, nonsense, senselessness, silliness, stupidity

wise aware, clever, discerning, enlightened, erudite, informed, intelligent, judicious, knowing, perceptive, politic, prudent, rational, reasonable, sagacious, sage, sapient, sensible, shrewd, sound, understanding, well-advised, well-informed

Antonyms daft, foolish, injudicious, rash, silly, stupid, unintelligent, unwise

wisecrack *n.* barb, funny (*Inf.*), gag (*Sl.*), jest, jibe, joke, pithy remark, quip, sardonic remark, smart remark, witticism

wish *v.* 1. aspire, covet, crave, desiderate, desire, hanker, hope, hunger, long, need, set one's heart on, sigh for, thirst, want, yearn 2. bid, greet with 3. ask, bid, command, desire, direct, instruct, order, require ~*n.* 4. aspiration, desire, hankering, hope, hunger, inclination, intention, liking, longing, thirst, urge, want, whim, will, yearning

Antonyms (*sense 4*) aversion, disinclination, dislike, distaste, loathing, reluctance, repulsion, revulsion

wistful contemplative, disconsolate, dreaming, dreamy, forlorn, longing, meditative, melancholy, mournful, musing, pensive, reflective, sad, thoughtful, yearning

wit 1. badinage, banter, drollery, facetiousness, fun, humour, jocularity, levity, pleasantry, raillery, repartee, wordplay 2. card (*Inf.*), comedian, epigrammatist, *farceur*, humorist, joker, punster, wag 3. acumen, brains, cleverness, common sense, comprehension, discernment, ingenuity, insight, intellect, judgment, mind, nous (*Brit. sl.*), perception, practical intelligence, reason, sense, understanding, wisdom

Antonyms dullness, folly, foolishness, gravity, humourlessness, ignorance, lack of perception,

obtuseness, seriousness, silliness, sobriety, solemnity, stupidity

witch enchantress, magician, necromancer, occultist, sorceress

witchcraft enchantment, incantation, magic, necromancy, occultism, sorcery, sortilege, spell, the black art, the occult, voodoo, witchery, witching, wizardry

withdraw 1. draw back, draw out, extract, pull out, remove, take away, take off 2. abjure, disavow, disclaim, recall, recant, rescind, retract, revoke, take back, unsay 3. absent oneself, back out, depart, detach oneself, disengage, drop out, fall back, go, leave, make oneself scarce (*Inf.*), pull back, pull out, retire, retreat, secede

Antonyms (*senses 1 & 3*) advance, forge ahead, go on, move forward, persist, press on, proceed, progress

withdrawal 1. extraction, removal 2. abjuration, disavowal, disclaimer, recall, recantation, repudiation, rescission, retraction, revocation 3. departure, disengagement, exit, exodus, retirement, retreat, secession

withdrawn aloof, detached, distant, introverted, quiet, reserved, retiring, shrinking, shy, silent, taciturn, timorous, uncommunicative, unforthcoming

Antonyms boisterous, bustling, busy, extrovert, forward, friendly, gregarious, open, outgoing, sociable

wither 1. blast, blight, decay, decline, desiccate, disintegrate, droop, dry, fade, languish, perish, shrink, shrivel, wane, waste, wilt 2. abash, blast, humiliate, mortify, put down (*Sl.*), shame, snub

Antonyms (*sense 1*) bloom, blossom, develop, flourish, increase, prosper, succeed, thrive, wax

withering 1. blasting, blighting, devastating, humiliating, hurtful, mortifying, scornful, snubbing 2. deadly, death-dealing, destruc~

tive, devastating, killing, murderous, slaughterous

withhold check, conceal, deduct, hide, hold back, keep, keep back, keep secret, refuse, repress, reserve, resist, restrain, retain, sit on (*Inf.*), suppress

Antonyms accord, expose, give, grant, hand over, let go, release, relinquish, reveal

witness n. 1. beholder, bystander, eyewitness, looker-on, observer, onlooker, spectator, viewer, watcher 2. attestant, corroborator, deponent, testifier 3. bear witness a. depone, depose, give evidence, give testimony, testify b. attest to, bear out, be evidence of, be proof of, betoken, confirm, constitute proof of, corroborate, demonstrate, evince, prove, show, testify to, vouch for ~v. 4. attend, be present at, look on, mark, note, notice, observe, perceive, see, view, watch 5. attest, authenticate, bear out, bear witness, confirm, corroborate, depone, depose, give evidence, give testimony, testify

wits acumen, astuteness, brains (*Inf.*), cleverness, comprehension, faculties, ingenuity, intelligence, judgment, nous (*Brit. sl.*), reason, sense, understanding

witty amusing, brilliant, clever, droll, epigrammatic, facetious, fanciful, funny, gay, humorous, ingenious, jocular, lively, original, piquant, sparkling, waggish, whimsical

Antonyms boring, dull, humourless, stupid, tedious, tiresome, unamusing, uninteresting, witless

wizard 1. conjurer, enchanter, mage (*Archaic*), magician, magus, necromancer, occultist, shaman, sorcerer, thaumaturge (*Rare*), warlock, witch 2. ace (*Inf.*), adept, expert, genius, hotshot (*Inf.*), maestro, master, prodigy, star, virtuoso, whiz (*Inf.*), whizz-kid (*Inf.*), wiz (*Inf.*)

wizened dried up, gnarled, lined, sere (*Archaic*), shrivelled,

shrunken, withered, worn, wrinkled

Antonyms bloated, plump, rounded, smooth, swollen, turgid

woe adversity, affliction, agony, anguish, burden, curse, dejection, depression, disaster, distress, gloom, grief, hardship, heartache, heartbreak, melancholy, misery, misfortune, pain, sadness, sorrow, suffering, trial, tribulation, trouble, unhappiness, wretchedness

Antonyms bliss, elation, felicity, fortune, happiness, joy, jubilation, pleasure, prosperity, rapture

woman 1. bird (*Sl.*), chick (*Sl.*), dame (*Sl.*), female, girl, lady, lass, lassie, maid (*Archaic*), maiden (*Archaic*), miss, she 2. chambermaid, char (*Inf.*), charwoman, domestic, female servant, handmaiden, housekeeper, lady-in-waiting, maid, maidservant

Antonyms (*sense 1*) bloke (*Brit. inf.*), boy, chap (*Inf.*), gentleman, guy (*Inf.*), lad, laddie, male, man

wonder n. 1. admiration, amazement, astonishment, awe, bewilderment, curiosity, fascination, stupefaction, surprise, wonderment 2. curiosity, marvel, miracle, nonpareil, phenomenon, portent, prodigy, rarity, sight, spectacle, wonderment ~v. 3. ask oneself, be curious, be inquisitive, conjecture, cudgel one's brains (*Inf.*), doubt, inquire, meditate, ponder, puzzle, query, question, speculate, think 4. be amazed (astonished, awed, dumbstruck), be flabbergasted (*Inf.*), boggle, gape, gawk, marvel, stand amazed, stare

wonderful 1. amazing, astonishing, astounding, awe-inspiring, awesome, extraordinary, fantastic, incredible, marvellous, miraculous, odd, peculiar, phenomenal, remarkable, staggering, startling, strange, surprising, unheard-of, wondrous 2. ace (*Inf.*), admirable, brilliant, excellent, fabulous (*Inf.*), fantastic (*Inf.*), great (*Inf.*), magnificent, marvellous, outstanding, sensational, smashing (*Inf.*), stupendous, super (*Inf.*), superb, terrific, tiptop, tremendous

Antonyms abominable, appalling, average, awful, bad, common, commonplace, depressing, dire, dreadful, frightful, grim, indifferent, lousy, mediocre, miserable, modest, ordinary, paltry, rotten, run-of-the-mill, terrible, uninteresting, unpleasant, unremarkable, usual, vile

woo chase, court, cultivate, importune, pay court to, pay one's addresses to, pay suit to, press one's suit with, pursue, seek after, seek the hand of, seek to win, solicit the good will of, spark (*Rare*)

wooden 1. ligneous, made of wood, of wood, timber, woody 2. awkward, clumsy, gauche, gawky, graceless, inelegant, maladroit, rigid, stiff, ungainly 3. blank, colourless, deadpan, dull, emotionless, empty, expressionless, glassy, lifeless, spiritless, unemotional, unresponsive, vacant 4. dense, dim, dim-witted (*Inf.*), dull, dull-witted, obtuse, slow, stupid, thick, witless, woodenheaded (*Inf.*) 5. dull, muffled

Antonyms (*sense 2*) agile, comely, elegant, flexible, flowing, graceful, lissom, nimble, supple

wool fleece, hair, yarn

woolly adj. 1. fleecy, flocculent, hairy, made of wool, shaggy, woollen 2. blurred, clouded, confused, foggy, hazy, ill-defined, indefinite, indistinct, muddled, nebulous, unclear, vague

Antonyms (*sense 2*) clear, clear-cut, definite, distinct, exact, obvious, precise, sharp, well-defined

word n. 1. brief conversation, chat, chitchat, colloquy, confab (*Inf.*), confabulation, consultation, discussion, talk, tête-à-tête 2. brief statement, comment, declaration, expression, remark, ut-

terance 3. expression, locution, name, term, vocable 4. account, advice, bulletin, communication, communiqué, dispatch, gen (*Brit. inf.*), information, intelligence, intimation, message, news, notice, report, tidings 5. command, go-ahead (*Inf.*), green light, order, signal 6. affirmation, assertion, assurance, guarantee, oath, parole, pledge, promise, solemn oath, solemn word, undertaking, vow, word of honour 7. bidding, command, commandment, decree, edict, mandate, order, ukase (*Rare*), will 8. countersign, password, slogan, watchword ~v. 9. couch, express, phrase, put, say, state, utter

words 1. lyrics, text 2. altercation, angry exchange, angry speech, argument, barney (*Inf.*), bickering, disagreement, dispute, falling-out (*Inf.*), quarrel, row, run-in (*Inf.*), set-to (*Inf.*), squabble

wordy diffuse, discursive, garrulous, long-winded, loquacious, pleonastic, prolix, rambling, verbose, windy

Antonyms brief, concise, laconic, pithy, short, succinct, terse, to the point

work n. 1. drudgery, effort, elbow grease (*Inf.*), exertion, grind (*Inf.*), industry, labour, slog, sweat, toil, travail (*Literary*) 2. business, calling, craft, duty, employment, job, line, livelihood, métier, occupation, office, profession, pursuit, trade 3. assignment, chore, commission, duty, job, stint, task, undertaking 4. achievement, composition, creation, handiwork, *oeuvre*, opus, performance, piece, production 5. art, craft, skill, workmanship 6. out of work idle, jobless, on the dole (*Brit. inf.*), on the street, out of a job, unemployed ~v. 7. drudge, exert oneself, labour, peg away, slave, slog (away), sweat, toil 8. be employed, be in work, do business, earn a living, have a job 9. act, control, direct, drive, handle, manage, manipulate, move, operate, ply, use, wield **10.** function, go, operate, perform, run **11.** cultivate, dig, farm, till **12.** *Often with* **up** arouse, excite, move, prompt, provoke, rouse, stir

Antonyms *n.* (*sense 1*) ease, leisure, relaxation, rest (*sense 2*) entertainment, hobby, holiday, play, recreation, retirement, spare time, unemployment (*sense 3*) child's play ~ *v.* (*sense 7*) have fun, mark time, play, relax, skive, take it easy (*sense 10*) be broken, be out of order

worker artisan, craftsman, employee, hand, labourer, proletarian, tradesman, wage earner, working man, working woman, workman

working *n.* **1.** action, functioning, manner, method, mode of operation, operation, running **2.** *Plural* diggings, excavations, mine, pit, quarry, shaft ~ *adj.* **3.** active, employed, in a job, in work, labouring **4.** functioning, going, operative, running **5.** effective, practical, useful, viable

workman artificer, artisan, craftsman, employee, hand, journeyman, labourer, mechanic, operative, tradesman, worker

work out 1. accomplish, achieve, attain, win **2.** calculate, clear up, figure out, find out, puzzle out, resolve, solve **3.** arrange, construct, contrive, develop, devise, elaborate, evolve, form, formulate, plan, put together **4.** be effective, flourish, go as planned, go well, prosper, prove satisfactory, succeed **5.** add up to, amount to, come to, reach, reach a total of

works 1. factory, mill, plant, shop, workshop **2.** canon, *oeuvre*, output, productions, writings **3.** actions, acts, deeds, doings **4.** action, guts (*Sl.*), innards (*Inf.*), insides (*Inf.*), machinery, mechanism, movement, moving parts, parts, workings

workshop atelier, factory, mill, plant, shop, studio, workroom, works

work up agitate, animate, arouse, enkindle, excite, foment, generate, get (someone) all steamed up (*Sl.*), incite, inflame, instigate, move, rouse, spur, stir up, wind up (*Inf.*)

world 1. earth, earthly sphere, globe **2.** everybody, everyone, humanity, humankind, human race, man, mankind, men, the public, the race of man **3.** cosmos, creation, existence, life, nature, universe **4.** heavenly body, planet, star **5.** area, domain, environment, field, kingdom, province, realm, sphere, system **6.** age, days, epoch, era, period, times **7. on top of the world** *Inf.* beside oneself with joy, ecstatic, elated, exultant, happy, in raptures, on cloud nine (*Inf.*), overjoyed, over the moon (*Inf.*) **8. out of this world** *Inf.* excellent, fabulous (*Inf.*), fantastic (*Inf.*), great (*Inf.*), incredible, indescribable, marvellous, superb, unbelievable, wonderful

worldly 1. carnal, earthly, fleshly, lay, mundane, physical, profane, secular, sublunary, temporal, terrestrial **2.** avaricious, covetous, grasping, greedy, materialistic, selfish, worldly-minded **3.** blasé, cosmopolitan, experienced, knowing, politic, sophisticated, urbane, well versed in the ways of the world, worldly-wise **Antonyms** (*sense 1*) divine, ethereal, heavenly, immaterial, noncorporeal, spiritual, transcendental, unworldly (*sense 2*) moral, nonmaterialistic, unworldly (*sense 3*) ingenuous, innocent, naive, unsophisticated, unworldly

worldwide general, global, international, omnipresent, pandemic, ubiquitous, universal **Antonyms** confined, insular, limited, local, narrow, national, parochial, provincial, restricted

worn 1. frayed, ragged, shabby, shiny, tattered, tatty, the worse

for wear, threadbare 2. care~
worn, drawn, haggard, lined,
pinched, wizened 3. exhausted,
fatigued, jaded, played-out (*Inf.*),
spent, tired, tired out, wearied,
weary, worn-out

worried afraid, anxious, appre~
hensive, bothered, concerned,
distracted, distraught, distressed,
disturbed, fearful, fretful, fright~
ened, ill at ease, nervous, on
edge, overwrought, perturbed,
tense, tormented, troubled, un~
easy, unquiet, upset
Antonyms calm, fearless, peace~
ful, quiet, tranquil, unafraid, un~
concerned, unworried

worry 1. *v.* agonize, annoy, badg~
er, be anxious, bother, brood,
disquiet, distress, disturb, feel
uneasy, fret, harass, harry, hassle
(*Inf.*), hector, importune, irritate,
make anxious, perturb, pester,
plague, tantalize, tease, torment,
trouble, unsettle, upset, vex 2. *n.*
annoyance, care, irritation, pest,
plague, problem, torment, trial,
trouble, vexation
Antonyms *v.* be apathetic, be
unconcerned, be unperturbed,
calm, comfort, console, solace,
soothe ~*n.* calm, comfort, con~
solation, peace of mind, reassur~
ance, serenity, solace, tranquil~
lity

worsen aggravate, damage, de~
cay, decline, degenerate, de~
teriorate, exacerbate, get worse,
go downhill (*Inf.*), go from bad to
worse, retrogress, sink, take a
turn for the worse
Antonyms ameliorate, better,
enhance, improve, mend, reco~
ver, rectify, upgrade

worship 1. *v.* adore, adulate, dei~
fy, exalt, glorify, honour, idolize,
laud, love, praise, pray to, put on
a pedestal, respect, revere, rever~
erence, venerate 2. *n.* adoration,
adulation, deification, devotion,
exaltation, glorification, glory,
homage, honour, laudation, love,
praise, prayer(s), regard, re~
spect, reverence
Antonyms *v.* blaspheme, deride,

despise, disdain, dishonour, flout,
mock, revile, ridicule, scoff at,
spurn

worst *v.* beat, best, conquer,
crush, defeat, gain the advantage
over, get the better of, master,
overcome, overpower, over~
throw, subdue, subjugate, van~
quish

worth 1. aid, assistance, avail,
benefit, credit, desert(s), estima~
tion, excellence, goodness, help,
importance, merit, quality, use~
fulness, utility, value, virtue,
worthiness 2. cost, price, rate,
valuation, value
Antonyms (*sense 1*) futility, in~
significance, paltriness, triviality,
unworthiness, uselessness,
worthlessness, wretchedness

worthless 1. futile, ineffectual,
insignificant, inutile, meaning~
less, miserable, no use, nugatory,
paltry, pointless, poor, rubbishy,
trashy, trifling, trivial, unavail~
ing, unimportant, unusable, use~
less, valueless, wretched 2. aban~
doned, abject, base, contempt~
ible, depraved, despicable, good-
for-nothing, ignoble, useless, vile
Antonyms consequential, decent,
effective, fruitful, honourable,
important, noble, precious, pro~
ductive, profitable, significant,
upright, useful, valuable, worth~
while, worthy

worthwhile beneficial, construc~
tive, gainful, good, helpful, justi~
fiable, productive, profitable,
useful, valuable, worthy
Antonyms inconsequential,
pointless, trivial, unimportant,
unworthy, useless, vain, value~
less, wasteful, worthless

worthy 1. *adj.* admirable, com~
mendable, creditable, decent,
dependable, deserving, esti~
mable, excellent, good, honest,
honourable, laudable, merito~
rious, praiseworthy, reliable,
reputable, respectable, righteous,
upright, valuable, virtuous,
worthwhile 2. *n.* big shot (*Sl.*),
bigwig (*Sl.*), dignitary, luminary,
notable, personage

Antonyms *adj.* demeaning, disreputable, dubious, ignoble, undeserving, unproductive, untrustworthy, unworthy, useless ~*n.* member of the rank and file, nobody, pleb, punter

wound *n.* **1.** cut, damage, gash, harm, hurt, injury, laceration, lesion, slash **2.** anguish, distress, grief, heartbreak, injury, insult, offence, pain, pang, sense of loss, shock, slight, torment, torture, trauma ~*v.* **3.** cut, damage, gash, harm, hit, hurt, injure, irritate, lacerate, pierce, slash, wing **4.** annoy, cut (someone) to the quick, distress, grieve, hurt, hurt the feelings of, mortify, offend, pain, shock, sting, traumatize

wrangle 1. *v.* altercate, argue, bicker, brawl, contend, disagree, dispute, fall out (*Inf.*), fight, have words, quarrel, row, scrap, squabble **2.** *n.* altercation, angry exchange, argy-bargy (*Brit. inf.*), barney (*Inf.*), bickering, brawl, clash, contest, controversy, dispute, falling-out (*Inf.*), quarrel, row, set-to (*Inf.*), slanging match (*Brit.*), squabble, tiff

wrap *v.* absorb, bind, bundle up, cloak, cover, encase, enclose, enfold, envelop, fold, immerse, muffle, pack, package, roll up, sheathe, shroud, surround, swathe, wind

Antonyms *v.* disclose, open, strip, uncover, unfold, unpack, unwind, unwrap

wrapper case, cover, envelope, jacket, packaging, paper, sheath, sleeve, wrapping

wrath anger, choler, displeasure, exasperation, fury, indignation, ire, irritation, passion, rage, resentment, temper

Antonyms amusement, contentment, delight, enjoyment, gladness, gratification, happiness, joy, pleasure, satisfaction

wreath band, chaplet, coronet, crown, festoon, garland, loop, ring

wreathe adorn, coil, crown, encircle, enfold, entwine, envelop, enwrap, festoon, intertwine, interweave, surround, twine, twist, wind, wrap, writhe

wreck *v.* **1.** break, dash to pieces, demolish, destroy, devastate, mar, play havoc with, ravage, ruin, shatter, smash, spoil **2.** founder, go *or* run aground, run onto the rocks, shipwreck, strand ~*n.* **3.** derelict, hulk, shipwreck, sunken vessel

Antonyms *v.* build, conserve, create, fulfil, make possible, preserve, reconstruct, save, salvage

wreckage debris, fragments, hulk, pieces, remains, rubble, ruin, wrack

wrench *v.* **1.** force, jerk, pull, rip, tear, tug, twist, wrest, wring, yank **2.** distort, rick, sprain, strain ~*n.* **3.** jerk, pull, rip, tug, twist, yank **4.** sprain, strain, twist **5.** ache, blow, pain, pang, shock, upheaval, uprooting

wrestle battle, combat, contend, fight, grapple, scuffle, strive, struggle, tussle

wretch 1. blackguard, cur, good-for-nothing, miscreant, outcast, profligate, rascal, rat (*Inf.*), rogue, rotter (*Sl.*), ruffian, scoundrel, swine, vagabond, villain, worm **2.** poor thing, unfortunate

wretched 1. abject, broken-hearted, cheerless, comfortless, crestfallen, dejected, deplorable, depressed, disconsolate, distressed, doleful, downcast, forlorn, gloomy, hapless, hopeless, melancholy, miserable, pathetic, pitiable, pitiful, poor, sorry, unfortunate, unhappy, woebegone, woeful, worthless **2.** calamitous, deplorable, inferior, miserable, paltry, pathetic, poor, sorry, worthless

Antonyms admirable, carefree, cheerful, contented, decent, enviable, excellent, flourishing, fortunate, great, happy, jovial, light-hearted, noble, prosperous, splendid, successful, thriving, untroubled, wonderful, worthy

wriggle *v.* **1.** jerk, jiggle, squirm, turn, twist, wag, waggle, wiggle, writhe **2.** crawl, slink, snake, twist and turn, worm, zigzag **3.** crawl, dodge, extricate oneself, manoeuvre, sneak, talk one's way out, worm ~*n.* **4.** jerk, jiggle, squirm, turn, twist, wag, waggle, wiggle

wring 1. coerce, extort, extract, force, screw, squeeze, twist, wrench, wrest **2.** distress, hurt, lacerate, pain, pierce, rack, rend, stab, tear at, wound

wrinkle 1. *n.* corrugation, crease, crinkle, crow's-foot, crumple, fold, furrow, gather, line, pucker, rumple **2.** *v.* corrugate, crease, crinkle, crumple, fold, furrow, gather, line, pucker, ruck, rumple

Antonyms *v.* even out, flatten, iron, level, press, smooth, straighten, unfold

writ court order, decree, document, summons

write author (*Nonstandard*), commit to paper, compose, copy, correspond, create, draft, draw up, indite, inscribe, jot down, pen, put down in black and white, put in writing, record, scribble, set down, take down, tell, transcribe

write off 1. cancel, cross out, disregard, forget about, give up for lost, score out, shelve **2.** *Inf.* crash, damage beyond repair, destroy, smash up, total (*U.S. sl.*), wreck

writer author, columnist, essayist, hack, littérateur, man of letters, novelist, penman, penny-a-liner (*Rare*), penpusher, scribbler, scribe, wordsmith

writhe contort, distort, jerk, squirm, struggle, thrash, thresh, toss, twist, wiggle, wriggle

writing 1. calligraphy, chirography, hand, handwriting, penmanship, print, scrawl, scribble, script **2.** book, composition, document, letter, opus, publication, work

wrong *adj.* **1.** erroneous, fallacious, false, faulty, inaccurate, incorrect, in error, mistaken, off beam (*Inf.*), off target, out, un-

sound, untrue, wide of the mark **2.** bad, blameworthy, criminal, crooked, dishonest, dishonourable, evil, felonious, illegal, illicit, immoral, iniquitous, reprehensible, sinful, unethical, unfair, unjust, unlawful, wicked, wrongful **3.** funny, improper, inappropriate, inapt, incongruous, incorrect, indecorous, infelicitous, malapropos, not done, unacceptable, unbecoming, unconventional, undesirable, unfitting, unhappy, unseemly, unsuitable **4.** amiss, askew, awry, defective, faulty, not working, out of commission, out of order **5.** inside, inverse, opposite, reverse ~*adv.* **6.** amiss, askew, astray, awry, badly, erroneously, inaccurately, incorrectly, mistakenly, wrongly **7. go wrong a.** come to grief (*Inf.*), come to nothing, fail, fall through, flop (*Inf.*), miscarry, misfire **b.** boob (*Brit. sl.*), err, go astray, make a mistake, slip up (*Inf.*) **c.** break down, cease to function, conk out (*Inf.*), fail, go kaput (*Inf.*), go on the blink (*Sl.*), go phut (*Inf.*), malfunction, misfire **d.** err, fall from grace, go astray, go off the straight and narrow (*Inf.*), go to the bad, lapse, sin ~*n.* **8.** abuse, bad or evil deed, crime, error, grievance, immorality, inequity, infraction, infringement, iniquity, injury, injustice, misdeed, offence, sin, sinfulness, transgression, trespass, unfairness, wickedness ~*v.* **9.** abuse, cheat, discredit, dishonour, harm, hurt, illtreat, ill-use, impose upon, injure, malign, maltreat, misrepresent, mistreat, oppress, take advantage of

Antonyms *adj.* accurate, appropriate, apt, becoming, commendable, correct, ethical, fair, fitting, godly, honest, honourable, just, laudable, lawful, legal, moral, praiseworthy, precise, proper, righteous, rightful, seemly, sensible, square, suitable, true, upright, virtuous ~*adv.* accurately, correctly, exactly, precisely, properly, squarely, truly ~*n*. decency, fairness, favour, good, good deed, goodness, good turn, high-mindedness, honesty, lawfulness, legality, morality, propriety, virtue ~*v*. aid, do a favour, help, support, treat well

wrongdoer criminal, culprit, delinquent, evildoer, lawbreaker, malefactor, miscreant, offender, sinner, transgressor, trespasser (*Archaic*)

wrongful blameworthy, criminal, dishonest, dishonourable, evil, felonious, illegal, illegitimate, illicit, immoral, improper, reprehensible, unethical, unfair, unjust, unlawful, wicked

Antonyms ethical, fair, honest, honourable, just, lawful, legal, legitimate, moral, proper, rightful

wry 1. askew, aslant, awry, contorted, crooked, deformed, distorted, off the level, twisted, uneven, warped **2.** droll, dry, ironic, mocking, pawky (*Scot.*), sarcastic, sardonic

Antonyms (*sense 1*) aligned, even, level, smooth, straight, unbent

XYZ

X-rays Röntgen rays (*Old name*)

yardstick benchmark, criterion, gauge, measure, standard, touchstone

yarn *n.* 1. fibre, thread 2. *Inf.* anecdote, cock-and-bull story (*Inf.*), fable, story, tale, tall story

yawning cavernous, chasmal, gaping, vast, wide, wide-open

yearly annual, annually, every year, once a year, per annum

yearn ache, covet, crave, desire, hanker, have a yen for (*Inf.*), hunger, itch, languish, long, lust, pant, pine, set one's heart upon

yell 1. *v.* bawl, holler (*Inf.*), howl, scream, screech, shout, shriek, squeal 2. *n.* cry, howl, scream, screech, shriek, whoop

Antonyms *v.* mumble, murmur, mutter, say softly, whisper

yes man bootlicker (*Inf.*), bosses' lackey, company man, crawler (*Sl.*), creature, minion, sycophant, timeserver, toady

yet 1. as yet, so far, thus far, until now, up to now 2. however, nevertheless, notwithstanding, still 3. additionally, as well, besides, further, in addition, into the bargain, moreover, over and above, still, to boot 4. already, just now, now, right now, so soon

yield *v.* 1. afford, bear, bring forth, bring in, earn, furnish, generate, give, net, pay, produce, provide, return, supply ~*n.* 2. crop, earnings, harvest, income, output, produce, profit, return, revenue, takings ~*v.* 3. abandon, abdicate, admit defeat, bow, capitulate, cave in (*Inf.*), cede, cry quits, give in, give up the struggle, give way, knuckle under, lay down one's arms, part with, raise the white flag, relinquish, resign, resign oneself, submit, succumb,

surrender, throw in the towel 4. accede, agree, allow, bow, comply, concede, consent, go along with, grant, permit

Antonyms *v.* appropriate, attack, combat, commandeer, consume, counterattack, defy, grab, hold on to, hold out, keep, lose, maintain, oppose, reserve, resist, retain, seize, struggle, use, use up ~*n.* consumption, input, loss

yielding 1. accommodating, acquiescent, biddable, compliant, docile, easy, flexible, obedient, pliant, submissive, tractable 2. elastic, pliable, quaggy, resilient, soft, spongy, springy, supple, unresisting

Antonyms (*sense 1*) dogged, headstrong, mulish, obstinate, opinionated, perverse, stubborn, tenacious, wilful

yoke *n.* 1. bond, chain, coupling, ligament, link, tie 2. bondage, burden, enslavement, helotry, oppression, serfdom, service, servility, servitude, slavery, thraldom, vassalage ~*v.* 3. bracket, connect, couple, harness, hitch, join, link, tie, unite

yokel boor, bucolic, clodhopper (*Inf.*), (country) bumpkin, countrycousin, countryman, hick (*Inf., chiefly U.S.*), hillbilly, hind (*Obsolete*), peasant (*Inf.*), rustic

young *adj.* 1. adolescent, callow, green, growing, immature, infant, in the springtime of life, junior, juvenile, little, unfledged, youthful 2. at an early stage, early, fledgling, new, newish, not far advanced, recent, undeveloped

Antonyms *adj.* adult, advanced, aged, developed, elderly, experienced, full-grown, grown-up, mature, old, ripe, senior, venerable

youngster boy, cub, girl, juvenile,

kid (*Inf.*), lad, lass, pup (*Inf.*), teenager, teenybopper (*Sl.*), urchin, young adult, young hopeful, young person, young shaver (*Inf.*), young 'un (*Inf.*), youth

youth 1. adolescence, boyhood, early life, girlhood, immaturity, juvenescence, salad days, young days 2. adolescent, boy, kid (*Inf.*), lad, shaveling (*Archaic*), stripling, teenager, young man, young shaver (*Inf.*), youngster
Antonyms adult, adulthood, age, grown-up, later life, manhood, maturity, OAP, old age, pensioner, senior citizen, the aged, the elderly, the old, womanhood

youthful 1. boyish, childish, girlish, immature, inexperienced, juvenile, pubescent, puerile, young 2. active, fresh, spry, vigorous, young at heart, young looking
Antonyms adult, aged, ageing, ancient, careworn, decaying, decrepit, elderly, grown-up, hoary, old, over the hill, mature, senile, senior, tired, waning, weary

zeal ardour, devotion, eagerness, earnestness, enthusiasm, fanaticism, fervency, fervour, fire, gusto, keenness, militancy, passion, spirit, verve, warmth, zest
Antonyms apathy, coolness, indifference, passivity, stoicism, torpor, unresponsiveness

zealous afire, ardent, burning, devoted, eager, earnest, enthusiastic, fanatical, fervent, fervid, impassioned, keen, militant, passionate, rabid, spirited
Antonyms apathetic, cold, cool, half-hearted, indifferent, lackadaisical, lacklustre, languorous, listless, low-key, sceptical, torpid, unenthusiastic, unimpassioned

zero cipher, naught, nil, nothing, nought

zest 1. appetite, delectation, enjoyment, gusto, keenness, relish, zeal, zing (*Inf.*) 2. charm, flavour, interest, kick (*Inf.*), piquancy, pungency, relish, savour, smack, spice, tang, taste
Antonyms abhorrence, apathy, aversion, disinclination, distaste, indifference, lack of enthusiasm, loathing, repugnance, weariness

zone area, belt, district, region, section, sector, sphere

CLASSICAL AND FOREIGN WORDS AND PHRASES

Abbreviations - L. Latin; G. Greek; F. French; It. Italian; Ger. German.

à bas [F.] down with.

ab initio [L.] from the beginning.

ab ovo [L.] from the beginning.

absit omen [L.] may there be no ill omen.

accouchement [F.] childbirth, confinement.

à cheval [F.] on horseback, astride.

à deux [F.] of, for two persons.

ad hoc [L.] for this special object.

ad hominem [L.] to the man.

ad infinitum [L.] to infinity.

ad interim [L.] in the meanwhile.

ad majorem Dei gloriam [L.] for the greater glory of God.

ad nauseam [L.] to the point of disgust.

ad referendum [L.] for consideration.

ad rem [L.] to the point.

adsum [L.] I am here; present!

ad valorem [L.] according to value.

affaire d'amour [F.] a love affair.

affaire d'honneur [F.] an affair of honour, a duel.

affaire du coeur [F.] an affair of the heart.

a fortiori [L.] with stronger reason.

agent provocateur [F.] a police or secret service spy.

aide mémoire [F.] memorandum; summary.

à la carte [F.] picking from the bill of fare; *see* **table d'hote**.

à la française [F.] in the French style.

à la mode [F.] in the fashion.

al dente [It.] cooked so as to be firm when eaten.

al fresco [It.] in the open air.

alma mater [L.] benign mother; the term is used by former students in referring to their university.

alter ego [L.] another self, a close friend.

alto relievo [It.] high relief.

amende honorable [F.] apology.

amor patriae [L.] love of country.

amour propre [F.] self-esteem.

ancien régime [F.] the old order.

anglice [L.] in English.

anno Domini [L.] in the year of our Lord.

anno regni [L.] in the year of the reign.

anno urbis conditae [L.] (**A.U.C.**) in the year from the time of the building of the City (Rome).

annus mirabilis [L.] year of wonder.

ante meridiem [L.] before noon.

aperçu [F.] summary; insight.

à propos [F.] to the point.

arrière-pensée [F.] mental reservation.

arrivederci [It.] goodbye.

au contraire [F.] on the contrary.

609

CLASSICAL AND FOREIGN WORDS AND PHRASES

au courant [F.] fully acquainted (with).

au fait [F.] fully informed; expert.

au fond [F.] fundamentally; essentially.

au naturel [F.] naked; uncooked or plainly cooked.

au revoir [F.] good-bye, till we meet again.

auf wiedersehen [Ger.] good-bye, till we meet again.

auto da fé [Portuguese] act of faith, the public burning of heretics.

beau geste [F.] noble or gracious act.

beau idéal [F.] ideal excellence, imagined state of perfection.

beau monde [F.] fashionable world.

bel esprit [F.] a man of wit.

bête noire [F.] an object of special detestation, pet aversion.

billet doux [F.] a love-letter.

blitzkrieg [Ger.] lightning war.

bona fide [L.] in good faith.

bonhomie [F.] good nature.

bonjour [F.] good-morning, good-day.

bon marché [F.] cheaply.

bonne bouche [F.] titbit.

bonsoir [F.] good-evening, good-night.

bon ton [F.] good breeding.

carpe diem [L.] enjoy the present day.

carte blanche [F.] full powers.

casus belli [L.] something which involves war.

cause célèbre [F.] famous lawsuit or controversy.

ça va sans dire [F.] that is a matter of course.

caveat emptor [L.] let the buyer beware.

cave canem [L.] beware of the dog.

c'est la vie [F.] that's life.

chacun à son gout [F.] every one to his taste.

ceteris paribus [L.] other things being equal.

chef-d'oeuvre [F.] masterpiece.

cherchez la femme [F.] look for the woman; there is a woman at the bottom of the business.

che sarà, sarà [It.] what will be, will be.

ciao [It.] hello, goodbye.

ci-devant [F.] former.

cogito, ergo sum [L.] I think, therefore I am.

comme il faut [F.] as it should be .

compos mentis [L.] sane.

compte rendu [F.] a report.

con amore [It.] with love, earnestly.

concierge [F.] a porter or doorkeeper.

coram populo [L.] in the presence of the people, openly.

corpus delicti [L.] the substance of the offence; the body of the victim of murder.

corrigenda [L.] things to be corrected.

coup d'état [F.] a stroke of policy, a sudden decisive political move, an abuse of authority.

coup de foudre [F.] sudden amazing event.

coup de grâce [F.] a finishing blow.

coup de théâtre [F.] a theatrical effect, a sudden change in a situation.

cui bono? [L.] for whose benefit is it? (i.e. the crime - in a law-case).

cum grano salis [L.] with a grain of salt, with reservation.

de facto [L.] actually, in fact.

Dei gratia [L.] by the grace of God.

de jure [L.] in law, by right.

de mortuis nil nisi bonum [L.] say nothing but good about the dead.

de novo [L.] anew.

Deo gratias [L.] thanks to God.

Deo volente [L.] (**D.V.**) God willing.

de profundis [L.] out of the depths. (The first words of the Latin version of Psalm 130.)

de rigueur [F.] indispensable, obligatory.

dernier cri [F.] latest fashion.

de trop [F.] superfluous, intrusive.

deus ex machina [L.] literally, a god out of the (theatrical) machine, i.e. a too obvious device in the plot of a play or story.

dies non [L.] a day on which judges do not sit.

Dieu et mon droit [F.] God and my right; motto of the British crown.

disjecta membra [L.] the scattered remains.

distingué [F.] of distinguished appearance.

distrait [F.] absent-minded.

dolce far niente [It.] pleasant idleness.

double entendre [F.] double meaning.

douceur [F.] a tip, a bribe.

dramatis personae [L.] the characters in a drama.

ecce homo! [L.] behold the man! (Spoken by Pilate; St. John, c.19, v.5.)

embarras de richesses [F.] perplexing wealth.

emeritus [L.] retired from office.

éminence grise [F.] person who wields power unofficially or behind the scenes.

en famille [F.] with one's family; at home; informally.

enfant terrible [F.] literally, "a terrible child."

en fête [F.] on holiday, in a state of festivity.

en masse [F.] in a body.

en passant [F.] in passing, by the way.

en rapport [F.] in sympathy with.

en règle [F.] in due order.

en route [F.] on the way; march!

entente cordiale [F.] friendly understanding between two nations.

entre nous [F.] between ourselves.

e pluribus unum [L.] one out of many. (Motto of the U.S.A.)

erratum (*pl.* **errata**) [L.] error.

esprit de corps [F.] team-spirit.

CLASSICAL AND FOREIGN WORDS AND PHRASES

eureka! (heureka) [G.] I have found it! (The exclamation of Archimedes.)

ex cathedra [L.] from the chair of office, hence, authoritatively.

exeat [L.] literally, "let him go out"; formal leave of absence.

exempli gratia [L.] (**e.g.**) for example.

exeunt omnes [L.] all go out.

exit [L.] goes out.

ex libris [L.] from the books ... (followed by the name of the owner).

ex officio [L.] by virtue of his office.

ex parte [L.] on one side, partisan.

facile princeps [L.] an easy first.

fait accompli [F.] a thing done.

faute de mieux [F.] for lack of anything better.

faux pas [F.] a false step, a mistake.

felo de se [L.] a suicide, literally, a "felon of himself."

femme fatale [F.] seductive woman.

festina lente [L.] hasten slowly.

fête champêtre [F.] a rural festival.

feu de joie [F.] a bonfire; gun salute.

fiat lux [L.] let there be light.

fidei defensor [L.] defender of the faith.

fille de joie [F.] prostitute.

fin de siècle [F.] end of the 19th century; decadent.

finis [L.] the end.

flagrante delicto [L.] in the very act, red-handed.

folie de grandeur [F.] delusions of grandeur.

fons et origo [L.] the source and origin.

gaudeamus igitur [L.] let us then rejoice.

gendarme [F.] one of the *gendarmerie*, a body of armed police in France.

haute couture [F.] high fashion.

haute cuisine [F.] high-class cooking.

hic jacet [L.] here lies.

honi soit qui mal y pense [Old F.] shame to him who thinks ill of it.

horribile dictu [L.] horrible to relate.

hors de combat [F.] out of condition to fight.

ibidem (abbreviated as **ib**; or **ibid**) [L.] in the same place.

ich dien [Ger.] I serve.

idée fixe [F.] an obsession, monomania.

id est [L.] (usually **i.e.**) that is.

idem [L.] the same.

ignis fatuus [L.] a will-o'-the-wisp.

imprimatur [L.] literally, "let it be printed", a licence to print, sanction.

in camera [L.] in a (judge's private) room.

in extremis [L.] at the point of death.

infra dignitatem [L.] (**infra dig.**) below one's dignity.

in loco parentis [L.] in the place of a parent.

in medias res [L.] into the midst of things.

in memoriam [L.] to the memory of.

in perpetuum [L.] for ever.

in re [L.] in the matter of.

in situ [L.] in its original position.

in statu quo [L.] in the former state.

inter alia [L.] among other things.

in toto [L.] entirely.

in vino veritas [L.] in wine the truth (comes out).

ipse dixit [L.] "he himself said it"; his unsupported word.

ipsissima verba [L.] the very words.

ipso facto [L.] by the fact itself.

je ne sais quoi [F.] "I don't know what", a something or other.

jeu d'esprit [F.] a witticism.

joie de vivre [F.] joy of living; ebullience.

laissez faire [F.] policy of inaction.

lapsus linguae [L.] a slip of the tongue.

lares et penates [L.] household gods.

leitmotif [Ger.] a theme used to indicate a person, idea, etc. in opera, etc.

lèse-majesté [F.] high treason.

l'état, c'est moi [F.] I am the state. (Saying of Louis XIV.)

lettre de cachet [F.] a sealed letter; a royal warrant for imprisonment.

locum tenens [L.] "one occupying the place", a deputy or substitute.

magnum opus [L.] a great work.

mal à propos [F.] ill-timed.

mal de mer [F.] sea-sickness.

malentendu [F.] a misunderstanding.

manqué [F.] potential; would-be.

mariage de convenance [F.] a marriage from motives of interest rather than love.

mauvaise honte [F.] false modesty, bashfulness.

mauvais quart d'heure [F.] a brief unpleasant experience.

mea culpa [L.] by my fault.

memento mori [L.] remember death.

ménage à trois [F.] sexual arrangement involving a married couple and the lover of one of them.

mens sana in corpore sano [L.] a sound mind in a sound body.

mésalliance [F.] marriage with someone of lower social status.

meum et tuum [L.] mine and thine.

mirabile dictu [L.] wonderful to relate.

mise en scène [F.] scenic setting.

modus operandi [L.] manner of working.

mot juste [F.] the exact right word.

moue [F.] a disdainful or pouting look.

multum in parvo [L.] much in little.

mutatis mutandis [L.] with the necessary changes.

née [F.] "born", her maiden name being; e.g. *Mrs. Brown née Smith*.

nemine contradicente [L.] (often as **nem.con.**) without opposition.

nemo me impune lacessit [L.] no one hurts me with impunity.

ne plus ultra [L.] nothing further; the uttermost point.

nihil obstat [L.] there is no obstacle.

nil desperandum [L.] despair of nothing.

noblesse oblige [F.] nobility imposes obligations.

nolens volens [L.] whether he will or not.

noli me tangere [L.] don't touch me.

nom de guerre [F.] an assumed name. (**nom de plume** is hardly used in French.)

non compos mentis [L.] insane.

non sequitur [L.] it does not follow.

nota bene [L.] (**N.B.**) note well.

nous avons changé tout cela [F.] we have changed all that.

nouveau riche [F.] one newly enriched, an upstart.

nulli secundus [L.] second to none.

obiit [L.] he (or she) died.

obiter dictum [L.] (*pl.* **obiter dicta**) something said by the way.

on dit [F.] they say; a rumour.

ora pro nobis [L.] pray for us.

O tempora! O mores! [L.] literally, "O the times! O the manners!"; what dreadful times and doings.

pace [L.] by leave of.

par avion [F.] by aeroplane (of mail sent by air).

par excellence [F.] pre-eminently.

pari passu [L.] with equal pace; together.

passim [L.] here and there, everywhere.

pax vobiscum [L.] peace be with you.

peccavi [L.] I have sinned.

per ardua ad astra [L.] through difficulties to the stars.

persona non grata [L.] unacceptable or unwelcome person.

post hoc, ergo propter hoc [L.] after this, therefore because of this (a fallacy in reasoning.)

pour encourager les autres [F.] in order to encourage the others.

prima facie [L.] at a first view.

primus inter pares [L.] first among equals.

pro patria [L.] for one's country.

pro tempore [L.] for the time being.

quis custodiet ipsos custodes? [L.] who will guard the guards?

qui vive? [F.] who goes there?

quod erat demonstrandum [L.] (**Q.E.D.**) which was to be proved.

quot homines, tot sententiae [L.] as many men as there are opinions.

quo vadis? [L.] whither goest thou?

rara avis [L.] a rare bird, something prodigious.

reductio ad absurdum [L.] a reducing to the absurd.

répondez s'il vous plait [F.] (**R.S.V.P.**) please reply.

requiescat in pace [L.] (**R.I.P.**) may he (or she) rest in peace.

rus in urbe [L.] the country in the town.

sans peur et sans reproche [F.] without fear and without reproach.

sans souci [F.] without care.

sauve qui peut [F.] save himself who can - the cry of disorderly retreat.

semper fidelis [L.] always faithful.

seriatim [L.] in order.

sic [L.] thus. Often used to call attention to some quoted mistake.

sic transit gloria mundi [L.] so passes the glory of the world.

sine die [L.] without date, indefinitely postponed.

si monumentum requiris, circumspice [L.] if you seek (his) monument, look around you. (The inscription on the architect Wren's tomb in St. Paul's.)

sine qua non [L.] an indispensable condition.

soi-disant [F.] so-called; self-styled.

status quo [L.] "the state in which", the pre-existing state of affairs.

stet [L.] let it stand.

Sturm und Drang [Ger.] storm and stress.

sub judice [L.] under consideration.

sub rosa [L.] "under the rose", secretly.

sub voce [L.] under that heading.

sursum corda [L.] lift up your hearts (to God).

table d'hôte [F.] general guest-table, meal at a fixed price.

tant mieux [F.] so much the better.

tant pis [F.] so much the worse.

tempore [L.] in the time of.

tempus fugit [L.] time flies.

terra firma [L.] solid earth.

terra incognita [L.] unexplored land or area of study.

tour de force [F.] a feat of strength or skill.

tout de suite [F.] at once.

tout ensemble [F.] the whole taken together, the general effect.

tout le monde [F.] all the world, everyone.

ubique [L.] everywhere.

ultima Thule [L.] the utmost boundary or limit.

ultra vires [L.] beyond one's powers.

vade in pace [L.] go in peace.

vade mecum [L.] go with me; a constant companion, work of reference.

vale [L.] farewell.

veni, vidi, vici [L.] I came, I saw, I conquered.

ventre à terre [F.] belly to the ground; at high speed.

verbum sapienti satis [L.] (**verb.sap.**) a word is enough for a wise man.

via media [L.] a middle course.

videlicet [L.] (**viz.**) namely, to wit.

volente Deo [L.] God willing.

Weltschmerz [Ger.] world-weariness; sentimental pessimism.

Zeitgeist [Ger.] the spirit of the times.

GROUP NAMES AND COLLECTIVE NOUNS

barren of mules
bevy of quails
bevy of roes
brace or lease of bucks
brood or covey of grouse
brood of hens or chickens
building or clamour of
  rooks
bunch, company or knob of
  wigeon (in the water)
bunch, knob or spring of
  teal
cast of hawks
cete of badgers
charm of gold-finches
chattering of choughs
clowder of cats
colony of gulls (breeding)
covert of coots
covey of partridges
cowardice of curs
desert of lapwings
dopping of sheldrakes
down or husk of hares
drove or herd of cattle
  (kine)
exaltation of larks
fall of woodcocks
field or string of racehorses
flight of wigeon (in the air)
flight or dule of doves
flight of swallows
flight of dunlins
flight, rush, bunch or knob
  of pochards
flock or flight of pigeons
flock of sheep
flock of swifts
flock or gaggle of geese
flock, congregation, flight or
  volery of birds
gaggle of geese (on the
  ground)
gang of elk

haras (stud) of horses
herd of antelopes
herd of buffaloes
herd, sedge or siege of
  cranes
herd of curlews
herd of deer
herd of giraffes
herd or tribe of goats
herd or pod of seals
herd or bevy of swans
herd of ponies
herd of swine
hill of ruffs
host of sparrows
kindle of kittens
labour of moles
leap of leopards
litter of cubs
litter of pups or pigs
litter of whelps
murmuration of starlings
muster of peacocks
nest of rabbits
nye or nide of pheasants
pace or herd of asses
pack of grouse
pack, mute or cry of hounds
pack, rout or herd of wolves
paddling of ducks
plump, sord or sute of wild
  fowl
pod of whiting
pride or troop of lions
rag of colts
richesse of martens
run of poultry
school or run of whales
school or gam of porpoises
sedge or siege of bitterns
sedge or siege of herons
shoal or glean of herrings
shoal, draught, haul, run or
  catch of fish

616

GROUP NAMES AND COLLECTIVE NOUNS

shrewdness of apes
skein of geese (in flight)
skulk of foxes
sleuth of bears
sord or sute of mallards
sounder of boars
sounder or dryft of swine
stand or wing of plovers
stud of mares
swarm of insects

swarm or grist of bees, or flies
swarm or cloud of gnats
tok of capercailzies
team of ducks (in flight)
troop of kangaroos
troop of monkeys
walk or wisp of snipe
watch of nightingales
yoke, drove, team or herd of
    oxen

PLANETS OF THE SOLAR SYSTEM

Earth • Jupiter • Mars • Mercury • Neptune
Pluto • Saturn • Uranus • Venus

CHARACTERS IN CLASSICAL MYTHOLOGY

Achilles
Actaeon
Adonis
Aeneas
Agamemnon
Ajax
Amazons
Andromeda
Antigone
Aphrodite
Apollo
Arachne
Ares
Argonauts
Ariadne
Artemis
Atalanta
Athena / Athene
Atlas
Aurora
Bacchus
Bellona
Boreas
Cassandra
Cassiopeia
centaurs
Charon
Charybdis
Chimaera
Circe
Cronus
Cupid
Cybele
Cyclopes
Daedalus
Demeter
Diana
Dido
Dionysus
dryads
Echidna

Electra
Eros
Eurydice
Galatea
Ganymede
Gorgons
Hades
hamadryads
Harpies
Hebe
Hecate
Hector
Hecuba
Helen
Hephaestus
Hera
Heracles /
   Hercules
Hermaphroditus
Hermes
Hydra
Icarus
Iris
Janus
Jason
Jocasta
Juno
Jupiter
Leda
Mars
Medea
Medusa
Mercury
Midas
Minerva
Minotaur
Muses
Narcissus
Nemesis
Neptune
Nereids

Niobe
Oceanids
Odysseus
Oedipus
oreads
Orestes
Orion
Orpheus
Pallas
Pan
Pandora
Paris
Pegasus
Penelope
Persephone
Perseus
Phoebus
Pleiades
Pluto
Poseidon
Priam
Prometheus
Psyche
Pygmalion
Remus
Romulus
Saturn
satyrs
Selene
sibyl
Sirens
Sisyphus
Sphinx
Tantalus
Tiresias
Titans
Triton
Uranus
Venus
Vulcan
Zeus

CHEMICAL ELEMENTS

actinium
aluminium
americium
antimony
argon
arsenic
astatine
barium
berkelium
beryllium
bismuth
boron
bromine
cadmium
caesium
calcium
californium
carbon
cerium
chlorine
chromium
cobalt
copper
curium
dysprosium
einsteinium
erbium
europium
fermium
fluorine
francium
gadolinium
gallium
germanium
gold

hafnium
hahnium
helium
holmium
hydrogen
indium
iodine
iridium
iron
krypton
lanthanum
lawrencium
lead
lithium
lutetium
magnesium
manganese
mendelevium
mercury
molybdenum
neodymium
neon
neptunium
nickel
niobium
nitrogen
nobelium
osmium
oxygen
palladium
phosphorus
platinum
plutonium
polonium
potassium

praseodymium
proactinium
promethium
radium
radon
rhenium
rhodium
rubidium
ruthenium
rutherfordium
samarium
scandium
selenium
silicon
silver
sodium
strontium
sulphur
tantalum
technetium
tellurium
terbium
thallium
thorium
thulium
tin
titanium
tungsten
uranium
vanadium
xenon
ytterbium
zinc
zirconium

BOOKS OF THE BIBLE
(including the Apocrypha)

Acts of the Apostles
Amos
Baruch
Chronicles
Colossians
Corinthians
Daniel
Daniel and
  Susanna
Daniel, Bel, and
  the Snake
Deuteronomy
Ecclesiastes
Ecclesiasticus
Ephesians
Esdras
Esther
Exodus
Ezekiel
Ezra
Galatians
Genesis
Habbakuk

Haggai
Hebrews
Hosea
Isaiah
James
Jeremiah
Job
Joel
John
Jonah
Joshua
Jude
Judges
Judith
Kings
Lamentations
Leviticus
Luke
Maccabees
Malachi
Manasseh
Mark
Matthew

Micah
Nahum
Nehemiah
Numbers
Obadiah
Peter
Philemon
Philippians
Proverbs
Psalms
Revelations
Romans
Ruth
Samuel
Solomon
Song of Songs
Song of the Three
Thessalonians
Timothy
Titus
Tobit
Zechariah
Zephaniah

WEDDING ANNIVERSARIES

YEAR	TRADITIONAL	MODERN
1st	Paper	Clocks
2nd	Cotton	China
3rd	Leather	Crystal, glass
4th	Linen (silk)	Electrical appliances
5th	Wood	Silverware
6th	Iron	Wood
7th	Wool (copper)	Desk sets
8th	Bronze	Linen, lace
9th	Pottery (china)	Leather
10th	Tin (aluminium)	Diamond jewellery
11th	Steel	Fashion jewellery, accessories
12th	Silk	Pearls or coloured gems
13th	Lace	Textile, furs
14th	Ivory	Gold jewellery
15th	Crystal	Watches
20th	China	Platinum
25th	Silver	Sterling silver jubilee
30th	Pearl	Diamond
35th	Coral (jade)	Jade
40th	Ruby	Ruby
45th	Sapphire	Sapphire
50th	Gold	Gold
55th	Emerald	Emerald
60th	Diamond	Diamond

TYPES OF CALENDAR

The number of days in a year varies among cultures and from year to year.

GREGORIAN

The Gregorian calendar is a 16th-century adaptation of the Julian calendar devised in the 1st century BC. The year in this calendar is based on the solar year, which lasts about 365 1/4 days. In this system, years whose number is not divisible by 4 have 365 days, as do centennial years unless the figures before the noughts are divisible by 4. All other years have 366 days; these are leap years.

Below are the names of the months and number of days for a non-leap year.

> January 31
> February 28*
> March 31
> April 30
> May 31
> June 30
> July 31
> August 31
> September 30
> October 31
> November 30
> December 31
>
> * 29 in leap years

JEWISH

A year in the Jewish calendar has 13 months if its number, when divided by 9, leaves 0, 3, 6, 8, 11, 14 or 17; otherwise, it has 12 months. The year is based on the lunar year, but its number of months varies to keep broadly in line with the solar cycle. Its precise number of days is fixed with reference to particular festivals that must not fall on certain days of the week.

Below are the names of the months and number of days in each for the year 5471, a 12-month year (1980 AD in Gregorian).

Tishri 30
Cheshvan 29*
Kislev 29*
Tevet 29
Shevat 30
Adar 29
Nisan 30
Iyar 29
Sivan 30
Tammuz 29
Av 30
Elul 29

* 30 in some years.

In 13-month years, the month Veadar, with 29 days, falls between Adar and Nisan.

MUSLIM

A year in the Muslim calendar has 355 days if its number, when divided by 30, leaves 2, 5, 7, 10, 13, 16, 18, 21, 24, 26 or 29; otherwise it has 354 days. As in the Jewish calendar, years are based on the lunar cycle.

Below are the names of the months and number of days in each for the Muslim year 1401 (1980 AD in Gregorian).

Muharram 30
Safar 29
Rabi'I 30
Rabi'II 29
Jumada I 30
Jumada II 29
Rajab 30
Sha'ban 29
Ramadan 30
Shawwal 29
Dhu 1-Qa'dah 30
Dhu 1-Hijja 30*

* 29 in some years.

BEVERAGE MEASURES

BEER MEASURES

1 nip = 1/4 pint
1 small = 1/2 pint
1 large = 1 pint
1 flagon = 1 quart
1 anker = 10 gallons
1 firkin = 9 gallons
1 kilderkin = 2 firkins
1 barrel = 2 kilderkins
1 hogshead = 1 1/2 barrels
1 butt = 2 hogsheads
1 tun = 2 butts
      216 gallons

HANDY MEASURES

small jigger = 1 fl oz
small wine glass = 2 fl oz
cocktail glass = 1/4 pint
sherry glass = 1/4 pint
large wine glass = 1/4 pint
tumbler = 1/2 pint

US SPIRITS MEASURES

1 pony = 1/2 jigger
1 jigger = 1 1/2 shot
1 shot = 1 fl oz
1 pint = 16 shots
1 fifth = 25.6 shots
      1.6 pints
      0.8 quart
      0.758 litre
1 quart = 32 shots
      1 1/4 fifths
1 magnum of wine = 2 quarts
      2 1/2 bottles

WINE MEASURES

10 gallons = 1 anker
1 hogshead = 63 gallons
2 hogsheads = 1 pipe
2 pipes = 1 tun
1 puncheon = 84 gallons
1 butt (sherry) = 110 gallons

COLLINS
ENGLISH
Mini
DICTIONARY

- Up-to-date text

- All entry words in colour

- Special supplement of new words

- Clearly worded definitions

- Attractive easy-to-read page

The perfect companion to
Collins English Mini Thesaurus